KAREN MacNEIL

THE WINE BIBLE

REVISED SECOND EDITION

WORKMAN PUBLISHING | NEW YORK

Copyright © 2001, 2015 by Karen MacNeil

All rights reserved. No portion of this book may be reproduced—
mechanically, electronically, or by any other means,
including photocopying—without written permission of the publisher.
Published simultaneously in Canada by Thomas Allen & Son Limited.

Library of Congress Cataloging-in-Publication Data is available.

ISBN 978-0-7611-8083-8 (pb)
ISBN 978-0-7611-8572-7 (hc)

Cover and interior design by Jean-Marc Troadec

COVER PHOTO: DAVID ARKY
GLASS: EISCH SKY SENSIS PLUS BURGUNDY GLASS
AUTHOR PHOTO: LOWELL DOWNEY OF ART & CLARITY
MAPS BY ACCURAT
PHOTO CREDITS CAN BE FOUND ON PAGES 995–996

Workman books are available at special discounts when purchased in bulk
for premiums and sales promotions as well as for fund-raising or educational use.
Special editions or book excerpts also can be created to specification.
For details, contact the Special Sales Director at the address below,
or send an email to specialmarkets@workman.com.

WORKMAN PUBLISHING CO., INC.
225 VARICK ST.
NEW YORK, NY 10014-4381
WORKMAN.COM

WORKMAN is a registered trademark of Workman Publishing Co., Inc.

Printed in the United States of America
First printing October 2015

10 9 8 7

To *Emma*,
who has taught me the meaning of love

And to *Harvey*,
who has taught me the meaning of friendship

And to the lesson of red tulips . . .

ACKNOWLEDGMENTS

The process of writing a book involves a contradiction. For years, the writer breathes the thin air of solitude and lives within the isolation of her own mind. Yet at the same time, she is surrounded by hundreds of people without whose help—large and small—the book simply would not be.

Over the four years it took to research, write, and taste my way to this second edition of *The Wine Bible*, I was helped by a group of smart, dynamic, dedicated wine pros who conducted endless amounts of research, unearthed thousands of facts, tasted and evaluated nearly 10,000 wines with me and were, in every way imaginable, the buttresses that allowed *The Wine Bible* to be built.

ABOVE ALL WAS Elizabeth Caravati, my assistant for the years during which I wrote the second edition. Elizabeth was there with me in the writing trenches when the trenches got very deep and numerous. For her brilliant mind, impeccable organization, and amazing dedication, I will always be grateful.

ALONG WITH ELIZABETH, a core team of talented wine pros worked tirelessly and brilliantly on research, photos, wines, and support structure. I am deeply indebted to Lauren Marsh Banks, Lauren Watters, Linda Schmitt, Alexandra Shimizu, Lauren Cadwallader, Stacey Carlo, Rebecca Fletcher, Emma Thomas, Jessi Moyle, Elizabeth Hemphill, Kort van Bronkhorst, Jacqueline Rogers, Jonathan Williams, Christina Hieb, and Michael Hoefling. You are all extraordinary people whose hard work (and fantastic palates) were indispensable.

OF COURSE NO BOOK is ever really a good book without the deep belief and demands of an editor and a publisher. To Suzanne Rafer, editor and visionary *extraordinaire*, thank you. I am, as ever, grateful for your guiding grace and amazing intellect. And to the late, much-missed Peter Workman—one of the titans of publishing and the first person who believed in this book—I know you are right this moment in heaven, working on the real bible.

WHEN I HANDED OVER the 4,000-something page manuscript, I held my breath. What would it look like? Jean-Marc Troadec is a brilliant designer, and the fact that he fell in love with the wines of Burgundy (and this project) was a great bit of luck for me. Michael Dimascio, thank you for agonizing over the 1,500 photos we sent you and rounding up even more. Sarah Brady—you're the only person I can email at midnight saying, "Can you fix the comma we messed up on page 923?" Enormous thanks, too, to Beth Levy for guiding the manuscript through its many editing passes, and to Barbara Peragine for perfecting the page layouts. Thanks also to Selina Meere, Chloe Puton, Jessica Wiener, Moira Kerrigan, Doug Wolff, and David Schiller, and the whole fantastic team at Workman Publishing—you're the best.

ALL WRITERS WRITE within a world created by their colleagues. The writers below are not only friends—they are among the inspired people who have helped make the wine industry rich and dynamic. Thank you to Gerald Asher, Andy Blue, Mary Ewing-Mulligan MW, Antonio Galloni, Howard G. Goldberg, Evan Goldstein, Jim Gordon, Sarah Kemp, Matt Kramer, Rick Kushman, Meredith May, Ed McCarthy, Elin McCoy, Jay McInerney, Sophie Menin, Robert M. Parker, Lisa Perrotti-Brown MW, Andrea Robinson MS, Jancis Robinson MW, Steven Spurrier, Brian St. Pierre, Terry Theise, Alder Yarrow, and Kevin Zraly.

AND THEN THERE were the hundreds of wine professionals who answered endless research questions in painstaking detail, and photographers who provided us with stellar imagery.

FOR THEIR EXPERTISE, professionalism, talent and sheer massive knowledge, I am thankful to: Ana Abreu, Greg Allen, Janine Allen, Sao Anash, Holly Anderson, Maggie Anderson, Gail Appleson, Travis Arnesen, Susan Auler, Christopher Barefoot, Xavier Barlier, Daniel Baron, Alfredo Bartholomaus, Meaghan Becker, Didier Bedu, Danene Beedle, Jeremy Benson, Marybeth Bentwood, Jennifer Berry, Bob Bertheau, Tania Bicknell, Anna Boatwright, Angela Bortugno, Dr. Roger B. Boulton, Katia Braithwaite, Jennifer Brown, Catherine Bugue, Kimberly Burfiend, Lacey Burke, Steve Burns, Karel Bush, Barbara Cacao, George Caloyannidis, Robert Camuto, Jean-Louis Carbonnier, Kristen Carrillo, Beth Cash, Doug Caskey, Kate Chaplin, Kimberly Charles, Pierre Cheval, Molly Choi, Steffen Christmann, Andrea Mingfai Chu, Tracy Clark, John Concannon, Alex Conison, Allison Conway, Rogelio Cortés Ricárdez, Tom Cosentino, Susan-Anne Cosgrove, Bobby Cox, Eileen Crane, Jean-Charles Cuvelier, Allison Dallas, Eric Danch, Mark Davidson, Sarah Davis, Eric Dench, Frank Dietrich, Sara Dirks, Joanne Dow, Yannick Doyard, David Duncan, Jennifer Eckinger, Tom Elliot, Michèle Ellner, Maria Ferri, Michelle Fleming, Véronique Foureur, Frederick Frank, Owen Franken, Jon Fredrikson, Lacey Fussel, Linsey Gallagher, Robin Garr, Emil Gaspari, Axel Gillery, John Gillespie, Anthony Gismondi, Marlène Gloaguen, Cécile Gonzalez, Charlotte Good, Penelope Goodsall, Randall Grahm, Nigel Greening, Chryssa Gribabi, Shannon Gunier, Eva Gurfein, Robert Haas, Barbara Handl, Timothy Hartley, Sam Heitner, Dr. Ed Hellman, Oscar Henquet, Dr. Hildegarde Heymann, Robert Hill-Smith, Olivia Hoffman, Tom Hogue, Gladys Horiuchi, Glenn Hugo, Patrick Hunt, Mitzi Inglis, Tim Irwin, Gene Ivester, Elisabeth Jaubert, Karla Jensen, Christopher Jones, Magdalena Kaiser, Leon Karatsalos, Vincenza Kelly, Lindsay Kelm, Molly Kennedy, Jane Kettlewell, Tina Kezeli, Sue Kibbe, Dr. Aaron Kingsbury, Don Kinnan, Shae Kinsman, Chris Kissack, Kerstin Klamm, Suzie Kukaj, Fran Kysela, Valerie Lailheugue, Kara Larmie, Jason Lett, Jeff Leve, Matthew Levy, Nancy Light, Zach Long, Pedro Lopes Vieira, Kat Luna, Kermit Lynch, Avis Mandel, Jeff Marazoni, Augusto Marchini, Jean-Pierre Mareigner, May Matta-Aliah, Jarrod McCann, Sharron McCarthy, Patsy McGaughy, Stephanie McIntyre, Beth McMahon, Dr. Carole Meredith, Jan Mettler, Janis Miglavs, Amber Mihna, Catherine Miles, Arnie Millan, Alexia Moore, Christian Moya, Heather Muhleman, Megan Murphy, Katrin Naelapaa, Jonathan Nahrgang, Charles Neal, Mariana Nedic, Grant Newton, Heather Thompson Noll, Erica Nonni, Dieter Odendaal, Kathy O'Neal, Betty O'Shaughnessy Woolls, Jennifer Pagano, Elpida Palamida, Marsha Palanci, Frédéric Panaïotis, Sarah Papenfus, Lluís Pellejà Serra, Ryan Pennington, Sofia Perpera, Bridget Perrault, Susan Piovesan, Thomas Pothmann, Marla Priest, Julie-Adele Provansal, Alain Puginier, Erik Quam, Sona Rai, Alyssa Rapp, Linda Reiff, Dr. Thomas J. Rice, Georg Riedel, George Rose, Louisa Rose, Monica Rosenthal, Leslie Rudd, Ronnie Sanders, Carla Sarabia, Bethany Scherline, Emily Schindler, Meredith Schlacter, Thea Schlendorf, Claire Schmitt, Frank Schulz, Marie-Louise Schÿler, Jami Segoria, Johannes Selbach, Robert Shack, Doug Shafer, John Shafer, Hiram Simon, Monica Simpson, Katie Sims, Nicki Sizemore, Anthony Smith, Jim Smith, Wendy Lane Stevens, Tom Stevenson, Sabine Stock, Sherry Stolar, Guy Stout, David Strada, Jordi Suárez Baldrís, Jim Sweeney, Tracy Sweeney, Rupert Symington, Dr. Ludger Tekampe, Clark Z. Terry, Elaine Testa, Stephanie Teuwen, Karen Thornton, Lori Tieszen, Jim Trezise, Maru Valdés, Joanna Vlahos, Paul Wagner, Teresa Wall, Karli Warner, Ross Wasserman, Belinda Weber, Rebecca Weber, Wilhelm Weil, Diego Weiss, Shannon Wesley, Peter Weygandt, Bryce Wiatrak, Philippe Wibrotte, Jen Wilkinson, Paul Woolls, Alan Zalayet and the Eisch Glass team, Annette Zangrandi, and Joco Znidarsic.

CONTENTS

INTRODUCTION

WHY WINE MATTERS

During the ten years it took to write the first edition of *The Wine Bible* and the four years it took to write this second edition, I have often asked myself why wine matters. What is it about wine that I hold so deeply? What is this endless attachment?

I have always known what it is not. It's not about scoring or competitive analysis, though like any wine pro, I'm game for the next blind tasting. And it's not about the need to retell what I have learned, though I can lie awake for hours thinking about how to capture a wine in words.

Perhaps it is this: I love wine because it is one of the last true things. In a world digitized to distraction, a world where you can't get out of your pajamas without your cell phone, wine remains utterly primary. Unrushed. The silent music of nature. For eight thousand years, vines clutching the earth have thrust themselves upward toward the sun and given us juicy berries, and ultimately wine. In every sip taken in the present, we drink in the past—the moment in time when those berries were picked; a moment gone but recaptured—and so vivid that our bond with nature is welded deep.

Wine matters because of this ineluctable connection. Wine and food cradle us in our own communal humanity. Anthropologically, they are the pleasures that carried life forward and sustained us through the sometimes dark days of our own evolution.

Drinking wine then—as small as that action can seem—is both grounding and transformative. It reminds us of other things that matter, too: love, friendship, generosity.

The Wine Bible has taken me a long time to write—in some ways I've spent the better part of my last twenty years on it. It has taken this long not because it takes a long time to accumulate the facts, but because it takes a long time to *feel* a place—culturally, historically, aesthetically.

And so, on my mission to understand the wine regions of the world, I've danced the tango (awkwardly) with Argentinian men to try to understand malbec; drunk amarone while eating horsemeat (a tradition) in the Veneto; sipped wine from hairy goatskin bags in northern Greece (much as the ancients would have); and been strapped into a contraption that lowers pickers down into perilously steep German vineyards (an experience that momentarily convinces you your life is over).

I've shared wine and cigars with bullfighters in Rioja; ridden through the vineyards of Texas on horseback; eaten octopus and drunk assyrtiko with Greek fishermen in Santorini (considered by some to be the lost Atlantis); and picked tiny oyster shells from among the fossilized sea creatures that make up the moonscape soils of Chablis.

I've waltzed among wine barrels with winemakers in Vienna; stomped grapes with Portuguese picking crews until my legs were purple, and worked for weeks with a Mexican harvest crew in California, one of the hardest and most rewarding experiences I've ever had.

These encounters brought wine so vividly into my life that I ultimately moved to Napa Valley on the sheer belief that living near vines would touch my heart in ways imaginable and not.

And so it has.

—Karen MacNeil

HOW TO USE THIS BOOK

Every author writing about wine has to make decisions about what to include, what to exclude (a harder choice), and how to present information that can be technical, complex, or just plain messy in scope. Here are my decisions and the thinking behind them.

● **WHERE TO BEGIN** Acquiring knowledge about wine doesn't usually occur in a linear fashion and neither, I suspect, does reading about wine. So *The Wine Bible* is written in a way that allows you to begin anywhere. You can, of course, start with the section I call Mastering Wine, but if you want to read about Spain first, by all means, go ahead. Some readers may read this work cover to cover, but you can also dip into it over time as your fascination with a given topic, country, or type of wine takes hold.

● **THE COUNTRIES AND THEIR MOST IMPORTANT WINES** This second edition of *The Wine Bible* covers every major wine region in the world and most of the minor ones. That said, regrettably, because of lack of space, I was not able to include Israel, Turkey, Bulgaria, Romania, or Croatia.

For every major wine region that's included, you'll find a Most Important Wines box. The wines listed are divided into Leading Wines and Wines of Note. My hope is that the Most Important Wines boxes will give you a quick idea of the wines that most deserve your attention. For example, if you're going to Tuscany, which wines should you be sure not to miss? Those are designated as Leading Wines. And which wines are absolutely worth trying even though they aren't as important as a Leading Wine? Those are the Wines of Note.

● **ABOUT THE WINES TO KNOW** For every major country and every significant region within it, there's also a section called The Wines to Know. The Wines to Know are highly personal choices that I recommend you try because I think they'll tell you, within a few sips, the story of that place in a way that words

barely can. (Just as an aside, looking for the wines that tell the story of a place is slightly different from looking only for "great" wines that might score high in a critic's notebook.) To arrive at the Wines to Know for this edition of *The Wine Bible*, I tasted close to ten thousand wines. Still, finalizing the specific wines to be included was often difficult, and I know I've left out some deserving wines.

Most of the Wines to Know are available either from a wine retailer, directly from the winery or via the Internet. Alas, because of high demand, a few wines may prove difficult to locate through standard retail channels. I've included them anyway because you may very well encounter them on a restaurant wine list or find them while traveling in wine country.

● **ABOUT VINTAGES** *The Wine Bible* does not include information on specific vintages. Not because vintages of a given wine aren't different—of course they are—but my hope was to present wines that are worth your knowing about in *any* vintage.

I also hope that the whole concept of vintages is something that you'll take in stride because most vintages aren't nearly as cut and dry, black or white, good or bad as they are often made out to be. In this spirit, I hope you'll find How Much Do Vintages Matter? (page 124) evocative and worthy of consideration.

● **ABOUT COST** I also haven't given prices in this book. That sort of information often changes so rapidly that only newsletters, newspapers, magazines, and the Internet can attempt to be accurate. But I have sometimes indicated that a wine is a steal, or moderately priced, or super-expensive, and so on.

● ABOUT FOOD What would a wine book be without food—wine's ineluctable companion? I've included dozens of boxes and sections on the traditional foods of a given wine region. Want to know the history of croissants? (Hint: The story doesn't begin in France.) Or why Sherry's soulmate is tapas? Or why you need to eat chinchilla while drinking malbec in Argentina? It's all here. You'll also find lots and lots of information on wine and food marriages including a section in the Mastering Wine chapter outlining strategies for pairing wine and food (page 115).

● ABOUT THE MAPS AND PHOTOS The maps created for this second edition are not overly complex or overly simple. They include, I believe, what every wine lover needs to know—that is, how wine regions relate to one another in terms of their locations. Each region has a slightly different color shading, allowing you to easily tell them apart. (Note that the color of the shading does not indicate the color of the wine in that region).

Dozens of individuals helped me by sharing their photos—some were professional photographers; others, wine pros on a wine country excursion. I thank them all for allowing us to use their works. Their names are listed in the acknowledgments or in the photo credits.

● ABOUT THE SEVEN GLOSSARIES In addition to a comprehensive general glossary of wine terms in English, there are seven other glossaries for wine terms in other languages—a glossary each for terms in French, Italian, Spanish, German and Austrian, Portuguese, Hungarian, and Greek. So a word like *cosecha* ("vintage," in Spanish) appears not in the main glossary, but in the Spanish one.

● ABOUT GRAPE GENETICS This edition of *The Wine Bible* includes fascinating information on the genetic parentage of all the leading grapes. In all cases, my information comes from Dr. José Vouillamoz and the writers Jancis Robinson MW and Julia Harding MW.

● ABOUT STATISTICS There are several companies and organizations that track worldwide wine statistics, but they often have widely differing formats and provide information that is often not comprehensive. To maintain consistency throughout this book, my figures for wine production and vineyard acreage come from the OIV, *Organisation Internationale de la Vigne et du Vin,* and for consumption, from the Wine Institute. Both are highly respected organizations.

● ABOUT NAMES, SPELLING, AND PUNCTUATION As seemingly prosaic as this topic is, it can galvanize you as you attempt to write a book of this scope. Grape varieties are called different things or spelled different ways in different countries. Throughout, I've tried to be as clear as possible, always tipping you off about synonyms and local spellings. As for punctuation, you'll find that I've capitalized all wines that are named after places (this is standard), and put all grape varieties (and wines named after grape varieties) in lowercase. Thus in Piedmont, Italy, two of the leading wines are Barolo and barbera; the first capped because it takes its name from a place, the second appearing in lowercase because it's named after the grape. The only exception to this practice is grapes named after people, such as Müller-Thurgau and Palomino, both of which are capitalized.

● AND FINALLY, LEARNING MORE ABOUT WINE Some topics may be a bit boring to study. Not wine. It's quite possibly the most engaging, fun, and fascinating subject a learner could ever want. I hope *The Wine Bible* plays a role in your process of understanding wine and that you'll also give wine courses and certification a try. WSET (Wine and Spirits Education Trust), the Master Sommelier program, and the Society of Wine Educators are all top-notch organizations that will help your study of wine develop and evolve. In addition, there are countless wine courses and wine schools in cities large and small around the world. Happy tasting.

THE WINE BIBLE

MASTERING WINE

WHAT MAKES GREAT WINE GREAT?

ost wine books begin with what wine is, how it's made, where it comes from. And we'll definitely get into each of those.

But I wanted to lead off the first section of *The Wine Bible* with the bottom line, the big question, and the final paradox: What makes great wine great? Intentionally or not, many of us spend our entire "wine lives" tasting in pursuit of the answer (or answers), and it's a delicious journey to be sure. But it seems to me that this, the most intriguing of important wine questions, also deserves some thoughts put down on paper. So to begin, in this chapter

◀ *Wine has a way of pulling you into it—of making you want to taste and experience more.*

I'll share mine. From there, we'll get down to the specifics, and I'll take you through all the essentials: what wine is; the building blocks that make it taste the way it does; the stunning role that place plays in a wine's flavor; how wine is made; the professional method of tasting in a way that magnifies a wine's flavor; the vast world of grape varieties and how to get to know them; pairing wine with food; plus all the practical particulars, from how to feel more comfortable in a wine shop to how to choose the best wineglasses to how to know when a wine is ready to drink.

A final thought: When I was first learning about wine, I remember thinking that wine wouldn't be so hard to understand if I could just find someone to explain it well. Above all, I wanted to understand the concepts in *this* chapter—the concepts that give each of

Among wine's central mysteries: How is it that mere grapes can become a beverage of profound depth and complexity? How is it that this simple fruit can tell the story of a place?

us the grounding we need to think about wine more meaningfully and know it better. I hope I can be that good explainer for you. For it's by understanding this chapter—wine in all of its magnificent, paradoxical, and elemental details—that we enhance our awe and enjoyment of what is, after all, the world's most captivating beverage.

THE NINE ATTRIBUTES OF GREATNESS

No one needs a wine book to tell them what they *like* to drink. Subjectivity in wine is pretty easy. But a wine is not great merely because we like it. Liking a wine is simply liking a wine—it tells you something about what you take pleasure in.

I would argue that to really know wine—and to consider its potential greatness—requires that we move beyond what we know we like. It

requires that we attempt a larger understanding of the aesthetics behind wines that have garnered respect, wines that have consistently been singled out for their merit, wines that have, again and again over time, been cherished for their integrity and beauty. I'll call this our best attempt at wine objectivity. And by attempting to objectively understand wine, we begin to inch toward the underlying principles that make great wine great.

Like literature, then, wine encourages two assessments: one subjective, the other, objective. You may not like reading Shakespeare, but agree nonetheless that Shakespeare was a great writer. You may have loved that carafe of wine in the Parisian café . . . and yet know that it was not, in the end, a great wine.

What does it take to have as objective an opinion as possible about a wine? Discernment, an open mind, and usually some experience in repeatedly tasting the wine so you have a feel for how it classically presents itself. Experience with the wine is, I think, especially critical. My own best example of this is Sherry. The first time I tasted Sherry I envisioned writing an article called "Death by Sherry." I could not imagine why anyone would drink the stuff.

Today, I consider Sherry one of the greatest wines in the world, and it has become one of my favorites. By tasting it over and over again with "the willing suspension of disbelief" (to borrow a literary concept), I came to a closer understanding of it. One day while tasting it, the light switched flipped. In that moment, I "got" Sherry. Many, many wines require this sort of pursuit. (As do foods. Who can say they had a good idea of how to evaluate sushi the first time they tasted it?)

So, open-minded tasting experience is key. Assembling all that experience is also the fun part. After years of doing that, here are the nine attributes that I believe matter most in determining whether a wine is great: distinctiveness, balance, precision, complexity, beyond fruitness, length, choreography, connectedness, and the ability to evoke an emotional response.

DISTINCTIVENESS

In the simplest sense, consider: If you buy a Granny Smith apple, you want it to taste like one. If it tastes simply generic—like any old apple—you'd probably be disappointed. In fact, the more Granny Smith-ish the Granny Smith apple is, the more it can be appreciated and savored for what it is. Great wines are great because they are distinctive; not because they exhibit sameness. This is true first of all for wines based on single grape varieties. Each variety of grape presents itself in an individual way (see Getting to Know the Grapes, page 53). Wines that fully and precisely express those individual grapes are said to have "varietal character." A good thing. (As a quick aside and perhaps needless to say, not all varietal characteristics have mass appeal. Some wine drinkers, for example, think the edgy, "wild girl," tangy green herb character of some sauvignon blancs is hard to love. And indeed it can be. But think about cheese. Just because some people cannot bear intensely flavored cheese, is blue cheese awful? Should every cheese be remade in the image of American singles? I hope not.)

Then there are wines that are blends, including many of the most remarkable types of wine in the world: Champagne, Bordeaux, Rioja, Chianti, Châteauneuf-du-Pape—and many others. A blend does not, cannot, demonstrate varietal character. But it should demonstrate distinctiveness. Tasting a great Châteauneuf-du-Pape should tell you above all that *this* is a Châteauneuf-du-Pape and cannot be anything else. (And, of course, we'll address what great Châteauneuf-du-Pape tastes like in the Rhône Valley section of the French chapter.)

Finally, great wines are distinctive not only in their aromas and flavors, but also distinctive in their textures. Great wine does not lie amorphously on the palate. It has a feel that is exciting. That feel can be as soft as cashmere, as minerally as mountain water, as brisk and crisp as fresh lime juice, or as downy as falling snow (which is the texture of many great Champagnes). The nature of the texture doesn't matter. What's important with great wine is that it have a discernible and distinctive texture.

In the end, distinctiveness is perhaps the highest attribute of great wine. It's the sense that this wine could not be just *anything*; it is *something*.

BALANCE

One of the most commonly used words to describe a great wine is *balance*, along with its cousin, *integration*. The two words mean slightly different things. Balance is the characteristic a wine possesses when all of its major components (acid, alcohol, fruit, and tannin) are in equilibrium (see What Makes Wine, Wine?, page 9). Because no single component sticks out more than any of the others, a balanced wine has a kind of harmonious tension of opposites. I often think of a Thai soup when I think of balance. Sweetness, heat, acidity, spice—they're all there in perfect contrapuntal tension with

> "Great wine is about nuance, surprise, subtlety, expression, qualities that keep you coming back for another taste. Rejecting a wine because it is not big enough is like rejecting a book because it is not long enough, or a piece of music because it is not loud enough."
>
> —**KERMIT LYNCH,**
> *Adventures on the Wine Route*

one another, and as a result the soup tastes harmonious.

Integration takes this concept one step further. When a wine is integrated, its components and flavors have coalesced in a way that seems almost magical. Instead of various components and flavors that are all separate and discernible, an integrated wine possesses a unique and stunning character that comes from the synthesis of the independent parts. A wine that is balanced when young has the potential to become integrated when it's older.

Balance or integration is essential in great wine. That said, they are difficult characteristics to describe. Wine that is not balanced or integrated is far easier to talk about. It presents itself like a broken star on the palate, with a few points sticking out. When oakiness is out of balance, for example, it's easy to taste because, from a sensory perspective, it sticks out like a sore thumb. It's worth noting that great wines usually leave wine critics literally speechless.

PRECISION

Great wines do not have flavors that are muddled or blurry. Great wines have flavors—whatever those flavors are—that are precise, well defined, and expressive. Imagine an old-style radio where you can dial in the frequency. If you don't adjust the dial perfectly, you can still hear the music, but its integrity is lost in static. When you get the frequency just right, the music takes on a special beauty because it is precise.

Interestingly, sensory scientists often analogize flavor to sound. Is flavor X a whisper or a shout?, they will ask in an experiment. Using this as a metaphor, I would offer that a great wine has a flavor that is the precision equivalent of a church bell in the mountains.

Given two well-made wines from two above-average vineyards in the same good year, it is not clear why one wine might be more precise in flavor than the other. There are many ways in which winemaking could be at fault (overhandling a wine, for example, can discombobulate it; too much oak could blur its flavors). But it is also well known that certain vineyards, mostly year in and year out—for reasons immensely complex to fathom—simply produce precise wines.

COMPLEXITY

Wines fall along a spectrum from simple to complex. Simple wines are monochromatic in flavor and monodimensional in appeal. They may be delightful, but in a sense they have only one thing to say.

By comparison, complex wines have multifaceted aromas and flavors—and here's the most important part: Those layers of aroma and flavor reveal themselves sequentially over time. Tasting a complex wine is a head trip. Just when you think you've grasped the flavors, the kaleidoscope turns and new flavors emerge, revealing different facets of the wine. A complex wine is therefore not knowable in one sip. A complex wine almost pulls you into it, compelling you to take sip after sip in order

> "There's volumes to be said for a wine that takes you three glasses to decide whether you find it compelling or repellent."
>
> —**EVAN AND BRIAN MITCHELL,**
> *The Psychology of Wine*

LITTLE RED RIDING HOOD

"One day her mother said to her, 'Come, Little Red Riding Hood, here is a piece of cake and a bottle of wine. Take them to your grandmother, she is ill and weak, and they will do her good.' "

—"ROTKÄPPCHEN"

(Little Red Riding Hood, or Little Red-Cap) printed in Kinder und Hausmärchen, *a collection of German fairy tales first published in 1812 by the Brothers Grimm*

In 1989 and 1990, two California school districts, in Culver City and Empire, respectively, banned this version of the tale over concern about the mention of alcohol in the story.

to understand it (or at least follow what's going on!). I like to think that, as humans, we are somehow hardwired to like complexity; that the not-knowing-what-is-coming-next quality of a thing is inherently gravitational.

It's important to note that complex wines don't have to be powerful, full-bodied wines. As Jurgen Wagner, the winemaker of Capçanes winery in Spain, once said to me, "If someone tells me a wine is fragile, I consider it a good thing. Fragility is complex. I love introverted wines because, like introverted people, they know they are good; they don't have to show off."

BEYOND FRUITNESS

The description "fruity" has become such a positive in the past two decades that what I'm about to suggest may seem surprising, even sacrilegious. But the fact remains: The great wines of the world are not merely fruity. Fruitiness alone often comes off in a juvenile, sophomoric way—like wearing an all-pink dress. Great

wines go beyond fruit and are woven through with complicated aromas and flavors—things like tar, bitter espresso, roasted meats, blood, worn leather, exotic spices, minerals, rocks, wet bark, and dead leaves, to name a few. These beyond-fruit characteristics give wine an even broader and deeper sensory impact and make it more intellectually stimulating.

LENGTH

The persistence of a wine on your palate, even after you've swallowed, is called its length or finish. The better the wine, the longer the length. By contrast, the flavor of a common wine disappears almost as soon as you swallow it. (This can be a blessing.)

In Sensual Geography: Tasting Wine Like a Professional (page 101), I talk about the method professionals use to get a good sense of the length. But here I simply want to state the importance of long persistence on the palate as a hallmark of great wines.

As an aside, no one knows why certain wines possess a long finish. Is it a vineyard characteristic? Something about certain vintages? A quality associated with physiological states like ripeness? There is no definitive thinking on this.

CHOREOGRAPHY

Since writing the first edition of *The Wine Bible* (2001), I have thought a lot about this aspect of great wine. Yet, what I'm about to describe has no agreed-upon language. Indeed, it's virtually never addressed in wine books. It's an added facet that great wine appears to possess—a kind of fifth dimension. To me, that extra dimension might be thought of as the choreographic character of a wine—the way its flavors appear to move physically and spatially. Does the wine appear to "grow" or blossom in the mouth? Does the wine almost attack the palate with explosive flavors, then crescendo and fade out in a slow ooze? Does the wine move with broad, sweeping brushstrokes? Or is it precise and pointillistic, like the tiny dots in certain Impressionist paintings? As my friend the importer Terry Theise would say, does it feel like Swedish massage or shiatsu?

One thing would appear true: The finest wines are multidimensional on the palate. There are wavelengths of flavor, force, volume, and velocity. In my experience, when the fifth dimension of a wine is spellbinding, you're in the midst of a great wine.

CONNECTEDNESS

Connectedness is perhaps the most elusive of these concepts and the most difficult quality to ascertain. It is the sense you get from the wine's aroma and flavor that it is the embodiment of a particular place. Connectedness is the bond between a wine and the land it was born in.

Connectedness, like cultural identity, makes a thing different from other things and therefore worthy of appreciation. It was, for example, innately satisfying when, not so long ago, Frenchmen still wore berets, when you could find only olive oil (not butter) in the south of Italy, when Spanish children were given wine-dipped bread sprinkled with sugar as a snack. Each of these things, small as they were, revealed the links between people and their cultures and homes. Wine without connectedness to the ground from which it came may be of good quality but, like a chain hotel in Rome, there is a limit to how deep one's aesthetic appreciation of it can be.

Connectedness, though hard to describe, is easy to find. Try a Côte-Rôtie (syrah) from the northern Rhône, with its almost savage peppery, gamey flavors, or a shimmeringly tart riesling from the Mosel region of Germany. Neither of these wines could come from anywhere other than the place it did.

ABILITY TO EVOKE AN EMOTIONAL RESPONSE

This is the final hallmark of greatness and, in many ways, it's the combined result of everything I've talked about so far. Great wines incite emotion. They stop you in your tracks. Send chills down your spine. Make you write things like "oh my God" as a tasting note.

Great wines appeal not only to the intellect; they have the rare power to make us *feel*.

Throughout its history, wine has always been a communal beverage. Drinking it implies sharing, generosity, and friendship. There's a reason wine is rarely sold in single-serving bottles!

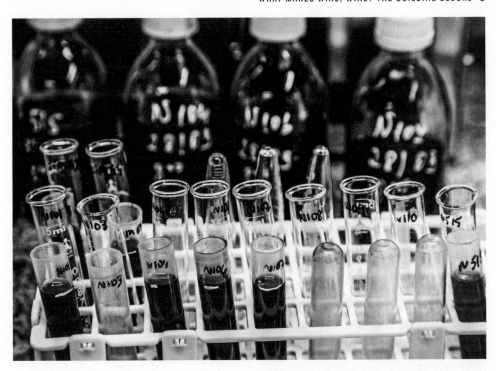

WHAT MAKES WINE, WINE? THE BUILDING BLOCKS

or all of wine's complexity, it is born of something utterly simple: a grape. A grape berry is, by weight, 75 percent pulp, 20 percent skin, and 5 percent seeds (there are usually two to four of them). Pulp is the soft, juicy center of the grape, and is what will become the wine. Mostly water and, after that, sugar, the pulp of a ripe grape contains minuscule amounts of acids, minerals, and pectin compounds, plus a trace of vitamins. It's the sugar in the pulp that is crucial to vinification, since it's the sugar that will be converted to alcohol. As for the skins, they get to play the sexy part. They're largely responsible for the wine's aroma and flavor, as well as its color and tannin, the compound that makes some wines feel slightly dry and taste bitter (more on this soon). But a bunch of grapes has a way to go before it can be called wine. And once it's transformed, there will be several components to consider: alcohol, acid, tannin, fruitiness, and dryness and sweetness. These are the structural building blocks of any wine. Let's look at each of them.

▲ *Wine is, of course, more than the sum of its parts. But today all wineries have laboratories to analyze a wine's components.*

HANG TIME

Let's say a grape variety normally takes 120 days to ripen. In an especially hot year, it may ripen after only 100 days; in a cooler year, after 130 days. Which situation would a viticulturist prefer? All other things being equal, viticulturists want a long growing season. Long ripening (a long hang time) allows components in the grape other than sugar—tannin, for example—to reach greater physiological maturity. Fully developed grapes, of course, hold more promise for a wine with fully developed flavors. Historically, perfectly ripe grapes that took a long time getting ripe often produced superior wines with more complex aromas and flavors. (For complexity, I always imagine the deep flavor of freshly squeezed orange juice from ripe oranges versus the shallow flavor of powdered mixes.) There's one important distinction here. Long hang time in the pursuit of ripeness (a good thing) is not the same as overripeness (a bad thing). When a wine has all the charm of prune juice crossed with flat cola, it isn't pretty.

ALCOHOL

Alcohol is a critical constituent in wine, not because of the genial mood it can evoke (although that's surely part of its charm), but rather because of the complex role it plays in the wine's structure, and the profound effect it can have on aroma and flavor. Alcohol occurs in wine as a result of yeasts. During fermentation, a yeast cell takes one sugar molecule in the grape pulp and turns it into two ethanol (alcohol) molecules. In the process, two carbon dioxide molecules and some heat are thrown off. (Tiny amounts of a few by-products are also created. One of the most important of these is glycerol, which gives wine a sweetness and may contribute a slightly viscous, mouth-coating texture.) The more sugar the grapes contain (that is, the riper they are), the higher the alcohol content of the final wine will be.

How does alcohol manifest itself in the wine? First and most important, alcohol determines the body of the wine. Quite simply: The more alcohol, the fuller the body. Thus, high alcohol wines feel weighty on the palate. They are the sensory equivalent of heavy cream, not skim milk. By comparison, very low-alcohol wines are so light in body they almost seem weightless (dry German rieslings are a good example).

Alcohol can also influence aroma and flavor. In a wine with very high alcohol, the aromas of the wine may be masked by the more dominant smell of the alcohol. What we call alcohol's aroma is actually more of a nasal burn. Put your nose directly over a bottle of rubbing alcohol and you'll probably instinctively and quickly want to turn away. When a wine has so much alcohol that all you get when you smell it is the burn, the wine is said to be "hot."

As for taste, alcohol can impact wine in two ways that are negative. First, high alcohol can mask the flavors of the wine, rendering them virtually meaningless because you can't taste them anyway. Second, a wine that's very high in alcohol is a wine that has come from very ripe grapes. If the grapes are so ripe they border on raisins, the wine can have a dull, "overcooked" fruit character. In the worst cases, very high-alcohol wines can come with flavors that are so mind-numbing and lifeless, one might as well mix grape jam with vodka and call it a day.

You notice I keep qualifying the alcohol as being "very" high. There is no agreement on what defines this. Moreover, it's true that the impression of alcohol may be mitigated by a significant level of other components—tannin, acidity, and fruit. All of this said, my sense is that many wine professionals (including me) would argue that once a table wine exceeds 15 percent alcohol by volume, the chances of it being elegant, being reflective of its place, and being distinctive, diminish considerably.

Today, ripe grapes the world over are generally picked quickly and put into small, squat boxes so that the weight of the grapes on top won't crush or bruise the fruit underneath.

ACID

As a grape ripens, its acid content decreases from around 3 percent usually to less than 1 percent, and its sugar content increases from 4 percent usually to more than 24 percent. The challenge is to harvest precisely when an optimal balance between the two is struck, for acidity is critical to the final balance, flavor, and feel of the wine.

Acidity gives wine liveliness, snappiness, freshness, and, to a certain extent, makes it thirst quenching. Acidity also "frames" the fruit, and gives the wine a sense of precision and clarity.

Without a sufficient amount of acidity, a dry wine seems languid, dull, flabby, amorphous, and flat. A sweet wine that doesn't have enough acidity will, in addition, taste overly saccharin and candied. In the end, having just the right amount of acidity is as pivotal in wine as it is in lemonade (actually more so).

Another concern: Wines that lack acidity do not age well and may be susceptible to spoilage. The vast majority of California and Australian chardonnays, for example, are not candidates for long keeping precisely because of their fairly low acidity. In fact, in warm wine regions where grapes quickly lose their natural acidity, winemakers commonly "adjust" the acid by adding 2 to 3 grams of tartaric acid per liter (.2 percent to .3 percent) to the fermenting wine. (Tartaric acid is one of the natural acids in grapes). Small as it is, this bit of natural acid can help a wine taste more focused.

But there's more to acidity than just the amount. While we have no good language to describe acidity in depth, many pros agree that what's important about acidity is not just the quantity but the quality of it. For example, German winemakers (acid experts if ever there were any), distinguish between harsh acidity (the sensory equivalent of shattering glass), round acidity (harmonious crispness), and candied acidity (the sweet, crystalline taste of powdered sour candies or drinks like Crystal Light).

One type of acidity, volatile acidity (often called V.A.), is not an inherent part of the grape, but instead is acetic acid formed by bacteria during or after fermentation. A tiny amount of volatile acidity is neither harmful nor perceptible. If, however, the bacteria are exposed to air and allowed to multiply, the resulting volatile acidity will make the wine smell vinegary and taste somewhat dank and sour. A wine with very noticeable volatile acidity is considered flawed.

TANNIN

Tannin is among the most intellectually intriguing components in wine. The amount of tannin, its physiological maturity, and the extent to which it is counterbalanced by other building blocks can all contribute to (or detract from) a wine's greatness, structure, and ageability.

Plants build tannins for protection, preservation, and defense. (Since Neolithic times, plant tannins have been used to prevent the spoilage of animal skins—when "tanning" hides into leather, for example). Tannin belongs to a class of complex compounds called phenols and comes primarily from the grapes' skins and seeds (stems, too, have tannin, but stems usually are not used in winemaking). Because

NICE LEGS . . .

The rivulets of wine that roll down the inside of the glass after a wine has been swirled are called *legs* in the United States, Canada, and Britain. The Spanish call them *tears*; the Germans, *church windows*. Some wine drinkers look for great legs, falsely believing that nicely shaped legs (and who knows what that means?) portend great flavor. In fact, legs are a complex phenomenon related to the rate at which liquids evaporate and the difference in surface tension between the wine's water and alcohol contents. Legs have nothing to do with greatness.

With wine, as with women, there is very little meaningful information one can deduce by looking at the legs.

THE TANNIN TABLE

On the facing page is my view of how various major red grape varieties compare in the amount of tannin they generally display. Climate, place, and factors such as vine yield, vine age, and winemaking can shift these relationships a bit. But in general, I think, this is a good guide.

red wines are fermented with their skins, and whites are not, tannin is a consideration primarily with red wines.

To begin with, different varieties of grapes are predisposed to having different amounts of tannin. Cabernet sauvignon, for example, generally has a lot of tannin; pinot noir has comparatively little.

What does tannin do for a wine? It provides two things: structure and ageability. Structure—which, in wine, is difficult to describe—is the sense that the wine has an underlying "architecture." The French sometimes refer to structure as the skeleton or backbone of the wine. With a well-defined structure, a wine takes on a certain formidableness and beauty. Structured wines feel impressive on the palate. Tannin is also, as just noted, a natural preservative. All other things being equal, wines with significant amounts of tannin live longer than wines without. Look at any collector's cellar and you're likely to see wines like cabernet sauvignon and Bordeaux—wines that have a lot of tannin and therefore have a good chance of living well into the future.

From a sensory standpoint, tannin has both a taste and a feel. The taste of tannin is bitterness—good bitterness, like espresso or dark chocolate. The feel of tannin is astringency or dryness. When tannin in the grapes is physiologically mature or "ripe," the feeling of dryness in the final wine is slight, and the taster simply senses that the wine has a commanding structure. If, on the other hand, the tannin in

GAMAY PINOT NOIR SANGIOVESE GRENACHE ZINFANDEL SYRAH MALBEC MERLOT MOURVÈDRE CABERNET FRANC CABERNET SAUVIGNON PETITE SIRAH NEBBIOLO

LEAST TANNIC VARIETIES   MOST TANNIC VARIETIES

the grapes is completely unripe, the dryness in the wine can be so gripping and harsh it feels like your palate has been shrink-wrapped. If you've ever bitten into an unripe persimmon, you know the severely drying, puckery feeling of immature tannin.

So, what causes tannin to be ripe or unripe? In a word: sun. As grapes become ripe, in general, the sugar in them builds, the acidity drops, and slowly the tannin matures.

Imagine the ideal situation: Sugar would build just enough to provide ripe (but not over-ripe) fruit flavors in the final wine; the acidity would drop but not disappear (remember, some acidity is essential); and the tannin would evolve from something harsh-feeling to mellow. Alas, it's difficult to get this timing down perfectly. Say, for example, bad weather forces

a vintner to pick his grapes before the tannin has had a chance to mature fully. The wine he makes in this case will certainly be drinkable—even, perhaps, enjoyable. But it will definitely have a rough grip to it. The vinous equivalent of Clint Eastwood with a five-o'clock shadow.

Critical as ripe tannin is to the final texture of the wine, you'd think there would be a high-tech way to test grapes to see if the tannin is ripe. There isn't. The only device that exists is the oldest tool of all: one's senses. Watch a winemaker as harvest approaches, and if that winemaker makes red wine, it's a sure bet he walks the vineyards constantly, tasting hundreds of grape berries and squeezing them open to look at the seeds. The seeds turn a nutty brown as the tannin ripens. But most

THE CLINT EASTWOOD
FIVE-O'CLOCK-SHADOW EFFECT

Why does tannin sometimes come across with such grip? Why is it sometimes so drying? Short of an organic chemistry course, here's what's happening. Tannin molecules in wine are hugely attracted to the protein in saliva (of which there is a copious amount). In effect, it's not that tannin itself is drying. It's that saliva, bound up by tannin molecules, can no longer lubricate the palate, and as result, your mouth tissues rub against one another, causing your palate to feel dry. At this

point, the story gets complex, and chemists aren't sure what happens to tannins to cause some of them to glide over the palate (causing you to perhaps describe the wine as "silky"). Do tannin molecules get longer and slip more easily across the palate? Until recently, scientists thought so. But new research describes tannin as complex structures that form, re-form, and combine with all manner of other molecules, sometimes with soft, tactile results. In the end, no one is sure why some wines come across as Clint Eastwood with a five o'clock shadow.

HOW SWEET IT IS (OR ISN'T)

Amazingly, there is no international, or even national, consensus on the meaning of terms like dry, off-dry, medium dry, medium sweet, semisweet, and so on. In 2002, the European Union did legislate the definition of some of these terms. But the definitions depend on the wines' acidity levels. So, for example, a "dry" European wine cannot have any more than .4 percent residual sugar, unless that wine has "suitable acidity," in which case it can have up to .9 percent residual sugar and still be considered dry. From a taste perception standpoint, this does make sense; but it also makes it next to impossible to grasp where one term ends and another begins. In the United States and much of the New World, producers decide for themselves what

terms to use and what those terms mean. The only simple guideline in the U.S. (and it's not law) is suggested by the Sweet and Fortified Wine Association. Here are their definitions:

DRY: Less than .5 percent residual sugar

OFF-DRY: .5 percent to 1.9 percent residual sugar

SEMISWEET: 2 percent to 6 percent residual sugar

SWEET: More than 6 percent residual sugar

Note that if these definitions were legally adopted in the United States, most chardonnays would probably need to be labeled "off-dry."

---

important, he's tasting for that moment when the feel of the grape skins changes, when the tannin switches from unripe to ripe.

For any good taster, then, there are two dimensions to consider when thinking about tannin in a wine. First, how much tannin does one perceive? Second, what is the quality, or ripeness, of that tannin?

Finally, the perception of tannin can be changed by food. In other words, to some extent tannin can be "solved" by a lamb chop. For more thoughts on this, see Marrying Well: Wine and Food, page 115.

FRUITINESS

As the word suggests, fruitiness is simply the propensity of a wine to display ripe, fruitlike aromas and flavors. Fruitiness is most marked in young wines and is rarely found in mature ones. Some varieties—gewürztraminer and gamay, for example—are characteristically very fruity. Gewürztraminer, a white wine

made notably in the Alsace region of France, has effusive lychee aromas and flavors; drinking gamay (the red grape of Beaujolais) is like diving into a pool of black cherries. Fruitiness is often confused with sweetness, but the two are distinctly different.

DRYNESS AND SWEETNESS

Dryness is a funny word to apply to wine, which, after all, is wet. But in the world of wine, *dry* means that the wine has no more natural grape sugar that could be converted into alcohol during fermentation. (Don't confuse the term dry here with the idea of a wine displaying a drying or astringent sensation as a result of tannin.) If a wine has any natural grape sugar left—that is, if some of the sugar was not converted to alcohol during fermentation—then the wine is said to have residual sugar. Importantly, a little bit of residual sugar does not necessarily make the wine as sweet as dessert wine. In fact, most of us would not be

In the "quiet" winter months after the harvest, wineries are busy analyzing and repeatedly tasting the different lots of wine that they've fermented. Preliminary blends—often many dozens of them—will be painstakingly made.

> Colas, by the way, clock in at about 11 percent residual sugar; most wines that you'd have with dinner would be 0 to perhaps 2 percent residual sugar.

able to detect a small amount of residual sugar in wine. A lot of so-called "dry" California chardonnays, for example, actually have a little residual sugar to make them taste mellow. Ironically, of course, many people swear they like only dry wines (even while happily drinking one of those chardonnays). In fact, the presence of sweetness in beverages appears to be uniquely a wine problem. After all, no one says, "I don't want any sweetness in my Coke." (Colas, by the way, clock in at about 11 percent residual sugar; most wines that you'd have with dinner would be 0 to perhaps 2 percent residual sugar.)

In order to be considered a sweet wine (not a dinner wine), a wine has to have quite a lot of residual sugar. According to European Union legislation, for example, a wine labeled sweet must have at least 4.5 percent residual sugar. Most of Europe's great sweet wines, however, have considerably more than that. Port, for example, generally has approximately 8 percent residual sugar; Sauternes, 10 to 15 percent; German *trockenbeerenauslesen* (TBAs), as much as 30 percent; and some of Spain's fabled, opulent Pedro Ximénezes have over 40 percent residual sugar.

There are also several notable styles of wine where a tiny bit of sweetness is critical to balance the poignancy of the wine's acidity. This is true, for example, with Champagne, some German rieslings, and some French Vouvrays (chenin blanc). With these wines, a little sweetness is used to counterbalance the wines' soaringly high acidity. By way of an analogy, think about a really bitter espresso. A quarter teaspoon of sugar in the espresso would not make the espresso sweet. But it would mollify the edges of the bitterness.

Sweetness, then, can either be a goal, as in dessert wines, or it can be a counterpoint, something used in small amounts to create overall balance and harmony.

WHERE IT ALL BEGINS

n the drama of wine, the land itself is a character—rough and brutal sometimes, but also tender and, ultimately, fragile. The wine that comes from it in any given year will never exist again. How is it that the land gives us this continual gift? It is an unanswerable question, for in a literal sense, great wine is not made, but rather revealed and released from the land. I often think of the story of Michelangelo's *Pietà*, depicting the Madonna holding her crucified son in her arms. When asked how he could sculpt such divine beauty, Michelangelo is said to have replied that he did not make it; he *freed* it from the block of stone.

Great wines don't come from just anywhere. The Earth has her own vinous erogenous zones—a few places of harmonic

Vit, the Latin root of the word *viticulture,* is also the source of *vita*—life itself.

convergence, where every facet of the vineyard and every nuance of the grape fit together like chromosomes on a DNA helix. In these rare places, grapes and ground are transformed into thrilling wine. Indeed, it is grapes' ability to reflect the character of the place where they were grown that separates wine from beer and

▲ *Whether their farming approach is high-tech or traditional (as with Alta Vista's malbec vineyard in Mendoza, Argentina, above), all vintners work within the demands of a vineyard's microclimate and soils. Here, the canopy of leaves helps shade the grapes from too much heat and potential sunburn.*

TERROIR

The French word *terroir* has no single-word equivalent in English. Historically, terroir has been defined as the sum of every environmental force affecting a given vineyard site. Soil, slope, orientation to the sun, and elevation are all part of a vineyard's terroir, as is every nuance of climate, including rainfall, wind velocity, frequency of fog, cumulative hours of sunshine, average high and low temperatures, and so forth. The late twentieth and early twenty-first centuries have been a time of profound discussion about the importance of terroir versus winemaking. Is a wine great because of natural forces that have come together in near Platonic perfection? Or must all great wines be "realized" by the skilled hand of a winemaker? Can human intervention itself—from the way the grapes are farmed to the way the wine is aged—be considered part of terroir? Indeed, does terroir even exist? "It's the question of our time— the enological equivalent of 'Is God dead?'" says Randall Grahm, proprietor and winemaker of Bonny Doon Vineyard in California.

"What single cloudless day, what soft late rainfall decides that a vintage shall be great among the others? Human care can do almost nothing towards it. It is all celestial wizardry, the orbits of planets, sunspots. . . ."

—COLETTE,
Prisons et Paradis

a comfortable constant, while technologies are fascinatingly new.

As the twenty-first century emerged, however, the picture in the foreground was already changing. The ancient idea that "wine is made in the vineyard" began once again to take prominence. In the New World especially, it seemed as if wineries were going back to the future. For the first time in modern memory, the person who grew the grapes was given as much credit for the wine as the person who made it.

In this chapter, we'll consider wine from the perspective of viticulture, the science of grape growing. Although a vineyard may appear passive and pastoral to the casual observer, to the viticulturist it is a powerful, animate ecosphere full of complexities. Independently and synergistically, such factors as climate, soil, grape variety and clone, rootstock, spacing, and many others push and pull wine in different directions. Like the colors in a kaleidoscope, these elements are swirled together in thousands of intricate, unique patterns, profoundly influencing the aroma, flavor, body, and finish of a wine. It's these nuances of individuality that viticulture celebrates. In the end, fine wines are compelling not because they are the same, but because they are different.

spirits. Wheat and potatoes do not give "voice" to their environments. But grapes do.

The last three decades of the twentieth century were a time when sweeping advancements in winemaking commanded much of the wine world's attention. And rightfully so. With new technologies and scientifically trained winemakers, entire countries—Portugal, Spain, Argentina—were lifted out of what might be called "peasant winemaking." Others, such as New Zealand, sprang, already sophisticated, onto the scene. But if technology has sometimes seemed more sexy than dirt, it is only because in the history of wine, dirt has been

CLIMATE

ature influences wine quality conspicuously and dauntlessly through climate. For starters,

Flowering, as it is known, is that fragile time in spring when grape clusters pollinate themselves. Every fertilized flower will become a grape.

climate determines whether grapes can exist at all. Grapevines thrive in temperate regions where long, warm, frost-free periods allow them to develop. Specifically, vines begin to grow when the ambient temperature reaches about 50°F (the precise temperature varies from one grape variety to another). Below 50°F (10°C), the vines remain dormant. When the average daily temperature reaches 63°F to 68°F (17°C to 20°C), vines will bud and then flower. Flowering is critical, for only those flowers that become pollinated and "set" on the cluster become individual grape berries. As crucial as it is, set is an extremely fragile phenomenon. Even under favorable climatic conditions, up to 85 percent of a vine's flowers never set at all and are destined to die as "shatter." As the temperature moves into the mid-80s, (28°C to 30°C) vines hit their growth stride and flourish.

If you narrow your field of vision, you find "climates" within climates, created by such factors as the proximity of oceans and bays; the presence of hills and mountains; the slope, orientation, and altitude of the vineyard; plus wind, cloudiness, and precipitation.

In fact, while we use the general term *climate* to describe most situations, viticulturists distinguish between macroclimate, mesoclimate, and microclimate. Macroclimate (often just called climate) is the weather patterns of a general area over a long period of time, usually the average of thirty years or more. Mesoclimate, the climate of a small area, is caused by local variations in topography and vegetation, as well as by human actions. Mesoclimates are found over lakes and in big cities. Vineyards often have unique mesoclimates. Far smaller in scale is a microclimate, or the climate in which a vine exists. A microclimate is defined as that area around a vine that extends 6 feet (2 meters) above the ground and about 3 feet (1 meter) into the soil, below the ground.

Climates can be counterintuitive. Take, as an example, the Napa Valley—a small wine region and yet one that has multiple distinct temperature zones. Calistoga—the warmest part of the Napa Valley—is, surprisingly, the farthest north. Carneros—as much as 30°F (17°C) cooler than Calistoga—is nonetheless the farthest south. Another even more dramatic reversal of the expected: Several of the wine regions in Santa Barbara County, nearly 300 miles (483 kilometers) to the south of Napa, are some of the coolest in California.

A YEAR AS A GRAPE

During the course of a single year, grapes and vines go through several important stages. The life cycle begins in the spring, around April 1 in the northern hemisphere (the dates are six months later in the southern hemisphere), when new shoots—small, green, feathery branches—emerge from dormant buds on the vine. This is called bud break. As May arrives, the shoots lengthen and tiny flowers appear which "set," that is, pollinate themselves (helpfully, cultivated grapevines are hermaphroditic). The pollinated flowers grow into tiny berries that stay green and hard until midsummer. In July, the berries begin to soften, swell, and change color (called veraison). The skins of white varieties will turn shades of yellow, gray, and light pink; red varieties will turn purple and some will appear almost blue-black. Come fall—usually September through October—the grapes will be harvested. Finally, in November and December, the vine loses its leaves and goes into dormancy until the following spring when the cycle will begin anew.

In both of these cases, proximity to the ocean matters more than latitude when it comes to climate. Santa Barbara's wine regions, for example, are east-west-running valleys that form virtual wind tunnels for bracing breezes and fog drawn in off the Pacific Ocean.

Ironically, bodies of water can have a cooling effect or a warming effect, or both, at different times. Water tempers and stabilizes the climate. A marine breeze can cool down a hot vineyard, but it can also warm a vineyard where temperatures are dropping and frost threatens.

One of the most intriguing aspects of any wine region's climate is the impact hillsides and mountains can have and how that subsequently affects the ripeness of the grapes. A mountain's creased face contains crevices, caverns, and canyons that become nichelike mesoclimates on their own. Mountains can block cold winds, acting as shields behind which grapes can mature. They can also impede ripeness, acting as huge slides that cause frost and cold air to pool in vineyards on the valley floor. If high enough, mountains also force clouds to give up their moisture as frequent rain on one side, while the other side basks in the sun. A perfect example of this is found in Washington State, where the Cascade mountain range causes the western part of the state near Seattle to be extremely overcast and rainy, while in the eastern part, grapes—with the help of irrigation—thrive in sunny, near desert conditions. Mountains also offer the

The old zinfandel vines of the Napa Valley have never grown on trellises. Their stark, twisted trunks are especially striking in spring when all around them grow stems of vivid yellow wild mustard.

For every winery in the world, the most important decision of the year is when to pick. Once the decision is made, crews work relentlessly and quickly to harvest the grapes at optimal ripeness.

possibility of different vineyard altitudes. A vineyard at 2,500 feet (762 meters) will generally (but not always) be cooler overall than one at 500 feet (152 meters) on the same mountain. Not surprisingly, the wines will usually be strikingly different.

In general, in very cool regions like northern Germany, the most prized vineyards are always on mountainsides, since slopes angled precisely southward act like huge solar panels catching every ray of the sun. (In the southern hemisphere, cold-climate vineyards face north.) Sometimes even the name of a vineyard reveals this importance. On the cool alpine foothills of Piedmont, Italy, famous vineyards often contain the words *bricco* or *sorì*, as in the Bricco Asili vineyard of the producer Ceretto or the Sorì Tildìn vineyard of Angelo Gaja. A *bricco* is the sun-catching crest of a hill; *sorì* in Piedmontese dialect means a south-facing slope where the sun melts the snow first.

Alas, sun can be a double-edged sword. In some wine regions, too little sun is not the problem—too much is. Intense sun can cause grapes to lose considerable acidity through respiration, leading to flat, flabby wine, or cause hyperactive leaf growth, which shades the grapes and may lead to vegetal and other off flavors in the wine. As heat becomes excessive, unprotected grapes begin to scorch and their leaves wither and burn. At about 104°F (40°C), sustained heat becomes intolerable for most grapevines, and the grapes start to shrivel into raisins. Thus, wine producers in hot, sunny climates often face hurdles that are the complete opposite of those faced by wine producers in cooler climates.

But no matter where they are located, viticulturists are trying to find balance in the vineyard, in much the same way that a winemaker aims for balance in a wine. When this is achieved, the vines reach a healthy medium between what viticulturists call vigor (growth of leaves and shoots), and fruitfulness (number of grape clusters and size of grapes).

Finally, the biggest current concern regarding the impact of climate on viticulture is the issue of climate change. It is fair to say that winemakers nearly the world over name climate change as a major—if not *the* major—worry facing wine regions today. The effects of climate change on viticulture can already be felt in many parts of the world, including Spain, where new plantings are focused on high-heat-tolerant varieties, and Germany, where a decade of warm temperatures has led winemakers to experiment with warm-loving red varieties as well as cold-tolerant varieties such as riesling. What climate change ultimately means for wine regions around the world is not fully known, but some of those

THE BANE OF RAIN AND THE HELL OF HAIL

Rain, especially just before or during harvest, is dreaded throughout the wine world. Why? Absorbed quickly through the roots, rainwater can bloat the grapes, diluting their flavors. Severe rain can actually tear open grapes or even break off the bunches, destroying the crop. If the rain is followed by warm temperatures, high humidity, and no wind, rot or mildew can easily take hold. Finally, trying to pick grapes when the vineyard is a foot deep in mud is no picnic.

Hail is even worse. Defined as large, irregular clumps of icy frozen water (sometimes as large as golf balls), hail can occur as part of a thunderstorm and wreak devastating damage. A hail storm in 2013 that swept through Bordeaux, Burgundy, and Champagne (in each region it lasted no longer than ten minutes) turned hundreds of acres of vineyard into wasteland. The damage in Bordeaux alone was estimated at over 100 million euros.

what is ideal is not a perfect environment but, rather, something less than consummate. A perfectly sunny, hot climate augmented by moisture and fertile soils with ample nutrients may be good for many plants (as jungles testify), but is usually too much for grapevines. All of the world's great vineyards are in places that are in some way marginal. Assuming that the stress (from lack of sun, water, and/ or nutrients) is not so severe that the vines shut down, go into shock, or die, an endurable amount of adversity forces grapevines to struggle, adapt, and put their energy into their reproductive system to ensure survival. The essential element of a vine's reproductive system is, of course, its grapes. When healthy vines are forced to concentrate their sugars in a limited number of grape clusters, the result is grapes and wine of greater character and concentration.

TEMPERATURE SWINGS

Many winegrowers believe that good stress can come in the form of wide temperature fluctuations, either from spring to fall or from day to night or both. Temperature swings can help create balance.

The difference between average daytime and average nighttime temperatures is called diurnal temperature fluctuation. For example, wine regions that are extremely hot during the day, like Ribera del Duero, on the north-central plains of Spain, benefit from nights that can be as much as 40°F (22°C) cooler, effectively shutting down the ripening process and helping grapes to preserve essential acidity. By delaying ripening, cool nights also extend the span of time from bud break to harvest, leading to better total physiological maturity.

As for seasonal change, grapevines don't like ambiguity. Vines need definitive temperature cues so that bud break and grape development and maturation proceed steadily and uniformly, ensuring (all other things being

regions are taking an active approach to the issue. The Napa Valley vintners, for example, employ climate scientists from the Scripps Institute to conduct research and collect data on the effect of climate change on viticulture within the valley.

STRESS

One of the few monodimensional rules is one of wine's wonderful curiosities. In making fine wine,

ROCK GROUP

Grapevines are impacted not only by the soils they grow in, but also by the type of rock that may be present. The basic rock forms are:

SEDIMENTARY ROCK: It includes arenaceous (e.g., sandstone), argillaceous (e.g., clay), calcareous (e.g., limestone), carbonaceous (e.g., peat, lignite, or coal), and siliceous (e.g., quartz).

IGNEOUS ROCK: Formed from molten or partially molten material, most igneous rocks are crystalline.

METAMORPHIC: Sedimentary or igneous rock that has been transformed by heat or pressure. Examples of metamorphic rock include marble and slate.

equal) a good harvest. Very warm winters can awaken vines. With nutrients being pumped into their shoots, vines soon become confused and begin to bud in the wrong season. Uneven or untimely budding can wreak havoc on a vineyard, creating a patchwork quilt of mixed-up vines, all maturing at different rates and times. A definitively cold winter, followed by its opposite, a definitively warm spring and summer, is the optimal viticultural scenario.

WATER AND FROST

Like sunlight, the water that vines receive must be part of an overall balanced environment. There is no optimal amount. How much water vines need (and when they need it) depends on a number of factors, including the age and size of the vines, the length of the growing season, the temperatures during the growing season, wind, humidity, the drainage and water-holding capacity of the soil, and the spacing of the vines, to name a few.

Vines are not arbitrary in the way they grow; they search for water. Well-drained soils encourage the roots to burrow deeper into the earth, where they find a more stable environment of moisture and nutrients. Vines with fully developed root systems can handle drought or other climatic difficulties better.

In the world's generally dry wine regions—including parts of California, Washington State, Australia, Chile, Spain, and Portugal—lack of rainfall can be exacerbated by long, droughtlike summers. In the New World, these wine growing regions generally allow irrigation, although increasing limitations on water resources are destined to make viticulture more difficult in these places.

In most of Europe, irrigation is forbidden (under severe vintage circumstances, restrictions are sometimes temporarily lifted). In Europe, natural rainfall and moisture is often sufficient to grow healthy vines. Prohibiting irrigation is seen as a way of ensuring quality, since vines given excess water can produce swollen grapes with diluted flavors. This "dilution effect" is also, of course, one of the reasons winemakers fear too much rain.

Not surprisingly, timing is everything. In the spring, right before flowering, vines need some water to jump-start growth. Without water at this critical moment, the flowers will not set properly—and therefore will not create grape berries. Water is also critical during veraison, that time in summer when the grapes begin to change color. A lack of water then can lead to excessively small grapes that never achieve maturity.

One form of water—frost—is unconditionally a threat to grapes and grapevines. Spring frosts may kill buds and shoots and thus destroy the potential for a crop. Early fall frosts can destroy entire swaths of vineyards, or ravage foliage enough that ripening is impeded, resulting in weakly flavored wines. Even in winter, when the vine is dormant, an

In the mountainous Priorat region of northeastern Spain, old, low-yielding carignan vines are almost entirely covered by snow in winter. With their deep roots and sturdy trunks, old vines are generally able to withstand extremely cold temperatures.

excessive cold snap can be ruinous. Below 25°F (-4°C), the vine's trunk may split, leaving it open to infection. After prolonged below-freezing temperatures, the entire vine and root system can die.

The methods used to counter frost are often desperate and generally expensive, but vintners have no choice; the financial repercussions of losing an entire year's crop are too severe. Giant windmill-like frost protectors are fixtures in many cold areas. These help stir up the warm air hovering above the vineyard and mix it with the colder air that has settled like a thick blanket under the vines. A more expensive takeoff on the windmill idea is to hire helicopters to fly low over the vineyards, zigzagging back and forth until the threat of frost has passed. And finally, there's a solution that seems crazy, but works: spraying the vines with water, using overhead sprinklers. The water coats the leaves, shoots, and buds, forming a thin glove of ice that insulates the vines from windchill and traps the plant's natural heat. That incremental amount of insulation, coupled with the tiny amount of heat thrown off when water turns to ice, is enough to keep the leaves, shoots, and buds from freezing unless it gets significantly colder.

WIND

On the Aegean Islands of Greece—one of the most windswept wine regions of the world—not even the mostly-impervious-to-everything olive tree can grow. Vines survive only because they are trained in a circular manner so close to the ground that they look like large doughnuts, with the grapes crouching even lower in the center hole. Each vine is called a *stefáni* (crown); it will grow that way for twenty years, after which time the trunk becomes strong enough to withstand the whipping wind, and the vine can be trained somewhat more upright.

Most wine regions are not subject to such gales, but wind still torments grapevines in many parts of the world. Although a gentle breeze is almost always good (it cools the grapes and promotes air circulation as a guard against rot), a slashing wind is another story. Right after flowering, a severe wind can prevent flowers from setting properly, scattering them in the air so that they never fertilize and become grapes.

The Soils to Know

Exactly how a wine's flavors are influenced by the type of soil the grapes are grown in remains one of wine's central mysteries. Yet, for the past millennium, winemakers everywhere have considered soil a critical factor in the character of any given wine. Soil not only retains heat (or not), reflects sunlight (or not), and holds nutrients for the vines, soil also importantly influences water drainage. A good soil must retain enough water to steadily supply the vine, but not so much water that the roots become saturated. Below you'll find basic descriptions of some of the main types of soil that vines are known to live in (and often thrive in).

ALLUVIAL SOIL Fertile soil that has been transported down a slope, usually by a river or stream. At the bottom of the slope, alluvial soil usually forms a fan that contains gravel, sand, and silt. Alluvial soils are found, for example, in the Napa Valley, especially near the area of western Oakville at the foot of the Mayacamas Mountains.

BASALT Cooled lava from volcanic rock that is high in calcium, iron, and magnesium. Very evident in the Willamette Valley of Oregon, to name one place.

CALCAREOUS SOIL Alkaline soil with high levels of calcium and magnesium carbonate. Often calcareous soils are "cool," which means they retain water and delay ripening, thereby leading to more acidic wines.

CHALK Very porous, soft limestone soil that vine roots can easily penetrate. A classic soil in Champagne, France, among other places.

CLAY Sedimentary rock–based soil that has good water retention ability but poor drainage. The soil is often very "cool" and high in acidity. The Right Bank of Bordeaux is dominated by clay-based soils.

FLINT Siliceous stone (sedimentary rocks that contain silica from silica-secreting organisms such as diatoms and some types of sea sponges) that reflects sun and heat well. The Pouilly-Fumé wines of the Loire Valley are generally produced from flint-based soils.

GALESTRO Schist-based soil found in the Tuscany region of Italy.

GNEISS A coarse-grained form of granite.

GRANITE A hard, mineral-rich soil that is composed of 40 percent to 60 percent quartz. The soil warms quickly and retains heat well. Thus, granite soils are ideal with acidic grapes like gamay. Granite is found in Beaujolais, as well as in the Cornas region of the northern Rhône Valley.

GRAVEL Soil that is loose and pebbly and has good drainage and poor fertility. Vines planted in this type of soil must penetrate deeply to find nutrients in the subsoil. The Graves and Sauternes regions of Bordeaux consist predominantly of gravel-based soil.

GREYWACKE Sedimentary soil formed by rivers depositing quartz, mudstone, and feldspar. It is found in vineyards of Germany, New Zealand, and South Africa.

HARDPAN A dense layer of clay or other material that is impermeable to water. In some areas of Bordeaux, a sandy, iron-rich layer is located deep enough below the surface to act as the bottom of a water table for the vines.

LIMESTONE A wide range of sedimentary-based soils consisting of calcium carbonates, many of which are formed from the skeletal fragments of marine organisms. Limestone is consistently alkaline and is generally planted with grapes of high acidity levels. This is a main soil type in Burgundy, Champagne, and several parts of the Loire Valley. Because limestone is a remnant of some ancient seabeds, certain islands (including the Florida Keys) are made from limestone.

LLICORELLA A soil type found in the Priorat appellation of Spain. The soil is a mix of slate and quartz that is very porous and drains well.

LOAM Warm, soft, fertile soil composed of roughly equal amounts of silt, sand, and clay. It is typically too fertile for high-quality wines.

LOESS very fine, silt-based soil composed of wind-borne sediment that is typically angular and decalcified. The soil has good water retention and warming properties. Loess is a common soil type in top Austrian and Washington State vineyards.

MARL Calcareous clay–based soil that is "cool" and thus delays ripening, resulting in wines with prominent acidity. Marl is typically deep and lacking in stone fragments; it is the main soil type in the Piedmont wine region of Italy.

QUARTZ A common material found in sand- and silt-based soils. The high soil pH of quartz can reduce the acidity of the resulting wines. But quartz also stores heat, so it can increase ripening of the grapes. Quartz is very notable in the vineyards of the lower Nahe in Germany, where the wines have stone-fruit and wet stone flavors.

SAND Warm, airy soil that is composed of tiny particles of weathered rocks. One of the few soils that the insect phylloxera does not thrive in (see page 30). The soil drains well but does not have good water retention. Sand is a main component in the soils of California's south central coast near Santa Barbara. Sandstone is a sedimentary soil composed of sand particles that has been pressure-bound by various iron-based minerals.

SCHIST Laminated, crystalline rock–based soil that retains heat well and is rich in magnesium and potassium, but is poor in organic nutrients and nitrogen. The upper slopes of Alsace's Andlau region are planted on schist-based soils.

SHALE Fine-grain sedimentary-based soil that can turn into slate when under geologic pressure. The soil is moderately fertile and retains heat well. New York State's Finger Lakes region boasts shale-rich soil, brought by glacial deposits hundreds of thousands of years ago.

SILEX A flint- and sand-based soil type, found primarily in the Loire Valley, that is formed from a mixture of clay, limestone, and silica.

SILT Soil type consisting of fine-grain deposits that offer good water retention but poor drainage. It is more fertile than sand.

SLATE The most common soil type of the Mosel region of Germany. Slate is a metamorphic, platelike rock formed when shale, clay, or siltstone is subjected to pressure deep within the earth. The soil retains heat well and warms up relatively quickly.

TERRA ROSSA A sedimentary soil, known as "red earth," that is formed after carbonates have been leached out of limestone. The breakdown leaves behind iron deposits that oxidize and turn the soil a rustic red color. This soil type is found in some areas along the Mediterranean and in Coonawarra, Australia.

TUFA A highly friable calcareous soil created from exploding volcanic rock flung into the air. Common in the Loire Valley of France.

VOLCANIC Soil that is derived from one of two volcanic activities. 1) Vent-based volcanic soil is formed from rock material or molten globules that have been ejected at high velocity into the air and then have cooled before settling to the earth (such as tufa). 2) Lava-based volcanic soil is the product of molten lava flows from a volcano. Ninety percent of lava-based soil is basalt.

For a more extensive list of soils in which grapevines grow, I recommend Tom Stevenson's excellent *New Sotheby's Wine Encyclopedia*.

WHERE WERE THE WORLD'S FIRST WINE GRAPES GROWN?

Turkey may not have as much cachet as Bordeaux, but Anatolia, in southern Turkey, is in effect the world's first wine appellation, according to research conducted by Swiss grape geneticist Dr. José Vouillamoz, of the University of Neuchâtel in Switzerland, and Dr. Patrick McGovern, scientific director of the Biomolecular Archaeology Laboratory at the University of Pennsylvania Museum in Philadelphia. The teams' research, published in 2012, indicates that people in Anatolia—part of the historic Fertile Crescent—grew and harvested grapevines to make wine as long ago as 8000 B.C., and possibly before.

Vouillamoz and McGovern unearthed the origin of domesticated wine grapes by comparing the DNA sequences of cultivated grapevines with the DNA sequences of wild grapevines all over the world. The greatest similarities between the two were found in wild grapevines growing in Anatolia, although areas of Iran, Georgia, Armenia, and Azerbaijan also tell tales of early domestication and wine drinking. Clay jars used to store and age wine have been found in all of these areas, some dating to 5400 B.C.

Wild grapevines were abundant in Anatolia around the same time that Stone Age farmers settled into villages and domesticated wild grains. Vouillamoz and McGovern hypothesize that the Anatolians collected the berries from the vines they found growing freely along the ground and high up into trees. When it was discovered that the fermented juice of these wild grapes was delicious (not to mention euphorically mind-altering), the farmers appear to have begun planting wild grapevines alongside their grains. Ten thousand years later, the wines you sip are made from distant descendants of these early vines.

One of the fascinating facts revealed by the research is that many popular grape varieties, all from the grape species *Vitis vinifera*, are more closely related than previously thought. For example, dense, peppery syrah is the unexpected great-grand-child of subtle, delicate pinot noir. Pinot (responsible for pinot noir, pinot blanc, and pinot gris grapes) is closely related to the French grape savagnin, but so far no one can tell which grape descended from the other. And although it makes only a neutral-tasting quaffing wine, gouais blanc, the surprising Casanova of wine grapes, is the parent of more than eighty other grape varieties, including chardonnay, riesling, and gamay.

Bludgeoning wind can break off tender parts of the vines, damage the canes, bruise the leaves, and even rip away the fruit. Lastly, a harsh wind may cause the vine to close its stomata, microscopic holes in the undersides of the leaves that are responsible for evaporation. With the stomata closed, the vine ceases to draw water through its root tips. Eventually, all growth comes to a halt.

SOIL

The ground has always been seductive—the smell of it, the feel of it, the sight of it, and certainly the possession of it. The history of civilization is in large part a running commentary on man's relationship to the land. Soil's allure is very evident in the world of wine. There is something

Soil is undeniably seductive. For thousands of years, it has also been the intellectual assumption behind a wine's character—that is, the notion that a given wine tastes the way it does because of the soil it was born in.

strangely beautiful about the white chalk of Champagne, the legacy of ancient seabeds and sea fossils; or the jet-black, pitted stones of Santorini in Greece, the relics of a massive volcanic explosion; or the cool, blue-gray slate shards of the Mosel in Germany, remnants of the path of glaciers. Remarkably, vines grow contentedly in all of these.

Soil is defined as the naturally occurring loose particles that cover the Earth's surface. Soil is composed of tiny bits of broken rock, the pore spaces of air between them, water, minerals, and organic matter. There are five main factors in the creation of soil: parent material, climate, topography, biota, and time.

Scientists classify soil into six categories. The broadest category are soil orders, and there are twelve in the world (interestingly, in the small Napa Valley, six of the world's twelve soil orders can be found). From orders, soils are more and more finely categorized. Ultimately, the most specific classification is called a soil series. In the U.S., for one example, there are some seventeen thousand soil series, each marked by a unique set of characteristics based on the arrangement of the soil's layers, its color, texture, structure, consistency, and chemical and mineralogical properties.

As far as grapevines are concerned, one of the important factors of any soil is the size of the soil's particles. Larger particles such as sand (relatively loose, large grains of weathered rock) can be important for good drainage. But smaller particles such as silt and clay are also important, for these may help hold just enough water to support the vine's growth. Other particles, such as rocks and organic matter, also help create the delicate balance of water drainage versus water retention. In addition, rocks and organic matter aerate the soil and contribute minerals and nutrients.

Most viticulturalists today believe that the most important soil characteristic is its capacity to drain water. Nothing could seem less exciting, yet good drainage is critical in viticulture, ensuring that vines push their roots deep into the ground (sometimes 20 feet/6 meters or more) to find a stable source of water and nutrients.

The geologic formation of the land is another important element in drainage. Limestone and schist have large vertical planes sliced by fissures—perfect for vine roots tunneling in search of water. Conversely, dense subsoil or some sort of impenetrable

In the remarkable vineyards of Châteauneuf-du-Pape, the "soil" is composed of large round rocks deposited over millennia by the receding Rhône River. Barely a speck of dirt can be seen.

horizontal formation may cause the roots to remain closer to the surface, where they can soak up water in heavy rains, or more easily suffer from drought.

One of the most important—if curious—aspects of soil is its color and ability to reflect sunlight or absorb heat. In the cool, northern region of Champagne, vines are trained low so that the ripening grapes can take advantage of the warm sun bouncing off the white, chalky ground. (At one time the thrifty Champenois used to accentuate this phenomenon by scattering bits of white plastic garbage bags in the vineyards which, despite the PR drawbacks, did reflect the sun.) In equally cool Germany, dark gray and blue slate rocks help hold the sun's heat, even after the sunlight is beginning to retreat.

The big question, of course, concerns flavor. Taste two pinot noirs from the same small Burgundian domaine, for example, and it would seem almost self-evident that soil profoundly affects flavor. The two wines were made from the same variety, by the same person, using the same process and the same minimal equipment. The wines have been aged and stored identically, and yet they taste remarkably different. How else can one account for so intriguing a phenomenon except through the mysteries of soil?

Yet, while soil is undoubtedly the soul of wine, there is no absolute correlation between certain soil types and specific wine flavors. (At least not that we yet know of.) A vineyard with, say, granite soils, does not have a *predictive* flavor effect because of those soils. Moreover, while it's tempting to think of the soil as a kind of underground spice shop in which a vine can literally root around for flavors, that's not how a vine works. The roots of grapevines can suck up only molecules, ions, and some available forms of minerals. These compounds are then metabolized for vine and grape growth. How soils "work" is, in the end, one of wine's greatest unanswered questions. I can't resist the pun of saying: We've only just begun to scratch the surface.

MATCHING GRAPES TO GROUND

owever omnipotent climate and soil may seem, they cannot be considered apart from the variety of grape being grown. A climate too warm for successful pinot noir is one that can be perfect for syrah. Varieties respond differently to heat, hours of sun, water, wind, and every other facet of climate and soil. Great wine can result only when the grape variety is tuned in, like the signal on a radio dial, to the "channel" of its terroir. To continue the metaphor, when a grape variety is less perfectly suited to its environment, you can still hear the music, but it doesn't have the same sound quality. This is why a vineyard that produces extraordinary riesling should not be pulled up and replanted with merlot simply because merlot has become popular. Clearly, it can be pulled up and replanted, and some vintners do chase trends. However, mediocre merlot is not better than excellent riesling, even though it might very well make the vintner more money.

In general, certain grape varieties (cabernet sauvignon, zinfandel, sauvignon blanc) prefer relatively warm temperatures; others (pinot noir, riesling), cool ones. And some grapes can dance to almost any beat. Chardonnay is mind-boggling in its flexibility. It is as happy in the warm regions of Australia as it is in nippy Chablis, France. Miraculously, it can produce good wine in either climate, although admittedly, the style of the chardonnay will be different. Great chardonnay, however, still appears to be the province of selected sites within cooler environments.

There is an old rule of thumb in Bordeaux that vines need one hundred critical days for proper ripening. In fact, different grape varieties may take as few as ninety days or nearly twice that to ripen. The time required dictates where certain varieties can successfully be planted. Clearly, it would make no sense to plant a variety that needs 150 days to ripen in a place with a growing season 120 days long.

If grape varieties are sensitive to their sites, does that mean that every site is ideal for only one grape variety? It depends on the site and its size. Many of the world's top winegrowing sites—for example, the Burgundy vineyard called Romanée-Conti (pinot noir) or the Mosel vineyard Bernkasteler Doctor (riesling)—are each planted with a single variety that appears to supremely express the

IT'S A DOG'S LIFE . . . NO, REALLY

In most places, a dog is a dog. But in a California vineyard, you might as well spell dog backward. In a vineyard, a dog realizes her higher calling. A good vineyard dog is, first and foremost, in charge of overall public relations. She (or he) greets—and loudly announces—all visitors. She then attends all wine tastings, pre-sampling the baguettes for freshness and occasionally resting her head in the lap of the taster so as to inspire creative descriptions of the wines being tasted. A vineyard dog is, of course, faithfully dusty from stalking mice, moles, wild turkeys, rabbits, and deer in the vineyard. She knows exactly when the vineyard crew stops for lunch, so as to help in the consumption of *burritos con pollo* and *tacos al pastor*. Above all, a good vineyard dog knows (this is true) when the grapes are ripe and will nibble a cluster right off the vine when the time is right.

uniqueness of that small swath of ground. The wines from these sites become something more than just great tasting. They become legendary—masterpieces of Nature.

On the other hand, many sites the world over provide excellent environments for two or more grape varieties that are fairly similar in their needs. For example, in both Bordeaux

PHYLLOXERA: THE BUG OF THE CENTURY

In the latter part of the nineteenth century, phylloxera—a tiny, yellow, aphid-like bug one-thirtieth of an inch long and one-sixtieth of an inch wide—spread throughout Europe, destroying vineyards in its path. From Europe, phylloxera (*phi-LOX-er-ah*) moved around the world, killing vineyards in South Africa, Australia, New Zealand, and California. So swift and sure was the annihilation that many vintners believed the world's vineyards were doomed, and that wine would cease to exist. Originally named *Phylloxera vastatrix* (the "dry leaf devastator") and now specifically identified as the insect *Daktulosphaira vitifoliae,* phylloxera feeds on a vine's roots, ultimately sucking life out of the vine. Although native to America, the bug remained harmless and unknown for centuries. The reason? Indigenous American vines belong to several species that are tolerant of the insect. Native European vines, however, belong to the species *vinifera* (vin-IF-er-ah), which is susceptible to the pest.

In the 1860s, when native American vines were sent to southern France for experimentation, phylloxera, unbeknownst to anyone, hitched a ride on the roots. Within two decades, the "phylloxera plague" had destroyed vineyards throughout Europe. If phylloxera was deadly, it was also eerie. Too minuscule to be seen, the insect wrought havoc totally undetected. European growers watched in maddening frustration as their vines yellowed, shriveled, and then slowly perished. If the grapes managed to ripen at all, the wine made from them was often weak and watery. Eventually the vine would simply collapse.

Countless remedies were tried. French vineyards were doused with chemicals, flooded with water, and irrigated with white wine. By 1873, the French government even offered a prize—30,000 francs (about $10,000 today)—to anyone who could come up with a solution. Nothing worked.

While phylloxera was waging war in Europe, the young California wine industry was unknowingly setting itself up to become phylloxera's next victim. California's first vintners busily began planting vineyards with European vines, which were considered superior to native American ones. Once phylloxera struck, some 17,000 acres (6,880 hectares)

---

and northern California, cabernet sauvignon and merlot are often planted in adjoining vineyard blocks. If a site can support two or more similar varieties well, then planting those there can have advantages both in the vineyard and in the cellar. In the vineyard, multiple varieties can be an asset because grapes ripen at different rates. If the earlier-ripening grape is already picked when a devastating storm hits, the grower loses only a percentage of the crop. Many Old World vineyards, including the vineyards of Bordeaux, are planted with several varieties precisely as an economic hedge against bad weather. And in the cellar, the winemaker has more colors on the palette with which to paint.

CLONES

When most of us think about wines, we think about various grape varieties. Chardonnay tastes different from sauvignon blanc, pinot noir tastes different from merlot, and so forth. Moreover, we think about a grape variety as a single thing. But grape varieties are not quite that simple.

Grapevines, it turns out, are not genetically stable; they spontaneously mutate over time. Each grape variety, therefore, is actually a collection of numerous subtypes called clones.

of California vineyard were ruined before the only known remedy was discovered. By grafting European vines onto the roots of American varieties, the aphidlike creature can be rendered powerless.

As the twentieth century approached, vineyards around the world were painstakingly uprooted, vine by vine, and replanted on American rootstocks. Today, most wines worldwide come from vines growing from American roots.

Growers and winemakers undoubtedly thought they'd seen the last of phylloxera. But when a second wave of the pest spontaneously erupted in the Napa Valley in 1983, the wine industry knew it was up against an extremely formidable foe. Known as biotype B, the new phylloxera began moving at lightning speed through vineyards planted with a specific type of rootstock called AxR1. Throughout the California wine boom of the 1960s and 1970s, AxR1 had been the rootstock of choice. By 1980, nearly two-thirds of Napa and Sonoma vineyards were planted with it.

The fatal flaw was genetic: AxR1, a hybrid, had one American species parent and one *vinifera* parent. California plant biologists knew this, but in early experimental trials, AxR1 had performed well against phylloxera—so well that California scientists felt safe in recommending it. (Interestingly, European scientists remained skeptical about AxR1 and suggested that European growers use other American rootstocks instead.) By 1995, biotype B had spread throughout much of California and into Washington State and Oregon. As of 1997 (the final year statistics were collected), replanting costs in California alone were estimated at about $10,000 (in 1997 dollars) an acre as tens of thousands of acres of Napa and Sonoma vineyards were pulled up and replanted with different rootstocks.

It takes at least three years before new vines can be commercially harvested. For every California winery with vineyards planted on AxR1, the staggering financial burden of replanting was exacerbated by the loss of income from vineyards that were not fully productive for several years.

There is a small silver lining to the story, however. The replanting that has taken place has been done with the benefit of several decades' worth of knowledge. As a result, vineyards have been replanted with varieties, clones, and rootstocks better suited to each site. Have even better California wines resulted? Most winemakers and viticulturists say yes.

A clone is a genetic variation that has been singled out and reproduced. All clones are identical to their mother vine, because cultivated grapevines are reproduced by cuttings (not from seed.)

To explain clones in a very simplistic but helpful way, let's say it's the beginning of time. Adam has a vineyard and Eve has a vineyard (seems right given that this is *The Wine Bible*). Adam and Eve each grow pinot noir. Their son Abel grows up and decides he, too, wants to plant a vineyard. Abel tastes his mother's pinot noir and his father's pinot noir and decides his mother's is better. He scrutinizes both vineyards. In his mother's vineyard, every now and then, he sees a vine that somehow looks better, more healthy, the grapes smaller and more uniformly shaped. To plant his vineyard, Abel takes a cutting from one of these special vines in his mother's vineyard. He grows all of his vines from this cutting. Today, we'd say that Abel planted "Eve's Clone" of pinot noir.

Different clones of a variety make wines that smell and taste different, which is why winemakers are so focused on them. One clone of pinot noir may have a strong strawberry jam character; another clone may be suggestive of mushrooms. Some clones have more intensity of flavor in general, while others can be fairly neutral tasting. All of this is important for wine producers, for a wine's ultimate flavor

Virtually everywhere in the world, the scion (the upper part of the vine) is grafted onto a disease-resistant rootstock. Grafting is a time-consuming, delicate process that requires considerable skill.

and character will be affected by the clone or clones the producer chooses to plant.

There's a catch, however, and it's an important (and frustrating) one. No clone is ever superior in all sites. In other words, the fact that clone X produces great wine from a given piece of ground does not mean clone X will necessarily produce the best wine in a vineyard a half mile away. Clone and site are inextricably and inevitably bound together in a complex dance. And the results are not always predictable.

How many clones of any given variety are there? It depends on two factors: How old the variety is and how genetically erratic it is. Pinot noir, for example, is an ancient vine probably two or more millennia old. It has had a lot of time to mutate compared to, say, cabernet sauvignon, which is only several hundred years old. Moreover, pinot noir is highly unstable genetically, which is not so true for cabernet sauvignon. Thus, there are hundreds of clones of pinot noir, but only a dozen or so well-known clones of cabernet sauvignon.

All of this said, clonal research is relatively new. The discovery of clones dates back just to the 1920s, and practically speaking, it has been only in the past couple of decades that producers have been able to request the specific clone or clones they want when they purchase cuttings from a nursery. Most vineyards worldwide remain as they always have been, a mixture of clones. Often, this is a good thing. After all, by blending several clones of a given variety, a winemaker may have a better chance of producing a wine with nuance and complexity.

ROOTSTOCKS

One of the simple but rather amazing facts about grapevines is that most of those growing in the world today are not growing from their own roots. Instead, most grapevines are grafted onto one of a handful of different rootstocks that are tolerant of specific pests or soil conditions. This might not seem particularly compelling news, but if it were not for rootstocks, the main species of grapes used for wine would have become extinct in most parts of the world about a century ago.

THE SEX LIFE OF WINE GRAPES

Each spring, there's a lot of sex in the vineyards. Strictly between the vines, of course. Cultivated vines are hermaphroditic (the reproductive organs of both sexes are simultaneously present). Thus, come spring, grapevines pollinate themselves. But only if the moment is right. Grapevines, as it turns out, are rather particular. Too much wind? Forget it. A little chill in the air? The grapevines get a headache. Rain? May as well take a cold shower. Only when it's calm, peaceful, and perfectly warm, will grapevines procreate. The tender process is called flowering, and indeed, if all goes well, tiny white flowers will result. With time, these tiny white flowers will become clusters of grapes. But if circumstances go awry and no flowers appear, there will be no grapes. (Sorry, buddy.) With wild grapevines (as opposed to cultivated ones), the situation is different. Wild vines are usually either female or male, although a small percentage are naturally hermaphroditic. As a result, wild female plants can produce fruit only if there is a wild male nearby that can provide pollen. (Male plants, alas, are barren and fruitless.)

Botanists suspect that the first peoples to have cultivated grapevines—perhaps as long ago as 7000 to 5000 B.C.—would have initially selected only female plants, since these would have been the fruitful ones. Ultimately, however, the females, without any males whatsoever, would have been unproductive too. Thus, over time, the vines chosen for cultivation (and propagation) would have been the vines that naturally possessed both female and male sex organs. It's good to be a hermaphrodite.

The rootstock is simply the root system beneath the soil. And that rootstock has nothing to do with the variety of grapes produced. The grapes come from the variety grafted *onto* the rootstock (called the scion). Varieties as different as chardonnay, sangiovese, and riesling can all be grafted onto the same type of rootstock. It's also possible to change the variety growing on a rootstock. If a grower who has planted sauvignon blanc on a rootstock later decides he would do better with chardonnay, he can usually scalp off the sauvignon blanc and graft chardonnay onto that same rootstock instead.

It might seem as though the roots are merely a channel through which water and nutrients flow. In actuality, rootstocks play a far more complex and important role. They have the power to affect a vine's vigor, fruitfulness, and resistance to drought and disease.

Let's backtrack a moment. Until the mid-1800s, most vines grew on their own original roots. However, when phylloxera, a root-eating aphidlike insect, began to ravage vineyards around the world, rootstocks took on new importance. The minuscule yellow bug is native to North America. Native American vines, which belong to several dozen different species, are tolerant of the pest. Unfortunately, European vines, all of which belong to the single species *vinifera*, are not. In the mid-1800s, when American vines were first brought to France for experimental purposes, phylloxera rode along, clinging to the roots.

Between 1860 and 1890, the American pest laid siege to Europe's vineyards. Ironically, the roots of American grapevines proved to be their saviors. French botanist Jules-Émile Planchon and American entomologist Charles Valentine Riley were two of the key figures whose detective work over two decades and subsequent lobbying led to the planting of American rootstocks in France, so that the last living French vines could be grafted onto them and thereby saved. Later, Texas vine expert T. V. Munson helped by introducing American rootstocks that were especially well suited to French soils. Eventually, most vineyards worldwide were pulled out and the vines replanted on American rootstocks.

Today, most rootstocks can be traced back to three major native American grape species: *Vitis riparia*, *Vitis rupestris* (also known as St. George), and *Vitis berlandieri*. Many of the rootstocks used throughout the world are crosses, or hybrids, of these that were bred to tolerate certain vine pests or soil conditions. They have exciting names like 3309, 110R, and SO4.

How does rootstock affect vine growth? Rootstocks can be high vigor or low vigor, can have shallow or deep roots, can be drought resistant or tolerate wetter conditions, and can be more or less tolerant of certain soil pests or other soil conditions. Selecting the best rootstock for a given location can therefore be one of the most critical decisions the grower must make. Of all the subjects currently being aggressively researched, rootstock is considered by many viticulturists to be one of the next big keys to understanding why a given wine tastes the way it does.

FARMING FOR FLAVOR: PRUNING, TRELLISING, SPACING, PICKING, YIELD

Americans traveling in Europe for the first time often drive past vineyards having no idea what they are. Unlike something immediately recognizable no matter where you are—say, a rose bush—vines can come in a dizzying array of shapes and sizes. Vineyards in Burgundy, France; Sonoma, California; and the province of Galicia, in Spain, look about as similar as Abraham Lincoln, Winston Churchill, and Julia Roberts (not necessarily in that order).

The size and shape of the vine is the result primarily of the grape variety and the climate, but the way vines are pruned, trellised, and spaced is also critical. Pruning is the exhausting

BIODYNAMIC VITICULTURE

While biodynamic methods have been used by farmers for centuries, the term *biodynamics* came into use in the 1920s and was based on the teachings of the Austrian philosopher Rudolf Steiner and his student Maria Thun. Sometimes described as a "spiritual science," biodynamic farming involves managing a farm holistically as a regenerative living organism. Vines are fertilized using compost created on the farm, and soils are regenerated naturally through the waste droppings of farm and ranch animals. Harmful pests are controlled by encouraging a population of beneficial pests that feed on them, creating a "living balance." Biodynamic practioners envision plants as existing in a "middle kingdom" influenced from below by the forces of the earth and governed from above by solar and astral forces. Thus, vineyard practices such as pruning are done according to the movement of the moon through the twelve houses of the zodiac. The goal of biodynamics is to align all of the forces of Nature, creating a natural harmony.

process of cutting back the vines while they are dormant during the winter. Although nothing might seem more boring, viticulturists consider pruning to be both an art and a science, and experienced pruners often adopt a zenlike contentment after spending several cold and rather solitary weeks in a starkly barren vineyard during the winter. What the pruner decides to leave becomes the basis for the next year's crop. If pruned too severely, the vines' fruitfulness and strength may be compromised. Conversely, if pruned too little, the

SUSTAINABLE AND ORGANIC: A FARM FOR THE FUTURE

In the first decade of the twenty-first century, the movement toward eco-friendly grape-growing accelerated worldwide. "Green viticulture," as it's known, generally falls under one of three concepts: sustainable, organic, or biodynamic (see box on the facing page).

SUSTAINABLE VITICULTURE Voluntarily practiced by conscientious winegrowers worldwide, sustainable viticulture has no single definition or legal requirements. Vintners decide for themselves which farming practices to implement, and which to avoid, in order to create an integrated farming system capable of sustaining itself indefinitely.

ORGANIC VITICULTURE Organically grown grapes are those grown without the use of artificial fertilizers, engineered plant materials, or synthetic chemicals, including pesticides, fungicides, herbicides, or soil fumigants. In many countries, vineyards and farms that have met organic standards for a given period of time may subsequently be certified as having done so. "Organic wine" is different. In the United States, for example, USDA regulations stipulate that organic wine must be made from organic grapes and, in addition, sulfites cannot be added to the wine. (Sulfites, natural antimicrobial agents, help prevent spoilage and act as a preservative.) Winemakers who grow grapes organically but use small amounts of sulfites cannot use the term *organic wine,* but can say their wine has been made with organically grown grapes.

---

vines will push out too many shoots and leaves and produce too much fruit and become unbalanced. The overabundance of fruit will mean the crop will have a hard time ripening, and this in turn could lead to fewer shoots and stunted growth in subsequent seasons.

In many parts of the world, especially where there are old vineyards, vines still grow out of the ground like short, stubby bushes. In most modern vineyards, however, the vines are trellised up on wires. The rationale behind trellising is simple. By lifting the vines up and spreading the canopy along wires, the leaves get the sun they need for photosynthesis, but at the same time, the grapes hang freely in the air where, less shaded, they get enough sunlight for ripeness, and good air circulation to mitigate against rot.

The spacing of vines, like trellising, has become something of a mini science that must take into consideration the site. In the past, vines were spaced with only one factor in mind: economics. In Europe, this often meant only as much space between the vines or rows as necessary to admit a man with a basket on his back, or a horse-drawn plow. By the 1960s in California, spacing at larger intervals, usually 8 feet (2 meters) between vines and 12 feet (4 meters) between rows, neatly accommodated all sorts of machines and tractors, including those pulling gondolas into which the harvested grapes would be dumped.

But spacing has implications far beyond such simple economic issues as size or type of tractor and equipment. The closer vines are spaced, the more their roots may have to compete for the same soil, nutrients, and water. If the vines are too vigorous, this competition may be beneficial, acting to slow down the vines' growth, limit the number of grape clusters produced, and bring the vines into a better balance. The better balanced the vineyard, of course, the better the grapes and, all things being equal, the better the wine.

In California, the vines in many new and replanted vineyards are now placed much closer together. Twenty years ago, an acre of California vineyard typically contained four hundred to six hundred or so vines. With closer planting, the range is now from six hundred to nearly three thousand vines per acre (and sometimes even more). Importantly however, the overall yield of grapes is about the same because in closely spaced vineyards, the vines are kept quite small. The goal, in other words, is not to increase yield (more on this in a moment) but rather to increase competition between vines and hence quality.

The romantic vision of grapes lovingly picked by hand is, in many cases, just that—a romantic vision. Mechanical harvesting is being used with increasing frequency throughout the world. It has both drawbacks and advantages over handpicking. First, a machine can never be as selective or careful as a person. Mechanical harvesters can break and damage the skins of grapes, as well as the vines themselves if the plants are young. Second, even though modern mechanical harvesters are calibrated to distinguish between ripe and unripe grapes, some unripe grapes and material other than grapes (MOG) still get picked.

On the other hand, mechanical harvesters have some very real assets. They can operate twenty-four hours a day, ensuring that large vineyards can be picked swiftly once the grapes reach ripeness. A mechanical harvester can pick up to 300 tons of grapes in an eight-hour day, compared to the 2 tons picked by the average California harvest worker (admittedly still a breathtaking amount for one person in just one day). Speed is critical if bad weather is about to break. And with machines, large tracts of vineyard can be harvested at night, a real advantage in very warm climates, since cool nighttime temperatures help preserve the fruit's freshness. (Handpickers with appropriate lights can also work at night, but on a smaller scale.) Finally, apart from the initial outlay of capital to purchase a mechanical harvester (in 2012, they cost about half a million U.S. dollars each), mechanical harvesting is usually less expensive than handpicking, and is critical in wine regions with limited availability of labor, such as Australia.

And finally in this chapter, we come to yield. Are quantity and quality mutually exclusive? This is a very complex question, the answer to which can only be: sometimes. On the one hand, it does sound reasonable that growing, say, 3 tons of grapes on an acre of land rather than 10 tons would result in more intensely flavored grapes. And to support this, many of the greatest wine estates in the world limit (to some degree) the yield from their vineyards, though it can seem counterintuitive, if not sacrilegious, to discard what Nature and man have together worked so hard to foster.

Even so, there is no perfect linear correlation between yield and flavor. In the Napa Valley, for example, fantastic cabernet sauvignons are made from vineyards that yield 2 tons per acre—as well as from vineyards with yields double that. Another good example is the Champagne region of France, where top wines often come from vineyards that yield more than 5 tons per acre.

All of this said, "tons per acre" may eventually fade from the lexicon of quality. Today, viticulturists worldwide have telescoped down to finer measurements based on each individual vine. How many clusters does the vine support? What is the weight of each cluster? Most important, what size are the berries? (A high ratio of skin to juice promises lots of concentrated aroma, flavor, and structure.) As one viticulturist told me during harvest, "They may be grapes, but when they're great, they look like blueberries."

In the end, each vineyard must be viewed as its own entity and every factor must be considered before any specific assessments can be made of yield. How strong the vines are, how old the vineyard is, the characteristics of the vineyard's terroir, the intensity of prevailing stress factors, the type of grapes grown—all of these dramatically influence the quality that can be derived from any given yield. Despite all other contingencies, we do know this: For every vineyard, there is a breaking point—a point where too many grapes will cause the vineyard to be out of balance and where the subsequent quality of the wine will plummet.

HOW WINE IS MADE

Wine has been with us for more than six thousand years. Yet the natural, complex process by which it is made—fermentation—has been understood for only a little more than 160 years. It was not until the 1850s, when Louis Pasteur's research in microbiology linked sugar's conversion to alcohol (fermentation) to the living organisms called yeasts, that winemaking moved out of the realm of the occult and into the realm of science. More than a century more would pass before the next significant advances in winemaking occurred.

Up until World War II, most wines were made according to two classic methods, one for white wine, the other for red. The only exceptions were fortified wines, such as Sherry and Port, and sparkling wines, such as Champagne—all of which were made in specialized, complex ways of their own. By the 1960s, advances in winemaking around the world, plus the advent of more sophisticated winemaking equipment—especially temperature-controlled stainless steel tanks—meant that winemakers possessed a far greater ability to influence a wine's aromas, flavors, texture, and finish. A powerful new world of

▲ *They may look a little industrial, but stainless-steel tanks transformed winemaking when they first began to be widely used in the 1960s. Eventually, the tanks were "jacketed" (like the ones above), allowing them to be cooled or heated to control fermentations more precisely.*

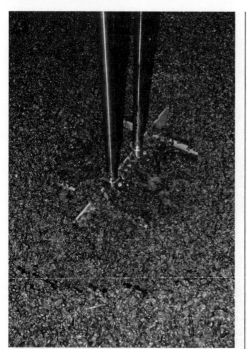

Heat and alcohol generated during fermentation act as solvents, pulling red color out of the skins and tinting the juice red.

winemaking was born. In this chapter we look at how mere grape juice becomes the stuff of poetry and legend.

WHY IS WHITE WINE WHITE AND RED WINE RED?

While starting this section with the question above might seem almost too basic, over the years I've found that most people don't get the answer quite right. It isn't just "because of the skins."

The juice of all grapes, red and white, is almost colorless (with a few rare exceptions). Thus, red skins alone do not make red wine red. The big difference between red wine and white wine is this: For red wine, the juice is *fermented with* the red grape skins. During fermentation, heat and alcohol are generated.

Both are solvents that help leach out the reddish-purple color pigments from the skins, tinting the surrounding wine. In the absence of this heat and alcohol, "red" wine in a fermentation vessel would actually be a pinkish liquid with red skins floating around in it.

With white wine, the skins aren't necessary to tint the juice (it's already clear), plus the skins might add tannin, an undesirable element in white wine. So, in making white wine, the skins are quickly separated from the juice *before* the juice is fermented.

MAKING DRY RED WINE

As we've just seen, since red wines are fermented with the grape skins present, red wines contain substantially more tannin than white wines (see the tannin section in What Makes Wine, Wine?, page 9). Tannin figures into the first decision that must be made in red winemaking, namely: Should the stems be removed from the grapes before they are crushed? It's important to know that grape stems also contain tannin. With grapes that already have a lot of tannin in their skins (cabernet sauvignon, for example), stems can add excessive tannin to the juice. As a result, the stems are usually removed by putting the grape bunches into a machine called a crusher-destemmer. With less-tannic varieties, such as grenache from the Rhône Valley or pinot noir from Burgundy, winemakers may choose to leave the stems on precisely because they do add a bit of tannic strength.

The soupy mass of crushed grapes, juice, skins, pulp, seeds, and possibly stems is called the must. In the old days before stainless steel tanks were invented, this would be fermented in large wooden vats, which would be used over and over again. Today, most red wine is fermented in stainless steel or concrete tanks, which are both easier to control in terms of temperature and easier to clean—someone, after all, is going to have to muck out all those skins and seeds when the whole process is done. (As an aside, a small number

A FEAST OF YEASTS

Yeasts, forty thousand of which could fit on the head of a pin, are single-cell organisms that are part of the fungus family. Yeasts reproduce by "budding." One mother cell will bud about twelve times, creating a new daughter cell each time, before the mother eventually dies. Various strains of yeasts exist naturally in vineyard soils, cling to grapes as they grow, and are present in the air and on the surfaces of wine cellars. As winemakers unknowingly did throughout most of history, some winemakers today allow these ambient, or "native," strains of yeasts to carry out fermentation. In effect, the strains slowly compete with one another to consume the sugar in the juice. This process takes time (often weeks), during which desirable aromas and flavors in the wine may be created. But the opposite may be true, too: Ambient yeasts may produce funky, "off" aromas. They are often not just slow, but sluggish about fermenting. If a fermentation takes too much time getting started, the juice may be harmed by spoilage bacteria or other microorganisms. To end-run these worries, many winemakers prefer to use a strain of cultured yeasts, which can be depended on to multiply quickly at a given temperature. There are many strains of cultured yeasts. A winemaker's choice depends on how fast and intense he wants the fermentation to be. This, in turn, may subtly affect the flavors and aromas of the wine.

of prestigious, expensive cabernet sauvignons and Bordeaux-style wines are now being fermented in new wooden barrels or new wooden vats. Though very labor intensive, fermenting a red wine in a barrel allows oxygen to have a role in the process, and is thought to result in a more soft-textured wine.)

Before fermentation begins, the winemaker has another choice to make. Instead of proceeding immediately, he may decide to chill the tank down and let the juice "cold soak" for a few hours or days. During this time, the skins will ever so slowly and gently release a small amount of tannin, aroma, and flavor compounds. Since fermentation has not yet begun, no heat or alcohol are present, and the extraction effect is therefore subtle. That said, putting a wine through a cold soak is definitely intended to make the wine a bit more intense than it otherwise would have been.

Like any place where regular fermentations occur, a cellar is full of ambient yeasts. With the help of these yeasts, a mass of crushed grapes left alone will turn itself into wine. A winemaker, however, may choose to use cultured yeasts, thereby gaining control over the onset and rate of fermentation. Something as simple as the speed at which fermentation proceeds can profoundly affect the flavor of the wine. Slower fermentations, for example, often produce more complex and aromatic wines.

The next step is the actual fermentation, a furious chemical reaction during which the wine can almost look like it's boiling (you can actually hear it). As the yeasts begin to convert the grape sugar into alcohol, heat is thrown off and carbon dioxide bubbles up from the fermenting mass, pushing the skins to the surface, where they form a thick "cap" over the liquid.

Unattended, the skins will remain at the surface of the liquid, pushed from underneath by the tremendous pressure of the CO_2 for as long as fermentation continues. This presents a problem. Since the skins contain the wine's potential color and tannin, as well as compounds that become aromas and flavors, it's critical that they be mixed with the pinkish-white juice below. Indeed, the more the cap is broken up, pushed apart and squished down

Small amounts of wine evaporate through the oak staves of a barrel, creating a dangerous "head space" of air which could cause the wine to oxidize. To keep the barrels full to the top (and keep air out), winemakers regularly "top off" the barrels.

into the juice, the more color, tannin, flavor, and aroma can be extracted.

Sometimes (especially with fragile grapes like pinot noir), winemakers do this by "punching down," which, despite its name, is considered a gentle method. The winemaker simply takes a pizza paddle–like pole and pushes the skins under the surface of the liquid, breaking up the cap in the process. A similar technique, stripping off most of one's clothes, hopping into the tank, and using one's feet and legs as paddles, worked for centuries.

The cap can also be broken up by a technique called pumping over. In this case, a large hose is run from the bottom of the tank to the top, where the juice is sprayed over the thick mantle of skins and percolates through the cap, picking up color, tannin, aroma, and flavor.

During fermentation, the temperature of the must rises to between 60°F (16°C) and 85°F (29°C). The winemaker does not want it to rise above 85°F, for at higher temperatures the delicate aromas and flavors of the wine may be volatilized, or burned off.

After virtually all of the sugar has become alcohol (a process that usually takes from several days to a few weeks) the wine is said to be dry. At this point, the wine will usually contain anywhere from 10 to 16 percent alcohol. In any case, wine cannot, by natural methods, be much more than 16.5 percent alcohol. At about this concentration, the yeasts die by being poisoned by the very alcohol they created. Near the end of or after the alcoholic fermentation, all red wines go through a months' long transformation called malolactic fermentation. The process is crucial to a red wine's softness and microbial stability. (I've described it in full in the section on Making Dry White Wine, page 43, because I think it's easier to understand in the context of white wine.)

Once a red wine has finished fermenting, the winemaker once again has a decision to make. Should the wine be drained off the skins or be allowed to sit with those skins for several more hours, or even days. This post-fermentation maceration (sometimes called extended maceration) is a little like letting a warm homemade stock sit and "marinate" longer with the meat bones and vegetables. In the case of wine, even more color, tannin, aroma, and flavor are extracted from the skins. The

WARNING: THIS LABEL IS MISLEADING

"Contains Sulfites." With the initiation of that federally mandated warning label in 1988, wine drinkers began to worry. What were sulfites and why were they suddenly being put into wine? In the confusion that followed, wine was blamed for everything from headaches to rashes.

The facts are these: Wine has always contained sulfites. The compounds occur as a natural by-product of fermentation. Historically, winemakers have also added small, controlled amounts of sulfites to wine to prevent oxidation and spoilage.

Widespread concern over sulfites first occurred in the late 1970s and early 1980s, with the dawn of the salad bar. Cut vegetables and fruits were routinely sprayed with large amounts of sulfites (up to 2,000 parts per million—[ppm]) to keep them from wilting and turning brown. The FDA received reports of cases of adverse reactions from several hundred people. In response, strict regulations were enacted to protect the estimated 0.4 percent to 1 percent of the population, most of them severe asthmatics, who are considered at risk.

Historically, however, the regulations on sulfites in wine have been stricter than those applied to salad bars. In wine the upper limit is 350 ppm. In practice, most wines today contain 100 ppm or less. In wineries where the grapes are healthy and unbruised, and where sterilized equipment is used, the amount of sulfites in the wine may be far less. Several wines around the world are now made entirely without added sulfites. And, of course, wine isn't the only product in the sulfite discussion.

Sulfites are found in beer, cocktail mixes, cookies, crackers, pizza crust, flour tortillas, pickles, relishes, salad dressings, olives, vinegar, sugar, shrimp, scallops, dried fruit, and fruit juice, among other foods and beverages.

When sulphur is used in winemaking in small, judicious doses, it cannot be smelled or tasted. Nor is it responsible for headaches, according to scientists. Current research suggests that wine-related headaches are probably more often the result of a simple imbalance: More alcohol has been consumed than water. And there's another possibility as the culprit—glycoproteins. Discovered in 2010 by Italian scientists, glycoproteins are proteins coated with sugars and are produced naturally as grapes ferment. The Italian research team found that many grape glycoproteins have structures similar to known allergens, including proteins that trigger allergic reactions to ragweed and latex.

---

winemaker must be extremely careful, however, because at this point the wine is indeed wine, meaning that it contains alcohol, which will act as a powerful solvent. A little too much maceration at this point could mean a wine that is teeth-grittingly tannic and bitter beyond words.

Finally ready to be separated from the skins for good, the wine is drained off to begin the aging process. This wine, known as free run, is the best possible, and all luxury wines are made from it. The remaining mixture of wine and solids is gently pressed to release additional wine. This lightly pressed juice (called first press) may not be as virginal as free run, but it often contains valuable tannin, as well as flavor and aroma components.

Fruity red wines meant to be quaffed but not contemplated will usually be kept for a few months in a tank or vat, then bottled. More serious reds will go into small barrels for periods ranging from several months to a few years, depending on the potential complexity and structure of the wine. The barrels are virtually always oak. In them, complex chemical interactions will take place that gradually and subtly alter the wine's aroma, flavor, and texture (see What Oak Does, page 48).

An important part of barrel aging is the racking of the wine. Racking is simply the process of allowing solids to settle to the bottom of the vat or barrel, then pouring or drawing the clear wine off. Depending on the grape variety, a red wine may be racked numerous times as various types of solids continue to precipitate out. Racking also aerates the wine, helping it mature.

During aging, there's another winemaking process that is sometimes utilized: fining. Fining helps remove excessive tannin, thus, hopefully, making the wine softer and less bitter, and improving its balance. Fining can also clarify minute solids such as unstable proteins, which may be suspended in the wine. There are several types of fining agents, most of which are protein coagulants—egg whites, casein (a milk protein), gelatin (made from skin, tendon, and muscle), and—hardest of all to imagine—isinglass (a gelatinous substance derived from the air bladders of sturgeon). To fine a wine, the coagulant is stirred into the wine. Like one half of a Velcro patch, the coagulant immediately attaches itself (in this case, chemically) to the tannin, which acts like the other piece of the Velcro. Together, the coagulant and the tannin form molecules that are too heavy to remain in suspension, and thus fall to the bottom of the barrel. The wine can then be racked. (So, in case you were wondering, no egg whites, milk, gelatin, or fish bladders remain in the wine.) The choice of which type of fining agent to use is an important one. A wine fined with egg whites may taste entirely different from the same wine fined with gelatin—not because the fining agent itself contributes flavor, but because each fining agent is made up of different-size protein molecules that attach themselves to different things in

NOT ROMANTIC BUT REVOLUTIONARY

No single entity has had a more profound impact on white wine than the temperature-controlled stainless steel tank. In such tanks, fermentation can take place slowly and at a cool temperature, resulting in white wines with fruity aromas and great delicacy.

Before the tank's invention in the latter half of the twentieth century, many of the world's white wines tasted slightly oxidized and flat. The best white wines came, virtually without exception, from Germany, and from Champagne and northern Burgundy in France, where the naturally cold climates preserved the wines' freshness and finesse.

In 1912, the giant German industrial conglomerate Krupp filed for a patent on the first chrome-nickel-steel-molybdenum tank. This stainless steel tank was not refrigerated, but it resisted corrosion from acids far better than its predecessor, the simple chrome-steel tank. Still, it would be several decades before the technology to cool such huge tanks would be invented and the temperature-controlled stainless steel tank would become a common sight in European wineries.

In the United States, the first non-refrigerated stainless steel tanks were probably those commissioned by Gallo after World War II. Finally, in the 1950s, advanced rotary compressors capable of refrigerating 25,000-gallon tanks became commercially available (and affordable). By the late 1960s, temperature-controlled stainless steel tanks were a fixture in every American winery serious about white wine.

In addition to stainless-steel vessels and oak barrels, wines are sometimes made in concrete eggs, which look like giant Easter eggs.

the wine. Egg whites, for example, are widely used in Bordeaux and are considered excellent at pulling out excessive tannin. Another fining agent—activated carbon (derived from charcoal)—pulls out so many things, it can leave a wine stripped down to the point where it smells and tastes completely neutral. Indeed, activated carbon is usually used only in extreme cases, as when a wine has been adversely affected by smoke (so-called smoke taint has been problematic a few times in the past decade in wine areas prone to massive forest fires).

After oak aging and (possibly) fining, but before bottling, a wine may be filtered. Highly controversial, filtering has generated so many invectives you'd think the subject was taxes. The facts are these: There are times when a wine must be filtered to avoid being spoiled by bacteria, and other times when filtering is undesirable as it may result in a lesser wine. The art is knowing whether to filter, and exactly which method to use so that the wine is improved, not harmed. Filtering helps to stabilize a wine microbiologically and helps clarify

it by removing suspended particles. Excessive filtering, however, also removes desirable particles and thus strips the wine of some of its flavor and aroma.

There are several types of filters, most of which work in a similar manner. In one commonly used type, the wine is pumped through a series of porous pads made of simple cellulose fibers. The pores of the pads may be wide or narrow. In what is called a loose polish filtration, wide-pore pads are used to clarify a wine without removing flavors and aromas. Pads with smaller pores remove smaller particles. Filtered tightly enough, a wine can be made to taste as bland and boring as sliced white bread.

Finally, after filtering (or not), the wine is bottled, often to be aged yet again. In a bottle, the water and alcohol can't evaporate and, assuming the cork is sound, oxygen cannot readily penetrate. The bottle itself, unlike a barrel, is sterile and chemically inert. In the bottle, the components in the wine interact alone, slowly coalescing into harmony. Together, barrel and bottle aging work synergistically toward a level of optimal maturity. The greatest red wines in the world always experience both barrel (oxidative) and bottle (reductive) aging.

Before moving on to how white wine is made, let me add that most red wines in the world roughly follow the process outlined above. There's one well-known exception: Beaujolais, which is made according to a second method called carbonic maceration (see the Beaujolais chapter for how carbonic maceration works, page 228).

MAKING DRY WHITE WINE

Although conscientious winemakers everywhere take enormous care to harvest all types of grapes quickly and as carefully as possible, white grapes require special speed and handling. Crushing grapes on the way to the winery can cause the skins to leak tannin into the juice, which can make a white wine taste coarse.

Bruised, warm, sun-beaten white grapes also risk losing their delicate range of fresh aromas and flavors. As a result, winemakers in warm climates like much of Australia and California are often adamant about harvesting white grapes when the grapes themselves are coolest—at night or in the early morning. Once at the winery, the grapes may be chilled before any winemaking process begins.

As we've seen, in making red wine, the color-packed skins remain with the juice during fermentation and are only removed when fermentation is finished. With white wine, however, the juice is separated from its skins immediately, well before fermentation begins. To obtain the juice, whole bunches of white grapes are put directly into a press, or may be put into a crusher-destemmer that removes the stems first. The press itself is often what is called a bladder press—a large cylinder in the center of which a pliable air tube is suspended (the bladder). As the bladder is inflated with air, it slowly pushes the grapes against the fine screen inside the press. The grapes are squeezed so gently that the stems and seeds are not broken.

Once the grapes are pressed, the juice is transferred to a settling tank so that particles in suspension (mostly minute pieces of grape pulp) can sink to the bottom. In large wineries, this may be done more quickly by filtering or centrifuging the juice instead. Regardless of the method used, once the settling process is finished, the clean juice is ready to be fermented.

As is true of red wine, white wine will ferment on its own as a result of ambient yeasts in the environment. Some winemakers, however, prefer to introduce a yeast culture, making the process of fermentation a surer, faster bet, and easier to control.

Either way, much effort is made to keep the fermenting juice cold (again, the idea is to preserve freshness and aroma). Thus, white wines are often fermented in temperature-controlled fermentation tanks, so they ferment at 50°F to 65°F (10°C to 18°C)—as opposed to 75°F to 85°F (24°C to 29°C) for red wines. Temperature-controlled stainless steel tanks are usually double-skinned, wrapped on the outside with a cooling jacket through which glycol runs.

Although temperature-controlled stainless steel tanks preserve a white wine's freshness and delicacy, some grapes—notably chardonnay—can benefit from being fermented in small oak barrels.

During barrel fermentation, the barrel is filled about three-quarters full to prevent the wine from foaming over. As the wine ferments, the temperature rises to 70°F (21°C) or more. Some fresh fruit aromas and flavors are sacrificed, but in the warm tango of fermentation, the yeasts help pull toasty, sweet, vanillin flavors from the wood, creating the barrel-fermented style. (To keep the white wine from getting too hot during barrel fermentation, you can bet winemakers in warm climates have the AC cranked way up in the fermentation room.)

At first thought, it might seem as though a barrel-fermented white wine would also take on an undesirable amount of tannin from the barrel itself. Curiously, this is not the case. During fermentation the developing wine does extract tannin lodged in the staves. But when fermentation is complete and the spent yeast cells (lees) are removed from the wine, many of the wood tannins cling to them and are removed as well.

When a white wine fermentation is nearly or totally complete, and the sugar in the juice has been mostly converted to alcohol, the winemaker may decide to initiate another

BLUEPRINT

Lail Vineyards

SAUVIGNON BLANC
NAPA VALLEY

Having put so much meticulous work into growing grapes well, then transforming them into fine wine, few vintners want to see their wines served in anything less than a generous, well-shaped glass. Above, Riedel's Sommelier Series glasses for white wine.

amazing chemical transformation: malolactic fermentation (ML for short). Importantly, this months-long process is carried out by bacteria (*Oenococcus oeni*)—unlike the alcoholic fermentation, which is done by yeasts. What happens is simple: The bacteria convert the malic acid in the wine to lactic acid. Why do we care? Because malic acid has an extremely tart mouthfeel (imagine the crunchy acid in a crisp green apple). Lactic acid, on the other hand, has a mouthfeel that is much softer (imagine the acidity in milk). Thus, the goal of malolactic fermentation is to change the way the wine will *feel* on the palate. A wine that has undergone malolactic fermentation has a texture that's creamy.

The story doesn't stop there. During malolactic fermentation, a by-product called diacetyl (die-ASS-i-tuhl) is produced. Diacetyl is the molecule that makes butter taste buttery. So, wines that have experienced malolactic fermentation—like chardonnay—are often buttery. Or, to turn the binoculars around: When a wine is described as tasting like buttered popcorn, that flavor came not from the grapes themselves, but from malolactic fermentation.

Mashed potatoes aside, not everything is better when it's creamy and buttery. Malolactic fermentation is intentionally *not* done with grape varieties like riesling, that take their character from piercing snappiness and the purity of their fruit flavors. Would anyone slather butter on a fresh, lively fruit salad?

In addition, even with wines that have gone through malolactic fermentation and become softer, the winemaker may be able to lessen the buttery diacetyl flavor. (Really expensive chardonnays, for example, are often creamy but don't taste like buttered popcorn). The technique involves leaving the wine in the barrel for several days after the malolactic fermentation is complete, but before the wine is dosed with the antimicrobial agent sulfur dioxide (most wine usually is given a bit of SO_2 immediately after malolactic fermentation). During this few-day period, the yeasts remaining in the juice will metabolize the diacetyl, eating it up as a food source. Thus, diacetyl can disappear from a wine as naturally as it appeared. As an aside, I've used chardonnay as an example here, but it's worth noting that red wines can also taste buttery. Most do not, since the diacetyl flavor is masked by stronger flavors such as those contributed by tannin. But occasionally a red wine will taste buttery and the effect is, to me, unpleasantly jarring.

So, how do you know for sure if a wine has gone through malolactic fermentation? You don't. Its flavor and texture may inspire a hunch. But the technique is usually not listed on the label.

In addition to being barrel fermented, full-bodied white wines, such as chardonnay, may also be left *sur lie,* a French term meaning "on the lees," or "on the spent yeast cells." (As a result of the hard work of fermentation, yeasts partially disintegrate and become what is known in English as lees.) During this process, the wine rests in contact with a thick layer of lees that have settled at the bottom of the barrel. In effect, the wines are marinating on the yeasts. This process adds a slightly richer texture and sometimes more complexity to the wine. To accentuate the effect, the lees may also be regularly stirred up into the wine. (Continuing the culinary metaphor, this would be like basting.) A white wine such as a good-quality chardonnay typically spends four to

HOW BARRELS ARE MADE

I t's estimated that approximately 100,000 to 200,000 new wine barrels are sold each year in North America alone. The story of how each was made begins with the tree from which the wood came.

A tree, like a grapevine, is affected by climate. In cold, dry climates, a tree grows slowly, forming a narrow growth ring for that year. In wetter, warmer climates, a tree grows more quickly and the growth ring is wider. The widths of all the rings together become the wood's grain.

In addition to the species of oak used (French or American), the manner in which a barrel is made significantly affects the flavor of a wine. An oak tree is generally harvested when it is 150 to 250 years old. In practical terms, this means that some forests being harvested today are made up of trees that were growing when the U.S. Constitution was signed in 1787.

For centuries, the traditional European practice—still used today by the best coopers—has been to hand split the oak into

Barrels, like great wine, are made in an artisanal manner.

Pieces of oak wood are used for the fire over which the barrel is made.

As far as wine is concerned, oak flavors are extracted more gradually from tight grained (narrow ring) oak trees. And these, as noted, always come from cool, dry forests. Winemakers generally prefer barrels made from tight-grained oak, since the oak's impact on the wine is usually better integrated and more mellow.

Thus, barrels made from trees that grow in the cool, dry French forests of Tronçais, Vosges, and Nevers are highly sought after. The forest of Tronçais, in particular, was planted in the late 1600s as a source of superior ship masts for the French navy. Although American oak is not designated by the forest from which it came, the best American oak also comes from cool places, such as Minnesota, Missouri, Wisconsin, and Iowa.

staves along natural grain lines, then air-dry the staves by leaving them stacked outdoors in a stave yard, exposed to air, sun, rain, snow, wind, fungi, and microbes for two to four years. Traditionally, the stacks are dismantled and restacked once a year so that all of the staves have similar exposure to the elements. During this seasoning period, the wood's physio-chemical composition changes and, among other benefits, the harshest tannin is gradually leached out of the wood.

After years of seasoning, the staves will be built into barrels. Historically this was done entirely by hand, but today machinery is used for parts of the process. First, the large staves will be planed into slightly smaller staves that can be fit together as tightly as possible, since an imperfect seam could result in a leaky barrel. To make the wood pliable enough to bend into a barrel shape, a cooper uses the traditional method and heats the staves over an open fire pot. Since the fire in the pot can reach 800°F to 1,000°F (430°C to 540°C), and the temperature of the wood, 350°F to 400°F (180°C to 200°C), the outside of the staves are constantly swabbed with a wet mop, ensuring that the wood doesn't burst into flames. As the wood groans and softens, it is pulled into a barrel shape with the help of winches and chains, as well as iron hoops that must be hammered into place and act like belts holding the staves together. It is backbreaking, hot,

The fire reaches temperatures of 800°F to 1,000°F (427°C to 538°C).

deafening work. (The saws are extremely loud.) If he does everything by hand, a top cooper working swiftly can make just one barrel a day.

After the barrel is built, it will be exposed to a fire again, this time to "toast" the inside. The fire caramelizes the wood's natural carbohydrates (think of a tree as a giant vegetable), bringing out compounds such as vanillin, a molecule that occurs naturally in oak. Vanillin in oak tastes remarkably like vanilla (which comes from the pods of a tropical plant). From this caramelization, the wine will ultimately take on a complex repertoire of flavors that are toasty, charred, spicy, and sweet. Depending on the degree and character of the flavors they want to impart, winemakers can order their barrels—like breakfast toast in a coffee shop—lightly, moderately, or heavily

toasted. A lightly toasted barrel spends about twenty-five minutes over the fire; heavily toasted, up to an hour.

In addition to this traditional European method, there is a second method—one which, while sharply criticized today, has been used extensively, especially in the past for American oak barrels. In this method, the staves are dried over a few months in a kiln rather than outdoors over the course of years. Although expeditious, kiln drying does not have the tannin-leaching or seasoning effect that air drying has. As a result, kiln-dried barrels tend to impart coarse flavors. This doesn't matter too much if the liquid inside

Iron hoops hold the staves together. The hoops are hammered into place using a medieval-looking tool.

is bourbon, but if it's pinot noir, the result can taste terrible.

In addition, the staves for American barrels were traditionally bent over steam rather than fire. Barrels with steam-bent staves impart a raw, less complex, less toasty character to wine than barrels made from fire-bent staves. (Think of the difference between boiled beef and grilled beef.)

The world of American oak barrel making has changed, however. Since the mid-1990s, some American oak barrels (the best ones) have been made according to the traditional European method. American oak remains, of course, a different species than French oak, and thus the core flavors will always be slightly different. But American oak barrels are no longer the stepchildren they once were.

ENCHANTED FORESTS

At the beginning of the Middle Ages, more than two thirds of France was covered in oak forests. Alas, these began to rapidly disappear as the twelfth century dawned. The population was growing; wood was the fuel of iron smiths; wars meant the French navy needed a continual supply of wood for ships and masts. In 1285, Philippe I nationalized the country's forests and established the Bureau of Water and Forestry to ensure a steady supply of materials for national defense. Over the next seven centuries, France's oak forests (many of which were geographically defined and given specific names) were among the country's greatest economic assets. Today, 25 percent of the land in France is still covered by nationally owned oak forest—some 35 million acres (14 million hectares). Preserved and painstakingly managed by the Office National des Forêts, these forests show no signs of declining—nor does the price of a French oak barrel.

twelve months in contact with its lees before the wine is finally racked off. The lees themselves will then be filtered to recover as much wine as possible. As for the lees solids (which now look like a thick brown milkshake), they will be thrown away.

At this point, most white wines are cold stabilized—quickly chilled down to a point slightly above freezing for a period of several days. The purpose of this process is to shock the wine just enough for tartaric acid to precipitate out of the wine in the form of solid, small, snowflake-like crystals. The clear wine can then be racked off the crystals. If you've ever seen these crystals on the underside of a cork or in the bottom of your glass, you have encountered a wine that has not been cold stabilized by the winemaker. No matter, really: The crystals are harmless and tasteless. (If you pulverized them, you'd have cream of tartar.)

After cold stabilization, some white wines, like red wines, are aged in oak, although for considerably shorter periods. Oak aging (especially when the barrels are new) can profoundly change the flavor of white wines (see What Oak Does, below). When aged in wood too long, a white wine loses delicacy and the purity of its fruit, and instead takes on the brazen flavor of wood and overt vanilla. In anthropomorphic terms, such a wine can seem like the equivalent of a small-built woman wearing tons of makeup and a huge fur coat. Conversely, when oak aged with care and restraint, such full-fruit grapes as chardonnay can acquire greater lushness and complexity.

Finally, white wine, like red, may be fined or filtered to stabilize and further clarify it. It is then bottled and, again like red wine, may be given further aging in bottle.

WHAT OAK DOES

Without oak, many wines as we know them would not exist. They would not taste the same, smell the same, or have the same texture or structure. Nor are there good substitutes for oak. Cherry, walnut, chestnut, pine, and many other woods can all be made into barrels; none, however, enhances wine the way oak does. Nor has technology devised an oak alternative. In short, wine and oak—inseparable for the past two millennia of winemaking—show every sign of remaining married.

Why is there a special affinity between oak and wine? Oak has the ability to transform wine, to coax it out of the genre of simple fermented juice and give it depth, length, volume, and sometimes, more complexity and intensity. Oak wood is composed of several classes of complex chemical compounds, which leave their mark on virtually every aspect of a wine's character. The most noticeable of these are phenols, some of

CHIPS, BEANS, AND BLOCKS—
OAK WITHOUT BARRELS

Consider the cost of a tree grown for two centuries, and the price of barrels made, largely by hand, from that pristine wood. Not surprisingly, barrels are time consuming to make and breathtakingly expensive. After salaries, they're often the second biggest yearly expense for a winery. (In 2011, one of the largest American wine companies spent a reported $22 million on barrels alone.) Yet, today, barrels are used virtually exclusively for fairly expensive wines. For their part, modestly priced wines rarely, if ever, rest inside barrels. Enter the brave new world of chips, powders, beans, blocks, and interstaves. Made from oak wood that's unsuitable for barrels, these barrel alternatives, as they are known, are a fraction of the cost of barrels (and,

of course, the time and labor involved in making them is less). How are they used? Oak chips, beans, and blocks are added directly to the fermenting tank—either loose or enclosed in a giant mesh teabag. Staves can be inserted into frames that can be dropped into older barrels or suspended in stainless steel tanks. Finally, most barrel alternatives come toasted in a variety of ways and flavors worthy of a Starbucks menu. Spicy staves, anyone? How about premium dark-roast chips with extra vanilla and caramel?

No matter their range of flavors, barrel alternatives never achieve the subtle, complex effects of barrels. And while such alternatives are an asset in the making of inexpensive wines, as of this writing, I know of no great wine in the world that is made using them.

---

which impart vanilla-like flavors, notes of tea and tobacco, and impressions of sweetness. One of the most important classes of phenols are the substances commonly called tannins.

I do want to quickly add that not every wine benefits from time in a barrel. For some wines—whites in particular—the weighty, sweet vanilla and toasted oak flavors of new wood can be like a glob of sauce masking the purity of the fruit itself. Moreover, some wines with oaky flavors haven't actually spent time in barrels. It's highly unlikely, for example, that an $18 chardonnay was fermented in a new French oak barrel that cost $1,300. The economics just don't work. To get its oaky character, the chardonnay was probably made with a "barrel alternative." For more about this, see Chips, Beans, and Blocks—Oak Without Barrels, above.

Although open wooden buckets were used to hold and transport wine more than two thousand years before the Christian Era, closed oak barrels first came into use during

the Roman Empire. Oak, extremely plentiful in the forests of Europe, had many desirable qualities: It was strong enough to withstand considerable wear and tear without busting apart, yet sufficiently malleable to be shaped into barrels that could be rolled and moved. Moreover, oak barrels were leakproof, despite the fact that nothing was (or is) used between the staves to seal them.

Lastly, oak usually had a desirable effect on the wine itself. Early winemakers discerned that wine grew softer, and in many cases tasted richer and more substantial, after oak aging. During the last third of the twentieth century, research on oak aging began to unravel the reason why.

At least as far as wine is concerned, oak wood is porous to a perfect degree. Both water and alcohol evaporate outward through the barrel's staves and bunghole (the small access hole, closed with a stopper, or bung). A 60-gallon (230 liter) barrel of cabernet sauvignon,

KOSHER WINE

The word *kosher* means "fit," thus, in Jewish tradition, kosher wines are considered fit to drink. There are two types—non-mevushal and mevushal.

Non-mevushal kosher wine must be made, handled, bottled, certified, opened, poured, and drunk only by Sabbath-observant Jews. If a non-Jew touches the wine, the wine loses its non-mevushal kosher status, is considered unfit for sacramental use, and will be rejected by strict observant Jews, who will not drink it. The second, and far more common type of kosher wine is mevushal (literally, "cooked"). Mevushal wines are made like non-mevushal wines, with one exception—they are pasteurized and can therefore be bought, opened, and shared among Jews and non-Jews, as well as non-observant Jews and observant Jews.

Religious scholars speculate that the reason for the two types goes far back in history. Traditionally, of course, Jewish religious authorities knew that wine was used not just for sacramental purposes, but also socially. Wine eased and encouraged social interaction. It's thought that early Jewish intellectuals may have feared such socializing, viewing it as the first step toward the disintegration of Jewish culture and the assimilation of Jews into other cultures. To mitigate against this, two versions of kosher wine would be made. Mevushal wine would be, quite literally, boiled, making it in a sense morally sterilized. Although mevushal wine would therefore be less palatable than non-mevushal wine, it could be shared by non-Jews and non-observant Jews with observant Jews.

Until recently in the United States, the wines were also produced from foxy-tasting native grapes, such as Concord (of jelly fame). Such grapes thrived along the East Coast, where the largest centers of Jewish population were to be found. Over time, American-made kosher wine became inextricably linked with low-quality, syrupy-sweet wines that tasted like adult Kool-Aid.

Today kosher wines—non-mevushal and mevushal—are in an entirely different league, and compete with fine wines made anywhere in the world. They are made around the world from classic European grape varieties, such as cabernet sauvignon and chardonnay. Importantly, mevushal wines are no longer boiled, but flash pasteurized—a gentler form of sterilization—and the wine is then aged. According to KosherWine.com, a leading kosher wine retail site, as of 2010, annual sales of kosher wine in the United States alone had a value of approximately $45 million.

---

for example, may lose as much as 5 to 6 gallons (19 to 23 liters) of liquid per year—about thirty bottles of wine. At the same time, minute amounts of oxygen from outside are seeping through the grain and into the barrel, helping to weave together the elements of the wine and giving it a softer dimension. Oxygen also becomes a factor in the equation each time the winemaker removes the bung from the barrel and tops up the wine or partially clarifies it by racking it into another barrel.

The impact oak has on wine depends, among other things, on the type of oak used. Of the approximately three hundred species of oak that grow around the world, just three main types are used in winemaking: the American oak *Quercus alba* (mainly from the Midwest) and the French oaks *Quercus robur* and *Quercus sessiliflora* (also called *Quercus petraea*).

The flavor American oak imparts to wine is different from the flavor French oak imparts. American oak, which is heavier, denser, and less porous than French oak, also tends to be less tannic and have more pronounced vanilla and sometimes coconut-like flavors. French oak is more subtle in terms of flavor, somewhat more tannic, and allows for slightly greater—but still gentle—oxidation. Neither is necessarily better than the other, in the same way that basil isn't necessarily better than rosemary. The idea is to find a type of oak that will best support the fruit flavors in a given wine. To determine this, winemakers generally age small lots of their wines experimentally in many different oak barrels representing different oak species, different forests, and a variety of coopers, and then decide which ones work best.

The age of the barrels also matters. A winemaker can choose to put a wine into new barrels, used barrels, or a combination of new and used barrels. (Note that sometimes used barrels are euphemistically referred to as seasoned barrels—as in a "seasoned" person.) New barrels have the strongest impact on a wine's aroma and flavor (and for that reason, some winemakers prefer not to use them). Second-use barrels have considerably less impact, since most things that can be extracted from a barrel are extracted the first time that barrel is used. After four uses or so, a barrel is generally considered "neutral"—though it can still be used (for decades) to store and age wine. In a neutral barrel, a small amount of oxygenation will still occur, but little if any barrel flavor is left to be imparted to the wine.

Aging in oak is not the same as fermenting in oak. The two distinctly different processes have different consequences. Imagine, for example, a batch of chardonnay that is fermented in oak and then aged in oak for six months. Imagine a second batch that is fermented in stainless steel and then aged in oak for the same period. Although you might expect that the wine receiving two doses of oak (during fermentation and aging) would have the most pronounced oak and vanilla flavors and the strongest impression of tannin, the opposite is usually true. When a wine is fermented in oak, the yeasts also interact with the wood. When the spent yeast cells (lees) are ultimately removed from the wine, a measure of the wood tannin (and wood flavors) may be removed with them. By comparison, a

The oak forests of France have been carefully maintained by continual replanting since the 13th century.

white wine fermented in stainless steel and then put without the lees into oak barrels readily absorbs the wood flavors and tannins to which it is exposed.

So, in the end, in using oak judiciously, a winemaker can opt to: ferment the wine in oak but not age it in it; age the wine in oak but not ferment it in it; use some of both; or use none of either.

MAKING OFF-DRY AND SWEET WINE

As noted in What Makes Wine, Wine? (page 9), there are no internationally agreed-upon definitions for terms such as off-dry and semisweet. Still, we could probably all recognize a wine that's just a touch sweet, in other words, a wine that's not dessert-level opulent.

How are these wines—I'll group them all together under the banner "off-dry"—made? As you know, during the fermentation of dry wines, yeasts convert the sugar in grapes to alcohol. However, in making an off-dry wine, fermentation is stopped, usually by giving the wine a small dose of SO_2 (sulfur dioxide), which kills the yeasts before they have converted all the sugar to alcohol. This leaves a wine with a touch of natural sweetness and a slightly lower level of alcohol. In this scenario, the wine is not sweet enough to be a dessert wine; in fact, the tiny bit of residual sugar may be just barely perceptible. Usually, the goal of leaving this small snippet of sugar is simply to buttress the fruitiness of the wine. Many rieslings are made in this way.

So, how does a wine come to be sweet enough to be dessert in itself? The process starts with grapes that are very high in sugar because they were:

---

1 PICKED WHEN THEIR sugar content is very high; or

---

2 PICKED, LAID OUT on mats, and allowed to raisinate, thereby concentrating their sugar; or

---

3 PERMITTED TO FREEZE on the vine (as in *eiswein*) so that water can be separated from the sugary juice; or

---

4 ATTACKED BY THE fungus *Botrytis cinerea* (the "noble rot" of French Sauternes), which consumes some of the water in the grapes and helps more to evaporate, again concentrating the sugar.

Each of these methods is explained in more depth later (the *Botrytis cinerea* responsible for Sauternes, for example, is addressed fully in the Bordeaux section, page 157). What's important to know here is that all of these options are extremely risky—animals may eat the sweet grapes, the grapes may be attacked by unfavorable molds or diseases, weather may destroy the grapes before the crop can be picked, and so on. Moreover, each of these processes is very labor intensive. Sweet wines, as a result, are almost universally rare and expensive.

No matter which of the four methods is used, the resulting grape juice has a higher sugar content than usual. Before the yeasts can convert all this sugar to alcohol, either the winemaker stops the fermentation early, as for an off-dry wine, or the yeasts' action is halted by the very alcohol they have produced. (As you'll recall, once the alcohol level has reached about 16 percent, most yeasts die from "alcohol poisoning," and whatever natural sugar is left remains.)

CHAPTALIZATION

Many people think sweet wines are made by adding sugar to them, but as you see from the previous section, that's not the case. Adding sugar—chaptalization—has a different purpose. Named after Jean-Antoine Chaptal, minister of agriculture under Napoleon, who first sanctioned the process, chaptalization is the act of adding sugar to a low-alcohol wine before and/or during fermentation so the yeasts will have more sugar to convert to alcohol. Thus, the goal is not to make the wine sweeter—it's to make it higher in alcohol and therefore fuller in body.

Importantly, you cannot taste sugar in the chaptalized wine; the process does not increase the wine's sweetness. Critics, however, contend that chaptalized wines take on a blowsy, out-of-balance character, since the final alcohol has been artificially jacked up.

Many wines in northern Europe are chaptalized when the grapes do not get ripe enough to produce a wine with sufficient body. Even though this process is usually illegal, it's rather easy—just by accident of course—to spill a huge sack of sugar into the fermenting vat. *Quel domage!* Conversely, wines made in such sunny places as Australia and California are rarely chaptalized because grapes in those places virtually always get ripe enough to produce more than enough alcohol.

GETTING TO KNOW THE GRAPES

 irén (i-WREN) is a good place to begin. Recognize the name? What about rkatsiteli (are-cat-si-TELL-ee) or savagnin (sa-va-NYEN)? They are, respectively, one of the most widely planted grape varieties in the world; the most widely planted grape in the former Soviet Union (it also grows in the United States, in New York State); and the "mother" of sauvignon blanc. But you may never have drunk wine made from airén or rkatsiteli or savagnin.

There are five thousand to ten thousand varieties of grapes (see Drinking DNA, page 55). Scientists do not have an exact figure because many varieties are thought to exist solely in laboratory collections, and are no longer cultivated. Of this large number, about 150 are planted in commercially significant amounts. I've chosen twenty-five of those—the ones I think we are most likely to encounter—and have included here a profile of each. You'll find them on the following pages, followed by a glossary of virtually every other important grape worldwide.

One last note: I have tried, when it seemed appropriate (or just plain fascinating), to include information on the parents or genetic relationships of the grapes in this chapter. Hundreds of today's grapes are, in fact, natural crosses (that is, they spontaneously occurred in nature) of other grapes, and hundreds more are intentional crosses (made by growers or

▲ *Cabernet sauvignon grapes ripen in the Napa Valley sunshine. Each grape variety is subtly unique in the shape and size of its berries and clusters, as well as its leaves.*

scientists). My leading resource for this information has been the authoritative and quite phenomenal reference work *Wine Grapes* by Jancis Robinson, Julia Harding, and Dr. José Vouillamoz (2012).

THE TOP TWENTY-FIVE GRAPES TO KNOW

ALBARIÑO

One of the liveliest white wines in Europe and considered one of the best wines for seafood, albariño (al-bar-EEN-yo) comes from the region of Rías Baixas (REE-az BUY-shaz), along northeastern Spain's ruggedly beautiful and very green northwestern coast (it looks like Ireland). In the past decade, albariño has become Spain's most notable and delicious dry white table wine, even though the dry whites of Rioja (made from the grape variety viura) were once better known. Albariño is floral and citrusy, but not quite as aromatic as, say, riesling or gewürztraminer. It is rarely made or aged in oak and is best when young and snappy. Interestingly, unlike most Spanish (or European) wines, which are named for the place from which they come, albariño is always labeled just that—albariño. (See also Rías Baixas, page 485). Albariño, for all its fame in Spain, probably originated in northeastern Portugal, where it has grown for centuries and where it is known as alvarinho. It is still grown widely there and is the core grape in vinho verde.

Ripe cabernet franc grapes, amazingly formed in a heart-shaped cluster.

BARBERA

Barbera (bar-BEAR-a), the most widely planted red grape in the northwestern Italian region of Piedmont, rose to prominence there after the phylloxera epidemic (page 30). Genetic research suggests it probably originated someplace else and was brought to Piedmont. Its parents are not known.

Even though nebbiolo (the grape used to make Barolo and Barbaresco) is more renowned, it's barbera, not nebbiolo, that Piedmontese winemakers invariably drink with dinner. Beginning in the mid 1980s, the quality of barbera rose dramatically. By planting it in better sites, limiting the yield, and aging the wine in better barrels, Piedmontese winemakers began making superbly mouthfilling, rich wines packed with flavor. Top barberas also have a natural vivacity—a precision and vibrancy that comes from the grapes' relatively high acidity. Today, all of the great barberas come from Piedmont, and the grape is rarely planted elsewhere, although there is a small amount grown in northern California. A century ago, Italian immigrants in California planted it in poor, usually hot areas, hoping to make a hearty, low-cost red wine. After a brief resurgence as part of the "Cal-Ital" movement of the early 1990s, barbera sadly began to decline in importance there.

CABERNET FRANC

While not as well known as its offspring, cabernet sauvignon and merlot, cabernet franc (CAB-er-nay FRONK) plays an important role in many of the world's top Bordeaux and Bordeaux-style blends. Indeed, on the so-called "Right Bank" of Bordeaux, in the appellations Pomerol and St.-Émilion, cabernet franc can make up 50 percent of the blend or more as is often the case with the legendary Bordeaux wine Château Cheval Blanc.

Compared to its Bordeaux confreres, cabernet franc is generally not as fleshy as merlot, nor is it as structured and intense as cabernet sauvignon. For many wineries, it thus sits in perfect mid-prance between the two. If it gets ripe, that is. When the grapes are unripe

DRINKING DNA

Throughout the entire history of winemaking—and indeed right up until the early 1990s—the only way to try to tell, say, merlot from mourvèdre was by ampelography, the science of identifying vines by measuring and characterizing their shoots, canes, leaves, buds, flowers, clusters, seeds, and grapes. Not surprisingly, farmers sometimes got it wrong, growing renowned "pinot blanc" that turned out to be chardonnay, and so on.

Since the early 1990s, however, grapevine identification has had quite a bit in common with, say, an FBI forensic laboratory. Just as DNA (deoxyribonucleic acid, the chemical composition of genes) obtained from a crime scene can be compared with the DNA of a suspect, so the DNA of a grape variety being researched can be compared to the DNA of known varieties. Scientists, using complex techniques, attempt to find genetic messages encoded in certain sequences of the grape variety's DNA. These then become the identification markers for any individual variety.

In groundbreaking research in 1997, such DNA typing was also used for the first time to reveal the parentage of grapes. According to top genetic researchers such as Dr. José Vouillamoz, author, with Jancis Robinson and Julia Harding, of *Wine Grapes,* the most authoritative reference work on vine genetics, a small number of grape varieties have given birth to all of the varieties in the world today. Chief among these "founder varieties" are pinot noir, gouais blanc, and savagnin (also known as traminer). The first two together have begotten more than twenty different varieties over time, including chardonnay and gamay. For its part, the Casanova-like gouais blanc has crossed with scores of varieties (some of which no longer exist), resulting in the creation of more than eighty different varieties, including riesling, blaufränkisch, and muscadelle, to name three very different progeny. The idea that all of the important varieties—red and white—can be traced back to perhaps fewer than ten founder varieties, and a few primary domestication sites (some of which are probably in modern-day Turkey) is startlingly new.

Finally, the very first original varieties that gave rise to the founder varieties were probably all red. It's thought that the first white variety was a mutation that occurred when pieces of DNA moved within the gene, interrupting the coding for anthocyanins, molecules that create color. In early wine-drinking civilizations, the rarity of white wines gave them social value and led to the perception that white wines were more refined than reds, and as such, more desirable as upper-class drinks.

(and it's a challenge to ripen cabernet franc), the wine has a distinct green bell pepper character—the result of compounds in the wine known as pyrazines. But in warmer years, when sugars are high and pyrazines fall, cabernet franc can be fantastic, with its violet or irislike aromas and minerally, dark chocolaty flavors. Loire Valley Chinon (100 percent cabernet franc) is the most well-known, delicious example. But the grape has also made quiet but stunning progress in California, as wines like Vineyard 29's cabernet franc attest.

Most French grape varieties came from the east: France got its initial vines from Italy, which in turn got them via Lebanon (historically, Phoenicia), which probably got them from southern Turkey. But surprising genetic research in the 2010s revealed that cabernet

The highest quality wines come from clusters of grapes that are sometimes painstakingly destemmed by hand. Only the most perfect grapes will be picked off the cluster; the rest are discarded.

franc originated to the southwest of France, in Spain's Basque country, and from there was brought northeast to Bordeaux.

CABERNET SAUVIGNON

The preeminent classic red grape variety, cabernet sauvignon (CAB-er-nay sew-vin-YAWN) is capable of making some of the most structured, complex, majestic, and ageworthy reds in the world. It's astounding that a wine so often angular and powerful when young can metamorphose into a velvety, rich, elegant, and complex wine with several years' aging. Cabernet can be like the awkward kid who grows up to be a Nobel laureate, and sexy to boot. Not all cabernet sauvignons have this ability, of course. Many modestly priced cabernets are made in an easy-drinking style that is simply simple. These wines bear little of the depth, power, and intense concentration of, say, Château Latour from Bordeaux, Sassicaia from Italy, or Harlan Estate from the Napa Valley.

But there's something else that makes great cabernets like these so compelling. Few other red wines in the world have cabernet's counterintuitive ability to combine two of the characteristics mentioned above—power and

HOW MUCH CABERNET IN THE CABERNET?

*L*abeling a wine based on the variety of grape used to make the wine has been commonplace in the New World since the late 1960s. (In Europe, wines are far more commonly labeled according to the place where the grapes were grown.) In the United States, the first varietally labeled wines were required by federal law to be composed of 51 percent of the variety named. In 1983, the minimum was raised to the current level of 75 percent. Specific appellations can choose to exceed (but not lessen) the federal regulations (for example, in the Willamette Valley of Oregon, all pinot noirs with that grape name on the front label must be at least 90 percent pinot noir).

elegance. I think it's this capacity to embody, in one split second, two contrapuntal ideas that makes the great cabernets so intellectually fascinating . . . a yin-yang of flavor.

Cabernet sauvignon's aromas and flavors are well known and easy to indentify: blackberry, black currant, cassis, mint, cedar, graphite, licorice, leather, green tobacco, cigar, black plums, dark chocolate, sandalwood, and so on. These sensations are then swirled into a delicious amalgam as the wine ages. I should add that unripe, poorly made cabernet sauvignon, like poorly made sauvignon blanc, usually tastes vegetal—a dank mixture of bell peppers, canned green beans, and cabbage water. This shared tendency toward vegetative green flavors if the grapes are not ripe comes as no surprise, since cabernet sauvignon is the offspring of sauvignon blanc (which, one day, thought to be in the mid-1700s, had a nice moment in nature with cabernet franc, resulting in cabernet sauvignon). Both cabernet sauvignon and sauvignon blanc are high in pyrazines—compounds in grape skins that give the final wine a bell pepper flavor.

Because cabernet sauvignon is one of the most tannic of all the major red grapes, it has, over the past few decades, been a prime focus in the study of tannin and tannin ripeness. Twenty five years ago, for example, it was commonly thought that cabernet required decades of aging to feel soft. Today, many cabernet sauvignons packed with large amounts of tannin nonetheless possess a soft mouthfeel right off the bat. This is possible because harvest decisions are now often based on the physiological maturity of the tannin in cabernet grapes, rather than sugar (see the tannin section in What Makes Wine, Wine?, page 12). So, even though it may seem like a public relations pitch: It is indeed possible for the best cabernet sauvignons today to be ready to drink now *and* delicious decades in the future.

Finally, historically, the world's most prized cabernet sauvignons were cabernets blended with merlot, cabernet franc, and perhaps malbec and petite verdot. They came from the Médoc communes of Margaux, St.-Julien, Pauillac, and St.-Estèphe in Bordeaux, where the wines were (and still are) ranked

THE MYTH OF CABERNET AND CHOCOLATE

It may sound romantic—even inspired—but as marriages go, cabernet and chocolate are a match made in hell (or in the depths of the marketing department). Chocolate is an extremely powerful, profound, and complex flavor. Its deep bitterness accentuates the tannin in cabernet sauvignon, making the wine taste severe and angular. Chocolate's rich fruitiness blows away cabernet's graceful fruity nuances, making the wine taste drab and hollow. Moreover, chocolate's profound sweetness makes most dry wines taste sour. In short, the would-be dominatrix chocolate needs a partner more powerful and sweeter than herself. Which may be one of the reasons sweet, luscious, opulent Port is a life necessity.

into "growths," from First Growth, the most renowned, down to Fifth Growth. However, world-class cabernets are now regularly being made in California (especially the Napa Valley), Italy, Australia, and Washington State.

CHARDONNAY

To any wine drinker, it comes as no surprise that, for several decades, chardonnay (shar-doe-NAY) has been one of the most successful white wines in the world. The wine's easily understood, appealing flavors—vanilla, butter, butterscotch, buttered toast, custard, minerals, green apples, exotic citrus fruits—are matched by equally effusive textures—creamy, lush, and full-bodied. (It's the Marilyn Monroe of white grapes, to be sure.) We are talking here about the majority of chardonnays in the world; of course, lean, racy, lightning-crisp Chablis (100

IT'S ALL ABOUT SPECIES

All grapevines belong to the genus *Vitis* (VIT-tis). Sometime in the late Tertiary Period, 66 million to 2.58 million years ago, climatic changes caused the genus to split into about sixty separate species. The most important species for wine drinkers is *vinifera* (vin-IF-er-a). Today 99.99 percent of the wines in the world are made from grapes belonging to *Vitis vinifera*. Interestingly, this was and is the only species native to Europe and Asia. Chardonnay, cabernet sauvignon, merlot, pinot noir, riesling, sauvignon blanc, and zinfandel, for example, are all *Vitis vinifera* grapes. The other dozens of species were and are all native to North America. Among these, the best known among wine drinkers is *Vitis labrusca*, native to New England and Canada. Concord belongs to this species. It was probably *Vitis labrusca* vines that inspired Leif Eriksson to name North America Vinland in 1001. Wines (not to mention jelly and jam) are still made from this species, especially in upper New York State.

percent chardonnay) remains a brilliant sensorial exception to the norm.

But chardonnay's popularity is, indeed, relatively recent. Wine drinkers are often surprised to learn that, as of the mid-1960s, there were but a few hundred acres of it in all of California (by 2011, there were 95,000 acres /38,445 hectares!). Ditto for most of the rest of the world. Little, if any, chardonnay existed in Chile, Argentina, Australia, South Africa, Spain, or Italy, not to mention Oregon, Washington State, and other parts of the United States. In fact, the only places chardonnay reigned were its homeland, the small Burgundy region of France, and Burgundy's northern neighbor, Champagne. (See Burgundy, page 197.) It was

in Burgundy, probably sometime in the early Middle Ages, that chardonnay arose as a seedling—a natural cross of the white grape gouais blanc with the red grape pinot noir.

Small as it was in terms of production, Burgundian chardonnay proved prodigious in its ability to inspire winemakers worldwide. Today, chardonnay is virtually ubiquitous. (Although I think it's fair to say that few wines among the millions of cases now produced ever manage to hold a candle to the best Burgundian versions.)

Stylistically, chardonnay is often said to be a "winemaker's wine"—meaning that winemakers like it for its capacity to be transformed by lots of winemaking techniques. Barrel fermentation, malolactic fermentation, *sur lie* aging, and so on—chardonnay often gets the whole nine yards of technical possibility. Of course, there's a hitch. Today, too much chardonnay tastes manipulated, diffused, flabby, overoaked, and overdone. In a sea of these sad behemoths, however, the finest chardonnays remain among the world's most luscious and complex dry white wines.

CHENIN BLANC

The most famous, vibrant chenin blancs (SHEN-in BLAHNK) of the world come from the Loire Valley of France, specifically from the appellations Vouvray and Savennières. The Loire Valley is also the ancestral home of this grape, which arose as a natural cross of savagnin and an unknown parent.

The best examples of chenin blanc are stunningly complex wines with a flavor of apples and honey (although not necessarily honey's sweetness). They are shimmering with acidity, minerally, and long-lived. If modern life allowed for such seemingly lost pleasures as sitting in a meadow reading *Madame Bovary* or *The Age of Innocence*, chenin blanc would be the fitting wine to drink.

Loire Valley chenin blanc is made in a variety of degrees of sweetness, from bone-dry to just a touch of sweetness (to balance the wine's dramatic acidity) to fully sweet. The latter can make for phenomenal dessert wines, as evidenced by the most legendary and luscious of all, Quarts de Chaume, from a tiny area in the middle of the Loire Valley.

Chenin blanc is also a well-known white grape in South Africa, where it is sometimes known as steen. There, however, it is unfortunately made mostly into a simple, innocuous quaffing wine. In California, chenin blanc was a major white grape prior to the 1960s. Today, most California chenin blanc grapes are over-cropped for high yields and are destined for jug wines, a sad fate given the grapes' potential character.

GAMAY

Gamay (gam-AY), or more properly gamay noir, is the source of the French wine Beaujolais (including Beaujolais Nouveau), oceans of which are washed down in Parisian bistros every year. Of all the well-known red grapes, gamay is perhaps the lowest in tannin and thus, structurally speaking, more like a white wine than a red. It's also exuberantly fruity. In the hands of a great producer, and from grapes grown on a great site, this fruitiness spirals around flavors that exude a sense of crushed rock and minerals, and the total flavor effect can be dazzling. (Alas, gamay from a mediocre site, grown at high yields, and then made

Though they make white wine, gewürztraminer grapes are deep pink in color.

in a commercial style, is fruitiness that's back-fired. Indeed, cheap commercial gamays are dead ringers for melted black cherry Jell-O and bubble gum.) The most serious, best gamays in the world are from small producers in one of the ten "cru" villages within the Beaujolais region. See the Beaujolais section (page 227) for more on these.

Gamay noir's parents are pinot noir and gouais blanc, making it a sibling of many grapes, including chardonnay, Auxerrois, and melon de Bourgogne. It has existed in its homeland, Burgundy, France, since the four-teenth century. Late in that century, however, it was banned by one of the powerful dukes of Burgundy, and banished to the Beaujolais region, south of Burgundy proper.

Several decades ago, so-called gamay (probably actually the French grape valdiguié, or sometimes an undistinguished clone of pinot noir) was commonly grown in California to be used in jug wines. Today, however, outside France, gamay is virtually nonexistent as a varietal wine.

GEWÜRZTRAMINER

More than almost any other wine we might regularly encounter, gewürztraminer's (guh-VURZ-tra-meen-er) nose is heady (sorry, couldn't resist). In fact, the explosive aromas of gewürztraminer—roses, lychees, gingerbread, orange marmalade, grapefruit pith, fruit-cocktail syrup—come vaulting out of the glass. Gewürztraminer is nothing if not extroverted. Even novice drinkers easily recognize it.

The prefix *gewürz-* means spice in German, although the meaning is more along the lines of "outrageously perfumed" than anything that might come out of a kitchen spice rack. The grape is not actually a distinct variety, but rather savagnin rosé—a pink-berried, highly aromatic clone of savagnin, one of the so-called "founder varieties." (Traminer aromatico, a specialty of the northern Italian province of Trentino-Alto Adige, is another clone of savagnin.)

It's important to note that gewürztraminer's pungent aromatics and massive fruitiness can be confusing, leading you to think that the

In very warm years, grapes of all types can shrivel and dessicate. Most "raisined" bunches will be sorted out and removed, though a small percentage can contribute extra sweetness, leading to a fuller-bodied wine.

wine you're drinking is sweet. That's usually not the case (the telltale edge of bitterness at the finish is evidence). Indeed, the world's best gewürztraminers are decidedly dry (unless, of course, the wine in question is specifically a dessert wine made from this grape).

The most intense and breathtaking gewürztraminers are made in France, in the northeastern region of Alsace. Here the wine is legendary—deeply yellow with a coppery cast, superbly concentrated, exquisitely balanced, full-bodied, full of extract, with just enough acidity to hold it all together, and a megamouthful of flavor. (Because the wine tends to be naturally low in acidity, poor-quality examples can come off oily.) No surprise that top gewürztraminer is usually drunk with rich, complex pork dishes.

Outside of Alsace, there's only one place in the world where gewürztraminer is reliably sensational: the region of Trentino-Alto Adige in Italy.

GRENACHE

Grenache (gren-AHSH) is well known both as a white grape (grenache blanc) and a red

(grenache noir). The red grenache noir is especially valued and makes a slew of stunning wines around the world. It is, for example, the lead grape in many southern French wines, including Châteauneuf-du-Pape, Côtes-du-Rhône, and Gigondas, as well as the top grape in many northern regions of Spain, including Campo de Borja and Priorat. And, when the vines are old, grenache makes devastatingly great wine in Australia. In California and Washington State, the grape continues to inspire many avant-garde winemakers, and there are now remarkable examples of grenache and grenache blends in both states.

Although France is often thought of as grenache's ancestral home, the grape is Spanish in origin and rightfully ought to be known by its Spanish name, garnacha (gar-NA-cha). While garnacha's parents are not known, it is thought to have arisen in Aragon, one of the seventeen autonomous communities in Spain.

That said, until recently, a strong scientific hypothesis had grenache originating in Italy, first as a white grape called vernaccia (later the pronounciation was corrupted to garnaccia or garnacha) and later brought to Spain (where it mutated to form a red clone) and from there to

France. But as similar sounding as the names vernaccia and garnacha are, molecular analyses show no genetic relationship between the two grapes. The Italian connection is not without merit, however, since DNA typing shows Sardinia's important grape cannonau to be garnacha tinta/grenache noir.

Like pinot noir, grenache is genetically unstable, is difficult to grow, and challenging to make into wine. From less than ideal vineyards, grenache noir can be heavy-handed, simple, and fairly alcoholic (there are countless examples of this in central and southern Spain, southern France, and the Central Valley of California). But when grenache is at its best, the wines that result have an unmistakable purity, richness, and beauty, plus the evocative aroma and flavor of cherry preserves. Grenache is not particularly high in tannin, and thus great examples have a sappy, luxurious texture.

In most places where it is grown, grenache is blended with other varieties—carignan, syrah, and mourvèdre in particular.

GRÜNER VELTLINER

A decade ago, grüner veltliner (GREW-ner VELT-leaner) would not have made a top-25 list like this. But its place today is a testament to the quality of the variety and the surging success of Austrian wine. Grüner veltliner is, in fact, the leading white wine of Austria—more acres are planted with it than with any other variety. It's also the vinous signature of the country; the grape especially excels in the pristine vineyards along the flowing Danube river north and west of Vienna. With the exception of the Czech Republic, Hungary, and a few other, smaller areas in Eastern Europe, grüner veltliner is grown virtually no place else.

The grape is an ancient natural cross of savagnin and a nearly extinct German variety, St. Georgener. Going back even further in the family tree, grüner veltliner is related to pinot noir (possibly as a grandchild), since pinot noir and savagnin are related.

Grüner veltliner has a forward personality. Precise, lively, bold, dry, and minerally,

As autumn approaches, a swallow has found a perfect spot to make her nest.

it's legendary for its lightening-strike of white pepper aroma and flavor, along with a subtle hint of green legumes. Like riesling, grüner is virtually never blended with other grapes and is made in a purist manner, which almost never involves new oak. Also like riesling, the grape tends to be high in natural acidity, giving it a mouthwatering quality, as well as considerable advantages when it comes to pairing with food.

MALBEC

Indigenous to southwestern France, malbec (MAL-beck), the now-popular name for the grape variety cot, is the offspring of two obscure French grapes—magdeleine noire des Charentes and prunelard. While malbec is one of the five main red grapes that can be blended to make red Bordeaux, plantings of it there have been declining for a long time (the grape is prone to frost, and thus has steadily fallen out of favor in Bordeaux's maritime climate). Today, malbec generally makes up less than 10 percent of any Bordeaux wine—if it's used at all.

Half a world away, however, malbec is a star. In the mid-nineteenth century, the grape was brought from Bordeaux to Argentina, where it is now the leading grape for fine red wines.

MUSKRAT LOVE

The place:
My wine classroom in the Napa Valley.

The scene:
An exchange with a middle-aged CEO from abroad, during a class on and tasting of California chardonnays.

The dialogue:
HIM: Number three chardonnay is, umm . . . a little musky.

ME, hoping he's referring to muscat grapes: You mean like muscat blanc or moscato?

HIM: No. Not moscato. Musky.

ME: As in, ahem, the testicles of a male deer?

HIM: I think it's the ducts in their legs.

Alas, we were both wrong on the anatomy. The word *musk,* probably originally derived from the Sanskrit *mushká* ("scrotum"), refers to a strong-smelling substance secreted in a glandular sac under the skin of the abdomen of the male musk deer, or a similar secretion of civets, otters, and muskrats. Interestingly, despite the word's rather sobering definition, the term *musky* is most often used to describe fruity, feminine wines with aromatic allure.

There, it is grown in the dry, sunny, extremely high-altitude vineyards that, like steps, descend from the peaks of the Andes. And, in contrast to Bordeaux, malbec in Argentina (pronounced, in that country, mal-BEC) is almost always made as a varietal wine, rather than part of a blend.

Malbec tends to be low in acidity and slightly less tannic than cabernet sauvignon. Indeed, it's prized for its soft, mouthfilling texture (the wine equivalent of molten chocolate cake), its deep, inky color, and its plummy, mocha, earthy aromas and flavors.

Outside of Argentina and Bordeaux, malbec is the historic grape of Cahors, in southwestern France, where it has traditionally been known by its original name, cot. (In an interesting marketing twist, Cahors now refers to its wine as the "French malbec," although in Cahors the grape makes a rough-edged, tannic wine.)

Malbec shows good promise in the Napa Valley of California, where it is increasingly grown to be used as part of top-notch cabernet blends.

MERLOT

Very similar in flavor and texture to cabernet sauvignon, merlot (mehr-LOW) is easily confused with it in blind tastings. Indeed, the two share the same father—cabernet franc. But merlot's mother is the grape magdeleine noire des Charentes, while cabernet's mother is sauvignon blanc.

In the regional French dialect of Bordeaux, the name *merlot* means "little blackbird" (after the blackbirds—spelled "merlau"—who reportedly love to eat the grapes). Merlot's aromas and flavors include blackberry, cassis, baked cherries, plums, licorice, dark chocolate, and mocha. What merlot usually lacks is cabernet sauvignon's occasional hint of green tobacco or dried mint.

Much is made of merlot's relative roundness, plumpness, and lack of tannin compared to cabernet sauvignon. I think the idea is largely misleading. When merlot is planted in rocky, well-drained soils in top appellations, it can be every bit as structured, commanding, complex, and tannic as cabernet sauvignon. The problem is that too often wine drinkers buy fairly innocuous, inexpensive merlot (sure it's soft; maybe limp would be a better word), then compare it with expensive cabernet sauvignon from a top site. That's apples to oranges.

As for cabernet sauvignon, the most famous region for merlot has historically been the Bordeaux region of France, where merlot (not cabernet sauvignon) is the leading grape in

Merlot grapes growing in an unexpected place: Austria.

MOURVÈDRE

If you were ever an English major, you'll know what I mean by this: Mourvèdre (moor-VED-rah) is the Heathcliff of red grapes. Its dark, hard-edged, almost brooding flavors are never light, juicy, or lively. Mourvèdre has gravitas.

Like carignan and grenache, the grape is Spanish in origin. It should properly be known by its Spanish name, monastrell (or mataró, as it's called in northern Spain and in the Pyrenees). Today, it is grown in numerous provinces in the south-central region of Castilla-La Mancha (especially in the denomination of Jumilla), where it's used to make delicious, sometimes muscular wines with dry, bitter espresso-like flavors (red meat is helpful when consuming them).

The variety is thought to have originated next door to Castilla-La Mancha, in the province of Valencia, where it was propagated by monks. The name derives from the Latin *monasteriellu,* a diminutive of *monasteriu,* meaning "monastery."

In southern France, a small amount of mourvèdre is often used to give depth, color, and kick to Rhône blends such as Châteauneuf-du-Pape and Côtes-du-Rhône. Indeed, before the phylloxera epidemic, mourvèdre was widely planted throughout the south and was the main red grape in Provence. Today, only the small Provençal appellation of Bandol remains steadfast mourvèdre territory.

Mourvèdre was first brought to California from Spain in the mid-1800s, and sparse plots of old-vine "mataro" can still be found. The grape became popular once again in the 1980s as a blending grape in California's Rhône-style blends.

MUSCAT

No matter what anyone says, I doubt Eve was tempted by an apple in the Garden of Eden. A cataclysm of original sin . . . all for a plain apple? It makes no sense. Some muscat (MUScat) grapes, on the other hand, could have done it. Intensely aromatic and awesomely delicious, muscat is irresistible. If every luscious, ripe fruit in the world were compressed

terms of total production. Merlot in Bordeaux is planted mostly outside of the Médoc, and is especially renowned on the Right Bank—in the appellations of Pomerol and St.-Émilion. Here, merlot, too, is almost always blended with cabernet sauvignon, cabernet franc, and possibly malbec and/or petit verdot. There is one extremely famous exception to the blending notion—Château Pétrus (from Pomerol), one of the most expensive wines in the world, is 99 percent merlot.

In addition to rich, complex, structured merlots from top regions, another compelling style of merlot also exists: I'll call it the sleek style. Northern Italy has many such merlots, as does Long Island, in New York State. But some of the best in this style come from two places: Chile and Washington State. The sheer number of exciting, deeply concentrated merlots coming from Washington State is astounding, and is growing larger year after year. In Chile, merlots like Casa Lapostolle's Cuvée Alexandre show the riveting potential this grape has in the New World.

into one phantasmagoric flavor, it would come close to evoking muscat.

Or muscats to be more precise. For, muscat is not a single variety, but rather, a large group of different ancient grapes that have grown around the Mediterranean for centuries. Many scientists and anthrobiologists, in fact, think that some form of muscat may have been the first domesticated variety of grape.

What most of these muscats share is the distinct, awesomely fruity muscat aroma. But that's where the easy part stops, for there are hundreds of named muscat-something-or-others. To take but one example, muscat of Alexandria alone is known by approximately two hundred different names around the Mediterranean.

Some of the varieties in the muscat group are genetically related, but not all. The two main muscats that gave rise to numerous progenitors are muscat blanc à petits grains, a high-quality, small-berried variety, and its daughter, the aforementioned muscat of Alexandria.

Within the muscat group are varieties that can be and are made in virtually every style imaginable: dry, sweet, still, sparkling, and fortified. In Alsace, France, and in Austria, they are made into fantastic dry still wines (and are often served with asparagus). In southern Italy and Spain, various muscats are dried on mats (*passito*) then made into dessert wines.

GRIS AREA

Pinot gris is not the same as **vin gris**. *The French term* **vin gris** *(literally, "gray wine") refers to any number of slightly pinkish-tinted white wines made from red grapes. Vins gris are usually not as deeply colored as rosé or blush wines. While there are dozens of pinot gris made in the United States, there are only a few* **vins gris**.

In northern Italy, muscat blanc à petits grains is made into the sweet bubbly wine almost everyone has had at some time in their lives (moscato d'Asti). In parts of southern France, the same grape is made into a fortified sweet wine: muscat de Beaumes-de-Venise. And the list goes on.

Today, some type of muscat is grown virtually everywhere in the world—from Cyprus, South Africa, and Slovenia to Israel, Oregon, and Greece.

NEBBIOLO

One of the oldest and most important varieties in Piedmont, Italy, *nibiol* was first mentioned in Piedmontese documents in the early thirteenth century. Its parents are presumed extinct, but its origin does appear to be either Piedmont, or perhaps the Valtellina region of Lombardy, next door.

Massively structured and adamantly tannic when young, nebbiolo (neb-ee-OH-low) from anything less than a fantastic vineyard can simply slam your palate closed and cause your taste buds to shrink away. The finest nebbiolos, however, possess a combination of complexity and power that's unequaled. Those wines come only from certain spots within the province of Piedmont, in northwestern Italy. Nebbiolo, alas, is the poster child for grapes that don't travel well. (Outside of Piedmont, there is only one place that has shown even modest success with this difficult grape, and it's a place that's not on many people's wine radar: the Guadalupe Valley of Mexico.)

In the minds of Italians, nebbiolo is, in status and kingly reputation, equal to the great cabernet sauvignons of France. The grape makes the exalted Piedmontese wines Barolo and Barbaresco. Of course, expensive Barolo and Barbaresco are never better than when served with Piedmont's other jaw-droppingly expensive specialty: white truffles.

The word *nebbiolo* derives from *nebbia*, fog, a reference to the thick, whitish bloom of yeasts that forms on the grapes when they are ripe (although many say the name may also refer to the wisps of fog that envelop the Piedmontese hills in late fall, when the grapes are picked).

At Ata Rangi estate in Martinborough, New Zealand, wildflowers grow as part of the cover crop between rows of vines. The flowers draw up moisture from the soil, making sure the vines don't have "wet feet."

The wine has very particular flavors and aromas reminiscent of tar, violets, and often a rich, espresso-like bitterness from the wine's pronounced tannin.

Lastly, until relatively recently, it was an unwritten but adamant rule within the wine world that all great nebbiolos needed to be aged a decade or more before they could be consumed (never mind enjoyed). Modern winemaking techniques (see the Piedmont section, page 331) have changed that, and while the great Barolos and Barbarescos remain utterly long-lived wines, they are also, when young, more delicious than ever.

PINOT GRIS

Depending on where it is grown, pinot gris (PEE-no GREE)—"gray" pinot—can taste strikingly different. Ironically, the best-known pinot gris—Italian pinot grigio—is unquestionably usually the lowest in quality. It's often utterly neutral stuff—serviceable but not significant; the wine version of a white T-shirt. Of course, there's no shame in making basic wine. The crime is in charging a lot for it. (Hello, Santa Margherita.) As always with wine, there are some delicious exceptions. I've always loved the purity and freshness of the

pinot grigios from Jermann (Friuli) and Alois Lageder (Alto Adige), for example.

Then there are the pinot gris from Alsace, France—as opposite of pinot grigios as a wine could be and still be from the same grape. The best Alsace pinot gris is complex, opulent, often a bit smoky and spicy, but still precise and crisp. It's considered one of the four so-called "noble" varieties of Alsace, and is often the perfect wine if you don't want something as aromatic as riesling or gewürztraminer. In Germany, pinot gris (called grauburgunder) can be something else again—broad, even Rubenesque by German wine standards.

In Oregon, where pinot gris began to be planted in the 1990s, the best wines are very tasty, with pear and spice-cake flavors. As for California pinot gris (some of which are called pinot grigio), most are crisp, fresh wines, sometimes with an intriguing edge of pepperiness or arugula-like bitterness. But undoubtedly, the most dependably delicious pinot gris in North America are made in Canada—in the cold, sunny, dry, northern-latitude Oakanagan Valley of British Columbia.

Although I have included it here because of its global popularity, pinot gris is not, technically speaking, its own variety. Like pinot blanc, pinot gris is a clone of pinot noir that includes a color mutation. As such, in the vineyard, pinot gris grapes can be any color from bluish silver to mauve-pink to ashen yellow. As a result, this white wine varies in color, too, although subtly.

PINOT NOIR

Thought to be more than two thousand years old, pinot noir (along with savagnin and gouais blanc) is considered one of the "founder varieties"—the great great grandparent of scores of other well-known grapes, from chardonnay and gamay to corvina and garganega. It is also, according to geneticist Dr. José Vouillamoz, the likely grandparent of syrah. While the parents and exact origin of pinot noir (PEE-no NWAHR) itself are not known, the grape is thought to have come into existence in northeastern France. The name, by the way, is generally thought to derive from *pin*, meaning pine, because the small clusters resemble a pine cone.

By virtue of its old age and its genetic instability, pinot noir has also begotten hundreds of clones of itself. The most well known is undoubtedly pinot meunier, the so-called third variety grown in Champagne, France, but actually a clone of pinot noir that ripens earlier (an asset in a cold region) and exhibits more fruity flavors. Two other main clones are color mutations: pinot blanc and pinot gris (pinot grigio).

If a computer search were conducted on the words and phrases used to describe pinot noir, this detail would emerge: More than any other wine, pinot is described in sensual terms. Pinot noir's association with sensuality derives from the remarkably supple, silky textures and erotically earthy aromas that great pinot noirs

> If a computer search were conducted on the words and phrases used to describe pinot noir, this detail would emerge: More than any other wine, pinot is described in sensual terms.

Clos de Tart, one of the greatest pinot noirs, comes from the very small Burgundian Grand Cru vineyard Clos de Tart. The estate was founded in 1141 by nuns.

display. Aromatically and in terms of flavor, the best pinots can exude not only fruit flavors—warm baked cherries, plums, rhubarb, pomegranate, strawberry jam—but also the sense of damp earth and rotting leaves (the French call this *sous bois*, or forest floor), plus mushrooms, worn leather, and what's sometimes in Europe called *animali*—a highly attractive male sweaty smell (like the smell of a man who has run one mile; I personally find that five miles is a whole different situation). An old friend of mine who, for many years, was the winemaker of California's famous Etude pinot noir, used to say that great pinot noir always possesses a "hint of corruption."

Pinot noir is lighter in body and far less tannic than cabernet sauvignon, merlot, or syrah. It is lighter in color, too, leading beginning wine drinkers to assume that pinot noir's flavors are feeble. For the great pinots, just the reverse is true. Although they are often frail in color, their aromas and flavors can be deep and riveting.

Of all the well-known grapes, pinot noir is considered the most difficult to grow and make into wine. For example, pinot noir is highly sensitive to climate changes and variations in soil composition, and it oxidizes easily during winemaking. This makes pinot noir a riskier (and more expensive) proposition for the winegrower, the winemaker, and the wine drinker than, say, cabernet sauvignon. But it's precisely this enological gamble that often makes pinot noir all the more fascinating and irresistible.

The region of Burgundy, in France, where all the red wines (except Beaujolais), are made from pinot noir is, historically, the most renowned area for the variety. The most expensive pinots still come from this small place, including the most expensive and legendary pinot noir of all: Romanée-Conti from the Domaine de la Romanée-Conti. Prices for this wine can be significantly different based on the quality of the vintage, but even modest vintages command double-take prices. A few years after they were released, two vintages in the late 2000s, for example, carried price tags of $4,800 and $12,900. That's *per bottle*.

In the New World, Oregon has specialized in pinot noir since the 1970s, and many of the best delicate pinots in the United States come from here. And New Zealand is fast emerging as the southern hemisphere's Oregon. Yet, I'd argue that no place beats California in terms of the sheer diversity, complexity, and deliciousness of pinot noir. From the Sta. Rita Hills, Santa Maria Valley, and Santa Ynez Valley in south-central California to the Santa Lucia Highlands in central California to Carneros, the Sonoma Coast, and the Russian River Valley in the north (plus many other top small appellations in between), California is a hotbed of fantastic pinot.

RIESLING

Riesling (REEZ-ling) is considered by many—possibly even most—wine experts to be the most noble and unique white grape variety in the world. The grape is thought to have originated in the Rheingau region of Germany, probably as one of the offspring of gouais blanc and an unknown father.

Great riesling has soaring acidity, an incomparable sense of purity and vividness, plus considerable extract (the nonsoluble substances in wine that add to its flavor). Yet the wine is wonderfully graceful on the palate and has a sense of energy that makes it seem light. Indeed, great riesling is dangerously easy to drink.

Given the right soil and winemaking methods, the triad of high acidity, high extract, and relatively low alcohol leads to intensely flavorful wines of ravishing delicacy, transparency,

and gracefulness. Riesling's refined structure is complemented by the mouthwateringly delicate flavors of fresh ripe peaches, apricots, and melons, often pierced with a vibrant mineral quality, like the taste of water running over stones in a mountain stream.

More than almost any other white grape, riesling is temperamental about where it is planted. It doesn't grow well in very warm places, and even in cooler sites, the quality and character of the wine can vary enormously. The most elegant and precise rieslings come from cool to cold climates—Germany, the Alsace region of France, Austria, Slovenia, Canada, and upstate New York. Rieslings from a warmer climate, such as in Washington State or California, are usually softer, slightly fuller, and can have less-precise, less-minerally flavors. *Usually* is a key word here. Australia, for example, has a generally warm climate. But in the cooler districts of the Clare and Eden valleys of Australia, rieslings are usually ethereal, minerally, vibrantly fresh, and as taut as a tightrope.

On the topic of dryness and sweetness, it's not correct to assume that any given riesling is probably going to be sweet. That's not the case. In fact, most of the rieslings in the world are dry. The exception, of course, are intentionally sweet styles such as beerenauslese (BA) and trockenbeerenauslese (TBA).

Admittedly some of the confusion about the sweetness level of riesling happens because the wine is so fruity—that is, it tastes like fruits, especially peaches and apricots. And in riesling's case, the taster (you or me) confuses this dramatic fruitiness with sweetness. To help clarify where a riesling stands in terms of the taste perception of sweetness, the International Riesling Foundation (IRF), a global educational initiative, created a Riesling Taste Profile chart. The chart, which producers use on the wine's back label, shows a spectrum from dry to medium dry to medium sweet to fully sweet. It then pinpoints where that wine falls in terms of how sweet or dry it tastes. Importantly, producers don't just guess when it comes to their wine's sweetness level. The IRF developed sophisticated technical guidelines, which include the sugar-to-acid ratio and the pH of the wine.

SANGIOVESE

Italy's most famous grape, sangiovese (san-gee-oh-VAY-zee) is responsible for the three great wines of Tuscany: Chianti Classico, vino nobile di Montepulciano, and brunello di Montalcino. It's also a major grape (if not *the* grape) in many of the prestigious wines known as Super Tuscans. Outside Tuscany, sangiovese is used to make red wines in the neighboring regions of Umbria and Emilia-Romagna (and there's a bit in California), but with a few notable exceptions, great sangiovese comes only from Tuscany, in central Italy.

This said, surprising DNA research in 2004 revealed one of the parents of sangiovese to be southern Italian—Calabrese di Montenuovo (presumed to be from Calabria).

The other parent, ciliegiolo (Italian for "small cherry"), is cultivated all over Italy but today is especially well known in Tuscany. It appears, then, that sangiovese may have originated in southern Italy and only later spread to Tuscany.

Sangiovese, like pinot noir, is old enough (and possibly genetically unstable enough) to have mutated considerably, leading to hundreds (perhaps thousands) of clones. The differences among these clones, coupled with differences in the sites where sangiovese is planted, mean that the wines made from the

> A glass of great sangiovese, with its salty sensations, has historically been the perfect partner to Tuscany's other great classic—peppery extra virgin olive oil.

grape vary widely in style and quality. Indeed, from poor clones in poor sites, sangiovese can be as thin and dreary as red-stained, watery alcohol. The top sangioveses, however, are as earthy, rich, and complex as a great sauce.

In flavor and structure, sangiovese is, again, closer to pinot noir than it is to cabernet sauvignon. Sangiovese, for example, takes its structure primarily from acidity, rather than tannin. When it's young, sangiovese has the wonderful appeal of a fresh, warm cherry pie. As it ages, the wine takes on dried leaf, dried orange peel, tea, mocha, spicy, peaty, earthy flavors, and a fabulous sensation of minerality, even saltiness. (The latter is just a metaphor; wine never contains significant sodium per se.) In fact, a glass of great sangiovese, with its salty sensations, has historically been the perfect partner to Tuscany's other great classic—peppery extra virgin olive oil. Indeed, as any visitor to Tuscany can attest, sangiovese-based wines seem to taste so much better *in* Tuscany. Is this as simple as salt and pepper, perhaps?

SAUVIGNON BLANC

The name *sauvignon* comes from the French *sauvage,* meaning "wild." It's a fitting name for a vine that, if left to its own devices, would grow with riotous abandon. Riotous, untamed, and wild can also describe sauvignon blanc's (SEW-vin-yawn BLAHNK) flavors. Straw, hay, grass, smoke, green tea, green herbs, lime, and gunflint charge around in your mouth with wonderful intensity. The wine appears almost linear on the palate, with a clean, keen stiletto of acidity that vibrates through its center.

Some sauvignons push the envelope even further, taking on a feral, acrid character wine

Sauvignon blanc grapes ripening in the summer sun.

WHAT GREEN CAN MEAN

One of the words most frequently used to describe the aroma and flavor of sauvignon blanc is *green*. The theme of green can, however, have many permutations. Here are the ones I think you're most likely to find.

GREEN IDEA What you might smell or taste in the wine

GREEN FRUITS Green fig, honeydew melon

BITTER GREEN Arugula, green tea

EXOTIC GREEN Lemongrass, lime leaf

SMOKY GREEN Lapsang souchong tea

CITRUSY GREEN Lime pith

GREEN VEGETABLES Snap peas, lettuce, green beans

GREEN HERBS Sage, thyme, mint

GREEN SPICE Green peppercorns

PIQUANT GREEN Jalapeño peppers

GREEN OUTDOORS Mown grass, meadows

OCEANIC GREEN Seaweed, sea spray, briny saltwater

---

pros describe as cat pee. (This is usually considered a positive attribute.)

The best, most outrageous, tangy sauvignons come from the Loire Valley of France (Sancerre and Pouilly-Fumé), from New Zealand, and from Austria. On the heels of these come the sauvignons from South Africa and Chile. In Bordeaux, virtually all white wines are made from a blend of sauvignon blanc plus sémillon. In blending the two, sauvignon's tart herbalness is mellowed by sémillon's broad, clean character. Blending the two is also sometimes done in California and Australia.

Despite the assumption that sauvignon blanc probably originated in Bordeaux, most leading geneticists believe the grape to have begun life in the Loire Valley. One of its parents was probably savagnin; the other is unknown. (For its part, sauvignon blanc, with the help of co-parent cabernet franc, begot cabernet sauvignon.)

One of the widespread synonyms for sauvignon blanc is blanc fumé or fumé blanc (the latter term is widely used in California, for example). This is purely a synonym; and it's not

true that as a group, wines labeled fumé blanc have an especially smoky (fumé) character.

When sauvignon blanc is poorly made, it tastes vegetal—like canned asparagus, or the water that artichokes have been boiled in. Sauvignon blanc can become vegetal if it's made from unripe grapes. This could happen, for example, if the vines were planted in wet, fertile, poorly drained soil, or if the vines were allowed to grow out of control, or if the grapes simply did not receive enough sunlight for proper photosynthesis.

SÉMILLON

A friend once told me that sémillon (SEM-ee-yawn) always brought back his childhood memories of the smell and flavor of cotton sheets as he ran under the clothesline on a summer day. Whimsical as that description might seem, there can indeed be something pure, clean, and starched about many sémillons, especially when they are young.

In Bordeaux (sémillon's birthplace), the grape is often blended with a bit of sauvignon blanc (which is thought to be genetically

A bottle of red wine and two glasses—the historic makings of a great evening.

linked, but the relationship between the two is not yet clear). Sémillon's broad, mouthfilling character gets a perfect lift from the lean tartness of sauvignon blanc. In fact, the blend of sémillon and sauvignon is true not only for dry white Bordeaux, but also for the region's sweet wines, such as Sauternes. Sémillon is ideal for Sauternes, as the grapes' thin skins and loose bunches are readily attacked by the noble rot, *Botrytis cinerea* (see page 157).

The name *sémillon*, by the way, may be derived from the old pronunciation of St.-Émilion, the well-known commune in Bordeaux now devoted to merlot and cabernet franc, and no longer a place where sémillon is commercially made.

With all due respect to Bordeaux, some of the greatest dry sémillons in the world are made in Australia, where the wines are considered national treasures. Fascinatingly, Australian sémillon (the Aussies pronounce it "SEM-i-lawn") bears almost no resemblance to the broad, lush sémillons of Bordeaux. Instead, Australian versions are howlingly tart and full of almost tensile energy when young. With age, they become radically transformed—taking on rich, honeyed flavors, a cashewlike nuttiness,

WHAT AMERICANS DRINK

A ccording to The Wine Regions of America, *by John J. Baxevanis, for most of history, in nearly every wine-producing country, red wines have been more popular than whites. Reds were easier to make in most parts of the world, and seemed better suited to hearty meals and the hard physical labor that agriculturally based economies required. Between the end of World War II and the early 1990s, however, white wine consumption in America increased thirty-four times. Changing lifestyles, the drastic reduction in agricultural employment, the rise in economic activity, central air-conditioning, refrigeration, and the dietary shift away from red meat to lighter meats, fish, and vegetables all helped transform the United States into a white-wine-drinking country. Today, however, the color split among wine drinkers in the United States is moving back to red. As of 2010, for example, among those who drank wine once a week or more, about 50 percent of what they drank was red, about 30 percent was white, and the rest was blush and rosé.*

and an almost lanolin-like texture. I will never forget being at Tyrrell's, in the Hunter Valley of New South Wales, and tasting their legendary "Vat 1" sémillons going back to the mid-1960s. The wines were nothing short of mesmerizing.

SYRAH

Syrah (sear-AH) has always reminded me of the kind of guy who wears cowboy boots with a tuxedo. Manly yet elegant. In fact, at the turn of the twentieth century, the British scholar and wine writer George Saintsbury described the famous Rhône wine Hermitage (made exclusively from syrah) as the "manliest wine" he'd ever drunk.

In France (where plantings are on the dramatic increase), syrah's potent and exuberant aromas and flavors lean toward leather, smoke, roasted meats, bacon, game, coffee, spices, iron, black olive, and especially white and black pepper. The best wines have a kinetic mouthfeel, with flavors that detonate on the palate like tiny grenades. The most dramatic syrahs in the world come from the northern Rhône Valley. There, in exclusive, small wine districts, such as Hermitage, Côte-Rôtie, and Cornas, the only red grape allowed is syrah. In the southern Rhône Valley, syrah is usually part of the blends that make up Châteauneuf-du-Pape and Gigondas. It is also planted throughout the Languedoc-Roussillon. In Australia and California, syrah takes on a less gamey, more fruity, syrupy character, but remarkably often possesses the same potent pepper spice character (in 2007, Australian

A long, conical cluster of shiraz (syrah) grapes.

researchers isolated this as the aromatic compound rotundone).

THE NOT-SO-PETITE PETITE

What Californians call petite sirah (sometimes spelled petite syrah) is not the same as syrah, but the histories of the two are interwoven. Vines called petite sirah have grown in California since the 1880s. In the early days some of those vines were probably a type of syrah that had small—petite—grapes. (All things being equal, winemakers prefer small grapes because there's a high ratio of skin to juice. Since color, flavor, and tannin come primarily from a grape's skin, small grapes yield the most concentrated, flavorful wines.) Indeed, there is nothing petite about petite sirah. The wine is mouthfilling and often hugely tannic. Over the course of many decades in California's early history, other vine types were often mixed in with petite sirah vines, creating what are known as field blends in the same vineyard. As more and different varieties found their way into California, and as new vineyards were begun with unidentified cuttings from older vineyards, petite sirah's true identity grew more and more obscure. Then, in the 1990s, DNA typing revealed that most California petite sirah is actually the French grape durif, a cross of peloursin and syrah created in the 1880s. Today, some of the oldest "petite sirah" vineyards remain field blends of many varieties, including true syrah, durif, carignan, zinfandel, barbera, and even grenache.

At Cloudy Bay estate in Marlborough, New Zealand, the flavors of sauvignon blanc are explored in the context of food. Now this is the sort of research you want to be in charge of.

In the seventeenth century, French Huguenots brought syrah from France to South Africa's Cape of Good Hope. From South Africa, it was brought to Australia, although, as of the 1830s, Australian explorers were also bringing syrah to the Australian continent directly from France. Australia, of course, calls syrah shiraz. For its part, South Africa uses both syrah and shiraz, depending on the preference of the winery. Most scholars think the name shiraz is a corruption of one of the colloquial French names for the grape. (Frustratingly, many wine articles continue to reproduce the erroneous legends that syrah/shiraz somehow came from the Iranian city of Shiraz, the Greek island of Syra, or the city of Syracuse in Sicily. All false.) Today, of course, shiraz is Australia's most famous red wine. Indeed, in appellations such as the Barossa Valley, McLaren Vale, and a half dozen others, shiraz can be a spellbinding, spicy blockbuster of a wine.

Syrah was brought to California three times, first in 1936, and then again in the early 1970s (see Syrah in California: Mysterious Beginnings, page 689). But syrah and other Rhône grapes only began to grip the imaginations of maverick winemakers in California in the 1980s, and a decade later, the same thing happened in Washington State. Today syrah is well established in both places, although no single appellation has emerged as *the* appellation of excellence. From a consumer standpoint, it's important to know that syrah producers in the United States can call their wine syrah or shiraz (depending on whether the marketing department wants to channel its inner Aussie).

Syrah is the progeny of two fairly obscure French grapes—dureza (cultivated in the Ardèche) and mondeuse blanche (cultivated in the Savoie). For its part, dureza appears to be the grandchild of pinot noir, which would make pinot noir the great grandfather of syrah.

TEMPRANILLO

Spain's most famous red grape, tempranillo (tem-pra-KNEE-oh), makes a huge range of wine styles depending on where it is grown in Spain—and it's grown in dozens of places. Tempranillo is, for example, the main grape in the country's famous wine region of Rioja.

> When young, tempranillo's flavors are a burst of cherries. After aging, the wine tends to take on a deep, complex earthiness.

Traditionally styled Rioja can resemble red Burgundy (pinot noir) in its refinement, earthiness, and complexity. At the same time, tempranillo is also the grape that makes blockbuster dense reds like tinta del Toro, of the Toro region, and the tinta del país of Ribera del Duero. In short, various clones of tempranillo have, over time, adapted to Spain's diverse regions, and the wines that have resulted often have such highly differentiated characters that they almost seem like separate varieties. Indeed, tempranillo has a slew of different names in Spain, including ull de llebre ("eye of the hare"), cencibel, tinto aragónez, and escobera, in addition to those named above.

Only one probable parent of tempranillo has been identified—the grape variety albillo mayor, which today grows in Ribera del Duero. That said, tempranillo itself is thought to have originated somewhere in the provinces of Rioja and Navarra, in northern Spain.

Tempranillo is usually well structured and well balanced. Its significant amount of tannin allows it to age for long periods, although the wine is generally not as firm on the palate as cabernet sauvignon. Tempranillo's level of acidity gives the wines made from it a sense of precision, yet tempranillo is not as high in acidity as pinot noir. When young, tempranillo's flavors are a burst of cherries. After aging, the wine tends to take on a deep, complex earthiness.

Tempranillo also grows in Portugal, where it's known as tinta roriz and is one of the grapes that make up Port wine. Additionally, the grape is grown in Argentina and California.

VIOGNIER

A Los Angeles restaurateur once described viognier (vee-oh-NYAY) this way: "If a good German riesling is like an ice skater (fast, racy, with a cutting edge), and chardonnay is like a middle-heavyweight boxer (punchy, solid, powerful), then viognier would have to be described as a female gymnast—beautiful and perfectly shaped, with muscle but superb agility and elegance."

Viognier is one of the finest but rarest French white grapes. The grape nearly went extinct in the 1960s, until it became fashionable in California and in Languedoc-Roussillon. Today, fewer than 300 acres are planted in the grape's home, the northern Rhône. Through DNA analysis, it appears that viognier is related to mondeuse blanche, and thus may be either a half sibling of syrah or possibly a grandparent of syrah.

In the northern Rhône, viognier makes the prestigious wines Condrieu and Château-Grillet. (A minuscule appellation, Château-Grillet has just one estate, also called Château-Grillet. It is now owned by the Artemis Groupe, proprietors of Bordeaux's Château Latour). A small amount is also planted in among the syrah vines of the Côte-Rôtie. These white viognier grapes are harvested, crushed, and fermented along with the syrah grapes, giving Côte-Rôtie (which is a red wine after all) a slightly more exotic aroma than it might otherwise have.

Viognier is usually a full-bodied wine with honeysuckle, apricot, gingerbread, and musky aromas and flavors, and a mesmerizingly lanolinish texture. Like gewürztraminer, its extroverted fruity/floral aromas mean that many drinkers assume it's a little sweet, even when it's bone-dry.

Come early winter, a few last grapes, now frozen, still cling to the vine.

In Condrieu, in the northern Rhône Valley of France, the finicky viognier excels. The wines made here have aromas that are simply ravishing.

Viognier exploded in popularity in the United States in the 1990s. In half a decade, the number of California producers went from a mere few to more than thirty. By 1998 there were more than a thousand acres of this variety planted in California. But the demand has since ebbed there, and plantings are now in decline. One of the reasons may be that few California viogniers have the beauty and purity of Condrieu. In California, viognier often suffers from having too little acidity to give it definition, and the wine is too often oaked to within an inch of its life (not true of Condrieu).

Besides in France's Rhône Valley and California (and a few other U.S. states such as Virginia), viognier is also well known in Australia. Among the most exquisite viogniers I've ever tasted have been those from the Australian producer Yalumba.

ZINFANDEL

For decades, zinfandel (ZIN-fan-dell) was the most widely planted red grape in California, until cabernet sauvignon surpassed it in 1998. Now number two in acreage, zinfandel is a chameleon. It can be (and is) made into everything from blush wine to sweet fortified wine. But the zinfandel that knowledgeable wine drinkers love—true zinfandel—is a soft-textured dry red wine crammed with jammy blackberry, boysenberry, and plummy fruit. Made in this style, it's usually concentrated, medium to full in body, and notorious for (temporarily) staining one's teeth crimson if you drink enough of it.

Until 1972, zinfandel was always a hearty, rustic red wine. But in that year, the large

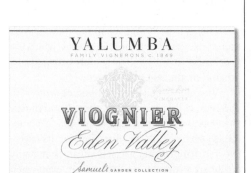

California winery Sutter Home made the first "white zinfandel"—actually light pink—by quickly removing zinfandel's red skins before much color was imparted to the wine.

Soon after its invention, white zinfandel began to outsell true (red) zinfandel—a fact that remains the case today. Yet because it is often slightly sweet and almost always mass-produced from less-than-top-quality grapes, white zinfandel is considered a beginner's wine by serious wine drinkers.

The zinfandel grape's history in California goes back to the 1830s, when it was imported from Croatia (then a part of the Austro-Hungarian Empire). In the 1990s, DNA typing revealed zinfandel to be the Croatian grape called, in modern times, crljenak kaštelanski. During the Middle Ages and earlier, however, the grape was called tribidrag and was grown all over the Dalmatian coast of Croatia. Linguistically speaking, it's not known how *tribidrag* evolved to *crljenak kaštelanski* evolved to *zinfandel*. Moreover, in southern Italy, where it grows predominantly in the region of Apulia, the same grape has yet another distinct name: primitivo.

Zinfandel vineyards are some of the oldest in California. Zinfandel vines well over a hundred years old still thrive in Amador County and Sonoma County, for example. Wines

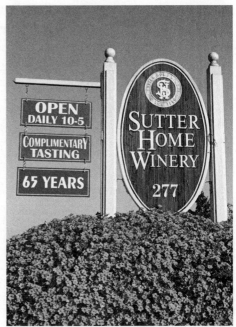

For over sixty-five years, Sutter Home has played a key role in the history of zinfandel In California.

from old zinfandel vines are, in fact, especially prized, and many producers use the term "old vine" on their zinfandel labels. The term has no legal definition, but many winemakers suggest that a zinfandel vine—like a person—turns the corner, becoming "old," after forty.

A GLOSSARY OF OTHER
GRAPE VARIETIES WORLDWIDE

With five thousand to ten thousand grape varieties in the world, there are dozens a wine lover is bound to (and should) discover. Following is a small handbook of the most noteworthy. While some of these grape varieties are usually the sources of wines on their own—Spain's verdejo and Italy's dolcetto, for example—others, such as France's clairette, are very important as grapes used in blends. The list contains both red and white wine grapes, designated as ● and ○ respectively.

A

● **AGIORGITIKO (AH-YOUR-*YEE*-TEE-KOH):** The name, in Greek, means St. George's grape. An important, widely planted Greek grape, it is the source of Nemea, a spicy, earthy wine from the Peloponnese peninsula. The grape variety has nothing to do with the rootstock called St. George.

● **AGLIANICO (A-LEE-*ANN*-EE-CO):** Ancient grape planted almost exclusively in southern Italy. In Campania, it makes the famous wine called Taurasi, and in Basilicata, the wine aglianico del Vulture. Aglianico appears to be related to several southern Italian grapes, but its parents are not known.

○ **AÏDANI (A-*DAN*-EE):** Indigenous to Greece, this aromatic variety is mostly planted in Santorini and is used in the island's white blends.

○ **AIRÉN (I-*WREN*):** The most widely planted grape of Spain, grown mainly on the central plains of Castilla-La Mancha that were immortalized in *Don Quixote.* Used in blending (it's often the base for inexpensive sparkling wine around Europe) and on its own. Grown and made by small family wineries, it can make a fresh, lively, minerally white (not unlike pinot grigio, only better) that's a steal.

○ **ALBANA (AAL-*BAAN*-AAH):** Ancient variety grown in the region of Emilia-Romagna, Italy, albana is thought to be a descendant of garganega. The neutral, somewhat fruity, low-alcohol albana di Romagna was (rather shockingly) the first wine to have been awarded the prestigious DOCG designation in Italy.

○ **ALBARIÑO:** See page 54.

● **ALBAROSSA (AL-BAR-*OSS*-A):** A minor grape grown in the Piedmont region of Italy, a cross of barbera and an obscure grape called chatus.

● **ALEATICO (AL-EE-*AT*-I-KO):** A fascinating, aromatic red possibly related to the white grapes greco and muscat blanc à petits grains. Native to Tuscany, it is especially famous on the island of Elba, off the coast of Tuscany, and the third largest island in Italy, after Sicily and Sardinia. Also grown in southern Italy.

● **ALFROCHEIRO PRETO (AL-FRO-*SHAY*-ROO PRAY-TOH):** Native to central or southern Portugal, high-quality alfrocheiro preto is one of the important grapes in the red table wines of the Dão region.

● **ALICANTE BOUSCHET (AL-I-*KAN*-TAY BOO-SHAY):** The name for one of the last extant crosses of garnacha (grenache) with petit Bouschet, crossed in France by Henri Bouschet in the mid-1800s. In Spain, sometimes called garnacha tintorera. Innocuous in flavor but thick skinned, high yielding, and deeply colored. It is, in fact, one of the very few grapes (red or white) in the entire *Vitis vinifera* family to have red flesh (known as teinturier grapes). As such, alicante Bouschet has been used for decades in southern France to give light red wines more color and the appearance of more flavor intensity. In California, it was used extensively during Prohibition to make thin, watery wines seem like standard reds. Alicante Bouschet is still used in California, mainly in the Central Valley, where it is a useful extender in jug wines. Should not be confused with the denomination Alicante in southeastern Spain, where the main grape is monastrell (mourvèdre).

○ ALIGOTÉ (AL-I-GO-*TAY*): Fairly rare grape of Burgundy, France, and a sibling of chardonnay (both grapes are the progeny of pinot noir and gouais blanc). The light, tart white wine made from it is used with crème de cassis in the Kir cocktail.

○ ALVARINHO (AL-VAR-*EEN*-YO):The main grape of the light, low-alcohol, slightly spritzy wine known as vinho verde, a specialty of northern Portugal. The same as the Spanish grape albariño (see page 54).

○ ANSONICA (AN-*SON*-EE-CA): Also known as inzolia. Floral, high-acid variety considered one of the best native white varieties in Sicily, Italy, and also grown in southern Tuscany. In Sicily, it was once used for Marsala, but is now part of the blend for many white table wines.

● ARAGONEZ (AIR-AH-GO-*NEZ*): One of the Portuguese names for tempranillo. Grown primarily in southern Portugal, where it is used in the red wines of the Alentejo region.

○ ARINTO (AR-*IN*-TOE): More correctly known as arinto de Bucelas. High-quality Portuguese grape from the area of Bucelas, north of Lisbon. Planted throughout Portugal because of its attractive ability to retain acidity. Known as pederña in the Minho region, it is one of the grapes used in vinho verde.

○ ARNEIS (AR-*NACE*): One of the three top white grapes of Italy's Piedmont region, the other two being cortese and moscato (muscat blanc à petits grains). Makes refreshing dry wines.

○ ASPRINIO (AZ-PRIN-*EE*-O): Commonly known as asprinio bianco, it is indigenous to southern Italy's Campania region. Strikingly, the grape is still grown by the ancient method of allowing the vines to climb up local poplar trees so that the vines rise 30 feet or more in the air.

○ ASSYRTIKO (A-*SEAR*-TI-KO): Greek grape with lively acidity. A specialty of the volcanic island of Santorini, in the Aegean.

○ ATHIRI (AH-*THEE*-REE): Greek grape variety that is easy to grow and produces simple, pleasant wines even at high yields.

○ AUXERROIS (AUCHS-AIR-*WAA*): Fairly common grape in Alsace, France, where it originated as a progeny of pinot noir and gouais blanc, making auxerrois a sibling of chardonnay. Usually blended into pinot blanc in Alsace. Confusingly, in southwest France, auxerrois is a synonym for the red variety côt, or malbec.

● AUXERROIS (AUCHS-EAR-*WAH*): A confusing synonym for cot (also known as malbec) in southwestern France—confusing because auxerrois is also the name of a white grape grown in Alsace, France.

● AZAL TINTO (AH-*ZAL TEEN*-TOE): A Portuguese variety with considerable acidity, used to make the strident, rare red version of Portugal's vinho verde. Its more proper name is amaral.

B

○ BACO BLANC (*BAA*-CO *BLAHNK*): A French-American hybrid, also known as Baco 22A, it was developed in 1898 by French nurseryman François Baco. Used as the basis for Armagnac until the 1970s, it continues to be used in that distilled spirit, although to a lesser extent.

● BACO NOIR (BAA-*KO NWAHR*): One of the most famous French-American hybrids, created in 1902 by French nurseryman François Baco. To obtain it, Baco crossed folle blanche with grand glabre (a variety belonging to the American species *Vitis riparia*). It was cultivated in Burgundy and the Loire Valley until France officially barred all hybrids from being grown in French vineyards. Baco noir is now principally found in New York State and Canada.

● BAGA (*BA*-GAH):The word *baga* means berry in Portuguese. One of Portugal's most widely planted red grapes and the leading grape of the region of Bairrada.

● BARBERA: See page 54.

● BASTARDO (BAHS-*TAR*-DOE): Yes, the name means bastard (in Portuguese). A common workhorse grape for dry Portuguese reds, including those made in the Douro and to a lesser extent, the Dão. Bastardo was brought to Portugal some two centuries ago from its native homeland, the Jura region of France, where it is known as trousseau.

○ BLANC DU BOIS (*BLAHNK* DUE *BWAA*): A white hybrid developed in 1968 at the University of Florida and now grown in Florida, Texas, and throughout the Gulf states. Unlike many grapes, it is well suited to humid climates. Blanc du bois also has good resistance to Pierce's disease, a fatal infliction, and one with no known remedy to date, caused by insects known as sharpshooters. Blanc du bois' genetic parentage is complex. The grape is a cross of an American hybrid belonging to the muscadine family with the red grape cardinal, itself a cross of two *vinifera* grapes, flame seedless and ribier.

● BLAUBURGUNDER (BLAUW-BRR-*GUN*-DER): The Austrian name for pinot noir; see page 594.

● BLAUER PORTUGIESER (*BLAUW*-ER POR-CHEW-GAY-ZER): A prolific vine that has nothing to do with Portugal. Very widely planted in Austria (its probable home) and elsewhere in Eastern Europe, including, notably, Hungary. Also used in many simple red German blends.

● BLAUFRÄNKISCH (*BLAUW-FRANK*-ISH): A highly esteemed Austrian variety—probably of Austrian or Hungarian origin—that can make delicious, spicy, precise, earthy, deeply colored reds, especially in Burgenland (the warmest of the Austrian wine regions). Also the leading red in Hungary (where it is called kékfrankos) and grown in Washington State, where it is called by its German name, Lemberger. DNA analysis indicates it is probably the progeny of gouais blanc.

● BOBAL (BO-*BAAL*): Indigenous Spanish red that is grown principally in the Utiel-Requena region of north central Spain. Historically used in blending, but increasingly made into fascinating, spicy, delicious wines that are not unlike grenache.

● BONARDA (BO-*NAR*-DA): The second most popular variety in Argentina after malbec. Although it is called bonarda, this grape is not the same as the relatively rare, indigenous Italian variety bonarda Piedmontese that is grown in Piedmont. Rather, Argentine bonarda has been shown to be the French grape douce noir (sweet black), which originated in the Savoie region of France. In France, the grape is also known as corbeau (meaning crow, a reference to the grape's black color) and charbonneau, which was shortened in California to charbono. (Cult followers of California's now rare charbono will be happy to know they can switch to Argentine bonarda.)

○ BOURBOULENC (BORE-BOO-*LAHNK*): Ancient, simple-tasting Provençal variety, today used in blends throughout the South of France, in the white wines of appellations such as Châteauneuf-du-Pape, Côtes-du-Rhône, Corbières, Minervois, and Bandol.

● BRACHETTO (BRA-*KET*-OH): Native to and found primarily in Piedmont, Italy, around the towns of Asti and Alessandria, where it is used to make brachetto d'Acqui, a deep-red-colored and delicious, if somewhat soda pop–like, sparkling wine.

○ BUAL (BOO-*ALL*): Cultivated on the island of Madeira, bual—sometimes spelled boal—is the grape that makes the rich, sweet style of Madeira also known as bual or boal. The grape is the same as malvasia fina and is also used for dry white table wines in the Dão region of Portugal.

C

● CABERNET FRANC: See page 54.

● CABERNET SAUVIGNON: See page 56.

● CALITOR (*CAL*-I-TOR): One of the lesser red grapes used in France's southern Rhône. Calitor is virtually always blended.

● CANAIOLO (CAN-AYE-*OH*-LOW): An important blending grape in Tuscany and throughout central Italy. Canaiolo is used as part of the blend in making Chianti, where it serves to soften sangiovese's tannic firmness and acidic bite.

● CANNONAU (CAN-AN-*OW*): The famous red grape of the Italian island of Sardinia. The same grape as grenache/garnacha (see page 60).

○ CAPE RIESLING (CAPE REEZ LING): A widely planted grape in South Africa, where it is used mostly in cheap blends. Not the same as true riesling, Cape riesling is thought to be related to the obscure French grape crouchen blanc.

● CARDINAL (CAR-DIN-*AHL*): A vigorous, high-yielding cross of a Hungarian table grape and a French table grape, in which both grapes were themselves obscure crosses. Grown in Texas and Florida.

● CARIGNAN (*CARE*-I-NYAN): The French name for the Spanish grape mazuelo, which originated in northeastern Spain, probably in Aragón, and is used today in Rioja as part of the blend. In some parts of Spain (such as Priorat, which also grows a lot of the grape), mazuelo carries the name cariñena. (The French name carignan is probably derived from cariñena.) Despite being an important grape in Spain, there is far more carignan growing in France. Earthy-flavored and powerful, with dark color, relatively high acidity, and high tannin, it is mostly used for blending in the Languedoc-Roussillon, and to a lesser extent in Provence and the Rhône. In Italy, on the island of Sardinia, it's known as carignano. Also grown in California, where it is spelled carignane and is often a part of inexpensive blends.

● CARMENÈRE (CAR-MEN-*AIR*): An ancient Bordeaux variety (also known in Bordeaux as grande vidure) whose parents are cabernet franc and gros cabernet. Carmenère's half siblings are cabernet sauvignon and merlot.

While virtually extinct in Bordeaux today, the grape is now widespread in Chile, where it is considered the leading red and can make complex, intensely red-hued wines. The name may derive from the word *carmin*—crimson in Latin—and is a reference to the vivid red color of the variety's leaves come harvest time. In China, carmenère is known as cabernet gernischt or cabernet shelongzhu (literally cabernet snake pearl).

○ CARRICANTE (CARE-I-*CAHN*-TAY): A white grape indigenous to Sicily and known for its high yield and acidity. Also known as catarrato.

○ CATARRATTO BIANCO (CAT-A-*RHAT*-O BEE-*AHN*-CO): Bland but hearty Italian variety grown widely in Sicily and used as a blending grape, especially for Marsala. At lower yields it makes a more interesting wine. On Mt. Etna in Sicily, it is called carricante. The grape is probably the progeny of garganega.

● CATAWBA (CA-*TAW*-BA): Found mostly in the northeastern part of the United States, where it is used for juice, jams, and jellies, as well as wine. With its hard-to-describe grapey/animal fur aroma and flavor, often called "foxy," the grape may be a hybrid or a cross; its parents are unknown. Made into light red and rosé wines, especially in New York State.

○ CAYUGA (KAI-*OOO*-GA): An important French-American hybrid, especially in the Finger Lakes region of New York State, where it is made into off-dry and sweet wines.

● CHAMBOURCIN (SHAM-BORE-*SAIN*): A French-American hybrid created (through multiple crossings of crossings) sometime in the late 1940s, but available only since the 1960s. Highly thought of thanks to its "lack of hybrid taste"— in other words, no pronounced grapey/animal fur aromas and flavors. Makes good and very good wines in many eastern and midwestern states of the United States, including Missouri, New Jersey, New York, and Virginia.

● CHARBONO (SHAR-*BO*-NO): Native to the Savoie region of France, where it is properly known as douce noir ("sweet black"), but is also known by the names corbeau and charbonneaux (in California this was later shortened to charbono). Tiny amounts are still grown in California, where the wine has a small but cult following. In Argentina, douce noir is called bonarda, which means that California's charbono and Argentina's bonarda are the same variety.

○ CHARDONNAY: See page 57.

○ CHASSELAS (SHAAS-I-LAS): Ancient, low-acid variety also known as fendant. Best known in the French-speaking part of Switzerland, where it probably originated near Lake Geneva. Also cultivated to a smaller extent in Alsace. In Germany it is referred to as gutedel.

○ CHENIN BLANC: See page 58.

● CILIEGIOLO (CHEE-LEE-EH-JOE-LOW): If you aren't Italian, don't try to say this three times fast. Once only used sparingly in low-cost Italian red blends, ciliegiolo's popularity has increased dramatically in the past ten years, and this grape, with its fresh, cherrylike flavors (ciliegiolo means "cherry" in Italian), is now a component of many DOC wines, especially in Tuscany. Ciliegiolo and Calabrese di Montenuovo are thought to be the parents of sangiovese.

● CINSAUT (SIN-SO): Southern French grape today grown all over the south of France and in the southern Rhône; most frequently used in blends, where it adds a slight spiciness. It can also be found in Algeria, Morocco, and Tunisia. In South Africa, where the grape was confusingly called Hermitage (a region in the Rhône Valley, in France), it was crossed with pinot noir to create pinotage. Sometimes spelled cinsault.

○ CLAIRETTE (CLARE-ET): At low yields this variety is beautifully fresh and aromatic. A common blending component in many white wines of southern France, including those of Provence, Châteauneuf-du-Pape, and Côtes-du-Rhône.

○ COLOMBARD: See French colombard.

● CONCORD (CON-CORD): The most well-known American grape variety in New York State. It belongs to the species *Vitis labrusca* and was first found growing wild near the Concord River in Concord, Massachusetts. Makes distinctly flavored but not very highly esteemed wines with brazen, candylike aromas and flavors. Although it is used in basic kosher wines like Manischewitz, Concord is much more appreciated as juice and jelly than as wine.

● CORNALIN (CORE-NA-LAN): Ancient variety from the Val d'Aosta of northwest Italy, but now virtually extinct there. Better known today in Switzerland, where it grows in the Valais, and is sometimes called humagne rouge. Considered the top red in a country better known for its whites.

○ CORTESE (CORE-TAYS-AY): Northwestern Italian grape that makes the medium-bodied wine Gavi, historically the most prized white wine of Piedmont, Italy.

● CORVINA (CORE-VEE-NA): Considered the most important red grape in the blends that make the well-known Italian wines Amarone and Valpolicella, in the Veneto. It probably originated in the area around Verona; one of its parents is refosco dal peduncolo rosso (refosco with the red stem). The name *corvina* may derive from *corvo* (crow, a reference to the color of the grapes). Usually blended with its progeny, rondinella, and with molinara.

● CÔT (CO): The enologically correct name for malbec. An old variety that originated near the southern French region of Cahors, where it is still the specialty. In Cahors, côt makes a strapping, highly tannic wine that could not be more different from plush Argentine malbec. Côt's parents are prunelard and magdeleine noire des Charentes. The latter is also the mother of merlot.

● COUNOISE (COON-WAZ): One of the common, if lesser, red grapes in France's southern

Rhône Valley. Used in Gigondas and sometimes in Châteauneuf-du-Pape.

● CRIOLLA (CREE-*OH*-LA): Criolla, Spanish for creole, is a group of several *Vitis vinifera* varieties that are historically important in the Americas, especially South America. Their story is convoluted. To begin with, the criollas may have originated naturally in South America as the progeny of European varieties brought earlier, or they may have been cultivated from seeds or cuttings brought by Spanish and Portuguese *conquistadores*. Here are a few of the important criollas: Criolla grande is a pinkish-skinned grape that probably originated in Argentina, where it is still used to make neutral cheap wine. Another criolla called cereza (the word means "cherry" in Spanish) also originated in Argentina, as the progeny of criolla chica and muscat of Alexandria. For its part, criolla chica (Creole girl) is the same as the Spanish grape listán prieto, an old variety from Castilla La Mancha. It was brought to Argentina and Chile in the mid-sixteenth century. By the nineteenth century, criolla chica had, in Chile, been renamed país ("country"). Around the same time, listán prieto was brought from Spain to Argentina and Chile, it was also brought to Mexico by Franciscan missionaries, and there it was renamed misión. Later, in California, misión's spelling was changed to mission. Thus, in the end, Chile's criolla chica (país) and California's mission are the same, and both are the Spanish grape listán prieto. Argentina's criolla grande is related, but it's not known how. And Argentina's cereza is a cross of criolla chica (aka país, aka listán prieto) and muscat of Alexandria. See also Listán prieto.

D

● DELAWARE (*DELL*-A-WARE): More pink-skinned than truly red, this French-American hybrid (whose parentage is cloudy) is grown primarily in the Lake Erie region of New York State, but also in Michigan and Ohio, where it was created. Makes soda pop-ish wines. Curiously, Delaware is also grown in Japan.

● DOLCETTO (DOLE-*CHET*-OH): A fruity, low-acid grape (the name means "little sweet") made into a delicious, fruity, licoricey, bitter-edged everyday wine—the quaffing wine of northern Italy's Piedmont region, although barbera is, more and more, taking over that role.

● DORNFELDER (DORN-*FELL*-DER): German cross of two crosses (Helfensteiner and Heroldrebe) bred in 1956 and honorifically named for an important eighteenth-century viticulturist—Immanuel August Ludwig Dornfeld. Makes darkly colored, soft wines, mostly in the Rheinhessen and Pfalz.

● DOUCE NOIR (*DUE-SAY NWAHR*): Old French variety from the Savoie region, often called corbeau ("crow"). In California, the now rare variety called charbono is douce noir, and in Argentina, the variety bonarda is douce noir.

● DURIF (DUR-*EEF*): A variety created sometime just before the 1860s by French botanist François Durif. A cross of syrah and the now obscure French grape peloursin. Although Durif has virtually disappeared in France, it lives on in California, where it is known as petite sirah. Alas, some (but a minority) of so-called petite sirah vineyards in California are simply peloursin, and some may be extensive field blends that include peloursin and Durif.

E

○ EHRENFELSER (*ERRAN*-FELL-SIR): A German cross of riesling and silvaner now popular in Canada, where it's often made into *eiswein*.

○ EMERALD RIESLING (EM-ER-ELD REEZ-LING): A cross of muscadelle and garnacha developed at the University of California at Davis. Now only tiny amounts are grown, and the grapes are used mostly for jug wines.

○ ENCRUZADO (EN-CREW-*ZAH*-DOH): Important grape in the dry white wines of Portugal's Dão region.

F

○ **FALANGHINA** (*FAA*-LAN-*GHEE*-NA): More properly falanghina flegrea, this is an ancient grape made into white wines in southern Italy's Campania region, in the districts of Falerno del Massico and Sannio. The name may derive from the Latin *falangae,* for the stakes that support vines.

○ **FENDANT** (FEN-*DAHNT*): See Chasselas.

○ **FIANO** (FEE-*AH*-NO): An ancient grape cultivated near Avellino, in Campania, in southern Italy. The fiano of Apulia is thought to be an entirely separate variety.

○ **FOLLE BLANCHE** (FOAL *BLONCH*): Once, but no longer, a leading grape in Cognac and Armagnac. Today used mostly in the western Loire to produce the extremely tart, thin Gros Plant. Also known as mune mahatsa in Spain's Basque region, it is one of the varieties used to make the tart, dry white wine Txakoli.

● **FREISA** (*FRAY*-ZHAH): Bitter, acidic, aromatic red grape of the northwestern Italian province of Piedmont. Thought to be an offspring of nebbiolo, it was traditionally made into a frothy, slightly sparkling, pale red wine with a touch of sweetness. Today, it is often made in a still, dry style.

○ **FRENCH COLOMBARD** (FRENCH CALL-UM-BARD): More correctly known simply as colombard, it is widely planted in the southwest of France, where it is mostly distilled into eaux-de-vie, Cognac, and Armagnac. In California, it is a high-yielding grape made into jug wines. Known as colombar in South Africa, where it is also made into jug wines.

○ **FRIULANO** (FREE-OO-LAHN-OH): Formerly known in Italy as tocai Friulano and planted mostly in the northeastern Italian region of Friuli-Venezia Giulia, it is the source of somewhat spicy, lightly floral, medium-bodied wines that are considered among the region's best. The same grape as sauvignonasse, sometimes

called sauvignon vert, a grape well established in Chile.

○ **FURMINT** (*FUR*-MINT): Native to Hungary and the major grape in the famous Hungarian botrytized sweet wine Tokaji aszú. Furmint is also used for dry wine. Also grown in Austria.

G

● **GAGLIOPPO** (GAL-EE-*OH*-PO): An ancient grape variety and natural cross of sangiovese and mantonico bianco, an obscure variety from the region of Calabria. Gaglioppo is the main grape today in Calabria, where it is the source of the grapey red Italian wine Cirò.

● **GAMAY**: See page 59.

○ **GARGANEGA** (GAR-*GAN*-I-GA): An ancient variety most closely associated with the northern Italian region of the Veneto, and the major grape of Soave. Garganega is thought to be one of the parents of many other Italian white varieties, including trebbiano Toscana, malvasia bianca di Candida, albana, and catarratto bianco.

● **GARNACHA**: See Grenache, page 60.

○ **GARNACHA BLANCA** (GAR-*NA*-CHA *BLAHNK*-A): See Grenache blanc.

○ **GELBER MUSKATELLER** (*GEL*-BER *MUS*-CA-TELLER): Sometimes simply muskateller, this is the Austrian name for muscat blanc à petits grains. See Muscat, page 63.

○ **GEWÜRZTRAMINER**: See page 59.

● **GIRÒ** (JEER-*OH*): An ancient grape variety that is grown on the large Italian island of Sardinia. Girò may be of Spanish origin.

○ **GLERA** (*GLARE*-AH): Ancient northern Italian grape also known as prosecco, and used to make the Italian sparkling wine Prosecco. In 2009, when the wine Prosecco was awarded DOCG status (the highest rank for an Italian wine), the grape name prosecco was officially discontinued to avoid confusion. Glera, which had been an old synonym for the prosecco grape, henceforth came into official use.

O **GODELLO (GO-DAY-YO):** Major white grape made into wines in northwestern Spain, in the remote mountainous region of Valdeorras, although the grape's origin is probably in Galicia, next door. Makes wines that can have a full body and a viscous, almost lanolin-like mouthfeel.

O **GOUAIS BLANC (GOO-AY BLAHNK):** One of the prolific ancient "founder varieties," and as such, a parent and grandparent to a slew of other varieties, including such disparate varieties as riesling, muscadelle, blaufränkisch, and colombard. No known wine from gouais blanc is made today, though a few isolated vines may still exist in the Haute-Savoie region of France.

O **GOUVEIO (GOH-VAI-YOU):** One of the grapes used to make the dry white wines of the Dão and the Douro Valley in Portugal, and also used in the making of white Port. The same grape as Spain's godello.

● **GRACIANO (GRA-SEE-AN-OH):** High-quality, late-ripening Spanish grape, with delicate, slightly spicy flavors and an ability to hold onto its acidity even in warm places. Used primarily in Rioja, as part of traditional Rioja blends. Also found to a small extent in the Languedoc-Roussillon, where it is confusingly called morrastel (which sounds like monastrell, but the grape is entirely different). On the Italian island of Sardinia, it's known as bovale sardo, and is much appreciated as an addition to blends.

O **GRAŠEVINA (GRAH-SHEH-VINA):** The most widely planted white grape in Croatia. Known in Austria as welschriesling and in northern Italy as riesling Italico, although it is not related to riesling.

O **GRAUBURGUNDER (GRAOW BUR-GUND-ER):** One of the German names for the grape pinot gris, which is also known as ruländer.

O **GRECHETTO (GREH-CHET-OH):** Grown in the central Italian province of Umbria, it is one of the grapes that make the medium-bodied Italian wine Orvieto.

O **GRECO (GREC-OH):** An ancient variety now grown primarily in the southern Italian region of Campania, where it is made into distinctive white wines, the most famous of which is greco di Tufo.

● **GRENACHE:** See page 60.

O **GRENACHE BLANC (GREN-AHSH BLAHNK):** A white-berried clonal mutation of the red grape grenache. Grenache blanc is a leading blending grape in the white wines of southern France, including the whites of Provence, the Languedoc-Roussillon, and the southern Rhône. More properly known as garnacha blanca, since it originated in Spain.

● **GRIGNOLINO (GREE-NO-LEE-NO):** Native to Piedmont, Italy, where it is the source of light-reddish, frothy, crisp wines that can also have a tannic bite. The name may come from *grignòle,* a Piedmontese dialect word for pips or seeds, because grignolino is known for the high number of seeds in each berry.

O **GRILLO (GREE-LOH):** One of the main white grapes of Sicily, where it can make fantastically refreshing, floral, peppery dry white wines. Also, along with catarratto bianco, one of the two grapes used in Sicily to make Marsala. Grillo's parents were catarratto bianco and muscat of Alexandria.

● **GROLLEAU (GROW-LOH):** A mostly uninspired grape used primarily in France's Loire Valley, in the red and rosé wines of Anjou.

O **GRÜNER VELTLINER:** See page 61.

O **GUTEDEL (GOOT-I-DEL):** German name for the Swiss grape chasselas. In Germany, it is planted mostly in the Baden region, where it makes basic wines.

H

○ HANEPOOT (*HAHN*-E-POOT): See Muscat, page 63.

○ HÁRSLEVELŰ (*HARSH*-LEH-VEH-LOO): Aromatic Hungarian grape that lends a smooth, spicy character to the renowned botrytized sweet wine Tokaji aszú. Native to Hungary, hárslevelű is a progeny of furmint.

● HONDARRIBI BELTZA (HONDA-*REE*-BEE *BELT*-ZA): Beltza means black in Basque. Used to make the somewhat rare, light, lively, crisp red Txakolí (shah-co-LEE) of Spain's Basque region. Like cabernet sauvignon and carmenère, hondarribi beltza is one of the decendents of cabernet franc. Despite its name, it is not related to hondarribi zuri (white hondarribi).

○ HONDARRIBI ZURI (HONDA-*REE*-BEE *ZURI*): Indigenous to Spain's Basque region, this is the name given to the leading variety of grape in the region's sassy, high-acid white Txakolí (shah-co-LEE) wines (*zuri* means white in Basque). However, DNA analysis has revealed that what is called hondarribi zuri is actually not a single variety but rather any one of three white grapes planted in the Basque region: courbu blanc, crouchen, or the hybrid noah.

○ HUXELREBE (HOUKS-EL-*RAY*-BA): Developed in Germany, this unusual cross of chasselas (also known as gutedel) and the obscure grape courtillier musqué makes aromatic wines, especially in Germany's Pfalz and Rheinhessen regions.

I

○ INZOLIA (IN-*ZOL*-EE-AH): See Ansonica.

○ IRSAI OLIVÉR (*EER*-SHA-EE *OH*-EYE-VEHR): A white Hungarian grape that was originally bred to be a table grape but is now often used to produce soft, aromatic wines that are best drunk young.

○ ISABELLA (IS-A-*BELL*-AH): An American hybrid probably derived from a seedling that occurred in nature when an unknown variety within the species *Vitis labrusa* crossed with an unknown variety of the *Vitis vinifera* species. The grape was brought from South Carolina to New York in the early 1800s by a grower, George Gibbs, whose wife was named Isabella. Now planted in places as disparate as Japan, New York State, India, and Brazil. Unlike most grape varieties, Isabella grows well in semitropical and humid conditions.

○ IZKIRIOT TTIPI (EE-*SKEE*-REE-OT *TEE*-PEE): The Basque name for petit manseng, which is grown in Spain's Basque region to make the tart, dry white wine known as Txakolí.

J

● JAEN (JAI-*EN*): See Mencía.

○ JUHFARK (*YOO*-FARK): A minor white grape mostly grown in the volcanic soils of the Somló region of Hungary. It makes wines that are high in acid and often more salty and minerally than fruity.

K

● KADARKA (KAH-*DAR*-KAH): An Eastern European variety, especially important in Hungary, where it is grown throughout the country. Makes light-colored, spicy, earthy wines that have a similarity to simple pinot noir.

● KÉKFRANKOS (*KEK*-FRANK-OSH): A leading red grape in Hungary, probably of Hungarian or Austrian origin. It makes spicy, earthy, deeply colored reds in Hungary, Austria's Burgenland, and in Washington State, where it is called by its German name, Lemberger. DNA analysis indicates it is probably the progeny of gouais blanc.

○ KERNER (*KER*-NER): A popular and often delicious German variety created by crossing the red trollinger (schiava) grape with the white riesling grape. Named after a nineteenth-century medical doctor and songwriter, Justinius Kerner, who prescribed wine as good natural medicine.

○ KHIKHVI (*KEEK*-VEE): Rare variety from the Republic of Georgia, where it is still grown and made into highly thought of dry and sweet wines.

○ KIRÁLYLEÁNKYA (*KEE*-RAH-LEE-*LEE*-ANK-YA): Widely planted white Hungarian grape with fresh acidity and citrus flavors, whose name means "little princess."

○ KOSHU (*KO*-SHOO): Widely planted Japanese variety grown in several areas of that country, including the Mt. Fuji area. Legend has it that the grape is a cross of a native, wild Japanese grape with a *vinifera* variety that was brought from the Caucasus to China and then, by Buddhist monks, to Japan approximately a thousand years ago. But DNA typing has revealed no relationships with other known varieties, and thus koshu's origins remain a mystery. The first mentions of the variety being made into wine in Japan go back to the 1870s. Historically the wine was produced in a sweet style; today it is made as a dry, delicate, low-alcohol, crisp white, not unlike Muscadet.

● KOTSIFALI (KOT-SI-*FAHL*-EE): Unique to the Greek island of Crete, its home. Kotsifali makes a light, strawberry-scented red, and is one of the varieties in the Greek wines Achárnes and Pezá.

● KRASSATO (KRAH-*SAH*-TOE): Fairly full-bodied Greek variety thought to be indigenous to the area around Mt. Olympus, on the Greek mainland. Blended with xinomavro and stavroto to make the wine Rapsáni.

L

● LACRIMA DI MORRO D'ALBA (*LAK*-REE-MA DEE *MORE*-O *DAL*-BA): The word *lacrima* (meaning "tears") is used for several different Italian varieties and wines. The most important of the grape varieties is lacrima di Morro d'Alba, which is the dominant variety in the wine also called lacrima di Morro d'Alba, a fruity red of Italy's Marche region (not the same as Alba in Piedmont).

● LAGREIN (LAH-*GRAYNE*): A distinctive, fruity, bitter northern Italian variety probably indigenous to the Alto Adige region, where most of it grows today. One of its parents is teroldego; the other is unknown. It is sometimes blended with schiava.

● LAMBRUSCO (LAM-*BRUCE*-KO): The name *lambrusco* means wild grape. There are more than thirteen different varieties with the word *lambrusco* or *lambrusca* in their names. A small number are cultivated in Piedmont, but the majority are more famously in Emilia-Romagna, where the refreshing, very slightly sweet or dry fizzy wine called lambrusco is a specialty. Because of its fizz and acidity, lambrusco is traditionally drunk as a counterpoint to Emilia-Romagna's famous salumi and rich meat pasta sauces.

○ LAŠKI RIZLING (*LASH*-KEE *REEZ*-LING): See Welschriesling.

● LEMBERGER (*LEM* BRR GER): The German name for the dark, spicy, Austrian grape blaufränkisch. Grown in small amounts in Washington State, where it is called Lemberger. See also Blaufränkisch.

● LENOIR (LEN-*NWAHR*): A complex American hybrid originally created in the southeastern part of the United States and named after Lenoir County, in South Carolina. It was eventually taken further south, to Mississippi, by a Spanish man named Jacquez; hence Jacquez is a synonym, as is black Spanish, thanks to the deep color of the grape's skin. (Note that several different varieties have black Spanish as a synonym.) Widely planted in southeast and central Texas, where it has appeared to evolve a natural resistance to Pierce's disease (a potentially fatal vine disease caused by insects known as sharpshooters) despite the heat and humidity of the climate. Also widely planted in Brazil, where it is used for juice, jelly, and jug wines.

● LIATIKO (LEE-*AT*-E-KO): The most widely planted grape on the Greek island of Crete. Makes floral, spicy, pale reds with relatively high acidity. Used for dry and sweet wines.

● LIMNIO (*LIM*-KNEE-OH): Ancient Greek variety said to have been appreciated by Aristotle. Native to the island of Limnos, in the northern Aegean, and now planted all over northern Greece. Sometimes blended with cabernet sauvignon and cabernet franc.

● LISTÁN PRIETO (LEE-*STAN* PRE-*ET*-OH): A dark-skinned grape (*prieto* means dark in Spanish) native to the region of Castilla La Mancha in central Spain. In the sixteenth century, listán was brought on several occasions to the Americas, where the grape had a profound influence on the early viticultural history of many countries. Indeed, listán prieto was the first European (*Vitis vinifera*) variety to be cultivated in the Americas. The grape was brought directly and independently to Argentina, Chile, and Mexico. In Chile, listán came to be known as criolla chica, "Creole girl" (see Criolla, page 81), and was later renamed país. In Mexico, listán was introduced by Franciscan missionaries, who renamed it misión. It traveled eventually to Baja California (present day Mexico), then up to Alta California, where it was planted (spelled mission) at the Mission San Diego de Alcalá around 1770. In Argentina, listán prieto crossed naturally with muscat of Alexandria to create several grapes, including cereza, torrontés Riojano, and possibly torrontés Sanjuanino. A small amount of listán prieto is still grown on the Canary Islands in Spain, and a huge amount is still grown in Chile as país. In California, as mission, 600 acres (242 hectares) are left.

M

○ MACABEO (MAC-A-*BAY*-OH): Northern Spanish grape also known as viura. One of the three grapes used in cava, Spanish sparkling wine, and the primary grape in the white wines of Rioja. A small amount is grown in the Rhône, in France, where it is used in the appellation of Lirac; it is also used to a small extent in the Languedoc-Roussillon.

○ MADELEINE ANGEVINE (*MAD*-EH-LIN AN-JE-*VINE*): A cross of a cross of a cross created in the Loire Valley in the mid-nineteenth century and now grown in extremely limited amounts, mostly in British Columbia, Canada. A seedling of madeleine angevine crossed with an unknown parent—so-called madeleine x angevine 7672—is somewhat more famous as a pleasantly floral grape variety grown principally in England.

● MAGDELEINE NOIRE DES CHARENTES (*MAG*-DEH-LIN *NWAHR* DAY SHAR-*AWNT*): This obscure, rare French variety is the parent (with cabernet franc) of merlot, and (with prunelard) of malbec grapes. Thought to have been cultivated since the Middle Ages, magdeleine noire des Charentes was rediscovered in the 1990s in the Charente department of southwestern France, where it was known as raisin de la madeleine. But DNA typing revealed no genetic relationship to other varieties with the word *madeleine* in the name. In the 2000s, the scientists renamed the variety magdeleine noire des Charentes in a not-completely-successful attempt to distinguish it from other magdeleines. (As part of a grape's name, "magdeleine" is thought to refer to the feast day of Mary Magdalene—July 22—a recognition of the fact that all the "madeleines" are extremely early ripeners and are often harvested in July.)

○ MALAGOUSIA (MAH-LAH-GOU-*ZYAH*): Historic variety native to central Greece. Lively and perfumed, it is grown with success in Macedonia in particular.

● MALBEC: See page 61.

○ MALMSEY (*MALM*-ZEE): See Malvasia.

○ MALVASIA (MAHL-VA-*ZEE*-AH): Like muscat, malvasia is not a single variety but a collective name for a wide variety of Mediterranean grapes (white, pink, and black skinned), most of which are not actually related. What some of them do share, however, is an ability to result in sweet wines that are high in alcohol. Greece has been put forward as the original home of malvasia, but DNA testing does not support this idea. Among the different varieties—all with malvasia in the name—are malvasia bianca di Candia (the most planted type of malvasia, and common in Italy); malvasia bianca lunga (used in Tuscany for vin santo, and historically in Chianti, where it was part of the original Chianti "formula"); malvasia branca de São Jorge (the malvasia used to make malmsey Madeira); and malvasia di Lipari (which makes the famous Sicilian passito dessert wine of the same name; confusingly, this is also known as malvasia candida, which sounds awfully close to malvasia bianca di Candia). Malmsey is an English corruption of the word *malvasia*.

○ MALVOISIE (MAHL-VWA-*ZEE*): See Vermentino.

● MAMMOLO (MAM-*MO*-LOW): Old Tuscan variety grown in central Italy as well as on the island of Corsica, where it is known as sciaccarello ("crunchy"). In Tuscany, it is often blended with sangiovese.

● MANDILARIA (MAN-DELL-*ARE*-EE-AH): A darkly colored, tannic grape native to the Greek islands of the eastern Aegean. Blended in small amounts with kotsifali to make the wines Arhánes and Pezá, on Crete. Also grown on numerous other Greek islands, including Santorini and Pylos, and all over the southern Peloponnese peninsula.

● MARÉCHAL FOCH (*MAR*-EH-SHAWL FOSHE): A complex hybrid created in France in 1911 and named after Maréchal Ferdinand Foch, a general in the French army during World War I. Deeply colored, tannic, and somewhat herbaceous, and well suited to cold climates. Grown today in small amounts in Canada and the northeastern United States.

○ MARSANNE (MAR-*SAHN*): The main white grape of the northern Rhône in France. Makes big-bodied wines and is often blended with the aromatic and elegant grape roussanne, which may be either its parent or its offspring. It is also grown in the Languedoc-Roussillon, as well as in California.

● MARSELAN (MAR-SE-*LAN*): A recent cross (1961) of cabernet sauvignon and garnacha/grenache, cultivated in the Languedoc and the southern Rhône. The name refers to Marseille, the well-known city near the agronomy institute in Montpellier, where the cross was developed.

○ MAUZAC (MAO-*ZAHK*): In the Languedoc-Roussillon, in France, the grape used to make sparkling Crémant de Limoux.

● MAVRODAPHNE (MAV-RO-*DAFF*-KNEE): Also spelled mavrodaphni, the name means "black laurel." Probably native to Cephalonia (Kefalonia in Greek), one of the Ionian islands of western Greece, or the Peloponnese peninsula. It is the leading grape in the famous Greek wines mavrodaphne de Patras and mavrodaphne de Kefalonia, which are long-aged, sweet, fortified red wines made in Patras on the Peloponnese peninsula and in Cephalonia, the largest of the Ionian islands in western Greece.

● MAVROTRAGANO (MAV-RO-*TRAG*-AH-NOH): Indigenous to the Greek island of Santorini, mavrotragano produces wines with high tannin, and berry and spice characteristics. Once almost extinct, it is now experiencing a renaissance.

● MAVROUDA (MAV-*ROO*-DAH): The name (also spelled mavroudi or mavroudia) for several unrelated dark-skinned grape varieties grown all over Greece.

● MAZUELO (MA-*ZWAY*-LO): Native to northeastern Spain—probably the region of Aragón, mazuelo has dozens of synonyms in Spain and elsewhere. In Spain, in Rioja, it is known as mazuelo and is used in many Rioja blends for its acidity, tannin, and earthy flavors. But in Priorat and elsewhere in Spain, it is known as cariñena. In France, especially in the Languedoc-Roussillon, Provence, and Rhône regions of southern France, it's known as carignan. Indeed, today, despite this grape's

Spanish origins, more of it is grown in France. In the United States, carignan is often spelled *carignane*.

● **MELON DE BOURGOGNE** (MEL-*AWN* DE BORE-*GOY*-NYA): An ancient Burgundian variety, melon was subsequently banned in Burgundy, but found a centuries-long home in the Loire Valley, where it's the grape that makes the light, tart, dry French wine Muscadet, considered the working man's accompaniment to oysters.

● **MENCÍA** (*MEN*-THEE-AH): A spicy grape native to the area around Bierzo, in the province of León, in northwestern Spain, that is currently undergoing a small revival. Also grown in Portugal's Dão region, where it is known as jaen.

● **MERLOT:** See page 62.

● **MISSION** (*MI*-SHEN): The first *Vitis vinifera* variety planted in California. Originally from Spain, and brought to California by Franciscan missionaries traveling north from Mexico in the 1700s. Determined in the 1990s to be the Spanish grape listán prieto. Mission remained the mainstay of the California wine industry until the Gold Rush of 1848. There are still some 600 acres (242 hectares) of mission planted in California, mostly in the hot San Joaquin valley. See also Listán prieto.

● **MOLINARA** (MOLE-IN-*ARE*-AH): A high-acid red grape probably native to the Veneto. It is not as high in quality as corvina or rondinella, the grapes it is blended with (albeit in small amounts) to make Italy's powerful wine Amarone, as well as for the lighter wines Valpolicella and Bardolino.

● **MONASTRELL** (MON-AH-*STRELL*): A widely planted, very late-ripening grape that originated in Valencia, Spain. Today it is used mostly in the central part of that country, in provinces such as Jumilla, to make powerful, dark, dense red wines. See Mourvèdre (the French name of the grape), page 63.

○ **MONEMVASIA** (MO-NEM-*VASE*-EE-A): Greek variety found mainly on the Cyclades Islands in the Aegean, notably Paros, and in the southern Peloponnese Peninsula. Makes both dry and sweet wines. The name is said to come from the fortified medieval port city Monemvasia, which, thanks to an earthquake in A.D. 375, is now an island connected to the mainland by one bridge. In Greek *moni emvassis* means single entrance.

● **MONTEPULCIANO** (MON-TI-PULL-CHEE-*AH*-NO): Confusingly, this is not the grape of the Tuscan wine vino nobile di Montepulciano, which is made from sangiovese. Instead, the grape montepulciano is widespread throughout central and southern Italy, and is especially well known in Abruzzi, where it makes the good, rustic montepulciano d'Abruzzo.

○ **MORIO-MUSKAT** (*MOOR*-EE-OH *MUS*-CAT): A German cross of unknown parentage found mostly in Germany's Pfalz and Rheinhessen regions. Makes a somewhat perfumed wine that can often be a bit too much like cheap perfume.

○ **MOSCATEL** (MOSS-CA-*TELL*): The general name used in Spain and parts of Portugal for both muscat blanc à petits grains and muscat of Alexandria. In Jerez, moscatel bianco (muscat of Alexandria) is the third most important grape, after Palomino and Pedro Ximénez, and there, it is made into a sweet, fortified wine that is sometimes made by the solera system of fractional blending that is used to make Sherry. It is also made into intriguing dry, aromatic still wines (both alone and as part of a blend) in several other parts of Spain.

○ **MOSCHOFILERO** (MOW-SHO-FEE-*YER*-OH): Highly aromatic Peloponnesian grape that is the source of the light, fresh Greek Peloponnesian wine Mantineia.

● **MOURVÈDRE:** See page 63.

○ **MTSVANE KAKHURI** (MUTZ-VAH-NEH KAH-KOO-REE): An old variety from southeastern Georgia, but also grown in Ukraine, Russia, and the Republic of Moldova. Usually just called mtsvane. Used to make dry and sweet wines, some of which are made in the traditional clay *qvevri,* a kind of large amphora without handles that is buried in the ground.

○ **MÜLLER-THURGAU** (*MOO*-LER *TER*-GAO): Well-known German grape variety that makes rather neutral-tasting, undistinguished wine in Germany (but very good wine in surrounding countries, such as Italy and Hungary). Recent DNA typing has established it as a cross between riesling and madeleine royale, a table grape of unknown parentage. Müller-Thurgau was widely planted after World War II and became the leading grape in Germany in the 1990s. Today, it has been supplanted by riesling, which makes vastly superior wine.

○ **MUSCADEL** (*MUS*-CA-DELL): South African name for muscat blanc à petits grains. See Muscat, page 63. See also Muscadelle.

○ **MUSCADELLE** (*MUS*-CA-DELL): Perfumed grape blended in tiny amounts with sémillon and sauvignon blanc to make some white Bordeaux. It's more famous, however, in Australia, where it is used to make the famous Australian fortified wine topaque (formerly known as tokay) in the Rutherglen region of Victoria. It is not the same variety as any of the varieties called muscat. Confusingly, South African muscadel *is* a muscat.

○ **MUSCADET** (*MUS*-CA-DAY): The name sometimes used for melon de Bourgogne, the grape that is the source of the sharp, light, dry French wine Muscadet.

● **MUSCARDIN** (MUS-CAR-*DEN*): A relatively rare, fairly neutral grape used in France's southern Rhône, in such wines as Châteauneuf-du-Pape and Gigondas.

○ **MUSCAT:** See page 63.

○ **MUSKATELLER** (*MUS*-CA-TELLER): Austrian name for muscat blanc à petits grains. See Muscat, page 63. Also known as gelber muskateller.

N

● **NEBBIOLO:** See page 64.

● **NEGOSKA** (NE-*GOES*-KA): A northern Greek variety used with xynomavro to make the popular, full-bodied Greek wine Goumenissa.

● **NEGRAMOLL** (NEG-RA-*MOL*): An old variety that probably originated in Andalucía, Spain, and from there was brought to Spain's Canary Islands, where it still is grown today and where it makes light aromatic reds. It is better known, as tinta negra mole, on the Portuguese island of Madeira, where it is the leading grape planted and is used for much of the basic Madeira produced.

● **NEGRARA** (NE-*GRA*-RA): A minor blending grape in the powerful Italian wine amarone and the lighter-bodied Valpolicella. Considered lower in quality than corvina and rondinella, with which it is blended.

● **NEGRETTE** (NE-*GRET*): A variety that grows north of Toulouse, in southwestern France, where it is fruity and simple, and not as popular as the other local variety, tannat.

● **NEGROAMARO** (*NEG*-RO A-*MAR*-OH): Negro (black) and amaro (bitter) tell it all. An appealing, southern Italian grape with slight bitter espresso-like flavors and yet a soft texture. Widely grown in the Apulia region, especially in the hot, dry Salento peninsula, the spur of the Italian boot. No parental relationships have yet been established for this main variety.

● **NERELLO CAPPUCCIO** (NER-*ELLO* CA-*POO*-CHO): Grown on Mt. Etna, in Sicily, and is thought to be related to sangiovese, much like nerello Mascalese, but produces a lower-quality wine that is mostly used to add color and alcohol to red blends.

● **NERELLO MASCALESE** (NER-*ELLO* MAS-CA-*LAY*-ZE): Grown on the volcanic slopes of Sicily's Mt. Etna and thought to be distantly related to sangiovese. It is often bottled on its own, as well as being blended. Produces wines with good acid and tannin content.

● NERO D'AVOLA (*NER*-O *DA*-VO-LA): This widely planted black (*nero*) grape was probably named after the city of Avola, on the Italian island of Sicily. It's the aristocratic red grape of Sicily, making wines that are mouthfilling, structured, chocolaty, and often complex. It is sometimes called Calabrese. DNA analysis suggests there are several clones of nero d'Avola, and possibly several different varieties that fall under the name.

● NERO DI TROIA (*NER*-O DEE *TROY*-A): Also known as uva di Troia. Rustic, tannic, productive variety grown primarily in the Apulia region of Italy, in the province of Bari. The name translates as "black of Troy," but DNA analysis shows no relationship to Greek varieties.

○ NEUBURGER (*NOY*-BURGER): Austrian grape known to make golden-colored dry wines and some good sweet wines. A natural cross between roter veltliner and silvaner that probably took place in Austria.

○ NIAGARA (NIGH-*AG*-RA): A very pungently aromatic American cross of two *Vitis labrusca* varieties, named after Niagara, New York, where it was developed in the 1860s. Still best known in New York State, where it is the source of off-dry and sweet wines.

● NORTON (*NOR*-TEN): One of the oldest hybrids cultivated in the United States, having been discovered in Virginia sometime around 1820. DNA typing suggests it is a natural cross that occurred in the wild of a *Vitis vinifera* variety with a *Vitis aestivalis* variety. Today, it is grown in the Midwest and mid-Atlantic states, and is especially successful in Missouri and Virginia, where it is the source of some surprisingly good zinfandel-like wines.

O

● OSELETA (OH-SEH-*LET*-TAH): Used in small amounts in some amarone and Valpolicella blends, in northeastern Italy. Originally thought to be extinct, it was revived by producers in the Veneto in the 1990s.

P

● PAÍS (PIE-*EECE*): The name means country in Spanish. A prolific variety in Chile, where it is the source of common, undistinguished table wine. Originally known as criolla chica, país is the same as California's mission grape. In the mid-2000s, DNA typing revealed both país and misson to be the Spanish grape listán prieto, brought to Mexico, Argentina, and Chile in the sixteenth and seventeenth centuries by Spanish conquistadores and missionaries.

○ PALOMINO (PAL-OH-*ME*-NO): More correctly known as Palomino fino and grown in southern and central Spain, this is the major grape of Spain's famous fortified wine, Sherry. When just harvested, it has a fairly neutral character, which is desirable for the solera process of making Sherry.

○ PARELLADA (PAR-AH-*YA*-DA): The most refined of the three grapes used to make cava, Spanish sparkling wine.

○ PEDERNÃ (PEY-DARE-*NYA*): One of the minor grapes sometimes included in the blend to make the Portuguese wine vinho verde. The same grape as arinto.

○ PEDRO XIMÉNEZ (PEY-*DRO* HE-*MEN*-EZ): An Andalusian variety cultivated throughout the south of Spain. Nicknamed PX, it's the second most important grape for making Sherry. Aged unblended in a solera, it makes an unreal, delicious dessert Sherry that has the deep mahogany color and sticky viscosity of molasses.

● PELOURSIN (*PELL*-OR-ZAN): An ancient French variety native to eastern France and now a minor grape in the southern Rhône Valley. One of the parents (the other is syrah) of the grape Durif, commonly known in California as petite sirah.

● PERIQUITA (PEAR-IH-*KEY*-TA): The name of this hearty grape means parakeet. One of most widely planted grapes in Portugal, it is particularly successful in the south of the country, but grown as far north as the Douro. Also known as castelão, periquita is a natural cross of the Portuguese grapes cayetana blanca and alfrocheiro. Periquita is also the brand name of a popular Portuguese red table wine that is a blend of the grape periquita with touriga nacional and touriga franca.

○ PETIT CORBU (PEH-*TEET* CORE-*BOO*): An ancient grape grown primarily in the Gascony region of southwest France and also grown in the Basque regions of France and Spain. Contributes a note of honey to blends. Sometimes spelled petit courbut.

● PETITE SIRAH/PETITE SYRAH (PE-*TEET* SEAR-*AH*): The name is easy to remember, for nothing is petite about the wines that come from petite sirah. Instead, the "variety" makes a blockbuster, blackish, peppery, spicy, tannic wine. Most commonly grown in northern California, petite sirah is sometimes not a single variety. DNA typing indicates that wines labeled petite sirah are most often the Rhône grape Durif (a cross of peloursin and syrah), but they may also be a field blend of many varieties, including syrah, zinfandel, and several varieties common to southern France.

○ PETIT MANSENG (PEH-*TEET* MAN-*SANG*): Primarily used in the sweet wine Jurançon, a rare specialty of southwestern France. Commonly, the grapes are left on the vine until they are shriveled and their sugar is concentrated, although the noble mold *Botrytis cinerea* may also take hold. Also known as izakiriot ttipi in Spain's Basque region, where it is one of the varieties used to make the tart, dry white Txakolí.

● PETIT VERDOT (PE-*TEET* VER-*DOE*): Important, late-ripening Bordeaux grape, traditionally blended in small amounts with cabernet sauvignon and merlot, for spice, depth, and color. In California, it is sometimes made into powerful wines on its own. While petit verdot appears to have originated in or near Bordeaux, its parents are not known.

○ PICARDAN (PEE-CAR-*DAN*): One of the minor white grapes sometimes used in the wines of France's southern Rhône, especially in Côtes-du-Rhône and white Châteauneuf-du-Pape. On its own, picardan makes neutral-tasting, fairly uninteresting wine.

○ PICOLIT (PEE-KO-*LEE*): Highly regarded, rare grape native to the Friuli-Venezia Giulia region of northeastern Italy, where it is the source of the prized dessert wine also known as picolit. The name is derived from the small size of the clusters—*piccolo* in Italian means "small."

○ PICQUEPOUL BLANC (*PEEK*-POOL *BLAHNK*): Also spelled picpoul. One of the minor grapes of southern France, where it is used in the southern Rhône as part of the blend in Côtes-du-Rhône, Tavel, and Châteauneuf-du-Pape. See also piquepoul noir.

● PIGNOLO (PIG-*NYO*-LOW): Rare Friulian (northeastern Italian) variety that was almost extinct before being rescued and actively cultivated in the region since the 1970s. Makes distinctive, structured wines on its own, but is often used in red Friuli blends.

○ PINOT BLANC (*PEE*-NO *BLAHNK*): Generally makes good, not great, wines reminiscent of modest versions of chardonnay. The best worldwide come from small producers in northeastern Italy; Alsace, France; and in Austria (where it can be made into gorgeous sweet wines). In the New World, Oregon shows promise with the grape. Like pinot gris, pinot blanc is not actually a separate variety; it is an ancient clone (based on a color mutation) of pinot noir. Known as pinot bianco in Italy.

○ PINOT GRIS (*PEE*-NO *GREE*): See page 65.

● PINOT MEUNIER (*PEE*-NO *MOON*-YAY): The word *meunier* means miller, a reference to the thin layer of white hairs on the underside of the vine leaves, which gives them a downy, floury appearance. Pinot meunier is a clone of pinot noir, although in the classic Champagne triumvirate of chardonnay, pinot noir, and pinot meunier, it is usually presented as a variety in and of itself. The clone is valued for its early ripening, making it less susceptible to winter frosts, and for its ability to ripen well in soils that have clay in them (as along the Marne river valley of Champagne). See also Pinot noir, page 66.

● PINOT NOIR: See page 66.

● PINOTAGE (*PEE-NO-TAJ*): A South African cross, in 1925, of pinot noir and cinsaut (which at the time in South Africa was called Hermitage). Makes a rustic red wine (opinions vary on its potential quality) often consumed with South African barbecue.

● PIQUEPOUL NOIR (*PEEK-POOL NWAHR*): This black clonal mutation of piquepoul is now very rare, but still allowed as a blending grape in several appellations of the southern Rhône Valley and Languedoc-Roussillon regions of France.

● PLAVAC MALI (*PLA-VATZ MA-LEE*): The most highly regarded ancient red grape native to Croatia; a specialty of the Dalmatian coast, as well as other parts of Eastern Europe. A cross between crljenak kaštelanski (also known as zinfandel and tribidrag) and dobričić, another Croatian variety. The name refers to the small, blue grapes that the vines produce; in Croatian, *plavo* means blue and *mali* means "small."

● PRIÉ (PREE-*EH*): Native to the Valle d'Aosta region of northwest Italy, near Mont Blanc, and cultivated almost exclusively there. A complex set of family relationships suggests this northern Italian variety is somehow connected to northern Spain, but the exact genetic footprint is not known.

● PRIMITIVO (PRE-MA-*TEE*-VOH): The southern Italian twin of Croatia's tribidrag, where it is more commonly called crljenak kaštelanski.

○ PROSECCO (PRO-*SEC*-OH): Common name for the grape grown especially in the Conegliano area of the Veneto region of Italy, and used to make the bubbly Italian sparkling wine also known as prosecco. In 2009, the grape was officially renamed glera to distinguish it from the DOC zone for the wine, called prosecco. The grape is thought to have originated in the Istrian area of northern Croatia, a short distance from the Italian city of Trieste. Prosecco wine is the traditional sparkler (along with white peach juice) in the Italian cocktail the Bellini.

R

○ RAVAT BLANC (RA-*VAHT BLAHNK*): See Vignoles.

○ REBULA (REH-*BOO*-LAH): See Ribolla gialla.

● REFOSCO (REH-*FOSS*-CO): The collective name for several distinct varieties grown in the Friuli-Venezia Giulia region of Italy, and in Slovenia, where it is spelled refosko. The major one—refosco dal peduncolo rosso (refosco with the red stem)—makes tasty everyday red wines. A more rare variety, refosco del botton, is another name for tazzelenghe.

● REFOSKO (REH-*FOHSK*-OH): See Refosco.

○ RENSKI RIZLING (*RENZ*-KEE *REEZ*-LING): Slovenian for riesling; see page 67.

○ RHODITIS (ROW-*DEE*-TIS): An old Greek variety with pink berries that has begotten many clones. While no conclusive DNA analysis is yet available, many scientists think that what is called roditis may actually be field blends of various white varieties. It is the source of the simple white wine Patras, which is made on the Peloponnese Peninsula of Greece.

○ RIBOLLA GIALLA (REE-*BO*-LA GEE-*AH*-LA): A very old variety from the Friuli-Venezia Giulia region of Italy, which makes high-quality, lemony white wines. The same grape as the Slovenian variety rebula.

○ RIESLANER (REEZ-*LAHN*-ER): A German cross of riesling and silvaner, which is the source of good zesty wines, especially in Germany's Pfalz and Franken regions.

○ RIESLING: See page 67.

○ RIESLING ITALICO (*REEZ*-LING EE-*TAL*-I-CO): Grown in northern Italy, especially in Lombardy, to make basic dry whites; not a true riesling but rather the Croatian grape graševina.

○ RKATSITELI (ARE-CAT-SI-*TELL*-EE): The most planted grape of the former Soviet Union, and a specialty of the Republic of Georgia, where the grape originated and is still widely grown. Also well known in Ukraine and the Republic of Moldova, and in Eastern Europe. There are even historic plantings in New York State. Made into fascinating, spicy, floral, dry wines as well as sweet and fortified wines.

○ ROBOLA (ROW-*BO*-LA): Grown principally on several Ionian islands of Greece. Makes powerful, lemony dry wines.

○ ROLLE (*ROLL*): Native to Italy, where it is known as vermentino. Grown in southern France, in particular in the Languedoc-Roussillon and Provence (where it's used for blending) and on the island of Corsica (where it is the most important variety).

● RONDINELLA (RON-DIH-*NELL*-AH): With corvina and molinara, used to make the powerful Italian wine amarone and the lighter-bodied wines Valpolicella and Bardolina. Corvina, which is a higher-quality grape, is one of rondinella's parents; the other is unknown.

● ROSSESE (ROH-*SEH*-ZEH): The name rossese is used in Liguria, Italy, for several different varieties. The leading one, rossese di Dolceacqua (used to make the light red wine Dolceacqua), is the same as the Provençal grape tibouren.

○ ROTER VELTLINER (*ROW*-TER *VELT*-LEANER): Ancient, rather rare Austrian variety that can make powerful spicy whites (despite its name; roter means red) not unlike grüner veltliner (though the two are not related). One of the parents of rotgipfler.

○ ROTGIPFLER (*ROT*-GIP-FLUR): Austrian variety, the result of a natural cross between roter veltliner and savagnin. A specialty of the Thermenregion, south of Vienna, where it is often blended with zierfandler.

○ ROUSSANNE (RUE-*SAHN*): A variety of France's northern Rhône, appreciated for its greater elegance in comparison to its sister marsanne, with which it is often blended and to which it is genetically related, although scientists aren't sure which is the parent of the other. Also grown in the Languedoc-Roussillon and in California.

● RUBY CABERNET (*RUBY CAB*-ER-NAY): A cross of cabernet sauvignon and carignan, created in 1936 by the famous University of California at Davis scientist Harold Olmo, PhD. Olmo's intention, to make a grape that combined cabernet sauvignon's quality and carignan's drought tolerance, was not realized. Ruby cabernet does, however, make good jug wines.

○ RULÄNDER (*RUE*-LAHN-DER): See Grauburgunder.

S

● SAGRANTINO (SA-GRAN-*TEE*-NO): Native to the Montefalco area of Umbria, Italy, sagrantino is the delicious, bold-tasting grape used in one of Umbria's top wines, sagrantino di Montefalco.

○ ST.-ÉMILION (*SANT*-EH-MILL-E-*YAWN*): A name sometimes used in the Cognac region of France for the grape ugni blanc, also known as trebbiano Toscano. Today, St.-Émilion grapes are no longer grown in the town of St.-Émilion in Bordeaux, where merlot and cabernet franc are the reigning varieties.

● ST. GEORGE: See Agiorgitiko.

● ST. LAURENT (*SAINT* LOR-*ONT*): Probably native to Austria, and grown there to make velvety reds with lovely cherry flavors. Also grown extensively in the Czech Republic, where it is known as svatovavřinecké. St. Laurent's parents are not known, but it is one of the parents of another Austrian red, zweigelt.

● **ST. MACAIRE (*SAINT* MA-*CARE*):** An obscure Bordeaux variety now virtually extinct in Bordeaux, but planted in limited amounts in California.

○ **SÄMLING (*SAM*-LING):** Also known as sämling 88, it is a cross of riesling and an unknown grape, and is grown in small amounts, principally in Austria. In Germany, it is known as scheurebe. Can make very good *eiswein*.

● **SANGIOVESE:** See page 68.

● **SAPERAVI (SAH-PER-*RAV*-EE):** A very old Georgian variety whose name means "dye"— a reference to the dark color of the grape's skins, which immediately turn their white juice pink. The most widely planted grape in Georgia today, and widely planted in the former Soviet Union. Makes rich, darkly colored, full-bodied, savory dry wines. Some producers ferment the wines in the traditional manner, underground in *qvevri,* large clay vessels that look like amphorae without handles.

○ **SAUVIGNON BLANC:** See page 68.

○ **SAUVIGNON GRIS (*SEW*-VIN-YAWN *GREE*):** A grayish-pink-skinned genetic mutation of sauvignon blanc (*gris* means "gray" in French). Somewhat more floral and less "green" tasting than sauvignon blanc, and less edgy on the palate. It is grown primarily in Bordeaux and Chile, although there are also experimental plantings in California.

○ **SAUVIGNON VERT (SEW-VIN-YAWN VERT):** A lightly floral, slightly spicy grape that is not related to sauvignon blanc, but rather is the same as Italy's friulano, planted in the northeastern Italian region of Friuli-Venezia Giulia. In the New World, the grape (also known as sauvignonasse) was popular in Chile right up through the 1980s. Indeed many old-style Chilean wines labeled sauvignon blanc were actually sauvignon vert. Today, sauvignon vert is rarely planted in Chile—its place having been taken by true sauvignon blanc and sauvignon gris, though sauvignon vert has much to recommend it.

○ **SAUVIGNONASSE (SEW-VIN-YAWN-*AHSS*):** See Sauvignon vert.

○ **SAVAGNIN (SA-VA-*NYEN*):** An ancient variety indigenous to the area covering northeast France and southwest Germany. One of the ancestral "founder varieties" that gave rise to scores of others throughout Europe, including verdelho, grüner veltliner, sauvignon blanc, and chenin blanc. Also known as traminer in Germany and in Italy's Trentino-Alto Adige region. The pink-berried clone savagnin rosé is better known as gewürztraminer. Savagnin has a genetic relationship with pinot noir—either as its progeny or its parent, but geneticists are not sure which.

○ **SAVATIANO (SA-VA-*TEE*-ANO):** Widely planted in Greece, it is the grape most frequently used to make the wine retsina.

○ **SCHEUREBE (SHOY-*RAY*-BA):** Germany's best-kept secret—especially in the Pfalz and Rheinhessen regions—scheurebe has an unusual spicy/grapefruity/red currant flavor. A cross of riesling and an unknown grape.

● **SCHIAVA (SKI-*AH*-VA):** Italian name for a group of different varieties, all of which are grown in the north, usually near the Alps. The name may come from *schiavo,* slave in Italian, a reference to the way the vines are often trellised to limit their vigorous growth. The most widespread schiava is schiava grossa, grown in Trentino-Alto Adige, where it makes light-colored, fruity wines. The grape is also called vernatsch. In Germany, schiava is known as trollinger.

● **SCHIOPPETTINO (SKI-OH-PE-*TEE*-NO):** Fascinating though fairly rare grape native to northeastern Italy; a specialty of the region of Friuli-Venezia Giulia, where it makes medium-bodied, spicy, aromatic wines.

○ SCUPPERNONG (*SCUPPER*-NONG):The name in Native American Algonquin language means "place where magnolias grow"—a reference to the area near the mid-Atlantic U.S. island called Roanoke Island, and near the Atlantic coasts of Virginia and North Carolina, where scuppernong is thought to have originated as one of the first American wines. It belongs to the native American species *Vitis rotundifolia*. Around 1607, the Jamestown colonists are thought to have made wine from scuppernong grapes they found growing in Virginia. By the nineteenth century, the wine was so popular that North Carolina, where the vine grew rampantly, became the leading grape producer in the United States.

○ SÉMILLON: See page 69.

○ SERCIAL (SIR-SEE-*AHL*): Esteemed Portuguese grape, today best known for making the lightest, driest style of Madeira.

○ SEYVAL BLANC (*SAY*-VAL *BLAHNK*): One of the most popular French-American hybrids, originally developed in France for its disease resistance and ability to ripen early in cold climates, but now outlawed in that country (as are all hybrids). Still planted in England, Canada, and the eastern United States, particularly in New York State and Michigan.

○ SILVANER (SIL-*VAHN*-ER): Austrian variety, mostly neutral in character, that is a cross of savagnin with österreichisch weiss, an ancient white variety grown near Vienna. In Germany, silvaner makes a somewhat more characterful, dry, firm, bold wine, especially in the Franken region. In Alsace, France, silvaner is known as sylvaner, and some very good wines are made from the grape, although acreage in Alsace is declining.

○ SIVI PINOT (*SEE*-VEE *PEE*-NOH): Slovenian for pinot gris; see page 65.

● SOUSÃO (SUE-*SHAOW*): Portuguese grape probably native to the Minho, where it is called vinhão and used as the basis for good red vinho verde. Also used in small amounts in

the Douro, as a part of the Port blend, for its immensely saturated color and for the fact that it retains its acidity well and therefore contributes a sense of freshness.

● SPANNA (*SPAHN*-AH): Synonym for nebbiolo in various districts of Piedmont, Italy; see page 333.

● SPÄTBURGUNDER (*SHPATE*-BRR-GUN-DER): German name for pinot noir; see page 550.

● STAVROTO (STA-*VROW*-TOE): Native to eastern Greece, mostly grown in the Rapsáni appellation, where it is a required component (along with xinomavro and krassato) of blends labeled Rapsáni.

○ SUBIRAT PARENT (*SOO*-BEE-RAHT PARE-*ENT*): A minor variety best known in Catalonia, Spain. While it is sometimes said to be a malvasia, subirat parent is actually the same as the old Spanish variety alarije, which originated in Extramadura. Occasionally used in cava, Spanish sparkling wine.

○ SULTANIYE (SOOL-*TAHN*-EE-AY): A seedless variety, and one of the most wirely planted grape varieties in the world. The vast majority of it is planted for table grapes and raisins, not for wine (a good thing, since wines made from it are rather neutral and lack character). Named after the Ottoman (Turkish) sultans, for whom it was widely grown. Its origin is unclear, but Turkey, Greece, Iran, and Afghanistan have all been suggested. In California, it is called Thompson seedless.

● SYRAH: See page 70.

○ SZÜRKEBARÁT (*SOOR*-KEH-BARAT): Hungarian name for pinot gris; see page 65.

T

● TANNAT (TAN-*AHT*): One of the leading grapes in southwest France, particularly used in the wines Madiran and Irrouléguy. Robust, tannic, and deeply colored. Brought, probably, from the

Basque region to Uruguay in the 1870s. Today, it is the main grape of Uruguay, where it makes softer, fleshier wines.

● TAZZELENGHE (TAZ-EH-*LEN*-GAY): In Italian, the name means "cut the tongue"—a reference to the sharp acidity of the wine made from this grape. A specialty of Italy's Friuli-Venezia Giulia region. DNA analysis reveals it to be the variety also known as refosco del botton.

● TEMPRANILLO: See page 72.

● TERAN (TARE-*AHN*): See Terrano.

● TEROLDEGO (TARE-*OL*-DIH-GO): One of the leading red grapes of Trentino-Alto Adige, the northernmost region in Italy. The grape makes fascinating, highly structured wines with lively blackberry fruit and tar character. Teroldego is a grandchild of pinot noir and an unknown variety, and itself has spontaneously crossed with an unknown variety to produce lagrein.

● TERRANO (TARE-*AH*-NOH): Grown on the Italy-Slovenia border, and in Croatia (where it is known as teran), it is part of the refosco group. The wines have firm tannins and elegant fruit flavors, and often age well.

○ TERRANTEZ (TER-AHN-*TZSH*): Rare Portuguese grape historically grown on the island of Madeira, where it was once used to make the highly appreciated, rare style of Madeira also known as terrantez. While bottles of old terrantez Madeira still come up at rare wine auctions, the variety is virtually extinct as a commercial variety.

● TERRET NOIR (TARE-*ETTE* NWAHR): Grown in southern France, in the Languedoc-Roussillon, Provence, and in the southern Rhône. Of good but rarely great quality, terret noir is often a minor part of the blend in southern French appellations such as Fitou, Minervois, Cassis, Côtes-du-Rhône, Gigondas, and Châteauneuf-du-Pape.

○ THOMPSON SEEDLESS (TOMP-*SON* SEED-LESS): The California name for the seedless table grape variety sultaniye, one of the world's most widely planted varieties, but consumed vastly more as table grapes or dried for raisins than made into wine. A prolific grower, it was used in California jug wine blends after World War II.

● TIBOUREN (*TIB*-OU-REN): A well-known variety all along the French Riviera, and especially along the gulf of St. Tropez, where it is used primarily to make rosé wines. The same as rossesse di Dolceacqua, in Liguria, across the Italian border.

● TINTA BARROCA (*TIN*-TAH BAR-*OCA*): The name means "black baroque." Native to the Douro region of northern Portugal, where it is one of the grapes commonly used as part of the blend to make Port, as well as in dry table wines.

● TINTA DEL PAÍS (TIN-TAH DEL PIE-*EESE*): A group of clones of tempranillo grown in Spain in Ribera del Duero; see Tempranillo, page 72.

● TINTA DEL TORO (*TIN*-TAH DEL *TOR*-OH): A group of clones of tempranillo grown in Spain's Toro region; see Tempranillo, page 72.

● TINTA FRANCISCA (*TIN*-TAH FRAN-*CEASE*-KA): Native to the Duoro region of Portugal, where its name means "French black," although DNA analysis reveals the grape has no links with France. Used as one of the minor grapes in the blends to make Port.

● TINTA NEGRA MOLE (*TIN*-TAH *NEG*-RA MOLE-AY): Most often used on the Portuguese island of Madeira for basic Madeiras of modest quality. The grape is Spanish in origin and its more proper name is negramoll.

● TINTA RORIZ (TIN-TAH RO-*REEZ*): Spanish grape also known as tempranillo. One of the grapes commonly used as part of the blend to make Port, as well as in the dry table wines of Portugal's Douro region. See Tempranillo, page 72.

● TINTO CÃO (*TIN*-TOE *COW*): The name means "red dog," but it's not clear why a grape would be so named. An old Portuguese variety native to the Douro and Dão regions, commonly used as part of the blend to make Port, as well as in the dry table wines of those regions.

● TINTO FINO (*TIN*-TOE *FEE*-NO): A group of clones of tempranillo grown in Spain's Ribera del Duero region; see Tempranillo, page 72.

○ TOCAI FRIULANO (TOE-*KIGH* FREE-OO-*LAN*-OH): See Friulano.

○ TORRONTÉS (TORE-ON-*TEZ*): A specialty of Argentina, where it can make beautifully aromatic, slightly viscous dry wines that are drunk as aperitifs. Yet torrontés is not a single variety, but three distinctly different ones all indigenous to Argentina: torrontés Mendocino (not highly thought of); torrontés Sanjuanino (also unexceptional, planted mostly in the province of San Juan); and torrontés Riojana (the most aromatic and highest-quality torrontés, often grown in the high-elevation vineyards of the province of Salta). DNA typing suggests that torrontés Riojana is a white-skinned natural cross of muscat of Alexandria and the red grape mission (listán prieto), both of which had been brought to the Americas in the sixteenth century by Spanish missionaries and conquistadores. In Spain and Portugal, the name torrontés is used for several other distinctly different varieties, causing complete confusion.

● TOURIGA FRANCA (TORE-*EE*-GAH *FRANK*-AH): High-quality variety native to the Duoro region of Portugal, even though the word *franca* might seem to imply it came from France. Used as one of the leading grapes in the blend to make Port, it has somewhat more finesse and a more refined aroma than touriga nacional, which is one of its parents. The other is a Portuguese grape called marufo. Touriga franca is also used in the dry table wines of Portugal's Douro region.

● TOURIGA NACIONAL (TORE-*EE*-GAH NA-SEE-ON-*AHL*): Probably native to Portugal's Dão region, but today widely known as the leading powerhouse grape in many of the blends that make

Port. The grape has many attributes, including richness, depth, a commanding tannic structure, good deep coloring, and good aromas. Also used in the dry wines of the Douro.

○ TRAJADURA (TRA-JAH-*DOO*-RAH): Probably native to northern Portugal, and still grown in the Douro and Minho and used as part of the blend for vinho verde, the grape was brought across the border into Spain. Today it is more famous as one of the grapes (known as treixadura) grown in Galicia, Spain, where it's used in the wine regions of Ribiero and Rías Baixas. Makes dry, fresh whites with a slightly exotic character. Sometimes blended in small amounts (along with loureira), into albariño.

○ TRAMINER (*TRAM*-I-NER): Also known as savagnin, one of the "founder varieties" that led to dozens of others. In the northern Italian region of Trentino-Alto Adige, a special clone of traminer—traminer aromatico—is the source of delicious, exotically aromatic wines. It is also grown in Austria and other parts of eastern Europe. In France, savagnin rosé—the pink-berried clone of savagnin (aka traminer)—is better known as gewürztraminer.

○ TREBBIANO (TREB-EE-*AHN*-OH): The name given to a whole group of different varieties that share the traits of large clusters and mostly vigorous growth. Varieties called trebbiano this or trebbiano that are among the most prolific vines in the world, yielding millions of gallons of neutral, bland wine yearly. Grown principally in Italy (where it is listed as one of the permissible grapes in more than eighty DOCs). There is a trebbiano in Abruzzi, a trebbiano in Lazio, a trebbiano in Emilia-Romagna, a trebbiano in Umbria, and a trebbiano in Tuscany—and genetically, they are all different varieties. (In Italy, so-called trebbiano is also part of the blend that makes up the popular wine Soave, though *that* trebbiano is actually the better-quality grape verdicchio bianco.) In France, trebbiano Toscano is also known as ugni blanc, and the grape is used in distillation to make both Cognac and Armagnac. Trebbiano Modenese is the main grape in the top balsamic vinegars of Emilia-Romagna.

○ TREIXADURA (TRAY-SHA-*DUR*-AH): See Trajadura.

● TREPAT (*TRAY*-PAHT): Native to Catalonia, in northeast Spain. Mostly used for making rosé cavas.

● TRINCADEIRA PRETA (TRIN-KA-*DARE*-RAH *PRAY*-TA): A darkly colored grape that probably originated in central Portugal and is now grown all over southern Portugal, where it makes rustic wines. Sometimes known by the synonym tinta amarela, "black yellow."

● TROLLINGER (*TRAWL*-IN-JER): Common German variety making mostly undistinguished wines, especially in the Württemberg area. Known in its homeland of northern Italy as schiava.

U

○ UGNI BLANC (OO-KNEE *BLAHNK*): One of the leading grapes of France in terms of production, it is the same as the variety known in Italy as trebbiano Toscano. Makes a thin, neutral-tasting wine that is the basis for Cognac, and is one of the grapes used to make Armagnac. Also known as St.-Émilion.

V

● VACCARÈSE (VACK-ARE-*EZ*): One of the common, if minor, red grapes in France's southern Rhône Valley. Sometimes used in Châteauneuf-du-Pape. Also known as brun argenté.

● VALDIGUIÉ (*VAL*-DIH-GAY): Southwestern French variety, now virtually extinct there, but growing in tiny amounts in California, where, in the past, it was the source of some wines known confusingly as Napa gamay.

○ VERDEJO (VER-*DAY*-HO): Grown in (and probably native to) the north-central Spanish province of Rueda. Makes one of Spain's top dry whites, popular for its bay laurel and bitter almond flavors. Verdejo (from *verde*, green

in Spanish) can also show a slightly piquant green character in the manner of sauvignon blanc. Indeed, some Rueda wineries blend the two grapes with successful results.

○ VERDELHO (VER-*DEL*-YO): The most planted white grape on the Portuguese island of Madeira, where the grape probably originated. The name is used on the label to indicate a medium-dry, nutty style of Madeira, which falls between the styles sercial and bual. Verdelho is also grown in Australia. It is not the same as the Italian grape verdello.

○ VERDELLO (VER-*DEL*-OH): One of the minor blending grapes in the Italian wine Orvieto. Despite its virtually identical-sounding name, it is not the same as verdelho, a key grape in making a medium-dry style of Madeira.

○ VERDICCHIO BIANCO (VER-*DICK*-EE-O BEE-*AHN*-CO): Usually simply known as verdicchio. Cultivated principally in central Italy, where it's usually made into simple, clean white wines in the region known as the Marche. But in the top sites and at low yields, it can make a racy, bold, crisp wine with more personality. This is the grape used in the Veneto, with garganega, to make the best Soaves (although there, it is confusingly called trebbiano di Soave).

○ VERDUZZO (VER-*DOOTS*-OH): More accurately verduzzo Friulano, it is grown in northeastern Italy, primarily in Friuli-Venezia Giulia, where it makes both dry and deliciously honeyed sweet wines. The most famous of the latter is verduzzo di Ramandolo.

○ VERMENTINO (VER-MEN-*TEEN*-OH): Well known along the Italian Riviera, where it is the source of dry, floral white wines considered indispensable partners for Ligurian fish soups. Also grown on the Italian island of Sardinia and the French island of Corsica, where it's sometimes called malvoisie. Grown in southern France, vermentino is often known as rolle.

○ VERNACCIA (VER-*NAHT*-CHA): Lively light, slightly bitter-tasting Italian wine grape grown around the touristic Tuscan hilltop town of San Gimignano. Vernaccia di San Gimignano was the first Italian wine to be awarded, in 1966, Denominazione di Origine Controllata (DOC) status. The grape has a long history in Italy and was praised in the fourteenth-century poem, *The Divine Comedy—The Vision of Paradise, Purgatory, and Hell* by Dante Alighieri. Italy's other famous vernaccia—vernaccia di Oristano, grown on the island of Sardinia—is a completely different variety and is used to make Sherry-like wines.

○ VESPAIOLA (VES-PIE-OH-LA): Native grape of the Veneto region of Italy, where it is the source primarily of honeyed sweet wines.

○ VIDAL (VEE-*DAHL*): French-American hybrid created in France in the 1930s by Jean-Louis Vidal, who was hoping to invent a hearty variety that could be used in making Cognac. Vidal's parents are trebbiano Toscano (ugni blanc) and rayon d'or, itself a hybrid. Now it is grown primarily in Virginia, New York State, and Canada. In the latter two places, it is made not only into dry wines but also into some terrific *eisweins*. Also known as Vidal blanc.

○ VIDIANO (VID-EE-*AH*-NOH): A Greek variety that almost became extinct in the twentieth century, but is now seeing a revival on the island of Crete.

○ VIGNOLES (VEEN-*YOLE*): A French-American hybrid also known as Ravat 51. The biggest plantings in the United States are in Missouri, where it is used to make both dry and sweet wines.

● VINHÃO (VEEN-*YOW*): Along with azal tinto, a high-acid Portuguese variety used in the rare red versions of vinho verde.

○ VIOGNIER: See page 73.

○ VIOSINHO (VEE-OH-*ZEEN*-YO): A relatively old variety native to the Douro Valley of Portugal. One of the grapes used in white Port and in the dry table wines of the Douro Valley region.

○ VITOVSKA (VEE-*TOVE*-SKAH): Grown in the Isonzo and Carso regions of eastern Friuli-Venezia Giulia and across the border in the Carso/Kras region of Slovenia. Makes fascinating, fleshy dry white wines with elegant, floral, herbal, and fruit flavors. A surprising natural cross of Tuscany's malvasia bianca lunga and the grape variety glera, which is used to make Prosecco.

○ VIURA (*VYOUR*-A): The leading white variety in Spain's Rioja region, where it is the source of simple, dry whites. In the Penedès region, where it's used to make Spanish sparkling wine (cava), it's known as macabeo. A far smaller amount is grown in France, in the Languedoc-Roussillon, where it is known as maccabeu.

W

○ WEISSBURGUNDER (*VICE*-BRR-GUN-DER): In Germany and Austria, the name for pinot blanc; see page 91.

○ WELSCHRIESLING (*WELSH REEZ*-LING): The name Austrians use for the grape graševina, which is thought to have originated in Croatia (where it is the leading white grape variety). Used in Austria, especially in Burgenland, to make delicious late-harvest, botrytized wines. Also widely grown in Slovenia (laški rizling) and in Hungary (olasz rizling). In Italy it's known as riesling italico and makes dry, light wines in Lombardy. Despite the word *riesling* in its names, the grape is not directly related to riesling genetically.

X

○ XAREL-LO (SHA-*REL*-OH): Highly regarded Catalan grape grown in the Penedès for cava, Spanish sparkling wine. Used for cava, it contributes body, flavor, and structure. Also made into good, bold-flavored still table wine in the Penedès.

● XINOMAVRO (*ZEE*-NO-MAV-RO): Sometimes spelled xynomavro. From *xyno*, acid, and *mavro*, black. Greece's most intense, well-respected red grape, it probably originated near the Náoussa region, in northern Greece, and is still used to make the wine called Náoussa, one of the best Greek reds. Also used in blends to make many other impressive Greek wines, including Gouménissa and Rapsáni.

Z

● **ŽAMETOVKA** (ZAH-MEH-*TOV*-KAH): An ancient Slovenian variety used as part of the blend in the crisp, pale-red Slovenian wine called cviček. Known worldwide for a different reason—namely, that the presumed oldest vine in the world, a 450-year-old vine in the Slovenian town of Maribor, is Žametovka. The vine's nickname is, logically enough, *stara trta,* Slovenian for "old grapevine."

○ **ZÉTA** (*ZEH*-TAH): One of the four recommended varieties in the Hungarian sweet wine Tokaji aszú. It ripens early and is highly susceptible to botrytis. Zéta was called oremus until 1999.

○ **ZIBIBBO** (*ZEE-BEE*-BOH): The name, on the island of Sicily, for the ancient variety muscat of Alexandria, and the source of several famous Sicilian dessert wines.

○ **ZIERFANDLER** (*ZEER*-FAND-LER): An Austrian variety with powerful orange/spice flavors and considerable body weight. It is blended with rotgipfler to make a powerful, spicy white that is a specialty of Austria's Thermenregion.

● **ZINFANDEL:** See page 74.

● **ZWEIGELT** (*ZVEYE*-GELT): An Austrian cross of blaufränkisch and St. Laurent made in 1922 by an Austrian researcher named Fritz Zweigelt. It is now one of the most widely planted red grapes in Austria, and is the source of grapey, fruity, purple/red wines in that country.

SENSUAL GEOGRAPHY: TASTING WINE LIKE A PROFESSIONAL

think of this chapter as an exploration of sensual geography. (For that evocative term, I thank super-chef Mark Miller, who first mentioned it to me in the mid-2000s.) We've already addressed *what* to look for in wine; in this section, we'll deal with *how* to do that.

To begin, suppose you were asked to write a ten-word description of a wine you drank three nights ago. Could you? Unfortunately, it is possible (easy, in fact) to go for years drinking wine without tasting it in a way that helps you understand and remember it. Most of us—even those of us who are committed food and wine lovers—don't really taste with conscious intent, nor do we take time to concentrate on

what we smell. Tasting and smelling are often virtually mindless tasks. Yet, without sensory focus and without a systematic method of smelling and tasting, it's just about impossible to develop a taste memory and, ultimately, impossible to understand anything significant about wine.

Most experts did not begin to develop sensory focus as soon as they started drinking wine. Years of drinking wine—however enjoyable—do not automatically lead to an increase in knowledge, or gratification. To gain expertise and—even more significantly—to heighten

▲ *Scientific research suggests that the more you know about flavor, the more intense all flavors become.*

Guests compare wines at one of my seminars at the Napa Valley Reserve.

the pleasure and impact of what you drink, you must learn to be a deliberate taster. Moreover, wine expertise takes (remember those piano lessons?) practice.

How much practice? Here I have to thank my fellow wine writer Matt Kramer, who reveals the research of cognitive psychologist Daniel Levitin, who runs the Laboratory for Music Perception, Cognition and Expertise at McGill University in Montreal, Canada. According to Levitin, it takes a minimum of ten thousand hours of practice (equivalent to three hours a day for ten years) to achieve the level of mastery associated with being a world-class expert—in anything. So no matter if you're a concert pianist, a gymnast, a poker player, or someone who really knows wine, ten thousand hours appears to be the magic number. As it turns out, the brain learns through assimilation and consolidation in neural tissues. Levitin's work firmly suggests that the more experiences you have with something, the stronger the learning becomes. But there's one critical qualifier. You can't just practice something—you have to actually *care about*

Of the one million genes in the human genome, thirty thousand are solely dedicated to encoding smells.

what you practice. The research suggests that the more emotional weight you bring to your practice, the more effective it will be.

So if you're charged up, here we go. In this chapter, we'll explore the six critical steps pros go through when trying to determine the personality of a wine:

1	ASSESS THE AROMA
2	GAUGE THE BODY WEIGHT
3	FEEL THE TEXTURE
4	CONSIDER THE TASTE
5	FOCUS ON THE FINISH
6	CONFIRM THE COLOR

One last thought before we get started: Professional tasters usually spend a second getting mentally prepared before they taste. (Okay, maybe not when they're drinking some quaffer in a beachside café in Hawaii . . . but short of those kinds of experiences.) So, before you begin, remind yourself what you're looking for in any wine. And what *are* you looking for? It's all in The Nine Attributes of Greatness (page 4).

ASSESSING THE AROMA

At the turn of the twentieth century, only a handful of elements in wine were known. Today, more than thirteen hundred volatile (smellable) compounds have been identified in alcoholic beverages. In wine, the perception of these aromas is exceedingly complex. Wine aromas are more than the sum of their parts. It's the interactions between them that count. Aromatically, wine is more like a symphony than a series of instruments being played at the same time.

Moreover, as sensory scientists point out, the genes that encode for olfaction are the largest group of genes in the body. Of the one million genes in the human genome, thirty thousand are solely dedicated to encoding smells. That's a staggering number. Every bit of evidence we have suggests that smelling a wine is critical to tasting it.

What many wine drinkers may not realize is that there are two centers of olfaction. (Humans are thought to be the only creatures to possess two sensory locations for the perception of smell.) The first, obviously, is the nose. Smelling via the nose is what scientists refer to as orthonasal olfaction. But olfaction also happens at the back of the mouth—or, as it is technically called, retronasal olfaction. When wine is mixed with your saliva and warmed, volatile compounds in the wine are released and waft back through the retronasal passage at the back of your mouth and up to the cavity behind the bridge of your nose. There, they are registered by receptor nerve cells, five million of which flash information to the olfactory bulb of the brain. These cells,

stimulated by everything you breathe in and out, are the most exposed nerves in the body.

Amazingly enough, the two centers of olfaction do not appear to do the same job. Some molecules may be smelled via the nose, while others may only be smelled retronasally, giving you an oblique sense that you just "tasted" something.

What is especially remarkable is the intensity with which smell can be registered. Dr. Marian W. Baldy, PhD, writing in the *American Wine Society Journal* ("How the Nose Knows"),

> "As soon as I attempt to distinguish the share of any one sense from that of the others, I inevitably sever the full participation of my sensing body from the sensuous terrain. Many indigenous peoples construe awareness, or "mind," not as a power that resides inside their heads, but rather as a quality that they themselves are inside of along with the other animals and plants, the mountains, and the clouds."
>
> — DAVID ABRAM,
> *The Spell of the Sensuous*

WINE CONUNDRUM #1

Sensory scientists have always suspected that the order in which you taste wines affects your judgment of them. In 2009, Canadian research confirmed the idea. As reported in the journal *Psychological Science*, Antonia Mantonakis, PhD, of Brock University in Ontario, Canada, and her colleagues had volunteers taste two, three, four, or five wines whose identities had been hidden and select their favorite. Some volunteers were novices and others were wine professionals. Unbeknownst to the participants, all of the wine samples were identical. Every group of volunteers preferred wine #1 over wines #2 and #3. However, among wine experts in the study who tried four or five samples, there was also a "recency effect"—that is, wine #5 was preferred over #4 and #3. Dr. Mantonakis believes that her study suggests that connoisseurs may compare wines in such a way that each new wine has a chance to beat the current favorite (setting up the possibility of selecting the last sample). Novice wine drinkers, on the other hand, get overwhelmed with choices early on, and feel happy sticking by wine #1.

It helps to have good "equipment" when smelling a wine. This includes a generous glass and a big . . . well, let's say, the right anatomy.

says, "The sensitivity of our sense of smell for some molecules is astonishing. We can detect the off-odor of hydrogen sulfide in concentrations of three parts per billion—the equivalent of locating a particular family of three in China—and even smaller amounts—one to five parts per trillion—of the compound pyrazine which accounts for the bell pepper aroma in cabernet sauvignon. This is like sniffing out a one-cent error in your ten billion dollar checking account."

Alas, depending on the compound, the sensitivity to smell is also highly individual. Take, for example, the roselike aroma in gewürztraminer. In a group of eight to ten people, there is greater than a ten thousand-fold difference in sensitivity between the most sensitive and least sensitive sniffers. That means that there would need to be ten thousand times more of this compound in the wine for the least sensitive person to smell it compared to the most sensitive person.

Aroma is also highly dependent on temperature. A good example: Warm garlic smells more garlicky than cold garlic. While some wines should be served cool to accentuate their acidity, it's also true that a wine can be

> "I do not like broccoli. And I haven't liked it since I was a little kid and my mother made me eat it. And I'm President of the United States, and I'm not going to eat any more broccoli."
>
> —**FORMER U.S. PRESIDENT GEORGE H.W. BUSH,**
> relaying evidence that the perception of taste is highly individual

chilled to the point that it appears to have no aroma at all.

In the end, if you do not smell a wine, or simply take a brief cursory whiff, very little information goes to the brain and, not surprisingly, you have trouble deciding what the wine "tastes" like.

How do you smell correctly? Start by swirling the wine in the glass. Swirling aerates wine, helping to volatilize the aromas. The best way to do this is to rest the glass on a table and, holding it by the stem, rapidly move it as if you were drawing small circles. (All wines—whites, reds, and rosés—should be swirled.)

As for actually sniffing the wine, nothing is achieved by holding your nose 2 inches above the glass and taking a polite whiff. You must get your nose (a big one is an asset) into the glass near the liquid. Then take a series of short, quick sniffs.

Why not one long inhale? Imagine putting a grilled steak at one end of the room, and tying up a dog at the other. The dog wouldn't take one long deep breath. Instead, its nose would virtually vibrate as it figured out what that aroma meant. Sniffing, the corollary to swirling, creates tiny air currents in the nose that carry aroma molecules up to the nerve receptors, and ultimately to the brain for interpretation.

But beware of what I call the "Macy's effect." As anyone who has stood in the cosmetic section of a department store knows, the perfumed aromas are almost overwhelmingly strong—initially. Within seconds, however, you smell nothing. That's because the nose fatigues amazingly quickly. The moral of the story for a wine taster: Don't acclimate your nose by keeping it in the glass for a long time. Put your nose into the glass only when you're absolutely ready to concentrate, and then try to put names to the aromas. This is harder than it sounds. Although the nose "knows" and can distinguish thousands of smells, most people, when presented with many aromas at once, can actually name only a handful. Scientists hypothesize that smell is elusive because it is the most primitive of the senses. Having evolved millions of years ago as a survival mechanism for guiding eating and sexual behavior, smell is not easily grasped by the verbal-semantic parts of the brain.

If you give someone a list of multiple choices, however, their ability to name aromas improves dramatically. Again, there's a wine lesson in this. Rather than tasting a wine and

UMAMI

The fifth taste—in addition to sweet, sour, salty, and bitter—is umami (oo-MA-mee), a word that literally translates as "deliciousness" in Japanese. Discovered in 1908 by Japanese scientist Kikunae Ikeda, umami is based on the presence of glutamates, also known as glutamic acid, the most abundant type of amino acid in certain foods and, as such, indicators of protein. In 2000, University of Miami researchers found receptors in our taste buds designed to receive the umami compounds, and named the specific receptors T1R1 and T1R3 in 2009. With that discovery, umami became the fifth official taste. Since then, further research has revealed that umami exists in several forms. For example, as a simple compound, umami is present in foods such as blue cheese, tomatoes, and fermented soy products like soy sauce. But it is also present in a more complex, or what scientists call "synergizing" form, in foods like mushrooms, truffles, and seaweed. Umami is also synergized in food by aging, fermenting, or long, slow cooking. When the two types are combined, the experience is exponentially more satisfying—the so-called umami "yum factor."

Although amino acids are present in grapes, it's not clear if glutamates are powerfully at work in wine. (Some research suggests that glutamates in wine are created by winemaking techniques such as *sur lie* aging, or leaving wine in contact with the decomposed yeast cells after fermentation.) Of course, from an empirical standpoint, what wine drinker doesn't instinctively recognize the yum factor in wines that are well made?

It's all in the wrist. A sommelier pours wine for a guest in the Priorat, Spain.

then trying to think of what it smells like, run lists of possibilities (lemons? apple pie? cowboy boots?) through your mind. By suggesting ideas to yourself, you'll often have an easier time hitting upon the aroma you're searching for.

Finally, the smell of a wine is today often referred to as its aroma, bouquet, or a combination of the two, the wine's so-called "nose" (an old Britishism). Technically, however, aroma and bouquet are completely different. *Aroma* is used to describe smells associated with a young wine. A young merlot, for example, can have a cherry aroma. *Bouquet*, on the other hand, describes the smell of a wine that has been aged for a considerable period of time, and thus all of the early smells have evolved and coalesced. Bouquets (unlike aromas) are almost impossible to describe. Which is why, when it comes to old wine, you'll often read a comment like "phenomenal bouquet," but no list of specific adjectives.

TASTEVINS

Silver, shallow-sided tastevins (tasting cups) were invented possibly as far back as the fifteenth century, for tasting in dark cellars. The cups are more portable and less fragile than glass would be. More important, they have circular indentations in their sides that reflect candlelight across the metal base of the cup and make it possible to determine, in a dark cellar, the clarity of a wine just drawn from the barrel.

GAUGING THE BODY WEIGHT

The term *body* is used to describe the weight of a wine on your palate. A wine's body is described as light, medium, full, or some permutation in between. How do you decide? Imagine the relative weights of skim milk, whole milk, and half-and-half in your mouth. A light-bodied wine, like skim milk, sits lightly on the palate. A medium-bodied wine has more weight, like whole milk. A full-bodied wine seems heavier still, like half-and-half.

Body is often poorly understood and misconstrued. For example, body tells you nothing about the quality of a wine or the intensity of its flavors or how long the finish will be. Think about great sorbet. It's very light in body, but the quality, flavor intensity, and sustained impact of its taste can be riveting.

So where does body come from, and why is it important?

Body comes primarily from alcohol. Low-alcohol wines have a light body. High-alcohol wines have a full body. Alcohol, in turn, comes from sugar, or essentially, from the sun. (See Alcohol, page 10.)

Thus, a wine's body can tip you off to where the wine comes from. Here's how it works: Say you taste a wine and you decide it has a full body (it has the weight of half-and-half). You could then say to yourself: Aha, this wine

THE MYSTERY OF MINERALITY

The word *minerality* is used to describe all sorts of different wines, from Sancerre to Chianti, yet curiously, there is no agreement among the world's winemakers and scientists about what minerality is, how it is perceived, where it comes from, or even whether it exists.

Metaphorically, the word is often said to describe wines that smell and/or taste of crushed minerals, stones, wet stones, or even ocean water. For many wine professionals, however, a minerally wine is not only a wine with stony/minerally aromas and flavors; it's also a wine that's remarkable for its relative absence of fruit aromas and flavors. For example, the greatest French Chablis and Austrian rieslings (to name two types of wines often said to be minerally) do not exude significant fruitiness.

Apart from aroma and flavor, however, the term *minerally* is also often used to describe wines that carry a distinct tactile sensation (that is, they stimulate the trigeminal nerve). And while some tasters associate this feeling with acidity, there is general agreement that the mouthfeel of minerality is not quite the same as the mouthfeel of acidity. The two can be easily confused, however, because sometimes minerality and acidity are found together in the same wine. This is the case with many white Burgundies, for example. Yet there are also notable examples of low-acid wines that possess distinct minerality—wines from Châteauneuf-du-Pape, for example, or tempranillos from central Spain.

In Europe, minerality in wine is often explained as the result of certain soils, especially limestone. In this view, the roots take up minerals from the ground, and these are then expressed as aromas and flavors in the wine. But, as logical as this idea seems, many geologists take issue with it. The problem is that minerals in rocks and soils—geological minerals—are intricate, complex compounds that are not easily broken down to yield their constituent elements. And even if a geological mineral were to decompose, thus freeing its component elements, there's no guarantee these elements could be absorbed by the vine's roots. Vinification adds to the already multipart problem. Yeasts eat various inorganic compounds in order to ferment sugars into alcohol. Processes such as fining, filtering, and aging add and subtract other compounds. In the end, the inorganic chemical profile of the matured wine is virtually unrelated to the geological minerals in the vineyard. And then there's the final icing on the scientific cake: Most inorganic elements occur in amounts measured in mere hundreds of milligrams per liter—which is to say, amounts that are not detectable by analytics and theoretically not tasteable.

None of this, of course, sways wine tasters for whom minerality is one of wine's assets, no matter how difficult it may be to explain.

I have shared with two sensory scientists, from Cornell and Yale universities, my own theory about minerally wines, both white and red. Here it is: Minerally wines—whatever they are and wherever they come from—activate the salt receptor taste buds. That is, they are picked up on the palate as salt is. As such, minerally wines magnify other flavors and make them more lively; they make them "jump." So, even though there's never any actual salt in any wine, minerally wines enhance the foods around them by acting as the "salt" in a meal equation. The scientists heard me out. Their conclusion? Said one of them: "I think you're on to something."

"To know is to be able to name."

— ÉMILE PEYNAUD,

Le Goût du Vin (The Taste of Wine)

must have a lot of alcohol. A lot of alcohol, in turn, means that there must have been a lot of sugar in the fermentation tank for the yeasts to eat (and convert to alcohol). A lot of sugar in the tank means those grapes must have gotten quite ripe. Very ripe grapes means that the grapes must have grown in a very warm place. Therefore, this full-bodied wine probably came from some place that's relatively warm, like Australia or California. It could not have come from Austria, Burgundy, Germany, or any other place that's very cool.

FEELING THE TEXTURE

Closely related to body is texture, sometimes called mouthfeel. A wine's texture is the tactile impression it has in your mouth. This impression is the result of stimulation of the trigeminal nerve. (The largest of the cranial nerves, the trigeminal nerve is responsible for sensations in the face and mouth.) Fabrics are often used as metaphors for texture or mouthfeel. A wine can be as soft as flannel (an Australian shiraz, for example), as seamlessly smooth as silk (a pinot noir), or as coarse and scratchy as wool (some southern French reds feel this way). It can also feel syrupy, gritty, crackling crisp, or have any of dozens of other textures. In order to assess a wine's texture, you must roll it around in your mouth and feel it. And what's causing a wine's texture in the first place? Acidity, tannin, alcohol, ripeness, and sweetness, to name the major influencers.

Texture is probably the least talked-about dimension of wine, but I'd argue that, as with food, it's one of the key characteristics in determining preferences. Does anyone think that the texture of, say, steak is beside the point? That it's only the flavor of

HOW FAST ARE YOUR TASTEBUDS?

The human body can taste faster than it can see, touch, or hear. According to Dr. Hildegarde Heymann, professor and enologist in the Department of Viticulture and Enology at the University of California at Davis, taste perception is swift because the tongue and mouth (assisted by the nose) are the body's primary defenses against poison. Here's how fast perception occurs after initial stimulation, as measured in thousandths of a second, for our four main senses:

TASTE: 1.5–4.0 milliseconds

TOUCH: 2.4–8.9 milliseconds

HEARING: 13–22 milliseconds

VISION: 13–45 milliseconds

the steak that counts? Similarly, it's rarely just the lightly herbal, minerally flavors of Sancerre that someone loves, it's also Sancerre's spring-loaded snap of crispness.

CONSIDERING THE TASTES

Taste—along with aroma, appearance, and mouthfeel—make up what we call the flavor of a wine (or the flavor of a food) as perceived by the tongue. The world of taste is commonly described as encompassing five—possibly six—basic characteristics: sweetness, sourness, saltiness, bitterness, savoriness (umami), and possibly heartiness (kokumi). Note that although certain wines can seem to taste salty,

TASTE BUDS AND THE TOTALLY WRONG "TONGUE MAP"

Taste buds were first detected in the nineteenth century by two German scientists, Georg Meissner and Rudolf Wagner. We now know that these buds—which are shaped like onions—each contain between fifty and one hundred taste cells. The top of each taste bud has an opening called a taste pore. When we taste something, it's because chemical stimuli from that food have dissolved in our saliva and then come into contact with the taste cells by slipping through the taste pores. From there, the stimuli travel via cranial nerves to the medulla and then the thalamus and hypothalamus centers of the brain, where flavor is perceived. Taste buds, incidentally, can be found not only on the tongue, but on the soft palate, pharynx, larynx, and epiglottis as well.

The discovery of taste buds paved the way for the next step in taste research: determining the mechanisms by which taste cells carry out their work. From the 1940s through the 1970s, virtually every basic biology textbook—and certainly every wine book—perpetuated the myth that taste buds were grouped in the mouth according to specialty. Correspondingly, the tongue was diagrammed into separate areas where certain tastes were registered: sweetness at the tip; sourness on the sides, and bitterness at the back of the mouth.

In the 1980s and 1990s, however, research at Yale University, Monell Chemical Senses Center, in Philadelphia, and the University of Connecticut, and elsewhere demonstrated that the "tongue map" explanation of how we taste was, in fact, totally wrong. As it turns out, the map was a misinterpretation and mistranslation of research conducted in Germany at the turn of the twentieth century.

Today, leading taste researchers, such as Dr. Linda Bartoshuk of Yale University School of Medicine, believe that taste buds are not grouped according to specialty. According to Bartoshuk's research, sweetness, saltiness, bitterness, and sourness can be tasted everywhere in the mouth, although they may be perceived at slightly different intensities at different sites. Moreover, the mechanism at work is not place, but time. It's not that you taste sweetness at the tip of your tongue, but rather that you register that perception *first*. Similarly, bitterness is not perceived at the back of your mouth, rather, you taste it a few milliseconds after sweetness.

actual salt—sodium chloride—is never found in wine.

A word about umami and kokumi. Umami was discovered in 1908 by Japanese chemist Kikunae Ikeda. The word is Japanese for deliciousness or savoriness. Foods high in umami share a high concentration of glutamates, which tend to magnify the flavor of the food (see Umami, page 105). Kokumi (ko-KEW-mee) was first reported in 2009. Scientists disagree on the taste (if any) of kokumi, but

report that kokumi enhances taste by triggering calcium receptors in the tongue. Kokumi is thought to be behind the fact that meat slow-roasted for five hours tastes better than meat cooked for one, for example, or why aged Gouda tastes better than new, young Gouda.

The ability to taste is fully developed in utero (except for saltiness, which develops postnatally, at about four months). But despite our entire-life experiences tasting, the basic tastes take a wine drinker only so far. For

TIMING THE FINISH

The finish of a wine is the extent to which its aromas and flavors persist in your mouth, even after you've swallowed. All truly great wines have a long finish. By contrast, the flavor of, say, a jug wine disappears almost as soon as you swallow it (a blessing of sorts).

You can get a good sense of the length of the finish by using a technique called retronasal breathing. To do this: Take a sip, hold the wine in your mouth, swirl it around, and swallow it, keeping your mouth closed. With your mouth still closed, breathe out forcefully through your nose. (Make sure you swallow before breathing out, or you'll be in for a dry-cleaning bill.) Now notice the sensation. If the wine has a long finish, you'll still be able to smell and taste it even though you've swallowed. If it has a short finish, you'll sense very little, if any, flavor or aroma.

How long is a long finish? Using a stopwatch to time the finish may be a little too geeky for most of us, but you can expect a really long finish to hang in for up to a minute, and occasionally even longer.

ARE WOMEN BETTER WINE TASTERS THAN MEN?

Wouldn't that be nice. Alas, there's no scientific proof that women are categorically superior to men when it comes to wine tasting. According to Dr. Ann Noble, who, until her retirement, was one of the leading sensory scientists in the Department of Viticulture and Enology at the University of California at Davis, women do not have better sensory skills, but they may, at least initially, have better language skills. Noble theorizes that, because women spend more time in the kitchen and at the market working with food, they have "larger aroma libraries in their brains" and are therefore more adept at describing what they taste.

So why is taste so hard to pin down and seemingly so different for each of us? Moreover, why does every wine lover, at least some of the time, experience "language block," that moment when you know for sure what you think about a wine but just can't *say* it?

Interestingly, language does describe other things quite well. Linguists point out, for example, that we do have fairly accurate words to describe shape, size, color, and spatial relationships. If I say that, in front of me, there's a blue square plate 6 inches by 6 inches, and on it is sitting a scoop of lemon sherbet about 2 inches in diameter, you can easily and accurately visualize the dessert even if you never actually see it. But if I say the wine that I'm tasting is elegant, well, it's virtually impossible for you to share in that experience because you can only guess at what I mean by elegant, and, moreover, you might use the same word to describe a very different sensation.

example, as a teacher, I know that fifty people in that classroom, all tasting the same wine at the same time in the same circumstances, will nonetheless generate dozens of different metaphorical ideas about what the wine tastes like and how intense or mild those sensations are. Moreover, some people in the group will say they taste only a scant few things, while others will go off into a long list of evocative descriptors: puppy's breath, old women sitting in the wooden pews in church, nice baby throw up (all are actual quotes; the single wine in question was a pinot noir).

Because there's no good way to describe how a wine tastes, most of us resort to comparing a wine's flavors to objects whose meanings are generally agreed upon. We might say, for example, that a wine tastes "like cherries" or "like chocolate." But food isn't the only arena that offers metaphorical possibilities. So does music, contemporary culture, architecture, and so on. Of course, you might find some descriptions a bit over-the-top ("it's a precocious little wine and its femininity is alluring . . ."). But the truth is that these creative, if idiosyncratic, attempts to describe how a wine tastes do carry some meaning that can orient the taster. Most people, for example, know what's meant when a wine is described as lemony. Describing a wine as "warm lemon meringue pie with bits of burnt crust" is just going one step farther in the attempt to telescope down to what the experience of tasting the wine was actually like, and to create a "memory note" so the wine can be remembered later.

As with aroma, pros tend to suggest taste ideas to themselves as they are tasting, rather

Conducting a private wine seminar for a corporate client. I lead several such wine events each year.

than wait for specific flavors to occur to them (and risk that absolutely nothing will occur to them). That is, while the wine is in his mouth, the professional taster is running possible flavors through his mind—apples? caramel? grass? tobacco?—and in a sense, checking off those flavors that are present.

ARE YOU A SUPERTASTER?

How intensely you experience a given taste sensation depends on whether you're what scientists call a "nontaster," a "taster," or a "supertaster." About a quarter of the population are nontasters, a quarter are supertasters, and half are regular tasters. Looking at the data by gender, interestingly, 35 percent of women are supertasters while just 10 percent of men are. Supertaster abilities are also more common in Asians and in African Americans than in Caucasians. To determine if a person is a nontaster, taster, or supertaster, researchers give the subject a small taste of the nontoxic compounds 6-n-propylthiouracil (known as PROP) or phenyl thio carbamate (known as PTC).

Supertasters experience this compound as so bitter they want to gag, while tasters detect a faint whisper of bitterness and nontasters experience no taste sensation at all. Finally, but importantly, the term *supertaster* sounds thoroughly desirable (who doesn't want to be super at most things?)—but it is not. Supertasters live in a neon taste world where many flavor impressions are just too intense to enjoy. According to Dr. Hildegarde Heymann, professor and enologist in the Department of Viticulture and Enology at the University of California at Davis, supertasters usually dislike the taste of broccoli, spinach, cabbage, and sprouts; hot curry and chili; grapefruit and lemon; cigarettes; coffee; and (oh no) alcohol. Good-bye wine.

SAUERKRAUT, SKUNKS, AND SWEATY SOCKS

You bought a bottle of wine that you'd been wanting to try. Finally, the moment arrived and you pulled the cork. What greeted you was a smell one step away from sweaty socks. What went wrong?

Wines can develop foul odors and tastes for a wide variety of reasons, ranging from the presence of offensive-smelling bacteria to overexposure to oxygen to unclean barrels. A full understanding of these aromas would require mastery of organic chemistry. Here, instead, I've provided some simple explanations of why you might think that the wine you just opened is not like anything you'd want to drink. Keep in mind that the number of wines with off-putting aromas is a small fraction of the total number of wines produced each year. Still, when you come across such a wine, can you return it to the shop where you bought it? For most of the entries below, the answer is yes. A wine that smells like nail polish remover or wet cardboard will immediately be taken back by any reputable wine shop. But keep in mind that some of the concerns below are a matter of degree—*brettanomyces* (breh-tan-o-MY-seas) for example. With *brettanomyces,* an amount that you consider objectionable may well seem just fine for another wine drinker.

BANANA AROMAS: A by-product of malolactic fermentation, a process during which malic acid, which has a crisp mouthfeel, is converted to lactic acid, which is softer. While a small amount of banana aroma and flavor is not objectionable, a significant amount tastes odd, especially in red wines.

BAND-AID AROMAS: One of the manifestations of *brettanomyces* (see Barnyard).

BARNYARD/HORSE BLANKET/MANURE AROMAS: A sign of *brettanomyces,* sometimes called *brett,* a strain of yeast that robs wine of its fruity aromas and flavors. While many winemakers—especially in the New World—abhor even the faintest aroma of *brettanomyces,* other winemakers find a faint suggestion of the barnyard aroma attractive. *Brettanomyces* can generally be prevented in wine by scrupulous sanitation in the winery and during the winemaking process.

BURNING MATCH AROMAS: A sign of excessive sulfur dioxide. Sulfur has been used as a preservative for centuries. It is used in the vineyard to protect vines from mildew and mold, and in the winery to protect grapes and grape juice from oxygen, unwanted yeasts, and bacteria that may cause them to spoil. It is impossible to produce a wine entirely without sulfur dioxide since, even when it is not added by winemakers, the compound is a natural by-product of fermentation (see Warming: This Label Is Misleading on page 41). Burning match aromas usually dissipate as the wine opens up in the presence of oxygen.

CANNED ASPARAGUS AROMAS: Often a sign that the vines were not carefully farmed and that the grapes were picked unripe.

DIRTY SOCK AROMAS: Could be the result of myriad problems, anything from bacterial contamination to unclean barrels.

FAKE BUTTER/OILY AROMAS: The result of excessive diacetyl, the buttery compound formed during malolactic fermentation, when the wine's crisp-tasting malic acid is converted to softer-tasting lactic acid. Although a small amount of diacetyl can be attractive, a large amount tastes very offensive.

MOLDY AROMAS: Bacterial spoilage, moldy grapes, or unclean barrels can all produce a moldy aroma.

NAIL POLISH REMOVER/PAINT THINNER AROMAS: A sign of ethyl acetate, a

When it's not right, you know (usually right away).

harsh-smelling compound that can be formed when acetic acid bacteria (also known as acetobacter) combines with ethanol, the most common type of alcohol in wine. Acetic acid bacteria are the bacteria that eventually turn wine into vinegar.

OXYDIZED AROMAS: A sign that the wine has been excessively exposed to oxygen. It's important to note that a little bit of oxygen can help a wine taste open and evolved. In addition, certain wines—notably Sherry, tawny Port, and Madeira—take their characters from intentional exposure to oxygen in a controlled manner. But a table wine that has been damaged by too much oxygen is a different story. In the winery, oxidation can be minimized by careful and quick handling of both the grapes and the wine. At home, oxidation can be prevented by storing bottles on their sides, so that the cork remains moist and forms a tight seal with the neck of the bottle. Oxidized wines take on a brownish or burnt orange color, which is especially noticeable in whites.

ROTTEN EGG AROMAS: Hydrogen sulfide, a foul-smelling gas that can be created during or at the end of fermentation, has the odor of rotten eggs or a dirty fish tank. Hydrogen sulfide can be the result of an excessive amount of sulfur applied late to grapevines, usually to prevent mildew or rot. The formation of hydrogen sulfide is exacerbated when the grape juice is deficient in nitrogen, which is present naturally in the juice, as a result of nitrogen compounds in soil.

ROTTING ONION AROMAS: A sign of mercaptan compounds. These horrible-smelling compounds can be created after fermentation, when hydrogen sulfide and other basic sulfur compounds combine to create larger compounds that smell like rotting onions or spoiled garlic. Mild skunky aromas, on the other hand, may indicate the wine is temporarily "reduced" and needs oxygen (vigorous swirling in the glass will do), which will then dissipate the aroma.

RUBBING ALCOHOL AROMAS: Usually experienced as a hit high up in the nostrils, the aroma of rubbing alcohol indicates that the wine's alcohol is out of balance with its fruit and acidity. A wine that is too high in alcohol feels caustic in the mouth and is described as "hot" (see What Makes Wine, Wine? on page 9).

VINEGARY AROMAS: A sign of volatile acidity (VA) caused by acetic acid bacteria, which can begin to grow in wines in which the fermentation is not handled properly, or at any time when alcohol, oxygen, and acetic acid bacteria find themselves together, especially in a warm environment.

WET CARDBOARD AROMAS: A dank, wet cardboard aroma indicates that the cork and subsequently the wine have been contaminated by one of a series of compounds, the lead one of which is trichloroanisole (commonly called TCA), perceptible when present in amounts as minuscule as 5 to 10 parts per trillion (equal to a drop of water in an Olympic-size swimming pool). This fault in wine is referred to as "corked." While a corked wine won't hurt you, it smells unattractive—rather like a wet sheepdog sitting on damp cardboard in a dank basement. The leading industry solution to corkiness is closing wine bottles with a modern screw cap, rather than cork bark.

SEDIMENT AND TARTRATES

Every now and then you may come across a wine that has small particles in it. Chances are, this is either sediment or tartrates. Sediment occurs only in older red wines—wines that are usually ten years old or more. As red wine ages, color pigments in the wine combine with tannin to form long chains of molecules too heavy to stay in solution. These sometimes precipitate out, forming a sediment—a group of rather large dark red particles that appear in the wine. Sediment is tasteless and harmless, but it can feel a little gritty on your teeth, which is one of the reasons red wines with sediment are decanted.

So-called tartrates (actually potassium bitartrate crystals) are also tasteless and harmless. These are the whitish/clear snowflakelike crystals that are sometimes found floating in white wine or sticking to the bottom of the cork. These crystals (which are the same as cream of tartar) are bits of natural tartaric acid that have precipitated out of the wine, usually because of a quick and extreme drop in temperature.

For my part, I start by imagining about fifty different common flavors as I taste a wine.

Finally, if there's one practical aspect of tasting that's important, it is this: Don't swallow too quickly. As with medicine, if you swallow a wine superquickly, you won't taste it at all. "Down the hatch" is an idea best saved for cheap tequila.

CONFIRMING THE COLOR

Most wine books deal with color first. Indeed, the color of a wine "sets us up," giving us some basis (or so we think) for anticipating a wine's aromas and flavors.

But color is *not* necessarily tied to aroma or flavor. For me, in fact, the color of a wine (beautiful though it may be) is the last thing I think about when I evaluate a wine. I've therefore chosen to put color last in this discussion.

The color of a given wine comes from a group of pigments in grape skins called anthocyanins. The correct way to look at color is not to hold the glass up in the air, but rather to look down and across the wine-filled glass while holding it at a 45-degree angle.

Different grape varieties have different hues. Pinot noir makes a wine that is usually light brick in color; gamay can be lipstick red; zinfandel, electric purple; and nebbiolo, almost black. When an experienced taster is given an unidentified wine, color is often the final icing on the cake as to the wine's identity. Color is also a clue to age. White and red wines behave inversely: White wines get darker as they get older; red wines get lighter as they get older.

Beware the common mistake of thinking that the intensity of a wine's color is related to the intensity of its flavor. Despite how counterintuitive this seems, deeply red wines (like cabernet sauvignon) are not necessarily more flavorful than pale red wines (like pinot noir).

Finally, clarity of color—often called limpidity—is also important. Today, improved winemaking means that virtually all well-made white wines have clarity. For red wine, clarity is neither wholly good nor bad. Many great reds have perfect clarity, and others (those that have not been filtered, for example) may seem more opaque.

MARRYING WELL: WINE AND FOOD

Since its origins approximately eight thousand years ago, wine has always had a constant, delicious companion: food. For most of European history, little distinction was drawn between the two. Wine *was* food. A solace. A source of calories. As intimate a part of life as breathing.

That we've come to a time when we need guidance on the marrying of these two primal forces is an intriguing conversation in itself. But here, my purpose is different. Here, I hope to remind us all about affinities. And set the course for some thrilling combinations.

Let me begin by admitting that I don't think every wine always needs to be perfectly matched to a food, or vice versa. And I don't say this because I lack passion for food. Flavor is flavor. It doesn't matter to me if it's liquid or solid in my mouth. Moreover, I started out as a food (not a wine) writer; I love to cook, and as you will perhaps deduce from the many food sections scattered throughout the chapters of this book, I have a deep appreciation for the historic connection between the foods of a place and the wines of a place. Together the two allow us, however briefly, to actually participate in the culture of a place. And that, it seems to me, is one of the true gifts wine and food offer us.

▲ *The delicious triumvirate of wine, food, and great friends.*

> "The food was average but the meal was great."
>
> —ANDREW JEFFORD,
> writing about a meal in
> *The New France*

Wine and food matching is a bit different. In the United States, beginning in the 1980s, wine and food pairing became something of a national sport. Restaurants offered wine and food dinners; food magazines began to suggest wines with certain recipes; the back labels on bottles of American wines began to suggest accompanying dishes (although one of the first wineries to do this in the world was Napa Valley's Beaulieu Vineyard, back in the 1960s). It was all very exciting.

But as time went on, what started out as an exploration meant to heighten enjoyment began to take the form of just another set of "rules" complex enough to make anyone dizzy. Acidity contrasts with salt. Salt fights with fat. Umami decreases bitterness. And on and on.

The problem with this sort of approach is that it has very little connection—today or historically—to how we actually behave when we cook, eat, and drink. A hundred years ago, did an Italian grandmother stop to consider the acidity level in her pasta sauce before choosing a wine for dinner? I doubt it. Admittedly, she had very little choice; only a limited selection of wines would have been available to her. But it's also true that, both then and now, we sometimes choose wines as much to match the *mood* as the food. Sometimes maybe more so. All of this is simply to point out that wine and food don't always have to be technically perfect together to be delicious anyway.

That said, it's certainly true that extraordinary flavor affinities do exist, and that most of us have had at least a few of those "wow" moments when the wine-and-food combination was unbelievably good.

How do you create those moments? It isn't easy. A meal, after all, rarely highlights the flavor of a single food, and many dishes present countless variables. Say you were trying to

Lamb may be the most versatile meat for the world's greatest reds. Historically in Europe, it was the traditional accompaniment to everything from great Bordeaux to fine Rioja to the powerful Naoussas of Greece.

choose a wine to go with grilled chicken breasts with spicy coconut sauce. What exactly would you be matching? The chicken? The coconut milk? The spices and chiles in the sauce? And what if those chicken breasts were just one part of the dish? What if they were accompanied by a rice pilaf seasoned with coriander, cumin, and toasted almonds?

There's simply no absolute way to predict what might happen when all these flavors, plus the multiple flavors in a wine, are all swirled together, like in a giant kaleidoscope. And even if you could predict the result, would we really all agree on whether it was delicious? Ultimately, taste preferences are highly individual.

So where does that leave us? To me, it leaves us squarely in the realm of instinct. People who pair wine and food together well don't have a set of rules as much as they have good instincts. And good instincts can be acquired. It's simply a matter of drinking lots of different kinds of wines with different kinds of dishes and paying attention to the principles that emerge. After years of doing precisely that, here's what I've discovered.

RISKY RELATIONSHIPS

The following foods can be a challenge to pair with wine. Incorporate them carefully, using cooking techniques like grilling and/or combining them with other ingredients, like bacon or cream, to minimize the impact these foods can have on wines.

ARTICHOKES: Artichokes contain cynarin, an amino acid that can produce the impression of cloying sweetness and an unpleasant, metallic taste in wines.

ASPARAGUS: Asparagus contains mercaptan, a skunky-smelling compound associated with a fault in wine.

CHILES: Hot chiles contain capsaicin, which can make wines high in alcohol taste unpleasantly hot, and accentuate astringency in tannic wines.

CRUCIFEROUS VEGETABLES: Broccoli, cauliflower, kale, and cabbage are examples of cruciferous vegetables. All members of this healthy family contain sulfur and release sulfur compounds when cooked, often contributing an off-flavor impression to wines.

EGGS: Eggs also contain sulfur, and release sulfur compounds when cooked, often contributing an off-flavor impression to wines.

VINEGAR: Vinegar and foods pickled in vinegar contain high concentrations of acetic acid, which can rob wines of their fruit flavors, and often create a bitter or astringent taste impression.

THE TEN MOST IMPORTANT PRINCIPLES BEHIND GREAT MARRIAGES

THIS MIGHT SEEM LIKE THE MOST ELEMENTAL OF IDEAS, BUT FOR ME, THE FIRST IMPORTANT PRINCIPLE IS SIMPLY: Pair great with great, humble with humble. A hot turkey sandwich doesn't need a pricey merlot to accompany it. On the other hand, an expensive crown rib roast may just present the perfect moment for opening that powerful, opulent Napa Valley cabernet sauvignon you've been saving.

SECOND, MATCH DELICATE TO DELICATE, BOLD TO BOLD. It only makes sense that a delicate wine like a red Burgundy will end up

"It takes me twelve minutes to eat a good plate of food and two hours to drink a good bottle of wine, so who cares about the food?"

— **PETER BARRY,**
owner of Australia's Jim Barry winery, renowned for its shirazes

tasting like water if you serve it with a dramatically bold dish like curry. Dishes with bold, piquant, spicy, and hot flavors are perfectly cut out for bold, spicy, big-flavored wines. Which is why various shirazes are terrific with many "hot and spicy" cuisines.

DECIDE IF YOU WANT TO MIRROR A GIVEN FLAVOR, OR SET UP A CONTRAST. Chardonnay with lobster in cream sauce would be an

THE WHITE-WINE-WITH-FISH RULE

The old chestnut "white wine with fish; red wine with meat" is based on matching body (the weight of the wine in the mouth) and color. The adage dates from the days when many white wines were light in body and whitish in color (like fish), and many red wines were weighty and, obviously, red (like meat). It is, however, the body and components of the wine—not its color—that are important in matching wine with food. Some red wines, for example, are far lighter in body than white wines (compare, say, an Oregon pinot noir with a Sonoma chardonnay). Today, many wine lovers have abandoned the old rule and have begun drinking red wine with fish. Red Burgundy and sushi?—yes.

Salmon works well with both red wine and white. Here, green beans dictate the final decision.

example of mirroring. Both the lobster and the chardonnay are opulent, rich, and creamy. But delicious matches also happen when you go in exactly the opposite direction and create contrast and juxtaposition. That lobster in cream sauce would also be fascinating with Champagne, which is sleek, crisp, and sharply tingling because of the bubbles.

THINK ABOUT A WINE'S FLEXIBILITY. Although chardonnay is wildly popular in many parts of the world, it's one of the least flexible white wines with food. Chardonnays often have so much toasty oak and high alcohol that they taste hard and dull when accompanied by food. For maximum flexibility, go with a sauvignon blanc or a dry riesling, both of which have cleansing acidity. Wines with high acidity leave you wanting to take a bite of food, and after taking a bite of food, you'll want a sip of

wine. The perfect seesaw. The most flexible red wines either have good acidity, such as Chianti, red Burgundy, and California and Oregon pinot noir, or they have loads of fruit and not a lot of tannin. For the latter reason, zinfandel, lots of simple Italian reds, and southern Rhône wines, such as Châteauneuf-du-Pape, are naturals with a wide range of dishes, from such simple comfort foods as grilled chicken to more complex dishes like pasta Bolognese.

NOT SURPRISINGLY, DISHES WITH FRUIT IN THEM OR A FRUIT COMPONENT TO THEM— pork with sautéed apples, roasted chicken with apricot glaze, duck with figs, and so forth—often pair beautifully with very fruit-driven wines that have super-fruity aromas. Gewürztraminer, muscat, viognier, and riesling are in this camp.

SALTINESS IN FOOD IS A GREAT CONTRAST TO ACIDITY IN WINE. Think about smoked salmon and Champagne, or Parmigiano-Reggiano cheese and Chianti. Asian dishes that have soy sauce in them often pair well with high-acid wines like riesling.

COOKING WITH WINE

Anywhere wine is made, it is used, usually liberally, in cooking. And for good reason. Wine layers in more flavor and richness than water. In addition, wine is often included as a final splash of flavor in sauces and various dishes.

The concern (if that's the right word) has always been: What happens to the alcohol? And the conventional wisdom has been that after a few minutes of cooking, the alcohol in wine evaporates and is therefore eliminated.

That's not exactly the case. Research conducted by the U.S. Department of Agriculture in the mid-1990s showed that 85 percent of the alcohol remained when alcohol was added to a boiling liquid that was then removed from the heat. The longer something is cooked, however, the less alcohol remains. When a food is baked or simmered for 15 minutes, about 40 percent of the alcohol remains. After one hour, only 25 percent remains and after 2½ hours, just 5 percent will be present. (Remember that wine does not have huge amounts of alcohol to begin with—most wines are between 12 and 15 percent alcohol by volume—so for most people, the final amount of alcohol remaining in a dish is usually not a problem.)

As for cooking with wine, here are the most important guidelines:

NEVER use poor-quality wine. If you wouldn't drink it, don't pour it into the stew. A poor-quality wine with sour or bitter flavors will only contribute those flavors to the dish.

NEVER use "cooking sherry" or other wines billed for cooking. These wretched liquids are horrible-tasting, cheap, thin base wines to which salt and food coloring have been added.

> "I cook with wine; sometimes I even add it to the food."
> — **W. C. FIELDS**

IF A RECIPE calls for dry white wine, many whites from all over the world will work, but one of the best and easiest choices is a good-quality sauvignon blanc or Sancerre, which will contribute a fresh, light herbal lift.

IF THE RECIPE calls for dry red wine, think about the heartiness of the dish. A rustic, long-cooked casserole or a substantial stew often needs a correspondingly hearty wine. Use a big-bodied shiraz, zinfandel, or red from the south of Spain, Italy, or France.

DON'T pass up Port, Madeira, Marsala, and the nutty styles of Sherry, such as amontillado and oloroso. I could not cook without these scrumptious wines. All four are fortified, which means they have slightly more alcohol, but they all pack a bigger wallop of flavor, too. Plus, opened, they can be used for cooking for several months or more. Be sure to use the real thing. Port from Portugal, Sherry from Spain, and so on. Most ersatz New World versions are far weaker in flavor. Port has a rich, sweet, winey flavor, a real plus in meat casseroles. Sherry's complex, roasted, nutty flavors can transform just about any soup, stew, or sautéed dish. Madeira can be mesmerizingly lush, with toffee and caramel flavors; use the medium-rich style known as bual. And Marsala's light, caramel-like fruitiness is incomparable in Mediterranean sautés. I like to use dry Marsala rather than sweet.

A savory cheese tart. White wines high in acidity work best to balance the salt and fat in cheese.

SALTINESS IS ALSO A STUNNINGLY DELI-CIOUS CONTRAST TO SWEETNESS. Try that Asian dish seasoned with soy sauce with an American riesling that's slightly sweet, and watch both the food and the wine pull together in a new way. This is the principle behind that great old European custom of serving Stilton cheese (something salty) with Port (something sweet).

A HIGH-FAT FOOD, SOMETHING WITH A LOT OF ANIMAL FAT, BUTTER, OR CREAM, USUALLY CALLS OUT FOR AN EQUALLY RICH, INTENSE, STRUCTURED, AND CON-CENTRATED WINE. Here's where a well-balanced red wine with tannin, such as a good-quality cabernet sauvignon or merlot, works wonders. The immense structure of the wine stands up to the formidableness of the meat. And at the same time, the meat's richness and fat serves to soften the impact of the wine's tannin. A powerful California cabernet sauvignon with a grilled steak is pretty hard to beat. This same principle is at work when a Bordeaux wine (made primarily from cabernet sauvignon and merlot) is served with roasted lamb. And pairing richness with richness is also the principle behind what is perhaps the most decadent French wine and food marriage of all: Sauternes and foie gras.

BUT NONE FROM FAT

One 5-ounce glass of typical white wine contains about 104 calories; a typical red contains about 110. Wines that have a small touch of sweetness may have an additional 5 to 10 calories. By comparison, the same amount of grape juice has about the same number of calories—102.

CONSIDER UMAMI (see Umami, page 105), the fifth taste, which is responsible for a sense of deliciousness in foods. Chefs increasingly use foods high in umami, such as Parmigiano-Reggiano cheese, soy sauce, wild mushrooms, and most red meats, to build a dish, and potentially make it sensational with wine. When wine and food are paired well together, adding an umami component to the food often serves to heighten the overall experience. So, for example, we know steak and cabernet sauvignon to be a successful match. Topping the steak with grilled mushrooms gives the overall combination even more punch.

WITH DESSERTS, CONSIDER SWEETNESS CAREFULLY. Desserts that are sweeter than the wine they accompany make the wine taste dull and blank. In effect, the sweetness of the dessert can knock out the character of the wine. Wedding cake, for example, can ruin just about anything in a glass, although happily, no one's paying attention anyway. The best dessert and dessert wine marriages are usually based on pairing a not-too-sweet dessert, such as a fruit or nut tart, with a sweeter wine.

So there they are, a group of pretty simple principles, meant only as a guide. The real excitement is in the experimentation, and only you can do that.

THE TEN QUESTIONS ALL WINE DRINKERS ASK

 hat makes wine continually fascinating is that, apart from the hedonistic pleasure it provides, it appeals to the intellect in a way that, say, root beer or vodka do not. And because wine entices the mind, wine lovers are always beset by questions: Should you let a wine breathe? How much do vintages matter? How long does wine need to age? Even simple issues present challenges: What constitutes a good wineglass? What's the right temperature at which to serve a wine?

I hope this final section will provide you with solid answers. I'll begin with my own first question/conundrum: How to feel comfortable in a wine shop.

HOW CAN I BUY WINE MORE COMFORTABLY?

I n such a complex world, buying a bottle of wine for dinner should be one of life's easier (and happier) tasks. Unfortunately, it often doesn't seem that way.

▲ *I love this photo . . . memories of countless dinner parties and dining tables full of wineglasses. Why serve one wine with a dish when two is so much better for conversation?*

A thousand points of deliciousness. That's how I think of a wine shop. But having a shopping strategy is always helpful.

When I first started buying wine, I was so overwhelmed by the sheer number of bottles in my local wine shop that for a good six months, I simply chose from a cache of assorted wines on sale, all sitting in a bin positioned near the cash register (allowing at the very least for a quick getaway should embarrassment set in). I was about twenty-one and, as I recall, I wound up drinking a lot of cheap Bulgarian wine, which was (somewhat inexplicably) what the bin usually contained. The fact is, navigating a wine shop isn't a snap. Even a medium-size wine shop might have seven hundred or so different wines and a large store, four thousand or more. So how do you make buying wine a comfortable experience? Here are some insider tips.

CHOOSE THE RIGHT WINE SHOP. Forget the stuffy places. At the same time, don't necessarily opt for a big, impersonal discount store. Many discount stores employ people who know next to nothing about wine. You want someplace different from either of these—a place that lets you browse, ask questions (and get answers)—a place where, over time, you can get to know one or two of the staff well

enough to trust them to point out new and exciting wines.

DON'T LET THAT LITTLE VOICE IN YOUR HEAD SAY, "YOU'LL NEVER UNDERSTAND THIS." Don't forget, there was a time when you didn't know what avocados, sushi, or peach ice cream tasted like either. But you decided to give each of them a try anyway, and in so doing, you expanded your knowledge about different foods and their flavors. Trying a wine you don't yet know is really the same thing.

TACKLE THE WINE WORLD ONE PLACE AT A TIME. Choose a single country—any country—and for six months, drink *only* wines from that country, avoiding everything else. Let's say you choose Spain. What you'll find, surprisingly enough, is that after six months of choosing bottles only from Spain, you'll have a feel for the flavors and textures of Spanish wine. Once you've got country number one under your belt, move to the next country. In this systematic way, you'll build up a reservoir of wine experiences associated with certain places and, best of all, in a controlled way you'll begin to know the flavors you love, the flavors you like, and the flavors you'd just as soon let somebody else have.

THE BEGINNINGS OF BOOZE

*T**he word** booze, once spelled* bouse, *comes from the medieval Dutch word* büsen, *meaning "to drink to excess." Bouse dates back almost one thousand years, to medieval English, but was most commonly used in the sixteenth century by unsavory characters— thieves and beggars—before becoming used more frequently as general slang.*

THE TWELVE APOSTLES, A DOZEN EGGS, AND . . . THE TWELVE-BOTTLE CASE

One could make a case against cases. Why are the damn things so heavy? Why, for that matter, do they contain twelve bottles? When it comes to the latter, surprisingly, no one seems to know. The leading theory is that twelve bottles of wine (weighing 30 to 35 pounds/13 to 15 kilograms) is the upper limit of what most people can lift and carry at one time. The configuration of three bottles by four bottles renders the nearly-square case stable and therefore easy to stack in a warehouse or store. Stable stacking is much harder, for example, when the case is configured six bottles by two bottles, though admittedly a minority of cases are constructed this way. While it's not clear when wine began to be shipped in case boxes, various types of goods have been packaged in multiples of six for as long as wine has been bottled (which is slightly more than three centuries). Indeed, a dozen is thought to be one of the most primitive groupings, perhaps because there are a dozen cycles of the moon, and a dozen months in a year. A dozen is also easily split up as $\frac{1}{2}$, $\frac{1}{3}$, $\frac{1}{4}$, $\frac{1}{6}$, and $\frac{1}{12}$. The Romans, in fact, first used twelve as a way of subdividing their money. No matter how deeply embedded a dozen is in Western culture, however, the twelve-bottle wine case may soon be a memory. Already several European countries, including France, have banned twelve-bottle cases as being too heavy to lift and therefore potentially injurious to health. The French now package and buy their wine in tidy boxes of six bottles. And thus, no longer does *un six-pack, s'il vous plaît* just mean beer.

PUT PRICE IN PERSPECTIVE. A bottle of wine serves five. So that $25 wine is, per serving, about what many people spend without a second thought on, say, a latte. In addition, there are many very good, inexpensive wines—you just have to taste more widely to find them. Wine professionals themselves often buy very reasonably priced wines for every-night drinking.

THAT SAID, DON'T BE AFRAID TO TREAT YOURSELF. There are extraordinary wine experiences to be had, and you should have them! Occasionally springing for a special, expensive bottle enriches your wine knowledge and can be very satisfying.

SET ASIDE A MODEST BUDGET FOR NEW WINE EXPERIENCES. Then, once every week or two, spend that money on a wine you've never had before. Remember: The best way to learn nothing about wine is to continue to drink what you already know you like.

THINK OF WINE AS A WAY TO TRAVEL. You may not be able to get to Tuscany or the south of France next summer, but you can certainly have a lot of fun experimenting with Tuscan or southern French wines anyway. Again, it doesn't matter where you begin. If you're fascinated by Australia, start there. If you've never tried a wine from Argentina, try one now.

BE ENDLESSLY CURIOUS. You're not the only one who doesn't know what's inside all those bottles. Most people don't. The wine drinkers who have the most fun and learn the most are those who have the courage to be curious.

FINALLY, USE FOOD AS A LANGUAGE. If you're trying to describe to the wine shop staff the kinds of wines you like and you're at a loss for

The great Burgundian Grand Cru red, Le Corton. To drink this wine would be to drink a moment in time—in 1964. Capturing time and nature in this way is a mind-blowing experience that only wine provides.

words, think about foods. Wines can be big and juicy like a steak; fresh and light like a salad; or spicy and bold like a Thai soup. It isn't necessary to use technical wine terms. One day, wanting an adventure, I asked a salesperson to give me a wine like the late comedian Robin Williams. Amazingly enough, and without a minute's hesitation, he did just that.

HOW MUCH DO VINTAGES MATTER?

Imagine this scenario: A waiter comes back to a group of diners and explains that the restaurant is out of the 2010 Château Pavie but has the 2012; would the customers like that? Eyebrows furrow. No one wants to make a mistake. Someone tries a Google search under the table. Should vintages be so troubling?

Consider the reason behind giving wines vintage dates to begin with. Originally, vintages were stated in order to give the buyer a date to count from. By knowing the vintage, one could tell how old the wine was, and since old wines were often not very good, this information was valuable.

The second premise of vintage dating is that, as a rule (especially in the Old World), weather is not necessarily on a grapevine's side. Historically, listing the vintage was a way of alerting consumers to certain years when very bad weather led to wines that were disappointingly thin. Such wines would generally be priced cheaply. People would drink the poor vintage until a better vintage came along, but no one would buy up cases of the wine and cellar it away to age.

Winemakers played a very small role in this annual drama. No matter how talented they were, Nature had the upper hand and the final say. From both the winemakers' and the wine drinkers' standpoints, vintages had to be accepted for what they were. Some were poor, some were good, most were somewhere in between . . . and were happily drunk.

In the past thirty plus years, however, the picture has changed. Both winemaking technology and viticultural science have advanced to such a degree that talented winemakers can sometimes turn out delicious wines even when Nature is working against them. The fact is, weather can now have a less detrimental

LEAD CRYSTAL

An English glassmaker named George Ravenscroft discovered, in 1674, that adding lead oxide to molten glass made it softer and easier to work. As a result, lead crystal could be cut into elaborate designs. But even more important, lead made glass more durable and more brilliant.

In 1991, researchers at Columbia University found that wine and other acidic beverages left in lead crystal decanters for several months could absorb possibly dangerous amounts of lead. Subsequently, the FDA recommended against storing acidic foods and beverages for long periods of time in lead-glazed pottery or lead crystal decanters. The specific health hazards, however, are still not known. Since wine does not stay in a crystal glass long enough to leach lead from it, drinking wine from lead crystal glasses is considered safe.

magnificent at first, only later to be declared not as good as originally thought, as well as the opposite—vintages proclaimed average at first and later awarded praise. From a wine drinker's standpoint, what is the point of memorizing the pluses and minuses of vintages if the pluses and minuses change? The final, sensible approach can only be to have an open mind. Remember that wines evolve and that one-shot vintage proclamations are entirely too superficial. Remember, too, that talented winemakers can surprise us even when Nature has worked against them.

WHERE AND HOW SHOULD I STORE WINE?

The ancient Greeks mixed wine with honey (sugar acts as a preservative), poured olive oil on top of it (as a barrier to air), and stored it in large ceramic amphorae buried in the ground to keep the wine cool. For thousands of years, wine lovers have been motivated to store wine in a way that keeps it as wine, rather than expensive vinegar.

By the sixteenth century, much of the wine traded throughout Europe was high in alcohol and further fortified with brandy to preserve it. The base wine itself may have come from any warm place along the Mediterranean, from southern Spain to Crete. In many cases, the origin did not matter; what was important was that the raw wine be fortified sufficiently that it would still be drinkable when it reached England, Ireland, or northern Europe. Any wine that was not fortified was drunk immediately. These young, fresh wines were highly desirable. For most of history, in fact, young wine was always more expensive than old. Intentionally storing wine to age it came into practice only after the eighteenth century, when bottles came into widespread use. When aged in a bottle with a tight-fitting cork, wine not only did not turn to vinegar, but some of it actually improved—sometimes markedly so, especially if it was red. For the first time,

impact on the final wine than it once did. This is not to say that wines taste the same every year; they clearly do not. But given the knowledge, skill, and access to technology winemakers now have, vintage differences are often differences of character. For example, in a hot year many wines will be packed with bigger, jammier fruit flavors. In a cool year they will be more austere, lighter in body, and perhaps more elegant. Are any of these qualities terrible? Isn't it at least theoretically possible to like both kinds of wine? Unfortunately, vintage assessments assume that, for all wines and all wine drinkers everywhere, greatness comes in one form. But that is simply not true.

There is another problem: Vintages are generally categorized by the media once—when the new wine is tasted in the spring following the harvest. But wine changes over time. There are many examples of vintages deemed

Cork—the historic closure for wine—is a miraculous material. But the 20th century gave us an additional asset: well-made, expensive screw caps.

First off, it's important to recognize that wine doesn't care if it's stored in a $20,000 custom-built cellar, in the basement, or between shoes in the closet, as long as three things are true:

- The environment is cool
- The bottle is lying on its side or upside down (not standing upright)
- There is no direct sunlight

Storage temperature matters because it can dramatically affect the rate at which various chemical changes will take place as the wine matures. Wines forced to mature too quickly show a sharp, exaggerated curve of awkward development, followed by dramatic deterioration. In a hot room, a fine wine can be shoved so quickly through the stages of aging that it begins to unravel. In order to develop properly and with stability, a fine wine must mature slowly over a long period of time. Scientists say this happens best when wines are kept at about 55°F (13°C). For less expensive, everynight wines, a constant temperature of 70°F (21°C) or lower is fine.

What now comes to mind for many people is the wine-in-the-trunk question. How long can a wine be exposed to imperfect temperatures and still remain good? Professor Cornelius Ough, of the Department of Viticulture and Enology at the University of California at Davis, notes that most wines *of average quality* could be heated to 120°F (49°C) for a few hours (as in the trunk of a car in summer) and remain unscathed. However, several days at such temperatures would cause the wines to taste cooked or stewed. Speaking personally, I wouldn't leave a rare, older, or great wine in a hot trunk for even ten minutes.

Scientists also insist that violent swings of temperature are detrimental—as, for example, when a wine is alternately taken out of a hot closet and put into a cold refrigerator several times because plans to drink it have changed. Extreme fluctuations in temperature can affect both how the wine matures and the pressure inside the bottle, which in turn shifts the cork and thus may allow air to enter, oxidizing the wine. So once you've chilled that bottle, drink it!

certain older wines began to command a higher price than young wines. And "laying a wine down" to better it began to take on sophisticated connotations.

The legacy remains. Aging a wine still seems like the right thing to do with a moderately expensive wine, even though the fact that most modern wine is actually not meant to be aged for long periods of time. Virtually all white wines and rosé wines are made to be drunk fresh and young. Even among red wines, only those with firm structure and impeccable balance are meant for the long haul. The French make a distinction between wines intended for current drinking and the far smaller universe of wines they call *vins de garde*—wines to save.

In reality, of course, many wines—even *vins de garde*—are "saved" just about as long as it takes to get them home from the store. Still, despite the pull of immediate gratification, most of us will eventually be faced with the issue of wine storage.

SMELLING THE CORK

You order a bottle of wine in a restaurant and the waiter puts the cork down beside you. Are you supposed to:
• Smell it?
• Feel it?
• Glance at it, then ignore it?

The answer is the third option. The practice of placing the cork on the table dates from the eighteenth century, when wineries began branding corks to prevent unscrupulous restaurateurs from filling an empty bottle of Château Expensive with inferior wine, recorking it, then reselling it as Château Expensive. In honest restaurants, the cork was placed on the table so the diner could see that the name on it matched that on the label, a guarantee that the wine had not been tampered with. Admittedly, feeling the cork tells you if the wine was stored on its side, and that can be a clue to its soundness. But a moist cork is no guarantee that the wine is in good condition; similarly, a dry cork does not necessarily portend a wine gone awry. As for smelling the cork, alas, many flaws—such as cork taint—can be detected only by smelling the actual wine. The smell of the cork itself is never a reliable indicator of a fault or of a wine's character or quality.

Similarly, when a wine is stored upright, the cork begins to dry out and shrink. After a few months, air may begin to slip between the cork and the neck of the bottle, oxidizing the wine. A bottle is best kept on its side or upside down, so that the cork, moist with the wine, stays swollen against the neck of the bottle.

Sunlight is harmful because ultraviolet light in particular causes free radicals (basically, atoms with unpaired electrons) to develop in wine, resulting in rapid oxidation. This is why the best wine stores don't display wine in the windows, unless those bottles are dummies that are not going to be sold.

Finally, vibration may be detrimental, although scientists have not seen conclusive evidence for this. Before Les Caves de Taillevent, one of the most famous wine shops in central Paris, was built, the owners embarked on an extensive and nearly impossible search to find a neighborhood location far away from all metros. Although the rumble of Parisian trains is barely discernible anywhere beyond the train platform itself, the owners decided not to take any chances with their multimillion-dollar inventory.

WHAT ALLOWS A WINE TO LAST?

In order to withstand time and age well, wine must have the right amount of sugar, acid, or tannin. These are the three preservatives in wine. Without a significant amount of any of them, most wines are better off being drunk at the next opportunity.

Sugar is clearly a preservative. If you needed some honey and found a jar that had been sitting in the back of your kitchen cabinet for ten years, you'd nonetheless (rightfully) use it. (And a bottle of French Sauternes in your cellar is destined to go the long run.)

Like a jar of honey, an old bottle of vinegar (acid) could always be employed in a salad dressing. Wines high in acid—German rieslings for example—have amazing aging potential.

Tannin is the third preservative, but since it comes from the grapes' skins, it is a factor mainly in red wines. Yet it's the most obvious entity in most collectors' cellars, filled as they are with high-tannin wines such as Bordeaux, Napa Valley cabernet sauvignon, and Barolo, for example.

To take wine from a barrel, winemakers use a tool called a "thief" that can be inserted into the bung hole. A "barrel sample" is usually not fully ready to drink, but it can give the taster an inkling of the wine's character and what's to come.

WHEN IS IT READY?

The question of readiness is a frustrating one. Drinking a wine when its most interesting flavors are being fully expressed is clearly preferable to drinking a wine that's too young to have anything much to say. On the other hand, opening a bottle you have patiently saved only to find the wine has wizened and dried up in old age is sad, to say the least.

So, let's suppose you were given a bottle of Château Latour (current vintage) as a birthday present. How would you know when to drink it? The first important realization is this: Drinking wine is not like baking a cake. There is no magic moment when the wine is ready. Most very good to great red wines evolve and soften progressively. They start out with rather "tight" fruit that seems difficult to discern and, bit by bit, slowly metamorphose into a supple, more complex drink with flavors that seem more vivid. Where a wine lies along this spectrum at any point in time is a matter of conjecture.

Interestingly, a wine somewhere in its midlife can also go into what winemakers call a dumb phase, where it may actually taste almost blank—without charm, without depth.

In Bordeaux, this is called the wine's *age ingrat,* difficult age. Like adolescence, it is not permanent. And some wines never go through it. At some unknown point, however, every wine turns its own corner and begins to move toward maturity.

Predicting the arrival of that maturation remains anything but easy. Each wine is a living substance that changes according to its own rhythms. This should not be disillusioning. In fact, it is just the opposite. The unpredictability of wine makes it all the more compelling. Never truly knowing what to expect is part of the attraction; it is why wine appeals to the intellect in a way that, say, vodka does not. Best of all, the incontrovertibly inexact nature of readiness is a good excuse for buying more than one bottle of a fine wine, then opening them at several stages to see how they're developing.

I know. You still want a specific idea of when that bottle of Château Latour might be ready, right? Use this as a bold-stroke guiding principle: The firmer and more structured the wine (i.e., the more tannin or acid it has), the longer it can be kept. Drink inexpensive and moderately priced wines now. With a very expensive, high-quality cabernet sauvignon, merlot, nebbiolo, or other structured wines, the simplest rule of thumb is to wait at least five years, and ten is better. If you want to get

SERVING DESSERT WINES

Here are the major dessert wines from around the world, as well as information about how to serve them. (Note that the dry styles of Madeira and Sherry are not included, since the dry styles are usually served as aperitifs or with savory dishes.) Although some dessert wines are traditionally served in specially designed glasses, the standard glass for white wine works fine for most dessert wines. A typical serving is 2 to 3 ounces.

WINE	CHILL BOTTLE*	DECANT
Sparkling dessert wine and demi-sec Champagne	Yes	No
Sweet muscat (including orange muscat, black muscat, moscato, moscato d'Asti, muscat canelli, and muscat de Beaumes-de-Venise)	Yes	No
Icewine and *eiswein*	Yes	No
Late-harvest white wine and botrytized wine (including Sauternes, Barsac, late-harvest riesling, German *beerenauslese* (BA) and *trockenbeerenauslese* (TBA), late-harvest sémillon, Austrian *ausbruch,* sweet Vouvray, Quarts de Chaume, Coteaux du Layon, Alsace *vendange tardive,* and *sélection de grains nobles*)	Yes	No
Tokaji aszú	Slightly chilled	No
Dried grape wines (including *vin santo* and recioto della Valpolicella)	No	No
Banyuls	Yes	No
Sherry (amontillado, palo cortado, oloroso, Pedro Ximénez)	No	No
Madeira (bual, malmsey)	In summer, slightly chilled	No
Australian Port-style wines (Australian tawny, topaque, and muscat)	No	No
Port		
Tawny	Slightly chilled	No
Reserve, Late-Bottled Vintage	No	No
Vintage, Single Quinta	No	Yes

*No dessert wine should be served icy chilled. Most dessert wines taste best with a moderate chill of 45°F to 55°F (7°C to 13°C). One to two hours in the refrigerator should be sufficient.

a sneak peek and drink it in three years, you'll probably still have a terrific experience (even though you will have knowingly decided to forgo the additional nuances the wine might have slipped into given more time).

DOES SERVING TEMPERATURE MATTER?

On the first day of my wine classes, I serve two red wines, the identities of which have been concealed, and ask the participants to pick the one they like better and describe why. Invariably, most people like B, but there are always votes for both wines and a lively discussion of how different the two wines are. In fact, wines A and B are the same red wine—with one difference: B is about three degrees cooler than A.

The class is always surprised, but perception of alcohol, acidity, fruitiness, and balance are all influenced by small differences in a wine's temperature. Temperature, in fact, can make the difference between enthusiasm and indifference for the same wine.

At cool temperatures, a white wine's acidity is highlighted and the wine seems to taste lighter and fresher. It is also possible, however, to chill a white down to the point where it is so cold, it can barely be tasted at all since extreme cold anesthetizes the taste buds. Increases in temperature have a different effect. As the temperature of a white wine rises, its alcohol becomes more obvious and the wine begins to taste coarse. An already high-alcohol chardonnay can taste almost caustic at too warm a temperature.

Red wines are more tricky. While a red wine served too warm can also taste alcoholic and coarse, the same wine overchilled can taste thin. Historically, the solution for red wines has been simple: Serve them at room temperature—European room temperature prior to central heating, that is. In other words, 60°F to 65°F (15°C to 18°C). Room temperature today is, of course, generally far warmer, and many

red wines don't taste their best as a result. You can easily demonstrate this for yourself. Pour a glass of good red wine from a bottle that has been kept in a warm room. Now chill the rest of the bottle in a bucket of ice and water for five to ten minutes. The idea is not to make the red wine cold, but simply to bring its temperature down to about 65°F (18°C). At that temperature, good red wines taste balanced, focused, and full of fruit. Because most of us don't get a thermometer out when we open a bottle of wine, a good rule of thumb is this: Imagine the temperature of a movie theater in summer. That's where most red wines need to be.

There are, of course, exceptions to the idea above. Extremely fruity, low-tannin red wines—Beaujolais is the main example—should be cooled almost as much as white wines, so that their fruitiness is magnified.

MAN'S BEST FRIEND: A GOOD CORKSCREW

Canines aside, man's best friend is surely an obliging corkscrew—one that does not require the user to have bell-shaped biceps; one that does not shred the cork to smithereens half the time. Today, decent corkscrews exist. For most of history, however, they have been frustrating, imperfectly designed tools.

Originally called bottle-screws, corkscrews were invented in England between 1630 and 1675, where they were used not for wine but for beer and cider. Both sparklers required tight-fitting corks (often tied on) capable of trapping fermenting gas (which would have quickly dissipated had the cider or beer been stored in casks). Such corks, forced deep into the neck of the bottle, often proved impossible to extract without the help of some kind of tool.

The first tool took its inspiration from a gun. Manufacturing records from the 1630s describe a bullet-extracting "worm" that was to be used with muskets and pistols. By the 1800s, several English firms that manufactured

The Ah-So cork remover, invented in 1879, is especially helpful with older wines that have fragile, crumbling corks.

> "During one of my treks through Afghanistan, we lost our corkscrew. We were compelled to live on food and water for several days."
>
> —CUTHBERT J. TWILLIE
> (played by W. C. Fields) in
> *My Little Chickadee*

steel worms for muzzle-loaded firearms also made corkscrews.

Corkscrews went from being helpful to being essential with the discovery that wine matures favorably in bottles, as well as in casks. New, cylindrical aging bottles, meant to be laid on their side and stacked for long periods of time by the winery or merchant selling the wine, were designed. The cork now had to be fully driven into the neck of the bottle for a leakproof fit. Corkscrews became a necessity.

The early T-shaped corkscrew, with its simple handle and worm, spawned thousands of design variations. Double-wormed, folding, left-handed, brush-tipped, and combination corkscrews (walking-stick corkscrews, cigar-cutter corkscrews, and so on) were made of a variety of materials: silver, gold, bronze, steel, gilt on copper, wood, mother-of-pearl, ivory, horn, teeth, tusks, seashells, bone, and later, plastic. Decorative handle shapes knew no bounds, from a cardinal's cap to a woman's legs.

The flat, lever-type waiter's corkscrew was invented in Germany in 1883, by Carl Wienke, a civil engineer. Its convenient, fold-up design and concealed knife has made it an artifact of virtually every restaurant in the world.

A somewhat less popular corkscrew—actually more of a cork puller—is the Ah-So, patented in 1879. Originally named the Magic Cork Extractor, the Ah-So has been so called since the 1960s. The derivation of the name is unclear, although some speculate that it describes the user's surprise at how the device works. The Ah-So has no worm, but rather two flat metal blades that are inserted down the side of the cork. This makes the Ah-So especially useful when trying to extract a disintegrating cork with a crumbling interior. In England, this cork puller was nicknamed the butler's friend because it enabled a disaffected butler to remove a cork, sample some of his master's best, replace that with inferior wine, and then recork the bottle with no telltale hole as evidence.

The most important advance in corkscrew design occurred in 1979, with the birth of the Screwpull, the first nearly infallible corkscrew. Invented by the late Herbert Allen, a Texas oil field equipment engineer, the Screwpull's extremely long worm is coated with Teflon, so it glides without friction through the cork. As the worm descends, the cork is forced to climb up it and out of the bottle, requiring no effort (or expertise) on the part of the puller.

All good corkscrews have a helical worm with a thin, needle-sharp point. A helix is a straight line wrapped around an imaginary cylinder. Thus, the center of a good corkscrew is not its worm but the space framed by the worm. You can drop a toothpick into a helix-shaped worm. Such a design means that as the

CORK: A FUTURE OR FAREWELL?

In a technologically advanced civilization, sealing wine with a hunk of bark may seem hopelessly archaic. Indeed, cork has a growing number of critics. Yet the promising *thwock* as a cork leaves a bottle, a familiar sound for centuries, may continue to be heard for decades to come— at least with some expensive wines.

Cork, the bark of the cork oak tree (*Quercus suber*), is native to the poor, rocky soil of southern Portugal and Spain, as well as Sardinia, Algeria, Tunisia, Italy, and Morocco. Most top-quality corks used today come from Portuguese trees.

Cork's structural composition is remarkable. A cubic centimeter of cork contains roughly 40 million fourteen-sided cells arranged in rows and filled with a mixture of gases similar to oxygen. With a specific gravity of 0.25, it is four times lighter than water, yet highly elastic, capable of snapping back to its original shape after withstanding 14,000 pounds of pressure per cubic inch. Cork is impervious to air, almost impermeable by water, difficult to burn, resistant to temperature changes and vibration, does not rot, and has the ability to mold itself to the contour of the container it is put into (such as the neck of a wine bottle).

A cork tree is harvested, or stripped, for the first time when it is twenty-five years old, and thereafter once every nine years. Although stripping does no permanent damage, the tree will need two years or more to recover its vitality. A cork tree will be stripped, on average, sixteen times in its 150 to 200 years of life.

The stripping itself is grueling work. Using special wedge-shaped axes, workers peel four-foot planks from the bark during the intense summer heat when the tree's sap is circulating, making it possible to pry the bark off. Once the bark is stripped off, it is stored in rooms with concrete floors (not on the ground, where it could be contaminated by soil) and left to season and dry for

point spirals down through the cork, the rest of the worm follows the exact same path, minimizing damage to the surrounding cork cells. Because the cork is basically intact, it does not shred as you pull up. By comparison, a worm that is the central shaft of the corkscrew (as is true of most "rabbit ears" corkscrews) plows a hole through the belly of the cork, ripping apart cells and causing the cork to disintegrate into bits.

DOES WINE REALLY NEED TO BREATHE?

The idea that many wines soften and open up after breathing— being exposed to air—is true. To effectively aerate a wine, you have to pour it into a large glass, carafe, decanter, pitcher, or some other vessel so that it mixes with oxygen as it pours from the bottle. Allowed to breathe in this way, the flavors of many wines—especially young, tannic reds, such as cabernet sauvignon, merlot, nebbiolo, and petite sirah—will almost seem to unfurl. White wines, too, will open up as a result of exposure to oxygen.

Interestingly, this process of aerating a young wine is often called decanting, even though true decanting is entirely different (see next section).

Keep in mind that simply pulling the cork out of a bottle and letting the bottle sit, opened, for a few minutes is not an effective way to aerate a wine (even though you often see this done in restaurants). The amount of air in the tiny space of the neck of an opened

several months. The bark is then boiled or steamed to improve its elasticity and flatten it, and then dried again and left in a dark cellar to dry out for three to four weeks. Finally, the bark is trimmed into rectangular planks and separated according to quality and thickness. Wine corks are shaped from the planks, graded, and washed in a mild hydrogen peroxide solution to remove dust, sanitize them, and lighten their color.

Before the mid-1990s, most corks were washed in a chlorine solution. Chlorine, alas, can react with moisture and fungi inside the cork to facilitate the growth of 2,4,6-trichloroanisole (TCA) and related compounds, chemicals responsible for the "wet dog sitting on damp newspapers in a dank cellar" aroma wine can pick up from corks. A wine tainted with TCA is said to be "corked" (see page 113). Although chlorine is no longer used in cleaning corks, the problem of corked wines has not gone away, in part because wineries use water to clean barrels and equipment, and municipal water contains chlorine. Indeed, the average incidence of corked wine is now estimated at 2.5 percent. TCA can also be generated by other means. Sometimes the compound exists naturally in raw cork bark. But it has also been found in soil, inside barrels, on cardboard boxes, on wooden pallets, even just in the air—and from there, it can contaminate corks, which in turn taint the wine.

Today, cork's future is anything but clear. While the Portuguese government has taken measures to encourage improvements in cork manufacture and cork oak tree reforestation, wine producers around the world appear to be increasingly fed up with the cost and loss of reputation associated with tainted bottles. In response to the problem, a modern screw-cap initiative began in the Clare Valley of Australia as far back as 2000, with New Zealand soon following. (Wines with screw caps do not get tainted by TCA.) Today, about 45 percent of all Australian wine is stoppered by screw cap, as is 85 percent of all New Zealand wine. Worldwide, the number of wine bottles with screw caps continues to grow.

bottle is simply much too little, relative to the volume of wine, to have an effect—unless, perhaps, you left it open for nearly a day. Of course, many devices on the market purport to aerate wine perfectly. As of this writing, I have found that most of them jostle the wine so vigorously as to discombobulate it. For me, the tried and true method of using one's hand to swirl the glass (at no cost whatsoever) is still the best.

Also keep in mind that there are some wines that should never be aerated. These reds are too sensitive to oxygen and, splashed into a carafe or decanter, will fall apart and taste dull and lifeless. The wines that should never be aerated include older pinot noirs and red Burgundies, along with older gran reserva Riojas (made from tempranillo) and older Chianti Classicos (made from sangiovese).

WHEN DOES A WINE NEED TO BE DECANTED?

Decanting a wine, a more complex procedure than aerating, means pouring the wine off any sediment in the bottom of the bottle. So, in order to truly decant a wine, there has to be sediment in the first place.

Sediment—long, chain molecules of color and tannin that have precipitated out of solution—is generally present only in older red wines (10-plus years old) that were once deeply colored, such as cabernet sauvignon, Bordeaux, and vintage Port. If you carefully take an older cabernet out of its resting place and hold it up to a light, you'll often see a sort of crusty material clinging to the inside

Decanters can be useful for very old wines (which have thrown a sediment) or very young wines (to help "open up" the wine's aromas and flavors).

of the bottle. That's sediment. (It's more difficult to see the sediment in an old vintage Port, since many Port bottles are traditionally made from dark, opaque glass.) Of course, you could drink an old wine that has thrown some sediment without decanting it; the sediment is not harmful, just slightly teeth-clinging.

Decanting a wine is not difficult. First, the wine bottle must be placed standing upright for a day or two to let all the suspended sediment gently settle to the bottom of the bottle. Without picking the bottle up or turning it around, remove the cork slowly. Now pick the bottle up and begin pouring the clear wine slowly into a decanter. It's best not to shake the bottle too much or tilt it back and forth as you pour. (Note: You can do this with the help of a light source, like a candle or flashlight, behind the neck of the bottle, or not.) When less than 2 inches of wine is left, you should begin to see sediment coming into the neck of the bottle. That's when to stop. The clear wine is now all in the decanter; the sediment remains in the bottle.

Exactly when should a wine be decanted? To be on the safe side, the general rule of thumb is to decant older, tannic wines—vintage Port, cabernet sauvignon, Bordeaux, Barolo, and Rhône wines, for example—less

CLEANING WINEGLASSES

A wine that smells or tastes strange may be perfectly fine. The culprit could be (and often is) the glass. While glass looks perfectly smooth, the inside, examined under a microscope, looks like the surface of the moon. Bacteria and residue easily live in these microscopic pits, and these can react with components in the wine, making it smell stinky and taste odd. Additionally, less than perfectly clean glasses mean that sparkling wines and Champagnes will immediately appear flat and bubbleless.

The best way to wash wineglasses is by hand (I know, I know), using your hand (not a sponge) and a small amount of diluted soap and lukewarm water. Glasses should be rinsed several times in hot, but not scalding, water. Very hot water can cause the glass to expand rapidly and crack. Drain the glasses briefly upside down, then turn the glasses upright and let them dry in the air. Any drops or spots can be finished off with a clean, soft cloth. And once it's dry, a wineglass should be stored right side up, standing on its foot, not on its more fragile rim.

Interestingly, in Italy, in many homes and virtually all top restaurants, a washed wineglass is not yet considered ready for use. The Italians always pour a small amount of wine in the glass, swirl it around, then throw this wine rinse out—a process known as *avvinare i bicchieri,* preparing the glasses to receive the wine. A baptism of sorts.

than an hour before serving. Decant it earlier than that, and the wine may become tired and dull by the time it's drunk.

ARE SOME WINEGLASSES BETTER THAN OTHERS?

I n a word: Yes. Although wine can be happily drunk from just about anything, from Mason jars to Baccarat crystal, most wine drinkers would agree that a good wineglass can heighten the pleasure of wine drinking and actually enhance the aroma and flavor of wines. This is not just psychological. A well-designed glass allows the wine's aromas and flavors to evolve. Moreover, the wine itself will flow over the rim in a direct stream that focuses it on the palate.

How do you go about buying good wineglasses when there are dozens of glass manufacturers to choose from, and prices for wineglasses can range from five to a hundred dollars a glass? Here are some guidelines:

● BUY ONLY WINEGLASSES YOU CAN AFFORD TO BREAK. If spending fifty dollars per glass means you'd never use them, buy less expensive ones.

● BUY MORE GLASSES THAN YOU THINK YOU'LL NEED. Glasses break. And besides, there may be times when you want to serve two different wines side by side for comparison.

● NEVER BUY SMALL GLASSES. Drinking wine out of a small glass feels as awkward as sitting on a too-small chair or eating dinner off a bread plate.

● CONSIDER BUYING ONE GREAT GLASS TO USE FOR BOTH RED AND WHITE WINES. A well-designed, good wineglass—whether it will eventually hold red or white wine—should have a generous bowl. An ample bowl gives the wine's aromas and flavors room in which to evolve. Closer to the rim, however, the bowl should narrow, forcing the aromas to be focused toward your nose.

● BUY GLASSES THAT ARE ABSOLUTELY CLEAR AND SMOOTH, not faceted, to show off the depth and richness of the wine's color.

Colored and/or cut glass may be beautiful, but you cannot see the wine.

● MAKE SURE THE GLASS HAS A THIN RIM, so that the wine glides over it easily, and so that you don't feel like you have to chew on the glass to get to the wine.

● CHOOSE A GLASS WITH A STEM, to give you something to hold other than the bowl. Holding the glass around the bowl can warm the wine. And besides, without a stem, it's almost impossible to swirl the wine in the glass.

● IN ADDITION TO REGULAR WINEGLASSES, BUY TULIPS/FLUTES for serving Champagne and sparkling wines. The slightly tapered shape of a tulip/flute encourages a steady stream of bubbles, and with these wines, bubbles are part of the pleasure.

THE END . . . BUT REALLY THE BEGINNING

W hether you read Mastering Wine in its entirety, or flipped back and forth between sections, I want you to know that you've just finished what I think is the most important part of *The Wine Bible*. An intimate knowledge of anything necessarily begins with the fundamentals of that thing. With wine, I'd even go one step further and say that the capacity for pleasure—the capacity to be thrilled by wine—is ineluctably tied to understanding it in all its most basic details. Anyone can drink good wines, and anyone wealthy enough can drink super-expensive wines. But without knowledge, the soulful, satisfying part of the experience is lost. All of this is by way of saying, Bravo! You did it. This may be the last section of "Mastering Wine," but it's the beginning of many delicious things to come.

And now for the world of wine . . .

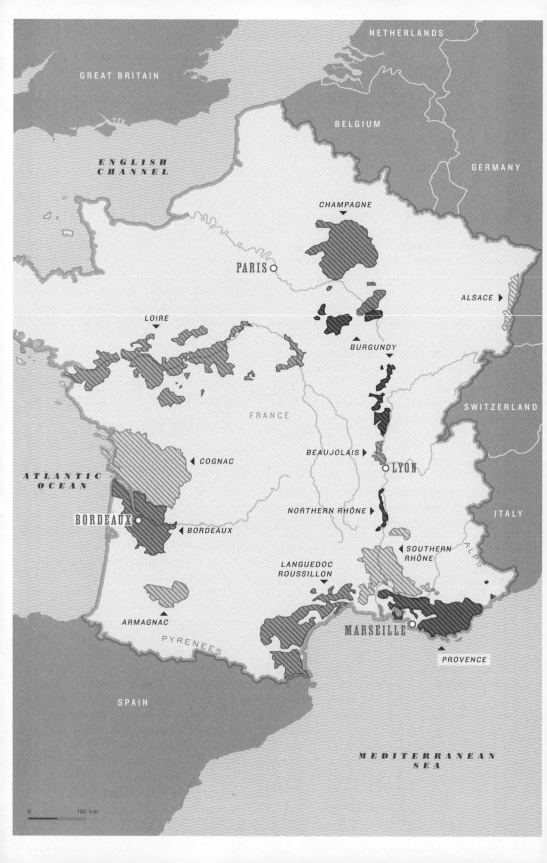

NETHERLANDS

GREAT BRITAIN

BELGIUM

GERMANY

ENGLISH
CHANNEL

CHAMPAGNE ▼

PARIS ○

ALSACE ▶

LOIRE ▼

BURGUNDY ▲

FRANCE

SWITZERLAND

BEAUJOLAIS ▶

LYON ○

ATLANTIC
OCEAN

◀ COGNAC

NORTHERN RHÔNE ▶

ITALY

BORDEAUX

○

◀ BORDEAUX

◀ SOUTHERN
RHÔNE

ALPS

LANGUEDOC
ROUSSILLON ▼

ARMAGNAC ▲

MARSEILLE ○

PYRENEES

▲ PROVENCE

SPAIN

MEDITERRANEAN
SEA

0   100 km

FRANCE

BORDEAUX | CHAMPAGNE | BURGUNDY | BEAUJOLAIS | THE RHÔNE
THE LOIRE | ALSACE | LANGUEDOC-ROUSSILLON | PROVENCE

FRANCE RANKS FIRST AMONG WINE-PRODUCING COUNTRIES WORLDWIDE. THE FRENCH DRINK AN AVERAGE OF 14 GALLONS (52 LITERS) OF WINE PER PERSON PER YEAR.

rance produces more fine wines than any other country in the world. This fact alone has elevated some French wines to almost mythic status. Indeed, French winemaking techniques, viticultural practices, even French grape varieties have been adopted by wine regions around the world. Like French food, French wine has been (and largely remains) the benchmark against which greatness elsewhere is judged.

But France's impact extends even further. The country has molded the very way we think about great wine. It was in France that the fundamental concept of terroir (the idea that the site determines the quality of the wine) became pervasive and flourished (see page 17). Traditionally the French have been so convinced that nature and geography make the wine that there has never been a French word for winemaker. Instead, the term commonly used, *vigneron*, portrays man's role as more humble. *Vigneron* means "grape grower."

France's near obsession with geography (plus numerous episodes of wine fraud, including cheap wine being passed off as more expensive wine) resulted, in the 1930s, in the development of a detailed system of regulations known as the *Appellation d'Origine Contrôlée* (AOC). This system designated those places where, today, most of the best wines in France are made, and then went on to define how those wines must be made. Given the emphasis on place of origin, most AOC wines are logically known by their geographic names (Sancerre, Côte-Rôtie, Volnay, and so on), not by the names of the grape varieties from which they are made (see France's Wine Laws in the Appendix on Wine Laws, pages 923–924).

WORDS ON WINE

While it's tempting to assume that, when it comes to wine, the French invented almost everything, there's one pursuit they largely overlooked: wine writing. For that, we first have to thank ancient Greek and Roman writers, then later, the English, for whom writing about wine has been a specialty for the last several centuries.

The first book on wine in the English language was *A New Boke of the Natures and Properties of All Wines,* written in 1568 by William Turner. Turner's book is thought to have been a guide for William Shakespeare, who laced his texts with numerous references to wine. Then, during the eighteenth century, dozens of major wine books were written—many of them, interestingly, by English physicians.

In 1775, Sir Edward Barry's *Observations—Historical, Critical, and Medical—on the Wines of the Ancients and the Analogy Between Them and Modern Wines* was published. The book's engraved illustrations are impressive and the beautiful text was printed on a wooden press not unlike the one Gutenberg used for his bibles. Later, in 1824, Alexander Henderson wrote *A History of Ancient and Modern Wines,* an opus devoted to French and German wines.

For the next century and a half, most English writers shared Henderson's view that no other countries need be included in a comprehensive wine book, since, as educated drinkers knew, fine wine wasn't and couldn't be produced anyplace else.

Luckily for the French, their homeland is blessed with numerous locations in which fine wines can be made. The first of these areas was established in southern France, near Montpellier. Here, at the archaeological site of Lattara on the French coast, wine was imported from Etruscan cities in central Italy. By approximately 500 B.C., the enterprising French had established a small wine culture all their own. Later, with Roman help, viticulture spread throughout what is now southern France. Indeed, Provence gets its name from the Romans, who called it *nostra provincia*—"our province."

By the fifth century A.D., with the collapse of the Roman Empire, the vineyards of France increasingly fell under the control of the Catholic Church. In particular, such powerful monastic orders as the Benedictines painstakingly and systematically planted vineyard after vineyard until vines stretched north beyond Paris.

From the Middle Ages until the eighteenth century, the vineyards of France flourished

SOMMELIERS

During the French Renaissance, a sommelier (so-mel-YAY) bought the title and paid to become part of the retinue of the king or a nobleman. The sommelier, responsible for stocking food and wine for journeys, kept the provisions in a carriage called a somme. Simply stocking provisions, however, was not the sommelier's most important job; ensuring the condition of the perishables was. He did this rather riskily, by taking a bite of each food and a sip of each wine before it was presented to his lord. If the food or wine had been poisoned by an enemy, the sommelier was the first to know.

COMMUNES

The term *commune* is used in France to denote a wine village, as in Burgundy's commune of Chambolle-Musigny, or Bordeaux's commune of Margaux. But a commune in France isn't necessarily only related to wine. In fact, communes are the lowest level of administrative division in France, and as such, the equivalent of incorporated cities in the U.S. Communes have revolutionary beginnings. Following the storming of the Bastille prison and the start of the French Revolution in 1789, the first commune—Paris—was created. The idea was to do away with the burdens of class and tradition and create a perfect society—one where everyone was equal, and reason, not tradition, ruled. Indeed, the word *commune* comes from the medieval Latin word *communia*, meaning "a small gathering of people sharing a common life." The actual size of a commune, however, can vary from millions, as with Paris, to a dozen or so. There are currently close to 38,000 communes throughout France—and their structure remains largely the same today as when they were set up two centuries ago.

under the guidance of hundreds of thousands of monks. But the French Revolution of 1789 to 1799 forever severed the intimate relationship between the Church and the country's vineyards. Under the orders of Napoléon I, vineyards were ousted from Church ownership and given away or sold, often to local peasants. In some areas where the Church's authority had been especially powerful (such as Burgundy) entire new systems were developed for owning and inheriting vineyards. This included the stipulation that all children must inherit equally (today, Burgundy's small vineyards have been so progressively divided that some family members now own mere rows of vines).

Perhaps the most dramatic period in France's wine history is the era it would most like to forget. Sometime between 1860 and 1866, the deadly, root-eating phylloxera insect arrived from America. The subsequent devastation it unleashed is thought to have begun in the southern Rhône Valley. From there, the microscopic insect spread throughout the country, throughout Europe, and eventually throughout much of the world (see box, page 30). Even after French vineyards recovered by planting phylloxera-tolerant American rootstock, the country's wine areas were never the

Vineyards are enclosed by hand-built stone terraces on the steep hillsides of Cornas in the northern Rhône Valley.

same. Many French regions today are half the size they were before the phylloxera epidemic.

The French take their food and wine very seriously. (The national school lunch program consists of a four-course meal that ends

The Café du Palais is a favorite people-watching spot in the center of Reims in Champagne. Behind the pedestrians, a few of the café chairs are occupied by dogs, content to sniff the occasional platter of frites as waiters whisk by, mostly with trays of wine.

with cheese!) Indeed, historically, under the auspices of the Ministry of Culture, French schoolchildren have gone on field trips to three-star restaurants in order to taste foods such as foie gras, Bresse chickens, Isigny butter, and other famous french products, including, sometimes, wines.

And, needless to say, the French are a proud people. Many of them spend their entire lives drinking wine from their local area alone. (The word *chauvinism*, perhaps not surprisingly, comes from the French.) Even today, it is not unusual to find Burgundians who have never tasted Bordeaux or Bordelais who have never tasted a wine from Alsace. And it's not as though France is that big; the whole country would fit inside Texas. Nonetheless, 204 different varieties of grapes are grown here and, with nearly 2 million acres (809,000 hectares) (now, perhaps more) planted with grapevines, France produces more wine than virtually every other country (although in some years, Italy produces a tiny bit more).

Climatically and geographically, France can be thought of as being divided into three parts. In the north, such regions as Champagne and Burgundy have a continental climate, with severe winters and cool, often rainy autumns, meaning that grapes may not fully ripen, and thus produce wines that can be delicate and refined. By comparison, southern France has a Mediterranean climate. Achieving ripeness presents little problem, and the wines are fleshier, fuller, more "sunny" in the mouth. Lastly, on the Atlantic coast, the wine regions of Bordeaux and the western Loire have a maritime climate. Here, the Gulf Stream tempers what might otherwise be too harsh an environment, but again, rain and humidity can present problems. There are some silver linings.

"La vie est trop courte pour boire du mauvais vin." ("Life is too short to drink bad wine.") Tellingly, the French were the first people to assert this now common bit of wisdom.

FRENCH WINE CULTURE BEGAN
IN (MON DIEU) . . . ITALY

The French may have been the undisputed masters of the art of winemaking for the past thousand years, but they learned it from the Italians. Indeed, startling research reported in 2013 suggests that French wine culture began about 600 B.C. when the Etruscans, a pre-Roman civilization based in central Italy, began shipping wine to southern France, and establishing a market for the beverage. The entrepreneurial French soon initiated their own winemaking industry by importing Etruscan grapevines and emulating Etruscan winemaking techniques (including mixing wine with basil, thyme, rosemary, and other herbs). For their part, the Etruscans learned about wine sometime around 800 B.C., from the Phoenicians (based in what is modern-day Lebanon), who themselves had learned how to grow vines and make wine from tribes in the area that, today, is Turkey. These tribes were the first to domesticate grapevines, more than eight thousand years ago.

The research team that made the discovery was headed by Dr. Patrick McGovern, Director of Biomolecular Archaeology at the University of Pennsylvania Museum of Archaeology and Anthropology, and the study was reported in the journal *Proceedings of the National Academy of Sciences*.

During the research, excavations at the ancient port site of Lattara (near Montpellier) in southern France unearthed well-preserved Etruscan amphorae, vessels used to transport wine and other goods in the ancient Mediterranean world. Using extremely sensitive chemical analytics, the scientists revealed that the amphorae contained the residues of wine, herbs, and pine resin (which was used to preserve wine during long journeys). Even more amazing was the discovery of an ancient limestone platform covered in wine residue—thought to be among the first French wine presses.

Bordeaux's muggy summers, for example, make the great sweet wine Sauternes possible.

About 90 percent of French wine is based on thirty-six grapes. The wines made from these varieties run the full gamut from dry to sweet and from still to sparkling. And in addition to wine, of course, two of the world's most famous grape-based spirits are French: Armagnac and Cognac (see pages 313 and 318, respectively).

Notwithstanding the worldwide prestige of several French white wines, the French themselves tend to drink red wine. Copious amounts of rosé are tossed down, too, especially in summer. Indeed, more rosé is consumed (27 percent of all wine) than white wine (16 percent of all wine).

Unlike the wines of most other European countries, French wine is known in virtually every corner of the globe. A thirsty traveler in Fiji, Nairobi, or Taipei can easily hunt down a bottle of Champagne, even when all other wine possibilities seem exhausted. Of course, the quality of French wine accounts for a good measure of its appeal, but so do various historic and geographic considerations. France was the first European country to develop significant international trade for its wines. This was possible thanks to the proximity of most French wine regions to large, navigable rivers. As early as the twelfth century, Bordeaux wines were being shipped down the massive Gironde Estuary and out to sea, headed for England and Scotland.

PDO, PGI—THE EUROPEAN UNION WINE LAWS

Each wine-producing country has its own wine laws (you'll find them in the Appendix on Wine Laws; see pages 923–930). But in Europe, somewhat confusingly, there are now two sets of wine laws: laws imposed by each country and, as of 2009, laws enacted by the European Union. The latter are applicable to all twenty-seven EU member countries, including the major wine-producing countries of France, Italy, Spain, and Portugal.

It's important to know that EU laws and national country laws exist in parallel and contemporaneously. For example, French wine regions continue to be governed by that country's *Appellation d'Origine Contrôlée* (AOC) laws; Italy by the *Denominazione di Origine Controllata* (DOC) laws, and so on. But there are now concomitant laws, designations, and even graphic logos that apply to wines across the EU. The main EU designations for wine are:

PROTECTED DESIGNATION OF ORIGIN (PDO)

PROTECTED GEOGRAPHICAL INDICATION (PGI)

Wineries can choose to use either their national designations or the European Union designations/logos. Thus wineries from AOC areas such as Bordeaux or Champagne can use the term AOC or the European Union term PDO plus the PDO logo.

Similarly, French wineries that have commonly been designated as *vin de pays* can now, at their discretion, use PGI instead. (To make matters extremely confusing, some producers that use the designation PGI invert the acronym to correspond with the local language. So in France, PGI is sometimes written as IGP, for *Indication Géographique Protégée*.) But even if a *vin de pays* producer chooses to stay with the term *vin de pays,* the PGI logo is now compulsory on the label.

The EU's goals—consumer protection and a single, unified system that identifies quality and origin—would appear to be sound. But for those who just mastered DOCG, DOC, AOC, DOP, and other national designations, adding two more possibilities—PDO and PGI—doesn't seem (at the moment anyway) to make the picture a lot clearer.

But France has given the world more than just her wine. From the seventeenth to the nineteenth centuries, as the New World began to be colonized, French vine cuttings—often from revered estates and châteaux—were shipped, smuggled, or lugged in suitcases to South Africa, the Americas, New Zealand, and Australia. For the settlers of those territories, French vines held out the hope that one day they, too, might bring into the world a great wine.

We'll look at France's most important wine regions in the order that, I believe, reflects their importance and prestige, although Bordeaux, Champagne, and Burgundy could arguably all be first in line.

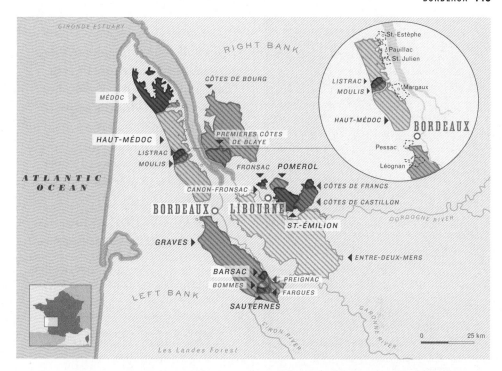

BORDEAUX

ordeaux—the word alone fires the mind with the anticipation of greatness. No other wine region is more powerful, more commercially successful, or more important as a source of profoundly complex, ageworthy wines. The challenge is to comprehend it all, for this single region—the largest *Appellation d'Origine Contrôlée* in France—covers more territory than all of the vineyard areas of Germany put together, and is three and a half times larger than the vineyard acreage of New Zealand. In Bordeaux, some 8,650 growers and dozens of top-class estates—plus thousands more of lesser standing—produce more than 661 million bottles of wine every year, including many of the priciest wines in the world.

While it makes stunning, long-lived white table wines and superb white sweet wines

The name Bordeaux derives from *au bord de l'eau,* meaning "along the waters." Bordeaux lies within the French region of Aquitaine, a word whose Latin roots mean a well-watered place.

(notably, Sauternes), Bordeaux is primarily a red-wine region. Nearly 90 percent of the wine made is red.

The range of red Bordeaux is astounding. At the most basic level there are scores of utterly simple Bordeaux stacked, by the case, on the floor of any large wine shop. Wines labeled simply Bordeaux or Bordeaux *Supérieur* fall into this category, and they can cost $20 a bottle or so. At the most rarefied level,

THE QUICK SIP ON BORDEAUX

MORE THAN PERHAPS any other wines in the world, the top Bordeaux wines have set the standard for greatness and commercial success. They are renowned and sought after by collectors everywhere on the globe. In addition to these iconic wines, Bordeaux is the source of large quantities of every-night dinner wine.

BORDEAUX'S TOP WINES are known for their ability to be elegant while still possessing concentrated, powerful flavors.

BOTH RED AND WHITE BORDEAUX are almost always blends of two or more varieties. Blending is used to achieve complex flavors. Plus, growing multiple varieties that ripen at different times is a practical way of spreading the agricultural risk in Bordeaux's sometimes difficult maritime climate.

"Terroir is a way by which man uses soil, vine, and climate to express a trait in wine. Terroir isn't a hierarchy for quality, but rather a mantle for the sense of identity. This notion is a sensitive one in times of changing fashions. Wine is diversity, and terroir is a real way to escape the monotony of daily life."

— JEAN-CLAUDE BERROUET, renowned French enologist and winemaker of Château Pétrus from 1964 to 2008

THE LAND, THE GRAPES, AND THE VINEYARDS

Just about halfway between the North Pole and the equator, Bordeaux is one of the largest fine wine regions in the world—some 290,350 acres (117,500 hectares), encompassing sixty different appellations. (For comparison's sake, Bordeaux is six times larger than Napa Valley and slightly more than four times larger than Burgundy.)

The region lies along the path of three important rivers—the mighty Gironde Estuary, plus the two large rivers that feed it, the Dordogne and the Garonne. To the immediate west, just an hour's drive away, is the Atlantic Ocean, and everywhere the region is crisscrossed by small streams. All of this water has played a critical role in the wines Bordeaux produces. Indeed, these waterways were partially responsible for the region's early success. As of the thirteenth and fourteenth centuries, barges would dock along the wharves of the Gironde, ever ready to ferry wine to and fro between merchants and ultimately to ships headed for England. This, at a time when most other wine regions in France were relatively unknown beyond their own borders.

however, the famous Bordeaux we all hear about—the First Growths and wines in their league—can be the apotheosis of refinement. While these wines represent just a fraction of all of the Bordeaux produced, their complexity and age-worthiness are legendary. As are their astronomical prices. Indeed, by 2013, the First Growths and wines in their orbit often cost up to $1,500 a bottle (and sometimes more) for current vintages. This has effectively (and sadly) removed them from the wine-drinking experiences of all but the most well-connected, high-net-worth wine lovers. A generation ago, an upper-middle-class person—say, a university professor—could have saved up and splurged on a First Growth once a year. Today, top Bordeaux exist in their own realm, far outside the culture of normal wine drinking.

THE GRAPES OF BORDEAUX

WHITES

MUSCADELLE: A minor native grape sometimes incorporated into modestly priced blends for its light floral character. Not related to varieties with the word *muscat* in their names.

SAUVIGNON BLANC: Major grape. Crisp, austere, lively. Has an herbal freshness. Usually blended with sémillon.

SÉMILLON: Major grape. Dry and clean. Provides weight and depth and, with age, a honied character. Usually blended with sauvignon blanc. The primary grape for Sauternes.

REDS

CABERNET FRANC: An important grape in Bordeaux, highly valued in blends even in small amounts. Often said to contribute aromatic intensity and notes of violets and spices. Especially important in the Right Bank communes of St.-Émilion and Pomerol. The only one of the major Bordeaux reds to have originated elsewhere. (Cabernet franc is native to the Basque region of Spain.)

CABERNET SAUVIGNON: The second leading red grape in terms of acreage, after merlot. At its best, intense, deeply flavored, and complex. Provides the framework and structure behind many of the top wines. Most of the wines of the Left Bank (the communes of Margaux, St.-Julien, Pauillac, and St.-Estèphe) are based on it.

CARMENÈRE: Ancient Bordeaux variety (also known as grande vidure). The progeny of cabernet franc, but nearly extinct in Bordeaux today.

MALBEC: Old southwestern French variety also known by its original name, côt. Planted in only tiny amounts in Bordeaux today, used to add touches of nuance.

MERLOT: Bordeaux's major grape in terms of production, constituting more than 60 percent of all planted acres. Along with cabernet sauvignon, one of the two main grapes in most blends. At its best, round and supple. Sometimes characterized as the flesh on cabernet sauvignon's bones.

PETIT VERDOT: A minor grape in terms of production, but even small amounts are highly valued in blends. Contributes vivid color, flavor intensity, and tannin.

Most important, the rivers and adjacent sea (warmed by the Gulf Stream) act to temper the region's climate, thereby providing the vineyards with a milder and more stable environment than would otherwise be the case. In addition, Bordeaux is edged on the south and west by Les Landes—2.5 million acres (1,012,000 hectares) of manmade pine forests that also help to shield the region from extreme weather. Were it not for the maritime climate and the presence of these forests, Bordeaux's vineyards would be at even greater risk of damage by storms, severe cold snaps, and potentially devastating frosts.

Many of the vineyards of Bordeaux—and especially of the Médoc, including Margaux, Pauillac, St.-Émilion, and St.-Estèphe—appear quite flat. And they are, if one compares them to, say, the steeply sloped vineyards of the northern Rhône, those of northern Portugal, or most precipitous of all, the vineyards of Germany's Mosel region. But although it's hard to see with the naked eye, Bordeaux does have gently rolling hills that create variations

CLARET

*T**he British often call red Bordeaux claret. The word comes from the French* claret, *which originally referred to a light red wine (to distinguish it from Port). Today, of course, the top red Bordeaux are anything but light in color or in body.*

in topography, orientation to the sun, soil, and drainage patterns.

Drainage is key, for the grape varieties that grow in Bordeaux are very sensitive to too much water, and water is everywhere around them. Thus, the best vineyards tend to be on very well-drained soils of gravel and stone, and sometimes (especially in St.-Émilion) limestone. In the Médoc, these deep gravel beds are frequently near the Gironde Estuary. An old Bordeaux saying has it that the best vineyards "can see the river," and not surprisingly, if you stand in the middle of the vines at Château Latour, at Château Pichon-Longueville Comtesse de Lalande, or at many of the other top estates, you can indeed watch the boats moving up and down the Gironde.

If the gods had been generous, every bit of Bordeaux would have been gravel and stone. Unfortunately they were not, and it is not. Many Bordeaux soils are based primarily on clay, which doesn't drain water as well. As a result, clay stays cool in the spring, delaying the vines' budbreak and slowing the start of ripening. If the grapes are to ripen fully and if the tannin is to be physiologically mature, the vines will need to make up for this slow start by benefiting from lots of warm weather throughout the growing season. Because of its slightly less tannic structure to begin with, and because it tends to ripen early, merlot is often thought to have a better chance of doing this than cabernet sauvignon. As result, merlot is often planted in areas with a high percentage

of clay. Of course, when clay is more abundant, being located on a good slope with significant drainage becomes critical.

In a moment, I'll address the specific regions within Bordeaux, but first, here's an overview of the grapes.

By law, red Bordeaux wines must be made from one or more of six red grapes: merlot, cabernet sauvignon, cabernet franc, petit verdot, carmenère, and malbec. Merlot is by far the most widely planted of these, constituting more than 60 percent of all the vineyard land planted with red grapes. In Bordeaux, merlot is often described as fleshy, mouthfilling, and supple. By comparison, cabernet sauvignon (which accounts for just over 20 percent of vineyard plantings) is more angular and gives many of the great red Bordeaux their framework, or structure. Structure comes principally from tannin, and both cabernet sauvignon and merlot have considerable amounts. Tannin also acts as a preservative in wine, which is why so many top Bordeaux can be aged for such long periods of time.

France takes her marriages seriously. Here, Atlantic oysters, a traditional partner for exuberant white Bordeaux.

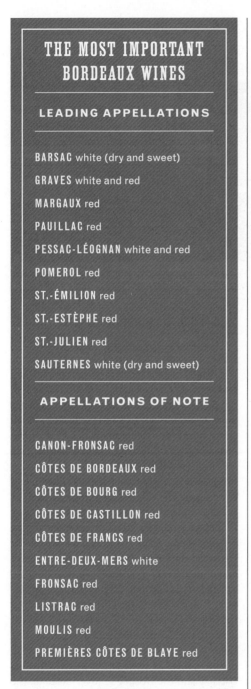

THE MOST IMPORTANT BORDEAUX WINES

LEADING APPELLATIONS

BARSAC white (dry and sweet)

GRAVES white and red

MARGAUX red

PAUILLAC red

PESSAC-LÉOGNAN white and red

POMEROL red

ST.-ÉMILION red

ST.-ESTÈPHE red

ST.-JULIEN red

SAUTERNES white (dry and sweet)

APPELLATIONS OF NOTE

CANON-FRONSAC red

CÔTES DE BORDEAUX red

CÔTES DE BOURG red

CÔTES DE CASTILLON red

CÔTES DE FRANCS red

ENTRE-DEUX-MERS white

FRONSAC red

LISTRAC red

MOULIS red

PREMIÈRES CÔTES DE BLAYE red

important variety, and all of the other reds (carmenère, malbec, petit verdot) are planted only in tiny amounts, and together constitute no more than 2 percent of red grapes grown.

As far as genetics, all of Bordeaux's red varieties appear to have originated in the southwestern quadrant of France, except cabernet franc, which is of Spanish Basque origin and was later brought to France. Cabernet franc is the father of merlot, cabernet sauvignon, and carmenère (each grape had a different mother), while malbec is a cross of prunelard and magdeleine noire des Charentes. For its part, petit verdot's parents are not known. For more on these varieties, see their descriptions in Getting to Know the Grapes (page 53).

For white Bordeaux wines, seven grapes are permitted: the main three—sémillon, sauvignon blanc, and muscadelle—plus ugni blanc, colombard, merlot blanc, and sauvignon gris, although these final four exist only in extremely tiny amounts and tend to be used only in the least expensive wines. Of the important three white grapes, sémillon, considered the soul of white Bordeaux, originated there and is the most widely planted. With age, sémillon takes on a wonderful honey flavor and a creamy, almost lanolinlike texture. Indeed, it is the high percentage of sémillon that allows legendary Bordeaux whites, such as Château Haut-Brion Blanc and Château La Mission Haut-Brion Blanc, to age so gracefully and deliciously.

Then there's sauvignon blanc, which, although widely assumed to have first appeared in Bordeaux, actually originated in the Loire Valley. Only one of its parents—savagnin—is known. Muscadelle appears to have originated somewhere in southwestern France, possibly Bordeaux, and again only one parent is known—gouais blanc (interestingly, gouais blanc is also chardonnay's mother). Muscadelle is not related to any of the varieties with *muscat* in their names.

The fact that three red and three white grape varieties are widely used in Bordeaux (and thirteen are actually grown and permitted) makes the practice and philosophy of winemaking extremely different from that in Burgundy, Bordeaux's northeastern neighbor,

Together, merlot and cabernet sauvignon make up more than 80 percent of all the vineyard land devoted to red grapes in Bordeaux. Cabernet franc (just over 10 percent of vineyard plantings) is Bordeaux's third most

Château Palmer, along with Château Margaux, makes one of the silkiest, most luscious wines in Margaux. The magnificent estate, built in 1748, was bought by Englishman General Charles Palmer in 1814 for about $17,000 (15,000 Euros).

CHÂTEAU, CUVERIE, AND CHAI

*T*hree of the most important words in Bordeaux are château, cuverie, and chai. Though we think of a château as a palatial estate, anything can be a château in Bordeaux—from a farmhouse to a garage. The word simply refers to a building attached to vineyards, with winemaking and storage facilities on the property. Within the château is the cuverie (coo-ver-EE), the building where the wine will be made, and the chai (pronounced shay), the cellar where it will be stored and aged.

where there is just one leading red and one white. For the Bordelais winemaker, blending is critical. And while thirteen permissible grape varieties may seem like a lot, that number is far fewer than in the past. As of the 1780s, for example, thirty-four red varieties and twenty-nine white varieties could still be found in parts of St.-Émilion and Pomerol.

AN OVERVIEW OF BORDEAUX'S MAJOR REGIONS

Bordeaux is divided into multiple subregions. I've listed here the most important ones; you'll find sections on each of these later in this chapter. Keep in mind, however, that Bordeaux has many less-well-known subregions from which come numerous delicious wines that represent good value. These include Listrac and Moulis, Entre-Deux-Mers, Fronsac and Canon-Fronsac, and the outlying districts known collectively as the Côtes. We'll look at each of these as well, although in less detail.

Before we begin, there are two terms that are important to know: Left Bank and Right Bank. To understand them, imagine you are standing in the city of Bordeaux, at the southern end of the Gironde Estuary. Looking northwest (toward where the Gironde empties into the Atlantic Ocean), all of the vineyards left (or west) of the Gironde Estuary and the Garonne River constitute the so-called Left Bank. All of the vineyards to the right of the Gironde Estuary and the Dordogne River make up the Right Bank. (In between these lies *Entre-Deux-Mers*—literally "between two seas.")

Starting on the Left Bank of the Gironde Estuary and then moving southward in a big U to end on the Right Bank, the most important subregions are:

MÉDOC AND HAUT-MÉDOC: Together referred to as the Médoc. Inside the Haut-Médoc (literally, the upper Médoc) are six communes, or smaller appellations. Four are famous. Starting from the north and going south to the city of Bordeaux, they are: St.-Estèphe, Pauillac, St.-Julien, and Margaux.

GRAVES: Inside Graves is one famous smaller appellation, Pessac-Léognan.

SAUTERNES AND BARSAC

ST.-ÉMILION

POMEROL

In the past, the wines from Bordeaux's different regional appellations manifested significant differences in flavor and texture. The wines of Pauillac, for example, shared characteristics of soil and climate that made them taste quite different from Pomerol wines. As is true in most places today, however, these regional distinctions have been considerably blurred by modern winemaking techniques that have become nearly global in reach.

In the impressive cellars of Haut-Brion, one of the top Bordeaux châteaux, barrels are never stacked but rather laid out like showpieces.

THE MULTIPLE CLASSIFICATIONS

Fasten your seat belt. Bordeaux is an amalgam of regional classifications that can seem insanely complicated. To begin with, the classifications are different from one region to the next, even though the terms used may be the same or similar. Thus, the words *Grand Cru Classé* mean one thing in St.-Émilion, something slightly different in Graves, and nothing at all a few miles away in Pomerol.

What do the classifications classify? It might seem like an odd question, but it's important to know that in Bordeaux, the main classifications (those that apply in the Médoc and in Graves) are based on the estate, not on the land (as is true in Burgundy). Thus, when a famous grand château in either of these regions buys a neighboring lesser château, the lesser château could be elevated to the higher rank. This is quite at odds with the philosophy that terroir makes the wine, but it is nonetheless the way the Médoc and Graves classifications are legally structured.

Finally, before we tunnel down into the specifics of the rankings, it's important to know that the classifications are highly politically charged. The entire 2006 classification of St.-Émilion, for example, was annulled in a tumult of legal action following the demotion of some châteaux and the ascendancy of others. This is no surprise, for more than pride is at stake. When a château's ranking changes, the value of the property changes astronomically, with a higher rank resulting in hundreds of millions of euros in added value for the château owner. For example, in 2012, a Grand Cru property elevated one step up to Premier Grand Cru Classé B status was immediately worth nearly ten times what it had been just the day before.

As for the classifications and rankings themselves, the classification of the Médoc was the first and remains the most famous classification. It occurred in 1855 and is called, logically enough, the 1855 Classification (see The Immutable 1855 Classification, page 151). It ranked sixty top châteaux in the Médoc, plus

CLASSIFICATIONS: THE CHEAT SHEET

Here's a quick take on the confusing world of Bordeaux classifications. Each area has its own system as well as its own terminology. Unfortunately, wine labels don't always indicate a wine's classification.

THE MÉDOC: In 1855, sixty châteaux in the Médoc and one château in Pessac-Léognan, in Graves, were classified from Premiers Crus (First Growths), down to Cinquièmes Crus (Fifth Growths).

SAUTERNES AND BARSAC: Also classified in 1855. One château was designated as Premier Cru Supérieur Classé (Château d'Yquem), the next best as Premiers Crus Classés, followed by Deuxièmes Crus Classés.

GRAVES: In 1953, and revised in 1959, the top châteaux in Graves were not ranked but all given the same title: Grands Crus Classés for their red wine, white wine, or both.

ST.-ÉMILION: In 1954, the châteaux of St.-Émilion were classified, with the provision that the classification be revised every ten years. The top level is Premiers Grands Crus Classés, divided between an A level (the very best) and a B level. Below these two come the Grands Crus Classés. As a result of various amendments and annulments over the decades, the last revision was in 2012.

POMEROL: Pomerol, as well as outlying areas such as Fronsac and Canon-Fronsac were never classified.

one, Château Haut-Brion, in Pessac-Léognan, in Graves. The châteaux were ranked into five categories, from Premier Cru, or First Growth (the best) down to Cinquième Cru, or Fifth Growth. (In Bordeaux, the French word *cru*, translated as "growth," is used to indicate a wine estate, vineyard, or château. Thus a Premier Cru, or First Growth, is a wine estate of the top rank. The word is the past participle of the French verb *croître*, meaning "to grow.")

The châteaux of Sauternes and Barsac were also part of the 1855 Classification, although they were categorized differently. Here, the best château (there was only one—Château d'Yquem) was called Premier Cru Supérieur Classé, First Great Classified Growth. The second-best châteaux were called First Growths and the third-best, Second Growths.

(If you're on the verge of skipping the next couple of paragraphs, I understand.)

The wines of Graves, including Haut-Brion, were classified in 1953 and revised in 1959. (Because it was already classified as part of

Château Pétrus, unranked in the 1855 Classification because it was a Pomerol, is today one of the world's most expensive wines.

the Médoc's 1855 Classification, Haut-Brion today boasts two different classifications.) In both the original and revised classifications, no hierarchical order was established. The sixteen châteaux recognized for their red wines, white wines, or both were simply given the legal right to call themselves Grand Cru Classé, Great Classified Growth.

THE IMMUTABLE 1855 CLASSIFICATION AND THE FIRST GROWTHS

The legendary treatise known as the 1855 Classification established four First Growths—the elegant Château Margaux and Château Lafite-Rothschild, the powerful Château Latour, and the earthy, sensual Château Haut-Brion. (As we'll see, Château Mouton-Rothschild was added later.) Here's how it happened: In 1855, Napoléon III asked Bordeaux's top château owners to rate their wines from best to worst for the Paris Universal Exhibition, a fair. One imagines that the château owners cringed. The prospect of rating the wines, one against the other, was nightmarish. The château owners stalled.

Eventually, the Bordeaux Chamber of Commerce was invested with the job. There was no fretful hand-wringing about terroir. The Chamber members ranked the châteaux based on one stark quantitative measure: how much the wine sold for. The wines that sold for the most were called Premiers Crus, or First Growths. The Deuxièmes Crus, Second Growths, sold for a little less. The system continued down to Fifth Growths. In all, sixty-one châteaux were classified. The hundreds of châteaux whose wines cost less than the Fifth Growths were apparently not worth bothering about and were not classified at all.

There was one other provision: The classification—clearly immutable as far as its authors were concerned—was never to be revised.

As you would expect, since that time, entire books have been written on the 1855 Classification and the validity (or lack thereof) of its now-controversial rankings. For their part, château owners have, for decades, reasoned that the market will ultimately establish value. And that's what has happened. In 2009, for example, the electronic wine exchange company Liv-ex reclassified the top châteaux using the same parameter—price—that was used in 1855. In the latest Liv-ex list (2011), Château Palmer, ranked twenty-eighth in 1855 (a Third Growth) has moved into seventh position (it would be a Second Growth today). Château Duhart-Milon, ranked thirty-eighth in 1855 (a Fourth Growth), would now be number eleven (it would also be a Second Growth today). And, seemingly against all odds, Château Lynch-Bages, ranked fiftieth in 1855 (a Fourth Growth), would now be number twelve (making it, too, a Second Growth today). In addition to the three châteaux just mentioned, a slew of others have climbed up to a higher rank, including Clerc-Milon, Pontet-Canet, Beychevelle, Grand-Puy-Lacoste, d'Armailhac, Cos d'Estournel, and Ducru-Beaucaillou.

An important footnote: One man did challenge, and ultimately change, the classification of his château: Baron Philippe de Rothschild. Obstinate and relentless, he petitioned the government for twenty years to upgrade Mouton-Rothschild from a Second Growth to a First. His persistence paid off in 1973; Château Mouton-Rothschild was moved up to First Growth rank. The classification was thereby changed for the first and last time.

In the end, rankings and ratings are intellectually fascinating, but they remain temporal things. If the 1855 Classification has taught us anything, it's that wines can soar above (and below) their historic reputations. Rankings, in other words, can never fully replace the best evaluation method of all—tasting.

FUTURES

The most expensive red Bordeaux wines are commonly sold as futures. Under this system, referred to in France as selling *en primeur,* the châteaux set (much anticipated) opening prices for the wines produced each year. During the spring after the harvest, these wines go on sale for the opening amounts. The wine itself will not be delivered for another two or more years, when it is done aging and is ready to be released for the first time. For their part, châteaux get cash flow out of the deal, and customers—usually negociants, importers, and ultimately retailers, who may then in turn sell futures to their customers— secure wines they might otherwise not, at what is usually (but not always) a better price than if they'd waited for the wine's release. Buying futures is, in effect, buying on speculation. In a global, fast-paced, wine-as-profitable-investment marketplace, some Bordeaux may be traded multiple times through middlemen before the wine even leaves the château. The system, well entrenched in Bordeaux for decades, exists virtually no place else. In 2012, Château Latour stunned the world by being the first top château to discontinue the practice of selling futures, saying it preferred to sell the wine directly to the consumer and only when it was deemed ready to actually drink.

St.-Émilion was first classified in 1954, with the provision that the classification be revised every ten years (this is not true for the Médoc or Graves classifications, which, by current law, are never revised). In St.-Émilion, the best wines were termed Premier Grand Cru Classé, First Great Classified Growth. The second-best were named Grand Cru Classé, Great Classified Growth. Below that came Grand Cru, Great Growth. The top level, Premier Grand Cru Classé, was further divided into an "A" group and a "B" group. As of 2012, and in the midst of ongoing legal challenges, four wines are in the "A" league: Château Angélus, Château Ausone, Château Pavie, and Château Cheval Blanc. All other Premiers Grands Crus Classés are designated "B," although these are still, of course, considered above the Grands Crus Classés. The St.-Émilion classification in particular has experienced considerable turmoil, including many legal battles that have resulted from demotions made when the original rankings have been revised. In the midst of so many classifications, the vineyards of Pomerol were, sanely enough, never ranked. For a complete list of the Bordeaux châteaux classified in 1855, see the Appendix, pages 965–967.

Finally, it's interesting and a little startling to realize that, even in those regions with classifications, most of the châteaux within those regions were never classified. Which brings us to the Cru Bourgeois.

In the Médoc, there's a collective name for the châteaux (now numbering 250 estates) that were not classified. They are called the Crus Bourgeois du Médoc, and since 2010, a new list of them is published each year by the Alliance des Crus Bourgeois du Médoc. For the most

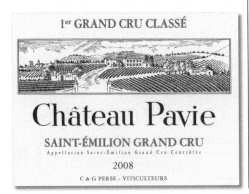

1er GRAND CRU CLASSÉ

Château Pavie

SAINT-ÉMILION GRAND CRU
Appellation Saint-Émilion Grand Cru Contrôlée

2008

C & G PERSE - VITICULTEURS

The vineyards of Château Mouton Rothschild. In 1855, the estate was classified as a Second Growth. But in 1973, thanks to the relentless lobbying by Baron Philippe de Rothschild, the rankings were changed for the first and last time. Mouton was elevated to First Growth status.

part, Cru Bourgeois are extremely well priced. Today, a well-regarded Cru Bourgeois, for example, costs ⅓₅ the price of a First Growth, the latter, of course, being stratospherically priced.

THE MÉDOC

The largest of the famous regions of Bordeaux, the Médoc starts at the city of Bordeaux (a UNESCO World Heritage Site) and stretches northward like a snake for fifty miles along the left bank of the Gironde Estuary. The Médoc is made up of two smaller appellations. One is, confusingly, also called the Médoc (the northern third of low-lying land, near where the Gironde empties into the Atlantic), and the other is called the Haut-Médoc (literally the upper Médoc; the part closest to the city of Bordeaux and farthest away from the Atlantic). It is in the Haut-Médoc, all at the river's gravelly edge, that you find the famous communes

(villages) of Margaux, St.-Julien, Pauillac, and St.-Estèphe. Virtually all the châteaux rated in the 1855 Classification are scattered throughout these four communes. Farther inland are the Haut-Médoc's two less important communes, Listrac and Moulis. Here, away from the river, the heavier, less-well-drained soils often result in less refined wines.

Almost all the Médoc's wines are red. The dominant grape is cabernet sauvignon (forming up to 70 percent of all blends), followed by merlot. Both do well in the Médoc's stony soil, which, here and there, is interspersed with clay.

Amazingly, the flat plateaus of the Médoc were originally marshlands—low-lying semiswamps badly suited to making any wine at all, never mind great wine. In the seventeenth century, however, the Bordeaux nobility brought in Dutch engineers to cut huge drains in the land, effectively lowering the water table and creating riverside gravel banks. With the marshes drained, Bordeaux's emerging class of wealthy lawyers and merchants seized the opportunity to become significant landowners. Huge parcels of land along the banks of the Gironde

The ancient cobblestoned streets of St.-Émilion. The medieval village is a UNESCO World Heritage Site.

were purchased, grand estates were built, and a vine-growing revolution ensued. During the seventeenth and early eighteenth centuries, many of the most prestigious châteaux and vineyards were established, including Lafite-Rothschild, Latour, and Mouton-Rothschild.

MARGAUX

The southernmost and largest commune of the Médoc, Margaux (mar-GO) has more classified estates than St.-Estèphe, Pauillac, or St.-Julien. The aristocratic Château Margaux is here, of course, plus twenty other well-known properties.

The soil in Margaux is among the lightest and most gravelly in the Médoc, giving the best wines in the best years a sort of soaring elegance and refinement, plus wonderful, generous aromas. Margaux are often described as being like an iron fist in a velvet glove. It is this combination of power with delicacy that has given these wines their vaunted reputation.

The two most renowned Margaux are the First Growth Château Margaux, and the Third Growth Château Palmer. In top years these wines can be superbly elegant, with long, silky, hedonistic flavors. Other exceptional Margaux to consider: Château Rauzan-Ségla, Château Lascombes, Château Kirwan, and Château Giscours.

ST.-JULIEN

Just north of the largest commune, Margaux, is the smallest, St.-Julien (SAN ZHU-lee-ahn).

It's easy to drive right through it and not realize you've been there. Of all the communes, St.-Julien has the highest percentage of classified growths—about 95 percent of the wines here are Second, Third, or Fourth Growths, although there are no Firsts. If you were to drink only the wines from this commune for the rest of your life, you could be very happy.

Among St.-Julien's most well-known wines are the three Léovilles (Léo is from the Latin *leon*, meaning "lion"): Léoville-Barton, Léoville-Las Cases, and Léoville-Poyferré. All are classified as Second Growths and all are structured and intense, although in many years, Léoville-Las Cases and Léoville-Poyferré in particular can broach First Growth status.

Like those of Margaux, the leading wines of St.-Julien are known for their precision and refinement. Others not to miss: Château Ducru-Beaucaillou, Château Gruaud-Larose, Château Branaire-Ducru, Château Langoa-Barton, and Château Clerc-Milon.

PAUILLAC

This word is music to the ears of Bordeaux lovers. Pauillac (POY-yack), just north of St.-Julien, is where much of the excitement in Bordeaux is centered. Three of the five First Growths are born in this soil: Château Lafite-Rothschild, Château Mouton-Rothschild, and Château Latour. In all, Pauillac has eighteen of the sixty-one classified wines, including many of the best.

Pauillac wines can lean several ways. Some have a sort of full-bodied luxuriousness; others, a bold structure; still others, a subtle, precise refinement. The best are always complex, with rich black currant and cranberry flavors, often overlaid with cedary and graphite notes. The range of styles within this commune is due to variable terroir and marked differences among the châteaux in the composition of their blends. In the north, Lafite-Rothschild sits on bits of limestone scattered through the gravel (its wine exudes elegance). Farther south, Pichon-Longueville Comtesse de Lalande (often called

IN PRAISE OF DELAYED GRATIFICATION

No matter how delicious a young top Bordeaux is, it will almost always be more thrilling when it's older, after it's had a chance to evolve and reveal other facets and nuances of its personality. How much older? No one can say for sure. There is never one magic moment when a wine is ready. Most Bordeaux—most structured red wines—evolve and soften progressively. If they are very good, they usually go from being slightly tight to being supple and having a wider range of more complex flavors. But where a wine is along this spectrum at any point in time is a matter of conjecture. (And no matter where it stands on this spectrum, it will have its positive points.) Generally, the more structured the wine when young (i.e., the more tannin it has), the more slowly it will evolve. Since most top Bordeaux are very structured wines, they usually take at least eight or ten years of aging before beginning to soften and show more complex nuances. For a truly great Bordeaux, however, a good rule of thumb is to wait a decade before you think about opening it. Then add on another year (or however much you can bear) of delayed gratification time.

simply Pichon-Lalande) is situated on gravel and clay (its wine is often more fleshy).

If money is no object and one has the sort of access usually reserved for those in the Fortune 100, then drinking one of the Pauillac First Growths is certainly the best introduction possible to Pauillac flavors. But the cost of the Pauillac First Growths—in 2013, about $1,500 a bottle or more for a current vintage—effectively removes these wines from many people's "must-try" list. There are, luckily, many other very good Pauillacs, including: Château Pichon-Longueville Comtesse de Lalande, Château Pichon-Longueville Baron, Château Lynch-Bages, Château Duhart-Milon, Château Pontet-Canet, Château Beychevelle, and Château Clerc-Milon.

ST.-ESTÈPHE

Stacked on top of Pauillac is the northernmost Médoc commune of St.-Estèphe (SAN es-TEFF), known for wines that, at least by Bordeaux standards, have the staunchness of an army general and a sense of ruggedness from the commune's heavier soil, closer to the mouth of the Gironde Estuary. (Many wines, as a result, are simply good, hearty Cru Bourgeois.) Only a few of the very top wines—notably Cos d'Estournel (which is so close to the border with Pauillac, you could hit a golf ball into the courtyard of Château Lafite-Rothschild)—have captivating intensity and exquisite concentration and profundity of flavor. Cos (the *s* is pronounced; the word is an old Gascon term for "hill") makes a blatantly sensuous wine (about 65 percent merlot), with waves of chocolaty, pipe-tobacco-like, earthy, black currant fruit flavors that, when the wine is young, often seem to be bursting at the seams. The Asian-inspired nineteenth-century château itself, with its show-stopping copper pagoda roof and massive carved door, is one of the most intriguing in Bordeaux. Other top St.-Estèphes to seek out: Château Calon-Ségur and Château Montrose.

GRAVES

South of the city of Bordeaux, Graves (GRAHV) extends like a sleeve dangling off the arm of the Médoc. It is named for its famous gravelly soil, the gift

Château Haut-Brion, the only estate outside the Médoc (it's in Graves) to be ranked a First Growth in the 1855 Classification. The wine has a distinct, complex earthiness and exquisite texture.

of Ice Age glaciers. The glaciers also deposited tiny white quartz pebbles easily found in all the best vineyards.

Graves holds the distinction of being the only part of Bordeaux where both red and white wines are made by most châteaux. The vineyards, some of the most ancient in the region, were the first to be known internationally. Casks of wine from the region were shipped to England as early as the twelfth century, and by the sixteenth century several important estates were already established, including Graves's most famous château, Haut-Brion. Spelled "Ho Bryan" at the time, the wine it produced was praised by the seventeenth-century British. A century later, Thomas Jefferson, third president of the United States, wrote about how delicious "Obrion" was and purchased six cases to be sent from the château in Graves to Virginia.

So stunning was Château Haut-Brion that it was the sole Graves wine to be included in the 1855 Classification. Powerful yet hauntingly supple, Haut-Brion has an almost primordial earthy character. The other top wines of Graves were first classified in 1953 and the classification was revised in 1959.

Within Graves is the appellation Pessac-Léognan. Many of the best red and white Graves come from this area of ten tiny communes, grouped together by the French government in 1987.

Although many wine drinkers think of dry white wines when they think of Graves, slightly more red wine than white comes from here, and in fact, about a dozen of the region's most stunning wines, all of which, incidentally, carry the Pessac-Léognan appellation, are red. Cabernet sauvignon, merlot, and cabernet franc are all used extensively. Château Haut-Brion has by far the most merlot (often as much as 45 percent) and the most cabernet franc (sometimes up to 20 percent) of any of the First Growths.

In addition to the voluptuous Château Haut-Brion, Château La Mission-Haut Brion, Château Domaine de Chevalier, Château Pape-Clément, and Château Haut-Bailly all make outstanding red wines, with rich, earthy, chocolaty, plummy, cherry, spicy flavors and, sometimes, a very appealing earthy/animal quality.

Classically, all white Graves are blends of sémillon and sauvignon blanc. From sémillon comes richness, body, depth, and the ability to age with honeyed overtones. From sauvignon comes sprightly acidity and a fresh snap of flavor. Indeed, simple white Graves has undergone an enormous revolution in quality since the late 1980s, and the wines are more concentrated as a result.

But within Graves, a step even farther up are the top white Pessac-Léognan wines. These range from very good wines, such as Château Carbonnieux, with its minerally vibrancy and satiny mouthfilling texture, to outstanding. (White Pessac-Léognan wines are considered the classic companions for the icy cold, briny oysters caught off Bordeaux's Atlantic coast.) Among the most outstanding, the whites of Château La Mission Haut-Brion, Château Haut-Brion, and Domaine de Chevalier, for example, are mind-boggling in their intensity and complexity, and with age, take on ravishing flavors that are unlike any other white wines in France, indeed, unlike any other white wines in the world.

SAUTERNES AND BARSAC

Quite a bit south of Graves, along the Garonne River, are Bordeaux's five sweet-wine-producing communes, the two most important of which are Sauternes and Barsac (the other three are Bommes, Fargues, and Preignac). Sauternes and Barsac are not simply two unique, small places within Bordeaux; they are among the few regions in the world devoted to sweet wines. Sauternes, the more famous of the two, is about four times larger than tiny Barsac, but the wines from each can be extraordinary. At their best, these are wines with an apricotish opulence that detonates in your mouth and then spreads over your taste buds like liquefied honey. The British wine expert Hugh Johnson has described them best. Of one Sauternes, he wrote, "It was glorious in its youth; a creamy, stinging, orange-scented, head-filling quintessence of *pourriture noble*. It is still awesome: now deep gold and smelling of crème brûlée, but still racily potent and endlessly sweet."

Needless to say, it takes merely a sip of a great Sauternes or Barsac to create a convert. The great examples are wonderful not because of their sweetness, however, but because of their extraordinary balance. The best are luscious without being cloying, richly honeyed without tasting like candy. To achieve this, the wines must have just the right acidity and alcohol and must be complex.

How is this done? Sauternes and Barsac are made mostly from sémillon and, to a lesser extent, sauvignon blanc grapes left on the vine well into the fall, whereupon they usually become infected with the benevolent fungus *Botrytis cinerea*, also known as *pourriture noble* or noble rot. Sémillon, the leading grape in the area, is especially susceptible to the fungus because of its large bunches of thin-skinned grapes with a high sugar content.

> Graves is the only region of Bordeaux where almost every château produces both a red and a white wine.

Although it seems unlikely that grapes left to decay into furry, moldy raisins will become magnificent wine, they can. In Sauternes and Barsac the process occurs naturally, though erratically, by virtue of the region's singular climate. For the botrytis fungus to take hold on healthy, ripe grapes, the region must have just the right amount of humidity and warmth (too little or too much can produce problems). Sauternes and Barsac, the farthest south of all the important regions of Bordeaux, are ideally situated. Here, the Ciron River meets the Garonne River, creating gentle morning mists. If all goes well, nearby forests will help to hold the moisture in the air. When the day warms up and grows drier, a perfect stage is set for botrytis to appear.

As the beneficial mold punctures the grapes' skins in search of water to germinate its spores, the water begins to evaporate and the grapes dehydrate. Inside the shriveled berries, the sugar in the juice becomes progressively more concentrated. The botrytis also alters the structure of the grapes' acids, but the amount of acidity in the wine is not diminished.

Beyond a technical approach. Caroline Frey, winemaker of Chateau La Lagune.

Château d'Yquem, that ranked a Premier Cru Supérieur Classe in the 1855 Classification, is the only estate to be given this super status. D'Yquem makes what is arguably the best known sweet wine—Château d'Yquem Sauternes.

The process begins in late September, but the rate at which botrytis takes hold is unpredictable. In great years, the berries will begin to desiccate, forming a tiny amount of liquorous sweet juice by late October. In other years, the process may be painfully slower. Throughout, the château owner is sitting on pins and needles. First, he or she hopes for a good warm growing season so that as fall approaches, the grape bunches are healthy and ripe. Next, he prays for just the right balance of moisture, dryness, and warmth so that the bunches will become botrytized as evenly and uniformly as possible. But the most nerve-wracking part is the race against winter. Day by day as winter approaches, the risk of losing the crop increases. One cold snap, one heavy rain, one winter storm could knock the fragile berries off the vine, swell them with water, or freeze them before the botrytis has fully taken hold. In each case the crop could be ruined, and the château could conceivably be left with nothing. (About twice a decade, the weather is so borderline that Château d'Yquem [pronounced dee-KEM]—of all the châteaux specializing in sweet wine, the one ranked the highest in the 1855 Classification—chooses not to make any sweet wine at all.)

As the botrytis spreads through the vineyard, the château owner is keenly aware of its growth pattern. Botrytis that takes hold sporadically means a difficult, laborious harvest, for only perfectly rotted berries with concentrated juice can be picked and pressed. Grapes only partially infected by the mold can give diluted juice or juice with funky off-flavors.

Unfortunately, the fragile and erratic botrytis rarely reaches readiness at one moment throughout an entire vineyard. To harvest each grape at perfect "rottenness," therefore, pickers must go into the vineyards four to ten times over the course of several weeks in October and November, sometimes picking whole clusters, but sometimes picking individual botrytized grapes out of the clusters. The cost of such painstaking repetition is considerable. In the end, for the greatest of estates, like Château d'Yquem, the grapes picked from one vine may ultimately yield just one glass of wine.

The individually handpicked grapes and whole bunches are brought into the cellar. There, they are pressed with great difficulty since the grapes are so dehydrated, and the must is transferred into oak barrels, where it will ferment. Because of the concentration of sugar in the must, fermentation is difficult and takes a long time—up to a year (by comparison, a dry white wine generally ferments in two weeks to one month).

During fermentation, yeasts convert the sugar in the must into alcohol (see How Wine

EATING SAUTERNES

Sauternes is one of the most magical things you can drink—and (as it turns out) eat. Now, you may have yet to come across dark chocolate–covered, Sauternes-soaked raisins, and indeed there are only a scant few places (both in Paris) where you can get these little nubbins of hedonism. But get them you must. They will look innocent enough. But the minute you take a tiny bite and the mind-blowing flavor of Sauternes seeps into the luscious dark chocolate, well, this is when (as with everyone else who experiences them) your eyes will go wide and you momentarily won't know what to do with yourself. I have been told that Parisians think it's quite romantic to spend rainy mornings in bed, eating dark chocolate–covered Sauternes raisins with a loved one. You will have to test this for yourself.

Only a few *confiserie* (candy shops) in France sell chocolate-covered Sauternes, requiring that you keep a close lookout for the delicious nuggets when you are in that country. For decades, the best of these (and a temple of gastronomy for anyone with a sweet tooth) was L'Etoile d'Or, in Paris's 9th Arrondissement. (Alas, the historic shop closed in 2014 after a fire.) Today, luckily, a French shop called Oulala (sweet.oulala@gmail.com), sells them by mail order. Oulala indeed.

Is Made, page 37). As you know, a dry wine is dry because the yeasts convert all but the merest trace of sugar into alcohol. With Sauternes and Barsac, the yeasts begin to convert the sugar as usual. At a certain point, however, the concentration of alcohol is so great, it kills the yeasts. Fermentation stops, even though there is unconverted natural grape sugar left in the must. What remains, in other words, is a wine with leftover, or residual, sugar—a naturally sweet wine. Sauternes and Barsac usually have 10 to 15 percent residual sugar.

These are not feeble wines. The sensory impact of a wine with 14 percent alcohol and 10 to 15 percent residual sugar is formidable. Plus, another factor comes into play: the botrytis itself. When the grapes being pressed have been perfectly infected, the mold, as well as the alcohol, can help kill the yeasts. As a result, the fermenting must may reach only 13 percent alcohol before the mold and alcohol working in tandem destroy the yeasts and cause fermentation to stop. At 13 percent alcohol, a sweet wine tastes more refined, elegant, and in balance than it does at a higher level of alcohol. Thus, with Sauternes and Barsac the finesse and complexity of the wines is directly related to how thoroughly and uniformly the botrytis takes hold in the vineyard.

Can you taste botrytis in the wine? An experienced taster can. The mold is not washed off or in any other way removed from the grapes and bunches, and it does contribute to the flavor. That flavor, however, is not like something that was left too long in the back of the refrigerator. Botrytis adds an extra dimension,

Botrytized sémillon grapes about to be harvested at Château Lafaurie-Peyraguey.

BON APERITIF

The word *aperitif* comes from the Latin *aperire,* meaning to open, and indeed, a variety of fresh, slightly bitter drinks have traditionally been used to open both meals and appetites. More than mere cocktail-hour stimulants, however, wine aperitifs are also thought to be healthful because many contain minute amounts of quinine, an ingredient thought to have beneficial anti-inflammatory properties and one that was originally added to aperitifs to protect French soldiers from malaria (for most of history, French soldiers have been given—even paid with—considerable amounts of wine).

Currently, one of the bestselling French aperitifs in the United States (thank you, James Bond) is Lillet, first created in 1872, when two French brothers blended white Bordeaux wine with a mixture of macerated fruits and a small amount of quinine. Today, numerous fruits—some of which are a well-kept secret—along with green oranges from Morocco, sweet oranges from Valencia, Spain, bitter oranges from Haiti, and cinchona bark (quinine) from the Peruvian Andes are cold-macerated in French brandy for four to six months before the brandy is mixed with wine and aged.

Two types of Lillet are made: nonvintage, also called classic, and vintage, known as Jean de Lillet, the only vintaged aperitif in the world. Vintage Lillet is aged in newer oak barrels than nonvintage. Lillet Blanc, both vintage and nonvintage, is produced from Bordeaux-grown sauvignon blanc, sémillon, and muscadelle grapes. Lillet Rouge, whether vintage or nonvintage, is a blend of merlot and cabernet sauvignon.

---

sometimes described as being faintly like sweet corn or mushrooms, to the overall complexity of the wines.

After a Sauternes or Barsac has completed fermentation, it remains in a cask for at least two years of aging. It then goes on to age in the bottle. After thirty or more years, a top Sauternes or Barsac can still be remarkably alive. Which is not to say you have to age these wines for three decades. The wines' honeyed apricot flavors are almost irresistible when the wine is young, say, five years after the vintage date. But it's only after about ten years, once the obvious hit of sweetness has passed and the flavors have totally coalesced, that the wines' mesmerizing opulence comes into full force.

In France, this vinous opulence is usually juxtaposed against a food that's equally intense and flamboyant. Historically, for example, Sauternes was often served with foie gras—a hedonistic marriage if ever there was one—astoundingly, often as a first course (in my opinion, making every wine and dish that followed pale by comparison).

The wines of Sauternes and Barsac were the only ones rated, along with the Médoc, in the famous 1855 Classification. One Sauternes was singled out and given the highest rating of Premier Cru Supérieur Classé: Château d'Yquem. Yquem is still the ultimate, richest, most perfectly balanced Sauternes. After Yquem, eleven châteaux are classified as Premier Cru and fifteen as Deuxième Cru.

Dry white wines are also made in Sauternes and Barsac, although they are not as well known. Château d'Yquem named its dry wine Y (*ygrec,* pronounced E-GREK, the French name for that letter of the alphabet). This set off a trend. Now, most dry Sauternes are named after the first letter of the château's name. Château Rieussec's is called R; Château Guiraud makes G. Dry Sauternes have an unusual, bold flavor. Made principally from sémillon, they are very full-bodied, thick-textured, and relatively high in alcohol.

Among the most exceptional Sauternes (and one Barsac) to try, in addition to Château d'Yquem, are: Château Suduiraut, Château Rieussec, Château Climens (Barsac), Château Lafaurie-Peyraguey, Château Guiraud, and Château de Fargues.

ST.-ÉMILION

Like Pomerol, its soul mate nearby, St.-Émilion is not a part of the Médoc or Graves but, instead, is on the other side of the Gironde Estuary, on Bordeaux's Right Bank. It is a region that, in every way, is as different from the Médoc as it can be. The vineyards of St.-Émilion tend to be smaller than those in the Médoc, and the châteaux more modest. Often, much of the work, both in the vineyard and in the cellar, is done by the proprietor and his family.

The first thing that strikes most visitors is the village of St.-Émilion itself. A small, fortresslike medieval town carved out of limestone, it is by far the most stunning Old World village in the Bordeaux region, and it, like Bordeaux city, is a UNESCO World Heritage Site. In the center of the village is the twelfth-century Église Monolithe, one of Europe's only underground churches, carved by hand by Benedictine monks out of one massive block of limestone. The church, which is quite large, is built on the site of a cave said to be the hermitage of an eighth-century saint. Visitors to the church can see two blocks of stone, each with shallow indentations, said to be the saint's chair and bed. (A local superstition has it that women who sit on the saint's chair will become pregnant.)

From the Middle Ages on, St.-Émilion was the home of several monastic orders. Community life was extremely religious. All governing power was exercised by the Jurade, a coterie of men given complete authority through a charter granted them in 1199 by King John of England. Part of the Jurade's mandate was ensuring the quality and prominence of St.-Émilion wine.

Unlike the long, flat stretch of the Médoc, or the long, gently rolling landscape of Graves, St.-Émilion has hillsides (the *côtes*)—limestone outcroppings and plateaus, plus gravelly terraces. Over centuries of geologic upheaval, clay, sand, quartz, and chalk have been intermixed there. The twists and turns and different soil compositions make St.-Émilion, small as it is, a patchwork quilt of varying terroir. A fairly wide range in the style and quality of the

THE JURADE

The Jurade de Saint-Émilion, a fraternity of *jurats,* or aldermen, traces its beginnings back to 1199, when a royal charter issued in England gave local notables and magistrates the power to govern the region and its wines. Banned after the French Revolution of 1789, the Jurade was revived in 1948 as a wine brotherhood dedicated to the advancement and promotion of St.-Émilion wines. Twice a year, during the first flowering of the vines in spring, and again during the autumn harvest, the Jurade conducts a majestic pageant. Members, wearing flowing red robes, white gloves, and puffy red caps, proceed through the streets of St.-Émilion to a solemn, candlelit mass in the cloister of the town's monolithic church. As part of the pageant, visiting dignitaries—princes, ambassadors, politicians, famous artists—are inducted into the Jurade. Alan Shepard, the first American astronaut in space, has been made a member, as has the cellist Mstislav Rostropovich. The Jurade tries not to take itself too seriously, however. It has also inducted the comedian Mel Brooks.

The Jurade de Saint-Émilion, a fraternal organization, parading in red robes through the cobbled streets of St.-Émilion.

wines is the result. Merlot and cabernet franc are the dominant grape varieties.

Only red wines are made in St.-Émilion, and the wine community is extremely chauvinistic about them—there are more than fifty wine shops in the village! The pride is justified; in very good years, the top wines can be positively riveting.

Arguably, the very best St.-Émilion is the super-elegant Château Cheval Blanc. Along with Château Ausone, Château Angélus, and Château Pavie, it is one of the four wines designated in 2012 as "A" among St.-Émilion's Premier Grand Cru Classé.

Cheval Blanc has the highest percentage of cabernet franc of any well-known Bordeaux estate—40 to 50 percent in recent vintages, with the remainder of the blend being merlot. In great years the wine can have an almost unnerving texture—it is, all at the same time, deep, luxuriant, and kinetically alive in the mouth. When young, the wine fairly oozes with decadent blackberry fruit laced with

vanilla, rather like eating a bowl of squashed, ripe blackberries drizzled with crème anglaise. (One of the greatest Bordeaux—indeed, one of the greatest wines—I have ever drunk was a 1947 Cheval Blanc, considered among the most majestic wines Bordeaux produced in the twentieth century.)

The vineyard of Cheval Blanc is on a mostly gravelly terrace several miles north of St.-Émilion, almost in Pomerol. However, many of the châteaux producing the best St.-Émilion are those on the southwestern limestone hillsides hugging the village. Château Ausone, Château Canon, Château Magdelaine, and Château Pavie are all here. In addition to wines from these vineyards, some others to try include: Château La Dominique, Château Figeac, Château Trotte Vieille, Château l'Arrosée, and Château Troplong Mondot.

POMEROL

The tiniest of all the major Bordeaux wine regions, Pomerol has definite cachet. This wasn't always so. The area was obscure and the wines were unknown in the nineteenth century (and were not ranked in the 1855 Classification). At the turn of the twentieth century, Pomerol's wines were considered merely average. The region's current fame is based, in part, on the ascendency of Château Pétrus, which produces Pomerol's most famous, expensive, and sought-after wines. Often ravishing, opulent, and complex, it sets the aesthetic criteria for other Pomerols.

Like its neighbor, St.-Émilion, Pomerol is on the Right Bank of the Gironde Estuary. The wines here are exclusively red, and the majority are based on merlot and cabernet franc. Merlot alone accounts for more than 80 percent of all the grapes planted in Pomerol, and not surprisingly, it is extremely well suited to the region's gravel and clay beds. Cabernet sauvignon is rarely part of a Pomerol blend.

Pomerols from the best sites stand out with a velvetlike texture and a plum/cocoa/violet

LOCATION, LOCATION, LOCATION

Pomerol and St.-Émilion remained far less well known than the Médoc even after the first bridges over the Gironde Estuary and the Garonne and Dordogne rivers were built in the mid-1800s. Wine estates in the two regions were small; no château had an established, bankable reputation; and for Bordeaux's wine brokers, it was difficult to get to these inland vineyards and even harder to transport the wine out. It made much more sense for the brokers to do business with the larger, well-known Médoc châteaux in Margaux, Pauillac, St.-Julien, and St.-Estèphe, which were also far more accessible thanks to their proximity to the Gironde Estuary just north of the city of Bordeaux.

richness. This is Bordeaux's harmonic convergence of intensity and elegance at its best. Their relative softness make Pomerols fairly easy to drink young.

As noted, Pomerol was, until the 1980s, a fairly unknown region that only began to emerge from its obscurity in the 1940s and 1950s. It was then that Jean-Pierre Moueix, a talented businessman with a keen palate, began buying exclusive sales and marketing rights to Pomerol's best châteaux. In 1964, he bought a 50-percent share of what was to become the most prized property of all, Pétrus.

Improving quality was an obsession for Moueix. Soon, news of the supple, rich, plummy character of the wines under his direction spread by word of mouth. By the mid-1960s, Pomerols began to develop a cult following among collectors. Today, the firm is headed by Jean-Pierre Moueix's son Christian.

In addition to the portfolio of Moueix wines in Pomerol and in neighboring Fronsac, Moueix owns Dominus, a top estate in the Napa Valley of California.

The tiny town of Pomerol encompasses the square around the small church and not much more. Similarly, most Pomerol properties are small, especially compared to those in the Médoc. In general, a proprietor here owns a vineyard less than 10 acres (4 hectares) in size, and eighty Pomerol châteaux have fewer than 2 acres (under 1 hectare). By comparison, vineyards in the Médoc span dozens and sometimes hundreds of acres/hectares. Finally, Pomerol châteaux are extremely modest; there are no breathtaking mansions.

If price and availability were indeed no object, the Pomerol we should all experience would be Pétrus. In the best vintages, the wine's exotic aromas of licorice and rich fruits leap out of the glass, after which, a creamy, black raspberry explosion fills your mouth. It is hard to imagine a more luxurious red wine, where each of the components is so seamlessly integrated into the whole.

But Pétrus aside, there are a number of other terrific, seductive Pomerols. Unfortunately, many of these are, like Pétrus, made in small quantities and thus hard to find. Nonetheless, among the ones to seek out: Château Le Pin, Château La Fleur de Gay, Château Lafleur, Château L'Évangile, Château La Conseillante, Château Certan de May, and Château Trotanoy.

OTHER REGIONS OF BORDEAUX

The less-important wine districts of Bordeaux are less important for a good reason. Without the benefit of coming from the best terroirs, much of the wine made there is simply simplistic. That said, some wines are definitely diamonds in the rough. And, importantly, the regions that follow are good hunting grounds for wines that don't give you sticker shock.

I'll begin with Listrac and Moulis, which are the other regions of the Médoc, and then

IF MONEY WERE NO OBJECT

Let's say you were willing to pay $20,000 to $36,000 per case for Château Pétrus (the cost for contemporary vintages). How would you go about buying it? Alas, the process wouldn't be easy—Pétrus is rarely available. Here's why.

Each year, 2,500 to 3,000 cases of Pétrus are made. In the United States, as one example, about four hundred of these cases are allocated to Pétrus's United States importer. The importer, in turn, offers the wine to a small, select group of wholesalers around the country who have consistently bought Pétrus in the past. These wholesalers, in turn, offer their limited allotments only to a small, select group of exclusive wine shops and a few prestigious restaurants that have seniority based on their past record of purchases.

A wine shop or restaurant will offer the wine, often personally, to a select group of customers, mostly collectors who buy Pétrus every year regardless of the cost.

It can be next to impossible to break into this loop.

---

move on to Entre-Deux-Mers, east and south of the city of Bordeaux, over to Fronsac and Canon-Fronsac, near Pomerol, and finally to the Côtes. There are many other outlying districts making simple, good table wines (Entre-Deux-Mers-Haut-Benauge, Lussac-St.-Émilion, Montagne-St.-Émilion, Lalande de Pomerol, Puisseguin-St.-Émilion, Ste.-Foy-Bordeaux, and St.-Georges-St.-Émilion), plus a number of outlying appellations producing mostly sweet wines—Cadillac, Cérons, Côtes de Bordeaux-Saint-Macaire, Loupiac, and Ste.-Croix-du-Mont among them. Yet the districts below have, I think, a bit better track record for making wines worthy of discovery.

LISTRAC AND MOULIS

Listrac and Moulis are inland communes of the Médoc, that is, they are not positioned on the gravelly banks of the Gironde Estuary like their more famous sisters, Margaux, St.-Julien, Pauillac, and St.-Estèphe. Away from the riverbanks, the soil tends to be heavier and to hold more water. As a result, the wines of Listrac and Moulis (based on cabernet sauvignon, with merlot and cabernet franc added) are generally rougher-textured and less polished, but also a fraction of the cost. They can sometimes seem straitjacketed by tannin.

There are exceptions. Several of the best Crus Bourgeois, for example, are here, including Château Poujeaux, Château Chasse-Spleen, and Château Fourcas-Hosten.

ENTRE-DEUX-MERS

Entre-Deux-Mers (literally "between two seas") is the vast expanse of rolling hills and forested land between the Dordogne and Garonne tributaries of the Gironde Estuary. Although it is a large wine region and a picturesque one, the wines are generally very simple and are never as high in quality as the wines of the Médoc, Graves, Pomerol, or St.-Émilion.

It's important to know that the appellation Entre-Deux-Mers applies to dry white

The wine harvest at Château Figeac. Everyone—young and old; male and female—helps with the work.

WHEN YOU VISIT . . . BORDEAUX

BORDEAUX IS A VERY LARGE REGION, and traffic—especially near the cities—can be staggering. Concentrate your visits day by day in a given area (today Pomerol, tomorrow Graves, and so on).

STAYING IN BORDEAUX CITY? Check out the charming Le Boutique Hotel Bordeaux. Housed in an eighteenth-century UNESCO World Heritage building, this gem boasts everything luxe right down to the Hermès bath amenities. Out in the country, one of the most impressive hotels is Cordeillan-Bages (cordeillanbages.com) which is housed in a seventeenth-century mansion. The hotel's wines are made at Château Lynch-Bages.

FOR A BREAK FROM WINE TASTING, the spa at Château Smith Haut Lafitte is famous for its relaxing treatments, including spa products made with extracts from local grapes.

BORDEAUX TENDS TO BE a somewhat formal region. Leave the shorts and flip-flops home.

AN ADVANCE APPOINTMENT (not to mention your best manners) are essential.

FINALLY, don't miss a meal at La Tupina, the legendary restaurant in Bordeaux's old quarter. Besides the roast chicken (acclaimed by many as the best roast chicken in France), the must-have specialties include hand-cut potatoes deep-fried in duck fat, and country French bread soaked in chicken fat, then fried. You only live once.

---

wines only. These are primarily sauvignon blanc, sometimes with a bit of sémillon and muscadelle, which adds a faint spicy-flowery quality. They are fresh, zesty, and light—perfect for pairing with fish and shellfish, or just for plain pleasure. A significant amount of red wine is made here, too, but because these wines are often lower in quality than the region's whites, they must carry the appellation Bordeaux or Bordeaux Supérieur, not Entre-Deux-Mers.

Entre-Deux-Mers wines have never been classified. Among the Entre-Deux-Mers worth seeking out are: Château Bonnet, Château Turcaud, Château Nardique la Gravière, Château de Camarsac, and Château Peyrebon.

FRONSAC AND CANON-FRONSAC

Over the past decade Fronsac and Canon-Fronsac have gained some momentum and risen out of "lesser-dom" into greater recognition. The two communes are spread over the hillsides just north and slightly west of Pomerol and St.-Émilion, and they sometimes share a similar topography with their famous cousins, as well as clay/sand soils interlaced with limestone. At their best, the wines can be full of black raspberry flavors and have a kind of edgy power and rusticity.

The wines are all red. Merlot is the dominant grape, followed by cabernet franc, with a bit of cabernet sauvignon sometimes blended in for strength and balance.

This is similar to the grape profile in St.-Émilion and Pomerol, yet the wines from Fronsac and Canon-Fronsac tend to be far more rustic. Among the wines worth seeking out: Château La Vieille-Cure and Château Dalem.

THE CÔTES

Outlying the four communes of Pomerol, St.-Émilion, Fronsac, and Canon-Fronsac are a handful of satellite regions called the *côtes*

SECOND IN LINE

To make the best possible wine, a top château will blend together only its very finest lots of wine. These generally come from the most mature and well-sited vineyard plots. What happens to all the other wine? In many cases, the château makes a second wine, which will have its own brand name and its own distinct label. (A second wine is different from a Second Growth.)

A second wine is usually made by the same winemaker in essentially the same manner as the famous wine, and it will usually come from the same vineyard, although the age of the vines will generally be younger. Although the second wine may not be as complex or ageworthy as the *grand vin,* it will also be a lot less expensive. Of course, for many experienced wine drinkers, the second wine of a great château like Château Lafite-Rothschild may be preferable to the top wine from a far less well-known château.

Châteaux rarely promote their second wines, preferring to be known for their famous ones. Often, the label on a second wine does not reveal the château it came from, but the name may be close enough to tell.

Some of the best second wines and the châteaux they come from:

LE CARILLON DE L'ANGÉLUS (Château Angélus)

CARRUADES DE LAFITE (Château Lafite-Rothschild)

LE CLARENCE DE HAUT-BRION (Château Haut-Brion)

CLOS DU MARQUIS (Château Léoville-Las Cases)

LA CROIX DE BEAUCAILLOU (Château Ducru-Beaucaillou)

ECHO DE LYNCH-BAGES (Château Lynch-Bages)

LES FORTS DE LATOUR (Château Latour)

LES PAGODES DE COS (Château Cos d'Estournel)

PAVILLON ROUGE DU CHÂTEAU MARGAUX (Château Margaux)

LE PETIT CHEVAL (Château Cheval Blanc)

RESERVE DE LA COMTESSE (Château Pichon-Longueville Comtesse de Lalande)

(hillsides): the Côtes de Bourg, Côtes de Castillon, Côtes de Francs, and Premières Côtes de Blaye. With the 2008 vintage, these wines were also allowed to use the broader, simpler name Côtes de Bordeaux if they preferrred.

The rural, hilly *côtes* are some of the oldest wine regions in Bordeaux. Vines were planted here by the Romans. The wines are mostly reds for everyday drinking—medium-bodied and juicy when they are good, shallow when they are not. Merlot is the leading grape variety, but *côtes* wines very rarely have the plummy depth and lushness of merlot planted in, say, Pomerol or St.-Émilion. Often, this is due to the fact that the grapes are planted in more fertile soil and harvested at higher yields.

Among the best red *côtes* are Château Puygueraud (Côtes de Francs), Château Roc de Cambes (Côtes de Bourg), Château Les Jonqueyres (Côtes de Blaye), and Château de Francs (Côtes de Francs).

SWEET SUCCESS:
MACARONS AND *CANELÉS*

Who would imagine that two of the famous food specialties in the world's most prestigious wine region are a chewy cookie and a miniature, cakelike sweet? What's more, no one seems to know how these simple items became so legendary. Nonetheless, you have not truly experienced Bordeaux until you go on an expedition in search of the ultimate example of each.

Macarons won't present a problem. These almond cookies, thought to date from the early 1600s, are a specialty of just one place: the ancient walled village of St.-Émilion. Virtually every *pâtisserie* in the village sells them.

Then there are *canelés,* which are often eaten accompanied by a glass of red wine on a Sunday afternoon. If anything can drive a Bordeaux pastry chef to fits of fanaticism, these homey, much-loved sweets can, for they are a challenge to make perfectly (and easy to make poorly). Nonetheless, virtually all top Bordelais pastry chefs are members of the *Confrérie du Canelé de Bordeaux,* an organization of *pâtissiers* devoted to the tradition of baking them.

A *canelé* looks like a molded cream puff. The center is sort of custardy; the outside, crunchy and caramelly. But a *canelé* is not a pastry per se, not a cookie, and not really a cake either. If they weren't French, *canelés* would be perfect as part of English afternoon tea. The confection's origin is not clear, although one historical account suggests that the first *canelé* may have been baked by a nun who accidentally overcooked her pastry cream sometime in the thirteenth century.

Chewy yet delicate macarons, *a specialty of St.-Émilion, were created sometime in the 17th century and now come in myriad flavors.*

THE FOODS OF BORDEAUX

Bordeaux may have many of France's most impressive wines but, on the whole, it comes nowhere close to having France's most impressive food. Admittedly, describing French food, any morsel of it, as less than stellar seems gastronomically sacrilegious. After all, French food at its lowest ebb is still French food. And so goes the cooking in Bordeaux. It is French; it is good. Yet, the paradox is nagging. How can a region of France produce wine so incredibly inspired and food that, for the most part, is so incredibly "un"?

My first suspicion that Bordeaux might not be as electrifying culinarily as enologically came while dining at a renowned château. The regal eighteenth-century dining room was

Not cookies exactly; not cakes; not pastries, canelés *are the star "sweet" of Bordeaux, often nibbled with a glass of red wine alongside.*

dominated by a 20-foot-long table on which rested heirloom silver and three antique crystal decanters containing some of the château's older vintages. Dinner consisted of potatoes, green beans, and chicken.

Potatoes, green beans, and chicken? To be sure, these were delicious, waxy French potatoes, pencil-thin *haricots verts*, and chicken that was scrumptious. But still.

When I asked why Bordeaux had such simple food compared to other parts of France, several hypotheses were suggested. The first was that cooking in Bordeaux is partly Anglo-Saxon in orientation, thanks to the long-standing, deep ties between the Bordelais and the British. In fact, for three centuries, beginning with the marriage of Eleanor of Aquitaine to Henry II in 1152, the people of Bordeaux considered themselves citizens of England, not France. The bonds that formed were so strong that, to this day, Britain remains one of Bordeaux's most important markets, and a large percentage of château owners speak flawless English.

Several Bordelais, however, rejected this theory. The simple cooking of Bordeaux, they said, reflected the region's close-knit, hard-working, conservative families who prefer locally grown, unadorned cooking. By way of evidence, they pointed out that many of the best restaurants in the region are the simplest ones that serve local specialties like lamprey (large, fatty, eel-like fish caught from nearby rivers and usually baked in casseroles, often with red wine), or—more appealingly—roast lamb. Indeed, before the 1970s, sheep were often taken from the rural areas ringing Bordeaux to graze over the winter in the vineyards of Pauillac, St.-Julien, St.-Estèphe, and Margaux. There, they would feed on the grasses that grew between the rows of vines—grasses said to give their meat an especially delicious flavor. And there, too, among the dormant vines, lambs would be born.

The Bordeaux Wines to Know

I won't include any of the First Growths here, although in great vintages they are all truly stunning experiences. There are wines like the 1966 Château Latour, or the 2000 Château Margaux, that, for me, had such beauty they were impossible to believe. But those are (and should be) rare experiences, and they are surely rare opportunities. So here are some other incredible wines. Admittedly, most, like all great Bordeaux, are still expensive and much in demand.

WHITES

CHÂTEAU CARBONNIEUX

PESSAC-LÉOGNAN | GRAND CRU CLASSÉ

Approximately 75% sauvignon blanc, 25% sémillon

This is one of the great classic white Pessac-Léognans, and because it is relatively affordable, you see the bottle, wet and chilled, being opened next to huge platters of iced local oysters in brasseries all over Bordeaux. Very good white Bordeaux like Carbonnieux has a distinctive, smooth, broad texture—it reminds me of the feel of cool cotton sheets on a hot night. The aromas and flavors are completely atypical of so much white wine drunk today—they evoke chamomile tea, dried flowers, hay, nuts, beeswax, minerals, and the flavor (but not the sweetness) of honey. Château Carbonnieux was founded in the thirteenth century by the Benedictine monks of the Abbey of Sainte-Croix, and is among the oldest châteaux in Bordeaux.

DOMAINE DE CHEVALIER

PESSAC-LÉOGNAN | GRAND CRU CLASSÉ

70% sauvignon blanc, 30% sémillon

If there were only ten wines left to drink in the world, I'd want this to be one of them. It is, for me, a wine of great sophistication, a wine that ignites imagination and emotion. Once, I wrote about Domaine de Chevalier that drinking it was "like being washed out to sea; your senses exquisitely alive with the freshness of the ocean air; the purity of the sunlight, the saline taste of the minerally seawater." With age, Domaine de Chevalier takes on a honeyed complexity that even honey would envy. The estate is one of the few in Bordeaux to be called a domaine rather than a château.

CHATEAU
LA MISSION HAUT-BRION

2009

MIS EN BOUTEILLE AU CHATEAU

DOMAINE CLARENCE DILLON
PROPRIETAIRE

CHÂTEAU LA MISSION HAUT-BRION

PESSAC-LÉOGNAN | GRAND CRU CLASSÉ

Approximately 80% sémillon, 20% sauvignon blanc

Bordeaux has but a handful of regal white wines. This is my vote for the best of them. Racy yet sublime, elegant, and deeply complex, La Mission Haut-Brion is one of the world's most stunning examples of the mesmerizing richness that can be achieved by blending exquisite-quality sémillon and exquisite-quality sauvignon blanc. The white wine has existed only as of the 2009 vintage (before that, the estate produced only its stupendous red). The white was made possible when the grapes that had been used to make Laville Haut-Brion wine henceforth were designated for La Mission Haut-Brion Blanc (and the Laville wine ceased to exist). Given the near perfection of both its red and white wines, La Mission Haut-Brion has often been named as an estate that deserves to move to First Growth status (as Mouton-Rothschild did in 1973). The château is owned by Domaine Clarence Dillon, which also owns Château Haut-Brion.

REDS

CHÂTEAU LA CONSEILLANTE

POMEROL

Approximately 80% merlot, 20% cabernet franc

CHATEAU
LA CONSEILLANTE
POMEROL

2008

HÉRITIERS LOUIS NICOLAS
PROPRIÉTAIRES DEPUIS 1871

I have always loved Conseillante's grace, yet underlying power. The wine is supple and cocoa-y on the one hand (so very like Pomerol), yet full of fascinating dark bitters and waves of exotic spices on the other. Best of all, it moves like a pendulum across the full range of the palate. The finish fades and flickers out slowly, like some old French film. The estate, located near the border with St.-Émilion, has the famed Château Cheval Blanc for a neighbor. For the last 140 years, La Conseillante (and now its modern, new, ovoid-shaped winery) has been owned and cared for by the Nicolas family.

CHÂTEAU ANGÉLUS

ST.-ÉMILION | PREMIER GRAND CRU CLASSÉ "A"

Approximately 55% merlot, 45% cabernet franc

Angélus is as majestic and thunderingly impressive as a French cathedral. But when it's young, it's wound tight with espresso bean, dark plum, earth, and exotic spice aromas and flavors. With time (and this is a wine that can teach one about time), there's a slow reveal, and you can almost feel the surrender in the wine—a kind of descent (or ascent) into loveliness. In 2012, Château Angélus was promoted to "A" status among St.-Émilion's Grand Cru Classés. The estate has been owned by the de Boüard de Laforest family for more than a century. The name refers to the three bells still rung for the custom of Angélus (the eleventh-century monastic practice of reciting three Hail Marys during the evening bell), which are audible from the château's vineyards. The bells are located in the nearby chapel at Mazerat, the church in Saint-Martin de Mazeret, and the church in St.-Émilion.

CHÂTEAU PICHON LONGUEVILLE, COMTESSE DE LALANDE

PAUILLAC | SECOND GROWTH

45% to 70% cabernet sauvignon (depending on the vintage) followed by merlot, with tiny amounts of cabernet franc and petit verdot

Pichon Lalande, as it is simply called, is located beside Château Latour and across the road from its deeply powerful and intense cousin Château Pichon Longueville Baron (usually just called Pichon Baron). Pichon Lalande is the more feminine and elegant of the two, indeed the wine almost lifts off the palate, with cassis and cocoa flavors infused with spices, minerals, and a sense of beautiful fresh pine trees. Yet, for all of its flavor, the wine is never weighty or ponderous. It knows how to creep up on you. Pichon Longueville Comtesse de Lalande is owned by the Champagne house Louis Roederer.

CHÂTEAU BRANAIRE-DUCRU

ST.-JULIEN | FOURTH GROWTH

Mostly cabernet sauvignon, with merlot, cabernet franc, petit verdot

Branaire-Ducru has steadily climbed the charts in reputation and price over the past several years. Although a Fourth Growth in 1855, the wine sells on par with many Second Growths today. And it's a stunner. Exquisite richness. Structurally immaculate. Intense. Focused. Enduring. And possessing a rarified kind of beauty. It's a wine that Colette or Hemingway would have admired.

CHÂTEAU LÉOVILLE-POYFERRÉ

ST.-JULIEN | SECOND GROWTH

Mostly cabernet sauvignon, with merlot, petit verdot, cabernet franc

Imagine eating milk chocolate candy bars your whole life and then someone gives you a piece of intense, 80 percent cacao dark chocolate. A whole new sensory universe opens in the chocolate center of your brain. That's how I've felt about the last several vintages of Léoville-Poyferré. The structure and intensity are formidable. The flavor is molecularly dense. The texture is molten softness. And yet the wine is not bombastic or out of balance. Indeed, it is thrilling to see the flavors of Bordeaux taken to the nth power. At the time of the French Revolution, there was one grand Léoville (Lion) estate. It was subsequently broken up into two estates, Château Léoville-Las Cases and Château Léoville-Barton. Eventually Léoville Las Cases was again divided and Château Léoville-Poyferré was created on the unnamed piece of land.

CHÂTEAU COS D'ESTOURNEL

ST.-ESTÈPHE | SECOND GROWTH

Approximately 65% merlot, plus cabernet sauvignon

The boundary line between the tiny communes of Pauillac and St.-Estèphe finds Château Lafite in the former, Cos d'Estournel in the latter. Yet Cos, as it is known (the *s* is pronounced), is indisputably one of the most distinctive Bordeaux. In great years it has an exotic, earthy, you-just-opened-a-humidor sensuality to its aroma (not unlike Château Haut-Brion), but the classic, soaring structure, deep concentration, and supple elegance of Lafite-Rothschild. In great years (1985, 1995, 2000) and with some age, the wine's savory richness and almost creamy tannin leave most tasters awestruck. The château was one of the first in Bordeaux to develop an Asian market—in the 1820s!

CHAMPAGNE

or many wine drinkers, Champagne is not simply a wine; it is also a state of mind. Handed a glass, we simply abandon ourselves to its dizzying pleasure. How a mere beverage achieved such distinction is a complex story, made all the more rewarding because of its unlikeliness.

The story begins 70 million years ago, in the Mesozoic era, when a vast prehistoric sea covered northern France and Britain. As the waters receded and the so-called Paris Basin sank, a great crescent of limestone, rich with minerals and marine fossils, was left behind. From this geologic legacy would eventually emerge the beautiful, chilly vineyards of Champagne. Sunlight here is painfully scarce, and vines exist at their limits of cold tolerance—the average temperature, amazingly, is no more than 50°F (10°C).

> "Remember gentlemen, it's not just France we are fighting for, it's Champagne!"
> — SIR WINSTON CHURCHILL

The wine Champagne comes from the region of Champagne, 90 miles northeast of Paris. Here, the vineyard land—considered among the most expensive in the world—is owned, primarily, by fifteen thousand small growers. A majority of the grapes they raise will be made into Champagne by nearly 350 wine firms, known as houses (Moët & Chandon, Veuve Clicquot, and Taittinger are famous examples). In addition, more than

▲ *In Champagne, a traditional basket press is often still used for grapes.*

4,500 of the 15,000 growers make their own limited-production, often stellar, Champagnes. And there are also 136 cooperatives, several of which, like Collet and Nicolas Feuillate, boast Champagnes of very good quality.

Well-known wines have been made in the Champagne region since Roman times. Those wines (both red and white) were, for much of their history, only slightly effervescent, not bubbly. By the Middle Ages, the wines had found a receptive audience among affluent locals, for Champagne was a wealthy region known for its superb and expensive textiles. Indeed, many Champagne houses were eventually begun by the well-to-do German accountants of textile firms—men with names like Krug, Heidsieck, Mumm, and Deutz.

> The name *Champagne* was first used in the sixth century and is derived from *campagnia remensis*, a Latin term for the countryside around the city of Reims.

As the seventeenth century drew to a close, the blended sparkling wine we recognize as Champagne began to emerge. It was not suddenly invented, as the story goes, by a monk named Dom Pérignon (although he was important in its development). Rather, Champagne was the curious result of decades of work by many Champenois, based on a happenstance of nature.

Climate is key to the explanation. Champagne is one of the coolest wine-producing areas in the world. Historically, wines would be made in the fall and left to settle over the winter. The cold temperatures would generally paralyze the yeasts, temporarily halting the fermentation before all of the grape sugar had been turned into alcohol. Once spring arrived and the wines (and yeasts) warmed up, the wines would gently bubble or sparkle—a sign that fermentation had resumed. For centuries, the Champenois were not amused. At a time before Louis Pasteur's

---

THE QUICK SIP ON CHAMPAGNE

CHAMPAGNE IS AROMATICALLY, texturally, and in terms of flavor, one of the most distinct wines in the world. It comes from only one region, also called Champagne, where the cold temperatures and limestone soils help to create a definitive terroir.

ALL CHAMPAGNES ARE BLENDS of as many as a hundred separate still wines and, among winemakers in the region, the art of blending is considered paramount.

THE COMPLEX AND PAINSTAKING process by which Champagnes are made involves a secondary fermentation during which natural carbon dioxide gas is trapped inside each bottle. The trapped CO_2 will eventually become Champagne's bubbles.

---

discovery (in 1860) of yeasts and the actions of fermentation, wines that foamed were frightening. Worse, it seemed that only the wines of Champagne behaved so strangely. Wines made in Burgundy—Champagne's archrival to the south—never bubbled.

Frustrated by Champagne's foam, many clerical winemakers of the seventeenth century, including Dom Pérignon, strove painstakingly to develop techniques that would quell the fizziness. By today's standards, their Champagnes would have been unrecognizable. They were cloudy, gritty, pinkish wines, often oxidized and heavily sweetened (probably with a molasses-like product) to disguise their tartness.

One possible improvement, experimented with by some Champenois, was to keep the wine in glass bottles, where it might remain fresher, longer. Most Champagnes at the time were, by law, sold in barrels, since the liquid,

DOM PÉRIGNON

Although no one person invented Champagne, Pierre Pérignon (Dom is an honorific title for a monk) was among a group of innovative clerics whose techniques furthered Champagne's evolution.

Pérignon was sent, at the age of twenty-nine, to the Abbey of Hautvillers (now owned by Moët & Chandon). Soon thereafter, he became its *procureur,* the administrator in charge of all the goods that provided a living for the monks, including wine.

Pérignon (who may not have drunk wine himself) was an avid winemaker and savvy businessman. He increased both the size of the abbey's vineyard holdings and the value of the wine produced. By 1700, the wines of Hautvillers were worth four times that of basic Champagne.

Pérignon and his monk/winemaker colleagues were the first to master the art of making a clear white wine from red grapes. Although this is easily done today, all white wine made at the turn of the seventeenth century either came from white grapes, or the "white" wine was actually gray from skin contact with red grapes. Pérignon was fanatical about consistency, precision, and discipline in grape-growing and winemaking. He insisted that vines be pruned severely and only sparingly fertilized, thus lowering the yield of each grapevine and improving the concentration of the wine. He mandated that grapes be picked early in the morning so that their delicate aromas and flavors would not be compromised by the afternoon sun. And he had *pressoirs* (wine-presses) built in the vineyards, so that the grapes could be pressed as quickly as possible.

Pérignon was also the first to keep the wines from different vineyard lots separate and the first to realize that blending several still wines ultimately leads to a more interesting Champagne. Most important, he was the first to experiment with glass flasks as a way to preserve Champagne's freshness, instead of leaving it in wooden barrels, where it easily oxidized.

All of these innovations made Champagne a vastly better wine. What we don't know for sure is how Dom Pérignon felt about Champagne's sparkle. He was, of course, never able to prevent it, despite his initial attempts. Champagne historians believe that Pérignon, renowned for his business acumen, eventually came to see that sparkle as the key to Champagne's future commercial success.

"The sparkling froth of this fresh wine is the dazzling image of us, the French."

—VOLTAIRE

contained in that manner, was easily measured and therefore easily taxed. Barrels would then be shipped by boat down Champagne's Marne River to the Seine River, and on to Paris, and often to Great Britain.

In Britain, where the Industrial Revolution was about to begin, sturdy glass was widely available. Indeed, British wine merchants were already beginning to transfer the barrels of Champagne they imported into British bottles. Soon, to satisfy the national sweet tooth, many British merchants began adding sugar to the bottles before sealing them. That bit of added sugar, eagerly consumed by yeasts in the air and exisiting naturally inside the bottles, restarted fermentation, throwing off even more CO_2—this time, trapped

THE LOOK OF LUXURY

For centuries, artistically arresting bottles have been part of many houses' strategies to inspire desire for the "art" within. But no bottle is more stunning or renowned than Perrier-Jouët's art-nouveau-style "flower bottle," with its enameled arabesque of white anemones. Meant to celebrate the period known as the Belle Époque (1840s to 1914) the bottle was designed by renowned art-nouveau glassmaker Émile Gallé. Soon after its creation in 1902, the flower bottle was abandoned due to the difficulty in manufacturing it. To fire the design, Gallé had to heat the enamel to 1,112°F (600°C), just below the melting point of glass. In the early 1960s, Pierre Ernst, then president of Perrier-Jouët, found one of the original Gallé bottles and resolved to recreate it for Maxim's, the legendary Parisian nightclub. Ernst found an artisan enamel specialist who created a technique for manufacturing the bottles en masse. The modern flower bottle premiered in 1969 and held the 1964 vintage of the house's prestige wine, logically named cuvée Belle Epoque. The very first of those bottles was opened in Paris at a seventieth birthday party for jazz musician Duke Ellington. In 2012, a hundred years after its creation, the famous flower bottle was exquisitely updated by Japanese floral designer Makoto Azuma, who added golden vines and delicate dotted flowers to the classic pattern of anemones. A mere one hundred bottles (containing the 2004 vintage) were produced.

---

inside each bottle. The coincidental result—a bigger pop when the bottle was eventually opened—was, as far as the Brits were concerned—amusing, not to mention wonderfully distinctive.

The Champenois started to think the same way. In 1728, French King Louis XV standardized bottle sizes and allowed Champagne's wines to be shipped in glass bottles for the first time. The product met with extraordinary success abroad. Although bottled Champagne cost twice as much as barreled Champagne (at the time, as many as 20 percent of glass bottles exploded from the pressure of the bubbles inside, and moving hundreds of thousands of bottles from place to place was long, tedious work), the drama of Champagne's quivering bubbles and effusive pop had become unquestionably chic. Soon, the forests ringing Champagne were replete with giant, wood-fired kilns where beautiful French glass bottles were made.

There were still problems, however. Although glass had improved and wineglasses themselves were now clear, Champagne remained a cloudy liquid because of the spent yeast cells in it. Increasingly, drinkers wanted to be able to see those curious bubbles. By the early 1800s, Champagnes were sometimes being decanted from bottle to bottle to remove the cloudy sediment of spent yeast cells. Of course, the more a Champagne was decanted, the more likely it was to go flat.

The solution was a process called *rémuage* (from the verb *remuer*, to move something several times), known in English as riddling, which allows the yeasts to be removed from the wine in one frozen clump. The process was developed in 1816 by Antoine de Müller, the *chef du cave* (head of the wine cellar) of Nicole Ponsardin Clicquot, owner of the Champagne house eventually known as Veuve Clicquot.

Slowly, more improvements ensued. The flavor of Champagne was getting better, thanks

Moët & Chandon, founded in 1743 by Claude Moët. One of the preeminent Champagne houses today, the company owns 2,840 acres (1,150 hectares) of vineyards and produces approximately 26,000,000 bottles of Champagne each year.

to better work in the vineyards, and, as a result, there was less need to camouflage it with sweetness. Champagnes began to get drier. More and more, houses hoping to capture new markets and increase sales positioned Champagne as an aperitif perfect to begin an evening, rather than a sweet wine suited to the end of one. First came half-dry Champagnes—demi-sec. When these proved successful, producers began making sec, or dry, Champagnes (these were actually fairly sweet by today's standards). By the 1840s, the British in particular began to covet decidedly dry Champagnes. Very dry Champagnes intended just for them were made and sold with the designation extra-dry, a term in English rather than French. Finally, as time passed, an even drier version—called brut— was made (which is how extra-dry turns out to be, in effect, slightly sweeter than brut).

In 1846, in a radical move at the time, Perrier-Jouët made a Champagne without any sugar at all. But Champagne drinkers found it too severe—too brutelike, indeed. It took another generation before brut wine gained widespread acclaim. In 1874, the Pommery wine called Nature was the first to establish Champagne as a dry wine. It's interesting to note that the evolution of Champagne as a drier and drier wine continues to this day. Two decades ago, most brut Champagnes had a *dosage* of 12 to 15 grams of residual sugar. Today, the *dosage* of most top houses' brut

Champagnes is 9 or 10 grams. (Read about how *dosage* works in Making Champagne, page 181.)

Champagne's improvements in the nineteenth century were met with such success (and sales) that the houses launched elite promotional campaigns aimed at aristocrats, royalty, and the world's most wealthy individuals. By the beginning of the twentieth century, Champagne's luxury status was nothing short of legendary.

THE LAND, THE GRAPES, AND THE VINEYARDS

Three billion bottles of sparkling wine are made every year in the world. But no matter where they are from, these sparklers are always distinguished from Champagne (see California Sparklers and French Champagne: Comparisons, page 691).

Mapped out by the Institut National des Appellations d'Origine (INAO) in 1927, the Champagne region includes some 85,000 acres (34,000 hectares), which is about half the size it was prior to phylloxera (see page 30). Of this total area, 97 percent (82,800 acres; 33,500 hectares) is already planted. Thus, all the vines of Champagne would easily fit into, say, the city limits of Denver, Colorado.

The harvest at Taittinger, one of Champagne's great traditional houses. In the cold northern climate of the region, harvesting is chilly work.

THE GRAPES OF CHAMPAGNE

WHITE

CHARDONNAY: Major grape and the only white grape grown in the region. Used in virtually all Champagnes generally for its finesse. Champagnes called *blanc de blancs* are based exclusively on chardonnay.

REDS

PINOT MEUNIER: Major grape, although the least ageworthy of Champagne's three grapes. It usually contributes fruitiness and body. Technically not a separate variety, but rather a clone of pinot noir.

PINOT NOIR: The more revered of Champagne's two red grapes. It often contributes body, texture, and aroma.

Unlike Burgundy, which has more than one hundred controlled and specified appellations (AOCs) within it, and Bordeaux, which has more than fifty AOCs, all of Champagne falls into just one appellation—Champagne. (The appellation is governed by some of the strictest self-imposed regulations of any area in the world.) The region comprises 320 villages, boasting some 275,000 separate vineyard plots. These villages are ranked as either Grand Cru (17 villages), Premier Cru (42 villages), or Cru (258 villages). Every vineyard in a village holds the same rank. Collectively, the villages produce about 320 million bottles of Champagne a year.

The region has two phenomenal natural assets that are key to the style of wine made here: its iffy, northerly climate and its limestone-laced soils. Climatically, Champagne lives life on the edge. As noted, the average temperature is just 50°F (10°C), a bare minimum for photosynthesis. It can be wet and rainy at the worst possible time—in late summer, when rot can erupt and the grapes themselves can become waterlogged or attacked by the mold *Botrytis cinerea*. It's also very cold in the winter, and annihilating spring frosts and summer hailstorms are not unusual. In short, the grapes usually have a difficult time surviving and then ripening evenly. In fact, the small vines are intentionally trained low to the ground so they can absorb whatever warmth might be reflected off the white soil.

The famous white soil of Champagne is more than 75 percent limestone, and in many parts, a specific type of porous limestone known as chalk. Like a great white crescent, the area that spans from Britain's White Cliffs of Dover to Champagne was once the basin of a vast prehistoric sea. Some 70 million years ago, the waters receded, leaving behind minerals, such as quartz and zircon, plus fossils of sea urchins, sea sponges, and other sea animals. These fossils helped form the chalk. Millions of years later, violent earthquakes erupted, mixing the chalk with material from within the earth and creating the sloping hills over which the best Champagne vineyards now lie.

Walking in the countryside, it is not unusual to see stark white outcroppings, bare slices of ashen-colored earth pierced by the ends of deeply burrowed grapevine roots. The soft and porous chalk encourages the roots to delve deeply into the earth in search of water. Chalk drains well but also acts as a reservoir that can provide water back to the vines, even in very dry summers.

Champagne may only be made from three varieties of grapes: chardonnay, pinot noir,

> For me, a great Champagne possesses the contrapuntal tension of opposites—like a sword enveloped in whipped cream. The sword is the Champagne's dramatic acidity. The whipped cream is the hedonic texture that comes from *sur lie* aging.

and pinot meunier (the "fourth grape" of Champagne is often said to be time itself, in recognition of how long the wine is aged). Of the three, pinot meunier is technically not a separate variety but rather a clone of pinot noir. Each of these grapes has its own assets—and its own needs in terms of soils and sunlight. Thus, each tends to be planted in certain areas within Champagne, but not in others.

In general, chardonnay tends to be planted in the chalkiest sites, and when well made, contributes an almost unreal sense of purity, laciness, linearity, and finesse to the blend. Chardonnay grown on chalk also contributes

IS IT CHALK OR IS IT LIMESTONE?

In wine conversations, the words *chalk* and *limestone* are often used interchangeably to refer to especially prized soils. But the two are not exactly the same. Chalk is limestone, but limestone is not necessarily chalk.

Limestone, a soil type found in Champagne, Burgundy, parts of the Loire Valley, central Spain, and several other wine regions, is a marine sedimentary rock made from decomposed seashells and marine skeletons that are extremely high in calcium. Limestone can form under a variety of conditions; thus, there are many different types, including chalk, marble, marl, coquina (a sedimentary rock composed of fragments of mollusk and invertebrate shells), and oolitic limestone (a carbonate rock made up of ooliths or ooids, which are sand-size carbonate particles that have concentric rings of calcium carbonate). Not all types of limestone are conducive to grape-growing— but chalk, in particular, is. Defined as soft limestone that is porous and cool, chalk allows for easy root penetration. It provides good drainage, and works well with high-acid grapes. It is, as a result, especially appreciated in Champagne and Burgundy, where the grapes are indeed high in acid and the significant rainfall means good drainage is a must.

THE INCREDIBLE *CRAYÈRES*

In order to have enough stone to construct the city of Reims in what was then Gaul, in the fourth century, the Romans dug three hundred immensely deep quarries in the chalky rock. These same vertical chalk pits, called *crayères,* are used today by the Champagne houses to age Champagne. They are miracles of construction that seem to defy physics, and descending into their eerily quiet, cold, dark, humid chambers is an otherworldly experience that no wine drinker should miss. Because the best chalk was often well underground, the *crayères* often go down as far as 120 feet (36 meters). They are shaped like pyramids, so the deepest parts of the *crayères* are also the widest and the tops of the pits are narrow (this limited air exposure in the quarry and kept the chalk moist and soft, and thus easier to cut into large construction blocks). During World War I, when Reims was extensively bombed, twenty thousand people lived for years in the dark *crayères* (no sunlight penetrates). Indeed, the *crayères* under Veuve Clicquot and Ruinart were makeshift hospitals, and under Pommery, a school.

---

a flavor often described as chalky or minerally. Indeed, the Champenois believe firmly that minerality in wine is a flavor derived specifically from chalk.

Pinot noir has more gravitas, more structure. In famous Grand Cru villages such as Aÿ, on the Montagne de Reims, pinot noir can be rich and complex. (As an aside, no Champagne village is more cherished or lauded than Aÿ. Indeed, the name of the Champagne town Epernay evolved from *après Aÿ*, or "after Aÿ.")

And pinot meunier is a savior. Less prone to frost and botrytis than the other two, it can be planted in the Marne Valley nearer the low-lying river, and thus in more humid conditions. Pinot meunier has a supple, fresh fruitiness to it and is often used in nonvintage blends for that reason. It's considered the variety least capable of long aging, and thus tends not to be used in vintage and prestige cuvée Champagnes.

Finally, while, as I've said, there is only one AOC in Champagne—that is, Champagne—the region encompasses five main vineyard areas (below). These are usually not listed on the label, but in investigating any wine, you'll find references to them.

---

1 MONTAGNE DE REIMS, the "mountain of Reims"; an essentially south-facing slope where the chalk layer is deep. Mostly planted with pinots noir and meunier.

---

2 CÔTE DES BLANCS, the "hillside of whites"; named for the chalky outcroppings near the surface of the ground here. Planted almost exclusively with chardonnay. Mostly east facing.

---

3 VALLÉE DE LA MARNE, "valley of the Marne River"; mostly planted with pinot meunier. Soils tend more toward marl, clay, and sand.

---

4 CÔTE DE SÉZANNE, just south of the Côte des Blancs, and like it, mostly east facing and planted with chardonnay.

The Grand Cru vineyard of Aÿ, in the Vallée de la Marne.

THE CATHEDRAL OF KINGS—THE WINE OF KINGS

Champagne's characterization as the wine of kings is based on its association with the Cathedral of Reims, the coronation site of virtually every French king. Built in the thirteenth century, the cathedral (which is dedicated to the Virgin Mary) marks the site of the baptism of Clovis I, King of the Franks, in 496. (The year of Clovis's baptism is also considered the birth of modern France.)

Construction of the cathedral began in 1211 on the site of two former Romanesque cathedrals. By the time it was completed almost 100 years later, the cathedral, with its dramatic, 114-foot-high (35-meter) great rose stained-glass window, and its 2,300 (originally, brightly painted) statues, was considered among the most stunning Gothic cathedrals of all time.

Ranking with those at Chartres, the cathedral's immense stained glass windows have remained under the care of one family of glassmakers—the Simon family—since the seventeenth century. During the bombings of World War II, the main stained glass windows were, piece by piece, painstakingly removed and hidden, and thereby saved from the destruction suffered by the rest of the city. In 1954, Jacques Simon was commissioned by the Champagne producers to create three additional triptych windows portraying the art of vine growing and winemaking in Champagne.

The facade's portals contain some of the most impressive statuary to be seen in any Gothic cathedral, including figures representing David and Goliath, the coronation of the Virgin, the kings of France, and the famous Smiling Angel, *l'ange au sourire*. The local Champenois expression for joy—the smile of Reims—is based on the statue's beaming countenance.

5 CÔTE DES BAR (also known as the Aube), a region relatively far to the south of the other regions; mostly planted with pinot noir. Many young growers are making exciting small-production wines there.

Of these areas, Montagne de Reims, Côte des Blancs, and Vallée de la Marne are the three most important. The first two between them share all seventeen Grand Cru villages.

MAKING CHAMPAGNE

Champagne, along with Sherry, Port, and Madeira, is one of the world's most complicated wines to make. Not only are the steps involved numerous and demanding, but the winemaking itself requires a specific type of intellectual dexterity that can be daunting.

The Champagne maker makes not one or even ten wines, but hundreds of still wines. These are sometimes referred to as the base wines, and they look like typical white wines. They are all made from one of Champagne's three grapes: chardonnay, pinot noir, or pinot meunier. All will eventually be blended. And that is where the plot thickens.

The Champagne maker's goal is not to make a blend of wines that immediately tastes good. This, in any case, would be difficult, for the base wines used to make Champagne are virtually vibrating with acidity and often taste rather simple at first. Instead, the Champagne maker blends these base wines with an idea, an imagining of what the blended wine will taste like years later, once it has undergone a long period *sur lie*, plus a second fermentation, has possibly been sweetened by some *dosage*, and

HOW DRY IS THAT CHAMPAGNE?

After the yeasts are removed from each bottle, Champagnes may be topped up with sweetened reserve wine, or *liqueur d'expédition.* The number of grams of sugar in this liqueur—known as the *dosage*—will determine the category of Champagne made.

The vast majority of Champagnes now produced are brut (less than 1.2 percent sugar), and some Champagnes (known as *dosage* zero) have no added sugar whatsoever. As for the categories sec, demi-sec, and doux—while they are treasured in some countries, these Champagnes are increasingly rare, and constitute only a tiny percentage of the Champagnes now made.

Below are the categories of Champagne based on their *dosage.* Keep in mind that, relative to, say, a luscious dessert wine, no Champagne today is extremely sweet. Sauternes, for example, often contains 120 grams of sugar per liter, making it 12 percent sugar.

BRUT NATURE: less than 3 grams of sugar per liter (.3 percent sugar)

EXTRA BRUT: 0 to 6 grams per liter (0 to .6 percent sugar)

BRUT: less than 12 grams per liter (less than 1.2 percent sugar)

EXTRA-DRY: 12 to 17 grams per liter (1.2 to 1.7 percent sugar)

SEC: 17 to 32 grams per liter (1.7 to 3.2 percent sugar)

DEMI-SEC: 32 to 50 grams per liter (3.2 to 5 percent sugar)

SWEET: more than 50 grams per liter (5 percent sugar)

---

has developed bubbles. Years of skill, experimentation, and experience are needed to understand what a given blend might taste like post-transformation. (The sensory demands are so complex that few houses employ just one winemaker. Most have a team of individuals, often headed by a senior winemaker, the so-called "memory of the house," who remembers distant vintages, how the wines were made, and how they turned out decades after aging.)

The process begins with the harvest. To ensure elegance in the final wine, the grapes must be harvested gently and quickly by hand so that the juice doesn't pick up any tannic coarseness from the skins. The grapes are often therefore not transported to a winery to be pressed, but rather pressed right in the vineyard in some two thousand pressing houses. Each lot of grapes is kept separate.

In most cases, the juice is fermented in stainless steel vats, which allows the winemaker to control the temperature and pace of the fermentation and completely inhibits oxidation. However, a few houses (notably Krug, Bollinger, Louis Roederer, and Jacquesson) still ferment some of their wines in used wooden barrels, as was historically done. Champagnes that have been fermented in barrels often take on a slight nuttiness and a fuller mouthfeel as a result of slight oxygen exposure. And since the barrels are never even close to new, there is never any oak flavor. After fermenting their wines, most producers (but not all) will put those wines through malolactic fermentation to soften the impression of the wines' acidity.

The actual number of separate lots of base wine can be astounding. A typical house, for example, will have hundreds of separate lots of

In a region of architectural majesty, the Cathedral of Reims is perhaps the most majestic building of all. Construction of the cathedral began in 1211. When it was finished 100 years later, the cathedral became the coronation site of French kings.

THE SOUND OF TASTE

I think I like Champagne because of its taste and the way it feels. But Oxford University professor Charles Spence has shown that sound also plays a major role in what any of us think about flavor. Some of Spence's research, for example, showed that potato chips taste better if they sound noisier when you bite into them. (And who can deny the charming hiss of Champagne being poured into the glass?) Moreover, even the sound of a food's or drink's packaging can influence our perceptions. (The pop of a Champagne cork?—totally appealing.) Interestingly, according to Spence, the perceived flavor of a substance can also be affected by background sounds— bacon tastes more bacony if you can hear the sound of it sizzling in a pan; eggs are more eggy if you hear chickens.

base wines available for use. The largest house, Moët & Chandon has some eight hundred separate base wines available for use each year.

In addition, every producer also has a stock of reserve wines held back from former years, principally the past three years. (As a matter of law, a small amount of reserve wine is held back each year to ensure consistency of flavor year to year and as a hedge against tiny crop yields in difficult vintages.) Even a small amount of this reserve wine can give a Champagne blend extra depth and complexity, although it might mitigate against a sense of freshness.

In the spring after the harvest, the winemakers for a given house will start the process of making that house's nonvintage wine by blending dozens of base wines from different years. The blend finally arrived at (still a still wine) is called the *assemblage*. The flavor of every Champagne hinges on its blend. Thus, in the region, blending is considered not only a phenomenal skill, but also a high art.

If the weather has been particularly good, certain lots of wine will be set aside as blending material for the house's vintage Champagne (a type of Champagne in which the blend is composed only from the wines of a single year) and other lots for a prestige cuvée (the house's top, most expensive wine). However, no house will

COMPARING NONVINTAGE, VINTAGE, AND PRESTIGE CUVÉES

onvintage Champagnes differ from vintage and prestige cuvée Champagnes in a number of ways, detailed below.

VINEYARDS

In Champagne, some forty-two villages (and all of the vineyards in them) are considered superior and are ranked Premier Cru. Seventeen more villages (and the vineyards within those) carry an even higher status: Grand Cru.

NONVINTAGE CHAMPAGNE: Grapes come from good vineyards (neither Premier Cru nor Grand Cru) although some Premier Cru wine may be blended in.

VINTAGE CHAMPAGNE: Grapes come from good to great vineyards, many of which are ranked Premier Cru or Grand Cru.

PRESTIGE CUVÉE: Grapes come from the greatest vineyards, historically, ranked Grand Cru exclusively.

GRAPES

Most Champagnes are a blend of chardonnay, pinot noir, and pinot meunier. However, because pinot meunier is usually not as capable of long aging as chardonnay and pinot noir, some houses prefer to use it only in nonvintage Champagnes, which tend to be drunk early, not cellared for many years.

NONVINTAGE CHAMPAGNE: Pinot meunier is almost always included in the blend.

VINTAGE CHAMPAGNE: Pinot meunier is sometimes included in the blend.

PRESTIGE CUVÉE: For most—but not all—houses, pinot meunier is rarely included in the blend.

BLENDING

All Champagnes are blends. Blending, in fact, is considered the most critical skill a Champagne maker must possess.

NONVINTAGE CHAMPAGNE: Dozens—sometimes hundreds—of still wines are used, from several different years.

VINTAGE CHAMPAGNE: Dozens of still wines are used, from a single year that was considered exceptional.

PRESTIGE CUVÉE: A blend of only the best wines from the best vineyards to which the producer has access.

AGING ON THE YEASTS

Most houses far exceed the legal minimums below.

NONVINTAGE CHAMPAGNE: fifteen months *sur lie.*

VINTAGE CHAMPAGNE: three years *sur lie.*

PRESTIGE CUVÉE: No requirement; common practice is four to ten years *sur lie.*

use up all of its great lots making a vintage or a prestige cuvée wine at the expense of turning out a mediocre nonvintage. Since the lion's share of what every house makes every year is nonvintage, making an inferior one would make no business sense.

Next, the nonvintage blend will be mixed with a small amount of yeasts plus a *liqueur de tirage*—a combination of sugar and wine—and then bottled and capped. The predictable happens. The yeasts eat the sugar (this constitutes a second fermentation), forming a bit more alcohol and throwing off carbon dioxide gas. Or trying to. Because the bottles are capped, the CO_2 cannot escape. It becomes physically trapped in the wine as dissolved gas. When the bottles are eventually opened, this trapped gas will explode and become bubbles.

Legally, the bottles must rest in the cellars for at least fifteen months at this point, but in practice, most producers leave them there for about three years. Because the yeasts are still inside the bottles, the wine is said to be resting *sur lie* (on the yeasts). Although it may seem as if the yeasts' job is done, they continue to have a profound effect on the wine inside the bottle. Through a process called autolysis, the yeasts' cell walls begin to disintegrate, spilling the contents of each yeast cell (amino acids, lipids, and enzymes) into the wine. The effect is to give the wine an almost magical sense of creaminess, and greater complexity. Indeed, it is Champagne's long aging on the yeasts that gives the wine what I call contrapuntal tension. In the same split second, Champagne's sensory impact is lightning crisp (from acidity) yet lusciously creamy (from *sur lie* aging).

If the nonvintage Champagne was sold at this point, it would be cloudy with yeast cells. To remove the yeasts and create a clear Champagne, the bottles are riddled—turned upside down, then slightly rotated some twenty-five times. Traditionally, bottles to be riddled were placed in an A-shaped frame known as a *pupitre,* and turned by hand by a person called a *rémueur.* A good *rémueur* can riddle thirty thousand to forty thousand bottles a day, and *pupitres* are still used, primarily for prestige cuvée Champagnes. Most nonvintage Champagnes today are riddled equally

Magnums of Ruinart Blanc de Blancs lie in the house's spectacular crayères.

THE PUNT

While it's tempting to pour a Champagne by holding the bottle with one's thumb inserted in the punt, the indentation in the bottom of the bottle was never intended for such a purpose. Originally, the punt was a way of preventing the jagged pontil mark—the point left over after a glass bottle was blown and shaped—from scratching the surface of a table. By pushing the pontil up into the interior of the bottle, a punt was formed and the table was saved. When mold-made wine bottles were introduced, the punt remained, since it adds stability to the bottle when the bottle is upright. With Champagne bottles, however, the punt has even greater purpose. During the second fermentation, which ultimately gives Champagne its bubbles, six atmospheres of pressure are built up inside the glass wall of the bottle. The Champagne bottle's prominent punt allows for a more even distribution of pressure inside the bottle, preventing the disastrous explosions that were a common and serious problem for early Champagne makers.

The vin clairs *(base wines) at Veuve Clicquot. In the late fall after the harvest, houses taste each of their wines from different villages and vineyards in order to begin making the* assemblage *or master blend.*

effectively, but more efficiently, by large machines called gyropalettes. At work twenty-four hours a day, seven days a week, a gyropalette can riddle a Champagne in one to two weeks, versus two months or more when the wine is in *pupitre.*

As the bottles are riddled, the yeast cells collect in the necks of the bottles. Now removal is easy. In a process called *dégorgement,* each bottle is placed, still upside-down, in a glycol solution, which freezes the entire length of the neck and its contents. When the bottle is then quickly turned upright and the cap removed, the frozen plug of yeasts shoots out. This leaves a clear, bone-dry wine.

But it also leaves about ¼ inch (½ centimeter) of space unoccupied. Immediately, the Champagne is topped up with the *liqueur d'expédition,* a combination of reserve wine and sugar. The number of grams of sugar in the liqueur, also known as the *dosage,* determines how dry or sweet the Champagne will be (see How Dry Is That Champagne?, page 182).

During the time the Champagne stays in contact with the yeast lees, it is aging reductively—that is, without the presence of oxygen—because the broken down yeast cells bind any oxygen present. Once the wine is disgorged, however, and the yeasts are removed, the wine begins to age oxidatively—that is,

oxygen is present. These two types of aging are radically different. You could easily experience the difference by tasting two bottles of the same vintage Champagne that have been disgorged at different times. Let's say bottle A is a 2005 Veuve Clicquot that was disgorged in 2009 (after four years on the yeasts) and you drank it in 2013. Bottle B is 2005 Veuve Clicquot that was disgorged in 2012 (seven years on the yeasts) and, again, you drank it in 2013. Although the bottles are the same age, and you opened them at the same time, they'd taste very different. In the first case, the wine was aged for four years oxidatively, without yeast lees present. In the second case, the wine aged oxidatively, without the yeasts, for just one year.

Many (but not all) Champagne connoisseurs would prefer the bottle B scenario—aging as long as possible with the yeasts and disgorging only at the relative last minute before the wine goes to market. For that reason, a handful of Champagne firms now mark their Champagnes with a disgorgement date on the wine label. Doing so is controversial in the region, however. Several houses, for example, point out that some consumers, confused by the concept of disgorgement, read the date and think it's a "drink by" date, which it most certainly is not.

BIBLICAL BOTTLES

The smallest Champagne bottles hold about one glass of bubbly; the largest, about one hundred glasses. Large Champagne bottles are rarities and are individually handblown.

For unknown reasons, in the late 1800s, such bottles were given the names of biblical kings.

SIZE	EQUIVALENT
SPLIT	187.5 milliliters, about 1½ glasses
HALF-BOTTLE	375 milliliters, about 2½ glasses
BOTTLE	750 milliliters, about 5 glasses
MAGNUM	2 bottles, about 10 glasses
JEROBOAM	4 bottles, about 20 glasses
METHUSELAH	8 bottles, about 40 glasses
SALMANAZAR	12 bottles, about 60 glasses
BALTHAZAR	16 bottles, about 80 glasses
NEBUCHADNEZZAR	20 bottles, about 100 glasses

Jeroboam was a king of the northern kingdom of Israel. Methuselah, not an ancient king, was distinguished by his incredible longevity, living 969 years. The Assyrian king Salmanazar ruled over the Judean kingdom. Balthazar was the name of one of the Three Wise Men, known as the Lord of the Treasury and also considered to be a grandson of Nebuchadnezzar. The king of Babylon, Nebuchadnezzar was a prominent and powerful ruler who destroyed Jerusalem.

THE BUBBLES

For starters, how many bubbles does a bottle of Champagne have? The answer, for a standard 750-milliliter bottle, is approximately 100 million. But that's only if the bottle is open; in an unopened bottle, the gas is still dissolved in the wine and thus, in an unopened bottle, there is only the *potential* for bubbles. The 100 million figure comes from Gérard Liger-Belair, PhD, in the department of physics at the University of Reims Champagne-Ardenne, in France, where he has been conducting bubble research for more than a decade.

Through the use of special high-speed cameras, Liger-Belair has also discovered that bubbles play a part in determining the aromas a drinker smells. Each bubble appears to contain hundreds of chemical components, some of

Research in the cold cellars 120 feet (36 meters) underground. I think I was wearing four layers of clothing.

which can affect taste, aroma, and feel. When the bubble bursts on the surface of the wine, tiny droplets of Champagne are projected into the air, allowing the drinker to smell the wine more acutely.

In Champagne, bubble size and persistency are signs of quality. Tiny bubbles, considered the best, are the result of a long aging on the yeasts and the temperature of the aging cellar (the cooler the smaller). Equally important is how the bubbles behave in the glass. A high-quality Champagne will have streams of bubbles arising from different spots in the liquid (as many as fifty bubbles per second), coming together to create a spiraling cascade. At the top of the glass, these collect to form a snowy layer called the mousse. Champagne makers insist that the feel of the bubbles should be extremely delicate (nothing like, for example, the harsh, large bubbles in, say, a cola).

TYPES OF CHAMPAGNE

By far, most Champagne produced is golden in color and made from all three Champagne grapes: chardonnay, pinot noir, and pinot meunier. However, there are two somewhat less well-known types of Champagne that can be quite special: *blanc de blancs* and rosé. (A type of sparkling wine known as *blanc de noirs* also exists but, as you'll see, it is virtually nonexistent in Champagne.)

MY FAIR BUBBLY

Just 80 miles (129 kilometers) north of Champagne is a cool, fairly sunny region with white, chalky limestone soils—soils that are strikingly similar to those found in Champagne. Indeed the region is so close to Champagne and seems so ideal for making sparkling wine that you'd think the Champenois would want to annex it. There's just one problem. The region in question is in England.

The English, of course, have always loved bubbles. The country continues to be, as it has been for decades, the leading export market for Champagne. But sometime in the 1990s, the English began to think big. Why merely buy bubbly? Why not try to make it . . . especially since southeast England—near Sussex, Kent, and of course the White Cliffs of Dover—bears a remarkable resemblance to the Champagne region?

They've done just that. More than a dozen British companies, including Ridgeview Estate, Nyetimber, Rathfinny, Camel Valley, Hush Heath, and Chapel Down, all make English sparkling wines, and several more ventures are in the works. For their part, numerous Champagne houses have scouted the region in anticipation of future deals.

They've had a royal welcome. Camilla Parker Bowles, Duchess of Cornwall (and second wife of Charles, Prince of Wales) is the current president of the United Kingdom Vineyards Association.

BLANC DE BLANCS CHAMPAGNE

Literally "white from whites," *blanc de blancs* Champagne is made entirely from chardonnay grapes. This type of Champagne was created in 1921 by Eugène-Aimé Salon, founder of the Champagne house Salon, whose intention was to create a Champagne with maximum finesse, lightness, and elegance. Easy to say, but exceedingly difficult to do, since the winemaker limited to one grape variety has fewer overall wines with which to work.

The best *blanc de blancs* are treasured for their lightnesss and their gymnastic lift on the palate. They, among all Champagnes, are the sopranos, capable of hitting the high notes of flavor and displaying an especially filigreed sense of texture. *Blanc de blancs* generally come from the chalky slopes of the Côte des Blancs, one of the premier grape-growing regions in Champagne and the one planted almost exclusively with chardonnay. Within the Côte des Blancs is the grand cru village of Le Mesnil-sur-Oger, home to two of the most extraordinary *blanc de blancs* Champagnes in the world: Krug's Clos du Mesnil and Salon's Le Mesnil. *Blanc de blancs* Champagnes may be nonvintage or vintage. They are generally expensive.

BLANC DE NOIRS CHAMPAGNE

Blanc de noirs ("white from reds"), is the opposite of *blanc de blancs,* an ever-so-slightly pink-tinged golden Champagne made entirely from red grapes (pinot noir and/or pinot meunier). *Blanc de noirs* Champagnes are extremely rare in Champagne itself (although common in, for example, California). Champagne makers seem to like definitiveness when it comes to color; if they're not making a golden Champagne, then they're making an unapologetically rosy pink rosé.

ROSÉ CHAMPAGNE

Among wine drinkers who know their Champagne, rosé Champagnes, which are richer and fuller-bodied than goldens, are considered the crème de la crème. They are usually significantly more expensive than golden Champagnes, a reflection of the fact that they are more difficult to produce, and they're more rare, forming just over 6 percent of all exports. There are two methods for making them. The first—and historical—method (called *saignée*) involves letting some of the base wine sit in contact with pinot noir skins until it picks up enough color to tint the wine pink. The other method, more modern and more common, involves adding a small amount of still pinot noir wine into each Champagne bottle before the second fermentation. Both processes are complex, and achieving a certain exact coloration is difficult, as a lineup of rosé Champagnes will attest.

A rosé Champagne needn't be made mostly from red grapes. The *assemblage* (blend of base wines) might be a blend of 80 percent pinot noir and 20 percent chardonnay—or just the opposite, 80 percent chardonnay and only 20 percent pinot noir. A rosé can be made either way, but when you drink them the impressions the two wines make will be quite different.

SERVING CHAMPAGNE–NOT WITH A BANG BUT A WHISPER

Champagne is classically served well chilled, and a cold temperature helps maintain the bubbles when the Champagne is poured. Because Champagne bottles are made with thicker glass than regular wine bottles, the time required to chill them is longer. Allow twenty to forty minutes in a bucket of ice and water.

"The pop of the cork should sound like a gunshot with a silencer."

—CLOVIS TAITTINGER,
Taittinger Champagne

Opening Champagne is not difficult, but it is different—and far more exciting—than opening a bottle of still wine. Each Champagne bottle is under six atmospheres of pressure, about the same as a truck tire. With so much pressure behind it, a cork can fly an astounding distance. But that's only if you open the bottle incorrectly. The correct, safe, and controlled way to open and serve Champagne is:

1 BREAK AND REMOVE the foil, not the wire cage, from around the cork.

2 PLACE YOUR THUMB firmly on top of the cork to keep the cork from flying.

3 WITH YOUR OTHER hand, unscrew the wire (it takes about six turns) and loosen the cage. You actually don't have to take the cage off completely.

4 HOLDING THE CORK firmly, begin to twist it in one direction as, from the bottom, you twist the bottle in the other direction. Contrary to popular opinion, a Champagne cork should not make a loud *thwock!* You're supposed to ease the cork out, so that it makes just a light hissing sound. Unbidden, more than one older Frenchman has advised me that a Champagne bottle, correctly opened, should make a sound no greater than that of a contented woman's sigh. Frenchmen are French men after all.

5 FILL EACH GLASS with about 2 inches (5 centimeters) of Champagne. Then go back and top them all up. Do not immediately top up glasses with fresh Champagne every time a sip or two has been taken. Just as topping up a half-filled cup of coffee ensures that you'll never have the satisfaction of a fresh, steaming hot cup, so too, frequent topping up of Champagne can mean the wine is never nicely chilled.

WHEN YOU VISIT . . . CHAMPAGNE

CHAMPAGNE IS A SOLEMN, spiritual place—a place of great religious and historic significance. It has none of the carefree abandon of, say, Tuscany; none of the sunny energy of the Napa Valley. Indeed, for all its joyfulness as a wine, the region itself has been continually torn apart by tragedy, especially during World Wars I and II, when it was a gruesome battlefield. As a result, there's a soulfulness here that's as palpable as the dazzling bubbles in every glass you'll have.

OF CHAMPAGNE'S TWO MOST IMPORTANT cities, the larger one, Reims, boasts many of the great houses, including Ruinart, Veuve Clicquot, and Taittinger, plus the majestic underground cellars called *crayères.* Reims is also the home of one of the most breathtaking cathedrals of the world—the Cathedral of Reims, site of the coronations of French kings. Don't miss

Maison Fossier (fossier.fr) in the center of the city. Founded in 1756, this jewel of a shop (decorated entirely in pink) is famous for *Biscuits Roses de Reims,* tiny, crunchy, pink-colored biscuits that are traditionally eaten by first dipping them in Champagne.

THE SMALLER TOWN OF EPERNAY is considered the unofficial capital of Champagne. Here, along the Rue de Champagne, are the side-by-side gleaming mansions and cellars of Perrier-Jouët, Moët & Chandon, and Pol Roger. Just outside the town is the Abbey of Hautvillers, where Dom Pérignon lived and worked.

AS IS TRUE IN BORDEAUX, Champagne is a fairly formal region, and it's mandatory to have an appointment to visit the Champagne houses. (This is not the time to be wearing running shoes, unless you want to feel vastly underdressed.)

GROWER CHAMPAGNES

Most wine drinkers are familiar with at least a few Champagnes made by the famous houses. But fewer know or have tasted many of the so-called grower Champagnes. From the top producers, grower Champagnes are distinctive, exquisite, and often mind-blowingly delicious.

Grower Champagnes are, as the name implies, made by small growers, often family firms who make what might be called artisanal Champagnes. Growers do not buy grapes or wine as the houses do. Rather, they make Champagnes exclusively from the grapes they grow themselves. As a result, a grower's Champagne is usually based on a very much smaller number of base wines that are blended together before the wine undergoes the second, bubble-inducing fermentation. Because a grower is using just his own grapes from a small area, grower Champagnes tend to reflect the place where they are made. In a sense, grower Champagnes exhibit what might be thought of as a more Burgundian approach, wherein individual terroirs are prized above all. Among my favorite grower Champagnes are those made by: Pierre Peters, René Geoffroy, Pierre Gimonnet, Gatinois, Doyard, Michel Loriot, Jean Milan, Varnier-Fannière, Chartogne-Taillet, and Jean Lallement.

THE RIGHT GLASS

Ever watch people being handed glasses of Champagne? At least half of them immediately stand up straighter and adopt a sexier tone of voice. The elegant and long-lined Champagne glass is about as sophisticated as glassware gets.

Tall, tulip-shaped glasses evolved from conical glasses made between 1300 and 1500 in Venice. These, in turn, were inspired by some of the earliest drinking vessels, such as animal horns. Serendipitously, the art of glassmaking was reaching its apex just as Champagne making was at its pivotal beginnings. By the late seventeenth century, Venetian glassmakers were capable of creating fragile goblets that possessed remarkable clarity. Historians theorize that the transparent beauty of such glass may have been one of the considerations that ultimately led winemakers to develop techniques for making crystal-clear, sediment-free Champagne.

Tall Champagne glasses allow the wine's bubbles to swell as they rise in long, spiraling streams to the surface. However, the glass

Riddling Cristal, the first prestige cuvée, in the cellars of Louis Roederer.

A Champagne cellar worker stacking barrels at Krug, one of the few houses that vinifies some of its base wines in oak barrels.

THE STARS AMONG THE CHAMPAGNES

*P*restige cuvées are the most expensive and highest-quality category of Champagne. Nearly every house and significant grower makes a golden prestige cuvée, and several make a rosé version as well. The first prestige cuvée was made in 1876 by the house of Roederer for Czar Alexander II of Russia, who wanted an exclusive Champagne not available to (god forbid) the lower aristocracy. The czar further dictated that it be shipped in leaded crystal bottles. Roederer's prestige cuvée was hence named Cristal. Among the other well-known and exquisite prestige cuvées are Bollinger's "La Grande Année," Perrier-Jouët's "Belle Epoque Fleur de Champagne," Pol Roger's "Cuvée Sir Winston Churchill," Veuve Clicquot's "La Grande Dame," and Taittinger's "Comtes de Champagne." Note that Dom Pérignon and Krug consider all of their wines prestige cuvées. Dom Pérignon also produces Oenothèque, two rare, breathtakingly expensive bottlings— one golden, one rosé—that have been aged fifteen to thirty years on the yeast lees.

should be slightly wide in the middle so that a bowl is formed within which aromas can congregate. (Severely narrow flutes are not ideal Champagne glasses.)

As for the wide, shallow, saucer-shaped Champagne coupe (often used at weddings), legend has it that the first was a porcelain version invented by Marie Antoinette, who used her breast (reportedly the left breast because it was closer to her heart) as the mold. Notwithstanding so compelling a beginning, the coupe is terrible for Champagne. In it, bubbles dissipate quickly, the Champagne is easily warmed by the drinker's hand, and, frustratingly, the vessel itself hardly holds more than two sips.

The Champagnes to Know

Champagne is my downfall. While other people might spend money on really nice clothes, the latest technology, exotic travel, and so on, I spend money on bubbles. Champagne has always seemed to me to be the most affordable luxury. Below are several of my favorite exquisite Champagnes—from large houses to small growers. Had I more room to write, this list could have easily been three times as long.

WHITES

PIERRE PETERS

CUVÉE DE RÉSERVE | BLANC DE BLANCS | GRAND CRU | NONVINTAGE | BRUT

100% chardonnay

The grower Champagnes from Pierre Peters are jewels—ravishingly beautiful, exquisite, crystalline. Their animated minerality plays on your palate like high notes on a piano. Yet the flavors are deeply resonant and complex. There's something salty, like the breeze on a pure white beach; something evanescent, like the lure of a delicate white flower; and something familiar yet exotic, like citrus tied up in ribbons of vanilla. Virtually all of the Pierre Peters vineyards are in the Côte des Blancs, with many in the heralded village of Le Mesnil-sur-Oger.

J. LASSALLE

BLANC DE BLANCS | VINTAGE | BRUT

100% chardonnay

One of the first grower Champagnes to be brought into the United States (by importer Kermit Lynch, in 1976), J. Lassalle is a small, family-run business in the village of Chigny-les-Roses on the Montagne de Reims. Since 1982, the company has been run by three generations of the women in the family, giving rise to the firm's unofficial adage, *une femme, un esprit, un style* (one woman, one spirit, one style). The Lassalle Champagnes—all of which undergo malolactic fermentation and are based entirely on Premier Cru vineyards—have exquisite balance. Their intensity of flavor fills your head like music floating in a room. The Blanc de Blancs is somewhat unusual in that the chardonnay is grown on the Montagne de Reims, which is prime pinot territory. Is it just my imagination that this leads to resonance and depth?

RUINART

BLANC DE BLANCS | NONVINTAGE | BRUT

100% chardonnay

Ruinart's Blanc de Blancs, in its rounded, ancient-shaped bottle, is the house's signature Champagne and a wine of such elegance and weightlessness that it seems to float around you and then eventually melt on your palate . . . a snowflake of sensation, then gone. Yet the wine's flavors are intense—juicy pears, whipped cream, spices, star fruit, minerals. Interestingly, there's a coolness to these flavors, in the way that mint is cooling, no matter what its actual temperature. Ruinart, founded in 1729 by Dom Ruinart, a contemporary of Dom Pérignon, was the first Champagne house. Its *crayères*, vast amphitheaters 60 to 120 feet (18 to 37 meters) deep, are the region's most impressive. The house's prestige cuvée, Dom Ruinart, is another not-to-be-missed wine—an exotic, primordial-tasting wine that, with age, can smell like truffles.

PIERRE GIMONNET ET FILS

BLANC DE BLANCS | PREMIER CRU | NONVINTAGE | BRUT

100% chardonnay

The top Pierre Gimonnet Champagnes taste as if chalk itself underwent some wizardly molecular transformation and emerged as exquisitely delicious froth and foam. In the Gimonnet playbook, the Blanc de Blancs is my favorite wine—an exotic riot of quince and bergamot, with a fresh, green note like lemongrass and a tingling minerality. At the same time, the wine is very suave, gentle, and creamy. It feels soft yet refreshing, like cool water on a hot day. Pierre Gimonnet, a relatively large grower Champagne firm, is family owned, with almost all of its vineyards in the Côte des Blancs.

POL ROGER

EXTRA CUVÉE DE RÉSERVE | NONVINTAGE | BRUT

Approximately 33% each of chardonnay, pinot noir, and pinot meunier

Pol Roger is a Champagne drinker's Champagne—winey, rich, citrusy, yet a bit custardy, with a sublimeness and seriousness on the palate. The house's Champagnes have always been favorites in England (Winston Churchill, a huge admirer, had cases delivered to 10 Downing Street on a regular basis). For me, the Pol Roger Champagnes always feel like just fallen snow, light yet clingy. And the balance of creaminess versus acidity is impeccable. In particular, their nonvintage brut, known as Extra Cuvée de Réserve, is an exquisite wine with tiny beads of bubbles and the wispy elegance that make the top bruts so compelling.

TAITTINGER

VINTAGE | BRUT

50% chardonnay, 50% pinot noir

Taittinger's vintage bruts have an exquisite sense of choreography—they dance and spark on the palate like beams of light. The wine begins with a rush of crème brûlée-like richness, then moves on to a fierce crispness, with flashes of wet stone—as if the wine could rain with chalky minerality. Only the most deliciously complex Champagnes move like this through different worlds of flavor and texture, all in one sip. The house of Taittinger is located on the site of the ancient Benedictine Abbey of Saint Nicaise, begun in 1231, and a locus of artistic and intellectual activity for monks until it was destroyed in the French Revolution.

KRUG

GRANDE CUVÉE | NONVINTAGE PRESTIGE CUVÉE | BRUT

Approximately 50% pinot noir, 30% chardonnay, and 20% pinot meunier

Krug, broodingly rich and positively Rubenesque in its fullness, is a Champagne with such a distinct style that no one who has tasted it has ever forgotten it. Every molecule aches with density and intensity. (I always imagine what roasted nuts would taste like if each little one could be filled with pastry cream.) But the wine is stunning not only because of its gravitas, but also because of its exquisite balance. Indeed, the contrapuntal tension of Krug—the simultaneous weight and lightness, impact and stillness—is what makes it such a connoisseur's wine.

BOLLINGER

LA GRANDE ANNÉE | VINTAGE PRESTIGE CUVÉE | BRUT

Approximately 66% pinot noir and 33% chardonnay

Founded in 1829, Bollinger is one of the best-known of the grand historic Champagne houses—and the wines are always round, rich, winey, luxurious, and toasty. More like lemon curd than fresh lemons; more like caramelized apple tart than fresh apples. The richness is the result of extremely long aging periods on the yeast lees, as well as micro-oxygenation. The latter occurs because Bollinger is one of the last remaining houses to vinify their best wines in impeccably-cared-for old oak barrels. (Indeed, the house has its own cooper and cooperage—the last ones to exist in Champagne.) La Grande Année, Bollinger's prestige cuvée, always has a low *dosage* (just 7 or 8 grams of sugar per liter, .7 to .8 percent) and comes entirely from Premier Cru and Grand Cru vineyards.

ROSÉS

GATINOIS

ROSÉ | GRAND CRU | NONVINTAGE | BRUT

90% pinot noir, 10% chardonnay

The Gatinois family—*père, maman,* and *fils*—are the twelfth generation of growers to make Champagnes from 14 acres (5 hectares) of Grand Cru vineyards in the famous village of Aÿ. (Father Pierre, a lawyer by training, is also the former deputy mayor of the village.) In their tiny dirt-floor cellar behind the village church, everything is done by hand—even the disgorging of every single one of the fifty thousand bottles they produce each year. The Gatinois Champagnes are all finely etched and full of personality, but I love the rosé especially—a winey, spicy, minerally Champagne redolent of kirsch and crushed strawberries that finishes with beautiful richness on the palate.

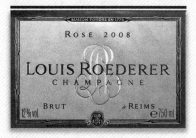

LOUIS ROEDERER

ROSÉ | NONVINTAGE | BRUT

65% pinot noir, 35% chardonnay

While many Champagne houses in the nineteenth century counted the Russian nobility among their best customers, the firm of Louis Roederer was especially successful, for the czar himself was its best customer. In 1876, at the request of Alexander II, Louis Roederer's son created Cristal, then a sweet Champagne (it's now dry) presented in a custom-designed crystal bottle. Cristal became the first prestige cuvée, and it is still the house's most famous and expensive wine (both golden and rosé Cristal are made). While Cristal is certainly a Champagne to have at least once in one's life, Louis Roederer's nonvintage brut rosé—made by the old *saignée* method and a rare wine in and of itself—is, for me, the can't-resist wine. Among rosé Champagnes, it is especially stunning, and has a sumptuousness that is nothing short of all-enveloping. The complex aromatics of pinot noir surge through the wine until the end, when a beam of bright crispness shatters all sensations. Great rosés such as this must be made from ripe grapes (difficult to come by in Champagne), and thus the grapes for this wine are sourced on a steep limestone/clay slope that benefits from light bouncing off the Marne River.

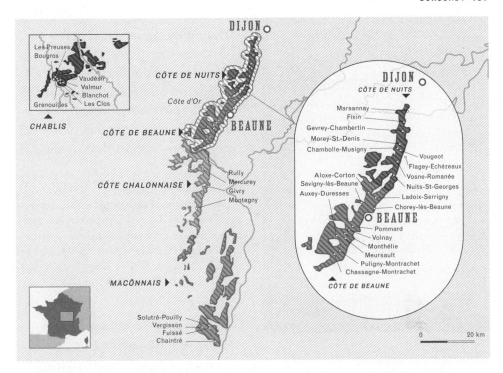

BURGUNDY

"What else do we have, in the end, except Nature?"
— FRANÇOIS MILLET,
winemaker,
Domaine Comte Georges de Vogüé

urgundy is not what most people choose to begin their journey with wine; but Burgundy is often where many of us find ourselves at the end. For Burgundy—*Bourgognes* in French—is the most spiritual of wines. Of all the wines in the world, it is the one that poses the deepest questions, and reminds us that the answers still lie in mystery.

What is it about this wine from a small, almost secluded region that makes it so compelling? Above all, great Burgundies are stunningly complex. Drinking them can be an exercise in discernment, refinement, and delicious patience as subtle layer of flavor after subtle layer of flavor reveals itself. Indeed, Burgundy is most certainly the "quiet music" of wine—not the rap.

The great Burgundies are also indisputably sensual. For centuries they have been described in the most erotic of ways, and sipping them has been compared, among other things, to falling in love. This sensuality extends beyond the wines' provocatively primal aromas and flavors. The top Burgundies, white and red, have beguiling textures that melt over or dance upon the palate in ways that make them unforgettable. Unlike many types of wine, Burgundy's physicality is trenchant.

While a small handful of grape varieties are grown in Burgundy, just two dominate

THE QUICK SIP ON BURGUNDY

BURGUNDY, a fairly small wine region in northeastern France, makes some of the world's most sought-after, expensive, and exquisite wines.

THE SYSTEM OF LAND OWNERSHIP is complex. Burgundy has thousands of tiny vineyards, each of which has dozens of owners.

TWO GRAPE VARIETIES DOMINATE. All top white Burgundies are made from chardonnay. All top reds come from pinot noir.

Burgundy got its name in the sixth century, in the aftermath of the fall of the Roman Empire, when the wandering Germanic tribe known as the Burgondes established a settlement in the area. They called it Burgundia.

the Côte Chalonnaise, and the Mâconnais. While legally, from a governmental standpoint, Beaujolais is also considered part of Burgundy, everything about Beaujolais—from soils and grapes to winemaking and philosophy—is entirely different. So I've given Beaujolais its own chapter, following this one.

production: chardonnay and pinot noir. Both grapes achieve their greatest elegance when planted in a cool climate, and that Burgundy has. Of all the wine regions in the world that are famous for red wine, Burgundy is the coolest and northernmost. The downside of Burgundy's marginal climate is that there are years when the lack of sun and/or the frequency of rain results in grapes that are not fully ripened and mature, leading to considerably leaner, less flavorful wines. These less-than-ideal years are not uncommon, and as a result, there are very apparent differences among vintages of Burgundy. Thus, even the priciest and most pedigreed Burgundies can occasionally be very disappointing. As spellbinding as a great Burgundy is, a poor one is almost depressing.

Later in this chapter, we will explore how (and why) Burgundy is an infinitesimally detailed study in terroir. But for now, it's important to know that of France's approximately five hundred designated appellations (AOCs, or *Appellations d'Origine Contrôlée*), just over one hundred are in Burgundy alone.

Lastly, this chapter addresses the four main regions that wine drinkers think of when they think about Burgundy—Chablis, the Côte d'Or,

HISTORY, MONKS, THE ESTABLISHMENT OF TERROIR, AND THE FRENCH REVOLUTION

Burgundy's first documented vineyard was planted in the village of Meursault in the first century A.D. But the population was minuscule and grape growing did not expand. With the Romans came a somewhat greater emphasis on wine, but Rome's ties were never as strong here in the north as they were in southern France. By the fifth century, as the Roman Empire collapsed, the region was repeatedly plundered by wandering barbarian tribes. Eventually, in the year 450, the Germanic Burgondes settled in the area, calling it Burgundia. In 534, Burgundia was absorbed into another Germanic entity, the Frankish kingdom established by Clovis, the king of the Franks. Clovis eventually went on to unify the numerous barbaric Germanic tribes that operated throughout what was then called Gaul. With Clovis's coronation, modern France (the name is derived from *Franks*) was born, and Clovis's eventual conversion to Christianity established France as a Christian nation. With Christianity in place, the course of Burgundy's history changed, as it went on to become a nucleus for Catholicism and monastic power.

But the period most crucial in the region's history was the thousand-year period from the eighth century to the French Revolution, when much of the land and most of its wines were under the powerful command of Benedictine and Cistercian monks.

The Benedictine Abbey of Cluny, founded in the year 909 near Mâcon, was the most well-endowed order in Europe and the largest landowner in Burgundy until the French Revolution. At the height of their dominance, the Benedictines controlled more than fifteen hundred monasteries. The magnificent Abbey of Cluny remained the largest cathedral in Europe until it was surpassed by the "new" magnificent St. Peter's in Rome, consecrated in 1626 (built on the spot of the original small St. Peter's basilica, dating from the fourth century).

At the end of the eleventh century, a reform movement within the Benedictines resulted in the formation of a second order, the Cistercians. The Cistercian Abbey of Citeaux, founded in 1098, was one of Europe's most magnificent workshops devoted to the creation of books, with monks serving as copyists, illuminators, and book binders. By the time of the Revolution, its library boasted more than ten thousand volumes.

Contemplative by nature, patient in temperament, systematic in approach, committed

A gray stone cross towers over the renowned Grand Cru vineyard Romanée-Conti.

BURGUNDY'S DOMAINES

*I*n Burgundy, the term domaine *is not precisely equivalent to that of* château *in Bordeaux. In Bordeaux, a château is a single estate composed of vineyards surrounding a building or house that is sometimes quite palatial. In Burgundy, a domaine is a collection of vineyard parcels, often extremely small, owned by the same family or entity (Domaine Leroy, Domaine Dujac, Domaine Leflaive, and so on). Usually these parcels are scattered throughout many villages and appellations, and the domaine will make a separate wine from each. A typical Burgundian domaine produces many wines, all in tiny quantities. There are six thousand domaines in Burgundy today. Interestingly, some domaines are now dropping the word* domaine *from their labels, in favor of just the producer's name.*

to grueling physical labor, well bestowed with land, and most important, literate, the monks were uniquely prepared for their mission: to delineate and codify Burgundy's vineyards. Plot by plot, they cleared and cultivated the most difficult limestone slopes of the Côte d'Or, studiously comparing vineyards and the wines made from them, recording their impressions over centuries. Tantamount to a millennium-long research project, the work of these monks not only revealed Burgundy's greatest vineyards—but, in fact, for the first time, established terroir as the critical core of viticulture.

Burgundy's monastic orders shared their power with a series of flamboyant and wealthy dukes who, in return for religious approbation, bestowed even more land upon the monks.

THE VILLAGES OF BURGUNDY

To name every important appellation in Burgundy would take pages because, in addition to all the villages, there are no fewer than 629 Premier Cru vineyards and 33 Grand Cru vineyards (see The 33 Grand Cru Vineyards of Burgundy, page 209). Here's a list of Burgundy's four main regions (in capital letters) and the most significant villages within them listed from north to south, and the type of wine each specializes in.

CHABLIS

CHABLIS white

CÔTE D'OR

Côte de Nuits

MARSANNAY red

FIXIN red

GEVREY-CHAMBERTIN red

MOREY-ST.-DENIS red

CHAMBOLLE-MUSIGNY red

VOUGEOT red

FLAGEY-ECHÉZEAUX red

VOSNE-ROMANÉE red

NUITS-ST.-GEORGES red

Côte de Beaune

LADOIX-SERRIGNY red

ALOXE-CORTON white and red

CHOREY-LÈS-BEAUNE red

SAVIGNY-LÈS-BEAUNE red

BEAUNE white and red

POMMARD red

VOLNAY red

MONTHÉLIE red

MEURSAULT white

AUXEY-DURESSES white and red

PULIGNY-MONTRACHET white

CHASSAGNE-MONTRACHET white and red

SANTENAY red

CÔTE CHALONNAISE

RULLY white and red

MERCUREY predominantly red

GIVRY predominantly red

MONTAGNY white

MÂCONNAIS

VERGISSON* white

SOLUTRÉ-POUILLY* white

FUISSÉ* white

CHAINTRÉ* white

ST.-VÉRAND** white

*One of the villages that produces the well-known wine Pouilly-Fuissé.

**The village that produces St.-Véran.

IT TAKES A RIVER . . . OR A POPE

Burgundy has always been comparatively less well known than Bordeaux, largely due to its inland location. For most of history, wine has been transported over water—that is, if it hasn't been completely consumed by the population at hand. As early as the thirteenth century, barrels of Bordeaux were being shipped down the Gironde Estuary, then out to sea, headed for England. But Burgundy, deep in France's interior, was without a great waterway. Transporting its wines meant hauling heavy loads over potholed dirt roads. It wasn't until the fourteenth century, when the papal court and residence moved from Rome to Avignon, in southern France, that Burgundy began to achieve recognition. Not surprisingly, the newly arrived pope and entourage of clerics were keen to drink the wines so intimately cared for by Burgundy's monks. Demand soared. Later, as towns grew and roads got somewhat better, Burgundy's fame spread.

The dukes served as strong promoters for Burgundy; their connections put Burgundian wines on the tables of popes, French kings, and the nobility. When the pious among the nobility began donating land to the monks as well, it seemed as though the fortunes of the church would know no bounds.

In 1789, the French Revolution ended forever the hegemony of the church and Burgundy's infamous dukes. Immense tracts of land were confiscated, split up, and redistributed to the farmers who had worked those lands. Later, these small plots were further fragmented as a result of the Napoleonic Code

of 1804, which stipulated that upon the death of a parent, all children must inherit equally. As a result of this successive fragmentation, it's not unusual today for a Burgundian to own just a few scant rows of vines.

PLACE, NOT PERSON

The idea of terroir is a kind of mental construct that, at least in Burgundy, is inescapable. You cannot think of the region simply in terms of pinot noir and chardonnay, for in the most elemental sense, Burgundy is not about pinot noir and chardonnay. Pinot noir and chardonnay are merely the voices through which the message of a site is expressed. Indeed, it's important to remember that there is no exact word in French for winemaker. In Burgundy, the term most often used is *vigneron,* which means "vine grower."

To some, this distinction might seem awfully precious. Yet terroir—and, in Burgundy, the incredible specificity of terroir—cannot be easily dismissed or avoided. Taste two wines from the same domaine and you may find enormous differences between them. How can these be explained when both wines were made by the same person, in the same exact manner, from the same variety of grapes grown in the same way? The clearly apparent variable, and the factor that reasonably seems responsible for those differences, is place.

UNDERSTANDING HOW BURGUNDY WORKS

Burgundy is often thought of as one of the world's most difficult wine regions to understand (a distinction it shares with Germany). And it is complicated—especially when compared to, say, California or Australia. But understanding Burgundy is a "road in" to thinking about all

LIEU-DIT AND CLIMAT

Two special wine terms are used in Burgundy (although only rarely elsewhere in France): *lieu-dit* (leh DEE) and *climat* (KLEE ma). *Lieu-dit* (literally, "said location") is the term used for a specific vineyard that has an established name. A *lieu-dit* is usually tiny (smaller than an appellation or AOC) and usually not inhabited. Sometimes the *lieu-dit* appears on the wine's label along with the AOC. *Lieux-dits* do not necessarily carry a rank, such as Premier or Grand Cru.

The term *climat* is sometimes used interchangeably with *lieu-dit*, but the two are actually slightly different. A *climat* is a specific parcel within a vineyard that has unique terroir characteristics. Most *climats* are within classified vineyards. For example, the Grand Cru vineyard Clos de Vougeot has sixteen *climats* that make it up. The name of a *climat* may appear on the label, as is the case with the seven *climats* that make up the single vineyard Chablis Grand Cru (see Chablis, page 212).

fine wine at a deeper, more philosophical level. Here are eight key points essential to beginning to understand Burgundy.

1 VIRTUALLY ALL WHITE BURGUNDY is made exclusively from chardonnay, and virtually all red Burgundy is made exclusively from pinot noir. (This said, the wines are so distinctive that white Burgundy in particular has very little flavor resemblance with most of the chardonnay made in the world today.) In Burgundy, at least for the top wines, chardonnay is never blended with another variety, and neither is pinot noir.

2 AS MENTIONED, BURGUNDY comprises four major regions—Chablis, the Côte d'Or, the Côte Chalonnaise, and the Mâconnais (again, Beaujolais, the fifth region, technically speaking, is given its own chapter following this chapter). The wines in these regions are grouped into four levels. Starting with the most basic (least expensive) wine and moving to the most sophisticated (and most expensive), the levels are:

- *Burgundy Red and White:* Bourgogne Rouge and Bourgogne Blanc, as they are known to the French, are usually simple, basic regional wines, generally blends of various lots of wine made from grapes of the same variety grown anywhere in the entire region of Burgundy. Often, wines such as these lack the specificity of terroir that Burgundy is acclaimed for, although they do have a basic regional character. These basic regional wines account for 52 percent of Burgundy's total production, and they are the most affordable Burgundies. Finally, while basic white and red Burgundy have historically been considered "entry wines" for the budget conscious, the quality of basic Burgundy has risen dramatically in the past ten years, and wines like the basic Bourgogne Blanc of, say, Domaine Leflaive or Pierre Matrot, are fantastic.

- *Village Wine:* This is where Burgundy begins to get dependably interesting. As the name implies, a village wine is made entirely from grapes grown in and around that village. This is a step up in price (and usually quality) from a regional wine because the grapes come from a smaller, more well-defined place. The name of the village—Beaune, Volnay, Gevrey-Chambertin, Pommard, Meursault, Nuits-St.-Georges, Chambolle-Musigny, and so on—will appear on the label. There are forty-four villages, and the wines that come from these account for 36 percent of Burgundy's total production.

- *Premier Cru:* The smallest, most well-defined place of all is a vineyard. In 1861, the top vineyards of Burgundy were classified as either Premier Cru—First Growth—or given an even higher designation, Grand Cru. There

Chambertin-Clos de Bèze, a Grand Cru vineyard in the village of Gevrey-Chambertin. A knockout in terms of its beauty, the wine has sophistication, nuance, and restraint.

are 629 Premier Cru vineyards. Wines from these vineyards are invariably expensive. The name of the vineyard (which I have put in quotes here for clarity) will appear on the label, after the name of the village; for example, Beaune "Clos de la Mousse" or Gevrey-Chambertin "Aux Combottes." Premier Cru wines account for 10 percent of Burgundy's total production.

• *Grand Cru:* The highest designation a Burgundian vineyard can hold is Grand Cru—Great Growth. Wines made from Grand Cru vineyards are the most treasured and expensive wines in Burgundy and rank among the most costly wines in the world. In the Côte d'Or, there are only thirty-two vineyards designated as Grand Cru, and there is one Grand Cru in Chablis (more on this in a moment), for a final total of thirty-three Grands Crus in the entire Burgundy region (see The 33 Grand Cru Vineyards of Burgundy, page 209). The Grands Crus are so famous that their names alone appear on the labels, along with the words *Grand Cru.* Thus, for example, La Tâche and Le Musigny are Grand Cru vineyards, but the label won't mention the villages (Vosne-Romanée and Chambolle-Musigny, respectively) where those vineyards are located. Wines from Grand Cru vineyards account for just 2 percent of Burgundy's total production.

THE ECCLESIASTIC WISDOM OF A SLOPE

Long before the French appellation system was established in the twentieth century, the Benedictine and Cistercian monks of Burgundy had already begun to define, differentiate, and characterize the region's vineyards and the quality of the wines that came from them. The wines from the lower part of the slope, which had the heaviest soils and suffered most in the rain, were known as the cuvées des moines ("wines for the monks"). Wines from the top of the slope, which had the least rain but where the sun did not have solar-panel-like focus, were called cuvées des cardinals ("wines for the cardinals"). Wines from the preferred, middle "thermal belt" of the slope, which had perfect sun orientation and where rain runs off, were called the cuvées des papes ("wines for the popes").

THE GRAPES OF BURGUNDY

WHITES

ALIGOTÉ: Very minor grape. Grown principally in the Mâconnais, where it is used to make inexpensive quaffing wines, although some surprising examples can be found. This is the classic white with which a traditional Kir cocktail is made. Also a frequent component in the sparkling wine Crémant de Bourgogne.

CHARDONNAY: Major grape. Used to make everything from simple wines like Pouilly-Fuissé and St.-Véran to Burgundy's most profound and lush whites, including the wines of Chassagne-Montrachet, Puligny-Montrachet, and Meursault.

RED

PINOT NOIR: Major grape. All of the red wines discussed in this chapter are made from this variety, including humble reds, such as Montagny and Givry, as well as the world-renowned wines from such villages as Chambolle-Musigny, Aloxe-Corton, and Vosne-Romanée.

How would you know if the name on the label is a village name or a vineyard name? Short of memorizing every village and vineyard in Burgundy, there's no foolproof method. However, a fairly good way of guessing is to know that vineyards are sometimes (but admittedly not always) preceded by "the" (le or la in French). Thus, La Tâche, Le Montrachet, and Le Chambertin are all vineyards, but Pommard, Beaune, and Volnay are all villages.

It's also helpful to know that many Burgundian villages (but not vineyards) have hyphenated names—like Chambolle-Musigny, Gevrey-Chambertin, and so on. Interestingly, these hyphenated names have a purpose—the village has annexed the name of its top vineyard in order to benefit from the prestige of that vineyard. Thus, Chambolle-Musigny was originally called just Chambolle until it appended the name of its most famous vineyard, Le Musigny, to its own name. Similarly, the village Aloxe added the name of its renowned vineyard, Le Corton, to become the village of Aloxe-Corton, and the village of Gevrey became Gevrey-Chambertin by incorporating the vineyard Le Chambertin into its name. A hyphenated name on the label invariably means a village wine.

3 YOU PROBABLY THINK of a vineyard as that piece of land owned by a single vintner. In other words, vineyards are commonly defined by the legal construct of ownership. Even though the property within a vineyard may contain highly variable terroir, it is still considered one vineyard when it's owned by one person. The opposite holds true in Burgundy. There, the boundaries of most vineyards were established centuries ago by monks attempting to define parcels of ground solely on the basis of terroir. To the monks, what in the modern world would be considered one vineyard could be two, four, ten, or more vineyards, depending upon the number of different terroirs the monks observed. Each of those distinct vineyards, an entity unto itself, would have been different—sometimes decidedly so—from neighboring vineyards.

4 SINCE VINEYARDS IN BURGUNDY are defined by their terroirs, not necessarily by who owns them, ownership itself takes on a different spin. Although it's a bit hard to picture at first, most vineyards in Burgundy, even the tiniest ones, have more than one owner. Perhaps the most well-known example is the Grand Cru vineyard Clos de Vougeot. At 125

Domaine J. Grivot's entrance to their section of Burgundy's Grand Cru vineyard Clos de Vougeot. The vineyard has 80 owners in all.

n the New World, wines are sometimes said to be made using "Burgundian methods." What does that mean exactly? In general, it involves the following:

HARVESTING THE WINE in small lots and then making each lot separately

USING INDIGENOUS YEASTS (that is, not adding commercial yeasts)

BARREL FERMENTATION OF WHITE WINES

MALOLACTIC FERMENTATION OF WHITE WINES

LONG LEES CONTACT (*sur lie*) and stirring of the lees (*bâtonnage*) of white wines

SMALL, OPEN-TOPPED FERMENTERS for red wine

VERY GENTLE and minimal handling of the wine after it is made

FINING WITH CASEIN OR ISINGLASS for chardonnay; egg whites for pinot noir

FIFTEEN TO EIGHTEEN MONTHS OF AGING in small oak barrels, usually not 100 percent new

acres (50 hectares; less than half the size of, say, Château Lafite-Rothschild in Bordeaux), Clos de Vougeot has eighty owners. Each of these owners makes a wine called Clos de Vougeot. By way of a simple analogy, a Burgundian vineyard is like a condominium. There are several owners, all of whom own distinct parts of the condominium. Still, each of the separate parts is a portion of the same condominium.

5 A HANDFUL OF VINEYARDS have only one owner. These vineyards are known as *monopoles*. They are rare.

6 AS YOU CAN SEE, the conventional, tidy image of a wine estate surrounded by vineyards isn't really applicable to Burgundy. Instead, most growers own many small parcels of many different vineyards in many different villages. For the top wines, although not for the basic ones, the grapes from those parcels will almost never be blended together, even though they might all be the same variety—say, pinot noir. Instead, the grower will make a separate pinot noir from each village and/or vineyard. Indeed, growers often own parcels of several different vineyards within the same village. The grower Domaine Roumier, for example, makes three wines from the village of Chambolle-Musigny: a village wine—Domaine Roumier Chambolle-Musigny; a Premier Cru—Domaine Roumier Chambolle-Musigny "Les Amoureuses"; and a Grand Cru—Domaine Roumier Le Musigny.

And those are just the wines the domaine makes from one village. Domaine Roumier also has vineyard holdings in several other villages.

Why go to the added trouble and expense of making, aging, bottling, marketing, and selling multiple pinot noirs when you could blend them together and make just one pinot noir, as

The "backyard" of pinot noir vines behind Domaine de L'Arlot in Nuits-St.-Georges. Below the house are some of the most enchanting old cellars in the village.

much of the rest of the world does? It's a matter of philosophy and purpose. For wines above the level of basic Bourgogne, the Burgundian grower's goal is to let the personality of the place emanate through the wine. Making one large blend would obliterate the differences in flavor and aroma derived from place. Still, it's a decision with practical consequences, for vineyard parcels can be tiny. It is not unusual for a grower to own just a few rows of vines, enough perhaps to make but a single barrel (twenty-five cases) of wine from that appellation.

THE D'OR IN CÔTE D'OR

*T**he name* Côte d'Or *is often translated as "golden slope," perhaps because the wines from here cost a ransom, or perhaps because the vineyards turn golden in autumn. However, the term is actually a contraction of* Côte d'Orient, *"eastern-facing slope"—a reference to the fact that the vineyards face east to catch each day's morning sun.*

7 IN TERMS OF their sensory characteristics, Burgundies don't lend themselves to quick evaluation. The wines are extremely elegant, highly nuanced, and often rather ethereal. They require a lot of concentration on the part of the taster. It's not uncommon (even for professional tasters) to have to delve deep into their sensory aptitude in order to grasp each wine.

8 UNTIL THE 1980s, most of the commerce in Burgundian wine was controlled by powerful brokers known as *négociants*. The *négociants* rose to power after the French Revolution, when fragmented ownership of small parcels of land in Burgundy made it economically and physically difficult for small growers to bottle, market, and sell their own wine.

Traditionally, *négociants* bought (negotiated for) dozens if not hundreds of small lots of wine from numerous growers, then blended these lots into several wines, bottled them, and sold them under their own labels. A *négociant* house, such as Louis Jadot, would buy many tiny lots of Gevrey-Chambertin to bottle a Louis Jadot Gevrey-Chambertin, and many lots of Pommard to bottle a Louis Jadot Pommard. The *négociant* would, of course, also buy many lots of a Premier Cru vineyard. For example, Louis Jadot might buy

REVOLUTION RECOVERY: BURGUNDY BROKEN; BORDEAUX BACK IN BUSINESS

Burgundy is full of tiny vineyard estates—some less than 3 acres (1.2 hectares) in size. Bordeaux, on the other hand, is made up of many large estates—Château Mouton-Rothschild, for example, is 208 acres (84 hectares); Château Lafite-Rothschild is 272 acres (110 hectares). Why are Burgundy's vineyards so small, and Bordeaux's so large comparatively?

Burgundy's far smaller geography and remote location deep in the center of France are certainly both factors. But a far greater one was this: By the end of the seventeenth century, Burgundy's vineyards were owned primarily by the Roman Catholic Church. This made Burgundy distinctly different from Bordeaux, a large, commercially successful, sophisticated area where vineyard estates were owned by wealthy merchants and aristocrats. With the French Revolution of 1789 to 1799, the course of Burgundy's future changed radically. To establish principles of equality and redistribute wealth, the new state ended the French monarchy and confiscated the church's holdings, breaking up vineyards into tiny parcels and auctioning them off to local peasants. To further strengthen the new state, in 1804, Napoléon Bonaparte issued the Napoleonic Code, a set of sweeping civil laws, including one that barred privilege based on birth order, and mandated that all children must inherit equally. (As a result, in Burgundy today, some members of a family each own just a few rows of vines.)

In Bordeaux, the revolution and its tumultuous Reign of Terror had a different impact. All four of the most prestigious châteaux (Margaux, Lafite-Rothschild, Latour, and Haut-Brion) were confiscated, divided, and, in three cases, their owners beheaded. But Bordeaux's properties had been important financial institutions (the equivalent of the corporations that today are deemed too big to fail). In the wake of the Revolution—and often through graft and insider deals among the bankers and architects of the new French state—the properties were reassembled more or less to their original size. Eventually these were resold to rich merchants or, in the case of Lafite, a foreign corporation that sold shares (at the time a radical idea) to acquire it. By the third decade of the nineteenth century, Bordeaux was back in business, but Burgundy, broken up, was more isolated than ever.

several lots of the Premier Cru vineyard Les Amoureuses (the name means "the women in love") and make a Louis Jadot Chambolle-Musigny "Les Amoureuses." Generally speaking, the *négociants* of the past owned few—if any—vineyards themselves.

By the 1960s and 1970s, however, the *négociant* business began to change. Many small growers—even the tiniest ones—decided to bottle their wines under their own labels, leaving fewer available sources of grapes for *négociants* to buy. The wines many *négociants* produced began to suffer in quality. To remedy this, *négociant* houses increasingly became growers themselves. Louis Jadot, for example, owned one small vineyard when it was founded in 1859. Today the firm has 519 acres (210 hectares) of vineyards and makes wines from more than ninety appellations. However, with the exception of a few top *négociant* houses, such as Louis Jadot (which makes extraordinary Burgundies), large *négociant* wines are often considered far less exciting than the wines from small domaines.

THE LAND, THE GRAPES, AND THE VINEYARDS

J ust driving down the Côte d'Or's famous main wine road—RN74— reveals how intimately connected growers are to the land and portends just how site specific the wines can be. On the slopes above each tiny village, instead of vast tracts of vineyards, the thick carpet of vines is parcelled into paddocklike plots, often enclosed by fieldstone walls. To encourage competition among them, the vines are closely spaced—about 4,000 plants per acre (.4 hectare). As astounding as this seems, it is not as dense as plantings once were. Before phylloxera, for example, vines in Burgundy were not planted in rows, but simply helter skelter in a tight fashion— a manner that suited the monks who tended the vines by hand. It wasn't until horses were employed in the work that planting in straight rows became commonplace. Today, thanks to the huge number of tiny plots owned by different growers, the visual effect of the vineyards, even from a short distance, is that of a patchwork quilt of vibrant green. Together, all of these tiny vineyards amount to just over 66,000 acres (26,700 hectares) of vines. By comparison, Bordeaux, with over 290,000 acres (117,400 hectares), is nearly four and a half times larger.

The region is composed of four main subregions. We'll look at these individually, beginning on page 212, but for now, here's a very brief overview:

CHABLIS This is the northernmost subregion of Burgundy, just 100 or so miles (160 kilometers) southeast of Paris. Chablis is entirely devoted to growing chardonnay grapes.

CÔTE D'OR Most of Burgundy's legendary wines (and most of the Grand Crus) come from the Côte d'Or, the collective name for the Côte de Nuits and the Côte de Beaune. The Côte d'Or is a 30-mile-long (48-kilometer) limestone escarpment, or ridge, with villages on the eastern side of the slope. Because the vines primarily face east, they are perfectly oriented to catch the morning sun each day. The Côte de Nuits (the northern half of the escarpment) is planted virtually entirely with pinot noir, and hence makes red wines only. The Côte de Beaune (the southern half) is planted with both pinot noir and chardonnay, and makes both red and white wines.

CÔTE CHALONNAISE Just south of the Côte d'Or is the Côte Chalonnaise, which while not as famous as its sisters, nonetheless produces some quite good, reasonably priced red and white wines.

MÂCONNAIS Moving south from the Côte Chalonnaise, you come next to the Mâconnais, a fairly large region devoted to making oceans of good, everyday, inexpensive chardonnay, as well as a handful of finer chardonnays. The three most well-known wines are Mâcon-Villages, Pouilly-Fuissé, and St.-Véran.

PLUS BEAUJOLAIS From a government administration point of view, Beaujolais is also considered a subregion within Burgundy. But because Beaujolais has little in common with the rest of Burgundy, it has its own chapter, beginning on page 227.

Because the entire Burgundy region is 140 miles (225 kilometers) from north to south, each of these subregions has many specific characteristics of climate and soil that

In Burgundy, pinot noir is held in absolute reverence.

THE 33 GRAND CRU VINEYARDS OF BURGUNDY

There are thirty-two Grand Cru vineyards in the Côte d'Or, plus one in Chablis, for a total of thirty-three. They are listed here from north to south. The village where each Grand Cru vineyard is located follows in parentheses.

CHABLIS GRAND CRU (Chablis)

CHAMBERTIN CLOS-DE-BÈZE
(Gevrey-Chambertin)

CHAPELLE-CHAMBERTIN
(Gevrey-Chambertin)

CHARMES-CHAMBERTIN
(Gevrey-Chambertin)

GRIOTTE-CHAMBERTIN
(Gevrey-Chambertin)

LATRICIÈRES-CHAMBERTIN
(Gevrey-Chambertin)

LE CHAMBERTIN (Gevrey-Chambertin)

MAZIS-CHAMBERTIN
(Gevrey-Chambertin)

MAZOYÈRES-CHAMBERTIN
(Gevrey-Chambertin)

RUCHOTTES-CHAMBERTIN
(Gevrey-Chambertin)

BONNES MARES (part in Morey-St.-Denis; part in Chambolle-Musigny)

CLOS DE LA ROCHE (Morey-St.-Denis)

CLOS DES LAMBRAYS (Morey-St.-Denis)

CLOS DE TART (Morey-St.-Denis)

CLOS ST.-DENIS (Morey-St.-Denis)

LE MUSIGNY (Chambolle-Musigny)

CLOS DE VOUGEOT (Vougeot)

ECHÉZEAUX (Vosne-Romanée)

GRANDS ECHÉZEAUX (Vosne-Romanée)

LA ROMANÉE (Vosne-Romanée)

LA TÂCHE (Vosne-Romanée)

LA GRANDE RUE (Vosne-Romanée)

RICHEBOURG (Vosne-Romanée)

ROMANÉE-CONTI (Vosne-Romanée)

ROMANÉE-ST.-VIVANT (Vosne-Romanée)

CHARLEMAGNE (Aloxe-Corton)

CORTON-CHARLEMAGNE (part in Pernand-Vergelesses; part in Aloxe-Corton; part in Ladoix-Serrigny)

LE CORTON (part in Pernand-Vergelesses; part in Aloxe-Corton; part in Ladoix-Serrigny)

BÂTARD-MONTRACHET (part in Puligny-Montrachet; part in Chassagne-Montrachet)

BIENVENUES-BÂTARD-MONTRACHET (Puligny-Montrachet)

CHEVALIER-MONTRACHET (Puligny-Montrachet)

LE MONTRACHET (part in Puligny-Montrachet; part in Chassagne-Montrachet)

CRIOTS-BÂTARD-MONTRACHET (Chassagne-Montrachet)

DOMAINE DE LA ROMANÉE-CONTI

The most-renowned estate in Burgundy, perhaps in all of France, Domaine de la Romanée-Conti, has been the subject of entire books. The DRC, as it is referred to, is owned by the de Villaine and Leroy families and is made up of parcels of seven vineyards, all of which are Grands Crus and all of which have been considered exemplary for centuries. These include one vineyard devoted to white wine, Le Montrachet, and six devoted to red: Romanée-Conti and La Tâche (both of which are *monopoles,* owned exclusively by the domaine), as well as Richebourg, Romanée-St.-Vivant, Echézeaux, and Grands Echézeaux. Together these seven holdings make up just a little more than 62 acres (25 hectares) of vines. Because the yields from these vineyards are kept extremely low, production is minuscule. The entire production of the DRC's wine from the Romanée-Conti vineyard is a mere six thousand bottles (five hundred cases) a year. This is about 1/40 the production of Château Lafite-Rothschild in Bordeaux. As for cost, year in and year out the wines of the DRC are the most expensive in Burgundy. Vintages in the mid-2000s (2004–2007) sold at auction for $6,500 to $10,500 a bottle.

define it. But in general, what makes Burgundy Burgundy are two enormously important realities. First, it is a cool place. As I mentioned earlier, of all the regions in the world that are famous for red wine, Burgundy is the most northern. Summers here are generally cooler than in Bordeaux and much cooler than in most of California. And because Burgundy is a cool place, its wines are not massive, syrupy, and overtly fruity. Instead, at their best they are intensely flavored but have a light to medium body and an almost gossamer gracefulness.

Burgundy's cool climate also means that the region is well suited to pinot noir and chardonnay. Worldwide experience with pinot noir suggests that the grape will produce wines that possess finesse, nuance, and complexity only when it is planted in a cool place, so that the grapes are allowed to ripen slowly and methodically over a relatively long period of time. (Pinot noir planted in hot, sun-drenched areas produces unfocused, dull wines that taste like flat cola.) As for white Burgundies, while chardonnay can be, and is, planted in quite warm places around the world, many knowledgeable chardonnay lovers would argue that the most nuanced and elegant wines come from grapes that are grown in cooler spots.

Because of Burgundy's cool northern climate, achieving ripeness is a concern, and thus it's no surprise that for the best wines, yields must be kept low (vineyards maxed out by trying to ripen too much fruit end up not ripening any of it very well).

Another concern is deciding when to pick. In Burgundy, it often rains in early fall. Growers who pick early in the season might avoid rain, but the slightly underripe grapes they harvest might also produce thin, bland wines that no amount of winemaking wizardry will improve. Growers who pick late are gambling that they can dodge the rain, thus letting the grapes benefit from a longer ripening

> "[Chambolle Musigny] is a wine of silk and lace; supremely delicate with no hint of violence yet much hidden strength."
>
> — GASTON ROUPNEL
> French poet (1871–1946)

In the small, cool, damp, dark, often earthen-floored cellars of Burgundy, pinot noir ages gracefully.

time, with richer wines as the result. But such growers are also betting that if it does indeed rain, they'll be able to harvest the crop before the grapes get waterlogged or before a serious rot sets in.

Of course, growers who pick early can chaptalize—a practice that's legal in Burgundy. Chaptalization involves adding plain old sugar to the fermenting vat. This, in turn, gives the yeasts more material to ferment. And the more sugar the yeasts have to ferment, the fuller in body (and higher in alcohol) the wine will be. It's safe to say that top producers avoid chaptalization, since wines with high alcohol but meek flavors can often taste out of balance and discombobulated.

What else makes Burgundy Burgundy? Limestone and limestone-rich clays called marls. In many areas—especially in the Côte d'Or and in Chablis—limestone rocks embedded with visible sea fossils are scattered everywhere in the vineyards, and outcroppings reveal entire blocks of fractured limestone underneath the barest minimum of topsoil. This particular limestone dates from the middle and lower Jurassic period, approximately 201 to 145 million years ago. (In Chablis, the limestone formed specifically during the Kimmeridgian stage within the Jurassic, and is therefore known as Kimmeridgian limestone.) Tiny filaments of roots burrow between the crevices of these limestone blocks, going down to depths reaching 70 feet (20 meters) or more. In Burgundy, it is common wisdom that such limestone is the source of both red and white wines' vivid minerality.

No one describes the soil more poetically than Anthony Hanson, in his authoritative book *Burgundy*:

During the Jurassic period, the whole of Burgundy sank beneath shallow seas. Archaeopteryx, or some other ancestral bird, took wing, great dinosaurs roamed the land, while on the sea bed, marine sediments were slowly laid down. The shells of myriads of baby oysters piled one on another, while the skeletons of countless crinoids or sea lilies were compacted together; from such petrified remains, limestone is formed. Jurassic limestone rocks, interspersed with marlstones, are fundamental keys to the excellence and variety of Burgundy's wines.

And finally, a few more words about the grapes.

Although it's hard to imagine now, until the modern wine revolution of the 1950s and 1960s, chardonnay and pinot noir were hardly heard of outside central France. Just a smattering of acres/hectares existed in the entire New World. Today, of course, that has all changed. California alone has slightly more than 95,000 acres (38,400 hectares) of chardonnay and nearly 40,000 acres (16,200 hectares) of pinot noir. Factor in Australia, New

Zealand, South America, and other U.S. states like Oregon and Washington, and both of these once rare Burgundian varieties are very much on wine's contemporary world stage.

Yet chardonnay and pinot noir don't merely grow in Burgundy; Burgundy is where chardonnay and pinot noir reach dizzying heights of beauty and individuality. Indeed, the Burgundian versions of both of these grapes stand distinctly apart from wines elsewhere that are made from the same varieties. A lifetime of experience with California chardonnay, for example, would give you little idea of what to expect from a white Burgundy. And it's not a matter of a special group of clones. Vineyards in Burgundy today are planted and replanted as they have been for centuries—not by planting selected individual clones, but rather by the method known as massale selection (taking cuttings from numerous vines within a vineyard and using buds from all of them to begin a new vineyard, thus replicating the original vineyard's genetic diversity).

CHABLIS

The northernmost subregion of Burgundy, Chablis sits like an isolated island far north of the Côte d'Or and the rest of Burgundy. In fact, the vineyards of Chablis are closer to Champagne, about 20 miles (32 kilometers) away, than they are to the rest of Burgundy, more than 60 miles (97 kilometers) away. This far north, Chablis's harsh, wet, and very cold temperatures are influenced by the Atlantic Ocean, and frosts in both spring and fall shorten the growing season. The wines, not surprisingly, are so crisp and racy that they vibrate with spring-loaded acidity.

The place itself is amazing looking. Vineyards roll this way and that, as if they grew on ocean waves. The whitish, crusty limestone soil—full of baby oyster shells and crinoids *entroques* (cousins of sea lilies and starfish)—is so stark that at twilight you feel as though you're on the moon.

CHARDONNAY— THE PLACE

One of the historic, tiny villages in the Mâconnais region of Burgundy is called Chardonnay. The name is derived from the Latin **Cardonnacum**, which in turn comes from **carduus**, Latin for "a place with thistles." (**Carduus** is the genus for ninety species of thistles.) Interestingly, during the Roman era, a nobleman named Cardus is also thought to have owned the area where the village now exists. The village of Chardonnay and the surrounding Mâconnais region may indeed be where chardonnay was born as a natural crossing. DNA typing reveals chardonnay's parents to be the red grape pinot noir and the white grape gouais blanc.

While Chablis was justifiably famous in the late nineteenth century (its proximity to Paris ensured its reputation as a brasserie favorite), the wine is perhaps less well known today. The area, which suffered tremendously during the phylloxera crisis, had a difficult time regaining financial stability, and with the establishment of France's major railway systems, cheaper, heartier wines were easily shipped north, weakening Chablis's position even further. That said, the 2000s saw a resurgence of its popularity, perhaps because the minerally, steely flavors, exuberant freshness, and kinetic feel of Chablis are wholly different from chardonnay made anywhere else in the world, and thus the wine has, in a commercial sense, little competition. The French often call the unique flavors of a good Chablis *goût de pierre à fusil*—gunflint. When, with a great Premier or Grand Cru Chablis, these gunflint flavors are spliced by edgy minerality, the effect can be sensational.

Most Chablis are made entirely in stainless steel to preserve the purity of their flavors. Some domaines ferment in stainless steel but go on to briefly age their Chablis in small, used oak barrels in order to deepen the wine's flavors. Still other producers (a small number) barrel ferment their Chablis, especially their Grands Crus, which are thought to be intense enough to stand up to the oak's impact.

Chablis has numerous Premier Crus and one Grand Cru—a magnificent sweeping hillside of Kimmeridgian limestone and marl covering 247 acres (100 hectares). Somewhat confusingly, the Grand Cru is known by the seven contiguous parcels—*climats*—situated along the hillside (leading some to imagine there are seven Grands Crus). These parcels are Blanchot, Bougros, Grenouilles, Les Clos, Les Preuses, Valmur, and Vaudésir. A bottle of Grand Cru Chablis will list one of these names on the label along with the words "Chablis Grand Cru."

SOME OF THE BEST
PRODUCERS OF CHABLIS

Alice et Olivier de Moor • Billaud-Simon • Christian Moreau Père et Fils • Jean Dauvissat • Jean-Marc Brocard • Jean-Paul & Benoît Droin • Laroche • Louis Michel et Fils • Pattes Loup • Raveneau • René et Vincent Dauvissat • Servin • Verget • Vocoret et Fils • William Fèvre

THE CÔTE D'OR

The 30-mile-long, 1,000-foot-high (48-kilometer, 305-meter) escarpment known as the Côte d'Or is Burgundy's most renowned wine region. When wine drinkers talk about being left spellbound by Burgundy, they are almost assuredly talking about wines from here.

The Côte d'Or is a narrow ridge of limestone, divided almost equally in half. The northern part, known as the Côte de Nuits, produces red wines almost exclusively. The southern half, the Côte de Beaune, produces both red and white wines, although whites—including the ultra-famous wines Puligny-Montrachet and Chassagne-Montrachet—dominate. (For the villages in each part, see The Villages of Burgundy, page 200.) In between the Côte de Nuits and the Côte de Beaune is the village of

WHEN YOU VISIT . . . BURGUNDY

BURGUNDY IS FILLED WITH QUIET, charming villages, many of which surround impressive medieval churches or cathedrals. There are scores of fabulous tiny restaurants specializing in the region's humble, delicious cooking, and dozens of small, comfortable hotels.

ALL OF THIS NOTWITHSTANDING, Burgundian domaines can be very difficult to visit, since they are so tiny and there is nothing that resembles a winery in the California sense. Small producers are simply not set up to receive visitors, and even if you call in advance and speak in French, your request may be refused. If luck is on your side however, you'll end up going with the proprietor down into a cold, damp cellar, and tasting great Burgundies out of the barrel. No wine experience is more thrilling.

TWO MAGNIFICENT, HISTORIC buildings are must-sees: the château of Clos de Vougeot, sitting like a jewel in the middle of a walled vineyard in the village of Vougeot, and in the city of Beaune, the impressive fifteenth-century Hôtel Dieu, with its colorful glazed tile roof and breathtaking grand hall. Each year, this is where the prestigious Hospices de Beaune wine auction is held.

SERVING BURGUNDY—
A FEW SPECIAL CONSIDERATIONS

Serving a great Burgundy, white or red, in too small a glass is considered a crime. Burgundies are, by their nature, aromatic wines. The only way to experience the full impact of these wines is to drink them from generous glasses with ample bowls that taper toward the top.

Know, too, that Burgundies are among the wines in the world that change a lot after being poured. In fact, it's almost impossible to accurately assess a great Burgundy after the first one or two sips. In twenty minutes, the wine may be transformed substantially, offering a whole new world of flavors and aromas. For many wine drinkers, this propensity to evolve in the glass is part of what makes top Burgundy intellectually intriguing.

With a fine red Burgundy, the wine's inclination to evolve and the relative fragility of the pinot noir grape mean that, in general, you should not open the bottle many hours before dinner or, worse, decant it. Pinot noir is the complete opposite of cabernet sauvignon in this regard. When pinot noir, especially a pinot that is ten years old or more, is given too much oxygen, its flavors can seem to fade and fall apart. So pour red Burgundy from the bottle (not a decanter) and drink it soon after it's opened.

Tasting in the cellars of Aurelien Verdet. Every Burgundian domaine, no matter how humble, serves their Burgundies in good, thin-rimmed, generous glasses.

Comblanchien—famous not for wine, but for its dusty quarries full of Comblanchien limestone and marble.

Every village in the Côte d'Or is said to have its own character—the wines of Chambolle-Musigny, for example, are frequently considered among the most elegant pinot noirs, while the pinots of Nuits-St.-Georges are thought to be more structured.

There is one broad generalization that can be made concerning red wines: The top reds from the Côte de Nuits (Gevrey-Chambertin, Flagey-Echézeaux, Vosne-Romanée, Nuits-St.-Georges, and others) often have greater intensity and a firmer structure than red wines from the Côte de Beaune (Aloxe-Corton, Beaune, Volnay, Pommard, and so on). By contrast, the top Côte de Beaune reds are frequently softer and sometimes more lush. In general, reds from all over the Côte d'Or are prized for their soaring, earthy flavors, often laced with minerals, exotic spices, licorice, or truffles. Of all the red wines in the world, these are some of the most heady in aroma and long in the mouth. They are also some of the most frail in color. (As with all pinot noirs, the intensity of

The church spire and bell tower in Savigny-lès-Beaune in the Côte de Beaune. The long and intimate relationship between wine and religion is evident in every Burgundian village.

a red Burgundy's color is not a reflection of the intensity of its flavor.)

As for white wines (again, all of which come from the Côte de Beaune), the most famous villages are Meursault, Puligny-Montrachet, Chassagne-Montrachet, Ladoix-Serrigny, and Beaune. The top Premier and Grand Cru wines from these villages can be amazingly rich and concentrated without being heavy or ponderous. Their tightly woven flavors are dripping with hints of toasted nuts, truffles, and vanilla. A wine such as the Grand Cru Corton-Charlemagne from Domaine Bonneau du Martray, for example, can have such exquisite elegance, it's toe curling.

The word *côte* is translated as "slope," and where a vineyard is located on the slope of the Côte d'Or is usually a clue to its rank. The humblest place to be on the slope is at the bottom. Village wines generally come from these bottom-slope or flatland vineyards. Here the soil is heaviest, least well drained, and most full of clay. A better place to be on the slope is on the top third. The soil is thinner and there's more limestone, but the sun is not entirely ideal (many Premier Cru vineyards are on the top third of the slope). The best vineyards of all—and where the Grands Crus are located—are those vineyards that are mid-slope. Here, the limestone and marl is abundant and there's

WHITE BURGUNDY AND LOBSTER

Move over Champagne and caviar. Among the world's most indulgent and sensational food-and-wine combinations is surely a Premier Cru or Grand Cru white Burgundy, especially an opulent Puligny-Montrachet or Chassagne-Montrachet, with Maine lobster drizzled with butter. When the sweet, rich creaminess of the wine meets the sweet, rich meatiness of the lobster, well, if you don't die of poverty first, you'll die from the pleasure.

a solar-panel-like 45-degree exposure to sun throughout the day. This midslope area is often called the thermal belt.

CÔTE CHALONNAISE

A few miles/kilometers south of the Côte d'Or is the Côte Chalonnaise, also devoted to both chardonnay and pinot noir wines. There are five main wine villages here: Mercurey, Bouzeron, Rully, Givry, and Montagny. In addition to wines from these villages, much basic Bourgogne is also produced here. There are no Grand Cru vineyards in the Côte Chalonnaise. There are, however, numerous Premiers Crus.

The wines of the Côte Chalonnaise are almost always less expensive than the wines of the Côte d'Or, so this is the subregion bargain hunters love to explore. Of course, Chalonnaise wines generally don't match the Côte d'Or in quality either. But delicious surprises can crop up, especially from the top producers.

The area's best-known and largest village, Mercurey, can produce very good pinot noirs with lots of spicy cherry character (although there are also Mercureys that are watery and weak). And while Mercurey is thought of as a red-wine village, it also produces a

The winemakers of Domaine Laroche taste their exquisite Chablis. The domaine makes filigreed, minerally Chablis that taste of ocean air and ancient seabeds. Their Grand Cru Chablis in particular are show stoppers.

THE HÔTEL DIEU AND
THE HOSPICES DE BEAUNE

One of the most prestigious wine events anywhere is the Hospices de Beaune, a charity auction held each November in Beaune's stunning Hôtel Dieu (literally, "God's House"). Built in 1443 by Nicolas Rolin, chancellor of the duchy of Burgundy, and his wife, Guigone de Salins, the Hôtel Dieu is perhaps the most magnificent refuge ever created for the sick and the destitute. Its numerous enormous rooms include large galleries with curtained bed chambers where the sick slept, two to a bed (for warmth), chapels for the bedridden to attend daily Mass, grand kitchens, and a pharmacy outfitted with distillation stills for the making of medicines. The building's steep roof is covered in dazzlingly colored glazed tiles and can be seen from miles away. Sunlight hitting the roof creates a halo of amazing light. The Hôtel Dieu (now a museum and wine domaine) owns almost 150 acres (60 hectares) of vineyards (much of it classified as Premier or Grand Cru), which have been donated to it over centuries. Each year since 1851, the wines made from these vineyards have been sold in a highly publicized auction that brings in considerable sums to benefit the hospitals of Beaune.

small amount of lovely, appley, minerally chardonnay.

Bouzeron is the northernmost village of the Côte Chalonnaise. It is known primarily for aligoté. In fact, perhaps the best wine made from aligoté in France is produced here, by Aubert de Villaine, codirector of the prestigious Domaine de la Romanée-Conti in the Côte d'Or.

The village of Rully used to be one of the centers of sparkling wine production in Burgundy, and a fair amount of Crémant de Bourgogne (a sparkling wine produced using the Champagne method) is still produced there. Otherwise, the village is known mostly for its simple pinot noirs and somewhat better chardonnays, which can be crisp and lemony, with nutty overtones.

Givry is better known for its pinot noirs, although chardonnays also come from there. Quality, of course, depends on the producer, but there are some very good wines with earthy and cherry flavors.

Finally, Montagny, the small, southernmost village of the Côte Chalonnaise, is exclusively devoted to chardonnay. Many Burgundy insiders consider Montagnys the best-value white Burgundies going, and this village has the highest number of Premiers Crus in the Côte Chalonnaise—forty-nine. Indeed, about two-thirds of the 740 acres (300 hectares) here are ranked Premier Cru and encompass more than fifty named sites. Because of the high proportion of top-rated vineyards within this single, small appellation, the significance of naming the individual vineyard is diluted. Thus, unlike the rest of Burgundy, a majority of Montagny Premier Cru wine is sold without reference to a specific vineyard.

SOME OF THE BEST
PRODUCERS OF THE CÔTE
CHALONNAISE

A. & P. de Villaine • Dureuil-Janthial • François Raquillet • J. M. Boillot • Joblot • Louis Jadot • Louis Latour • Meix-Foulot

Perhaps more than any other place in the world, Burgundy is vulnerable to vintages of widely differing quality. Nonetheless, to come upon a stash of really old Burgundy excites the imagination in a way few other wines ever do.

MÂCONNAIS

outh of the Côte Chalonnaise is the Mâconnais, a large area of low-lying hills, woodlands, farmland, and meadows. Some soils here are limestone and marl, but toward the southern end, granite and schist are also found. The top three Mâconnais (all made from chardonnay) are: Mâcon, Pouilly-Fuissé, and St.-Véran. Oceans of basic, serviceable chardonnay are also made. There are no Grands Crus or Premiers Crus in the Mâconnais.

Mâcon is found as either simple Mâcon (about 80 percent of production; much of it from cooperatives) or the even better Mâcon-Villages. And, in one further step up, twenty-six villages have the right to append their names to the word Mâcon: Mâcon-Lugny, Mâcon-Viré, Mâcon-Fuissé, and so on.

Pouilly-Fuissé, the most highly thought of appellation within the Mâconnais thanks to its generous limestone soils, comes from the area around the four small hamlets of Vergisson, Solutré-Pouilly, Fuissé, and Chaintré. PR got to Pouilly-Fuissé early on, and some producers' wines are dreadful and overpriced. But the top Pouilly-Fuissés are bold, dense chardonnays—delicious, although never as elegant as the hugely more expensive top whites of the Côte d'Or. (Don't confuse Pouilly-Fuissé with Pouilly-Fumé. The latter is a sauvignon blanc from France's Loire Valley.) And last, from the village of St.-Vérand comes the wine St.-Véran (minus the *d* in its name), which is usually less expensive than Pouilly-Fuissé, and sometimes better.

SOME OF THE BEST PRODUCERS OF THE MÂCONNAIS

Château Fuissé • Daniel Barraud • de Bongran • des Comtes Lafon • Guffens-Heynen • J. A. Ferret • Joseph Drouhin • Louis Jadot • Robert Denogent • Roger Lassarat • Valette

WHERE'S THE BOEUF?

Burgundy's famous boeuf bourguignon *is a slowly braised beef stew made with local Charolais beef, pearl onions, mushrooms, bits of fried bacon, and a whole bottle of Burgundy wine. Needless to say, no sane cook—and certainly no Burgundian cook, since most of them are known for their thriftiness—would pour a Premier Cru or Grand Cru into the pot. No, the stew is made with a basic Burgundy, something that won't require the cook to pawn the family silver. The Burgundy you drink with the stew, well, that's a different story. In the end, however, it's the combination that counts, and a rich, winey stew of slowly braised beef is one of the most stunning partners a bottle of great Burgundy could have.*

BUYING BURGUNDY AND THE QUESTION OF VINTAGES

Depending on your viewpoint (and the amount of money you can afford to lose on some wines that may prove disappointing), buying Burgundy is either frightening or exciting, for there are few absolutes that can be counted on. Indeed, buying Burgundy is a matter of trial and error, luck, intuition, and, you hope, some good advice. Actually, there is one absolute: Bargain Burgundies do not exist. Like caviar, the top Burgundies are dependably expensive.

You might logically think that Grands Crus are better than Premiers Crus and that Premiers Crus are better than village wines. While this is a solid, historically based idea that

often proves to be the case, there are also times when it's a wrong assumption. Burgundy, alas, is the ultimate moving target.

Then there's the issue of aging. Burgundies can take on remarkably different qualities as they age. There is no good rule of thumb for knowing when a given Burgundy will move into the scrumptious zone (or even if it will), for Burgundy rarely ages in a linear, predictable way.

And, of course, buying Burgundy encourages you to consider the place as much as, if not more than, the producer. A wine from the village of Chambolle-Musigny traditionally tastes quite different from a wine from the village of Nuits-St.-Georges. It's fascinating to try to taste these "flavors of place" and see if you can recognize the commonalities among wines from the same village, just minutes down the road from another village and its wines.

As for producers, remembering which producer is which in Burgundy can be daunting, since many growers are siblings or cousins with the same last name. For example, in the small, sleepy village of Chassagne-Montrachet alone, there are three producers with the last name

A wine shop and tasting room in the ancient walled city of Beaune.

At the celebrated bistro Ma Cuisine in Beaune, chef Fabienne Escoffier writes her daily menu on a blackboard. Roast pigeon and boeuf Bourguignon *are specialties.*

Morey (Domaine Bernard Morey, Domaine Jean-Marc Morey, and Domaine Marc Morey), two producers with Ramonet in their name (Domaine Ramonet and Domaine Bachelet-Ramonet), and four producers with the name Gagnard—and that's just in tiny Chassagne-Montrachet! It's easy to see why taking notes on the name of a Burgundy is essential if you ever want to find it again.

As for vintages, Burgundy—more than most of the rest of the world—is a place where the differences among vintages are clearly apparent. The region's coolish, rain-prone continental climate, the variations in sites and soils, and the exigencies of growing pinot noir and chardonnay in such a place mean that harvest conditions and wines can vary considerably. While all of this is true, it misses the most important truth of all: Most vintages are neither great nor poor. They are someplace in between. It doesn't make sense to think about Burgundian vintages in such black-and-white terms when, in fact, that sort of thinking has little basis in reality. Years ago, François Millet, the winemaker at Comte Georges de Vogüé, told me something I've never forgotten. Vintages, he said, are simply the mood of the wine. Some years the wine is in an exuberant mood; some years it is shy. And, of course, there are countless moods in between.

THE FOODS OF BURGUNDY

I f any one dish epitomizes the intimate connection of wine and food in Burgundy, it is coq au vin (hen or rooster cooked in Burgundy wine). Rustic, hearty, and slow cooked, it is soulful, humble fare that speaks of the earth, not of artifice. Burgundian cooking may not be cutting edge or elaborate, but it is honest and true to centuries of good home cooks who knew how to take snails, rabbits, and guinea hens and make them irresistible.

Burgundy's most famous vineyards are bracketed by two of the legendary food capitals of France—Dijon and Lyon. Dijon calls itself the mustard capital of the world, and mustard, simple as it is, is France's best-loved condiment. You can find a little pot on every table of virtually every bistro in the country. About 70 percent of France's mustard is *moutarde de Dijon*, which refers to the style—a creamy, smooth, especially pungent mustard—originally developed in Dijon. Today, many Burgundian villages have their own *moutarderie*, or mustard shop, where artisanal mustards are made, sometimes with slightly fermented white grape juice rather than vinegar.

Although snails are cooked and eaten all over France, no snail preparation is better known than *escargots à la bourguignonne*, snails cooked Burgundy style. Today, canned and frozen snails from Turkey and Algeria show up in many restaurants worldwide, but in Burgundy, wild snails can still be collected in the vineyards. Traditionally, these are stuffed with garlic butter, cooked, and served piping hot.

The beef dishes of Burgundy are also much acclaimed, especially the slowly braised beef stew known as *boeuf bourguignon*. But the most exciting beef of all is Charolais, named for the town of Charoles in southwestern Burgundy, and one of Europe's finest breeds. These massive cattle have meat that is tender and succulent, with an incomparable full, rich flavor. A hunk of roasted Charolais and a glass of Pommard or Volnay is Burgundy gift-wrapped. With Charolais cattle, meat is just the beginning, however. From the Charolais's milk come cylinders of rich Charolais cheese, which are also prized.

But the most legendary Burgundian cheese of all must be the pungent, runny Époisses de Bourgogne, named after the village Époisses. Sought after all over the world, Époisses is aged slowly and given a daily washing with *marc de Bourgogne*, the local *eau-de-vie*.

A mural on a wall in the old city of Beaune depicts a young Dionysus.

Finally, there's *pain d'épice*, Burgundy's spice bread. In Gallo-Roman times, Burgundy was one of the corridors of the spice trade to the northern countries. Dijon's love of mustard resulted from this propitious positioning, and so did spice bread. The dense loaves, made with honey, cinnamon, cloves, nutmeg, coriander, aniseed, and orange peel, are not exactly sweet; they're more of a hearty snack. Who knows how many generations of *vignerons*, come winter, have devoured an entire *pain d'épice* after a day spent pruning in the damp, cold vineyards of Burgundy.

The Burgundies to Know

When I approached the writing of this section, I had all the enthusiasm of a woman going to have a root canal. Frankly, recommending Burgundies is fraught with problems, chief among them the knowledge that, thanks to their infinitesimally small quantities in a global marketplace, great Burgundies are hard to get one's hands on (which doesn't mean you shouldn't try).

Then there's the worry over the wines themselves—the wines of Burgundy are fragile. Vintages, the age of the wine, and how the wine was handled all dramatically leave their stamp. Despite these hesitations, the wines here have all provided me with stellar experiences, and I've loved them to the very last drop. I offer them in the hope that these bottles will also find their way to you, and that you'll be equally pleased.

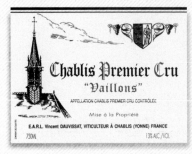

WHITES

RENÉ ET VINCENT DAUVISSAT

CHABLIS | VAILLONS | PREMIER CRU

100% chardonnay

Shiveringly vibrant with acidity, René and Vincent Dauvissat's Chablis always seems to personify the stark cold, white landscape that is Burgundy's most northern enclave. Chablis should never be unfocused, and this one, from the Premier Cru vineyard known as Vaillons, certainly isn't. Although this Chablis can have a honey-peach aroma that sets you up for something mellow and lush, it's almost savagely exact, pure, and cleansing. Vaillons is one of the finest Premier Cru vineyards, and no one makes better wines from this small parcel than the Dauvissat family.

DOMAINE LAROCHE

CHABLIS | LES BLANCHOTS | GRAND CRU |
RESERVE DE L'OBÉDIENCE

100% chardonnay

Can Nature speak more vividly than this? Domaine Laroche's Chablis from the Grand Cru vineyard Les Blanchots is as pristine as a deep mountain lake, and the tension in the wine—the electricity between its acid and its fruit—is haunting. I love this wine's aroma, a smell that takes you back to ancient seabeds, ocean air, fresh brineyness. Massively chalky on the palate at first, the wine turns ethereal, with notes of chamomile tea, lime, honey, and rocks. I've always thought of this as the soprano of wines—high notes that linger and hold you, suspended in a state of sensory purity. Domaine Laroche is one of the oldest domaines in Chablis and is built on an ancient cellar that dates from the ninth century. The Reserve de l'Obédience is a special bottling of the Blanchots. *L'obédience* is an old French term for a monastery.

DOMAINE RAMONET

CHASSAGNE-MONTRACHET | LES RUCHOTTES | PREMIER CRU

100% chardonnay

All-enveloping, rich and powerful, Ramonet's wines make stunning statements. (A friend describes this wine as, "like James Bond—elegant and a badass at the same time.") What I've always loved about Ramonet's Chassagne-Montrachet is its midpalate density . . . a ticking atomic bomb of chalk, salt, and citrus that washes over the taster in waves of minerality and fruit. And then lasts and lasts. Ramonet is a legendary estate in the Côte de Beaune. The late Pierre Ramonet—known simply as the *père* ("father")—was an eccentric peasant farmer who, at age seventy-two, reportedly paid for a tiny sliver of the Le Montrachet vineyard by taking massive wads of French francs out of his pockets and handing them to the lawyer conducting the transaction. The estate is now run by his grandsons Noël and Jean-Claude.

LAFON

DOMAINES DES COMTES | MEURSAULT | LES PERRIÈRES | PREMIER CRU

100% chardonnay

Like spun filaments of gold, Lafon's Meursault from the Les Perrières vineyard is a wine of great intricacy and great opulence. The aromas, not of simple fruits, plunge you down into a deeper world of chalk beds, sassafras, hazelnuts, caramel, and the flavor of honey as if all of the sweetness were removed from it and you were left with the taste of gold and earth. Lafon is known for having an exquisite touch with Meursault, for capturing its sensuality and elegance.

DOMAINE LEFLAIVE

BÂTARD-MONTRACHET | GRAND CRU

100% chardonnay

Bâtard-Montrachet is never an understated wine. Year in and year out, this Grand Cru vineyard makes some of the most dramatic, bold chardonnays in Burgundy, indeed in the whole world. The arc of flavor on the palate is mind-blowing. The first sensation is one of massive richness, but then the wine seems to lift off in wave after wave of chalky, minerally, honeyed flavors. Just when you think the wine can't get any more intense, the subtle, exquisite finish comes and saves you. Domaine Leflaive, headed by Anne-Claude Leflaive, practices biodynamic viticulture. The domaine dates from from the sixteenth century, although many of the family's vineyards were cultivated by monks as far back as two thousand years ago.

BONNEAU DU MARTRAY

CORTON-CHARLEMAGNE | GRAND CRU

100% chardonnay

Possibly the most sought-after white Burgundy of all, Corton-Charlemagne is the world's greatest chardonnay, and Bonneau du Martray is the largest owner of vines within the Grand Cru Corton-Charlemagne vineyard, which lies partly in the village of Pernand-Vergelesses. The centuries-old vineyard is thought to have been owned in the late 700s by Charlemagne himself. With the vineyard's perfect exposure and soil, Corton-Charlemagne is a wine that ought to be mind-blowing, and it is. In the hands of the prestigious, small estate Bonneau du Martray (the only estate in Burgundy to produce wines exclusively from Grand Cru vineyards), the wine is as exquisite, vibrant, sensual, and long as Corton-Charlemagne can be. I love the way the wine lifts out of the glass and seems to levitate on some higher plane of flavor. Chardonnay doesn't get more poetic, more ethereal, than this.

REDS

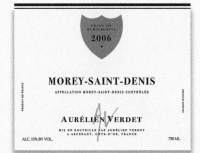

AURÉLIEN VERDET

MOREY-ST.-DENIS | EN LA RUE DE VERGY

100% pinot noir

In the Côte de Nuits village of Morey-St.-Denis, right below the Grand Cru vineyard Clos de Tart, lies a *lieu-dit* called En la Rue de Vergy, considered one of the best vineyards in Morey-St.-Denis. From a tiny 3.5-acre (1.4-hectare) parcel within En la Rue de Vergey, Aurélien Verdet makes an ethereal pinot noir with a velvety, sappy texture and exquisite balance. The wine is rich and alive with morello cherry and cinnamon notes, plus undercurrents of something that exudes umami—black truffles maybe, or fine miso. Driven and enthusiastic, Aurélien Verdet is one of Burgundy's young (born in 1981) star *vignerons* and was a race car driver when his father asked him to come back to the vineyards.

DOMAINE DANIEL RION & FILS

CHAMBOLLE-MUSIGNY | LES CHARMES | PREMIER CRU

100% pinot noir

Great Burgundy is often the equivalent of quiet but insistent music. Something about it pulls you back again and again—as if the mystery of its taste could be solved with just one more sip. The Daniel Rion Chambolle-Musigny from the Premier Cru vineyard Les Charmes can be like this. Seamless and supple, in great years it displays a beautiful core of delicious things evocative of grenadine, cherry syrup, Asian spices, and earth. And all so impeccably balanced, silky, and understated, it's unnerving. In general, Chambolle-Musignys are more about grace than power, as Rion's Les Charmes charmingly shows. The Rion family, considered to be among Burgundy's top-ranking producers, is also known for their sumptuous Nuits-St.-Georges.

DOMAINE DUJAC

CHAMBOLLE-MUSIGNY | LES GRUENCHERS | PREMIER CRU

100% pinot noir

This domaine, begun in 1967 by the influential, highly praised winemaker Jacques Seysses, is now run by his two sons, Alec and Jeremy, and Jeremy's wife, Diana. The domaine's wines are among the most sublime from Burgundy. As a village, Chambolle-Musigny is known for the almost lacy elegance of its wines. Add to that a top Premier Cru vineyard like Les Gruenchers (just down the slope from the Grand Cru Bonnes Mares) and an artist family like the Seysses', and you have magic. When I have tasted it, Les Gruenchers has been the epitome of sensuality, with long, creamy mocha and earth flavors.

COMTE GEORGES DE VOGÜÉ

CHAMBOLLE-MUSIGNY | LES AMOUREUSES | PREMIER CRU

100% pinot noir

The name of this vineyard—Les Amoureuses (women in love)—says it all, for the wine's comingling of femininity and sensuality is complex and beautiful. The rich flavors of raspberry and pomegranate are driven deep into the wine and entwined there with a fresh, pure sense of minerality. Drinking this wine is, I must say, an ethereal experience, as if every one of one's senses has taken flight. The cellars of Comte Georges de Vogüé are mesmerizing and hypnotic—a silent sanctuary for exquisite wines resting until they slowly unfurl themselves. There is no doubt that these cellars are among the most spiritual places in all of Burgundy.

DOMAINE LEROY

CLOS DE LA ROCHE | GRAND CRU

100% pinot noir

In top vintages, this wine is incomparable and as close to sheer perfection as Burgundy gets. Its sappy cherry quality—like fruits drenched in syrup—is pure hedonism. Its smell, like a damp forest—sweet, fresh, dying and yet vividly alive—is sensual. Spices and minerals form a kind of intricate lacework within the wine. The texture is silk against your cheek. All in all, the wine leaves you exhausted with pleasure. It is from the great Grand Cru vineyard Clos de la Roche, in the village of Morey-St.-Denis. And the woman who makes it—Lalou Bize Leroy, the owner of Domaine Leroy—is something of a legend in Burgundy, and one of its most flamboyant and influential winemakers.

CLOS DE TART

CLOS DE TART | GRAND CRU

100% pinot noir

The *monopole* Clos de Tart, in Morey-St.-Denis, is a 17-acre (7-hectare) Grand Cru vineyard. The original estate, founded by medieval nuns, once belonged to the Abbaye de Tart, itself part of the famous Abbaye de Cîteaux. The wine is sumptuous, with a vivid, fresh richness evocative of pomegranates, cranberry compote, and raspberry jam, plus whorls of spice and sassafras. Clos de Tart is known for its profound and incredible structure—qualities that carry it for decades of aging. But I like it when it is young, when the pent-up power is palpable.

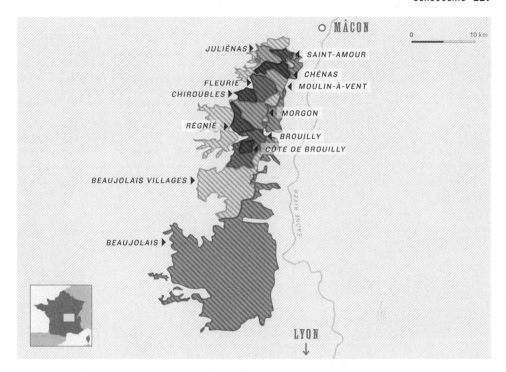

BEAUJOLAIS

The vineyards of Beaujolais extend for some 35 miles (56 kilometers) over low granite hills to the south of Burgundy. For French administrative purposes, Beaujolais is considered part of Burgundy, even though, aside from proximity, the two regions have almost nothing in common. The climates are dissimilar; the soils and geology are different; the grapes are not the same; the way the wines are made varies radically. Even the spirit of each place is singular. Beaujolais is fruit and joy; Burgundy is earth and solemnity.

Beaujolais is both the name of the place and the wine made there. For several decades now, the sad misconception about the wine Beaujolais has been that it's a once-a-year experience, drunk around the end of November when signs in restaurants and wine shops from Paris to Tokyo trumpet *Le Beaujolais Est Arrivé!* ("The Beaujolais Has Arrived!") What has arrived, to be exact, is the PR exploit Beaujolais Nouveau, a grapey young red wine made immediately after the harvest. Beaujolais Nouveau—with its bubble-gum-like flavors—can be amusing (kids in France get to drink it), but as wines go, old-style, traditional Beaujolais is infinitely better.

Beaujolais has been called the only white wine that happens to be red. Indeed, despite its vivid magenta color, Beaujolais can seem like white wine in its expressiveness, freshness, and thirst-quenching qualities. The wine's personality begins with the gamay noir grape (usually known simply as gamay), virtually the only one used in Beaujolais's production. Gamay's flavors are unmistakable: a rush of black cherry and black raspberry, then a hint of peaches, violets, and roses, often followed by peppery

With its rush of vivid cherry, raspberry, and peach flavors, good Beaujolais is irresistible and as exuberant-tasting as childhood itself.

spiciness at the end. And because gamay is naturally low in tannin, its already profuse fruitiness seems even more dramatic.

THE QUICK SIP ON BEAUJOLAIS

TWO WORLDS OF BEAUJOLAIS exist—old-style Beaujolais wines made in a traditional manner, and contrived Beaujolais that are very commercial. The marketing phenomenon known as Beaujolais Nouveau belongs to the latter group.

ALL BEAUJOLAIS is made from gamay, a deliciously, deeply fruity grape.

MOST BEAUJOLAIS is made by a special fermentation technique—carbonic maceration—that maximizes the wine's inherent fruitiness.

Beaujolais's character comes, however, not solely from gamay, but also from the unusual, traditional manner in which many of the wines are made. Called carbonic maceration, the process enhances fruity aromas and fruity flavors in wine. During this process, entire clusters of grapes (usually hand-harvested so that the clusters are rot-free and perfectly intact) are put whole into the fermenting tank. The grapes on the bottom, crushed by the weight of the grapes on top, release their juice, which immediately starts fermenting naturally due to wild yeasts on the grape skins, bathing the grapes on top in carbon dioxide gas (a by-product of fermentation). Those top-layer grapes eventually explode from the pressure of the CO_2, exposing them to yeasts in the tank and thus causing them to ferment as well. Carbonic maceration could theoretically be used with any grape, but it is particularly successful with ultrafruity grapes, such as gamay.

After Beaujolais is fermented, it rests in tanks (a few growers also put it briefly in small, relatively new oak) for several months or more before being sold.

COMMERCIAL VS. OLD-STYLE BEAUJOLAIS

Several decades ago, all Beaujolais was what I'll call old-style—meaning, made as a serious wine. But fueled by the popularity of Beaujolais Nouveau in the 1960s and 1970s, growers and producers began to increase their productions, making cheap, cheerful wines that—in the beginning—were easy to sell and a cash-flow dream come true. As the hype wore away, the practice turned in on itself and became a self-fulfilling prophecy. Growers, paid increasingly little, were forced to take more and more shortcuts, increasing yields; chaptalizing thin, unripe wines; filtering the wines severely; and releasing them early. Beaujolais made in this large-scale, commercial way tasted more tutti-frutti than truly fruity. Its bouncy, sophomoric flavor was often a dead ringer for Jell-O.

Today, while commercial Beaujolais is widely available, so are wines from the serious, old-style producers. Traditionally made Beaujolais from small estates often costs more, but the pure deliciousness of the wines is incomparable. In many cases, they possess an almost electric richness of fruit, floral, and spice notes that's like drinking happiness. Among the old-style producers to search out: Marcel Lapierre, Jean-Paul Thévenet, Jean-Paul Brun, Guy Breton, Dominique Piron, Michel Tête, Jean Foillard, Domaine du Granit, and Julien Sunier.

In total, there are some three thousand growers and eighteen cooperatives in Beaujolais today. Many growers sell to the region's well-established *négociants,* including the largest well known *négociant,* the firm Georges Duboeuf.

Finally, like chardonnay, its sibling, gamay is the progeny of pinot noir and gouais blanc. The grape originated in Burgundy in the fourteenth century, but was harshly (and unfairly) judged by one of Burgundy's powerful dukes (Philippe the Bold) who issued an edict in 1395 banishing the grape from the Côte d'Or to the southern Burgundian region of Beaujolais. His edict read, in part, "a very bad and disloyal variety called Gaamez (the old name of gamay), from which come abundant quantities of wine . . . And this wine of Gaamez is of such a kind that it is very harmful to human creatures, so much so that many people who had it in the past were infested by serious diseases, as we've heard; because said wine from said plant of said nature is full of significant and horrible bitterness. For this reason we solemnly command you . . . all who have said vines of said Gaamez to cut them down or have them cut down, wherever they may be in our country, within five months."

THE GRAPES OF BEAUJOLAIS

RED

GAMAY: More correctly called gamay noir, gamay is effectively the sole grape of Beaujolais, where it makes everything from utterly simple quaffs to more sophisticated fruity wines.

CATEGORIES OF BEAUJOLAIS

By law, Beaujolais is made in three ascending categories of quality (and price). They are:

BEAUJOLAIS

BEAUJOLAIS-VILLAGES

BEAUJOLAIS CRU

Basic Beaujolais—about 50 percent of all the Beaujolais made—is the result of grapes grown mainly in less distinguished (less granitic) vineyards in the south. Soil here is more

THE BEAUJOLAIS CRUS

From north to south, here are the ten villages—*crus*—that produce the most distinctive Beaujolais. The labels on bottles of Beaujolais Cru will usually name the producer and the *cru* only. The word *Beaujolais* will not appear.

ST.-AMOUR: Rich, silky, and sometimes spicy wines; the aroma can suggest peaches. St.-Amour means "holy love." One theory suggests the name is derived from a Roman soldier who, after escaping death, converted to Christianity and set up a mission. He was canonized as St. Amour.

JULIÉNAS: Rich and relatively powerful, the aroma and flavor of Juliénas is floral and spicy. Named after Julius Caesar.

CHÉNAS: A supple and graceful wine, with a subtle bouquet of wild roses. At just under 700 acres (280 hectares), Chénas is the smallest Beaujolais *cru.*

MOULIN-À-VENT: Hearty, rich, and well-balanced in texture, bouquet, and flavor. With Fleurie and Morgon, Moulin-à-Vent is one of the *crus* said to age the best. The name means "windmill," in honor of a three-hundred-year-old stone one that rises above the vines.

FLEURIE: Velvety in texture, with a bouquet both floral and fruity. Fleurie, situated on east-facing slopes that get gentle morning sun, is considered the most feminine of the Beaujolais *crus.*

CHIROUBLES: Grapes for Chiroubles come from some of the vineyards located at the highest altitudes in Beaujolais. The wines are very low in tannin and light-bodied, often with a bouquet of violets.

MORGON: With its soils rich in iron and manganese, Morgon has a personality that stands apart from all the other *crus.* Rich, masculine, and deep purple in color, it's rather full in body for a Beaujolais. It tastes of apricots, peaches, and the earth.

RÉGNIÉ: The newest *cru,* established in 1988, Régnié is relatively full-bodied and round, with red currant and raspberry flavors.

BROUILLY: The wines of Brouilly are fruity with aromas of raspberries, cherries, blueberries, and currants. The pinkish-colored granite soils here yield light-bodied wines. At more than 3,000 acres (1,200 hectares), this is the largest *cru.*

CÔTE DE BROUILLY: Wines from the Côte de Brouilly are heady and lively, with a deep fruity quality. The more powerful expression of fruit is said to be the result of the Côte de Brouilly's elevated location on the slopes of Mont Brouilly, an extinct volcano.

---

fertile, the land is flatter, and the wines tend to be lighter and less concentrated.

Beaujolais-Villages—25 percent of production—is a notch better in quality, and comes from thirty-nine villages in the hilly midsection of the region. Soil here is poorer, composed of granite and sand, forcing the vines to yield better, riper grapes.

Better still are the Beaujolais Crus—the final 25 percent of production. In Beaujolais the word *cru* does not indicate a vineyard as it does in other French regions, but instead refers to ten distinguished villages. Beaujolais Cru wines come from these villages, all of which are located on steep granite hills (about 1,000 feet/305 meters in elevation) in the northern part

Nicole Chanrion (left), shown with her sister Michèle, runs her family's winery Domaine de la Voûte des Crozes in Côte-de-Brouilly. Chanrion does every task herself—from pruning the vines and driving the tractor to making the wine and bottling it.

of Beaujolais. Cru wines are denser, richer, and more expressive than basic Beaujolais. Not surprisingly, they are also capable of aging, thanks to their greater structures.

THE LAND, THE GRAPES, AND THE VINEYARDS

The 42,000 acres (17,000 hectares) of Beaujolais vineyards carpet a corridor 35 miles (56 kilometers) long and about 9 miles (14 kilometers) wide. On the east is the Saône River valley, on the west, the Monts de Beaujolais, a mountainous spur of the Massif Central. The climate is continental, with cold winters and hot, mostly dry summers. The region is divided in two. The northern (Haut) Beaujolais is where the highly desirable granite soils are found. All ten of the Cru Beaujolais villages are located in the north. The southern (Bas) Beaujolais is dominated by sedimentary rock and clay soils. Basic Beaujolais tends to come from vineyards in the south.

WHEN YOU VISIT . . . BEAUJOLAIS

WINEMAKERS IN BEAUJOLAIS are warm and welcoming, and the region is unpretentious and joyfully focused on eating and drinking. It's been said that Beaujolais flows in the veins of every cook here, and indeed the region is full of terrific country restaurants specializing in home cooking. Lyon—considered the gastronomic capital of France and the place where bistros first began—is less than 15 miles (24 kilometers) from the southern part of Beaujolais and just north of where the Rhône Valley begins. Many lovers of French cuisine consider a meal in Lyon worth the price of an international plane ticket.

TWO OF THE CRUS especially worth visiting are Moulin-à-Vent with its famous windmill (the unofficial symbol of Beaujolais) and Chiroubles. the highest in elevation, so hikers take note, this is the hill to climb. At the top is the reward—a panoramic view of the Haut Beaujolais and an excellent tasting cellar where you can taste an array of local wines.

BEAUJOLAIS NOUVEAU

Beaujolais Nouveau is regular Beaujolais, from the lesser districts, that is seven to nine weeks old. Nearly a century ago, casks of the just-made, grapey wine would be shipped by paddleboat down the Saône River to the bars and bistros of Lyon (and later, Paris). By the 1960s, the wine had become a successful PR campaign—a way of getting quick recognition (and cash), all under the guise of celebrating

The church of Régnié la Durette amid the gamay vines of Régnié. The westernmost of the Beaujolais cru, Régnié became the tenth cru in 1988.

TO CHILL OR NOT TO CHILL?

*C*hill it—but just a little. When Beaujolais is served just below room temperature, but not cold to the touch (fifteen minutes in the refrigerator will work), its flavors explode with fruit and spice. Chilling the wine is also customary in the region. Historically in Beaujolais, on summer Sundays, jugs of the wine would be set in buckets of cold water and placed under the shade of a tree in the center of the village so that men playing boules would have something to slake their thirst.

the harvest. Nearly half a million cases of Nouveau were being sold. Today, Beaujolais Nouveau still accounts for about half of all basic Beaujolais made.

In 1985, France's Institut National des Appellations d'Origine (INAO) established the third Thursday in November as the wine's uniform release date. (Interestingly, in the rush to release Nouveau on the official date, growers sometimes have to pick early, before the grapes are ripe, thus undermining the quality of the wine.) While theoretically there is better and worse Nouveau, in fact, much of the wine tastes merely like melted purple Popsicles. Drinking it gives you the same kind of silly pleasure as eating cookie dough.

The Beaujolais to Know

The wines below are all what might be called "serious" Beaujolais—made by small-scale producers using artisanal methods. (Nothing reminiscent of Popsicles and melted Jell-O here.) Beaujolais such as these are utterly delicious fruit-driven, mineral-spiked wines waiting for food.

DOMINIQUE PIRON

MORGON | CÔTE DU PY

100% gamay

Dominique Piron's Morgon makes me envision black raspberries nudged against chocolate cake. It's joyful, hedonistic wine to be sure. But the structure is also serious and impeccable, and the light waves of sandalwood-like spice add an especially enticing note to the aroma. The Piron family has been growing grapes here since the sixteenth century, making Dominique a fourteenth-generation winemaker. The Côte de Py is a small hill within Morgon that produces especially concentrated flavors.

MARCEL LAPIERRE

MORGON

100% gamay

Deliciously spicy, the Morgons of Marcel Lapierre are also very pure and racy. The gorgeous burst of gamay fruit in the wines is counterbalanced by high notes of flowers and deep notes of minerals, creating a very complex sensory experience. Marcel Lapierre became legendary for spearheading the Gang of Four, a group of four Beaujolais winemakers who, starting in the 1970s, fought against the use of pesticides and argued for a return to the old days of high-quality wine production.

JULIEN SUNIER

RÉGNIÉ

100% gamay

Julien Sunier is a small producer whose elegant Régniés have intense floral and spicy notes. One could, for all the world, be standing in a sunny field of wildflowers on the hills of Beaujolais. The wines' textures are so silky, the fruit in the wine is so seductive, that it's nearly impossible to stop drinking. The son of a hairdresser, Julien caught the wine bug from his mother's client Christophe Roumier (of Domaine Georges Roumier) and traveled the world learning about wine before settling down on his tiny estate to make his magnetic wines.

JEAN-PAUL BRUN

FLEURIE | DOMAINES DES TERRES DORÉES

100% gamay

Although granite soils do not yield granite-tasting wines (the mechanisms by which minerality in wine occur are intricate and poorly understood), the stony flavors in this wine, coupled with the lively, fresh, palate-drenching splashes of cherry fruit, are in a word, sensational. Lipsmacking yet sophisticated. My kind of wine.

MICHEL TÊTE

JULIÉNAS | DOMAINE DU CLOS DU FIEF

100% gamay

Deliciousness hit dead-on. The mineral-strewn, rich cherry fruit in this wine seems so deeply embedded that the wine just keeps evolving for hours after the bottle is opened. (If it lasts for hours, that is.) I love the synthesis of flowers, minerals, and fruits; and the texture is utterly silky. Michel Tête, grandson of a barrel manufacturer who started the estate, uses Burgundian techniques to create his concentrated wines.

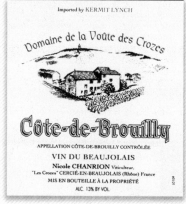

DOMAINE DE LA VOÛTE DES CROZES

CÔTE DE BROUILLY

100% gamay

This wine changed the way I view Beaujolais. Its serious aromas of rocks, minerals, granite, and salt are anything but frivolous. But then, a split second later, a firehose of gushing fruit (pomegranates, peaches, and raspberries) comes at you. And in their wake, you feel as if the sky just rained down violets. In a way that is totally charming, this irresistible Beaujolais has both impact and beauty. The domaine is owned and worked by Nicole Chanrion, one of the few women winemakers in the region, who tends all 16 acres entirely by herself, from pruning the vineyards and driving the tractors to making and bottling the wine.

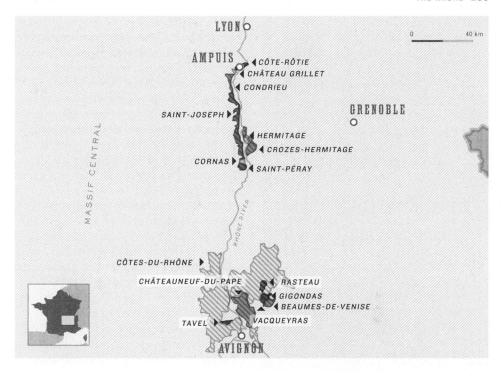

THE RHÔNE

f I had to name France's three greatest regions, I would say: Bordeaux
(for the aristocracy of the best
wines made there); Burgundy (for
what it teaches us about elegance
in wine); and the Rhône (for the uninhibited, fearless, almost savage flavors that the
top wines possess). There is no question that
among the world's greatest *red* wines, Rhônes
are the most untamed. Their howlingly spicy,
dark flavors can seem almost caged, ready to
explode with fierceness. Rhônes are the wine
equivalent of a primal scream.

The Rhône Valley takes its name from the
Rhône River, which begins high in the Swiss
Alps and flows into France through the canyons of the Jura Mountains. South of Lyon
and just north of Ampuis, where the vineyards
begin, the river makes a sharp turn and plunges
southward for 250 miles (400 kilometers)

until it washes into the Mediterranean, just
west of Marseille.

The valley is divided into two parts: the
northern Rhône, smaller and a bit more prestigious, and the southern Rhône, larger and
better known. It takes about an hour to drive
between the two, and along the way, you see
only patches of isolated vineyards. In fact, the
northern and southern Rhône are so distinct
and different that, were it not for the river that
connects them, they would almost certainly be
considered separate wine regions.

In both the north and the south there
are multiple wine districts, or appellations.
The most renowned northern reds are Côte-
Rôtie and Hermitage; the most famous southern red is Châteauneuf-du-Pape. The popular,
well-priced wines known as Côtes-du-Rhône—
staples in French cafés and many others worldwide—can come from either part of the valley,

THE QUICK SIP
ON THE RHÔNE

THE RHÔNE VALLEY in southeastern France is divided into two parts: the northern Rhône and the southern Rhône. Wines from each are distinctly different.

RED WINES DOMINATE THE REGION, although whites and rosés are also made in the Rhône. The most famous northern Rhône reds are Côte-Rôtie and Hermitage; the most famous southern red is Châteauneuf-du-Pape.

SYRAH IS THE SOLE RED GRAPE in the north. Southern Rhône reds are usually blends of many grapes, the most important of which are grenache and mourvèdre.

The southern Rhône is just the opposite. In such appellations as Châteauneuf-du-Pape, Gigondas, and Vacqueyras, a small chorus of red and white grapes come out to sing, including grenache and syrah, as well as mourvèdre. As we'll see, there is a good reason northern Rhône reds are the expression of one grape and southern Rhônes the expression of many.

The Rhône Valley is one of the oldest wine regions in France. When the Romans arrived some two thousand years ago, the inhabitants of what was then Gaul were drinking wines that the Roman writer Pliny described as excellent. Indeed, wine had been introduced to southern France well before—sometime around 500 B.C.—by the Etruscans (a pre-Roman Italian tribe), and the French had quickly learned the art of winemaking themselves.

All of this said, Rhône wines are not a singular idea. Among the top wines, the large number of small growers here, plus the huge differences in the terroirs, plus the wide range of grape varieties, all add up to a mountain of highly individual, exciting wines.

although most come from tracts of vineyards in the south.

Although twenty-seven varieties of grapes are grown in the Rhône Valley, only a handful of these are of major importance. The others—many of them grapes that have grown in the Rhône for centuries and are simply interplanted with the main varieties—are today used almost nostalgically, to add nuance and what winemakers sometimes call the flavors of tradition. As a matter of law, each appellation specifies which of the twenty-seven grapes can be used within its borders (see The Major Appellations, Wines, and Principal Grapes of the Northern Rhône, page 241, and The Major Appellations, Wines, and Principal Grapes of the Southern Rhône, page 249). Winemakers are then free to create their "personal recipe" blend from the permissible varieties.

The grapes of the northern Rhône are the easiest to remember. All red wines come from only one red grape—syrah. All white wines in the north are made from either viognier or a blend of marsanne and roussanne.

THE NORTHERN RHÔNE

The northern Rhône is where many of the Rhône Valley's rarest and most expensive reds and whites are made. The region begins with Côte-Rôtie, the northernmost appellation, and extends about 50 miles (80 kilometers) south, as far as Cornas and the small, inconsequential St.-Péray. In between are the five appellations: Condrieu, Château-Grillet, St.-Joseph, Hermitage, and Crozes-Hermitage.

The best vineyards cling to narrow, rocky terraces on the steep slopes that loom over the river. The ancient, shallow granite and slate soil there is poor. Erosion is such a threat that, were it not for the terraces and the hand-built stone walls that wearily hold them in place, the vines would slide down the hillsides. Even so, some of this weathered, crumbly soil usually does wash down the slopes in the winter rain, and when it does, Rhône winemakers do what

Harvesting marsanne grapes in the steep vineyards of Hermitage above the city of Tain.

they've always done: haul the precious stuff back up in small buckets.

The climate in the northern Rhône is continental, entirely unlike the climate in the south, which is Mediterranean. In the north, the winters are hard, cold, and wet; the summers are hot. Late spring and early fall fog make the southern orientation of the vineyards critical. Without this good southern exposure, the grapes would not receive enough sunlight and heat to ripen properly. It helps that the well-drained, fractured granite soils retain heat, for the howling, icy northern wind, known as Le Mistral (in the Occitan dialect of southern France, the word means master), can quickly cool the vines.

The only red grape permitted in the northern Rhône is syrah, a natural cross of the white grape mondeuse blanche and the red grape dureza (which itself is a descendent of pinot noir). The cross is thought to have occurred in the Rhône-Alps region of eastern France.

Divine enological wisdom must have been operating when the northern Rhône settled on syrah, for syrah planted there makes what are unquestionably some of the world's most intense wines. Darkly savage and dramatic, they exude corruption, and almost pant with gamy, meaty, animal flavors. (Then there's blood and offal. You can count on Rhône syrahs taking you down into realms of flavor that can't be talked about in polite company.) Plus the flavor that tips you off that you're in the northern Rhône—white pepper, which is evident in virtually every wine here. But pepper is just the beginning. From there, the wines explode with aromas of exotic smoky incense, forest, and leather, while the flavors of black plums, blackberries, and blueberries pile on. The fervor of these flavors is due in part to the age of the vines. Many are at least forty years old, and some broach a hundred. These centurians don't produce many bunches of grapes, but the grapes they do produce are packed with power and concentration.

As for white wine, only a small amount is made here. Condrieu and Château-Grillet are the most renowned and expensive northern

THE GRAPES OF THE RHÔNE

WHITES

BOURBOULENC: A component in southern Rhône blends, especially in white Côtes-du-Rhône, where it adds acidity.

CLAIRETTE: Fresh and beautifully aromatic when grown at low yields, clairette plays a leading role in virtually all of the white Côtes-du-Rhône.

GRENACHE BLANC: The white mutation of grenache and the workhorse white grape of the southern Rhône. Has high alcohol and low acidity.

MACCABEO, PICARDAN, PICPOUL, AND ROLLE (AKA VERMENTINO): Blending grapes of modest quality that are used in southern Rhône blends.

MARSANNE: Important white grape of the northern Rhône. Makes up the majority percentage in Hermitage Blanc, Crozes-Hermitage Blanc, and St.-Joseph Blanc. Also used widely in the south. Usually blended with other white grapes.

MUSCAT BLANC À PETITS GRAINS: The deeply aromatic grape that makes the Rhône's famous fortified dessert wine, Muscat de Beaumes-de-Venise. Considered one of the best grapes among the varieties with muscat in the name.

ROUSSANNE: Elegant, aromatic white of the northern Rhône. Often added to marsanne for finesse. Difficult and hence expensive to grow.

UGNI BLANC: French name for the grape trebbiano Toscano, a prolific white grape grown all over southern and central France. Used as filler in inexpensive southern blends.

VIOGNIER: The most perfumed white of the Rhône. Grown in small quantities in the north, where it becomes Condrieu and Château-Grillet. Small amounts of viognier are also grown in the southern Rhône, where it makes its way into some of the top Côtes-du-Rhône.

REDS

CALITOR: Relatively neutral red used in blends but declining in importance.

CARIGNAN: Used mostly in the south in Côtes-du-Rhône and rosé wines.

CINSAUT: Blending grape in southern Rhônes. Adds finesse and cherry nuances and can make especially lovely rosés.

CLAIRETTE ROSE, COUNOISE, MARSELAN, MUSCARDIN, MUSCAT NOIR, PICPOUL NOIR, TERRET NOIR, AND VACCARÈSE: Minor blending grapes used in many southern Rhônes for aromatic and flavor nuances.

GRENACHE: Leading grape of the southern Rhône. Makes up the dominant percentage of virtually all red blends. Has elegant cherry and raspberry confiture flavors. (A mutation known as grenache gris [gray grenache] is not as high in quality.)

MOURVÈDRE: Major blending grape in southern Rhônes. Gives structure, acidity, and leather and game flavors. It also originated in Spain, where it is called monastrell, or sometimes mataro.

SYRAH: Star grape of the northern Rhône, where it is used alone to make bold, spicy, peppery wines. In the south, it is an important part of such blends as Châteauneuf-du-Pape, Gigondas, and Côtes-du-Rhône.

whites. Both are made exclusively from the perfumed, lush white grape viognier (also indigenous to the Rhône and also the progeny of mondeuse blanche). All other northern Rhône whites—Hermitage Blanc, Crozes-Hermitage Blanc, St.-Joseph Blanc, and so on—are made from two other white grapes: marsanne, the heartbeat of the blend, and roussanne, added for its finesse and exotic aromas and flavors of quince, peaches, and lime blossoms. And finally, no rosés are made in the northern Rhône, although as we'll see, the southern Rhône is well known for them.

Northern Rhône wines are made by tiny, family-owned estates; by larger, well-known, family-owned firms such as M. Chapoutier and E. Guigal; by *négociants* who buy wine, blend it, and then bottle it under their own brand label; and by a few cooperatives (which make the least interesting wines). The small producers are very small. In Côte-Rôtie, for example, there are only sixty vineyards, but more than a hundred producers who make wine from those vineyards.

As they are most everywhere else, winemaking styles in the northern Rhône are moving in a modern direction. Yet certain traditional methods live on. Key among these is the old custom of including the stems along with the grapes during fermentation. Stems profoundly affect a wine, imbuing its aroma and flavor with notes of sandalwood, spice, and a briary character. In addition, since stems as well as grape skins contain tannin, not removing the stems increases the tannin and gives the wines more edge, more grip.

Because the production of most northern Rhônes is limited, and because many vineyards are extremely difficult to work, the wines—especially the top Côte-Rôties and Hermitages—are expensive.

CÔTE-RÔTIE

Some of the most thrilling wines of the Rhône carry the appellation Côte-Rôtie (literally, "roasted hillside"). They are dramatic wines with incisive, earthy, and gamy flavors. Pepper seems to pace back and forth in the glass like a caged animal. All Côte-Rôties are red and based on syrah. No white wine is made in this appellation.

There are slightly less than 600 acres (240 hectares) of Côte-Rôtie vineyards, the best of which are on precipitous granite slopes with grades of up to 60 degrees, facing due south. There are other Côte-Rôtie vineyards on the plateaus above the slopes (the ironic "non-côtes" Côtes). These newer vineyards were permitted to be established when the original appellation was slightly expanded several times in the 1970s and 1980s. In acknowledgment of the inferiority of certain plateau vineyards, some producers willingly declassify the wines made from those vineyards, labeling them Côtes-du-Rhône, rather than the more prestigious Côte-Rôtie.

Wherever they are found, steep vineyards that happen to fall in direct sun are coveted, for the grapes are drenched in light (for ripeness) but cooled by the altitude and breezes (preserving acidity and finesse). Syrah, in particular, needs this yin and yang of warmth and coolness. When it is grown in the hotter, southern Rhône, syrah can be fatter on the palate, but it loses the savage precision and striking ferocity of a great Côte-Rôtie.

Within the Côte-Rôtie are two famous slopes: the Côte Brune and the Côte Blonde. According to a predictable legend, these were named after the daughters—one brunette, one blonde—of an aristocratic feudal lord. The wines are just what the stereotypes suggest. Côte Brunes are generally more tannic and powerful; Côte Blondes, more elegant and racy. If a Côte-Rôtie comes from one of these slopes, or is a blend of the two, the label will say so.

Producers in Côte-Rôtie, and in the Rhône in general, commonly blend grapes from different vineyard sites to achieve complexity. Occasionally, if the vineyard is extraordinary, grapes from it may be vinified separately and made into a wine labeled with the name of the vineyard. Such wines are expensive and ravishing. Among the top vineyards are La Mouline, La Landonne, La Chatillone, La Garde, La Chevalière, and La Turque.

Côte-Rôtie is one of only two top French red wines that, by law, may be made with a small quantity of white grapes blended in (the

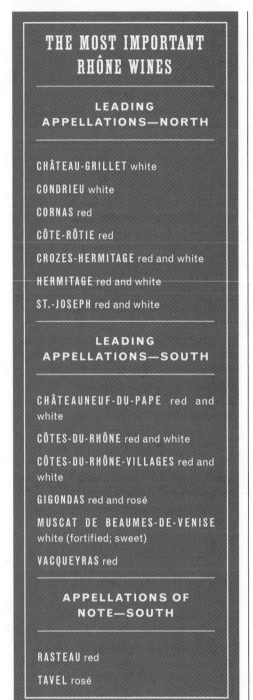

THE MOST IMPORTANT RHÔNE WINES

LEADING APPELLATIONS—NORTH

CHÂTEAU-GRILLET white

CONDRIEU white

CORNAS red

CÔTE-RÔTIE red

CROZES-HERMITAGE red and white

HERMITAGE red and white

ST.-JOSEPH red and white

LEADING APPELLATIONS—SOUTH

CHÂTEAUNEUF-DU-PAPE red and white

CÔTES-DU-RHÔNE red and white

CÔTES-DU-RHÔNE-VILLAGES red and white

GIGONDAS red and rosé

MUSCAT DE BEAUMES-DE-VENISE white (fortified; sweet)

VACQUEYRAS red

APPELLATIONS OF NOTE—SOUTH

RASTEAU red

TAVEL rosé

The tiny appellation of Côte-Rôtie (literally, "Roasted Slope") makes some of the most treasured and hauntingly delicious wines of the Rhône.

many vineyards. Historically, viognier's creamy texture (the result of its high glycerine and low acid levels) was thought to soften the sometimes blunt edges of syrah. Today viognier is included for its exotic aroma as well, making Côte-Rôtie more fascinating. Although up to 20 percent viognier can, by law, be included in red Côte-Rôtie, most producers include less than 5 percent.

The four fairly large, well-known firms in Côte-Rôtie are Guigal, M. Chapoutier, Paul Jaboulet Aîné, and Delas Frères (today owned by the Champagne house of Louis Roederer). In the 1970s, Guigal was one of the first Rhône wineries to age wines partially in new French oak. In the 1990s, Chapoutier wines, in particular, soared in quality as the family firm was taken over by the ambitious son, Michel Chapoutier. In addition to the four impressive firms above, some of the most exciting Côte-Rôties are made by tiny producers, including René Rostaing, Robert Jasmin, Henri Gallet, Jamet, Michel Ogier, J. M. Gerin, Benjamin et David Duclaux, and Château de St. Cosme.

CONDRIEU AND CHÂTEAU-GRILLET

Condrieu and Château-Grillet are the northern Rhône's most famous white wines appellations. One is tiny; the other, microscopic. Château-Grillet, of course, sounds as though it

other being Hermitage). The reason for this is largely practical, since in Côte-Rôtie viognier vines are scattered in among the syrah vines in

THE MAJOR APPELLATIONS, WINES, AND PRINCIPAL GRAPES OF THE NORTHERN RHÔNE

The appellations are listed following the Rhône River north to south. All of the red wines of the northern Rhône are made from one red grape exclusively—syrah. While the region is primarily devoted to red wine, the two small appellations Condrieu and Château-Grillet are both devoted entirely to white wines made from viognier. (No rosés are made in the northern Rhône.)

APPELLATION	WINE(S) MADE	PRINCIPAL RED GRAPE	PRINCIPAL WHITE GRAPE(S)
CÔTE-RÔTIE	red	syrah	none
CONDRIEU	white	none	viognier
CHÂTEAU-GRILLET	white	none	viognier
ST.-JOSEPH	red and white	syrah	roussanne, marsanne
HERMITAGE	red and white	syrah	roussanne, marsanne
CROZES-HERMITAGE	red and white	syrah	roussanne, marsanne
CORNAS	red	syrah	none

is one producer, not an appellation. It is both. Within the appellation Château-Grillet there is but one producer: Château-Grillet. At 8.6 acres (3.5 hectares), it is one of the smallest appellations in France and sits like an enclave within Condrieu. Today it is owned by the Artemis Group, the parent company of Bordeaux's Château Latour.

Both Condrieu and Château-Grillet are made from viognier, an exotically aromatic variety that, to its admirers, is one of the most drippingly sensual white grapes in the world. In great years, and when it's perfectly made, viognier explodes with the heady aromas of honeysuckle, peaches, white melons, lychees, fresh orange peel, and gardenias. The wine's texture is as soothing as fresh whipped cream.

But, the grape is notoriously fickle, sensitive to its site, low in acidity, and difficult to grow. If the producer isn't careful, the wine can seem like cheap perfume.

There is very little viognier in France. In addition to the 270 or so acres (100 hectares) in Condrieu and the 8.6 acres (3.5 hectares) in Château-Grillet, there are smatterings in other

> The village of Condrieu sits at a curve in the Rhône River. The name comes from the French *coin de ruisseau,* "corner of the brook."

At the summit of the Hermitage hill is La Chapelle—a small stone chapel built as a sanctuary in 1235 by the knight Gaspard de Stérimberg. Today, La Chapelle and the renowned vineyards surrounding it are owned by Paul Jaboulet Aîné.

parts of the Rhône, as well as a small amount in the Languedoc-Roussillon. Outside of France, California is the leading producer—growing ten times more viognier than is grown in the Rhone.

The most well-known, top producer of Condrieu is Georges Vernay. Look also for excellent Condrieu from E. Guigal, René Rostaing, André Perret, Dumazet, Yves Cuilleron, Philippe Faury, and Robert Niero.

ST.-JOSEPH

When it was first established in 1956, St.-Joseph was a small, hilly appellation directly across the river from Hermitage. The red wines in particular had a very good reputation. Today, while some St.-Josephs are dynamite, many others lack stuffing, seeming coarse and thin. One reason for this is the appellation's expansion. St.-Joseph has grown into a long, 2,500-acre (1,000-hectare) corridor stretching from Condrieu to the bottom tip of the northern Rhône. Vineyards are now planted where the exposure to the sun is less ideal.

Today as in the past, most St.-Joseph wines are red and based on syrah, with up to 10 percent of the white grapes marsanne and roussanne blended in. About 10 percent of the production of the appellation is white; St.-Joseph Blanc logically is made from marsanne, with touches of roussanne. One of the best, Roger Blachon's, has, in great years, the ethereal texture of the finest honey.

Among the top producers of white and red St.-Joseph are M. Chapoutier, Jean-Louis Chave, Yves Cuilleron, Jean-Louis Grippat, Alain Graillot, and André Perret.

HERMITAGE

In the eighteenth and nineteenth centuries, Hermitage was France's costliest red wine. Not only was it more expensive than the best Bordeaux, but the best Bordeaux (including the First Growths) were often—if secretly—"hermitaged," meaning that Hermitage was secretly blended in to give the Bordeaux extra depth, color, and richness.

The appellation Hermitage is a single 1,000-foot-high (300-meter) hill, with just 300 acres (120 hectares) of vineyards clinging to its mostly southern-facing slope. The whole of Hermitage is smaller than some wine properties in California. The famous soils here are mostly granite, interspersed with gravel, flint, and limestone.

BISTRO LESSONS

*T*he vineyards of the Rhône Valley lie just south of the city Lyon, known as the gastronomic capital of France (north of Lyon, the vineyards of Beaujolais begin). In a country that takes its belly seriously, this unofficial title is no small feat, and Lyon lives up to the challenge with 1,500 restaurants (one restaurant for every 333 residents!). It's no surprise that France's first bistros—and their simpler predecessors, known as bouchons—originated here as family-owned taverns where working men could eat and drink cheaply but well. Even today, a no-frills, roll-up-your-sleeves approach to food remains the city's signature. And no one gets too uppity about wine either—carafes of Côtes-du-Rhône and Beaujolais are never more than an arm's length away. And what better way to wash down poached pork offal sausages (andouillettes), cold chicken liver salad, cheesy potato gratin, curly endive with chunks of salty bacon, or a wine-soaked chicken fricassee?

Predictably, there are many legends concerning hermits who supposedly gave Hermitage its name. The one most often told concerns a medieval crusader, Gaspard de Stérimberg, who, after being wounded in war, was granted, by Queen Blanche de Castille, the right to establish a sanctuary on top of the hill. A small, ancient stone chapel still marks the spot. It is for this chapel that La Chapelle, the impressive top wine of Paul Jaboulet Aîné, is named.

Along with Côte-Rôtie, red Hermitage is the most revered wine of the northern Rhône. In great years, Hermitage is a leathery, meaty red, packed with blackberry and black cherry fruits and smoky, damp earth flavors. The famous English scholar and wine writer George Saintsbury once described Hermitage as "the manliest wine" he'd ever drunk.

As in Côte-Rôtie, the only red grape in Hermitage is syrah. It is generally vinified in a traditional manner and aged either in large casks for up to three years or in small oak barrels, some percentage of which are new. Up to 15 percent white grapes (marsanne and/or roussanne) are allowed in red Hermitage, but few producers add them.

The rare white wine Hermitage Blanc, made from marsanne and roussanne, tends to be a full-throttle, full-bodied, bold-tasting, rich, almost masculine white wine, sometimes with a fascinating oily, resiny texture. In the best wines, the roussanne lifts the wine and adds hints of peaches, quince, almonds, honeysuckle, and lime. The two best examples of Hermitage Blanc are Jean-Louis Chave's Hermitage Blanc and M. Chapoutier's Ermitage l'Ermite Blanc. Both are massive wines with swaths of flavor so bold they seem like brushstrokes on an Impressionist painting.

The top Hermitage producers, some of whom make both red and white wine, include E. Guigal, Jean-Louis Chave, Marc Sorrel, M. Chapoutier, and Paul Jaboulet Aîné.

CROZES-HERMITAGE

Following Hermitage tradition, Crozes-Hermitage makes red wines from syrah, as well as a tiny amount of white wine from marsanne and a bit of roussanne. The Crozes-Hermitage vineyards, however, are mostly on the flatlands that spread out south and east of the hill of Hermitage. The area they cover is ten times larger than Hermitage; indeed Crozes-Hermitage is the largest appellation in the northern Rhône.

Because Crozes-Hermitage comes from less distinguished, higher-yielding vineyards, it is usually less concentrated than either Côte-Rôtie or Hermitage. That said, there are a few top-notch producers of Crozes-Hermitage, notably Alain Graillot, whose wine—vibrant, complex, severe, and peppery—is easily

The Rhône Valley takes many of its culinary cues from the city just north of it—Lyon (known as the gastronomic capital of France). The restaurant Le Petit Glouton specializes in crepes and traditional bistro fare.

the equal of many Hermitages, at less than half the price. Other top producers to know are Albert Belle, M. Chapoutier, and Domaine Combier.

CORNAS

Cornas, from the old Celtic word for burnt or scorched earth, is a tiny region that sits at the southern end of the northern Rhône. Only red wines are made here, all of them exclusively from syrah. At their best, Cornas are dense, edgy, masculine wines with a phalanx of white pepper that hits you in the teeth. A split second later, a briary character explodes on your palate, and, if the Cornas is especially untamed, that may be followed by what can only be described as the sense that your tongue is being lashed by strips of black leather. Cornas is not everyone's cup of tea, but those of us who love it, love it madly. Aging is a critical factor. In the Rhône Valley, Cornas is generally drunk after it has been aged for seven to ten years and has taken on a fine leatheriness and earthiness.

As in Côte-Rôtie and Hermitage, Cornas's best vineyards are on dangerously steep hillsides precariously held in place by ancient terraces with stone walls. The vineyards, interspersed with patches of oak and juniper forest, face due south. The hills above block cool winds from the north. Both the light and the heat of the sun are intense. It's a perfect equation for powerful wine. Top Cornas producers include Auguste Clape, Jean-Luc Colombo, Thierry Allemand, and Franck Balthazar.

The Northern Rhône Wines to Know

Be prepared. The wines below are a collective primal scream. Northern Rhône wines are tempests of wild flavor . . . and for those of us who love them, the wilder, the better. In particular, the daringly intense syrahs here have no equivalent elsewhere in the wine world. Falling in love with them isn't easy at first, but it is a right of passage.

WHITES

M. CHAPOUTIER

ERMITAGE | L'ERMITE

100% marsanne

This is my vote for the most massive white wine of France. So strong and "present," its impact (though not its flavor) is like Cognac—a full-throttle experience to be sure. Great Hermitage whites, such as L'Ermite (spelled without the *H*, the way it was before the nineteenth century, when the British, who had a monopoly on distribution, added the *H*), are hard to describe. They are relatively low in acid, not fruity, not spicy, and not sweet, although, like this one, they often taste a bit like honey or caramel, absent the sugar. Bold and broad on the palate, L'Ermite can only be described as commanding, with a gravitas that rivals the most intense red. The Chapoutier family also makes wines in the southern Rhône, and their Châteauneuf-du-Pape, called Barbe Rac, is sensational.

YVES CUILLERON

CONDRIEU | LES CHAILLETS

100% viognier

Yves Cuilleron is one of the Rhône's shining lights. His exquisite Condrieu fills your mouth as opulently as a spoonful of whipped cream. The incredible honeysuckle and soft vanilla flavors are utterly refined, yet rich. More than many other producers, Cuilleron has enormous talent when it comes to weaving lushness together with elegance.

REDS

ALAIN GRAILLOT

CROZES-HERMITAGE | LA GUIRAUDE

100% syrah

Graillot makes one of the few great Crozes-Hermitages, a wine many believe is the equal of Hermitage—at less than half the cost. This is a dark, brooding, edgy, Clint Eastwood of a wine, with flavors that wrestle each other in the glass. Spices, pepper, earth, blackberries, and violets all collide in a delicious explosion. La Guiraude, a special selection of the best lots of wine, is made only in very good years. Not to worry. Graillot's regular Crozes-Hermitage is also pretty wonderful.

DOMAINE JEAN-LOUIS CHAVE

HERMITAGE

100% syrah

Hermitage has been called the manliest of wines, and this one has the sort of sensual darkness that fits the bill precisely. At first, the huge, mesmerizing aromas and flavors suggest smoking meat, leather, sweat, and damp earth. But Chave's wines are so complex, they can pour forth new flavors by the minute. The Chave family has been making Hermitage since the fifteenth century, and over those centuries very little about the winemaking has changed.

E. GUIGAL

CÔTE-RÔTIE | LA MOULINE

Almost entirely syrah, with a trace of viognier

Guigal is one of the most outstanding producers in the Rhône, year in and year out making textbook Rhônes, sensuous wines of profound depth and concentration. When I was just beginning my wine career, it was a Guigal Côte-Rôtie, Brune et Blonde, (a blend of grapes from two vineyards evocatively named the brunette and the blonde), that convinced me that nothing on earth was quite as mesmerizing, as intellectually riveting as a great wine. I still love Brune et Blonde, but if one of Guigal's stars shines just a little bit brighter than all the others, it is its Côte-Rôtie known as La Mouline, one of three esteemed single-vineyard wines in the Guigal portfolio (the other two are La Turque and La Landonne, leading collectors to give them the nickname "the La La's"). Sweetly rich and ripe, a great La Mouline is fat with velvety-textured boysenberry/cassis fruit interwoven with violets and exotic spices, and buttressed against a dramatic, almost primal gaminess. The heady aroma alone is enough to stop you in your tracks.

JEAN-LUC COLOMBO

CORNAS | LES RUCHETS

100% syrah

Here it is—quintessential Cornas: brooding, black, massive, earthy, leathery, and yet somehow voluptuous at the same time. Jean-Luc Colombo, restless, driven, and impatient, turns out some of the most sensational Cornas today. In Colombo's hands, Les Ruchets (the beehives) sacrifices none of its power, but there's an elegance, a sweet ripeness here, too, that's seductive. Colombo's mother was a chef, and he makes all of his wines, he says, with food in mind. So what did he have in mind with this? Wild hare.

PAUL JABOULET AÎNÉ

HERMITAGE | LA CHAPELLE

100% syrah

Named for the thirteenth-century chapel on the top of the Hermitage hill, this is a legendary wine, and a wine every syrah lover should have at least once. As with all great wines, you can lose yourself in it. The animal fur and campfire aromas have savage appeal, and the texture—like black licorice melting on your palate—is hedonistic to be sure. Despite its suppleness and grace, La Chapelle has enormous structure and is one of the most age-worthy of all Rhônes.

RENE ROSTAING

CÔTE-RÔTIE

100% syrah

The flavors in Rostaing's Côte-Rôties usually begin quietly, like a whisper, then crash in wave after wave of delicious intensity. Taste buds need seat belts for this wine. All of the quintessential northern Rhône flavors and aromas are here: white pepper and exotic spices, incense, roasted meat, gaminess, plowed earth, blueberries, and blackberries. Rostaing, a small producer, is known for wines full of energy and personality.

The forbidding, impossible-to-farm vineyards of the southern Rhône Valley defy belief. Pieces of rock sheared off Alpine glaciers tumbled and rolled as they were carried down the Rhône River, ultimately becoming the rounded "galets" in which the vineyards of Châteauneuf-du-Pape are planted.

THE SOUTHERN RHÔNE

No one can resist the charm of southern France—especially the magical place known as Châteauneuf-du-Pape ("new castle of the Pope"). The southern Rhône's best-known appellation, Châteauneuf-du-Pape is close by the striking historic walled city of Avignon, and has some of the most rocky, breathtaking vineyards in France. And the wine—the wine is sheer sensuality.

Châteauneuf, however, is just one of several wine regions in the southern Rhône. The other two major ones are Gigondas and Vacqueyras, followed by southern France's self-styled capital of rosé, Tavel. In addition, most of the Côtes-du-Rhône and Côtes-du-Rhône-Villages wines come from southern vineyards.

The southern Rhône does not begin where the north leaves off but about an hour's drive farther south. In between, only a few patches of vineyard can be found. The gulf of separation is significant. The southern and northern Rhône have little in common, except the river that gives them their names. The differences in climate are major. The southern Rhône is part

"The inseparable connection in southern France between wine, food, and the earth reminds me that wine is a gift from God. In a visceral sense, drinking Châteauneuf-du-Pape and eating local sausages becomes a way of transcending time, of experiencing that which, though it may seem temporal, is, in fact, timeless."

— STEVE EDMUNDS,
co-owner, Edmunds St. John Winery, which specializes in Rhône wines made in California

of the sunny, herb-scented, lavender-strewn, olive-growing Mediterranean. Hot days are pierced by Le Mistral, the savage, cold wind that blows down from the Alps and through the Rhône River valley, gathering speed and ferocity as it goes. Although you can barely stand up when the mistral is blowing hard, it nonetheless is often a grape grower's friend.

THE MAJOR APPELLATIONS, WINES, AND PRINCIPAL GRAPES OF THE SOUTHERN RHÔNE

Twenty-three grape varieties are permitted in the southern Rhône, although not all of them are legal in all appellations. The twenty-three fall into two groups: principal varieties and secondary varieties. The principal varieties are listed below. Today, many of the secondary varieties are used only in tiny amounts, if they are used at all. These secondary varieties include, for red wines: calitor, carignan, counoise, gamay, muscardin, pinot noir, terret noir, and vaccarèse; and for white wines: marsanne, roussanne, picardan, picpoul, viognier, ugni blanc, macabeo, and muscat blanc à petits grains. Rosé wines can be made from a combination of any of the grapes, red and white. As always with wine, however, there are some notable exceptions. Roussanne, for example, is the grape on which Château de Beaucastel's famous white Châteauneuf-du-Pape Vieilles Vignes is based. There are also interesting peculiarities. Muscat is grown only in Beaumes-de-Venise. And only Châteauneuf-du-Pape allows slightly more than half of all the twenty-three varieties (see The Châteauneuf "Thirteen," page 251).

APPELLATION	WINE(S) MADE	PRINCIPAL RED GRAPE(S)	PRINCIPAL WHITE GRAPE(S)
CHÂTEAUNEUF-DU-PAPE	red and white	grenache, syrah, mourvèdre, cinsaut	grenache blanc, clairette, bourboulenc
GIGONDAS	red and rosé	grenache, syrah, mourvèdre, cinsaut	none
VACQUEYRAS	red, white, and rosé	grenache, syrah, mourvèdre, cinsaut	grenache blanc, clairette, bourboulenc
RASTEAU	red	grenache, syrah, mourvèdre	none
TAVEL	rosé	grenache, syrah, mourvèdre, cinsaut	clairette, bourboulenc
CÔTES-DU-RHÔNE AND CÔTES-DU-RHÔNE-VILLAGES	red, white, and rosé	grenache, syrah, mourvèdre, cinsaut, carignan	grenache blanc, clairette, bourboulenc, roussanne, viognier
MUSCAT DE BEAUMES-DE-VENISE	fortified sweet white	none	muscat blanc à petits grains

LE MISTRAL

No one who has ever experienced Le Mistral will ever forget it. The treacherous wind (named after the Occitan—Provençal—dialect word for masterly, or master) barrels out of the Alps unexpectedly, traveling hundreds of miles/kilometers south, picking up speed as it goes. The mistral is especially treacherous by the time it gets to the southern Rhône, and caught in it, you can be lifted into the air or slammed to the ground.

The mistral is helpful for vines in some ways; detrimental in others. During the growing season, it cools down the vines, helping the grapes retain acidity. Near harvest time it acts like a giant blow-dryer, making sure the grapes are free of humidity and mold. The wind also causes substantial evaporation, which then concentrates the sugar and acid inside the grapes. The mistral can be so violent, however, that it can rip apart the vines. As a result, the best vineyards are found in partly sheltered pockets of land, and the vines are pruned low to the ground. The older, gnarled ones look like twisted black dwarfs slanted sideways from years of trying to hang on to the earth despite the strong, cold wind whipping through.

There are significant differences between northern and southern Rhône in the proximity and orientation of the vineyards to the river. In the north, vineyards are poised above and so close to the river they almost seem as though they could fall into it. In the south, they spread out from the river for 20 to 30 miles (32 to 48 kilometers) over flatter land and gentler hillocks.

Soil in the south is also fundamentally different from the granitic soils of the north. In many parts of the south, vines are planted in what looks like a vast carpet of riverbed rocks, some the size of cantaloupes. Elsewhere, the soils are either clay, sandy limestone, or gravel.

Grenache, not syrah, is the leading red grape of the south. But what is even more significant is that, unlike northern Rhône wines, which are intense wines based on a single grape variety, southern Rhône wines are almost always, like rainbows of flavor, combinations of many different varieties. The reason? In the southern Rhône's hot, dry climate, such classic grapes as syrah can lose their focus and intensity. Other, less noble grapes may adapt well to the heat, but they rarely possess enough character on their own to make a satisfactory wine. Blending is a way of creating a whole wine that is more than the sum of its parts (see The Major Appellations, Wines, and Principal Grapes of the Southern Rhône, page 249).

The southern Rhône has almost sixty cooperatives, and they have amazing clout. They make dozens—sometimes hundreds—of

À droit ou à gauche? *A street corner with helpful advice for visiting the wineries of Châteauneuf-du-Pape.*

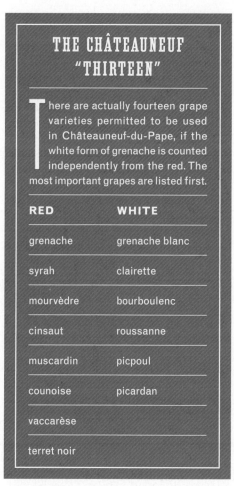

THE CHÂTEAUNEUF "THIRTEEN"

There are actually fourteen grape varieties permitted to be used in Châteauneuf-du-Pape, if the white form of grenache is counted independently from the red. The most important grapes are listed first.

RED	WHITE
grenache	grenache blanc
syrah	clairette
mourvèdre	bourboulenc
cinsaut	roussanne
muscardin	picpoul
counoise	picardan
vaccarèse	
terret noir	

CHÂTEAUNEUF-DU-PAPE

The most southern of the major southern Rhône wine appellations, Châteauneuf-du-Pape is just a fifteen-minute drive from the historic city of Avignon. The region, which encompasses the plateaus and slopes around the town of Châteauneuf-du-Pape, plus four adjacent villages, is large by Rhône standards—slightly more than 8,000 acres (3,200 hectares) (Hermitage has only about 300 acres/ 120 hectares). More wine is made in this one place than in all of the northern Rhône. To put Châteauneuf in perspective, however, the Napa Valley is more than four times larger, and Bordeaux is thirty-four times larger.

Before World War I, much of the Châteauneuf-du-Pape harvest was sold in bulk to Burgundy, to be used as *vin de médecine*—a quick fix of alcohol to boost Burgundy's

CHÂTEAUNEUF-DU-EXTRATERRESTRIAL

The vintners of Châteauneuf-du-Pape have always been fastidious when it comes to creating laws that will protect their vineyards. In a legendary 1954 municipal decree, they mandated the following:

ARTICLE 1. *The flying overhead, landing, and taking off of aeronautical machines called "flying saucers" or "flying cigars," of whatever nationality they may be, is strictly forbidden on the territory of the commune of Châteauneuf-du-Pape.*

ARTICLE 2. *Any aeronautical machine—"flying saucer" or "flying cigar"—that lands on the territory of the commune will be immediately taken off to the jail.* (No joke.)

different blends that they bottle under scores of brand names, some of which, cleverly, seem like the names of estates. In addition, the cooperatives sell to dozens of *négociants* who do the same thing on a smaller scale.

Two additional types of wine are made in the south that, with minor exceptions, cannot be found in the north: rosés and sweet wines. Tavel, the leading rosé of the southern Rhône, is also (thanks to tourism in southern France) one of the most well-known rosés in the world. The south's sweet wine is equally famous: muscat de Beaumes-de-Venise.

Of all the southern Rhône's important wine appellations, the one that can rival the north's Côte-Rôtie or Hermitage is Châteauneuf-du-Pape, so it leads off our exploration of the southern Rhône.

THE NAME
CHÂTEAUNEUF-DU-PAPE

C
*hâteauneuf-du-Pape, "new cas-
tle of the pope," refers to the
time in the fourteenth century
when the pope resided not in Rome but
in the walled city of Avignon, just south
of these vineyards. (At the time, what we
call Châteauneuf-du-Pape was called
Châteauneuf-Calcernier, after a nearby
village and its limestone quarry.) The
pope who instigated this startling change
in residence was the Frenchman Clement V
(in Bordeaux, Château Pape-Clément
is named after him). Later, his succes-
sor, John XXII, built a new papal summer home out among the vineyards. It
wasn't until the twentieth century, after
vast improvements were made in the vineyards and winemaking, that the new name
Châteauneuf-du-Pape took hold. Today
most bottles of estate-grown Châteauneuf-
du-Pape are embossed with the papal
crown and St. Peter's keys, as an acknowledgment of the region's holy history.*

strength. Decades later, the practice was still
commonplace. Only since the 1970s has the
number of quality-minded southern Rhône
producers increased significantly, and today
more than any other wines, the top reds of
Châteauneuf-du-Pape define the southern
Rhône. They are often not the big, blowsy,
easygoing wines you might expect from a warm
Mediterranean region. Just the opposite. These
are penetrating, sassy wines that can come at
you with a dagger of earthy, gamy flavors. They
have a wildness to them, a fascinating edge of
tar, leather, and rough stone. They beg for a hot
night, chewy bread, and a dish loaded with garlic, black olives, and wild herbs.

Of all the things that set Châteauneuf apart,
the most startling is its "soil" composed largely
of smooth, rolled stones. They are everywhere.
Many vineyards are simply vast rock beds with
no visible dirt whatsoever. The stones and
rocks—known as *galets*—which range from
fist-size to the size of a small pumpkin, are the
remnants of ancient Alpine glaciers. The with-
drawal of these glaciers, along with temperature increases, ripped quartzite off the flanks
of the Alps. Over many millennia, these chunks
of quartzite were rolled, broken, and rounded
by the tumultuous waters of the then larger
Rhône River. As the river receded, the stones
were left scattered over the plateaus and terraces. Although there is soil underneath the
stones, varying from clay to sandy limestone to
gravel, the land is extremely difficult to work,
and tending the vineyards is a painstakingly
slow process.

What southern Rhône vineyards do not
lack is heat. Unfortunately, the stones retain
this heat and therefore hasten ripening. At the
same time, however, the stones protect the
ground from becoming parched and dry and
help hold moisture in the soil, a boon for the
vines, especially as summer proceeds.

Approximately 95 percent of Châteauneuf-
du-Pape is red, although there are white and
rosé wines. The grapes that can be used are
the so-called Châteauneuf thirteen (actually
fourteen)—eight reds and six whites. Almost
no producer other than Château de Beaucastel
grows and makes wine from the whole gamut.
The majority of Châteauneufs are based on
grenache grown until it is sweetly ripe and
tasting like homemade jam. Blended into
the grenache are syrah, to deepen the color
and add spice, as well as mourvèdre, which
adds structure. Other red grapes may play
a role, too, but none are as important as
these three.

Among the top Châteauneuf-du-Pape
whites are two from Château de Beaucastel:
their leading wine, known as Cuvée Classique,
and the rarer Vieilles Vignes (remarkably, made
solely from roussanne); as well as those from
Château Rayas, Clos des Papes, Château La
Nerthe, Château de la Gardine, Les Cailloux,
and Domaine du Vieux Télégraphe.

Old bottles lying in the cellars of Vieux Télégraphe in Châteauneuf-du-Pape. The estate was named after an old telegraph station that stood on the hill of the Le Crau plateau where the winery was eventually established in 1898.

Two important factors in the making of Châteauneuf-du-Pape are yield and oak (actually, the absence of oak). Yield is pivotal because at high yields, the grapes that make up Châteauneuf all taste terrible and thin. As a result, and not surprisingly, by law, Châteauneuf-du-Pape is required to have the lowest yields in France—35 hectoliters per hectare (368 gallons per acre). This is about half the yield at most Bordeaux estates, for example.

As for oak, you don't see many small, new oak barrels in the southern Rhône, and there's a reason for that. Grenache is usually vinified in large cement tanks (grenache is easily susceptible to oxidation, so wooden barrels, which are porous, are not ideal). Wines made from other grapes, such as syrah and mourvèdre, are usually made in large, old barrels called *foudres*. Because the wines are generally not put in small, new oak barrels, they don't have the unmistakable toast/vanilla character that new oak imparts. Instead, you taste what Châteauneuf-du-Papes (as well as Gigondas and Vacqueyras) are truly about: stones and soil—the unadorned flavors of their terroir.

MADE FOR FROMAGE

Maybe it's their dark intensity, or the way they evoke an almost primordial earthiness, but Châteauneuf-du-Pape, Vacqueyras, and Gigondas all beg for a good—a really sensual—cheese. If you visit these wine regions, there is no better place to find one (or several) than La Fromagerie du Comtat, in the center of the old walled city of Carpentras, which is about ten minutes from Châteauneuf-du-Pape. The aroma that hits you as you open the door of the *fromagerie* assures you that you're in the right place, for it's unmistakably the sort of aroma that would make a U.S. health department inspector blanch. The cheeses, all handmade raw milk cheeses from local, small farms, are sensational. Don't miss the tiny chèvres (goat's milk cheese) wrapped in chestnut leaves, or the utterly amazing sheep's milk cheese wrapped in crushed white wine grapes that have been affected by *Botrytis cinerea,* or "noble rot."

ONE OF THE PLACES WHERE PHYLLOXERA BEGAN

Just north of Tavel is Lirac, a modest place that makes even more modest wines. But Lirac does have one claim to fame: It's thought to be one of the areas where the European phylloxera epidemic began. According to John Livingstone-Learmonth, in *The Wines of the Rhône,* sometime around 1863 the innovative owner of Château de Clary decided to plant a few California vine cuttings to see how they'd fare in the south of France. The cuttings, unable to adapt, died. The microscopic insects (phylloxera) clinging to the cuttings' roots survived. Phylloxera destroyed the vineyards at Château de Clary and from there spread through neighboring vineyards. But phylloxera's presence already extended beyond the southern Rhône, for at that time Europe permitted extensive importation of living plants. Also in 1863, a professor at Oxford University reported finding phylloxera in plants growing outside London. Within a few years, there were several reports of the pest in the Languedoc, and by 1869, there was evidence of phylloxera in Bordeaux.

Finally, it's interesting to note that, in the wake of phylloxera and World War I, regulations enacted in the early 1920s to improve Châteauneuf-du-Pape later became the basis for France's monumental *Appellation d'Origine Contrôlée* (AOC) laws.

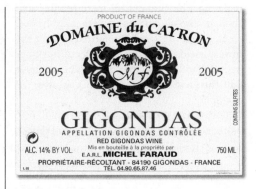

SOME OF THE BEST PRODUCERS OF CHÂTEAUNEUF-DU-PAPE

Château de Beaucastel • Château de la Gardine • Château La Nerthe • Château Rayas • Clos des Papes • Clos du Mont Olivet • Domaine de Beaurenard • Domaine de Chante-Perdrix • Domaine de la Charbonnière • Domaine de la Janasse • Domaine du Pégau • Font de Michelle • Le Bosquet des Papes • Le Vieux Donjon • Les Cailloux • M. Chapoutier • Vieux Télégraphe

GIGONDAS

The Gigondas vineyards cover a series of hills just below the jagged spurs of rock known as the Dentelles de Montmirail. This is the most northern of the important southern Rhône appellations. A few miles/kilometers south of it is Vacqueyras, and south of that and to the west is Châteauneuf-du-Pape.

Maybe Gigondas took its cue from the rugged Dentelles, for its wines are as strong and appealing as a firm handshake. The best have explosive raspberry, leather, and spice aromas and flavors and chewy textures. They are often characterized as robust versions of Châteauneuf, but the truth is they have an altogether different personality. To drink Gigondas is to go back to a time when great red wines were muscular—a time before

The Pont-Saint Bénezet—better known as the Pont d'Avignon—about which many poems and songs have been written. The bridge spans the Rhône River within the famous medieval town of Avignon to which the papacy was temporarily relocated (from Rome) in the 14th century.

winemakers knew how to soften up wine and give it polish.

Ninety-nine percent of Gigondas is red; 1 percent is rosé. By law, the reds must be no more than 80 percent grenache, with no less than 15 percent syrah and/or mourvèdre blended in. The remaining fraction is often cinsaut, but may be made up of any other red Rhône grape except carignan.

The top producers include Domaine du Cayron, Domaine la Garrigue, Les Hauts de Montmirail, Grand Bourjassot, Domaine Santa Duc, St. Cosme, and Domaine les Pallières.

VACQUEYRAS

Just south of Gigondas, Vacqueyras became an appellation in 1990. Before that, wines from this area were labeled Côtes-du-Rhône-Villages. Vacqueyras are sturdy, bold red wines—rather like even more rustic versions of Gigondas. The best smell and taste like the land itself; there's the aroma of sun on the hot, stony ground, of scrappy dried brush and wild herbs. Charging through this is the flavor of black currants, blueberries, and pepper.

Grenache, syrah, mourvèdre, and cinsaut are the dominant grapes. But whereas Gigondas are weighted toward grenache, most

BEAUMES-DE-VENISE

Beaumes-de-Venise, one of the top small villages of the southern Rhône, is associated with two types of wine. The wine simply called Beaumes-de-Venise is a dry red, like its better-known sisters Vacqueyras and Gigondas. But the village is more famous for its historic fortified sweet wine, muscat de Beaumes-de-Venise, made from the brazenly aromatic grape muscat blanc à petits grains.

Drinking a glass of it is a powerful experience thanks to the fortification, and while peach, apricot, and orange flavors dance in the glass, the wine is not sugary sweet. Indeed, southern Rhône locals often drink it as an aperitif. Among the best muscats de Beaumes-de-Venise are those from Paul Jaboulet Aîné, Domaine Durban, Domaine Coyeux, and Vidal-Fleury.

AN ANCIENT MEDITERRANEAN MARRIAGE

Throughout the Mediterranean, the affinity between lamb and wine is centuries old. And for good reason. Historically, much of the Mediterranean's ancient, arid, impoverished soils could support only the least demanding crops and livestock. And thus, in regions as diverse as Bordeaux, Greece, north-central Spain (Rioja and Ribera del Duero), and southern France (the Rhône and Provence), grazing sheep and planting vineyards became a way of life. Today, in each of those wine regions, lamb is considered the quintessential accompaniment for the local wine. Which of those wines is best with lamb? An immediate answer would be: all of them. Yet, there is something especially satisfying about the rich, gamy flavors of lamb fed on the wild herbs and grasses of southern France, then crusted with herbs and roasted, when it is mirrored by the Rhône's rich, wild, gamy wines made from syrah, grenache, and mourvèdre.

Vacqueyras have significantly higher percentages of syrah. A minuscule number of white wines and rosés are also made.

Among the producers to try are Domaine de la Charbonnière, Domaine le Sang des Cailloux, and, most especially, the sensational Domaine des Amouriers (which seems like it

A stone religious niche in the vineyards of Tardieu-Laurent, Châteauneuf-du-Pape.

ought to mean the domain of lovers, but *amouriers* are actually mulberry trees).

TAVEL

Tavel—one of France's most famous rosés—is precisely the kind of wine you fall in love with on vacation. What better color than pink when you're on a beach in St.-Tropez?

Despite their pretty pink colors, most Tavels are rugged wines with robust, spicy berry flavors. Bone dry, they have an appealing roughness, an edge that makes them perfect for washing down southern French dishes laden with garlic, olive oil, and fresh, wild herbs.

Tavel rosés are made in the tiny, sleepy village of the same name, less than 10 miles (16 kilometers) southwest and across the river from Châteauneuf-du-Pape. No red or white wines come from here—just rosé. Nine Rhône grapes, both red and white, can be used, but grenache is generally the leader. Interestingly, the wine is usually made by putting whole red and white grapes together in a single tank. The weight of the grapes on top begins to crush the ones below. The pink color comes as the juice sits in contact with the red skins. As seemingly straightforward as Tavel rosé is, it is not easy to make a good one—one that has freshness and bright flavors.

WHEN YOU VISIT . . . THE RHÔNE VALLEY

THE OLD CELLARS of the Rhône Valley were built on sites dating back to the Romans. The wineries themselves are generally small, modest, and practical: often with dirt floors and lots of cobwebs. The tasting table may be an old board balanced between two barrels. It is almost always necessary to have an appointment, and it is greatly helpful to speak French.

IN THE SOUTHERN RHÔNE, visit the historic city of Avignon, the papal seat in the fourteenth century, and be sure to see the massive gothic palace, the Palais des Papes. In addition, the old city of Orange boasts some of the best-preserved Roman ruins in the world. Indeed, the Ancient Theater is the most intact Roman theater in the world, and the acoustics are still so perfect that the internationally acclaimed opera festival, Les Chorégies d'Orange, is held there every summer.

THE RHÔNE VALLEY is full of small country restaurants that make you feel as though you've stepped into the France of a half century ago where *la cuisine de grand-mère* still deliciously dominates. And if you're in the mood to smell and "taste" the sea, Marseilles, and its many restaurants specializing in bouillabaisse, is less than 70 miles (110 kilometers) away from Châteauneuf.

Tavel should be drunk young and chilled, so that its exuberant flavors explode in your mouth. A delicious one to try: the rosé from Prieuré de Montézargues, a former abbey founded by monks in the twelfth century.

CÔTES-DU-RHÔNE AND CÔTES-DU-RHÔNE-VILLAGES

Amazingly, 70 percent of all Rhône wines are Côtes-du-Rhône and Côtes-du-Rhône-Villages. Unlike Côte-Rôtie, Hermitage, or Châteauneuf-du-Pape, however, wines with these two designations do not come from a single place. Instead, the terms refer to wines made from grapes that, in the case of Côtes-du-Rhône specifically, are grown on vast, noncontiguous tracts of less prestigious vineyards totaling more than 148,000 acres (59,900 hectares). You'll find both appellations all over the Rhône Valley, although most vineyards are in the south. Alas, the quality of these wines ranges all over the board, from wines that have little going for them to sensational, juicy, spicy wines with real character.

The relatively large, reputable Rhône producers like E. Guigal, M. Chapoutier, and Beaucastel all make dependable Côtes-du-Rhône, and so do a number of small producers.

So just what are the differences between Côtes-du-Rhône and Côtes-du-Rhône-Villages? Côtes-du-Rhône is the basic appellation; theoretically, Côtes-du-Rhône-Villages is a step up in quality. Generally speaking, this is true. However, several of the very best wines of all are simply Côtes-du-Rhône, so no hard-and-fast rules can be made. You should know this, however: Of the ninety-five tiny villages legally entitled to make Côtes-du-Rhône-Villages, fewer than twenty are considered superior, and in recognition of that fact, they are allowed to append their name to the appellation as, for example, with Cairanne Côtes-du-Rhône-Villages.

As for top producers, look for Château de Fonsalette (made by Château Rayas), Domaine Gramenon (especially its wine called Cuvée de Laurentides), St.-Cosme, Domaine Santa Duc, Domaine du Trignon, Domaine Le Clos des Lumières, Jean-Luc Colombo (especially the red Les Forots and white Les Figuières), and Domaine de la Renjarde.

The Southern Rhône Wines to Know

Southern Rhône wines have a sumptuousness that is undeniable. From aroma to flavor to texture, the wines below are uninhibited, sophisticated, and sensual—just what you'd expect from the south of France. I'd be happy to spend years drinking the wines of just this one place, for place speaks explosively and deliciously here.

WHITES

CHÂTEAU DE BEAUCASTEL

CHÂTEAUNEUF-DU-PAPE | VIEILLES VIGNES

100% roussanne

If ever there was a wine that you'd like to smell for eternity, this is it. The utterly refined, totally sensual top white from Château de Beaucastel has no equal in Châteauneuf-du-Pape. Made entirely from roussanne from a patch of eighty-year-old vines, it's unearthly in its complexity and in the way the flavors of honey, roasted nuts, quince, and crème brûlée embrace your tongue. And this is a dry wine! When young—and with age—it's a showstopper. Beaucastel's owners, the Perrin family, drink this, drinks this with another southern Rhône masterpiece: buttery scrambled eggs cooked with the local black truffles.

REDS

CHÂTEAU DE SAINT COSME

GIGONDAS

80% grenache, 15% syrah, 5% cinsaut

In medieval times, doctors regularly prescribed wine for various ailments, including the wine Saint Cosme (pronounced comb), a nice coincidence since St. Cosme is the patron saint of medicine. I'm not sure if this wine is healing, but it's wonderfully hedonistic and very evocative of its terroir. Imagine leather and cherry jam somehow combined and then poured over minerals and black earth, and you've got this gripping Gigondas.

CHÂTEAU LA NERTHE

CHÂTEAUNEUF-DU-PAPE

Approximately 50% grenache, 20% mourvèdre, 20% syrah, 5% cinsaut, 5% other

Château La Nerthe (pronounced la NAIRT) was built in 1760, and it is unquestionably one of the most majestic sites in Châteauneuf-du-Pape. The precious old vineyards ring the graceful, grand château, which also houses immaculate (rather rare in France) winemaking cellars. And the wine is stupendous. Long and saturated on the palate, it is suffused with the flavors of chocolate, espresso, grenadine, game, spices, and stones. As with all top Châteauneufs, there's real grip here, but also real elegance. In addition, La Nerthe makes a special (more expensive) Châteauneuf called Cuvée des Cadettes. One of the rare Châteauneufs to be aged in 100 percent new oak, it's a massive wine that has a dark, minerally lusciousness, as if rocks were coated in black licorice. Cuvée des Cadettes is often most expressive after a decade of aging.

CHÂTEAU DE BEAUCASTEL

CHÂTEAUNEUF-DU-PAPE

Approximately 30% grenache, 60% mourvèdre, 10% syrah

In what seems like an impossibility, Beaucastel's Châteauneuf-du-Pape hits the palate with all five basic tastes moving at full throttle—salty, bitter, sour, sweet, and savory. It's a shocking first sip. But maybe not as shocking as the aroma—a feral immersion into leather, offal, and animal notes. Some love this about Beaucastel and find the wine distinctive and complex; for other tasters, it's the most unsettling Châteauneuf. I promise you this: Tasting it, you won't be bored.

DOMAINE DU VIEUX TÉLÉGRAPHE

CHÂTEAUNEUF-DU-PAPE

Approximately 70% grenache, 15% syrah, 15% mourvèdre

Known for wines with grip, complexity, and elegance, Vieux Télégraphe ("old telegraph") is one of the great historic estates of Châteauneuf. When first poured, the wine seems almost biting, with its sharp tar, earth, and spice aromas and flavors. But after a short time in the glass, the texture begins to turn to cashmere and a wealth of other gamy and boysenberry jam flavors emerge. Vieux Télégraphe's vineyards are beds of stone.

DOMAINE LE SANG DES CAILLOUX

VACQUEYRAS

Approximately 65% grenache, 20% syrah, 10% mourvèdre, 5% cinsaut

Translated, the name of the domaine is the blood of stones. No title could be more perfect, for while juicy and sensual, this Vacqueyras nonetheless smells and tastes like hard stone. At first. Then, right behind the stoniness, comes a mouthful of what the southern French call *garrigue*—that flavor of the Rhône and Provence, reminiscent of wild thyme and rosemary, dry scrub brush, and warm earth. Did I forget to mention blueberries? This is one of the most complex, satisfying Vacqueyras around.

DOMAINE LES PALLIÈRES

GIGONDAS

80% grenache, 10% syrah, 5% mourvèdre, 5% other

On the beautiful, sloping hills of Gigondas sits the old estate Les Pallières. In 1998, just about the best thing possible happened to this estate: It was bought by the Brunier family (owners of Vieux Télégraphe) and the American wine importer Kermit Lynch. Under their direction, the wines have become stunning. Gamy, peppery, sweetly rich, explosively fruity, and with a soaring structure, Pallières is once again one of the top Gigondas.

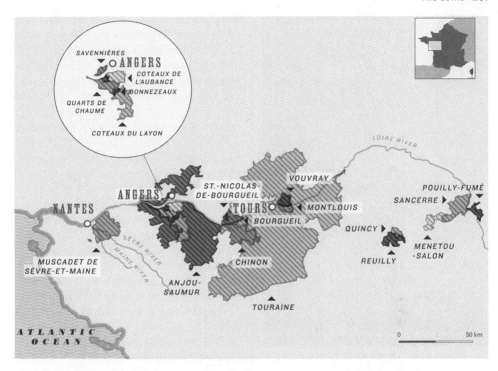

THE LOIRE

he Loire is the most diverse wine region in France. Just about every style of wine is made here, from dry still wines to snappy sparkling wines to elegant, long-lived sweet wines. The most familiar of these are the white still wines Sancerre, Pouilly-Fumé, Muscadet, and Vouvray. Yet the Loire is also well known for rosés, reds, and sparkling wines. Indeed, rosé d'Anjou and reds such as Chinon are comforting fixtures in Parisian bistros, where they are served with everything from grilled sausages to onion soup.

The Loire is defined by the massive, often writhing Loire River—France's longest—as well as the surreal pastoral valley (known as the garden of France) that extends along its banks. Thanks to silt, the river is now too shallow to be navigated, but it was once a flowing engine of transport. Thus, even as early as the Middle Ages, Loire Valley wines were being shipped north to Flanders and Britain.

For its part, the river erupts from deep within the volcanic peaks of the Massif Central, in the heart of France. From there, it flows north for about 300 miles (480 kilometers), makes a left turn, and then flows west for another 300 miles until it pushes out into the Atlantic. It is in this east-west, 300-mile stretch that all of the Loire's best wine regions are found. Farthest east is Pouilly-Fumé and its neighbor, Sancerre. Farthest west, a five-hour drive away, is Muscadet, bordering the Atlantic Ocean. In between are more than sixty-three appellations. Indeed, were it not for the wild river connecting them, the diverse wine areas of the Loire would never share the same pages in a book. In the pages that follow, we will examine the Loire in the above direction.

THE QUICK SIP ON THE LOIRE

THE LOIRE is one of the largest and most diverse wine regions in France. Virtually every type of wine is made there—still and sparkling; dry and sweet; red, white, and rosé.

THE SIGNATURE characteristic of all Loire wines is their zesty freshness.

THE LEADING WHITE GRAPES of the Loire—chenin blanc and sauvignon blanc—make wines that are so extraordinary, they are, in many cases, the world's standard-bearers for these grapes.

We'll start with the far inland, eastern Loire (Sancerre and Pouilly-Fumé), then look at the middle Loire (Vouvray, Savennières, Quarts de Chaume, Chinon, and Bourgueil, among others), and finally end with the western Loire (Muscadet).

But before delving into these three main areas, here are a few more important points to know. The Loire is one of France's larger wine regions (although it is smaller than in times past, when it was the main supplier of wine to Paris and northern countries). Slightly more than 124,000 acres (50,200 hectares) are planted with vines, making the region just less than half the size of Bordeaux. Of France's wine regions, however, the Loire is the least easy to characterize. Those sixty-three appellations produce wines that, in almost every way, are more different than they are similar. Except for one thing: The wines all share a taut, wiry freshness thanks to the region's cool, northern climate. Like Champagne, the Loire exists on the fringe of the lowest temperatures at which grapes can ripen. Often the vines have not even begun to flower (that is, produce tiny flowers that, once fertilized, will become grapes)

until June 1, a month and a half behind warmer places like the Napa Valley, in California. While in difficult, rainy years, this can be agonizing for local growers (and result in chaptalization of the wines, see page 52), the cool climate can also be a plus, leading to elegant, lacy wines with haunting precision (the result of high acidity). In great years, the best wines can have such dynamic tension they seem poised on a tightrope, or even spring loaded. In French, their refreshing vigor is described as *nervosité*.

Wine estates in the Loire Valley are generally small and often family owned. In the past, little capital was available for expansion or major improvements. This opened the door for the creation of cooperatives, as well as a widespread network of *négociants*, who buy wines, blend them, and then bottle them under their own labels. As of 2013, there were about a hundred *négociants* and some twenty cooperatives in the Loire.

The two leading white grapes of the Loire are sauvignon blanc and chenin blanc. Both originated in the Loire Valley, and as both have savagnin as a parent, they are most likely siblings or half siblings. For its part, sauvignon blanc has gone on to make inspired wines everywhere from New Zealand to Austria. But chenin blanc is a different story; it has seemingly retreated back to its homeland. Today, chenin blanc achieves extraordinary heights only in the Loire Valley—especially in the top,

Peter Hahn, owner of Le Clos de la Meslerie, holds a chunk of flint from his vineyard in Vouvray.

THE GRAPES OF THE LOIRE

WHITES

ARBOIS: Minor grape native to the Loire. The use of arbois (in small amounts in blends) is declining.

CHARDONNAY: Minor grape. Found in blends for both white and sparkling wines of the middle Loire.

CHENIN BLANC: Major grape, also called pineau de la Loire. Historically, the most important grape of the middle Loire, used for numerous wines, including Savennières and Vouvray. Wines made from it may be still or sparkling, dry or sweet.

FOLLE BLANCHE: Minor grape. Used to make the wine called Gros Plant in the Muscadet region of the western Loire.

MELON DE BOURGOGNE: The source of Muscadet, in the western Loire.

SAUVIGNON BLANC: Major indigenous grape. Used to make the famous wines Sancerre and Pouilly-Fumé, as well as Menetou-Salon, Reuilly, and Quincy, plus many simple whites from the middle Loire.

REDS

CABERNET FRANC: Major grape. The source of the best Loire reds, Chinon, Bourgueil, and St.-Nicolas-de-Bourgueil. Also used as a blending grape in the reds, rosés, and sparkling wines of the middle Loire.

CABERNET SAUVIGNON, CÔT (MALBEC), PINEAU D'AUNIS, AND PINOT MEUNIER: Minor grapes. Used as blending components in the red, rosé, and sparkling wines of the middle Loire.

GAMAY: The grape that makes Anjou and Touraine gamay. Also a blending grape for red, rosé, and sparkling wines of the middle and eastern Loire.

GROLLEAU: Native grape. Usually the dominant grape in Rosé d'Anjou. Also blended into other rosé, red, and sparkling wines of the middle Loire.

PINOT NOIR: Used for the red wines of Sancerre and the eastern Loire, and as a blending grape in the reds, rosés, and sparkling wines of the middle Loire.

---

mesmerizing wines from Vouvray, Savennières, Coteaux du Layon, Coteaux de l'Aubance, and Quarts de Chaume.

Most of the best Loire reds and rosés are made from cabernet franc, although seven other red grapes are grown, including cabernet sauvignon, pinot noir, gamay, and native varieties, such as grolleau. Loire reds are unmistakably stamped by their northern climate. Zesty and vivid, they are appreciated precisely because they are energetic and fresh, not weighty or full-bodied.

THE EASTERN LOIRE:
SANCERRE, POUILLY-FUMÉ, AND MENETOU-SALON

The eastern Loire may be 300 miles (480 kilometers) from Muscadet and the Atlantic coast, but it's less than half that distance from Paris, and the region's main wines—Sancerre and Pouilly-Fumé—are accordingly well known.

THE MOST IMPORTANT LOIRE WINES

LEADING APPELLATIONS	APPELLATIONS OF NOTE
BOURGUEIL red	ANJOU-VILLAGES red
CHINON red	BONNEZEAUX white (sweet)
CRÉMANT DE LOIRE white (sparkling)	COTEAUX DE L'AUBANCE white (sweet)
MENETOU-SALON white	COTEAUX DU LAYON white (sweet)
MONTLOUIS white (dry and sweet)	QUINCY white
MUSCADET white	REUILLY white, red, and rosé
POUILLY-FUMÉ white	ROSÉ D'ANJOU rosé
QUARTS DE CHAUME white (sweet)	ST.-NICOLAS-DE-BOURGUEIL red
SANCERRE white	SAUMUR-CHAMPIGNY red
SAVENNIÈRES white	SPARKLING SAUMUR white (sparkling)
VOUVRAY white (dry, sweet, and sparkling)	SPARKLING TOURAINE white (sparkling)
	SPARKLING VOUVRAY white (sparkling)
	TOURAINE white and red

The dry whites from Menetou-Salon are also from this easternmost part of the Loire, as are the less well-known regions of Reuilly and Quincy. All are made from sauvignon blanc.

But that's saying it too simply, for Loire sauvignon blancs are in no way routine, herbal-inflected sauvignon blancs. With their racy, flinty, tangy, and smoky flavors, the best of these wines are true to the word *sauvignon*'s root, *sauvage,* meaning "untamed." They are the world's model for frisky, nervy, pinpoint-focused sauvignon blanc, and are considered some of the best white wine matches for food. (Most are fermented in stainless steel and undergo no malolactic fermentation, although some are made or aged in barrel.)

The vineyards of Sancerre are spread over chalky limestone and flint hills near the small town of the same name on the western bank of the river. (In the late spring, the rolling green hills are covered in red poppies, making the whole area appear like the fall-asleep scene in *The Wizard of Oz.*) While the soils here are disparate, thanks to abrupt fault lines running through the region, many of the soils are highly valued for what growers say is the mineral-ity they contribute to the wines. These soils include Kimmeridgian-era limestone (lime-stone and clay imbedded with sea fossils);

The village of Sancerre and its vineyards. Lying on well-drained, perfectly sunlit slopes, the vineyards are located slightly lower on the hillsides than the domes of the hills (which, more exposed to the climate, are better for forests).

IT TAKES TWO TO BE TANGY

*A*lthough many of us immediately think of red wine when we think of cheese, the tangy, *creamy, chalky, salty, and fatty flavors of most goat cheeses can neutralize the flavor of many red wines. Sancerre and Pouilly-Fumé, on the other hand, are perfect counterpoints, in part because they are so tangy themselves. In particular, the combination of Sancerre and Crottin de Chavignol, a small disk of goat cheese from the nearby village of Chavignol, is considered to be a French classic. (Crottin is French slang for goat turd.)*

Portlandian-era limestone (straight limestone without many sea fossils); the so-called *terres blanches* ("white earth"), which is chalk on top of clay; and *les caillottes*, gravel intermixed with limestone. In addition, about 30 percent of the vineyards here contain silex, a flint- and sand-based soil that combines clay, limestone, and silica. Highly desired locally, silex is said to give the best wines their especially vivid minerality and dramatic freshness.

There are a number of excellent vineyards here, but the three called Le Grand Chemarin, Chêne Marchand, and Clos de la Poussie are especially exemplary. As of the mid-1990s, however, a curious Sancerre ruling prevented wine producers from using the name of the vineyard on their labels. Wine producers therefore resorted to "creative" ways of letting consumers know where the grapes came from. The producer Jean-Max Roger, for example, calls his tangy and deliciously exotic top Sancerre "Cuvée GC" (meaning Grand Chemarin). There are many first-rate Sancerre producers. Among them: Cotat Frères,

Pascal Cotat, Lucien Crochet, Henry Pellé, Domaine Laporte, Reverdy-Ducroux, Matthias et Emile Roblin, Domaine Prieur Pierre et Fils, Domaine Vincent Delaporte, Pascal Jolivet, André Neveu, and as just mentioned, Jean-Max Roger.

A final word on Sancerre: Although the very word brings to mind white wine, red and rosé Sancerres are also made. Red Sancerre, in fact, accounts for about 12 percent of the total production. Both red and rosé Sancerres are made from pinot noir with some gamay.

Opposite Sancerre, on the eastern bank of the Loire, is the town of Pouilly-sur-Loire. In Pouilly (poo YEE) the landscape is more gentle and the soil contains slightly more limestone and flint. This soil, it was believed, gave the wine a more pronounced gunflint or smoky

Crottins of goat cheese from the village of Chavignol, one of the culinary treasures of the Loire Valley.

flavor, hence the name of the wine—Pouilly-Fumé. (The word *fumé* means "smoke;" Pouilly is a reference to the Roman general Paulus, who presided here.) In truth, few people except perhaps local experts can tell Pouilly-Fumé and Sancerre apart in a blind tasting.

As noted, a small number of new-wave Sancerres and Pouilly-Fumés, made in small oak barrels, have appeared since the 1980s. The best producer of this style was the late so-called "wild man of Pouilly," Didier Dagueneau (an ex–motorcycle racer with no formal training as a winemaker), whose intensely delicious barrel-fermented and barrel-aged Pouilly-Fumés set off a quiet storm of controversy in the Loire. The wines, now made by Dagueneau's son Louis-Benjamin Dagueneau (under whose name the wines are now labeled), are complex, lush, super-rich, full-bodied, and expensive—especially the ones called Pur Sang (the name means "pure blood") and Silex ("flint"). These are not to be missed by anyone who loves Loire wines. Along with the Louis-Benjamin Dagueneau wines, other top producers include: Ladoucette, Francis Blanchet, Domaine Seguin et Fils, and Domaine Serge Dagueneau et Filles (second cousins of the Didier/Louis-Benjamin clan).

The eastern Loire has three other appellations that are perhaps less well known outside of France itself. Menetou-Salon, just west of Sancerre, can make sauvignon blanc with all

THE SECRET TO MARRIAGE: ACIDITY

*T*wo of the Loire's most famous wines, Sancerre and Pouilly-Fumé, are among the world's most flexible when it comes to pairing wine with food. The reason is: acidity. Bone-dry and refreshing, both Sancerre and Pouilly-Fumé possess the kind of clean, bracing acidity that can counterbalance a surprising ethnic diversity of dishes, from Chinese chicken salad to shrimp tacos with guacamole. At the same time, both of these sauvignon blanc–based wines are dramatic enough so that their own flavors are not subdued by most foods. As for a time-honored partnership, Sancerre or Pouilly-Fumé with seafood is certainly one. (The Loire boasts a number of seafood festivals, including an oyster fair, a crayfish fair, and even a deep-fried fish fair.)

COULÉE DE SERRANT—
MODEL BIODYNAMICS

One of the Loire's most famous and longest-lived whites, Clos de la Coulée de Serrant, comes from a 17-acre (7-hectare) vineyard that was one of the first vineyards in the modern era to be farmed according to biodynamic principles. First propounded by the Austrian philosopher Rudolf Steiner in the 1920s, and later developed by his followers, biodynamics is a holistic system of "living agriculture" whereby the soil and plants growing in it are nurtured through natural forces. Biodynamics envisions soils and plants as living in a "middle world" influenced from below by the forces of the earth and elements, and influenced from above by the cosmos (see Biodynamic Viticulture in the Mastering Wine section, page 34).

The Joly family, owners of Coulée de Serrant since 1959, believe that modern agricultural methods have thoroughly ravaged the earth's soils. They have become the leading proponents of biodynamics worldwide and have influenced a number of other famous French producers to adopt the practice, including Domaine Leroy in Vosne-Romanée, Burgundy, and M. Chapoutier in the Rhône.

---

the fireworks of the best Sancerre and Pouilly-Fumé. Among the top producers are Henry Pellé (also known for his Sancerres), Domaine Jean Teiller, and Domaine de Chatenoy.

Quincy and Reuilly are two tiny appellations near the river Cher, a tributary of the Loire. Again, the sauvignons can be quite crisp and delicious—and less expensive than Sancerre or Pouilly-Fumé.

THE MIDDLE LOIRE:
SAVENNIÈRES, QUARTS DE CHAUME, COTEAUX DU LAYON, ROSÉS D'ANJOU, VOUVRAY, CHINON, BOURGUEIL, AND OTHERS

The middle Loire is where the Loire can get especially confusing, because there are so many (often overlapping) appellations and wine styles. This is where the best rosés and reds are made (Rosé d'Anjou and Chinon, for example), as well as sparkling wines (Crémant de Loire) and whites that are sometimes dry, sometimes medium-sweet, and sometimes sweet (Vouvray). While several grape varieties are grown, the leading white grape is chenin blanc, and the leading red, cabernet franc.

Château de Brissac in Anjou, built in 1621. Privately held today by the 14th Duke of Brissac, the château still produces a range of wines.

The middle Loire is divided into two general, broad areas known as Anjou-Saumur and Touraine. Anjou-Saumur, in the west near the city of Angers, includes the appellations Savennières, Quarts de Chaume, Bonnezeaux, Coteaux du Layon, and Coteaux de l'Aubance, all of which produce white wines.

Touraine, in the east near the city of Tours, includes the appellations Chinon, Bourgueil, and St.-Nicolas-de-Bourgueil, which produce red wines, and Vouvray and Montlouis, which produce white wines.

SAVENNIÈRES

The middle Loire's most extraordinary dry white wine, Savennières, is possibly the greatest dry chenin blanc in the world. Made in a tiny area just southwest of the city of Angers, in Anjou-Samur, Savennières are densely flavored wines with such intensity, grip, minerality, and taut acidity that they can be aged for decades. The vineyards are spread over steep, south-facing slopes of volcanic schist. Yields from these vineyards are among the lowest in the Loire,

SIDETRACKED BY TARTE TATIN

One of the most famous rustic desserts of France, tarte tatin originated in the Touraine region of the Loire, in the tiny village of Lamotte-Beuvron. An upside-down caramelized apple tart, it was created in the nineteenth century by two sisters, Stephanie and Caroline Tatin, owners of the Hôtel-Terminus Tatin, a wayside stop for travelers across from the train station. Tarte tatin is the perfect accompaniment for one of the Loire's other prizes—Quarts de Chaume, the gorgeously sweet, lightly honeyed dessert wine made from chenin blanc grapes.

LOIRE SPARKLING AND CRÉMANT DE LOIRE

One of the middle Loire Valley's specialties is French bubbles at an unfussy price. Indeed, more sparkling wine is made in the Loire than in any other French region except Champagne. Loire sparkling wines fall into two categories: first, the large general category known as Crémant de Loire, and second, sparkling wines from a specific smaller appellation—sparkling Saumur, sparkling Vouvray, sparkling Touraine, and so forth. All are made according to the traditional (Champagne) method of secondary fermentation inside each bottle.

Crémant de Loire—a simple splash of a wine—is usually based on chardonnay, but chenin blanc and cabernet franc are also often used and the law allows for any other grape grown in the Loire Valley. Crémant de Loire is aged just a year on the yeast lees (far less than in Champagne), and is generally made in a dry (brut) style. As for sparklers from small appellations, such as sparkling Samur, a grab bag of different grape varieties can be used, including chenin blanc, chardonnay, sauvignon blanc, cabernet franc, cabernet sauvignon, côt (malbec), gamay, pinot noir, pineau d'Aunis, and grolleau. Idiosyncratic but fun, these sparklers are also dry and aged only briefly on the yeast lees.

which accounts, in part, for Savennières' concentration and depth of flavor. The Loire wine expert Jacqueline Friedrich calls Savennières the most cerebral wine in the world. But sheer hedonistic flavors are operating here, too, for Savennières tastes like nothing else. It's a whirlwind of quince, chamomile, honey, and cream, all pierced by a lightning bolt of citrus.

Among the great producers of Savennières are Domaine des Baumard, Château d'Epiré, Château de Chamboureau, and Domaine du Closel. But the most famous of all Savennières is Clos de la Coulée de Serrant, considered one of the greatest white wines in the world. Coulée de Serrant is made on the single estate also called Coulée de Serrant. The prized vineyard (first planted by monks in the year 1130) is owned by the Joly family (see box Coulée de Serrant—Model Biodynamics, page 267). Though it is just 17 acres (7 hectares) in size, Coulée de Serrant has its own appellation. (Only a handful of other appellations in France are made up of a single property, including Romanée-Conti, La Tâche, and Clos de Tart, all in Burgundy, and Château-Grillet in the Rhône.)

QUARTS DE CHAUME AND THE SWEET WINES OF THE MIDDLE LOIRE

The Anjou-Samur part of the middle Loire is devoted to a slew of medium-sweet or fully sweet whites that carry the appellations Quarts de Chaume, Bonnezeaux, Coteaux du Layon, or Coteaux de l'Aubance. The vineyards for these sweet wine appellations are spread out along the steep slate, schist, and clay slopes that form the banks of the Layon River, a tributary of the Loire. In good years, the grapes receive just the right combination of morning moisture from the river, followed by afternoon sun, for *Botrytis cinerea*, or "noble rot," to form. Thus, each of these wines gets much of its complexity from botrytis (as does Sauternes).

In all four appellations the wines are always made from chenin blanc, which, here in the middle Loire (although virtually no place else in the world), exudes gorgeous floral, peach, apricot, and ripe red apple flavors. Yet the wines, even when made in a sweet style, are also naturally taut and energetic thanks to

high acidity in the grapes and the "cool" soils. The smallest appellation and most prestigious of these wines, Quarts de Chaume, can be an absolute masterpiece, with soaring elegance, lightness, sheerness, and purity of fruit.

Among the wonderful wines to try from this part of the Loire are the Quarts de Chaume from Domaine des Baumard and Château de Bellerive, as well as the Bonnezeaux from Domaine de la Sansonnière.

THE ROSÉS OF ANJOU

Just over half the wine produced in the Anjou-Samur part of the middle Loire is not white, but delicious rosé—the kind of rosé meant to be chilled cold and then disappear quickly over a family meal. Rosé d'Anjou is usually low in alcohol (often no more than 11.5 percent) and ever so slightly "tender," as the locals say (meaning it has 1 to 1.5 percent residual sugar). It's usually made primarily from the local red grolleau grape, although five other red grapes can be part of the blend: gamay, cabernet franc, cabernet sauvignon, côt (aka malbec), and pineau d'Aunis.

A curious version of rosé d'Anjou is rosé Cabernet d'Anjou—made solely from cabernet

Wines from two of the great sweet wine appellations of the Loire: Coteaux de L'Aubance and Quarts de Chaume.

VOUVRAY—DRY TO SWEET

Vouvray can be made at four official levels of dryness/sweetness, according to the amount of residual sugar in the wine. Like Champagne or German riesling, however, the actual impression of sweetness for any given Vouvray is based not only on the quantity of residual sugar present, but also on the degree of acidity. Thus, a Vouvray with, say, 1 percent residual sugar (the classic, main style) generally tastes totally dry, since Vouvray possesses a soaring level of acidity. A Vouvray label may not indicate the level of sweetness of the wine.

SEC (VERY DRY)

0% TO 0.8% RESIDUAL SUGAR (8 grams or less of sugar per liter)

CLASSIC OR DEMI-SEC (PERCEIVED AS DRY ON THE PALATE)

0.8% TO 1.2% RESIDUAL SUGAR (8 to 12 grams of sugar per liter)

As you can see, the classic version of Vouvray has some minor sweetness to balance the wine's high acidity. These are sometimes called by the French term *demi-sec,* which means "half dry."

MOELLEUX (MEDIUM SWEET; LITERALLY, "MELLOW")

1.2% TO 4.5% RESIDUAL SUGAR (12 to 45 grams of sugar per liter)

DOUX (QUITE SWEET)

MORE THAN 4.5% RESIDUAL SUGAR (more than 45 grams of sugar per liter)

Château de la Grille, one of the top Chinons.

franc or cabernet sauvignon. Although the thought of cabernet is appealing, a rosé with green flavors (a characteristic of cabernet) is something of an acquired taste. To counterbalance the "gherkin" effect, more residual sugar is left in rosé cabernet d'Anjou than in rosé d'Anjou.

CHINON, BOURGUEIL, AND ST.-NICOLAS-DE-BOURGUEIL

The Touraine, a fairly large area in the middle Loire, due east of Anjou-Saumur, surrounds the city of Tours. It is a wine region befitting Cinderella. Centuries-old storybook châteaux, replete with turrets, moats, and drawbridges, rise up from verdant rolling fields and vineyards. The châteaux were built by seventeenth- and eighteenth-century aristocrats attracted

Chinon and its famous cabernet franc vineyards as viewed from the Château Chinon, built in the 10th century on the site of earlier castles. Chinon lies along the Vienne River, a tributary of the Loire River.

by the agricultural wealth and abundance of the region.

Touraine is where the climate shifts from the milder western Loire (Muscadet), influenced by the Atlantic, to the eastern Loire (Sancerre, etc.), with its hot summers and extremely cold winters. The top vineyards in Touraine seem to have gotten the best of both worlds—mildness as well as warmth, a situation ideal for red wines.

The three most famous red wine appellations of the Loire are found here: Chinon, Bourgueil (it only looks hard to pronounce; it's bore-GOY), and St.-Nicolas-de-Bourgueil. All three types of wine are almost always made entirely from cabernet franc. Of the three, Chinon is generally the fullest and most elegant. But the quality of all three has increased greatly in recent years, as top estates incorporate more gentle maceration techniques, helping the wines achieve richness and freshness, while avoiding a hard tannic grippiness. No bona fide bistro is ever without red wines from at least one of these three places, especially in summer, when they are served cool.

WHEN YOU VISIT . . . THE LOIRE VALLEY

THE LOIRE VALLEY can be reached in about two hours by car from Paris. The region (known as the garden of France) is beautiful, full of forests and fields, plus stunning châteaux.

THE EASTERN PART OF THE LOIRE, around Sancerre, is known for its artisanal goat cheeses; the western part of the Loire, where Muscadet is made, is known for oysters and fish dishes.

IN ANGIERS, do not miss a chance to visit Chenonceau, the most famous castle in France (in addition to Versailles), and site of the Apocalypse Tapestries, considered among the masterpieces of French art.

Among the most delicious of these reds are the Chinons from Charles Joguet, Domaine Bernard Baudry, Domaine du Roncée, Château de la Grille, Philippe Alliet, and Domaine de la Perrière, and the Bourgueils from Pierre-Jacques Druet.

Chinon, Bourgueil, and St.-Nicolas-de-Bourgueil can vary quite a bit with the vintage. In good years, when the cabernet franc grapes ripen fully, the wines burst with raspberry, violet, cassis, licorice, and briary/spicy flavors, but in poor years, the wines that are not from the very best producers can be on the thin side.

Two final notes: If you are in the Loire, you'll also encounter basic Touraine Rouge (largely forgettable generic red), and you may encounter a fantastic specialty that you should not miss tasting: white Chinon made from chenin blanc. From a top producer, such as Trois Coteaux or Domaine de la Noblaie, it's an exquisite, complex, minerally, dry white wine that can be quite exotic.

The chenin blanc vineyards of Gaston Huet sit peacefully in front of the bell tower of Vouvray.

VOUVRAY AND MONTLOUIS

One white wine appellation of the middle Loire is well known the world over: Vouvray, made from 100 percent chenin blanc. No other place in the world produces chenin blancs that are so gossamer, richly flavored, and honeyed—even when dry. (Just across the Loire River is Vouvray's "little sister," Montlouis—also all chenin blanc—although the wines here are not as exciting.) Most astonishing of all is how long a great Vouvray lasts. It would seem counterintuitive that a white wine could taste vibrant and luxurious after half a century or more, but the top Vouvrays can and do (the wines' ultra-high level of acidity preserves them). Not surprisingly, these have always been collector's wines. *Top* is an important word here, for truly great Vouvray exists alongside a small ocean of basic, nice-tasting commercial examples for which a low price is the main attraction. Among the top Vouvrays I love are those from Domaine le Haut Lieu (Gaston Huet), Domaine de la Fontainerie, Domaine des Aubuisières, Philippe Foreau, Champalou, and Le Clos de Meslerie.

Vouvray can be dry (sec), medium dry (demi-sec; sometimes called classic), or medium sweet (*moelleux*). Medium dry is the traditional main style, but even with a modest amount of residual sugar, classic Vouvray generally tastes completely dry and balanced thanks to its dramatic acidity. In addition, a share of the total production is sometimes, but not always, made into sparkling Vouvray. The amount of sparkling wine depends on the weather. Vouvray has one of the coolest climates in the Loire. Harvests here are some of the latest in Europe—as late as in, say, Germany, often well into November. Thus, in extremely cool years when the acidity in the grapes remains high, some producers may make twice as much sparkling wine as still. In warmer years with riper grapes, the situation flip-flops and more still wines are made—both dry and sweet.

The best medium-sweet (*moelleux*, literally "mellow") Vouvrays are always the product of *Botrytis cinerea*, the beneficial fungus that also produces Sauternes. As in many areas of the

Château Chenonceau, was built in 1513 on the Cher River, a tributary of the Loire, to make it easily accessible to Parisian royalty who often came to stay. Still private, it is considered the most impressive castle in France after Versailles. The château is owned by the Menier family, who were once well known for their chocolate business.

middle Loire, the vineyards of Vouvray get just the right proportion and progression of sun, moisture, and dryness to be infected with the "noble rot."

Because they are also full of daggerlike acidity, Vouvray's greatest sweet wines are an extraordinary taste sensation. When the tension of opposites—sweetness and acidity—is perfectly balanced in these wines, they can be otherworldly in their vibrancy and richness. Often they must be aged for three to seven years before the counterpoint tastes harmonious. *Moelleux* (pronounced moi-LE) Vouvrays are traditionally drunk with rich dishes, especially those with complex sauces, or served as dessert wines. Finally, though rarely, you may also come across an extremely sweet "Doux" Vouvray. With more than 45 grams per liter of residual sugar, these Vouvrays have mind-blowing opulence.

Some of the vineyards and cellars of Vouvray almost defy existence. Vineyards cling to the tops of cliffs, with cellars and houses below them, cut into the soft, *tuffeau* rock, a type of limestone, that forms the face of the cliff. Many cellars were chiseled into the caves left behind long ago, after the *tuffeau* was quarried for building materials for châteaux.

As for Montlouis, as I mentioned, in general it tends to be softer and less dramatically focused than Vouvray. That said, certain producers, such as Domaine Deletang, make extraordinary Montlouis that is every bit the equal of Vouvray.

In addition to Vouvray and Montlouis, the middle Loire is also home to simple whites that can come from anywhere in the region. These can be made from a variety of grapes, including chenin blanc, sauvignon blanc, and even a minority percentage of chardonnay. The

> It would seem counterintuitive that a white wine could taste vibrant and luxurious after half a century, but the top Vouvrays can and do.

most popular of these wines is Touraine sauvignon, made from sauvignon blanc grapes, which tastes like an extremely simple relative of Sancerre and makes for good carafe wines.

THE WESTERN LOIRE: MUSCADET

The westernmost part of the Loire, hard up against the cold, wet Atlantic coast, is known for one wine alone—Muscadet, the leading wine of the Loire by volume. A dry, lean, fresh, stainless-steel-fermented white meant for drinking (not thinking), Muscadet's claim to fame has always been its easy partnership with seafood—especially homey French classics like *moules frites* (a pot of mussels steamed in wine with a tangle of thin French fries on top). It is made from the melon de Bourgogne grape, often referred to simply as melon. The grape's name refers to Burgundy (Bourgogne), not the Loire, thanks to an especially destructive frost in 1709, which destroyed most of the Loire's vineyards. Afterward, Burgundian monks came to help replant, bringing with them a local, frost-hearty Burgundy variety—melon de Bourgogne. Recent DNA analysis indicates the grape is a cross of pinot blanc and gouais blanc. As of the early eighteenth century, the grape was forbidden in Burgundy in favor of chardonnay, and today, melon is extinct there.

The Muscadet area is a sea of vines, some 30,000 acres (12,100 hectares) of them, spread over gently rolling terrain (the vineyards of Sancerre, by comparison, cover just 6,700 acres/2,700 hectares). Like an upside-down fan, the region spreads in a vast arc west, south, east, and northeast of the city of Nantes. The soil here is highly variable, but the best vineyards tend to be planted on mixtures of granite, gneiss, and/or schist. Within this area is one important subzone: Muscadet de Sèvre-et-Maine, named for the small Sèvre and Maine Rivers that flow through the district. Virtually all of the tastiest Muscadet wines come from Muscadet de Sèvre-et-Maine, or from one of the three small areas allowed to append their name to Muscadet de Sèvre-et-Maine: Gorges, Clisson, and Le Pallet.

The labels of most of the top Muscadets read *sur lie*, on the lees, meaning that the wine was left in contact with the yeast lees for several months—theoretically until it was bottled. A Muscadet made this way takes on extra flavor and a bit more "baby fat" on its lean frame, plus, sometimes, a very slight refreshing spritzyness. The practice dates from the beginning of the twentieth century, when producers would put aside an especially good barrel of Muscadet for family celebrations. Over time, they noticed that the wine in this barrel, known as the honeymoon barrel, got even better thanks to its longer contact with the yeasts.

Muscadet is made by six hundred growers, most of whom sell their wines to some forty *négociants*, who blend and bottle the wines under their own labels. Many of these wines are quite good as well as inexpensive. Should you ever encounter them, here are the Muscadets to buy: Domaine de l'Ecu, Louis Métaireau, Chéreau-Carré, Château de la Cassemichère, Domaine de la Grange, Domaine de la Pépière, Domaine Luneau-Papin, and Château du Cléray.

Crates of older Muscadet in a cellar. Because of its high acidity, fine Muscadet can age amazingly well.

The Loire Wines to Know

I love wines that have precision and snap, wines that seem spring-loaded with freshness. That characteristic is a calling card for the Loire, and in particular for the lively dramatic wines below. The Loire is a big region, of course, but the through-line for the wines is a certain "thirst-quenchingness"—true of reds, as well as whites.

WHITES

DOMAINE PELLÉ

SANCERRE | LA CROIX AU GARDE

100% sauvignon blanc

This is the Ingrid Bergman of Sancerres—ravishing, polished, and effortlessly elegant. In great years, besides having perfect tension between acidity and fruit, the wine has a unique kind of purity and clarity, with absolutely vivid smoky/minerally flavors. Henry Pellé himself was considered one of the legendary masters of the sauvignon blanc grape, and now his family carries on, making wines that are widely admired. The Pellé estate is perhaps best known for its extraordinary, rich, dramatic Menetou-Salon, which is also where the estate is located.

MATTHIAS ET EMILE ROBLIN

SANCERRE | AMMONITES

100% sauvignon blanc

I could not write notes fast enough when I tasted the Matthias and Emile Roblin wines—creamy yet tight; spicy yet herbal; peppery yet salty; turbulent yet refined; flashy and focused, with not a whit of fat on their bones. Best of all, the wines were evocative of the ocean—with rolling waves of seawater-like, briny flavors. Among the slew of terrific wines they make, this one, named Ammonites for the large seashell fossils in the vineyard, is most memorable.

DOMAINE PRIEUR PIERRE ET FILS

SANCERRE | LES COINCHES

100% sauvignon blanc

Whenever I taste this wine, I feel like someone has just slammed a door made of chalk and flint, and molecules of aroma and flavor are flying in all directions. Vivid, sharp, starched, and mouth-filling, yet all the while, lacy, it's Sancerre to the core. Domaine Prieur Pierre et Fils—a 42-acre (17-hectare) estate dominated by *caillottes* and silex—is run by brothers Bruno and Thierry Prieur. The vines are planted on a hillside so steep, a winch is needed to harvest the grapes. Les Coinches is a corner of sorts, where rows of vines meet.

DOMAINE LAPORTE

SANCERRE | LE ROCHOY

100% sauvignon blanc

Nothing soft or mellow going on here. Domaine Laporte's Le Rochoy is a firecracker of a Sancerre. Spicy, edgy, zingy, and smelling like you just put your nose into a dynamited cliff (or perhaps smelled the barrel of a gun), it's invariably loaded with all the wild, tangy, flinty flavors hard-core sauvignon blanc drinkers love. Not for the timid. Le Rochoy, a single vineyard owned by the Laporte family, is one of the vineyards closest to the Loire River.

LOUIS-BENJAMIN DAGUENEAU

POUILLY-FUMÉ | SILEX

100% sauvignon blanc

The late Didier Dagueneau was considered both a renegade and a genius in the Loire. In the 1990s and 2000s, Dagueneau, an ex-motorcycle racer with no formal winemaking training, upended conventional winemaking in Pouilly-Fumé by, among other practices, severely reducing yields, allowing his grapes to get very ripe, and then making several of his sauvignon blancs in oak. The results were racy, tightly wound, super-concentrated, expensive sauvignon blancs that often took years of aging before the full extent of their flavors unfurled. The wines are now being made by Dagueneau's son, Louis-Benjamin (whose name is now the brand). Of the Dagueneau cuvées, the one called Silex (flint) is my favorite—dramatically aromatic, thrillingly vibrant, and sophisticated, it has flavors so alive the wine dances in your mouth. For pure, opulent hedonism, however, the Louis-Benjamin Dagueneau Pur Sang ("Pure Blood") has few competitors for its profoundly complex matrix of stone, saline, chalk, spice, and citrus flavors.

CLOS DE LA COULÉE DE SERRANT

SAVENNIÈRES

100% chenin blanc

The most famous Savennières, Coulée de Serrant, is also one of the most famous white wines in the world. In great years, it is chenin blanc from another galaxy. The wine can be so suffused with apple-caramel flavors, you feel as though you're inside a tarte tatin. The finesse, the nuance, the incisive focus, the gripping flavors that melt into a silky, honeyed body—it's all here in great years. The 17-acre (7-hectare) Coulée de Serrant vineyard is cared for by the Joly family, the world's leading proponents of the biodynamic approach to viticulture (see page 267).

LE CLOS DE LA MESLERIE

VOUVRAY

100% chenin blanc

In the first decade of the 2000s, expat American Peter Hahn restored by hand a rundown old stone house built in the 1600s, and the few hectares of clay-chalk vineyard surrounding it, naming the wine Le Clos de la Meslerie. Hahn's Vouvrays are massive, intense, very ripe, full-bodied wines, yet they manage to have an amazing tightness and through-line of energy. And while *energy* may seem like an odd word, there's no better term for their explosive quince, citrus, honey cake, and minerally character.

CHÂTEAU DE LA CASSEMICHÈRE

MUSCADET SÈVRE-ET-MAINE | CLOS DU BON CURÉ | SUR LIE

100% melon de Bourgogne

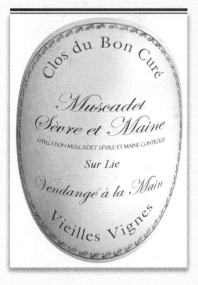

From fifty-year-old vines comes this pretty, lacy, delicate Muscadet that's gentle and fresh and makes you want to drink a ton of it. When Muscadet is in top form, as this one is, it has a light minerality to it that's thirst quenching. The impressive castle of Château de la Cassemichère was built in the early 1700s. Alas, like many royals, the family that owned the estate at the end of the 1700s, the Cottineaus, were beheaded during the French Revolution.

REDS

DOMAINE DE LA PERRIÈRE

CHINON

100% cabernet franc

This serious Chinon, with its beautiful streak of spiciness, opened my mind about Chinon. When Chinon is very good, as this is, it has a trim, fit body (it could be in a health club commercial), plus a pure, lively drive of freshness more often associated with white wine than red. Best of all, great Chinon, such as Domaine de la Perrière's, has an almost miraculous structure—one senses the tannin from the cabernet franc—yet there's no bitterness, dryness, or raspyness. Just vivid, licoricey, violety fruit.

CHÂTEAU DE LA GRILLE

CHINON

100% cabernet franc

Château de la Grille is one of the most masculine and muscular Chinons. It's usually jet-black in color and bursting with pent-up flavors evocative of licorice, violets, and something like café au lait. The way this wine unfurls itself on the palate is especially captivating. Tightly wound at first, it unleashes itself in a whirlwind of moves, as though it were, itself, a martial art. Built in the fifteenth century, the château grows only cabernet franc on its 69 acres (28 hectares) of land. Today owned by Baudry-Dutour, the estate's reputation was firmly established by Albert Gosset, of Champagne fame, who purchased it in 1951 and installed state-of-the-art equipment and updated the viticultural practices.

ALSACE

 lsace is one of the rare wine regions in the world devoted almost exclusively to white wine. More than seven different varieties are common and, with few exceptions, they are whites rarely made in other parts of France. Although by law (and in spirit), Alsace is a French wine region, it has also at various times in its past belonged to Germany. Indeed, within one seventy-five-year period in the nineteenth and twentieth centuries, the two superpowers exchanged ownership of the region four times, for Alsace is one of Europe's strategic geopolitical crossroads.

It is also a wine region so charming it may as well have emerged straight out of a fairy tale. The vineyards are sun dappled, the half-timbered houses are cheerfully adorned with flower boxes, the 119 villages—centuries old—are immaculate. All are set against the grand backdrop of the Vosges Mountains. Perhaps it was all of this beauty that inspired the Alsatian artist Frédéric Auguste Bartholdi; he sculpted the Statue of Liberty, a gift from France to the United States.

The most important grapes are the four white varieties: riesling, gewürztraminer, pinot gris, and muscat. A fifth white, pinot blanc, is used to make basic quaffing wine. The lone red grape, of which only a tiny amount is grown, is pinot noir. And interestingly, unlike the practice in most of the rest of France, Alsace wines are labeled according to these varieties, rather than by the place where the grapes grow.

▲ *Quite possibly the most beautiful wine region in France, Alsace has it all—gorgeous scenery, quaint villages and towns, exquisite wines, and dozens upon dozens of top-rated restaurants.*

Founded in the 7th century, the village of Hunawhir (officially considered one of the "most beautiful villages of France") is set among the vines. In the center is the 15th-century church of St Jacques le Majeur, named for one of Christ's twelve apostles.

THE QUICK SIP ON ALSACE

THE TOP WINES of Alsace are the dry, aromatic whites: riesling, gewürztraminer, muscat, and pinot gris.

A SINGLE, PASSIONATE PHILOSOPHY pervades Alsace winemaking: to create wines with pure fruit flavors. New oak is almost never used.

THANKS TO THE FAR NORTHERN but immensely sunny climate, Alsace wines are usually medium- to full-bodied. The best are concentrated wines, often with a dramatic streak of acidity.

The great unsung heroes of France, Alsace whites are not the demure wines that you might imagine. Nor do they usually taste sweet, a common misconception (unless, of course, a sweet late-harvest wine is intentionally being made). The best among them are powerful, bold, and dramatic. They virtually always taste dry. For some wines, a tiny amount of residual sugar may be left in the wine, but this is balanced out—and, in effect, negated—by a considerable amount of acidity. Moreover, they are made according to a single, deeply held philosophy—namely, that great wine should be the purest possible expression of two factors: the grapes it is made from and the ground it is grown in. An Alsace winemaker's goal is not to craft a wine with certain flavors, it's to showcase the inherent character of the grape itself when grown in a certain plot of earth. The emphasis on the grape is so strong that blending is (almost) unthinkable. The most highly regarded wines are almost always 100 percent of the variety named on the label.

For wines to be truly expressive of grape and ground, the winemaking must be hands-off. In Alsace, the top wines are fermented with indigenous yeasts instead of commercial yeasts, and the wines are usually made in neutral containers—either stainless steel or cement tanks, or older, inert casks called *foudres*. The lightning bolt of natural acidity in the wines is rarely mollified by letting them go through malolactic fermentation, a process that would soften the impression of acid. The combination of lively acidity, dryness, and unhampered, uninhibited, unleashed fruit and minerality is what defines the great Alsace wines and makes them some of the best all-around marriage partners for food.

Besides dry table wines, two other categories of wine are made in Alsace: *Vendange tardive* wines and wines known as *sélection de grains nobles. Vendange tardive* wines are made from super-ripe, late-harvested grapes. Powerful and concentrated, VT wines, as they are known, can taste slightly sweet. The second category, even more rare than VT, is *sélection de grains nobles* (SGN). These are ravishingly unctuous wines made from super-concentrated, late-harvested, botrytis-affected grapes. Curiously, the final taste impression of both VT and SGN wines is not of sugariness but of hauntingly dense concentration.

Finally, many of the top Alsace wine estates are family-owned firms. Some own all of their own vineyards, others supplement their grapes with those bought from the region's 4,600 small growers. As luck would have it, many wines that are exported from Alsace—especially the rieslings and gewürztraminers—are of very high quality. This makes buying them a pretty safe bet even if you don't know the producer.

A rocky outcrop of the Kitterle Vineyard, Domaines Schlumberger. The vineyard is nicknamed the "calf breaker," because its steep slopes can reach inclines of 50 degrees.

TYPES OF WINE

Amazingly, most leading Alsace producers—even small producers—make twenty to thirty different wines. The majority of these can be broken down into three types: regular, reserve, and late harvest.

The regular bottlings are the producer's standard bread-and-butter wines. A typical producer will make regular bottlings of all five leading grapes—riesling, gewürztraminer, pinot gris, pinot blanc, and muscat.

Next are the reserve bottlings. Although the word *reserve* might cause you to imagine a single, special wine, in Alsace producers usually make multiple reserve wines. There can be three reserve rieslings, four reserve gewürztraminers, and so on, all from the same producer.

Alas, reserve wines may be labeled in a number of ways. The label may carry the name of a special, well-known vineyard, such as Zind Humbrecht's Clos St.-Urbain. Or, if the reserve wine happens to come from a Grand Cru vineyard (not all do), it may be labeled with the words *Grand Cru* plus the name of the vineyard. And finally, a reserve wine may be given a title such as *réserve personelle* or *réserve exceptionnelle.*

The third type of wine—late-harvest wine—is made when the harvest permits. A producer may make up to six of the rare specialties, *vendange tardive* and *sélection de grains nobles.* They will be among the estate's most precious and expensive offerings.

On top of all this, just for the fun of it, many producers also make a pinot noir or a sparkling wine or an inexpensive blended quaffing wine—or all three. It's easy to see how all these wines add up. From the perspective of an Alsace producer, more wines mean the ability to show off how distinctly different the flavors derived from different sites can be.

CRÉMANT D'ALSACE

ll of the sparkling wine made in Alsace is called Crémant d'Alsace, and like all *crémants,* it is made in the same, painstaking way as Champagne. A blend of grapes is used, including pinot blanc, Auxerrois, pinot noir, pinot gris, and/or chardonnay (which by law is permitted only in Crémant d'Alsace; it cannot be made into a still table wine on its own). All of the grapes used for Crémant d'Alsace are harvested earlier than grapes for Alsace still wines, so that their acidity is pronounced. It's this vivid acidity, of course, that will give the final wine its snap, crackle, and pop.

Crémant d'Alsace, which is an official appellation, accounts for more than 20 percent of all Alsace wine. Indeed, thanks to its terrific quality and very affordable price, the bubbly is getting more and more popular. In 1979, fewer than one million bottles of Crémant d'Alsace were made. Today, that figure is more than 30 million bottles a year. Try the ones from Pierre Sparr and Lucien Albrecht.

THE MOST IMPORTANT ALSACE WINES

LEADING WINES

GEWÜRZTRAMINER white (dry and sweet)

MUSCAT white (dry and sweet)

PINOT GRIS white (dry and sweet)

RIESLING white (dry and sweet)

WINES OF NOTE

CRÉMANT D'ALSACE white (sparkling)

PINOT BLANC white

PINOT NOIR red

THE LAND AND THE VINEYARDS

Alsace lies about 300 miles (480 kilometers) due east of Paris. The vineyards run north to south in one long, thin strip over the foothills along the eastern flank of the Vosges Mountains. Germany's Rhine River is about 12 miles (19 kilometers) to the east, and even closer (about 6 miles/10 kilometers to the east) is Alsace's river, Ill (pronounced EEL).

After Champagne, this is France's northernmost wine region, yet it is not generally overcast and cool, as one might presume, but surprisingly sunny and dry. Thanks to the protective mantle of the Vosges Mountains, less rain falls on the vineyards here than on vineyards elsewhere in France.

The best vineyards are south-facing for maximum sun, and most are located in the southern part of the region, known as the Haut Rhine or upper Rhine. The growing season is long, ensuring that even at this northern latitude, grapes growing in the best, sunniest sites develop full physiological maturity.

Soil in Alsace is varied enough to be a geologist's dream. Wide variations in soil often mean wide variations in the flavor and quality of the wines. And, in fact, there is an enormous difference in flavor between an average wine from a nondescript vineyard and a wine from an extraordinary vineyard, such as Trimbach's Clos Ste.-Hune, which produces one of the greatest rieslings in the world.

The checkerboard of soil types in Alsace includes chalk combined with clay, limestone, granite, schist, volcanic rock sediment, and sandstone. Alsace's pinkish-colored sandstone, called *grès de Vosges,* is a favorite building material for local cathedrals.

THE GRAND CRU

In 1983, twenty-five of the very best vineyard sites in Alsace were, for the first time, legally recognized as

SURPRISING AGING POTENTIAL

O nly exceptional white grapes can be made into wines that will stand up to long aging— say, twenty years or more. Riesling is the world's preeminent white grape in this regard, followed by (in no particular order) sémillon, pinot gris, gewürztraminer, and chardonnay from cold climates. In general, for a white wine to age, it must have an impeccable balance of fruit and alcohol, and it helps if the wine has high acidity. When made by the best producers, three of the most important Alsace whites—riesling, gewürztraminer, and pinot gris—all age remarkably well. Alsace rieslings, in particular, have an amazing ability to become graceful and honeyed the older they get.

superior, and designated as Grand Cru. The act, however, was wildly controversial. For two decades prior to this designation, Alsace producers and growers had debated not only which vineyards were indeed the crème de la crème, but also what the boundaries of those vineyards should be and what, if any, limits should be set on a Grand Cru's yield. Clearly, the stricter the requirements, the more impact and validity the designation Alsace Grand Cru would have.

As it turned out, the standards set were not as stringent as many producers would have liked. To add fuel to the fire, twenty-six more vineyards were later added to the original twenty-five, bringing the total number of Grand Cru vineyards to fifty-one. That's far too many to suit a number of producers. Moreover, the yield set for Grand Cru vineyards 686 gallons per acre (65 hectoliters per hectare), is considered by many to be too high for the production of great wine.

On the other hand, just because the regulations could be stricter does not mean that no great Grand Cru wines are being made. They are. In fact, most wines labeled Grand Cru are far more intense, elegant, complex, and structured than the producers' regular bottlings. But, some top producers, as a quiet form of protest, refuse to use the term Grand Cru even though they own Grand Cru vineyards. Instead, they call their best wines by a vineyard name or a proprietary name. The producer Hugel simply uses the word *Jubilee* (as in Hugel Riesling Jubilee) to designate wines that come from Grand Cru vineyards.

By law, only wines made from four grape varieties are allowed to be called Grand Cru, and they are the varieties that, over many decades, producers have deemed capable of greatness: riesling, gewürztraminer, pinot gris, and muscat. If a producer chooses to label his wine Grand Cru, the label must also state the specific Grand Cru vineyard from which the wine came. Grand Cru wines are several times more expensive than regular bottlings,

"True quality is that which succeeds in surprising and moving us. It is not locked inside a formula. Its essence is subtle (subjective) and never rational. It resides in the unique, the singular, but it is ultimately connected to something more universal. A great wine is one in which quality is contained. Such a wine will necessarily be uncommon and decidedly unique because it cannot be like any other, and because of this fact it will be atypical, or only typical of itself."

—ANDRÉ OSTERTAG, winemaker, as quoted in Kermit Lynch's *Inspiring Thirst*

Half-timbered houses are one of Alsace's architectural signatures. Here, houses in Colmar, the "capital" of Alsace wine country.

THEY BRING BABIES, DON'T THEY?

I n Alsace, everyone looks up. Not only because they're admiring the architecture, but also because they're hoping to spot a white stork—or a whole nest of them. The animal best known as a baby-delivery agent is, in fact, the official bird of Alsace. Indeed, the species was in rapid decline until Alsace's activists initiated successful repopulation efforts. The bird itself has enchanted humans for centuries. Storks are referenced in everything from Egyptian hieroglyphics to Greek mythology. To this day, they symbolize good luck and fertility. Their posture and size are quite striking in flight, so have your camera ready.

and production of them is small. Indeed, only 4 percent of the total production of Alsace wines are Grands Crus.

THE GRAPES AND WINES OF ALSACE

lsace wines are based on and named after the grapes from which they've come. Here are the main wines.

RIESLING

Riesling is Alsace's most prestigious grape, although the wine made from it is as thoroughly different from German riesling as a wine can be and still come from the same grape—and grown virtually next door to boot! The best German rieslings are fruity, finely etched, exquisitely nuanced wines, low in alcohol, vibrating with acidity, and usually balanced with a softening pinch of sweetness.

Alsace rieslings are not nearly as dainty. These are mostly very dry, broad wines with palate-coating flavors that lean toward gunflint, steel, and minerals, with a limey sort of citrus. Tight and austere when young, the wines begin to come around after two to three years. With a decade or more of age, they take on a richness, as well as a viscosity, that can be stunning.

Riesling is known to be a grape sensitive to its terroir, and this is as true in Alsace as it is elsewhere. Grown in a merely decent vineyard, it makes merely okay wine. Extraordinary riesling requires near-perfect vineyard conditions.

No discussion of great Alsace riesling could fail to include Trimbach's Clos Ste.-Hune and Cuvée Frédéric Emile; as well as Domaine Zind Humbrecht's Clos Saint Urbain Rangen de Thann; Domaine Weinbach's Cuvée Ste.-Cathérine; Domaine Ostertag's Fronholz; and Domaine Marcel Deiss's Altenberg de Bergheim.

THE GRAPES OF ALSACE

WHITES

CHARDONNAY: Legally permitted to be used only in the sparkling wine Crémant d'Alsace, where it adds finesse and body.

GEWÜRZTRAMINER: A major grape. Makes flamboyant, dry wines full of personality, plus extraordinary late-harvest wines.

MUSCAT: Two types grow in Alsace, muscat blanc à petits grains and muscat ottonel. These are often blended to make stunningly aromatic wines usually drunk as aperitifs.

PINOT BLANC: Makes medium-bodied quaffing wines of good, not usually great, character. Also known as klevner.

PINOT GRIS: A major grape. The source of unique, full-bodied wines, totally unlike pinot gris planted elsewhere in the world. Very old vintages may carry pinot gris's former name, tokay or tokay-pinot gris.

RIESLING: A major grape and the most prestigious one. Alsace rieslings can have remarkable complexity and aging potential. Also used for late-harvest wines.

SYLVANER: A minor grape. Can make very good wines in Alsace, especially when the sylvaner vines are old. The same as the grape silvaner in Germany.

RED

PINOT NOIR: A minor grape, but noteworthy because it is Alsace's only red. Occasionally makes fascinating wine.

GEWÜRZTRAMINER

It's often said that gewürztraminer (or, gewurztraminer without the umlaut, as you'll almost always see it, this being France) is something you either really like or really don't. I suspect that the people who "really don't" have never had a Grand Cru gewürztraminer from Alsace. In fact, gewürztraminer (like nebbiolo) is one of the grapes that simply doesn't travel well. Virtually all of the great ones—the ones with gripping flavors, finesse, and complexity—come from Alsace (the gewürztraminers from Italy's Trentino-Alto Adige region are their only competitors).

The aromas and flavors are extroverted. Lychees, gingerbread, vanilla, fruit-cocktail syrup, grapefruit, smoke, spice, stones, minerals, honeysuckle, and a wonderful bittersweet character rather like marmalade, do not simply rest in the glass—they rage about in it. Such massive fruitiness is sometimes mistaken for sweetness, but as already noted, most Alsace gewürztraminers are dry or nearly so (unless a late-harvest wine, a *vendange tardive*, is being made).

To go along with their big 3-D fruit, Alsace gewürztraminers have an enormous body and low natural acidity. The existing acidity therefore must be carefully protected by the winemaker. With age, Alsace gewürztraminer seems—if this is possible—even bigger-flavored. Made as a *vendange tardive*, it can be a knockout.

The grape gewürztraminer is a rose-colored mutation—that is, a clone—of the ancient grape savagnin, which originated centuries ago somewhere in what is today the area of northeastern France and southwestern Germany.

Many Alsace producers make excellent gewürztraminers. Some of my favorites:

Domaines Schlumberger Kessler Grand Cru; Kuentz-Bas Pfersigberg Grand Cru; Domaine Zind Humbrecht Goldert Grand Cru; Domaine Weinbach Altenberg Grand Cru Cuvée Laurence; Hugel et Fils Hommage à Jean Hugel; and Domaine Marcel Deiss Altenberg Grand Cru.

PINOT GRIS

Riesling may be the most prestigious grape in Alsace, but pinot gris is the well-loved hometown girl. The variety is, technically speaking, not a variety, but a clone of pinot noir, and originated in Burgundy. Indeed, in Alsace, pinot gris has such depth and richness it's reminiscent of white Burgundy. What it is generally *not* like, however, is pinot gris from Italy (pinot grigio) or from Oregon. Both of those are usually lighter in body and somewhat more subtle in flavor. Alsace pinot gris, on the other hand, is a high-impact wine, with a full body and bold, concentrated flavors of bitter

ASPARAGUS, MEET WINE

*I*f opening a restaurant for just three months a year seems crazy, consider a three-month-only restaurant that also serves only one food. In Alsace, from April until June, small restaurants dedicated to asparagus alone open their doors. Every single dish on the menu will be composed of the fat, juicy spears. Asparagus aficionados believe there to be only one perfect wine accompaniment: dry muscat. Indeed, after a long winter, the most sensational way to celebrate the arrival of spring is with a huge platter of asparagus drizzled with hollandaise sauce, and a cold bottle of a great Alsace muscat like Domaine Zind Humbrecht Goldert Grand Cru.

almonds, peach, ginger, smoke, vanilla, and earth.

Among the great pinot gris are those from Kuentz-Bas, Léon Beyer, Domaine Marcel Deiss, Domaine Ernest Burn (especially the Clos St.-Imer), and Zind Humbrecht. Pinot gris is often made into lush *vendange tardive* wines.

MUSCAT

Grapes with the word *muscat* in the name have been grown around the Mediterranean (and indeed, around the world) for centuries, and represent many different varieties, only some of which are related.

In Alsace, two types of muscat are grown, then blended. Muscat blanc à petits grains (literally, "white muscat with the small berries"), with its outrageously floral and citrus flavors, is considered the best of the named muscats. The other muscat, muscat ottonel, is more delicate, earlier ripening (an advantage in a northern climate), and has lower acidity. But muscat ottonel (a cross of chasselas and another cross called muscat d'Eistenstadt) is somewhat rare, since it can have problems with *coulure* (a condition whereby the buds lose their flowers before those flowers can be fertilized to become grapes).

Alsace is one of the few places where muscat is made in a dry style. Indeed, Alsace muscat is a bone-dry, dramatically aromatic wine redolent of peaches, orange peel, tangerine, and musk. It is one of the world's most evocative aperitifs.

The muscats to search out? Those from Domaine Albert Boxler, Domaine Ernest Burn, Léon Beyer, Domaine Ostertag, and Zind Humbrecht.

PINOT BLANC

Just like pinot gris, pinot blanc is, genetically speaking, a clone of pinot noir. Alsace's pinot blanc (also known as klevner) is easy to like, dependable, and safe. It's never as thrilling as riesling, as dramatic as gewürztraminer, or as novel as pinot gris; nonetheless, the top Alsace pinot blancs are tasty wines with baked-apple flavors and a light texture. Unfortunately, there are also many bland versions.

Historically, some older pinot blanc vineyards also contained a small percentage of vines later identified as the Burgundian white grape Auxerrois. Thus, some Alsace pinot blancs may be, technically speaking, field blends. Top producers of pinot blanc include Domaine Albert Boxler, Josmeyer, and Domaine Weinbach.

PINOT NOIR

The only red wine made in Alsace is pinot noir. In the past, the quality was so variable that much of it ended up looking like rosé. Then, in the 1990s, a few of the top wineries began rethinking their approach, planting pinot noir in better sites, lowering the yields, using better equipment and aging the wine in new barrels. As expected, the wine got better. A lot better. In good vintages Marcel Deiss's Bergheim Burlenberg pinot noir, Ostertag's Fronholz pinot noir, and Hugel's Jubilee pinot noir show earthy, complex, almost Burgundy-like flavors.

Like all other Alsace wines, pinot noir must, by law, be bottled in tall, Germanic flute bottles. Because it's surprising, if not a little unnerving, to see red wine flow from what looks like a bottle of riesling, several producers are battling the bottle law, in hopes of having the rule changed.

VENDANGE TARDIVE AND SÉLECTION DE GRAINS NOBLES

Two sensational types of late-harvest wines, *vendange tardive* (VT) and *sélection de grains nobles* (SGN), can be made only in certain favorable years (sometimes only once or twice a decade) and even then they generally make up less than 1 percent of the region's production.

But sensational isn't nearly adequate as an adjective. These wines can be astonishing in the depth and vividness of their flavors. By law, only the four grape varieties allowed for Grand Cru wines may be used: riesling, gewürztraminer, pinot gris, and muscat. By the time they are picked, the grapes for VT wines may be (but don't have to be) infected with *Botrytis cinerea*, the noble rot responsible for Sauternes.

The rolling vineyards of Alsace lie over the foothills of the Vosges Mountains.

Vendange tardive wines are not exactly dessert wines but, rather, wines of such profound concentration that they seem to have atomic density. Lush but underscored by exuberant acidity, they may be a touch sweet or dry. (Unfortunately, there's no way to tell from the label.) VTs are so spellbinding, they are generally drunk by themselves or with something utterly simple. (I always skip the pie, and drink one as the finale to Thanksgiving dinner.)

Sélections de grains nobles are late-harvested wines that are always sweet and always infected with botrytis. To say that the wines are sweet, however, is an understatement. SGN wines can make Sauternes seem shy. Wines of ravishing unctuousness, SGNs are balanced by such soaring acidity, profound alcohol, and huge extract that they actually finish in a way that is exquisitely balanced.

Because a significant amount of botrytis does not appear in Alsace vineyards every year (or even very easily in any year), the production of SGNs can range from nothing to a barely commercial amount.

A producer's VTs and SGNs will often come from the same vineyard, usually one of the best. First, the pickers will go through the vineyard choosing, berry by berry, only

Deiss, Hugel et Fils, Kuentz-Bas, Trimbach, Domaines Schlumberger, Domaine Weinbach, or Domaine Zind Humbrecht.

WHEN YOU VISIT . . . ALSACE

THE BEST WAY TO VISIT the wineries of Alsace is to follow the wine route of Alsace, which winds for 75 miles (120 kilometers) along the eastern side of the Vosges Mountains, over the vineyard-covered hillsides, and along the floors of deep valleys. The close-to-poetic atmosphere includes charming old-world towns with bell towers and ramparts, storybook inns, and lovely churches. Castles overlook the plain, paths run through the vineyards, and everywhere, wine taverns and cellars invite you to drop in on the spur of the moment.

IN THE HEART OF THE VINEYARDS, a few miles/kilometers from Colmar, is the Kintzheim castle, headquarters of the fascinating Alsace Wine Museum and the Confrérie Saint-Etienne, a society dating from the 1400s, which now acts as a promotional organization, hosting, among other events, some of the most lavish banquets in France.

---

the botrytis-infected grapes for SGN. Then, they'll go back and pick the remaining super-ripe grapes for VT.

VT and SGN wines are governed by extremely strict regulations. Producers must officially declare their intentions to produce them; the grapes must be handpicked and analyzed as they are being pressed. The wines cannot be chaptalized. Once they are made, they are subjected to a taste test before they can be sold. In some years, up to 35 percent of the wines fail to pass the test! VT and SGN wines are expensive, but they are unequaled in the world. Do not miss a VT or SGN from any of the following producers: Léon Beyer, Domaine Albert Boxler, Domaine Marcel

THE FOODS OF ALSACE

After a few days in Alsace, even the most insatiable food and wine lover is ready to beg for mercy. The sheer number of delicious regional dishes is daunting, and the number of great restaurants—both humble and grand—is second only to that of Paris.

Kugelhopf is a good example of the irresistibility of Alsace specialties. These mildly sweet, turban-shaped rolls, rich with eggs and butter, are dusted with sugar or flecked with walnut pieces and sometimes diced bacon. In every bakery, they line the shelves like perfect soldiers, along with *pains paysans,* golden, crusty loaves studded with raisins and almonds, and *petits pains au lait,* soft, doughy milk rolls.

Alsace's most stunning "bread," however, is *flammekueche,* also known as *tarte flambée*—best described as pizza meets the onion tart. First, a thin layer of bread dough is stretched across a chopping board; it's then smeared with *fromage blanc* (a fresh white cheese) and heavy cream. Next it's topped with smoked bacon and onions, and finally it's baked in a fiery, wood-burning oven until blistered. In *winstubs* ("wine bars") all over Alsace, *flammekuechen* can't be baked fast enough for the hoardes of happy families and friends who come to share it.

Since roughly the tenth century, Alsace has been the capital of Munster, a creamy, pungent cheese. Almost as important as driving along the Route du Vin is driving along a smaller side road, the so-called Route du Fromage (cheese route), where country restaurants offer home-made Munster, baked with potatoes and onions and served with bacon and ham.

With due respect to the Romans, who fattened snails on choice tidbits and housed them in special snail boxes, the French, and especially the Alsatians, have raised the eating of

WHITE WINE AND THE OTHER WHITE MEAT

Among all the world's rieslings, pinot gris, and gewürztraminers, those of Alsace are usually the most full-bodied and concentrated. This makes them great choices when you're having meat but want to drink a white wine. Which is what happens in Alsace all the time. The region's robust, down-to-earth, cold-weather food revolves around pork and game that are often cooked with hearty vegetables, such as potatoes, onions, and cabbage. The region's specialty, *choucroute garni,* a dish of sauerkraut, pork, sausages, bacon, and potatoes, is stellar with riesling. But *choucroute* aside, even a simple pork roast is raised to new heights when it's served with a powerfully fruit-packed, crisp Alsace riesling.

An irresistible kugelhopf, *rich with eggs and butter, and dusted lightly with sugar. Alsace is for those with insatiable appetites.*

escargots to a fine art. Drizzling snails with garlic butter is merely the tip of the iceberg. There are dozens of ways of preparing snails, including a famous one in which the mollusks are simmered with wild chanterelle mushrooms, garlic, and shallots in a wine and whipped cream stock, then served with a chilled riesling.

In Alsace, April is not the cruelest month; it is the time for unrestrained asparagus madness. The vegetable inspires such devotion that there are restaurants open only from mid-April until the end of June that serve nothing but asparagus and dry muscat (see Asparagus, Meet Wine, page 286).

Alsace is one of the two capitals of foie gras (the other is southwestern France). While many animal activists would see the food universally banned, it is still allowed here, and many consider it one of the treasures of French gastronomy. Geese are force-fattened until their livers are large and rich. The livers are then seasoned with salt, pepper, and a touch of Cognac and coddled in a *bain-marie.* In pâté de foie gras, the liver is flecked with truffles and wrapped in a rich pastry crust, then cooked. But Alsatian chefs also stuff game birds with it, sauté it in gewürztraminer, and even top plebeian sauerkraut with it.

Speaking of cabbage, although its exact origins are not known, *choucroute* is so undeniably Alsatian that locals are often referred to as choucroute-eaters by the rest of France. *Choucroute* is prepared by shredding young white cabbage and layering it with salt in large crocks until it ferments. The fermented cabbage is then cooked in wine—usually a riesling—and served with a stunning array of potatoes, several cuts of pork, sausages, and if the *choucroute* is fancy, suckling pig.

Given the heartiness of Alsace cooking, it might seem as though only the lightest of sorbets should be in order for dessert. Fat chance. Dense, creamy cheesecakes are common, as are apple tarts, plum pies, and soufflés made with the local kirsch (cherry brandy). One thing never shows up with dessert, however. That is a *vendange tardive* or *sélection de grains nobles.* These rare, late-harvest wines are so extraordinary and complex that dessert only seems to get in the way.

The Alsace Wines to Know

I t's almost impossible to go wrong drinking Alsace wine. The quality of the wines is so high and the deliciousness factor so great that you are virtually guaranteed to be happy, impressed (and sometimes blown away). Unlike Burgundy, in Alsace, the Grand Cru wines are often *not* stratospherically more expensive than regular bottling . . . a reason to indulge.

SPARKLING

LUCIEN ALBRECHT

CRÉMANT D'ALSACE | BRUT ROSÉ

100% pinot noir

One of the best-known producers of Crémant d'Alsace, the family-owned firm of Lucien Albrecht was founded in 1425. The winery's *blanc de blancs* is widely known, and deservedly so. But it's this rare rosé—made entirely from pinot noir—that's extra special. Beautifully made according to the traditional (Champagne) method, the wine is a slice of cold, spiced-strawberry freshness.

WHITES

DOMAINE MARCEL DEISS

RIESLING | ALTENBERG DE BERGHEIM | GRAND CRU

100% riesling

All of the best Alsace rieslings have lift. They are like Gothic arches, soaring in their elegance, never heavy, never weighted down. Marcel Deiss's rieslings are a prime example. These are wines of impeccable elegance. In the best years, they are thoroughly concentrated with fruit but so carefully balanced by a tightrope of acidity that the overall impression is not of fruit or acid, but simply of beauty and delicacy.

DOMAINE OSTERTAG

RIESLING | FRONHOLZ

100% riesling

The wines of André Ostertag have a cult following for their distinctive, mesmerizing character and for the flavors that ignite like sparks against your palate. The riesling from the vineyard known as Fronholz is amazing, with thrusts of minerals, cool jets of citrus, damp swaths of earthiness, and an almost levitating sense of spiciness. After tasting this wine, I usually can't get the memory out of my head for hours.

DOMAINE WEINBACH

PINOT GRIS | CUVÉE LAURENCE

100% pinot gris

Built in the early eighteenth century as a Capucin monastery, Domaine Weinbach is now owned and run by two women, Madame Colette Faller and her daughter, Catherine, who is in charge of marketing. (In 2014, daughter Laurence—for decades the estate's winemaker—died unexpectedly at an early age.) The wines from this estate are among the most expressive, powerful, and elegant in all of Alsace. They have a purity to them that can seem absolutely regal. The domaine's pinot gris Cuvée Laurence is a stunning example. Rich, minerally, spicy, creamy, and utterly dense with flavor, it is nonetheless a wine with a long, refined finish. The Cuvée Laurence gewürztraminer from the estate's best gewürztraminer vineyards is also mind-bending in concentration.

DOMAINE ZIND HUMBRECHT

GEWÜRZTRAMINER | GOLDERT | GRAND CRU

100% gewürztraminer

From the Grand Cru vineyard Goldert comes this richly dense and opulent, yet refined and intriguing, gewürztraminer, evocative of tropical fruits fused with roses and exotic spices. Few white grapes are more expressive and powerful than gewürztraminer, and gewürztraminer is nowhere more expressive or powerful than in Alsace, especially from a top Grand Cru vineyard such as Goldert. This wine has it all. But then, virtually all Zind Humbrecht wines are massively lush and fleshy, with bold, extroverted flavors. Not for the faint of heart.

KUENTZ-BAS

GEWÜRZTRAMINER | PFERSIGBERG | GRAND CRU

100% gewürztraminer

Kuentz-Bas makes some of the most stunning gewürztraminers in the world. This one, from the Grand Cru vineyard Pfersigberg ("hill of peach trees"), is so taut, hard, and sleek, the sensation is akin to running your hand over the biceps of a bodybuilder. In great years, the creamy, spicy flavors are massively concentrated, and yet the wine is also ravishingly elegant. The aroma is so heady, you'd swear you're lying in a bed of acacia and honeysuckle blossoms.

TRIMBACH

RIESLING | CUVÉE FRÉDÉRIC EMILE

100% riesling

A family-owned estate, Trimbach makes scrumptious gewürztraminer and pinot gris, but their rieslings can be simply devastating in their elegance and concentration. The Cuvée Frédéric Emile, named after an ancestor, comes from old vines in two Grand Cru vineyards: Osterberg and Geisberg. The aroma is quintessentially riesling—like cold stone that has been rubbed with peaches and apricots—and the vivid acidity is almost crunchy.

SWEET WINES

DOMAINE WEINBACH

PINOT GRIS | ALTENBOURG | VENDANGES TARDIVES

100% pinot gris

One of the best wineries in Alsace, Domaine Weinbach is an extraordinary producer of VTs and SGNs. This is the domaine's least expensive (though still pricey) *vendange tardive*, yet it is a masterpiece. Sensationally pure and deep aromas and flavors of orange marmalade and dried peaches predominate. The texture is like cool silk, though the body is opulent. Although sweet, the wine does not come off sugary but has a refinement that is both beautiful and memorable.

DOMAINES SCHLUMBERGER

GEWÜRZTRAMINER | CUVÉE ANNE | SÉLECTION DE GRAINS NOBLES

100% gewürztraminer

The largest of the top producers, Domaines Schlumberger has 350 contiguous acres (140 hectares), half of which are classified Grand Cru. The rieslings from this family-owned estate are delicious, but the gewürztraminers truly leave you dazzled. Cuvée Anne, a rare, late-harvest gewürztraminer SGN, is produced on average only twice a decade. The wine is so opulent and powerful it tastes as though every molecule of water has been siphoned out of it, leaving only the utter essence of fruit. The flavors and aromas zigzag among ginger, apricots, and wet granite, with flying sparks of acidity.

LANGUEDOC-
ROUSSILLON

pread over an immense crescent of land along the Mediterranean coast from Spain in the west to Provence in the east, the Languedoc-Roussillon is, in many ways, France's best-kept secret. Despite its considerable size (700,000 acres/283,000 hectares), historical importance, and innovative winemaking, the region is still relatively unknown in the New World. Yet, a century ago, almost half of all French wine was made in this one place. Today about 25 percent still is.

The wines of the Languedoc-Roussillon cover a broad spectrum, from white to red, dry to sweet, still to sparkling, and even fortified (the famous fortified wine Banyuls is made

The Languedoc-Roussillon is sometimes called *le Midi*, loosely translated as "the land of the midday sun."

here). But the region's best wines are its reds, which possess a rustic, juicy, earthy/minerally/fruity "south of France flavor" that's irresistible.

During the Middle Ages, when most vineyards here were in the care of monks, the wines

▲ *Harvesting grapes in the Languedoc-Roussillon, the large, strikingly beautiful swath of land in southern France, along the Mediterranean.*

THE QUICK SIP ON LANGUEDOC-ROUSSILLON

THE WINES of Languedoc-Roussillon are the quintessential wines of southern France and represent the most exciting, best-value French wines.

THE LANGUEDOC is the largest wine-producing region in France. More wine is produced in this one area than in the entire United States.

DOZENS OF GRAPE VARIETIES are grown, from carignan, mourvèdre, and grenache (all of which originated next door in Spain), to French varieties such as syrah, cabernet sauvignon, and chardonnay.

The Languedoc-Roussillon is bordered and sheltered by mountains on two sides—the rugged Pyrenées to the southwest, and the Cévennes Mountains part of the Massif Central, in the north.

were prized. In the fourteenth century, wines from certain parts of the Languedoc-Roussillon were so famous that the hospitals of Paris prescribed them for their healing powers. But for most of the twentieth century, the Languedoc (as it is often simply called) produced mostly the sort of no-name, no-frills *vin ordinaire* that was bought in bulk and cost less than water. (During the world wars, the ration of wine given daily to French soldiers usually came from here.) In fairness, there were small enclaves where making fine wine had always been important, but they were just that—small enclaves.

A transformation began in the 1980s, as the Languedoc became an insider's paradise for bargain hunters seeking easy-to-drink French wines that go well with Mediterranean foods. The transformation was initiated at all levels of the industry, from small producers like Borie de Maurel, Domaine de Villemajou, Domaine de l'Hortus, Gilbert Alquier, Domaine de l'Arjolle, and Mas de Daumas Gassac; to large companies, such as Fortant de France; and to very large (27 million gallons/102 million liters of wine a year!), quality-oriented cooperatives, such as Val d'Orbieu/UCCOAR.

Languedoc-Roussillon reds are often blends based on several of the same traditional grapes used in the southern Rhône Valley: syrah, mourvèdre, grenache, and carignan. (Interestingly, the latter three are all Spanish in origin, and were brought from Spain over the Pyrenees and into the Roussillon part of the Languedoc-Roussillon.) These red wines are known, as are most wines in France, by their appellations—Corbières, Faugères, St.-Chinian, and so on. However, the Languedoc is also one of the few regions in France where wines can be named after a grape variety. More on this in a moment, in The Categories of Languedoc-Roussillon Wine, page 297.

THE LAND OF YES

T he Languedoc region is named after a group of languages and dialects spoken in southern France during the Middle Ages, known collectively as the langue d'oc, or "language of oc," oc being the word for "yes" in the Occitan language of southern France. In the north of France, the word for "yes" was oïl, which later evolved to oui.

THE MOST IMPORTANT LANGUEDOC-ROUSSILLON WINES

LEADING APPELLATION-DESIGNATED WINES

BANYULS red (fortified; sweet)

CORBIÈRES red

CÔTES DU ROUSSILLON VILLAGES red

FAUGÈRES red

LA CLAPE red

LANGUEDOC white, rosé, red

MINERVOIS red

MONTPEYROUX red

MUSCAT DE FRONTIGNAN white (fortified; sweet)

MUSCAT DE RIVESALTES white (fortified; sweet)

MUSCAT DE ST.-JEAN-DE-MINERVOIS white (fortified; sweet)

PIC SAINT LOUP red

PICPOUL DE PINET white

QUATOURZE red

ST.-CHINIAN red

ST.-SATURNIN red

TERRASSES DU LARZAC red

LEADING VARIETALLY DESIGNATED WINES—PAYS D'OC IGP

CABERNET SAUVIGNON red

CHARDONNAY white

MERLOT red

PINOT NOIR red

SAUVIGNON BLANC white

SYRAH red

VIOGNIER white

APPELLATIONS OF NOTE

BLANQUETTE DE LIMOUX white (sparkling)

COLLIOURE red

CÔTES DU ROUSSILLON red

CRÉMANT DE LIMOUX white (sparkling)

FITOU red

The Languedoc and Roussillon were two separate provinces for most of history. The Languedoc became part of France in the late thirteenth century, but Roussillon belonged to Spain until the mid-seventeenth century. Nonetheless, the regions have always been entwined culturally and financially; they were finally joined administratively in the late 1980s. Today, while the province is French, threads of Spanish culture (such as the local passion for bullfighting) are still evident.

Like Provence and the southern Rhône, the Languedoc is warm, arid, and so luminously full of light it can seem as though the sky

THE GRAPES OF LANGUEDOC-ROUSSILLON

WHITES

BOURBOULENC, CLAIRETTE, GRENACHE BLANC, PICPOUL, MARSANNE, MACCABEU, ROLLE (VERMENTINO), AND ROUSSANNE: Used in numerous traditional white wines throughout the region. When yields are low and winemaking is skillful, blends of these grapes can be delicious.

CHARDONNAY: Major grape for international-style Vin de Pays d'Oc. Also used in the traditional sparkling wine Crémant de Limoux, and in the still wine Limoux.

CHENIN BLANC: Minor grape used primarily in the traditional sparkling wine Crémant de Limoux.

MAUZAC: Native Languedoc grape used mainly in the sparkling wines Blanquette de Limoux and Crémant de Limoux.

MUSCAT BLANC À PETITS GRAINS: Considered the greatest of the muscat grapes in terms of quality. Used to make the sweet fortified wines Muscat de Frontignan and Muscat de St.-Jean-de-Minervois.

MUSCAT OF ALEXANDRIA: One of the dozens of grapes with muscat in the name. Considered less prestigious than muscat blanc à petits grains. Used to make the popular sweet fortified wine Muscat de Rivesaltes, among others.

SAUVIGNON BLANC: Used for international-style Vin de Pays d'Oc.

VIOGNIER: Major grape. Source of some of the best white Vin de Pays d'Oc.

REDS

CABERNET SAUVIGNON: Major grape. Used for high-quality Vin de Pays d'Oc.

CARIGNAN: Historically a major grape, but declining in importance. Used in small amounts in numerous traditional red wines, including Corbières, Faugères, Minervois, and others. Although widely grown in the Languedoc-Roussillon, the grape originated in Spain, where it is referred to as mazuelo and cariñena.

CÔT (MALBEC), LLADONER PELUT, PICPOUL NOIR, AND TERRET NOIR: Minor grapes. Used in small amounts in traditional reds and rosés, although plantings are mostly on the decline.

CINSAUT: Workhorse grape used in inexpensive traditional red table wines and rosés.

GRENACHE: Major grape. Used for blending in traditional dry red wines, but also famous as the principal grape in the renowned, sweet fortified red wine Banyuls. Known in Spain, its original home, as garnacha.

MERLOT: Major grape for international-style Vin de Pays d'Oc.

MOURVÈDRE: Major grape. Used in numerous traditional red wines, including Corbières, Faugères, Fitou, Minervois, and others. Like grenache and carignan, Spanish in origin (referred to in Spain as monastrell).

SYRAH: Major grape. Used in numerous modern and traditional red wines, including those of Corbières, Faugères, Minervois, and others.

A masterpiece of ancient Roman architecture, the Pont du Gard was built halfway through the 1st century A.D. *It is the principal construction in 27-mile-long (50-kilometer), three-level-high limestone aqueducts that supplied the Languedoc-Roussillon city of Nîmes with water.*

itself is somehow bigger there. Compared to the vineyards of northern France, it is an easy place in which to grow grapes. The landscape is dominated by the scratchy patchwork of low bushes, resinous plants, and wild herbs known as garigue. Indeed, the wines themselves are often described as exuding garigue, a heady commingled aroma of wild, resinous thyme, rosemary, and lavender, intermixed with scrub brush and broom.

THE CATEGORIES OF LANGUEDOC-ROUSSILLON WINE

I n most French wine regions, wines are labeled according to the appellation from which they come, not the grape variety (or varieties) from which they are made. Sancerre, St.-Émilion, and Meursault, for example, are all French appellations—specific, delimited areas where wines are made in a traditional way according to strict regulations. For most of modern history, these wines were known as *Appellation d'Origine Contrôlée* (AOC) wines; as of 2009, however, appellation wines in France may also now use the European Union's designation, Protected Designation of Origin (PDO).

Appellation wines are meant to reflect their terroir, to taste of their place. In the Languedoc-Roussillon, such wines as Corbières, Faugères, and Minervois, for example, are traditional appellation wines. The best of them can be downright sensational. Indeed, within these traditional appellations, the wines from four places have been singled out as the best of the best. Known on their labels as "Crus de Languedoc," the four are Corbières-Boutenac, Minervois La Livinière, St.-Chinian Roquebrun, and St.-Chinian Berlou. More *crus* are awaiting official approval.

But the Languedoc can be confusing, because coexisting with these appellation wines are wines labeled according to the variety of grape from which they are made (chardonnay, merlot, and the like). These fall into the all-encompassing category of Vin de Pays d'Oc, which has smaller *vins de pays* inside it, such as Vin de Pays de l'Hérault. For wines labeled simply Vin de Pays d'Oc, the grapes may be sourced from anywhere in the entire Languedoc-Roussillon region, so the wines may or may not, in the conventional sense, reflect the flavors associated with a place. Among the most famous *vins de*

CRÉMANT DE LIMOUX

The word *crémant* is used to describe a French sparkling wine that is made outside the Champagne district but according to the traditional (Champagne) method. *Crémants* come from all over France; some of the best-known include Crémant d'Alsace, Crémant de Bourgogne, Crémant de Loire, and Crémant de Limoux.

Crémants de Limoux are simple, tasty sparkling wines made in some forty-one small villages surrounding the town of Limoux. The wines must be made primarily from chardonnay and chenin blanc grapes, although together the two cannot exceed 90 percent of the blend. The rest can be made up of the local grape mauzac and/or pinot noir. In the end, Crémants de Limoux are 40 to 70 percent chardonnay, 20 to 40 percent chenin blanc, 10 to 20 percent mauzac, and 0 to 10 percent pinot noir. Crémant de Limoux must spend at least fifteen months aging on the yeast lees.

A more traditional style of sparkling Limoux is called Blanquette de Limoux. It is made by the traditional method but consists of at least 90 percent mauzac and is aged just nine months on the lees, thus less than *crémant*. Interestingly, *blanquette* is the Occitan word for the mauzac grape and also refers to the dusty, white, powdery appearance of the leaves on mauzac vines.

Medieval villages dot the western hills of the Languedoc-Roussillon.

Prior to European Union legislation in 2009, these wines were always referred to as Vin de Pays d'Oc. Today they may still be referred to that way, but in some cases, wineries choose instead to use the European Union designation Pays d'Oc IGP (*Indication Géographique Protégée*), written in English as Pays d'Oc PGI (Protected Geographical Indication).

THE LAND, THE GRAPES, AND THE VINEYARDS

The majority of the vineyards of the Languedoc-Roussillon are planted on a curved plain that forms a giant, sunny semicircle facing the Mediterranean Sea. In so dependably warm a climate, the best wines generally come from vineyards on slopes or on high, cool plateaus along the foothills of the Pyrenees or the Cévennes Mountains. Soils in the region vary from alluvial soils near the sea to chalk, gravel, and limestone farther inland. Some of the best vineyards are filled with round, ancient riverbed stones, similar to those in Châteauneuf-du-Pape.

pays are those from the estate Mas de Daumas Gassac, the red wine of which (principally cabernet sauvignon) costs as much as very good quality Bordeaux. (This estate gained even greater fame in the 2000s when it was prominently featured in the "underground" wine film, *Mondovino*.)

VINS DOUX NATURELS AND BANYULS

The Languedoc-Roussillon has a long tradition of producing sweet fortified wines, known collectively as *vins doux naturels.* Translated, this means natural sweet wines, although they achieve their sweetness by human intervention, specifically by being fortified with clear brandy (grape spirits) in order to stop fermentation early, thereby leaving the sweetness of unfermented grape sugar in the wines. There are expensive versions, and very affordable ones.

Several of the best-known *vins doux naturels* are based on muscat grapes, including the locally famous wines Muscat de Frontignan and Muscat de St.-Jean-de-Minervois, both of which are made from the best type of muscat—muscat blanc à petits grains—which was cultivated by the Romans around the historic cities of Narbonne and Frontignan, on the Languedoc coast. A third fortified sweet wine, Muscat de Rivesaltes, is made with the somewhat less distinguished grape muscat of Alexandria.

With many *vins doux naturels* (especially the less expensive versions), you can taste a strong alcoholic punch, even though they are often no higher than 16 to 17 percent alcohol by volume. They are certainly sweet, but not sugary, at 8 to 10 percent residual sugar. In the past, inexpensive *vins doux naturels* were often drunk as hearty aperitifs (or, the truck driver's preference—with a shot of coffee in the morning). For most everyone else today, they are commonly drunk with (or as) dessert.

Although the muscat-based *vins doux naturels* are the most pervasive of the Languedoc's sweet fortified wines, the most unusual one is Banyuls, a reddish-colored wine made principally from grenache. When you think about sweet fortified reds, Port might spring to mind, but Banyuls is not Portlike. Neither massive in size nor dense in texture, it's deceptively (even dangerously) elegant and easy to drink, thanks to its heady flavors of coffee, chestnut, mocha, and tea, which can be irresistible. Then there's the chocolate-compatability factor. Banyuls is one of the small handful of wines in the world that pairs well with chocolate and chocolate desserts.

Before phylloxera invaded southern France in the latter part of the nineteenth century, the Languedoc-Roussillon was home to more than 150 different varieties of grapes. Today, more than fifty grape varieties still grow here, but the lesser grapes that once dominated production—aramon, macabeo, and the like—have been in a free-fall decline for more than three decades in favor of the well-regarded Mediterranean varieties syrah, mourvèdre, grenache, and others grown in the Rhône Valley and Provence, as well as international varieties. It's interesting to note, for example, that in 1968 there was no merlot in the Languedoc. Today there are 76,000 acres (30,800 hectares) of it.

THE TOP VILLAGES OF THE LANGUEDOC-ROUSSILLON

If you go into a neighborhood wine shop in Paris, you'll see numerous shelves sporting wines from villages such as Corbières, Faugères, Minervois, St.-Chinian, and others, alongside wines from the large area known simply as Languedoc. In addition, within the Languedoc are many *cru* or especially high-rated villages, some of which are pending appellation status of their

The fortified village of Carcassonne, recognized since pre-Roman times for its strategic location along two axes—linking the Atlantic and the Mediterranean and linking the Pyrenees and the Massif Central.

THE CAPITAL OF MUSSELS

C ulinarily speaking, the Languedoc is not as famous as its next-door neighbor, Provence, with perhaps one exception: mussels. The Languedoc's tiny hamlet of Bouzigues, near the town of Sète, is considered the unofficial mussel capital of France. Bouzigues, in fact, is really just a string of no-frills seafood cafés that jut out over the glistening blue saltwater lagoon called Bassin de Thau. Here in the lagoon's slow-moving current, fat, juicy mussels are cultivated in special nets or clinging to wooden frames. In just about every café, the mussels show up, often strewn with bits of grilled sausage, along with bottles of red Corbières, Faugères, Minervois, and St.-Chinian. While on first consideration mussels may seem exclusively white wine fare, the cafés of Bouzigues prove otherwise. Juicy, rustic Languedoc reds, with their supple, earthy, slightly spicy flavors, can be real winners in this combination.

own. These include Pic Saint Loup, Picpoul de Pinet, La Clape, Quatourze, Montpeyroux, St.-Saturnin, and others. Wines from any of these well-known villages—especially from small producers—are usually steals.

Corbières is spread over the undulating northern foothills of the Pyrenees, in the western part of the Languedoc-Roussillon. This fairly large region (about 34,000 acres/13,800 hectares) specializes in dense, juicy, slightly spicy, rustic, garigue-infused red blends based on carignan. One of the four *crus* of the Languedoc is here—Corbières-Boutenac. Top small Corbières producers include Domaine du Grand Crès, Gérard Bertrand, Ollieux Romanis, Domaine de Villemajou, and Château Mansenoble.

Faugères, in the center of the Languedoc-Roussillon, near the little town of Béziers, is about one-eighth the size of Corbières and makes spicy, earthy, and powerful reds, especially from old carignan vines. Faugères' top producers include Leon Barral, Château La Liquière, and Gilbert Alquier.

North of Corbières, in the hilly western Languedoc, Minervois (about 12,000 acres/4,900 hectares) is known for well-priced red wines that, at their best, have outrageously good flavor. That's especially true of the cru de Languedoc called Minervois La Livinière, which is up in the rocky hills above the flat plateau. Here, old, low-yield vines of carignan, along with grenache, syrah, and other southern

WHEN YOU VISIT . . . THE LANGUEDOC-ROUSSILLON

THE LANGUEDOC-ROUSSILLON is one of France's most compelling regions from the standpoints of history, architecture, and religion. Ancient monasteries and magnificent Roman ruins exist side by side with sun-drenched vineyards, creating a cultural tapestry that is both fascinating and poignant.

ONE OF THE BEST EXAMPLES OF MEDIEVAL ARCHITECTURE IN THE WORLD IS HERE: the ancient Cité de Carcassonne, a medieval town located within the core of the modern city of Carcassonne. The Cité has been named a UNESCO World Heritage Site for its impeccably preserved stone walls and citadel.

THE LANGUEDOC-ROUSSILLION'S annual extravaganza—the raucous Féria de Béziers—takes place every August in the city of Béziers (the French equivalent of Pamplona in Spain). A four-day festival of bullfighting, eating, drinking, and dancing, it's attended by more than one million people.

AND DON'T MISS THE STUNNING, 24,000-seat amphitheater in the ancient city of Nîmes. Built around A.D. 1 by the Romans, using stones but no mortar, it remains one of the best-preserved amphitheaters in existence. Nearby is the Roman stone temple La Maison Carrée, originally dedicated to the adopted sons of Augustus Caesar.

AND FINALLY, A GASTRONOMIC MUST: the tiny coastal village of Bouzigues, near Sète, where extraordinary oysters and mussels are farmed in saltwater lagoons. The only establishments in Bouzigues are no-frills seafood cafés, where the platters of shellfish are incomparable.

French varieties, are made into wines that are dense, rich, and for all the world taste like blackberry syrup poured over stones. Among the best producers here are Borie de Maurel, Domaine Anne Gros, Château Massamier la Mignarde, Gérard Bertrand, and Domaine Combe Blanche.

Between Minervois and Faugères lies the small (about 6,000 acres/2,400 hectares) red wine appellation of St.-Chinian. From the northern part of the region come gutsy red wines with sharp-edged grip, while wines from the southern part are usually softer. As is true in Corbières, Faugères, and Minervois, carignan is still a player in the blends here, but increasingly it is being supplanted by syrah, grenache, and mourvèdre. Two of the *crus* de Languedoc are here: St.-Chinian Roquebrun and St.-Chinian Berlou. Look for the producers Clos Bagatelle, Canet-Valette, Domaine de

Bouzigues, a tiny village on the Mediterranean, is one of France's top spots for fresh-out-of-water mussels and oysters.

Viranel, Laurent Miquel, and Château Maurel Fonsalade.

The Languedoc-Roussillon Wines to Know

The most spectacular wines of the Languedoc-Roussillon are generally not the easy-to-find Vin de Pays d'Oc wines (Mas de Daumas Gassac excepted) but, rather, the region's great traditional reds from villages like St. Chinian, Faugères, and Minervos. These wines—often made from old vine carignan, syrah, and mourvèdre—have beautiful richness and spiciness, and I've focused on them below.

WHITE

MAS DE DAUMAS GASSAC

VIN DE PAYS DE L'HÉRAULT

Approximately one-third each of chardonnay, viognier, and petit manseng, plus a touch of muscat, marsanne, and roussanne

Mas de Daumas Gassac is widely acknowledged as one of the first estates to prove that wines without AOC status (such as this *vin de pays*) could nonetheless be serious, complex wines capable of long aging (and of commanding high prices). Indeed, the estate's first wine was produced in 1978 under the guidance of the famous French enologist Émile Peynaud, who considered the estate's geography and terroir exemplary for fine wine production. Mas de Daumas Gassac was founded by the irascible Aimé Guibert, who still owns it (Guibert was prominantly featured in the documentary film, *Mondovino*). The Mas de Daumas Gassac red is a beauty of a wine, structured much like a fine Bordeaux. But I also love the estate's white, made in smaller amounts, and perhaps more distinctive. The richness of chardonnay, the floral-ness of viognier, and the exotic-ness of petit manseng make a fascinating combination, and the wine possesses an uncanny elegance.

REDS

DOMAINE RIMBERT

ST.-CHINIAN | LE MAS AU SCHISTE

40% carignan, 30% syrah, 30% grenache

The old vineyards of Jean-Marie Rimbert (some with vines broaching a century of age) are in the scenic foothills of the Cévennes Mountains, part of France's huge Massif Central. (The area of the Cévennes is one of the original homes of the French Protestants known as Huguenots.) This wine is unmistakable as a St.-Chinian, and evidence that carignan, at least in the Languedoc, can be coaxed to great heights. Violety and minerally, with dark berry flavors, it belongs to the school of red wines that have huge, savory intensity without heaviness. Immaculately "on point," the flavor of this wine is not diffused by broad vanilla strokes of oak, nor is the fruit dulled down to mush from overripeness. Instead it has that sexy, vivid, floral/earthy character that makes the traditional appellations of the Languedoc-Roussillon so desirable.

HECHT & BANNIER

FAUGÈRES

55% syrah, 35% mourvèdre, 10% carignan

In 2012, Gregory Hecht and François Bannier formed a *négociant* business focused on extraordinary small vineyards in the best traditional appellations of the Languedoc-Roussillon. Their wines seem to hit the mark every time—loaded with character, they exude a southern French sophistication. This Faugères, for example, is massive and masculine in structure and vividly alive, with notes of peat, violets, minerals, black tea, savory dried herbs, and a salty/iodine-like character. Plus, of course, waves of dense fruit that seem like a tasty fabric woven from black and red cherries. The partners' other signature wine—the Côtes du Roussillon—is a savory, gamy, berry-infused implosion of earth, spice, and fruit.

DOMAINE DE L'HORTUS

PIC SAINT LOUP

Approximately 50% syrah, 30% grenache, 20% mourvèdre

Domaine de l'Hortus is known for soft, dense reds with waves of wild resinous herbs (garigue) and the scent of woodlands floating through them. At their best, they are dark reds with a delicious savoriness reminiscent of meat juices. This wine comes into your mouth with a big arc of flavor and finishes with a spicy/minerally bang. The domaine is a family estate lying in a valley between two facing limestone cliffs, the Pic Saint Loup and the Montagne de l'Hortus. The word *hortus* is Latin for "garden," a reference to the many gardens the Romans found, to their surprise, when they arrived in the area. Long before then, this valley and the many natural caves embedded in the surrounding, protective mountains are thought to have been one of the areas where Neanderthals found refuge.

GÉRARD BERTRAND

MINERVOIS LA LIVINIÈRE | LE VIALA

60% syrah, 25% grenache, 15% carignan

Gérard Bertrand makes several terrific, honest wines in the Languedoc-Roussillon, but it's this wine—his Minervois La Livinière called Le Viala—that I find the most special. Loaded with sexy, spicy, sweaty, firm, and powerful aromas and flavors, it sits on a delicious precipice between flavors reminiscent of the earth (rocks, minerals, bark) and flavors evocative of darkness (dark plums, black figs, bitter chocolate). As in so many really good Languedoc wines, there's also a sophisticated hint of gaminess and animal fur. The small, 15-acre (6-hectare) vineyard for Le Viala sits on a south-facing, clay- and limestone-covered hillside of the Montagne Noire—Black Mountains.

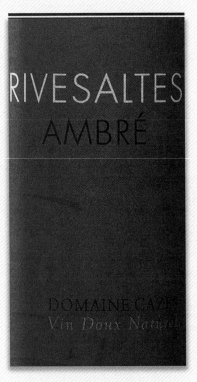

SWEET WINES

DOMAINE CAZES

RIVESALTES | AMBRÉ

100% grenache blanc

A completely unique, elegant, complex, orange/amber–colored wine, the ravishingly distinct Ambré is reminiscent of exotic spices, tea, caramel, brown sugar, dried fruits, mushrooms, and brandy. It is made by Domaine Cazes, founded in 1895 and one of the leading estates making *vin doux naturel* (the estate has no relationship with the well known Cazes family of Bordeaux). The grapes grow in a brilliantly sunny, limestone/clay amphitheater halfway between the Pyrenees Mountains to the west and the Mediterranean Sea to the east. Often served chilled as an aperitif, the wine is somewhat like amontillado Sherry, and somewhat like tawny Port. Its complexity and unreal color come in part from its aging for seven to ten years or more in large oak casks (*foudres*) before release.

LES PETITS GRAINS

MUSCAT DE SAINT JEAN DE MINERVOIS | SAINT JEAN DE MINERVOIS

100% muscat blanc à petits grains

This *vin doux natural* is one of the most lip-smacking wines of the Languedoc—and a wine so abuzz with fresh, delicious apricot flavors that you feel like you've just fallen into a pool of cool apricot and orange puree. The wine is not syrupy sweet, not heavy, not viscous, and nothing like, say, Sauternes. And there's no punch of alcohol (even though the wine is lightly fortified). Instead, this dessert wine floats over to you on a cloud of fruit, then opens up and drenches you with irresistible flavor. Located on a high limestone plateau above Minervois proper, the small appellation Saint Jean de Minervois makes some of the most luscious fortified sweet wines of France.

PROVENCE

he word *Provence* induces hunger, not thirst. One hardly thinks of wine at all, except as something to brace you for the oncoming wave of a great, garlicky aioli. It's not that the wines of Provence do not deserve attention. The problem is getting sidetracked by bouillabaisse—or by landscapes so beautiful that van Gogh, Renoir, Matisse, Picasso, and Cézanne could not stop painting them. Yet Provence's wines are both special and delicious. Provençal rosés (what everyone drinks with the local cuisine) are famous for their refreshing slash of flavor. The region's reds—bold and distinctive—are creating a small surge of new excitement. And although the quality of the white wines ranges across the board, the best of them are perfect with a plate of grilled

> The Romans called this region *nostra provincia,* our province, hence Provence.

Mediterranean fish. One thing is for sure: Provençal foods do throw the switch that makes Provençal wines come alive.

Provence encompasses the vast, rambling countryside of far southeastern France. In fact, one can't get any farther south, for Provence dead-ends on the beaches of the French Riviera. From the coast, with its famous seaside towns of Marseille, Bandol, and

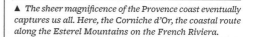
▲ *The sheer magnificence of the Provence coast eventually captures us all. Here, the Corniche d'Or, the coastal route along the Esterel Mountains on the French Riviera.*

THE QUICK SIP ON PROVENCE

PROVENCE, in the far southeastern corner of France, along the Mediterranean Sea, has only recently emerged as a region producing serious wines.

THE MAJORITY OF PROVENÇAL WINES are blends based on a curious array of international as well as Rhône grape varieties.

PROVENCE MAKES DELICIOUS red wines, but the most popular Provençal wines are zesty, refreshing rosés, which are the gold standard for rosés everywhere.

Viognier grapes bask in the warmth that emanates from the rocky soils of the famous Domaine Trévallon near Les Baux.

ROSÉ, JUST RIGHT

If there's a lesson to learn from Provence in matching wine and food, it's the amazing versatility of snappy fruity rosés in complementing countless Mediterranean dishes. In particular, Provençal rosés are delicious with the region's seafood dishes, seasoned as they usually are with generous amounts of olive oil, garlic, herbs, and spices. The supreme example is bouillabaisse, the traditional Provençal fish stew flavored with olive oil, saffron, and dried orange peel, and then usually served with croutons and rouille, a super-garlicky, pepper-spiked mayonnaise. The flavor of many wines would disappear or be distorted by such dramatic ingredients. Not so with Provençal rosés. Boldly fruity and substantial in body, they are tailor-made for bouillabaisse and other hearty seafood dishes.

St.-Tropez, Provence extends inland. How far is hard to say; it sometimes overlaps with the Rhône Valley. Indeed, the French often define Provence more by its remarkable landscape—which is to say, by the presence of garigue. The word describes the character of the land: sunbaked, low, rolling hills covered in thin, rocky soils of limestone, schist, and quartz, plus old oaks and dry, scrubby, resiny plants—especially wild rosemary, wild thyme, and wild lavender. The best Provençal wines are said to smell and taste of garigue.

Provence's four most important wine appellations all fall in the far south, with some bordering on the Mediterranean. They are: Bandol, Cassis, Coteaux d'Aix-en-Provence (and its terrific, tiny subregion, Les Baux de Provence), and Côtes de Provence. Bandol is the most prestigious; Côtes de Provence is the largest.

Provence's eclectic hodgepodge of grape varieties reflects the region's rich history of political affiliations with just about every Mediterranean power, large and small. Most of the Rhône grapes are grown, as well as traditional Provençal grapes; Italian grapes, such as vermentino; and even Bordeaux grapes, such as cabernet sauvignon.

The climate of Provence is dramatic. The sun (three thousand hours of sunlight a year!) bounces off the land and sea, creating

THE GRAPES OF PROVENCE

Provençal wines have historically been blends of many grape varieties that on their own would be undistinguished.

WHITES

BOURBOULENC: Commonly used in blending. Rustic and undistinguished on its own.

CHARDONNAY, MARSANNE, SAUVIGNON BLANC, SÉMILLON, AND VIOGNIER: Commonly used in blends, especially in more modern avant-garde wines.

CLAIRETTE: Very common blending grape in traditional white wines. Can have pretty aromas and good acidity.

GRENACHE BLANC: White clone of grenache. Very common blending grape in traditional white wines. Can make delicious, citrusy wines of personality.

ROLLE: Also known as vermentino. Adds freshness and vivacity to blends.

UGNI BLANC: Undistinguished, common blending grape.

REDS

BRAQUET, CALITOR, CARIGNAN, CINSAUT, FOLLE NOIRE, AND TIBOUREN: Grapes used in blending. At low yields, carignan can have real character, and cinsaut is a major force in many rosés.

CABERNET SAUVIGNON: Used in some of the best reds and rosés, especially in the appellations Coteaux d'Aix-en-Provence and Côtes de Provence.

GRENACHE: Common blending grape used in many reds and most rosés. Can add delicious berry flavors.

MOURVÈDRE: Major grape, used in many of the top reds and rosés for structure.

SYRAH: Fairly minor grape in Provence, but used in some of the very best reds.

---

relentless light—no wonder painters love it. As in the Rhône, the aggressive wind from the north, known as Le Mistral, cools the vines and helps prevent rot, but it can also tear the vines apart. The best vineyards are therefore located in protected pockets, mostly facing south toward the Mediterranean, with the hills at their backs.

BANDOL

The best appellation in Provence, Bandol is a relatively small seaside region about a 30-mile (48-kilometer) drive southeast from the center of Marseille. The best Bandol rosés (Domaines Ott's Cuvée Marine, for example) usually have a higher percentage of spicy, structured mourvèdre than less well-favored examples. But red wines are where the real action is. These are deep, wild, leathery, spicy wines. By law, they must be 50 percent mourvèdre, and some producers use as much as 100 percent.

There are dozens of small producers in Bandol, as well as cooperatives. The most famous producer is Domaine Tempier, owned by the Peyraud family. Like romantic characters out of a novel on the alluring back-to-basics Provençal lifestyle, the Peyrauds not only make some of Provence's most ravishing red and rosé wines on their humble, charming estate but they are also among the region's best cooks. The matriarch of the family, Lulu Peyraud, was a mentor to the famous California chef Alice Waters.

Butter and cheese. The king and queen of French gastronomy in a region that lives to eat (and drink).

WHEN YOU VISIT . . . PROVENCE

Provence is undoubtedly one of the world's most charming wine regions, conducive to aimless wanderlust and weeks spent crisscrossing the countryside, visiting wine estates, and making a habit of cold carafes of rosé twice a day in countless cafés. Most Provençal wine estates are small and fairly humble. It's good to make an appointment in advance and very helpful to speak French.

COTEAUX D'AIX-EN-PROVENCE

North and west of the old town of Aix, in the heart of Provence, is the wine region of Coteaux d'Aix-en-Provence. At about 9,100 acres (3,700 hectares), it's roughly twenty times larger than Cassis. Within this large appellation is a smaller, renowned appellation

PASTIS

*T*he most well-loved aperitif in Provence is pastis, a greenish-yellow, licorice-flavored liqueur served with a carafe of ice water. When the water is added to the pastis, the drink immediately turns ominously cloudy. The licoricey forerunner of pastis, absinthe, was outlawed by the French government in 1915 because of the toxicity of the wormwood leaves from which it was made. Today, pastis, which does not include wormwood and is not toxic, is made by infusing either licorice or aniseed in a distilled spirit.

known as Les Baux de Provence. Here, the limestone soils and hot days are perfect for red grapes (the surrounding valley is known as the Val d'Enfer—"Valley of Hell").

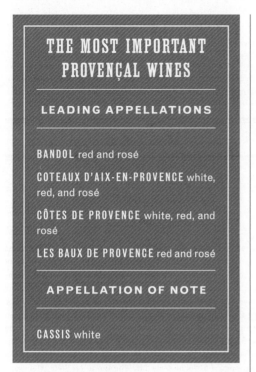

THE MOST IMPORTANT PROVENÇAL WINES

LEADING APPELLATIONS

BANDOL red and rosé

COTEAUX D'AIX-EN-PROVENCE white, red, and rosé

CÔTES DE PROVENCE white, red, and rosé

LES BAUX DE PROVENCE red and rosé

APPELLATION OF NOTE

CASSIS white

The best wines are made from grenache, cinsaut, mourvèdre, and syrah, with cabernet sauvignon and carignan allowed to make up 30 percent of the blend, but no more. Cabernet is the surprise here, for it's not a Mediterranean grape and is extremely rare in other parts of Provence, and nonexistent in the Rhône. Less rosé (and far less white wine) is made in Coteaux d'Aix, although some local finds are surprisingly good.

Among the top producers are Mas de la Dame, Domaine de Trévallon, and Château Vignelaure. It was the former owner of Château Vignelaure, Georges Brunet, who, among others, brought cabernet sauvignon to Provence from Bordeaux in the 1960s. Brunet had once owned Bordeaux's Château La Lagune.

CÔTES DE PROVENCE

Like Côtes-du-Rhône, the appellation Côtes de Provence is not a single place but rather many vast tracts (almost 50,000 acres/20,200 hectares in all) of noncontiguous vineyards. These are found in every part of Provence except the west. Côtes de Provence wines are therefore the product of numerous small, individual climates and terrains. They range a lot in quality.

Almost 90 percent of the wine is dry rosé, based on grenache, cinsaut, and the local red grape tibouren. A lion's share of this is simply chugalug co-op pink. But there are also a few fine estates concentrating on making serious rosés from the grapes listed above, as well as reds based increasingly on cabernet sauvignon or syrah.

The most famous and largest of the top estates is the family-owned firm of Domaines Ott, the wines of which are sold in unique, amphora-shaped (some say bowling-pin-shaped) bottles. The Otts own several properties in the Côtes de Provence, plus one in Bandol. Although white wines are fairly rare in the Côtes de Provence, the Otts make three, as well as two earthy, spicy reds. But most famous are the Ott rosés. The regular one, called Clair de Noirs, is a wine you could easily drink all summer long, and the sharper, more bracing one, called La Déesse, is just waiting for any food slathered in aioli.

CASSIS

*T*he cassis most of us first knew is a black-currant liqueur, which, when added to white wine, makes an aperitif called a Kir. Although the names are the same, Cassis, the wine region, has nothing to do with the liqueur. A popular (but minor) appellation of Provence, Cassis is a small fishing village a few miles southeast of Marseille. Stories are told about how the prostitutes of Marseille, in times past, helped pick the grapes at harvest. Surrounding the fishing village are the vineyards, fewer than 400 acres 160 hectares) in all. Most of the wine is mouthfilling dry white, made principally from clairette and marsanne grapes.

The Provençal Wines to Know

Sitting in a café, you could drink the best wines of Provence all day long. They are mostly not intellectual wines, but wines of pleasure . . . wines that remind us of the time when reaching for a gulp of wine was as natural and common as reaching for a hunk of bread.

WHITE

MAS DE LA DAME

LES BAUX DE PROVENCE | LA STÈLE

80% rolle, 20% roussanne

Mas de la Dame ("Farm of the Women") makes some of the most distinctive (and good-value) wines of Provence—wines that speak of the luminous sun and of the hard scrabble of the wild, herb-covered, stony escarpment called the Alpilles. This wine—their white—smells like a southern French kitchen with sage and thyme hanging from the rafters and wild anise and lavender growing in flowerpots on the windows. It's a weighty white in terms of body (all the better when in the company of garlic), but has no oakiness or sweetness. The La Stèle Rouge (grenache and syrah)—a spicy/peppery red—is also stellar. The name *La Stèle* (the word is Latin for a stone erected for funereal or commemorative purposes) comes from a quote by Nostradamus, "*un jour, la mer recouvrira la terre et s'arrêtera à la stèle du Mas de la Dame*" ("One day, the sea will once again cover the land and will stop at the stele of Mas de la Dame"). Nostrodamus, a sixteenth-century Provençal apothecary and healer during one of Europe's worst plagues, was also purported to be a "seer" of the future (he made 6,338 prophecies). The original fifteenth-century estate (upon which the current Mas de la Dame was founded in the early 1900s) was owned by a woman named Hélène Hugolène, the first "dame." It is not known exactly how Nostrodamus came to be familiar with the estate and its wines, though the property would probably have been known to any educated inhabitant of Provence at the time.

ROSÉS

CHÂTEAU D'ESCLANS

CÔTES DE PROVENCE | ROSÉ

Mostly grenache with some rolle (vermentino)

The beautiful, unreal color of this rosé could not be characterized as pink, exactly—it's more like light with a translucent copper/silver sheen. The wine itself is fantastically fresh—chalky and palate coating, with a bracingly dry finish. It's a bold wine, with dramatic impact on the palate—a character all the best Provençal rosés possess. It deserves to be served unabashedly cold, next to cold poached lobster. Owned by Sacha Lichine, whose family is the former owner of Bordeaux's Château Prieuré-Lichine, and Patrick Léon, the former managing director of Château Mouton-Rothschild, the estate also produces a less-pricey rosé called Whispering Angel, and what may be the only $100 bottle of rosé in the world—called Garrus—but I find this wine, known as the estate wine, so much more pure and true.

CHÂTEAU BEAULIEU

COTEAUX D'AIX-EN-PROVENCE | ROSÉ

40% grenache, 40% syrah, 20% cabernet sauvignon

The color of this superb wine—an ever-so-delicate neon orange-pink—could set off a fashion rage. But the flavor—utterly refined, with a starburst of pure watermelon and strawberry—is the best part. Then there's the way the wine moves on the palate, a sort of zoom/splash/bite effect. Vivid yet elegant rosés such as this seem to encapsulate happiness.

REDS

DOMAINE TEMPIER

BANDOL | LA TOURTINE

Approximately 80% mourvèdre, plus cinsaut and grenache

From a single chalky-clay hillside vineyard above the village of Le Castellet comes Domaine Tempier's almost menacingly powerful La Tourtine. It is a textbook example of the dark, masculine wines that emerge from mourvèdre, one of the latest-ripening grapes in the world (and thus a grape that absolutely needs the massively sunny, dry climate of Bandol). The edge and grip of this wine is astounding, as is its savory Provençal meaty character—a flavor not unlike the crust of a lamb chop that has been covered in olive oil and herbs and then roasted (a dish, by the way, that a wine like this really needs). The four-hundred-year-old Domaine Tempier is a legendary estate in Provence. In 1936, Lucie Tempier married Lucien Peyraud, and throughout their marriage, the Peyrauds worked tirelessly to elevate the wines of Bandol and the status of mourvèdre as one of France's great grapes. Their impact also extended into cuisine. Lucie Tempier (known as Lulu), a highly accomplished French cook, was a mentor to California's famous chef Alice Waters, whom many credit with ushering in a new culinary era in the United States.

CHÂTEAU DE PIBARNON

BANDOL

100% mourvèdre

This is what I think of as an honest wine—a wine that mirrors its landscape and offers it back as something to be tasted and taken into the body. The edgy, minerally, rocky flavors are animated, and the sense of fresh red cherries and raspberries gives the wine a brightness. But there's intrigue here, too . . . notes of animal fur, strange spices, coffee, roasted meats—the kind of primordial aromas and flavors that are the apogee of mourvèdre, and that take our senses to a darker side. One of the top estates of Provence, Pibarnon sits above the rocky limestone amphitheater that is Bandol, on hillsides facing the sea.

DOMAINE DE TRÉVALLON

VIN DE PAYS DES BOUCHES DU RHÔNE

Approximately 50% cabernet sauvignon, 50% syrah

This absolutely scrumptious and legendary wine is not to be missed. Black, thick, and silky, in most years it's got an almost hauntingly masculine, earthy, minerally aroma. The flavors all suggest wildness—wild blackberries and brambles; wild resiny herbs; wild tangles of dried brush; wild exotic spices. Domaine de Trévallon's vineyards are on the edge of the rocky Alpilles Mountains, surrounded by the eerie, desolate landscape of the Val d'Enfer ("Valley of Hell"). The domaine specializes in cabernet sauvignon, which here turns into wines as startling and dramatic as the land itself. Indeed, were it not for the large percentage of cabernet, the wine would carry the AOC designation Les Baux de Provence. But Les Baux limits the amount of cabernet a wine can have, and thus the appellation of this fantastic red is Vin de Pays des Bouches du Rhône.

ARMAGNAC & COGNAC

THE TWO FAMOUS GRAPE-BASED SPIRITS OF FRANCE

ARMAGNAC

Deep in France's southwest corner, about 100 miles (160 kilometers) south of Bordeaux, lies Gascony, a bucolic farming region and an enclave for perhaps the most sensual, rich, rustic cooking in France. Indulgences (if not contraband) elsewhere, foie gras and confit of duck are virtually daily fare here, and the propensity to sauté the accompanying potatoes (or just about any other vegetable) in duck fat, too, leaves French nutritionists wondering why the local

▲ *Autumn in Gascony, Armagnac's home in the southwestern corner of France.*

Monsieur Gessler sits among his oldest Armagnacs at Domaine de Joÿ.

population isn't keeling over. But in Gascony, eating traditionally matters. Not surprisingly, so does drinking well.

As the local desserts—soufflé of prunes in Armagnac and fruit strudel laced with Armagnac—reveal, this is the home of one of France's most well-loved brandies. Armagnac (ARE-ma-nyack) is far less famous than its sister, Cognac, and the two are usually assumed to be quite similar, since both are distilled from grapes. Not so. In everything from how it tastes to how it is made, Armagnac is distinct and unique. It is decidedly not Cognac, and when you're in Gascony, you get the feeling that the Armagnacais, as the people of the region are called, like it that way. Proud and somewhat stubborn, they quickly remind you that this, after all, is the home of d'Artagnan, the most famed of the fictionalized king's musketeers who, in the nineteenth century, were immortalized by Alexandre Dumas.

Armagnac has the longest history of any French brandy. By the thirteenth century, simple distilling techniques first used in the Arab world (primarily for perfumes) had spread into Spain and over the Pyrenees into southwest France. Like distillations of local herbs and flowers, the first distillations of the region's grapes, thought to have occurred in the early fifteenth century, were for medical purposes. The clear brandies that resulted—the seminal Armagnacs—were said to inspire a sense of well-being, relieve toothaches, diminish mental anguish, and promote courage. (Joan of Arc, although not from the region, came to be known as l'Armagnacaise, because of her courage.)

Being first didn't guarantee Armagnac the prominence you might expect. Unlike the region of Cognac, Armagnac was isolated inland, with no navigable river that could serve as an easy means of promoting commerce. Nonetheless, by the seventeenth century Dutch traders installed themselves in Gascony, as they did in Cognac, and the production of Armagnac increased, even though it had to be transported overland before it could

> **The top Armagnacs are masculine spirits—more rustic, robust, and full-bodied than the top Cognacs.**

CALVADOS

Unlike its French cousins Cognac and Armagnac, both of which are distilled from grapes, Calvados (CAL-va-dose) is distilled from apples (and sometimes pears)—but not just any apples. Approximately 800 or so heirloom varieties of apples grow in Normandy, the French region most famous for this drink. Of these, most producers would grow 20 to 25 different varieties, among them, Douce Moen, Kermerrien, Douce Coet Ligne, Bedan, Binet Rouge, Frequin Rouge, Marie Menard, and Petit Jaune. The apples fall into four flavor categories: sweet, bittersweet, bitter, and acidic. By distilling different kinds of apples in different proportions, the Calvados maker crafts a subtle, complex apple spirit. About 17 pounds of apples are needed to make one bottle of Calvados.

By law, Calvados can be made only in Normandy. It's a staunch tradition for diners in the region to imbibe a shot of Calvados in the middle of a long, rich meal. The shot, called a *trou Normand* (Norman hole), supposedly creates a hole in the stomach, temporarily halting digestion and allowing even more food to be eaten!

The most famous district within the Calvados region is the Pays d'Auge, known for its chalky soil and superior apples. All Calvados Pays d'Auge is double-distilled in a pot still and aged in oak casks for a minimum of twenty-four months, although some of the finest spirits may be aged in oak for more than six years. (Calvados made in a sister region of the Pays d'Auge—Calvados Domfrontais—is made from at least 30 percent pears in addition to apples.) Notable producers include Michel Huard, Boulard, Busnel, Christian Drouin, and Roger Groult, as well as the artisanal producer/growers Domaine de Montreuil, Lemorton, and Adrien Camut.

be loaded on ships destined for northern markets. By the middle of the nineteenth century, a canal built on a local river connected Armagnac to Bordeaux, and for the first time its brandy became readily accessible.

The vineyards dedicated to the production of Armagnac cover some 11,776 acres (4,766 hectares) and are divided into three subdistricts: the Bas Armagnac, Armagnac-Ténarèze, and the Haut Armagnac. Of the three, the Bas Armagnac (lower Armagnac, so named for its lesser altitude) not only produces the most wine for distillation (67 percent), but it's also home to most of the top producers and best Armagnacs, with their flavor notes of plums and prunes. Situated in western Gascony, near the immense pine forests of the Landes, the Bas Armagnac is noted for its sand-based soil, often with a high iron content, plus small pieces of clay. Armagnacs from Ténarèze can

A farmhouse in Normandy where Calvados is distilled from heirloom apples.

be more floral, lively, and sharp when young, although they develop finesse with age. Some 32 percent of the wine destined for distillation is made in this subregion. As for the Haut Armagnac, only 1 percent of all Armagnacs are

The old copper still of the Samalens Distillery, one of the top producers of Armagnac. Most Armagnacs are distilled only once, giving the spirit a robust character.

produced there today. If an Armagnac is from the Bas Armagnac, it will say so on the label. Armagnacs from Ténarèze are sometimes labeled as such, but more often the label will simply read Armagnac.

The top Armagnacs are more rustic, robust, fragrant, and full-bodied than the top Cognacs, and the reason begins with the grapes. In Cognac, the neutral-tasting grape ugni blanc makes up most of the blend. In Armagnac, ugni blanc is only about 55 percent of the blend to be distilled. The rest comes from up to eleven other white grapes, although just four—folle blanche, colombard, ugni blanc, and to a declining extent, Baco blanc—are of importance. While all provide a so-called "neutral foundation" for Armagnac, folle blanche is also thought to contribute some faint elegance, plus floral and fruity notes, and colombard is said to add a slightly herbal note. As for Baco blanc, or Baco 22A, as it is more technically known, the grape is a hybrid. It was developed after the phylloxera epidemic and was well appreciated for its resistance to rot and mildew. In Armagnac it adds such fullness and character to the blend that the resulting *eau-de-vie* is almost fat. Armagnacs made with a

significant amount of Baco are instantly loved for their rich fruitiness, even if they do lack a little elegance. Interesting, in the 1990s the French government stipulated that wines and brandies with Appellation d'Origine Contrôlée status (which Armagnac has) must, as of 2010, discontinue any use of hybrids and instead be based exclusively on *vinifera* varieties. The outcry in Armagnac was so strong that in 2005 a legal exception was made. Today, Armagnac is the only AOC wine in France that may legally include hybrid grapes.

Armagnac is distilled in a way that accentuates its already bold character. Rather than being double distilled, as Cognacs are, most (but not all) Armagnacs are distilled only once. Single distillation results in a more gutsy, aromatic, and less polished *eau-de-vie* when it is young. The distillation takes place in what is known as a continuous still. The process (simplified) goes like this: The base wine enters a gas-fired still and is heated in a chamber. From there it passes into the main column of the still, where it cascades over a number of hot plates. When it reaches the bottom, it begins to evaporate. The alcoholic vapors then rise back up through the incoming wine, causing the *eau-de-vie* to take on more flavors and aromas. Finally, the vapors exit through the top of the column into a condensing coil (where they become liquid as they cool). This liquid is ultimately collected in wooden casks where it will remain to age, becoming, in time, Armagnac.

Since Cognac's double distillation results in a more polished, elegant brandy that can ultimately be drunk younger, you might wonder why single distillation is appealing to most Armagnac producers. The answer is historic. Armagnac producers tend to be tiny (there are no large firms equivalent to Cognac's Courvoisier, Martell, Rémy Martin, or Hennessy) and comparatively poor. Many never had the capital required to own their own stills. Producers traditionally relied on distillers who, with movable stills (*alambics ambulants*), went from farm to farm from November to January. The continuous still was, and is, both easier to transport and cheaper to run.

The *eau-de-vie* that emerges from the still in precious drops is not yet an Armagnac, however. What turns the *eau-de-vie* into brandy is aging in oak barrels, in this case 106- to 111-gallon (400- to 420-liter) casks, often from the black oak of the Monlezun forest in Bas Armagnac, or from the Limousin forest of southern France. While the Armagnac-to-be is left in wood to mature, evaporation of both water and, to a somewhat lesser extent, alcohol concentrates the liquid. Because of this, Armagnacs, like Cognacs, are gradually cut with water or *petites eaux*, a weak mixture of water and Armagnac, to bring their final alcohol level down to 40 percent, or 80 proof.

Armagnacs are sold in three ways: by such terms as VSOP and XO, by age designations, and by vintage. Armagnacs that carry designations like VSOP are blends of a variety of *eaux-de-vie* of different ages. As in Cognac, the designations indicate the age of the youngest *eau-de-vie* in the blend but the average age of the Armagnac is usually older. Here are the lengths of time the youngest *eau-de-vie* in an Armagnac blend must be aged in barrel:

VS (VERY SUPERIOR) OR THREE STAR (***): one to three years

VSOP (VERY SUPERIOR OLD PALE): four to nine years

NAPOLÉON: six to nine years

XO (EXTRA OLD) AND HORS D'AGE: ten to nineteen years

XO PREMIUM: more than twenty years

Finally, Armagnacs are often labeled according to vintage, something that's rare in Cognac. The *eau-de-vie* in a vintage Armagnac must come entirely from that vintage and be aged for a minimum of ten years in barrel prior to release. (The bottle must indicate a bottling date so that you know when the Armagnac was taken out of the barrel.)

Armagnacs don't really age once they are removed from the barrel and put in glass bottles, where they're protected from oxygen. A 1947 Armagnac that stayed in the barrel for twenty years, for example, is different from a 1947 Armagnac that stayed in the barrel for forty years before being bottled. But an Armagnac distilled in 1947 and put in bottles in, say, 1975, and one distilled in 1970 and bottled in 1998 are equally mature—twenty-eight years—even though they bear different vintage dates.

A great Armagnac has a complex flavor reminiscent of prunes, quince, dried apricots, vanilla, earth, caramel, roasted walnuts, and toffee, and it is best when it is well aged, which is to say ten years old or older. Younger Armagnacs have not developed any of the extraordinary nuances of older ones, and they often taste too blatantly fiery. It's easy to tell how old a vintage Armagnac is; ditto for an Armagnac labeled *trente ans d'age* (thirty years old). But it's not so easy to tell when the Armagnac is labeled with letters or names, such as Extra or Napoléon, since those letters and names tell you only the minimum age of the youngest *eau-de-vie* in the blend, not the average age of blend as a whole. The best advice here is to let price be your guide. There's no such thing as a cheap, well-aged Armagnac. Among the top producers of Armagnac are the *négociants* Sempé, Larressingle, Samalens,

Marquis de Caussade, Darroze, Château de Laubade, and Tariquet, as well as the artisanal producers Château de Ravignan, Domaine d'Ognoas, Domaine Boingnères, Delord, Domaine du Miquer, Château de Briat, and Pellehaut.

COGNAC

I'm not sure I knew what to expect the first time I visited the Cognac region, but the throttling potency of the (not-very-high-quality) Cognacs I had drunk up until then certainly did not prepare me for so gentle, so pastoral, so enchanting a landscape. This is France at her most timeless—waves of green vineyards, thick cornfields, and meadows noisy with birds are dotted here and there with stone farmhouses and unassuming hamlets. The region, 197,000 acres (79,700 hectares) of vines, is about a one-and-a-half hour drive north of Bordeaux and worlds apart in character.

Technically, the Cognac (CON-nyack) region falls into two French administrative *départements* (the rough equivalent of states): Charente-Maritime on the Atlantic coast and, just inland from that, Charente. (Besides Cognac, this part of France is renowned for its butter, snails, and *fleur de sel,* the finest type of natural French sea salt.) Both *départements* take their name from the Charente River, which meanders through them, and on whose banks are the two important towns, Cognac and Jarnac. Cognac, of course, has given the brandy its name, and about 10 miles (16 kilometers) away, Jarnac, the other hub of Cognac activity, is home to such prestigious firms as Courvoisier, Hine, and Delamain.

As the saying goes, all Cognac is brandy, but not all brandy is Cognac. Good-quality Cognacs can cost $200 or more a bottle, and the dozen or so most expensive cost about $5,000 a bottle. (The single most expensive Cognac—of which there is only one bottle—is the Henri IV Dudognon Heritage, valued at 2 million dollars. It was aged in barrel for more than 100 years and, for good measure, the bottle is dipped in 24-karat gold and sterling platinum, and decorated with 6,500 diamonds.)

Poised between the ocean and the Massif Central, where maritime and continental climates collide, Cognac straddles a northern French climate and a southern one. These factors, combined with wide variations in the soil, have led Cognac to be divided into six smaller subdistricts, or *crus,* each of which

The Rémy Martin distillery, founded in 1724. The house makes its Cognacs from grapes grown in the very best districts within Cognac, the areas known as Grande Champagne and Petite Champagne.

STORING, SERVING, AND TASTING FRANCE'S SPIRITS

Cognac and Armagnac are very different from wine when it comes to storing, serving, and drinking. First, none of them improve with age after they are bottled; each is ready to drink when you buy it. Not drinking the entire bottle immediately, however, presents no problem. An open bottle of Cognac or Armagnac will remain in good condition for about a year.

Bottles of Cognac and Armagnac should be stored upright, not on their sides. The high alcohol content in the spirits can rot the cork, causing unpleasant aromas to form.

As for giant balloon snifters, forget them. Impressive as they may appear, such snifters dissipate brandy's aroma, meanwhile propelling alcohol vapors toward you so forcefully that you may feel like you've been smacked between the eyes. In the regions of Cognac and Armagnac, the preferred glass is a relatively small (it should be easy to cradle in your hand), chimney-shaped glass with a thin rim. And, all the Hollywood portrayals to the contrary, neither the glass nor the spirit should be warmed over a flame; direct heating discombobulates the brandy's aroma and flavors. Generally speaking, a 1- to 2-ounce serving is customary.

Wine tasters commonly plunge their noses into wineglasses and inhale deeply—not a good idea with any of these spirits. They are meant to be sniffed gently and at a slight distance. Similarly, taking tiny, not large, sips accentuates the spirits' smoothness. Finally, don't assume that a deep, rich color indicates that the spirit has been aged a long time. Caramel is allowed as a coloring agent, enabling some Cognacs and Armagnacs to appear older than they really are.

---

produces a Cognac of a different character and quality. (The name of the subdistrict usually appears on the label; if there is no subdistrict name, then the Cognac is a blend of different crus.) The top three *crus*, in descending order of quality, are Grande Champagne, Petite Champagne, and Borderies. The word *champagne* here has no relationship to the region of the same name. Rather, champagne in Cognac derives from the Latin *campagna*, meaning "open fields," as distinguished from the French *bois*, "woods." Cognac's three less-highly-regarded subdistricts, Fins Bois, Bons Bois, and Bois Ordinaires ("fine woods," "good woods," and "ordinary woods," respectively) were all once forests. Grande Champagne is indisputably the most renowned of the districts, and its porous chalky soil is thought to produce the richest-tasting Cognacs with the most elegance and finesse. (A confusing designation you might come across—Fine Champagne—is not a subdistrict itself, but rather the term for a Cognac distilled from wines made exclusively in Grande and Petite Champagne.)

Cognac is made from the most innocuous of grape varieties. The leading one by far is ugni blanc, which in the Cognac region is called St.-Émilion, even though it has nothing to do with the wine district of that name in Bordeaux. Colombard and folle blanche are used in much smaller amounts. (By law, six other varieties—sémillon and five very obscure varieties—may be included, but none can account for more than 10 percent of the grapes grown and used.) All of these grapes are grown to produce enormous yields, resulting in a thin, high-acid blended wine that is barely palatable on its own. Distillation changes everything. Indeed, a high-acid blend is ideal for distillation, for acidity contributes to the brandy's structure.

The vineyards of Cognac stretch over the bucolic landscape north of Bordeaux. This is pastoral France at her best. In Cognac, time takes on another dimension.

Distillation involves boiling a liquid and then condensing the vapors that form. These condensed vapors are a highly concentrated form of the original liquid. The first distillers were Egyptians who, as early as 3000 B.C., used crude stills to make perfumes. But in the Cognac region, distillation—and the birth of Cognac as we know it today—was the result of Dutch intervention. From the end of the Roman Empire until the sixteenth century, the area surrounding the Charente River was known for neutral-tasting wine, most of it white and low in alcohol. The Dutch traded in the area, primarily for salt, and despite their disappointment with the wine's proclivity to deteriorate during the sea voyage, they began to purchase it and ship it to England and other northern countries. Eventually, to delay the deterioration, they began to distill the wine once it reached the Netherlands, and then sell the more durable result, which they called burnt wine—*brandewijn*. By the seventeenth century, the Dutch began to install stills in the Charente region itself. Today more than three hundred firms distill Cognac, although just six—Hennessy, Martell, Rémy Martin, Camus, Otard, and Courvoisier—account for about 90 percent of the sales.

Cognac is distilled twice (unlike most of the world's other brandies) in small copper pot stills, known as *alambics charentais*.

The first distillation produces a cloudy liquid that is roughly 30 percent alcohol (the *brouillis*). This is distilled a second time (*la bonne chauffe*, literally, the good heating) to produce a clear Cognac that is 70 percent alcohol, or 140 proof, about twice what it will be once it's bottled. During each distillation the distiller must expertly make *la coupe*, the cut, separating the "heads," the liquid distilled first, and the "tails," what is distilled last, from the *coeur*, or "heart." The heads and tails contain off odors and flavors; only the heart is used to make Cognac.

The heart at this point is a clear, rather harsh brandy traditionally called *eau-de-vie*— "water of life." What transforms this into Cognac is long aging in moderately large barrels that hold between 71 and 119 gallons (270 and 450 liters) and are made of oak from one of two famous French forests, Tronçais or Limousin. Immediately as it leaves the still, the brandy is put into barrels (either new or old depending on the firm's preference for intense or delicate flavors). Left in these barrels for years, the water in the brandy gradually evaporates, as does, usually to a lesser extent, the alcohol. Between 2 and 5 percent of pure alcohol, called the angel's share, evaporates from each barrel each year. (Given the vast number of barrels in the region, it's estimated that about 20 million bottles' worth of brandy evaporates yearly.) During this process, the level of humidity in a firm's huge barrel-holding warehouse, or *chai*, is crucially important. Too little humidity and the brandy loses its alcohol more slowly because more water evaporates. This hardens and dries out the brandy. Too much humidity and the Cognac will be flabby and lack structure. The perfect level of humidity is found right beside the Charente River, where many of the old warehouses are located. Throughout the process of evaporation and concentration, the brandy is also acted on by oxygen, which, through numerous natural chemical reactions, causes the brandy to soften and become more fragrant. All the while, the brandy is also absorbing the subtle vanilla and crème brûlée–like flavors of the oak, and taking on a rich brownish amber color.

Although the brandy progressively loses alcohol as it rests in the barrel, it does so slowly. Its strength must still be brought down to the level stipulated by law for bottling, 40 percent alcohol, or 80 proof. This is done by gradually adding distilled water to the brandy as it ages in barrel, or by adding *faible*, a weak mixture of distilled water and Cognac that has been aged.

Unlike most wines, most Cognacs are expected to be consistent year after year, so most don't carry a vintage date. Each Cognac firm achieves consistency by a complex and continual process of blending different lots of brandy, each of which may be a different age. In practice, many brandies are aged in barrels for twenty-five to sixty years. (After sixty years, most brandy is thought to decline rather than improve.) It's said that no truly great Cognac can be produced without including a proportion of very old brandy, which contributes a pungent, earthy character known as *rancio*.

When a Cognac firm advertises that its Cognac has been aged thirty-five years, that figure is the average age of all the brandies that went into the blend. This is not, however, what you will see on the label. Such label designations as XO or VSOP refer to the youngest *eau-de-vie* in the blend, not the average age of all of them. In Courvoisier XO, for example, the youngest *eau-de-vie* must be aged

six-and-a-half years. (The average age of the *eaux-de-vie* in this Cognac, however, is thirty-five to fifty years. The average age of the eaux-de-vie in any Cognac blend does not appear on the label.)

Here are the lengths of time the youngest *eau-de-vie* in a Cognac blend must be aged in barrel:

VS (VERY SUPERIOR) OR THREE STAR (***): not less than two-and-a-half years

---

VSOP (VERY SUPERIOR OLD PALE), VO (VERY OLD), AND RÉSERVE: at least four-and-a-half years

---

XO (EXTRA OLD), NAPOLÉON, EXTRA, VIEUX, VIEILLE RÉSERVE, AND HORS D'AGE: at least six-and-a-half years

---

As for vintage Cognacs, although they're a rarity, they do exist. Initially prohibited by law, they were often made anyway by houses who set aside lots of especially good harvests to watch the evolution of those brandies. In 1987 French law changed, and vintage Cognac is now legal. To prevent fraud, barrels of vintage Cognac must be aged in special locked cellars, which can only be opened with two keys, one of which is kept by the government, the other by the Cognac firm.

At its best, Cognac should taste complex, balanced, and smooth, and have long-lasting aromas and flavors that subtly suggest flowers, citrus, honey, vanilla, smoke, and earth. Among the top Cognacs (their average age is noted in parentheses) are: A. de Fussigny Fine Champagne Vieille Réserve (thirty years); A. E. Dor XO (twenty-five years); Courvoisier XO (thirty-five to fifty years); Delamain Très Vénérable (forty-five to fifty years); Martell Extra (forty to fifty years); Rémy Martin XO (twenty-two years); and Hine Triomphe (forty to fifty years).

> About 20 million bottles' worth of Cognac—called the angel's share—evaporate annually.

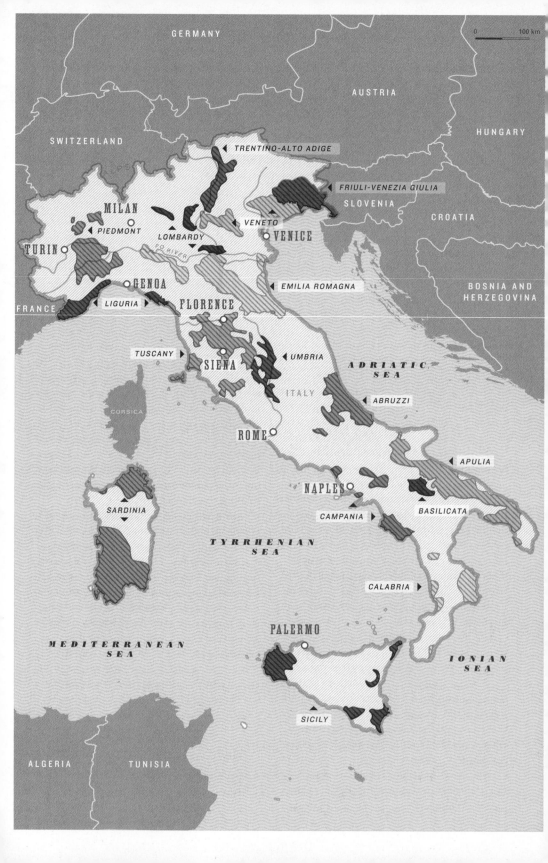

GERMANY

AUSTRIA

SWITZERLAND

HUNGARY

0   100 km

TRENTINO-ALTO ADIGE

FRIULI-VENEZIA GIULIA

SLOVENIA

MILAN

CROATIA

◄ PIEDMONT

LOMBARDY

VENETO

VENICE

TURIN

PO RIVER

BOSNIA AND
HERZEGOVINA

GENOA

LIGURIA ►

EMILIA ROMAGNA

FRANCE

FLORENCE

TUSCANY ►

ADRIATIC
SEA

SIENA

UMBRIA ►

CORSICA

ITALY

ABRUZZI ►

ROME

APULIA ►

NAPLES

SARDINIA

CAMPANIA ►

BASILICATA

TYRRHENIAN
SEA

CALABRIA ►

PALERMO

IONIAN
SEA

MEDITERRANEAN
SEA

PALERMO

SICILY

ALGERIA

TUNISIA

ITALY

PIEDMONT | VENETO | FRIULI-VENEZIA GIULIA | TUSCANY

TRENTINO-ALTO ADIGE | LOMBARDY | LIGURIA | EMILIA-ROMAGNA | UMBRIA | ABRUZZI |
THE SOUTHERN PENINSULA: CAMPANIA, APULIA, BASILICATA, AND CALABRIA | SICILY AND SARDINIA

ITALY RANKS SECOND AMONG WINE-PRODUCING COUNTRIES WORLDWIDE. THE ITALIANS DRINK AN AVERAGE OF 13 GALLONS (50 LITERS) OF WINE PER PERSON PER YEAR.

I n Italy, making wine—like eating or breathing—is so utterly natural it almost seems instinctive. Grapevines grow everywhere; they are Italy's version of the American lawn. There is simply no region, no district, virtually no cranny of the country that does not produce wine. The numbers are astonishing: 1.9 million acres (769,000 hectares) of vineyard; 384,000 wineries; and some 377 different grape varieties cultivated (more varieties than in any other country), leading to a dizzying number of wines.

Wine at this order of magnitude can seem unfathomable—but of course, not all of these wines are considered to be of major importance. Scores of Italian wines are simple quaffing wines consumed almost entirely in or near the villages where they are made.

The Italian wines that knowledgeable wine drinkers get excited about come predominantly from a few major areas. These include Piedmont, Veneto, Friuli-Venezia Giulia, and Tuscany. I'll cover these in the most depth, but I'll also provide overviews of numerous other wine regions. North to south, these include Trentino-Alto Adige, the Alpine home of some of Italy's most pristine white wines; Lombardy, the source of Italy's best sparklers; Liguria, the crescent-shaped region known for wines that are easily paired with fresh seafood; Emilia-Romagna, one of the greatest regions in the world for food, and the birthplace of cheerful, fizzy lambrusco; Umbria, the home of dry, refreshing Orvietos; Abruzzi (the English name for Abruzzo), memorable for such soft, thick, mouthfilling reds as montepulciano d'Abruzzo, a wine just waiting to be paired with rustic

CHAOS ON THE BOTTLE—
ITALIAN WINE LABELS

To learn about Italian wine, it is necessary to abandon yourself to the chaos of Italian wine labels. Here's one: Feudi di San Gregorio Piano di Montevergine Riserva Taurasi. Okay, um . . . This happens to be a delicious wine, but unless you already know what's what, it's nearly impossible to look at a label like this and understand it. And also understand what it doesn't say. For example, this label does not mention the grape variety used to make the wine (it's aglianico; you'd just have to have that part memorized). Moreover, who is the producer here? To drive one really crazy, the name of the producer, the name of the estate or villa, the name of the brand, and the proper name of the wine may all be listed. (In this case, by the way, the name of the producer is Feudi di San Gregorio). Even the simplest Italian wine labels can be confusing, because sometimes the wine may be named after the grape variety used to make it (such as barbera) and at other times named after the place where the grapes grew (such as Barolo). To make matters even more internecine, the names of some Italian wines (and even some grapes) combine both grape and place. The wine named montepulciano d'Abruzzo, for example, pairs montepulciano, the grape, with Abruzzo, the place. And, you'd just have to know that that wine is different from the wine vino nobile di Montepulciano, which isn't made from montepulciano at all (it's made from sangiovese). And finally, with characteristic Italianness, some Italian vintners simply abandon the whole system and just give the wine a fantasy name like "W... Dreams," the name of a famous Friulian chardonnay (it's up to you to figure out what it means).

> The ancient Greeks called Italy *Oenotria*, the land of wine.

pasta dishes; and finally, Italy's most southern regions: Campania, Apulia, Basilicata, and Calabria, plus the islands of Sicily and Sardinia, all of which are sources of delicious wines that are good values, and several make wines from rare, ancient grape varieties as well.

Although wine and food are inextricably linked in most parts of the world, in Italy they are fervently wedded. Wines that seem slightly lean, tart, or bitter to some are highly appreciated by the Italians precisely because they have the grip and edge to slice through the dauntless flavors of Italian food. But it goes even further than that. In Italy, wine *is* food. Not so long ago, a daily supply of basic village wine cost Italians less than their daily supply of bread, according to Italian wine expert Burton Anderson, and both were as essential to an Italian diner as a fork and knife (probably more so). Along with olive oil, wine and bread make up what the Italians call the Santa

St. Peter's Square in Vatican City. The Vatican consumes more wine per capita than any other country.

Villa Sparina in the Gavi DOC in Piedmont, which lies over the foothills of the Alps. Go 736 miles (1,185 kilometers) south, and you can stand on Italian soil and see North Africa.

THE VATICAN: IN VINO VERITAS

Vatican City, with a population of fewer than one thousand people, confined in a mere .27 square mile (.7 square kilometer) within Rome, consumes more wine per capita than any other country in the world—more than 16 gallons (61 liters) per person in recent years. By comparison, U.S. per capita consumption is about 3 gallons (11 liters). The Vatican's voluminous wine usage is, in part, the result of an important Catholic ritual—the celebration of the Holy Eucharist, in which bread and wine are consecrated during Mass and thus believed to be transubstantiated into the body and blood of Jesus Christ.

Trinità Mediterranea—the Mediterranean Holy Trinity. An Italian friend once summed up the special affinity between Italian wine and food this way: "In Italy, if someone drinks a little too much wine, the Italians don't say he has drunk too much; they say he hasn't eaten enough food yet."

Italian wines can vary substantially in flavor, texture, and body—even when the wines being compared are the same type. Two Chianti Classicos from estates less than a half mile apart can taste remarkably dissimilar. Some of this variability is due to differences in winemaking, for Italy is a country of fiercely maintained ancient traditions and, at the same time, extremely sophisticated modern methods. But an equally compelling reason is this: Italy is a tangle of different, tiny mesoclimates that powerfully influence the character of any given wine.

What creates those mesoclimates? The geography and variable climates of the land itself. You can stand on Italian soil and look at the Alps, but you can also stand on Italian soil and look at North Africa. The country is

Men and women harvest chardonnay at Ferrari in Trentino-Alto Adige. The winery, founded in 1902, has become one of Italy's top producers of metodo classico *(Champagne method) sparkling wine.*

> In Italy, if someone drinks a little too much wine, the Italians don't say he has drunk too much; they say he hasn't eaten enough food yet.

about 40 percent mountains (even Sicily has them!) and another 40 percent hills. As any drive from one village to the next proves, straight lines don't seem to exist in this country. The combined zigzagging slopes of hills and mountains, plus the close proximity of four seas (the Tyrrhenian, Adriatic, Ligurian, and Mediterranean), plus the geologic impact of numerous earthquakes has produced an almost pointillistic profusion of environments in which grapes grow.

Although Italy's most revered wines are known worldwide, the grape varieties that constitute them are rarely found outside the country. You won't find sangiovese, the leading grape of Chianti, or nebbiolo, the grape that makes Barolo, growing in France, Spain, or Australia (except perhaps as an oddity).

THE ULTIMATE GIFT

In ancient Rome, wine was linked with authority. Of all the pleasures and privileges of power, none was rated more highly than the possession of a vineyard. The highest favor bestowed by the Roman emperor Julian was the gift of a vineyard prepared—actually planted and pruned—by his own hands.

Even in the United States, the brief, so-called "Cal-Ital movement" of the late 1980s and early 1990s has been largely abandoned as California wineries have acknowledged that Italy grows her own indigenous grapes so much better.

As of the 1980s, the Italians, however, adopted cabernet sauvignon and other international varieties with lightning speed and total confidence. (The first wave of cabernet

HOW THE ITALIANS EAT PASTA

Pasta became commonplace in Italy in the thirteenth and fourteenth centuries. Early pasta dishes all had a similar sauce: melted butter and some type of hard cheese, such as Parmigiano-Reggiano. To make the dish even more special, the pasta would often be sprinkled with sugar and spices as well. (Tomato sauces did not appear until sometime after the tomato was brought from the New World, in the sixteenth century.) The difficulty of eating buttery pasta with the fingers may have contributed to the early use of the fork in Italy.

Watch Italians eat slender pasta, such as spaghetti, and you will not see them twirling the strands around a fork set into the bowl of a spoon. Italians eat pasta with a fork only. The correct technique involves stabbing some pasta near the edge of the bowl, usually at the twelve o'clock position (not in the center of the mound), and then twirling the fork while bracing it against the inside rim of the bowl. It's considered appropriate to have a few strands hanging down from the fork as you lift it to your mouth.

The American habit of twirling the fork against a soup spoon is thought to have originated around the turn of the twentieth century, when poor Italian immigrants came to the United States and found bountiful supplies of affordable food. As the ratio of sauce to pasta increased, a spoon became necessary to scoop it all up. Inevitably, someone got the cunning idea of using the spoon to assist in eating the pasta as well.

sauvignon plantings in Italy actually occurred in the late eighteenth century, although the appeal of this *uva francesca*—French grape, as the Italians called it—was initially found to be limited.) Today, Italian wine is a dual world where ancestral grape varieties and contemporary grape varieties easily exist side by side.

ITALY'S FINE WINE REVOLUTION

To gain insight into Italian wine today and to understand the revolution in quality that Italian wine underwent in the latter part of the twentieth century, it's important to understand something of the history that led up to Italy's current wine laws. (For the laws themselves, see the Appendix on Wine Laws, page 924). Admittedly, governmental regulations usually make for pretty dry reading but, in Italy's

In Italy, pasta and wine are made with a loving hand.

GRAPPA

You can always tell when Italians don't want the night to end. Out comes the grappa. This, in turn, causes everyone to recount their most infamous grappa-drinking stories—which leads to the pouring of more grappa, which leads to more stories. Although today grappa is made and drunk all over Italy, historically it was a specialty of the northern part of the country, where a small shot in the morning coffee helped one get going on a freezing day.

Grappa is the clear brandy that results when grape pomace (the pulpy mash of stems, seeds, and skins left over from winemaking) is refermented and distilled. Depending on the quality of the raw material and the method of distillation, the final product can taste as though a grenade has just ignited in your throat, or it can taste smooth, winey, and powerful. *Ue,* a softer, lighter type of grappa invented and made famous by the firm Nonino, is a distillate of actual grapes rather than pomace. And *grappa di monovitigno* is a grappa from a single grape variety, such as riesling, moscato, gewürztraminer, or picolit. These grappas are considered superior because the result carries a faint suggestion of the aroma and flavor of the original grapes. Expensive and rare, such grappas incite cult worship. In fact, grappa fans are called *tifosi di grappa,* a phrase that implies almost feverish allegiance (the word *tifosi* also refers to people suffering from typhoid).

The bottles are part of the attraction. Since the late 1980s, the dazzling, avant-garde designs of grappa bottles have been nothing less than astounding. No northern Italian *enoteca* is without an astonishing display of these elegant bottles, each holding a grappa that looks far more innocent than it tastes.

When grappa seems like a good idea, it usually means I should have already gone home.

case, it's almost impossible to comprehend the country's wines without a grasp of how the wines are categorized by the Italian government and by the Italians themselves.

Italy's wine revolution was provoked by a set of regulations defining the areas where specific wines can be made. These laws—*Denominazione di Origine Controllata, Denominazione di Origine Controllata e Garantita,* and *Indicazione Geografica Tipica*—are known by their acronyms, DOC, DOCG, and IGT. More than 330 wine zones have been designated as DOCs and 73 as DOCGs, yet the wines from these zones, widely regarded as many of the best wines in the country, represent only a small percentage of all the Italian wines produced. Some 118 wine areas have been named IGTs, a more humble designation. (These same laws are the ones that ensure that cheeses such as Parmigiano, hams such as

Piero Antinori and his successors—daughters Albiera, Allegra, and Alessia. The family has been in the wine business since Giovanni di Piero Antinori joined the Florentine Guild of Vintners in 1385.

> Most Italians think about wine the way they think about a Ferrari. It ought to be red. That said, white wines account for 50 percent of the production of Italian wine, and most of the best of those come from the northeastern part of the country, bordering the Alps.

prosciutto, condiments such as balsamic vinegar, and a host of other foods can come only from their designated traditional areas.)

The story behind these pivotal regulations begins in the 1960s. Although great wine families, such as the Antinoris, Frescobaldis, Contini-Bonacossis, and Boscainis, had all been making fine wine for centuries, many Italian wines were still the product of peasant winemaking. But with the enactment of the DOC laws in 1963, an official regulation stipulated standards for certain types of wine. The first wine given DOC status was the Tuscan

white vernaccia di San Gimignano, in 1966. The course of Italian wine changed dramatically.

No sooner had the DOC commandments been handed down than innovative Italian winemakers began to chafe against them. As comprehensive and protective as the DOC laws sought to be, they failed to take into consideration a key reality—advances in wine quality often come through creativity, innovation, and the introduction of new techniques. The DOC stipulations for any given type of wine were formed around what was traditional practice in that region. Traditional practice reflected traditional taste. And traditional taste was, in many cases, that of palates rarely exposed to anything more than the wine from vineyards within a 20-mile (32-kilometer) radius. By the 1970s, Italian winemakers were restless.

Piero Antinori, head of a centuries-old Tuscan winemaking family and a prominent force within the Italian wine industry, made the first well-publicized break with DOC regulations in 1971. Antinori's wine, called Tignanello, was modeled after a wine that virtually no one had ever heard of or tasted: Sassicaia. Although Sassicaia was made in

The 1974 vintage of Castello di Nipozzano Chianti Rufina Riserva, aging gracefully in the cellars of Marchesi de Frescobaldi.

Tuscany, it was neither a Chianti nor any other familiar type of Tuscan wine. It wasn't even based on the traditional Tuscan grape, sangiovese. Sassicaia was a cabernet sauvignon; the inspiration behind it was French Bordeaux. Sassicaia was then a quiet, "underground" project, but Antinori knew about it because his cousins were its creators (see the section on Tuscany, page 382).

Like Sassicaia, Antinori's Tignanello was made in the Chianti region, but it was not—as far as the Italian government was concerned—a Chianti, since it had not been made according to the DOC regulations. Therefore, like Sassicaia, it could officially be considered only a *vino da tavola* (table wine), the lowest status an Italian wine can hold. Tignanello and Sassicaia thus became the first two *vini da tavola* to cost a small fortune in an ocean of *vini da tavola* that cost peanuts. None of this seemed to bother wine drinkers or the wine press, who bestowed on these wines (and the others like them that followed) their lasting nickname, the Super Tuscans.

Then, in 1980, just as the first steps toward better-quality wine were being taken in many parts of Italy, the government enacted the DOCG—*Denominazione di Origine Controllata e Garantita*—for wines of exceptional quality and renown. The DOCG regulations were even more strict than the DOC. The first four DOCGs were brunello di Montalcino and vino nobile di Montepulciano, in Tuscany; and

Barolo and Barbaresco, in Piedmont, all designated in 1980. By 1999, there were twenty-one DOCGs. And by 2013, there were, as mentioned, seventy-three.

Most of the initial DOCGs were red. Alas, the first of the white DOCGs, albana di Romagna, granted in 1987, made the government look silly. Albana, a fairly neutral wine from the Emilia-Romagna region, comes nowhere close to being one of Italy's top white wines. Albana's status as the first white DOCG threw a cloak of suspicion over the whole system.

A more serious flaw in the DOCG, however, was the misleading word *garantita* (guarantee) in its title. In fact, the DOCG designation does not guarantee the quality of the wine. A DOCG is applied to an entire region. Both the greatest wine in that region and the worst get to say they are DOCG.

Finally, neither the DOC nor DOCG addressed the growing number of creative, nonconformist Italian wines, many of which came from places outside DOC and DOCG wine areas, and all of which continued to be officially considered mere *vini da tavola*. Therefore, in 1992, the third designation, *Indicazione Geografica Tipica* (Typical Geographic Indication), was created. While IGT wine zones include many places that make good, even great, wines, they are places that historically have never been considered as prestigious as the areas awarded DOC and DOCG status. Most IGT wines are the equivalent of French *vins de pays*, or country wines.

So what does all this mean in the end? From a practical standpoint, knowing that a wine has IGT, DOC, or DOCG status doesn't guarantee that that particular wine will be exemplary. Nor are these designations a classification system (like, say, the Grand Cru/Premier Cru classification of Burgundy, France). But Italy's designations are a tip-off to the places that are recognized for the quality or prestige of their wines. Think of the designations as forming a pyramid of Italy's wines. *Vini da tavola* constitute the broad base; IGT are next, in the middle; DOC wines are nearer the top; and DOCG wines are at the apex. Fantastic wines are to be found at every level.

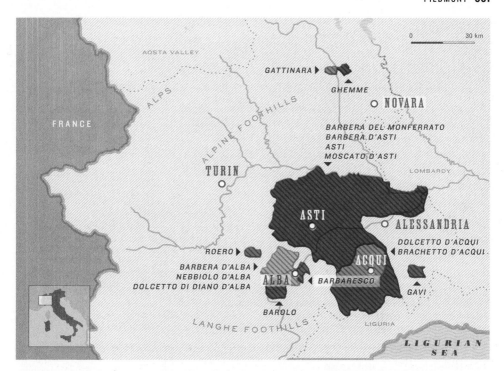

PIEDMONT

ying in a remote white amphitheater created by the Alps, Piedmont is Italy's preeminent wine region. Barolo and Barbaresco—two of the country's most legendary and serious reds—are born here. (So is the world's least serious sparkling wine, the playful *spumante* known as Asti.)

If Italy is sometimes thought of as the cradle of Bacchanalian frivolity, you'd never know it in Piedmont. Winemakers here are prudent and diligent about their work. Shake a Piedmontese vintner's hand, and it's the rough, heavy, calloused hand of someone who has worked forever in a vineyard. The wine-making style in Piedmont (as well as the culinary traditions of the region) has strong links to that of their closest neighbor, France. Indeed, if Piedmont has an enological soul

mate, it is not Tuscany, as one might expect, but France's Burgundy. In both regions, wine estates are meticulously cared for and mostly small (the average vineyard estate in Piedmont is 3 to 5 acres/1.2 to 2 hectares). The wine traditions of both were firmly molded by centuries of monastic (Benedictine) rule. Most important of all, Piedmont and Burgundy share the philosophic belief that great wine is the progeny of a single, perfectly adapted grape variety (nebbiolo in Piedmont; pinot noir in Burgundy). This is in complete opposition to most of the rest of Italy, and indeed most of France, where wines tend to be made from a blend of grapes.

It's difficult to describe just how esteemed Piedmont's leading wines Barolo and Barbaresco are, not just in Piedmont, but in Italy as a whole. At their best, these wines are supremely complex and riveting. But Barolo

Old Italian farms usually engaged in "promiscuous agriculture." Each farm would have vineyards, orchards, olive groves, vegetable gardens, and livestock—everything a family needs to subsist on. Here, barbera vineyards on a farm in the Monferrato hills of Piedmont.

THE QUICK SIP ON PIEDMONT

TWO OF ITALY'S MOST MAJESTIC, powerful red wines—Barolo and Barbaresco—come from Piedmont. Like great red Bordeaux, they can be and often are aged a decade or more before being drunk.

BAROLO AND BARBARESCO are made from the nebbiolo grape, a highly site-specific variety known for its forceful tannin.

PIEDMONT is also known for Asti—a playful, delicious, semisweet sparkler that is the complete opposite of serious Barolo and Barbaresco.

and Barbaresco are also lauded because nebbiolo, one of the world's most site-specific grape varieties, is, in terms of viticulture and

winemaking, one of the most difficult to master. Indeed only 8 percent of all plantings in Piedmont are nebbiolo. Yet no place in the world has more nebbiolo than this one place, and no place in the world has had more success with this complicated, demanding, challenging grape.

Like the great red Bordeaux, Barolo and Barbaresco are highly structured, expensive wines that can be aged for years, even decades. Until the 1990s, Piedmontese winemakers routinely advised waiting no less than fifteen years, and sometimes as many as twenty-five years, before drinking them. Today most Barolos and Barbarescos are made in a way that renders them softer (but not soft, exactly) at a younger age, and thus enjoyable earlier. Still, as we'll see, Barolo and Barbaresco are not casual, happy wines. They aren't good for taking to the beach. They aren't good with salads. But in their cultural context, the wines make utter sense. These formidable, firm, black-red wines are meant for carnivorous drama—for whole roasted pigs or lambs—or with grand pastas showered with white truffles and costing a ransom.

Needless to say, Barolo and Barbaresco

are decidedly not what the Piedmontese drink with dinner every night. That distinction goes to two other red wines that stand next in the hierarchy of importance: barbera and dolcetto. Barbera, made from the barbera grape, is a vibrant, sometimes rustic wine, oozing with a wealth of fruit flavors. The grape is Piedmont's most widely planted variety, but genetic research suggests it was probably brought there from someplace else. Dolcetto is a juicy quaffing wine and often has an attractive, bitter edge. It's made from the dolcetto grape.

In addition to these important wines, there are a number of others that, like Barolo and Barbaresco, are made from nebbiolo, although they are usually less polished, less complex, and generally more rough and lean. The best known and most important of these wines is Gattinara, followed by Ghemme, nebbiolo d'Alba, and wines called spanna, spanna being a synonym for nebbiolo.

Piedmont is also home to four principal white wines: the dry whites Gavi and arneis; the slightly sweet, refined moscato d'Asti; and, as already mentioned, the irrepressibly popular semisweet sparkler Asti.

THE MOST IMPORTANT PIEDMONT WINES

LEADING WINES

ARNEIS white

ASTI white (sparkling; semisweet)

BARBARESCO red

BARBERA red

BAROLO red

DOLCETTO red

GAVI white

MOSCATO D'ASTI white (semisweet)

WINES OF NOTE

GATTINARA red

GHEMME red

NEBBIOLO D'ALBA red

SPANNA red

THE LAND, THE GRAPES, AND THE VINEYARDS

Piedmont, meaning "foot of the mountain," is the largest region of the Italian mainland. As its name suggests, Piedmont is comprised of mountains and rolling foothills. Since much of this land is too steep or too cold for vines, Piedmont, despite its size, is not Italy's leading producer of wine. If only fine wines are considered, however, it excels. More than 15 percent of all the DOC and DOCG wines in Italy are made here. (This is more than any other region except for Tuscany.) Indeed, 84 percent of all the wines made in Piedmont are either DOC or DOCG.

Nearly all of Piedmont's best vineyards are located in the eastern and southern parts of the region, where it is warmer than in the more Alpine northern part. The best vineyards lie over two hilly, southeastern ranges known as the Langhe (from *lingue*—tongue—a reference to the mountains, which are said to be shaped like tongues) and Monferrato. Here are found the important wine towns of Alba, Asti, and Alessandria. Of them, the most treasured is Alba.

The tiny villages of Barolo and Barbaresco (from which the wines take their names) lie about a dozen miles (19 kilometers) apart on either side of Alba, which, despite being a

THE GRAPES OF PIEDMONT

WHITES

ARNEIS: Makes a bold, fresh wine of the same name. The variety, once nearly extinct, was rediscovered and "rescued" in the late 1960s and is now planted mainly in the Roero area north of Barolo.

CORTESE: Source of the dry, crisp, but neutral-tasting wine Gavi.

MOSCATO: The Italian word for muscat. In Piedmont, the main type of muscat used is muscat blanc à petits grains, an ancient variety with extremely fruity, floral, and musky aromas and flavors. Used to make sparkling Asti and moscato d'Asti. Sometimes called moscato bianco (white muscat) or moscato Canelli (Canelli is a reference to the village, south of Asti, which is famous for the grape).

REDS

BARBERA: The most widely planted grape in Piedmont; the source of a vibrant, mouthfilling, often slightly rustic wine of the same name; it's a favorite local dinner wine and an easy companion to food, thanks to its relatively high acidity and low tannin.

BONARDA AND VESPOLINA: Two minor blending grapes used with nebbiolo in the wines Gattinara and Ghemme.

DOLCETTO: Makes a simple, fruity quaffing wine also called dolcetto.

NEBBIOLO: Piedmont's star grape and one of the most renowned red grapes in all of Italy. Known for power, structure, and tannin; makes the legendary reds Barolo and Barbaresco; and is the primary grape in Gattinara and Ghemme. In some parts of Piedmont, nebbiolo is known as spanna.

---

rather humble town, holds an almost mythic place in the minds of food and wine lovers—not solely for mighty Barolo and Barbaresco, but also for the world's most astonishing white truffles, which are unearthed here each fall. Just imagining autumn in Alba—drinking sumptuous Barolos and dining on homemade taglierini generously mounded (this is Piedmont, after all) with white truffles—is enough to send shivers up my spine.

The soil around Alba is clay, limestone, and sand. The best vineyards, most of which are planted with nebbiolo, are located on the domes of hills that are tilted south, resulting in maximum exposure to the sun, and hence ripeness. The names of the vineyards underscore the

sun's importance. The producer Ceretto, for example, makes a famous Barolo from a vineyard called Bricco Rocche; in Piedmontese dialect a *bricco* is the sun-catching crest of a hill. Similarly, the producer Angelo Gaja makes an extraordinary Barbaresco from a vineyard called Sorì Tildìn; a *sorì* is the south-facing part of a slope where, in winter, the snow melts first.

Piedmontese vintners are as obsessed with the individual characteristics of vineyards as are their Burgundian counterparts. Rather than making a single Barolo or Barbaresco, most top producers make tiny amounts of multiple versions of both, designating each according to the specific vineyard from which it came (such wines are, not surprisingly,

The word *nebbiolo* derives from *nebbia,* "fog," a reference to the thick, whitish bloom of yeasts that forms on the grapes when they are ripe (although many say the name may also refer to the wisps of fog that envelop the Piedmontese hills in late fall when the grapes are picked).

there was one). Piedmont's most important and most traditional white grape, moscato, accounts for 22 percent of all plantings in the region.

And finally, the town of Alessandria, the farthest east, near the border with Lombardy, lies in the limestone-laced hills of the Monferrato range. This area is well known for the red wines barbera and dolcetto.

BAROLO AND BARBARESCO

expensive). In a nod to France, the top vineyards are often referred to as cru vineyards. Among the most famous Barolo vineyards are Rocche, Cannubi, Cerequio, Brunate, and Bussia-Soprana. Top Barbaresco vineyards include Rabajà, Sorì Tildìn, and Asili.

About 20 miles (30 kilometers) northeast of Alba, the town of Asti will forever be linked with moscato (muscat blanc à petit grains). Two moscato-based wines take their names from Asti: the gorgeously refined, low-alcohol wine moscato d'Asti, which the Piedmontese adore, and the widely popular, slightly sweet sparkling wine Asti, formerly known as Asti Spumante (a non-collector's wine if ever

Close your eyes and imagine it is evening in the cold, dark, hard foothills of the Alps. A fire smolders in the hearth of a stone farmhouse; game is being roasted in the old oven. Wine in this setting becomes more than wine. It is reassurance; it is solace.

Barolo and Barbaresco are located in the Langhe hills of southeastern Piedmont. Both wines can be powerful and both are made solely from nebbiolo, an ancient variety that originated in Piedmont (or possibly in Lombardy next door) but whose parents are presumed extinct. Nebbiolo has very specific aromas and flavors, often characterized by Italian wine experts as "tar and roses," along with licorice, violets, leather, chocolate, prunes, and black figs. None of these characteristics emerges gently and in an orderly fashion from the wines. With most Barolos and Barbarescos, flavors hurl themselves over you like a stormy ocean wave.

Grown on steeper, cooler sites, Barolo is generally the more robust, austere, and masculine of the two wines. Barbaresco tends to be slightly more graceful, even though it, too, is often described as having brooding power. Another difference concerns supply. Each year, about a third as much Barbaresco is produced as Barolo. While Barbaresco is made in three tiny villages—Barbaresco itself, plus Neive and Treiso—Barolo is made in eleven, the most important of which are Barolo, La Morra, Castiglione Falletto, Monforte d'Alba, and Serralunga d'Alba. Because Barolo spans a

Tiny, compact clusters of nebbiolo in the vineyards of the Barolo producer Roberto Voerzio.

GAJA

No man has heralded the virtues of Piedmont more than the dynamic, ambitious, and inventive Angelo Gaja (pronounced GUY-ah). For decades he has traveled around the world, talking about Barbaresco and Barolo to every journalist and restaurateur who would listen (and making converts of most of them).

Gaja's wines can have spellbinding intensity and power. The best seem not simply great but virtually unreal in their ability to be massively opulent and yet finely etched at the same time. They are also gaspingly expensive.

Gaja made his mark with his estate-grown Barbarescos, especially his intense single-vineyard Barbarescos called Sorì Tildìn and Sorì San Lorenzo. Later, he bought a famous but rundown property outside Alba and began making the now legendary single-vineyard wine called Sperss (dialect for *nostalgia*) in the Barolo region (but not labeled Barolo because it contains a small amount of barbera blended in with the nebbiolo).

For all of his inventive vineyard and cellar practices, Gaja is a traditionalist in his devotion to nebbiolo. When he made Piedmont's first cabernet sauvignon in 1978, he called it Darmagi, in honor of his father. In the local dialect, *darmagi* means "what a pity"; this was what Gaja's father mumbled every time he passed the cabernet vineyard and thought about the nebbiolo vines that had been pulled out to plant the cabernet. Although Darmagi was highly praised internationally (as were Gaja's two chardonnays, Rossj-Bass and Gaia & Rey), Gaja maintains that it was merely a marketing ploy. Making a cabernet that could rival the great Bordeaux, he says, was just a clever way of drawing the world's attention to Barbaresco and Barolo, and to Piedmont.

larger number of mesoclimates, it is said to be more variable in quality and style, from producer to producer, than Barbaresco.

The ancient small town of Barolo gave its name to the wine Barolo, long considered one of Italy's most magnificent wines.

Until the late 1980s, Barolo and Barbaresco were almost unpalatable unless they had been aged fifteen to twenty years, whereupon the wines' fierce tannin might begin to mellow. Often they required a twenty-five- or thirty-year wait. Daring (or foolish) drinkers who opened the wines earlier often ended up with tongues that felt as though they'd been sheathed in shrink-wrap.

The wines' severity was the result of several factors. First, nebbiolo is genetically high in tannin. (The common Barolo descriptor "tarry" is not just a flavor, but a reference to the way the tannin feels.) Second, and to make matters worse, nebbiolo is a late-ripening variety, often harvested on the brink of winter when the ambient temperature is cold. Two problems are embedded here. Late-ripening grapes often don't get ripe, so the wines, rather than having a soft texture, end up feeling like

The vaulted cellars of Ceretto. Historically, Barolo was deemed drinkable only after it had aged 15 to 20 years in barrel. Today, thanks to improved viticultural and winemaking techniques, the wines are drinkable (but maybe not as heavenly) when they are far younger.

sandpaper. In addition, historically, Piedmont's small cellars would be very cold by the time the grapes were brought in. As a result, fermentation would choke along in fits and starts (yeasts work best in warm environments, not cold ones), often for months, before it got rolling effectively. Piedmontese winemakers of the past were forced to stand by and let nebbiolo run its course, even though, in the long process, hard, bitter tannins were extracted from the grape skins. Many winemakers then inadvertently exacerbated that harshness by leaving the wine for years in large oak or chestnut casks, often desiccating any little fruitiness the wine might have had, and sometimes oxidizing the wine in the process.

As modern tastes swung toward soft, flavorful wines that could be drunk the night they were bought, consumers began bypassing Barolo and Barbaresco. It seemed as if Italy's two greatest wines were on their way to becoming the dinosaurs of fine red wine. But eventually, using modern technology, winemakers in the 1980s began making Barolos and Barbarescos that possessed a certain suppleness, even while they remained majestic, monolithic wines. Most notably, the introduction of temperature-controlled tanks meant that fermentation could be immediately

warmer and quicker, thereby avoiding astringent tannins. Juice could be pumped over the grape skins in a way that imparted maximum color to the wine but, again, minimized harsh tannin. Finally, winemakers began to understand how to divide the aging of nebbiolo between small French barrels and bottles so that the lush fruit quality of the wine would not be sacrificed. By the 1990s, a new era for nebbiolo had been born.

Of course, although most Barolos and Barbarescos are now made to be drunk sooner, sooner is a relative term. A Barolo or Barbaresco less than five years old may still be imprisoned by tannin and may taste closed, and not particularly complex. With these wines, you simply must make yourself wait, for with time, the wines reward you. They unfurl themselves, revealing layers of flavor and richness of texture that weren't even hinted at when the wines were young. Perhaps more than any other wines, Barolo and Barbaresco need at least half a decade (and a decade is better) to evolve into themselves.

Finally, by law, Barolo and Barbaresco are among the longest-aged wines in Italy. Barolo must be aged a total of thirty-eight months, eighteen of which must be in oak, and for Barolo riserva, the total is sixty-two months, eighteen of which must be in oak. Barbaresco must be aged a total of twenty-six months, nine of which must be in oak, and for Barbaresco riserva, the requirement is fifty months of aging, nine of which must be in oak.

SOME OF THE BEST PRODUCERS OF BAROLO

Aldo Conterno • Bruno Giacosa • Ceretto • Domenico Clerico • Elio Altare • Elio Grasso • Gaja • Giacomo Conterno • Giuseppe Mascarello • Giuseppe Rinaldi • Luciano Sandrone • Luigi Einaudi • Marcarini • Paolo Scavino • Renato Ratti • Roberto Voerzio • Vietti

---

SOME OF THE BEST PRODUCERS OF BARBARESCO

Bruno Giacosa • Ceretto • Cigliuti • Gaja • La Spinetta • Marchesi di Gresy • Moccagatta • Renato Ratti • Sottimano • Vietti

---

GATTINARA, GHEMME, NEBBIOLO D'ALBA, AND SPANNA

A slew of wines besides Barolo and Barbaresco are made from nebbiolo, including Gattinara, Ghemme, nebbiolo d'Alba, and spanna. Nebbiolo d'Alba is slightly different from the others in that, like Barolo and Barbaresco, it is produced in the famous Langhe foothills near the town of Alba. But the grapes that go into nebbiolo d'Alba come from outlying areas and don't quite have the finesse and power that nebbiolo intended for Barolo and Barbaresco possesses. Still, nebbiolo d'Alba is a good, lower-priced "starter" wine before one jumps into the deep end of the pool with Barolo and Barbaresco, and because it's less powerful, it doesn't require the same aging that its more famous sisters do.

Gattinara and Ghemme are produced far north of Alba, in colder Alpine foothills with glacial soil and terrain. Although Gattinara in particular can occasionally seem like a mini Barolo, with fairly powerful flavors, both Gattinara and Ghemme are generally leaner than Barolo or Barbaresco, with simpler flavors and tannin that is sometimes aggressive. The Italians would never drink these wines without food (they'd taste too harsh), and indeed the wines can taste entirely transformed if drunk with a juicy roast or creamy risotto. Gattinara and Ghemme are frequently made with a small percentage of bonarda or vespolina, two minor blending grapes that help tone down and soften the northern-grown nebbiolo. The best known of these wines in the United States is the Gattinara made by Travaglini, shipped in an almost square-shaped black bottle.

DOLCETTO—EAT, DRINK, DO A LITTLE BUSINESS

Dolcetto, a model of versatility, has been used by the Piedmontese in a number of creative (and commercial) ways. The wine is a traditional accompaniment to dishes such as tajarin (thin, gold-colored pasta made with up to forty egg yolks) with butter and sage. But the grapes themselves—unlike most wine grapes—can also be delicious eaten raw as table grapes. They are even cooked down and made into cognà, a jam served with local hard cheeses such as Murazzano, from sheep's milk, and Castelmagno, mainly from cow's milk. And why not do a little business while you are eating? Historically, the commercially savvy Piedmontese also used dolcetto grapes to barter with neighboring Ligurians for their famous green-tinged olive oil, salt, and anchovies.

The Vietti family has made stellar single-vineyard Barolos and Barbarescos for decades. But the family's barbera is the sort of wine that's so irresistible and delicious you just can't put the glass down.

Curiously, in northern Piedmont nebbiolo is called *spanna*. Thus, both Gattinara and Ghemme are usually said to be made from spanna, not nebbiolo. Wines labeled simply with the word *spanna* are basic wines made from nebbiolo grown in northern Piedmont. Rustic defines them best.

BARBERA

The word *barbera* may sound as though it could be related to barbaric, but in reality, this is Piedmont's most juicy, straightforwardly delicious red wine. Scan any Piedmontese restaurant around dinnertime; a bottle of barbera will be on most tables. In many ways, barbera is the antithesis of Barolo and Barbaresco. It usually does not have hard, tannic edges, nor does it require super-long aging. Instead of Barolo's blackish hue, barbera is almost shockingly magenta. And unlike Barolo and Barbaresco, it is not considered a classic. Barbera, at its best, is simply a captivating wine with lots of flavor muscle.

The barbera grape is Piedmont's most widely planted variety (it was brought to Piedmont after the phylloxera epidemic and met with good success). Historically it was grown almost everywhere—everywhere, that is, except in the best soil on the best south-facing slopes. Those went to Barolo or Barbaresco. In the winery, barbera received stepsister treatment as well. The best barrels were reserved for Barolo and Barbaresco, which also got more winemaking attention. Worst of all, barbera was often cultivated for quantity. Instead of limiting yields, producers stretched them. Given barbera's second-class treatment in the past, it's surprising that the wine was as good as it was.

In the 1980s, however, the forward-thinking Piedmontese vintners Giacomo Bologna and Renato Ratti began to view barbera as a diamond in the rough. Planting it on better sites, they limited yields, vinified it more carefully, and began aging it in small, new French oak barrels. Quality soared. Today, many producers make very tasty modern barberas with supple, feltlike textures, and mouthfilling chocolaty, licoricey, cherry, figgy fruit. And because the barbera grape is naturally high in acid, the wines also have a kind of vibrancy

PIEDMONT'S OTHER TREASURE: WHITE TRUFFLES

I think I can say this: No food in the world is more riveting than the Piedmontese white truffle. Its aroma and flavor is, in a word, narcotic. Of the more than seventy species of truffles that can be found throughout the world, white truffles are the most cherished and highly sought after. They grow in unpredictable spots, a foot or more underground, generally near oak, chestnut, or beech trees. They ripen throughout the late fall; their harvest corresponds with that of Piedmont's grapes.

Ugly. But to every food and wine lover, a thing of beauty.

No one knows why white truffles grow mainly in Piedmont or why the Piedmontese type is superior in flavor to the small quantity that can be unearthed in Tuscany, Umbria, Emilia-Romagna, and Croatia. White truffles have never been successfully cultivated, and even in Piedmont, their existence varies greatly year to year based on the weather.

Because white truffles that are buried underground cannot be detected by humans, dogs and pigs are trained to sniff them out. The truffle hunter (*trifalao*) must be careful to pull the animal away at just the right moment lest the truffle become pet chow. White truffles are always hunted under the cover of night, so that the location of the truffle bed remains secret. This, in turn, is important because white truffles command exceedingly high prices—$4,000 to $5,600 per pound most recently—and are bought and sold almost like illicit drugs.

According to research conducted in Germany and England, truffles are profoundly and appealingly aromatic because they contain a special substance that is also found in the testes of men and boars. This substance is secreted by the sweat glands in a man's armpit and can be detected in the urine of women. Researchers report that the substance has a powerful psychological effect on human beings.

White truffles are ugly things—gray, knobbed balls that look as though they have been deformed by some especially evil bit of witchcraft. They range in size from marbles to baseballs, although the larger ones are exceedingly rare. And although they are breathtakingly expensive, only a tiny amount is needed to transform a dish. In Piedmont, white truffles are shaved raw over homemade pasta, risotto, polenta, soft scrambled eggs, veal carpaccio, or veal tartare. The earthy pungency of the truffle seems to intensify the earthiness of the Barbaresco or Barolo that is usually served alongside.

Each autumn in Alba, a truffle market is held under a long medieval arcade. Truffle hunters with scales at their sides display their finds. The air is heady with the collective aroma of thousands of truffles. Restaurateurs, buying in quantity, have sometimes been accompanied by bodyguards.

A final note: Tartufi Ponzio, in the center of Alba, is a tiny shop that sells products related exclusively to truffles and wine. There are white-truffle oils, pâtés with truffles, truffle sauces, truffle slicers, and so forth, plus a small but stunning collection of Piedmontese wines (tartufiponzio.com).

and zip that make them great counterpoints to food.

Today, barbera is grown everywhere in Piedmont, although the two places that produce most of the outstanding wines are the area around the town of Alba (barbera d'Alba) and near Asti (barbera d'Asti). A small number of producers have begun to blend barbera and nebbiolo in the hopes of fusing barbera's blackberry-fruit vibrancy with nebbiolo's structure and complexity. Some of these blends, like Conterno Fantino's Monprà, are delicious.

SOME OF THE BEST PRODUCERS OF BARBERA

Aldo Conterno · Coppo Camp du Rouss · Elio Altare · Elio Grasso · Gaja · Giacomo Bologna · Giacomo Conterno · Giuseppe Mascarello · La Spinetta · Marcarini · Moccagatta · Paolo Scavino · Pio Cesare · Prunotto · Renato Ratti · Vietti

---

DOLCETTO

The appealing simplicity of dolcetto (the name means "little sweet") has caused it to be misleadingly pegged as Italy's Beaujolais. In fact, the two wines taste quite different. Dolcetto, made from dolcetto grapes, has firm, spicy fruitiness set off against a subtle bitter-chocolate background. Beaujolais, made from gamay, has a grapey fruitiness and at its best, a minerally edge.

Dolcetto has relatively little acid, not much tannin, and is lighter in body than barbera, making it so easy to drink it becomes almost gulpable. It, too, is a favorite every-night wine in Piedmont, and is often served with the gargantuan Piedmontese *antipasto misto*. Though most dolcetto is made to be merely easy-drinking stuff, a few producers make serious versions—wines with such forthright grip, structure, and depth that they hardly seem like dolcetto. These producers include Chionetti, Marcarini, and Vietti.

VERMOUTH

The indispensable ingredient in a martini, vermouth was first created and commercially sold in Piedmont in the 1700s. Vermouth is red or white wine that has been infused with a secret blend of more than a hundred aromatic spices, barks, bitter herbs, and flavorings, among them angelica, anise, bitter almond, chamomile, cinnamon, coriander, ginger, nutmeg, peach, quinine, rhubarb, and saffron. Until it was banned in the early twentieth century because of its potential psychoactive toxicity, wormwood was also included. In fact, the word *vermouth* comes from the German *wermut,* "wormwood." Historically, the Piedmontese used muscat grapes for their base wine, and thus most vermouth was white. Today, cheap red or white bulk wine from the south of Italy is usually used as the base, and as a result, the quality of vermouth is not as high as it once was. After the wine has been infused, it is then fortified to raise the alcohol content to 15 to 21 percent (table wine is usually 12 to 14 percent). Red vermouth is generally sweet; white vermouth may be dry or semisweet. Both are consumed solo, as aperitifs, or mixed into various cocktails, including Manhattans. The large, commercial vermouth firms, such as Cinzano, Martini & Rossi, and Punt e Mes, are all headquartered around Turin, the capital of Piedmont.

The Gothic-Romanesque Abbey of Vezzolano in Asti, the region made famous by the semi-sweet sparkler also known as Asti (once called Asti Spumante). Dizzingly fruity and a joy to drink, Asti is made from moscato (muscat blanc à petits grains) grapes.

Dolcetto is made in selected spots all around Piedmont, but the best wines generally come from near Alba (dolcetto d'Alba) and from around the small village of Dogliani (dolcetto di Dogliani), which calls itself the birthplace of dolcetto thanks to sixteenth-century documents that reference the grape, though the origin and parentage of the variety has not been established by DNA typing.

GAVI AND ARNEIS

In Piedmont, red wine has always been a religion, and white wine, something of a postscript. Nonetheless, a small number of good (and moderately expensive) white wines are being made in the region, notably those called Gavi and arneis. Gavi, the wine made around the village of Gavi, in the southeast, near the border with Liguria, once had more than just a local reputation. During the 1960s and 1970s, when Italy was in the midst of its fine wine revolution, many wine experts considered it the best dry white wine in the entire country. (Pinot grigio, at the time, was considered so characterless it didn't warrant

consideration.) By the 1980s, however, the stunning whites of Friuli-Venezia Giulia and Trentino-Alto Adige began to challenge Gavi's standing, and today they are far more highly thought of.

Gavi is made from the cortese grape, presumed to be native to Piedmont, and mentioned in early-seventeenth-century literature. At its best the wine is bone-dry and crisp, with citrus and mineral notes—pleasant enough, to be sure. About thirty estates specialize in Gavi, most in and around the small village of that name. The area's proximity to the Ligurian coast, the Italian Riviera, has made Gavi a natural partner for seafood.

Arneis, which means "rascal" in the Piedmontese dialect, has gone through several fashion cycles. For decades, plantings were in decline, and there still isn't very much produced, but in the mid-1980s arneis began to acquire underground cult status as another chic match for seafood in fashionable restaurants along the Ligurian coast. The vagaries of fashion notwithstanding, this can be a delicious wine—dry, lively (like that rascal), and fairly full in body, with light pear and apricot flavors. Arneis is made mostly in the hills of Roero, northwest of Alba. The best producers include Vietti, Ceretto, Bruno Giacosa, and Castello di Neive.

ASTI

Italy produces sparkling wines from more different grape varieties than any other country in the world. The best known is Asti, formerly known as Asti Spumante, an aromatic, semisweet sparkler made from moscato grapes grown all over southeastern Piedmont but especially around the famous wine towns of Asti and Alba. South of Asti and east of Alba is the tiny village of Canelli, where Asti production began in the latter part of the 1800s. The village is such a hub of Asti production that this particular type of moscato is sometimes called moscato Canelli. It has another name, too—moscato bianco, white muscat. Both of these names refer to the same grape that in French is known as muscat blanc à petits grains.

If everyone in the world were sitting down together for one immense lunch party and only one wine could be served, a top Asti might be a good choice. The frothy *spumante* (the word *spumante* means "foaming") is as irresistible as chilled peaches on a hot day. Yet the wine has anything but a good public relations image. Lots of poorly made, commercial Asti Spumante exported after World War II gave it a cheap-fizz reputation that has been slow to die. The best modern Astis are far from that. They are not sugary sweet like candy but, rather, dizzyingly fruity and evocative of perfectly ripe peaches and apricots. Plus, there's the wine's intriguing muskiness—a hallmark of moscato grapes. Asti is also quite light—7 to 9 percent alcohol (standard wines are 12 to 14 percent). It should be served very well chilled—cold, in fact, and in a tall, narrow glass.

There are dozens of grape varieties that have the word *muscat* (or *moscato*) in their names, and they are some of the oldest vines around the Mediterranean. Indeed, moscato may well have been the first grape cultivated in Piedmont, although nebbiolo, too, is an ancient variety. Despite moscato's long sojourn in Piedmont, its use in sparkling wine is relatively recent. The first Asti is attributed to Carlo Gancia, who introduced sparkling wine

BRACHETTO . . . RUBY FIZZ

Legend has it that both Julius Caesar and Mark Antony presented gourds of sparkling brachetto to Cleopatra, as the wine was an aphrodisiac. While that last idea is hard to fact-check, the sparkler has undeniable charm. Brilliant ruby red in color, with intense floral and fruity notes, brachetto is made exclusively from brachetto grapes in the Acqui region of Piedmont, hence its full name, brachetto d'Acqui. The wine is frizzante ("lightly sparkling"), very low in alcohol, fresh, and loaded with sweet raspberry and black cherry flavors. It is the perfect ending to a meal, and is one of the few wines in the world that pairs extremely well with chocolate.*

to the region around 1870. Gancia is still a leading commercial maker of the wine.

Most Asti is not made according to the traditional (Champagne) method (with secondary fermentation in the bottle) but by the Charmat, or tank, method. In this type of fermentation, the grapes are crushed and the must is put in large vats and chilled to near freezing to prevent immediate fermentation. The wine is then fermented in batches as needed, which preserves the sensational fruitiness of the grapes. The process takes place in enormous, pressurized, sealed tanks that trap the natural carbon dioxide gas and cause it to dissolve back into the wine (the trapped carbon dioxide will become the wine's bubbles). When the wine has reached about 7 to 9 percent alcohol, and about 3 to 5 percent of the natural grape sugar (residual sugar) remains, it is chilled down to stabilize it, centrifuged to remove all remaining yeasts, and bottled. At that point the sparkler is immediately shipped, so that it can be consumed at its freshest and liveliest. Asti producers do not generally put vintage dates on bottles, since the wines for sale should always (you hope) be from the immediate past harvest.

Each year, 68 million bottles of Asti are made by a handful of giant companies, including Cinzano, Contratto, Gancia, Fontanafredda, and Martini & Rossi. In fact, more than five times as much Asti is made yearly than Barolo.

MOSCATO D'ASTI

Asti's more prestigious cousin, moscato d'Asti is generally made in tiny batches and in limited quantities by small Piedmontese producers using selected muscat blanc à petit grains grapes. Delicate, lightly sweet, and gorgeously fruity, moscato d'Asti is particularly low in alcohol—no more than 5.5 percent by law (Asti is usually 7 to 9 percent alcohol). This makes moscato d'Asti a fairly fragile wine, which in turn has made it highly desirable among Italian wine connoisseurs.

Moscato d'Asti is also less effervescent than Asti. It is not considered *spumante* (foaming) at all, just a bit *frizzante* (fizzy). Since it is under less pressure than Asti, it is stoppered with a regular cork, not a sparkling wine cork with a wire cage. Moscato d'Asti is vintage dated and is served well chilled, generally in regular wineglasses, not flutes. It should be drunk while fresh, soon after release. In Piedmont it's traditional to drink a glass on Christmas morning.

SOME OF THE
BEST PRODUCERS OF
MOSCATO D'ASTI

Cascina La Spinetta-Rivetti • Icardi •
I Vignaioli di Santo Stefano
• Marchesi di Gresy • Vietti Cascinetta

THE FOODS OF PIEDMONT

Northern Italian food, including the food of Piedmont, is not what many people imagine it to be—and for a good historical reason. The great wave of Italian emigrants who left Italy at the beginning of the twentieth century consisted mostly of extremely poor people from southern villages. To their new home countries, they brought a modest repertoire of regional peasant dishes that revolved around pasta, olive oil, tomatoes, and vegetables. Dishes like "spaghetti and meatballs" were among the immigrant inventions that bore little resemblance to what was being cooked and eaten in southern Italy itself.

The cuisines of northern Italy went largely unknown around the world until the past few decades. And then, their appeal was said to be their lightness. Whoever suggested that, however, certainly wasn't thinking about Piedmontese food. Here, hearty, copious dishes evolved as the logical sustenance of people who lived in the cold shadow of the Alps and drank robust red wines to keep warm.

WHEN YOU VISIT . . . PIEDMONT

Virtually all of the best wine estates in Piedmont are small and family-run. Visiting is by appointment only. Luckily, most are also within easy driving distance from Alba, a charming small town as famous for white truffles as it is for wine. (Late November is white truffle season.) Conveniently, many of Piedmont's best restaurants, such as Guido, Boccondivino, Cacciatori, Piazza Duomo, La Rei, and La Ciau del Tornavento, are also located in this part of the wine country.

Thanks to Piedmont's cold winters and its inland location on the foothills of the Alps, the local cuisine is meat-based and hearty.

Moreover, Piedmont, on the border of France, was once part of the Kingdom of Savoy. As the cuisines clanged together, Piedmont adopted the most luxurious French ingredients. Butter, cream, and eggs are used more extensively here than in any other region of Italy, with the possible exception of Emilia-Romagna.

Perhaps the most startling difference between the cooking of Piedmont and that of the rest of Italy is the prominence of meat. In no other region are diners presented with such he-man-size hunks of roasted game, veal, and lamb. Remarkably, the carnivorous feast is usually preceded by a herculean Piedmontese *antipasto misto*—a series of up to twenty dishes (egg frittatas, sausages with beans, veal tartare, and so on) that could feed at least a dozen people more than are at the table.

One of the single most compelling Piedmontese appetizers is *bagna cauda*

(literally, "hot bath"), a hearty fall specialty always served during the grape harvest. Extra virgin olive oil, butter, anchovies, and garlic are whisked together, heated to near boiling, and served with a variety of vegetables that you dip in the hot oil. These include cardoons (a member of the artichoke family), red peppers, fennel, leeks, radishes, onions, cabbage, beets, and bitter lettuces. Bread is put to use as an edible plate, helping to convey the vegetables from the pot to the mouth without dripping oil all over the tablecloth.

The two famous Piedmontese pasta dishes are tagliatelle and agnolotti. Tagliatelle are long, thin, handmade egg noodles lavishly but simply dressed with nothing more than melted butter and sage. In the fall, white truffles will be shaved over the pasta, falling like snowflakes on top of the glistening yellow strands. (Heaven when accompanied by Barolo.) Agnolotti are small, half-moon-shaped ravioli, frequently stuffed with veal and sage, or such vegetables as pumpkin or spinach and, again, drizzled lightly with melted butter.

Stretching across the north of Italy is a vast corn and rice belt, with the result that polenta and risotto are as customary as pasta. Piedmontese risottos, made with rich meat broths and the region's earthy wild mushrooms, are irresistible. Polenta (cornmeal as art) is often pan sautéed in butter and served (like American mashed potatoes) as a foil for roasts.

In Piedmontese restaurants, large breadsticks—*grissini*—are immediately brought to the table, lest anyone go hungry in the first few seconds after arrival. These impressive specimens can be as long as the width of the table, or just big and fat. Baking in general is more significant in the north thanks to both French and Austrian influences.

Above all else, however, the food that immortalizes Piedmont is the white truffle—one of the world's most rarified specialties and a tribute to Italian hedonism.

The Piedmontese Wines to Know

WHITES

VIETTI

MOSCATO D'ASTI | CASCINETTA VIETTI

100% muscat blanc à petits grains

For sheer abandon, nothing beats this wine. The flavor is a juicy riot of peaches, apricots, oranges, and ginger, all framed by effusive bubbles. I could drink this all day. (I think I really could; it's only 5.5 percent alcohol.) Much of the moscato d'Asti made today (especially by very large wine companies) is little more than a cheap, fruity fizz. But the small-estate moscatos d'Asti made by quality-oriented producers, such as the Vietti family, are wholly different. Their artisanal flavor and pure scrumptiousness are irresistible. In fact, well-made moscato d'Asti is a wine nobody doesn't like.

GAJA

CHARDONNAY | ROSSJ-BASS

100% chardonnay

Angelo Gaja makes two delicious chardonnays: Rossj-Bass and Gaia & Rey. Although the latter is more famous and more voluptuous, the Rossj-Bass is the more pure, high-toned, elegant wine. (The wine is named after Angelo Gaja's youngest daughter, Rossana, Rossj for short.) There's just a hint of oak to enrich the fruit, plus a dense, creamy pear-nectar quality, always spiked with jazzy, appley acidity.

REDS

MARCARINI

DOLCETTO D'ALBA | BOSCHI DI BERRI

100% dolcetto

Marcarini makes seriously delicious dolcetto from the century-old, pre-phylloxera vineyard known as Boschi di Berri. The wine is a vibrating bowl full of burstingly ripe, maddeningly red cherries laced with violets and vanilla crème anglaise. The fruit is effusive, the balance is perfect, the finish is remarkably long, and the crave factor is at an all-time high.

VIETTI

BARBERA D'ALBA | SCARRONE

100% barbera

The spirited Vietti family is intensely hardworking, and their passion shows in their wines. The family members are considered barbera experts, although their Barolos and even their moscatos are delicious wines full of personality. They make several single-vineyard barberas and each has explosive, rich fruit. The most profound, refined, and ageworthy is the Scarrone, which, with even a few years of age, can stop you in your tracks. This is a kinetic barbera, a barbera where berry, licorice, citrus, leather, and vanilla flavors rage around, tempestlike, in the glass.

GAJA

BARBARESCO | SORÌ TILDÌN

100% nebbiolo

Gaja makes a number of stunning Piedmontese wines, including his four Barbarescos, which are the heart and soul of the winery. Although all are richly flavored, complex wines, the single-vineyard Sorì Tildìn is incomparable. The sensation of sipping this wine is rather like coming in from the cold and being wrapped up in a warm blanket. The wine unleashes a torrent of compelling aromas and flavors—violets, chocolate, roses, tar, and figs, and the tannin broaches silk in its ability to be strong and soft at the same time.

PIO CESARE

BARBARESCO

100% nebbiolo

Founded in 1881, in the center of Alba, the estate of Pio Cesare has been one of the pillars of winemaking in the Langhe for more than a century. The Barolos and Barbarescos here are especially sumptuous and long, For me, the Barbaresco is a poem to the earth . . . to the scents of fallen leaves, tobacco, worn leather, and summer as it descends into the decay of fall. For all the gentility of the fruit flavors, the wine's severe and majestic structure is classic nebbiolo. The grapes for this Barbaresco come in part from the Pio Cesare family's Il Bricco vineyard, in the village of Treiso.

LUCIANO SANDRONE

BAROLO | CANNUBI BOSCHIS

100% nebbiolo

Luciano Sandrone makes some of the most texturally rich Barolos in Piedmont. Indeed, texture is so important to Sandrone that he heats his cellars during the harvest so that the just-picked nebbiolo grapes can immediately begin to ferment (yeasts work more quickly in a warm environment), rather than sit for an extended period in contact with the highly tannic nebbiolo skins. The effect is amazing, especially with Sandrone's Barolo from the famous Cannubi Boschis section of the Cannubi vineyard. Suppleness—a word not often used with Barolo—is the right word here. Plus the flavors—tar, incense, dark plums—soar, giving one the uncanny sense that the wine is somehow flying across one's palate.

CERETTO

BAROLO | BRICCO ROCCHE BRICCO ROCCHE

100% nebbiolo

Bricco Rocche Bricco Rocche (the name of the wine and the name of the tiny, 3.7-acre/1.5-hectare vineyard are the same) is above all a graceful wine of intense concentration, with a flawless, suede-like texture. The irresistible aromas of earth, sea salt, dried leaves, incense, and something evocative of the human body are mesmerizing. This is the most expensive and refined of the three Ceretto single-vineyard Barolos, and it is from extremely steep vineyards at the crest of a hill. Ceretto produces Bricco Rocche Bricco Rocche only four or five times a decade.

GIACOMO CONTERNO

BAROLO | CASCINA FRANCIA

100% nebbiolo

One of the most traditional wine estates of Piedmont, Giacomo Conterno still makes some of the greatest Barolos. No modern hand with oak or fermentation temperatures here, just a very fine sense of how to coax finesse out of nebbiolo. The effect is dazzling. In great vintages, the Giacomo Conterno wines from the family's 35-acre (14-hectare) Cascina Francia estate in Serralunga are beautiful, lingering wines evocative of roses, tar, licorice, sage, rosemary, and salt. These are Barolos for laying away until, on some dark, cold night, with a roast in the oven, you can't bear it any longer.

THE VENETO

he leading wine-producing region of the north in terms of volume, the Veneto is, in some years, the most prolific region in all of Italy. Unfortunately, oceans of Veneto wine are entirely forgettable, obscuring the fact that the region is also home to some great classics, such as amarone, considered by many Italian wine experts to be the greatest traditional red wine of northern Italy.

Both the Veneto and its beloved city of Venice take their names from the Veneti, the tribe that settled in the area around 1000 B.C. As one of the leading ports and commercial centers of the medieval world, Venice was a link between the Byzantine Empire in the East and the emerging countries of northern Europe. Its trade in wines, spices, and food, as well as its wealth and accomplishments in art, architecture, and glass production, laid the groundwork for Venice to become one of the most sophisticated cities in all of Italy.

From Venice and the Adriatic coast, the plains of the Veneto stretch inland through fairly flat farmland until they come to the lower foothills of the Alps and the border with Trentino-Alto Adige in the northwest. Much of this land is fertile and extremely productive, which helped set the scene for the ambitious scale of viticulture that has ensued.

The Veneto's big-business stance began in the 1960s and 1970s when the region geared up to produce industrial amounts of the whites Soave and pinot grigio and the reds Valpolicella

▲ *Venice's strategic position has afforded it both protection and power. From the 9th to the 12th centuries, it was a key center of trade between western Europe and the Byzantine Empire.*

Just-harvested black-purple corvina grapes at Bertani Winery. Corvina is the leading variety in many of the Veneto's best-known red wines, including amarone and Valpolicella.

and Bardolino. Much of this was intended for the United States and Great Britain, where undemanding, inexpensive, innocuous Italian wines had begun to sell like hotcakes.

It's tempting, of course, to dismiss the wines just mentioned, for the commercial version of each can be truly awful. But nothing Italian is ever that simple. Take Soave. While most of it is a mass-produced liquid with only slightly more flavor than water, there are a number of quite extraordinary Soaves—wines you'd never guess were Soave if you didn't know. Thus, for many Veneto wines, two versions exist: the casual cheap version, and a giant step up in quality (and price), the really terrific version.

The Veneto also produces several wines made by a method called *appassimento*, in which grapes are spread on mats or left to hang in cool lofts, in order to raisinate and concentrate them. The dry wine amarone is made this way, as are sweet wines labeled *recioto* (as in recioto di Valpolicella). The word *recioto* derives from *recie*, dialect for "ears," in this case referring to the protruding lobes, or ears of a bunch of grapes. Since they are the part of the bunch that is most exposed to the sun, the ears often have the ripest grapes. To make a

THE QUICK SIP ON THE VENETO

TWO OF ITALY'S most well-known and widely exported wines come from the Veneto: Soave, a white, and Valpolicella, a red. Both are available as low- and high-quality wines.

SOME VENETO WINES, both dry and sweet, are made by a special process known as *appassimento*, which concentrates the sugars in the grapes. The two best known of these are the dry red amarone and the sweet red recioto di Valpolicella.

ONE OF THE VENETO'S MOST POPULAR wines is Prosecco, a very chic, casual Italian *spumante,* and the sparkling wine behind the legendary cocktail, the Bellini.

recioto wine, either the ears or, if they are ripe enough, entire bunches of grapes are dried until the sugar is very concentrated. When the grapes are fermented, a percentage of the natural residual grape sugar is allowed to remain in the wine. The wine that results can be rich indeed. Opulent yet elegant sweet versions of both Soave and Valpolicella are made in this way.

Against the backdrop of such extremely well-known wines as Soave and Valpolicella, you'll find several Veneto wines with almost cultlike followings. Among them are those of the producer Maculan, made near the village of Breganze. Maculan was one of the first to approach chardonnay and cabernet sauvignon with quality (and higher prices) in mind. But Maculan's most renowned wine is Torcolato, the most famous dessert wine of the Veneto. Torcolato is made primarily from native vespaiolo grapes that have been lightly affected by botrytis and then, after picking, put into special drying lofts and allowed to shrivel and raisinate (the *appassimento* method). The wine is gorgeously balanced, with striking raisin, orange, vanilla, green tea, and roasted nut flavors. The name Torcolato ("twisted" in Italian) refers to the special way the winery's workers tie bunches of grapes with twine, twisting them so that each bunch hangs freely, completely surrounded by air, ensuring perfect drying.

Lastly, the Veneto is home to Prosecco, an easy-drinking sparkling wine and the bubbly that's traditionally blended with the juice of fresh white peaches to make Venice's most famous cocktail, the Bellini.

THE MOST IMPORTANT VENETO WINES

LEADING WINES

AMARONE red

PINOT GRIGIO white

PROSECCO white (sparkling)

SOAVE white

VALPOLICELLA red

WINES OF NOTE

BARDOLINO red

BIANCO DI CUSTOZA white

CABERNET SAUVIGNON red

CHARDONNAY white

MERLOT red

RECIOTO DELLA VALPOLICELLA red (sweet)

RECIOTO DI SOAVE white (sweet)

THE LAND, THE GRAPES, AND THE VINEYARDS

Though the northern and western parts of the Veneto can be quite mountainous, the region is less influenced by the Alps than either of its neighbors, Trentino-Alto Adige or Friuli-Venezia Giulia. Both the Adige and Po rivers, on their way to the Adriatic Sea, flow across the broad plains of the Veneto, creating large expanses of rich, sun-drenched farmland where vegetables and fruits, including grapes, grow profusely. Since great wines in general come not from fertile soil but from the opposite, the Veneto's best vines tend to be planted near hills, on well-drained volcanic soil interspersed with sand, clay, and gravel.

The Veneto can be divided into three zones. In the far west, near Lake Garda and the

THE GRAPES OF THE VENETO

WHITES

CHARDONNAY: Can make some attractive New World–style wines, but more often they are merely decent.

GARGANEGA: Leading grape grown in the Veneto since the Rennaissance. The dominant grape in Soave, where it is blended with so-called trebbiano di Soave (verdicchio bianco).

GLERA: Probably originally native to the Istrian peninsula (now part of Croatia) near Friuli-Venezia Giulia's far eastern border. Today grown almost exclusively in the Veneto. The principal grape in the popular sparkling wine Prosecco.

PINOT BIANCO: A minor grape in terms of production, but when pinot bianco (pinot blanc) is used, as it often is, as part of a blend, it contributes good body and character.

PINOT GRIGIO: Also known as pinot gris, pinot grigio makes volumes of decent light wine (with a few exceptions, most are usually not as good as the pinot grigios of Friuli or the Alto Adige).

TREBBIANO DI SOAVE: Despite its local name, not actually a trebbiano, but rather, the grape verdicchio bianco. Good-quality grape blended with garganega to make Soave and bianco di Custoza.

TREBBIANO TOSCANO: A neutral-tasting grape used in cheaper versions of Soave and other Veneto whites.

VESPAIOLA: Native grape. The source of some interesting dry white wines, and more-famous sweet ones.

REDS

CABERNET SAUVIGNON: With a few notable exceptions, made into relatively insubstantial wines.

CORVINA VERONESE: Leading native red grape. Thanks to its good structure, it's the lion's share of the blend in amarone, Valpolicella, and most Bardolinos. The name may be derived from *corvo* ("crow," a reference to the black color of the grapes).

MERLOT: Mostly made into simple, serviceable, but uninspired wines.

MOLINARA: A minor blending component in the wines amarone, Valpolicella, and Bardolino. Considered generally lower in quality than corvina and rondinella.

NEGRARA: A minor blending component in the wines amarone, Valpolicella, and Bardolino.

OSELETA: Rare blending grape thought to be extinct but rescued and revived in the 1990s and now used in very small amounts by some producers in their amarones and Valpolicellas.

RONDINELLA: The second most important grape, after corvina (which is one of its parents), in amarone, Valpolicella, and Bardolino.

volcanic mountain range of Monte Lessini, the traditional wines Soave, Valpolicella, Bardolino, and amarone are produced, as well as Bianco di Custoza, one of those simple sorts of white wines that taste best when drunk in a bar (the wine, not you) in the region where

The fortresslike medieval castle of Soave, built in the 10th century in the western Veneto. The countryside around the castle is well known for garganega and trebbiano di Soave grapes and the simple, easy-drinking white wine made from them.

they're made. Verona, the major city, is one of Italy's wine capitals; each year, the country's largest wine fair, Vinitaly, is held here. (Spread over five or more coliseum-size buildings, the fair includes so many thousands of Italian wines that tasting them all could take weeks.) In the Veneto's northern hills above Treviso (held to be the radicchio capital of Italy), Prosecco is made. What is considered more or less the center of the Veneto, from Venice to Vicenza, is the source of several different types of wine, ranging from simple merlots, cabernet sauvignons, chardonnays, and pinot grigios of no particular distinction (Santa Margherita pinot grigio comes from here) to more exciting wines, especially from around Breganze, Colli Berici, and Colli Euganei.

As with Friuli and Trentino-Alto Adige, the Veneto was once home to dozens of grape varieties and many of them are still grown today, though in smaller amounts. In addition to the international varieties already mentioned, several native grapes are key. The leading native red grape by far is corvina, more accurately corvina Veronese, the major grape in amarone, Valpolicella, and Bardolino. Corvina is usually blended with smaller amounts of rondinella (its progeny), molinara, and sometimes negrara.

The leading white grape for the traditional wine Soave is an old Veneto variety—garganega, almost always blended with what is locally called trebbiano di Soave. (While it may be called a trebbiano, this old Veronese grape has been shown by DNA typing to be the grape verdicchio bianco.) Then there is vespaiola, a far more rare grape than garganega or trebbiano, that makes some fascinating wines, especially sweet wines. The grape owes its name to the word *vespa* (Italian for "wasp"), because when ripe, the grapes attract large numbers of these insects.

A HISTORY OF WINEGLASSES: ITALY'S MAJOR ROLE

From the beginning of time, drinking vessels have taken their inspiration from natural forms: hands cupped together, the conical horn of an animal, a gourd split into two bowls, a flower and its stem. Such simple images as these have given rise to an incredible number of objects used throughout history from which to drink wine. These range from the animal skins of the ancient world to the plastic tumblers of today.

But if any one substance was meant to carry wine, it is glass. Wineglasses are not a modern invention. In the first century B.C., mouth-blown goblets, beakers, and bottles were being made in the Mediterranean and Near East. These early vessels were extremely precious and rare.

Remarkably, modern glasses are made in essentially the same way ancient ones were. Basically, common sand—which contains silica—is combined with ashes from trees—potash. The mixture is then fired at intense heat—up to 2,500°F (1,371°C)—causing the substances to melt together. After firing, the molten blob is blown by mouth (or machine) and shaped.

Glassmaking reached its zenith in the sixteenth and seventeenth centuries on the island of Murano, near Venice, Italy. There, glassmakers were held as virtual captives of their guild. Any glassblower caught trying to escape from the island or revealing the secret of Venetian glassmaking was punished by death. (Murano glass is still considered among the finest in Europe.)

Meanwhile, in England, perhaps the single greatest innovation in glassmaking had been stumbled upon. In 1674, a glassblower named George Ravenscroft discovered that adding a small amount of lead oxide to molten glass made it more malleable. Elaborate designs could now be etched and cut into the lead crystal. Moreover, after being formed, lead crystal was more brilliant and durable than simple glass.

In propitious, yin-yang fashion, more beautiful glasses became an incentive to create better wines and beverages. These, in turn, inspired ever more beautiful glasses. One of the best examples of this is Champagne. First made in the late 1600s, Champagne was hazy with sediment, viscous, and sweet. When advances

SOAVE

One of Italy's best-known, exported white wines, Soave comes from the castle-topped hillside town of the same name, just east of Verona, in the western part of the Veneto. Traditionally, Soaves—made from garganega and "trebbiano" (verdicchio bianco)—were light, fresh, and at their best, smooth and *soave* ("suave" or "smooth" in Italian). Since the early 1970s, however, a lot of the Soave produced has been commercial, bland, cheap jug wine based on a neutral-tasting grape—an actual trebbiano variety—called trebbiano Toscano and produced from vineyards that have enormous yields.

Basic, featherweight Soave is never aged and can come from anywhere in the Soave denomination, which was greatly expanded in the 1970s. A step up in quality is Soave Classico, wine that comes from the original, smaller Soave zone on the steep hills above the towns of Soave and Monteforte d'Alpone. An even greater step up in quality is Soave Classico Superiore, which cannot be released until a year after the harvest.

Finally, each year a tiny amount of sweet Soave is made from garganega

in glassmaking led to glasses with a transparent brilliance and elegance never before thought possible, the new, graceful glasses inspired improvements in Champagne making. In turn, improvements in the clarity of Champagne inspired ever more stunning glasses into which beautiful Champagne could be poured.

From their invention until the beginning of the nineteenth century, glasses were used mainly by royalty, and principally on special occasions. The purchase of a single wineglass was considered a serious investment, and at the most prestigious banquets, one glass might be shared by several dinner guests. If the host was especially wealthy, the banquet glasses might include some intentionally designed with a rounded bottom and no stem. Such glasses made the party livelier, since only cups that had been drained of their contents could be put down, lest the liquid spill out. These glass cups were the forerunners of our tumblers.

In the nineteenth century, glass production soared as blowing techniques improved. Glass houses capable of large-scale manufacturing began to emerge. The process of making glasses in molds was invented. Glassmaking quickly achieved a scale of production that allowed sets to become affordable. Glasses became status symbols. At all of the best dinner parties, each guest's place would be set with numerous goblets: one for Champagne, one for red wine, one for white, one for Sherry, and so on.

Modern molds and techniques also allowed greater variation in bottle shapes and colors. Glass houses throughout Europe began producing signature bottles meant to be identified with certain wines. Bottles with sloping shoulders were used for Burgundy; extremely tapered bottles held German wines. High-shouldered bottles (helpful in blocking sediment while decanting) were used for Bordeaux.

As the twentieth century drew to a close, a renewed sense of creativity gripped the world of glassmaking. Wineglass design ranged from dramatically whimsical to almost exaggeratedly classic. And for the first time in decades, wine bottles again became a vehicle for avant-garde design. Witness the utterly fragile, delicately curved modern shapes of grappa bottles. As much as the liquid inside, the beauty of these bottles has inspired a whole new generation at least to buy (if not to drink) Italian grappa.

A glassblower in Murano, where, in the 16th century, glassmaking was raised to a high art.

grapes, using the *appassimento* method. Like amarone and recioto della Valpolicella, recioto di Soave is made from very ripe grapes that have been put in special drying rooms, allowing the grapes to dry out and their sugars to concentrate. Since fermentation is halted before all of the sugar is converted into alcohol, recioto di Soave is sweet. Although made in small amounts, it is one of the true specialties of the Veneto and can be a stunningly delicious wine. (Try the recioto di Soave from Pieropan.)

The three absolute champions when it comes to Soave are the producers Anselmi (which actually renounced the designation Soave years ago to protest the commercial versions, and now labels its wines with proprietary names such as Capitel Croce), Gini, and Pieropan (whose La Rocca is a terrific Soave). Other top producers to look for include Bertani and Guerrieri Rizzardi.

PROSECCO

The Veneto's ubiquitous *spumante* ("sparkling wine"), Prosecco is made principally from glera grapes, sometimes with small amounts of pinot bianco, pinot grigio, or an indigenous grape such as verdiso added. The grape glera used to be referred to as Prosecco (so, historically, Prosecco the wine was made from prosecco grapes), but in 2009, when Prosecco di Conegliano-Valdobbiadene was elevated to DOCG status, producers changed the name to avoid confusion between the name of the grape and the name of the wine.

Basic, inexpensive Prosecco is made from grapes grown at fairly high yields over a very large area. A step up in quality are Proseccos made from the best glera grapes grown in the original Prosecco Superiore zone, just north of Venice, in the rambling hills between the villages of Conegliano and Valdobbiadene.

Originally, Prosecco was only slightly fizzy. Today, most examples are fully sparkling and dry (brut), with a simple fruity flavor and an appealing bitter edge. (Hence the Bellini's brilliance—sweet white peach juice as a counterpoint to glera's bitterness.) Prosecco, however, does not get its bubbles via the traditional (Champagne) method. Rather, Prosecco is made by the Charmat process, in which the wine undergoes a second fermentation in pressurized tanks rather than bottles. Most versions are not vintage dated. That said, a new very high level of Prosecco has recently come to be. This level, called *rive* (local dialect for "hillside"), is made up of small-production Proseccos that are vintage dated and based on grapes grown in a single town.

In the late afternoon, virtually every bar in Venice pours glass after glass of Prosecco, which the civilized, chic Venetians consider revitalizing after working all day. (In the 2010s, with Prosecco

sales soaring, it seemed like New Yorkers felt the same way.) Top producers include Adriano Adami, Bisol Jeio, Bellenda, Carpenè Malvolti, Nino Franco, Col Vetoraz, Sorelle Bronca, Mionetto, and Ruggeri.

AMARONE

Big, dense red wines the world over are unquestionably the product of very ripe grapes, and very ripe grapes in turn are the product of warm, sunny places. Historically, this simple fact meant that most relatively cool regions, and the Veneto is one, learned to be satisfied making lighter reds or settling for whites. How, then, did the Veneto get to be famous for amarone, an intense wine with a syrupy thickness? By the special style of winemaking called *appassimento*. Here's what happens.

Amarone (the name means "great bitter one") is made in the Valpolicella

---

AMARONE: SAY CHEESE

*D*espite the common assumption that all red wines taste good with cheese, many cheeses can make red wines taste flat and hollow. One exception is amarone—which stands up to even dramatic cheeses. At 15 to 16 percent alcohol and with a Portlike body and deep bitter chocolate, mocha, dried fig, and earthy flavors, amarone is a powerhouse. In his authoritative books on Italian wine, the Italian wine expert Victor Hazan (husband of the late, famed cookbook author Marcella Hazan) suggests that amarone is the perfect wine to drink with a roast, being careful to save the last glasses to sip during the finale: a plate of walnuts and bite-size chunks of Parmigiano-Reggiano.

Corvina and rondinella grapes lose 30 percent of their weight as they dry on wooden or bamboo slats. Once concentrated in this way, the grapes will be used to make lush, full-bodied amarone.

region, near Verona, from the same grapes as Valpolicella: mainly corvina, with rondinella, molinara, and sometimes negrara. But while the grapes for Valpolicella are picked during the regular harvest, a small percentage of grapes (historically about 40 percent) are left to hang on the vine a little longer, achieving extra ripeness before they are picked. These are the grapes that can become amarone. Next, the best whole bunches of these ripe grapes are spread on bamboo shelving or left hanging in the air in cool drying lofts for three to four months, although the exact amount of time varies from producer to producer. This causes the grapes to shrivel, further concentrating their sugar and flavors. As they dry and raisinate, the grapes lose up to a third of their weight, mostly water. When the grapes are finally crushed and fermented, the resulting wine is opulent, full-bodied, and, at 15 to 16 percent alcohol, higher in alcohol than a regular Valpolicella, which averages around 12 percent. Amarones are then aged for two years or more (four years for the riserva) before release. Today, some of that aging may take

place in small, new oak barrels, giving the wine even broader and more powerful flavors.

The labor-intensive method of concentrating grape sugar not only adds to the wine's cost, but the process itself is also fairly risky. Even a small amount of wet autumn weather

Venice is spread over 118 small islands connected by bridges and canals.

Lake Garda, the largest lake in Italy, was formed by glaciers at the end of the last Ice Age. The lake water is known for its intense hues of blue. Around the lake, corvina, rondinella, molinara, and negrara vines thrive and are used to make the light red Bardolino.

can cause the bunches to rot rather than dry out. As a result, producers who are less than scrupulously careful and clean in their wine-making can end up with amarones with flavors that seem to hint of mold and a certain dankness. But when the winemaking is above reproach and the grapes selected for drying are only of the highest level and come from a good vineyard, an amarone can be spellbinding—powerful almost to the point of Portlike concentration, and packed with mocha and earthy flavors at the same time.

WHEN YOU VISIT . . . THE VENETO

Start out in the magical city of Venice, and make day trips to the Veneto's vine-covered hills, which stretch from the Austrian border through Prosecco country to the eastern shores of Lake Garda. The landscape is beautiful; the food stellar. Lovers of sparkling wine should not miss the Strada del Vino Prosecco (Prosecco wine route) that winds through the Treviso hills. For most wineries, appointments are necessary, and it helps to have a working knowledge of Italian.

SOME OF THE BEST PRODUCERS OF AMARONE

Allegrini • Bertani • Corte Sant'Alda • Le Ragose • Le Salette • Masi • Quintarelli • Romano dal Forno • Serègo Alighieri • Speri • Tedeschi • Tommasi • Tommaso Bussola • Zenato

VALPOLICELLA AND BARDOLINO

Like amarone, Valpolicella is made from corvina, along with rondinella, molinara, and sometimes negrara grapes. Five distinct styles of Valpolicella (the name means "valley of many wine cellars") are made. First is the basic, lightweight, grapey stuff, which is usually not aged and can come from anywhere in the Valpolicella denomination. Like Soave, this area was greatly expanded in the 1970s to meet increasing demand for inexpensive wine. Better quality is Valpolicella Classico, which refers to wines that come from the original, smaller Valpolicella zone. Better still is Valpolicella Classico Superiore, which must be aged a year before release and, in practice, commands better grapes. In the hands of a great producer like Allegrini, Valpolicella Classico Superiore can be a sensational wine, with rich, minerally, dried cherry and licorice flavors.

But there's an even higher-quality, more intensely flavored, and thicker-textured kind of Valpolicella yet. Called Valpolicella ripasso, it is made by taking the newly fermented Valpolicella wine and adding it to amarone pomace, which is the pulpy mass of seeds and skins leftover after the amarone has fermented. The Valpolicella is left in contact with the powerfully flavorful amarone pomace for a couple of weeks, during which time the wine picks up extra color, tannin, flavor, and structure from the pomace. In the end, the wine can possess an almost zinfandel-like jamminess. The word *ripasso* comes from the verb *ripassare*—"to pass over" or "do something again." In particular, the producer Masi has been at the forefront of making Valpolicella ripasso. Theirs, which was the first, is called Campo Fiorin.

Finally, there's the fifth kind of Valpolicella, recioto della Valpolicella. Like amarone, recioto della Valpolicella is made from the ripest grapes, which have been put in special drying rooms, allowing the grapes to raisinate and their sugar to concentrate. But while, in the case of amarone, all that sugar is converted into alcohol, thereby making the wine dry, fermentation is halted for recioto della Valpolicella before all of the sugar is converted into alcohol, so the wine is sweet. Only a tiny amount of recioto della Valpolicella is made, and it can be utterly sensational—a rich, sweet, but not saccharine red wine that is supple and complex and just waiting for an oozingly creamy Italian cheese, like a ripe Taleggio.

THE BELLINI

*I*taly's legendary summertime cocktail, the Bellini, is a combination of icy-cold sparkling Prosecco and fresh white peach juice. The drink was invented in the 1930s at Harry's Bar, in Venice, which employed one man each summer—when peaches were ripe—to do nothing but cut and pit small, fragile Italian white peaches (never the yellow variety) and then squeeze them by hand to extract the juice. Today, many Bellinis are made with frozen white peach juice exported from France and any sort of sparkling wine, but in the Veneto, every Bellini is the real thing.*

The top producers of Valpolicella, in addition to Allegrini and Masi, are Bertani, Tedeschi, Quintarelli, and Tommasi.

Though often thought of as a stand-in for Valpolicella, Bardolino is quite different, although it's made from the same grapes. Named after the town of Bardolino, on Lake Garda, the wine—more pink than red—is very light-bodied, with faint cherry flavors and sometimes an edge of spiciness. (It is drunk by the carafe with pizza in the modest trattorias along the lake.) Bardolino Classico, from the original district surrounding the town, is a more interesting wine than simple Bardolino. When turned into an inexpensive rosé sparkling wine, Bardolino is called chiaretto, which is a popular summertime quaff. In the fall, basic Bardolino is also made as a *novello* wine, a takeoff on commercial-tasting Beaujolais Nouveau. All types of Bardolino are best drunk slightly chilled. The top producer of Bardolino is Guerrieri-Rizzardi.

The Veneto Wines to Know

SPARKLING

ADRIANO ADAMI

PROSECCO | GARBÈL | BRUT

100% glera

This is one of the freshest, loveliest Proseccos around, despite being the Adami family's "basic" Prosecco. (Its big sister, called Vigneto Giardino, is masterful.) The Garbèl's beautiful tinge of briochelike yeastiness gives it a flavor that's deeper and a little more sophisticated than that of most other Proseccos. And while many moderately priced Proseccos are rather thin and slightly bitter (making them cry out for a Bellini-Band-Aid of peach juice), the Adriano Adami Garbèl is gingery and creamy on the palate. The word *garbèl*, in the old Venetian dialect, means "crisp and dry."

REDS

ALLEGRINI

LA GROLA

80% corvina, 10% syrah, 10% oseleta

This is my favorite "Valpolicella," although, since it is made outside the specific requirements for the Valpolicella DOC, it's designated an IGT. La Grola comes from the high-elevation, chalky-clay vineyard La Grola, and a richer, more lively, flavor-packed Veronese red does not exist (apart, of course, from amarone). The wine's silky texture and heady aromatics are immediately seductive, but the whirlwind of racy flavors—spices, tobacco, tar, raspberries, graphite, minerals, and licorice—is unbeatable. Best of all, La Grola always possesses a distinctive character that's not unlike the sweet-bitter quality of Italian bitters, making it a very sophisticated wine at the table.

ALLEGRINI

AMARONE DELLA VALPOLICELLA CLASSICO

80% corvina, 15% rondinella, 5% oseleta

If you could only ever drink one superb amarone, this should be the one. Indeed, Allegrini's amarone reaches heights of complexity that few others do. It's hard to say exactly what the wine is like. The intense aromas and flavors are equal parts fruity, salty, savory, acidic, and bitter. Tasting this not long ago, my mind flashed through: cherry-filled chocolate truffles; the saline taste of blood; the umami of a chunk of Parmigiano-Reggiano cheese; the high soprano notes of a great balsamic vinegar; the complex bitters of, say, Fernet-Branca. Not surprisingly, the way the wine feels is also irresistible. Ribbons of cashmere richness seem to weave through the center of the wine. And the finish appears never ready to surrender. In the end, I am stunned—but not stunned, for just about everything the Allegrini family touches turns to vinous magic. Their sweet *recioto* is a masterpiece (fewer and fewer producers today attempt to make this complex red dessert wine) and their single-vineyard wines, like La Grola, show just how rich and delicious great Veneto wine can be.

ZENATO

AMARONE DELLA VALPOLICELLA

70% corvina, 20% rondinella, 10% molinara

No wine is more perfect during the long, raw, cold winters in northern Italy (or anywhere, for that matter) than amarone. Big, lustful, and earthy, amarone is warming and satisfying. Zenato's amarone fits this bill exactly, but in great years it's also among the softest and most hedonistic of amarones, with deep, luscious, earthy, chocolate, balsamic, and fruit flavors. The complexity of Zenato's amarones always reminds me of Venetian cooking, where sweet, sour, and savory flavors are used with exquisite balance.

MASI

AMARONE DELLA VALPOLICELLA | CLASSICO RISERVA | COSTASERA

Approximately 70% corvina, with rondinella, molinara, and a tiny amount of oseleta

If you don't know amarone, Masi is a good place to begin for its lush, ripe, almost Portlike texture. Costasera is one of the winery's top amarones and comes from vineyards that the winery says "face the sunset." The riserva version contains the rare native Venetian grape oseleta, once thought to be extinct, but rescued, due in large part to the efforts of Masi. This is a muscular amarone, and one that is utterly fascinating, with flavors and aromas suggestive of leather, grenadine, plums, violets, exotic spices, and black licorice. In the small restaurants of northern Italy, amarones like Masi's are drunk with hearty slabs of roasted meat.

SWEET WINE

MACULAN

TORCOLATO

100% vespaiola

Italian desserts and sweet wines are generally not as sweet as their French counterparts. Torcolato is a great example of this. Devastatingly intense in flavor, it's only faintly sweet, and it's certainly not syrupy. Instead, this forceful neon-yellow/orange wine is bursting with flavors (exotic oranges, bitter walnut skin, dried citrus peel, apricot, bergamot-infused tea, cardamom, honey) that, mingled together, taste strangely beautiful and refined. In Italy, Torcolato is called a wine for meditation. Its hypnotic persuasion is certainly undeniable.

FRIULI-VENEZIA GIULIA

ticking out like a small ear from the northeastern corner of Italy, Friuli-Venezia Giulia (usually just called Friuli) is culturally and historically rich. For centuries, northern European and Near Eastern tribes moved through the region on their way to the Mediterranean. The overland spice routes ran through Friuli from the markets of the Byzantine Empire to Venice. Much later—before it became part of the newly formed country of Italy in 1866—Friuli was the strategic Mediterranean port province of the Austro-Hungarian Empire. Even today, the region seems psychologically much closer to Austria than, say, to Rome. And you can almost taste the proximity in the wines. More than any other wines in Italy, they have Teutonic precision, focus, and grip.

After so many centuries of exposure to eclectic ethnic influences, cultural diversity, political jockeying, and mercantile bustle, the

---

▲ *Friuli-Venezia Giulia, on the cusp of the Alps, is renowned for fresh, lively wines that possess almost Teutonic precision.*

THE QUICK SIP ON FRIULI-VENEZIA GIULIA

MANY OF ITALY'S MOST VIBRANT, racy white wines are produced here.

FRIULI-VENEZIA GIULIA'S TOP whites are sometimes 100% varietal wines, made entirely from such varieties as Friulano and ribolla gialla, and sometimes they are blends made from those varieties plus international varieties like pinot grigio (pinot gris), sauvignon blanc, and chardonnay.

DESPITE THE RENOWN ACCORDED the region's whites, red wines account for almost half of the total production in Friuli. The most prestigious red grapes are merlot, cabernet sauvignon, and cabernet franc, as well as the native grape schioppettino, all of which are turned into stunning wines.

Trieste, a vibrant port city on Friuli's Adriatic Coast, is a city that understands how to eat and drink.

Friulians have been left with a sense of dynamism, a can-do spirit, and a healthy attitude when it comes to change. You can taste this, too, in the wines. As a group, Friulian wines are spirited, creative, highly varied, and wholly individualistic.

In a country where "real" wine generally means red wine, Friuli is acclaimed as one of the top places in the world for racy whites. In particular, Friuli's pinot grigios, sauvignon blancs, and ribolla giallas can be stunning, as can its chardonnays. But if any white wine has captured the Friulian heart, it is one that is theirs alone: Friulano. (Before legislation in 2007 shortened its name, Friulano was called tocai Friulano, a term that confusingly implied a connection—where none exists—with Hungarian Tokaji.) Each of the grape varieties above is made into single-varietal wines and is used in the region's numerous white blends, such as Vintage Tunina, a blend of sauvignon blanc, chardonnay, ribolla gialla,

malvasia, and picolit (the percentage of each grape variety in the composition is a secret) by the producer Jermann.

Notwithstanding the popularity and success of Friuli's white wines, the region makes some stunning reds. Indeed, more than 40 percent of the region's wines are red. Most of this is merlot, which, grown in Friuli's warmer pockets, can be fantastic. But three other local grape varieties can also be stellar:

THE NAME FRIULI-VENEZIA GIULIA

Friuli and Venezia Giulia were once two separate provinces. The "Giulia" of Venezia Giulia refers to Julius Caesar. So does Friuli, which is derived from the Latin Forum Julii, now the city of Cividale, in the renowned eastern wine district of Colli Orientali.

THE TRE VENEZIE

Friuli-Venezia Giulia, Trentino-Alto Adige, and the Veneto, the three northeastern regions of Italy, are known collectively as the Tre Venezie—"Three Venices"—because of their historical relationship to the Republic of Venice. Today, they are united by more than history alone. With only a handful of exceptions, Italy's most stylish, highest-quality white wines come from this area. Bordered on the north by the majestic Alps, the regions share a northern climate and a way of doing things that doesn't quite seem Mediterranean in spirit. Germanic, Austrian, Swiss, Croatian, and Slovenian influences go back centuries. The cultural ties crop up in local dialects, local dishes, and even in the precise and decisive way winemakers go about making their wines. Not surprisingly, two of the best wine schools in Italy are located in the Tre Venezie, and one of Europe's largest vine nurseries is in Friuli-Venezia Giulia. More than half the vines planted in Italy originated there.

schioppettino, tazzelenghe, and pignolo. (In the local dialect, *scoppiettio* means "to pop" or "crackle;" *tazzelenghe* translates as "cuts the tongue"; and *pignolo* means "fussy.")

Then there are sweet wines. As any knowledgeable Italian wine lover probably knows, two of Italy's most exquisite dessert wines, verduzzo di Ramandolo and picolit, are both made in Friuli (although admittedly in tiny quantities).

Finally, Friuli is one of the most ambitious and successful winemaking regions of Italy. Premium wines (those with DOC or DOCG status) constitute more than 50 percent of its total production. Moreover, in less than three decades Friuli's white wines have gained an international following. No other region of Italy has moved so quickly from near obscurity to distinction.

SOME OF THE BEST PRODUCERS OF FRIULIAN PINOT GRIGIO

Jermann • Marco Felluga • Pierpaolo Pecorari • Renato Keber • Ronco dei Tassi • Ronco del Gnemiz • Schiopetto • Števerjan • Villa Russiz

THE LAND, THE GRAPES, AND THE VINEYARDS

Friuli-Venezia Giulia is a small place—some 3,000 square miles (7,780 square kilometers)—considerably smaller than the metropolitan area of Los Angeles (about 4,800 square miles/12,430 square kilometers), for example. Despite its small size, the region is known for more than a dozen grape varieties. (While a lot, this is far fewer than in the past. Before phylloxera arrived in Friuli at the end of the nineteenth century, more than 350 varieties were grown here!)

The Alps form Friuli's northern border, and the northern half of the region is extremely mountainous. As a result, nearly all of the vineyards—about 49,000 acres (19,800 hectares)—are located in the southern half. The best are situated on sloping Alpine foothills, but the vast majority of Friulian vineyards are on the plains that stretch inland from the Adriatic Sea. It is this juxtaposition of mountains and sea that creates the cool nights and warm days that contribute to the exhilaratingly taut structure and pinpoint balance of Friuli's best wines. It is important that the vineyards

THE GRAPES OF FRIULI-VENEZIA GIULIA

WHITES

CHARDONNAY: An important grape. Can make monodimensional wines or lush, highly complex ones, depending on the producer and the site.

FRIULANO: A very important local favorite. The same as the grape sauvignon vert (which is distinctly different from sauvignon blanc). The wines made from it can be stunningly complex and creamy.

PICOLIT: A native grape used to make interesting, rare dessert wines. Only a tiny amount is produced due to the vines' genetic predisposition to abort their berries for no good reason.

PINOT BIANCO: Also known as pinot blanc. Wines from it are usually good, not great. Often blended with chardonnay.

PINOT GRIGIO: Also known as pinot gris. A popular variety. Makes light- to medium-bodied wines that range from decent to delicious.

RIBOLLA GIALLA: An important variety. In Friuli, makes very attractive, aromatic wines with delicious, exotic, citrusy, peachy flavors.

SAUVIGNON BLANC: A popular variety. Turned into zesty, wild, dramatic wines, the best of which could be confused with the zesty, wild sauvignon blancs of South Africa.

VERDUZZO FRIULANO: A special native grape that is used to make Friuli's most stunning dessert wine, verduzzo di Ramandolo.

VITOVSKA: Grown near the border with Slovenia, in the Isonzo and Carso region of Friuli-Venezia Giulia. Makes fascinating, fleshy, dry white wines with elegant, rich, floral, herbal, and fruit flavors.

REDS

CABERNET FRANC: The second most popular red variety. First planted in Friuli in the late nineteenth century. Often high in acidity and lean in body, but can make good cranberry-flavored wines.

CABERNET SAUVIGNON: While less widespread than cabernet franc, cabernet sauvignon was planted in Friuli even earlier. The wines are usually lean and tight.

MERLOT: The most widely planted red. Makes wines that range in quality from lean and austere to rich and silky.

PIGNOLO: A rare, indigenous variety making distinctive wines especially near the towns of Buttrio and Rosazzo.

REFOSCO: The collective name for a handful of different varieties, the main one of which is refosco dal peduncolo rosso, which makes a popular, zesty, inky, easy-drinking red in Friuli.

SCHIOPPETTINO: The most sophisticated local red variety. Wines made from it are sharp and concentrated, with multiple fruit and spice flavors.

TAZZELENGHE: Translates literally as "cuts the tongue." Makes unusually bold, high-acid wines. Native to the larger region encompassing Friuli-Venezia Giulia and western Slovenia.

Cividale, a Friulian town in the foothills of the Alps, was founded by Julius Caesar as a municipality of Rome.

THE MOST IMPORTANT FRIULIAN WINES

LEADING WINES

CABERNET FRANC red

CABERNET SAUVIGNON red

CHARDONNAY white

FRIULANO white

MERLOT red

PINOT BIANCO white

PINOT GRIGIO white

REFOSCO red

RIBOLLA GIALLA white

SAUVIGNON BLANC white

SCHIOPPETTINO red

WINES OF NOTE

PICOLIT white (sweet)

PIGNOLO red

TAZZELENGHE red

VERDUZZO DI RAMANDOLO white (sweet)

The two most prestigious wine districts in Friuli are Colli Orientali del Friuli and Collio (technically known as Collio Goriziano). Both are in the far east, just short of the Slovenian border. Here, the best hilly vineyards are located on terraces, where the well-drained, crumbly, calcium-rich marl and sandstone soil is known as flysch. The soil in the valleys tends more toward clay, sand, and gravel.

In the local Friulian dialect, the tops of the terraced hillsides are called *ronchi*. The word *ronchi*—or the singular, *ronco*—is often the first word of the name of a vineyard or wine estate, such as Ronco dei Tassi (hilltop of the badgers). As for the word *colli*, it means "small hills" in Friulian dialect. Colli Orientali refers to eastern hills.

Sophisticated white wine was Friuli's toe up in the world, but characteristically, the Friulians took their own approach to making it. During the 1970s and 1980s, while almost every up-and-coming wine region in the world was focused on creating unctuous, barrel-fermented, oak-aged wines, especially chardonnays, Friulian producers (especially Schiopetto and Livio Felluga) were committed to making the opposite—taut, kinetic whites with a spring-loaded urgency of acidity, and flavors devoted to the purity of the grapes. Among the other places that share this philosophy of purity are Alsace and the Loire Valley

lie across hillsides and plains on the sunny south side of the Alps. Here, exposed to the heat and light of the sun, the grapes have time to ripen fully. As a result, Friuli can grow both white and red varieties well, and the whites are not fragile; they are whites with body and a determined grip.

WHERE DREAMS CAN HAPPEN

Among the most legendary Friulian wines are those of the artistic winemaker Silvio Jermann. In 1977, at the age of twenty-one, Jermann created Italy's first cult white wine—Vintage Tunina, a then secret blend made up of sauvignon blanc, chardonnay, ribolla gialla, malvasia, and picolit, among other grapes. Vintage Tunina was so voluptuous and nuanced (many Italian wine pros consider it the perfect white with truffles), it set off the modern trend for sophisticated Friulian white blends. (Tunina was the name of the old woman who originally owned the vineyard from which the grapes came . . . as well as the name of one of Casanova's lovers.) Jermann's genius is the ability to pull deep facets of personality from each grape. Every Jermann wine, from sauvignon blanc and ribolla gialla to Friulano and chardonnay, is clearly focused, powerfully flavored, and impeccably balanced. Until 1987, no Jermann wine was made or aged in new oak. In that year, Jermann created a barrel-fermented chardonnay originally called "Where the Dreams Have No End." The name, a takeoff on the song "Where the Streets Have No Name" by the Irish rock group U2, was later changed to just "W . . . Dreams." To Jermann (who says that his dreams help inform his winemaking), the "W dot dot dot" means "where dreams can happen."

in France, and the wine regions of Germany and Austria, New Zealand, and Friuli's eastern neighbor, Slovenia.

Above all, Friulian whites have presence. Rarely plain-Jane or frail, these are concentrated, complex whites with enticing aromas and pronounced fruity-spicy-earthy flavors. And while many pinot grigios are about as exciting as tap water, the top Friulian pinot grigios can soar with delicate peach, almond, and green apple flavors (Števerjan's, for example) or be so voluptuous and rich they seem to be descended from ice cream (Jermann's).

Friulano, the local favorite, is probably the hardest Friulian wine to describe. It ranges from smoky, resinous, and white peppery to lush and vanilla-y to spiked with minerals, exotic spices, and something like honey cake (or in some cases, it combines all of these sensations, as does the extraordinary Friulano called "Plus," from the producer Bastianich). Because of its intensity, many Friulian winemakers refer to it as the most masculine of the white grapes.

Wines made from ribolla gialla can be so pretty, so exuberantly fresh, so delightfully peachy, floral, and citrusy, and so simply satisfying that it's amazing this grape is not grown anywhere else in any significant amounts except in Slovenia, next door. Villa Russiz and Josko Gravner make especially appealing ones.

Silvio Jermann, one of the innovative Friulian winemakers who revolutionized white winemaking in Italy in the 1980s.

The hilly Collio region of Friuli-Venezia Guilia. The Collio and the Colli Orientali del Friuli are the province's two most important wine districts. Both lie near Italy's eastern border with Slovenia.

The sauvignon blancs (the name is usually shortened to just sauvignon) are usually terrific wines—lean, zesty, peppery, and smoky, with a green, resiny end reminiscent of capers. As for Friulian chardonnays, their quality and style vary greatly, but from a master like Jermann, chardonnay—even in a voluptuous style—is utter elegance.

It would seem counterintuitive that a relatively cool region known for vivacious white wines would also produce a significant number of delicious reds. Yet, as noted, a significant amount of Friulian wine is red, and much of that is structured, concentrated merlot. Other dynamic reds here are made from grape varieties thought to have originated in Friuli, or in Slovenia, next door. Schioppettino, one of the best, nearly disappeared from Friuli in the wake of phylloxera, but was rescued in the 1970s when Paolo Rapuzzi, owner of Ronchi di Cialla winery, collected one hundred extant vines and clandestinely had them grafted to make them available for propagation (schioppettino was not an officially allowed variety in Friuli at the time). Wines made from schioppettino can be startling—hauntingly dry with sharp peppery, spicy, black cherry flavors and a tight, angular body. The word *schioppettino* comes from *scoppiettio,* to "crackle" or "pop," a possible reference to the grape's or wine's texture. Like schioppettino, pignolo, too, was almost extinct until a few vines discovered in the 1970s were painstakingly nurtured and the variety was recultivated. The name *pignolo* means "fussy"—a reference to its low yields and the difficulty of growing it. Refosco is actually the collective name for a handful of different local varieties, the most widespread of which is refosco dal peduncolo rosso (literally, "refosco with the red stem"). In Friuli it makes a great everyday drinking wine, with dense blueberry and blackberry flavors and vivid acidity. As for *tazzelenghe* ("cuts the tongue"), it is dagger sharp. The grape is native to the area encompassing Friuli as well as western Slovenia, and is also known as refosco del botton (not the same variety as refosco dal peduncolo rosso).

Only 999 left to massage. A worker rubs, pats, and pounds haunches of prosciutto di San Daniele, made from Lambrea pigs raised in Friuli. The meat is rubbed with salt and naturally cured over 400 days.

Merlot and cabernet have been made in Friuli for more than a century. In the past, these were sometimes austere, light, and lean wines. Not so today. As winemakers have better understood the nuances of making red wines in fairly cool climates, Friuli's merlots and cabernets have become far more flavorful and concentrated. There are a score of great merlots made here, including those from Moschioni, Miani, Meroi, Schiopetto, Damijan, Vie de Romans, and La Castellada. And, as is true of the white wines, the reds of Friuli are often unpredictably intriguing blends. Le Vigne di Zamo's Ronco dei Roseti, for example, takes on a sharply spicy, forest-floor character, thanks to the tazzelenghe and refosco that are added to the blend of cabernet sauvignon, merlot, and cabernet franc.

WHEN YOU VISIT . . . FRIULI-VENEZIA GIULIA

Most wineries in the Collio and Colli Orientali districts are an easy drive from the ancient port city of Trieste. (Coffee lovers take note: This is where the espresso maker Illy has its headquarters; thus, the coffee around town is magnificent.) Farther inland, the wine town of Udine, with its Venetian Renaissance-style piazza, serves as an unofficial headquarters for traveling wine lovers who want to make day trips in all directions. Appointments are necessary.

SOME OF THE BEST PRODUCERS OF FRIULANO

Abbazia di Rosazzo • Bastianich • EnoFriulia • Francesco Pecorari • Jermann • Livio Felluga • Marco Felluga • Miani • Pierpaolo Pecorari • Ronco dei Tassi • Števerjan • Villa Russiz • Le Vigne di Zamò

THE FAMOUS PROSCIUTTO OF FRIULI

Prosciutto is so much a part of the culinary landscape, it's hard to believe that certain countries, including the United States, once banned the importation of the famous ham. In the U.S., that changed on September 6, 1989, when six thousand haunches of prosciutto were cradled aboard jets and flown to New York.

Prosciutto is made all over Italy, but the best comes from just one type of pig: the massive (350-pound/160-kilogram) Lambrea pig, raised either in Friuli, near the town of San Daniele (for prosciutto di San Daniele), or in Emilia-Romagna, near the town of Parma (for prosciutto di Parma). The pigs are fed natural grains and the rich whey from such famous cheeses as Parmigiano-Reggiano.

The raw ham is cured without smoke or heat over the course of four hundred days. (By contrast, some American hams are processed in one day.) First, the meat is thickly salted, then the hams are massaged, pounded, rubbed, and eventually washed with water and a stiff wire brush. The haunches are hung to air cure slowly in specially designed buildings with long vertical windows. In Friuli, it is said that the warm, salty sea air mixed with the cold Alpine air is a perfect combination—the result is a coral-pink ham with a silky texture and a sweet, meaty taste that is exceedingly complex. In Friuli, prosciutto combined with melon or figs is served with a fruity, floral white wine, often a glass of Friulano or ribolla gialla.

FRIULI'S SWEET WINES

Italy makes more diverse, fascinating dessert wines than any other country in the world, and two of the most intriguing are Friulian—verduzzo di Ramandolo, made from verduzzo Friulano grapes, and picolit, made from picolit grapes. Both grape varieties are grown on the Alpine hillsides of the Colli Orientali.

Verduzzo di Ramandolo is made near the tiny village of Ramandolo. This is one of the lightest-bodied, most exquisite dessert wines made anywhere. Often it has a beautiful coppery sheen and touches of herbal flavors. The best producers are Giovanni Dri, Ronchi di Manzano, Livon, and Ronchi di Cialla.

Picolit (from *piccolo*, "small" in Italian, a reference to the tiny size of the clusters) probably shouldn't even exist. The grape variety has a genetic mutation that causes it to spontaneously abort the flowers on its newly formed clusters (the flowers that ultimately would become grapes). Even in good years, less than half of picolit's flowers survive to become pollinated and evolve into grapes. The wine, as a result, is very expensive. The best picolits are gossamer, with a delicate honeyed flavor (try the picolits from Livio Felluga, Ronchi di Cialla, and Dorigo). Indeed, picolit was one of Friuli's first internationally successful wines and—bottled in handmade Murano glass—was sought after by European nobility in the eighteenth century.

The Friulian Wines to Know

WHITES

SCHIOPETTO

PINOT GRIGIO

100% pinot grigio

This is not your standard pinot grigio. In fact, Schiopetto's pinot grigio towers above most other Italian versions. For one thing, the wine is complex (not usually true) and for another, it has a sophisticated weight and presence on the palate (very rare for pinot grigio). But above all, this wine has fascinating choreography; it moves with energy. From a core of dense fruit, sparks of flavor fly out in all directions. It's like tasting a sunburst.

BASTIANICH

PLUS | VENEZIA GIULIA

100% Friulano

It's safe to say the Bastianich family understands flavor. The mother, Lidia, is one of the foremost experts on Italian food in the United States and is an author and television host. The son, Joe, is a wine expert and a business partner with his mother and with United States super chef Mario Batali. Together they are the primary owners of a slew of famous restaurants, including New York's Del Posto. The family's ties to Friuli-Venezia Giulia go back generations, so it's no surprise that their wine ventures are based there. And what wine they make! In a lineup of Bastianich wines, the taster simply runs out of superlatives, if not adjectives. But the wine that I find most stunning is their Friulano called Plus. The grapes come from a single vineyard of sixty-year-old vines. Ten percent of the wine is made *appassimento*, that is, by drying the grapes over a period of months to raisinate and shrivel them, thereby concentrating their sugars. (This is the process used to make amarone in the Veneto.) The intense richness of the wine is matched only by its impeccable elegance. The core of fruit has near atomic density. And the flavors are sweet, savory, and minerally all at once. As oxymoronic as it may sound, Plus explodes slowly on the palate.

JERMANN

VINTAGE TUNINA

Chardonnay and sauvignon blanc with small amounts of ribolla gialla, malvasia, and sometimes picolit; percentages not disclosed

One of the greatest Italian white wines from one of the greatest Friulian winemakers, Vintage Tunina proved early on that the sky was the limit for Friulian whites. The wine—a blend of multiple grapes—is a huge, voluptuous riot of juicy flavors, the equivalent of an Impressionist painting.

VILLA RUSSIZ

RIBOLLA GIALLA

100% ribolla gialla

Not as patently aromatic as, say, muscat or riesling, ribolla gialla has a smell that's delicately intoxicating. Did someone just walk into the room holding a vase of jasmine? A pear tart just whisked from the oven? But aroma is only one of this grape's strong suits. When made impeccably, as is this Villa Russiz, the wine sweeps across the palate with waves of fruit, minerals, exotic spices, and delicious zestlike bitters. Ribolla gialla, one of Italy's most underrated, fantastic whites, is thought to have come to Friuli from Slovenia, next door. Also highly notable is Villa Russiz's fantastic sauvignon—Sauvignon de la Tour—which also possesses flavors that sweep over the palate in rushes of intensity.

REDS

BASTIANICH

CALABRONE ROSSO

70% refosco, 10% schioppettino, 10% pignolo, 10% merlot

Made like amarone (harvested grapes are hung or laid on mats in special rooms to dry and concentrate their sugars), Calabrone Rosso is a knockout of a wine. Its get-outta-my-way force and driving power would make it ideal for, say, Wall Street. Every aspect of the wine—from the aroma to the texture to the finish—is massive and masculine, and built to age well. Naturally somewhat tannic, the refosco here takes on an almost syrahlike, delicious corruptness, tasting of earth, peat, cigars, espresso, and Scotch.

VIE DI ROMANS

VOOS DAI CIAMPS

100% merlot

The proprietor of Vie di Romans, Gianfranco Gallo, makes some of the lushest, ripest reds in Friuli—wines of great power and exactitude that burst from the glass in a flurry of dense chocolate flavors, minerals, wild berries, and a lacy note of vanilla given their considerable time in oak. This is no casual sipper of a merlot, but rather an intense, structured wine that commands a few years of aging and then a great meal.

MOSCHIONI

SCHIOPPETTINO

100% schioppettino

This is the real deal . . . a stunning, opulent schioppettino that shows how sensational the indigenous reds of northern Italy can be. Generally, the Moschioni family allows the grapes to dry for several weeks (amarone style) before fermenting them. The result is a spicy, earthy, minerally red with a core of dense cherry preserve flavors, and a vibrancy on the palate that is worthy of an electric current. One of Friuli's most lip-smacking reds, like all good schioppettinos, it begs for food.

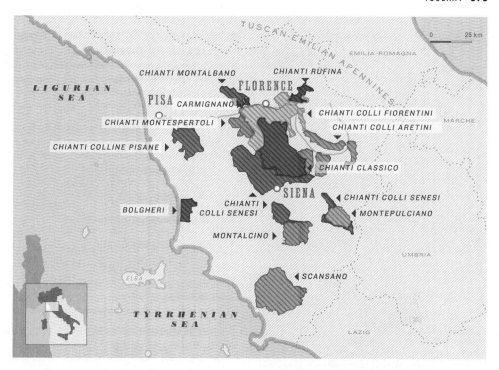

TUSCANY

oscana to the Italians, Tuscany is the quintessential Italian wine region. Here, where the Renaissance was born and where the church has reigned with near omnipotent power, wine has strong ties to both art and religion. Yet at the same time, wine has always been the most humble of Tuscan comforts—on the table at every meal (breakfast excepted); sometimes, with a piece of bread, a meal in itself.

Tuscany is also the birthplace of four of Italy's most important red wines: Chianti, Chianti Classico, brunello di Montalcino, and vino nobile di Montepulciano. Though all are made from the variety sangiovese, the wines taste quite different. One reason is that Tuscany is a plethora of distinct mesoclimates. These are created by an endless succession of twisting, turning, undulating hills and low mountains. Another reason is that sangiovese, a finicky and demanding grape, has begotten hundreds of clones or genetic variations of itself. Over time, these variations have adapted to their local environments and taken on distinct flavor characteristics. In addition, it's fascinating to know that while sangiovese is today inextricably linked to Tuscany, the variety appears to have originated in southern Italy. Surprising DNA

> "Sangiovese, to be a great wine, needs a good connection with God."
>
> —**LAMBERTO FRESCOBALDI**,
> Marc hesi de'Frescobaldi

THE QUICK SIP ON TUSCANY

TUSCANY IS THE HOME of four of Italy's most important, well-known red wines: Chianti, Chianti Classico, brunello di Montalcino, and vino nobile di Montepulciano.

THE LEADING RED GRAPE, used in every major traditional wine, is sangiovese, considered one of the greatest red grapes of Italy.

A WINE REVOLUTION in the 1970s and 1980s led to wines of an immensely higher quality, as well as the creation of the so-called Super Tuscans, a group of avant-garde, expensive wines made in an untraditional manner.

research in 2004 revealed one of sangiovese's parents to be Calabrese di Montenuovo (from Calabria), and the other parent to be ciliegiolo (Italian for "small cherry"), now cultivated all over Italy.

For English-speaking wine drinkers and food lovers in the 1960s, Tuscany seemed to symbolize a kind of cultural chic. Chianti wines, in particular, were romantic, earthy, "European," and fit the bohemian esthetic (and budget). But the old Chianti of red checkered tablecloths and amorous evenings was, for the most part, not very good wine. By the 1970s the market for Chianti—and the wine's international reputation—had reached an all-time low. As the full impact of this realization began to sink in, Tuscans were shocked into action. With the help of new wine laws (see the Appendix on Wine Laws, page 924), the Tuscan wine industry bounced back with what is considered one of the most dramatic revolutions in the world of modern wine. The result was vastly superior, exciting wines, including a slew of internationally acclaimed, expensive Super Tuscans.

All of this said, from a 35,000-foot (10,700-meter) view, there's a flavor and feel to Tuscan wine—red wine in particular—that, to me, is dramatically different from wines made almost anywhere else. There's a firmness and espresso-like bitterness to the wines—the result of acidity coupled with tannin. Sangiovese is, like pinot noir, a grape relatively high in acidity. At the same time, modern winemaking methods have coaxed more color, power, and tannin from the grape. Significant acidity and tannin, when found together in the same wine, is not always easy to take. The best wines pull off the marriage. For lower quality wines, the combination can be a train wreck. (Top Tuscan wines never taste better than they do in Tuscany itself because one's palate is usually coated in olive oil—a countermeasure against the firm, bitter bite of the wine.)

So much red wine has always been made in Tuscany that, with the exception of the famous dessert wine vin santo, white wine has been mostly an afterthought. Yet some high-quality, dry white Tuscan wine is made—mostly modern-style sauvignon blancs and chardonnays. As for Tuscany's standby traditional dry white, vernaccia di San Gimignano, there now exist many more high-quality examples than in the past.

Many Tuscan vineyards are lined with the region's stunning, tall cypress trees.

The interior courtyard of the Palazzo Chigi-Saracini in central Siena. Built in the Gothic style in the 12th century as a private urban palace, its curved exterior façade traces the ancient, narrow, curving streets of the city.

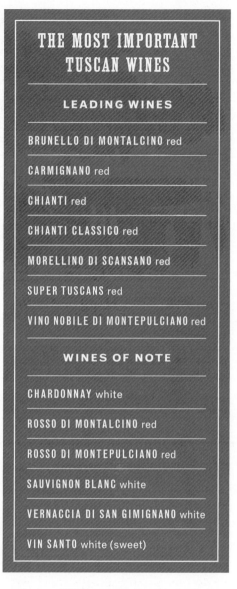

THE MOST IMPORTANT TUSCAN WINES

LEADING WINES

BRUNELLO DI MONTALCINO red

CARMIGNANO red

CHIANTI red

CHIANTI CLASSICO red

MORELLINO DI SCANSANO red

SUPER TUSCANS red

VINO NOBILE DI MONTEPULCIANO red

WINES OF NOTE

CHARDONNAY white

ROSSO DI MONTALCINO red

ROSSO DI MONTEPULCIANO red

SAUVIGNON BLANC white

VERNACCIA DI SAN GIMIGNANO white

VIN SANTO white (sweet)

THE LAND, THE GRAPES, AND THE VINEYARDS

As visitors to Tuscany quickly discover, there doesn't seem to be a straight line in the entire region. Winding back and forth and up and down along Tuscany's rural roads, it's impossible not to fall in love with the patchwork of vineyards that cover a landscape undulating so magically. To any driver, it comes as no surprise that the region is roughly 68 percent hills. The paucity of flat land means that nearly every vineyard is on a slope of some kind, gentle or steep, and that even two vineyards that are only a stone's throw apart often produce wines of very different character.

Tuscany stretches from the Tyrrhenian Sea in the west to the low mountains that separate the region from Emilia-Romagna, the Marche, and Umbria, its neighbors to the east. At nearly 9,000 square miles (23,300 square kilometers), it is the fifth largest region in Italy. Yet most of the important wine zones are more or less in the middle of the region, from Florence in the north to Siena in the center and then south to the tiny hill town of Montalcino (famous for brunello). The climate in this central zone is warm, although not as warm or humid as along the Tyrrhenian coast. Nights are cool, helping to preserve the natural acidity of the grapes, particularly in sangiovese. Soil varies considerably, but the well-drained slopes of the central hills tend to be sandy or stony, calcareous, and interspersed with schist and galestro (a crumbly, stony marl).

Like many Italian wine regions, Tuscany was once home to dozens of grape varieties (in the

THE GRAPES OF TUSCANY

WHITES

CHARDONNAY: A minor grape accounting for a small production of expensive white wines.

MALVASIA BIANCA LUNGA: One of the many different varieties in the world that have *malvasia* as part of the name. In the past, it was the white grape blended into Chianti in small amounts to lighten it. Now it is the grape best known for vin santo, the famous Tuscan dessert wine.

SAUVIGNON BLANC: Limited amounts are grown, but wines made from this grape show promise.

TREBBIANO: Technically, trebbiano Toscano. Formerly used with malvasia in Chianti, and now used for vin santo as well as for dry white wines generally of neutral character.

VERNACCIA: Makes Tuscany's most traditional, simple white wine; grown around the hill town of San Gimignano.

REDS

CABERNET SAUVIGNON: Often a significant part of the blend in Carmignano, and sometimes blended in very tiny amounts with sangiovese to make contemporary Chianti and Chianti Classico. It is the sole grape variety or a component in some Super Tuscan wines.

CANAIOLO: Historically the second red grape, besides sangiovese, in the traditional Chianti blend.

COLORINO: One of the historic blending grapes in the traditional Chianti blend. Contributes structure and a deep color (much as petit verdot does in a Bordeaux blend).

MERLOT: Sometimes blended in small amounts with sangiovese to make contemporary Chianti and Chianti Classico. Also used in a limited number of Super Tuscans.

SANGIOVESE: The major Tuscan grape used for all the important traditional red wines of the region—Chianti, Chianti Classico, brunello di Montalcino, and vino nobile di Montepulciano.

mid-eighteenth century, more than two hundred were officially recognized). But in modern times, the region has been identified almost exclusively with two grapes: sangiovese, for centuries Tuscany's single greatest grape, and cabernet sauvignon, responsible for making up, in whole or as part of the blend, numerous famous Super Tuscan wines.

Sangiovese is, like pinot noir, an exacting, troublesome grape. It doesn't ripen easily or uniformly. In sites that are not consistently sunny, or in rainy, overcast years, it's common around harvest time to see bunches with soft, purple, ripe grapes as well as slightly green, underripe ones. Unevenly ripe bunches can lead to thin, unbalanced wines that taste like sweet-and-sour sauce if the grower doesn't pick out (often by hand) all of the green, unripe berries.

There's another vexing issue: Italy is literally strewn with multiple clones of sangiovese. Although no one knows precisely how many different clones there are, winemakers

Hand sorting sangiovese grapes at Castello di Fonterutoli. The estate, owned by the Mazzei family since 1435, includes a villa, a small church, and 1,600 acres (650 hectares) of forest, vineyards, and olive groves.

are convinced that the main ones vary enormously in flavor, and that the future of Tuscan wine lies in clonal research. The world's most ambitious study of grape clones was begun in Chianti Classico in 1987. Known as the Chianti Classico 2000 project, it was financed by the European Union and took sixteen years to complete. In just the small Chianti Classico region alone, 239 clones of sangiovese were identified and studied, along with other viticultural factors (rootstock, trellising methods, and so on). From this research, seven clones of sangiovese were selected, officially registered, and named "Chianti Classico 2000" clones for their superior quality and viral resistance.

As for cabernet sauvignon, although it was brought to Tuscany in the eighteenth century, reportedly by Grand Duke Cosimo de' Medici III, the variety was largely unimportant for centuries except as a component in Carmignano (see page 392). In the late 1970s and 1980s, however, cabernet achieved greater prominence as one of the varieties of grapes used in the Super Tuscans.

White grapes have never been very important in Tuscany, although, in the past, an enormous number of neutral trebbiano Toscano and somewhat more interesting malvasia (malvasia bianca lunga, specifically) vines were planted. The best of these grapes were (and still are) used to make vin santo, while the remainder were mostly used in red wines—in particular, Chianti and vino nobile di Montepulciano. Even vernaccia, the grape of vernaccia di San Gimignano and the only white grape of any character, still makes what most Italian experts consider a serviceable, occasionally charming white at best.

As for chardonnay and other international whites, there are far fewer examples in Tuscany than there are in Friuli-Venezia Giulia or Trentino-Alto Adige. That said, unlike in those regions, chardonnay is relatively new in Tuscany. Beginning in the 1980s,

> The word *sangiovese* is thought to derive from the Latin *sanguis Jovis*—"the blood of Jupiter." The name is said to have been given to the wine by monks residing near Monte Giove (Mount Jupiter), in Emilia-Romagna.

A FIASCO BY ANY OTHER NAME . . .

If you were of a certain age in the U.S. in the 1960s, you remember Woodstock, the early Beatles, and putting candles into the round, straw-covered bottle nearly every Chianti used to come in—called, technically, a *fiasco.* The word, probably of medieval Italian origin, described a glass bottle or flask with a long neck and a bulbous body, usually covered in wicker or straw for protection. Historically, both wine and olive oil came in *fiaschi.* According to *The Oxford English Dictionary,* the word *fiasco*—meaning "a failure or complete breakdown"—comes from the Italian expression *fare fiasco,* to make a bottle. How this Italian expression came to mean a foul-up is unknown. Some wine experts have speculated that the poor quality of past Chianti may be the reason. Today in Tuscany one still finds old trattorias called *fiaschetterias*—working men's taverns known initially for cheap, hearty Tuscan wines and later for the homey Tuscan specialties that went with them.

several Tuscan winemakers decided to make what they called "serious" white wines, which turned out to mean big-bodied, oaky, buttery chardonnays and fruit-packed sauvignon blancs. These wines are not made on a large scale. The most impressive of them include the rich Capannelle chardonnay, as well as Poggio alle Gazze (hill of the magpies), the sauvignon blanc from Ornellaia (where magpies do live in the vineyard).

Old-style Chianti *fiaschi—memories of a former time.*

CHIANTI, CHIANTI CLASSICO, AND THE SUPER TUSCANS

What is called the Chianti zone (including all of the subdistricts of Chianti and Chianti Classico) covers a vast territory encompassing most of central Tuscany—more than 38,000 acres (15,400 hectares). Wines were made here as far back as the thirteenth century, when records document "Chianti wine" being made in the "Chianti Mountains" around Florence. Interestingly, some records suggest that this first Chianti wine may have been white.

This is a place of inspiring beauty. Vineyards share the hillsides with olive groves, cypresses, umbrella pines, castles, and centuries-old stone farmhouses. Since ancient times, artists and poets have been captivated by the lucid softness of the daylight, which seems as though it has been brushed onto the sky with a feather.

In this section, we will look at Chianti and its subdistricts, as well as Chianti Classico. I know that it might seem as if Chianti Classico is simply the "top level" of Chianti, but the two wines are distinctly different. Indeed, each has its own DOCG and thus its own set of stringent rules. This means that you can't make Chianti in Chianti Classico, and you can't make Chianti Classico in Chianti.

SOME OF THE TOP SUPER TUSCANS

Many of what are considered Italy's superstar wines were first made in Tuscany in the 1970s and 1980s. Generally flamboyant, powerful, highly structured, and wrapped in the vanilla robe of flavor that new oak imparts, they are wines that try to be international, yet evoke Italianness at the same time. The collective name for these wines, the Super Tuscans, is a consumer term, not an official designation. Each wine listed below has its own proprietary name; the words *Super Tuscan* never appear on the label. Note that some producers make more than one Super Tuscan wine.

PROPRIETARY NAME	PRODUCER	MAIN GRAPE
Cepparello	Isole e Olena	sangiovese
Coltassala	Castello di Volpaia	sangiovese
Excelsus	Castello Banfi	merlot
Flaccianello della Pieve	Fontodi	sangiovese
Fontalloro	Fèlsina	sangiovese
Grosso Sanese	Il Palazzino	sangiovese
I Sodi di San Niccolò	Castellare	sangiovese
Il Sodaccio	Montevertine	sangiovese
Le Pergole Torte	Montevertine	sangiovese
Masseto	Ornellaia	merlot
Monte Antico	Monte Antico	sangiovese
Olmaia	Col d'Orcia	cabernet sauvignon
Ornellaia	Ornellaia	cabernet sauvignon
Percarlo	San Giusto	sangiovese
Sammarco	Castello dei Rampolla	cabernet sauvignon
Sassicaia	Marchesi Incisa della Rocchetta	cabernet sauvignon
Solaia	Antinori	cabernet sauvignon
Summus	Castello Banfi	cabernet sauvignon
Terrine	Castello della Paneretta	canaiolo
Tignanello	Antinori	sangiovese
Tinscvil	Monsanto	sangiovese
Vigna d'Alceo	Castello dei Rampolla	cabernet sauvignon

BOLGHERI: BIRTHPLACE OF SASSICAIA

In 1944, a nobleman named Mario Incisa della Rocchetta planted Tuscany's first cabernet sauvignon vineyard on a stony/sandy hill (1,200 feet/366 meters in altitude) in a sunny commune called Castiglioncello. It was, in every way, unusual. First, there was the fact that the vines were cabernet (reportedly from Chateau Lafite Rothschild) not sangiovese. Second, the wine was aged in small, new French oak barrels. Third, the vineyard wasn't anywhere near the Chianti zone, nor near the brunello town of Montalcino, nor the vino nobile town of Montepulciano.

The vineyard was in the far west of Tuscany, along the coast of the Tyrrhenian Sea in an area known as the Maremma, in a district then known for peach orchards—Bolgheri. (Tuscan viticultural wisdom at the time held that no great red wine could be made from vineyards close to the sea.) Incisa della Rochetta called the wine Sassicaia—from Tuscan dialect, *sasso* for rock, and *aia,* used like the letter *y* is, in English, to make the word an adjective—that is, rocky. Thus, Sassicaia—rocky place. For twenty years, it was a wine produced only for the family's use. Finally, in 1968, Sassicaia was released commercially, bearing the blue-and-white label we know today. Quiet Bolgheri achieved considerable notoriety, but it was just the beginning. Today, several top producers in the region make remarkable wine. The top estates include Ornellaia, Guado al Tasso, Grattamacco, Macchiole, and Michele Satta. Cabernet sauvignon remains the leading red grape, with merlot and cabernet franc following. Several Bolgheri estates also make simple but fantastic vermentinos for every-night drinking.

CHIANTI AND THE SUPER TUSCANS

A modern memoir of basic Chianti would probably begin with its role as the companion to spaghetti and (if you were well-to-do) meatballs. Not that this association is necessarily pejorative. After World War II, especially, being cheap and gulpable was pretty ideal. But as the mid decades of the twentieth century went on, Chianti grew increasingly disappointing. Part of the problem was the historic so-called Chianti formula.

Traditionally Chianti was a blend of grapes: red—sangiovese, canaiolo, and colorino—and white—malvasia and/or trebbiano. The formula was formalized in the mid-1800s by Baron Bettino Ricasoli (second prime minister of the united Italy), whose family had been making Tuscan wine since the twelfth century. Ricasoli posited that adding a small amount of white malvasia bianca lunga (known simply as malvasia in Tuscany) to Chianti would heighten its vivacity, boost its flavor, and make it more drinkable when young. Embedded in this notion were the beginnings of disaster.

The more popular Chianti became, the more it was lightened with white grapes—and not

The moody sky over a villa in Bolgheri, near the western coast of Tuscany.

just malvasia, as Ricasoli had intended, but also the fairly dull type of trebbiano known as trebbiano Toscano (which, in France, was and still is used as neutral distilling material for Cognac). Far from adding character to Chianti, trebbiano turned it into an anorexic red. Yet, by World War II, trebbiano made up more than 30 percent of some Chiantis. In 1967, the Italian government used the "Ricasoli formula" of a sangiovese-based blend with 10 percent to 30 percent malvasia and trebbiano as the legal foundation for the Chianti DOC (it wasn't until 1984, after numerous changes in the regulations, that Chianti was given the higher designation of DOCG).

Meanwhile, trouble was brewing in the vineyards. In the economic aftermath of the war, winegrowers were given agricultural development funds by the government, and the Chianti area was enlarged. And, to quickly meet the demand for affordable Chianti, winegrowers (often unknowingly) planted easily accessible, different types of sangiovese, clones collectively known as sangiovese di Romagna brought in from the nearby region of Emilia-Romagna (which is not, for the most part, known for excellent red wine). Given overproduction, poorly situated vineyards, ill-suited clonal types, and dilution with weak-flavored white grapes, the quality of Chianti collapsed. By the 1970s, Italian romance notwithstanding, Chianti was bought as much for its straw-covered bottle (the candleholder of the era) as for the liquid inside.

Faced with the possibility of the industry's demise, a handful of innovative, iconoclastic producers in the mid-1970s began taking the first steps toward making wines that would be the polar opposites of "spaghetti Chianti." Their inspiration was Sassicaia (dialect for "rocky place"), made by Marchese Mario Incisa della Rocchetta at his estate, Tenuta San Guido, near the Tuscan coast, in Bolgheri (see box, facing page).

The first Sassicaias—a tiny production made in the late 1940s—were awkward, even coarse wines. But by the late 1960s, Incisa della Rocchetta had refined his techniques considerably and the wine, defying expectation, turned out to be very impressive. Among the wine's admirers was Piero Antinori; the Incisa della Rocchettas were his cousins. Antinori himself was the head of a centuries-old Tuscan winemaking family. Thus, Sassicaia became the catalyst for Antinori's Tignanello—the first well-known non-Chianti Chianti.

THE ETRUSCANS

From 800 to 300 B.C. the Etruscans, an ancient civilization of highly cultured people, lived in what is now Tuscany. Many of the hilltops where they built their flourishing villages are now blanketed by a pastoral carpet of vines. Some historians believe the Etruscans were the first purely indigenous Italian race. But their almond-shaped eyes and slanting eyebrows led others to suggest that they may have migrated from Asia Minor. Elaborate Etruscan tombs, funerary drawings, and grave artifacts depict a vibrant society of aristocrats and slaves that formed a culture that was both obsessed with ceremony and superstitious. Divination, for example, was performed by "reading" the entrails of freshly slaughtered animals, the flight of birds, or flashes of lightning during thunderstorms. Tomb murals portray sybaritic banquets, full of wine drinking, dancing, and athletic contests. Later, this hedonism, along with Etruscan military pageantry, would profoundly affect the Romans who, by the end of the third century B.C., defeated and dissolved the Etruscan world.

Barrels in the old cellars of Castello di Volpaia. More than an estate, Castello di Volpaia was built in the 11th century as a fortified village on the border between Florence and Siena. Part of the original protective walls and two of the village's six medieval towers are still standing.

Made in 1971, Tignanello contained no white grapes, was based almost entirely on sangiovese (later, cabernet sauvignon and cabernet franc were added), and was aged in small, new French oak barrels. Tignanello was like a flashlight in the dark. Other top producers immediately followed suit, making expensive proprietary wines of their own, sometimes from sangiovese blended with cabernet sauvignon, sometimes from either grape alone. What unified these wines was what they were not: They were not made according to the traditional Chianti formula specified at that time in the DOC laws (see the Appendix on Wine Laws, page 924). As a result, the government considered them mere *vini da tavola* ("table wines"); the press nicknamed them the Super Tuscans.

The eclectic group of Super Tuscans motivated winemakers to further improve the quality of Chianti. In 1984, Chianti was elevated from DOC to DOCG status, paving the way for additional improvements and many subsequent changes. Still, basic Chianti—especially when it's moderately priced—is often a lean, old-fashioned wine, tasting less of fruit than of earth, dried leaves, wet rocks, and damp bark, and possessing a characteristic, appealing bitterness. No longer are white grapes a mandatory part of the Chianti formula. Indeed, basic modern Chianti can be anywhere from 75 percent to up to 100 percent sangiovese, should the winemaker choose. Canaiolo can comprise no more than 10 percent of the blend, and so-called "other authorized reds" (like cabernet sauvignon and merlot) can make up no more than 15 percent of the blend. The white grapes malvasia and trebbiano can still be used (although they rarely are) for up to 10 percent of the blend.

Thus far we've been talking about basic Chianti, but within the large Chianti zone are eight subzones. One of these—Chianti Classico—is so distinct, it has its own DOCG, and we'll explore it in a moment. But the other seven are very much worth knowing, for the wines are usually a big step up in quality from basic Chianti, and many of the top wines from these regions have a delicious, Old World Italian flavor—what might be called a traditional high-quality Chianti flavor. This is, in part, a result of the fact that many producers

VIRGINAL VALUE

For centuries around the Mediterranean, vines and olive trees have grown side by side (sometimes literally entwined), often in soil so arid little else will grow there. The bond between the two crops is especially strong in Tuscany, where many wine estates double as top olive oil producers, and where the extra virgin olive oil is considered among the best in the world. The three varieties of olives used—frantoio, maraiolo, and lecciono—are known respectively for their fruitiness, spiciness, and richness. Because Tuscany is cold in the fall, the olives are harvested early, before potential frosts—so early that Tuscan olives are picked green, before they are fully ripe (most other olives worldwide are harvested after they ripen, when they are black). Olives that are not fully ripe give Tuscan oil its classic lime green color, an almost herbal freshness, an explosive fruitiness, and a kind of peppery bite. Among the finest producers of Tuscan extra virgin olive oil are the wine producers Antinori, Avignonesi, Caparzo, Castellare, Castello di Ama, Castello di Fonterutoli, Castello di Volpaia, and Fattoria di Fèlsina.

in these zones still use the traditional barrels used in Chianti—large Slavonian oak casks rather than small French oak barrels. The percentages in the blend for Chianti with a named subzone are slightly different than for basic Chianti. These wines can be up to 20 percent of "other authorized reds," not 15 percent.

Also, you'll see the names of the subzone on the wine's label. The subzones are (clockwise from the north): Colli Fiorentini, south of the city of Florence; Montespertoli, located within Colli Fiorentini around the commune of Montespertoli; Chianti Rufina, in the northeastern part of the zone around the commune of Rufina; Colli Aretini, in the Arezzo province to the east; Colli Senesi, in the Siena hills; Colline Pisane, the westernmost subzone in the province of Pisa; and Montalbano, in the northwest part of the zone.

The best wines from these zones are very fine, and in particular, wines from Chianti Rufina can be stunning. Among the best Rufinas are those produced by Castello di Nipozzano, the estate owned by the Frescobaldi family (one such Frescobaldi wine, Montesodi, is renowned), as well as those produced by Selvapiana. Finally, by definition, Chianti today is always a red wine. There is no such thing as white Chianti.

Filippo and Francesco Mazzei, the 24th generation of the Mazzei family to own Castello di Fonterutoli, one of the top estates in Chianti Classico.

CHIANTI CLASSICO

Historically, the area that yielded the richest, fullest Chianti was the original, small, hilly central region known as Chianti Classico. In 1984, the uniqueness of Chianti Classico was underscored when it was given a DOCG of its own.

THE LAW OF MEZZADRIA

As late as 1960, the relationship of landowners to land workers in Italy was feudal in nature and governed by the law of *mezzadria*. For centuries, much of the Italian countryside had been divided into many *fattorie* ("large farms") owned by wealthy, aristocratic, often absent landowners. Each *fattoria* was made up of ten to twelve *poderi* ("small farms"). Each *podere* covered about 20 acres and was worked by one peasant family (the *mezzadri*). The agriculture of the *podere* was *promiscuo*—a mixture of olives, corn, wheat, wine grapes, vegetables, fruit trees, sheep, and chickens—virtually everything the literally penniless working family needed to survive. Of the total production, 51 percent went to the landowner; the *mezzadri* (from *mezza,* meaning "half") kept 49 percent as payment for their labor. The system—essentially sharecropping—kept the *mezzadri* in a constant state of poverty, and ensured an incapacitating status quo among landowners who relied on unpaid labor to keep agriculture afloat.

In the 1950s and 1960s the system of *mezzadria* slowly dissolved, but not without a huge impact on Italian farms (many of which were abandoned), agriculture (which subsequently became far more industrialized), and social structure (farmers moved to better-paying jobs in cities). In Tuscany, where many deserted properties were later bought and restored as second homes for upper-middle-class city dwellers, wine estates are often still known as either *fattorie* or *poderi* (Fattoria di Fèlsina, Fattoria di Montevertine, Podere Il Palazzino). And some small Tuscan vineyards remain as they have been for decades, planted not only with several varieties of grapes but also with fruit and olive trees scattered among the vines.

The mesoclimates of Chianti Classico are multiple and diverse, thanks to the undulating hills and the variations in geology. The ancient communes of Panzano, Radda, Gaiole, and Castellina, for example, slope toward the basin of Siena—once a prehistoric lake. The Tyrrhenian Sea is close enough to bring cooling, dry breezes that help minimize the humidity. The grapes, the best of which are planted on south- and southwest-facing slopes, mature gradually over a long summer of warm Mediterranean days and cool nights.

If the mesoclimates are diverse, so are the soils. Many of what are considered the best sites are on well-drained, fractured rock and stone, including the schist locally known as galestro. These give the most structured wines. But there are also sites interspersed with limestone, which tend to yield wines higher in acidity, and sites with more clay, which is less well drained and tends to lead to gentler, softer wines.

By law, Chianti Classico can be composed of 80 to 100 percent sangiovese, and up to 20 percent canaiolo, colorino, cabernet sauvignon, and/or merlot. *Riservas*—Chianti Classicos that have been aged for an extra period of time (see facing page)—must abide by these percentages as well.

A word about cabernet sauvignon, which sometimes figures in small amounts in the Chianti Classico blend. Unlike sangiovese, cabernet is relatively easy to grow and make into wine, and it's a known commodity in the international wine marketplace. But from a flavor standpoint, the two grapes are odd bedfellows. Sangiovese, after all, tends to be delicate and high in acidity; cabernet is dense, bold, and high in tannin. It's easy for even small amounts of cabernet to take over a wine's flavor, leaving the delicate nuances of sangiovese far behind. Tuscan winemakers have been well aware of this challenge for a good three decades. In every wine where cabernet is part of the blend, the goal is to allow the flavors of sangiovese to shine through, and indeed, some of the most balanced and nuanced Chianti Classicos are now being made.

The best basic Chianti Classicos have plum and dried cherry flavors and sometimes a touch of salt and spice. The more structured, complex, and elegant wines from this region are the Chianti Classico Riservas—aged, by law, at least two years in wood and three months in bottle. Many are aged longer and most are aged, at least partially, in small, new French oak barrels. *Riservas* are generally made only in the best vintage years, from grapes that come from selected vineyard sites. Produced in these great years, *riservas* can develop mesmerizing waves of refined, savory aromas and flavors: fig, chocolate, cedar, dried orange, earth, smoke, saddle leather, prune, minerals, salt, and exotic spices. Paradoxically, these flavors can seem both supple and explosive at the same time. They are flavors that linger long after you've swallowed.

And finally, in 2013, the Chianti Classico producers created an even higher category of quality than *riserva*. Called Gran Selezione, it is only for wines made from estate-grown grapes, and the wine must be aged thirty months (including three months in bottle) before it is sold.

Franco Biondi Santi, whose family discovered the highly flavorful brunello clone of sangiovese. This and other efforts by the family helped establish brunello di Montalcino as one of Italy's great wines.

SOME OF THE BEST PRODUCERS OF CHIANTI CLASSICO RISERVA

Antinori • Badia a Coltibuono • Castellare • Castello dei Rampolla • Castello della Paneretta • Castello di Ama • Castello di Volpaia • Fattoria di Fèlsina • Fattoria Selvapiana • Fonterutoli • Fontodi • Il Molino di Grace • Monsanto • Rocca di Castagnoli • Ruffino • San Felice • Villa Cafaggio

---

BRUNELLO DI MONTALCINO

Brunello (dialect for "the nice dark one") is Tuscany's most revered wine. It is also Tuscany's rarest, most expensive, and longest lived. It is made around Montalcino, a walled medieval village clinging to a rocky hilltop, about an hour's drive south of Chianti Classico. (Montalcino is a UNESCO World Heritage Site.) This southern region is warmer and, as a result, the wines have historically been fuller-bodied, more powerful, and sometimes more dramatic than Chiantis. They have always been based on sangiovese alone, which in these hilltop vineyards seems to possess all the nuance of aroma and flavor needed to make a layered, complex, lavish, decadent wine, even without the help of other varieties.

The vineyards of brunello di Montalcino cover a modest area of approximately 5,200 acres (2,100 hectares). (The total Chianti zone, including Chianti Classico, by comparison, covers more than 38,000 acres/15,400 hectares.) The best vineyards, as well as the village, are some 1,800 feet (550 meters) above sea level, where they are blanketed by a luminous swatch of sunshine. In the spring, the light in Montalcino is unlike any in the rest of Tuscany. There is more limestone in the soil than there is in Chianti, and there are strips of clay, schist, volcanic soil, and plots of the crumbly marl called galestro. The best vineyards are planted on slopes facing south and southwest. Like a giant rock curtain, the Monte Amiata range to the southeast helps to protect the vineyards from sudden rain and hail.

Brunello di Montalcino is not made from the clones of sangiovese that are typically the source of Chianti but, instead, from a series of special clones collectively called brunello. (Historically, brunello was thought to be a single clone, but is now considered to be a collection of related clones.) In good years, the brunello clones yield a lavish wine, fleshier in texture than Chianti, with complex, "dark" aromas and flavors of blackberry, black cherry, and black raspberry fruit, and chocolate, violet, tar, cinnamon, and leather. By law, brunello di Montalcino must be aged longer than most other Italian wines. Regular brunello can be released only after five years of aging; riserva brunello, only after six. How the wine is aged is also dictated. For regular brunello, at least two of the five years must be in oak and the wine must spend four months in the bottle. For riserva brunello, two of the six years must be in oak, and the wine must spend at least six months in bottle.

The kinds of barrels used for aging vary, resulting in two extremely different styles of wine. Traditional producers still use large, old Slavonian oak casks, which allow the wine to age and evolve but which do not impart significant character themselves. More modern producers use small, new French oak barrels, which give the wine more structure and an unmistakable note of sweet vanilla. And many producers, creating a third style, use a combination of both, so that oak flavors are present but more subtle.

In great vintages, brunello can take on stunning elegance, suppleness, and concentration. The flavors seem almost animate as they somersault over themselves and out of the glass. The combination of unctuous textures and deep, savory aromas and flavors is, needless to say, captivating.

Brunello di Montalcino has a reputation for longevity, and indeed many brunello di Montalcino producers feel the wine attains its full potential for complexity and a velvety texture only after significant aging. One of the most legendary wines in this regard—not just in Tuscany, but in Italy—is the Biondi-Santi brunello di Montalcino. After a hundred years of aging, it can still be remarkable, with fragile but complex flavors that almost tremble in the

No road in Tuscany follows a straight line. All the twisting and turning helps demarcate subtle shifts in terroir. Here, rolling fields of grain in the countryside between Montalcino and Montepulciano.

WHEN YOU VISIT . . . TUSCANY

IT WAS IN FLORENCE that the Renaissance was born, and Tuscany is still a haven for every sort of artisan— cabinetmakers, sculptors, silversmiths, gilders, and of course, winemakers.

TUSCANY'S SMALL VILLAGES and hill towns seem untouched by time. Here, no road even remotely resembles a straight line. One of the most beautiful is the Chiantigiana, the country road that twists and turns, rises and falls through the vineyards and woodlands that connect Florence with Siena.

WINE ESTATES IN TUSCANY vary tremendously in size, from small farms that have been converted into working wine villas to large wineries. Many of these offer a full palette of gastronomical possibilities, so in addition to tasting the estate's wines, you might be able to taste its olive oils and honey, or take a cooking class, or sample the local cheeses.

TUSCAN WINE ESTATES are almost always a challenge to find. There are rarely any signs or street addresses on the properties themselves, and you can forget the GPS. The best bet is to meander around the nearest village and ask for specific directions from a waiter in a local bar or café. Of course, it's hard to get truly lost in Tuscany: Dirt paths off the main road almost always end at some wine estate.

MOST WINE TOWNS have a local *consorzio*, or governing body, for that wine region. The *consorzio* can give you an overview of winemaking in the region, provide you with maps, and suggest producers to visit.

ABOVE ALL, NO WINE TRIP to Tuscany would be complete without a visit to the *enoteca* in Siena, a former de'Medici fortress. Hundreds of wines from all over the country are available there for tasting.

---

mouth. Brunello di Montalcino was initially the vision and creation of Ferruccio Biondi Santi who, in the 1870s, isolated a brunello clone of sangiovese and planted it throughout the vineyards at his estate, Il Greppo, some 1,790 feet (550 meters) above sea level. Biondi Santi's brunello could not have been more unconventional. At the time, most of the wine made in Montalcino was sweet and white. Those who preferred red drank Chianti, much of which was light in style and not very ageworthy. Biondi Santi's brunello di Montalcino was the exact opposite: ample in body, packed with flavor, intensely colored, and capable of being cellared for decades. Having isolated the clone he wanted, Biondi Santi went on to limit the yields of his vines and then, during fermentation, to let the grape skins sit with the juice for maximum color extraction. He aged the resulting wines for years before releasing them. Although common today, each of these practices was virtually unheard of in the mid-nineteenth century, especially in a rural village in agrarian central Italy. (The first paved road to Montalcino was completed in 1960!) In 1980, brunello di Montalcino was awarded DOCG status; it was one of the first Italian reds to be given the designation.

Today, slightly more than two hundred producers continue to improve what has been considered a venerable wine for the past hundred years. Most of these producers are small. However, one producer—the American-owned firm of Banfi—is colossal. The estate, spread

The Casottino Vineyard of Conti Costanti, one of the top "old guard" producers of brunello di Montalcino. In the late 19th century, the Costanti family, along with the Biondi Santi family, were early proponents of a clone of sangiovese they called brunello *("nice dark one").*

over more than 7,000 acres (2,800 hectares), includes a state-of-the-art winery that makes several wines, including a good brunello.

SOME OF THE BEST PRODUCERS OF BRUNELLO DI MONTALCINO

Altesino • Antinori • Argiano • Biondi-Santi • Casanova di Neri • Casanuovo della Cerbaie • Case Basse • Cerbaiona di Diego Molinari • Ciacci Piccolomini d'Aragona • Col d'Orcia • Conti Costanti • Fattoria dei Barbi • Ferro di Burroni Carlo • Fornacina • Gaja • Gorelli • I Due Cipressi • La Fortuna • La Serena • Pieve di Santa Restituta • Pinino • Poggio Antico • Poggio di Sotto • Uccelliera

ROSSO DI MONTALCINO

Sometimes thought of as brunello di Montalcino's younger sibling, rosso di Montalcino is a lighter, fruitier, less complex wine than brunello di Montalcino; it's also a lot less expensive. Rosso di Montalcino is usually made from grapes from the younger and/or less ideal vineyards in Montalcino; the older and better ones are reserved for brunello di Montalcino. The yields of rosso are not as limited as those for brunello di Montalcino. And, by law, rosso di Montalcino must be aged one year, compared to brunello di Montalcino's four. In poor vintages, however, rosso di Montalcino can be a smart choice, since many brunello di Montalcino producers declassify their brunello grapes and make rosso di Montalcino with them instead. Only a few producers consistently make truly exciting rosso di Montalcino. In many cases, these producers give near brunello-like treatment to their rosso, leaving the juice in contact with the skins for a longer period than usual and aging the wine in small oak barrels. Among the best producers of rosso di Montalcino are Argiano, Case Basse, Conti Costanti, I Due Cipressi, and Poggio Antico.

VINO NOBILE DI MONTEPULCIANO

Wine has been made in and around the Tuscan town of Montepulciano since Etruscan times. It was not until the eighteenth century, however, that the wine was given the name *vino nobile*, a reference not literally to the nobleness of the wine, but rather to the noblemen, poets, and popes who regularly drank it. Today vino nobile sometimes lives up to the quality suggested by its name—but not always. When at their best, vino nobiles have a spicy concentration and wonderful savory bitterness, underscored by fresh acidity. But too many are just plain thin and tart, without sufficient structure, fruit, or flavor. In all fairness, proponents contend that a golden period for vino nobile may dawn once producers get a firmer grasp on clones and begin to understand better how to tame vino nobile's difficult combination of acidity and tannin.

Like brunello di Montalcino and Chianti, vino nobile is made primarily from its own set of clones of sangiovese. These are collectively

Chianina—a breed of white cattle—is the secret behind Tuscany's phenomenally delicious T-bone steaks.

called *prugnolo* (the word means "little prune," a reference to the prunelike shape, color, and aroma of the grapes). Often the grapes are, as they are in Chianti, blended with a small amount of canaiolo, malvasia, and/or trebbiano.

The vineyards of Montepulciano ring the city of Siena, near the southern end of the Valley of Chiana. Curiously enough, Chiana may partly explain vino nobile's prestige. The valley is famous for a special breed of white cattle, Chianina, which is the source of Tuscany's renowned specialty: mammoth T-bone steaks called *bistecca alla fiorentina*. Perhaps the utter perfection of these steaks led people to assume that the accompanying wine had to be pretty incredible, too.

Montepulciano's vineyards are planted on broad, open slopes. At about 600 feet (180 meters) above sea level, they stand at less than half the altitude of the brunello di Montalcino vineyards. The soil is mostly sandy clay. By law, the wines must be aged for two years; *riservas* must be aged for three years. Vino nobile di Montepulciano was granted DOCG status in 1980. Avignonesi, Poliziano, and Poderi Boscarelli are among the best producers.

Finally, don't confuse vino nobile di Montepulciano, a Tuscan wine made principally from the prugnolo clones of sangiovese, with the grape montepulciano, which is planted throughout central and southern Italy and is a specialty of the region of Abruzzi. (Italy—profusion of confusion!) Indeed, because these are easily mixed up, vino nobile di Montepulciano producers are considering renaming their wine simply vino nobile.

ROSSO DI MONTEPULCIANO

As rosso di Montalcino is to brunello di Montalcino, so rosso di Montepulciano is to vino nobile di Montepulciano, which is to say, the less expensive "younger sister." Rosso di Montepulciano is made from prugnolo clones of sangiovese, but the vineyards are usually younger than the vineyards dedicated to vino nobile. The yields of rosso are not as limited as those for vino nobile, and rosso di Montepulciano is generally aged for a shorter period of time. All of this would seem to make rosso di Montepulciano pale in comparison to vino nobile, but the quality is entirely dependent on the producer. The immediate splash of fruit in some rossos can be very appealing. A bottle of Gattavecchi's rosso di Montepulciano served with a juicy *bistecca alla fiorentina* will prove the point.

CARMIGNANO

I t may lack the prestige of brunello di Montalcino, the popularity of Chianti, and the lucky name of *vino nobile*, but Carmignano nonetheless has an important claim to fame: cabernet sauvignon. In this tiny wine region just west of Florence, cabernet sauvignon has been part of the Carmignano blend since the eighteenth century. Today, by law, Carmignano must be composed of a minimum of 50 percent sangiovese, plus 10 percent

THE BEST WINE BARS IN FLORENCE

F lorence has a number of extremely casual wine bars, often just marble counters, which are perfect for a glass of Chianti plus a snack of focaccia, some pecorino cheese, or finocchiona *("fennel sausage") heaped on Tuscan bread. Prices are reasonable. A few to experience: L'Antico Noè, Cantinetta da Verrazzano, Fuori Porta, and Le Volpi e l'Uva.*

to 20 percent cabernet sauvignon and cabernet franc (up to 20 percent canaiolo, 10 percent white grapes, and 10 percent "other reds" are also allowed).

In a sea of Tuscan sangiovese, it's surprising to come upon vineyards planted with cabernet sauvignon and cabernet franc. Yet both grapes have been part of the Carmignano blend since the 18th century.

At La Taverna di San Guiseppe in Siena, a wine tasting means multiple glasses.

Carmignano, which has a reputation for finesse and structure, comes from a tiny area. There are fewer than twenty producers, most of them minuscule. In fact, the wine drinker is likely to encounter only one or two producers, and most probably the first will be the famous estate of Villa de Cappezzana, which makes what many Italian wine lovers consider the very best Carmignano. The estate was originally a de' Medici villa.

VERNACCIA DI SAN GIMIGNANO

Although everything about Tuscany seems to put a person in the mood to drink red wine, there is a historic white wine to consider: vernaccia di San Gimignano, traditionally referred to as the wine that kisses, licks, bites, and stings. Actually, only the best vernaccia di San Gimignanos do that; plenty of others—which are utterly neutral—just don't appear to be good at romance.

As its name suggests, vernaccia di San Gimignano is made from vernaccia grapes grown on the slopes surrounding the storybook medieval hill town of San Gimignano, roughly an hour's drive southwest of Florence. Although historically vernaccia di San Gimignano was made and aged in large, old wood casks, the best modern versions are young and fresh, and owe their charm to temperature-controlled stainless-steel tanks. There are about sixty relatively small producers. The best of these include Il Cipressino, Riccardo Falchini, Montenidoli, Pietrafitta, La Quercia di Racciano, San Quirico, and Teruzzi & Puthod.

VIN SANTO

Of the hundreds of different sweet wines produced in Italy, the best known may be *vin santo*, "holy wine," so named because priests have drunk it during Mass for centuries. Unlike many sweet wines, however, *vin santo* is not served solely on ceremonious occasions. It is the customary finale to even the humblest Tuscan meal, served after espresso, almost always with a plate of small biscotti called *cantucci*, stubby, twice-baked cookies meant for dunking.

Most *vin santo* does not taste as sweet as, say, Sauternes. The wine has a delicate, creamy, honey-roasted flavor, and the color can be unreal, from radiant amber to neon orange. The sweetness level, however, is entirely up to the producer, and there are even some rare *vin santos* that are bone-dry.

True *vin santo* is expensive because the ancient process of making it remains artisanal and labor intensive. First the grapes (generally malvasia bianca lunga or trebbiano) are partially dried for three to six months. Although there are several ways this can be accomplished, the preferred method is to hang them from rafters in an airy, dry attic or room. During the drying period, nearly half of the liquid (mostly water) in the grapes evaporates, concentrating the remaining sugar. The grapes are crushed, combined with a *madre*, or "mother" (a small remnant of the thick residue from a former

The vineyards of Marchesi de Frescobaldi, with the estate's renowned Castello di Nippozano in the background. The Frescobaldi family, one of the original banking families of medieval Florence, has made wine for seven hundred years.

STEAK ITALIAN STYLE

If the wine list in most steak houses is any evidence, cabernet sauvignon is a steak's best friend. Tuscany begs to differ. The region's specialty, **bistecca alla fiorentina**—*a huge, three-inch-thick slab of grilled Chianina beef*—is always served with a wine made principally from sangiovese—especially a top Chianti Classico Riserva, brunello di Montalcino, or vino nobile di Montepulciano. Sangiovese, with its underlying bright acidity and hint of saltiness, is stunning as a counterpoint to the richness and fat of the beef.

batch), and then the must is left to ferment slowly for three to five years in small, sealed barrels placed in a warm attic or loft called a *vinsantaia*. The barrels are commonly oak, but some producers give the wine greater complexity by using juniper, cherry, and chestnut as well, then blending the final lots. (This idea of using several different types of wood to contribute to the complexity of flavor is also used in neighboring Emilia-Romagna to make the best balsamic vinegars, and indeed, if everything does not go right, a Tuscan winemaker can end up with some very delicious vinegar rather than *vin santo*.)

Typically families make their own *vin santo* for home use and as a proud offering to guests. In addition, there are several dozen small commercial producers. Of them, these seven make the most stunning *vin santos*: Avignonesi, Badia a Coltibuono, Fontodi, Isole e Olena, San Giusto a Rentennano, Selvapiana, and I Selvatici.

In addition, the larger producers Antinori, Barone Ricasoli, Frescobaldi, and Lungarotti make very excellent *vin santos* that are not as limited in production and thus more easily found.

THE FOODS OF TUSCANY

Perhaps because it was the birthplace of the Renaissance, Tuscany is often associated with refinement, wealth, even ostentation. We assume that Tuscan cooking will exhibit these characteristics as well, and that the cuisine will be both sumptuous and elaborate.

Sumptuous it can be. Elaborate, almost never. Tuscan cooking is some of the humblest in Italy. It is quite definitively poor people's cuisine. In contrast to special-occasion dishes, such as *bistecca alla fiorentina* (mammoth slabs of grilled Chianina beef), everyday meals are more likely to be dominated by beans and bread. When other Italians want to be derogatory, they call the Tuscans by their age-old nickname: *mangiafagioli*, "bean eaters."

But if beans are commonplace in the region's culinary repertoire, bread is even more so. The entire *cucina* of Tuscany is said to revolve around this one essential food, and in no other region of Italy does bread seem more intimately tied to everyday life. The Tuscans may have been among the first people to regularly use forks, but bread is a Tuscan's oldest and most treasured utensil. At every meal, it is enlisted to help transport one thing or another to the mouth.

Tuscan bread, *pane toscano*, tastes like no other bread in Italy, mostly because it is made without salt. In restaurants and trattorias this bread is the first thing whisked to the table, even though great examples are, sadly enough, increasingly hard to find. (Many trattorias now serve a cardboardlike commercial version that discriminating pigeons would reject.) Traditionally, butter is never served alongside, nor is olive oil for dipping. Generally, and without regard for its quality, a small cover charge for *pane toscano* appears on the bill.

Tuscan children walking to school often munch on *schiacciata*, a piece of flat bread baked with olive oil and sometimes sweetened with sugar or wine grapes. Before lunch or dinner there are always crostini, thin slices of Tuscan bread traditionally spread with an earthy paste of chopped liver, but sometimes, in more creative cases, covered with grilled wild mushrooms or a puree of olives and garlic. Crostini are not the same as bruschetta—which, in any case, is not a Tuscan term but the Roman one for peasant bread that has been grilled over a fire, brushed with olive oil, rubbed with garlic, and then possibly topped with chopped fresh tomatoes.

But perhaps the most glorious way to serve bread is as *fettunta*, a piece of toasted *pane toscano* swathed with just-pressed, ripe, green, unfiltered Tuscan extra virgin olive oil. Technically you can only eat *fettunta* in late fall, right after the olives have been harvested, when the oil is at its apex. The name *fettunta* comes from *fetta*, the name workers used to describe the hunk of bread that they anointed with intensely flavorful extra virgin olive oil as it ran fresh from the press.

Tuscany revolves around olives and grapes.

Bread—the lifeblood of Tuscany and, along with wine, an indispensable part of the Tuscan table. Dozens of Tuscan specialties from panzella to crostini to ribollita depend on it when the bread is fresh, and even when it's stale.

In Tuscany, bread is also constantly used in cooking, especially good bread gone stale. The homiest Tuscan soup is *ribollita,* made with stale bread, black Tuscan cabbage, and beans. *Panzanella,* the humble and irresistibly delicious Tuscan salad, is made of stale bread moistened with a little water and then tossed with fresh tomatoes, chopped basil, onions, celery, and olive oil. A classic Tuscan cookbook, *Con Poco o Nulla ("With Little or Nothing"),* opens with ten suggestions for using day-old bread.

Bread made without salt has a muted, almost bland flavor. That Tuscan bakers would intentionally choose to make their bread this way seems surprising, until you consider that bread alone is not the issue. In the Tuscan triumvirate of bread, olive oil, and wine, the plain *pane toscano* is the perfect backdrop for the pepperiness of Tuscan olive oil, and both are delicious juxtaposed with the slight perception of saltiness in many wines made from sangiovese grapes. Salt and pepper. Wine and bread. Liquid and solid. What more could be asked for? Then again, perhaps this small but admirable bit of culinary compatibility was the result of more mundane considerations. Culinary historians point out that salt was always a precious, expensive commodity in Tuscany, and that often it was heavily taxed. *Pane toscano,* it seems, could also have been a simple method of tax-avoidance.

The Tuscan Wines to Know

 hile white wines are made in Tuscany, the wines of most importance, including the ones below, are all red.

FATTORIA DI FÈLSINA BERARDENGA

CHIANTI CLASSICO RISERVA | RANCIA

100% sangiovese

The Fèlsina estate is in the southeast corner of Chianti Classico, in the district of Castelnuovo Berardenga, where the soils are marine sediments and alberese, a type of marl limestone with a high concentration of calcium carbonate. Indeed, all of the wines have amazing aromas that suggest prehistoric sea beds, iodine, and minerals. They are sophisticated wines that start out subtle and then zoom forward on the palate, with bitter cherries steeped in liqueur, damp bark, spices, and dried rose petals. The winery's basic Chianti Classicos always have classic flavors and flair, but I especially like their *riserva* wine, called Rancia, the grapes for which come from a single parcel that used to be part of a Benedictine monastery.

BADIA A COLTIBUONO

CHIANTI CLASSICO RISERVA

90% sangiovese, 10% canaiolo

Badia a Coltibuono ("Abbey of the Good Harvest") dates from the eleventh century and was founded by the Vallombrosan order of reformed Benedictine monks. In the mid-1800s, the estate was acquired by the Giuntini family and eventually was passed down to an heir, Piero Stucchi Prinetti, who, with his family, set about transforming the estate into a superb modern property devoted to wine and food. (Lorenza de'Medici, the wife of the late Piero Stucchi Prinetti, and as close to a Renaissance woman as it gets, is a famous cookbook author and the founder of the estate's acclaimed cooking school.) The wines, of course, are the heart of the estate, and they are delicious—especially the Chianti Classico Riserva, with its autumnlike flavors of woods, mushrooms, withered leaves, wet bark, truffles, damp soil, and small wild berries. I have always loved the leathery grip of this wine, and the way it incites hunger for a richly sauced pasta.

FONTODI

FLACCIANELLO DELLA PIEVE

100% sangiovese

Flaccianello della Pieve is named for a Christian cross in the village of Pieve, but this wine comes from the village of Panzano, and specifically the impressive amphitheater of steep hillside vineyards outside the town. This is a wine you can drink once and remember forever. Precise in its delineated flavors, distinctive in character, and exuding finesse, it's one of the most exotic sangioveses made—syrupy-rich in texture, exceptionally complex, and dappled with uncommon flavors, such as incense, ginger, black licorice, and persimmon. Most impressive of all is the way the wine explodes on the palate with sappy juiciness. Fontodi, a small estate owned by Giovanni Manetti, also makes astounding Chianti Classico Riserva.

MONTEVERTINE

LE PERGOLE TORTE

100% sangiovese

From the small estate of Montevertine, in the commune of Radda—one of the coolest spots in Chianti Classico—comes Le Pergole Torte ("the twisted stake" in Italian, a reference to the old vine training method used in 1968, when the vineyards were planted). One of the first 100 percent sangioveses in Chianti Classico, Le Pergole Torte is a wine that incites sheer emotion in its drinkers. It is a selection of the estate's best lots, and is richly textured yet vividly precise. Its dramatic flavors—black cherry, black fig, vanilla, violets, and orange peel—flash across the palate like slashing knives. Like the stylized woman on its label, the wine seems powerful and yet mysteriously feminine at the same time.

ANTINORI

TIGNANELLO

Approximately 80% sangiovese, plus cabernet sauvignon and cabernet franc

Tignanello, the first well-known Super Tuscan, is the red wine that carved out a radically new direction for Tuscan winemaking and, in the process, galvanized the creative spirit of winemakers throughout Italy. When it was first made in 1971, Tignanello contained no cabernet, but from the beginning it was aged in small, French-oak barrels. By the early 1990s, after a few slight changes in the blend and the winemaking method, some of the best Tignanellos ever were being made. In the finest vintages, Tignanello possesses a fantastic aroma of bitter cherries and exotic spices. These open up into a wine that is primordial and dark (I always think of Joseph Conrad's *Heart of Darkness*). The savory, salty flavors have a deep deliciousness about them—like long-simmered meat juices. But best of all, Tignanello has vibrancy and energy, as if its concentration can't wait to be unleashed.

POLIZIANO

VINO NOBILE DI MONTEPULCIANO

85% sangiovese (prugnolo clones), plus colorino, canaiolo, and merlot

Poliziano's vino nobile is noble indeed. The wine's blast of savory, briny black olive and espresso flavors is delicious and just waiting for the traditional accompaniment to vino nobile—*bistecca alla fiorentina*, a huge, three-inch-thick slab of grilled Chianina beef. Like so many top Tuscan wines, Poliziano's vino nobile is beautifully structured and sophisticated. It is not about fruit, but rather, belongs to the sensory world of expensive Italian leather, fine espresso, and gourmet chocolate. The name Poliziano is an homage to humanist poet Angelo Ambrogini (1454–1494), known as Il Poliziano, who was born in Montepulciano.

CONTI COSTANTI

BRUNELLO DI MONTALCINO

100% sangiovese (brunello clones)

Andrea Costanti makes some of the richest, yet most elegant and completely fascinating, brunellos in Montalcino. The wine—as all great wines do—takes you on a taste journey. This one goes from savory grilled herbs and sea salt to violets and black licorice, to cranberries and blueberries. The explosive finish leaves you with echoes of rich fruits, espresso, and minerals. Costanti's wines always have a fineness, a pedigree, a beauty. They are sumptuous and sophisticated, and never overdone.

GAJA

BRUNELLO DI MONTALCINO | PIEVE SANTA RESTITUTA | RENNINA

100% sangiovese (brunello clones)

Angelo Gaja made his name in Piedmont working with (high-tannin) nebbiolo grapes, but in 1994 he acquired the Pieve Santa Restituta estate, and he has a deft hand with (high-acid) sangiovese as well. The Rennina, broad on the palate, shows a side of sangiovese that almost doesn't exist: sumptuousness. The wine is smooth and rich, but sangiovese's classic saline, spice, and forest floor flavors are there, too. The combination makes for a fascinating brunello. The estate itself is behind the seventh-century church Santa Restituta, which the Gaja family is restoring. The name of the wine—Rennina—is what the estate was called in the late Middle Ages.

BIONDI-SANTI

BRUNELLO DI MONTALCINO | RISERVA

100% sangiovese (brunello clones)

The brunello clone was first isolated and propagated by the Biondi Santi family around 1870. They were the only estate to produce brunello di Montalcino until after the Second World War, when several other producers joined the ranks. This is the most legendary estate in Montalcino and also the most traditional. Wines here (both the *riserva* and the regular Brunello) have been made in essentially the same manner for nearly a century, and the grapes come from a perfect, high-altitude vineyard. The Biondi-Santi wines age in large, old Slavonian oak casks, where they evolve painstakingly slowly. When they emerge, however, they are fascinating, complex wines with stunning elegance and balance.

OTHER IMPORTANT
WINE
REGIONS

TRENTINO-ALTO ADIGE | LOMBARDY | LIGURIA | EMILIA-ROMAGNA
UMBRIA | ABRUZZI | THE SOUTHERN PENINSULA: CAMPANIA,
APULIA, BASILICATA, AND CALABRIA | SICILY AND SARDINIA

---

taly is a treasure trove of vineyards, from Trentino-Alto Adige on the border of the Alps to the island of Sicily off the North African coast. No province here is *without* vines. I've covered the "big four" (Piedmont, Veneto, Friuli-Venezia Giulia, and Tuscany). Following are what I consider the next most important Italian regions to know, each of which has delicious wine specialties.

▲ *Mountain huts used by shepherds and farmers are scattered throughout the narrow alpine valleys of Trentino-Alto Adige with the majestic Dolomites towering above.*

TRENTINO-ALTO ADIGE

No Italian wine region extends farther north than Trentino-Alto Adige, where pristine vineyards carpet narrow Alpine valleys as high as 3,600 feet (1,100 meters) in elevation. The sheer rock faces of the forebodingly beautiful Dolomites (part of the Alps) rise up majestically and virtually perpendicularly behind the vines. These are some of the most breathtaking vineyards in the world (and the Alto Adige part of the region, in particular, gets my vote as one of the most gorgeous wine regions in all of Europe).

This is the sunny, south-facing side of the Alps and so, despite Trentino-Alto Adige's northern latitude, the vineyard-covered valleys are warm enough during summer to ripen grapes. The soil is also ideal. Well drained and laced with limestone, it was created by glacial and alluvial deposits of gravel, sand, and clay.

Trentino-Alto Adige, despite its hyphen, is really two distinct provinces. Trentino, in the south, is primarily Italian-speaking. But in Alto Adige, nestled beneath Austria in the north, German, not Italian, is the primary language (and both languages can appear on wine labels). The district takes its modern name from the river Adige, the second longest in Italy, which runs through its middle. But the area's historic name is the Südtirol (South Tyrol), a reference to its Austrian past. (Alto Adige was ceded to Italy by Austria after World War I.) Politics, however, don't always amend the ideology of a place, and for many residents of Alto Adige, the Südtirol is still the name of the place where they live, and goulash is a more familiar dish than polenta.

While cultural differences between Trentino and Alto Adige can run deep, the best producers in the two provinces share a common ideology when it comes to wine. Like Friuli-Venezia Giulia, Trentino-Alto Adige brings a northern, even Teutonic sensibility to winemaking. This is especially true of Alto Adige, where the top producers—such wineries as Alois Lageder, J. Hofstätter, Pojer e Sandri, Tiefenbrunner, Casòn Hirschprunn, Cantina Tramin, and Zeni, to name a few—make wines of ravishing beauty.

Trentino-Alto Adige is home to a vast range of local and international grape varieties. Among the most important white grapes are pinot grigio, traminer aromatico, gewürztraminer, sylvaner, Müller-Thurgau, pinot blanc, and chardonnay, the last having been grown in the region since the mid-nineteenth century. (Cantina Terlano's Nova Domus—a blend of pinot blanc and chardonnay—is one of the top white wines of the region.)

Interestingly, thanks to the chardonnay grown, a small ocean of *spumante* is made here. Indeed, sparkling wines were pioneered in the region in the early twentieth century by Giulio Ferrari (not of car fame), and Ferrari is still one of Trentino-Alto Adige's, indeed one of Italy's,

---

THE QUICK SIP ON TRENTINO-ALTO ADIGE

THE TOP TRENTINO-ALTO ADIGE white wines, including pinot grigios, kerners, traminers, Müller-Thurgaus, gewürztraminers, chardonnays, and sparkling wines, have precision, grip, and focus. The reds, including teroldego, lagrein, schiava, and cabernet sauvignon, are cool-climate, sleek reds with pure fruit flavors.

ONE OF THE MOST STUNNINGLY beautiful wine regions in Europe, Trentino-Alto Adige, is bordered by the Swiss and Austrian Alps in the north; to the southeast is the Veneto, and to the southwest, Lombardy.

THE REGION IS MADE UP of two distinctly different provinces. Trentino, to the south, is Italian in character, while Alto Adige, in the north, was once an area of Austria known as the Südtirol (South Tyrol). It is in Alto Adige that the very best wines are made.

Terraced vineyards near Trentino, the more southern, less mountainous, Italian-speaking part of the province Trentino-Alto Adige. The more northern, mountainous part, Alto Adige, once belonged to Austria, and German is still commonly spoken.

top sparkling wine houses and the best known from the region.

The grape variety called traminer (or more accurately, traminer aromatico) is a specialty here—especially in Alto Adige. (This is a clone of the ancient variety savagnin, one of the "founder varieties"; see Drinking DNA, page 55.) Gorgeously floral, flavorful, and yet light as a feather in body, traminer is a sister of the better-known grape gewürztraminer (a rose-colored clone of savagnin). In the hands of a producer like Pojer e Sandri, traminer is irresistible for its purity, liveliness, and brilliance. And speaking of gewürztraminer—Alto Adige has brilliant, vibrant, decadent, and yet elegant gewürztraminers that are as concentrated and vivid as the gewürztraminers of Alsace, only zestier and sleeker. If you want to be blown away by a gewürztraminer (not from Alsace), try the gewürztraminer called Nussbaumer, from the producer Cantina Tramin. And if Müller-Thurgau has always seemed a little drab (which it generally is in Germany), you must again taste Pojer e Sandri's sensationally spicy, minerally version, as well as the most famous Müller-Thurgau—Tiefenbrunner's Feldmarschall von Fenner zu Fennberg Müller-Thurgau, named after a

disciple of Kaiser Wilhelm II. It comes from the vineyard thought to have the highest elevation in Italy and tastes as fresh as water from an icy mountain stream.

But the northern Italian white grape that everyone seems to know—the grape that can make wines that hit remarkable depths of mediocrity—is pinot grigio. Here in Trentino-Alto Adige, pinot grigio saves its reputation. Somehow, in the glacial valleys of Alto Adige in particular, the wine finds its groove as a delicate, exquisite white of impeccable purity. The best example is Tenutae Lageder's Porer pinot grigio, an intense, cold-weather, utterly precise white wine made from biodynamically farmed grapes.

If you drink adventurously, you'll find Trentino-Alto Adige's indigenous reds to be captivating. One of the specialties of Trentino, in particular, is the brooding, super-spicy, tannic wine teroldego, a grape that grows best in the gravelly, glacial soil of the Rotaliano plain. Another Trentino specialty, schiava—from *schiavo*, "slave"—is turned into light, spicy wines with a slight bitter-almond character. In Alto Adige, schiava is often called vernatsch. Then there's lagrein—dark, sharp, bitter, robust. These grapes, along with Friuli's

Enthusiasm is a must. Bubbles hit the ceiling of the cellar at Ferrari in Trentino-Alto Adige.

tazzelenghe and schioppettino, make up a group of lean, sleek, bitter-edged, crisp, cold-climate Italian reds that have no parallel anywhere else in the world.

Finally, Trentino-Alto Adige is known for a luscious, amber-colored, silky dessert wine—*vino santo* ("holy wine;" probably a reference to its historic use as part of the Mass). Not the same as Tuscany's *vin santo*, which is generally made from trebbiano Toscano and/or malvasia bianca lunga grapes, Trentino-Alto Adige's *vino santo* is a specialty of the Valle dei Laghi, near the northern end of Lake Garda, and also of the hills west of Trento, where it is made by leaving native nosiola grapes on trays to dry for several months, before fermenting them and aging them in barrels for two to three years. The name *nosiola* most likely derives from *nocciola*, Italian for "hazelnut," and a reference to the slightly nutty aroma and flavor of the wine.

LOMBARDY

The north-central region of Lombardy—Lombardia in Italian—is Italy's most populous region and the country's leading industrial zone. Nowhere is the region's commercial flair more evident than in Milan, Lombardy's most important city and Italy's fast-paced capital of fashion and finance. With business so preeminent, there hardly seems room for a wine industry. But there is one; this is Italy, after all.

Unlike Piedmont or Tuscany, Lombardy is not associated with a single grape variety, but rather with dozens of them, as well as with several styles of wine, including the well-known sparkling wine Franciacorta. Wines in this region, including a number of DOCGs, are made in three principal areas located along the region's borders. In the north, just a short drive from Switzerland, is Valtellina; in the southwest corner, near Emilia-Romagna, is Oltrepò Pavese; and in the far east, near the Veneto, is the most important and famous of all three areas: the aforementioned Franciacorta, a DOCG. The name Franciacorta is said to derive from the region's towns—*curtes* in dialect—which were exempt—*francae*—from taxes during the Middle Ages.

Although sparkling wine is made in virtually every region of northern Italy, Lombardy's Franciacorta is the country's leading area for sophisticated, dry sparkling wines made by the traditional (Champagne) method. At their best, these are austerely elegant sparklers with a fine, creamy mousse of bubbles.

Historically a fairly bucolic place, and

THE QUICK SIP ON LOMBARDY

LOMBARDY (and its capital, Milan) are best known for industry and fashion, although some serious wines—especially sparklers—are made.

FRANCIACORTA—Italy's most prestigious traditional-method sparkling wine—is made here.

THE STILL WINES OF THE REGION—both white and red—are made from a great diversity of grape varieties.

VIN BRULÈ AND PANETTONE

On cold December mornings, there is nothing better than butter-slathered, toasted panettone, the large, cylindrical, Italian bread that is studded with candied fruits and raisins. With its church-dome-like, rounded top, panettone is traditional at Christmastime (and, come December, can be found in gourmet stores globally). Panettone is thought to have been created in Milan, in Lombardy, in the sixteenth century. The renowned bread is, in fact, now protected by a DOC for traditional Italian food products. Next door, in the Piedmont region of Italy, the bread is served in the late afternoon (or on Christmas Eve) with *vin brulè* (local dialect for "burnt wine"). Akin to English mulled wine, *vin brulè* is spiced and lightly sweetened wine, served steaming hot. To make it, the Italians combine a bottle of barbera or nebbiolo d'Alba with ¼ cup sugar, 2 cinnamon sticks, 4 pieces star anise, 2 cloves, several white peppercorns, and a couple of bay leaves. The mixture is heated almost to boiling, then put on very low heat and allowed to simmer for 30 minutes—whereupon it is drunk from mugs, with toasted panettone on the side.

home to many convents and monasteries, Franciacorta became Italy's premier sparkling wine zone in the 1970s largely because of the pioneering success of the producer Berlucchi. Today, a number of prestigious sparkling wine firms are located there, including Bellavista (try their elegant Gran Cuvée Pas Operé), Ca' del Bosco, and Cavalleri. As is true in Champagne, Franciacorta's sparkling wines are made from chardonnay and pinot noir (called pinot nero locally), although pinot blanc (pinot bianco) is also allowed. To distinguish them from *spumantes* that are made by the Charmat method (such as Asti), Franciacorta sparklers are labeled *metodo tradizionale* or *metodo classico*—synonyms for the traditional (Champagne) method (although, of course, their higher price automatically puts them in a different league).

Franciacortas are made as nonvintage wines as well as vintage-dated (known as Franciacorta *millesimato*). Rosé Franciacortas are also made, as well as a special category called Satèn (the word was chosen for its similarity to the English word *satin*). Satèn are sparklers with less carbon dioxide, and thus are slightly softer and less bubbly than traditional sparkling wines. Finally, like Champagne,

Franciacorta sparklers spend quite a long time on the yeast lees—from 18 months for Franciacorta non-vintage to 60 months for Franciacorta Riserva.

In the same general area as Franciacorta, but farther east, near Lake Garda, is the small region of Lugana, where the dry white wine based on trebbiano di Lugana, considered one of the most tasty, aromatic types of trebbiano, is made. Although most trebbiano-based wines are innocuous, Lugana—especially Lugana Superiore—can be nicely refreshing. Some of its appeal may be related to the fact that it's the wine usually served with the region's other specialty: fresh trout from the impressive Lake Garda.

The Oltrepò Pavese, known as the land of castles for the thirty-eight medieval fortresses that still stand imposingly across the landscape, is just a half hour's drive from Milan, but this is where the major share of Lombardian wine is made. The large (33,000 acres/13,400 hectares), hilly area is south of northern Italy's important Po River, hence the word Oltrepò ("on the other side of the Po"). Most of the wine here is of quaffing quality or just slightly better, based on a huge number of grape varieties. The reds, for example, are usually the

The town of Cinqueterre in Liguria, the coast of which is known as the Italian Riviera. The vineyards of Cinqueterre (literally "Five Lands") are located alongside five fishing villages.

product of barbera, cabernet sauvignon, pinot noir, and/or Croatina, a simple, indigenous red. The humble whites are based on riesling italico (also known as welschriesling, a grape also grown in Austria and eastern Europe and not the same as true riesling), cortese, chardonnay, moscato, malvasia, and/or pinot grigio. Quite a bit of easy-drinking, well-priced *spumante* also comes from here, as well as a relatively new, higher-priced category of sparklers called Cruasé. A Cruasé is always a rosé made by the traditional method (secondary fermentation in the bottle) predominantly (85 percent) from pinot noir. Like Franciacorta, Cruasé is a DOCG. The name comes from *crua*—a worthy piece of ground—and rosé.

Lombardy's third wine-producing area is the Valtellina, in the far north, on the precipitous, cold yet sunny foothills of the Alps. Vineyards here are on slopes so steep they must be terraced, and in some cases, as in Germany's Mosel region, harvested grapes are relayed down the mountainside in buckets attached to cables. This is the most northern wine-growing region in the world for nebbiolo. Regular Valtellina is a simple, rough-edged, lean red made principally from that grape. A notch higher in quality is Valtellina Superiore, made from 90 percent nebbiolo and aged at least two years (compared to

regular Valtellina's one). There are five subdistricts where Valtellina Superiore can be made: Grumello, Sassella, Inferno, Maroggia, and Valgella. Of the five, Inferno is where the tastiest and the biggest-bodied wines are made. The name *Inferno*, "hell" in Italian, refers to the summer sun, which beats down on the terraced mountainside vineyards, ripening the grapes.

And finally, there is Valtellina Sforzato, Lombardy's version of amarone. To make it, the best clusters of nebbiolo are harvested, then hung to dry for approximately four months in well-ventilated cellars. By the end of January, the grapes have lost 40 percent of their weight and the juices inside have become quite concentrated. After the grapes are fermented, the wine, inky and intense, is aged for two years before release.

LIGURIA

Known as the Italian Riviera, Liguria is the crescent-shaped region arcing from the French border down to Tuscany. Virtually in the center is Genoa, Liguria's capital and one of Italy's most historic and busiest ports. The steeply terraced vineyards, perched on the ridges of the Apennine mountain range, descend right to the Ligurian Sea. (Astoundingly, some of the vineyards can be reached only by boat.) So little land is available for these mountain-clinging vineyards that the production of Ligurian wine is necessarily minuscule. And the steep incline means that vineyards can be farmed only slowly and painstakingly by hand. Traditionally, much of the wine here was little more than a basic commodity, meant for washing down the local cuisine. (Pesto and olive oil, both Ligurian specialties, are especially famous.) But today, a new commitment to quality has taken hold.

Among Liguria's numerous DOCs are several types of easy-drinking wines that are important in the region. To Genoa's east is the wine known as Cinqueterre, which translates as "five lands" (so-called because the wine is made near five fishing villages). Cinqueterre, often a simple, somewhat neutral-tasting but nonetheless popular white, is made from bosco and albarola, two fairly innocuous varieties, plus vermentino, which has more character. Indeed, the best producers use as much vermentino as possible, making a wine that's crisp, lively, and great with the fresh fish caught in the villages where the grapes are grown. A sweet version—Cinqueterre Sciacchetrà—is made from grapes left in the sun to dry and concentrate. Delicious but nearly impossible to find on the export market, it's a must-try if you are in Liguria.

Here, east of Genoa, in the DOC known as Riviera Ligure di Ponente, you'll also find another rare local specialty—the white grape pigato (the name means "spotted," from the mottled appearance of the berries). At its best, pigato can make a lithe, minerally, bold white that's terrific with pesto.

West of Genoa, ormeasco, vermentino, and Dolceacqua are made. Ormeasco is Liguria's name for dolcetto; it is turned into fruity, quaffing reds. Vermentino grapes were probably brought to Italy from Spain, via Corsica, in the fourteenth century. The variety is the source of the dry, floral, somewhat resinous white wine also known as vermentino, a classic with Ligurian fish soups. Dolceacqua,

THE QUICK SIP ON LIGURIA

A MOUNTAINOUS REGION cantilevered over the Ligurian Sea, in the Mediterranean, Liguria is better known for dramatic landscapes than stellar wine.

AMONG THE TOP WINES in the region, the best known is Cinqueterre, a light-bodied, fresh wine from grapes grown on terraced hillsides overlooking the sea.

THE TWO MAIN GRAPE VARIETIES in the region are the white grape vermentino and the red rossese.

sometimes known by its more formal name, rossese di Dolceacqua, comes from rossese, the best red grape of the Italian Riviera. Reportedly a favorite of Napoléon, this wine is commonly used as an ingredient in one of the specialties of the region, rabbit braised with olives.

Estates in Liguria are small, many of them just local family operations, and often the smaller the property, the more interesting the wine. It's impossible to recommend producers under these circumstances and, in any case, the number of Ligurian wines exported is, as already mentioned, tiny. When in Liguria, the best strategy is an old European one: Find a good chef and ask what he or she drinks.

EMILIA-ROMAGNA

sk an Italian where to eat only one meal in Italy and, after recommending his mother's house, it is more than likely he will send you to the region of Emilia-Romagna." With this declaration, Lynne Rosetto Kasper opens her authoritative

BALSAMIC VINEGAR

Wine's "other self" is vinegar. And one of the best vinegars in the world is Italy's balsamic vinegar. (Its only competitor is Spain's Gran Reserva Sherry vinegar.) Both are unlike everything else called vinegar.

Standard vinegar (the word comes from the French *vin aigre,* sour wine) is created when bacteria convert the alcohol in a fermented liquid into acetic acid. The process is quick; the final liquid is blunt and sharp. Traditional balsamic vinegar, on the other hand, is an exquisitely mellow, deeply concentrated, syruplike liquid, sweet enough to drink on its own. In Italy it's often sipped from a small glass like a dessert wine. The adjective *traditional* is critical. There are countless inexpensive supermarket "balsamic vinegars" that are just ordinary red wine vinegar that has been sweetened and colored with caramel. They could come from Kansas.

Real balsamic vinegar is made only in Emilia-Romagna, just north of Tuscany, around the towns of Modena and Reggio. It's labeled *aceto balsamico tradizionale di Modena* or *di Reggio,* and recognizing its unique origin and authenticity, the EU and the Italian government grant it a DOP, Denomination of Protected Origin, equivalent to DOC status for wines. Price is always a tip-off: A small, 3-ounce (90-milliliter) vial of *balsamico tradizionale* can be three to five times the cost of a moderately expensive bottle of wine. The price reflects the painstaking, artisanal process by which traditional balsamic vinegar is made. First, the unfermented must of crushed grapes (usually trebbiano Modenese, but three others are also allowed) is boiled down to a sweet syrup, which then ferments and turns to vinegar. To condense the vinegar even more, the rich liquid is then aged a minimum of twelve years (it may be even decades) in a series of progressively smaller barrels made from different woods—oak, chestnut, cherry, linden, mulberry, juniper, ash, and so forth. As the water component of the liquid evaporates through the grain in the wood, the remaining liquid grows ever more dense and lush. Meanwhile, each wood imparts a different nuance to the final flavor of the vinegar. Although handcrafted, long-aged vinegars have been revered in Italian homes for centuries, the name *balsamic* was first used in the eighteenth century to refer to the "balmy" wood odors that would emanate from country farmhouses where the vinegar was patiently being made, usually in the attic.

Traditional balsamic vinegar is used very selectively in Italy. It is dribbled (it's too expensive to be poured) into a small amount of olive oil or butter and drizzled over cooked vegetables or fish. In the summer, it is dripped over fresh strawberries; in the fall, over fresh, thinly shaved, raw porcini mushrooms. For many Italians, however, the most godly of all culinary combinations is Parmigiano-Reggiano moistened with a few drops of an old, traditional balsamic vinegar.

cookbook *The Splendid Table,* and Kasper is right. Emilia-Romagna is Italy's ultimate food region and a place so consumed by its passion for gastronomy that even the name of its capital, Bologna, is telling: Bologna means "the fat one." Here in the land that gives the world such serious delicacies as Parmigiano-Reggiano, balsamic vinegar, and prosciutto di Parma, wine is, well, *playful* might be the best word. There are no wines of renown, nothing on a par with

THE QUICK SIP ON EMILIA-ROMAGNA

IN A COUNTRY WHERE EVERY REGION is known for its food, Emilia-Romagna is considered the culinary apex. Food comes first here; wine's sole purpose is to enhance whatever's on the plate.

SIMPLE, FROTHY (*frizzante*) lambrusco is what the region is known for, although more complex, artisanal versions of this wine are also now making their way onto the international scene.

THE REGION, WHICH SPANS almost the entire width of Italy, is made up of two distinctly separate provinces. Emilia focuses mostly on *frizzante* wines, while Romagna focuses on still table wines.

Chianti Classico, brunello di Montalcino, Barolo, or Barbaresco. What there is, however, is a seemingly endless sea of fizzy lambrusco. In many countries, in fact, lambrusco is among the top five imported Italian wines.

What makes Emilia-Romagna so culinarily rich is also what makes much of the wine so comparatively poor. Running across the width of the region is the fertile Po River basin. Readily available water and nutrients may be great for food crops, but for grapes it's a worrisome equation that usually results in high yields and thin, simple wines (although there are some fantastic examples from small producers working with top grapes from the best sites). The citizenry of Emilia-Romagna doesn't seem to mind. Go into any good restaurant, and rivers of lambrusco are being gulped down with pride.

As its name suggests, Emilia-Romagna is actually two regions. Emilia, to the west of Bologna, is the definitive home of lambrusco, and today also makes still wines, many of which are based on international varieties like sauvignon blanc, chardonnay, and cabernet sauvignon. In Romagna, to the east, most red wines are still, dry, and based on sangiovese. Romagna's leading white wine, albana di Romagna, is a fairly characterless white, although it does have the major claim to fame of being (illogically) the first Italian white wine granted DOCG status.

But above all, this is the land of lambrusco. Not surprisingly, the fizzy, slightly bitter, very fresh, and definitively purple wine tastes quite good with the region's hearty sausages, cured meats, and rich, meat-sauced pastas. Moreover, the people of Emilia-Romagna insist that the light, frothy, fairly high-acid wine is the perfect aid to digestion in a region that lives for its stomach.

Sadly, the only lambrusco most wine drinkers know is the highly commercial, slightly sweet stuff made by co-ops (and sometimes doctored into white and pink versions). Indeed, Riunite Lambrusco, made by the giant Riunite Co-op and introduced to America in 1967 was a huge success. By 1976, Riunite became America's number-one selling imported wine brand—a position it held, remarkably enough, for the next twenty-six years.

The top versions of lambrusco, however, are not sweet, but rather, dry and savory. Either way, all lambrusco wines are made from the grape variety also known as lambrusco. But here the going gets rough. There are at least thirteen different varieties (plus dozens of clones) with the word *lambrusco* (or *lambrusca*) in the name. In Emilia-Romagna, these different lambrusco varieties exist in close proximity—sometimes in the next village. The main three lambrusco varieties are lambrusco di Sorbara (with floral fresh flavors), lambrusco grasparossa (more intense wines with tannic grip), and lambrusco salamino (so named because the long, cylindrical clusters look like small salamis).

As noted, lambrusco is usually what the Italians call *frizzante,* slightly fizzy, not quite sparkling enough to be considered *spumante.* Generally speaking, most lambrusco gets its bubbles by being fermented in pressurized tanks, not by the traditional (Champagne) method. Top examples, however, do use the

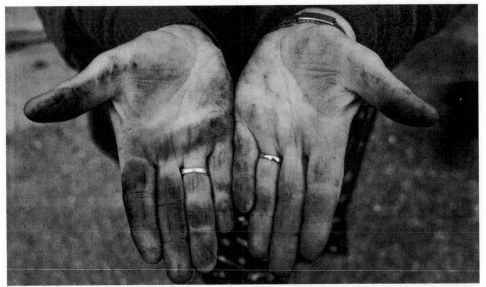

Hard work is evident everywhere in Emilia-Romagna, as the hands of a winemaker attest. In addition to wine, the region is famous for many artisanal food products, including aceto balsamico di Modena, prosciutto di Parma, *and* Parmigiano-Reggiano *cheese.*

traditional method of second fermentation in each bottle. Because of its frothy exuberance, lambrusco definitely tastes best when it is young, soon after its release.

There was a time, not long ago, when the zesty, artisanal lambruscos that any wine lover would prefer were available only in Emilia itself, and even then only in the four distinct zones that specialized in it. But today the picture has changed. A number of fantastic small-production versions are easy to find, including Cleto Chiarli, Fattoria Moretto, Fiorini, Francesco Vezzelli, Lini, and Tenuta Pederzana.

As for the wines of Romagna, albana di Romagna can be a soft and pleasant, if unremarkable, white. Most versions are dry, but in Romagna you will come across slightly sweet versions as well as *spumantes* made from the albana grape. The most popular red wine is sangiovese di Romagna, based on a clone of sangiovese, and usually considered simple at best. With some searching, it is possible to find more compelling versions made by small producers, including Fattoria Paradiso, Ferrucci, and Tenuta Zerbina.

UMBRIA

Compared to its neighbor Tuscany, the small region of Umbria is a serene, bucolic, understated sort of place. Here, smack in the center of Italy, the landscape is gentle and rolling, and the sunlight is almost as arrestingly gossamer as it is in Tuscany. It seems fitting that Saint Francis of Assisi, Umbria's most beloved son (and the patron saint of animals), lived here. Indeed, one of the most striking cathedrals in the region is the Basilica di San Francesco d'Assisi.

Umbria's best-known wine is Orvieto which, today, can be a white or red wine. Historically, however, Orvieto was a stylish, crisp, slightly peachy white wine produced around the medieval hill town of the same name, in the southern part of the region. Orvieto, the best versions of which can have real character, is made from trebbiano (specifically the local clones of trebbiano known as procanico), along with grechetto, verdello, drupeggio, and sometimes malvasia. A step up in quality from basic Orvietos are the Orvieto Classicos, wines that come from the original, small, central Orvieto zone. Although most Orvietos encountered today are dry, the wine was originally slightly sweet. While production is now limited, some of the most fascinating Orvietos are semisweet versions known as *amabile* or even sweeter still, *dolce*. Several large, important Tuscan firms, such as Antinori, Ruffino, and Barone Ricasoli, make dry Orvieto, and there are a number of very good, smaller Umbrian producers, including Barberani and Decugnano dei Barbi.

While the traditional white grapes of Umbria make delicious, every-night wines like Orvieto, there are also several more ambitious white wines coming from the region. The best known is Antinori's Cervaro della Sala, a rich, almost Burgundy-like blend of chardonnay and grechetto made at the family's breathtakingly beautiful, old Umbrian estate, Castello della Sala.

As for red wine, the relatively new red Orvieto (the DOC is known as Orvietano Rosso) takes the concept of blending to new heights, since some thirteen red varieties can be included, notably aleatico, cabernet franc, cabernet sauvignon, canaiolo, ciliegiolo, merlot, montepulciano, pinot noir, sangiovese, and several others, which can come from anywhere in the entire Orvieto zone. And just so that all bases are covered, the wine can also be made up entirely of any one of these (except montepulciano), as a single-varietal version.

Umbria's historic top red wines, however, are mostly made in the hills that surround Perugia. Two types in particular are considered among Umbria's best: Torgiano rosso riserva and sagrantino di Montefalco, both of which have DOCG status. Torgiano (from Torre di Giano, "tower of Janus," the Roman god of gates and the namesake of January) is a tiny village where the wine Torgiano is primarily made from sangiovese and canaiolo (as Chianti historically was). Three additional grapes are optional: trebbiano, montepulciano, and ciliegiolo.

The village and surrounding area are dominated by the family-run winery Lungarotti, founded by Giorgio Lungarotti in the 1960s. Lungarotti, a stately man, was instrumental in helping various wines in Umbria receive DOC

THE QUICK SIP ON UMBRIA

UMBRIA IS A LANDLOCKED REGION centrally located on the knee joint of the boot-shaped country.

WHILE PRODUCTION IS LIMITED compared to that of its neighbor Tuscany, Umbria produces the well-known, crisp white wine Orvieto, as well as two DOCGs: Torgiano rosso riserva and sagrantino di Montefalco.

THE MOST IMPORTANT GRAPES are the white grechetto, trebbiano, and verdello, and the red sangiovese and sagrantino.

and DOCG status, and the quality of his wines served as an inspiration to other Umbrian winemakers. Lungarotti's *museo del vino* ("wine museum"), known as "MUVIT" in the village of Torgiano, houses one of the most impressive personal collections of wine artifacts in Italy, and should not be missed by any traveler. Equally impressive is Lungarotti's Olive and Oil Museum, known as "MOO," also in

A basket of priceless, freshly harvested black truffles in Umbria.

THE EMPEROR'S WINE

Falernian was the Château Pétrus of ancient Rome—so sought after that you practically had to be the emperor of Rome to get a taste. Made from grapes grown in just three vineyards on Monte Massico, north of Naples, falernian symbolized the height of luxury and sophistication (so much so that counterfeits sprung up everywhere). It is not clear what variety of grapes were used to make the now-extinct wine. Indeed, scientists are not sure whether falernian was a white or red wine, although some writings by Pliny the Elder, and Petronius's play *Satyricon,* point to it being a white wine. The 121 B.C. vintage was so legendary that it was still being written about two hundred years after its release.

the village. Lungarotti's wines, especially the Torgiano rosso riserva called Rubesco, can be stunning and long-lived.

THE QUICK SIP ON ABRUZZI

LOCATED IN CENTRAL ITALY, Abruzzi is a somewhat isolated region along the Adriatic Sea. To the west, it is cut off from Lazio (Latium) and its capital, Rome, by the Apennine Mountains.

DESPITE VERY GOOD VITICULTURAL conditions, Abruzzi is best known for inexpensive wine, the vast majority of which is made by large cooperative wineries.

THE MOST NOTABLE WINE OF ABRUZZI is the rustic red montepulciano d'Abruzzo, made from the montepulciano grape. An often overlooked, easy-drinking, light-red style of montepulciano d'Abruzzo—cerasuolo d'Abruzzo—can also be delicious (it looks like a rosé but has a bit more oomph).

Sagrantino di Montefalco wines are quite the opposite of Torgiano wines. While most Torgiano reds have the medium weight and relative delicacy of Chianti Classicos, sagrantino di Montefalcos are inky-purple powerhouses—big, bold, gripping wines that have been compared to amarones. The wines are made from the indigenous sagrantino grape, and although the majority of examples today are dry, sweet versions made from dried grapes were far more common in the past. There aren't many producers of sagrantino di Montefalco; the top one is Adanti.

ABRUZZI

With its ample sunshine, dry climate, hilly terrain, coastal breezes off the Adriatic Sea, and high altitude (three-fourths of the vineyards are more than 2,000 feet/610 meters above sea level), Abruzzi appears to be tailor-made for vineyards. Indeed, this region in central Italy, with its nearly 80,000 acres (32,000 hectares) of vineyards, is one of the most productive in the country.

Alas, more than three-fourths of all the wine in the Abruzzi region is produced by large cooperative wineries, and a majority of that is made by the four co-ops that dominate

In Abruzzi, a grandmother picks grapes.

production: Cantina Tollo, Casal Thaulero, Casal Bordino, and Citra. These co-ops make oceans of wine labeled Abruzzi, but they also make oceans of bulk wine, some of it blended into wines from more famous neighboring regions.

The top wine here is montepulciano d'Abruzzo, made, as the name implies, from montepulciano grapes. (Note that the name of these grapes is very easily confused with the wine vino nobile de Montepulciano, which is made in Tuscany from sangiovese grapes.) Montepulciano d'Abruzzo, which is made all over the region, is usually an appealingly rustic wine, solidly built, with a soft texture and good, thick fruit flavors in the middle. Among the best wines are those labeled montepulciano d'Abruzzo Colline Teramane, a DOCG. Unfortunately, there's also a lot of characterless red made when montepulciano is grown at high yields. Let price be your guide.

A specialty here—especially suited to summer—is montepulciano d'Abruzzo cerasuolo (meaning "cherry red"). This fresh, tasty light red of montepulciano is best consumed cold and young, when its fruitiness is highlighted.

The best-known white wine of Abruzzi is trebbiano d'Abruzzo, which—with a handful of notable exceptions—usually makes a bland, dry, inexpensive quaffer meant to accompany the region's many fish dishes. The grapes behind most trebbiano d'Abruzzo were once thought to be poor-quality cousins of trebbiano Toscana, but it appears the Abruzzi trebbiano is a separate grape variety entirely. These grapes were also once thought to be the same as the neutral-tasting variety bombino bianco, but bombino, too, is now thought to be its own variety. In many cases, both varieties are part of the field blend that makes up the wine, so, in the end, the story behind trebbiano d'Abruzzo is not entirely clear.

What is clear, though, is that a tiny handful of small, artisanal producers in Abruzzi tower above all others and make extraordinary examples of these often uneventful wines. Working with small yields, and often in innovative ways, such producers have developed a cult following among Italian wine connoisseurs. Chief among them is the wine estate Valentini. The late Edoardo Valentini has been called the Angelo Gaja of Abruzzi.

THE SOUTHERN PENINSULA:
CAMPANIA, APULIA, BASILICATA, AND CALABRIA

When the ancient Greeks admiringly called Italy Oenotria, "the land of wine," they were referring specifically to the southern peninsula—the toe, heel, and ankle of the Italian boot. In this rugged, sunny, mountainous land, they found scores of fascinating grape varieties. To these they contributed some of their own, establishing an even richer foundation of viticulture. By the time of the ancient Romans, the south was a treasure trove of wines, including the wine the Romans esteemed most: falernian, a wine (reports differ on whether it was white or red) produced on the slopes of Monte Massico, in Campania.

As in Greece itself, however, this auspicious beginning never evolved into the kind of future it seemed to promise. Today, the four regions of the southern peninsula—Campania, Apulia, Basilicata, and Calabria—make many easy-drinking wines, but comparatively few high-quality, famous wines. Admittedly, these regions have historically been among Italy's

A statue of the Roman emperor Augustus stands on the limestone cliffs of Capri off the coast of Naples in Campania. Enthralled by the island's beauty, Augustus built temples, aqueducts, and private villas on the island.

poorest and most rural. The combination of poverty and a hot climate conducive to high yields has meant that quantity rather than quality has been the driving force behind the wines. Until recently, a lot of the wine here was not even bottled, but sold directly from the cask to local customers toting their own jugs.

Still, the southern peninsula can't be dismissed. Revolutions in quality have happened elsewhere, and there's at least some reason to believe one may happen here. Already, stirrings in that direction have begun, and more and more delicious southern Italian wines, especially from Campania and Apulia—many of them great values—are being exported.

CAMPANIA

Campania is certainly better known for the appealing cacophony of Naples, the beauty of the Amalfi Coast, and the cerulean blue waters of Capri than it is for wine, even though this is, along with Apulia, one of the two most exciting southern regions. While there were only three main wineries in Campania in 1970, today more than a hundred exist. Moreover, the number of grape varieties also tops one hundred, including three of the south's most impressive ancient grapes: the red aglianico and two whites—fiano and greco. All three of these important varieties thrive in the volcanic soils of Avellino, northeast of Mount

THE QUICK SIP ON THE SOUTHERN PENINSULA

CAMPANIA, APULIA, BASILICATA, and Calabria, on Italy's southern peninsula, form the toe, heel, and ankle of the Italian boot.

THESE SUNNY, LAID-BACK southern regions boast stunning coasts and imposing volcanic mountain ranges, although they remain some of the poorest and most rural regions of Italy.

MUCH OF THE WINE IN THESE REGIONS is simple and rustic, but there are also delicious and surprising wines from local varieties, including the white grapes fiano and greco di Tufo, and the red grapes aglianico and negroamaro.

Vesuvius, a still-active volcano that erupted violently in A.D. 79, destroying the nearby city of Pompeii (the remains of the city are perfectly preserved).

Preserving the three main grape varieties—often called the archaeological varieties—has been the mission of one of the south's most famous and important producers: Mastroberardino, founded in 1878 and still family run. In the late 1990s, the family, working with Italian archaeologists, developed a project to analyze the DNA from grape seeds buried in the volcanic ash and then replant the slopes of Mount Vesuvius with vineyards devoted to these ancient grape varieties, much as such vineyards might have existed in antiquity.

Aglianico, a red variety, is the basis for the south's most famous red wine, the DOCG known as Taurasi. Almost blackish in color and with fascinating bitter chocolate, leather, and tar aromas and flavors, Taurasi is also one of the only wines in the south noted for its capacity to age. Mastroberardino's sensational Taurasi, called Historia, is a dark, foreboding wine with delicious severity.

Aglianico aside, some of the most fascinating of Campania's top wines today are white. Their distinctiveness and quality result not only from the region's volcanic soils, but also from its hilly geography, which allows white varieties to be planted at higher, cooler elevations, preserving acidity in the grapes. For example, the greco di Tufos made by both Feudi di San Gregorio and Mastroberardino are bursting with freshness and are as cooling as homemade limeade. Mastroberardino's in particular (called Nova Serra) is a ballet dancer of a white—poised to spring into action, with lots of energy wrapped around a taut core.

Besides greco and the somewhat softer, less dramatic fiano, Campania is known for falanghina and coda di volpe. A mellow white wine with a hint of spice and bitter orange peel, falanghina is traditionally paired with seafood or buffalo mozzarella pizza, both local dishes. Coda di volpe (literally, "tail of the fox," a reference to the variety's elongated grape clusters, which can look like the bushy tails of

LACRYMA CHRISTI

Made primarily from the white grapes coda di volpe and verdeca and the red grapes piedirosso and aglianico, grown on the slopes of Mount Vesuvius, Lacryma Christi—"Tears of Christ"—is one of Campania's most recognized, simple, easy-drinking wines (red, white, and sparkling versions are all made). There are several stories behind the name. One says that as Jesus Christ ascended to heaven, he looked down and saw the Bay of Naples, and it was so beautiful that he cried. His tears landed on the slopes of Mount Vesuvius, where vines miraculously sprang up. Another story suggests that when Lucifer fell from heaven, Christ was sad and cried tears that landed on the slopes of Mount Vesuvius, again producing the miraculous vines. A third, far less miraculous, more pragmatic story recounts that local monks, lacking modern filtering equipment, passed the wine through canvas, causing it to fall in drops, like tears.

foxes) was once used primarily as a blending grape, but today is also used alone to make a fruity, spicy wine.

APULIA

A long, flat, sun-drenched, fertile strip of land across the Adriatic Sea from Greece, Apulia stretches from the spur of the Italian boot to its heel. For the past half decade, this region has produced more Italian wine than any other. Indeed, Apulia is so well suited to agriculture that it also produces more olive oil than any other region (almost half of Italy's total

Trulli, *the typical, conical-topped dwellings of Apulia. Made from limestone bricks stacked without mortar, the* trulli *were sometimes built over cisterns dug into the bedrock below. They were sometimes used as storehouses, but they also served as shelters for field and vineyard workers.*

production), and some of those olive trees are more than one thousand years old.

Much of the wine, alas, is basic, cheap table wine. Nonetheless, there are some very good, everyday red wines, the sort that would make perfect bargain-priced house reds. (With recent outside investments by well-known Italian producers, such as Tuscany's Antinori family, the quality of the basic table wines is rising.)

The leading grape varieties are negroamaro (based on the Latin name for black, *negro*, and probably on the Italian word for bitter, *amaro*, although some historians think *amaro* is derived from another reference to black, the Greek *maru*), malvasia nera di Brindisi, nero di Troia, and primitivo. All can be rustic and tasty. Negroamaro is the primary grape in Apulia's hot, arid, and most famous wine district, the Salento peninsula. Here it is made into the wine Salice Salentino, often one of the most popular low-priced wines on Italian restaurant wine lists, especially the dependably tasty Salice Salentino made by Taurino.

Uva di Troia (also known as nero di Troia) is the source of the robust red DOCG wine Castel del Monte Nero di Troia Riserva. (It is indigenous to Apulia, to the areas near the village of Troia, and has nothing to do with the Greek city of Troy.)

As for primitivo, it is (along with California's zinfandel) the same as the Croatian grape crljenak kaštelanski—historically known as tribidrag—and was brought from its home on the Dalmatian coast of Croatia to southern Italy. In Apulia, primitivo is made into dry and sweet wines. The dry is not unlike a light-bodied American zinfandel. The sweet primitivo is the DOCG known as primitivo di Manduria dolce naturale, a rare, sweet red (8 percent residual sugar) that can be made only in the best vintages and must be made entirely from primitivo grapes allowed to raisinate on the vine.

Finally, as a fascinating aside, because of Apulia's fertility and strategic location, dozens of groups and empires have ruled it over the past two thousand years. But the lack of ground water has been a constant limiting factor to the region's growth. That said, as of the seventeenth century, ingenious dwellings called *trulli* were constructed. Mortarless limestone huts with conical roofs, the trulli were usually built directly atop cisterns dug into the bedrock. They are still found today near the vineyards of the Itria Valley.

BASILICATA

Basilicata is the most mountainous region of southern Italy—almost half of the region is made up of the foothills and mountain peaks of the Apennines, one of the largest mountain ranges in Italy. Although the region has small coasts on the Ionian and Tyrrhenian Seas, it is, for the most part, landlocked and isolated. Overall, the region is extremely poor (it was completely deforested by the Romans two thousand years ago). Less than 5 percent of the wine here is DOC or DOCG. There is but one very important wine, the red DOCG known as aglianico del Vulture, named after Mount Vulture, an extinct local volcano on whose slopes the best grapes grow.

The aglianico grape variety is indigenous to southern Italy (there is no DNA evidence suggesting it is related to any Greek grape brought from Greece). The most highly regarded producers of aglianico del Vulture are Donato d'Angelo, Terre Degli Svevi, and Bisceglia (whose aglianico del Vulture, called Gudarrà, is an amazingly distinctive wine with the earthiness of dried porcinis).

CALABRIA

The toe of Italy's boot, Calabria, was a favorite place among ancient Greek adventurers. The arid, mountainous terrain has meant that Calabria has remained an impoverished region. While olive trees and orange orchards do well here, grape growing is a challenge. Nonetheless, some good wines are made. The most important of these is Cirò, a medium-bodied, grapey, spicy red made from the ancient variety gaglioppo. The top producer is Librandi. (Legend has it that Cirò was offered to the winners of the ancient Greek Olympics.)

Just east of Calabria's, and the country's, southernmost point is the remote seaside town of Bianco. This is the source of Calabria's other notable wine, the white wine greco di Bianco. A dessert wine made from partially dried greco grapes, it has a fascinating herbal, citrus flavor.

HOW OLD IS YOUR HOUSE?

In Basilicata, in the ancient city of Matera, the streets stacked against the hillsides are lined with cave dwellings, called *sassi*, that were part of a prehistoric troglodyte settlement, created by some of the first people to settle in Italy nine thousand years ago. The original cave dwellers ingeniously designed the caves to capture and direct the natural water channels in the rock, as water is scarce on the mountainside. These cave homes have been inhabited since they were constructed, although many people were forced out of these homes and into more modern houses by the Italian government in the 1950s (the caves were once rife with malaria). Today, you can have a drink at a café or rent a room for a night at a high-end hotel in a nine-thousand-year-old *sasso.*

SICILY AND SARDINIA

The Mediterranean's two largest islands, Sicily and Sardinia, have been the prized acquisitions of virtually every Mediterranean power in antiquity, from the Phoenicians, Byzantines, and Arabs to the Romans and Catalans. The two islands epitomize the sunny Mediterranean climate and share a long history of producing wines that range from simple and delicious to stunning.

SICILY

In terms of volume of wine produced, Sicily is one of the top regions in Italy, and it's also Italy's largest region—at 10,000 square miles

(26,000 square kilometers), it is larger than Tuscany, itself a fairly large region. Viticulture flourished here under the Greeks, and the island's wines soon became some of the most famous of the ancient world. By the time of the Roman Empire, the sweet Sicilian wine known as mamertine was highly admired by the ruling class and is said to have been the favorite wine of Julius Caesar.

In no place is the *Santa Trinità Mediterranea* —"Mediterranean Holy Trinity"—of wine, olive oil, and bread more evident than in Sicily. The island's hilly terrain, poor soil, and unfaltering sunlight are tailor-made for the production of all three Italian necessities. Moreover, Sicily's strategically located port cities have made the trading of all three relatively easy, both today and in the past.

For much of the twentieth century, Sicily suffered from the same wine mentality that handicapped Apulia, Campania, Basilicata, and Calabria—namely that quantity mattered more than quality. As in those regions, the yields in Sicilian vineyards were pushed to the limit and winemaking was haphazard at best; Sicilian wine grew predictably worse. Ironically, the island so famous for its wines in antiquity became, in the twentieth century, infamous for ultra-cheap *vino da tavola*. In the 1970s and 1980s, the decline of the reputation of Sicilian wines caused the top producers to launch a mini-revolution oriented toward quality. Today, more fascinating wines—white

The old, narrow streets of Sicily.

THE QUICK SIP ON SICILY AND SARDINIA

THROUGHOUT THEIR HISTORY, Italy's two largest islands have been conquered and claimed by numerous Mediterranean nations. Each of those countries left their stamp, creating what is today a richly diverse palette of foods and wines on each island.

MULTIPLE STYLES OF white and red wine are made on the islands, from such varied grapes as riesling, carricante, and nero d'Avola (Sicily) to cannanou, girò, and vernaccia di Oristano (Sardinia).

TWO OF THE MOST HAUNTINGLY delicious dessert wines in the world come from the tiny islands off Sicily's coast—moscato passito di Pantelleria and malvasia delle Lipari.

---

as well as red—are coming out of Sicily than ever before. The local grape variety grillo, for example, is made by top producers like Tenuta Rapitalà into dry, racy whites that detonate on the palate with spicy, peppery, exotic orange and herbal notes. Although, like grillo, the best of these local Sicilian varieties are still not widely known, many of them may eventually rank with the most distinctive and delicious wines produced in the entire country.

One of the areas generating excitement in Sicily today is Mt. Etna, a raging volcano that continues to erupt regularly. (The last series of massive eruptions, in 2012, resulted in spewing fountains of lava, some taller than the Eiffel Tower.) As improbable as it seems, in the past two decades, dozens of winemakers—Italian and foreign—have planted vineyards here, in the black lava soil on slopes that broach an astounding 45 degrees. (The vintners acknowledge the danger from eruptions, but so far the lava flows have descended on

The Piazza IX Aprile in the ancient coastal town of Taormina on Sicily's east coast. The square was named after April 9, 1860, when Mass in the nearby Taormina cathedral was interrupted to announce that Garibaldi had landed at Marsala (on the far side of the island) to begin a conquest that would ultimately make Sicily a part of Italy.

a side of the mountain not covered in vineyards.) Some of those vineyards lie at elevations greater than 3,300 feet (1,000 meters) above sea level. The sun here—as you might expect in Sicily—is bright. But what seem decidedly un-Sicilian are the cold temperatures. Indeed, Mt. Etna's chilly air and resulting late harvest (often as late as November) make the area ideal for snappy whites such as riesling and carricante, a local white grape that yields minerally, racy wines with resiny notes of fennel and citrusy notes of bergamot. In this extreme terroir, many vineyards are planted *alberello* ("little tree" or "bush") style, which is to say, without expensive trellising which, in any case, would be difficult to construct given the terrain. Graci's Etna Bianco, primarily carricante, is a fantastic example of a wine made from the variety. And the Mt. Etna white that must be tasted

for sheer exotic outrageousness is Frank Cornelissen's MunJebel Bianco, a bold, almost orange-colored wine that smells like orange-spiced tea and tastes of mangoes, spices, ash, and minerals.

Mt. Etna's reds are not for the faint of heart. They are generally based on two grapes—nerello Mascalese (which geneticists believe is a progency of sangiovese) and nerello cappuccio (parentage unknown; the name means "black hood").

Mt. Etna reds are often very delicately colored (lighter even than pinot noir). But beware; what awaits your palate is a massive onslaught of chalky, dusty dryness and the sort of bitterness that oversteeped tea possesses. (I always feel as if someone has just stuffed wet clay in my mouth.) As the Italians might say: You really need to drink them with food.

The coastal village of Naxos, the most ancient of the Greek colonies on Sicily. It was founded in 735 B.C., by a group of colonists from Chalcis (also spelled Chalkida) on Greece's Euripus Strait.

But Mt. Etna aside, Sicily generally makes good, concentrated reds based primarily on the grape variety nero d'Avola (also called Calabrese), a high-quality variety that can produce intensely black-colored wines of real depth, juiciness, and charm. Dozens of estates now focus on this variety, and some produce wines of surprising complexity and richness. Among the top producers: Feudo Principe di Butera, Tenuta Rapitalà, Abbazia Santa Anastasia, Duca di Salaparuta, Planeta, Fatascià, and the large firm Regaleali, for their nero d'Avola called Rosso del Conte.

But as good as all of these dry wines are, I have to say that two of the most wickedly delicious dessert wines in the world come from Sicily (actually, from two tiny islands off its coast)—moscato passito di Pantelleria and malvasia delle Lipari.

Moscato passito di Pantelleria is made just 37 miles (60 kilometers) off the coast of Tunisia, on the tiny (9 miles/14 kilometers long), active volcanic island of Pantelleria, a satellite island of Sicily and part of the same volcanic chain. (Pantelleria is currently sinking slightly, as the cooling magma under it deflates and degasses itself.) The Arabs, who ruled Pantelleria for four centuries (700 to 1123) and

were the first to bring grapevines here, called it *Bint al-Riyāh* ("the daughter of the winds"), a reference to the fierce, hot north African winds that rage over the island. The grapes the Arabs brought were zibibbo (from *zabib*, Arabic for "raisins"). Zibibbo is the local name for muscat of Alexandria.

Because of the ferocious winds, zibibbo on Pantelleria is trained low to the ground, small and bonsai-like, in shallow basins dug into the volcanic soil so that the vines are not ripped apart by the direct force of the winds. (A similar system is used on the windy Greek island of Santorini.)

In the sun-drenched vineyards of Pantelleria, zibibbo grapes have no trouble growing fat with sugar and being turned into ripe, effusively aromatic moscato wine. This is known simply as moscato di Pantelleria. Its more famous and complex sister—the syrupy, sensational moscato passito di Pantelleria— requires more involved winemaking and is made in minuscule quantities.

To produce it, part of the moscato is harvested when ripe, pressed, and the juice set aside, much like the grapes for the regular moscato di Pantelleria just mentioned. The remaining moscato grapes are handled as they would be for a *passito* wine; that is, the grapes are laid on mats and dried al fresco, in the sun for several weeks, until they've shriveled into supersweet raisins. Next, the sugary juice from the raisins is blended into the fresh moscato juice that was set aside, and the two are fermented together. Drinking the exquisite, neon-orange, langorous wine that results— moscato passito di Pantelleria—is tantamount to being on a roller coaster of luscious sensations. (Interestingly, Hungarian Tokaji aszú is made in a similar manner, whereby hyperconcentrated grapes—in the case of Hungary, the grapes are botrytized, not dried—are added to the juice of fresh grapes, then the whole is fermented into a sweet wine.)

The best moscatos passito di Pantelleria— both masterpieces of beauty—are Marco de Bartoli's Bukkuram (the name means "father of the vine") and Donnafugata's Ben Ryé (the name means "son of the wind").

And then there is Lipari, a chain of volcanic islands off Sicily's northeastern coast. Lipari forms part of the volcanic archipelago that straddles the gap between two other famous volcanoes—Mt. Vesuvius in Campania and Mt. Etna in Sicily. (The islands are famous for being covered in obsidian, a hard, black, volcanic glass.) This is where malvasia delle Lipari, Sicily's other stunning *passito* dessert wine, is made from malvasia di Lipari grapes (in the grape name, *di* replaces *delle*). Quantities of malvasia delle Lipari are minuscule. There are only a few small producers—notably Carlo Hauner and Lantieri. Both of their hauntingly orange-amber malvasia delle Lipari are so good, your mind hurts from tasting them.

Historically, one of Sicily's most famous wines was Marsala, a sweet fortified wine that, despite numerous cheap supermarket examples, can be extremely delicious when made by a first-rate producer. Marsala is made principally from grillo, catarratto bianco, and inzolia grapes, along with an occasional small amount of perricone, nero d'Avola, and/or nerello Mascalese. The wine takes its name from the ancient port city of Marsala, from which vineyards spread out on the plains and low hills of Sicily's Trapani province, in the far western part of the island.

Although well-regarded wines have been made in this region from classical times, Marsala as we know it today was "invented" in the 1770s by an Englishman, John Woodhouse, who predicted that the sweet and fortified wine would be an immediate hit in cold, rainy Britain, where the market for such warming wines as Port, cream Sherry, and Madeira had already proven gargantuan. Woodhouse was right; almost immediately, several large Marsala firms sprang up, and the fortunes of the city escalated. Over most of the subsequent two centuries, however, the quality of Marsala dropped to the point where it was relegated more to cooking than to collecting. In the 1980s, Marsala production experienced a small but significant turnaround, and today, high-quality Marsalas are again being made, though in minuscule amounts.

Marsala comes in three colors—*oro* ("golden"), *ambra* ("amber"), and *rubino* ("ruby"). *Rubino* is extremely rare. Each type can be made at three levels of sweetness: fairly dry (*secco*, 4 percent residual sugar), noticeably sweet (*semisecco*, 4 to 10 percent residual sugar), and very sweet (*dolce*, over 10 percent residual sugar). Each is fortified to 17 or 18 percent alcohol. Within each category, there is a hierarchy based on how long the wine is aged in oak (and sometimes in cherry wood). Fine Marsala is aged one year; *superiore* is aged two years; *superiore riserva* is aged four years; *vergine* is aged five years; and the oldest, *vergine stravecchio*, is aged ten years.

The multiple and intricate ways in which Marsala is made could easily take up a book in itself, since different production techniques are used depending on the type of Marsala being made. That said, many of the best versions are made by a method similar to the solera process of fractional blending used for Sherry (see page 458). In that process, younger wines are progressively blended with older wines, using a complex hierarchy of barrels. The least aged (and least expensive) Marsalas are those that sell the best, but the most stunning Marsalas are the *vergines* and *vergine stravecchios*, which in finesse and richness equal the best tawny Ports and oloroso Sherries. The single producer widely recognized for making a Marsala in a league of its own is Marco de Bartoli, whose Marsala is called Vecchio Samperi.

SARDINIA

Compared to the friendly, welcoming aura of Sicily's vineyards, vegetable markets, cities, hill towns, and fishing villages, Sardinia (*Sardegna* in Italian) is more remote. At 125 miles (200 kilometers) from the Italian mainland, the island is far more isolated, and its people more insular. Sardo, the local language, is a curious mix of Italian, Spanish, Basque, and Arabic. And despite the island's extensive coastline, the local inhabitants are far more likely to be descended from a long line of shepherds than from fishermen. Grazing animals is still a dominant activity on this rugged, sparse, mountainous island. Sardinians are known for their healthful lifestyle and Mediterranean diet. Indeed, Sardinia's Nuoro province is thought to have more people over the age of one hundred than anywhere else in the world.

Carignano grapes, undergoing veraison, at Agricola Punica in Sardinia.

Like Sicily, Sardinia was ruled by a succession of Mediterranean peoples, although the Spanish had more influence here than they did in Sicily. As a result, several of the grape varieties grown in Sardinia today are thought to be Spanish in origin, including cannonau (the same as Spain's garnacha), carignano (cariñena or carignan), and the ancient variety girò. Planted all over the island, cannonau is Sardinia's most important red grape.

Modern cannonau is a bold, dry, spicy red that has chaparral and dried herb flavors suggested by the parched island itself. Terrific on its own, it's also sometimes blended. Sella & Mosca's Tanca Farra—a blend of 50 percent cannonau and 50 percent cabernet sauvignon, is stellar. (The name Tanca Farra means "iron earth" in Sardinian dialect.) As for girò, it is planted mostly near Sardinia's major city Cagliari, and makes an interesting Portlike wine, though not a lot is produced. And carignano, grown in what was once known as Sulcis, in the far south of the island, makes a decent red that often has an appealing dirty, earthy flavor.

Two white wines are very much worth knowing about. First is the unusual vernaccia di Oristano, a fascinating, bone-dry, bitter-almond-like white, made in a way that allows the wine to partially oxidize so that it tastes rather like a simple Sherry. (Confusingly, Sardinia's vernaccia is not the same grape as the vernaccia of Tuscany's vernaccia di San Gimignano.) The other white is vermentino—a terrific dry white that could be any Italian wine lover's nightly house wine. No other dry white wine has a flavor that quite compares to vermentino. It's a simple wine to be sure. But the aromas and flavors mirror the dry, windswept island itself, and are evocative of wind-whipped dry brush and resinous herbs like wild rosemary, sage, and dried lavender. Add a platter of grilled Mediterranean fish dressed in pungent, fresh, extra virgin olive oil, and you're all set. Vermentino is often labeled simply vermentino di Sardegna (try the excellent one from the producer Argiolas), although those made in the area known as Gallura, in the far northern part of the island, near the neighboring island of Corsica, are labeled vermentino di Gallura.

SLOVENIA

SLOVENIA RANKS 27TH AMONG WINE PRODUCING COUNTRIES WORLDWIDE. THE SLOVENIANS DRINK AN AVERAGE OF 11 GALLONS (43 LITERS) OF WINE PER PERSON PER YEAR.

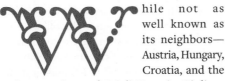 hile not as well known as its neighbors—Austria, Hungary, Croatia, and the Italian province of Friuli-Venezia Giulia—Slovenia has much in common with all of them, including similarities of climate, geography, and history and, importantly, the ability to produce phenomenal wines. This small country (half the size of Switzerland) currently ranks twenty-seventh in wine production volume worldwide, yet it's on track to become one of those old wine regions that emerges brilliantly new again.

Like many former Communist countries in Central Europe, Slovenia suffered under the political upheaval of the twentieth century. The country's fine wine industry—once centered around carefully cultivated vineyards and prestigious, historic wineries—was dismantled and neglected until little was left except cooperatives that produced cheap, low-quality wine in bulk. But like Hungary, Croatia, and the Republic of Georgia, Slovenia emerged from Communist rule with a fierce rededication to making the renowned wines of its past.

The first accounts of winemaking in Slovenia date from 500 B.C. to 400 B.C., when Celtic and Illyrian tribes here began growing grapes and making wine. From the fall of the Roman Empire, around A.D. 600, until the end of the Austro-Hungarian Empire (1918), Slovenian vineyards were mainly cultivated by monks and, as was true in

Northern Slovenian villages border Austria and the Alps. The country, at the same latitude as Piedmont, has a mixture of climates—from an alpine climate in the north to a more Mediterranean climate in the south near Slovenia's border with Italy.

Burgundy, much of the best vineyard land was under the control of monasteries. But the twentieth century brought vast changes. When the Austro-Hungarian Empire was dissolved in the aftermath of World War I, Slovenia declared independence and eventually became part of Yugoslavia. After World War II, Yugoslavia became a socialist state, and was folded into the so-called Eastern Bloc of the Soviet Union. Wine quality, which had taken a drastic dip after World War I, never recovered as Communist regulations kept production inexpensive and quality low. Revolutionary stirrings started in the 1980s, and in 1991 Slovenia gained independence through the Ten Day War with Yugoslavia. It joined the European Union in 2004, and has been on a mission to improve wine quality ever since.

Sometimes called "The Green Treasure of Europe" for its dense forests, Slovenia is the third-most-forested country in Europe, with over half of the country covered in trees. The country's climate is similar to its neighbors', with a Mediterranean influence near its border with Italy, an alpine climate on the border with Austria, and a continental zone in the middle of the country. Slovenia occupies the same band of latitude (40 to 46 degrees North) as many top winegrowing regions around the world, including Piedmont, Bordeaux, and Napa Valley, and faces similar weather challenges: spring frosts, summer drought, and, as happens occasionally in Bordeaux, devastating hail. A complex network of rivers runs across the plains and valleys of the country, supporting the vast forests and ubiquitous fruit orchards. Grapevines here

Vineyards on the limestone plateau of Kras, which extends over southwestern Slovenia and northeastern Italy.

HOW SLOVENIAN WINES ARE CLASSIFIED

Slovenian wines are classified by the ZGP (*Zaščiteno Geografsko Poreklo*), a government organization that has adopted a system similar to the European Union's. Basic table wine is labeled as *Namizno*, and the next step up, country wine, is called *Deželno PGO*. Fine wine dominates production in Slovenia—70 percent of all wine produced is classified as either *Kakovostno ZGP* (quality wine) or the highest quality designation, *Vrhunsko ZGP* (premium quality). Over Slovenia's long history of winemaking, however, unique traditional styles of wine have also developed within towns and communities. These are given the designation *Posebno Tradicionalno Poimenovanje* (PTP), and include the red wine known as teran (made from the grape refosco) from the Kras district of Primorska, and the pale red wine called cviček (made from red and white grapes including žametovka, blaufränkisch, and riesling) from the Dolenjska region of Posavje.

grow best on steep slopes above the rich and arable soil created by these river networks.

Slovenia has just over 25,000 growers, each of whom cultivates, on average, less than 2 acres (0.8 hectares) of vineyard land. (There are no current statistics on the number of brick-and-mortar wineries.) The country makes more white wine than red, and the range of grape varieties is astounding. Dozens of varieties are grown, from furmint and sauvignon blanc to cabernet sauvignon and blaufränkisch. Most of Slovenia's 40,000 acres (16,200 hectares) of vineyards fall into one of three regions: Primorska, Posavje, or Podravje.

Hugging the Italian border and the Adriatic coastline, Primorska has made the most progress in the past two decades. Forty percent of all Slovenian wine is now made here from a mix of native and international varieties, the most common of which are chardonnay, sauvignon blanc, sivi pinot (pinot gris), rebula (ribolla gialla), merlot, cabernet sauvignon, modri pinot (pinot noir), and refošk, also spelled refosko (refosco). Primorska consists of four districts, each marked by distinct geography: the Vipava Valley, Koper, Kras, and Goriška Brda. A few words on each follow.

The stunningly beautiful Vipava Valley acts as a corridor between northern Italy and Central Europe, and makes mostly white wines from the local varieties pinela and zelen. The family-owned winery Batič is located here, and the wines they make are nothing short of amazing. The family has strong philosophical and spiritual beliefs. They don't make wine when it is overcast because God can't see the wine. No one in the family has gone to viticultural

Harvest in Goriška Brda, in the region of Primorska.

THE QUICK SIP ON SLOVENIA

SLOVENIA is one of the most exciting "new" wine regions of the Old World.

SLOVENIAN WINE (and culture) has been highly influenced by its neighbors—Italy, Austria, Hungary, and Croatia—and by its position as a gateway between Central Europe and the ports of Italy.

SLOVENIA GROWS a huge variety of grapes: from furmint, sivi pinot (pinot gris), and rebula (ribolla gialla) to cabernet sauvignon, blaufränkisch, and refosko.

Zaria (a blend of pinela, zelen, and rebula) is one of the most distinctive and unusual wines of Central Europe—a profound commingling of orange zest, honeycomb, peach pits, sea salt, darjeeling tea, minerals, earth, and marmalade.

Koper, part of which hugs the Adriatic coast, is the warmest wine region in Slovenia, and produces white wines from refošk and malvazija (malvasia). The latter can be a real beauty—with spicy, peachy aromas and a wonderful minerality (try the malvazija from Vinakoper). The Kras region (also known as the Karst, or Carso in Italian), is a limestone plateau extending across the border of southwestern Slovenia and northeastern Italy. Here, the traditional wine is called teran, a dense, tannic, and acidic red wine made from refosco grapes (the grapes are known as refošk or refosko in Slovenia). Local tradition calls for teran makers to produce prosciutto (*pršut*), which is made by hanging it over the fermenting vat of teran until it, too, takes on a deep red color.

or winemaking school, in order to keep their intuitions and actions "pure" and profoundly connected to their natural environment. It may sound a bit out-there, but Batič's cloudy, orange-colored, bitter-fruity-salty wine called

The fourth region, Goriška Brda (sometimes known simply as Brda, which means hills), is Slovenia's most acclaimed wine region. Essentially an extension of Italy's Collio DOC in Friuli-Venezia Giulia, Goriška Brda is best

Family dinner in Podravje. Slovenians, like their neighbors the Italians and Austrians, live for flavor.

known for the white wine rebula, as well as for cabernet sauvignon–merlot blends. The rebula is sometimes fermented and aged on its skins in *kvevri*—large amphorae sealed closed for many months and buried underground—creating a dark, almost neon orange wine not unlike the orange wines of Georgia made in *qvevri* (spelled in that country with a *q*). The rebula-based orange wine called Amphora from the Kabaj winery is a great example. Brda is successful with numerous other grapes, too, including sauvignon blanc, sivi pinot, modri pinot, refošk, and zeleni sauvignon (Friulano). Some of the best producers in Brda include Kabaj, Movia, Edi Simčič, Marjan Simčič, and Kocijančič Zanut.

To the south and east of Primorska lies Posavje, the smallest of Slovenia's winegrowing regions. It is the only region in this white wine–dominated country to produce more red wine than white. Alas, much of this is inexpensive bulk wine. Yet the district known as Bela Krajina makes good modra frankinja (blaufränkisch) that is worth seeking out; and Dolenjska is known for a popular style of crisp, pale red wine called cviček, a blend of blaufränkisch and the local red žametovka with white grape varieties like riesling.

The largest wine region in Slovenia is Podravje, located in the northeast corner of the country and divided into seven districts. Simple white wines are produced here from laški rizling (welschriesling) and šipon (furmint), and a small amount of high-quality wine is made from renski rizling (riesling), chardonnay, sauvignon blanc, and sivi pinot. The best regions are Radgona-Kapela, Ljutomer-Ormož, and Maribor. As an aside, Maribor is home to the oldest living grapevine in the world. The vine (which was certified by Guinness World Records in 2004) is the native red variety

A winegrower in Kras.

žametovka, and is more than four hundred years old. Today, the vine produces less than a gallon of wine per year, which is bottled in one hundred tiny bottles and given to important figures around the world. Pope John Paul II and former United States President Bill Clinton both received tiny bottles of Maribor's miracle wine. Some of the best producers in Podravje are Marof, Pullus, and Črnko.

Finally, Slovenia's rich cultural heritage has been influenced by its neighbors—Italy, Austria, Hungary, and Croatia—and by its strategic position as a gateway between Central Europe and the ports of Italy. Feasts and festivals take place throughout the year, the apex being the Feasts of St. Martin, a week in November of eating, drinking, parades, and dances throughout all of Slovenia to celebrate St. Martin, the patron saint who turned water into wine.

ATLANTIC OCEAN

FRANCE

SAN
SEBASTIAN

SANTIAGO DE
COMPOSTELA

◄ RÍAS BAIXAS

BASQUE REGION ►

PYRENEES

◄ BIERZO

RIOJA ►

RIBERA DEL DUERO ▼

CAMPO
DEL BORJA ►

BARCELONA

TORO ►

PENEDÈS ►

◄ RUEDA

CALATAYUD ►

PRIORAT ►

SPAIN

MADRID ○

PORTUGAL

VALENCIA ○

CASTILLA-LA MANCHA ►

JUMILLA ►

MEDITERRANEAN
SEA

○ SEVILLE

◄ JEREZ

Strait of Gibraltar

MOROCCO

ALGERIA

CANARY ISLANDS ▼

100 km
to Africa

MOROCCO

0   100 km

SPAIN

RIOJA | RIBERA DEL DUERO | JEREZ: THE SHERRY REGION | PENEDÈS | RÍAS BAIXAS | PRIORAT

THE BASQUE REGION | BIERZO | CALATAYUD AND CAMPO DE BORJA | CASTILLA-LA MANCHA | JUMILLA | RUEDA | TORO

SPAIN RANKS THIRD AMONG WINE PRO-DUCING COUNTRIES WORLDWIDE. THE SPANISH DRINK AN AVERAGE OF 6 GALLONS (24 LITERS) OF WINE PER PERSON PER YEAR.

hen I began my career in wine, the first European country I explored was Spain (this was in the early 1970s and most of my colleagues had headed straight for Bordeaux). Like its wines, Spain itself, back then, was an enigma. Fiercely masculine, prideful, insular. As far away from the happy *ciao*-ness of Italy and the *joie de vivre* of France as any country could get. I remember going to my first bullfight, and at the end, when the bull was dead, the matador sliced off the animal's ear and threw it, bloody, into my lap. Spain was never

about emotional weakness. To this day, a sense of savagery and strength are the through-lines in many Spanish red wines.

Spain is a country of enormous history and tradition. Its former prowess is palpable.

Along the banks of the Duero River lie the vineyards of Toro in the Castilla y León area of Spain. Winemaking began here at the end of the 1st century B.C. In the 15th century, cuttings from Toro vines were some of the first brought to the Americas from Spain.

> "In Spain, no matter if you make screwdrivers, at some point after you have saved a little money, the first thing you want to do is own a winery. It is very important to the Spanish soul."
>
> — YOLANDA GARCÍA VIADERO,
> winemaker, Bodegas Valduero

When talking about making wine, Spaniards use the verb *elaborar*, to elaborate, not *fabricar*, to produce or manufacture. To elaborate something, Spain's winemakers say, implies consciousness, time, and the labor of creation and nurturance. It is different from mere production. More than at any other time in recent history, Spanish wines truly are being elaborated, and Spanish vintners have catapulted themselves to a far higher level of quality. Indeed, Spain has regained its position as one of the most exciting and vibrant gastronomic capitals of Europe. For Spanish wine (and food) a new golden age has begun.

Spain is a country in love with its bittersweet past; the land itself seems to quicken with the collective spirit of Cervantes, Ferdinand and Isabella, Goya, Franco, Picasso, El Cid, Dalí, and Saint Teresa. And so, to understand Spain you must consider history and tradition.

Spain (indeed the whole Iberian Peninsula) is thought to be one of the important early domestication sites for vines in Europe (Spanish grape varieties are genetically distinct from French and Italian varieties, leading scientists away from the theory that Spain acquired vines directly from either of those countries). Spain's first wine regions were probably established by proto-Celtic tribes who traveled out of North Africa around 2500 B.C. When the Phoenicians (seafaring groups of people—probably descended from Canaanite tribes—who occupied the coastal cities of what is today modern Lebanon) settled what would become the important southern Spanish trading port city of Cádiz in 1100 B.C., for example, they found grapevines already growing. But it was the ancient Romans who amped up the Spanish wine industry, introducing the stone *lagar* (large trough) so that significant amounts of grapes could be crushed (by foot) at the same time, yielding generous batches of wine. After the disintegration of the Roman Empire in the early fifth century, the entire Iberian Peninsula was overrun by successive tribes, especially the Visigoths. The chaos finally ended in the critical year A.D. 711, when the Moors (Muslims and Berbers of northwest Africa) advanced from the south and rapidly took over most of the peninsula. Muslim domination lasted more than seven centuries. The final defeat of the Moors at the southern village of Granada in 1492 (the same year Christopher Columbus sailed, ultimately encountering the New World) marked the beginning of Christian Spain under a single crown.

The massive bodegas in Jerez often house hundreds of thousands of barrels in which Sherry matures.

For many Spanish vintners making wine with shiny, high-tech equipment, it seems as if it was just yesterday that they were stripping down to shorts, hopping into the vats, and crushing the grapes by foot. For all of the modernization the country has experienced, Spanish winemakers continue to respect the wisdom of old ways—and the flavors that result from them.

Perhaps the biggest testament to this is the reverence accorded to indigenous varieties. While winemakers in other countries are often quick to cast off their idiosyncratic native grapes in favor of cabernet sauvignon, chardonnay, and other "global" varieties, Spanish vintners have ambitiously pursued mencía, godello, hondarrabi zuri, cariñena, verdejo, and a host of others. Spanish vintners are, quite simply, adamant about preserving their ancient lineage of grape varieties.

Another "flavor of tradition" is that imparted by long aging in barrels. Historically, Spanish reds and whites were aged in barrels longer than any other wines in the world. That could mean up to twenty-five years—a remarkable period of time. Modern tastes have changed, and Spanish wines are no longer kept nearly as long in barrels—but the flavor of, say, a Rioja *gran reserva* that has been aged in barrel for five years is still considered a thing of beauty in Spain, and indeed, around the world.

The singular image of Spain as a blisteringly hot country has given rise to the assumption that its wines must be big, coarse, and ponderous. This is patently not true in the top wine regions, where the best wines can be breathtaking in their complexity. The misunderstanding surely stems from Spain's latitude, which is farther south than much of Europe. But what many fail to realize is that the great Spanish vineyards are often at altitudes well surpassing 1,000 feet (300 meters) above sea level, where weather conditions are generally cooler. Geologically speaking, Spain is a giant rock lifted up out of the Atlantic. It is—to provide a mind-blowing vision—the second most mountainous country in Europe, after Switzerland.

According to European Economic Community statistics, Spain has more land planted with grapes than any other nation in the world—some 2.5 million acres (1 million

Spain has more land planted to vineyards than any other country in the world, and many of those vineyards are comprised of old "head trained" bush vines (not grown along a trellis). Here, the tempranillo vines of Bodega Numanthia.

hectares). It does not, however, produce the most wine. For more than a decade, Spain has ranked third in production, after Italy and France, due to the large number of old, low-yielding vines planted on extremely dry, infertile land. There are approximately 5,500 bodegas (as wineries are known) and cooperatives.

Eighty-seven different varieties of grapes exist in Spain. Surprisingly, in a country associated with red wine, the most widely planted grape by far is the white airén. Grown on the central high plains of Don Quixote's La Mancha, airén makes a snappy, crisp white that is Spain's answer to Italian pinot grigio. In contrast to simple airén, Spain's top grape varieties have even more personality. Such grapes as albariño and parellada (the white grapes of Rías Baixas and the Penedès, respectively) are revered for their regional character. But the country's best-loved and most-prized grape is decidedly tempranillo—the red grape that is the source of the legendary wines of Rioja and Ribera del Duero, plus numerous other wines made throughout the country. Tempranillo is to Spain what cabernet sauvignon is to Bordeaux or sangiovese is to Italy.

The six most important wine regions are Rioja, Ribera del Duero, Jerez (the region that produces Sherry), the Penedès, Rías Baixas, and Priorat. Following are sections on each of these regions. But there are also dozens of other smaller, fascinating wine regions, most of which are extremely old and now in the process of being revitalized. I've placed the most important of these at the end of this chapter. For an explanation of Spanish wine law, see the Appendix on Wine Laws, page 925.

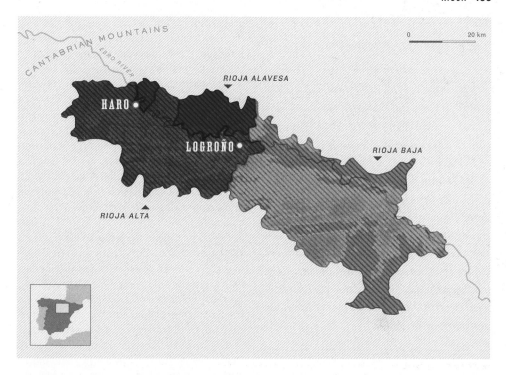

RIOJA

or more than a century, Rioja has been considered Spain's preeminent wine region. The vineyards, running for 75 miles (120 kilometers) along both banks of the Ebro River, cover more than 157,000 acres (63,500 hectares) in the remote interior of northern Spain. Behind them, craggy mountains stand in desolation. While white and rosé wines are made here, the region's fabled reputation is built almost exclusively on reds, all of which are based primarily on tempranillo grapes. Rioja is often referred to as Spain's Bordeaux, and the region's ties to France are multiple. They begin in the Middle Ages with the *camino Francés*, the French road, a route through Rioja named for French pilgrims who, with millions of other devout Europeans, walked across northern Spain to the shrine of the apostle James in

Santiago de Compostela, in the far western province of Galicia.

The signature of Rioja wines—long aging in oak barrels—was also inspired by French practice. In 1780, a Rioja winemaker named Manuel Quintano adopted the Bordelaise method of aging wine and began successfully maturing his wine in large French oak casks. Although much more expensive than stone *lagares*, oak casks transformed his wines in a way Quintano had never anticipated. By the 1850s, the Marqués de Murrieta and the Marqués de Riscal (founders of two bodegas that are still considered among the region's best producers) were both using French oak—this time, small barrels—to age their wines. Quickly, however, both Spaniards realized that the new "technology" of small oak barrels would prove more economical if they brought in oak trees from North America (a place toward which they felt a historical

THE NAME RIOJA

*T*he region of Rioja, so-called since the eleventh century, probably derived its name from the tiny Rio Oja, one of the seven tributaries of the Ebro River. A famous monastery, Santo Domingo de la Calzada, was located where the Rio Oja crossed the famous pilgrim's route, the Camino Francés. The importance of this monastery meant that countless pilgrims congregated there before continuing their walk across all of northern Spain. Thus did the area Rioja—near the Rio Oja—become one of the early destinations in Spain.

affinity) and coopered the wood themselves rather than importing French barrels.

The 1850s and 1860s were difficult times for French vintners, and the winemakers of both Rioja and the Penedès profited from the distress of their French counterparts. First oidium, a parasitic fungus, attacked French vineyards. In its wake came the fatal infestation of the insect phylloxera. To satisfy the demand for wine, French merchant/*négociants,* called *comisionados* in Spanish, traveled to Rioja. Wine sales there boomed. Within a single generation, the vineyard area in Rioja grew by 40,000 acres (16,200 hectares).

Some of the French who came to buy wine stayed and began bodegas of their own. By buying grapes (rather than wine) from small, local vineyard owners, then vinifying the grapes and aging the wine in traditional small oak barrels, the newcomers were able to create wines that tasted as close as possible to the French wines they were used to.

In 1880, with the first railroad link between the rural Rioja village of Haro and the village of Bilbao on the northern coast, Rioja wines became far easier to ship into France. Two years later, Haro got its first telephone; eight

years later, its first electric light. Haro became the nerve center of the wine community (which it remains), and Rioja wine became essential to the French market. Commerce flourished.

The party ended as the twentieth century dawned. Phylloxera crept into Rioja in 1901 and destroyed 70 percent of the vineyards. Meanwhile, the antidote—grafting native European vines onto tolerant American rootstock—had been discovered. French vintners quickly went about reestablishing their vineyards. Many of the French in Rioja returned home, and the booming market for Rioja wine collapsed.

The times ahead were Rioja's darkest. Left without a major market, the industry stagnated. A number of growers, financially destitute, simply sold their vineyards and left. World War I, and later the Spanish Civil War, the Great Depression, and World War II further impeded progress. Widespread hunger in Spain caused the government to decree that vines be torn out and vineyard land be replanted with wheat. It was not until the 1970s that Rioja began to regain its footing. Indeed, 1970, heralded as a major vintage of the century, was a turning point for the region's

THE QUICK SIP ON RIOJA

RIOJA, historically considered Spain's greatest wine region, is especially renowned for red wines made from the tempranillo grape.

IN GENERAL, Rioja's red wines are aged longer before release than most other wines in the world.

TWO STYLES OF RIOJA EXIST—so-called traditional wines aged for especially long periods, usually in used American oak barrels, and modern *alta expresión* (high expression) wines, made from riper grapes and aged for shorter periods in new French oak barrels.

Marques de Riscal, one of the oldest Rioja bodegas, was rebuilt in 2000 by world-famous architect Frank Gehry.

wine industry. Wines such as the 1970 R. López de Heredia Viña Tondonia Gran Reserva, the 1970 Faustino Gran Reserva, and the 1970 La Rioja Alta Viña Ardanza are still considered national treasures.

With the return of Spain's financial stability in the 1980s, investors turned their sights on the extraordinary wines coming out of Rioja. In half a decade, the region had more than a dozen new, well-capitalized bodegas. Many of the old bodegas modernized and expanded. By this time, the technique of aging wine for long periods of time in small oak barrels had been used for more than a century. The technique was not only ubiquitous, it had become the region's trademark.

Today in Rioja, there are two philosophies about oak, and they exist side by side. The traditionalists (whose numbers are dwindling) tend to use American oak and to cooper that oak in Spain in the traditional manner. Interestingly, traditionalists often use old barrels to mature their best wines, noting that older barrels impart a softer, gentler, less aggressive flavor. And then they leave the wine in the barrels—potentially for a very long time, as you'll see. Modernists do

the opposite—they tend to use high-impact brand-new French oak, then mature the wine in it for far shorter periods. The issue is important, for oak has an almost magical ability to transform wine, to lift it out of simple berryness and give it depth, length, complexity, and intensity (see What Oak Does, page 48). The care taken is key, since a wine kept in poor conditions for too long does not become mellow and complex but, instead, becomes dried out and thin—a shadow of its former self.

Thus, for wine drinkers today, two Riojas exist: an old world of well-aged, mellowed, earthy wines laced with faint notes of vanilla, and a new world of fruit-driven, more dramatically oaky wines in what might be called an extroverted style.

THE OLD MAN AND THE WINE

No American expatriot has loved Spain more than the novelist Ernest Hemingway (1899–1961). Although a legendary hard spirits drinker, Hemingway visited the famous old Rioja bodega Paternina every year for twenty-five years, generally with a bullfighter in tow. During his last visit, in 1959, the novelist was accompanied by the legendary bullfighter Antonio Ordóñez, who became the inspiration for *Death in the Afternoon.* In one of his best-loved works, *A Moveable Feast,* Hemingway wrote, "In Europe then we thought of wine as something as healthy and normal as food and also as a great giver of happiness and well being and delight. Drinking wine was not a snobbism nor a sign of sophistication nor a cult; it was as natural as eating and to me as necessary."

The old cellars of R. López de Heredia, one of the oldest bodegas in Rioja. Thanks in part to their long aging, the wines from the estate—both red and white—are considered quintessential examples of traditionally styled Rioja.

While the ranks of the modernists are growing, it is unlikely that Rioja's winemakers will ever fully abandon the practice of significant wood aging. Maturing a wine is almost a moral imperative for Spaniards. The sheer number of barrels in Rioja is a testimony to this; many bodegas have ten thousand or more, and the region as a whole is reported to possess just over 1.3 million barrels. And no matter the shift toward modernity, as a group, Riojas are still aged longer before release than almost any other wines in the world. While most Bordeaux and California reds are aged two years or less in oak, in Rioja, three to six years is common. As long as this is, by modern standards, it is far shorter than in the past, when the top Rioja reds were often aged at the bodega for fifteen to twenty years or more before they were sold to consumers. In an example that is almost unbelievable today but was quite common in Rioja not so many years ago, the renowned estate of Marqués de Murrieta released their 1942 *gran reserva* in 1983—forty-one years after it was made!

A word about price. Rioja's long-aged *gran reservas* remain among the best deals in the world. A supple, complex red Rioja with ten years of aging often

costs no more than a New World chardonnay made (and priced) by someone with a healthy ego. Nowhere else in the world can you drink so well, so reasonably. On the other hand, in recent years, what I'd call radically inexpensive Rioja has flowed onto the market. Most of these are *crianzas* at rock-bottom prices. Don't be tempted. The majority of these very low-end wines smell bad and taste murky. They are, I promise, not what you had in mind.

Finally, Rioja was the first region in Spain to carry the designation DOCa (*Denominación de Origen Calificada*), a status awarded it in 1991. To be granted DOCa status, a wine region must meet the highest standards in its winemaking and viticultural practices.

THE LAND, THE GRAPES, AND THE VINEYARDS

Although it is only 60 miles (97 kilometers) south of the Bay of Biscay and the northern coastal cities of San Sebastián and Bilbao, Rioja does not have a maritime climate. Several small mountain ranges

THE GRAPES OF RIOJA

WHITES

CHARDONNAY: Permissible as a blending component in white Rioja since 2007, but may not dominate the blend or constitute the entire wine. Contributes finesse.

GARNACHA BLANCA: Minor blending grape added for body.

MALVASIA: Minor blending grape added for aroma.

MATURANA BLANCA AND TURRUNTÉS: Minor grapes permitted by law but, in practice, yet to be widely used.

SAUVIGNON BLANC AND VERDEJO: Like chardonnay, these grapes are now allowed in white Rioja, but only in amounts less than 50 percent. Considered to have excellent potential as blending grapes with viura.

TEMPRANILLO BLANCO: A white mutation of tempranillo discovered in the late 1980s in the Baja district of Rioja. It shows promise in the making of snappy, lightly aromatic whites. Currently planted only in tiny amounts.

VIURA: A major grape in all Rioja white wines. It contributes aroma, mild fruit flavors, and good acidity. The same grape as macabeo in the Penedès.

REDS

GARNACHA: Important Spanish grape used to contribute juiciness and body. Known in France as grenache.

GRACIANO: An important grape for its intense color, flavor, and ability to retain acidity. Despite its qualities, it has fallen out of favor with some growers because it ripens very late. Represents less than 1 percent in most Rioja blends.

MATURANA TINTA AND MATURANO: Ancient native varieties allowed to be used in a blend. In practice, only tiny amounts are grown and available.

MAZUELO: Robust grape used in some red Riojas. Known in Priorat as cariñena and in France as carignan.

TEMPRANILLO: Major indigenous grape used in the vast majority of red Riojas. Contributes aroma, flavor, and aging potential.

---

and the outlying ridges of the Cantabrian Mountains—a spur of the Pyrenees—isolate the region from the moderating effects of the Atlantic Ocean, and they also help act as a shield, shutting out the harshest northern winds.

Although Spanish vineyards are often imagined to be at about sea level, Rioja rests on a vast plateau at an elevation of more than 1,500 feet (460 meters). The region is divided into three subregions: Rioja Alta, Rioja Alavesa, and Rioja Baja. The finest grapes come from Rioja Alta and Rioja Alavesa, which, being higher and farther north and west, toward the Atlantic, experience a cooler climate. The land then slopes downward to the warmer, lower, drier Rioja Baja, in the southeast—the only part of Rioja that experiences a more Mediterranean climate. Grapes there make wines that tend to be higher in alcohol and lower in acidity.

Three types of soil dominate: clay mixed with limestone and sandstone, iron-rich clay,

AGING REQUIREMENTS FOR RIOJA

While the law dictates the minimum length of time a Rioja must be aged, in practice many are aged for much longer.

CRIANZAS

WHITES: Must be aged for six months in oak barrels.

REDS: Must be aged for at least two years, one of which must be in oak barrels.

RESERVAS

WHITES: Must be aged for two years, six months of which must be in oak barrels.

REDS: Must be aged for at least three years, one of which must be in oak barrels.

GRAN RESERVAS

WHITES: Must be aged for four years, one year of which must be in oak barrels.

REDS: Must be aged for at least five years, two of which must be in oak barrels and the remaining three of which must be in bottles.

The old vines of Marques de Caceres are spaced far apart in the parched, infertile soil.

Alavesa and Rioja Alta. Many of these vineyards are forty years old or more. Though not very productive, old vines are treasured because their grapes usually have more concentrated flavors.

Like Bordeaux, after which they were modeled, Rioja wines have traditionally been blends of grapes. For reds, the finest grape, and the one that accounted for a lion's share of the blend, was tempranillo, a variety that originated somewhere in the province of Rioja, or in Navarra, next door. (Only one of tempranillo's parents has been identified—albillo mayor, a white grape from Ribera del Duero.)

In Rioja, three other grapes could be added to tempranillo: the native Spanish varieties garnacha (which the French call grenache), mazuelo (which the French call carignan), and graciano (the name means "graceful," but despite the quality of this grape, only minuscule amounts are now available because the grape is difficult to grow and ripens late). Today, while many Riojas continue to be blends, a growing number are made up entirely of tempranillo.

A word on tempranillo. The name of this early-ripening variety comes from *temprano* (Spanish for early). Depending on whether a

and loamy soil with alluvial silt from the Ebro. The best vineyards are planted in clay/limestone/sandstone soils found mostly in Rioja

THE WORLD'S BEST ROSÉS

French rosés may be more famous, but the best Spanish rosés *(rosados)* are usually better—lighter, fresher, less weighty, more elegant. Full of wild strawberry, ripe watermelon, and juniper berry flavors, they are like a cool shower on a hot day. Spanish rosés can be made from a number of different grapes, but most are made from either garnacha or tempranillo. Often they are made by *saignée*—*sangrado* in Spanish—the process of "bleeding" pink juice off a red wine-to-be. With the possible exception of the coastal northwest, they are made all over Spain, although many of the best known come from Rioja and Navarra. Garlicky seafood dishes and paella are especially good partners, but the wine is so delicious, all it really needs is a summer evening.

modern style or traditional style wine is being made, tempranillo grown in Rioja can either be powerfully structured, dark, and earthy, with notes of leather and a certain peatiness (the modern style), or elegant and very earthy—with an attractive dirtlike aroma—closer to pinot noir than to cabernet sauvignon (the traditional style).

Rioja is not known for its white wines (90 percent of the wine produced is red), although good basic white wines are made. These are simple, crisp, fresh wines, almost always made mainly from the grape variety viura (known as macabeo in other regions of Spain). The *New York Times* wine reporter and critic Eric Asimov may have captured white Rioja wines best when he called them "pinot grigios with a brain." Although it is rare now, one can also still occasionally come across the traditional style of white Rioja—viura that has been made in oak then aged in oak for years until it takes on a resiny, honied, waxy, oxidized character. These old-style white Riojas—today made principally by the two firms Marqués de Murietta and R. López de Heredia—can be spellbinding wines, though they are nothing if not an acquired taste.

In the past, most of Rioja's 375 or so bodegas owned no land at all, but instead bought grapes and/or wine from the region's 17,000 small growers, most of whom owned fewer than 10 acres (4 hectares) of land. Today, while the majority of bodegas still buy some grapes and wine from growers, there is a strong movement toward ownership of vineyards.

SOME OF THE BEST PRODUCERS OF RIOJA

Baron de Ley Finca Monasterio · Bodegas Artadi · Bodegas Breton · Bodegas Fernando Remirez de Ganuza · Compañía de Vinos Telmo Rodriguez · Contino · Coto de Imaz · CUNE · Finca Allende · Finca Valpiedra · La Granja Nuestra Señora de Remelluri · La Rioja Alta · Marqués de Cáceres · Marqués de Riscal · Martinez Bujanda · Muga · R. López de Heredia · Roda · Sierra Cantabria · Ysios

---

CRIANZA, RESERVA, AND GRAN RESERVA

While bodegas in Rioja are not legally obliged to use it, a hierarchy exists whereby wines are classified according to how long the wines are aged (see box page 438). The hierarchy includes *crianza* (the youngest; in Spanish the word refers to something that is raised or nursed), *reserva*, and *gran reserva*. When visiting Rioja, you might also encounter

The foods of Rioja are simple and simply prepared, reflecting the region's rural roots. Mushrooms sizzling on a grill will become a feast once bottles of earthy, complex Rioja reserva are opened and poured.

WET AND WILD

*A*lthough wild mushrooms (**setas**) *are more abundant and varied in Catalonia, they somehow seem more decadent in Rioja, where they are often each the size of a DVD, and where a glass of red wine and a huge plate of them sizzling in hot, garlicky, extra virgin olive oil is often the way a meal begins. The combination, straightforward as it is, can be magic. No wine accentuates the rich earthiness of wild mushrooms better than red Rioja, which is among the world's most beautifully earthy wines.*

very basic, very young wines known as *vinos jovenes* or *sin crianzas*. They are usually not exported.

Red *crianzas* are easy-drinking wines full of earth, spice, cherry, and vanilla. The bread-and-butter wines of every bodega, *crianzas* are generally made with grapes from good but not exceptional vineyards.

Made from superior grapes from prime sites, *reservas* are more than just simple, fruity wines, and although they are far more concentrated than *crianzas*, they are not necessarily powerhouses. In fact, just the opposite can be true. *Reservas* can be subtle, supple wines with quiet but intense echoes of earth, old saddle leather, and dried leaves. *Reservas* are made only in exceptional years.

Gran reservas, also made only in exceptional years, come from the very best vineyards of all and are extremely rare. In most years, *gran reservas* represent just 1 to 10 percent of the wines produced. In particular, white *gran reservas* are very uncommon and are now made only by a handful of bodegas. Red *gran reservas* are elegant, silky, and refined. They are aged the longest in the oldest, most neutral barrels. In fact, although five years of aging is required by law, in practice *gran reservas* may be aged far longer.

THE FOODS OF RIOJA

I f you are not vigilant, you can find yourself craving—and eating—roasted baby lamb and, if it's spring, fresh white asparagus every day in Rioja, a testimony to just how addictive these two specialties can be. Lamb and white asparagus, however, are just the beginning.

Rioja is a region of basic foodstuffs, straightforward cooking techniques, and hearty dishes. The success of any given dish is based solely on the integrity and freshness of the ingredients. Herbs and spices are rarely used. The simple homeyness of the food is beautifully in tune with the elegant, sweetly ripe flavors and silky textures of Rioja wines.

The fertile Ebro River valley is planted with a panoply of vegetables and fruits; the surrounding hills and mountains are home to goats, lambs, rabbits, quail, and large wild game. Rioja's goat cheeses are renowned. The *cabrito* (baby goat) roasted in a brick oven is to die for. And, as is true in many inland regions of Spain, the local *embutido* (charcuterie) is irresistible.

The names of many dishes include the words *a la riojana*—in the Rioja style. Generally, this means that tomatoes and fresh or dried sweet red peppers are part of the preparation. Rioja's classics include:

Chuletas al sarmiento: Lamb chops grilled over an open fire of vine shoots.

Menestra de verduras: A vegetable casserole that, depending on the season, includes artichokes, asparagus, Swiss chard, peas, carrots, leeks, or green beans tossed together with diced, cured ham and sautéed in olive oil.

Patatas a la riojana: Potatoes cooked in meat stock with spicy chorizo sausage.

Pochas a la riojana: A stew of young white beans, chorizo, peppers, and tomatoes, sometimes with roasted quail added.

Pimientos rellenos: Small, sweet local red peppers stuffed with minced meat or shrimp or puréed vegetables, then dipped in batter, fried, and cooked in a wine and tomato sauce. Sometimes cod, hake, or pig's feet are added to the stuffing.

WHEN YOU VISIT . . . RIOJA

S ome of the most impressive Rioja bodegas are a trip back in time. A century or more old, they have dark, damp cellars covered with mold and cobwebs and filled with bottles of decades-old Rioja. R. López de Heredia and Federico Paternina are good examples.

IF YOU LOVE ART or architecture, a must-visit is Marqués de Riscal. The bodega was rebuilt starting in 2000 by world-famous architect Frank Gehry (who also designed the Guggenheim Museum in Bilbao, Spain) and the bodega's soaring, rippled roof looks like giant curls of white chocolate on top of a layer cake.

IN THE CITY OF BRIONES, the bodega Dinastía Vivanco houses an impressive wine museum with permanent exhibits on the history, culture, and technology of winemaking, as well as rotating hands-on activities.

The Rioja Wines to Know

Riojas are among the most sophisticated wines of the Old World. They have a special place in my heart, for these were the wines that, at the beginning of my career, spoke to me about the *meaning* of wine. After being in and tasting Rioja, I understood that wine was the voice of a place and a culture.

WHITES

R. LÓPEZ DE HEREDIA

VIÑA TONDONIA | RESERVA

Approximately 90% viura, 10% malvasia

R. López de Heredia is one of the pillars of traditional winemaking in Rioja, and their reputation for quality is rock solid. The bodega makes both red and white Viña Tondonia (*reserva* and *gran reserva*), all of which are great classics. But I write about the white *reserva* here for, with just a few exceptions, it now stands alone as testament to a time long ago when aged white Riojas were considered jewels in the region's crown. Everything about this bone-dry wine, from the color (like wildflower honey) to the finish (extremely long), is mesmerizing. In top years, the aroma evokes fresh butter, roasted hazelnuts, candle wax, chamomile, sea salt, and sweet earth; the flavor adds a sense of exotic citrus and something at once nutty and honeyed, like baklava. And the texture, not to be dismissed, feels like ribbons of cream.

LA GRANJA NUESTRA SEÑORA DE REMELLURI

BLANCO

Approximately 25% garnacha blanca, 25% roussanne and marsanne, with 10% each of viognier, chardonnay, sauvignon blanc, and moscatel; plus small amounts petit courbut

While Remelluri's red Rioja is delicious and impeccable, the bodega's white Rioja is a contender for the most complex white wine of Spain. Made from an intriguing lineup of grapes, it's a wine of rare beauty and grace, which, when I have it, always reminds me of one of the most exquisite aged white Bordeaux (although the Remelluri costs a good deal less). The wine's aromas surge forward on wafts of candle wax, Danish pastry, sweet pineapple, dried herbs, and a resiny chaparral that smells like the Riojan countryside. The flavors follow the same complex trajectory, ending with something minerally that makes one crave a grilled fish. The estate's origins date back to the fourteenth century, when monks from the Toloño monastery founded a sanctuary and farm at the site. The modern winery was established in 1967, when Jaime Rodríguez Salís purchased the vineyards at the heart of the monastery's lands.

REDS

CUNE

IMPERIAL | RESERVA

Approximately 85% tempranillo, 10% graciano, 5% mazuelo

Founded in 1879, CUNE (the abbreviation for Compañía Vinicola del Norte de España; for ease of pronounciation, the V of Vinicola appears as a U on the label; pronounced COON-ay) makes *reservas* that perfectly demonstrate aged Rioja's delicacy. Subtle aromas and flavors of truffles, dried leaves, spices, cassis, rose petals, and old saddle leather seem to peek out from the wine. CUNE's Imperial Gran Reservas are also stunners—as complex in flavor as the best dark chocolates, with an equally hedonistic and elegant texture.

LA RIOJA ALTA

VIÑA ARDANZA | RESERVA ESPECIAL

Approximately 80% tempranillo, 20% garnacha

Viña Ardanza Reserva Especial is made only in the very greatest vintages—sometimes no more than once every ten years. The wine's refinement and superb quality are immediately apparent; indeed, the first sip of this wine is so comforting, it's akin to being wrapped up in a warm cashmere blanket. The aromas are rich and earthy—saddle leather, black truffles, and damp forest. They open up onto elegant flavors reminiscent of vanilla, plums, dark chocolate, and spiced tea, and the texture is lanolin soft.

MUGA

PRADO ENEA | GRAN RESERVA

Approximately 80% tempranillo, with 20% garnacha, mazuelo, and graciano

Dating from 1932, Muga is a highly respected family-owned bodega making some of the top traditional-style wines in Rioja. Like the best red Burgundies, these are Riojas with magnificent and complex aromas and a long finish. In the middle are sublime, if subtle, layers of earthy flavor. Prado Enea is the name of the winery's refined *gran reserva,* made only in great years and generally aged eight years, four of them in barrels that the Muga family makes themselves. The grapes for this wine come from vineyards that are among the highest in altitude in the region. In the 1990s, Muga also began making small quantities of what is now a highly sought-after modernist wine, Torre Muga. Big, muscular, concentrated, and oaky (it's aged in both American and French oak), Torre Muga is New World in style and very much the opposite of Prado Enea.

RODA

RODA I | RESERVA

100% tempranillo

The Roda bodega makes three modernist wines from among the largest selections of tempranillo clones in existence. Roda I has lovely, saturated, dramatic flavors reminiscent of dried cranberries, violets, exotic spices, licorice, and vanilla. Yet the underlying sexy earthiness of Rioja is also evident as aromas of bark, peat, cedar, and forest come alive in the glass. I especially love the blanket of cocoalike dustiness that Roda I leaves on one's palate—as if the wine were perfectly poised for the crusty, fatty edge of a grilled lamb chop. Roda I's big sister is Roda II, an even more concentrated (and more expensive) wine, and it's big *big* sister is called Cirsion, one of the most expensive and complex Riojas made.

R. LÓPEZ DE HEREDIA

VIÑA TONDONIA | GRAN RESERVA

Approximately 75% tempranillo, 15% garnacha, 10% mazuelo and graciano

The red Viña Tondonia *gran reservas* are nothing if not mindblowing for their elegance and finesse. In great vintages, drinking them is like being in that state before waking up when all sensations seem dreamlike. Both the aromas and flavors are exceedingly supple and complex, with hints of exotic spices, forests, damp mushrooms, and earth. Viña Tondonia is a quiet, refined, longaged wine, not a powerhouse (the wine is commonly aged nine to ten years in barrel, then at least another eight years in bottle before release). It's considered one of the great classic Riojas, and is renowned in Spain. The name of the wine—Tondonia—refers to a meander, or bend, along the banks of the Ebro near the bodega. Through this meander, known as Tondon (from the Latin *retondo*), ran the old medieval road that led from Rioja to the Basque country.

RIBERA DEL DUERO

 two-hour drive north of Madrid, Ribera del Duero is in the province of Castilla y León, a severe, dramatic land of rough mesas and rocky plateaus that stretch as far as the eye can see. Massive stone castles stand as fortresses atop the highest ridges. The masculine power and glory of medieval Spain is palpable.

On these high, dry, sunny plains, the vineyards, too, have a severity. Old vines, gnarled as if in agony, protrude from the rough ground. If the ground holds vines in place everywhere else in the world, in Ribera del Duero the opposite seems true. Earth herself clings to the muscular vines.

Ribera del Duero is almost exclusively a red wine region, although simple rosés are made for local consumption. The best reds are bold, concentrated, ripe, mouthfilling, structured, and packed with dark flavors reminiscent of roasted coffee, cocoa, peat, and black licorice. Yet the very best of them are also lusciously refined. Indeed, three Ribera del Duero wines—Unico (made by Vega-Sicilia), Pingus, and Pesquera—are among the most outstanding red wines anywhere in the world.

There are more than 250 wine estates in Ribera del Duero. The major grape variety, tinto fino (also known as tinta del país),

▲ *Counting sheep. In Ribera del Duero, it's a mule's lot in life.*

THE QUICK SIP ON RIBERA DEL DUERO

RIBERA DEL DUERO is the poster image of *conquistador* Spain, a land of rugged ocher mesas. All of its top wines are red and based on the grape tinto fino, the name of a group of clones of tempranillo.

THE MOST LEGENDARY and expensive red wine in Spain, Vega-Sicilia's Unico, is made here.

RIBERA DEL DUERO'S TOP WINES are concentrated, richly textured, and among the longest lived of all Spanish red wines.

centuries of adaptation, the tempranillo clones that exist in Ribera del Duero are quite different from those in Rioja. Thanks to Ribera del Duero's harsh, dramatic climate, tinto fino's smaller berries and tougher skins make wines that are often more powerful (but occasionally less polished) than Rioja.

Ribera del Duero is named for the river Duero, the third largest river on the Iberian Peninsula. The river crosses the great *meseta* (high plateau) of north central Spain, ultimately plunging down into Portugal, where it becomes the Douro (linked famously to Port wine) and finally empties into the Atlantic Ocean.

In Ribera del Duero, the river forms a 22-mile-wide (35-kilometer) valley with flat-topped mountains on either side. Vineyards, interspersed among fields of grain and sugar beets, are scattered along a 71-mile-long (115-kilometer) strip on the north and south sides of the valley. According to the region's official *Denominación de Origen* (DO), Ribera del Duero spans four districts within Castilla y León: Burgos, in the center of the DO, with the vast majority of vineyard land; Valladolid, to the west; and Segovia and Soria to the south and east, respectively.

is another name for the variety tempranillo. But, according to research by the Instituto Tecnológico Agrario de Castilla y León, there are, of course, clonal differences. After

OUNCE FOR OUNCE, MORE EXPENSIVE THAN WINE

Wine aside, perhaps the most prized agricultural product of the high plains of central Spain—especially in Castilla y León—is saffron, widely considered the most expensive spice in the world (Princesa de Minaya, considered one of the best brands of the highest grade of saffron, retails for more than $4,000 per pound). Indeed, saffron is one of Spain's most ancient crops—an indispensable seasoning (and source of vibrant color) in many classic dishes, including paella. The stigmas of the flowers of *Crocus sativus,* saffron

is harvested each fall by hand—usually by women whose fingers fly as they quickly pick the fields of delicate purple flowers and then, equally quickly (and gently), remove the three single, bright red threads that, once dried, become saffron. Between fifty thousand and seventy thousand flowers are required for one pound of saffron; amazingly, the fastest pickers harvest up to thirty thousand flowers in a day.

Besides Spain, the saffron crocus is also cultivated in Italy, Greece, Morocco, India, and Iran; the latter country now produces an estimated 90 percent of the world's saffron.

THE BODEGAS THAT SPARKED A REVOLUTION

Made in a remote and rocky part of the Duero, Vega-Sicilia is Spain's most legendary and expensive wine. Even Spanish schoolchildren know its name. While most other bodegas in Ribera del Duero were making innocuous wine throughout the 1950s, 1960s, and 1970s, Vega-Sicilia had long before embarked on making superb wine. This early commitment to quality in a region that was untested at the time—at least for fine wine—established Vega-Sicilia as an extremely serious estate. The fact that the wines were stunning only cemented the winery's reputation further. Vega-Sicilia wines would have been exceptional in most contexts, but against the backdrop of what was happening (or not happening) in Ribera del Duero for decades, they were otherworldly.

Then, in the 1970s, a second bodega, Pesquera, also began to build a reputation for remarkable wines. Pesquera is owned by Alejandro Fernández, an energetic maverick who is convinced that Ribera del Duero is potentially one of the world's best wine regions. After a full career making agricultural equipment, Fernández built Pesquera, planted vineyards, and started making what he called "masculine" wines. Tiny lot by tiny lot, he pressed the grapes in an old wooden press (used until 1982). The wines were put into barrels immediately after pressing and left to ferment and age. They were never filtered. Filtering a wine, Fernández said, was like "pushing a fat man through a keyhole." The body invariably got damaged.

Like Vega-Sicilia, Pesquera turned out to be a profoundly rich and complex wine. After both bodegas began to receive worldwide attention in the 1980s, new capital—and new talent—flooded into Ribera del Duero. Among the most influential winemakers to come in was the Danish-born, Bordeaux-trained winemaker Peter Sisseck. Hired first as a consultant in Ribera del Duero, Sisseck was so impressed by the region and its potential that he founded his own winery—Dominio de Pingus—in 1995. Pingus has gone on to be one of the stars of Spain, and a wine that, along with its "little" sister, Flor de Pingus, is frequently named as one of the most extraordinary wines in the world.

A new era for Ribera del Duero was born.

During much of the Middle Ages, Castilla was the battleground on which the Catholic kings fought the Moors, the Islamic conquerors who invaded Spain in 711. The stark, ponderous fortresses and castles along the Duero date from this time. Although grapes were grown throughout the upheavals, it was not until Spain was completely reconquered by the Catholic monarchs in the fifteenth century that Ribera del Duero, free of political conflict, could come into its own as a wine region. The city of Valladolid became the capital of Spain; Ferdinand and Isabella were married there in the late fifteenth century.

From the beginning of the twentieth century until the 1980s, Ribera del Duero was a wine region known primarily for cheap, gruff reds churned out by cooperatives that had been built with government subsidies after the 1950s. Mediocrity reigned. Most wines, even as late as 1970, were made in unclean barrels and left unattended to ferment at will. The wines were seldom racked off their lees, never filtered, and rarely bottled commercially. Customers simply arrived at the bodega with reusable containers and bought what they needed directly from the barrel.

Ribera del Duero reservas are made only in exceptional years and are aged at least three years before release.

As many drinkers of Ribera del Duero wines know, the main grape variety is, somewhat confusingly, called both tinta del país and tinto fino. Why? Historically, locals referred to these simple wines (and the grapes they were made from) as tinta del país—"red [wine] of the land." As time went on and higher-quality wines were made in Ribera del Duero, the term tinto fino—"fine red"—was increasingly used to describe both the wines and the grapes.

An enormous turnaround came in the 1980s. The success of two exceptional wineries, Vega-Sicilia and Pesquera, inspired an influx of capital and technical skill, plus a new passion for quality. By the mid-1990s, the wines coming out of the region were so shockingly good that some Spanish wine lovers suggested Ribera del Duero—rather than Rioja—might just be the finest wine region in Spain.

Today, the region contains some of Spain's most successful wineries—from the historic Vega-Sicilia, to lauded avant-garde estates such as Pingus, Abadía Retuerta, Alion, and Mauro. Indeed, these five estates, all lined up along Castilla's N22 highway, form Spanish wine country's so-called *milla de oro*, golden mile.

THE LAND, THE GRAPES, AND THE VINEYARDS

Despite its gentle-sounding name, Ribera del Duero is a region of harsh intensity; bodega owners call it the land of extremes. Sunlight—2,400 hours of it per year—is intense; rainfall is modest. Summers are blistering, with temperatures often exceeding 100°F (38°C). Winters are fiercely cold, sometimes reaching –20°F (–29°C). On any given day during the grapes' ripening cycle, the diurnal temperature fluctuation is dramatic—from scorchingly hot in the afternoon to cold at night. Grapes love this, for hot daytime temperatures allow the grapes to ripen at full speed, while cold nights temporarily shut down photosynthesis, letting the vine rest and preserving acidity.

Except for the bodegas built since the late 1980s, the landscape here seems unchanged by passing centuries. For much of the year Ribera del Duero is a brown, almost desolate place. Above ground, dirt fields stretch endlessly, hiding crops of sugar beets below. Villages appear subdued and turned inward, away from travelers. In some parts of the region, the only signs of life come from the omnipresent flocks of long-legged, black-eared Churra sheep crossing the road, bringing drivers to a dead halt no matter how late that driver might be for a winery appointment.

There are approximately 52,000 acres (21,000 hectares) of vines in Ribera del Duero—a modest amount compared, say, to Rioja, which has just over 157,000 acres (63,500

THE GRAPES OF RIBERA DEL DUERO

Ribera del Duero is planted almost exclusively with red grape varieties. The lone white variety, albillo mayor, is planted in tiny amounts and is not commercially significant. That said, albillo mayor does have a claim to fame: It is known to be one of the parents of tempranillo.

CABERNET SAUVIGNON: Makes up just 1 percent of the grapes planted in Ribera del Duero—and virtually all of that by the bodega Vega-Sicilia. The bodega also has minuscule plantings of merlot and malbec.

GARNACHA: A minor grape in this region, made into locally consumed, inexpensive rosés.

TINTO FINO: A major grape variety used almost exclusively in virtually all red wines. Also known locally as tinta del país. While the variety is the same as tempranillo, the clones that make up tinto fino are different from the clones of tempranillo that grow in Rioja and elsewhere in Spain.

hectares). And thanks to the number of old vines, yields tend to be very low (about 1.6 tons to the acre).

Then there are the vines themselves, which seem imbued with a life force all their own. Planted on Spain's grand high plateau, known as the *meseta*, 2,500 to 2,800 feet (760 to 850 meters) above sea level, the vines look like small, stunted arms protruding no more than a foot or two out of the earth. Most are still planted in the traditional manner, without posts, wires, or trellising of any sort. Many vines are thirty to fifty years old or more and thus produce grapes with concentrated flavor.

There are two general types of soil. Nearest the Duero River and its small tributaries, the soils are composed of sandy sediments, marl, and ancient riverbed stones. The higher vineyards—which are considered some of the best—are on slopes (known as *laderas*) above the riverbeds and contain more limestone and clay.

As for the Duero River itself, although it is neither wide nor deep nor particularly grand (at least as it flows through Ribera del Duero), it does help temper the region's dry, harsh climate. The river adds moisture to the air, and in summer the riverbanks buffer the hot, dry

winds that sweep through the valley. In fall and spring the river's stabilizing warmth helps protect against frost.

In Ribera del Duero, tinto fino accounts for the lion's share of all plantings, and all the top wines are made almost entirely from it.

Ribera del Duero is called a land of extremes. Old gnarled vines endure freezing cold winters and blistering summers.

Ribera del Duero is a vast agricultural area which, besides producing wine, is devoted to raising sheep. Spanish sheep have a particular talent for torpidly crossing the road when you're trying to get someplace fast.

WHEN YOU VISIT . . . RIBERA DEL DUERO

MOST TOURS OF BODEGAS in Ribera del Duero are in Spanish; to tour in English, it's important to make an appointment in advance. (Note that it's difficult to arrange a tour of Vega-Sicilia or Pesquera unless you have business with those bodegas; both are closed to the public.)

ALL OVER RIBERA DEL DUERO are little *asadores*—simple, tavernlike roast houses where roast baby lamb and roast suckling pig are not only specialties but are often the only things (besides a country salad) on the menu. You can't make reservations at such places . . . you just walk in. Any bodega will have a list of their favorites, so ask for recommendations.

SOME OF THE BEST PRODUCERS OF RIBERA DEL DUERO

Aalto • Abadía Retuerta • Alejandro Fernández/Pesquera • Alion • Alonso del Yerro • Arzuaga • Astrales • Condado de Haza • Dominio de Pingus • Emilio Moro • Ismael Arroyo • Legaris • Mauro • O. Fournier • Penalba Herraiz/Carravid • Pérez Pascuas/Viña Pedrosa • Protos • Reyes • Valdubón • Vega-Sicilia

CRIANZA, RESERVA, AND GRAN RESERVA

As is true in Rioja, Ribera del Duero wines can be classified according to the quality of the grapes and how long the wines are aged. I say "can be" because some modern producers choose not to

VEGA-SICILIA

Today, Vega-Sicilia, Ribera del Duero's most legendary estate is owned by the Alvarez family. (The name is a mystery. *Vega* is the word for the green part of a riverbank. *Sicilia* evolved from St. Cecilia and is not, as is commonly thought, a reference to the Italian island of Sicily.)

Vega-Sicilia's vineyards were first planted in 1864 by Don Eloy Lecanda, a winemaker who had studied in Bordeaux and returned to Castilla bringing eighteen thousand vine cuttings of cabernet sauvignon, merlot, malbec, and pinot noir with him. These grapes were combined with tinto fino to become the first Vega-Sicilia wines. Today, about 80 percent of Vega-Sicilia's 617 acres (250 hectares) of vineyards are planted with tinto fino, and the remainder with cabernet sauvignon, merlot, and malbec. Many of the vines are more than a century old.

Vega-Sicilia makes three wines: Valbuena 5, so named because it is sold after five years of aging; the very prestigious Reserva Especial (a blend of vintages); and the utterly rare Unico (Spanish for unique). Unico is aged in a succession of large and small oak barrels until the winemaker feels it is perfectly ready to drink, which, as it happens, is rarely in less than ten years and not according to any regular marketing schedule. Amazingly, the bodega released both its 1982 and 1968 Unicos in the same year—1991. That's after nine and twenty-three years of aging, respectively. This practice makes Unico one of the world's longest-aged reds before release. Among Unico's best customers are King Juan Carlos of Spain and England's Prince Charles, along with collectors around the world.

---

use the designations. For those that do, wines fall into the categories *crianza, reserva,* and *gran reserva.* (In Ribera del Duero itself, you might also come across simple, grapey wines known as *tintos joven*—young reds—but these are almost never exported.)

Crianzas are good, easy-drinking wines with cherry pie, spice, earth, and vanilla flavors and aromas. These wines generally come from good but not exceptional vineyards.

> In Ribera del Duero, old vines, gnarled as if in agony, protrude from the rough ground. If the ground holds vines in place everywhere else in the world, here, the opposite seems true. The earth herself clings to the muscular vines.

Made from superior grapes grown at better sites, *reservas* have a fuller, fleshier texture and greater overall depth, concentration, and intensity. Coming from the very best vineyards, *gran reservas* are the most polished and refined wines of all. *Reservas* and *gran reservas* are usually made only in above-average years. They represent just a small percentage of all the wine made in the region.

Here's what the categories mean:

CRIANZA: Aged a minimum of two years, at least one of which must be in oak barrels; the year starts October 1.

RESERVA: Aged a minimum of three years, at least one of which must be in oak barrels; the year starts December 1.

GRAN RESERVA: Wines of outstanding quality, made in select vintage years only. Aged

Lechazo—baby lamb cooked slowly in a wood-fired oven until the tender meat falls off the bone—is the quintessential meal in Ribera del Duero. An exercise in carnivorousness, the meat is accompanied by nothing but a little salad and a lot of tinto fino.

a minimum of five years, at least two of which must be in oak barrels; the year starts December 1.

THE FOODS OF RIBERA DEL DUERO

The legendary dish of Ribera del Duero is *lechazo*, a baby lamb fed only mother's milk and weighing less than 15 pounds (7 kilograms). In fact, *lechazo* is sometimes the only dish served in the best *asadores*—simple, tavernlike roast houses—which can be found throughout the region. The heavenly aroma of roast baby lamb can be smelled several blocks away from an *asador*, and it is hard to pass up.

The chef of each *asador*, who is usually also the owner, buys his lamb directly from shepherds, and butchers it himself. He seasons it with only a sprinkle of salt and pepper, then slowly roasts it in a *cuenco* (a ceramic roasting dish) over a hardwood fire in an old brick oven until the meat is seared crackling crisp on the outside and so meltingly tender on the inside that it falls off the bone.

Eating *lechazo* is an experience in pure carnivorousness. In rustic *asadores*, nothing is served with the central attraction except a sharp knife and a fork, a bottle or carafe of Ribera del Duero, and a small salad of lettuce and tomatoes. At slightly more upscale *asadores*, you might begin with a plate of garlicky grilled *setas* (wild mushrooms) or grilled *morcilla* (blood sausage stuffed with rice). Finally, there will be páramo de Guzmán, an artisanal cheese made from the milk of a special breed of Churra sheep, and *cuajada*, creamy, tangy sheep's milk yogurt served in an earthenware jar. Into the yogurt, you spoon the local honey.

The Ribera del Duero Wines to Know

Ribera del Duero is old, masculine Spain. If you close your eyes for a moment when you are there, you could be back in the sixteenth century: *conquistadores*; fortresses; walled cities. Today the wines bring us back, for the region's intense climate means that only earthy, powerful reds are made.

ALEJANDRO FERNÁNDEZ PESQUERA

RESERVA

100% tinto fino

Alejandro Fernández likes bold, masculine wines with lots of personality—a sure description of Pesquera Reserva. The wine explodes onto the palate with incredible blueberry and violet flavors, only to be replaced seconds later by a surge of bitter chocolate and espresso. As with all of the top Ribera del Dueros, there's a sexy sense of dirt and darkness here, and a long mineral-streaked finish.

O. FOURNIER

ALFA SPIGA

100% tinto fino

Alfa Spiga is a powerhouse—a rugged, meaty, dark wine that seems to embody Ribera del Duero's massive, gnarled vines themselves. The first to pull you in are the anything-but-dainty aromas—peat bog, coffee grounds, Scotch, wet bark. From there, the wine swallows you in a wave of intense black fruit flavor. It is massively structured, with a huge thrust of tannin—all the more reminder that Ribera del Duero wines can seem unyielding until you bring out the roast lamb.

DOMINIO DE PINGUS

100% tinto fino

Few wines broach the sheer power of this one. Pingus is, in a word, monolithic. When it's young, a curtain of tannin and oak often shroud the wine's beautiful core of complex, deep, cherry-laced fruit. But with time, the power and heaviness lift and notes of tobacco, leather, and minerals begin to emerge, giving the wine a more nuanced character, and allowing it to achieve a sense of harmony. Pingus is not for the faint of heart. Nor for those who require immediate gratification. *That* wine would be Flor de Pingus, theoretically Pingus's baby sister, but a wild tempest of a wine with amazing purity and vividness, a deep, concentrated core of fruit, and the hedonic texture of crushed velvet.

PÉREZ PASCUAS

VIÑA PEDROSA | RESERVA

100% tinto fino

Viña Pedrosa has always been a signature wine of Ribera del Duero. It's not as thick and Portlike as many of its brothers here, but it is a wonderfully sensual, harmonious wine packed with all those aromas and flavors that *sound* bad, yet taste really good (animal fur, manure, sweat, worn leather, gaminess). The first time I had this wine in Spain, I was eating a long-simmered, savory meat stew, and the two will always be entwined in my memory.

ABADIA RETUERTA

SARDÓN DE DUERO | PAGO NEGRALADA

100% tempranillo

Although technically just outside the region, Abadía Retuerta is nonetheless usually thought of as a bodega in Ribera del Duero—and not just any bodega, but one of the largest, most elaborate and expensive. The 500-acre (200-hectare) estate includes the twelfth century *abadía* (abbey) Santa Maria de Retuerta and now holds a luxury hotel plus a state-of-the-art winery. Famous Bordeaux winemaker Pascal Delbeck, who also makes the wines at Château Ausone, is the winemaker. Pago Negralada, the bodega's top wine, is utterly hedonistic and silky, packed with the aromas and flavors of cocoa, licorice, strawberries, dried figs, leather, and sweet pipe tobacco.

VEGA-SICILIA

UNICO

Mostly tinto fino with a small amount of cabernet sauvignon

It has been said of Unico that the more masculine vintages have the structure and depth of great Bordeaux and the more feminine vintages have the elegance and perfume of great Burgundy. Indeed, year after year, Vega-Sicilia produces exquisite wines with immaculate balance—wines that possess both finesse and raw power. Among the bodega's wines, Unico, from the estate's oldest vines, has a special appeal. A few years ago, in a vertical tasting going back to 1948, I was so stunned by the aliveness of the wines that I had the rather strange, out-of-body feeling that I was not drinking the wine—it was drinking me.

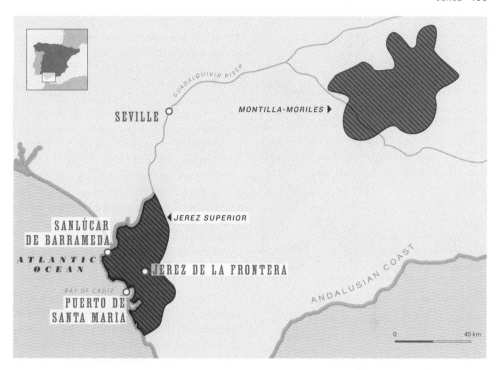

JEREZ
THE SHERRY REGION

he three words Jerez, Xérès, and Sherry that appear on every bottle of Sherry are a reflection of the diverse names for Spain's most spellbinding and fascinating fortified wine. Sherry is the English word, and Xérès the original Phoenician one, for the wines made in the Spanish wine region of Jerez. But no matter what you call it, if there were justice in the wine cosmos, Sherry would be one of the world's best-loved and oft-sipped wines. As it stands, Sherry—the unsung hero of five great wine classics (Sherry, Port, Madeira, Champagne, and Tokaji)—is largely misunderstood and underappreciated (at least in our time). That it is sometimes cast as the libation

of little old ladies is nothing if not amusing. Sherry, after all, is the daily drink of southern Spanish men—known for their machismo, love of bullfights, and prowess at horse racing, not to mention their predilection for bars and cigars.

As a fortified wine, Sherry's alcoholic strength has been raised to between 15 and 22 percent. (A standard table wine is usually 12 to 15 percent alcohol.) In addition to being fortified, Sherries are also given slow, careful, and systematic exposure to oxygen—the degree of which varies depending on the style of Sherry being made. But fortification and controlled oxidation do not begin to tell the whole hauntingly delicious and complex story of Sherry. No other wine in the world lights up the senses

Drying Pedro Ximénez grapes in the brilliant sunlight of Sherry country.

and the brain in the same way. Indeed, nowhere else in the world are so many radically different styles of wine made from the same grape variety. Much more on this to come.

Although vineyards and beaches would seem to make strange bedfellows, Sherry comes from a small wedge of land along the sea in southwest Spain, in the province of Andalusia. This is the Spain of a 1960s movie—a land of gypsies and heel-pounding flamenco dancers, guitars and prized horses, whitewashed villages, and perhaps the world's most mouthwatering array of shellfish. It was from these stark, chalky-white shores that Columbus began his westward sail. If he brought wine with him (and history suggests he did), Sherry was the first European wine drunk in America.

THE LAND, THE GRAPES, AND THE VINEYARDS

Sherry comes from an eerie, barren moonscape of blinding whiteness along Spain's southwestern Andalusian coast. The vineyards spread in triangular fashion from an inland point north of the charming town of Jerez de la Frontera to the small maritime towns of Puerto de Santa María, on the Bay of Cádiz, and Sanlúcar de Barrameda, on the Atlantic shore at the mouth of the Guadalquivir River.

The best vineyards lie in the heart of this triangle, a region designated as Jerez Superior by Sherry's Consejo Regulador, or governing body. Sherry's Consejo—legally constituted in 1935—was the first in Spain, and Sherry was the first DO, awarded that designation two years earlier, in 1933, by the national government. Within the Jerez Superior region, the vineyards of highest regard roll like waves over gentle hillocks. Looking at them, I am always reminded of the rippling landscape of the ocean floor. On these beautifully smooth and curved hills, the verdant vines glisten like emeralds in the glaring summer sun.

Millennia ago, the Sherry region was covered by a vast sea. Thus, not surprisingly today, the best soil type—usually found on the tops of the hillocks—is composed of the remnants of marine sediments mixed with chalky calcium

THE QUICK SIP ON SHERRY

AS CHAMPAGNE is in France or Port is in Portugal, Sherry is Spain's most complex and labor-intensive wine. The immense difficulty of producing this handcrafted wine has earned it its reputation as one of the world's most spellbinding wines.

SHERRY IS MADE in multiple styles. These range from hauntingly bone-dry to gorgeously sweet.

SHERRY COUNTRY is also one of Spain's most thrilling food regions and the place where the small dishes known as tapas were first created. Sherry is their quintessential accompaniment.

THE GRAPES OF SHERRY

Jerez is planted exclusively with white grape varieties.

MOSCATEL: Today, a relatively rare grape made into a wine on its own and used as a sweet blending wine.

PALOMINO: More correctly known as Palomino fino. Major grape for all styles of Sherry.

PEDRO XIMÉNEZ: A rare grape, picked and dried on mats in the sun to make the sensational dessert Sherry also called Pedro Ximénez.

carbonates (including limestone) and pre-historic sea fossils. Called *albariza,* the soil is stark white, crumbly, light as cake mix, and has very good water-holding capacity. The latter helps the vines endure southern Spain's long, often drought-ridden summers. In addition, since *albariza* soils tend to be the highest in elevation, vines planted in *albariza* tend to catch sea breezes—a boon for preserving acidity in the grapes. Less prized than *albariza* is *arena,* sand, often right beside the coast, and *barro,* a low-lying, brownish, more fertile clay where, today, mostly sugar beets and corn are planted.

The most widely planted grape in Jerez is Palomino fino (known simply as Palomino); 95 percent of Sherry is made from it. The name Palomino refers not to horses (as might be expected) but to Fernán Yáñez Palomino, a thirteenth-century knight to King Alfonso X. One of the least acidic grapes in the world, Palomino is also extremely high-yielding. Growers can easily reap the legal limit of 8,476 pounds per acre (9,500 kilos per hectare).

Even the bunches themselves are huge; a cluster of Palomino is equal in size to four or five bunches of Napa Valley cabernet sauvignon.

In terms of aroma, flavor, and character, Palomino won't turn any heads. As it happens, however, that very neutrality is sought. With a relatively simple grape as a blank canvas, a Sherry's individuality comes from the *albariza* soil in which its grapes are grown and the solera in which it is made. (More on the solera concept in a moment.)

Finally, completing the grape list, there are two other grapes—both white—found in Jerez. Both account for less and less acreage as time goes on, but both can make stunning wines. The first, moscatel bianco (muscat of Alexandria), is used to make a sweet wine for blending and, occasionally, a fantastic dessert wine on its own. Second, Pedro Ximénez (PEY-dro he-MEN-ez), or "PX," as it is known, is a local Andalusian variety used to make the style of sweet Sherry called Pedro Ximénez. This is a wine that any card-carrying wine lover *must* try, for it is one of the most sensual wine experiences to be had.

HOW SHERRY GOT ITS NAME

The name **Sherry** *has a long pedigree. The Greeks called the region Xera, the Romans, Ceret. By the early Middle Ages the Arabs called the region Sekeris, and northern Spanish Castilians called it Xérès, and later Xérèz. By the late nineteenth century, Xérèz had become Jerez, and the town that marked the frontier between the Arabs and the northern Spanish was called Jerez de la Frontera. The Spanish pronunciation of Jerez (hare-ETH) was corrupted by British importers of the wine, who pronounced it JER-rez, then JER-ee, and finally Sherry.*

TAPAS

No food is more associated with Sherry—and with southern Spain—than tapas. The little nibbles are thought to have originated in Andalusian bars in the late nineteenth century. Originally complimentary, they were served in the late morning, after breakfast coffee, but before lunch. Each nibble would be served on a small saucer, which would be placed atop one's mid-morning glass of Sherry, conveniently keeping the flies out. As the custom evolved, bar owners found tapas were a way to entice their patrons to stay longer and eat and drink more. And so they would; lunch after all, at least in this part of Spain, isn't usually served until 3:00 P.M.—a long time to wait for sustenance. The word *tapas* is derived from the verb *tapar,* which translates as "to cover." Today, tapas are rarely on the house, and the thousands of types range from simple to elaborate, with each small southern Spanish village claiming its own tapas specialty.

A glass of PX looks, for all the world, like a glass of molasses, and the wine—dense, syrupy, and dark mahogany in color—is the very epitome of artisanal creativity, opulence, and refined sweetness (at 44 percent, 440 grams per liter, residual sugar!).

HOW SHERRY IS MADE

Before I go into the specific wine-making processes by which Sherry is made and aged, it's important to know that Sherry is not a single entity, but rather seven distinct styles of wine, each of which is extremely individual. At one end of the spectrum are the manzanillas and finos, with their tangy, crisp, green earthiness; in the middle are the amontillados, palo cortados, and olorosos, with their lusty, roasted, nutty flavors; and finally come the creams, with their sweet, lush toffee, and fig flavors. None of these Sherry flavors, textures, and aromas ever quite falls into what we might think of as the galaxy of white or red wine. The flavor of Sherry is a world unto itself.

This is because of the unique way in which Sherry is progressively blended and aged in a complex network of old barrels, called a solera. Depending on how and the rate at which the wine moves through the solera, the different styles of Sherry can be made.

HOW THE SOLERA WORKS

The first important fact to know is that each style of Sherry has its own separate solera. What is a solera and how does the solera system work? The process, at its most simplistic, goes like this: Palomino grapes are picked early (often in August) when the grapes are just ripe (about 12 percent alcohol, potentially), but not overripe. They are then crushed, and the juice is fermented—usually in stainless-steel tanks—very much the way any other white wine might be made. At this point the wine is lightly fortified with grape spirits (fino will be fortified just a little; the fuller styles, like oloroso, will be fortified slightly more).

The fortified wine is then poured into barrels and set aside for six months to a year to develop a bit of initial complexity. This initial period in the wine's life is called the *sobretable*. When it is finished, the wine will enter the solera, where it will be progressively blended and aged until it eventually emerges as Sherry.

To form the solera, multiple rows of old 600-liter (160-gallon) American oak barrels, called *botas,* are lined up. Often these rows are stacked one row on top of the other, like children's building blocks. Generally the stack will be four or five rows of barrels high, but the solera may contain as many as fourteen rows of barrels. (In the case of fourteen rows, the barrels would not all be stacked one on top of the other, or the bottom barrels would burst from the weight.) Even at five barrels high, a solera is an impressive sight.

The barrels on the bottom row contain the oldest Sherry; from these barrels small amounts (known as the *saca*) will be drawn off and bottled when the Sherry is deemed ready—and usually only when an order is placed. This row is also called the solera row (from *suelo,* Spanish for "floor"). Each time Sherry is drawn off from the bottom row, bottled, and sent to market, the barrel is replenished with an equal quantity of wine from a barrel in the row above it. That row, second from the bottom, is called *criadera* #1, or the first nursery. It contains the second-oldest wine. When wine from *criadera* #1 is drawn off, it, in turn, is replenished with wine from a barrel in the row above it,

called *criadera* #2. *Criadera* #2 will be replenished with wine from the row above it, *criadera* #3, and so on. Thus, a tiny amount of wine is slowly, constantly being drawn off and added to older wine, moving progressively down through lower and lower barrels. (Some styles of Sherry are moved more slowly through the solera than others—a key factor in their final flavors.) At the very top, the solera is fed with the wine of the current year after it has undergone the initial *sobretable* period. The process of moving the wines from one *criadera* to the next has a lovely name—*rocíos.* The word means "morning dew" and is a reflection of how gently the wine must be handled when it is moved between *criaderas.*

Each bottle of Sherry is thus a complex molecular kaleidoscope of what can only be an estimated age. As a result of this constant fractional blending of younger wines into older wines, Sherry is not the product of any one year. By law, it never carries a vintage date, although it is not uncommon for a Sherry label to designate the year the solera was formed. Also by law, only 30 percent of a solera can be drawn off for bottling each year.

MONTILLA-MORILES

East and north of Jerez is the wine region Montilla-Moriles, near the old Moorish capital, Córdoba. Here, under the blazing summer sun, Pedro Ximénez grapes achieve such sugar-loaded ripeness that they easily result in wines that are 15.5 percent alcohol naturally, before (optional) fortification. Montillas are not technically Sherries, but like them, they develop flor, are aged in a solera, and are made in such similar styles as fino, amontillado, and so forth. Unlike Sherry, however, the naturally higher alcohol means that Montilla wines often do not have to be fortified with grape spirits. Even today, some Montillas are still fermented in tall clay vessels called *tinajas.*

The best producers of Montilla are the legendary bodegas Alvear, established in 1729, and Toro Albalá, founded in 1844. In particular, Alvear's fino seems to embody the intense and vibrant pulse of southern Spain, with its bursting flavors of lemon, chalk, olives, pepper, spices, almond cake, and roasted nuts. As for Toro Albalá's Pedro Ximénez, the English language does not possess sufficient descriptors. The black, oozy wine is one of the most surreal, luscious experiences any taster could ever have.

BARRELS—BLACK AND BROODING

Walking out of the cracklingly bright outdoor sunlight of southern Spain into the shadowy, dark interior of a Sherry bodega is an awesome experience. Often called cathedrals because of their unreal stillness and impressive size, Sherry bodegas are filled with large, imposing black barrels that sit like silent bulls in the dim light. A typical bodega might have a hundred thousand such casks (known as *botas,* or butts). Made from American oak, each is about three times the size of a standard Bordeaux barrel, and holds about 160 gallons (600 liters) of wine. The barrels are always painted with a water-based, jet-black matte paint, giving them a powerful, dramatic appearance. And why black? The answers most commonly given in Jerez are that: 1) the black paint discourages insects from nibbling on the wood, 2) the black paint keeps the sun from penetrating the wood and spoiling the wine, 3) because barrels are never thrown away in Jerez (many of those currently in use are 150 to 200 years old), they often look ragtag from years of being repaired; painting hides imperfections and makes the barrels look neat and uniform, and 4) any leakage could be easily detected because it would appear shiny against the matte black paint.

The labyrinthine solera process is especially remarkable because it is impossible to determine just how old a Sherry is when it finally emerges from the bottom row. The reason is twofold. First, once the solera is set up, the barrels are never completely emptied. Currently, Sherry barrels are, on average, one hundred years old, and many bodegas have barrels that average two hundred years old. Second, the small amount of wine drawn off and added to the wine in the barrel below is not stirred into that wine. The wine is therefore not fully homogenized. Each barrel will contain molecules of wine that were never drawn off, and thus date from when the solera was begun, as much as two centuries earlier.

For Sherry to become Sherry requires more than simply the physical movement of wine through a solera, however. Why does fino become fino and oloroso become oloroso? That metamorphosis is fairly well understood today. For most of history, however, Sherry was inexplicably supernatural.

MAKING FINO AND MANZANILLA— THE MAGIC OF FLOR

Each style of Sherry is ineluctably tied to the presence or absence of flor—a foamy, waxy film of yellow-white yeasts that appears on the surface of some styles of Sherry. (The word *flor* means "flower"—a reference to its ability to bloom.) To understand flor, let's imagine the winemaker is making a fino. First, he crushes, but does not press, the Palomino grapes. The free-run juice is then fermented and, after fermentation, fortified only slightly with spirits.

The wine is transferred into a Sherry *bota,* but instead of being filled to the top, the *bota* is filled only three-fourths full. Sherry makers call this space *dos puntos*—two fists (of air).

Next, a remarkable occurrence takes place. A film of flor appears on the surface of the wine. As they accumulate and grow, the yeasts form small curds. In a month's time, the flor will blanket the wine.

A century ago, horrified by the foul-looking flor, Sherry makers believed that certain barrels of wine simply got "sick." Slowly, opinion changed. The

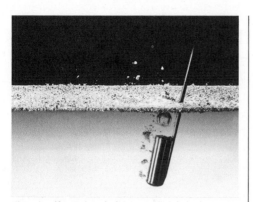

Flor—specific strains of wild yeasts that thrive in Jerez—float on the surface of wine, ultimately contributing to Sherry's unique flavor.

flor-covered wines, they noticed, emerged from the solera light, fresh, and very dry. This came to be seen as a blessing, for such a wine was, in fact, well suited to the sultry local climate. Enologists now know that flor is a family of four complex, wild strains of *Saccharomyces* yeasts (the leading one of which is called *Saccharomyces beticus*) that bloom spontaneously in Jerez's humid air.

Importantly, these yeasts have the metabolic capacity to consume alcohol and oxygen (rather than sugar). Indeed, the need for oxygen is in part why these strains of yeast evolved to float; by floating on the surface of a wine, they'd be closer to the air in the barrel. (The yeasts' need for oxygen is also why Sherry bodegas have famously large windows that are always open, and why most bodegas are situated facing the ocean to maximize sea breezes.) As they proliferate, the strains of flor yeasts also give off acetaldehyde, the aroma of which is a signature scent in certain styles of Sherry. Although it sounds awful, the smell of acetaldehyde is often compared to nail polish remover. Somehow, however, that aroma—when it emanates from Sherry—comes across in a singularly appealing way.

Interestingly, flor taken from Jerez to other parts of the world quickly mutates or dies, conveniently ensuring that true Sherry will never be made in California, Chile, Italy, or even anywhere else in Spain.

Flor is critical to a fino-to-be. Floating on the wine thanks to their waxy cells, the flor yeasts protect the developing fino from oxidizing by consuming the surrounding oxygen (remember, the barrel contents are one-quarter air). With fino, the flor ebbs and flows cyclically with the seasons. Thus, flor's shield is not absolutely impermeable. A small amount of oxidation will occur with fino—just enough to impart further complexity.

Flor is also critical to manzanilla. In the especially humid conditions under which manzanilla is made, flor will blanket the developing wine throughout the year. The result is a wine of finely etched delicacy that has the least possible exposure to oxidation. How is it that manzanilla is made in a significantly more humid environment than other Sherries when the entire Jerez region is humid? Manzanilla is, by law, only made by bodegas situated along the beach in the seaside town of Sanlúcar de Barrameda, where the salty air and average 78 percent humidity create a unique mesoclimate. So dependent is manzanilla on this oceanic mesoclimate that developing manzanillas taken to another bodega in the Sherry region (or even a bodega too far from the wet breezes off the beach) will turn into finos!

As for amontillados, they are made by taking fino Sherries, fortifying them a bit more to a higher alcohol content, and then putting them through another solera where they will *not* be protected by flor. The amontillado that results is darker in color (thanks to the air exposure), aged, nutty, and rich—and it has more alcohol than a fino.

MAKING OLOROSO, CREAM SHERRY, AND PEDRO XIMÉNEZ

Until quite recently, the mystical and unpredictable appearance of flor told Sherry makers whether they had emerging finos or manzanillas on their hands. If flor did not form in the *botas*, the Sherry makers knew the wines were destined to become olorosos and they would care for and age them accordingly.

Today an oloroso is usually made intentionally. Instead of using free-run juice and fortifying it only slightly, Sherry makers lightly press some of the juice from the grapes and fortify it enough so that flor is not able to form.

THE SEVEN STYLES OF SHERRY

Sherry falls along a spectrum of styles—from those (such as manzanilla and fino) that look like white wine and are light, dry, and crisp; to Sherries (such as palo cortado and oloroso) that are topaz to mahogany in color, fuller-bodied, and outrageously nutty. There are seven major styles.

MANZANILLA

A highly revered, light, elegant style of Sherry, manzanilla, by law, comes only from the tiny seaside town of Sanlúcar de Barrameda. There, the wet ocean air gives manzanilla a dry, salty tang as well as an iodine-like sea spray aroma, similar to the aroma of a freshly shucked oyster. Manzanilla has a delicate, crisp edge, and its flavors are often said to suggest chamomile, a plant that grows around Sanlúcar in the seaside marshes. (The name *manzanilla* translates as "chamomile.") Manzanilla is entirely dependent on the bloom of flor, the yellow foam of yeasts that forms on the surface of the wine as it develops. It is the presence of and exposure to flor (rather than long exposure to oxygen) that gives manzanilla its character. Because manzanillas are ultra-fragile, most bodegas bottle and ship them to order. They must be drunk chilled and fresh; opened bottles last no more than one or two days. Manzanillas are between 15 and 17 percent alcohol.

FINO

Fino is Sherry at the apex of refinement and complexity. Fino is pale in color and low in alcohol (for Sherry). Its unforgettable dry tang and aroma, reminiscent of a mossy garden after a rain, plus its pungent yeasty/almondy aroma, make it one of the world's great seafood wines. Like manzanillas, finos take their character from the presence of flor, not from extended oxidative aging. And although they are not quite as delicate as manzanillas, finos are still fragile and must be served well-chilled and at peak freshness. An open bottle should be drunk, like most white wines, within two to three days. Finos fall between 15 and 17 percent alcohol.

AMONTILLADO

Whereas mazanillas and finos take their character from flor and not from extended aging in the presence of oxygen, amontillados are the result of *both* flor and extended oxidative aging. They are a beautiful topaz/amber color. An amontillado starts out more or less as a fino. Then, after four to six years moving through its fino solera, the wine is fortified so that its alcohol content is slightly higher than that of manzanilla or fino. At this point, it is put into another solera where it will no longer be protected by flor. As a result, it will oxidize, taking on its classic topaz/amber color as well as rich, complex roasted hazelnut, fresh black tobacco, dried fruit, and spicy flavors, and a smooth, almost satiny texture—all in addition to the pungent character it already possessed by virtue of starting out in the presence of flor. For many people, this makes amontillado the perfect Sherry style. Some producers make bone-dry amontillados; others blend in a small percentage of sweet Pedro Ximénez to make a medium-dry wine. The label may or may not indicate the level of sweetness. Amontillados tend to fall between 16 and 22 percent alcohol.

PALO CORTADO

A rare, eccentric, and exceptionally profound and complex type of Sherry, palo cortado has a burnished mahogany color, sometimes with an unreal green glint at the edge of the wine. It is still something of a mystery, and even bodega owners don't always define palo cortados exactly the same way. The consensus, however, is this: Sometimes, what at first appears to be an oloroso develops in a manner that is more elegant and complex than oloroso typically is. Known henceforth as a palo cortado, the wine soars with aromas and flavors suggestive of roasted walnuts, dried leaves, fresh tobacco, animal fur, and exotic spices, and an almost primordially lush texture. The latter is the result of the wine's high level of glycerin, which gives it a sappy, silky, oozy texture. At the same time, palo cortados manifest the dry, slightly pungent aroma of amontillados and show a lactic (buttery) character (the possible result of a small amount of malolactic fermentation). This duplicitous curiosity, with the fragrance and finesse of a dry amontillado and a voluptuousness reminiscent of a dry oloroso, is quite simply an otherworldly experience to drink. Among Sherry connoisseurs, palo cortado is considered the apex of sophisticated drinking. The alcohol level of this style falls between 17 percent and 22 percent.

OLOROSO

The word *oloroso* means "intensely aromatic" in Spanish, and this style is indeed that. Olorosos are long-aged Sherries that have not been protected or influenced by flor. More than any other type of dry Sherry, olorosos are exposed to oxygen. This darkens the wine to a rich, deep mahogany and imparts a flavor ten orders of magnitude more nutty than nuts themselves. Olorosos are potent and full-bodied and have an unctuous feel on the palate—the result of their high level of glycerin. The initial raw material for an oloroso is usually pressed juice, which is slightly bolder than the free-run juice used to make fino. The wine is also more heavily fortified with grape spirits (18 to 20 percent) before it enters the oloroso solera and is moved more slowly through it. As a result, olorosos are meatier, denser Sherries. Classically, olorosos are hauntingly dry wines, but some producers today mellow the dry finish by blending in tiny amounts of Pedro Ximénez.

CREAM

Originally created for the British export market, mahogany-colored cream Sherries are made by sweetening oloroso—generally to at least 11 percent residual sugar (some cream Sherries are considerably sweeter). Cream Sherries range all over the board in quality—from inexpensive, mud-thick, saccharine quaffs to elegant, almost racy wines redolent of chocolate, licorice, figs, dried fruits, and roasted nuts. A vibrant and delicious Spanish cocktail calls for mixing good cream Sherry with Campari and red vermouth and then serving it over ice with a twist of lemon. Cream Sherries range from 15.5 to 22 percent alcohol. There's also a "white" version of cream Sherry. Known as a pale cream, it's a simple, sweet Sherry with less alcohol than regular cream Sherry.

PEDRO XIMÉNEZ

An ebony-colored sweet Sherry, Pedro Ximénez is often as dark and syrupy as blackstrap molasses. Unlike the vast majority of other Sherries, which are made from the Palomino grape, Pedro Ximénez is made from white Pedro Ximénez grapes (it continues to astound me that so black a wine can be made from white grapes!). The grapes achieve their sugary concentration by being dried on straw mats in the intense Spanish sun for about a week. (The mats are covered at night, so the grapes are spared from the morning dew.) Once made and aged in a solera, the wine will be 40 to 50 percent residual sugar—more than three times the sweetness of Sauternes, for example. Pedro Ximénez is served on its own as dessert, or with hard cheeses and *membrillo* (quince paste). As mentioned, small amounts of it are also used to sweeten other styles of Sherry. However, for a thorough dive into the deep end of hedonism, you can also do what the Spaniards do and employ it as an adult sundae topping, by pouring it over vanilla or rum raisin ice cream.

(Flor yeasts, like all yeasts, die in an environment that is greater than about 16.4 percent alcohol.) The extra bit of alcohol and tannin from the grape skins means that an oloroso will always have a rounder, fuller texture than the lighter, more elegant fino or manzanilla.

A Sherry maker moves the developing oloroso through its solera more slowly than fino or manzanilla go through theirs. By holding the oloroso longer in the solera, the Sherry maker allows it to take on a deep, caramel-toffee richness.

When the oloroso is removed from the solera, it is ready to be bottled as a dry wine. Or it may be lightly sweetened with a bit of ultra-sweet juice from Pedro Ximénez grapes, making it an off-dry oloroso. If the oloroso is sweetened to the extent that Pedro Ximénez makes up about 15 percent of the final blend, the oloroso becomes a cream Sherry.

The first cream Sherries were made at the turn of the twentieth century for the British export market. They were lush, warming wines perfectly suited to bitter, raw English winters. Such was the popularity of cream Sherries that shortcuts were sometimes taken to meet the

Black botas of Pedro Ximénez at Bodegas Tradicion. The bodega focuses exclusively on rare, old Sherries designated VOS or VORS.

demand for them and to make cheap versions. Today, the cheap cream Sherries on the market are little more than dull base wines that have been quickly passed through a few barrels, and then so heavily sweetened that they have virtually no character or complexity. But the best cream Sherries—like Lustau's East India Cream Sherry—are phenomenally hedonistic wines of profound richness and complexity.

As we've seen in The Seven Styles of Sherry (page 462), Pedro Ximénez is made into a rare Sherry of its own. Most Pedro Ximénez wines are nearly black in color and have a texture thicker than maple syrup. A thimbleful is more than dessert wine, it's dessert. To achieve this degree of sweetness and intensity, the grapes are picked and then laid out under the scorching sun for two to three weeks to dry and shrivel. Only when the sugar in them becomes very concentrated are the grapes slowly fermented into wine that will possess more than 40 percent (400 grams per liter) residual sugar.

THE THRILL OF THE CHILL

Sherry tastes best when it's drunk the way it is in Spanish bodegas—cold for certain styles; chilled for others. Manzanilla and fino, for example, should be served very cold (like Champagne). Nutty amontillado should be served well chilled. And even the deepest-colored Sherries—palo cortado, oloroso, cream, and Pedro Ximénez—taste best served at cool room temperature. Ice cubes aren't out of the question. In the south of Spain, one of the most refreshing and ubiquitous cocktails is cream Sherry served over ice with a twist of orange.

SOME OF THE BEST SHERRY PRODUCERS

Barbadillo · Bodegas Tradición · Emilio Lustau · González Byass · Hidalgo · Osborne · Pedro Domecq · Sandeman · Valdespino · Williams & Humbert

THE ARABIC THREADS
OF SHERRY HISTORY

For almost eight hundred years during the Middle Ages, while the rest of Europe was shrouded in cultural and intellectual darkness, the Moors controlled most of Spain. Progressive, powerful, and enlightened, they were not one people but a group of Middle Eastern and North African Muslim tribes that entered Europe through Andalusia. Their capital became the white-walled village of Córdoba, which under their caliphate became the most important city in Western Europe. By the tenth century, Córdoba had half a million people and was the first city in Europe with street lighting, a sewage system, and public fountains. There were fifty hospitals, three hundred public baths, sixty schools, twenty libraries, and more than a thousand mosques. Despite brief waves of religious fanaticism, the caliphate of Córdoba was remarkably secular. For centuries, Muslims, Christians, and Jews lived in harmony under its rule. Such was the atmosphere of liberalness, open-mindedness, and tolerance, in fact, that the Muslims largely ignored the Koranic prohibition against drinking. By the end of Arabic hegemony, Sherry was a well-established beverage—one that scholars believe was decidedly present at the caliph's table.

OLD AND RARE SHERRIES

As I've explained, traditionally, no style of Sherry has ever been vintage dated. That's because Sherry becomes Sherry by virtue of its slow movement through a solera (and some styles, as I've said, move more slowly than others). Since there's no way to know how long any molecule spends in any one barrel within the solera, the exact age of a Sherry remains a mystery. However, in 2000, Jerez's Consejo Regulador instituted legal age designations for four styles of Sherry—amontillado, oloroso, palo cortado, and Pedro Ximénez. (The regulations don't apply to manzanilla or fino because those styles move comparatively quickly through their soleras.) The designations are VOS and VORS. To achieve either of these designations, the wine must go through extensive sensory analysis and be carbon-14 dated!

VOS—Latin for *Vinum Optimum Signatum*, or Very Old Sherry—can be used on the label of a Sherry that went through a solera that's at least twenty years old, so the youngest possible molecule in the resulting Sherry is also at least twenty years old.

VORS—Latin for *Vinum Optimum Rare Signatum*, or Very Old Rare Sherry—can be used on the label of a Sherry that went through a solera that's at least thirty years old and thus the wine itself is at least thirty years old. In fact, many prized Sherries are far older than these designations suggest because they date from the time the individual solera for that wine was set up—sometimes as much as one hundred years ago.

THE IMPORTANCE OF FRESHNESS

For manzanilla and fino—the two light-colored styles of Sherry that experience flor—freshness is critical. Alas, in some restaurants and bars outside of Spain, it is not uncommon to be served from a bottle that has been open for months, and as a result has an almost rancid flavor.

In Jerez, an opened bottle of fino or manzanilla is served well chilled and kept no longer than a single day. More typically, the bottle is finished with the meal, which is why in Spain both types of Sherry are most often sold in half-bottles. By comparison, amontillados, olorosos, palo cortados, and creams (all served at cool room temperature) will last several months after the bottle has been opened, with only a slight diminution of flavor. Immediate consumption is not as critical with these Sherries because they are less fragile and slightly more oxidized to begin with. If they contain some Pedro Ximénez, their sugar content will also act as a preservative.

Freshness is not, however, solely a question of how long you keep an open bottle. Both fino and manzanilla begin to lose their zesty character six months after they leave the solera. Clearly, this presents a problem. Since Sherry, by law, cannot carry a bottled-on or drink-by date, there is no way of knowing whether any given bottle has been on the wine shop shelf

---

WHEN YOU VISIT . . . JEREZ

THE DARK, cathedral-like ambiance and the deep, incense-like smell of a Sherry bodega must be experienced to be believed. Plus the majestic sight of thousands of huge black barrels stacked up into soleras is nothing short of awe-inspiring. Be sure to bring sunglasses. Emerging from the dark bodegas into the white-bright Sherry sunshine is blinding.

SHERRY COUNTRY is full of great seafood bars—especially in the seaside cities of Puerto de Santa María and Sanlúcar de Barrameda. Bring your appetite!

---

ten weeks or ten months. The solution is to buy only top Sherries and only from the wine shops that are known to do a fairly good trade in Sherry and thus turn over their stock often.

SERRANO OR SHRIMP?

*I*n Jerez, there is not a more traditional pairing than a glass of bone-dry fino along with a small plate of thinly sliced serrano ham or, better yet, jamón de Jabugo. It's an unbeatable match. Until you consider gambas al ajillo (garlic shrimp) and a glass of manzanilla, which together just might constitute the single most satisfying appetizer/aperitif combination in the world. The salty, briny, olive-scented tang of a great manzanilla is the perfect dramatic counterpoint to fresh shrimp that have been quickly sautéed in a pool of ripe olive oil with a sprinkle of dried red chile and more garlic than you want to know.*

THE FOODS OF SHERRY

Andalusia's pulsating drama of bullfights and flamenco, of cathedrals and mosques, of fino and fiestas, whispers the promise of good things to eat. This is, first and foremost, the home of a huge, sensual, movable feast of seafood. Not the sort that is neat and tidy, either. No, this is the roll-up-your-sleeves, peel-crack-and-pull-apart, eat-the-heads, eat-the-tails, slurp-the-juice, lick-your-fingers sort of seafood eating.

The love affair with gutsy seafood occurs throughout the region, but it is especially poignant in the seaside towns of Sanlúcar de Barrameda and Puerto de Santa María, where the heady aroma of the ocean air puts everyone in the mood to eat fish. Sanlúcar is best experienced first around twilight, when the approach of evening brings cool air and the light over the sea fades to silver. The thing to do is eat platters of langoustines and drink Sanlúcar's famous manzanilla at a bar, such as Casa Bigote on the Bajo de Guía beach.

Later, go to Puerto de Santa María, where fishermen's bars, open-air cafés/markets, and *tascas* (taverns) are strung together as tightly as pearls along the waterfront roads of Ribera del Marisco and Ribero del Río. The idea is to stroll from place to place, drinking icy, fresh fino and eating a different assortment of fish at each: *langostinos, gambas,* and *cigalas* (spiny lobsters, prawns, and crayfish, respectively); then *boquerones* (fried fresh baby anchovies) and *percebes* (grotesque-looking gooseneck barnacles that are remarkably delicious and virtually worshipped by Spanish seafood lovers); next, *merluza* (ocean-sweet hake that is dipped in semolina flour and fried) and baby *salmonetes* (red mullet); then *calamares rellenos* (stuffed squid with fresh mayonnaise); and, if you are lucky, *angulas* (baby white eels, no longer than a matchstick, sautéed for mere seconds in sizzling, garlic-strewn olive oil).

Between bites of seafood and sips of Sherry, you nibble spicy green olives that have been gently cracked and then marinated in freshly pressed olive oil, garlic, and Sherry vinegar.

Jerezanos begin their nightly culinary pilgrimage through the taverns around 10:00 P.M., and by midnight the seafood-and-Sherry feast is in full swing. Before 10:00 P.M. the streets are as quiet as a convent. If bars and cafés offer such compelling food, you might imagine the restaurants to be thrilling. Not exactly. Over centuries, the hot climate, the proximity to the beach, the southern spirit of sensuality, and the open, relaxed lifestyle of the Jerezanos all came together in a way that was more suited to the vitality and conviviality of cafés and bars than to the formality of restaurants. Sherry country *is* its bars.

Eating in bars is different from eating in restaurants. Small dishes of many different simple foods (tapas)—most of which can be picked up with the fingers and eaten standing up—make more sense than full plates requiring correct utensils. Food historians suggest

ONE AWFUL; THE OTHER, AWESOME—COOKING "SHERRY" AND SHERRY VINEGAR

So-called cooking "sherry"—the kind found in every supermarket in the United States—is not true Sherry but rather cheap base wine that has been salted and then doctored to give it a baked, caramel flavor. Wretched stuff, it does nothing for the flavor of a dish but it does, sadly, tarnish the image of Sherry.

Sherry vinegar is a whole other story. Expensive and exquisite, the best Sherry vinegars (like the best balsamic vinegars) possess a complex, nutty, spicy, sweet flavor. With Sherry vinegar, this is the result of having been made from Sherries painstakingly aged and concentrated in old soleras. Sherry vinegar even has its own *Spanish Denominación de Origen* (DO) and must be made in the Jerez region of Spain. Really good Sherry vinegar is labeled *Reserva* and must be aged at least two years. But the elixir to absolutely get your hands on is called Gran Reserva Pedro Ximénez Sherry Vinegar. Aged at least ten years and dark mahogany in color, these *gran reserva* vinegars have such an otherworldly taste and velvety texture, they themselves are like drinking great old wine.

BRANDY DE JEREZ

Spain makes more brandy than any other country in the world, and most of it is made in Jerez. Every Jerez bodega that makes Sherry also makes brandy. All brandies, including Cognac, which is the type of brandy made in the region of the same name in France, are spirits distilled from grapes. This distinguishes them from, say, Scotch or vodka, which are distillates of grain.

Alembics, or pot stills, necessary for the process of distillation, were brought to Jerez in the early Middle Ages by Muslim tribes as they began their conquest of the Iberian Peninsula. The Arabs used alembics to distill fruit and plant essences for the making of medicines and perfumes. The Christians soon adopted the Arabic technique, applying it to grapes in particular. The result was a white distillate used first to fortify the local wine (the precursor of Sherry) and later to make a stronger beverage on its own. From southern Spain, stills and the technique for making brandy spread northward to France and ultimately to the rest of western Europe.

Like Sherry, top Jerez brandies are handcrafted, complex, and made in a solera (which is not true of Cognac, Armagnac, or brandies made elsewhere in the world). Since the solera is made up of oak casks that once held Sherry, brandy de Jerez takes on unique flavors that tend to be deep, rich, mellow, and less acidic than other brandies. Moreover, brandy makers in Jerez use different types of used Sherry barrels to steer the flavor of their brandies in different directions. The top brandy of González Byass, Lepanto, is matured in fino and dry oloroso barrels, resulting in a subtly nuanced, dry brandy. Cardenal Mendoza, from the bodega Sánchez Romate, uses sweet oloroso barrels, and the brandy that they produce is correspondingly more honeyed and vanilla-like.

Brandy de Jerez must be aged a minimum of one and a half years in a solera. The top brandies, however, far exceed this minimum and are aged in a solera ten to fifteen years. They are designated on the bottle as Brandy de Jerez Solera Gran Reserva. As a group, Solera Gran Reserva brandies are considerably less expensive than their cousins, the top Cognacs.

Among the most renowned *gran reservas*, in addition to the González Byass Lepanto and the Sánchez Romate Cardenal Mendoza, are Carlos I by Pedro Domecq, Conde de Osborne by Osborne, and Gran Duque d'Alba by Díez-Mérito.

---

that the custom of eating tapas, which can be found throughout Spain today, began in Jerez.

As for restaurants, some of the best are *ventas*—casual places that began as inns for travelers. In *ventas* and restaurants you can sometimes find special Andalusian dishes that emerged from the mingling of Christian and Arab culinary traditions. Local roasted game, such as duck, partridge, and quail, for example, might first be marinated in Sherry, then seasoned and/or combined with spices and foods introduced by the Arabs: saffron,

cumin, coriander, almonds, honey, figs, dates, and raisins.

The precursor to gazpacho, one of the most famous Andalusian dishes, was most probably the humble, Arabic-influenced cold soup *ajo blanco* (white garlic). For *ajo blanco,* almonds (brought to Spain from Jordan by the Arabs) are pounded and puréed together with garlic plus vinegar, bread, water, and olive oil. Centuries later, after Columbus brought tomatoes back to Spain from the Americas, gazpacho would be made using the same technique,

Paper-thin slices of silky Jabugo ham, from black-hoofed Ibérico pigs, are Sherry's soul mate.

BULL'S MEAT

Toro, the meat of a bull raised for bullfighting, is an Andalusian culinary specialty. In particular, the tenderloin, the tail, and the testicles are prized. Historically, the poor and uneducated believed that eating the meat of an especially powerful bullfighting bull would imbue the eater with the bull's strength, courage, and virility.

Small slaughterhouses were built just outside bullrings where you could (and still can) buy such meat. *Toro* is also sold in Andalusian markets, although this is usually the meat of bulls deemed too passive to fight well. While the meat of a bull that has fought is more expensive, the meat of a nonfighter is considered more tender, since the animal did not die under stress.

with tomatoes in place of almonds.

Soups, in general, are an important part of the cooking of southwest Spain, and they are always accompanied by a glass of Sherry. Some of the most traditional include *sopa de almejas y piñones* (soup made with black clams, garlic, and pine nuts), *caldo de perro gaditano* (Cádiz-style fish soup with the juice of bitter oranges), and *sopa de mariscos* (shellfish soup).

In Andalusia overall, and Jerez in particular, no eating establishment is without its haunch of *jamón*. The finest Spanish *jamón*, like fine Italian prosciutto, is the result of a long, painstaking process, during which the ham is rubbed with sea salt, then hung up to "sweat," first in rooms with long vertical windows that allow mountain breezes to mature and cure the ham, and later in underground cellars. Eventually the salt is washed off, resulting in a ham that is sweet and almost silky smooth in the mouth. No chemicals are involved. The entire, natural aging process can take up to eighteen months.

Spanish *jamón* comes from two different strains of pig—Ibérico and Landrace (the white pig that generally provides the ham known as serrano). The black-hoofed Ibéricos, thought to be related to a particular type of wild boar that once roamed the Iberian Peninsula, have a somewhat more complex, sweet, nutty, and profound flavor than the Landrace, thanks to their diet of wild roots, bulbs, corn, wheat, and especially acorns, on which the animals gorge themselves. The most prized Ibéricos come from the village of Jabugo, in the province of Huelva, just north of Sherry country. Many European connoisseurs consider *jamón de Jabugo* the world's ultimate cured ham, surpassing even the finest prosciutto. In the best restaurants, taverns, and bars of Jerez, *jamón de Jabugo* is sliced paper thin, fanned out on a plate, and eaten at room temperature. Purists accompany it with one thing only: a glass of Sherry.

The Sherries to Know

The styles of Sherry are so varied that I'm convinced no one can *not* like at least one them. Speaking for myself, I could spend days, weeks, months, in the cathedral-like bodegas of Jerez, just *smelling* what is one of the most complex wines of the world. The Sherries below are listed from the driest and lightest to the sweetest and fullest.

HIDALGO

MANZANILLA | LA GITANA

100% Palomino fino

Hidalgo's Manzanilla La Gitana (the gypsy) possesses a gossamer-like complexity that is evident every second you drink it—from the layered aroma of green moss, green olives, bitter almonds, and vanilla to the crisp, sea-fresh snap of minerally flavor to the wine's shimmering, nutty, minty finish. Manzanillas simply do not get more inspiring.

VALDESPINO

FINO | INOCENTE

100% Palomino fino

A ballet dancer of a fino—twirling on the palate with effortless grace. The wine starts out with a mossy, almondy aroma that draws you in with its elegance and complexity. Then the flavors emerge—waves of vanilla, almonds, minerals, crisp apples, and something that seems uncannily like honey dipped in cream. There's not a trace of the bitterness sometimes apparent in other finos. Before it is moved through the solera, the base wine is fermented in wood to give the flavors additional nuance. The Valdespino bodega is one of the oldest in Jerez and is still family owned and operated. This is a single-vineyard fino, a rarity in Spain.

BARBADILLO

AMONTILLADO | VERY OLD RARE SHERRY

100% Palomino fino

This amontillado started its life as a manzanilla, and as a result, it's an extremely elegant, pure, and aromatic amontillado. The wine surges with sublime flavors of bitter orange, black pepper, cocoa, toasted hazelnuts, brioche, and sea salt—indeed, it is so expressive and lively, it's almost kinetic on the palate. Despite their light body and refinement, amontillados have a dramatic character that comes from flor, and this Barbadillo is no exception. A fantastic aperitif, it's superbly long on the palate, and begging for some thin slices of sweet-salty *jamón*.

GONZÁLEZ BYASS

PALO CORTADO | APÓSTOLES | MUY VIEJO | VERY OLD RARE SHERRY

87% Palomino fino, 13% Pedro Ximénez

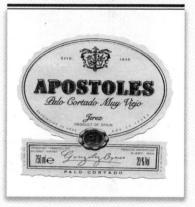

In 1862, with grapes specially pressed in honor of Spain's Queen Isabel II, González Byass founded a solera known as the Apóstoles. A century later, the solera was found among the more than 100,000 barrels in the bodega's cavernous cellars. And from that solera emerged a glorious elixir the color of burnt oranges, with a neon green tinge at the edge. Only very small amounts of Apóstoles are bottled (in half-bottles) every year and the wine is wildly seductive. Its flavors of roasted nuts, tangerine rind, brown butter, sea salt, crème brûlée, and caramel are so vivid and concentrated, they have an almost gravitational pull on the taster. The texture is pure satin. Sherries such as Apóstoles are primordial in their appeal, and no wine lover should miss them.

EMILIO LUSTAU

OLOROSO | EMPERATRIZ EUGENIA | SOLERA GRAN RESERVA | VERY OLD RARE SHERRY

100% Palomino fino

The best olorosos are a tsunami of profoundly lush flavors, and the Emperatriz Eugenia is the perfect example. Bone-dry and more nutty than any nut, the wine's complex, elegant flavors range over the whole sensory landscape of Sherry—from toffee and dates to dark chocolate, dark tobacco, and sea salt. The sheer depth of these flavors is mesmerizing. There are, in fact, many stupendous olorosos made in Jerez, but I consistently find Emperatriz Eugenia to be the most mind-blowing. The long, slow arc of sensation on the palate is not to be believed.

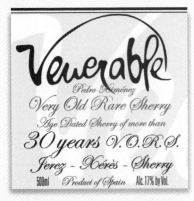

OSBORNE

PEDRO XIMÉNEZ | VENERABLE | VERY OLD RARE SHERRY

100% Pedro Ximénez

Here it is—the apotheosis of the PX style—as soft and hedonistic as velvet, with powerfully explosive flavors. Drinking this supercharged wine is an otherworldly experience. You almost feel as if the wine is consuming you, rather than the other way around. The flavors of dark chocolate, raisins, café au lait, fig jam, and licorice swirl around with abandon. In Jerez, it's not unusual to find men smoking cigars and eating ice cream over which a great Pedro Ximénez like this one has been (sacrilegiously) poured.

BODEGAS TORO ALBALÁ

PEDRO XIMÉNEZ | GRAN RESERVA

100% Pedro Ximénez

This wine, usually thought of as a Sherry, is actually from Montilla-Moriles, next door to Jerez and the source of most of the great Pedro Ximénez wines. Drinking it can only be described as a surreal experience. Black-mahogany in color, with greenish glints, it flows against the side of the glass like molasses or some wicked version of Christmas pudding. The flavors are as savory as they are sweet—black figs, miso, café au lait, tobacco, and dark fat raisins. Some Toro Albalá wines carry a vintage date (not allowed for Sherries, per se). Two Toro Albalás on the market currently are the 1910 and the 1982 Toro Albalá PX called Ginés Liébana.

PENEDÈS

he Penedès wine region is in Catalonia, arguably the most dynamic province in Spain and the epicenter of Spanish art, literature, philosophy, gastronomy, finance, and culture. Catalonia is a province fervent about politics and religion; a province where everyone speaks Catalan first, Spanish second; a province that cultivates creativity and genius. The painters Joan Miró, Salvador Dalí, and Pablo Picasso were all Catalan—as was the astoundingly avant-garde architect Antonio Gaudí, and the cellist Pablo Casals. The opera singers Montserrat Caballé and José Carreras, who still enchant live audiences, are also both Catalan. Catalonian artistry and exuberance is evident in the region's wines as well.

The region is anchored by one of the most spirited cities of the Mediterranean—Barcelona.

Indeed, the vibrant gastronomy, culture, and nightlife of Barcelona spill over into the Penedès, giving it an edge that many sleepy rural wine regions lack. Driving southwest out of the city, you pass through several miles of ugly industrial sprawl, but soon the sway of pine- and orchard-covered hills takes hold. Farther along, a patchwork quilt of vineyards unfolds across the rolling landscape. From the warm coastal land, the vineyards progress upward to higher and cooler elevations inland. Although relatively modest in surface area, the Penedès spans two mountain chains and a valley, and thus has a wide variety of climatic conditions and soil types.

The Penedès is only one of several *Denominaciones de Origen* within Catalonia, but

▲ *The Penèdes, on the outskirts of Barcelona, is where Spanish sparkling wine—cava—is born.*

THE QUICK SIP
ON THE PENEDÈS

THE PENEDÈS is best known for cava—Spanish sparkling wine made by the traditional (Champagne) method. Cava has been produced here since the 1870s.

IN ADDITION TO CAVA, a wide variety of still wines are made in the Penedès; many are simple wines made in a modern style.

THE PENEDÈS is a patchwork quilt of tradition and modernity. International grape varieties such as cabernet sauvignon are grown side by side with native Spanish varieties like macabeo and cariñena.

Codorníu, one of the large cava firms, was also the first to use chardonnay as part of the blend for its cavas.

it continues to be, along with Priorat, one of the most important.

Winemaking in the Penedès has deep roots. Amphorae and Egyptian wine jars uncovered at archaeological sites suggest that wine was introduced to Penedès by the Phoenicians some seven centuries before Christ. For the past two and a half millennia, the production of these still wines continued.

But when the very first cava (sparkling wine made in the same traditional manner as Champagne) was produced here in 1872, the course of Penedès winemaking changed forever. By the early part of the twentieth century, a handful of family bodegas had begun to specialize in it. Today, cava is Penedès's best-loved specialty, and there are just over 250 cava producers, including the two largest sparkling wine firms in the world, Freixenet and Codorníu, both of which are known today for their well-priced, commercial versions. During harvest each of these bodegas presses more than a thousand tons of grapes every day. There are a handful of smaller producers as well, and the most distinctive, highest

quality cavas come from these. Among them—Gramona, Recaredo, Castellroig, Raventós i Blanc, Mestres, and Bohigas. Ironically, the period during which cava was born was also a golden age for Catalonian still wines. Between 1868 and 1886, Catalonia produced nearly half of all the simple table wine in Spain. The best still wines were exported throughout Europe and as far away as Latin America. But it was French misfortune that catapulted Catalonian wines to their greatest recognition. As the vineyards of France were ravaged by oidium, a parasitic fungus, and phylloxera, an insect that destroys vines by attacking their roots, the production of Penedès and Rioja wines surged to accommodate French thirst.

The Penedès bodegas that specialize in still wines today are generally small and focused on making inexpensive wines from both indigenous and international varieties. The leading still wine firm, however, is not small at all—Torres, a family-owned company, is one of the largest and most innovative in Spain. (More on Torres can be found under Penedès Still Wines, page 482.)

THE LAND, THE GRAPES,
AND THE VINEYARDS

The Penedès region is set off by striking natural boundaries. To the north is the Montserrat Massif, an awe-inspiring geological formation of

THE GRAPES OF THE PENEDÈS

WHITES

CHARDONNAY: Increasingly used for cava, along with the native grapes listed below. Contributes finesse and aroma. Also used for still wines.

MACABEO: Spelled *macabeu* in Catalan. Major grape for cava and still wines; contributes fruity flavors and acidity. This is the grape known as viura in Rioja.

MUSCAT: Grown in small amounts and used for dry white wines that can be lovely and light, with amazing fruity aromas. The leading type of muscat in the area is muscat blanc à petits grains.

PARELLADA: Major grape for cava and still wines; contributes delicacy and aroma. Considered to be the key variety that contributes a sense of finesse to cava.

SUBIRAT PARENT: The Catalan name for the variety alarije, which originated in Extremadura, in southwest Spain. Used in the DO Penedès and sometimes used in cava.

XAREL-LO: Major grape for cava and still wines; xarel-lo contributes body and acidity. Xarel-lo has a resiny, citrus character that can be especially attractive in still wines.

REDS

CABERNET SAUVIGNON: Used alone and in blending to add depth, structure, complexity, and aging potential.

CARIÑENA: Major grape of Spanish origin; in blends, contributes alcohol, body, and tannin. Known as mazuelo in Rioja and as carignan in France.

GARNACHA: Spanish grape with minor importance in the Penedès. Contributes body and spiciness to still wines and rosé cava. Known as grenache in France.

MERLOT: Minor grape generally used in blending to add depth, complexity, and aging potential.

MONASTRELL: Spanish grape of minor importance in the Penedès. Adds substantial body to still wines and rosé cava. Known as mourvèdre in France.

PINOT NOIR: An important variety used in some cavas, although only a small amount is grown.

TREPAT: Indigenous red variety grown in small amounts to be used primarily in rosé cava.

ULL DE LLEBRE: Catalan for "eye of the hare," and the local name for tempranillo. A major grape, it contributes finesse, acidity, and aging potential.

mountains that, from a distance, resemble the teeth of a saw. To the east and south is the Mediterranean Sea. The terrain rises in a rugged, steplike fashion from warm coastal land (the Low Penedès) to cooler high plateaus more than 2,600 feet (790 meters) above sea level (the High Penedès). A great many different mesoclimates are wedged into this modestly sized area of some 64,000 acres (25,900 hectares).

The Montserrat mountain range acts as an umbrella against harsh northern winds, and the Mediterranean Sea warms and tempers the climate. The diverse geology means the soil varies considerably. Much of it is sedimentary in nature, with considerable sand and clay. Small deposits of limestone are scattered throughout the region.

The production of white wines far outweighs the production of red wines in the Penedès, and sparkling wines greatly outnumber still wines. As a result, the three leading grapes are the native white grapes parellada, macabeo, and xarel-lo. Increasingly, chardonnay is also used for cava, either on its own or blended with the native varieties. These four grape varieties are also blended together or used on their own to make white still wines.

As for grapes used to make red and rosé wines, ull de llebre (the local Catalan name for tempranillo, it translates as "eye of the hare") and cariñena are the most important traditional varieties—ull de llebre for its balance, good acidity, and aging potential; cariñena for its alcohol, body, and tannin. Among international varieties, cabernet sauvignon leads in importance. Again, all of these varieties are used together in blends as well as on their own. Other red varieties used mostly for blending include the native grapes garnacha (which the French call grenache) and monastrell (mourvèdre to the French), and the international variety merlot.

CAVA

Cava was the brainchild of Don José Raventós, head of the bodega Codorníu, who traveled throughout Europe during the 1860s selling red and white still wines, which the firm had been making since 1551. On one such mission, Raventós found himself in Champagne, where he was fascinated by the local sparkling wine. He returned to the Penedès keen to attempt his own sparkler. Using imported Champagne equipment and the

BILLIONS OF BUBBLES

More than 245 million bottles of cava are sold each year. While small bodegas may make fewer than 5,000 bottles a year, the two largest firms, Freixenet (FRESH-en-ette) and Codorníu (co-door-KNEW), make far more—96 million bottles a year and 48 million bottles a year, respectively—and most of that is every-night, inexpensive bubbly. This makes Freixenet and Codorníu the two largest sparkling wine producers in the world. In addition to being rivals in Spain, the firms also compete in California. Freixenet (the name derives from La Freixenada—"grove of ash trees," the name of the family's thirteenth-century home estate) owns the sparkling wine maker Gloria Ferrer; Codorníu owns Artesa Winery. Both California wineries are in the Carneros district, at the southern end of Napa and Sonoma.

three local white grapes still used in most cava today, Raventós produced Spain's first traditional method sparkler in 1872. The new wine was considered an intriguing triumph.

Around this time, a small group of successful, forward-thinking winemaking families, including the Raventós family, began meeting every Sunday after the ten o'clock Mass to discuss wine and share information. From these gatherings, an ambitious notion began to take shape. Why not convert all of the local still wines to sparkling and establish Penedès as Spain's Champagne region?

When cava was first produced, it was called *champán* or *xampany*. Penedès winemakers, however, later decided that the sparkler was different enough from Champagne to deserve its own name. They agreed on *cava*, Catalan for "cave" or "cellar."

The nascent Penedès sparkling wine industry had barely begun, however, before it was ravaged by phylloxera in 1887. Luckily, several cava firms were able to survive until the antidote to phylloxera—replanting European vines on American rootstock that can tolerate the insect—was discovered. Today, by law, cava can be made in any of six wine regions; however, 95 percent of all cava—and the best of it—is made in Penedès. Indeed, the heart and soul of its production is the sleepy town of Sant Sadurní d'Anoia (in Catalan, or San Sadurní de Noya in Spanish) about 27 miles (43 kilometers) southwest of Barcelona.

To be called cava, a Spanish sparkling wine must be made by the same process employed in making Champagne, in which the secondary fermentation (which creates the bubbles) takes place in each individual bottle (see page 181). (Lower-quality Spanish sparkling wines are made by the tank or bulk process method and cannot be called cava.) On each bottle of cava, you'll find the term Método Tradicional, indicating that the wine was made by the traditional (Champagne) method.

Less than 3 percent of all cava is rosé, but those rosés are exported and they can be delicious. Rosé cava tends to be fuller-bodied than the white. The pink tinge may come from the addition of pinot noir, garnacha, monastrell, or the local variety trepat.

Like Champagne, cava ranges in sweetness, and the residual sugar that defines each category (brut nature, brut, extra dry, and so on) is the same as in Champagne (see How Dry Is That Champagne?, page 182). With cava, the driest categories (especially brut nature and brut) are the most popular styles.

Also like Champagne, a cava can be either a nonvintage or a vintage wine. In nonvintage cava, the wines that constitute the blend may come from several different years. In vintage cava, all of the wines in the blend come from the same year. Finally, the terms *reserva* and *gran reserva* can be used on cava. *Reserva* indicates that the cava has been aged on its yeast lees at least fifteen months. *Gran Reserva*

Most cava today is riddled by gyropalette, though some small firms, such as Can Quetu, still use wooden racks and turn the bottles by hand.

THE GYROPALETTE

In the early 1970s, Freixenet invented the gyropalette, sometimes called a *girasol,* Spanish for "sunflower"—a spherical steel frame that mimics *rémuage,* the process of gradually moving the sediment down into the downturned neck of the wine bottle. For more than two centuries in the Champagne region, *rémuage* was done by hand, bottle by bottle, a process that is extremely time-consuming and costly. A typical gyropalette, by comparison, holds hundreds of bottles of sparkling wine, and the entire frame is tilted and rotated incrementally by computer. Many studies have shown that gyropalettes are as effective at moving the spent yeasts down into the neck as traditional *rémuage.* Gyropalettes are now widely used throughout Spain, and in California and France.

PAN CON COMFORT

Nothing could be more different than the behavior of the Spanish drinking cava and the behavior of the French drinking Champagne. Champagne is clearly a luxury sometimes accompanied by comparable indulgences, like caviar. Cava, on the other hand, is comfort wine, the perfect way to begin a summer evening, especially when the cava is accompanied by a humble appetizer like *pan con tomate,* the Catalonian specialty of thick slices of warm grilled country bread, rubbed on both sides with the cut side of a juicy, ripe tomato and then drizzled with extra virgin olive oil. Cava and *pan con tomate* is any-night fare—no special occasion required. Price, of course, has something to do with this, but then cava is nothing if not a steal.

means the wine spent at least thirty months on the yeast lees.

Cava must, by law, be made from one or more of seven grape varieties: parellada, xarello, macabeo, and chardonnay (the four most important); plus pinot noir; subirat, a white variety that belongs to the ancient malvasia family of grapes; and the native variety trepat, a high-acid red. The first three are the most common and are used in widely varying proportions depending on the bodega, but rarely is one included to the exclusion of the others. Xarel-lo contributes a generous, round body and good acidity and is considered by many cava producers to be the grape that contributes the most personality to cava. Macabeo is fruity and aromatic and also has good acidity. Parellada is the most delicate of the three Spanish grapes, and is grown in the higher, cooler vineyards. When chardonnay is added to these three varieties, the resulting cava often has more finesse. The first cava to include chardonnay was Codorníu's Anna de Codorníu, in 1981. Today, many cavas include chardonnay, and several are made entirely from it.

Lastly, even though Champagne was the inspiration for cava, there is an important line to be drawn between them. Cava does not hold the same "social standing" in Spain as Champagne does in France. An everyman's every-night beverage, cava is not necessarily a celebratory wine, as Champagne has remained—at least for some wine drinkers (this author excepted). I have been in restaurants in Barcelona where the waiter, without our realizing it, brought bottle after bottle of cava and poured it freely, for no other reason than we "looked thirsty."

WHO WOULDN'T WANT TO BE THE BABY?

Since its beginnings at the turn of the twentieth century, cava has been readily consumed by the middle classes. Barcelona has dozens of xampanyeria, wine bars specializing in Spanish sparklers. It is a Catalonian family tradition to drive to Sant Sadurní on Saturdays for a picnic of cava and grilled lamb. Bodegas sell locally raised lamb and rent outdoor stone fireplaces. Of course, the sparkler is also sipped ceremoniously. At a baptism, everyone drinks cava, even the baby, whose pacifier is dipped in the bubbly. Not to be left out (cava is a wine for everyone, after all), and possibly more important, other babies may be given the same treat as a way of keeping them quiet in church.

It's hard to imagine a more simple but more satisfying appetizer than the Catalan specialty pan con tomate. *Thick slices of warm, grilled country bread are rubbed with fresh tomato (and sometimes garlic), then drizzled with Spanish extra virgin olive oil. All kinds of wine work brilliantly with this humble dish, but I vote for cava.*

In addition, there's a vast difference in grapes used. The three main cava grapes have unique flavors and aromas that are different from those of chardonnay and pinot noir. Cava, moreover, is more often than not the product of all-white grapes, unlike most Champagne, which is a marriage of white and red grapes. The number of separate still wines blended to create cava is far smaller than the number of still wines in a Champagne blend (which includes dozens, sometimes hundreds of base wines). Most nonvintage cava is aged in contact with the yeasts for nine months, the legal minimum, while many nonvintage Champagnes are aged at least fifteen months and usually far longer. Finally, there is the critical issue of terroir. Climatically and geologically, Penedès and Champagne have almost nothing in common. How conceivable is it that the two wines could mirror each other in flavor?

All of this comes down to the fact that most cava tends to be fairly simple. Lemony, earthy, and somewhat mushroomy, it's fruitier and has less frothy foam than Champagne or sparkling wine from California. But, like California sparklers, the best cavas have a bright, citrusy streak of acidity running through them and are refreshing on the palate.

SOME OF THE BEST PRODUCERS OF CAVA

1 + 1 = 3 • Agustí Torelló Mata • Castellblanch • Cavas Hill • Chatel • Codorníu • D'Abbatis • Freixenet • Huguet • Jaume Serra • Maria Casanovas • Miro • Mont Marçal • Paul Cheneau • Segura Viudas • Vilarnau

The Cavas to Know

B ubbles for a steal. Is there anything better? I love the way the Spanish view cava—as a weekly necessity; no big deal. Here are some of my favorite cavas, all of them satisfyingly delicious.

WHITES

1 + 1 = 3

NONVINTAGE BRUT

Approximately 45% xarel-lo, 30% parellada, 25% macabeo

Like water bursting against a rock in a mountain stream, this cava has a vivacity and freshness that's immediately appealing. The wine is crisp and clean, with little of the earthy, mushroomy flavor that many traditional cavas possess. Instead, the wine is creamy and appley—the wine version of fresh, homemade applesauce.

PAUL CHENEAU

LADY OF SPAIN | NONVINTAGE BRUT

Approximately 45% macabeo, 40% xarel-lo, 15% parellada

The bold yellow and red graphics on Lady of Spain evoke the kind of passionate patriotism Spaniards are known for. The cava inside the bottle is equally bold—a refreshing splash of a wine that has the same kind of thirst-quenching attack as cold ginger ale. I love the light pear and apple notes that give the wine a touch more dimension. And don't miss the Paul Cheneau Blanc de Blancs Reserva Brut, with its appley/yeasty character that is reminiscent of a delicious Danish pastry.

HUGUET

GRAN RESERVA | VINTAGE BRUT NATURE

Approximately 56% parellada, 23% macabeo, 21% pinot noir

Complex is a word not often heard in relation to cava, but the Huguet cannot be described any other way. It manages to be both breathtakingly dry, taut, and focused, and at the same time, creamy, generous, and supple. The wine comes from parellada grapes grown in select vineyards above 1,200 feet (370 meters), and only when an importer or wine shop orders the wine is it riddled to remove the yeasts and disgorged, thereby giving the wine as much aging time in contact with the yeasts as possible.

AGUSTÍ TORELLÓ MATA

RESERVA | BRUT

Approximately 39% macabeo, 38% parellada, 23% xarel-lo

This is always one of my favorite cavas. Its strong citrus, ginger, and bitter notes are edgy and cleansing on the palate—almost in the way a Campari cocktail would be. Two other Agustí Torelló Mata wines are also worth seeking out: the Brut Rosat Trepat, a rosé cava made from the indigenous trepat grape (shimmering with strawberry flavor), and the creamy, complex Kripta, one of the most remarkable cavas around, made from very old macabeo, xarel-lo, and parellada vines.

SEGURA VIUDAS

ARIA | NONVINTAGE BRUT

Approximately 50% macabeo, 40% parellada, 10% xarel-lo

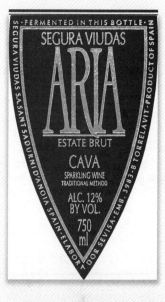

Made by the well known cava producer Segura Viudas, Aria is as alive, vibrant, and distinct as a saxophone solo. The usual earthiness and sometimes heavy fruitiness of cava is nowhere in evidence. Instead, there's a shower of lemon, and the tart snap at the end could challenge a Granny Smith apple.

SEGURA VIUDAS

HEREDAD | RESERVA | NONVINTAGE BRUT

Approximately 67% macabeo, 33% parellada

The Earth Mother of cavas, the Segura Viudas Heredad (Spanish for "estate") is the most satisfying example of the creamy/earthy/spicy/almondy style of cava. The wine's copious flavors reverberate in your mouth. Its texture is both effervescent and silky. Heredad comes in what is surely the most expensive custom-made bottle in the Penedès. Labeled with a pewter crest, it is anchored by a carved pewter base that acts as the bottle's coaster.

PENEDÈS STILL WINES

As the cava industry began to take serious form, Penedès still wines continued to evolve. The leading winery, Torres, was established in 1870. More than ever, this large (producing 3 million cases each year), family-owned dynasty epitomizes the maverick streak for which Catalans are known.

Torres has experimental plantings of over 250 different non-Penedès varieties, including roussanne, syrah, and chenin blanc from France; riesling and Müller-Thurgau from Germany; nebbiolo from Italy; and zinfandel from the United States. In addition to these, the winery has begun cultivating nearly extinct, ancient Catalan varieties that were common pre-phylloxera. In 1970, when virtually all other Spanish whites were flat, soft, and even partially oxidized from being made and aged in wood, Torres produced Viña Sol, a snappy, aromatic, fresh white, made from 100 percent parellada, and the first white wine in the country to be fermented in temperature-controlled, stainless-steel tanks. The winery is also environmentally conscious. Having shunned pesticides nearly two decades ago, they are today committed to reducing the winery's CO_2 emissions by 30 percent by 2020.

Torres went on to a number of other firsts, but their greatest achievement has always been the bodega's most prestigious wine, formerly called Gran Coronas Black Label (now known as Mas La Plana), made from 100 percent cabernet sauvignon. In 1979, when that wine (then a cabernet/tempranillo/monastrell blend) was slipped into a French blind tasting and came out on top, over a field of renowned classified Bordeaux, Torres's reputation for quality was sealed. Today, under the leadership of the hard-driving Miguel A. Torres, the family also owns wineries in Ribera del Duero and Rioja, as well as in Chile, where they were one of the early European investors in the modern era. In 1997, the ever-visionary bodega even established a joint venture in China, called Great Wall Torres. And, of course, Torres has a California operation—Marimar Estate, a prominent small winery in Sonoma, California, run by Marimar Torres, Miguel's sister. Indeed, the influential British magazine *Decanter* named Miguel the most influential Spanish winegrower of all, and placed him second on the "Power List" of vintners worldwide.

The impulse to be avant-garde and the penchant for experimentation is not, however, limited to such a large bodega as Torres. The far smaller bodega Jean León was the first to plant and then produce chardonnay and cabernet sauvignon in the late 1960s. Cuttings for the chardonnay came from the Corton-Charlemagne holdings of Louis Jadot, and the cabernet came from Château Lafite-Rothschild. I pulled a bottle of 1977 Jean León cabernet sauvignon from my cellar recently. It was thirty-five years old, and its aroma was as sensual as an old Bordeaux; the rich cassis fruit was mesmerizing. The Penedès may be best known for its every-night wines, but in the hands of a great producer, these still wines can be almost shockingly good. Besides Torres and Jean León, there are many other excellent small producers of still wines, including the

---

WHEN YOU VISIT . . . THE PENEDÈS

THE CAVA GIANTS, Freixenet and Codorníu, offer sophisticated educational tours in several languages, and Codorníu also has a striking wine museum. By comparison, at a small cava bodega, visitors are generally taken around by the owner/winemaker, and appointments must be made in advance. At small bodegas, it helps to speak Spanish.

BARCELONA is less than an hour's drive from the Penedès wine region, and boasts some fantastic wine bars. Three of the best are Monvínic, Vila Viniteca, and La Vinya del Senyor.

Zarzuela (*Spanish seafood stew*) *in a bar in Barcelona is pretty unbeatable.*

single-estate (*pago*) Can Rafòls dels Caus. The cava producer Segura Viudas also makes a very fine still Penedès wine called Creu de Lavit.

THE FOODS OF THE PENEDÈS

Catalonian cuisine is the most complex and richly seasoned in Spain. The province's proximity to France, as well as Barcelona's longstanding role as a pivotal Mediterranean port, have given Catalonian food a depth, dimension, and sophistication not found in the other, more provincial regions of Spain. Although it is sometimes suggested that Catalonian cooking is similar to the cooking of Provence and various regions of Italy, something closer to the reverse is true. During the twelfth and thirteenth centuries, before Spain financed the exploration of the Americas, the kingdom of Aragon, including what is now Catalonia, ruled part of France as well as the kingdoms of Sicily and Naples. The cuisine that flourished within these regions was a fertile mingling of Mediterranean ideas. Early on,

Catalonian cooking was infused with a certain worldliness.

If cooking can be thought of as the voice of a given land, then traditional Catalonian cooking tells the story of sea coast, farmland, and mountains. The larder includes shellfish, fish, lamb, wild game, veal, and pork, plus olive oil, garlic, tomatoes, onions, peppers, saffron, herbs, almonds, hazelnuts, fruits, and wine. Intriguingly, seafood is often combined with meat (spiny lobster and chicken in hazelnut sauce; baby squid stuffed with pork in chocolate sauce) as is meat with fruit (baby goose baked with pears; rabbit with quince and honey).

Four all-important sauces act as ties binding individual foods together. They are: *alioli*, *sofrito*, *picada*, and *romesco*. These are not truly sauces in the classic sense, however, but bold seasonings, unmasked by butter or cream. *Alioli* (or *allioli* in the Catalan spelling) is a mayonnaise-like emulsion of garlic and olive oil used as a condiment; *sofrito* (*sofregit* in Catalan), which is tomatoes and onion cooked in olive oil, is used as a flavor base; *picada*, a paste of garlic, almonds, olive oil, and possibly parsley, chocolate, saffron, and hazelnuts, is used as a seasoning and thickener; and *romesco* (*samfaina* in Catalan) is made from finely chopped almonds or hazelnuts combined with dried sweet peppers and tomatoes, and is used both as a base and as a sauce.

Though it is often dramatic, Catalonian food is never fussy. The best-loved traditional dish of all is *pan con tomate*, called in Catalan *pa amb tomàquet*—bread with tomato—grilled country bread rubbed with ripe tomato, then drizzled with olive oil and sprinkled with salt. *Pan con tomate*, along with a few grilled fresh anchovies or slices of mountain ham, often begins a meal.

Other Catalonian classics include: *canalones*, the Catalonian version of Italian cannelloni, which are stuffed with ground pork, ground duck, spinach, veal, game, or fish; *zarzuela* (*sarsuela* in Catalan), a full-blown stew of shellfish and seafood, rather like bouillabaisse; *bacalao* (*bacalla*), dried salt cod that is made into many dishes, including *brandade* (*brandada*), for

---

A MUST VISIT: THE MONASTERY OF MONTSERRAT

Built into the jagged peaks of one of the most awesome mountain ranges in the world is the monastery of Montserrat, poised like a guardian angel over the vineyards of the Penedès. Some say the mountains, which are shaped more like cylinders than pyramids, resemble contorted human forms; others, the ragged teeth of a saw. In fact, the words *mont serrat* in Catalan mean "sawtooth mountain." The monks say the range was sawn by God.

The large Benedictine order living at Montserrat is devoted to preserving Catalonian culture—a mission that endears them to the Catalans. (So much so that in tribute, thousands of Catalonian girls are named Montserrat—Montse for short.)

In the past, Montserrat served as a political refuge. Under Franco's rule, scholars, artists, politicians, and students went there to meet in rooms that the monks rented out for a small fee. It was not unusual for the military police to be waiting a few miles down the mountainside. The monks still rent rooms, mostly now to poets in need of solitude or artists who want to paint.

The monastery includes a museum of Catalonian art and a 200,000-volume library of rare manuscripts and engravings. There is also Montserrat's music school, Escolania, which dates from the thirteenth century, making it one of the oldest music schools in Europe. The fifty choir boys, who live and study with the monks, sing daily for visitors.

It is said that no Catalonian couple is ever truly married until they have come together to Montserrat, so the monastery is always full of wedding parties. On Sundays, these parties often break into the *sardana*, a gentle, rhythmic Catalonian round dance thought to be of Greek origin. Although it starts off as a small group of people holding hands, within minutes, the *sardana* is being danced by hundreds of people as everyone around joins in.

The monastery is dedicated to La Moreneta, "the little dark one"—a sculpted black Virgin dating from the twelfth century.

---

which it is desalted and whipped with potatoes, olive oil, and lots of garlic into a dish resembling mashed potatoes; and *mar i mutanya*, Catalan for "sea and mountain," a homey ragout of fish and meat—sometimes chicken and prawns, sometimes rabbit, monkfish, and snails.

And for dessert, there is *crema catalana*, the Catalonian version of the French dessert crème brûlée, a rich, creamy custard with a sheet of caramelized sugar on top. Catalans would wince to hear *crema catalana* thus described. The French dessert, they say, was inspired by theirs, not the other way around. Several food historians agree.

Lastly, and this may be the biggest statement of all regarding Catalonian gastronomy: Catalonia is where the modern world's most famous restaurant, El Bulli, was once to be found. A small, seaside restaurant on a bay on Catalonia's Costa Brava, El Bulli advanced the art and science of gastronomy perhaps more than any other restaurant in the past half century. Its founder, chef Ferran Adrià, has been described in the *New York Times* as "the most imaginative generator of haute cuisine on the planet." Although El Bulli closed in 2011, food lovers the world over are holding their collective breath, awaiting Adrià's next step behind a restaurant stove.

RÍAS BAIXAS

hen the small white wine region of Rías Baixas (RE-ez BUY-shez), in far northwestern Spain, came to prominence in the 1990s, a new era in Spanish white wine history was born. With the exception of Sherry, which is fortified, and cava, which is sparkling, the Spanish wines that have commanded world attention have almost exclusively been red—not white.

By the late 1980s and early 1990s, however, modern technology, including the use of temperature-controlled stainless-steel tanks, could be found in virtually all of the top wineries making white wine in Spain. Quality skyrocketed. Leading the way were the wines of Rías Baixas, a remote wine region poised on the Atlantic just above Portugal, in the southern part of the province of Galicia. Here, white grapes had been grown for centuries. But it wasn't until the technological revolution that the wines of Rías Baixas began to be considered among the best white wines in Spain.

Rías Baixas takes its name from the Galician *rías*, which are sharp, fjordlike estuaries that slice like cobalt swords into the *baixas*, or

---

▲ *The fishing village of San Gregorio de Raxó in Rías Baixas. The region's thriving coastal towns (and their taverns, cafés, and restaurants) underlie the question: Which came first—food or wine? Chicken or egg?*

lower part of southern Galicia. This is one of the world's most breathtaking wine regions, and definitely one of the most unusual looking in Spain. It would be easy to think you were in Ireland or Wales—until you take note of the eucalyptus forests that cover the steep hills and deep ravines. Wild scarlet roses grow out of ancient Roman stone walls. Orange trees dance in the breeze. The mountainous air is pristine; the sun is like a scoop of lemon sorbet moving in and out of the thick, coastal clouds. To find vineyards in the middle of this feels as though you've just uncovered a secret no one else knows.

The best Rías Baixas wines are made principally from the white albariño grape. In fact, albariño, not Rías Baixas, is the name by which the wines are commonly known and labeled. This is in complete contrast to other Spanish wine regions, where wines are typically referred to by region (Rioja), not according to the grape planted (tempranillo).

Albariño has a unique flavor profile. Not as zaftig as chardonnay, nor as minerally as riesling, nor as wild and herbal as sauvignon blanc, its flavors range from zingy citrus-peach to almond-honeysuckle. In texture, albariños are beautifully poised between light creaminess and crisp zestiness. Indeed, because most

THE QUICK SIP ON RÍAS BAIXAS

MANY OF SPAIN'S most exciting whites are produced in this tiny northwest wine region.

THE BEST RÍAS BAIXAS WHITES are made from the albariño grape. The word *albariño* appears on every bottle. By comparison, most other Spanish wines are referred to by their geographic region rather than by grape variety.

ALBARIÑO IS A RACY, refreshing wine considered one of the best matches in the world for seafood. It's meant to be drunk young.

albariños are neither fermented nor aged in wood, the best of them are as light as gossamer on the palate.

An ancient grape, albariño originated in northeastern Portugal and subsequently moved over the border to Galicia. (It is still grown in Portugal, where it is one of the grapes that is made into the Portuguese wine known as vinho verde.) Perhaps because it is so highly thought of, albariño inspired many folkloric tales before DNA-typing established it as having originated in Portugal. In one of these, it was brought from the Rhine, in Germany, in the twelfth century by Cistercian monks on their long pilgrimages to the tomb of the apostle James in the holy city of Santiago de

Albariño grapes ripen in the beautiful sunlight of Rías Baixas. Albariño is among Spain's top grapes.

Galicia's ancient Celtic heritage is apparent in its music. The traditional local instrument is a *gaita,* similar in appearance and sound to a Scottish bagpipe.

Compostela, in far western Spain. (During the Middle Ages, it was thought that that was where the world ended.)

Interestingly, although albariño and its local cousins were planted in Galicia for centuries (and some two-hundred-year-old albariño vines still exist there), the wines made from albariño were never more than humble quaffs. The Galegos—provincial, poor fishermen that they were—spent very little money on making their wine. Because they drank every drop, there was never any commercial impetus to improve it. At the bodega Santiago Ruiz, for example, the old wooden presses and primitive winemaking tools now displayed in the bodega's museum look as though they were used more than a century ago. They were. And they were still being used up until the 1980s.

Other modern winemaking techniques also came late here, long after such practices had been established for decades in parts of Europe and in the United States. It was not until the late 1970s that self-taught Galego winemakers employed processes as fundamental as settling and racking (allowing microscopic solids like yeasts and bits of grape skin to settle to the bottom of barrels, then pouring the clear wine on top into fresh, clean barrels). Statistics portray the radical turnaround best of all. When I first went to Rías Baixas in 1986, there were five commercial wineries. Just two years later, there were eighty-eight. And by 2011, there

THE GRAPES OF RÍAS BAIXAS

Rías Baixas is known exclusively for white wines.

ALBARIÑO: Major grape. Aromatic and flavorful, with a crisp/creamy texture.

LOUREIRA: Minor grape. Sometimes blended with albariño to add aroma.

TREIXADURA: Minor grape. Sometimes blended with albariño to add palate weight and aroma.

were just over 180 bodegas, and more than 6,500 grape growers (each of whom farms, on average, less than half an acre of vines).

The exhilarating boom has been driven by an emerging class of wealthy, well-educated Galegos with a profound sense of regional pride. Throughout the past two decades, small consortiums of lawyers, doctors,

THE GALEGOS

Rías Baixas is in the province of Galicia, which in numerous ways seems a world apart from Spain. The Galegos, as the people of Galicia are called, drink more wine and eat more seafood than any other Spaniards. They are hardworking, rural people of Celtic origin who, until the recent building of modern transportation routes, were geographically isolated from the rest of the country.

Like the Basques and the Catalans, the Galegos reinforced their separation and individuality by speaking their own distinct language, Galician. A Celtic-sounding quasi-marriage of Spanish and Portuguese, Galician is an officially recognized language in the province and is taught, along with Spanish, in the schools.

THE BEST SEASIDE TAVERN IN SPAIN

After countless pilgrimages (what else can they be called?) to the world's wine regions, I keep coming back to a final, ineluctable truth: The most blissful experiences with food and wine are utterly simple. They are experiences so pure they leave you helpless, speechless, and nearly mindless with joy—capable only of licking your fingers.

Restaurante Xeito, a humble tavern across the road from the sea in the village of Pontevedra, in the southernmost corner of Galicia, may be the best seaside tavern in Spain. The word *xeito* refers to the local art of fishing for sardines. And, as could only be true in a place where fish are revered, the word also means beauty or charm.

You walk through the bar to a small back room with no-nonsense red tablecloths, heavy wooden chairs, and Spanish ceramics on the walls. Nothing about the place prepares you for the fact that this is unquestionably one of the greatest seafood restaurants in Spain.

Over the years, the chefs here have been mostly women. And they have all followed a similar routine, each morning walking across the street to the sea and buying the day's fish directly off boats that have just returned with their catch.

If you like (and most people do), the chef will ask how hungry you are and then proceed to cook for you as though you were sitting at her kitchen table. She might begin by making miniature *croquetas de bueyes de mar* (sweet, creamy crab croquettes) or *pimientos del piquillo rellenos* (peppers stuffed with wild mushrooms, prawns, and salmon). Next might come a huge *langosta*—spiny lobster—with sweet, juicy, snow-white meat, followed by *lenguado a la plancha,* a pristine fresh sole broiled with a touch of ripe olive oil. Each fish is simply cooked and served. There are no adornments, no garnishes, and no sauces—just waves of oceanic flavor, so pure you could faint.

---

and businessmen have formed, buying and replanting family vineyards, building small state-of-the-art wineries, investing in modern equipment, and most important, hiring young, well-trained enologists from Europe's enology schools.

THE LAND, THE GRAPES, AND THE VINEYARDS

The western coast of Galicia is a wet place. Rainfall is heavy, some 45 to 65 inches (114 to 165 centimeters) each year. Yet, critically, the rains usually occur in winter, when the vines are

A man plays the gaita, *the traditional Galician guitar, outside the majestic cathedral of Santiago de Compostela.*

A promontory of coastline at A Coruña, Galicia, on the Atlantic Ocean, right before a storm. Many vineyard owners in Galicia come from families of fishermen.

dormant, not during early fall, around harvest. Still, moisture is a problem that can lead to mildew, mold, and fungal diseases. Luckily, albariño, with its small, thick-skinned berries, is not highly susceptible to moisture-induced disease. Additionally, many of the older vineyards are still trained high up on *parras*. These are canopies of support wires attached to 8- to 10-foot-high (2.4- to 3-meter high) granite columns. At harvest, tractors run under the *parras*, and pickers, working from stepladders, pick grapes that are over their heads. Lifted far above the land in this manner, not only are the grapes less affected by ground moisture but the increased air circulation also helps keep them dry. Dew and moisture notwithstanding, the presence of the ocean nearby is a positive force (as it is in Bordeaux), mitigating wide swings in temperature and otherwise extreme climatic conditions.

Although it is a tiny *Denominación de Origen*, comprising just over 9,000 acres (3,600 hectares), Rías Baixas is spread over five noncontiguous areas. The northernmost zones are Ribeira de Ulla and Val do Salnés; the most inland and more mountainous zone is Condado de Tea; Soutomaior is the tiniest; and O Rosal, named for the roses that grow everywhere, is

just over the border from Portugal. Each zone has its share of very good wines and top producers. The best vineyards have well-draining sandy/granitic soil, some of which has clay and limestone mixed in. They are planted on southwest-facing slopes to ensure the maximum number of hours of sun for ripening.

WHEN YOU VISIT . . . RÍAS BAIXAS

FOR ANYONE WHO LOVES history or architecture, it would be a big mistake to visit Rías Baixas without spending time in the cathedral of Santiago de Compostela, one of the most majestic cathedrals of Europe.

AS FOR THE BODEGAS, most are small, and it's possible to visit several in a day, but appointments are necessary. Chances are you will be shown around by the owner or winemaker. It helps to speak some Spanish.

Rías Baixas has some of the best and freshest seafood in Europe. Every fishing village boasts seaside taverns where platters of seafood and bottles of albariño are on every table, no exception.

Because it is a difficult grape to grow and is naturally low-yielding, albariño is one of the most expensive white grapes in Spain. As a result, the wines are never outright steals, but neither are they as pricey as, say, most well-known French whites. As for personality, albariño has a lot. Beautifully aromatic, it's a potpourri of citrus, lime, vanilla, peach, honey, and kiwi smells. (Interestingly, there are many kiwi orchards in Rías Baixas; indeed, kiwi was a major crop here until orchards were supplanted by vineyards.) The irresistible flavors range from almond and citrus to spice and quince. To underscore the freshness of these flavors, winemakers handle the grapes as little as possible. And because, historically, albariños were rarely barrel fermented, the flavors were dependably pure and vibrant. That said, several producers are now experimenting with barrel fermentation, hoping to make a fuller-bodied, oaky style. The results—literally and philosophically—have been mixed. Once, while visiting a tiny bodega in Rías Baixas, I noticed a life-size statue of the Virgin Mary in the corner. The statue was blindfolded. "What's with the Virgin?" I asked the winemaker. "Ah," she said, gesturing to some brand-new barrels on the other side of the room. "I'm sure the Holy Mother would not approve of those."

Virtually all Rías Baixas bodegas make only one albariño. Such categories as *reserva* or *gran reserva* do not exist. There are a few plantings of red grapes in Rías Baixas, but no superior red wines have been made.

SOME OF THE BEST PRODUCERS OF ALBARIÑO

Adegas Gran Vinum • As Laxas • Fillaboa • Lagar de Cervera • Lusco do Miño • Mar de Frades • Morgadío • Pazo de Señorans • Pazo San Mauro • Pazo Serantellos • Salnesur • Salneval • Santiago Ruiz • Terras Gauda • Vilariño-Cambados • Vionta

---

THE FOODS OF RÍAS BAIXAS

Seafood lovers go mad in Rías Baixas—in fact, anywhere in Galicia—for this is the single greatest seafood region in a country legendary for its fish. In the north, along the Cantabrian coast, and in the west, along the Atlantic coast, Galicia is splintered by deep estuaries (the Rías Altas and Rías Baixas, respectively). These fjordlike channels act as enormous funnels for fish. The seafood catch in Galicia is one of the largest in Europe.

Shellfish is pristine and dizzying in its variety: scallops, mussels, prawns, shrimp, lobster, crayfish, crabs, clams, spiny lobster, sea snails, oysters, cockles, barnacles, and more. Galicia is also famous for one of the ugliest and most delicious seafoods imaginable: *percebes*. Gooseneck gray barnacles the size of a man's thumb, *percebes* are harvested by divers who, wearing protective helmets, lower themselves into the crashing waves off the treacherous cliffs of Costa de la Muerte, "Death's Coast." Each year several divers die in their pursuit of *percebes*. The barnacle is, needless to say, expensive.

Grilled *pulpo* (octopus), sweet and tender, is another Galician specialty. On Sundays after church, the bars and *tavernas* are full of families eating *pulpo* drizzled with emerald olive oil and served with wondrously crusty country bread. Glasses of chilled albariño are found on every table.

For centuries, the Galegos have been renowned as particularly fearless fishermen who not only fish the *rías* but also venture far out into the ocean. Thus, the seafood kaleidoscope here also includes deep-sea fish, such as cod, hake, sardines, turbot, sole, and angler.

Fresh seafood lends itself to utterly simple cooking techniques. Over time, the simplicity afforded seafood came to define virtually every aspect of Galician cooking. The most complex Galician specialty, empanadas, is not particularly complicated at all. Empanadas are double-crusted pies usually filled with scallops, eel, potatoes, sardines, tuna, or pork. The filling is sautéed in olive oil with peppers, tomatoes, onions, and garlic. The crust is made from wheat flour or cornmeal. Empanadas are served in the humblest bars as well as in Galicia's best restaurants.

Finally, Galician cookery is also influenced by the region's Celtic roots. The potato is revered. In *caldo gallego,* the region's most famous peasant stew, potatoes are combined with kale, beans, pieces of pork (ear and tail), spicy sausage, and sometimes veal and chicken. Every Galician loves his or her mother's *caldo gallego.*

A BLESSED MARRIAGE

It hardly seems coincidental that Galicia, renowned in all of Europe for the abundance and variety of its seafood, would specialize in a wine considered one of the most compatible in the world with seafood, as albariño is. The wine's capacity to seem both crisp and creamy at the same time, plus its pure, clean flavors reminiscent of quince, almonds, ginger, and lemons make it a stunning partner for all sorts of simply prepared seafood dishes. But if there's one type of seafood made just for albariño, it's scallops. The sweet purity of scallops, often overwhelmed by other whites, is perfectly underscored by Spain's most famous white wine. In Galicia itself, scallops have been treasured for centuries. For more than a thousand years, the travelers who have walked across northern Spain on religious pilgrimages to the tomb of the apostle James in Galicia's Santiago de Compostela have taken the scallop shell as their religious symbol. The stone walls of Santiago's stunning cathedral are covered with carved scallop shells, and during the Middle Ages, the millions who made the pilgrimage each year decorated their cloaks and hats with badges in the shape of scallop shells.

The Rías Baixas Wines to Know

The cool maritime region of Rías Baixas along Spain's green, northwestern coastline specializes in just one wine. And it happens to be one of Europe's best wines for fresh seafood: albariño. The albariños below are all crisp, pure, bold wines that evoke the intensity of the Atlantic Ocean.

PAZO SERANTELLOS

ALBARIÑO

100% albariño

This estate (the term *pazo*, in Galician, designates a manor house, usually with a chapel, a granary, and a dovecote) makes albariños with an exotic flair. Lively tangerine and peach aromas waft out of the glass along with scents of tropical flowers. The flavors evoke mangoes and all sorts of citrus. The freshness here is unmistakable, and just the ticket for seafood dishes.

SALNEVAL

ALBARIÑO

100% albariño

Counterintuitively, albariño can be creamy and crisp at the same time (this is one of its assets in pairing with food). Salneval's albariño demonstrates this delicious textural duplicity. In addition, the fruit flavors here soar across the palate as if on a beam of light. And the hint of marmalade bitterness on the end gives the wine a terrific edginess.

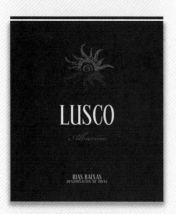

LUSCO DO MINO

ALBARIÑO

100% albariño

With albariño, purity and intensity of flavor is everything. *Lusco* (the word means "twilight" in Galician) possesses both. The wine's gorgeously concentrated quince, ginger, Asian pear, almond, and orange marmalade flavors are light but bold at the same time. And bright, focused acidity helps make Lusco irresistible. Best of all, there's an elegance and creaminess here that elevate this albariño to top rank.

AS LAXAS

ALBARIÑO | LAXAS

100% albariño

Lightly etched and yet deeply profound in flavor, the Laxas albariño is often one of the most full-bodied in Rías Baixas. The wine smells intriguingly of cream laced with lemon, and the feel on the palate is very much like the folds of whipped cream. Yet Laxas always has a definitive spiciness and minerally/saline snappiness (perhaps the result of the bodega's location near the Miño River). It's this final jolt that makes the wine such a great counterpoint to shellfish cooked in garlic and olive oil, as well as Galicia's other culinary treasures.

PAZO SAN MAURO

ALBARIÑO

100% albariño

In an almost Dolly Parton–like fashion, the Pazo San Mauro is tight and fleshy at the same time. In good years, the wine virtually bursts forward with seductive, lush vanilla-ness, yet it is so refreshing, crisp, and focused that the flavors seem magnified. The vineyard, which dates from 1591, rests on small, rolling hills along a tiny tributary of the Miño River. On the other side of the river is Portugal. For centuries, the Portuguese and Galegos have fought over the vineyard.

ADEGAS GRAN VINUM

ALBARIÑO | ESENCIA DIVIÑA

100% albariño

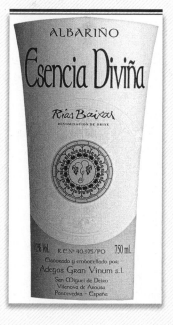

The best citrus marmalade never tasted as much like citrus marmalade as Esencia Diviña (Divine Essence) does. Highly aromatic (tangerines, peaches, mangoes), the wine has marmalade's snappy bittersweetness, and yet it's completely dry. At the same time, there's a light, creamy, lemon-meringue-pie texture here that's awesome.

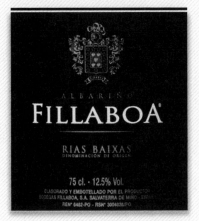

FILLABOA

ALBARIÑO

100% albariño

Everything about Fillaboa ("good daughter" in Galician) has energy, from the zesty aromas of lime and fresh apples to the tight, high-strung minerally flavors. Lots of wines are crisp, of course, but Fillaboa has a piercing sort of crispness that's underscored by notes of ginger ale, grapefruit, quince, and citrus.

PRIORAT

sually known by its Catalan name, Priorat (rather than the Spanish Priorato), Priorat is a tiny, isolated wine region just inland from Tarragona in Catalonia, on the Mediterranean coast. Barely heard of in the early part of the 1990s, the region emerged on the international scene in the latter part of that decade with a handful of exciting and highly sought-after wines, some of which upstaged even the most prestigious Riojas by costing four times as much. Priorat boasts the top classification: DOCa (*Denominación de Origen Calificada*, or "Qualified Denomination of Origin").

Priorat is what I like to call a "new old" wine region. Vines grew here for centuries before the ancient Romans arrived to mine lead and silver. But in the 1800s, the region was progressively abandoned. In the wake of phylloxera, it barely recovered. By the 1970s, the population had dwindled so much that the inhabitants in many villages were mostly the elderly. However, now Priorat has been reborn.

The region acquired its name during the Middle Ages when, as the story goes, a villager had a vision of angels ascending and descending a stairway to heaven. (So much for Led Zeppelin . . .) As a result, in 1163, Alfonso II of Aragón founded a Carthusian monastery on the spot. The monastery became known as Scala Dei ("God's stairway"), and given the important presence of the monks, the region was called Priorato, from the Spanish word for priory. Today, although the monastery has

▲ *The Carthusian monastery Scala Dei ("God's Stairway") built in Priorat in 1163 on the spot of a miraculous vision.*

THE QUICK SIP ON PRIORAT

THE BEST WINES OF PRIORAT are all red. Low-yielding old vines produce dense, inky wines that are some of the most powerful in Spain.

PRIORAT'S TWO NATIVE red grapes, garnacha and cariñena (known in France as grenache and carignan, respectively), are the region's main grapes and make intense, ageworthy wines.

PRIORAT'S RUGGED, mountainous terrain includes a distinctive stony, black slate soil.

been long abandoned, the little hamlet nearby is still known as Scala Dei, and one of the region's bodegas, Cellers de Scala Dei, operates in some of the old buildings that once belonged to the monastery. The wines from Cellers de Scala Dei have improved greatly in the past decade, and their wine called Cartoixa (the word means "charterhouse" in Catalan and is another name for a Carthusian monastery) is now one of the best in the region.

The region's most famous wines are all red and, when they are top notch, they are some of the most intense, inky, and powerful red wines in Spain. Massively structured, with considerable tannin that makes them ageworthy, they have thick, soft textures and are loaded with ripe blackberry fruit, dense chocolate, lively licorice, and mineral/rock flavors. The wines' concentration is a result of painfully low-yielding old vines (sometimes more than a century old), which protrude, gnarled and contorted, from the poor, stony, slate-laced soil called *llicorella* ("licorice") because of its blackish color. Days here are intensely hot; nights, very cool. In this dry, infertile, unforgiving landscape, few crops other than grapevines and olive trees have ever survived.

And perhaps for that reason, site and vintage are very important in Priorat. From a poor site or in an extremely hot vintage (or just when poor winemaking is at work), the wines can be aggressive and severe, with bite-your-head-off tannin and volatile acidity.

The 4,700 acres (1,900 hectares) of vineyards are scattered over a valley and up slopes more than 3,000 feet (900 meters) in elevation. Since much of the terrain is mountainous, many of these old vineyards are planted on terraces built centuries ago. Although the slate slopes are slippery and the heat in summer can be blistering, the vineyards are still worked by hand, with only mules and horses for assistance. Tractors haven't been invented that could negotiate such vineyards as these.

Priorat's wines are based primarily on two native red grapes, garnacha and cariñena (known in France as grenache and carignan, respectively). With the notable exceptions of Châteauneuf-du-Pape and the rest of the southern Rhône in the Old World, and Australia in the New World, garnacha and cariñena achieve their greatest heights in their homeland, Spain. Not surprisingly, in Priorat they have excelled for more than a century. Garnacha from the best vineyards here makes complex, luscious wines. For their part, the best cariñena vineyards result in wines with a sexy, sweaty, earthy quality that is undeniably appealing. In addition to these two varieties, some wines also contain smaller amounts of cabernet sauvignon, merlot, syrah, and tempranillo.

Like many vines in Priorat, those of Mas Doix are 75 to 100 years old.

The ancient village of Vilella Baixa is perched on cliffs above the point where the Montsant River meets the stream of Scala Dei. The houses in the village are 7 or 8 stories high, with the main door on the 4th or 5th floor. All around the town are old hillside vineyards.

Unlike the wines of Rioja or Ribera del Duero, the wines of Priorat are not categorized according to the hierarchy of *crianza, reserva,* and *gran reserva*. Nor, with few exceptions, are they ever aged in American oak (French oak is preferred). France has also inspired many of the wines' names. Clos Mogador, Clos de l'Obac, Clos Erasmus, and Clos Martinet all borrow the French concept of a *clos*, or a small, defined vineyard where, by inference, special high-quality wines are made. Most, but not all of the wine is dry; several Priorat bodegas also make sweet, fortified red wines called *vis dolçes* (Catalan for "sweet wines"). These sweet bombs, with their syrupy texture and flavors of chocolate-covered cherries, can be simply extraordinary and are priced accordingly.

Until the 1990s there were very few independent bodegas in Priorat. Because the vineyards were difficult to work and the region was isolated and poor, most vineyards were just small plots tended by farmers who worked the difficult ground by hand, usually with the sole help of a donkey. The farmers sold their grapes to the local cooperatives, and the cooperatives, in turn, made high-octane, rustic reds that were short on finesse.

Then, quietly, beginning in the early 1990s, a few ambitious growers as well as visionary winemakers decided that the region's potential for producing truly fine wine was just too great to ignore. Among the first pioneering bodegas to be founded were Costers del Siurana, Clos Mogador, Clos Martinet, Clos Erasmus, and Alvaro Palacios, the latter two of which, in particular, have built stellar global reputations for their complex, ageworthy, expensive wines. Clos Erasmus (owned by self-taught winemaker Daphne Glorian) makes profoundly spellbinding, rich wines that dance and move on the palate in waves of flavor. The wine is one of the most extraordinary expressions of garnacha anywhere. From Alvaro Palacios come two of the leading collector's wines from Priorat: the hugely concentrated and lush L'Ermita, made from 100 percent garnacha, and its (theoretically) less powerful little brother, Finca Dofí, although Finca Dofí, a blend of garnacha, cabernet sauvignon, syrah, and merlot, is massive and complex itself. The arrival of these pioneers—with their skill, energy, and ambition—turned Priorat completely around. One statistic sums up the story. According to the Priorat Consejo Regulador, between the mid-1980s and the mid-1990s, the price of a donkey rose 10,000 percent.

THE GRAPES OF PRIORAT

Priorat is home to red grapes almost exclusively, although some garnacha blanca is grown.

CABERNET SAUVIGNON: Used as an important blending grape, although usually in small amounts, in wines based primarily on cariñena and garnacha. Contributes structure.

CARIÑENA: A native Spanish grape and one of the two major grapes in Priorat, the other being garnacha, with which cariñena is blended. From the best vineyards and the oldest vines, it contributes intensity, depth, and concentrated fruit flavors. Known as mazuelo in Rioja, and as carignan in France.

GARNACHA: Along with cariñena, with which it is usually blended, one of the two major red grapes in the region. Contributes richness, juiciness, body, and density. Although it is a native Spanish grape, garnacha is better known in France, where it is called grenache. The white mutation of the grape, garnacha blanca, makes some straightforward white wines that are produced in very small amounts.

MERLOT: A minor grape used as part of the blend in wines based on cariñena and garnacha. Adds structure and roundness.

SYRAH: Like merlot, a minor grape used as part of the blend in wines based primarily on cariñena and garnacha. Adds depth and earthiness.

TEMPRANILLO: A minor grape used for blending. Contributes aroma and acidity.

Today, Priorat boasts more than ninety small bodegas. In addition to the pioneering bodegas mentioned above, the top Priorat producers include: Mas Doix, Mas Igneus, Nit de Nin, Celler Cal Pla, Celler Vall Llach, Clos Figueras, Mas Romani, Cellers Ripoll Sans, and Ferrer Bobet.

Finally, Priorat is almost completely encircled by another wine region to know—Montsant (the name means "holy mountain"). Montsant is a bit like Priorat's younger sibling. The vineyards of Montsant are generally lower in elevation than those of Priorat, and the wines are often not quite as complex. But Montsant wines are grown on similar granitic slate soils and, like Priorat, based on old-vine garnacha and cariñena grapes. No surprise, then, that Montsant's wines taste and feel a lot like the wines of Priorat, albeit usually at lower prices. Monsant wines such as Capçanes or Joan d'Anguera, for example, are terrific for their prices.

WHEN YOU VISIT . . . PRIORAT

PRIORAT IS AN EASY DAY TRIP from Barcelona or the city of Lleida, but to immerse yourself in its rugged remoteness, book one of the few hotels in Priorat's main town, Gratallops. Most of Priorat's other ten towns are very tiny (often with fewer than twenty-five inhabitants), but each has small wineries.

DO NOT MISS SCALA DEI, the monastery that started it all.

The Priorat Wines to Know

The best Priorat wines, like those below, are not for the timid. These are full throttle, deep dives into intense flavor. They are massively structured, complex reds that make it seems as though the earth herself has woken in a torrent of rage.

CELLERS RIPOLL SANS

CLOSA BATLLET

60% cariñena, 20% garnacha, 10% cabernet sauvignon,
plus merlot and syrah

Like many of the young vintners in Priorat today, Marc Ripoll left the region the first chance he got, but was ultimately drawn back. In 2000, Ripoll returned to his family's old vineyards near the village of Gratallops in order to restore them, and in the process, he founded Cellers Ripoll Sans. His very first vintage was a rich, delicious wine that, ten years later, had developed quite a seductive character. Indeed, wines such as Batllet (based on grapes from vines nearly ninety years old and grown on slate hillsides) show the kind of stateliness, purity, and complexity that fine Priorat achieves. (Before Ripoll returned to take over, his parents had sold the grapes for next to nothing to the local co-op.)

ALVARO PALACIOS

FINCA DOFÍ

Garnacha, cabernet sauvignon, merlot, and syrah,
unspecified percentages

One of the young pioneers of Priorat when he arrived at the region's largely abandoned vineyards in the early 1980s, Alvaro Palacios seemed to know intuitively which old plots would yield the most expressive, complex wines. Palacios's intense and precise L'Ermita ranks with the best wines in Spain. But L'Ermita's little brother, Finca Dofí, has also set the sommelier world on fire. The wine is contrapuntal in every way—rich yet with a rocky, lean edge; refined yet muscular; spicy yet coalesced around a puddle of fruit. It's the inherent sense of opposites that makes the wine so intellectually intriguing.

Cartoixa

Les vinyes, les millors de la propietat. El sòl de llicorella. El clima molt sec. El raïm Garnatxa negra, incorporant Cabernet Sauvignon i Syrah. La collita només en anys de qualitat excepcional. Les bótes de roure francès i americà. El vi negre. El Cartoixa de Scala Dei.

SCALA DEI

VINYES DE COSTER

IGNEUS

MAS

PRIORAT
denominació d'origen qualificada

EA
112

EMBOTELLAT PER
MAS IGNEUS
EMB. 29.006.00. CAT
POBOLEDA
CATALUNYA
PRODUCT OF SPAIN

75 CL
14%VOL

L·I

CLOS ERASMUS

PRIORAT
DENOMINACIO D'ORIGEN QUALIFICADA

PROPRIETARI DAPHNE GLORIAN

SCALA DEI

CARTOIXA

40% garnacha, 25% cariñena, 25% cabernet sauvignon, 10% syrah

I love this wine's peaty, rich, sweet, licoricey blackness, and the way its rocky firmness yields ever so gently to the violet notes that dance through the flavors. The first sip of a Priorat wine is often so dramatic that it's easy to forget to pay attention to what comes next. With this wine, what comes next is a beautiful rush of flavors suggestive of tar and soil, and a kind of crunchy sea-saltiness that calls out for grilled beef. The famous Scala Dei ("God's stairway") monastery where this wine is made was founded in 1163 by Carthusian monks. The name of the wine, Cartoixa, means "charterhouse," which is itself another name for a Carthusian monastery.

MAS IGNEUS

IGNEUS

60% garnacha, 30% cariñena, 10% cabernet sauvignon

When young, Mas Igneus, like most Priorat wines, is a ruggedly masculine behemoth—a wine that's so dense it's like a black hole of dark figs, black licorice, and black slate flavors. But with time, the massiveness melts away and the wine emerges as something superbly structured and majestic. All this said, Igneus—even when young—is a fantastic experience, especially in winter, and especially between bites of slow-roasted meat. The estate itself was the first organically certified estate in Priorat, and the vines for this wine are more than sixty years old.

CLOS ERASMUS

Approximately 70% garnacha, 30% syrah

Clos Erasmus is in a league by itself—the only wine that comes close is Alvaro Palacios's L'Ermita. What I find so extraordinary about the wine is its incredible freshness and liveliness, as if hard, black slate rock all of a sudden went fluid and danced. Each time I've drunk it, I feel I can't write fast enough, as chocolate, spices, licorice, fig, cherry, citrus, jam, and earth swirl together in a huge, whirling vortex of flavor. Rather amazingly for all this intensity, the wine has a minerally, slatey coolness that keeps it from being over-wrought. And the thick, silky texture is supple and sublime. Clos Erasmus was begun by self-taught winemaker Daphne Glorian, one of the original five pioneers of modern Priorat in the 1980s.

OTHER IMPORTANT
WINE
REGIONS

THE BASQUE REGION | BIERZO | CALATAYUD AND CAMPO DE
BORJA | CASTILLA-LA MANCHA | JUMILLA | RUEDA | TORO

THE BASQUE REGION

I n terms of both food and wine, the Basque region, in northern Spain, is fantastically idiosyncratic and highly celebrated. Here, just waiting for the adventurous eater/drinker, are a wealth of delicious things found nowhere else in the country.

The region itself lies on the Bay of Biscay, on the Atlantic coast, extending to the

▲ *In the Basque region, the txakoli vineyards of the Getaria district seem almost to hover over the Bay of Biscay in the Atlantic Ocean.*

mountainous border with France. Vineyards spill down dark, rocky limestone cliffs, often virtually cantilevered over the icy, slate-gray ocean below. It's no surprise that the most important wine here is white and crisp and made for seafood.

Brace yourself for the wine's name: txakoli (sha-ko-LEE). Alas, it is also referred to in Basque as txakolina (technically, "place of txakoli"); and chacoli, as it is sometimes written in Spanish and in French. The word comes from the Arabic *chacalet*, meaning "thinness." (We'll get to how sleek the wine is in a minute.)

Txakoli is made from the indigenous white grape called Hondurrabi zuri. *Zuri* means "white" in Basque; Hondurrabi is a village near the French border. There's also a red variety called Hondurrabi—Hondurrabi beltza (*beltza* means "black")—although this red grape is not related to the white, but instead may be another son of cabernet franc.

Once I got used to pronouncing *txakoli*, I felt I could take on the three main types: txakoli de Getaria, txakoli de Vizcaya, and txakoli Alava (from the small districts of Getaria, Vizcaya, and Alava, respectively).

In the Basque region, tapas are called pinxtos and are speared with a toothpick. You pay at the end by counting your toothpicks.

The wine itself has no parallel when it comes to bracing acidity. (Txakoli makes Champagne seem soft.) Dry as a bone, and extremely sleek on the palate, txakoli is often slightly carbonated and is served in a unique manner called "breaking." To break txakoli, the wine is poured from a height of several feet/meters into a little tumbler glass (splashing some on the floor seems to be standard operating procedure). The flight through the air is said to open up the txakoli and make it smell and taste more vivid.

The most renowned txakoli is Txomin Etxaniz. And now I dare every sommelier out there to say Txomin Etxaniz Txakolina de Getaria three times fast.

BIERZO

Bierzo is a remote, mountainous region in the province of León, within Castilla y León, in northwestern Spain. To the west is the region of Galicia (and its primary wine denomination, Rías Baixas). Indeed, the climate of Bierzo mingles some of the maritime influences of Galicia with the dry, hot, continental climate of the high plains of Castilla.

Like many of the wine regions of northern Spain, Bierzo's wine history dates to ancient Roman times, when the area was the largest gold mining center on the Iberian Peninsula. Ancient Roman mining sites are still visible in the area, one of the most spectacular being Las Médulas, a UNESCO World Heritage Site.

Soils in this mountainous region include mixtures of slate and quartz, which are thought to contribute to the unique flavor of the wines produced here. The main variety is mencía (men-THEE-a), a wildly spicy, gamey, minerally, dramatic red that, to me, often seems poised somewhere between syrah and pinot noir. For several years this fascinating, indigenous Spanish variety was said to have been brought from Bordeaux, where it was probably related to cabernet franc. Recent DNA typing, however, shows this to be untrue, although the exact parents of mencía are not known.

HIT BY A THOUSAND METEORITES?

In the arid, windy region of Geria on Lanzarote (one of the Canary Islands), the rocky volcanic soil traps moisture in the desertlike climate. Some of the original vine cuttings brought from Spain to the Americas were from vines growing on the Canary Islands.

On Lanzarote, the eastern-most island of Spain's Canary Islands, are more than ten thousand curious, dark pits spaced closely together. From a distance, it looks as if the entire region has been hit by thousands of meteorites. But in fact, these are some of the most bizarre vineyards in the world—vineyards that are an ingenious response to the island itself.

Lanzarote, and its most important wine district, La Geria, lie just 78 miles (130 kilometers) off the coast of Africa. Rainfall here is less than in some parts of the Sahara desert. In the 1700s, a volcanic eruption covered the island, including the best farming land, with ash and lava. Instead of giving up, local farm-ers invented a dry cultivation method called *enarenado* (literally, "covered with sand"). As it turns out, the island's volca-nic soil, called *picón,* is extremely good at absorbing and retaining moisture from the night air. To capture that mois-ture, each vine is individually planted in a hole about 13 feet (4 meters) wide and 6 feet (2 meters) deep. The pit is then filled with the hard granules of *picón.* These rocks are so absorbent that they can even draw water from a cloud passing by over-head. The pits are surrounded by 2-foot- (half-meter-) tall semicircular stone walls called *zocos.* The pits and the walls help to protect the vines (which, untrellised, spread along the ground laterally) from strong winds that blow in from the Atlantic Ocean across the Canary Islands.

Today, Lanzarote's vineyards are planted primarily with malvasia grapes— an ancient, hardy variety. Indeed, malva-sia, along with listan prieto (known as mission in the United States) were the grapes brought by Spanish explorers from the Canary Islands to Mexico in the 1500s. From Mexico, these grapes became the foundation of the wine industries in Chile, Argentina, and the U.S.

Windmills in Alcázar de San Juan, in Castilla-La Mancha, the setting for much of the famous novel Don Quixote.

Bierzo was launched on the modern Spanish wine scene in 1998, when famous Spanish winemaker Alvaro Palacios (who helped reestablish the Priorat region) began buying ancient vineyards near the village of Corullón. Palacios and his nephew Ricardo Pérez eventually established a tiny jewel of an estate, Descendientes de José Palacios, today considered among the best in the region. Another bodega to watch: the single estate (*pago*) Luna Beberide.

CALATAYUD AND CAMPO DE BORJA

Southeast of Rioja lie the two small, neighboring denominations of Calatayud and Campo de Borja. While they are separate DOs, I have chosen to address them together, for together these are Spain's equivalent of Châteauneuf-du-Pape—mini empires of astoundingly great garnacha.

The landscape of each is forbidding—high-altitude (1,000 to 3,000 feet (300 to 900 meters above sea level), dry-brush-strewn hills that look like they could be in the U.S. state of Nevada. The soils—a friable type of red and black slate—are interspersed with limestone, iron, and clay. Wild thyme and rosemary cling to the hot slate and give the air a refined, herbal, garigue-like aroma.

Fifty years ago, there was ten times as much vineyard acreage in Calatayud as there is today, and considerably more in Campo de Borja as well. But in the 1980s, the European Union provided generous grants to growers willing to grub up their vineyards here. Just over 9,000 acres (3,600 hectares) still exist in Calatayud; 18,000 acres (7,200 hectares) in Campo de Borja.

The grenaches of Calatayud and Campo de Borja are not delicate, restrained wines. Black, dense, chewy, and lip-smacking, they have irresistible, big thrusts of kirsch-berry fruit, minerals, and spice. (When is too much not enough?)

And although each is primarily a red wine region, some amazing whites are made, including zesty, aromatic macabeos from Calatayud vines more than fifty years old.

Among the wineries to watch for are Baltasar and Las Rocas, in Calatayud, and Borsao and Alto Moncayo, in Campo de Borja.

CASTILLA-LA MANCHA

Forming a semicircle south of Madrid, on the spectacular, grand high plateau of central Spain (the *meseta*), is the region known as Castilla-La Mancha. While enormous amounts of Spanish wine are made here, the region is, alas, somewhat better known to foreigners for its leading fictional character—Don Quixote.

Castilla-La Mancha is one of the largest wine regions in the world (one hundred times larger than Napa Valley, for example). Historically, it has been to Spain what the Languedoc-Roussillon has been to France—the comforting, dependable spigot for oceans of tasty, inexpensive wine. Today, the region is undergoing a transformation, as dozens of high-quality-oriented family wineries step up their game. Indeed, it is here, on these vast plains, that most of Spain's *pagos*—exemplary small estates devoted to top-notch wine—are to be found. But even the region's numerous cooperatives are making better wines than ever before.

Castilla-La Mancha has many natural assets as a wine region. The region is high in altitude—up to 3,500 feet (1,100 meters) above sea level. The nights are cool, thanks to huge diurnal temperature fluctuations. The days are sunny and dry. The soils are permeated by limestone (a somewhat shocking fact for those who associate limestone solely with Burgundy and Champagne). Many of the vines are old—sixty to eighty years is not uncommon. And to cap it all off, the wines remain steals in terms of their prices.

Thanks to what are more or less ideal viticultural conditions, more than forty grape varieties are grown—from indigenous varieties such as the white airén and the reds bobal and monastrell, to well-known Spanish varieties such as tempranillo, to global varieties like viognier, syrah, and cabernet sauvignon. (Speaking of global tendencies, one of the most surprising white wines from here is a blend of viognier, chardonnay, and riesling, which, as blends go, sounds like a train wreck, but is surprisingly delicious given the elegance of the local viognier and chardonnay.)

While I've had many delicious wines from this region recently (including some of Europe's best 100 percent petit verdots), I'd like to say a final word about airén, one of the leading grape varieties in the entire world in terms of production. For most of the twentieth century, airén was a wine you'd find in Spain's grittiest bars, and in places like truck stops. Lots of it was distilled into cheap brandy, and much of it is still sent to other countries in the European Union to be blended into sparkling wine. But today, dozens of producers in Castilla-La Mancha, convinced that airén can be more, are making it carefully, with an eye toward top quality. The result is a slew of new, fresh, racy, fruity, minerally airéns (still, not sparkling) that are terrific as every-night dinner whites. In a blind tasting, one of these airéns compared to, say, a typical, easily affordable pinot grigio, is no contest. The airén will win every time.

In Castilla-La Mancha, houses cling to the cliffs of the meseta, *the vast, rocky plateau of central Spain.*

JUMILLA

Many of Spain's exciting emerging wine regions are in the north. But Jumilla (pronounced who-ME-ah), south of Madrid and 50 miles (80 kilometers) inland from the Mediterranean coast, is a high-altitude, arid valley flanked by the southern towns Alicante, Albacete, and Murcia. Although they are scorchingly hot during the day, the vineyards benefit from cool nights, thanks to their location some 1,000 to 3,000 feet (300 to 900 meters) above sea level.

The main grape here is the red variety monastrell, a late-ripening variety that needs considerable heat. While monastrell is indigenous to Spain, it was brought to southern France, Australia, and California more than a century ago and rechristened mourvèdre or mataró. (French mourvèdre continues to be better known than Spanish monastrell.) The wines produced from it are usually rustic, easy-drinking, fruity, ripe, and lively, although occasionally you find a very serious, complex example that can be stunning. They are widely exported—often at bargain prices. Interestingly, in many of Jumilla's vineyards, these monastrell vines remain ungrafted (that is, on their own roots), phylloxera having never penetrated the arid soils here. Small amounts of syrah, tempranillo, merlot, and cabernet sauvignon are also grown—often for the purpose of blending with monastrell.

RUEDA

Poised between the regions Ribera del Duero to the northeast and Toro to the west, Rueda is one of the important, if small, white wine regions of Spain. Indeed, verdejo, the leading white wine of the region is, in terms of the volume produced, Spain's leading fine white wine.

Like Ribera del Duero, Rueda is spread over dramatic plateaus slashed by the Duero River before it flows into Portugal. This is a region of extremely cold winters and scorchingly hot summers. For centuries the principal grape was palomino, the heat-tolerant grape of Sherry. The ponderous, high-alcohol Rueda wines that resulted were turned into rather innocuous fortified wines that, sadly, never approached Sherry in quality.

Then, in the early 1970s, the historic Rioja firm Marqués de Riscal consulted with the legendary French enologist Émile Peynaud and came to the startling conclusion that Rueda (more than Rioja) had the potential to make lively white wines (Peynaud likened them to white Bordeaux). By using verdejo, a native Rueda grape; making the wine in temperature-controlled stainless-steel tanks; and bottling it young without wood aging, Riscal produced a fresh, vibrant, minerally wine that had splashes of bitter almond and herbal flavors, not unlike sauvignon blanc. Verdejo put Rueda on the map as an important Spanish white wine region.

Unusually for Europe, most Rueda wines are known primarily by their varietal name—verdejo—rather than their place (Rueda). Wines labeled verdejo must contain at least 85 percent verdejo. Wines labeled Rueda (and there are some) are generally only 50 percent

Harvesting viura grapes in Rueda, one of the best white wine regions of Spain.

The church of Santa María la Mayor in Toro is one of the most classic examples of transitional Romanesque architecture in Spain. Constructed of limestone and later sandstone, it was begun in 1170 and finished in the mid-13th century. Among the artistic works inside is an unusual sculpture depicting a pregnant Virgin Mary.

verdejo, with viura, the white grape of Rioja, or sometimes sauvignon blanc or Palomino making up the rest of the blend. In addition to Marqués de Riscal, other top producers include Compañía de Vinos Telmo Rodríguez, Buil and Giné, Marqués de Griñon, Oro de Castilla, and Viñedos de Nieva.

TORO

High on Spain's central plateau, on the banks of the Duero River in the province of Zamora, the small wine region of Toro encompasses slightly more than a dozen villages, the leading one of which is also named Toro. As is true in nearby Ribera del Duero, the climate here is dry and sunny, with very hot days and cold nights. Similarly, the soils here are sandy and mixed with ancient riverbed stones.

Toro is known for massively powerful, dense red wines based on tinta del Toro, locally adapted clones of tempranillo. (Some garnacha is also grown, as is a small amount of the white grape verdejo.) Often black in color, with a syrupy texture and flavors reminiscent of bitter chocolate, tobacco, dried spices, and dirt (sounds awful; tastes good), the best Toro wines come from old vineyards with vines that date back more than a century. But be warned, poor-quality, inexpensive wines from this region can tear your head off with their harsh tannin and high alcohol content.

Among Toro's most famous wineries are Campo Eliseo, a joint venture between the international wine consultant Michel Rolland and the Lurton family of France; as well as the grand winery Numanthia, today owned by the luxury group Moët Hennessey Louis Vuitton (LVMH). Of the bodega's 121 acres (49 hectares) of vineyards, half are composed of vines planted seventy to two hundred years ago. Numanthia makes two of the greatest cult wines in Spain: Numanthia Termanthia (which I call the "Burning Man" of red wine, it's so masculine) and the effortless-to-remember Numanthia Numanthia.

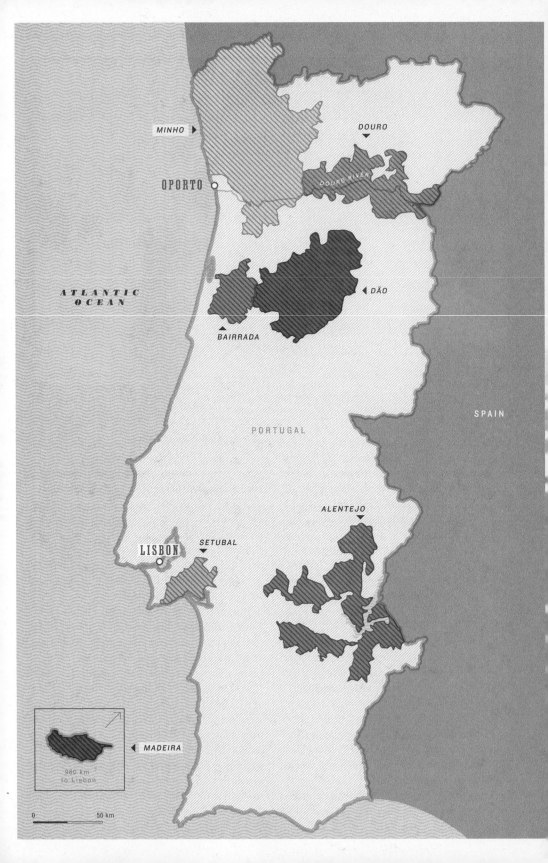

ATLANTIC
OCEAN

MINHO ▶

DOURO

OPORTO ○

DOURO RIVER

◀ DÃO

BAIRRADA ▲

SPAIN

PORTUGAL

ALENTEJO
▼

LISBON ○   SETUBAL
▼

◀ MADEIRA

960 km
to Lisbon

0   50 km

PORTUGAL

PORT | MADEIRA | PORTUGUESE TABLE WINES

PORTUGAL RANKS TENTH AMONG WINE PRODUCING COUNTRIES WORLDWIDE. THE PORTUGUESE DRINK AN AVERAGE OF 13 GALLONS (48 LITERS) OF WINE PER PERSON PER YEAR.

ore than any other western European country, Portugal has remained steeped in tradition even as it has modernized. Grapes for certain wines are still painstakingly trodden by foot in ancient stone *lagares,* and in the mountainous wine regions of the northeast, vineyards are still worked entirely by hand. Dirt paths that were used for oxcarts a decade ago are now, in some cases, sleek new highways (thanks to European Union membership and billions of euros worth of infrastructure). But adjacent to those highways, the vineyards remain almost exactly as they were centuries ago. The taste of Portugal's wines is, in many ways, the taste of a place where time has stopped.

The persistence of tradition in Portugal is due in large part to the importance of Port, Portugal's most famous wine and a wine that, like Spanish Sherry and French Champagne, is still meticulously handcrafted using ancient, artisanal methods. Port is a sweet, powerfully fortified wine, the drinking of which can only be described as a turbocharged experience. Since its evolution from the 1700s onward, it has been considered one of the most remarkable wines in the world. Because it is indeed Portugal's most extraordinary wine, Port leads off the chapter, followed by Madeira, an equally

Harvesting grapes in the Douro Valley of Portugal. The steep, terraced vineyards make the work hard and slow.

The Douro Valley, with its ancient hand-built rock terraces, is one of the most magnificently beautiful wine regions in the world.

Portugal, like its Iberian neighbor, Spain, is carpeted with vineyards—almost 600,000 acres (242,800 hectares) of them. In fact, although the country is just 370 miles (595 kilometers) long, 125 miles (200 kilometers) wide, and smaller than the state of Kentucky, it nonetheless ranks tenth in world wine production. Seventy-nine different grape varieties grow here, many of which can be found in the Douro alone. Many of these varieties are quite ancient and were probably brought to Portugal from Phoenicia (modern-day Lebanon) or Anatolia (Turkey), which were among the primary domestication sites for vines in the Old World. (As is true for Spanish grape varieties, Portuguese varieties are thought to be genetically distinct from varieties in France and Italy.) Since those early times, Portuguese vines have had to struggle formidably to survive. The varieties that exist today, for example, have, through natural genetic mutation, adapted to the dry, severely hot climate and impoverished landscape, and are surprisingly capable of producing well-balanced, elegant wines despite the climate challenges. For an explanation of Portuguese wine law, see the Appendix on Wine Laws, page 925.

spellbinding Portuguese treasure. Finally, Portugal's emerging class of good table wines should not be ignored. While I won't examine every one of Portugal's eleven wine regions in this chapter, I will look at the revolution in quality that is beginning to take place in the most important regions, such as the Douro, Dão, Bairrada, and Alentejo.

PORT

I f Portugal is the mother of Port, Britain is certainly its father. The famous Port firms were, for the most part, begun by men with such properly British names as Sandeman, Croft, Graham, Cockburn, Dow, and Warre. British men, in fact, were not only Port's founders but also its most ardent, if exclusionist, advocates. In fact, until recently Port might have been described as a rather sexist beverage. The quintessential man's drink, it was historically brought out (with great celebration and obligatory cigars) only after the women had left the room. Needless to say, women don't leave the room anymore (in fact, in some countries, including the United Kingdom, most Port today is purchased by women).

Although the ancient Romans prized the juicy red wines from the steep banks of the Douro River, in northeastern Portugal,

The name Port is derived from the city of Oporto, a major port on the Atlantic at the mouth of the Douro River—the golden river. Oporto is the second largest city in Portugal, after Lisbon.

centuries passed before the ingenious British transformed these wines from simple, tasty quaffs into Port, Britain's early version of central heating. There is a fable about Port's birth,

▲ *An aerial view of the twisting Douro River and on its banks, Croft's Quinta do Roeda, one of the great Port vineyards. Founded in 1588, Croft is the oldest Port shipper still operating in the Douro today.*

Historically, barrels of Port were transported from the inland vineyards of the Upper Douro to Oporto on the coast in narrow, shallow-bottomed boats known as barcos rabelos.

THE QUICK SIP ON PORT

THE SWEET FORTIFIED WINE known as Port is one of the most complex and ageworthy wines in the world.

TRUE PORT IS MADE only in the Douro River valley of Portugal, an ancient, forbidding wine region where vineyards cling to steep slopes and where the summer heat is intense.

PORT IS MADE in numerous styles, each of which is an extraordinarily different wine drinking experience.

even though in reality the wine's "invention" was more like a series of discoveries than a single creative act. As the apocryphal story goes, two young English wine merchants were traveling through Portugal in the late 1670s, looking for wines that would be saleable in the British market. (At the time, escalating political rivalry between Britain and France meant that, in Britain, French wines were increasingly met with great disfavor.) The two merchants supposedly found themselves at a monastery outside the town of Lamego, near the Douro River. The abbot there served them a wine that was smoother, sweeter, and more interesting than any they'd tasted. When pressed to explain, the abbot confided that he'd added brandy to the wine as it had fermented.

What actually happened was far less fanciful. By the seventeenth century, wine was regularly being fortified with grape spirits simply to make it more stable during the voyage to England. At first the amount of spirits was small, about 3 percent. But then an incredible vintage in the year of 1820 caused Port shippers to rethink their product. That year the wine was remarkably rich, ripe, and naturally sweet. Sales soared. The next year, hoping to recreate their success, Port shippers added more brandy and added it sooner, in order to arrest fermentation earlier and leave more sweetness in the wine. The idea worked. Gradually, over the course of many decades, the amount of grape spirits was incrementally increased, producing a sweet wine that is substantially fortified at the same time.

THE LAND, THE GRAPES, AND THE VINEYARDS

Port comes from only one place in the world, the 70-mile-long demarcated Port region, in the Douro River Valley, a region that is classified as a World Heritage site by UNESCO. The Rio Douro begins near Madrid, in Spain (where it's known as the Duero River), then carves a westward path through the rugged high plains until it finally forges its way across the border. In Portugal, the fjordlike river cuts a deep gorge through the arid, rocky, unforgiving land, ultimately crossing the entire country and washing into the Atlantic at the town of Oporto. The river is so massive that today, it supplies more than 30 percent of all the hydroelectric power in Portugal.

That vineyards are planted in the Douro is a testament to human will, for this is one of the most unmerciful environments in which grapes manage to grow. From a distance, the panoramic river valley appears as terraced amphitheaters of vines, stretched out as far as one can see. The terraces—tall, narrow, and all handmade—are cut into the extremely steep banks of schist that is occasionally interspliced

The forbiddingly steep hillsides of the Douro Valley range from 35 to 70 degrees in inclination. Terrace walls can be 15 feet (4.6 meters) high. These are some of the cruelest vineyards to work in Portugal's furnacelike summers.

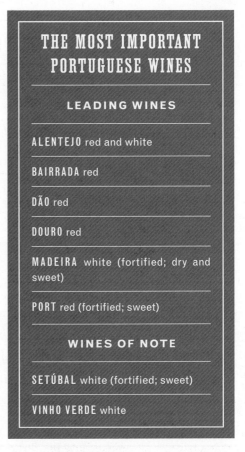

THE MOST IMPORTANT PORTUGUESE WINES

LEADING WINES

ALENTEJO red and white

BAIRRADA red

DÃO red

DOURO red

MADEIRA white (fortified; dry and sweet)

PORT red (fortified; sweet)

WINES OF NOTE

SETÚBAL white (fortified; sweet)

VINHO VERDE white

by granite. These hardened rock slopes originally contained so little soil that more had to be created by men who, almost inconceivably, over generations and by hand, chipped at the rock with hammers and pointed iron poles to break it down into small particles. (Later, blasting with dynamite became the common method.)

The presence of schist and granite is extremely important. Both drain water well, so the vines' roots must tunnel deeply (as far as 65 feet/20 meters down) within the rocky crevices for water. Roots that burrow deep into the earth find a stable environment there and thus become more stable themselves. This is critical in the Douro, where the vines must be hardy and supplied with enough water to survive the blazingly hot daytime temperatures.

The Douro's summers ("three months of hell," as they are locally referred to) are infamous. The temperatures can rise so high during the day—often to the hundred-teens Fahrenheit (mid-forties Celsius) for weeks at a time—that the vines temporarily shut down and wait until night to transport nutrients from the leaves to the grapes. The heat, luckily, is dry, thanks to the Serra do Marão mountain range, which separates the Douro from western Portugal's cooler, more humid Atlantic climate.

The hot climate, difficult terrain, and lack of paved roads also meant that, in the past— in fact, until the 1950s—young wines (Ports-to-be) were made in the Douro by the growers but then quickly transported down the river on colorful Phoenician-style boats (*barcos rabelos*) to Oporto and its sister city, Vila Nova de Gaia (villa nova de GUY-a). There, in a warren of warehouses known as lodges, the wines would be blended and matured by the shippers. Today, most Port is still blended, aged, and bottled in the shippers' warehouses, although the

Vineyards planted with touriga nacional, one of the leading varieties in the Douro, and a variety that contributes considerable power to wine.

THE GRAPES OF PORT

WHITES

CÓDEGA, GOUVEIO, MALVASIA FINA, RABIGATO, AND VIOSINHO: Obscure grapes used for only one style of Port—white. Also used for table wines.

REDS

SOUSÃO: Also known as vinhão. A darkly colored grape that retains its acidity well and is therefore used in small amounts to contribute a sense of freshness to the Port blend. (This is also the grape behind the best red vinho verdes.)

TINTA BARROCA: The name means "black baroque." Contributes alcohol, body, and an aroma and flavor reminiscent of chocolate. Like all of the Port grapes, it is also used for table wines.

TINTO CÃO: The name, inexplicably, means red dog. The grape has a delicate character and sometimes contributes spiciness. Like all of the Port grapes, it is also used for table wines.

TINTA RORIZ: Native to Spain, where it is known as tempranillo, it contributes body and red berry flavors and aroma. Like all of the Port grapes, it is also used for table wines.

TOURIGA FRANCA: Contributes floral, violety aromas and a sense of richness on the mid-palate (in the same way that merlot is said to do in the making of Bordeaux wines). Also used for table wines.

TOURIGA NACIONAL: Contributes color, tannin, structure, flavor, and aroma. Considered the cabernet sauvignon of Port grapes for its impressive structure. It is often used for its impact at the back of the palate. Also used for table wines throughout the country.

---

wine itself is brought down from the Douro by tanker trucks, a feat that hardly seems possible given the extremely narrow roads, hairpin turns, and general absence of shoulders on roads that, in some places, barely cling to the cliffs.

Until the mid-1980s, maturing wines in the lodges was not just standard practice, it was the law. In 1986, new regulations allowed Port to be aged, bottled, and shipped directly from the farm estate (the *quinta*). As a result, several growers who had formerly sold to large shippers—Quinta do Infantado, for example—began marketing their own Ports.

There are more than 135,000 vineyard properties in the Douro. These are owned by the shippers themselves, as well as the region's roughly forty thousand growers, each of whom owns, on average, no more than a scant acre of grapes. The region is divided into three subzones, and vineyards are planted in all three. From the Atlantic heading inland, or west to east, they are Baixo Corgo (Lower Corgo), Cima Corgo (Upper Corgo), and Douro Superior. (The name Corgo is a general designation for the area around the Corgo River, a main tributary of the Douro.)

The Lower Corgo, about 60 miles (100 kilometers) upriver from Oporto, is where basic-quality Ports are made. Better-quality Ports, including all vintage Ports, come from either the Upper Corgo or Douro Superior. The latter extends east to the Spanish border.

Despite these generalizations, the Douro remains difficult to categorize. Countless mesoclimates, each independent from the

Port is generally aged in large oak casks. Depending on the style of Port being made, the wine might spend as little as two years or as long as thirty years in barrels.

THE TERM *TOURIGA*

*G*rown in every wine region in Portugal, the grape touriga nacional is known by more than twenty different names, including simply touriga or tourigo. Unlike tinta which means red, the etymology of the word touriga is not clear, although it could be a reference to the small village Tourigo in the heart of the Dão, where the variety may have originated. Touriga nacional and its son, touriga franca, are now major grapes in the Douro, where they are used for Port production.

next, are created by the twisting and turning of the river, the changes in orientation to the sun, the variations in elevation (between 1,200 and 1,700 feet/370 and 520 meters), and numerous other factors. Vineyards may be close as the crow flies but vastly different in terms of the quality of grapes they produce.

In the early 1930s, in an attempt to make sense of all this and to figure out which vineyards were superior (thereby determining which grapes should be used for Port instead of table wine), a government commission rated the vineyards on a scale of A to F. Today, these vineyards remain the most intricately appraised in the world. Each is given points based on myriad factors, including altitude, type of soil, shelter from the wind, orientation to the sun, climate, age of vines, varieties planted, density of planting, and yield.

As for grapes, Port is virtually always a blend of different varieties. Blending, in fact, is what gives Port part of its complexity. While there are multiple dozens of both white and red grape varieties grown in the Douro, five—all red—are considered the most important for making Port. They are touriga franca, touriga nacional, tinta barroca, tinto cão, and tinta roriz. Of these, touriga franca and touriga nacional are preeminent, the first because of its finesse, richness, softness, and violet aroma; the latter because of its intense color, tannin, and boldness.

Yet, franca and nacional's special attributes aside, all five varieties have one characteristic in common. All are small-berried and thick-skinned, and are therefore able to withstand the Douro's heat spells and droughts. The small berries, of course, also mean very little juice. At painfully low yields, such grapes make concentrated wines indeed.

THE TOP PORT SHIPPERS

A. A. FERREIRA	QUINTA DO NOVAL
COCKBURN'S	QUINTA DO VESUVIO
CROFT	RAMOS PINTO
DOW'S	SANDEMAN
FONSECA GUIMARAENS (aka Fonseca)	SMITH WOODHOUSE
GRAHAM'S	TAYLOR, FLADGATE & YEATMAN (aka Taylor's)
NIEPOORT	WARRE'S
QUINTA DO INFANTADO	

To make Port, the top five Douro reds may be blended together in any combination, using any proportions. In most old vineyards, the blend is still "made" in the field—that is, the different vines themselves are interplanted. Only in modern vineyards are varieties kept separate.

MAKING PORT

The condensed version would go like this: Add one part grape spirits to four parts fermenting red wine. In truth, however, making Port is quite a bit more involved—and fascinating.

First, the red Port grapes are crushed. (Usually, this part of any winemaking story is pretty ho-hum. Not with Port.) Historically, crushing was done exclusively by hand—or rather, by feet—in *lagares*, shallow stone or cement troughs (about 2 feet/0.6 meters high) large enough to hold about a day's worth of picked grapes. After that exhausting day of picking, male vineyard workers would don shorts, hop into the *lagar* (yes, they washed their feet first), and tread the soupy, hot, purple mass of grapes for several hours. In the early part of the evening the workers would link arms and march with great solemnity and difficulty (the mass of grapes is very slippery) back and forth in military-style lines, to the clapping beat of a foreman (the *capataz*), who called out a rhythm. But as the night wore on, the time would come for the *liberdade*. This was the moment when the women—and musicians—arrived. As the women jumped into the *lagar*, men chose partners and everyone began to waltz, polka, or folk dance (depending on the music).

Amazingly, in the Douro, some grapes are still trodden by human feet—indeed many vintage Ports, in particular. I have fond memories (and pictures I'll never reveal) of dancing recently in the *lagar* at Quinta do Vesuvio until 2:00 a.m. Here's what no one tells you: Your legs are bright violet-colored for a month afterward.

As it happens, the human foot is ideally suited to crushing grapes. Treading breaks the grapes, crushes the skins, and then mixes the skins with the juice for good flavor and color extraction—all

> "Port wine cannot be produced in flat, easy vineyards. Here we engage in a fierce battle with the elements to produce top-quality wine with no help from God."
>
> — ARMONDO ALMEIDA, grape grower for Sandeman

without smashing the pips (the seeds), which contain bitter-tasting tannin.

But when electricity finally came to the Douro (in the 1970s!), the stage was set for a revolutionary invention: the mechanical, or "robotic," *lagar*. Invented by the Symington family and first used for the 2000 harvest, the robotic treader is a large stainless-steel trough with mechanical "feet" that plunge up and down through the grape skins, gently crushing them. The mechanical feet are heated to 98.6°F (37°C), which is the natural temperature of the human leg. These robotic *lagares* have profound advantages. Not only can they run all night, but they can be tipped up and quickly emptied so the grape juice and skins can be run off into a tank precisely when the treading is complete. Historically, it took hours

Crushing grapes by foot. The workers initially march through the mush, but as the night wears on everyone breaks out into dancing.

"PORTS" AROUND THE WORLD

For decades, fortified wines made in the United States, Australia, and South Africa used the word *Port on their labels, infuriating producers of authentic Port from the Douro River Valley of Portugal. As of the first decade of the twenty-first century, however, both Australia and South Africa have finally discontinued this practice out of respect for the original appellation. The United States remains the only major producer of "Port" not from Portugal.*

to do this by hand, and all that time the alcohol and tannin in the wine were building. In Portugal recently, I blind tasted the same exact Port, a portion of which had been foot trodden and the other portion trodden by mechanical *lagar*. Both were excellent, but if I had to vote, I'd say the latter may have had a bit more richness, softness, and density.

After the grapes have been trodden, the soupy mass is poured off into a tank so that fermentation can begin to turn the grapes' sugar into alcohol. At the same time, flavor, color, and aroma are being extracted from the skins. Thirty-six hours into the process, at the point when about half the natural sugar has been converted to alcohol, fermentation must be stopped. Thus, compared to most red table wines, Port is given about half the amount of time to ferment.

To stop fermentation, the wine is poured off into a vat containing neutral grape spirits (clear brandy) with an alcoholic strength of 77 percent (about 150 proof). The alcohol in the spirits causes the yeasts in the wine to die, and fermentation subsides. The result is a sweet wine with about 7 percent (70 grams per liter) residual sugar, fortified to about 20 percent alcohol.

THE BIRTH PRESENT

I t is an old tradition among the wealthy British upper classes to give a newborn child a *pipe* (about sixty-one cases, clearly a lifetime's supply) of Port from the newborn's birth year (or from the nearest great vintage year). In the past, only vintage Port and single-quinta vintage Port would be given. These would be shipped in cask to a British wine merchant, who would bottle the Port, after which it would be stored in the parents' cellar. By the time the child was old enough to drink, the Port would be matured and ready. Today the Port is bottled in Portugal, not Britain, but the tradition remains essentially the same.

Aging bottles of Port at the Graham's lodge in Vila Nova de Gaia.

Although this is the initial process by which all Port is made, it is only phase one. Phase two—maturing and aging the Port—is just as critical, if not more so. Each lot of Port is classified early, allowing each of the separate styles of Port to be matured and aged differently.

THE STYLES OF PORT

D epending on how you count them and whether you include the rarest types, there are as many as ten different styles of Port. While each is unique, their similar-sounding names can make it frustrating to tell them apart and remember them all. So in this next section, we'll examine just the top five Port styles; these are the ones I think any wine lover would want (or need) to know.

To begin, I want to share with you a tip that Port expert Paul Mugnier taught me. All Ports, he said, fall into one of two major categories: those that are more like crème brûlée and those that are more like chocolate cake. (It's kind of like dividing all meats into those that are more like chicken and those that are more like beef.)

The "crème brûlée" Ports are the ones that have been aged in wood a long time and thus have had exposure to air through the staves of the barrel. These Ports have brown sugar, almost crème brûléelike flavors. Tawny Port is the best example. (And, indeed, it tastes delicious *with* crème brûlée.)

The "chocolate" Ports have been aged a long time in bottle, with very little exposure to air. They are darker and denser in flavor and color, retain their red berry characteristics, and have an almost cocoalike or chocolaty flavor. Vintage Port is a perfect example of a bottle-aged Port. (Not surprisingly, it tastes phenomenal *with* chocolate.)

Given the above as a simple metaphor for thinking about the styles of Port in the broadest terms, let's now telescope down to the top five most important specific styles: aged tawny Port, reserve Port, late-bottled vintage Port (aka LBV), vintage Port, and single-quinta vintage Port.

IS PORT EVER WHITE?

Yes—*although white Port represents only a small fraction of the total production of Port. White Port is not expensive and it's not very complex. But it's absolutely delicious drunk in the Portuguese way: mixed with tonic water and a twist of lime, on the rocks. In the Douro in summer, you can count on this refresher appearing every night around five, when everyone needs the Portuguese equivalent of a gin and tonic. White Port is made from the Douro grapes códega, gouveio, malvasia fina, rabigato, and viosinho.*

1963—a fine year for current drinking. Most Vintage Port is consumed after decades of aging.

AGED TAWNY PORT

Aged tawny Port gets my vote for the most sublime style of Port. Its flavors—toasted nuts, brown sugar, and vanilla—are the adult version of cookie dough. And the texture of an aged tawny is pure silk.

Aged tawnies are blends of Ports from several years that are then kept for long periods in barrel. They are labeled as either ten, twenty, thirty, or more than forty years old, depending on the average age of the wines *by flavor*. In other words, a twenty-year-old tawny Port tastes, to an experienced Port maker, like it is made up of wines that are about twenty years old, but in fact aren't necessarily that old.

The wines used in the blend for an aged tawny are usually wines of the highest quality. In fact, these wines often go into vintage Port in years when a vintage Port is declared (see page 522). However, aged tawny Port and

PORT'S FLAVOR PARADOX

From a flavor standpoint, Port is one of the most paradoxical wines in the world. You would think that a wine made from very ripe grapes that have been grown in a severely hot climate (a wine that is then fortified with more alcohol!) would have thick, somewhat dull, raisiny flavors, and that the wine would be anything but fresh and lively. But great Ports are exactly that—fresh and vivid, often with "cool" blueberry and menthol flavors. Port winemakers attribute Port's paradoxical freshness to the centuries of adaptation the local grapes have undergone. Even in blistering heat, these varieties have "learned" to hold on to their acidity. In addition, Port's flavors are often given a tactile lift from a sense of minerality that Port winemakers say is evident in great years and may be in part related to the region's schist soils.

vintage Port taste nothing alike, since aged tawny Ports are generally kept a minimum of ten years in barrel (until they become tawny/auburn in color) and vintage Port spends only two years in barrel. Thus, aged tawny Ports are often about finesse, while vintage Port is about power.

Aged tawny Ports are among the best-loved Ports in Portugal, France, and Britain, where they are often drunk both as an aperitif and at the close of a meal.

A quick word about a sister style called *young* tawny Port (as opposed to aged tawny Port, described above). Basic and uncomplicated, young tawny is less than three years old (which is almost oxymoronic, since the word *tawny* implies the wine has been aged long enough for the color to brown). In the case of a young tawny, the grapes yield a lighter-colored wine. The wine may then be made even lighter by minimizing the time the juice stays on the skins during fermentation. Young tawnies, as a result, have a pale, onionskin color. In Europe, they are often drunk straight up, or on the rocks as an aperitif, although we don't see them much in the New World.

RESERVE PORT

Reserve Port is an easily affordable, good-quality, "every-night" Port. (Up until 2002, this was called "vintage character," but the term was subsequently determined to be confusing.) Reserve Ports have bold, red berry flavors that make them popular in the United States and Britain. Many have proprietary names. For example: Dow's AJS, Fonseca's Bin 27, Graham's Six Grapes, Sandeman's Founder's Reserve, and Warre's Warrior, are all reserve Ports. Reserve Ports are blends of good—but not great—quality wines that, on average, have spent four to six years aging in barrels before they are bottled and released.

Stacked barrels of Port in the old cellars of Warre's. Established in 1670, the firm was initially known as Burgoyne & Jackson. Besides wines, it exported Portuguese olive oil and fruit to England, while importing dried cod and English woolen goods to Portugal.

THREE SPECIALTY STYLES

There are three other, rather rare styles of Port that you may occasionally encounter. Each is a fascinating and rare drinking experience.

COLHEITA PORT

A tawny Port from a single vintage is called a colheita (col-YATE-ah) Port. It must be aged a minimum of seven years. In practice, many shippers release colheitas after they are ten, twenty, or even fifty years old. Colheitas are the rarest among rare Ports.

CRUSTED PORT

First made by British merchants who mixed together the leftover dregs from barrels of vintage Port and then aged it, crusted Port is designated as such because it leaves a heavy crust, or sediment, in the bottle. This is simply a gutsy, full-bodied, working man's Port, made from a blend of several different years (the average age of the wines in the blend is three to four years) that has been bottled unfiltered. As a result, it throws a sediment and must be decanted.

GARRAFEIRA PORT

Garrafeira (garra-FAY-ra) Ports come from a single exceptional year and are aged briefly in wood and then a long time—as many as twenty to forty years—in large glass bottles called *bonbonnes.* After aging, the garrafeira is decanted and transferred into standard 750-milliliter bottles and sold. This type of Port has the richness of a vintage Port yet the suppleness of an aged tawny. The word *garrafeira* means "wine cellar" or "bottle cellar" (from the Portuguese *garrafa*—"bottle"). The term *garrafeira* is also used to designate nonfortified Portuguese table wines of especially high quality.

LATE-BOTTLED VINTAGE PORT

Late-bottled vintage Ports—often called LBVs—are moderately priced Ports that are made every year and, yes, come from a single vintage. But the grapes don't come from the crème de la crème of grapes (in great years, those grapes go into vintage Port, the sine qua non). LBVs have been aged in the barrel for four to six years and then bottled. (So, they spend more time in barrel than vintage Port, but less time in bottle; see Vintage Port, below.) LBVs, importantly, are what most good restaurants serve. They are ready to drink when the shipper releases them, and require no decanting.

LBVs are satisfying, luscious wines, to be sure, but tasted side by side with a vintage Port, it would be clear to anyone that vintage possesses more richness, complexity, and sophistication. A small subset of LBV is called "traditional late-bottled vintage Port" or "bottle-matured late-bottled vintage Port." (I know; it can seem confusing to have so many names.) Unlike regular LBVs, these are not filtered and will therefore throw a sediment and need to be decanted.

VINTAGE PORT

Here it is: the style of Port that every wine lover hopes to experience (more than once!). No Port is more sought after—or expensive. Vintage Port represents only about 3 percent of the total production of Port. It is made only in exceptional years when Port shippers "declare" a vintage. All of the grapes in the

DECLARING A VINTAGE

The process of making a vintage Port begins with a judgment. How good were the grapes from this year? If they were excellent, if they possessed just the right structural balance, richness, power, and finesse, then a shipper will decide to "declare" the vintage. Each shipper makes this decision independently. However, the truly stunning years for vintage Port are usually those declared by 50 percent or more of all shippers. In the past hundred years, a vintage year for Port has been declared just twenty-five times.

Once a shipper declares a vintage, a formal procedure ensues. Before the wine can be bottled, the shipper must submit its intention and samples of the wine to the Port Wine Institute for tasting and approval.

The great vintage Port years from the second half of the twentieth century through the first decade of the twenty-first have been: 1955, 1958, 1960, 1963, 1966, 1970, 1975, 1977, 1980, 1983, 1985, 1991, 1992, 1994, 1995, 1997, 2000, 2003, 2007, and 2011.

---

blend will come only from that vintage, and only from the very top vineyards.

WHEN YOU VISIT . . . PORTUGAL

VIRTUALLY all of the Port shippers have lodges in Vila Nova de Gaia, across the river from Oporto. Most offer fascinating tours in English, plus tastings.

VISITING THE QUINTAS, far inland where the grapes are grown, is more difficult. Generally only members of the wine industry are allowed to do so. Plus, there aren't many hotels—although, for anyone who loves wine, the Douro's elegant vineyard estate and hotel known as Quinta da Romaneira is one of the most luxurious hotels in the whole country and worth the long drive on the nightmarishly narrow, steep roads of the inner Douro.

Vintage Ports are first aged just two years in barrel, to round off their powerful edges. Then—and this is the key—they are aged reductively (without oxygen) for a long time in the bottle. During bottle aging, the vintage Port matures slowly, becoming progressively more refined and integrated. A decade's worth of aging is standard, and several decades used to be fairly common. Indeed, Ports from the 1950s are still amazingly lively on the palate (the 1955 Cockburn's is one of the most hauntingly luscious wines I have ever tasted or felt . . . it was sheer silk).

But the concept of aging vintage Port is also changing. Thanks to highly improved viticultural and winemaking practices in the Douro, even very bold, young vintage Ports can be lip-smackingly delicious. In recent trips to the Douro, I have been astounded by the elegance of young vintage Port—its exuberance and power being, of course, givens.

To maintain the intensity, balance, and richness of vintage Port, it is neither fined nor filtered. This, coupled with the fact that Port grapes have thick skins and a lot of tannin, means that vintage Port throws a great deal of sediment, and always needs to be decanted (see Sediment and Tartrates, page 114). Finally, in the years a shipper chooses not to declare as

Astonishment awaits. Older vintages of Graham's, Dow's, Warre's, and other Ports are ready to be tasted in the Symington family lodges.

vintage quality, they take the grapes they might have used for vintage Port and, if they came from a great single quinta (vineyard estate), bottle them under the name of that quinta.

SINGLE-QUINTA VINTAGE PORT

The word *quinta* means farm, but in the Douro most quintas would be more accurately described as renowned vineyard estates. They range in size from a dozen to several hundred acres and usually include a house and sometimes gardens, in the manner of a French château. The grapes for a single-quinta vintage Port come, as the name implies, from a given quinta in a single year. The idea behind these Ports is that the very best vineyard estates are often located in special mesoclimates that allow exceptional wines to be made even in years when the vintage as a whole may not be declared.

Single quintas may be owned by small shipper-firms, such as Quinta do Infantado, which makes a single-quinta vintage Port by the same name. Or the quinta might be owned by a large shipper. The famous Quinta do Vesuvio, for example, is owned by the Symington

PORT'S CLASSIC PARTNERS

Port has several classic companions, all of which are, like Port itself, profoundly flavorful: blue cheese, chocolate, roasted nuts, and crème brûlée. Vintage Port, for example, is stellar with blue cheese—especially Stilton or Gorgonzola—although mountain cheeses from Portugal (most of which have the word *serra* in the name) are also extraordinary. Hedonists also pair vintage Ports (as well as LBVs) with anything made from bittersweet chocolate. Indeed, fine chocolate is such a complex flavor that Port is virtually the only wine that stands up to it. As for tawnies, these Ports are explosively scrumptious when paired with almond or walnut cakes or with crème brûlée. But my favorite pairing with tawny is the orange tea cake served every afternoon at the Symington family's Malvedos Estate.

family, which also owns the firms Graham's, Warre's, and Dow's. But in all cases, a single-quinta vintage Port will always be made exclusively from the grapes grown at that quinta. (Remember that, by contrast, a vintage Port may come from grapes from several quintas, as well as grapes grown by dozens of small, individual grape growers.) It's important to note that shippers may decide not to make a single-quinta vintage Port in the same year they make a vintage Port. In years declared for vintage Port, the quinta's grapes may be blended into the vintage Port and thus cannot be made into a wine of their own.

Apart from blending, single-quinta vintage Ports are made in the same manner as vintage Ports. They are not filtered, require significant bottle aging, and throw a sediment, so that the wine must

BLOODY HELL, COLLEGE WAS BRUTAL

Alas, it wasn't this way for me (or you either, probably), but in England historically, wine—and especially Port—played a notable part in college life. According to the Rare Wine Company (an importer/retailer specializing in Port and Madeira), in the early part of the nineteenth century, colleges had breathtakingly enormous wine cellars, and there was ten times as much Port in those cellars as any other wine. Far from being a mere hedonistic indulgence, Port was "currency"—often used by students to pay off wages, bets, and fines. Even after World War II, Port was still abundant in the cellars of universities like Cambridge, which bought the wine by the *pipe* (a traditional Port barrel holding the equivalent of about sixty-one cases), directly upon release, and then aged it for decades. Below is an excerpt from a student's letter, quoted in the 1949 edition of *The Custom of the Room: Early Wine Books of Christ's College Cambridge.*

"On Friday we dined in the hall of Trinity College. Everything on a grand scale . . . After partaking of a sumptuous dinner, which began at three, we retired with the fellows to the Combination Room, where we sat soaking Port til eight or nine. Cards were then introduced, and the entertainment concluded with a magnificent supper."

Port—served from a decanter—was a fixture in upper-class life in Britain in the 19th and early 20th centuries. The lower classes made do without the decanter.

eventually be decanted. Single-quinta vintage Ports are usually released after two years, just like vintage Ports. The wines are then aged a decade or more by the buyer. Single-quinta vintage Ports are generally slightly less expensive than vintage Ports.

DECANTING, DRINKING, AGING, AND STORING PORT

The only Ports that need decanting are those that throw a sediment. These include vintage Port, single-quinta vintage Port, traditional late-bottled vintage Port, and crusted Port. None of the other styles throw a sufficient sediment.

Decanting Port is very easy. Since Port sediment is heavy relative to the sediment thrown by other wines (see page 134 for more information on sediment), it tends to stick to the sides of a bottle lying on its side in a cellar. So, all you need to do is handle the bottle gently and pour slowly into the carafe or glasses, taking care not to shake up the contents of the bottle. If possible, it's helpful to stand the bottle of Port up for a day ahead so that much of the sediment sinks to the bottom of the bottle.

Depending on how old and delicate the wine is, it could be decanted many hours before it is to be served—or just before. This is a judgment call to be sure, but it is better to err on the side of less oxygen exposure, because the wine will get another big dose of oxygen when it's poured into the glasses.

As for serving, one of the oldest and most curious Port traditions concerns the direction in which a bottle is passed around the table. By custom, Port is always supposed to be passed from the right to the left, in a clockwise direction. Although the origins of the custom are obscure, research by the house of Sandeman suggests the practice is based on the old Celtic belief that all circular motions should be deiseal, that is, turning in a way such that a person moving in a circle would have his

The mind-blowing richness of Port starts with its hedonistic aromas.

THE FACTORY HOUSE

Built from 1786 to 1790, the majestic Factory House in Oporto is one of the last "factories" of its kind in Europe. In its original sense, a factory was a trading association made up of merchants called factors. From the early 1500s onward, the British built impressive, fortresslike factory houses all along their trade routes, from London to Africa, India, and China. The factories served as members-only meeting places, where British merchants conducted business in wine, gold, ivory, and spices. Importantly, the factory house was also the center of British social life, and many factory houses, like the one in Oporto, have lavish dining rooms, dessert rooms, libraries, drawing rooms, map rooms, writing rooms, and ballrooms. Interestingly, until 1843, women were forbidden from dining at the Factory House (and therefore not allowed to enjoy the copious amounts of Port—plus Bordeaux and Champagne—that flowed during and after the members' lengthy lunches and dinners). They were, however, always permitted to attend the balls, their presence there being somewhat more necessary. Today, thanks to consolidation within the Port industry, the Factory House in Oporto belongs to just a few Port shippers. To be a member, an individual must be British, and a director of a Port company. Members pay annual "dues" of twenty cases of vintage Port each year. And while the Factory House is not open to the public, the shippers who own it entertain frequently, allowing a considerable number of guest visitors to experience its history and splendor each year.

HOW LONG WILL AN OPENED BOTTLE OF PORT LAST?

Because Port is both fortified and sweet, an opened bottle lasts longer than an opened bottle of regular table wine. Precisely how long is dependent on a variety of factors including how old and fragile it is and whether or not it was exposed to considerable oxygen during its production. Here are some guidelines for the three leading styles:

TYPE OF PORT	WILL LAST
Aged Tawny	1 month to 6 months
Late-Bottled Vintage	1 week to 1 month
Vintage, Single-Quinta Vintage	From 1 day for an old, delicate vintage Port to 2 weeks or more for a younger, robust one

right hand toward the center. The word *deiseal* is derived from the Celtic *deas*, meaning "right hand," and *iul*, meaning "direction."

Drinking Port is the easiest part. Any good-size wineglass will do. (The glass should be large enough to allow the Port to be swirled.) Generally about 2½ to 3½ ounces (74 to 104 milliliters) of Port is poured in the glass—a slightly smaller amount, in other words, than you would pour of a table wine.

As for aging, some Ports are made so that they can be drunk right away; others will mature and improve if stored well. The two main styles of Port that improve with age are

Sandeman was founded in 1790 by George Sandeman, the son of a Scottish cabinetmaker. With a £30 loan from his father and the goal of making a "modest fortune," the younger Sandeman set up shop, ultimately establishing Sandeman as a leading producer of both Port and Sherry.

PORTUGAL'S NATIONAL DISH

Dried salted cod—*bacalhau*—is Portugal's national dish. Although the fish is also popular in Spain and the south of France, no place is more passionate about *bacalhau* than Portugal, where, it is said, there are at least a year's worth of different recipes for it.

By the time Columbus journeyed to America, the Portuguese were fishing for cod as far away as the Grand Banks of Newfoundland. The best *bacalhau* was salted at sea with sea salt from the area south of Lisbon, called Setúbal (an area also famous for its dessert wine), after which the salted cod would be dried onshore. The large, white, almost mummified fish can be seen hanging in *bacalerias,* shops that specialize in the fish. To prepare it, the fish is soaked for one to two days in several changes of water. This removes the salt and rehydrates the flesh. The fish is then cooked in any of a number of ways. In a very popular version, it's flaked, then whipped and cooked with extra virgin olive oil, potatoes, fried onions, and cream, until it has a thick, creamy texture somewhere between that of scrambled eggs and mashed potatoes. In my own experience, the *bacalhau* occasionally served to guests who visit Quinta do Vesuvio comes as close to perfection as any cod dish in the world.

THE BOTTLE'S BEGINNINGS

We have grown so used to bottled wine that we perhaps forget that wine bottles are a relatively recent invention. For most of wine's history, it was sold (and often consumed) directly from the barrel. The first wine in the world to be successfully sold in cylindrical bottles was Port, sometime around 1775. Indeed, the advent of the cylindrical bottle permitted the style of vintage Port to be born, since the wine could now be laid down in bins for long periods of maturing and aging in the bottle.

vintage Port and single-quinta vintage Port. These can be cellared a long time—as much as three decades or more.

All other Ports—tawny, reserve, and late-bottled vintage—are ready to drink when released, although they can also be stored for about two years (or sometimes more) without loss of quality. And here's a visual cue to aging: Ports that can be drunk right away generally have a stopper-type cork (a cork with a cap on top of it). This will be immediately obvious upon removing the foil. Ports that improve with age, such as vintage Port, are sealed with a regular cork (the kind that requires a corkscrew). These should be stored lying down. Notice that Port bottles themselves are generally black, to prevent oxidation and help preserve the freshness of the Port should it be kept for significantly long periods of time.

The Ports to Know

All of the wines below are blends of any combination of touriga nacional, touriga franca (these are usually the two leading varieties), plus tinta barroca, tinta roriz, tinta amarela, tinto cão, and other traditional grapes that are sometimes still interplanted in the vineyard. Often, the exact varietal breakdown of a wine is not available, and thus it is not listed below. (Instead, many shippers provide statistics on the percentage of a variety planted, as opposed to the percentage of that variety used in the wine.) In any case, the percentage of each grape variety used varies each year.

Note that the labels on Port bottles always refer to Porto, the Portuguese word for Port.

TAYLOR FLADGATE

10-Year-Old Tawny Port

A scrumptious tawny, full of walnut, brown sugar, and vanilla flavors, yet still young enough to have hints of spicy berry flavors as well. Ten-year-old tawnies are generally less complex than twenty-year-olds, but they can make up for it, as this one does, with zesty flavors. Taylor is also renowned for its rich, powerful vintage Ports and the stunningly delicious single-quinta Port, Quinta de Vargellas.

W. & J. GRAHAM'S

20-Year-Old Tawny Port

The wines of Graham's always evoke velvet and voluptuousness. Of all of the Port shippers, none is more dependable for making wines that always possess a hedonistic, mind-blowing richness. This hauntingly good twenty-year-old tawny is an example. You could tease apart the aromas and flavors (butter-roasted nuts, brown sugar, exotic spices, and crème brûlée) or you could just feel and sense the luxuriousness and be transported by the complexity.

RAMOS PINTO

Late-Bottled Vintage Port

One of the top Port shippers to be founded by a Portuguese family, Ramos Pinto makes some of the richest, raciest LBVs in the Douro. A typical Ramos Pinto LBV is very elegant, yet has remarkable tensile strength and torrents of plum, spice, and mocha flavors. The firm's vintage Ports are getting more stellar by the vintage. Adriano Ramos Pinto founded the house in 1880, when he was just twenty-one years old. Owned today by the French Champagne house of Louis Roederer, the firm is still run on a daily basis by the Ramos Pinto family, and houses a museum showcasing the art collection that the family has been building for over 130 years.

W. & J. GRAHAM'S

Vintage Port

Graham's is usually among the most sensuous of all vintage Ports. Typically, blueberry fruit soars in your mouth and then explodes over and over again—like a brilliant rush of fireworks. In great vintages, the combination of ultra-rich fruit, lots of chocolate and black tea flavors, plus supple, powerful tannin and the wine's impeccable balance is unbeatable. All of Graham's vintage Ports are trodden by foot.

NIEPOORT

Vintage Port

Niepoort is a small, family-owned firm producing what are usually thrilling vintage Ports since 1842. Rich and beautifully balanced, they are full of sweet, powerful fruit. The firm is known as well for its legendary colheita Ports, reserve aged tawnies with absolutely mesmerizing syrupy brown sugar and vanilla flavors.

QUINTA DO INFANTADO

Single-Quinta Vintage Port

The vintage Ports from the tiny firm Quinta do Infantado ("Quinta of the Prince") are chocolaty/spicy Ports with briary anise and nutmeg flavors. The fruit is lush, nuanced, almost feminine in its elegance. For years the wine made at Quinta do Infantado was sold to larger Port shippers such as Taylor Fladgate and Graham's. That changed in 1979, when the Roseira family, which has owned the estate for over one hundred years, led the region in fighting for changes in the law to allow small producers to bottle and sell their own wine. Today, all of the firm's production is estate bottled. Every grape used at the quinta is handpicked and trodden by foot.

DOW'S

SENHORA DA RIBEIRA

Single-Quinta Vintage Port

Owned by the important Port shipper Dow, the small Senhora da Ribeira (Lady of the River) estate makes extraordinary single-quinta Ports (in especially great years, the grapes go into Dow's vintage Port). These are Ports with a softness and smoothness that are so profound, one might imagine the touch of a baby's cheek. The flavors, however, are anything but subdued—a mad dance of bursting blueberries, violets, licorice, minerals, and the exotic taste of the menthol-like resinous shrub that grows wild over the mountains (*esteva*). The old estate includes a chapel right by the river, a place where travelers could be blessed (and pray) before they crossed the turbulent waters.

TAYLOR FLADGATE

Vintage Port

Highly sought after, Taylor's vintage Ports are always among the most expensive. They're also among the most difficult to drink young. Unlike many vintage Ports, Taylor's are initially secretive and cloaked by a dense curtain of tannin. But with fifteen or so years of maturation, the top Taylor vintage Ports undergo a transformation that defies prediction. Elegant and sophisticated, they exude finesse and richness. Taylor's history is filled with firsts: first Port shipper to purchase vineyards in the Douro Valley (in 1744), first to produce single-quinta vintage Port, and the inventor of late-bottled vintage Port. The estate is also the only Port company to have remained 100 percent family owned in its considerable—it was founded in 1692—history.

QUINTA DO VESUVIO

Vintage Port

Considered by many to be the most magnificent traditional estate in the Douro Valley, the remote Quinta do Vesuvio was founded in the mid-1500s on a brilliantly sunlit, south-facing bank, virtually cantilevered over the river's edge, with jaw-dropping views in all directions. For centuries, the hand-built terraced vineyards (which took hundreds of men decades to hew out of the schist and rock) were considered jewels of the Douro. Today, the vineyards (many of them old) and neo-Baroque manor house and chapel are owned by the Symington family. Only vintage Port is produced on the estate, and the grapes are entirely trodden by foot. The wine is immaculate. When young, it is explosive with blueberry, violet, cocoa powder, black fig, and mineral notes; when aged, it is langorously supple and silky, yet still vivid and pure.

MADEIRA

ortified, oxidized, maderized, and aged for as long as two hundred years, Madeira has no equal in the wine world. In fact, Madeira is unique and so hard to make, it's remarkable that the wine is still around today (a testament, surely, to its utter deliciousness). Here is Madeira's story.

The wine Madeira comes from a small cluster of volcanic islands, the largest and most important of which is also called Madeira—from *ilha da madeira*, "island of the woods." Although Madeira and its tiny sister islands are geographically part of Africa (about 310 miles/500 kilometers west of the Moroccan coast), they are nonetheless a province of Portugal, some 620 miles (1,000 kilometers) to the northeast. In fact, the islands were discovered in 1419 or 1420 (accounts differ), when the Portuguese explorer Prince Henry

the Navigator instructed the sea captain João Gonçalves Zarco to explore the coast of Africa and establish a port of call that could be used as a provisions stop by ships bound for the East Indies or the Americas.

Ultimately, no wine would become more a part of the United States' beginnings. Drunk by the founding fathers during the signing of the Declaration of Independence, Madeira was also what Francis Scott Key sipped as he composed "The Star-Spangled Banner." George Washington (who reportedly drank a pint every night with dinner), Thomas Jefferson, and Benjamin Franklin all adored it, as did John Adams (who wrote to his wife,

▲ *Old casks of verdelho aging in Blandy's lodge. Between the long heating process (which for the very best Madeiras takes place in barrels), then the subsequent long barrel aging process, the finest Madeiras may age a total of forty years or more.*

Abigail, about the copious amounts they consumed during the Continental Congress). By the end of the eighteenth century, nearly a fourth of all the Madeira produced was being exported to the American colonies. Among the colonial well-to-do, Madeira parties—forerunners of the American cocktail party—became commonplace.

The unbridled American passion for Madeira was certainly a testament to its compelling flavor. But Madeira's popularity was equally based on something far more mundane: taxes. As of 1665, British governing authorities in the colonies had banned the importation of European goods, unless they were shipped on British ships that had sailed from British ports (and paid British taxes). Merchandise shipped from Madeira was exempted. Merchants in Madeira took full advantage of the loophole, establishing close trading relationships with merchants in Baltimore, Boston, New York, Savannah, Charleston, and Philadelphia. As American corn and cotton flowed out of the colonies, Madeira wine flowed in.

THE LAND AND THE VINEYARDS

As is true in most of Portugal, growing grapes in Madeira is a herculean undertaking. The island's formidable terrain and maritime climate are significant obstacles to success, but then almost everything about Madeira is rather miraculous, including the intricate and painstaking manner by which the wine is made (more on this in a moment).

The main island and its minuscule sisters are the tops of a vast mountain range under the Atlantic Ocean (thought by some to be the lost continent of Atlantis). Volcanic in origin, these summits are deeply fissured peaks of basalt (cooled lava), stacked accordionlike one next to the other and separated by narrow ravines.

The main island (where all of the vineyards are located) possesses just over 1,000 acres (400 hectares) of grapevines. While bananas and sugarcane are grown extensively near the

THE FLAVOR OF HISTORY

If you want to taste something really old, Madeira is the answer. While finding a bottle of Bordeaux from, say, the 1960s can be daunting (not to mention fiscally dangerous), Madeiras that are a century old or more can easily be found in specialty wine shops. Indeed, vintage Madeiras that go back to the founding of the United States, in 1776, are known to exist. (For my part, I have tasted Blandy's Madeiras back to the awesome, luscious 1811, which redefined my notion of exquisite.) What makes these centurions especially outstanding is, of course, their spellbinding complexity and aliveness. Properly sealed, a bottle of Madeira will easily outlive its owner, and remain in excellent condition throughout its life. Importantly, because it's already been oxidized and maderized, Madeira is nearly indestructible. During colonial times (pre-refrigeration), this fact made Madeira especially appealing in the American South, where bottles could survive over decades of hot summers without any ill effects.

coasts, grapes tend to be grown higher up in the mountains, nearer the tops of the peaks—at altitudes from 600 to 1,300 feet (180 to 400 meters). Because the sheer cliff faces are difficult to cultivate, terraces were built by hand centuries ago (much as they were in the Douro). Necessarily, the vineyards themselves are often just tiny plots (locally referred to as *jardim*—gardens). Even today, they are tended and harvested by hand (at considerable expense), for machinery has proven virtually impossible to use in this landscape.

Although the islands are on the same parallel as Los Angeles and Jerusalem, they get a lot of rain—more, in fact, than London. But luckily, most of it falls in winter—between October and April, when the vines are mostly dormant. Nonetheless, mold and mildew are threats, and some vineyards are planted up on high trellises so that they are lifted way above the ground and dew. A potentially more serious danger is the *leste*, an intense heat wave blowing off the Sahara desert, which can cover the vines in sand and dust and raise the temperature to more than 100°F (38°C) for weeks at a time.

HOW MADEIRA IS MADE

Like Port, Madeira is a fortified wine (17 to 20 percent alcohol by volume) that started out unfortified. During the Age of Exploration (from the late fifteenth century into the sixteenth) unfortified Madeira was part of the provisions picked up by merchant ships traveling to Africa, the East Indies, and the New World. Baked in a sweltering hold, the unfortified wine spoiled quickly. Soon, small amounts of distilled alcohol (made from sugarcane) were being added to stabilize the wine. Later, by the late seventeenth century, brandy (rather than simple distilled alcohol) was added, which not only helped preserve the wine, but added a new dimension to its flavor.

Madeira fortified with brandy turned out to be a remarkable product. Aged over years on a rolling ship in the equatorial heat, this Madeira became a deliciously rich, velvety wine. In time, the most prized Madeiras of all were the so-called *vinhos da roda*, Madeiras that had taken a round-trip tropical cruise from Portugal to India and back again. As sensational as they were, they were also exorbitantly expensive to produce. Eventually, Madeira's winemakers thought of ways to replicate the effects of a trip halfway around the globe—without actually having to leave home.

To make Madeira, a winemaker starts out as he would with any wine. Grapes are harvested, crushed, pressed, and fermented in barrels or tanks.

In the case of Madeira, the grapes include the white grapes—sercial, verdelho, terrantez, bual (also known as boal and malvasia fina), and malmsey (technically the same as malvasia branca de São Jorge)—plus the red grape tinta negra mole (also known as negramoll). Historians believe that most of these grapes were brought to the island in the fifteenth century from northern Portugal. As we'll see, all but tinta negra mole are used independently to create a separate style of Madeira. (See The Grapes and Styles of Madeira, page 534.)

As with Port, brandy is added to the fermenting grapes at a very specific point. The brandy kills the yeasts, halts the fermentation, and leaves a fortified wine that has some of the sweetness of the original grapes. How much sweetness depends on when the brandy is added. If the brandy is added early in the fermentation, a lot of sweetness will be left. If the brandy is added at the tail end of fermentation, the Madeira will be almost dry.

But Madeira's toffee-caramel-butterscotch-cocoa-curry-like character comes not only as a result of the grapes used and the sweetness left in the wine. Next, the Madeira-to-be will be maderized and oxidized.

During maderization, the Madeira is heated—either slowly and naturally in hot attics (simulating months and sometimes years of heat in the hold of a ship sailing through the tropics), or by a process known as *estufagem* (esh-too-FAH-jaym) in specially designed tanks that can be heated. Indeed, the term for heating wine—maderization—originates from the word Madeira itself.

Several methods can be employed to maderize the wine, depending on the quality of the Madeira being made. For basic, inexpensive Madeira, the fortified base wine is placed in large vats fitted with serpentine stainless-steel heating coils. The wine is then slowly heated to a maximum temperature of 131°F (55°C) for three to six months—a method of *estufagem* called *cuba de calor*. Importantly, the wine is heated very, very slowly, for heated too quickly, the wine takes on a slightly burnt flavor and ages prematurely.

Another method—*armazém de calor*—involves storing large casks of the fortified

STENCILED BOTTLES

Just as they were hundreds of years ago, bottles of vintage Madeira continue to be stenciled, rather than labeled with a paper label. The process, done by hand by older women in the producers' lodges, dates from a time when the island was so poor and isolated that shipments of paper from the mainland could not be depended upon.

wine in specially designed rooms that can be heated like a sauna. This slightly more gentle process can last for six months to a year.

However, for the very finest Madeiras (a minuscule 3 percent of all Madeiras made) the heating is carried out naturally, more or less as it was done centuries ago. By this method (called *canteiro*), casks of the best wines are placed in rooms in the producers' lodges (warehouses), which, sitting under the hot Madeiran sun, eventually build up tremendous heat. There the casks remain undisturbed, usually for about twenty years, although sometimes as long as one hundred years or more.

Importantly, the casks are not filled to the brim, nor are they topped up. The combination of time, heat, and oxygen has a superb mellowing effect on the wine, creating an inimitable texture and flavor.

But the Madeira isn't quite done yet. After the heating process is complete, the wine is carefully and slowly cooled and allowed to rest (sometimes for a year or more, to recover from the sustained heat). When the wine is deemed well rested, it is aged even further.

For the finest Madeiras, this aging process is also lengthy and involved. The wines are put into casks made from various woods—usually American oak, but sometimes chestnut, Brazilian satinwood, or even mahogany. Again, the casks are not filled to the top; instead, a

head space is deliberately left so that the wine continues to slowly oxidize, mellowing the flavors even more.

Unbelievable as it may be, a fine Madeira is usually aged twenty years or more *after* the twenty-year heating process but before blending and bottling (and this doesn't count the time that it might be aged further in bottle in someone's cellar). Thus, many great Madeiras are at least forty years in the making!

THE GRAPES AND STYLES OF MADEIRA

The very best Madeiras—and the ones you should taste—are made from one of five white grapes designated as "noble" by the Madeira Wine Institute. These are sercial, verdelho, terrantez, bual, and malmsey. Conveniently, the names of these grapes are also used to designate the styles of Madeira (so I have not included a separate box on the grapes of this region). I'll start with the driest style (sercial) and move to the sweetest (malmsey).

But before I get to the big five styles, know that there are also inexpensive, basic Madeiras that have little of the refinement or complexity of sercial, verdelho, terrantez, bual (boal), or malmsey. Most of these basic-quality Madeiras are made from the red grape tinta negra mole (the name means "black soft"), and come designated as either dry, medium dry, medium sweet, or sweet. Among these basic Madeiras, the light style known as Rainwater (said to be the accidental result of casks left out in the rain) is fairly popular. But all of these basic Madeiras are, in my opinion, better for cooking than drinking, and in fact, because the wine is already maderized and oxidized, you can leave a bottle handy right beside the stove.

SERCIAL: The driest style (see The Sweetness Level of Each Madeira Style, page 535). Sercial grapes are grown in the coolest vineyards. The difficulties they encounter in ripening make for tart base wines. These in turn lead to tangy, elegant Madeiras with a bracing, almost salty grip and a dry, nutty flavor that I always imagine to be like caramel minus any sweetness.

VERDELHO: The medium-dry style. Verdelho grapes, grown in slightly warmer vineyards, ripen more easily, making for Madeiras that are exquisitely balanced and somewhat more full-bodied than sercials.

TERRANTEZ: A rare style based on a rare grape that is difficult to grow. It typically falls between verdelho and bual in sweetness and body.

BUAL: Another rare style; this one, medium-rich. Bual grapes (or boal, as it is sometimes spelled) are grown in warm vineyards, producing concentrated Madeiras with sweet richness. Bual was a great favorite in English officers' clubs in India because it was a lighter wine than either malmsey or Port. Bual/boal is the same as the grape variety malvasia fina.

MALMSEY: The richest, sweetest style. Also known as malvasia (once again, in this case, the malvasia is malvasia branca de São Jorge), these grapes are grown in the warmest locations, usually on the south side of the island, producing superripe grapes and ultimately, Madeiras of astonishing richness.

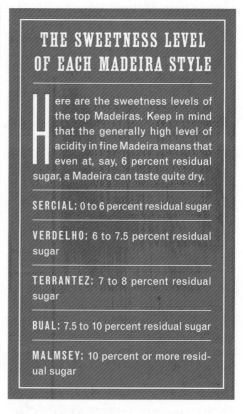

THE SWEETNESS LEVEL OF EACH MADEIRA STYLE

Here are the sweetness levels of the top Madeiras. Keep in mind that the generally high level of acidity in fine Madeira means that even at, say, 6 percent residual sugar, a Madeira can taste quite dry.

SERCIAL: 0 to 6 percent residual sugar

VERDELHO: 6 to 7.5 percent residual sugar

TERRANTEZ: 7 to 8 percent residual sugar

BUAL: 7.5 to 10 percent residual sugar

MALMSEY: 10 percent or more residual sugar

THE QUALITY LEVELS OF MADEIRA

In addition to styles of Madeira, there are also quality levels. In ascending order, they are three-year-old, five-year-old, ten-year-old, fifteen-year-old, solera, colheita, and vintage Madeiras, known as *frasqueira*.

THREE-YEAR-OLD MADEIRA: These are Madeiras made from tinta negra mole grapes that undergo a quick heating process and are then aged at least three years, usually in tanks, not casks. These are sometimes labeled "finest," and are totally fine . . . for cooking.

FIVE-YEAR-OLD RESERVE MADEIRA: This is the minimum quality level for a Madeira labeled with one of the noble varieties, sercial, verdelho, terrantez, bual, or malmsey. A five-year-old reserve is a blended Madeira in which the youngest component in the blend is aged at least five years in casks.

TEN-YEAR-OLD SPECIAL RESERVE MADEIRA: Higher still in quality are Madeiras, often made from the noble grapes, where the youngest component in the blend is aged at least ten years in casks. These special reserve Madeiras must go through the heating process naturally in casks, not tanks.

FIFTEEN-YEAR-OLD EXTRA RESERVE MADEIRA: Even better yet. The youngest component must be aged at least fifteen years. These wines are also maderized in casks (not in tanks) and are usually made from noble grapes.

MADEIRA PRODUCERS

Although there were more than two dozen producers exporting Madeira at the time of the American Revolution, by the second decade of the twenty-first century, fewer than ten remained. Today, the largest distinguished firm is the Madeira Wine Company, which owns most of the top brands, including Blandy's, Cossart Gordon, Leacock's, and Miles. The Madeira Wine Company is partly owned by the Symington family, which also owns many top Port firms, including Warre's, Dow's, Graham's, Quinta do Vesuvio, and Smith Woodhouse. In addition, the Rare Wine Company, based in Sonoma, California, in association with the Madeira firm Vinhos Barbeito, produces a historic series of Madeiras based on the top fine Madeiras once sold in Boston, New York, Savannah, and New Orleans.

SOLERA MADEIRA: While they can still be found on the market, these wines are very rare, and can no longer be produced, according to European Union law. Like Sherry, solera Madeiras are made by an intricate process of fractional blending (see How the Solera Works, page 458).

COLHEITA MADEIRA: Sometimes called "harvest" Madeiras, colheitas are a relatively new type of Madeira. They are made from grapes grown in a single year, then bottled after spending at least five years aging. The first colheita Madeira was a Blandy's 1994 Malmsey released in 2000. These are, in effect, early-bottled *frasqueira* wines. They must be made from the five noble varieties.

FRASQUEIRA OR VINTAGE MADEIRA: This is the ultimate quality level, and the wines can be ravishing in their complexity. Vintage Madeiras are wines of a single year. Remarkably, vintage Madeira must be aged at least twenty years in cask after the heating period, and then an additional two years in the bottle. Vintage Madeira must be made from one of the five noble grapes.

SERVING MADEIRA

Madeira is best served in a good-size white wine glass, so that there's enough room to swirl the wine. Sercials and verdelhos—the drier styles—are usually served cool; the sweeter styles—buals and malmseys—are served at coolish room temperature.

All styles of Madeira have a gripping backbone of natural acidity, making them refreshing to drink on their own but also exquisite counterpoints to food. Sercial and verdelho are dramatic aperitifs and delicious with first-course salads or soups. Bual and luscious malmsey can be desserts in themselves, but their racy acidity also means they are among the world's best juxtapositions to the richness of desserts made with cream or chocolate. One of my most favorite combinations in the world is chocolate chip cookies with Malmsey Madeira.

Finally, an opened bottle of Madeira lasts nearly forever. After everything it's been through—fortification, extreme heat, long aging in the presence of oxygen—Madeira is pretty indestructible.

PORTUGUESE TABLE WINES

THE MINHO | THE DOURO | DÃO | BAIRRADA | ALENTEJO

Historically, there have been two Portugals—the famous Portugal that made Port and the obscure Portugal that made dry table wines. The two worlds rarely overlapped, and the vast majority of producers made either one style of wine or the other, not both. Port was renowned but, with one or two exceptions, the country's table wines were less than inspired. Most were the cheap products of cooperatives.

But in the years following Portugal's entry into the European Economic Community in 1986, the picture slowly began to change. By the last decade of the twentieth century, some of the most underrated dry red and white table wines in Europe were coming from Portugal. Bold, distinctive reds and fresh, flavorful whites, they were delicious and often good values. And they still are. But for the first time, Portugal's top wine firms are now also taking higher aim and making phenomenal dry wines—reds in

▲ *The Ponte de Lima, a bridge in the Minho region of northern Portugal, leads to the church of San António. During the Middle Ages, the Minho was governed by Benedictine monks.*

THE GRAPES OF PORTUGAL—TABLE WINES

Portugal has more than 250 grape varieties, and most table wines are blends of several of them. Below are the major grapes, most of them native to the Iberian Peninsula.

WHITES

ALVARINHO: Portuguese grape, well known for being one of the main grapes used to make many vinho verdes, although more than twenty other white grapes are also permitted. It is known as albariño in Galicia, Spain, next door.

ARINTO: Used throughout Portugal in dozens of blended wines. Commonly used in vinho verde (where it is known as pederña) for its good balance of freshness and fruitiness.

AVESSO: A full-bodied white used in blends in the Minho region to produce white table wines and vinho verdes.

ENCRUZADO: A leading grape in the simple white wines of the Dão.

GOUVEIO AND VIOSINHO: Commonly blended together—sometimes along with malvasia fina—to make white table wines in the Douro. Also used for white Port.

LOUREIRO AND TRAJADURA: Along with pederña (arinto) frequently used in making vinho verde, usually blended with each other.

MALVASIA FINA: Portuguese grape native to either the Douro or the Dão and today a leading grape in the white wines of the Dão.

REDS

ALFROCHEIRO PRETO, BASTARDO, AND JAÉN: Important grapes in the Dão, where they contribute spice and acidity.

ARAGONEZ: One of the Portuguese names for the Spanish grape tempranillo. A leading grape used to make wines in the Alentejo region.

AZAL TINTO (AKA AMARAL) AND VINHÃO: Two of the leading grapes commonly blended together to make the sharp but fresh-tasting red vinho verde.

BAGA: The word means "berry" in Portuguese. Grown in almost all regions, but especially important in Bairrada. Tannic and acidic.

PERIQUITA: The word means "parakeet" in Portuguese. One of the leading grapes used to make wines in the Alentejo, and grown in other regions as well.

TINTA BARROCA, TOURIGA FRANCA, TINTA RORIZ, TINTO CÃO, AND TOURIGA NACIONAL: Well-established Portuguese grapes, often blended together to make table wines in the Douro and sometimes the Dão. Most are also used in the making of Port.

TRINCADEIRA PRETA: One of the leading grapes used to make wines in the Alentejo. Also known as tinta amarela.

particular—priced like top cabernet sauvignons from Napa Valley or Bordeaux.

Portuguese table wines are almost always blends of many grape varieties rarely found elsewhere. Most of these are thought to be Phoenician in origin, or varieties that are thought to have originated on the Iberian Peninsula. Indeed, some Portuguese table wines are still based on centuries-old field blends, with potentially a dozen or more varieties interplanted in the vineyard. For red wines (a majority of the table wines made are red), the most common varieties are also the major varieties used for Port (see page 514), but other varieties also show up, including jaén, alfrocheiro preto, periquita, and baga, among others.

As is true almost everywhere in Europe, Portuguese wines are named not by grape variety, but by region. Here are the top five wine regions, going from north to south. Historically, with the exception of the Minho, all of the regions were better known for red wines than white, although Portuguese table whites are now making great strides in quality and are thus attracting a following.

THE MINHO

In the far northwest, just below the Spanish border, the fertile, rolling green hills are crammed with orchards and farm crops (corn, potatoes, and beans). This is the Minho, one of the most agriculturally productive regions of the country, and the region where many bold, fresh-tasting white table wines are made. Among these is one of Portugal's most popular white wines—vinho verde.

Vinho verde (literally, "green wine") used to be a light, low-alcohol, inexpensive white with a touch of spritz meant for washing down humble fish dishes. Today, however, more serious vinho verdes are being made—wines with greater flavor intensity and no fizz. The word *verde* (green), by the way, refers not to the wine's color but to the fact that historically vinho verde was a young wine meant to be drunk soon after it was made. In days past, so immediate was the consumption of vinho verde that many producers

Quinta de Covela in the Minho. The 16th-century estate, which was recently restored, specializes in unique blends that combine Portuguese and French varieties.

Harvesting touriga nacional grapes in the Dão. Portugal's red table wines are loaded with personality.

didn't even bother to put a vintage date on the bottle.

Vinho verde can be made from any of twenty-five white grapes, or a combination of them. The best wines, however, come from alvarinho, trajadura, and loureiro (known as albariño, treixadura, and loureira in Rías Baixas, the Spanish wine region next door), as well as with the grape arinto, one of Portugal's fascinatingly fresh, citrusy whites. Indeed, in the past few years, the top vinho verdes have improved so much in quality that they seem very much like their Rías Baixas sisters—the vinho verde from Quinta das Arcas, for example. One of the most serious producers to watch here is Anselmo Mendes.

A large percentage of vinho verde is not white but red. Red "green" wine is usually not exported, but when you're in Portugal, don't pass up a chance to try it. A shocking magenta in color, red vinho verde can be fascinating, but it can also be as bitingly acidic as red wine gets. This is considered a plus, given the region's rustic bean, pork, and oily codfish dishes.

All of this said, know that vinho verde is only one of the DOs (denominations) in the Minho. For as good as the best vinho verdes are, some of the most avant-garde, intriguing whites are simply labeled Minho and are based on varieties not used for vinho verde. A good example is Quinta de Covela's terrific dry white that is a blend of avesso, chardonnay, viognier, and gewürztraminer.

YO, NEW YORKAS . . . WHO'S THE QUEEN IN QUEENS?

The borough of Queens, part of New York City, was named after the Princess of Portugal, Catherine of Braganza, who became Queen of England in 1662. It was during the reign of her husband, King Charles II, that the colony of New Amsterdam became New York, and Queens was named to honor Catherine.

THE DOURO

W hile the Douro is famous for Port (see page 511), it's also the up-and-coming region for Portugal's top dry red table wines—and there are many: Quinta do Vesuvio's Pombal do Vesuvio, Chryseia, Wine & Soul Pintas, Quinta do Malhô, Grande Escolha Piheiros, Quinta da Gricha, Quinta do Vallado, and Conceito among them. These are structured, powerful wines with dark, peaty flavors and a juicy black fig character (imagine Port if it wasn't fortified or sweet). They are aged in new French oak barrels and often possess a unique, resinous chaparral aroma not unlike the smell of *esteva*, a rock rose that grows along the terrace walls in the vineyards.

The vineyards for Douro table wines are, like the vineyards for Port, on rocky hillsides of schist. Of the nearly forty grapes allowed, some of the principal red grapes are the same as those used for Port: touriga franca, touriga nacional, tinta roriz, tinta barroca, tinto cão, sousão, and the spicy grape tinta da barca.

DÃO

A nother one of Portugal's most promising regions for red table wines, the Dão began to produce markedly better wines in the late 1980s, after the government rescinded the law requiring that all grapes grown in the region be sold to cooperatives. The region lies about 30 miles (48 kilometers) south of the Douro River. It is enclosed on three sides by mountains, which shelter the region from the chill and moisture of the Atlantic and give it a Mediterranean climate.

Nearly fifty grapes are authorized for use in the region. The best of them is the red touriga

THE WAY WE WERE: LANCERS AND MATEUS

F or any American in the baby boomer generation who began drinking wine in college, the two big date-night wines were Lancers and Mateus. Both wines are slightly sparkling, slightly sweet Portuguese rosés, and both played a phenomenally important role in the culture of wine in the U.S. in the 1950s, '60s, and '70s (both wines are still available today).

Lancers, produced by the historic Portuguese firm J. M. da Fonseca, was the 1944 brainchild of an American wine merchant named Henry Behar, who was looking for a rosé that would suit post-World War II American tastes. Behar named the wine after *Las Lanzas (The Lancers),* his favorite painting by the Spanish master Velázquez. From the beginning, it was bottled in the dark red crockery bottle that became its signature.

Mateus had been created two years earlier, in 1942, by Fernando van Zeller Guedes, founder of the Portuguese firm Sogrape. A blend of several grapes, including baga, tinta barroca, and touriga franca, Mateus came in squat, flask-shaped bottles, modeled on the water canteens soldiers carried during World War I. More than a billion bottles have been sold since the brand began. Finally, while it is said that Queen Elizabeth II regularly ordered Mateus as an accompaniment to her dinners at the Savoy Hotel, Mateus's most legendary customer may well have been Jimi Hendrix, who didn't bother with a glass, but drank it straight from the flask instead.

SETÚBAL

According to legend, Setúbal was settled by one of Noah's sons, Tubal, hence the region's name. The small peninsula, about 20 miles (32 kilometers) south of Lisbon, is known for only one wine, the famous dessert wine also known as Setúbal. A sweet fortified wine, like Port, Setúbal is made principally from two types of muscat grapes: moscatel de Setúbal (muscat of Alexandria) and moscatel roxo (purple muscat). Up to 30 percent of five other indigenous grapes may be blended in.

The best Setúbals are almost hauntingly aromatic, thanks to the extraordinarily long time the grape skins are left macerating in the wine—up to six months. The wine's flavor is outrageously irresistible, a rich, exotic mingling of mandarin oranges, caramel, molasses, and wild herbs. And the color can be mesmerizing, from vivid orange-red to rich chestnut. Setúbal is usually drunk with cakes made with nuts, such as walnut cake.

Setúbal may be vintage dated or may be a blend of wines of different ages. A Setúbal labeled twenty years old, for example, will be a blend of several wines, the youngest of which is twenty years old. Only a handful of companies make Setúbal, including the well-respected firm J. M. da Fonseca.

nacional, one of the major Port grapes. Other good-quality red grapes include alfrocheiro preto, jaén, and bastardo.

Among the leading Dão wines are Alvaro Castro Quinta da Pellada, Quinta dos Roques, and Quinta das Marias.

BAIRRADA

Bairrada derives its name from *barro,* the Portuguese word for clay, which constitutes a large percentage of the soil in the region. Bairrada is just west of the Dão, in central Portugal, and is not far from the Atlantic Ocean. The leading grape is the juicy, acidic baga, which by law must make up 50 percent of the blend of any red wine made there. Some fifteen other grapes are grown.

About 60 percent of Portugal's sparkling wines are made here, including rustic, grapey, red sparkling wines that are often paired with the region's specialty, roast suckling pig. Among the top Bairrada wines are those made by Luís Pato, Caves São João, and Campolargo.

ALENTEJO

The biggest wine region in Portugal, the Alentejo covers virtually all of the southeastern part of the country. The hot, dry, rolling plains produce, in addition to wine, olive oil, and cereal grains, more than half of the world's supply of cork.

The soil here is mostly volcanic in origin and includes granite, quartz, schist, and chalk. As in most of Portugal's other top regions, the finest wines are red (although, increasingly, a number of surprisingly refreshing whites are made). Among the popular red grapes are periquita, aragonez, and trincadeira preta. The Alentejo has historically been a poor region. Since ancient Roman times, the lack of forests here meant that wines were made in huge earthenware amphorae. A handful of producers continue to make wine this way today.

The top Alentejo red wines have a plummy/spicy/peppery character and come from near the Spanish border. Among the best are Herdade do Esporão, Herdade do Sobroso, and Herdade do Peso.

The Portuguese Table Wines to Know

WHITES

QUINTA DAS ARCAS

VINHO VERDE | MINHO

Loureiro, trajadura, and arinto

Fresh, limey, lively, and almost gingery in the way it refreshes the palate, Quinta das Arcas is among a group of estates moving away from the vinho verdes of the past and making more dramatically flavorful wines not unlike those of their next-door neighbor, the albariños of Rías Baixas, in Spain. The estate, founded in 1985, is one of four small estates in Minho and Alentejo owned by the Monteiro family. The family also produces handmade cheeses on the property.

Arca Nova

Alvarinho/Trajadura

QUINTA DE COVELA

COVELA BRANCO | MINHO

Avesso, chardonnay, viognier, and gewürztraminer

This very unusual regional blend of indigenous, modern, and aromatic grapes is phenomenally successful and has a unique flavor that's not quite like any single one of the grapes used to make it. Concentrated and lush (but not heavy), the wine has floral, tropical, and citrus notes that are pure and delicious. The Covela estate is in the area of the Minho where vinho verde is made, but the winery specializes in atypical white and red blends, some of which incorporate French grapes such as chardonnay, viognier, and cabernet sauvignon. The estate has passed through many hands over the years and most recently lay fallow, until it was purchased in the 2010s by a Brazilian businessman and British journalist who have restored it to its former glory. Parts of the main building date to the 1500s, when the stone Renaissance manor, Casa de Covela, ruled over the hillside.

HERDADE DO ESPORÃO

RESERVA | ALENTEJO

Antão vaz, arinto, roupeiro, and sémillon in varying proportions

The very warm-climate Alentejo region of southern Portugal does not seem like a place where crisp, racy whites could be made. But they are. Over thousands of years, grape varieties on the Iberian Peninsula have adapted to the severe climate, and the wines that result can often mimic wines from regions much farther north. This white *reserva* from Herdade do Esporão is a great example. Bone-dry, bracing, and full of personality, it has a spicy, citrusy tangerine and piquant green herb character that's cool and refreshing. Herdade do Esporão is one of the most stunning estates of southern Portugal and includes an important archaeological site and museum, as well as olive groves that yield some of Portugal's most renowned and sought-after olive oils.

REDS

PRATS & SYMINGTON

CHRYSEIA | DOURO

Tinta franca, touriga nacional, tinta roriz, tinto cão
in varying proportions

A 1998 joint venture by Portugal's Symington family and Bordeaux's Bruno Prats (former owner of Cos d'Estournel), Chryseia is widely regarded as a marriage of Portuguese tradition with modern Bordeaux winemaking. The wine is broodingly dark, sophisticated, structured, and evocative of bitter chocolate, cocoa, earth, and gamey meats. Yet for all its intensity, Chryseia has an elegance that comes across in its minerality and floral notes. The Symingtons and Prats are firm believers that the best grapes for Portuguese table wines are the intense, highly adapted great grapes that make Port. (Indeed, this table wine comes from blocks that are also used for vintage Port.) The name *Chryseia* means "golden" in Greek.

QUINTA DO VESUVIO

POMBAL DO VESUVIO | DOURO

Touriga franca, plus touriga nacional and tinta amarela

Despite their richness, Portuguese table wines have a wonderful freshness to them. Their freshness and precision remind me of cranberries, which are more fresh than, say, cherries. Quinta do Vesuvio's Pombal do Vesuvio (the name refers to the dovecote—*pombal*— in the middle of these vineyards) is a vivid wine with terrific, lightly bitter espresso flavors, plus notes of spice and peat, but also vanilla and chocolate. Quinta do Vesuvio, one of the most impressive estates of the Douro Valley, is famous for its Port. This is the second wine of the estate.

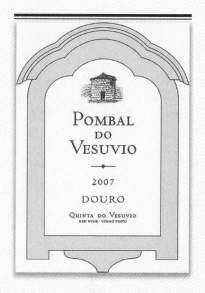

QUINTA DO VALLADO

RESERVA | DOURO

A field blend of more than twenty grape varieties

Duoro red table wines have a flavor evocative of the landscape—a wild chaparral, raspy scrub brush character—which tastes fantastic given the soft, dense core of black fig and tobacco flavors in these wines. Quinta do Vallado, which is also the home of the Port shipper Ferreira, is a perfect example of this, and a wine that de facto tastes more of its place than of a certain variety or varieties. Indeed, the wine is a field blend of old vines with more than twenty indigenous varieties interplanted, including tinta roriz, tinta amarela, and touriga franca. (Many such field blends of old vines remain in Portugal, and the often extraordinary wines that come from them are usually expensive.) Established in 1716, Quinta do Vallado is one of the oldest and most famous quintas in the Douro Valley, and today includes a stunning small hotel. It once belonged to Dona Antónia Adelaide Ferreira, a legendary businesswoman in the Port trade (historically completely dominated by men), and still belongs to her descendants.

0   100 km

DENMARK

SWEDEN

*NORTH
SEA*

*BALTIC
SEA*

○ HAMBURG

POLAND

BERLIN ○

NETHERLANDS

SAALE UNSTRUT ▼

GERMANY

SACHSEN ▶   DRESDEN

RHINE RIVER

BONN ○

▲
AHR

◀ *MITTELRHEIN*

MOSEL ▶

RHEINGAU
▼

FRANKFURT
○

BELGIUM

◀ *RHEINHESSEN*   ◀ *FRANKEN*

▲
NAHE

PFALZ ▶

◀ *BADEN*

CZECH REPUBLIC

FRANCE

MUNICH ○

AUSTRIA

SWITZERLAND

ITALY

GERMANY

MOSEL | RHEINGAU | PFALZ

AHR | BADEN | FRANKEN | MITTELRHEIN | NAHE | RHEINHESSEN

GERMANY RANKS NINTH AMONG WINE-PRODUCING COUNTRIES WORLDWIDE. THE GERMANS DRINK AN AVERAGE OF 10 GALLONS (38 LITERS) OF WINE PER PERSON PER YEAR.

ntil the twentieth century there were only two great wine-producing countries: France and Germany. While outstanding wines could occasionally be found elsewhere, no other country came close to these two for the supremacy of their wines. Indeed, in nineteenth-century London wine-auction and retail catalogs, German rieslings sold for more than First Growth Bordeaux and Grand Cru Burgundy.

Germany's vineyards lie at the northernmost extreme of where grapes can ripen dependably. At latitudes of 49 to 51 degrees, these vineyards are as far north as Mongolia and Newfoundland. Yet it is precisely this northern climate (along with many other factors I'll discuss) that gives German wines—especially rieslings—their shimmering beauty. The best German wines are, in many ways, what all wine aspires to be: an expression of fruit so vivid and pure that it is lifted up out of the ponderous, corporeal world of humanity and becomes a spiritual experience.

Of course, generic wines of no particular distinction are made in Germany, just as they

> The best German wines are, in many ways, what all wine aspires to be: an expression of fruit so vivid and pure that it is lifted up out of the ponderous, corporeal world of humanity and becomes a spiritual experience.

are everywhere else. Cheap and sweetish, these wines (sadly) constitute many wine drinkers' entire experience with German wines, and give rise to the gross misconception that German wine is categorically sweet. In fact, the top wines are just the opposite—they are dry. I'll address the confusion over dryness and sweetness momentarily, but for now, know that this chapter leaves generic wines aside and focuses on Germany's majestic wines—wines that should not be missed by anyone who loves flavor. For an explanation of German wine law, see the Appendix on Wine Laws, page 926.

THE TERRORS (AND THRILL) OF TERROIR

At northern extremes every nuance of terroir is magnified. Something as simple as being in the shadow of a ridge can ruin all hopes for ripeness, and hence all hopes of producing a wine of depth and intensity. As a result, Germany's vineyards—252,000 acres(102,000 hectares) in 2012—are the most precisely sited of any in the world. The best are always planted on south-, west-, or east-facing slopes to catch the light and warmth of every available sunbeam. (North-facing slopes are easy to identify; they're always vineless.) Most of the vineyards are planted in the river valleys of the Rhine and Mosel or their tributaries, since bodies of water act to moderate the severe climate.

Soil, too, must do its share. All of Germany's good vineyards are planted in places with heat-retaining soil and rocks, such as slate and

> The German word for vineyard is *weinberg,* literally, "wine hill." Many of the country's best vineyards are in fact on slopes, some of them as steep as 70 percent.

THE QUICK SIP ON GERMANY

GERMANY is considered one of the world's top producers of elegant white wines. The country's best rieslings, for example, have ravishing purity and concentration.

GERMAN VINEYARDS are at the northernmost extreme of where grapes can dependably ripen.

THE MAJORITY OF FINE German wines are dry or just a touch off-dry. The exceptions are the expensive late-harvest dessert wines *beerenauslesen* (BAs), *trockenbeerenauslesen* (TBAs), and eiseins, all of which are crafted to be sweet.

basalt. When each critical puzzle piece is fit together to form the whole picture, the wines will have just crested into ripeness, yet still be brimming—if not glistening—with acidity.

A word on ripeness. More than any other country in the world, Germany has benefited from climate change. For example, for most German wine regions in the 1960s and 1970s, only two or three vintages in a decade yielded ripe grapes and were considered a success. Today, virtually every vintage results in ripe grapes and is considered successful. To be sure, ripeness in Germany usually proceeds incrementally (there are few heat waves), but this is an advantage because grapes that ripen slowly have a better chance of developing complex flavors than grapes that get ripe fast. In short, Germany's changed climate has had a profound impact on the wines that are now made, and how those wines are categorized. I'll get to that later in this chapter.

If anything has been a German constant, however, it's acidity, and the levels are indeed high. For example, most Champagnes clock in at 5 or 6 grams of acidity per liter and are

FROM ROME TO BURGUNDY: GERMANY'S ROOTS

Curved wine pruning knives dating back to A.D. 100 have been found near the ruins of Roman garrisons along the Rhine River, suggesting that early wine-making in Germany was heavily influenced by Italy. But the first documentation of winegrowing in Germany comes from the Bordeaux writer Ausonius, whose poem "Mosella," written around A.D. 370, describes the meandering Rhine River and the vineyards clinging to the steep hills along it. By the time of the Middle Ages, monks were painstakingly planting and cultivating what are today considered the most famous vineyards. This ecclesiastical period was Germany's viticultural heyday, and the country is thought to have had four times as many acres of vineyard land then than exist there today. Around the 1500s, Germany's golden period waned due to a changing (colder) climate, greater wine imports, and perhaps the most persuasive reason of all: Better beer was being brewed. The final major change came in 1803, when Napoléon conquered the Rhine region and church ownership of the vineyards ended. As happened in Burgundy, vast sweeps of vineyard land were divided up, often into tiny parcels, and auctioned off to thousands of individuals. Indeed, today, the structure of the German wine industry resembles that of Burgundy more than any other place.

considered very fresh and crisp. German wines usually possess 6 to 8 grams per liter.

Because of their naturally high acidity, the top German wines often appear to be weightless on the palate. Indeed, instead of weight, most wines have tension, a dynamic energy coursing between the wine's acidity and fruit. Indeed, acidity is so important that German winemakers think of it qualitatively, not just quantitatively. When acidity is at its best, for example, it's often described as "round acidity" or "fine acidity"—a kind of harmonious crispness that comes across as tiny pinpoints of energy. But acidity can also be sour, garish, or hard—the sensory equivalent of shattering glass. My friend the vintner Johannes Selbach, of Selbach-Oster in the Mosel region, calls this loud acidity "Hollywood acidity."

Because of the wines' naturally high levels of acidity, it's impossible to think about (or evaluate) a German wine in the same way you would, say, a California wine. Big and powerful may be desirable adjectives when applied to wines from California, but German winemakers' mindsets are different. What they hope to achieve are precision, finesse, and a sense of transparency, meaning that the wine becomes a sheer reflection of the potential flavors bound up in a vineyard.

Transparency and tension are discernible in fine German wine only because the best winemakers are adamant purists. They do nothing that would alter or mold the inherent flavor of the grapes. They do not use commercial yeasts, adjust the acidity in the grapes, chaptalize, or ferment or age the wine in new oak. And many do not even fine the wines to clarify them.

THE LAND, THE GRAPES, AND THE VINEYARDS

Let's have a look at grapes first. Germany is mainly a producer of white wines, although red wines account for a surprising 40 percent of production and rosés (called *weissherbst*) are also made.

THE GRAPES OF GERMANY

WHITES

GEWÜRZTRAMINER: A very good quality grape, although not widely planted. It can make excellent wines, especially in the Pfalz.

GRAUBURGUNDER: The same as pinot gris. Makes fairly big, popular wines with good flavor, especially in Germany's more southern districts.

GUTEDEL: The same as chasselas in Switzerland. A minor grape made into simple wines. Mostly found in Baden.

HUXELREBE: A relatively new cross of gutedel and courtillier musqué. A very minor grape sometimes added to blends.

KERNER: A cross of riesling and the red grape trollinger. Although it can make delicious, simple wines, plantings in Germany are now in decline.

MÜLLER-THURGAU: One of the most widely planted grapes. DNA typing has established it as a cross between riesling and Madeleine royale, a table grape of unknown parentage. The vines produce larger yields than riesling, and the quality of the wine comes nowhere close.

MUSKATELLER: Sometimes called gelber muskateller (yellow muscat), this grape is actually the beautifully aromatic, fruity muscat blanc à petits grains. Germany's dry muskatellers, though not made in large quantities, rival the exquisite dry muscats of Alsace, France.

RIESLANER: A cross of riesling and silvaner, it can make good, zesty wines, especially in the Pfalz and Franken regions.

RIESLING: Considered Germany's greatest grape, it has remarkable finesse, elegance, and aging potential. Grown on all the best sites.

SCHEUREBE: A cross made in 1916 of riesling and an unknown grape, specifically for use in the Rheinhessen and Pfalz. Wines made from it have grapefruit overtones and racy acidity.

SILVANER: A major grape native to Austria, it is the same as sylvaner in the Alsace region of France. A source of dependably good but rarely great wines. In production, it is the leading grape of Franken.

WEISSBURGUNDER: The same as pinot blanc. A minor grape, it makes neutral to good, likable wines. The best are often from Baden, the Pfalz, and the Nahe.

REDS

BLAUER PORTUGIESER: Among reds, this grape is second in importance after spätburgunder. Makes light, acidic red wines.

DORNFELDER: Makes popular wines that are fruity and grapey. Germany's Beaujolais.

SPÄTBURGUNDER: The same as pinot noir. Germany's leading and best quality red grape in terms of production, it makes light, spicy, expensive wines.

SYRAH: Only a tiny amount is currently produced, but the potential is high.

THE MOST IMPORTANT GERMAN WINES

LEADING WINE

RIESLING white (dry and sweet)

WINES OF NOTE

GRAUBURGUNDER white

MÜLLER-THURGAU white

RIESLANER white (dry and sweet)

SCHEUREBE white (dry and sweet)

SEKT white (sparkling)

SILVANER white

SPÄTBURGUNDER red

WEISSBURGUNDER white

Of the nearly sixty grapes grown, riesling is the most prestigious. Nearly 60 percent of all the riesling in the world is grown in Germany, and virtually all of Germany's best wines are made from it. (This comes as no surprise, since the grape is thought to have originated in Germany's Rheingau region.) For the finest wines, riesling is never blended with another grape. Like the top pinot noirs in Burgundy, fine rieslings need to stand alone, for the grape's flavors are only diffused by blending.

After riesling, Germany's next most important white grape is Müller-Thurgau, which usually makes soft, decent, but rarely memorable wines. Müller-Thurgau was invented by Swiss vine breeder Hermann Müller at the famous Geisenheim viticultural station in 1882. It is a cross of riesling and Madeleine royale. Müller-Thurgau is not the only cross in Germany. In the late nineteenth and early twentieth centuries, plant scientists there developed a slew of them. The goal was to come up with a new variety that would be less fragile than riesling, ripen earlier, give higher yields, and at the same time have riesling's complexity and flavor. Today such crosses as Scheurebe and rieslaner make good and sometimes excellent wines, but they are rarely matches for riesling.

Germany's red wines are well loved—especially by the Germans. It is such a triumph to make red wines this far north that the best German reds are expensive and are immediately snapped up on the home turf. More than 35 percent of all German vineyard land is devoted to red grapes, the most important and widespread of which is spätburgunder (pinot noir), which, in Germany, makes a spicy/earthy, sleek red. (One of the most impressive and beautiful pinot noirs I have ever experienced was the 1943 pinot noir from Kloster Eberbach, a majestic monastery and wine estate in the Rheingau. Although it was thirty years old at the time, and the grapes were harvested—by women and children—in the extremely difficult years before the end of World War II, the pinot noir was as lively and vivid as a pinot noir one-fifth its age.) Dornfelder, blauer portugieser (a variety that has nothing to do with Portugal), and trollinger (the same as

Throughout the later Middle Ages, the impressive monolithic Kloster Eberbach, founded in 1136 in Eltville in the Rheingau, was one of the most economically successful Cistercian monasteries in Europe thanks to its remarkable wines.

WALL OF THE VIRGINS

Although Germany would seem like the last country to give its vineyards whimsical names, there are dozens of them. Here are the names of a few well-known vineyards.

ESELSHAUT: Donkey hide

GOLDTRÖPFCHEN: Little raindrops of gold

HIMMELREICH: Kingdom of heaven

HONIGSÄCKEL: Honey pot, with a sexual connotation

JESUITENGARTEN: Garden of the Jesuits

JUFFERMAUER: Wall of the virgins

KALB: Veal

KATZENBEISSER: The biter of cats

LUMP: Dope; idiot

NONNENGARTEN: Nun's garden

SAUMAGEN: Pig's stomach

SCHNECKENHOF: Home of the snails

SIEBEN JUNGFRAUEN: Seven virgins

UNGEHEUER: Monster

WÜRZHÖLLE: Spice hell

ZWEIFELBERG: Place of doubt

The steep-terraced vineyards of Herzöglicher Weinberg in Saale-Unstrut in far northern Germany. Vineyards here are often interspersed among stunning medieval castles.

surprisingly delicious reds evocative of wild herbs and game.

As for the land and the vineyards, while Germany's entire wine production amounts to well under 5 percent of the world's total, there are more than twenty thousand grape growers. The best estates are often minuscule. A top Bordeaux château produces more wine in a vintage than a top German estate produces in a decade. And yet, despite its small size, a first-rate German winery will produce ten or more wines, and thirty to forty wines is not uncommon. As we'll see, this is because most vintners are working with a number of different vineyard sites, different grape varieties, different ripeness levels, and different sweetness levels—and keeping every single one of those wines separate. Such exacting detail makes for dozens of different wines, and of course such exacting detail is what makes German wine, well . . . German.

Wineries are usually located in small villages at the edge of the vineyards. Indeed, German wine labels often give not only the winery name, but also the town and vineyard names. In the past, knowledgeable German wine drinkers (like Burgundy drinkers) bought

the Italian/Austrian Tyrolian variety schiava grossa) are also popular red grapes. But most surprising of all is syrah, which, while very new in Germany, has been made into some

wines based first on the reputation of the vineyard, then on the producer's name. But consider: Until 1971, there were more than thirty thousand individual vineyard names a wine drinker might encounter! These were reorganized by sweeping wine laws in 1971 and pared down to about 2,600 vineyards—still a mind-boggling number.

Germany is divided into thirteen wine regions. Two of these, Saale Unstrut and Sachsen, formerly in East Germany, were added after reunification in 1989. Of the thirteen, three are the most important—the Mosel, the Rheingau, and the Pfalz. These three are the main regions we will examine in the pages to come, followed by shorter briefs on six other regions. Lastly, just so you know these terms, Germany's thirteen wine regions are divided into thirty-nine districts called *bereiche,* which themselves are divided into 167 so-called collections of vineyards, each called a *grosslage.* Every *grosslage,* in turn, is made up of individual vineyard sites, each called an *einzellage.* As of 2013, there were 2,658 *einzellagen.*

UNDERSTANDING HOW GERMAN WINE IS ORGANIZED AND CATEGORIZED

Understanding how German wines are organized and categorized is not difficult, but it's not self-evident either. So, in my experience, it's helpful to have someone take you through, step by step in a logical manner. I'll do my best in the pages that follow. First, let me set the context, because in this case, context is critical.

In Germany, with vineyards so far north, ripeness has always been the fulcrum around which everything else revolves. As mentioned, however, climate change has thrown a wrench (a good one) into the old system. Over the past decade, contemporary German winemakers have been ecstatic to find themselves benefiting from a climate of which their fathers could have only dreamed. But the dramatic shift in climate has also turned Germany's fine wine industry upside down and, for some vintners, created a whole new way of thinking about and categorizing wines. Here lies the rub: Not all Germans have adopted the new thinking. And almost worse, some Germans have adopted it only partially.

So for now, there are two main independent systems that exist more or less side by side. I'll call them the traditional system and the modern system. The traditional system has been in place for many decades. The modern system was begun relatively recently by an organization of some two hundred prestigious estates called the VDP (*Verband Deutscher Prädikatsweingüter,* or Association of German Prädikat Wine Estates). Alas, to understand German wine, you have to know both systems. And most important of all, know that some wine estates are adopting the modern system bit by bit, creating a hybrid world of their own between the two systems.

One final point: In addition to the two main systems at work in Germany, some regions—the Rheingau is one—have associations of members who have set up their own internal regional systems, and their own classifications. While we won't telescope down to these small regional systems (many of which are currently in flux), I will address classification terms you might see on wine labels that could prove confusing.

Grapes being crushed during the harvest in Germany.

THE RIPENESS LEVELS

In the traditional system, fine German wine can be made at six levels of ascending ripeness. The ripeness levels are:

KABINETT: A wine made from grapes picked during the normal harvest; typically a light-bodied wine, low in alcohol, and usually dry or off-dry. *Kabinetts* are easy to drink and food friendly. German wine lovers typically drink them as casual dinner wines.

SPÄTLESE: *Spät* means "late." So *spätlese* wines are based on grapes harvested later than grapes for *kabinett.* They are fully ripened and make wines with greater fruit intensity and a slightly fuller body than *kabinett* wines. A *spätlese* may be dry or, like *kabinett,* may be off-dry. Even those with some sweetness, however, usually do not taste sweet because of the high level of acidity in the grapes, which offsets any impression of sweetness.

AUSLESE: *Aus* means "select." *Auslesen* are made from very ripe grapes harvested in select bunches—another step upward in richness and intensity. Generally, *auslesen* can be made only in the best years, which have been sufficiently warm. Picking individual bunches means that the wines are expensive. Most *auslesen* are lush, and today, they are often fairly sweet. But even two decades ago, most *auslesen* were made in a lighter, more elegant style. Back then, most were intensely flavored (and thus, a treat), but they weren't syrupy sweet. Today, both styles can be found, and the Germans sometimes drink them on Sunday afternoons as an aperitif with hard cheeses.

BEERENAUSLESE: Literally, "berry" *(beeren)* selected harvest. *Beerenauslesen* are rare and costly wines made from very ripe individual grapes selected by hand. Usually *beerenauslese* (called, conveniently, BA for short) grapes have been affected by noble

THE TRADITIONAL SYSTEM

Historically, because ripeness was not a given and because the climate was so marginal, fine German wines were categorized along two dimensions—ripeness and sweetness. This system is still in place for many German wines, so it's important to know the terms used to indicate ripeness as well as the terms used for sweetness. In the traditional system, these terms are usually indicated on the label.

THE RIPENESS CATEGORIES
(in ascending ripeness):

KABINETT: (CAB-i-net)

SPÄTLESE: (SCHPATE-lay-zeh)

AUSLESE: (OWSCH-lay-zeh)

BEERENAUSLESE (BA): (Bear-en-OWSCH-lay-zeh)

TROCKENBEERENAUSLESE (TBA): (TRAUK-en-bear-en-OWSCH-lay-zeh)

EISWEIN: (ICE-vine)

THE SWEETNESS CATEGORIES
(from dry to sweet):

TROCKEN: (bone dry; less than 0.9 percent residual sugar)

HALBTROCKEN; SOMETIMES CALLED FEINHERB: (half dry; less than 1.8 percent residual sugar)

LIEBLICH OR MILD: (some sweetness; up to 4.5 percent residual sugar)

rot, *Botrytis cinerea,* giving them a deep, honeyed richness. BAs are always sweet.

TROCKENBEERENAUSLESE: Literally, "dry berry" *(trocken beeren)* selected harvest, *trockenbeerenauslesen* (TBAs) are the richest, sweetest, rarest, and most expensive of all German wines. TBAs, produced only in exceptional years, are made from individual grapes shriveled to raisins by botrytis. It takes one person a full day to select and pick enough grapes for just one bottle. Because of the enormously concentrated sugar, the grapes have difficulty fermenting. As a result, many TBA wines are no more than 6 percent alcohol (less than half the alcohol of, say, Sauternes). TBAs are absolutely mesmerizing in their intensity and exquisite balance, and are rightfully pricey.

EISWEIN: Literally, "ice wine," so called because it is made from very ripe, frozen grapes that have been picked, often at daybreak, by workers wearing gloves so their hands don't freeze. As the frozen grapes are pressed, the sweet, high-acid, concentrated juice is separated from the ice (the water in the grapes). The wine, made solely from the concentrated juice (the ice is thrown away), is miraculously high in both sweetness and acidity, making drinking it an ethereal sensation.

Eiswein grapes must be frozen naturally on the vine. (Austria and Canada, two other countries famous for *eiswein,* also make it in this manner. In other countries, what is called *"eiswein"* is sometimes produced by freezing grapes in a commercial freezer. As far as purists are concerned, the freezer method is definitely cheating.) Interestingly, the climate change that has benefited German winemakers in so many ways may eventually prove detrimental to the production of *eiswein* because, under slightly warmer conditions, botrytis may occur first before temperatures turn cold enough for the *eiswein* to be made. In addition, under warmer conditions, the botrytis mold eventually consumes most of the water in the grapes, leaving little left to freeze!

Thus, any given ripeness level could potentially come at three levels of sweetness. A *kabinett,* say, could be *kabinett trocken* (bone dry), *kabinett halbtrocken* (half dry), or *kabinett lieblich* (slightly sweet). The same would be true for *spätlese,* and so on.

When you understand how this two dimensional approach to flavor works, you can easily imagine the sensory difference between a *kabinett halbtrocken* and an *auslese trocken.* The first is not very ripe, but there's some residual sugar in the wine. The second is quite ripe, but it's dry. The first wine, in other words, is like an unripe cantaloupe on which you've sprinkled a touch of sugar; the second, a very ripe cantaloupe with no sugar. Ripeness and sweetness are clearly different.

As a quick aside, sweetness is measured by the grams of residual sugar in the final wine. As for ripeness, it is measured in Germany by Oechsle (ERKS-leh)—the weight of the must, which is the thick, pulpy liquid of crushed grapes. Oechsle was named after the physicist Ferdinand Oechsle, who invented the scale in the 1830s. Interestingly, the Oechsle requirements for the ripeness categories change based on the region. So, for example, to make, say, a Rheingau *spätlese,* Rheingau producers must attain a higher Oechsle reading from the grapes than Mosel producers need to attain to make a Mosel *spätlese.* This is because in the Mosel, farther north and colder, it's harder to reach greater ripeness (which would result in a high Oechsle reading). So the system attempts to level the playing field.

Remember, the ripeness categories are based on the ripeness of the grapes when they were picked (not the final sugar content of the wine). What happens, for a top vineyard, is generally this: Come fall, the grower picks a percentage of the grapes early, well before snow and cold weather set in. These

READING A GERMAN WINE LABEL

Germany is in the process (anticipated to take several years) of changing how many of its wines are categorized and labeled. For now, to the right is an example of a traditional German label. (By contrast, modern VDP labels are usually simpler and often omit the village and/or vineyard name.) As you can see, traditional labels indicate the producer, village, vineyard, variety of grape, ripeness level, sweetness level, and vintage. In the wine Selbach-Oster Zeltinger Sonnenuhr Riesling Spätlese Trocken 2012, for example, Selbach-Oster is the producer; Zelting is the village (the *er* means "of"); Sonnenuhr is the vineyard; riesling is the grape variety; *spätlese* is the ripeness level; *trocken* is the dryness/sweetness level (*trocken* means "dry"); and 2012 is the vintage.

SELBACH-OSTER

2012

ZELTINGER SONNENUHR
RIESLING SPÄTLESE
TROCKEN

PRÄDIKATSWEIN - PRODUCT OF GERMANY
GUTSABFÜLLUNG WEINGUT SELBACH OSTER - D 54492 ZELTINGEN
LAP. NR. Z 606 319 022 13 - Enthält Sulfite

MOSEL

alc. 12,5 % vol.   750 ml e

are somewhat unripe, resulting in a very light wine (a *kabinett*). Despite the risk of worsening weather, certain bunches of grapes are allowed to continue to hang on the vine. Days or weeks later, the owner goes through the vineyard again and, if bad weather has not spoiled the bunches, he picks some percentage of them and uses those to make a separate, second wine (a *spätlese*), which will be riper and fuller-bodied than the first. During this second go-through, the owner again leaves some bunches to hang even longer. If freezing rain or snow doesn't get those, the bunches will be made into a third wine (an *auslese*), which will be fuller, richer, and riper than the second. And so the process goes. There are six degrees of ripeness, and a grower in a good year may make wines at all six levels from the same vineyard. Importantly, these categories

of ripeness often appear on the labels, allowing you to anticipate how lean or full the wine will be.

As for dryness/sweetness, traditional German winemakers fine-tune the balance of certain wines by leaving a little bit of sweetness in the wines or adding a touch of *süssreserve*—juice from the harvested grapes that has been held back, clarified, and left unfermented, so it's naturally sweet.

THE MODERN (VDP) SYSTEM

With the turning of the twenty-first century, many growers, including more than two hundred of the best and most prestigious estates of Germany, abandoned the traditional way of thinking about, organizing, and categorizing German wines. In its place they devised a modern system that, they believe, better reflects Germany's new climatic reality. Most of these wineries belong to a group called the VDP (*Verband Deutscher Prädikatsweingüter*). All VDP members display the VDP logo (a stylized eagle bearing a cluster of grapes) prominently on the bottle so it's easy to tell who they are.

WHAT IS PETROL, EXACTLY?

One of the characteristics displayed by some rieslings —especially some aged rieslings—is called petrol—a potent, distinctive aroma that some wine drinkers love and others find unpleasant. Petrol aroma is caused by trimethyldihydronaphthalene—TDN for short—and several scientific research studies have found that the molecule is up to six times more likely to occur in riesling than in other varieties. While several factors may be responsible for TDN formation, one of the leading ones is too much sun exposure on riesling grapes as they grow. (Top riesling growers are always careful to allow leaves to slightly shade riesling clusters.) With bottle age, concentrations of TDN in the wine increase, especially if the wine is high in acidity. Interestingly, cork can absorb as much as 50 percent of any TDN formed, and thus rieslings stoppered with a screw cap potentially show more TDN than wines stoppered with cork. Finally, aged riesling has wonderfully complex aromas that can be hard to describe. Many riesling winemakers point out that "that unusual aroma" in an old riesling is often not TDN at all, but a fascinating nexus of smells including sage, lemongrass, lime marmalade, honey, consommé, and toast.

The VDP's premise is that, thanks to climate change, all of Germany's best-sited, top vineyards can now achieve full (*spätlese*- to *auslese*-level) ripeness every year. Therefore, most wines will have a good measure of flavor intensity even when made in a dry style. So, under the modern VDP system, most wines are bone dry, that is, *trocken* (which, again, means less than .9 percent (9 grams per liter)—residual sugar).

Old bottles of riesling await their moment of opening. Thanks to its high natural acidity, riesling ages longer than any other white varietal in the world.

What happens, then, to terms like *spätlese, auslese,* and so on? Under the modern VDP system, these terms (*kabinett, spätlese, auslese, beerenauslese,* and *trockenbeerenauslese*) are used only to refer to sweet styles of wines. Thus, in the modern system, fine German wine is dry unless you see a term such as *kabinett, spätlese,* et cetera, in which case, the wine has some sweetness. (English majors and wine lovers will be driven crazy by the fact that what are *ripeness* terms in the traditional system have now become *sweetness* terms in the modern system.)

The modern VDP system also includes a hierarchy of vineyards based on their terroirs. The hierarchy is almost identical to the one in Burgundy, and has four levels. From the top down, they are:

GROSSES LAGE = GRAND CRU

ERSTE LAGE = PREMIER CRU

ORTSWEIN = VILLAGE WINE

GUTSWEIN = BASIC WINE FROM A BASIC-QUALITY VINEYARD OWNED BY THE ESTATE

(The terms for the top two levels—Grosses Lage and Erstes Lage—will always appear on either the label or the neck capsule. The terms Ortswein and Gutswein are optional according to VDP regulations. Some wineries list them; others do not.)

At the top level (equal to a Burgundy Grand Cru) is VDP Grosses Lage (pronounced grosses lah-geh). These are wines from vineyards that have consistently yielded the finest, most ageworthy wines. (As far back as the mideighteenth century, authoritative vineyard maps demarcate many of these vineyards, singling them out as being especially prized.) A Grosses Lage wine that is dry will usually carry an additional term on the label—Grosses Gewächs (literally, "Great Growth") or the initials GG. A Grosses Lage wine that is sweet would carry one of the traditional terms: *kabinett, spätlese, auslese, beerenauslese, trockenbeerenauslese,* or *eiswein.*

STUNNING AGING POTENTIAL

One of the benefits of acidity is that it acts to preserve flavor. Thus, German wines, among the highest in the world in acidity, are also among the longest-lived. If the wine in question also happens to be slightly sweet (sugar, too, is a preservative), it will age even longer. Probably every wine drinker familiar with German wine has been served a German wine and asked to guess its age. Say the wine in question has irresistible freshness; the fruit flavors (apricots and peaches) seem lively and poised for action; the minerality is vivid. Surely this wine cannot be more than a few years old. Then comes the reveal: It's twenty years old or more. No other wines come close to German wines in their ability to seem ageless.

The next step down (equal to a Burgundy Premier Cru) is VDP Erste Lage (urst lah-geh). Continuing down, come wines that would be equal to Burgundian "village wines." These are called VDP Ortswein (orts vine). Finally, at the base of the quality pyramid are VDP Gutswein (goots vine). These are good, entry-level wines made from grapes grown in modest-quality vineyards owned by the estate.

While the changes are frustrating to learn, the new system adopted by these top VDP estates is actually pretty easy. With it, German wine becomes like other high-quality wines around the word—dry—unless a sweet style is being made, in which case there's a term to let you know that. Moreover, the system includes terms that alert you to the best terroirs. Instead of having to know something about Kiedrich Gräfenberg (a village and vineyard) on a label, if you see *Grosses Lage,* you know that you are about to drink Grand Cru–level wine from one of Germany's top sites.

SEKT

P ossibly the easiest word to say in the German language, *sekt* (pronounced zekt) is the term for sparkling wine. Although all sparkling wine in Germany is called *sekt,* there are two distinct types—the bargain stuff and fine *sekt.*

Bargain *sekt*—which is most of the *sekt* made—is light, clean, and uncomplicated. Made with German grapes or with bulk wine from another European country, *sekt*'s fizziness is the result of the bulk process (the second fermentation takes place in large pressurized tanks, not in each individual bottle). Fine German *sekt*—a tiny portion of the German sparkling wine market—is entirely different

Many German churches, like this one in Oberwesel, are named Liebfraukirche ("Church of Our Blessed Lady"). The wine Liebfraumilch ("milk of our Blessed Lady") originally came from vineyards surrounding such churches.

BLUE NUN

T he first Liebfraumilch (literally, "milk of Our Blessed Lady") wines were produced several centuries ago, probably from vineyards surrounding the Liebfraukirche ("Church of Our Blessed Lady"). The church was founded by Capuchin monks in 1296, just outside the city of Worms. Liebfraumilch is a basic, slightly sweetish, inexpensive wine made from a blend of any combination of Müller-Thurgau, riesling, silvaner, kerner, plus "other grapes." For decades, the best-selling German wine in the English-speaking world was Sichel Liebfraumilch. By 1925, the wine had become so popular that the Sichels decided to create a more compelling label. It pictured a bunch of stern, nononsense, matronly German nuns in brown habits against a blue sky. (Nuns were used because of the close association, in Germany, of the church with wine.) Consumers began referring to the wine as the one with the blue label and the nuns. Slowly the label began to change. First there were fewer nuns; then the nuns were thinner; then the nuns smiled. By 1958, the nuns were clothed in blue habits. Today, the label of Blue Nun shows a coquettish blonde with blue eyes wearing a pastel blue and white habit, holding a basket of grapes, and smiling in a way that would make the Mona Lisa envious.

Tending to the vines in Germany usually means repeated (and exhausting) steep hikes up and down from the village below.

from the bargain stuff. These top-notch *sekte* are made in small lots by the traditional (Champagne) method. The grapes used are generally riesling, weissburgunder (pinot blanc), or blauburgunder (pinot gris), and the village and vineyard the grapes come from will usually be listed on the label.

These fine German *sekte* are sparklers with bite. Their crisp, streamlined flavors are vividly clear. The goal in making them is not to achieve the custardy, creamy roundness of Champagne but to make a wine that has the clarity and purity of flute music. Among the top producers: Darting, Theo Minges, Pfeffingen, Reichsrat von Buhl, and Bürklin-Wolf, from the Pfalz; Hubert Gänz, from the Rheinhessen; Künstler from the Rheingau; Schlossgut Diel from the Nahe; and Freiherr von Schleinitz and Kerpen, from the Mosel.

THE FOODS OF GERMANY

aybe it's the proximity of France and Italy, maybe it's the irresistible romanticism

the cuisines of both those countries possess, but somehow Germany has been overshadowed and undervalued as one of the great food cultures of Europe. This is definitely a mistake, for food is Germany's best-kept secret.

There are really two culinary worlds there. First, there's old-fashioned Germany, where meals can resemble a medieval feast of wursts (sausages), pig's knuckles, dumplings, potato salad, spaetzle, sauerkraut, and black bread. This is solid, sturdy fare, a straightforward response to the bodily needs imposed by a cold, damp northern climate. But there's also contemporary Germany, a land rich with game birds, wild mushrooms, a huge repertoire of river fish (including delicate pike and trout), the sweetest cherries, raspberries, and strawberries, plus bright green, tender garden cresses, mâche, and lettuces that simply have no equal anywhere. Clearly, the German penchant for perfection doesn't stop with Porsches and Mercedes.

To travel in Germany is to experience how deliciously and often these two worlds collide. Still, some things—German breads, for example—remain steadfastly traditional. As they should, for with the exception of Austria, there is no better bread in Europe. Before I tasted German *brot* ("bread"), I used to wonder how so many Europeans in centuries past supposedly lived on bread alone. One bite of *brot* was evidence enough. Dark, chewy, heavy, nutritious, and so packed with flavor that it's easily a meal in itself, German bread has muscle. The most well known is pumpernickel, which historically in Germany is leaden in weight, spicy-sour in flavor, and nearly black in color, thanks to the high percentage of dark rye flour used, plus a long, slow baking, during which the flour's starches caramelize. The bread most capable of inducing a nostalgia attack, however, is undoubtedly stollen, German Christmas bread, a yeast bread lavishly strewn with nuts and candied fruits and then generously topped after baking with butter and confectioners' sugar. Every region of Germany has its own version of stollen, including the fabulous *mohnstollen,* poppy seed stollen, a specialty of Bavaria.

From bread to soup seems only a short distance (culinarily if not philosophically), and Germany is a land of soups. There are the expected and sensational *kartoffelsuppen* ("potato soups") and many sturdy meat-and-vegetable-based soups (pheasant and lentil soup, for example, or *gulaschsuppe,* Germany's equivalent of Hungarian goulash), but most surprising, perhaps, is the wealth of fish soups, including *Hamburger aalsuppe* ("eel soup from Hamburg") and Black Forest trout soup.

The first time I visited Germany, I imagined that my vegetarian friends would find the

IT TAKES A WHOLE LOTTA BEER TO MAKE GREAT WINE

The German passion for wine is very strong, but beer has no peer. In recent years Germans drank, per capita each year, about 28 gallons (106 liters) of beer; and just over 5 gallons (19 liters) of wine. Interestingly, Americans also drink about 28 gallons (106 liters) of beer per capita each year, and some states (hello, North Dakota—46 gallons/174 liters of beer per capita per year!) take their six-packs very seriously. In the past, beer-making in Germany, like winemaking, was carried out by monks, who used the revenue from both to support their monasteries. Indeed, German monks made many of the most important discoveries in brewing, including the fact that hops could be used to add zestiness to beer and preserve its freshness.

so-called land of wursts to be their worst nightmare. Not true. Germany's passion for vegetables and fruits has the intensity that only a culture where sun is scarce can possess.

SOME OF THE MOST EXTRAORDINARY EISWEINS IN THE WORLD

The magnetic juxtaposition of lush sweetness and almost crinkly acidity gives German *eiswein* an electrified intensity. Made from frozen grapes picked in the dead of winter, *eiswein* tastes quite different from *beerenauslesen* and *trockenbeerenauslesen.* And unlike BAs and TBAs, *eiswein* is not made from grapes affected by *Botrytis cinerea.* Among the best German *eisweins* are those made by Darting, Eugen Müller, and Müller-Catoir, from the Pfalz; Hermann Dönnhoff and Schlossgut Diel, from the Nahe; and Joh. Jos. Prüm, Karlsmühle, Selbach-Oster, and Zilliken, from the Mosel.

WHEN YOU VISIT . . . GERMANY

GERMANY IS FULL OF SMALL, family-owned wine estates that are welcoming and charming to visit.

IN THE MOSEL there are impressive wine estates all along the Mosel Weinstrasse (Mosel Wine Route), which runs the entire length of the winding river. The best of them, and the most spectacular towering walls of vineyards, are concentrated in the middle stretch.

BESIDES SPECTACULAR WINE ESTATES in the Rheingau, do not miss Kloster Eberbach, in Eltville, a stunning, large monastery and wine estate founded in 1135 by Cistercian monks. One of the earliest known properties to be devoted to pinot noir, it was among the most successful, creative wine estates of the Middle Ages, a reputation it held for the subsequent seven centuries. Today, Kloster Eberbach is operated by the local state government and very good wines continue to be produced there. Also worth seeing are two very famous, beautiful old castle/wine estates, Schloss Johannisberg and Schloss Vollrads.

IN THE PFALZ, there are top estates strung all along the Deutsche Weinstrasse (German Wine Route), not to mention immaculate villages with cobbled streets and charming old houses. Try the Weinkastell Zum Weissen Ross, a charming inn and restaurant specializing in regional dishes. It's next door to the wine estate Koehler-Ruprecht and is owned by the same family.

A road sign you don't want to ignore—the Deutsche Weinstrasse (German Wine Route) in the Pflaz.

Among vegetables, cabbage (called *kraut* or *kohl*, depending on the region) and asparagus (*spargel*) stand out in such classic dishes as sauerkraut, the laborious authentic version (as in neighboring Alsace) for which cabbages are shredded, salted, and fermented until they are sweetly sour; braised red cabbage with onions and apples in wine sauce; and asparagus sautéed with morels, for which many Germans forage. Each May, at asparagus season (and asparagus mania), many chefs around Germany temporarily give up their regular menus to focus entirely on dozens of different asparagus dishes.

As for the humble potato (*kartoffel*), the number of compelling German potato dishes could make an Irish person (including this one) genuflect. There are infinite versions of *kartoffelklössen*, "potato dumplings," the classic accompaniment to Germany's national dish—sauerbraten, a "sour" pot roast in which the beef marinates in wine for up to four days before being slowly braised until meltingly tender. Other homey potato standbys include

Throughout Germany, towns are located on flatland, while vineyards are planted on slopes, angled (like solar panels) to catch the maximum amount of sun each day.

kartoffelpuffern, "potato pancakes," and *kartoffelsalat*, "potato salad" (usually served hot, often with bacon). When potatoes are not the accompaniment to a meal, *spätzle* often is. Germany's equivalent of gnocchi, these little squiggles of egg and flour batter are pressed through a *spätzle*-maker (which looks like a potato ricer) and then, like pasta, briefly boiled. Soft and rich, they are the perfect tool for sopping up sauces.

And those sauces often surround meat. It would be a bit of a shame not to indulge in meat in Germany, for the pork and beef are sumptuous. In addition to sauerbrauten, there are numerous hearty interpretations of beef stew, veal dishes simmered in riesling, and Wiener schnitzel (an Austrian dish, very popular in Germany, of pounded, breaded, and sautéed veal medallions). And wursts are so much a part of the German psyche that they figure into everyday language. (When a difficult decision must be made, the Germans say *Es geht um die Wurst*—"the wurst is at stake.") German wurst is rather like French cheese, a way of defining regions culinarily.

There are reportedly more than 1,500 different kinds of wursts in Germany, the most famous of which are frankfurters (authentic versions are still made in the city of Frankfurt, entirely from pork leg meat, and are served with hearty

CALLING ALL DOCTORS

Many German estates are named Doctor Something (Dr. Loosen, Dr. Bürklin-Wolf, Dr. von Bassermann-Jordan, and so on), as are many vineyards (the Doctor Vineyard in Bernkastel, owned by Dr. H. Thanisch, for example). For the Germans, taking pride in one's professional status is essential, and having a PhD or titled degree—that is, being a doctor—has been extremely important for generations.

mustard), *leberwurst* ("liverwurst;" made from pork or beef with a texture that ranges from coarse to as smooth and silky as pâté), and bratwurst (spicy, coarsely textured pork sausages seasoned with caraway). Finally, there's currywurst, Germany's über-loved, ubiquitous fast food. It's as simple as steamed, then fried, pork sausage seasoned with curry ketchup.

Germany, a country of immense forests, is known for the quality of its game as well, and Germans use it to create venison with chestnuts, wild rabbit braised in wine, pheasant with red currant gravy, and on and on.

Desserts would seem to be a German birthright, as the number and scope of *bäckereien* and *konditoreien* (bakeries and pastry shops) attest. Many of the best desserts are based on fruits, for stone fruits such as cherries, orchard fruits like apples, and all manner of berries—*himbeeren* (wild raspberries), *johannisbeeren* (fresh currants), and *preiselbeeren* (similar to cranberries), in particular—excel in Germany. Among the classic desserts are *apfelstrudel*, apple strudel, often made more like a cobbler than rolled in the Hungarian manner; *apfelpfannkuchen*, apple pancakes; and *zwetschgenkuchen*, a plum "cake" that looks like an open-faced pie, oozing with ripe, purple plums. Quark, often served with peaches or cherries, brings back childhood memories for virtually every German. Something like a cross between cream cheese and ricotta, quark is thick and tart, quintessential comfort food. Finally there are cherries—*kirschen*—harvested from the cherry orchards that flourish along the Rhine River. Distilled into a clear brandy, or *eau-de-vie*, cherries become *kirschwasser*, a favorite after-dinner digestif as well as an integral component in Germany's hedonistic chocolate dessert Black Forest cake. But cherries and *kirschwasser* know few limits. The Germans use them in everything from cherry tortes to cherry puddings to cherry pancakes served warm with whipped cream infused with, what else? *Kirschwasser.*

Above the village of Cochem, the Mosel River takes one of its breathtaking hairpin turns.

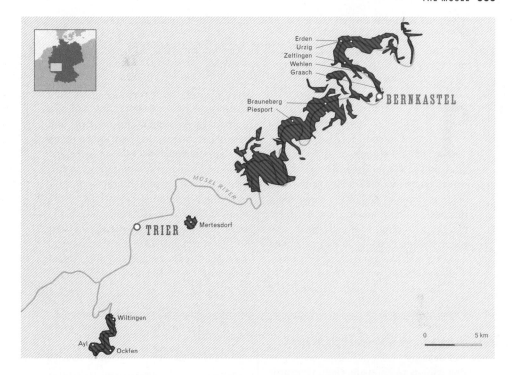

THE MOSEL

he Mosel is where Germany's most ravishingly elegant wines are made. The wine region— some 21,700 acres (8,800 hectares)—is defined by the hauntingly beautiful and eerily still Mosel River, which cuts a deep, snakelike gorge through the land. The river enters Germany where the country converges with Luxembourg and France, and then winds back and forth for about 145 miles (230 kilometers) northeast until it empties into the Rhine near the town of Koblenz. The Saar and the Ruwer are small tributaries of the Mosel.

The Mosel's greatest grape is riesling. But that states the case too simplistically, for along the Mosel, riesling is turned into wines that have such crystalline clarity, they are like glittering sunlight on a subzero day.

The reasons are several. The vineyards of the Mosel are the steepest in Germany and among the steepest in the world. Indeed, the expanse of vineyards from the village of Zelting to the village of Bernkastel is considered the longest stretch of near-vertical vineyards anywhere on the globe. (As an aside, the severe inclines make these vineyards the most treacherous, dangerous, and exhausting to work of vineyards anywhere. Picture the typical vineyard worker, often a woman of about sixty years of age, who climbs these perilously steep, icy slopes in the middle of frigid November.) The vineyards are also among the most northern vineyards in Germany. Steepness in a cold, northern wine region means that the sun is in contact with the vines for limited, precious hours each day. And, of course, the total number of sunlight hours during the growing season is also modest (the Mosel gets, in a good

THE STEEPEST VINEYARD IN THE WORLD

The steepest vineyard in Germany—and in the world— is Calmont, located between the villages of Bremm and Eller on the Mosel River. The vineyard, whose name roughly translates to rocky mountain, was carved by the Mosel more than 400 million years ago, and has been planted with grapes for more than 1,500 years. Calmont's 60- to 70-degree incline makes it look like a vertical wall of vines, all tenaciously gripping the slatey cliff. Terraces are built into the hill and fortified with rock walls, but they are constantly crumbling into the river and needing to be rebuilt. There are no roads through Calmont, only winding paths and one miniature monorail for bringing fertilizer up and harvested grapes down— everything else must be carried by the vineyard crew. In fact, because of the back-breaking labor required to harvest the vineyard, only 13 of its 20 acres (5 of its 8 hectares) are currently in production, and that number is decreasing every year.

year, about a third of the sunlight hours that Provence does).

If fine wine is to be made, then, vineyards must be nothing short of perfectly sited, so that each ray of light and warmth is maximized. As a result, the Mosel's vineyards hug only south-facing slopes. At each turn of the river where the banks face north, the slopes have no vines. In addition, the best vineyards are quite close to the river itself, for even the reflection of light off the water becomes one more increment in the quest for ripeness.

The famous grayish-blue slate of the Mosel holds heat well, helping riesling to ripen.

> On the palate, riesling is meant to move—to shimmer, to surge, to burst, to dance, to arc, to soar. Riesling has a rare trait— velocity. Of all varietals, it is the most kinetic and alive.

Then there's the issue of slate. The famous slate (sometimes blue-gray in color, sometimes burnt orange-red) of the Mosel is highly porous and heat retaining. The soil's porosity is an advantage in downpours, when powerful rains might otherwise cause mass erosion. (When some slate does wash down the slopes, the precious rocks, so necessary for ripeness, are immediately carried back up the hill.)

The slate's heat-retaining properties help advance ripeness. Indeed, in many of the best vineyards, there appears to be no soil at all, just broken slate. But, in ways that remain chemically and biologically mysterious, slate also appears to contribute to flavor. Wine drinkers throughout history have cherished Mosel wines specifically for their slatey, minerally, wet-rocks-in-a-cold-mountain-stream flavors. No other wines in Germany taste quite the same.

The vineyard of Würzgarten ("Spice Garden") in the village of Ürzig is among the most renowned vineyards of the Mosel. Just hearing the words Ürziger Würzgarten *is a promise of delicious things to come.*

Many of the top Mosel producers are clustered together in the middle section, known as the Mittelmosel (middle Mosel). Here is where the famous villages of Bernkastel, Piesport, Brauneberg, and Wehlen are found. Wines such as Piesporter Goldtröpfchen and Bernkasteler Doctor are just two of the renowned examples from this tiny stretch of the Mosel.

The three renowned *Sonnenuhr*—Sundial— vineyards are also in the Mittelmosel. They

VILLAGES AND VINEYARDS OF THE MOSEL

Wine labels for some top Mosel wines tell you where the grapes grew by listing the vineyard, or both the village and the vineyard, from which they come. Here are some to look for; the village names are in capital letters. More than one village may have a vineyard with the same name. For example, as this chapter suggests, many villages have a vineyard known as Sonnenuhr ("Sundial").

AYL: Kupp

BERNKASTEL: Bratenhöfchen, Doctor, Graben, Lay, and Matheisbildchen

BRAUNEBERG: Juffer and Juffer-Sonnenuhr

ERDEN: Prälat and Treppchen

GRAACH: Domprobst and Himmelreich

MERTESDORF: Abstberg and Herrenberg

OCKFEN: Bockstein and Herrenberg

PIESPORT: Goldtröpfchen

ÜRZIG: Würzgarten

WEHLEN: Sonnenuhr

WILTINGEN: Braune Kupp, Braunfels, and Gottesfuss

ZELTINGEN: Himmelreich, Scharzhofberg, Schlossberg, and Sonnenuhr

are the Wehlener Sonnenuhr, Brauneberger Juffer-Sonnenuhr, and Zeltinger Sonnenuhr. The huge sundials that give them their names were built as far back as the early 1600s in the sunniest part of three excellent slopes, so that vineyard workers would know when to stop for lunch or for the day. Because the vines in the vicinity of the sundial also got the most sun (and made the richest wine), the areas around the sundials soon came to be considered separate vineyards. Today the *Sonnenuhr* vineyards are among the best along the Mosel. As in Burgundy, each of these vineyards has multiple owners who possess tiny plots. Some two hundred wine estates own sections of the Wehlener Sonnenuhr, for example.

Because of the Mosel's far northern latitude, and the spine-tingling acidity that results, this is Germany's best region for fully sweet wines. Yes, sweet wines. Indeed, the BAs, TBAs, and eisweins from the Mosel never descend into gloppy sugar syrup. Instead, their sweetness is taut, lifted, and vibrant. They almost prance with energy, thanks to the counterpoint provided by acidity. This makes them unlike most other dessert wines in Germany, and indeed in the world. Wine drinkers who generally don't like dessert wines usually go mad for these.

SOME OF THE BEST PRODUCERS OF THE MOSEL

Alfred Merkelbach • Carl Loewen • Clemens Busch • C. Von Schubert • Daniel Vollenweider • Dr. H. Thanisch • Dr. Loosen • Egon Müller • Fritz Haag • Heymann Löwenstein • Joh. Jos. Christoffel • Joh. Jos. Prüm • Karlsmühle • Karp-Schreiber • Markus Molitor • Max Ferd Richter • Milz-Laurentiushof • Reichsgraf von Kesselstatt • Reinhard & Beate Knebel • Reinhold Haart • St. Urbans Hof • Schloss Lieser • Selbach-Oster • von Hovel • Willi Schaefer • Zilliken

---

The sonnenuhr *("sundial") in Zelting. In the Mosel, from medieval times onward, the vineyard around the sundial has always been considered exemplary thanks to its perfect sun exposure.*

The Mosel Wines to Know

T he wines of the Mosel—where sheer exquisiteness meets profound intensity—have no parallel anywhere else in the world. Some of the wines below are extremely bone dry; others are not quite as severely dry. But thanks to their soaring acidity, all are meant to accompany a meal (unless, of course, a sweet wine is intentionally being made).

WHITES

SELBACH-OSTER

ZELTINGER SONNENUHR | RIESLING | SPÄTLESE | TROCKEN

100% riesling

I have known the Selbach family for some twenty years, and each time I taste their wines I am brought back to the first, icy day, snow on the ground, that I walked (with their long-time U.S. importer, Terry Theise) into their parlor to taste their rieslings. The wines were then, and remain still, classic, exquisite, slatey, minerally rieslings humming with pinpoints of juicy acidity and imbued with mouthfuls of pristine fruit flavor. What I love most about them is their back palate "center of gravity," so that the biggest rush of flavors floods onto your palate a few seconds after you start to taste the wines. This taut, elegant dry riesling from the Sonnenuhr vineyard is a cool, fresh, beauty of a wine. Johannes Selbach is one of the most thoughtful winemakers on the Mosel and a great interpreter of the purity that is "Moselness."

ANNO 1668

SELBACH-OSTER

2012

ZELTINGER SONNENUHR
RIESLING SPÄTLESE
TROCKEN

PRÄDIKATSWEIN - PRODUCT OF GERMANY
GUTSABFÜLLUNG WEINGUT SELBACH-OSTER - D 54492 ZELTINGEN
LAP. NR. 2 606 319 022 13 - Enthält Sulfite

MOSEL
alc. 12,5 % vol.   750 ml e

REICHSGRAF VON KESSELSTATT

GRAACHER JOSEPHSHÖFER | RIESLING | KABINETT

100% riesling

The exquisite Josephshöfer riesling *kabinett* of Reichsgraf von Kesselstatt zooms in on a luscious kaleidoscope of fresh ripe peach, apricot, nectarine, and citrus flavors and then holds that flavor (like holding a music note) over the entire impact of the wine. This is a pure, filigreed, slatey, spicy, traditional *kabinett* from a jewel of a vineyard. Indeed, the tiny, steep Josephshöfer (with a slope inclination of 60 to 70 degrees!) was first planted 1,100 years ago and belonged to a local monastery until it was purchased by the Kesselstatt counts in 1858. Today, it is owned and run by the energetic Annegret Reh-Gartner.

2·0·12
JOSEPHSHÖFER
RIESLING KABINETT

REICHSGRAF von KESSELSTATT

VDP. GROSSE LAGE®

DR. LOOSEN

2012
Ürziger Würzgarten
Riesling Spätlese

PRÄDIKATSWEIN · PRODUCE OF GERMANY
ERZEUGERABFÜLLUNG WEINGUT DR. LOOSEN · D-54470 BERNKASTEL/MOSEL
A. P. NR. 2 576 162 33 13 · ENTHÄLT SULFITE

Alc. 7.5% / Vol.   Mosel   750 ml e

DR. LOOSEN

ÜRZIGER WÜRZGARTEN | RIESLING | SPÄTLESE

100% riesling

Every time I drink this wine, I wonder if there are enough super-latives in the world for it. So I'll stop saying it is great, exqui-site, refined, and majestic (although it is all of those). Instead, here's what it's like: Melted crystals of white light. Frozen peaches and apricots liquefied until they have no more weight than air. Minerals that have turned deliciously crunchy. High soprano notes that reverberate long after the song is finished. The Würzgarten (spice garden) vineyard in the village of Ürzig is, needless to say, renowned. Dr. Loosen is a two-hundred-year-old estate now run by the indefatigable Ernst Loosen. In 1999, Ernst Loosen formed a joint venture with Washington State's Chateau Ste. Michelle, and together the two produce Eroica, the best riesling made on the West Coast of the United States.

2012
Brauneberger Juffer-Sonnenuhr
Riesling Spätlese
Mosel

KARP-SCHREIBER

BRAUNEBERGER JUFFER SONNENUHR | RIESLING | SPÄTLESE

100% riesling

The dazzling acidity in Karp-Schreiber's riesling from the great Juffer Sonnenuhr vineyard in Brauneberg is like an arch held in perfect, seemingly weightless suspension, rendering everything around it graceful and light. Again, this is Mosel riesling that can't hold still. Flavors of nectarines and peaches splash around in the glass, giving the wine kinetic excitement. The Juffer Sonnenuhr (Virgin Sundial) vineyard of the village of Brauneberg (Brown Hill) is one of the three centuries-old sundials that still exist on the Mosel.

1624   1337
REUSCHER-HAART
Piesporter Goldtröpfchen
2011 Riesling Spätlese

REUSCHER-HAART

PIESPORTER GOLDTRÖPFCHEN | RIESLING | SPÄTLESE

100% riesling

The name of this vineyard, Goldtröpfchen, means drops of gold, and that describes how you feel drinking it—as if you're drink-ing plump golden drops of pure sunlight. As a village, Piesport is known for its rather fleshy, fruity rieslings, but the Schwang fam-ily, which owns Reuscher-Haart, must have a sixth sense of how to corset all that richness, for this Goldtröpfchen is elegant and laced with spices (teeing it right up for something like a Vietnamese pork, shrimp, and mint spring roll).

WILLI SCHAEFER

GRAACHER HIMMELREICH | RIESLING | AUSLESE

100% riesling

This mind-blowing wine is not as dry as the others listed in this section but it's definitely not a dessert wine. I've drunk it with everything from complex Shanghai seafood dishes to Southeast Asian appetizers to creamy French cheeses, and the experience has been nothing short of sensational. Willi Schaefer and his son Christophe and daughter-in-law Andrea date their winemaking ancestry back to 1121. Their wines have mesmerizing laser-like focus, and end with an explosion of flavor that always reminds me of cymbals clashing. From the famous Himmelreich (Kingdom of Heaven) vineyard in Graach, this *auslese* is a tight fist of minerals robed in apricot glaze.

SWEET

*The wines below are all definitely sweet
and are generally served with or as dessert.*

MILZ-LAURENTIUSHOF

TRITTENHEIMER FELSENKOPF | RIESLING | BEERENAUSLESE

100% riesling

The aroma of a great BA can be hypnotic—deep, rich, sweet fruits, of course, but also smells of the earth, like rain sprinkling down on mushrooms and stones (an indication of botrytis). This one, from the Milz family of Milz-Laurentiushof, is supercharged in every way. Indeed, the flavors of pears, tangerine, apricots, and minerals box their way into every corner of your mouth. All the while, the wine's dramatic, edgy acidity keeps unfolding and holding the sweetness in a suspended state of dazzling balance.

JOH. JOS. CHRISTOFFEL

ÜRZIGER WÜRZGARTEN | RIESLING | EISWEIN

100% riesling

The tiny estate of Joh. Jos. Christoffel makes digitally precise Mosel rieslings with wonderful rushes of slate, minerals, and restrained fruit that parcels itself out to you over many agonizingly delicious seconds. They are exquisitely classical in their structure—which bodes well when it comes to *eiswein*. There's nothing over-the-top and overwrought here. Instead, Christoffel's *eisweins*—especially this one from the fantastic Würzgarten vineyard in Ürzig—taste as though long, satin ribbons of honey, spice, and exotic citrus have twisted together and entwined themselves with crystalline acidity in an unnervingly luscious helix of sensation. Needless to say, these *eisweins* are made in minuscule amounts, and only in very special years when the climatic conditions are just right.

FRITZ HAAG

BRAUNEBERGER JUFFER-SONNENUHR | RIESLING | TROCKENBEERENAUSLESE

100% riesling

This wine has moved German men to tears—which, in a way, says it all. The sheer beauty of it is like the beauty of exquisite music that touches you so deeply that crying is the only rational response. Wines like Fritz Haag's TBA remind us that, at their pinnacle, the greatest wines of the world cannot be deconstructed into their component parts or described by adjectives. (Apricot, after all, is not as apricot as this. Honey, not as honeyed. Minerals, not as minerally.) Wines like this have what I'll call high-alert emotional purity. They are electrifying to the senses, and drinking them becomes an out-of-body experience.

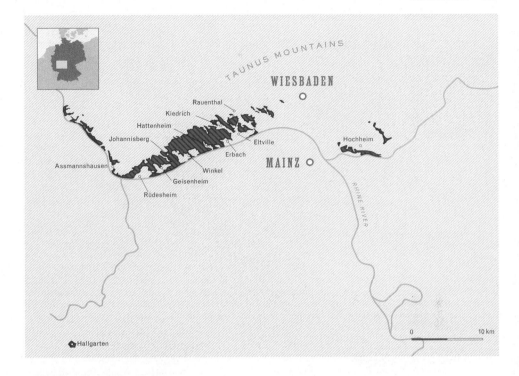

THE RHEINGAU

Germany's reputation as the greatest white-wine producing nation in the world was historically based largely on the Rheingau region. Today, the supremacy of this very small region (7,744 acres/3,134 hectares) is challenged by many delicious wines coming out of the Mosel and the Pfalz, yet the Rheingau has the longest history of quality winemaking of any region in Germany. It's also a hotbed for regional classification systems, more on which in a moment.

The Rheingau is a serene, aristocratic wine region—one long, virtually continuous horizontal slope, a rolling carpet of vines, with the densely forested Taunus Mountains rising up behind. In a sense, the mountains created the wine region, for they abruptly halted the Rhine's northward flow and forced it to veer straight west for 20 miles (32 kilometers) until it could again proceed north. The result was a nearly ideal, immense, south-facing bank backed by protective forests that block cold northern winds.

The leading grape of the Rheingau is riesling. Indeed, the first record of riesling being planted in Germany dates from 1435 at the wine estate (and former Benedictine abbey) Schloss Johannisberg in the village of Johannisberg near Geisenheim in the Rheingau. Today, of all the German wine regions, the Rheingau has the

The castle of Ehrenfels in Rüdesheim on the Rhine. Rüdesheim, one of the main wine towns in the Rheingau, is home to a number of legendary vineyards, including Berg Roseneck, Berg Rottland, Berg Schlossberg, and Bischofsberg. (The word berg *means "hill.")*

highest percentage of riesling—nearly 80 percent of its acreage. The rieslings here, however, are entirely different from Mosel rieslings—richer, rounder, earthier, and more voluptuous. Absent are the Mosel's icicle-like sharpness and slate flavors, and in their place is a near perfect gripping expression of lip-smacking fruit. The best Rheingau wines have amazing breadth; in a sip they can suggest everything from violets and cassis to apricots and honey.

Sun, soil, and latitude make the difference. To begin with, the Rheingau is farther south than the Mosel. Its long, south-facing bank rises up gently from the river, which for its part acts like a giant sunlight reflector. And the soil is not solely slate, but a vast mixture, including loess, loam, limestone, marl, sand, and quartzite.

THE FIRST BOTRYTIZED WINES

Four countries—Germany, France, Austria, and Hungary—are famous for their botrytized wines, and of the four, Hungary was the first to understand that grapes covered with the rather repulsive-looking mold *Botrytis cinerea* could lead to sensationally delicious wine. As of the early 1600s, the Tokaji Aszú wines of Hungary's Tokaj-Hegyalja region were well-established luxuries. And, although it is not clear if Austria adopted the technique from Hungary, the part of Austria famous for botrytized wines—Burgenland—borders Hungary, and indeed was once part of the vast Austro-Hungarian Empire. In Germany, the first botrytized wine, thought to have been a *spätlese,* was made in Rheingau at Schloss Johannisberg, in 1775. In Bordeaux, evidence is more sketchy, but the earliest accounts of botrytized wine are thought to date from 1847 at the famous Sauternes estate Château d'Yquem.

VILLAGES AND VINEYARDS OF THE RHEINGAU

Wine labels for some top Rheingau wines tell you where the grapes grew by listing the vineyard, or both the village and the vineyard, from which they come. Here are some to look for; the village names are in capital letters. As in the Mosel, more than one village may have a vineyard with the same name. For example, there's a Hölle vineyard in Hochheim and one in Johannisberg. Speaking of Johannisberg (named for Saint John the Baptist), such was the reputation of the village that, in the nineteenth century, German immigrants to the United States renamed the riesling vine cuttings they brought with them Johannisberg riesling.

ASSMANNSHAUSEN: Frankenthal, Hinterkirch, and Höllenberg

ELTVILLE: Langenstück, Rheinberg, and Sonnenberg

ERBACH: Marcobrunn, Schlossberg, and Siegelsberg

GEISENHEIM: Kläuserweg, Mönchspfad, and Rothenberg

HALLGARTEN: Jungfer and Schönhell

HATTENHEIM: Nussbrunnen, Pfaffenberg, and Wisselbrunnen

HOCHHEIM: Herrnberg, Hölle, and Königin Victoriaberg

JOHANNISBERG: Goldatzel, Hölle, Klaus, and Vogelsang

KIEDRICH: Gräfenberg and Wasseros

RAUENTHAL: Baiken, Gehrn, and Rothenberg

RÜDESHEIM: Berg Roseneck, Berg Rottland, Berg Schlossberg, and Bischofsberg

WINKEL: Hasensprung and Jesuitengarten

The slightly stronger sun, of course, leads to greater—or at least more reliable—ripeness, which in turn gives Rheingau wines their slightly fuller body and pronounced fruit. At the same time, high acidity in the grapes acts as a counterpoint, providing the wines with a kind of arching elegance. The potential for greater ripeness here bodes well for Rheingau *spätlesen, auslesen, beerenauslesen,* and *trockenbeerenauslesen.* These wines are legendary—the sort that make you want to lick the glass after swallowing the last drop.

The other important grape of the Rheingau is spätburgunder (pinot noir), which here makes a pale but spicy red with a kind of bitter-almond flavor. The most famous come

Founded in 1234, the Kloster Marienthal convent in the village of Geisenheim in the Rheingau is the oldest Cistercian nunnery in Germany.

The steep, 60-degree slopes of the Berg Schlossberg vineyard in Rüdesheim on the Rhine River. With its quartzite and slate soils, this vineyard is famous for its powerful, racy, dry rieslings.

HOCK

The British name for Rhine wine, hock, is an Anglicized reference to the famous village of Hochheim (pronounced HOE-hime) in the Rheingau. At first, hock implied a wine from Hochheim; later, it came to mean any Rheingau wine; and later still, any Rhine wine. Queen Victoria is credited with the line, "A bottle of hock keeps off the doc."

from the village of Assmannshausen and are expensive.

Finally, the Rheingau is where the long road to German wine classification began. In 1984, for example, Rheingau producers founded an association called Charta, which sought to classify the best vineyard sites in that region. After twenty-five years and many evolutions, a Germany-wide system of classification is now under the auspices of the VDP, *Verband Deutscher Prädikatsweingüter,* or Association of German Prädikat Wine Estates, an association of more than two hundred top estates throughout the country. But despite the VDP's prominence and strength, smaller regional Rheingau associations still exist. One such—the Rheingauer Weinbauverband (the Rheingau Winegrowers' Association)—classifies wines using terms very much like those of the VDP. For example, wineries that belong to the Rheingauer Weinbauverband, designate their top wines Erstes Gewächs ("First Growth"), a term that, confusingly, resembles two VDP terms: Erstes Lage (a First Class or "Premier Cru" vineyard) and Grosses Gewächs (a "Great Growth" wine that is dry).

SOME OF THE BEST PRODUCERS OF THE RHEINGAU

August Kesseler · Fred Prinz · Georg Breuer · Josef Leitz · Kloster Eberbach Hessische Staatsweinguter · Künstler · Peter Jakob Kühn · Robert Weil · Schloss Johannisberg · Schloss Schönborn · Spreitzer

The Rheingau Wines to Know

The Rheingau wines below are all vividly intense, humming with acidity, and all taste dry. Each has a profound depth of flavor. Historically, the Rheingau was Germany's first great wine region, and the wines have incomparable *gravitas*.

KÜNSTLER

HOCHHEIMER KIRCHENSTÜCK | RIESLING | GROSSES GEWÄCHS

100% riesling

Künstler, one of the stars of the Rheingau, is making some of the most exciting, precise, and filigreed rieslings in the region. From the Grosses Lage ("Grand Cru") vineyard Kirchenstück (literally "church song") in the famous village of Hochheim comes this Grosses Gewächs ("Great Growth") dry riesling. Suffused with peach, mirabelle, and kumquat flavors that rush out of the glass, it also fairly bursts with sophisticated notes of chalk, minerals, salts, and an ever-so-wonderful fruit-pit bitterness. The finish is a long beam of bright light. Künstler, a small, family-run estate, is headed by Gunter Künstler, a driving force in the Rheingau wine industry.

SPREITZER

OESTRICHER LENCHEN | RIESLING | SPÄTLESE "303"

100% riesling

I always think of this just off-dry wine as one of the most aristocratic of traditional Rheingau rieslings. Ribbons of ripe, sweet apricots and spice curl their way through pure minerals. The concentration of Spreitzer's "303" *spätlese* is always superb, and yet, for such concentration the wine reverberates with a sense of purity. The luxurious texture feels like a spoonful of fresh honey, although, of course, this is not a dessert wine. The name "303" refers to a subparcel of the Lenchen vineyard, called Eisenberg ("Iron Hill"). It was from this hill, in 1921, that the fruit for a TBA with one of the then-highest levels of Oechsle ever recorded—303 degrees Oechsle—was picked.

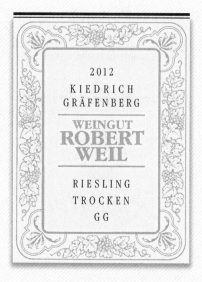

ROBERT WEIL

KIEDERICH GRÄFENBERG | RIESLING | GROSSES GEWÄCHS

100% riesling

The best dry rieslings of Robert Weil have immense power and depth, yet at the same time they possess a lusciousness and a vivid, crystalline sense of minerality. In particular, I love this riesling's exotic flavors, as if peaches were dipped in an especially bergamot-rich Earl Grey tea. And the way the opulent fruit wraps itself around the central spine of acidity is fantastic. Not surprisingly, this wine is ranked a Grosses Gewächs ("Great Growth"). The winery was founded in 1875 and is still run by the Weil family. Over the decades, the winery has been an official purveyor of riesling to the royal families of Germany, Austria, and Russia.

JOSEPH LEITZ

RÜDESHEIMER BERG ROSENECK | RIESLING | SPÄTLESE

100% riesling

Leitz's top rieslings are wines of razor-sharp precision, and this one from Berg Roseneck, in the village of Rüdesheim, builds on that precision with a blast of a cool, exotic aroma—something gingery maybe?—before the wine seems to drape itself like peach syrup over rocks. Leitz's wines often have a tightness and edginess that I love. Indeed, though this is just off-dry, it drinks like a dry wine. The Rüdesheimer *berg*, or "hill," is a south-facing, mountainlike slope that soaks up the sun. On it are three famous vineyards, one of which, Roseneck, is marked by quartzite with small shards of slate.

SCHLOSS REINHARTSHAUSEN

ERBACHER SCHLOSSBERG | RIESLING | ERSTES GEWÄCHS

100% riesling

Fresh. Lively. Slatey. Dry. A bullet train of intense fruit and rocky minerals that hurl themselves at you. I'm never sure if I should duck or drink. The finish is a bold exclamation point . . . but then, a second later, the wine comes whispering back. *I'm not done with you yet,* it seems to say. Schloss Reinhartshausen belongs to the *Rheingauer Weinbauverband* (Rheingau Winegrowers' Association), the members of which use the term Erstes Gewächs ("First Growth") for their top wines. The winery is one of the oldest in Rheingau, having been founded in the mid-fourteenth century, and today it is the largest privately owned winery in the region. Princess Marianne of Prussia founded Hotel Kempinski, the five-star hotel attached to the winery.

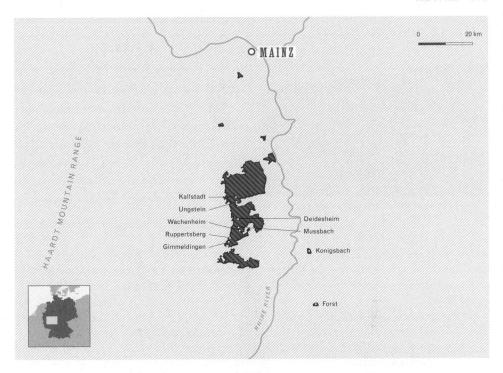

THE PFALZ

or two decades, the Pfalz has been among the most exciting, inventive wine regions in Germany. Pfalz growers have an irrepressible spirit and their own irreverent way of doing things. The buttoned-down image of German winemaking doesn't hold here. Individuality and creativity are prized above all. Not surprisingly, Pfalz winemakers make more great wines from more different types of grapes than winemakers anyplace else in Germany. Indeed, just 24 percent of Pfalz's 58,041 acres (23,488 hectares) is planted with riesling, although given this region's large size, that's still a considerable amount, as we'll see. The wide variability of soils here is another key to the diversity of wines and flavors. There is little slate; instead, limestone, loess, gravel, and well-drained red sandstone dominate.

Although it is technically part of Germany's Rhineland, the Pfalz does not take its climatic cues from the Rhine River, as the other regions do. The river is a couple of miles east; no important vineyards border it. The dominant influence instead is the Haardt mountain range, the northern flank of France's Vosges mountains. Just as the Vosges create a sunny, dry climate for Alsace wines, so the forested mountains of the Haardt create a protected environment for the vineyards of Pfalz.

Given its more southerly latitude and more generous sun, ripeness is more of a given. Pfalz wines, as a result, are almost extroverted with fruit. Acidity, the soul of German wine, comes across differently here, too. It's not harsh or piercing; it doesn't howl. Instead, the best Pfalz wines have an almost creamy acidity and a tensile energy that's palpable. Finally, because of the slightly greater levels of ripeness and

Weingut Pfeffingen in the Pfalz. Winemaking here dates back to the Roman Empire.

PFALZ

*T*he name *Pfalz derives from the Latin* palatinus, *meaning "palace." A palatine was a lord with royal privileges and the palatinate was the area he ruled. Today in Britain, the Pfalz is often called the Palatinate because it was once controlled by palatine counts.*

the softer impression of acidity, the bone-dry (*trocken*) wines of the Pfalz are far less starched and severe than the *trocken* wines of the Mosel.

Pfalz producers such as Müller-Catoir, Messmer, Darting, Lingenfelder, A. Christmann, and Eugen Müller make some of Germany's most sensational wines. In particular, words do not describe how fiercely vivid Müller-Catoir wines can be. But it's not vividness alone. There's a

precision in every Müller-Catoir wine that is breathtaking. Like flashing sushi knives. Like sunlight bouncing off icicles.

In actual acres, the Pfalz has, after the Mosel, the most vineyard area planted with riesling. But Pfalz riesling is different—perhaps more eccentric. Some of these wines possess exotic citrus flavors; others taste so gingery-peppery you want to grab a bottle and dash off to the nearest Thai restaurant.

VILLAGES AND VINEYARDS IN THE PFALZ

*W*ine labels for some top Pfalz wines tell you where the grapes grew by listing the vineyard, or both the village and the vineyard, from which they come. Here are some to look for; the village names are in capital letters. As in the Mosel and Rheingau, more than one village may have a vineyard with the same name.

DEIDESHEIM: Grainhübel, Hohenmorgen, Kieselberg, and Leinhöhle

FORST: Freundstück, Jesuitengarten, Kirchenstück, Musenhang, and Ungeheuer

GIMMELDINGEN: Langenmorgen, Mandelgarten

KALLSTADT: Saumagen

KONIGSBACH: Indig

MUSSBACH: Eselshaut

RUPPERTSBERG: Hoheburg, Nussbien, and Reiterpfad

UNGSTEIN: Bettelhaus and Herrenberg

WACHENHEIM: Böhlig, Gerümpel, Goldbächel, and Rechbächel

Pfalzgrafenstein Castle on the Rhine River, opposite the town of Kaub, was built in 1327 to collect tolls from ships and barges that used the river to transport and trade goods. Heavy chains from the castle walls to the shore helped force compliance. Resisting paying the toll could land the ship's crew in the castle's "dungeon"—wooden floats in a well.

SAUMAGEN

No visit to the Pfalz is complete without tasting the region's specialty, saumagen, the belly of a pig stuffed with pork, potatoes, and spices. Of course, saumagen *should be accompanied by a riesling from the Saumagen vineyard in Karlstadt, a famous— playfully named—Pfalz vineyard owned by the Koehler-Ruprecht estate.*

But riesling is only one of several successful grapes in the Pfalz. The top estates make small lots of many others, including gewürztraminer, weissburgunder (pinot blanc), grauburgunder (pinot gris), and spätburgunder (pinot noir). These can make very good to remarkably delicious wines, depending on the vintage and the winemaker. Several crosses— rieslaner and Scheurebe, notably—are grown in the Pfalz, too. Rieslaner (a cross of riesling and silvaner) makes pretty wines with pear and citrus flavors; and with its zany grapefruity- vanilla tang, Scheurebe (a cross of riesling and an unknown grape) has a cult following. The best producers of the latter include Müller- Catoir, Lingenfelder, and Pfeffingen.

SOME OF THE BEST PRODUCERS IN THE PFALZ

A. Christmann • Darting • Dr. Bürklin-Wolf • Dr. Deinhard • Dr. von Bassermann-Jordan • Dr. Wehrheim • Eugen Müller • Gies- Duppel • Klaus Neckerauer • Koehler- Ruprecht • Lingenfelder • Messmer • Müller- Catoir • Okonomierat Rebholz • Pfeffingen • Reichsrat von Buhl • Theo Minges

The Pfalz Wines to Know

A s the stunning dry wines below demonstrate, the Pfalz is Germany at her most creative. Although I could undoubtedly drink riesling every night of my life, the Pfalz has a few additional (delicious) ideas up her sleeve—in the form of rieslaner, muskateller, gewürztraminer, and more.

VON BUHL
2011 RIESLING
VINTAGE BRUT
TRADITIONAL METHOD

WEINGUT
EUGEN MÜLLER

FORST

KIRCHENSTÜCK

JA HR
GANG

Meßmer

SELEKTION

2008
RIESLANER
SPÄTLESE

ALTENFORST

PFALZ
Weingut Herbert Meßmer Burrweiler

SPARKLING

REICHSRAT VON BUHL

RIESLING | BRUT

100% riesling

Made by the traditional (Champagne) method, Reichsrat von Buhl's *sekt* is a foamy, delicious burst of freshness. With its fine mousse, the wine has a tingling elegance. And the aromas and flavors are more sophisticated than you find with many *sekte*. Indeed, the delicate white flower aromas are pretty, and on the palate there's a delicious, creamy nuttiness that suggests long contact with the lees. But it's the beautiful notes of fresh, cold nectarine (that's riesling speaking) that make you want to keep sipping.

WHITES

EUGEN MÜLLER

FORSTER KIRCHENSTÜCK | RIESLING | SPÄTLESE | TROCKEN

100% riesling

From the extraordinary Kirchenstück vineyard (full of limestone and basalt and considered one of the best, not just in the Pfalz but in all Germany), Eugen Müller makes rieslings that are simply otherworldly. This *spätlese*, for example, is mega-dry yet juicy, and as alive as an electrical current. The flavors are so tightly wound, they seem to spring out at you as flashes of cool nectarine, salt-crusted minerals, and feathery herbs. The finish—with its touches of spices and bitter marmalade made from exotic fruits—is extremely long.

MESSMER

BURRWEILER ALTENFORST | RIESLANER | SPÄTLESE

100% rieslaner

Rieslaner. The name suggests something rieslinglike, and indeed great rieslaner like this dry-ish one from Messmer shares riesling's sense of purity and freshness. But what happens next is all rieslaner. Namely, an onslaught of luscious flavor. Rieslaner is richer and weightier than riesling, with mouthfilling flavors reminiscent of poached pears, herbs, and wildflower honey if you remove most of the sweetness. And the texture—langorous right through the long finish. The Messmer family (the name is spelled using the "long s" of, it is thought, the script known as Fraktur; the letter ß looks like a capital *B* but indicates a double *s*) specializes in a slew of delicious non-riesling wines, including Scheurebe and gewürztraminer.

MÜLLER-CATOIR

HAARDTER BÜRGERGARTEN | MUSKATELLER | KABINETT | TROCKEN

100% muskateller

Most fans of German wine would happily drink anything from Müller-Catoir; the wines are mind-blowing across the board. But for sheer adventure, this ultra-dry muskateller (the name the Germans use for muscat blanc à petits grains) is beautiful, dense, and very pure. First come exotic, fruity notes (star fruit, cherimoya, kumquat) and then cool, herbal ones (spearmint and basil). A crunchy saltiness and a wild shiver of mineralty pierce through the whole package. This is one of the best dry muscats in the world—its only competitors are the sensational dry muscats of Alsace.

THEO MINGES

FROSCHKÖNIG | RIESLING | SPÄTLESE | TROCKEN

100% riesling

Great riesling is sheer; it is silk stockings—and in this case, the frog king (Froschkönig) is wearing them. Froschkönig is the playful name the Minges family gives to its dry (*trocken*) riesling. I love the aromas of forests, orchards, and rocks in this wine . . . as if many elements of nature had come together to sing in the glass. And while dry, the wine does not vaporize your taste buds with starched severity. The Minges family (now in its sixth generation as winegrowers) also makes beautiful, lightly sweet rieslings, especially the Flemingener Zechpeter, in which apricots, minerals, ginger, earth, and cream all come together in a wild, perfect balance.

DR. VON BASSERMANN-JORDAN

FORSTER JESUITENGARTEN | RIESLING | TROCKEN | GROSSES GEWÄCHS

100% riesling

Dr. von Bassermann-Jordan's riesling from the vineyard called Jesuitengarten ("Jesuit garden") is riesling at warp speed. The velocity behind the flavors in this wine is stunning. First, a hailstorm of spices and minerals. Then, coming up bold and fast, surges of freshness like gusts of wet wind after it rains. Then, high soprano-like notes of exotic citrus—kaffir lime, kumquat, and bergamot. Indeed, every element of the wine seems spring-loaded and ready to burst onto the scene. It's an enrapturing wine to drink because of its choreography. Also not to be missed: Dr. von Bassermann-Jordan's Deidesheimer Leinhöhle Riesling Auslese—an aria of apricots.

A. CHRISTMANN

IDIG | RIESLING | GROSSES GEWÄCHS

100% riesling

The vineyard Idig, in the village of Köngisbach, makes rich (almost Burgundian-style) dry rieslings with intense flavors reminiscent of candied orange peel, tropical fruits, and roasted nuts. The wines from Idig are classified Grosses Gewächs, which again, is the VDP designation for a dry wine from an exceptional Grosses Lage ("Grand Cru") site. The south-facing, basin-shaped vineyard catches and holds the warmth of the sun, contributing to the ripeness of the grapes. Also, importantly, the vineyard is laced with limestone, and indeed this wine possesses a minerally, starched, chalky character similar to one of the flavors of a great Champagne. The A. Christmann winery is now run by the seventh generation of the Christmann family.

THEO MINGES

EDITION ROSENDUFT | GEWÜRZTRAMINER | SPÄTLESE

100% gewürztraminer

I could not resist writing about Theo Minges's dry-ish gewürztraminer, as well as its riesling. Germany is not known for gewürztraminer, especially since the French region of Alsace—where dry gewürztraminer reigns as extraordinary—is virtually next door. But Theo Minges's gewürztraminer, called Edition Rosenduft, is every bit the equal of a top Alsace version. In fact, you might prefer it, since the high acidity in this wine lifts gewürztraminer up and gives the flavor more energy. And what flavor—an intricate and mesmerizing exotic tropical/spicy boldness. (Our whole office ordered out for Thai appetizers after we tasted this wine.) As is often true of the best German wines, the crystalline purity is fantastic.

OTHER IMPORTANT
WINE
REGIONS

AHR | BADEN | FRANKEN | MITTELRHEIN | NAHE | RHEINHESSEN

s some of the most historically significant white-wine regions in all of Europe, the Mosel, Rheingau, and Pfalz are deservedly Germany's best-known and most renowned wine regions. But good—occasionally very good—wines are made in several neighboring districts as well, including the Ahr, Baden, Franken, Mittelrhein, and especially the Nahe and the Rheinhessen.

▲ *The Mittelrhein—the beautiful stretch of river from Bingen to Bonn—is full of medieval castles and fortresses. Many vineyards here are so steep that workers must be transported up the slopes by cable. The difficulty and expense of working these vineyards has caused some to be abandoned.*

The old terraced vineyards of the Ahr. Each vine is bound to a separate pole.

AHR

One of Germany's smallest wine regions, the Ahr is also the most northerly, after Sachsen and Saale-Unstrut in the former East Germany. It is defined by the Ahr River, which flows into the Rhine just south of Bonn, in the Mittelrhein. The rough, rocky, forested terrain is beautiful. This region is a favorite wine country getaway for residents of Bonn.

Although counterintuitive, most of the wine made here is red. Specifically, it is pale, light spätburgunder (pinot noir)—decent enough but not usually remarkable. The top producers include Kreuzberg, J. J. Adeneuer, Meyer-Näkel, and Jean Stodden.

THE CASTLE IN THE RIVER

Among the most impressive sights along the Mittelrhein is Pfalzgrafenstein Castle, a medieval castle smack in the middle of the narrow river. French novelist Victor Hugo called it "a ship of stone, eternally afloat upon the Rhine." It was built on tiny Pfalz Island in 1327, with the purpose of collecting tolls (which it did until 1866). Working with fortified towns on either side of the river, the castle drew a giant chain across the Rhine to prevent boats that hadn't paid the toll from passing through. Captains who still refused to pay were often thrown in the dungeon, a wooden plank afloat in a well. Pfalzgrafenstein Castle played a role in the fall of Napoléon Bonaparte because Prussian Field Marshall Blücher crossed the Rhine at this spot in 1813 and went on to deal Napoléon's army a crushing blow.

BADEN

The wines of Baden do not—and could not—have one single character, for this extremely diverse region is made up of several large, noncontiguous chunks of land. One part of Baden is in central Germany, not all that far from Würzburg; another is on the Bodensee (Lake Constance) near Switzerland; and the biggest and most important part runs parallel to the Rhine from Heidelberg all the way south to Basel.

The southern part of this stretch—roughly from Basel to the famous spa town Baden-Baden—is where the very top wines are to be found. Immediately west of this district is France's Alsace region, and to the east, the Black Forest. In particular, wines from the area around the Kaiserstuhl (literally "emperor's throne"), an extinct volcano, are prized.

This is one of the warmest vineyard areas in Germany, and the wines taste like it. By German wine standards, they're very bosomy, big-bodied quaffs with considerable alcohol and only modest acidity. They are galaxies away from the Mosel wines in spirit and style.

The wide valley floor in Franken, on the northern edge of Bavaria. Wines here are sturdy, broad, and extremely crisp.

The leading grape in Baden is Müller-Thurgau, which makes wines for everyday drinking. You'll also find grauburgunder (pinot gris), gutedel (chasselas), silvaner, weissburgunder (pinot blanc), gewürztraminer, spätburgunder (pinot noir), and of course, riesling. (Very little of the latter is grown.)

The largest number of Baden wines are made by cooperatives (four out of every five growers sell their grapes to co-ops). The leading co-op is Badischer Winzerkeller. Even by cooperative standards, it is mammoth, making more than one-third of all of Baden's wine.

Baden is more famous for its food than for its wine. The forests of Baden abound with game, berries, and wild mushrooms. In particular, venison, country bacon, and ham from the Black Forest are legendary, as are *preiselbeeren* (a kind of small, sweet-tart cranberry) and *heidelbeeren* (huckleberries). Many Baden dishes combine kirsch, cream, and tart cherries, including, of course, the sine qua non of Baden cooking: Black Forest chocolate cake.

Among the top producers of Baden wine are Dr. Heger, Salwey, and Bercher.

FRANKEN

Just about due east of Rheingau, beyond the city of Frankfurt, is the W-shaped wine region known as Franken. Here, at the northern edge of Bavaria, the climate is severe, springtime frosts are common, and the size of the harvest fluctuates widely according to the weather.

By law, only Franken wine is bottled in a squat, plump flagon called a *bocksbeutel* (literally, a "goat scrotum"). Franken wines are broad, sharp, and sturdy, with little of the elegance, transparency, or brilliant fruit of those of the Rhineland or Mosel. Nonetheless, they are well loved by the Bavarians, who consume most of them. The top wines in Franken are usually made from silvaner; little riesling is planted there. Common, everyday wines tend to be made (often by cooperatives) from Müller-Thurgau or other crosses such as Scheurebe, bacchus, kerner, or rieslaner. Most are made in a very dry style. *Trockenbeerenauslesen* and *beerenauslesen* are very rare.

FOR ALL THE RIGHT RIESLINGS

The high acid in German rieslings, coupled with their clean, pure flavors and the absence of obfuscating oak, makes this the most exciting and versatile white wine when it comes to pairing with food. And—unusually for a white wine—the range of possibilities begins with meat. In Germany, riesling is drunk with every dish imaginable, from grilled sausages to pork roast. Talk about brilliant combinations! The wine's penetrating, rapier-like acidity is a dramatic counterpoint to the fat in meat. But riesling is also stunning with salads and simple vegetable dishes. Here, its light body and overall fresh character work to echo the light, fresh flavors of the food. The most inspired pairing of all, however, is that of riesling with complex Asian dishes, where soy sauce, garlic, and other bold and pungent seasonings create vivid contrasting flavors, often within the same dish. Many wines simply shut down in such company. But not riesling.

Among the best Franken producers are Staatlicher Hofkeller, Bürgerspital, Hans Wirsching, and Juliusspital.

MITTELRHEIN

The vineyards of Mittelrhein ("middle Rhine") lie, technically speaking, both north and south of where the Mosel flows into the Rhine. On the northern end, the region stretches almost to Bonn. But virtually all of the important vineyards are located along the southern stretch, from Koblenz to Bingen. At Bingen, where the Rhine makes an abrupt turn, Mittelrhein ends and Rheingau begins. Mittelrhein is a wine region right out of Hansel and Gretel. Fairytale medieval castles are poised above the steep vineyards; there are numerous quaint villages, such as Bacharach and Boppard; the half-timbered houses are postcard perfect. (The opera *Hänsel und Gretel*, based on the Grimm fairy tale, was actually composed in Boppard by Engelbert Humperdinck.)

Many Mittelrhein estates make wines geared to the tourist business. These simple, inexpensive quaffs (mostly based on Müller-Thurgau) are happily drunk up in the region's bustling restaurants and cafés. There are, however, a handful of top estates that make extremely good riesling and *sekt*. The best of these have a minerality and clarity reminiscent of the Mosel wines. This is not by chance. Like the Mosel's, the Mittelrhein's vineyards hover over the river on slate slopes that seem to soar skyward.

There are problems here. The vineyards, sadly, are diminishing in number and have been doing so for decades. The terrain is difficult to work, and for a variety of complex reasons, most Mittelrhein wines have never been able to command high enough prices to justify the cost of caring for and working the vineyards and making good wine. Any vineyard that is not absolutely stellar is eventually abandoned for lack of profit. (And it may never be used as a vineyard again. By EU law, if a vineyard has been abandoned for several years, it must revert to nature and can no longer be used for any commercial purpose.)

All this said, the top wine estates produce some very good wines. In particular, the rieslings that Jochen Ratzenberger makes are almost scary, they can be so intense, minerally, and majestic. Adolf Weingart's rieslings could blind you with their brilliant clarity. And for pure, uncomplicated scrumptiousness, the rieslings of Toni Jost are irresistible.

In spring, dandelions bloom in the vineyards above Nierstein in the Rheinhessen.

NAHE

The Nahe River, south of and parallel to the Mosel, flows into the Rhine near Bingen, close to where the Rheingau region ends. The region named after the Nahe is fairly large, but the top estates here make stunning wines, completely on par with the best of the Mosel. The rieslings in particular can be exceptionally complex, with beautiful arcs of stone-fruit flavors, as if peaches and apricots were riding atop a cresting wave of acidity. Nahe wines have an essential vividness and gracefulness; they can be exquisitely intense and nearly explosive—all at the same time. Theirs is a fiery and filigreed elegance, as one sip of a great *spätlese* from Dönnhoff, Hexamer, or Schlossgut Diel will attest. (The ravishing Dönnhoff rieslings have flavors so intricate and dense that they seem, like a Japanese sword, to be the fusion of hammered layers folded back into themselves.)

Of all of the Nahe's fine producers, I'd put the three just mentioned in a super-category of their own, based on their excellence. But just a step lower are many other fantastic producers, including Dr. Crusius, Hehner-Kiltz, Kruger-Rumpf, Schäfer-Fröhlich, Emrich-Schönleber, and Jakob Schneider. And for good though not great wine, there's also the Nahe State Domaine, a state-owned enterprise created in the early part of the twentieth century and called in German—get ready—*Staatliche Weinbaudomäne Niederhausen-Schlossböckelheim*. (OK, go for it: Say it three times, fast.)

RHEINHESSEN

Germany's largest wine area, Rheinhessen, spreads out over 65,000 acres (26,300 hectares) south of Rheingau. Most of it is rather flat, fertile farmland, good for asparagus, orchards, corn, and sugar beets. As for wine, everything depends on precisely where you are. Most parts of the region make wine that is merely okay, much of which is Liebfraumilch, a mild, inexpensive, generic wine (see page 559). Also produced—mostly by cooperatives—are buckets of bargain, bland, sweetish wines destined for European supermarkets. But there are delicious exceptions. The Scheurebe *spätlesen* from Ch. W. Bernhard, made near the village of Hackenheim, are exotic masterpieces. And the rieslings can be fantastic—especially from vineyards in one concentrated area, from Bodenheim to Mettenheim, along the steep west bank of the Rhine. Known as the Rheinterrasse (Rhine terrace), this brief stretch includes the well-known wine villages of Nackenheim, Oppenheim, and Nierstein. The soil here is unlike any in Germany—a reddish sandstone mixed with slate. The rieslings that come from this soil are earthy and juicy, with the kind of up-front fruit that catapults out of the glass. There are a handful of top producers, including Gunderloch, Keller, J. & H. A. Strub, Wagner Stempel, Wittmann, and Freiherr Heyl zu Herrnsheim.

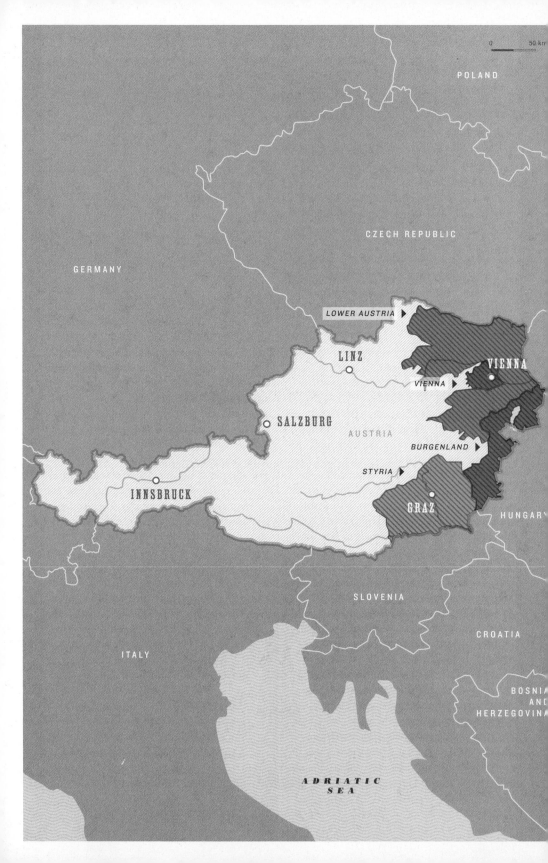

AUSTRIA

LOWER AUSTRIA | BURGENLAND | STYRIA | VIENNA

AUSTRIA RANKS THIRTEENTH AMONG WINE
PRODUCING COUNTRIES WORLDWIDE. THE
AUSTRIANS DRINK AN AVERAGE OF 8 GAL-
LONS (30 LITERS) OF WINE PER PERSON
PER YEAR.

ustria makes some of the raciest, most exciting wines in Europe. To taste them is to be easily convinced. These are wines—whites in particular—with an absolutely uncanny synergy (and energy) between power and elegance. Most of them are thoroughly dry, but Austria is also known for luscious sweet wines intended to accompany (or be) dessert.

Austrian viticulture is quite old. The Celts, discoverers of what would eventually become many of the top wine regions of central Europe, planted the first grapes here in the fourth century B.C. Later, the vineyards fell within the vast arc of the Roman Empire. By the Middle Ages, Austrian vineyards, like those of France, Germany, and Italy, were in the painstaking care of monks. But more than any other historical period, the twentieth century—and its tumultuous politics—shaped Austrian wine.

The modern country called Austria, about the size of Maine, dates from 1919, when the sprawling Austro-Hungarian Empire was dissolved by the Treaty of Saint-Germain. In its place, the post–World War I countries of Czechoslovakia, Hungary, Yugoslavia, and (a far smaller) Austria were formed.

The new Austria, economically unstable and enfeebled by war, could no longer afford to make the sort of handcrafted wines that were a hallmark of the empire past. Something serviceable and cheap was the order of the day. Austrian wine merchants began the mass manufacture of rather insipid, slightly sweet, cheap quaffs that sufficed locally, satisfied tourists, and could be exported easily to its main trading partner, Germany, which was also financially strapped. The market for such wines, notwithstanding their lack of character, grew. Austrian growers, paid peanuts for their

WHAT'S FREUD GOT TO DO WITH IT?

Austria is often wrongly assumed to be a sociocultural subset of Germany. Although they share more or less the same language, the two countries have national characters that are quite different. Austria, farther south and east than Germany, was often along the trade route taken by early travelers between Europe and Asia. As such, Austria has been influenced by both Western and Eastern thinking, philosophy, and art. The combination has given rise to a complex culture and national spirit. Austrians can seem more passionate, wilder, more spontaneous, and more melancholy than Germans. Austria is, after all, the homeland of both Sigmund Freud and Wolfgang Amadeus Mozart.

For their part, Austrian wines bear very little resemblance in flavor to German wines. Austria's dry whites are much fuller in body and bolder in character than Germany's filigreed, dry whites. The same is true with red wines. Austrian reds—juicy, lip-smacking, and often streaked with pepper and spice flavors—have almost nothing in common with the gentle, light-bodied reds of Germany.

That said, Austria and Germany do share a few things. Both countries are known for handcrafting some of the most decadent, small-production sweet wines in Europe, from mesmerizing eisweins to ethereal *trockenbeerenauslesen.* And finally, both countries make delicious *sekt,* sparkling wine that is happily popped open at the slightest provocation.

---

grapes, increasingly planted the highest-yielding, most innocuous varieties. Wine merchants and winemakers began taking every production shortcut they could find.

Then, in 1985, the downward spiral hit bottom. A small group of corrupt wine brokers doctored a batch of cheap wine with diethylene glycol (a component of antifreeze) to make it taste fuller and sweeter. Although the merchants were quickly caught and no one's health was compromised by the tainted wine, the news spread around the world.

In the end, the wine scandal proved to be what one winemaker called a cleansing thunderstorm. The mass market for inferior wine collapsed, leaving the few remaining quality producers—mostly small family estates—to build a new Austrian wine industry from the ground up. The turnaround has been dramatic. For the impassioned, knowledgeable winemakers of today's Austria, top-quality wine is a virtual religion, and respect for the land is paramount. (It's interesting to note that Austria has the largest percentage of

land under certified organic production of any country in the European Union.) For an explanation of Austrian wine law, see the Appendix on Wine Laws, page 926.

THE LAND, THE GRAPES, AND THE VINEYARDS

Austria, a landlocked country, is bordered by the Czech Republic, the Slovak Republic, Germany, Hungary, Slovenia, Italy, and Switzerland. Although the western part of the country, with its cities such as Salzburg and Innsbruck, is well known, the vineyards are all in the distant, more exotic eastern half. There, like a backward C, some 108,000 acres (43,700 hectares) of vineyards form a crescent along the country's eastern border. Just over 20,000 growers grow grapes here, and approximately 6,500 wineries make and bottle wine.

The rocky, terraced vineyards of F. X. Pichler in the Wachau. The Pichler family makes some of Austria's most stunning rieslings and grüner veltliners. Vines have been planted on these stark slopes since the 13th century.

There are four main wine regions, the two largest of which have several smaller regions within them. The two largest regions are Lower Austria and Burgenland; Styria and Vienna are the two smaller ones.

Lower Austria, the most important wine region in terms of size and reputation for high-quality wine, is in the north, along the Slovakian border, and includes the top subregion known as the Wachau. (The word *lower* in the name Lower Austria refers to the lower part of the Danube River, which flows through the region.) Burgenland is the easternmost Austrian wine region; much of it lies along the Hungarian border. Styria, the hilliest region, is in the south, along the Slovenian border. And Vienna is the only major city in the world that is considered a wine region.

Austria is mostly a white-wine producer; 60 percent of all its wine is white, although absolutely delicious reds are made (more on which in a moment). In total, some thirty-five grape varieties are planted. Grüner veltliner—still relatively unknown but capable of great quality—is the leading white grape in terms of wine production. That said, many Austrian wine experts consider riesling to be the country's greatest grape, albeit one that is far less planted. Austria can also excel with sauvignon blanc and pinot blanc, and the wonderfully expressive reds Zweigelt and blaufränkisch should not be missed by any wine lover. For the most part, all of the grapes I've just named stand alone in a wine; they are rarely blended.

THE QUICK SIP ON AUSTRIA

AUSTRIA MAKES some of the most purely riveting wines in Europe.

AUSTRIA IS DEVOTED primarily to dry white wines and magnificent sweet wines, although a surprising amount of delicious, food-friendly red wine is made.

THE BEST WHITE WINES of Austria are based either on the snappy, peppery grape grüner veltliner or on riesling; the best reds are Zweigelt and blaufränkisch.

THE GRAPES OF AUSTRIA

WHITES

FURMINT: A minor grape, but a common component in *ausbruch,* the famous sweet wine of Burgenland.

GRÜNER VELTLINER: Austria's most important grape in terms of both quality and the acreage devoted to it. The wines' unique flavor often begins with stone fruits and ends with a rush of white pepper.

MORILLON OR CHARDONNAY: Chardonnay is called by both names in Austria. A minor grape; the best dry wines from it are elegant, almost taut in style. It is also made into some good sweet wines.

MUSKATELLER: Locally also known as gelber muskateller, this is the same as muscat blanc à petits grains. Grown mainly in Styria, muskateller is extremely fragrant and lush.

NEUBURGER: Very simple workhorse grape; a source of pedestrian dry wine and some good sweet wines.

RIESLING: A major grape even though it is not widely planted in Austria. It is the source of lively, vibrant, often stunning wines, generally with more power than German rieslings.

SÄMLING: Minor grape; a cross between riesling and an unknown grape. Sometimes used for eiswein. Known in Germany as Scheurebe.

SAUVIGNON BLANC: Not widely planted except in the region of Styria, but important because of the quality of the exotically smoky and grassy wines made from it.

TRAMINER: Also known as savagnin. The aromatic ancestor of gewürztraminer; made into dry and sweet wines.

WEISSBURGUNDER: Major grape; known elsewhere as pinot blanc. Makes well-focused, dry wines that range from creamy to racy. In Burgenland, sweet wines are also made from the grape.

WELSCHRIESLING: Major grape; it is not a type of riesling, despite its name, but another name for the Croatian grape graševina. It makes simple, straightforward dry wines, sometimes with the aroma of fresh hay. In Burgenland, also used for late-harvest, botrytized wines.

REDS

BLAUBURGUNDER: Known elsewhere as pinot noir. Widely variable in quality; at best it produces light wines with raspberry overtones.

BLAUFRÄNKISCH: Major grape. Known in Germany, British Columbia, and Washington State by its other name—Lemberger. The source of bold, spicy, complex wines, often with commanding structures.

CABERNET SAUVIGNON: From great vineyards and winemakers it can make surprisingly rich, structured wines with good balance and deep flavors.

ST. LAURENT: Produces simple, hearty, and fruity wines.

ZWEIGELT: A cross between blaufränkisch and St. Laurent. Its wines are reminiscent of California's zinfandel; inky, fruity, with a briary edge.

THE MOST IMPORTANT AUSTRIAN WINES

LEADING WINES

GRÜNER VELTLINER white
(dry and sweet)

RIESLING white (dry and sweet)

SAUVIGNON BLANC white

WEISSBURGUNDER white
(dry and sweet)

WELSCHRIESLING white
(dry and sweet)

BLAUFRÄNKISCH red

ST. LAURENT red

ZWEIGELT red

WINES OF NOTE

GELBER MUSKATELLER white

TRAMINER white (dry and sweet)

The rolling vineyards of Burgenland are where most of the world's best blaufränkisch grapes are grown.

The Austrian philosophy of winemaking closely parallels that of top producers in Germany and Alsace—namely, that greatness resides in purity. Austrian winemakers are after the clearest possible expression of a given place and of a given grape's inherent flavors. Techniques that superimpose flavor (such as the barrel fermentation of white wines) are used infrequently and cautiously. For all their sophistication, Austrian winemakers have a firm respect for tradition and accumulated knowledge. Many of the extraordinary sweet wines, for example, are painstakingly made according to practices established hundreds of years ago.

These dessert wines notwithstanding, virtually all Austrian wines are bone dry. Technically and legally speaking, off-dry, half-dry, or semisweet wines could be made, but in reality, they aren't. Most Austrian winemakers are adamant about dryness. Of course, given the high acidity of most Austrian wines, dryness itself comes across in different ways that influence our perceptions of flavor. As the Austrian wine specialist Terry Theise points out, "[with Austrian wines] . . . there is soft creamy dry and there's accommodating dry and there's very crisp dry and there's fierce austere dry and there's even this-could-use-some-damn-sugar dry."

A few further words on the leading grape varieties themselves. As it does in Germany and Alsace, riesling thrives here, although it accounts for just 4 percent of vineyard plantings. Minerally, dramatic, and sheer, Austrian rieslings are unmasked. They show little fruit in the conventional sense. They are sophisticated, delicious sheets of glass.

Distinctive and vivid, grüner veltliner has not yet gotten the attention it deserves. For me, the flavors of grüner veltliner include a faint echo of something green, wonderful

THE ID OF COFFEE

Unlike cafés anywhere in the world, from Rome to Seattle, the Viennese coffeehouse is only tangentially about drinking coffee. Here, in the city where psychoanalysis was born, a coffeehouse is home to a complex ritual—more intimate than social, supremely private even within the public domain.

Traditionally, coffeehouses were more or less demarcated by profession or social ranking. There were coffeehouses for politicians, coffeehouses for artists, coffeehouses for scholars, and so on. Every person had a single place to which he or she went exclusively. At a minimum, you spent an hour at a coffeehouse (no quickly-downed espressos), but more commonly, you would spend several hours and possibly the entire day there. Coffee would be ordered by color—gold, light gold, blond, dark gold—according to the amount of milk added, and would be served on a small tray with a few sugar cubes and a glass of water. The main activity was, and still is, reading newspapers provided by the house, although you could also write or work in complete solitude, using the café table as a private desk. Since the waiters knew every customer and his or her preferred coffee, you never really had to utter a single word. When people did go to the coffeehouse in pairs, it was either to read in mutual silence or to discuss problems or personal intimacies. Still, private conversation, not social banter, was the custom.

Modern life has changed Viennese coffeehouses, but not by much. During the daytime, a respectful solemnity still prevails. People just sit, think, read, and sip coffee. At night, coffeehouses become somewhat more animated, serving goulash and then coffee and strudel to opera- and theatergoers.

In the late fall and winter, coffee can become more substantial, including a particularly fortifying rendition called a *fiaker*. Made with liberal amounts of rum and whipped cream, *fiakers* are named after the open horse-drawn carriages that once transported people through the streets of Vienna. Riding in a *fiaker* on a cold Austrian night made you want to stop and sip a *fiaker*.

Among Vienna's best coffeehouses: Café Hawelka, Café Landtmann, Café Sacher, Café Sperl, Demel Konditorei, and Heiner Konditorei.

exotic fruit, splashes of minerals, and a dramatic burst of white pepperiness. It is "cool," in the cucumber sense of having cool, refreshing flavors. It is also an ancient grape—according to DNA typing, it is a natural cross of savagnin and the nearly extinct German variety St. Georgener. Going back even further in the family tree, grüner veltliner is related to pinot noir (possibly as a grandchild), since pinot noir and savagnin are related.

If grüner veltliner is Austria's signature gift to the world of white wine, then blaufränkisch is its red gift. Undoubtedly noble in origin and very old (though its parentage isn't completely clear), blaufränkisch combines the words *blau*, meaning "blue;" and *fränkisch*, an old German designation for "a fine wine." Austrian blaufränkisch is precise and sleek—spicy, herbal, and floral—and all of this plus the flavors of delicious woodland berries and a sense of forestiness. Most of all, blaufränkisch has grip and bite. It is exactly what one so often wants in order to splice through the meatiness of meat. Despite its appeal, blaufränkisch is not the leading red grape of Austria. That would be Zweigelt. A cross of blaufränkisch and a usually

WHAT RIEDEL WROUGHT

If you're over 45 years old, you remember a time when wineglasses were just wineglasses. They were fairly small and sturdy and you didn't care if you broke one because they were cheap. (The *good* glasses—the Waterford crystal ones—were safely ensconced, still in their original boxes, up in the attic, where they'd been since your wedding day when you got them.) Then came the 1990s and a new word entered the wine vernacular—Riedel. Georg Riedel, the tenth-generation head of his family's Austrian crystal company, was a wine connoisseur. A man of strict and impeccable standards, Riedel had begun designing crystal wine glasses that would enhance the aromas and flavors of various varietals and types of wine. He soon became famous for his "Riedel Glass Tasting," in which the same wine was tasted in various glasses, and consumers and wine pros around the world were invited to judge the results. Winemakers and restaurateurs were especially convinced of the efficacy of Riedel glasses, and within a few years, no top winery or restaurant was without them. Riedel's success caused dozens of other top Austrian (Zalto) and German (Eisch, Schott Zwiesel) crystal companies to come out with competing lines of high-quality wineglasses. Today, no self-respecting wine lover thinks twice about having a cabinet full of good wineglasses and using them daily.

more simple grape called St. Laurent, zweigelt makes a juicy, fruity, easy wine.

Finally, Austria's top wine districts possess infertile, eroded, well-drained soils. Sand, gravel, slate, and loam are common, as are loess (fine sediment caused by wind-blown silt) and gneiss (foliated metamorphic rock with coarse mineral grains arranged in bands).

SWEETNESS AND RIPENESS: THE AUSTRIAN HIERARCHY

One of the obvious ways in which Austrian wine is different from German is its designations of ripeness. In Germany it's still common for some fine wines to be made at a variety of ripeness levels, starting with *kabinett* and *spätlese* and going up to BA and TBA. A very similar hierarchy of ripeness used to be used in Austria as well. No longer. Austrian fine wine producers all make *dry* wines from ripe grapes, end of story. The one exception where you will find designations of ripeness is sweet wine (that is, dessert wine). Here they are:

BEERENAUSLESE (BA): must be made from overripe and/or botrytized grapes

EISWEIN: must be made from overripe grapes naturally frozen on the vine

AUSBRUCH: this category, unique to Austria, applies to wines that must be made exclusively from botrytized and/or naturally dried grapes

TROCKENBEERENAUSLESE (TBA): produced only in exceptional years and must be made from predominatly botrytized grape bunches and extremely dried, raisinlike grape berries

To be called by any of the names above, a wine must reach a certain ripeness level measured in Austria by what is known as KMW, or the Klosterneuburger Mostwage scale. The KMW compares the specific gravity of the must (based on its sugar content) to the specific gravity of water. Austrian sweet wines

AUSTRIA'S CULINARY ICON

Pumpkinseed oil is to Austria what olive oil is to Italy— a culinary and cultural icon. Pumpkinseed oil comes from the seeds of a small, green-and-yellow striped pumpkin grown mainly in the southern Austrian province of Styria. The prized seeds are removed and washed by hand, then roasted, mashed, and pressed. (Far less valued, the pumpkin flesh becomes livestock feed.) Deep emerald green, the oil has an unctuous texture and an almost hauntingly intense, nutty flavor. Austrians drizzle it over lettuces, vegetables, and breads and pour small puddles into soups including, of course, pumpkin soup. Thanks to its high vitamin content and unsaturated fatty acids, pumpkinseed oil is considered very healthful. It's also quite expensive, and many of the best pumpkinseed oils are made by winegrowers.

make up just 1.8 percent of high-quality wine production in Austria.

In particular, Austrian sweet wines are a specialty of Burgenland, which is slightly warmer and more humid than the other regions (the better for botrytis to develop). But there may be something cultural at work, too, for Burgenland is nudged up against Hungary, which is known for one of the most sensational dessert wines in existence—Tokaji Aszú.

THE DAC

Ready for some controversy? In recent history, consumers of Austrian wine purchased it based on the grape variety and the place. If you were in the mood for a pristine, dry riesling and you knew the Wachau as one of the best

Winemaker Fred Loimer of Weingut Loimer, in his biodynamic vineyards in the renowned Langenlois area of the Kamptal. Loimer makes some of Austria's most ravishing and concentrated grüner veltliners.

Grüner veltliner grapes—the source of many of the best wines of Austria.

places in the world for riesling, you were all set. It was pretty simple. But as of the 1990s, Austria sought to align itself more closely with many parts of western Europe and introduce an appellation system (like France's) that encourages wines to be chosen based on the place where the grapes grew. (You, the wine drinker, would simply have to memorize the permissible grape varieties in that place, as for example, French Côte-Rôtie = syrah). Some have argued that Austria has taken a step backward by adopting an appellation system that restricts creativity among winemakers and forces memorization among wine consumers. Others have argued that an appellation system is the "grown-up" approach to wine, since it underscores the message of terroir.

In 2001, the Ministry of Agriculture adopted the latter thinking and instituted a new system called DAC (*Districtus Austriae Controllatus*, or "protected Austrian declaration of origin"). The first DAC was the Weinviertel, in Lower Austria (for grüner veltliner), in 2003. To date there are nine DACS, with more potentially to follow. For wines that use the DAC system, the appellation and the letters DAC are listed on the label, but usually not the grape variety. And therein lies the rub. When a DAC is known for just one variety, you're compelled to memorize which variety

it is, but at least the situation is not completely confusing. On the other hand, several DACs are known for multiple varieties, causing nothing if not consumer angst. Here are the nine, followed in parentheses by the grape that's allowed to be in the bottle.

In Lower Austria

WEINVIERTEL DAC: (grüner veltliner)

TRAISENTAL DAC: (grüner veltliner or riesling)

KREMSTAL DAC: (grüner veltliner or riesling)

KAMPTAL DAC: (grüner veltliner or riesling)

In Vienna

WIENER GEMISCHTER SATZ DAC: (At least three high-quality white wine grapes must be used, the leading one of which cannot constitute more than 50 percent of the blend. Among the twenty permissible grapes are grüner veltliner, riesling, pinot blanc, pinot gris, chardonnay, neuberger, and gewürztraminer.)

In Burgenland

EISENBERG DAC: (blaufränkisch)

MITTELBURGENLAND DAC: (blaufränkisch)

NEUSIEDLERSEE DAC: (Zweigelt or Zweigelt with other indigenous reds if the wine is reserve)

LEITHABERG DAC: (pinot blanc, chardonnay, neuberger, and grüner veltliner for white; blaufränkisch blended with up to 15 percent St. Laurent, Zweigelt, or pinot noir for red)

THE FOODS OF AUSTRIA

Austria's culinary traditions, along with Hungary's, are the most sophisticated and compelling in central Europe. Essays could be written on the soups alone. The gem of that genre is pumpkin

HEURIGE: THE WINEMAKER AS COOK

The best places in Austria in which to taste homestyle food, drink local wines, and immerse yourself in everyday Austrian life are not cafés or restaurants. They are *heurigen* (HOY-rig-en)—rustic eating and drinking rooms (it would be erroneous to call them dining rooms), which are often attached to winemakers' homes. *Heurigen* date from 1784, when a royal decree allowed every Austrian to "serve and sell their own produce including wine."

Traditionally, all of the food at a *heurige,* including the breads, soups, salads, strudels, and even the sausages, is made from scratch by the winemaker and his family. Similarly, the wine offered must be only the winemaker's. The word *heurige,* in fact, refers both to the wine of the latest

vintage and the place where it's drunk. In other words, you drink *heurige* at a *heurige.* By law, a winemaker may only keep his *heurige* open for business as long as his supply of *heurige* lasts.

Most *heurigen* are utterly modest gathering spots, with communal tables and often a small playground for the children of their patrons. People go as much to socialize as to eat or drink. Although wine is available by the bottle, lots of it is ordered and drunk by the glass, or is made into a spritzer and served in a mug. (Interestingly, no coffee or beer is allowed to be sold.) In the countryside outside Vienna, *heurigen* are often called *buschenschenken,* named after the swags of fir branches tied to the doors.

soup. Every top restaurant, every great home cook, has a personalized recipe, including decadent versions in which whipped cream is folded in and roasted pumpkinseed oil is drizzled on top. But there are also extraordinary potato soups that prove just how majestic that tuber can be. In wine country, one must also try a frothy *weinsuppe* ("wine soup"), usually made with riesling or grüner veltliner, beef stock, paprika, and cream.

Strudels are ubiquitous in Austria, as often savory (made with wild mushrooms, root vegetables, ham, shellfish, herbs, cheese, and so on) as sweet (made with apples, plums, nuts, cherries, apricots). Strudel dough, similar to phyllo dough, is rolled into ultrathin sheets and brushed lightly with butter before it is filled and rolled up. At the Heurige Schandl, in the village of Rust, in the wine region of Burgenland, the juicy baked red cabbage and caraway strudel comes with a pool of dill and sour cream sauce. (Peter Schandl, the owner, is also a winemaker, who makes an irresistible

pinot blanc.) Strudel is a venue for offal as well. Austrians are quite fond of wrapping the thin dough around lamb and veal tongues, hearts, sweetbreads, and brains.

The breads in Austria, like those in Germany, make bread in western Europe seem about as nutritious as Styrofoam. Austrian breads are usually multigrain and often include herbs, spices, and nuts; you'll find roasted onion and walnut bread, pumpkinseed bread, and anise and black pepper bread. The best bread I have ever had—anywhere in the world—is made by the Austrian baker Hubert Auer in the city of Graz, in Styria. The Auer breads are often made with ancient types of grain, custom cultivated for the company. The breads are available in Auer's shops in Graz as well as in Vienna.

When Austrians themselves are asked to name the quintessential Austrian dish, a majority answer Wiener schnitzel, pounded veal medallions that are coated in coarse whole-grain bread crumbs—to make the schnitzel crunchy—then fried.

Bread—in Austria, it's plentiful and irresistible. Even in a simple stall in the Naschtmarkt— Vienna's pulsing outdoor market—sweet and savory breads can be found in abundance.

The other well-loved meat specialties are venison, game birds, wild boar, all manner of pork, and *tafelspitz* (boiled beef), which tastes much better than it sounds and is usually served with *apfelkren*, fresh horseradish pureed with cooked apples, and roasted potatoes.

Meat and potatoes. Bread and soup. If these do not seem the stuff of culinary dreams, it is because we consider them common, too fundamental to be inspirational. But Austria's position as an Old World crossroads between East and West has meant that the cooking is anything but plebeian. The exotic and the familiar have been intriguingly mingled here for centuries. You can smell it. The aroma wafting out of any kitchen window is not just vegetables or meat, but a mesmerizing collective scent of those plus ginger, paprika, cumin, caraway, dill, garlic, poppy seed, nutmeg, cinnamon, and juniper.

The Austro-Hungarian monarchy left numerous culinary remnants, including the two most famous: dumplings (*knödel*) and goulash (*gulasch*). Dumplings can be made simply from potato flour or from crumbled bread rolls. But more intriguing is the invention of bread mixed with meat, herbs, and/or cheese

ABOUT THOSE "FRENCH" CROISSANTS

For centuries, imperialistic Turkish tribes hoping to invade western Europe considered Austria a militarily strategic foot in the door. Austria usually managed to defend itself against these periodic sieges, but occasionally the Turks prevailed. A brief occupation in the late 1600s had two redeeming results—both culinary. Coffee beans were brought to Vienna, instigating a revolutionary change in Austrian drinking habits, and Viennese bakers created the croissant to commemorate the end of the Turkish siege. The rich dough's shape was modeled after the crescent moon emblem on Turkish banners.

Viennese desserts—both simple and elaborate—are culinary high art and an inspiration for pastry chefs around the world. Here, a traditional Gugelhupf cake, just waiting to be accompanied by a cup of rich, dark Viennese coffee.

or, for sweet dumplings, fruit, jam, and/or sugar. *Knödel* are masterful and irresistible in Austria, and are often served with soup, meats, or dessert. As for goulash, it is still traditional in Vienna for friends to go out for this paprika-rich beef ragout after the opera or theater.

Another Austrian custom is wurst snacking. All over Vienna and other major cities, small kiosks sell dozens of different grilled sausages served with hot or sweet mustard, crisp pickles, and hot peppers.

Save room. Austrian desserts are so good that Austrians often have them for breakfast or with coffee at 10:00 A.M. or at 4:00 P.M. There are the classics: *apfelstrudel* (apple strudel) and *topfenstrudel* (strudel made with sweetened fresh cheese and raisins and served with a vanilla custard sauce), Linzertorte (a raspberry and nut torte named after the city of Linz), Sachertorte (a dense chocolate torte, after which the Hotel Sacher in Vienna is named), plus countless poppy seed puddings.

In Vienna, the most sumptuous spot for dessert—indeed, one of the premier café/pastry shops in the world—is Demel. It bakes some ninety-five types of cakes and tortes alone, plus perfect strudels bursting with fruit, and dark chocolate desserts that

beg you to order them. These are all grandly showcased along antique wooden sideboards and will be served to you by perfectly mannered Viennese waitresses. The accompaniment of choice is rich Viennese coffee served with whipped cream. Demel is on the elegant shopping street called (counterintuitively) Kohlmarkt—cabbage market—at number 14.

As for actual cabbages, the place to see them is Vienna's bustling outdoor market, the Naschmarkt, with its purple figs the size of apples, its wooden barrels of fresh sauerkraut, and the dizzying array of fragrant Turkish breads, olives, and cheeses. First-time visitors can be taken aback by finding Austrian *apfelstrudel* and Turkish baklava sold side by side, especially since the countries don't actually border one another. But the Naschmarkt clearly reflects the symbiosis that has existed for centuries (sometimes happily, most times not) between the two historic rivals. Today, Turkish immigrants make up a large part of the Austrian population, and their rich culinary traditions continue to be woven into the Austrian gastronomic mainstream with delicious results. One of the most magnificent examples: the croissant.

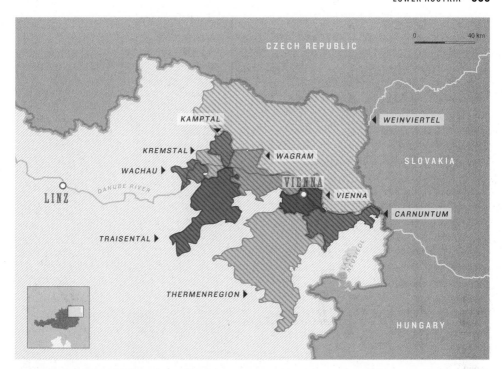

LOWER AUSTRIA

ower Austria (known locally as Niederosterriech) is made up of eight separate wine districts that loop in a grand arc around the city of Vienna. (Vienna is not included in these districts; it's a separate wine region of its own.) These are: the Wachau, Kremstal, Kamptal, Traisental, Wagram, Weinviertel, Carnuntum, and Thermenregion. Lower Austria is the most important wine region in Austria. More than 50 percent (67,000 acres/27,100 hectares) of Austria's vineyards are located here. The region is not in the south, as the name would seem to suggest, but rather is tucked into the northeastern corner of the country, along the lower part of the Danube River.

The Wachau (va-COW)—a UNESCO World Heritage site and the tiniest of the districts (just 3,334 acres/1,349 hectares)—is the most important. The whites here are unmatched in their sheer clarity of flavor, elegance, and balance (the vinous equivalent of perfect pitch). Through the middle of the Wachau, the Danube flows slowly and silently. Over millennia, it has gorged its way through granite gneiss (metamorphosed igneous rocks that are folated into layers) rich with quartz and feldspar, grinding them into drifting silt (loess) that settled on the east-facing terraces at the end of the last Ice Age. This is riesling and grüner veltliner territory at its best and wine country at its most serene, with storybook villages and country restaurants all along

In the cool cellars of Austria's best wineries, fermentation tanks are generally small, reflecting the fact that most top wineries make different wines from different vineyard sites.

THE BLUE MONASTERY OF DÜRNSTEIN

*T*he medieval village of Dürnstein is one of the prettiest in the Wachau. Along cobblestone streets sit houses outlined in flower boxes. The village itself can be seen from quite far away, thanks to the strikingly beautiful blue spire of the monastery's church, said to be the color of the Virgin Mary's robe.

the riverbanks. The climate, tempered by the river, is nonetheless cool, with strong variations in temperature between day and night. Both the soil and the climate give good structure and acidity to the grapes.

The Wachau is the only place in all of Austria where you'll find the three words *steinfeder, federspiel,* and *smaragd.* These terms were created by the Vinea Wachau, an association of the top Wachau producers, whose goal was to set their dry white wines apart. The categories (which must be listed on the wine labels) are defined as follows:

STEINFEDER: Natural unchaptalized wines with no more than 11.5 percent alcohol. (*Steinfeder* is the name of a local strain of feathery grass, and the association poetically describes these wines as "dainty.")

FEDERSPIEL: Natural unchaptalized wines with at least 11.5 but no more than 12.5 percent alcohol. The name *federspiel* derives from the local sport of falconry.

SMARAGD: The word *smaragd* (meaning "emerald") is also the name of a bright green lizard that suns itself in the vineyards here. *Smaragd* wines are the most physiologically ripe and are

The vineyards of Domaine Wachau in the Wachau region, along the Danube River.

despite its name, but the Croatian grape graševina), weissburgunder (pinot blanc), a small amount of chardonnay, and the slightly fat, somewhat neutral neuburger.

Just below Vienna, in the Thermenregion (named for the many hot springs there), two rare whites can be found: rotgipfler and zierfandler. Usually blended together to create the specialty wine of the region, the two make a massively fruity and rather heavy white with spicy orange overtones.

Although red wine is not Lower Austria's strong suit, there are some good ones, including a number of simple, spicy spätburgunders (pinot noirs) and Zweigelts. One of the most lip-smacking Zweigelts is that of Jamek, an excellent family-run winery, restaurant, and inn right on the banks of the Danube near the Old World village of Dürnstein (where, in 1192, the English king Richard the Lion-Hearted was imprisoned by Leopold V, Duke of Austria).

therefore considered the best. The wines must have a minimum of 12.5 percent alcohol; most are higher.

The other traditional white grapes in Lower Austria include welschriesling (not a riesling,

SOME OF THE BEST PRODUCERS OF GRÜNER VELTLINER

Bründlmayer • Emmerich Knoll • Franz Hirtzberger • F. X. Pichler • Hiedler • Hirsch • Holzapfel • Leo Alzinger • Loimer • Nigl • Prager • Schloss Gobelsburg

WHITES

SCHLOSS GOBELSBURG

RIESLING | TRADITION | RESERVE | KAMPTAL

100% riesling

One of the top producers in the Kamptal region, Schloss Gobelsburg makes exquisitely intense, shockingly pure rieslings and grüner veltliners. One of their rieslings—called Tradition—is a tightly wound molecule of energy waiting to explode into minerals, stone fruits, and waves of amazing freshness on your palate. But of course, there's more—a fragile whiff of flowers and an echo of exotic citrus peel savoriness, rather like preserved lemons. The wine comes from older vines on the slopes of the famous Gaisberg vineyard. Schloss Gobelsburg is the oldest winery in the Danube region, with a documented history back to 1171. The *schloss* (castle) itself is owned by the monks of the nearby Stift Zwettl monastery, and the winery is managed by the Moosbrugger family. "Tradition" is the name Michael Moosbrugger gives to bottlings he makes that honor a time before technology, and indeed this wine was made as it might have been at the turn of the twentieth century.

HIRSCH

GRÜNER VELTLINER | LAMM | RESERVE | KAMPTAL

100% grüner veltliner

Hirsch makes almost Baroque-style grüner veltliners—wines with curves of softness, fleshy peachiness, and gentle acidity that seem to lull you into a trance, until the end, when the wine hails with white pepper. I can think of a dozen things I'd like to eat with them right this moment. This is a small, family estate exclusively devoted to riesling and grüner veltliner, and this wine, from the famous Kamptal vineyard known as Lamm, is astonishing.

BRÜNDLMAYER

GRÜNER VELTLINER | LAMM | RESERVE | KAMPTAL

100% grüner veltliner

Willi Bründlmayer typifies the quality-obsessed New Wave generation of Austrian winemakers now at the helm of Austria's best estates. His rieslings, with their bright, powerful aromas and crystal-clear flavors, are like climbing into a lemon tree. But I love especially this grüner veltliner, from the same vineyard—Lamm—as the Hirsch. Once again, the vineyard offers up a shiatsu massage of white pepper, but Bründlmayer's wine also has a creamy core around which that pepper, plus minerals, circle like bees around the honey-rich hive. A simply fantastic grüner veltliner.

NIGL

GRÜNER VELTLINER | ALTE REBEN | LOWER AUSTRIA

100% grüner veltliner

The four letters N, I, G, L stand alone on the bare, white front label. Absolutely no adornment. It's as if everything is stripped away and you are left with one final essential. That idea also describes the Nigl wines. Crystalline, filigreed, precise, drenched in minerals, and possessing an atomic density of flavor, they are wines without an ounce of baby fat. Every molecule is lined up along a single trajectory of profound flavor. I would drink any Nigl wine anytime with pleasure, but I especially love this grüner veltliner from old vines (*alte reben*) for its operatic opener (minerals dipped in peach syrup) and its flourishing finale (cymbals of thundering white pepper).

LOIMER

GRÜNER VELTLINER | LANGENLOIS SPIEGEL | RESERVE | KAMPTAL

100% grüner veltliner

The Loimer family makes powerhouse grüner veltliners, racy wines with a sense of urgency to them. They are always vivid, but best of all is their tension of opposites—they are salty and peppery, light and dense, minerally and fruity, all at the same time. This wine is from the small Spiegel vineyard, near the town of Langenlois in the Kamptal (Kamp Valley), where the Kamp River has carved deep gorges (now covered in loess) in the bedrock. The Loimer family are ardent practitioners of biodynamics (see Biodynamic Viticulture, page 34).

DOMÄNE WACHAU

GRÜNER VELTLINER | TERRASSEN | SMARAGD | LOWER AUSTRIA

100% grüner veltliner

The massive wines of Domäne Wachau are known for their gravitas, and the sheer density and weight of this grüner veltliner is an astounding example. I once wrote, "It's like tasting howling sounds from the depths of the ocean; it makes you feel as if the entire earth welled up and gently put preserved lemons, spices, and rocks in your mouth." Domäne Wachau is a cooperative (certainly one of the top cooperatives in the world) that makes wines from dozens of small growers, who produce more than 30 percent of all the grapes in the Wachau. *Terrassen* ("terraces") refers to the fact that all of the grapes for this wine were grown on rocky, dry terraces where the elevation, orientation to the sun, and attenuated soils all lead to high-quality grapes.

RED

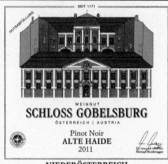

SCHLOSS GOBELSBURG

PINOT NOIR | ALTE HAIDE | LOWER AUSTRIA

100% pinot noir

Before I first tasted this wine, I would have said that Austrian and German pinot noir had a long way to go before they'd be put in the same company with Burgundy. This wine opened my eyes. It's as delicate, layered, precise, and filigreed as pinot noir can be, with long ribbons of spiciness and earthiness and a core of rich raspberry/cranberry fruit. The silky/creamy texture is sublime (for Burgundy lovers, it will seem like a page out of the Chambolle-Musigny playbook). I am not surprised that this wine comes from Schloss Gobelsburg, one of the great wine estates of the world, and an estate from which I've never had anything less than a stunning wine. As I noted in the description of its riesling, the castle of Schloss Gobelsburg is owned by the Cistercian monks of the adjoining Stift Zwettl monastery. It was these monks who brought pinot noir to the Langenlois region of Lower Austria from their homeland, Burgundy. In old German, *alte haide* means "old heath," a reference to land that was considered too dry or stony to grow things, and thus was left fallow or used for sheep.

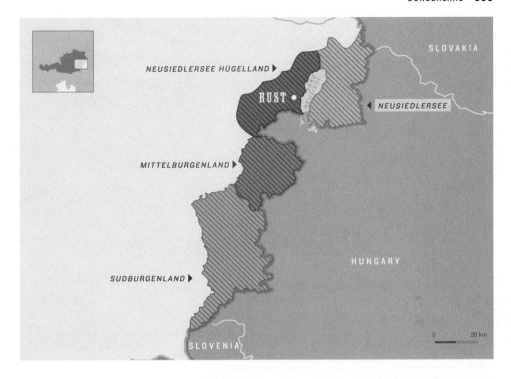

NEUSIEDLERSEE HÜGELLAND ▶

RUST •

NEUSIEDLERSEE ◀

SLOVAKIA

MITTELBURGENLAND ▶

SUDBURGENLAND ▶

HUNGARY

SLOVENIA

0   20 km

BURGENLAND

ustria's second-largest wine region after Lower Austria, Burgenland (13,840 acres/5,600 hectares) huddles against Hungary on the far eastern border (Budapest is only some 130 miles/210 kilometers away). The vineyards here, along with those in Hungary, formed a vast, uninterrupted sea of vines during the Austro-Hungarian monarchy. Burgenland is known primarily for its opulent sweet wines, as well as some remarkable reds.

Sweet wines have been the glory of this part of central Europe for eons. The most celebrated type—*ausbruch*—is made mostly from grapes infected by *Botrytis cinerea*, although some of the grapes can simply be dried and shriveled. For *ausbruch*, these grapes are then mixed with freshly pressed must from grapes that are only partially botrytized. (Reflecting Burgenland's proximity to Hungary, this process is similar to the manner in which Hungary's famous sweet wine, Tokaji Aszú, is made; see page 632.) Both the fully and partially botrytized grapes for *ausbruch* must come from the same vineyard. The grapes are sometimes foot-trodden, and the wine is aged in casks. *Ausbruch* is more baroque, outrageous, bruléed, and honeyed than *beerenauslese*, but has less residual sugar and more alcohol than *trockenbeerenauslese*.

The most famous *ausbrüche*, as well as BAs and TBAs, are made possible by a hauntingly beautiful natural entity: an almost supernatural lake poised between northern Burgenland and Hungary named Neusiedl (the Austrians call this the Neusiedlersee). More than 186 square miles (482 square kilometers) in size, it is only 2 to 7 feet (0.6 to 2 meters) deep. The shallow lake gives up so much humidity that it is threatened by constant evaporation.

Silvia Heinrich, who now runs her family's winery, J. Heinrich, in southern Burgenland. Her delicious blaufränkisch tastes as if it's poised halfway between the Old World and the New.

In fact, twice during the past century it dried up completely. Reeds and grasses love the lake. So many of them grow around it that thatching material developed into a local industry. Birds also love the lake. Indeed, the vast bird population has resulted in the area becoming one of Europe's largest wildlife preserves. And thanks to the thousands of storks that nest and feed here, the lake has been called a stork smorgasbord. But as much as the reeds or the birds, grapes love the lake. It's where they love to rot.

The wet air and the gentle climate make for a perfect macro petri dish in which botrytis can grow quickly, at the expense of other forms of rot and mold. Thus, the best Burgenland *ausbrüche*, BAs, and TBAs have luscious purity to them, and the echo of botrytis flavor is vivid. The tempting, sweet grapes do not go unnoticed by the birds, of course. Every last grape would be eaten by them were it not for the fact that growers here have set up programmed recordings of gun blasts that thunder through the tranquil vineyards every few minutes, keeping the flocks away (and shattering any romantic moment one might be having, communing with the vines).

A number of different grape varieties are used for Burgenland's sweet wines: welschriesling, chardonnay, traminer, Scheurebe, and others, including occasionally the principal grape used in Hungarian Tokaji Aszú, furmint. The vines are planted in sandy/stony/chalky soil all around the shallow lake. The pools of warm lake water at the edges of the vineyards are like natural humidifiers releasing their invisible mist, so critical for botrytis. Pickers generally go into the vineyards three separate times, hand harvesting only perfectly botrytized bunches each time.

The eastern shore of the Neusiedlersee is said to produce a more bountiful, fleshy, earthy style of sweet wine than the slightly more austere style of the hillier western shore. On the western side, called Neusiedlersee-Hügelland, is the charming village of Rust (pronounced roost), which along with Tokaj in Hungary, has been one of central Europe's most eminent wine towns since the Middle Ages. In 1681, Rust bought its political independence and religious freedom by paying Leopold I, who, at the time, was the reigning Holy Roman

Emperor, King of Hungary, King of Croatia, King of Bohemia, and Archduke of Austria, 60,000 gold guilders and 30,000 liters (7,900 gallons) of *ausbruch*.

In years when botrytis doesn't form as thoroughly, and thus when the production of *ausbruch*, BA, and TBA is small, growers in Burgenland may make other types of sweet wine—the rare *strohwein* ("straw wine") from grapes dried on mats made from the reeds of the lake; or, if the winter is especially cold, *eiswein*, the sweet outcome of grapes left on the vine until frozen. The long hang-time—well into the dead of winter—concentrates the grapes' sugar and acid. In the best Austrian *eisweins*, voluptuous sweetness is wrapped around an electrifying nucleus of acidity, making for an unparalleled taste sensation.

Then there are the reds. Specializing in ornate, sweet white wines and complex, dry reds may seem counterintuitive at first (until one considers Bordeaux). In any case, many Burgenland winemakers do both quite successfully.

As you move further south in Burgenland, away from Lake Neusiedl and toward Mittelburgenland (Middle Burgenland) and Südburgenland (South Burgenland), red wines

The ancient city of Rust in Burgenland on the western shore of Lake Neusiedl is celebrated for its ausbrüche.

take on greater prominence. Decent red wine has a long-established foundation here; superb red wine is a far more recent phenomenon. But already, Mittelburgenland is a DAC for blaufränkisch, as is the DAC Eisenberg within Südburgenland. In the latter, you find iron-rich schist soils, and the blaufränkisch that is grown in them has a distinct minerally spiciness all its own.

The foremost red grape is indeed blaufränkisch, and when it is good, it can become a daring wine—bold, dark in color, suffused with the unusual flavor of raspberries, blueberries, and sour cherries dusted with white pepper and minerals. The wine is usually structured and sleek, yet it has crushed-velvet softness and juiciness—imagine good cabernet franc crossed with good syrah crossed with malbec. In other words, blaufränkisch is the complete opposite of northern European red wines. Lastly, as red wine plantings have shot through the roof in recent years, so has the collective wisdom making the wines. Extremely delicious, Austrian blaufränkisch deserves (and well may get) much more serious attention from the world in years to come.

The two other well-loved local red grapes are Zweigelt and St. Laurent. Zweigelt, a cross between blaufränkisch and St. Laurent, is grapey, full of black cherry flavors, and uncomplicated. St. Laurent is usually also straightforward and satisfying—a combination of earth, mushrooms, and spices, not unlike a simple pinot noir.

In Burgenland, some winemakers also make dry whites, including chardonnay. The best are elegant, made entirely without wood, and brimming with creamy flavors balanced by just the right flash of acidity. Look for the producers Velich and Paul Achs.

SOME OF THE BEST PRODUCERS OF BLAUFRÄNKISCH

Ernst Triebaumer • Gesellmann • Hans Iby • Hans Igler • Hans Nittnaus • Krutzler • Prieler • Umathum • Wallner

The Burgenland Wines to Know

WHITE

UMATHUM

GELBER & ROTER TRAMINER | BURGENLAND

Approximately 60% roter traminer, 30% gelber traminer

This fantastic and unusual wine is made from the rare yellow (*gelber*) traminer and red (*roter*) traminer, both of which are versions of the grape savagnin. Beautifully aromatic, the wine has what can only be described as dazzling citrus bitterness—as if the skins of perfect grapefruits, limes, kumquats, and oranges were transmuted into wine. The effect is at once cool, sophisticated, refreshing, and begging for Southeast Asian appetizers. Umathum, which also makes one of the most fantastic rosés in Europe, is most widely known for its red wines, which are aged in bottle for three years before being released. The Umathum family has been growing grapes in Burgenland since the end of the eighteenth century, and began making their own wine in the 1980s.

REDS

SATTLER

ST. LAURENT | RESERVE | BURGENLAND

100% St. Laurent

St. Laurent is something of a mystery. Not as complex or distinctive as blaufränkisch, it's nonetheless a wine that, when it's good, is hugely satisfying. The kind of wine with a serious "yum" factor. Before you know it, you're on your third glass. Sattler, a small family winery that specializes in St. Laurent and Zweigelt, makes an explosively spicy, richly fruited, satiny textured reserve St. Laurent. It always reminds me of some wondrous vinous rendition of cranberries and Christmas spices. It's absolutely delicious with duck, turkey, and roast chicken.

J. HEINRICH

BLAUFRÄNKISCH | GOLDBERG | BURGENLAND

100% blaufränkisch

The loamy Goldberg vineyard is one of the oldest sites in southern Burgenland, and the wine, based on sixty-year-old vines, exudes a real purity of fresh fruit flavor. Great blaufränkisch like this tastes as if it's poised half in the Old World and half in the New World— on the one hand, there's a delicious Campari-like bitterness, but on the other, the core of the wine is vivid red cherry jam. This estate is run by the young Silvia Heinrich who, in 2002, left her career in Vienna to come back to the three-hundred-year-old family winery and learn alongside her father, the late Johann Heinrich.

PRIELER

BLAUFRÄNKISCH | LEITHABERG | BURGENLAND

100% blaufränkisch

Great blaufränkisch—and Prieler's is one—has an element of the savage in it, a howling, wild, gamy, pepper-and-salt character that you find in Northern Rhône syrahs. At the same time, the wine has a sleek structure and a blue-fruit coolness that's not unlike cabernet franc. Indeed, if someone told me blaufränkisch was a cross of syrah and cabernet franc, I'd believe it. (It's not.) Prieler's blaufränkisch called Leithaberg is a serious, untamed, dramatic red— tight, hard, and destined for a long life; as spicy as chai; as meaty as rare steak sitting in a pool of savory juices. An absolutely phenomenal example of this stellar variety.

SWEET WINES

FEILER-ARTINGER

JONATHAN | RUSTER AUSBRUCH | ESSENZ | NEUSIEDLERSEE-HÜGELLAND

50% welschriesling, 50% chardonnay

Feiler-Artinger's Ruster Ausbruch Essenz is a liquid caress, enveloping you and folding you into it. The wine quite simply has awesome beauty. It's unctuous, complex, and sweet but not saccharine. Dried fruits, nuts, and dried citrus peel explode on the palate, and all the while a gentle acidity hums in the background. The sense of refinement and exquisiteness (at just 6.5 percent alcohol) is crazy good. Feiler-Artinger is a family winery established in the early 1900s. This wine is named Jonathan in honor of the birth of the current winemaker's son. While all *ausbruch* must be made from botrytized grapes and reach a KMW (using the Klosterneuberg Mostwage scale) of 27 degrees, wines labeled Essenz are extremely concentrated and reach 35 degrees or more.

HEIDI SCHRÖCK

RUSTER AUSBRUCH | AUF DEN FLUGELN DER MORGENRÖTE | NEUSIEDLERSEE-HÜGELLAND

66% welschriesling, 34% weissburgunder

As beautiful as its name, *Auf den Flugeln der Morgenröte*, which means "on the wings of red dawn." Langorously sweet but not syrupy, and evocative of quince, exotic oranges, marmalade, and spices, Heidi Schröck's *ausbrüche* are always utterly elegant and have the ability to put their drinkers in a happy, satisfied, Zenlike state. The woman herself is a leading winemaker and innovator in Burgenland.

STYRIA

tyria, along Austria's mountainous, southern Alpine border, is the second smallest wine region in the country, with just 10,472 acres (4,238 hectares) of grapes. Yet this is arguably one of the world's top spots for sauvignon blanc, as well as Austria's most beautiful wine region. Behind the small houses with their lace curtains and flower boxes, the vineyards stretch over kelly-green hills. Many vineyards have a *klapotez*—a wooden windmill with hammers that make a loud clacking noise to scare off the birds (who, unfooled, sometimes sit right on top of the contraption).

Everywhere in Styria there are pumpkin patches, for this is the home of Austria's famous specialty, pumpkinseed oil. Made from the roasted seeds of a special green-and-yellow striped pumpkin, the dark green oil is mindblowingly delicious (see page 598).

As for Styrian wines, the best (almost all of them white because of the alpine climate) can be dazzling, with bright, focused flavors that have a keen, kinetic edge to them. Most of the top wines are found along the wine route (*weinstrasse*) in the hilly province of south Styria, Südersteiermark, where the lemon-yellow daylight is so vivid it almost seems polished. Vineyards here are among the steepest in the country, and the soils are varied—from slate, marl, and limestone, to gneiss, schist, basalt, sand, and loam.

Chardonnay (called morillon in Styria) has a long history here, the vines having been brought from the Champagne region of France

▲ *In a country full of exquisitely beautiful wine regions, Styria, in the southeastern corner of Austria, has a particular, pastoral charm. Sauvignon blanc is a specialty here as is artisanal pumpkinseed oil, Austria's equivalent of extra virgin olive oil.*

The Hannes brothers, who run the hotel and restaurant at Weingut Sattlerhof in Gamlitz in Styria, are known for making excellent wines.

EAU-DE-AUSTRIA

In Austria, schnapps is said to be made from every fruit and berry you have heard of and every fruit and berry you haven't. Schnapps, like *eau-de-vie* in France and grappa in Italy, is a clear, unaged distillate (about 40 proof) that is drunk after the meal. Often Austrian families proudly make their own schnapps from fruit they (also proudly) grow themselves, and it's frequently a delicious, relatively mild sweet liqueur. In restaurants you'll also find hundreds of handcrafted, limited-production, very expensive versions made by individual winemakers and artisanal distillers. Plum is the most common flavor, but more intriguing perhaps are schnapps made from elderberries, quince, juniper, apricots, cherries, blueberries, blackberries, and rowanberries from the mountain ash tree.

in the nineteenth century. For the most part, Styrian chardonnay is made in the style of French Chablis—taut and linear rather than fat and buttery. But the biggest surprise—and Austria's best-kept secret—is Styrian sauvignon blanc. These are racy, herbal, lemony wines, with a wild outdoorsy quality and a tanginess not unlike a good French Sancerre. In addition to sauvignon blanc and morillon, the varieties of note include welschriesling, weissburgunder, traminer, and beautifully taut, dry, refreshing muskateller (aka gelber muskateller), the Austrian name for muscat blanc à petits grains, the best of the extensive group of wines with muscat in their names.

Styria is also known for rosés—or rather, a single type of rosé called *schilcher*. Made from the blauer wildbacher grape, which grows almost exclusively in west Styria, *schilcher* is very high in acid. There is no better mate for the smoked, aged bacon that is also a specialty of the region.

Styrian wine estates tend to be very small but often have an adjoining restaurant, *buschenschenk*, or small inn. One not to be missed is Sattlerhof, a wine estate in Gamlitz, known for its extremely delicious sauvignon blanc and chardonnay and its adjoining restaurant, also called Sattlerhof, considered one of the best restaurants in Styria.

VIENNA

here is a vineyard of sorts in Paris. Someone in Rome must have a vine or two planted next to the tomatoes. But Vienna is the only major city in the world that is a commercially significant wine region unto itself. Within the city limits there are 1,512 acres (612 hectares) of grapes, all of which fall under a government protection program lest developers be tempted to put such valuable real estate to more profitable uses.

The name Vienna, or as it's spelled in Austria, Wien (pronounced veen), would seem to derive from *wein* ("wine"), but it does not. The word is of Celtic origin and means "white or wild river," a reference to the Danube. The city itself is romantic and exhilarating, the kind of place that makes you want to abandon yourself to its beauty. As in Paris, the very air seems to shimmer with the secrets of centuries past. Everywhere, stately buildings glow in the white sunlight. There is an aura of mystery and passion. That this also happens to be a wine region makes perfect sense to those for whom wine *is* mystery, beauty, and romance.

From the Middle Ages on, Viennese vineyards were planted to slake the thirst of the local citizenry. Many plots were in the care of either monks or nobles, who studied viticulture and built cellars, some of which are still in use. Vineyards were planted with different varieties of both white and red grapes side by side in the same plot. The grapes would be picked and pressed together as a field blend. This traditional style of wine, called *gemischter*

▲ *The Vienna State Opera on the Ringstrasse. Vienna, a stately but vividly passionate city, is the only major city in the world that is also a wine region.*

A heurige *is an Austrian institution, and Vienna is full of them. Part winery, part wine bar, part giant café,* heurigen *are where Austrians go to talk, argue, eat, kiss, and have a great time.*

WHEN YOU VISIT . . . AUSTRIA

AUSTRIAN WINE COUNTRY is immaculate and movingly beautiful. (You won't want to go home.) The vineyards are dotted with lovely small villages and historic towns, and the food everywhere is stunning. Many of the wineries have *heurigen* (restaurants) attached. Although most Austrian wineries do not have organized tours, proprietors, most of whom speak English, are accustomed to receiving guests by appointment.

IF YOU ARE IN LOWER AUSTRIA, don't miss the extraordinary wine academy known as Kloster Und, located just outside the historic city of Krems. A seventeenth-century Capuchin monastery, Kloster Und is not only a school but also a wine library, wine museum, and a luxury restaurant. In the vaulted stone cellar under the nave of the church, 150 Austrian wines are available for tasting.

satz—"mixed planting"—makes up about a third of all Viennese wine today, and as of 2013, the style has DAC status. Such wines are rarely very good, but they are always fascinating. Just try to imagine the flavor of a wine made from riesling, pinot blanc, neuburger, grüner veltliner, and gewürztraminer. Today, Vienna's better vineyards, of course, are planted variety by variety in the modern way. In the western part of the city, the mineral-rich limestone soils lead to very good riesling, chardonnay, and pinot blanc. In the southern part of the city, darker, heavier soils lead to fuller-bodied whites and are also planted with Zweigelt and other red varieties. Still, it can take you aback just a bit to see a plot of Zweigelt squeezed between two skyscrapers.

Viennese viticulture has also laid the foundation for the *heurigen*. These wineries-cum-cafés were where Austrian life was played out. People went to drink wine, eat, gossip, argue, and hold hands—sometimes concomitantly. *Heurigen* now exist all over the country, but some of the oldest and most infamous are in Vienna. The Heurige Franz Mayer is a good example. The Mayer family makes wines from one of the best city plots, the Alsegar vineyard, as well as from other, less distinguished urban vineyards. All of these wines, noble and lackluster alike, are cheerfully consumed at the family's boisterous, cacophonous, eight-hundred-seat *heurige*, where it is said Beethoven wrote part of his Ninth Symphony.

SWITZERLAND

SWITZERLAND RANKS SEVENTEENTH AMONG
WINE-PRODUCING COUNTRIES WORLDWIDE.
THE SWISS DRINK AN AVERAGE OF 12 GAL-
LONS (47 LITERS) OF WINE PER PERSON PER
YEAR.

Switzerland is surrounded on all sides by some of Europe's most prominent wine-producing countries, and although its wines are not nearly as renowned (or numerous), they are worthy of attention. To begin with, much of this small Alpine country (one-tenth the size of California) is just simply too high, and therefore too cold, for grapevines to grow successfully. Switzerland ranks seventeenth in the world in volume of wine production, just after Hungary and Canada. Most of its wines come from the western, predominantly French-speaking part of the country, and especially from the important provinces, or cantons, as they are known in Switzerland, of Valais, Vaud, Neuchâtel, and Geneva. Wine is also made, however, in the southern, Italian-speaking area known as Ticino, and in the more eastern, German-speaking Ostschweiz.

Switzerland (somewhat counterintuitively, given its climate) is mostly a red wine producing country. The leading variety, in fact, is pinot noir, called blauburgunder, a light, spicy, and often quite good wine, although rarely complex or nuanced in flavor. Some tasty, light red wines are also made from pinot noir-gamay blends, which are called Dôle. In the southern canton of Ticino, merlot has been growing since the early part of the twentieth

---

▲ *The tiny village of Aubonne surrounded by vineyards in the Vaud, a French-speaking part of Switzerland near Lake Geneva. Much of the wine produced in the Vaud is white, though counterintuitively, most Swiss wine is red.*

With the Alps as a backdrop, a picnic with bottles of Swiss wine is just right for contemplation. Here, First Lake, which can be reached only by cable car after a long hike. The lake, which is near Grindelwald, is 7,400 feet (2,260 meters) in altitude.

century, and again, the wines are light, sleek, fairly crisp, and sometimes spicy. But perhaps the most intriguing red variety of all in Switzerland is the indigenous *rouge du pays*

A tasting room near Lake Geneva specializes in wine from the terraced vineyards of Lavaux.

(incorrectly called cornalin locally), which can be the source of super-juicy, spicy wines redolent of black cherries and pomegranates.

The major white grape variety is chasselas (known in the Valais as fendant and known in German as gutedel), which makes light-bodied wines that range from neutral quaffing wines to crisp whites laced with citrus and almond flavors. Other Swiss white wines include sylvaner (the same as silvaner in Germany), pinot blanc, and pinot gris, plus numerous native varieties like amigne, humagne blanche, and petite arvine, an ancient grape that makes refreshing, floral, and exotically fruity wines.

The 38,000 acres (15,400 hectares) of vineyards in Switzerland can be enormously challenging to work because of their steepness. Along with the vineyards of Germany, these are some of the steepest vineyards in the world, some of them—at 40 to 50 degree

MILK'S HIGHER CALLING?

Some would say it's cheese. But every kid in the world would insist it's milk chocolate—a Swiss creation. In 1875, milk chocolate was invented by Swiss candle maker Daniel Peter, who lived in the city of Vevey. Thanks to increasing competition from oil-burning lamps in Europe, Peter gave up candle making to go into his wife's family business—chocolate.

An astute entrepreneur, Peter hypothesized that the chocolate market could be expanded by making chocolate more nourishing, especially for children. With the help of his friend Henri Nestlé, then a baby food manufacturer, Peter invented a method for blending cocoa and the milk from alpine cows without souring the milk in the process. Four years later, the two formed the Nestlé Company.

THE QUICK SIP ON SWITZERLAND

A COLD, MOUNTAINOUS country nestled in the Alps, Switzerland has obvious viticultural challenges. But despite these, the country boasts a small thriving wine industry.

MOST SWISS WINE IS LIGHT, tasty and red; the leading variety in terms of volume is pinot noir.

SWITZERLAND'S TOP WHITE is chasselas—a super-crisp wine, ideal for splicing through the rich flavors of the country's famous Alpine cheeses.

Harvesting fendant (chasselas) grapes on the steep slopes of the Valais.

slopes—appearing to be perilously close to vertical. As a result, terraces, called *tablars,* are cut into the mountainsides, and grapes are often transported up and down the slopes on monorails.

Swiss wines are governed by an appellation system not unlike France's, although the wines are usually labeled by variety, making them fairly easy to understand. While Swiss wines are not widely exported, here are a number of producers worth knowing on your next Swiss hiking or skiing vacation: Domaine des Muses, Domaine E. de Montmollin & Fils, Adrian Mathier, Rouvinez, and Angelo Delea.

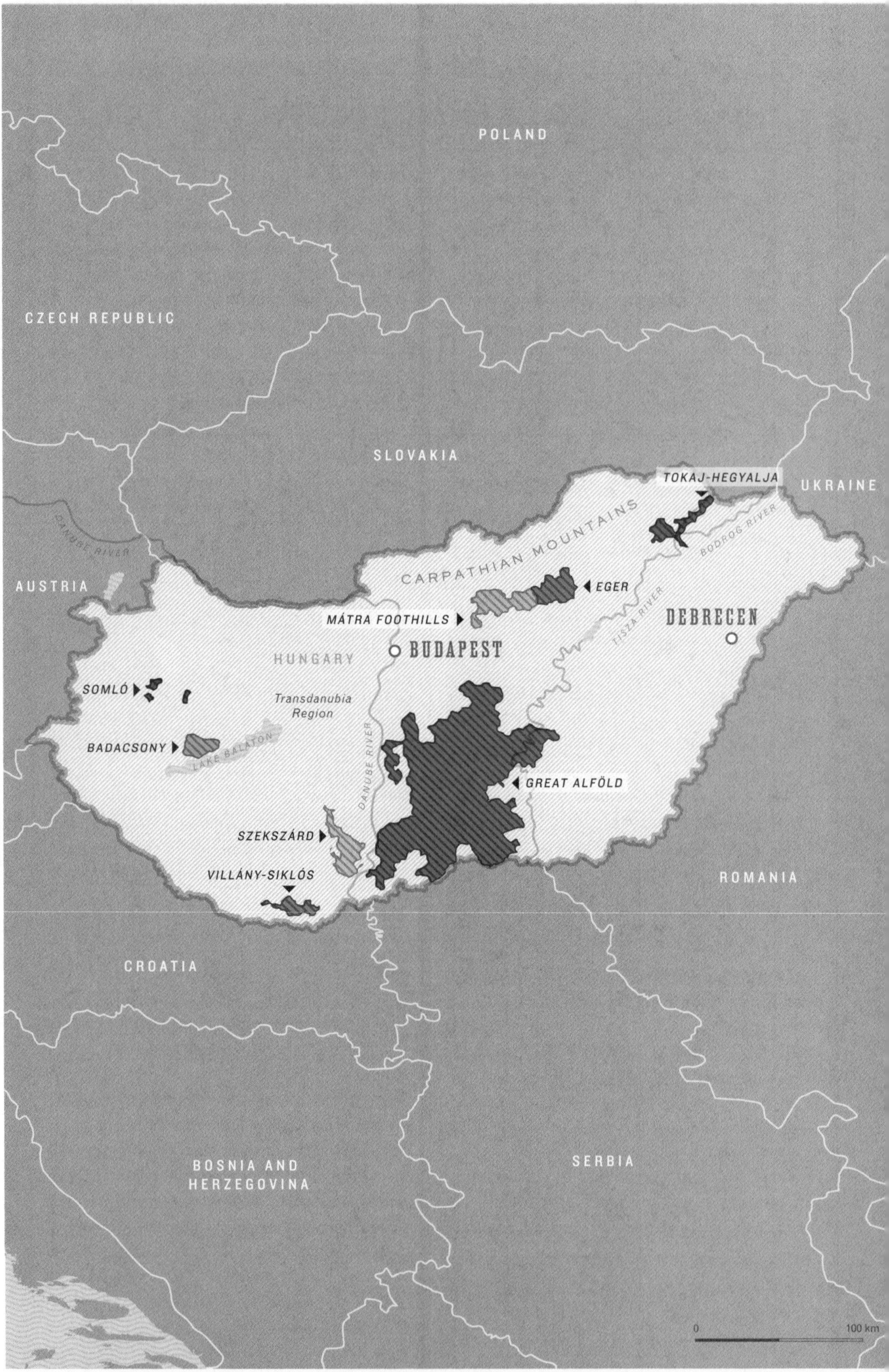
POLAND
CZECH REPUBLIC
SLOVAKIA
UKRAINE
AUSTRIA
TOKAJ-HEGYALJA
CARPATHIAN MOUNTAINS
BODROG RIVER
DANUBE RIVER
EGER
MÁTRA FOOTHILLS
TISZA RIVER
DEBRECEN
BUDAPEST
HUNGARY
SOMLÓ
Transdanubia Region
BADACSONY
LAKE BALATON
GREAT ALFÖLD
SZEKSZÁRD
VILLÁNY-SIKLÓS
ROMANIA
CROATIA
BOSNIA AND HERZEGOVINA
SERBIA
0
100 km

HUNGARY

HUNGARY RANKS FIFTEENTH AMONG WINE-PRODUCING COUNTRIES WORLDWIDE. THE HUNGARIANS DRINK AN AVERAGE OF 6 GAL-LONS (21 LITERS) OF WINE PER PERSON PER YEAR.

f all the countries in the eastern part of Europe, none has had a more solid tradition of producing great wines than Hungary. Its only possible rival is Austria, and although the wines of Austria are certainly soaring in recognition today, the wines of Hungary were for centuries the more esteemed of the two. In fact, from the seventeenth to the twentieth century, Hungary possessed what was arguably the third most sophisticated wine culture in Europe, after those of France and Germany. Among other distinctions, it was in the 1600s in Hungary's famous Tokaj-Hegyalja (TOKE-eye hedge-AL-ya) region—not in Bordeaux or Burgundy—that the first system for ranking wine on the basis of quality was developed. By 1700, the best plots in Tokaj-Hegyalja were designated First, Second, or Third Class, and strict royal decrees kept vineyard and winemaking practices at a very high level.

Modern Hungary, sitting virtually in the middle of eastern Europe, is a small country bordered on the north by Slovakia, on the northeast by the Ukraine, on the east by Romania, on the south by Croatia, Serbia, and Slovenia, and on the west by Austria. But it's worth noting that, from 1867 to the end of World War I, as the leading entity in the Austro-Hungarian Empire, Hungary was one of the most powerful forces on the globe and the second largest country in Europe, after the Russian Empire. At the height of its glory, the Austro-Hungarian Empire included not only every country that borders Hungary today, but also Bosnia and Herzegovina, the Czech Republic, and small parts of Italy, Montenegro, and Poland.

Vineyards have flourished in Hungary at least since Roman times. When the Magyars, an ancient tribe in the Ural Mountains, from whom modern Hungarians are descended, arrived in the region in the ninth century, they found vines growing everywhere and well-established viticultural and winemaking practices in place. (The Magyars brought something besides themselves to Hungary—namely their idiosyncratic language, which is one of the few languages in Europe today that does not belong to the Indo-European language family. As you're about to experience, trying to pronounce Hungarian, which belongs to the Uralic language family, can make you feel like you've got a mouth full of marbles. Indeed, Hungarian, Turkish, and Greek are the only European languages that have words for wine not derived from Latin; the Hungarian word for wine is *bor*. But in the seventeenth century, it was the emergence in Tokaj-Hegyalja of the rare, extraordinary wine Tokaji Aszú (TOKE-eye ah-SOO), commonly called simply Tokaji (spelled "Tokay" in English), that put Hungary on the international wine map. Tokaji became and remains not only the most stunning wine of eastern Europe, but one of the greatest dessert wines in the world. Precious, rare, and a wine whose creation hinges on just the right weather (more on this to follow), it represents just 4 to 6 percent of the country's total wine production each year. For an explanation of Hungarian wine law, see the Appendix on Wine Laws, page 927.

THE LAND, THE GRAPES, AND THE VINEYARDS

Hungary is a landlocked country of grassy plains, orchards, forests, and vineyards. The country is divided more or less in half by the Danube River, called the Duna in Hungarian, which runs north to south through the entire country, much like the Mississippi River does in the United States.

For a country just a bit larger than Scotland, Hungary grows a wide range of grape varieties. This is possible partly because Hungary sits at a relatively northern latitude (on par with Burgundy, France), so it is well suited to making crisp, light white wines from fairly cool-climate varieties, but at the same time, much of the country possesses a continental climate—warm to hot, sunny summers and very cold winters. This means that Hungary

BULL'S BLOOD

One of the most popular, well-known dry reds of Hungary is Egri bikavér—"bull's blood of Eger." It is made primarily from the kékfrankos and kadarka grapes, grown in Eger, which is about halfway between Budapest and Tokaj. The legend behind the wine dates back to the mid-1500s, when the fortress of Eger, which belonged to the Magyars (ancestors to modern Hungarians), was besieged by the Turks. The Magyars (men, women, and reportedly even children) fought fiercely, drinking huge amounts of red wine in the process. As the story goes, when the Turks encountered the Magyars' ferocious fighting skills and saw their red-stained faces, they retreated, fearing that the Magyars attained their prowess by drinking the blood of bulls.

can also ripen bold red varieties. Hungary's top varieties include some that many wine fans may not recognize, such as furmint (FUR-mint), hárslevelű (HARSH-leh-veh-loo), juhfark (YOO-fark), kadarka (kah-DAR-kah), and kékoportó (KEK-oh-PORT-oh). But Hungary is also home to many varieties such as olasz rizling (OH-lahs REEZ-ling), kékfrankos (KEK-frank-osh), and Zweigelt (ZVEYE-gelt) that are common throughout eastern Europe. Then there's a whole brigade of well-known varieties—everything from sauvignon blanc, gewürztraminer (known in Hungary as tramini), and pinot gris (known as szürkebarát) to cabernet sauvignon, cabernet franc, and pinot noir. As for the types of wine Hungary makes, more than 70 percent of total wine production is white. And finally, most Hungarian wines are labeled varietally, with the wine region noted

The Hungarian Parliament sits on the banks of the Danube River. Begun in 1885, it is Hungary's largest building and remains one of the most impressive legislative buildings in Europe.

on the label. It may also be helpful to know that many wine labels adhere to the Hungarian custom of listing a surname first, so the wine brand Demeter Zoltán is owned by the winemaker Zoltán Demeter.

Of Hungary's twenty-two wine regions, seven are considered the most important, based on the historic quality of their wines. By far, the most prestigious of these is Tokaj-Hegyalja, the region where Tokaji is produced, in the northeastern part of the country, known as the Northern Massif, along the Slovakian border. The six other important wine areas are Badacsony, Somló, Szekszárd, Villány-Siklós, Eger, and Mátra.

Badacsony and Somló are in the central, Transdanubia, region in the west, near Lake Balaton, one of the largest lakes in Europe. Badacsony produces primarily white wines from chardonnay, sauvignon blanc, szürkebarát (pinot gris), and olasz rizling (the same as welschriesling in Austria and graševina in Croatia). Somló, one of the smallest, most beautiful, and remote wine regions in Hungary (there are no paved roads and no electricity), has volcanic soils and is the source of traditional wood-aged, partially oxidized, powerful, dense white wines (from furmint, hárslevelű,

THE QUICK SIP ON HUNGARY

HUNGARY IS ONE OF THE MOST important wine regions in eastern Europe. For most of the modern era, however, Hungarian wines were little known outside of the Soviet Union and other Communist countries, thanks to forty years of Communist rule, from 1949 to 1989.

HUNGARY'S MOST IMPRESSIVE WINE is Tokaji Aszú, considered one of the great dessert wines of the world.

ALTHOUGH SMALL IN SIZE, Hungary boasts an enormous number of different grape varieties, including indigenous grapes, such as furmint and kékfrankos, and international varieties, such as chardonnay and cabernet sauvignon.

THE GRAPES OF HUNGARY

WHITES

CHARDONNAY AND SAUVIGNON BLANC: Important international grapes increasingly grown throughout Hungary.

CSERSZEGI FŰSZERES: Widely planted grape that makes crisp, citrusy whites for every-night drinking. The word *fűszeres* is the flavor term Hungarians use to mean "spicy," and is also used with paprika to differentiate spicy paprika from sweet or smoky.

FURMINT: The most important grape in Tokaji Aszú, Hungary's famous sweet wine. Also makes dry wines. Very high in acid.

HÁRSLEVELŰ: The second most important grape in Tokaji Aszú. Contributes a floral and fruity aroma.

IRSAI OLIVÉR: Important white grape for making soft, slightly aromatic every-night white wines.

JUHFARK: A rare but distinctive native grape that, blended with furmint and hárslevelű, is used to make the intentionally oxidized, powerful, dense white wines of Somló.

KIRÁLYLEÁNYKA: A popular, light, fresh, grapey wine. The name means "little princess."

MUSCAT LUNEL: See Sárga muskotály.

OLASZ RIZLING: A specialty of Transdanubia, west of the Danube River. Despite its name, it is not a true riesling, but rather another name for the Croatian grape graševina. In Austria, next door, olasz rizling is called welschriesling.

OTTONEL MUSKOTÁLY: Also known as muscat Ottonel. Grown mostly in Mátra and Eger, where it makes fine dry wines reminiscent of the muscat Ottonels made in Alsace, and serves as a blending partner in sweet wines.

SÁRGA MUSKOTÁLY: Literally, "yellow muscat." The Hungarian name for the grape

Anett and Attila Németh of Alana-Tokaj, a winery known for mind-blowingly delicious Tokaji.

juhfark, and others) that can be a challenge to appreciate if your palate is accustomed to fresh, light, modern-style whites. Nonetheless, Hungarians insist Somló whites are a specialty, and that they're especially perfect with heavy Hungarian dishes. The Hapsburgs believed that drinking the rare Somló wine juhfark (the name means "sheep's tail") guaranteed a pregnant woman that she would bear a boy.

In the southern part of Transdanubia are two more important wine regions, Szekszárd and Villány-Siklós. These are the two most dynamic wine regions in Hungary and the regions where you are most likely to find producers using modern equipment and new oak barrels. Each of these regions produces some of the country's best red wines. Kadarka, a specialty of Szekszárd, is said to be the ideal red

muscat blanc à petits grains; the third most important grape in Tokaji Aszú. Often referred to as muscat lunel in the Tokaji region.

SZÜRKEBARÁT: Also known as pinot gris; makes well-regarded wines, especially when grown near Lake Balaton.

TRAMINI: The same variety as gewürztraminer; imported from western Europe but now grown all over Hungary.

ZÉTA, KÖVÉRSZŐLŐ, AND KABAR: Minor grapes used in Tokaji Aszú thanks to their susceptibility to botrytis and their capacity to reach high sugar levels. Zéta was previously called orémus, but the name was changed because Oremus is also a brand of Tokaji.

REDS

CABERNET SAUVIGNON, CABERNET FRANC, MERLOT, AND PINOT NOIR: Important international grapes increasingly grown throughout Hungary.

KADARKA: Declining in importance in Hungary, although capable of making good, light-colored, medium-bodied, slightly spicy reds. Probably of Balkan origin; in Hungary, it is a specialty of Szekszárd and Eger.

KÉKFRANKOS: The same grape as blaufränkisch; sometimes blended with merlot and cabernet sauvignon. Kékfrankos is the major grape in the famous Hungarian wine Egri bikavér—"bull's blood" of Eger.

KÉKOPORTÓ: This red grape makes common, somewhat undistinguished wine, especially in Villány-Siklós. It's the same as Austria's blauer Portugieser.

ZWEIGELT: Like kékoportó, a red grape in Villány-Siklós, where it makes quite good red wine, but perhaps better known in Austria, where it's generally made into even better red wine.

---

wine for paprika-based dishes. In the warm area known as Villány-Siklós, several top small producers make what are, for Hungary, fairly full-bodied reds from cabernet sauvignon, kékfrankos, merlot, and Zweigelt.

Finally, there are Eger and Mátra, both of which are located, along with Tokaj-Hegyalja, in the Northern Massif. Eger is noted for light-bodied reds as well as Hungary's popular dry red wine Egri bikavér ("bull's blood"). Mátra, on the other hand, is white wine territory. Here, very good-quality wines are made from olasz rizling and yellow muscat, as well as chardonnay, sauvignon blanc, and sémillon. One of the best types of wine and a local specialty, királyleányka (pronounced kir-ALL-ee-lee-AN-ka) is slightly aromatic and tastes somewhat like gewürztraminer. Although it's most often

drunk by large Hungarian men, királyleányka means "little princess."

None of Hungary's most important wine regions are in the Great Alföld, the vast, hot, flat plain south of Budapest, where nonetheless more than half of the country's vineyards are found. Most of the simple, inexpensive quaffing wines produced here are based on international varieties, such as chardonnay and merlot, which were first planted in Hungary after phylloxera swept the country in the 1870s, and then later planted even more extensively in the 1970s and 1980s. In total, Hungary has about 158,000 acres (63,900 hectares) of vineyards, making it sixteenth in the world in terms of area under vine.

As for who makes Hungarian wines, for the forty years prior to the fall of Communism in

THE MOST IMPORTANT HUNGARIAN WINES

LEADING WINES

CABERNET SAUVIGNON red

CHARDONNAY white

EGRI BIKAVÉR red

FURMINT white (dry and sweet)

HÁRSLEVELŰ white (dry and sweet)

IRSAI OLIVÉR white

KÉKFRANKOS red

KÉKOPORTÓ red

KIRÁLYLEÁNYKA white

MERLOT red

MUSCAT white (dry and sweet)

OLASZ RIZLING white

OTTONEL MUSKOTÁLY white

PINOT NOIR red

SZÜRKEBARÁT white

TOKAJI ASZÚ white (sweet)

TOKAJI ASZÚ ESSZENCIA white (sweet)

TOKAJI ESSZENCIA white (sweet)

ZWEIGELT red

WINES OF NOTE

CSERSZEGI FŰSZERES white

JUHFARK white

SZAMORODNI white (dry and semisweet)

1989, the Hungarian wine industry was controlled by the state. Grapes were grown on enormous state-run farms, wines were made in large cooperatives, and all wine exports were controlled by a single large state-owned trading organization. Wines not consumed in Hungary were sold in bulk, by tanker truck, almost exclusively to the Soviet Union or East Germany. Wine quality was dismal, almost without exception. The post-Communist decade brought hope, but also confusion over vineyard ownership rights, foreign investments, and newly devised governmental regulations. Today, Hungary's wine industry is still taking the economically demanding steps toward modernization, and better wines are slowly claiming the spotlight. As of 2012, there were an estimated 515 wineries, but many grape growers—especially those with less than 2 acres (0.8 hectare) of vineyards—are still too economically disadvantaged to vinify and market their own wines. Yet, if Tokaji is any model, the country's wines might well undergo a significant revolution in quality as the twenty-first century unfolds.

TOKAJI

Over the millennia of wine's existence, there have been multiple occasions when politics, war, and/or disease have combined to nearly destroy a wine region and its wines. No more poignant example exists than the region Tokaj-Hegyalja (TOKE-eye hedge-AL-ya) and its wine, known as Tokaji (TOKE-eye). Yet despite the historic difficulties that it has endured, the wine that French King Louis XV offered to Madame de Pompadour, calling it *vinum regum, rex vinorum* —"the wine of kings and the king of wines"— is the most profound sweet wine in the world. To drink it means letting go of every assumption you may have of sweet wine, for Tokaji is a flavor world unto itself.

Tokaji's near demise began with the deadly pest phylloxera. As the twentieth century dawned, the vineyards of Tokaji lay in ruin as a result of the insect. Over the next several decades, vineyards were rebuilt only to be devastated again during World War I, the

break up of the Austro-Hungarian Empire, and World War II. But the biggest upheaval was yet to come. In 1949, as Hungary collapsed under Communist rule, wineries and vineyards were

HOW SWEET THEY ARE

Tokaji Aszú is one of the most decadent but well-balanced sweet wines in the world, thanks to the natural acidity in the grapes. The sweetness of Tokaji is measured in *puttonyos*. The word is a derivation of *puttony*, the name of the basket in which the *aszú* grapes were traditionally gathered. (See page 633 for details.) Below are the legal requirements for the sugar content that wines of the various numbers of *puttonyos* must have. (In 2014, the levels 3 *puttonyos* and 4 *puttonyos* were legally abolished, but given the longevity of Tokaji, wines with these designations will appear on the market well into the future, and so I have included them below.) In practice, many wineries make Tokaji Aszús that exceed the degree of sweetness required for a particular number of *puttonyos*. So, a wine labeled 5 *puttonyos* may contain 20 percent residual sugar even though the law requires only between 12 and 15 percent. Note the residual sugar of Tokaji Esszencia—an off-the-charts 450 to 900 grams of sugar per liter (45 to 90 percent)! (For comparison's sake, the residual sugar in

a French Sauternes is about 120 grams, or roughly equal to that of a 4-*puttonyos* Tokaji Aszú.)

3 PUTTONYOS
6 to 9 percent residual sugar
(60 to 90 grams per liter residual sugar)

4 PUTTONYOS
9 to 12 percent residual sugar
(90 to 120 grams per liter residual sugar)

5 PUTTONYOS
12 to 15 percent residual sugar
(120 to 150 grams per liter residual sugar)

6 PUTTONYOS
15 to 18 percent residual sugar
(150 to 180 grams per liter residual sugar)

TOKAJI ASZÚ ESSZENCIA
18 to 45 percent residual sugar
(180 to 450 grams per liter residual sugar)

TOKAJI ESSZENCIA
45 to 90 percent residual sugar
(450 to 900 grams per liter residual sugar)

confiscated and nationalized. The preciously refined and highly individual sweet wines of Tokaj were blended en masse in big coopera- tive cellars run by the state. Over subsequent years, vineyards were neglected, equipment deteriorated, the quality of grapes declined drastically, old winemaking traditions were abolished in favor of cheaper, easier short- cuts, and winemaking itself was degraded to the point where it was little more than bureau- cratic drudgery. By the mid-1980s, the innocu- ous wines called Tokaji bore no resemblance to the wines once considered so extraordinarily delicious (not to mention their purported ther- apeutic and aphrodisiacal properties) that a detachment of Russian soldiers was regularly stationed in the region to procure sufficient supplies and then escort them to the court of Czar Peter the Great.

Luckily Tokaji was not beyond redemption. When Hungary became a democratic repub- lic in 1989, the government invited prominent western European vintners to partner with them to resurrect Tokaji. Foreign investment in the region swiftly followed. By the fall of that year, a group of key investors, including Lord Jacob Rothschild, the British wine author- ity Hugh Johnson, and the noted Bordeaux

The ancient underground cellars of Royal Tokaji Wine Company, one of the first wine joint ventures in Hungary after the fall of Communism.

winemaker Peter Vinding-Diers, formed the Royal Tokaji Wine Company in conjunction with sixty-three of the best remaining wine- growers. Within three years, a slew of other foreign investors, consultants, winemakers, and businessmen acquired estates and vineyards. These included the Laborde family of Château

SERVING AND DRINKING TOKAJI ASZÚ

Tokaji Aszú is usually drunk in small amounts (a 2-ounce/ 60-milliliter serving is custom- ary) and the wine should always be lightly chilled, but not icy cold. Because Tokaji is considered ready to drink upon release, there is no need to age it. That said, you certainly can age it if you want to, since the wine's high concentrations of sugar and acid act as preservatives. (In a remarkable show of delayed grati- fication, eastern European royal families would sometimes age the wine for close to a hundred years.) And, because of its sweetness, an opened but unfinished bottle of Tokaji will last for many months, especially if you keep it in the refrigera- tor. While drinking Tokaji Aszú by itself can be perfect (the wine doesn't really *need* food), Tokaji's richness and underly- ing acidity do make it a fascinating partner for many dishes. In Hungary, it is tradi- tionally served with celebratory desserts, such as crêpes (*palacsinták,* literally "pan- cakes") filled with thick chocolate cream, apricot cake, or else paired hedonistically with foie gras, or a blue cheese like Roquefort or Stilton.

Clinet in Pomerol, Bordeaux, who helped found Château Pajzos; the Álvarez family, owners of Spain's most famous wine estate, Vega-Sicilia, who founded Oremus; and three French multinational insurance companies, one of which, AXA, also owns Bordeaux's Château Pichon-Longueville Baron and Château Suduiraut, as well as the famous Port wine firm Quinta do Noval. AXA's Tokaji firm is called Disznókő. The financial capital these companies brought was formidable. In less than half a decade, Tokaji was reborn.

Tokay, as formerly noted, is the English spelling of Tokaji, (the *i* means "of," so Tokaji means "from the place Tokaj"). The Tokaj region, known officially as Tokaj-Hegyalja ("Tokaj Hill"), is about 120 miles (190 kilometers) northeast of Budapest, close to the Slovakian border. It includes twenty-seven villages spread over sloping hills, the remnants of ancient volcanoes. As of 2014, there were just under 15,000 acres (6,070 hectares) of vines in the Tokaj region, making it about one-third the size of the tiny Napa Valley, for example. The vineyards belong to about fifty leading producers of Tokaji, as well as hundreds of family-run operations, many of which make very small amounts of wine for their own and local consumption. Indeed, the average size of a vineyard here is just 1.4 acres (.57 hectares).

The Tokaj region produces both dry and sweet wines, but it is the lusciously honeyed wine Tokaji Aszú for which it is world famous. Indeed, Tokaji Aszú has been called "the Sauternes of eastern Europe," but perhaps the phrase should be reversed and Sauternes should be called "the Tokaji Aszú of France," since it was in the Tokaj region, not Sauternes, that the world's first sweet, botrytized wines were made.

During the Middle Ages, wines from the region were highly regarded and many vineyards were owned by members of the royalty. The style of those wines, and whether they were sweet or dry, remains unknown. However, one of the first recorded mentions of *aszú* grapes appeared in the *Nomenklatura* of Fabricius Balázs Szikszai, which was completed in 1576. And a recently discovered inventory of *aszú* wines predates this reference by five years. By the mid-1600s, a chaplain named Máté Szepsi Laczkó had also begun experimenting with furmint grapes left to ripen to the point where they were shriveled and had begun rotting, before picking them. Miraculously, the small amount of liquid that oozed from them tasted like honey. When the chaplain blended this nectar with the regular table wine from the previous year, the prototype of Tokaji Aszú was born.

MAKING TOKAJI ASZÚ

Like all wines made with the help of *Botrytis cinerea*, Tokaji Aszú is dependent on a singular set of climatic conditions. For the botrytis

---

WHEN YOU VISIT . . . HUNGARY

The most fascinating (and easiest) Hungarian wineries to visit are those of Tokaj-Hegyalja, in northeast Hungary, about 120 miles (190 kilometers) from Budapest. The majority of Tokaj's leading wineries are located in or near the sleepy village of Mád (easy to remember). With an advance appointment, tours can usually be conducted in English.

IF, ON YOUR WAY TO OR FROM wine country, you stop overnight in Budapest, be sure to dine at Gundel, the palatial nineteenth-century restaurant restored in 1992 by international businessman Ronald Lauder (of Estée Lauder) and the late United States restaurant consultant George Lang. The menu is devoted entirely to traditional Hungarian classics, including legendary Hungarian pastries.

A PASSION FOR PAPRIKA

It's hard to imagine that three centuries ago, one of the (now) defining ingredients of the Hungarian kitchen—paprika—was not yet known in Hungary. But paprika, along with several other Hungarian culinary essentials—tomatoes, sour cherries, coffee, and phyllo (which the Hungarians immortalized by reinventing as strudel)—were all introduced by the Turks during their numerous occupations. Be that as it may, in Hungary, paprika found its truest admirers and its raison d'être. Fiery and passionate themselves, Hungarians like their dishes to have drama. Even something as simple as paprika chicken *(paprikás csirke)* is a kind of lusty and luscious duel between the tangy richness of sour cream on the one hand and the tantalizing bite of paprika on the other. Of course, in Hungary, paprika is not a single thing. The Hungarians classify it into eight types, starting with the mildest and sweetest, Különleges, which is bright red in color, and proceeding to Erős, a very spicy version that is light brown in color. The region of Szeged is generally considered to produce the best paprika in Hungary. Interestingly, the peppers used to make paprika have the highest vitamin C content of any vegetable. Indeed, paprika was used in numerous experiments by Hungarian physiologist Albert Szent-Györgyi, who won the Nobel Prize in Physiology and Medicine in 1937 for his discovery of vitamin C.

---

fungus to take hold on healthy, ripe grapes, the region must have just the right amount of humidity and warmth (too little or too much can produce problems). Tokaj-Hegyalja is well situated. The Carpathian mountains, which arc around the region, shelter it from cold winds from the east, north, and west, creating prolonged, gently warm autumns. The region, shaped like a check mark, lies along a range of volcanic hills topped with loess, fine-grained deposits of silt, as well as volcanic tufa, both of which warm easily. Following the length of these hills is the Bodrog River, which meets the Tisza River at the bottom point of the check mark, near the village of Tokaj. Mists and humidity rising from these rivers are held in place by the warm hills, creating the perfect environment for botrytis to form.

The three main white grapes used in Tokaji are ideally suited for this purpose. Furmint, which makes up about 60 percent of all grapes planted in the region, is high in acid, late-ripening, thin-skinned, and easily susceptible to botrytis. Hárslevelű—the name means "linden leaf"—is second in importance, and although slightly less susceptible to botrytis, it, too, is high in acid as well as very aromatic and rich-tasting. Third in importance, sárga muskotály, also known as muscat blanc à petits grains, is both highly aromatic and crisply acidic. It is used as a seasoning grape. The fact that all three of these grapes naturally possess a bracing level of acidity means that, even at its sweetest, Tokaji Aszú tastes beautifully balanced, not saccharine or candied. Since the 1990s, three other grapes—all of which are botrytis-prone and capable of attaining high sugar levels—are also allowed in Tokaji and are sometimes included in minor amounts: zéta (formerly called orémus), kövérszőlő, and kabar.

The beneficial botrytis mold punctures the grapes' skins in search of water to germinate its spores. This causes water in the grapes to evaporate, and the grapes begin to dehydrate. Inside the shriveled grapes, the sugar and acid in the juice become progressively more concentrated. It is a perfect system to foster sweetness, but it's not without challenges. Botrytis spreads erratically, affecting some grapes and

Botrytized grapes destined to become Hungary's elixir, Tokaji Aszú, one of the world's most sensational wines. Hungary was the first country in the world to make wine from grapes affected by noble rot. Each perfectly shriveled berry will be picked out of the cluster by hand.

not others, some bunches and not others. It also moves through the vineyards sporadically; in some years, when little or no botrytis takes hold, no Tokaji Aszú will be produced.

Producers differ slightly in how they make Tokaji Aszú, but generally speaking the process goes like this. First, throughout the fall, the shriveled *aszú* grapes are picked by hand, berry by berry—not cluster by cluster—from botrytis-affected bunches. These *aszú* grapes are then brought to the winery, where they are lightly crushed into a paste. Meanwhile, the rest of the crop (all the grapes and bunches not affected by botrytis) is picked separately and made into a base wine. The *aszú* paste is added in various proportions to the base wine of the same year. (In the past, *aszú* was sometimes added to a base wine held back from the previous year; this practice is now rare.)

The proportions of *aszú* added are measured in *puttonyos*. A *puttony* is a basket in which the *aszú* grapes were traditionally gathered. It holds 44 to 55 pounds (20 to 25 kilograms) of grapes, equal to about 5.2 gallons (20 liters) of *aszú* paste. The ratio of *puttonyos* to base wine in each barrel determined the sweetness of the wine. The traditional barrels, called *gönci* (after the village of Gönc, known for its barrel makers), hold about 140 liters of wine. Thus, based on 140 liters, and just for the sake of a simple example, a wine labeled, say, Tokaji Aszú 2 *Puttonyos* would have 40 liters of *aszú* paste and 100 liters of base wine. A wine labeled Tokaji Aszú 4 *Puttonyos* would be even richer and sweeter, as it would have 80 liters of *aszú* paste and 60 liters of base wine. A 4- or 5-*puttonyos* Tokaji would be about as sweet and concentrated as a German *beerenauslese*. The sweetest Tokaji Aszús are 6 *puttonyos* and they are technically much sweeter than Sauternes (but don't taste like they are, because of Tokaji's vibrant acidity). Today, Tokaji Aszú is usually made in stainless-steel tanks rather than in barrels, and the number of *puttonyos*

Classified as Pro Mensa Ceasaris Primus, *the Super First Class Mézes Mály vineyard is one of the two most renowned in the Tokaj region.*

assigned is now officially based on the amount of residual sugar the wine contains (see page 629) rather than picking baskets.

Depending on the concentration of sweetness in the *aszú* grapes when they were picked, the *aszú* paste will steep in the base wine for as little as eight hours or as long as three days. At this point, the sweetened wine will be drawn off the *aszú* paste and allowed to ferment again in Tokaj's small, narrow cellars, dug centuries ago as places to hide during Turkish invasions. In these single-vaulted, cold, damp, moldy cellars, the second fermentation can take months, even years, since the cold temperatures coupled with the high sugar content of the wine slow down the process. Under current law, Tokaji Aszú must be aged for at least three years in oak barrels and in bottle before being sold. The bottles are always the traditional, squat, 500-milliliter Tokaji Aszú bottles, three-quarters the size of a standard wine bottle.

In the past, as the Tokaji wines aged, the barrels would not be topped up, leaving air space in each. At the same time, a special strain of natural yeasts, which flourished in Tokaj's cool, dark cellars, would coat the surface of the wine with a fine film, rather like *flor* in Sherry. The combination of the yeasts and the partial, controlled oxidation of the wine would contribute yet another unique flavor to Tokaji Aszú. Today, most Tokaji Aszús are intentionally made in completely full barrels and tanks so that they are protected from oxygen and their fruity/floral character is preserved, although yeasts (omnipresent in these cellars) still contribute to the flavor.

There are two other categories of rare, super-concentrated Tokaji Aszús: Tokaji Aszú Esszencia and Tokaji Esszencia (the word Esszencia—"essence"—is also sometimes spelled with one *s*—eszencia—and sometimes spelled essencia). Let me address Tokaji Esszencia first, as it is the most luxurious, hedonistic Tokaji of all. Only a minuscule amount is made, and only in exceptionally good years. The wine is, of course, frighteningly expensive. To make it, *aszú* grapes are put in a cask and the juice that runs free from these grapes, out of the bottom of the cask (traditionally through a goose quill put in the bunghole of the cask), with no pressure other than the weight of the grapes on top, is Tokaji Esszencia. At 45 percent to 90 percent sugar, this liquid is so syrupy and sweet that the yeasts, slowed to a stupor, barely manage to do their work, and the luscious liquid ferments unbelievably slowly—sometimes barely at all. A Château Pajzos Tokaji Esszencia from the legendary vintage of 1993 took four years to ferment to 4.7 percent alcohol, and a Royal Tokaji Company Tokaji Esszencia from the same 1993 vintage was still fermenting in 1999! In the end most Tokaji Esszencias may only reach an alcohol level of 2 to 5 percent. But simply to say the wine is sweet does not do it justice. The color of honey, velvety rich, and tasting of molecularly dense apricots and peaches, Tokaji Esszencia is one of the world's most penetrating and profound taste sensations, rendering wine lovers (including this one) speechless. It is said to be one of the longest lasting of all wines, capable of aging for centuries. Historically it was reserved for royalty, who sometimes drank it on their deathbeds, hoping to be revived by its mysterious medical powers.

Tokaji Esszencia is so rare and precious that most of it is not bottled on its own but instead is blended sparingly into 6-*puttonyos* Tokaji Aszú to make the highly revered Tokaji Aszú Esszencia, itself a rare, super-expensive, extraordinary wine that is also made only in exceptional years. Tokaji Aszú Esszencia must be aged five years, of which three must be in the barrel.

THE TOKAJI CLASSIFICATION SYSTEM

The vineyards of Tokaj were the first in the world to be classified according to quality. In 1700, about a century and a half before Bordeaux's 1855 Classification, Prince Rákóczi issued a royal decree assigning the vineyards of Tokaj rankings of first, second, and third class, using the Latin designations *Primae Classis, Secunde Classis,* and so on. In addition, two vineyards, Csarfas and Mézes Mály, were given a special designation, a sort of super-first-class status called *Pro Mensa Caesaris Primus,* or "chosen for the royal table."

In total, 173 vineyards were classified, and others that were not particularly well sited were listed as unclassified. Throughout much of the forty-year Communist regime, with vineyards in poor condition, the classification system was largely meaningless. But in 1995, the top producers of Tokaji formed an association called Tokaj Renaissance, with the goal of reviving the significance of the old classification system. It is now common to see vineyard names such as Betsek and Szt. Tamás on Tokaji labels, along with their rankings; in this case, both are First Class.

OTHER WINES OF THE TOKAJ REGION

The enormous viticultural and winemaking improvements of the 1990s not only elevated the quality of Tokaji Aszú, but they also vastly improved the region's dry white wines. Dry furmint bottled as a single variety makes a crisp, complex white wine that's delicious and often minerally. Try the fantastic dry furmints of Balassa, Barta, and Gróf Degenfeld wineries. Hárslevelű is softer, slightly creamy, and has the added bonus of an

TOKAJI ALLURE

Perhaps more than any other wine in history, Tokaji has been the wine of the famous, the powerful, the pious, and the noble. Its description as "the king of wines and the wine of kings" comes from the early eighteenth century, after Francis II Rákóczi, Prince of Transylvania, gave Tokaji to King Louis XIV of France as a gift, resulting in the wine becoming a regular favorite of the French court at Versailles. Next, Louis XV made it a special gift for Madame de Pompadour. Later, Emperor Franz Josef (who was also king of Hungary) developed a tradition of sending Tokaji Aszú to England's Queen Victoria as a yearly birthday present—one bottle for every month she had lived. On her eighty-first, in 1900, she received 972 bottles (a significant present—and something of a shame, since this was her final birthday). Artists, writers, and musicians loved Tokaji—the wine was a favorite of Beethoven, Liszt, Schubert, Haydn, Goethe, Heinrich Heine, Friedrich von Schiller, Johann Strauss, and Voltaire. Emperor Peter the Great of Russia and Emperor Napoléon III of France both consumed Tokaji heavily—Napoléon, for example, bought thirty to forty full barrels of Tokaji every year. Needless to say, Tokaji was the near-religious elixir preferred by many popes.

appealingly fruity aroma. And Ottonel muskotály (the other muscat, besides ságra muskotály, that is grown in Tokaj) often has ripe peach, apricot, and quince flavors.

In addition to these dry wines, Tokaj is also now making late-harvest sweet wines that are not Tokaji Aszú. Late-harvest Tokaji, rather like German *beerenauslese*, is a late-harvest sweet wine that may have been made with the benefit of some botrytized bunches of grapes. But that is different than Tokaji Aszú where, as noted above, a paste is made from entirely botrytized berries, the paste is combined with wine, and then the whole is refermented. Two late-harvest wines to try include Oremus Tokaji Furmint Noble Late Harvest and Château Pajzos Muskotály.

Yet another type of wine made in the Tokaj region is *szamorodni,* which means "as it is grown" or "as it comes." When vineyards are not sufficiently affected by botrytis to produce enough *aszú* berries to make Tokaji Aszú, a blended wine from Tokaji's three main grapes is made. The *szamorodni* may be dry (*száraz*) or slightly sweet (*édes*). *Szamorodni* must be aged two years in the barrel, and most often barrels are not topped up, so the wine takes on a partially oxiydized, intriguing toasted-nut character similar to that of Sherry.

SOME OF THE BEST
PRODUCERS OF TOKAJI ASZÚ

Alana-Tokaj • Château Pajzos • Disznókő
• Dobogó • Hétszőlő • István Szepsy •
Oremus • Royal Tokaji Wine Company

Early morning mists over the Bodrog River encourage the development of Botrytis cinerea *in the surrounding vineyards of Tokaj-Hegyalja. The noble rot, along with the land itself and the painstaking way in which Tokaji is made, all conspire to make a wine that has unreal deliciousness and elegance.*

The Hungarian Wines to Know

ungary's dry white and red wines are not yet widely exported and thus are not always easy to find. So, while I have included a few outstanding dry wines here, most of the wines below are sweet Tokaji wines—Hungary's ultra-famous specialty.

WHITES

SZŐKE MÁTYÁS

IRSAI OLIVÉR | MÁTRA

100% irsai olivér

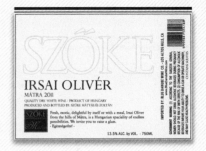

I knew nothing about irsai olivér (a cross created in Hungary in the 1930s) or the dry white wines made from it until late 2013, when I encountered this exploding bomb of fruit from the Szőke Mátyás winery. Although it's fantastically fruity and aromatic, with roselike notes, it also carefully skirts the problem of being too perfumed by having flashes of lime-skin bitterness and a distinct minerality. Irsai olivér is not as weighty or viscous as many other aromatic varieties can be, but it's weighty enough to invite any spicy dish to play along. The Szőke family's vineyards are in the Mátra foothills, about an hour and a half northeast of Budapest, near Hungary's highest extinct volcano, Kékes, which is part of a long-dormant volcanic chain that extends all the way to Tokaj. *Szőke* means "blond" in Hungarian, a reference to the proprietor Mátyás's mane of hair when he was younger.

DEMETER ZOLTÁN

HÁRSLEVELŰ | SZERELMI | TOKAJ-HEGYALJA

100% hárslevelű

Zoltán Demeter studied wine in France and the United States before returning to Hungary to be the assistant to the country's star winemaker, István Szepsy. It's been said that this was the first modern, dry hárslevelű to show that the grape is capable of greatness. The wine is based on sixty-year-old vines planted in the pure loess soils of the Szerelmi vineyard in Tokaj-Hegyalja. And what a wine. Massive, opulent, and softly creamy on the one hand, it is also spicy, sassy, and intense on the other. It's as if crème caramel met Kaffir lime. Thoroughly delicious.

DOMAINE KIRÁLYUDVAR

FURMINT SEC | TOKAJ-HEGYALJA

100% furmint

Domaine Királyudvar's (kee-RYE-oohd-var) is one of the best dry furmints I've ever tasted. Its gingery, minerally fresh aroma is pure and distinctive, and the wine's flavors—an exotic marriage of preserved lemons, baked pears, and brioche—are both lively and creamy at the same time. Although it's rich and satisfying, the wine is also airy, light, and ethereal. A stunning wine. Királyudvar (the name means "king's court") dates to the eleventh century, when the estate supplied wines to the Imperial Court of the Hapsburgs. In the modern era, it was purchased in 1997 by Anthony Hwang (an owner of the renowned French estate Domaine Huët in the Loire), who restored the vineyards and estate.

RED

GERE ATTILA

KOPÁR CUVÉE | VILLÁNY-SIKLÓS

Approximately 50% cabernet franc, 45% merlot,
5% cabernet sauvignon

From the Villány part of Villány-Siklós, where the soils are loess and red clay along with dolomite and limestone, comes Kopár Cuvée, Attila Gere's top wine. The fruit comes from vineyards on the extinct volcano Kopár, which means "barren" (a reference to the poor soils). Of all of the regions in Hungary, Villány is known for the commanding structure of its red wines, and for the ambitions of its winemakers, who closely follow the great wines of Bordeaux, Napa Valley, and Tuscany. Indeed, Kopár Cuvée's edgy, bitter grip, its wonderful tobacco notes, plus its aromas and flavors of cassis and cedar, are all very much in the jet stream of a good Bordeaux.

SWEET WINES

OREMUS

LATE HARVEST | TOKAJI | TOKAJ-HEGYALJA

100% furmint

Oremus was the first producer to make late-harvest Tokaji, which is slightly less concentrated and complex than Tokaji Aszú. Made from extremely ripe grapes (some clusters of which have botrytis), late-harvest Tokajis are not made with *aszú* paste in the traditional manner of Tokaji Aszú. But there's no lack of beauty here. Indeed, the wine's deep, honeyed-apricot richness has a crystalline purity and exquisite balance. Imagine the grown-up version of highly concentrated dried apricots, liquefied into nectar. Oremus is owned by the Álvarez family, proprietor's of Spain's most famous estate, Vega-Sicilia.

ALANA-TOKAJ

MUSCAT | BETSEK | TOKAJ-HEGYALJA

100% muscat blanc à petits grains

During my immersion into Hungarian wine, this was one of the most exquisite late-harvest wines I drank. The luscious flavors of lychee are so mesmerizing and intense that I'm convinced this wine tastes more like lychees than lychees do. But, far from monochromatic, Alana-Tokaj's sweet muscat (specifically muscat blanc à petit grains) from the Betsek vineyard (one of the vineyards historically ranked Primae Classis, First Class) soars into rushes of flowery meadows, wild lavender, orange marmalade, lemon curd, white pepper, and allspice. Fresh and vibrant, the wine seems thoroughly animated and alive. Winemaker Attila Gábor Németh and his family acquired the last Tokaji vineyard holdings of the royal Hapsburg family in 2005, all of which were ranked First Class. Attila immediately got down to work by severely cutting back the yields (now below those of Bordeaux's Château d'Yquem) and pushing the harvest as late as possible (into December/January in most years) to maximize the concentration of the grapes' flavors. Also not to be missed: Alana-Tokaj's Aszueszencia, a Tokaji Aszú Esszencia that's mind-blowingly silken in texture and hypnotically rich.

CHÂTEAU PAJZOS

TOKAJI ASZÚ | 5 PUTTONYOS | TOKAJ-HEGYALJA

Approximately 38% furmint, 27% muscat, 19% zéta, 16% hárslevelű

It's hard to imagine a 5-*puttonyos* Tokaji that is more sensual than that of Château Pajzos. In great vintages, the wine positively drips with the aromas and flavors of honeycomb, lavender, lilies, dried apricots, lime marmalade, saffron, white pepper, wild herbs, meadows (and such is the complexity of the wine, that one could go on with even more descriptors). Tasting it, it seems clear that every single exquisite molecule is lined up along the same intense trajectory of flavor. As for a finish, the wine simply refuses to stop emanating deliciousness. Château Pajzos's Tokaji may well have one of the longest finishes of any wine in the world. Château Pajzos is owned by the Laborde family, which also owns Bordeaux's Château Clinet, in Pomerol.

DOBOGÓ

TOKAJI ASZÚ | 6 PUTTONYOS | TOKAJ-HEGYALJA

60% furmint, 30% hárslevelű, 10% muscat lunel

Dobogó's Tokaji is sheer voluptuousness in a bottle. In the first split second of the first sip, you are drenched in the aromas and flavors of fresh pineapple, fresh tangerines, lemon curd, chamomile tea, and ginger. The very next second, waves of white pepper and exotic spices appear to lift the wine up into a vibrating freshness. Indeed, this wine is so intricate and light that the sweetness is very sheer and exquisite tasting. Dobogó (the name means "heartbeat") is a family winery begun in 1995 by Izabella Zwack and Attila Domokos.

ROYAL TOKAJI WINE COMPANY

TOKAJI ASZÚ | SZT. TAMÁS | 6 PUTTONYOS | TOKAJ-HEGYALJA

Approximately 70% furmint, 30% hárslevelű

From the Primae Classis (First Class) vineyard known as Szt. Tamás (St. Thomas) come distinctive Tokajis that stop you in your tracks, they are so fascinating, delicious, and long. Indeed, Szt. Tamás Tokajis often display aromas and flavors evocative of lemon verbena tea, roasted apricots, peach puree, minerals, sea salt, dried herbs, and honeycomb. They never come across as sweet, exactly, but rather as something refined, richly delicious, and so light that the flavors feel as if they are floating on a cloud. The Royal Tokaji Wine Company was founded in 1990 by a group of investors that included the prominent English wine expert Hugh Johnson.

REPUBLIC
OF GEORGIA

Qvevri *waiting to be filled with wine, then buried underground.*

t's not every day you get a call from a holy man. But in the summer of 2011, sitting in my office in the Napa Valley, I picked up the ringing phone and to my utter surprise, on the other end of the line was a monk and the winemaker of the eleventh-century Alaverdi Monastery in Kakheti, Republic of Georgia. He asked if he and his colleagues could meet with me and bring their wines to taste. There is only one answer to that question, and so the next day a bearded man clad in voluminous black robes with a large Orthodox Christian cross hanging from his neck and a rosary in his hand walked into my office, followed by ten other Georgian vintners. Before they sat down, they

The Georgians are very spiritual about the harvest and about wine, considering it a mystical beverage. Wine is always part of the country's frequent feasting rituals that involve much sipping and elaborate, contemplative toasts.

sang a folk song, for an old Georgian tradition insists that men sing before they drink.

Many of the wines they brought with them were so-called "orange wines"—almost neon orange in color—that had been made in *qvevri* (KEV-ree), large, egg-shaped clay vessels, lined with beeswax and buried entirely underground. Drinking these wines was like nothing I had ever experienced.

One of the oldest agricultural societies in the world, Georgia is nestled on the isthmus between the Black and Caspian Seas, and lies just north of Turkey and south of Russia and the great Caucasus Mountains. Wine has been made here for over eight thousand years, and Georgia, along with Turkey, Iran, Armenia, and Azerbaijan, is considered one of the world's earliest sites of grapevine domestication and winemaking. For millennia, much of that wine was renowned. But throughout the twentieth century, Georgia was caught in the political turmoil of the Soviet Union (of which it was a part) and wine quality suffered. Suppressed, the wine industry regressed. Then, in 1991, Georgia gained its political independence and began the long, slow road back to reestablishing its fine wine industry.

There are wine districts in every part of this small country, and the vineyards—which cover 112,000 acres (45,300 hectares)—are planted primarily with fascinating native varieties, and sometimes with international varieties, like cabernet sauvignon. The most important native grapes are the white grapes rkatsiteli (ARE-cats-i-tell-ee) and mtsvane (metz-VAH-neh), and the red grape saperavi (sah-per-RAV-ee).

A Georgian wine cellar with sealed qvevri buried underneath the floor.

Rkatsiteli is a hardy grape with significant acidity and delicate green apple flavors, while mtsvane is fruity and aromatic (the two are often blended). For its part, saperavi—one of the few grapes in the world with red pulp—produces deeply colored, dramatic wines with wild berry, peppery, and gamy flavors, not unlike syrah. The best examples of both of these grapes are grown in the highly regarded Kakheti region, in the foothills of the Caucasus, where the continental climate and well-drained slopes are ideal for wine-growing. Interestingly, a large portion of the grapes grown and harvested by small farmers each year is purchased by individual families who don't grow grapes but who make their own wine at home.

In Georgia, tradition is everything. Here, girls in Tbilisi perform centuries-old dances.

As mentioned, among the most famous Georgian wines—whites and reds—are those made in clay vessels known as *qvevri*, the smallest of which are large enough that a grown man can stand inside, and the largest of which can hold 10 tons (9 metric tons) of grapes. Unlike their historic cousins, the amphorae, *qvevri* were not used for transportation and were never moved. Instead, they were buried completely underground, where the stable, cool temperatures were an asset to fermentation and maturation. Today *qvevri* are still used to make and age Georgian wines, but not to transport them. The crushed grapes, usually along with their stems, are added to the vessels without the addition of commercial yeasts. (Fermentation takes place as a result of yeasts present on the grape skins and clinging to the inside walls of the vessels.) Afterward, the *qvevri* are sealed with wooden lids and clay or hot beeswax, then left undisturbed for up to six months. During the enzymatic breakdowns that follow this long contact with skins and stems, juice that was formerly white is turned into an orange-colored wine, and red juice becomes red wine shot through with beautiful glints of orange. In 2013, the Ancient Georgian Traditional Qvevri Wine-Making Method, as it is officially called, was added to the UNESCO Intangible Cultural Heritage list. Needless to say, the flavor of a wine made in *qvevri* is amazing—an attractive resiny-bittersweet amalgam, as if wild herbs, dried orange peel, and the skins of walnuts were macerated together with a bit of fruit and honey.

Finally, a few fascinating facts: Georgians are considered one of the main groups of native Caucasian peoples, but they do not fit into any of the main ethnic categories of Europe or Asia. The Georgian language, which belongs to the Kartvelian family of languages, is neither Indo-European, Turkic, nor Semitic. The present-day native population traces their history back to autochthonous inhabitants and immigrants who infiltrated into the South Caucasus from the direction of Anatolia, Turkey, in remote antiquity.

Lastly, Georgia is considered to have some of the most exciting food and culinary traditions in eastern Europe. Among the most prized and most often used foods are walnuts, garlic, coriander, pomegranates, and marigold flowers. Georgian culinary traditions center around the *supra*, or "feast," that is held on special occasions. The *supra* is presided over by the *tamada*, a sort of spiritual leader and toastmaster, who leads many emotional and philosophical toasts over large quantities of wine and food consumed over many hours. The *tamada*'s role is essential to Georgian culture and it is said that a good *tamada* must be eloquent, intelligent, smart, and quick-thinking, with a good sense of humor in order to prevail when guests try to out-toast him. During most toasts, all men are expected to stand up and drink wine in silence as they contemplate the ideas and lessons embedded in the toast the *tamada* has given.

SERBIA

BULGARIA

MACEDONIA

ALBANIA

◄ GOUMENISSA

THESSALONIKI

AMYNDEON ▶

NAOUSSA

HALKIDIKI

EPIRUS ▼

MOUNT
OLYMPUS

◄ RAPSANI

◄ THESSALY

AEGEAN
SEA

TURKEY

GREECE

CEPHALONIA
▼

PATRAS ▶

◄ NEMEA

ATTICA

SAMOS ▶

MANTINIA ▶

ATHENS

IONIAN
SEA

PELOPONNESE

SANTORINI ▶

MEDITERRANEAN
SEA

CRETE

CRETE ▼

ARCHARNES

0   100 km

LIBYA

GREECE

GREECE RANKS ELEVENTH AMONG WINE-PRODUCING COUNTRIES WORLDWIDE. THE GREEKS DRINK AN AVERAGE OF 7 GALLONS (25 LITERS) OF WINE PER PERSON PER YEAR.

he birthplace of western civilization, Greece is in many ways also the birthplace of our modern wine culture. For the ancient Greeks, wine was a gift to man from the god Dionysus, an offering of formidable importance since the recipient actually took it into his own body. Dionysus's gift established wine (not beer, the more common beverage of antiquity) as a symbol of worthiness, a luxurious blessing, and the beverage that would henceforth be inextricably woven into the very fabric of religious celebration. Homer, Plato, Aristotle, and Hippocrates all wrote of wine's virtues and its beneficial effects on thought, health, and creativity. For the ancient Greek man, the intellectual discussions that arose when drinking wine formed the central core of the symposia, animated get-togethers from which sprang the beginnings of Western philosophy.

Bordered by Bulgaria, Macedonia, and Albania to the north and by Turkey to the east, Greece nonetheless gives the impression of being a country made up as much of water as of land. Three seas—the Aegean, the Mediterranean, and the Ionian—nudge into the mountainous landmass, creating a tumble of islands, inlets, bays, and rugged peninsulas. The dominance and beauty of all this water and the 2,500 miles (4,000 kilometers) of coastline are inescapable. No part of Greece, except for a small portion in the northwest, is more than 50 miles (80 kilometers) from the sea.

Precisely when winemaking began here is not entirely clear. We know this, however: Grapevines were probably first domesticated around 8000 B.C. in the so-called Fertile Triangle—an area that extends from the Taurus Mountains (eastern Turkey) to the northern Zagros Mountains (western Iran) and the Caucasus Mountains (Republic of Georgia, Armenia, and Azerbaijan). From this triangle, grapevine cultivation spread to Syria, Iraq, Lebanon, Palestine, and Jordan. From Palestine, wine was exported to Eygpt, which according to the world's leading grapevine geneticist, Dr. José Vouillamoz, author, with Jancis Robinson and Julia Harding, of

Many of Greece's top wine regions border on (or are surrounded by) water. Here, the volcanic Aegean island of Santorini (imagined by some to be the lost island of Atlantis), is known for crisp white wines that are delicious with the local cuisine.

THE QUICK SIP ON GREECE

THE WINES OF GREECE were among the most important wines in antiquity. Thanks to Greece's extensive trade and colonization, wine became an integral part of the cultures of western Europe from their earliest beginnings.

GREECE'S WINE REGIONS range from inland, cold-climate, mountainous regions in northern Macedonia to beautiful Aegean islands, where vines are often mere miles from the sea.

GREECE IS KNOWN for producing a range of wines and styles, from whites like assyrtiko and moschofilero to robust reds made from xinomavro and agiorgitiko, to lusciously sweet white and red wines made from muscat blanc à petits grains and mavrodaphne, respectively.

Wine Grapes, developed its own extensive and sophisticated wine industry from 3200 to 2500 B.C. Finally, thanks to Greece's extensive trade with Egypt, grape cultivation spread to southern Greece and to the Minoan civilization on Crete by about 2200 to 2000 B.C. Eventually, of course, wine spread around the Mediterranean. (The evidence for this migration includes carbonized grape seeds; the residue of resinated wine found in jars and on stoppers; amphorae stamped with hieroglyphic signs indicating where the grapes were grown to make the wine inside [the first wine labels]; and drinking vessels painted with winemaking scenes found in tombs.) Indeed, it was primarily through trading in wine, and the subsequent social relationships wine encouraged, that ancient Greece's influence on everything from ethics to politics spread throughout the Mediterranean world.

The wines drunk in ancient Greece were sometimes flavored—intentionally and unintentionally—by pine resin, which was used to coat the otherwise porous insides of the amphorae, or jars, in which wines were stored and transported. Millennia later, the resinated wine known as retsina is still immensely popular in Greece (see page 653). During classical times, wines were also sometimes flavored with wildflowers and flower oils, giving them

THE MOST IMPORTANT GREEK WINES

LEADING WINES

AMYNDEON red, rosé, sparkling

ARCHARNES red

CEPHALONIA white

CRETE white and red

GOUMENISSA red

HALKIDIKI white and red

MANTINIA white and rosé

MAVRODAPHNE OF PATRAS red (sweet)

MUSCAT OF PATRAS white (sweet)

MUSCAT OF SAMOS white (sweet)

NAOUSSA red

NEMEA red

PATRAS white

RAPSANI red

RETSINA white

SANTORINI white

WINES OF NOTE

VINSÁNTO white (sweet)

what Plato considered to be even more positive aromas than they already possessed. In the ancient Greek view, the proper aromas were necessary for restoring the body to its natural harmony. The similarity between floral aromas and the aromas of certain wines raised the reputation of those wines, for floral smells

On the extremely windy islands of Greece, vines are sometimes trained to grow close to the ground and in a basket shape to protect the grapes.

were thought to be particularly beneficial to the brain and, in addition, were deemed capable of forestalling intoxication.

Intoxication itself was something the Greeks denounced for its harmful effects. Accordingly, wine was always diluted with water in proportions ranging from two parts wine and three parts water to one part wine and three parts water. In the eyes of the Greeks, only barbarians drank wine straight. Eubulus, the Greek poet of the fourth century B.C. known for his mythological burlesques, summarized the Greek penchant for moderation when he attributed these words to Dionysus:

Three kraters [bowls used for wine] do I mix for the temperate: one to health, which they empty first, the second to love and pleasure, the third to sleep. When this bowl is drunk up, wise guests go home. The fourth bowl is ours no longer, but belongs to hubris, the fifth to uproar, the sixth to prancing about, the seventh to black eyes, the eighth brings the police, the ninth belongs to vomiting, and the tenth to insanity and the hurling of furniture.

Reflecting on the Greek wisdom of taking no more than three drinks, Hugh Johnson, the esteemed British wine expert, notes that throughout history three drinks have been considered the model for moderation. Johnson goes on to suggest that from this historic counsel is derived the wine bottle, which just happens to contain 750 milliliters, or about three glasses each for two people.

For an explanation of Greek wine law, see the Appendix on Wine Laws, page 927.

THE MODERN GREEK
WINE INDUSTRY

For all its hegemony as one of the most important wine producers of antiquity, Greece has had an arduous climb into the modern world of fine wine. During the Middle Ages, the country was part of the Byzantine Empire, and the best Greek wines were made by monks following monastic traditions. But the fall of Byzantium and the subsequent occupation of Greece by the Ottoman Turks effectively brought an end to Greece's respected place among wine producers. The Turks did not formally forbid winemaking for the Christian population, but the strictures and taxes imposed during nearly four hundred years of Ottoman domination were severe enough to prevent Greece from developing a significant wine industry. Greek wine remained the work of peasants whose necessary goal was subsistence, not sophistication.

Greece's wine industry remained largely undeveloped until the twentieth century. As was true in virtually every other European country, the devastating effects of the insect phylloxera, which arrived in Greece in the late 1890s, lasted for several decades. This was followed by two world wars, and then Greece's own civil war, the combination of which left the country's wine industry in ruins. By the 1960s, most Greek wines were still being sold in bulk, directly from barrels,

The Boutari Winery's modern tasting room on Crete, one of the most ancient centers of civilization in Europe, dating from the Minoan period circa 2700 B.C.

to buyers who brought their own jugs to fill. It was not until the mid-1980s, with Greece's entry into the European Union, that the country's wine industry began to shift away from very inexpensive table wines intended for local consumption, toward wines of finer quality. This meant lowering grape yields substantially, improving viticultural techniques in the vineyards, employing more modern equipment, and in many cases, using expensive, small oak barrels.

Today there are some six hundred wineries in Greece, and the country's wine industry is composed of a handful of well-organized large firms, such as Boutari, D. Kourtakis, and Tsantali, as well as scores of newer, smaller, quality-oriented, family-run estates. In a country where land ownership is fragmented, most of these firms, large and small, both own their own vineyard land and buy grapes from thousands of very small-scale growers. All are more intent on making fine wine than they've been at any other time, and cheap bulk wine is now left to cooperatives.

TRANSPORTING WINE
IN THE ANCIENT WORLD

Other than goatskin bags, the earliest vessels for transporting wine in the ancient world were amphorae, terra-cotta jars with two looped handles and, usually, a pointed base. Although the exact date and place in the eastern Mediterranean where these distinctive jars originated has often been debated, their history can be traced back to at least 2000 B.C. Around this time, the so-called Canaanite jars that were used to ship a variety of goods, including wine, were used in Canaan's extensive trade with pharaonic Egypt. By the thirteenth century B.C., such vessels were being shipped as far afield as mainland Greece, where they were found in the tombs of Mycenaean royalty. The hundreds of thousands of amphora fragments that have been uncovered by anthropologists attest to the enormous volume of commerce in antiquity, including trade in wine.

While some small amphorae held about 2½ gallons (10 liters), the jars used in transporting wine were generally larger, holding 6½ gallons (25 liters) or more and weighing at least 22 pounds (10 kilograms) when empty. Filled with wine, an amphora would have been heavy, hence the practicality of two handles, allowing two people to carry the jar. Although the pointed base seems odd, it, too, was pragmatic, offering a third "handle" when necessary. Such a design was also very functional on ships, where the pointed bases could be buried deep in sand and the handles of the jars tied together for stability. When they weren't being carried, amphorae would be leaned against the wall of a room or placed in special ring stands to hold them erect.

Since different Greek city-states produced their own distinctive styles of amphorae, archaeologists theorize that the various jar shapes would have signaled different kinds of wine in the marketplace. In addition, before they were fired, the handles of many jars were stamped with information about the type, the origin, and often the date of the wine that the amphora contained.

In order to form an airtight seal and thereby prevent bacteria from turning the wine into vinegar, the narrow necks of ancient wine amphorae were sealed using one of a number of methods. Most commonly, the mouth of each amphora was filled with a clump of fibrous material, such as straw or grass, that had been soaked in pine resin, and was then capped with clay. Likewise, because the jars were porous, the insides of many amphorae were coated with resin in order to prevent or retard evaporation and oxidation. Since the resinous coating would have been soluble in alcohol, early Greek wines probably tasted as much of pine pitch as of the wine itself; in this way, they were the forerunners of modern retsina, the resinated Greek wine that is nothing if not an acquired taste. Sometime later, certainly by Roman times, lumps of pine pitch were also thrown into wine to help preserve it, or to disguise the flavor of a wine gone bad.

From an amphora, wine would be poured into a bronze or pottery bowl called a krater. From the krater the wine might then be scooped out with a ladle called a *kythos* into a shallow, two-handled, often beautifully decorated cup known as a *kylix*.

The vineyards of Rapsani lie over the foothills of Mount Olympus. Here, bold, tannic, dramatic wines are made from one of Greece's most important red grapes—xinomavro.

THE LAND, THE GRAPES, AND THE VINEYARDS

I n square miles, Greece is only slightly larger than the island of Cuba, and of its total land area, about 70 percent is mountains and 20 percent islands (making mechanical cultivation all but impossible). Mountainous regions are used primarily for grazing sheep and goats, although some vineyards are planted on the more moderate mountain slopes and high plateaus. The relatively small amount of land that is available for agriculture—some 326,000 acres (131,900 hectares; an amount only modestly greater than the acreage planted with grapes in Bordeaux)—is widely planted with grapevines and olive trees; both do well in Greece's mostly infertile, thin, dry soil.

Greece's climate is well adapted for grape growing. Rains come mainly in the winter, when the vines are dormant. There is bountiful sunlight, augmented by even more light reflected off the sea, to ripen the grapes fully.

If anything, too much sun and heat can be a problem, for grapes that ripen too quickly often have simple, monochromatic flavors. For this reason, some vineyards are planted on north-facing slopes to slow down the ripening process.

The proximity of Greek vineyards to the sea and cooling maritime breezes is usually an advantage. But strong sea winds can pose problems. To anyone accustomed to vines that stand 5 feet (1.5 meters) tall or more (as vines do in California), it's startling to see the vineyards on some of the most windswept Greek islands. There, the vines are trained in the circular *kouloura* method, close to the ground so that they form what look like wreaths or shallow baskets. Trained this way, each vine is called a *stefáni*, or crown. In the center of the *stefáni*, protected from the wind, lie the grapes.

Greece's peculiar geographic configuration, with its four thousand plus islands, allowed many different grape varieties to become established. As of this writing, seventy-seven ancient indigenous varieties have been identified, although others may have gone extinct over the past century due to the lack of a

THE GRAPES OF GREECE

Greece is home to seventy-seven known indigenous grape varieties. Here are the most important. (And don't forget, pronunciations can be found in the main grape glossary; see page 76.)

WHITE

ASSYRTIKO: A major grape native to Santorini, in the Aegean Islands. Makes dry wine in a crisp style and in a riper, oak-aged style. Also blended into Santorini's sweet wine, *vinsánto*.

MALAGOUSIA: An ancient grape that was saved from extinction in the 1980s. Makes aromatic, full-bodied wines with bitter citrus and exotic fruit flavors and aromas.

MOSCHOFILERO: Despite this grape's pinkish-red skin, only white wines and occasionally rosés are made from it. Aromatic, with a spicy character, moschofilero is the source of the Peloponnesian wine Mantinia.

MUSCAT BLANC Á PETITS GRAINS: Used in the famous, aromatic, sweet and often lightly fortified wines muscat of Patras, from Peloponnese, and muscat of Samos, from Samos, an Aegean island.

ROBOLA: Native to Greece's Ionian Islands or the Peloponnese, and not related to Italy's ribolla gialla despite the close spelling. Makes complex wines with lemon and mineral characteristics.

RODITIS: Makes the simple, dry white wine of Patras in Peloponnese.

SAVATIANO: A widely planted grape, including in the region of Attica, where Athens is located. Most retsina is made from savatiano.

REDS

AGIORGITIKO: One of Greece's two most important red varieties, also known as St. George. Makes the spicy, dried-cherry-flavored wine Nemea.

KOTSIFALI: Unique to the island of Crete, this is the main grape of Acharnes, the wines of which are soft and full-bodied.

LIMNIO: Ancient, unique variety mentioned by Aristotle. Spicy, earthy. Native to the island of Lemnos.

MANDILARIA: Unique to Crete and the Aegean Islands. Fairly tannic; blended in small amounts with kotsifali to make the Cretan wine Acharnes, and into Santorini's sweet wine, *vinsánto*.

MAVRODAPHNE: Major grape. The leading variety in mavrodaphne of Patras, a sweet, fortified, aged wine made in the Peloponnese.

NEGOSKA: Soft, low-acid variety blended with xinomavro to make Goumenissa.

STAVROTO AND KRASSATO: Minor grapes grown on Mount Olympus. Used in Rapsani.

XINOMAVRO: One of Greece's two most important red varieties. Makes the powerfully tannic, sexy/earthy wine Naoussa and is the leading grape in Goumenissa.

market for the wines made from them. (Several Greek winemakers, however, are determined to protect those indigenous varieties that currently exist from a similar fate.) At the same time, international varieties, such as chardonnay and cabernet sauvignon, have also been planted in recent years.

The country's most memorable and delicious wines are based about equally on white and red grape varieties, although approximately 60 percent of Greece's total wine production is white. Among the top white grapes are assyrtiko, muscat blanc à petits grains, robola (not related to the ribolla gialla grape of northern Italy, despite the close spelling), roditis, savatiano (the grape usually used to make the rustic Greek specialty retsina), and the popular, wonderfully aromatic grapes malagousia and moschofilero, which are said to make the best aperitifs in all of Greece. The most important red varieties include agiorgitiko (also known as St. George), kotsifali, mandelaria, limnio, mavrodaphne, and the bold xinomavro, whose gastronomically challenged name means "acid black."

Greece is made up of five broad winegrowing areas: northern Greece; mainland Greece; the Peloponnese and Ionian Islands; the Aegean Islands; and Crete. Each of these has been well known since antiquity, and each contains numerous important subregions. (One side note before we explore these regions. Greek place names can have multiple spellings, due to the lack of universal rules for converting from the phonetically based Greek alphabet into English, with its Roman alphabet. I have used the most common English spellings for the places mentioned below, but on a wine label, you might find a different spelling, or even Greek itself, of course.)

Northern Greece, along the northern coast of the Aegean Sea and far inland, comprises the large regions known as Macedonia, Thrace, and Epirus. Within these are several smaller wine regions, among them: Goumenissa, Naoussa, Amyndeon, Rapsani, and Halkidiki; the latter is a stunning peninsula that thrusts out into the Aegean like three fingers.

Among northern Greece's white wines, the rare, exotic, and deliciously bitter-citrus-tasting grape malagousia (which was rescued from extinction in the 1990s thanks to the efforts of Vangelis Gerovassiliou) thrives here, especially in Macedonia. Xinomavro, and the dark, brooding, very tannic reds it often makes, are also a specialty of northern Greece,

In Greece, every aspect of viticulture is done by hand, as it has been for centuries. The country's steep, undulating terrain and 2,500 miles (4,000 kilometers) of coastline effectively prohibit mechanization.

RETSINA OF ATTICA
TRADITIONAL APPELLATION

KOURTAKI

🐦 *From selected grape varieties grown in the finest vineyards of Attica* 🐦 *Shipped to 150 cities all over the world* 🐦 *By Kourtakis S.A., a company dedicated, since 1895, to maintaining the 5.000 year-old Greek winemaking tradition* 🐦

DRY WHITE WINE
BOTTLED BY GREEK WINE CELLARS D. KOURTAKIS S.A.
19003 MARKOPOULO GREECE

WINE OF  GREECE

e75cl   11,5%vol

especially in Naoussa, Goumenissa, Rapsani, and the far-inland, high-altitude region of Amyndeon. I often think of xinomavro—one of the few grapes that is high in both acid and tannin—as Greece's Barolo, and like Barolo, wines made from xinomavro resist oxidation and can take years to soften and come around. In Rapsani, xinomavro is blended with two other minor red grapes, stavroto and krassato, grown on the foothills of Mount Olympus, Greece's highest mountain. Krassato means "wine colored," a description used frequently in antiquity, including by Homer, who, in the *Odyssey*, describes Odysseus's journey on the "wine-dark sea." Finally, in Halkidiki, cabernet sauvignon and syrah have been especially successful. The Carras family, of Domaine Porto Carras, helped pioneer this region with the assistance of famous French enologist Émile Peynaud.

Mainland Greece encompasses two distinctly different areas—the northern, mountainous part near Thessalia (Thessaly), and the flatter plains, where the main wine region is Attiki (Attica). Most of the grapes here go into simple table wines, and this is the leading home of the native grape savatiano, the most cultivated wine-producing variety in Greece and the grape used for retsina.

RETSINA

Few visitors to Greece escape without either falling in love with or learning to abhor retsina, the pungent, pine-resin-flavored wine, the drinking of which is virtually a baptismal right in Greek tavernas. Today, retsina (which has protected appellation status in Greece) accounts for an impressive 15 percent of Greece's total production of table wine. Resinated wines have a long history in Greece; traces of pine resin have been found in Greek wine amphorae dating back to the thirteenth century B.C. Modern retsina can be made anywhere in the country, although most of it is made in Attica, the region that surrounds Athens. While many different white grape varieties can be used, and are, the most common variety is savatiano, a relatively neutral white grape. Small amounts of resin from the Aleppo pine are added to savatiano grape juice as it ferments, imparting retsina's inimitable piney flavor and unmistakable turpentine-like aroma. Among non-Greeks, retsina is often the subject of good-natured jokes. But a number of Greeks take the unique wine quite seriously, suggesting that it is the perfect accompaniment to many Greek meze (small dishes of appetizers served like Spanish tapas).

The southernmost region of the Greek mainland is the peninsula known as the Peloponnese, which in fact is so completely surrounded by water that, save for the 4-mile-wide (6.4-kilometer) and 20-mile-long (32-kilometer) Isthmus of Corinth, it would be a large island. The vineyards of the Peloponnese and the Ionian Islands that surround it are concentrated in the more mountainous areas, either on rugged plateaus or in valleys wedged in between the mountain massifs. The three most important wine regions here are Nemea, Mantinia, and Patras. The wines of Nemea, thought to have been the palace wines of Agamemnon, are made from the highly regarded agiorgitiko, a red grape. Nemea, firm and structured, can have a fascinating, spicy, and peppery flavor. The wine from Mantinia is usually a fantastic, dry, spicy, aromatic white, made from the pink-skinned grape moschofilero. And Patras is home to three different wines. In its most straightforward version, Patras is just a simple, dry white wine made from the roditis grape. More unusual and interesting is muscat of Patras, made from muscat blanc à petits grains, a viscous dessert wine that is sometimes fortified, sometimes not. Most idiosyncratic of all

HUNTING DOWN THE HOME OF EASTER EGGS

*D*evouring *a handful of milk chocolate Easter eggs or hunting around the backyard for plastic ones are two behaviors that are, well, all Greek to the Greeks. In Greece, where the practice of dyeing eggs for Easter originated, the custom continues to be a deeply felt religious ritual. The eggs (real ones, needless to say) are dyed on Holy Thursday (the Thursday preceding Easter Sunday) and are eaten after midnight mass on Holy Saturday as a way of breaking the Lenten fast. In Greece, Easter eggs are always dyed a deep red, symbolizing the blood of Christ, while the egg itself represents life and regeneration. In some parts of northern Greece, the eggs are not just dyed, they are also hand painted with figures, often of birds—a symbol of Christ's resurrection from the dead.*

is mavrodaphne of Patras, made (in the best cases) 100 percent from mavrodaphne grapes (the word *mavrodaphne* means "black laurel"). Cheaper versions of mavrodaphne of Patras include black Corinth grapes, which are better known as the source of dried currants. Amber to mahogany colored, sweet, thick, fortified, complex, and slightly oxidized, mavrodaphne of Patras is aged for several years in barrels in a manner somewhat like tawny Port. Traditionally, Greeks drink mavrodaphne of Patras in the afternoon with a small plate of figs or oranges (although it is also stunning with chocolate). It is the wine most often used in Greek Orthodox churches during Holy Communion.

The Aegean Islands are fascinating, small, enclavelike wine regions unto themselves. Extremely windy, with barren soils and minimal water, the islands require specialized forms of viticulture that have been used for millennia. In the northern Aegean, on islands such as Lemnos and Samos, muscat varieties—especially muscat blanc à petits grains—dominate. In particular, Samos, off the coast of Turkey, is well known for muscat of Samos, which can be aromatic and dry or a sweet, apricotish, lightly fortified wine. In the southern Aegean, on islands such as Rhodes and Santorini, the main varieties are the white assyrtiko, athiri, and monemvasia and the red variety of mandilaria.

Of all of these islands, the one that, in the modern era, has remained famous for wine is Santorini, considered by some Greeks to be the legendary Atlantis. A spectacular, almost surreal volcanic island, Santorini is a giant blackened crater poised between the shockingly blue sky and the equally blue sea, each of which can seem indistinguishable from the other. The soil that makes up many vineyards on the island is little more than eerie-looking, pockmarked, jet black lava rocks, the remnants of multiple ancient volcanic eruptions. One of these, which occurred sometime between 1627 and 1600 B.C., was one of the largest volcanic events on earth in recorded history, and was so catastrophic that it is thought to have destroyed the Minoan civilization on the nearby island of Crete.

WHEN YOU VISIT . . . GREECE

CONSISTENT WITH ITS REPUTATION as a generous and welcoming destination for tourists, Greece offers many opportunities for visiting wine lovers. Among the best are two programs, the Wine Roads of Northern Greece and the Wine Roads of Peloponnese. Each of these outlines specific routes, with directions to wineries, plus information on local food specialties, restaurants, archaeological sites, monasteries, museums, and churches.

Santorini's vineyards may be among the oldest under continuous cultivation in the world. The age of the vines themselves is difficult to specify because of the way the vines are grown and pruned. To protect the grapes from the sharp sun and the extreme winds, the vines are trained low to the ground, forming what look like wreaths or baskets—a method known as *kouloura* (meaning "coil"). After many years of such training, the nutrients must pass through the roots and several yards/meters of vine to finally reach the grapes, which greatly affects the yields of these old vines. Eventually the yields become so low that the "basket" is cut completely off at the root of the plant, near the surface of the soil. This is generally done when the vines approach seventy-five years of age. A new plant eventually sprouts from a dormant eye on the old roots, and a new basket will be formed that produces a harvest within two to three years. From historical records kept by Greek vintners, it's known that this procedure has been performed at least four or five times over the past few centuries, making some of the original roots hundreds of years old. So, how old are the vines? In Santorini it depends on whether you are speaking of the scion (the above-ground part of the vine) or the roots themselves.

Traditionally, most wines from Santorini were crisp, dry whites made from assyrtiko grapes. Their simple purity and freshness were perfectly suited to the island's simple, seafood-based cooking. In recent years, however, more and more of these have been made in a riper style and made or aged in oak. These wines have gained weight and broadness on the palate, but some have lost what, to me, was their traditional appeal.

The island is also famous for *vinsánto*, a sweet dessert wine reminiscent of the Tuscan dessert wine *vin santo*. (But while *vin santo* means "holy wine," *vinsánto*—without the space—is a contraction of wine [*vin*] from Santorini.) Both are made from grapes that have been dried to concentrate their sugar. In the case of Santorini *vinsánto*, assyrtiko and mandilaria grapes are first spread out on mats to dry in the sun for one to two weeks. When they achieve a state referred to as half-baked, the grapes are fermented. Afterward, the wine is aged in barrel for a decade, giving it a mellow, rich flavor.

And, finally, the island of Crete, the largest of all the Greek islands, was one of the first places in the world to develop a systematic approach to grape growing and winemaking,

Assyrtiko and mandilaria grapes drying on mats in the sun. Once fermented, they will become Greek vinsánto.

On Crete, a restored entrance to Knossos, considered Europe's oldest city.

and the varieties that grow there even today are unique to the island. Kotsifali (soft and full-bodied) and mandilaria (more structured), for example, are the two rare grapes that are blended together to make the famous red wines of Archarnes, the most important wine region on the island.

THE FOODS OF GREECE

I f the French can't wait to impress you with their cooking and the Italians want to romance you with theirs, the Greeks have decided to keep their cuisine—the real stuff, that is—mostly a secret. It's a shame, for the country can legitimately boast one of the most exciting (and healthful) cuisines in Europe. Greece's mountainous, arid terrain has always prohibited large-scale agriculture, and most good products—from cheeses and yogurts to olives and vegetables—are still made largely on an artisanal basis. Even today, working women and men who live in Greek cities often return to their families' villages in the fall to help with the olive and grape harvests and to put up fruits and vegetables.

Greek cuisine is also intrinsically tied to religion. In no other country that I know of is fasting (especially during Lent and Advent) still so much a part of contemporary life. For the typical Greek, fasting and feasting, frugality and wealth, are irrevocably interwoven. Greek cuisine encompasses both utterly humble dishes based on little more than vegetables and olive oil, and extravagant dishes served at Easter and Christmas, including a whole repertoire of elaborate, rich breads baked for holidays.

A Greek meal is adamantly languorous. Greeks do not plunge straightaway into a main course but rather begin with a deeply ingrained ritual known as the meze (the name refers to both the concept and the foods that make it up). A meze is a nugget of food, smaller than an American appetizer, more like a tapa in Spain. Typically many different *mezedes* are offered for the express purpose of accompanying wine or ouzo, the well-loved local anise-flavored liqueur. (The Greeks, who rarely drink without eating something, all seem to have an opinion on which *mezedes* are *krasomezedes,* "those that go better with wine"—*krasi*—and which are *ouzomezedes,* "those that go better with ouzo.") There might be bite-size golden triangles of crisp phyllo stuffed with cheese (*tyropittakia*) or small, mint-and-anise-flavored lamb meatballs (*keftedes*). Always, there's a rich dip like *tzatziki,* a tangy jolt of thick yogurt, garlic, dill, and cucumbers; *taramasalata,* a creamy swirl of carp roe, olive oil, and lemon; or my favorite, *skordalia,* a bracing puree of potatoes, olive oil, wine vinegar, and, depending on the cook, enough garlic to beat aioli at its own game. *Dolmadakia,* one of the most traditional *mezedes* (this should win over just about every wine lover) is made from tender grape leaves, usually picked in the spring and then rolled and stuffed with lemony, dill-scented rice.

There is a seemingly infinite number of *mezedes,* but the very simplest is one that no Greek would omit: olives. Since the days when it was the cradle of Western civilization, Greece has been renowned for the diversity and abundance of its olives, virtually all of which are stronger in flavor and more pungent in aroma than French or Italian olives, because of the low-tech, centuries-old ways in which they are still picked and cured.

The meze completed, Greeks may still not yet delve into the main meal, for next comes *pitta* (assuming that tiny *pittas* weren't served as *mezedes*). A *pitta* is not the same as the flatish pocket bread we know as pita but rather is a savory pie with a phyllo crust. The best known is *spanakopita,* stuffed with spinach, but there are also *melitzanopitta*—eggplant, cheese, and walnuts flavored with ouzo and oregano and wrapped up in a phyllo crust—and, perhaps closest to the Greek heart, *hortopitta*—a phyllo pie filled with wild greens, for which women forage around their villages. Everything from dandelion greens and sorrel to fennel and lemon balm might be included, making it difficult to put your finger on a *hortopitta*'s flavor, although all Greeks instantly recognize their mother's version. The most sensational (and sensuous) *pitta* I ever had was made with homemade phyllo dough stuffed with a creamy puree of a type of pumpkin that grows in the mountains of northern Greece.

Phyllo, for its part, is inescapable. Today, the ultrathin dough that turns golden, crisp, and flaky when baked is almost uniformly made commercially in Greece and sold in supermarkets. But there are women—usually old women in remote villages—who continue to make phyllo by hand, rolling the dough out to a seemingly impossible thinness using broom-handle-thin rolling pins that are several feet/meters long.

The long stretches of poverty that Greeks have experienced throughout their history make this a country where vegetables, salads, and legumes are prized, and where they often constitute the main part of the meal. Markets are piled high with shiny eggplants, tomatoes, cucumbers, zucchini, leeks, cauliflowers, fennel, and carrots, plus dozens of types of wild and cultivated greens. Vegetables like leeks and zucchini are often stuffed with a lemony rice mixture emboldened by fresh mint and dill. But they are also cooked as ragouts or baked and then laced with Greece's one famous and nearly ubiquitous sauce, *avgolemono,* a delicate, deep yellow sauce made with egg, lemon

Exciting and healthful, traditional Greek cuisine relies on artisanal products—mostly vegetables, fruits, and legumes. But when meat is in order, lamb—spit-roasted—is a favorite.

The harbor and fortress on the island of Rhodes, where the rare red grape mandilaria is grown.

baked in grape leaves, baked with feta cheese, fried in olive oil, and simmered in countless stews that recall bouillabaisse. But the seafood that truly epitomizes Greece is the world's most sumptuous cephalopods—octopus and squid (*htapothi* and *kalamaria*). In particular, the delicate, oceanic flavor of salt-crusted octopus grilled over hot coals, then dressed with lemon and olive oil, is incomparable.

Asked to name the one food they most associate with Greece, many people would name lamb, and lamb is indeed revered by the Greeks. The biggest testament to this is at Easter, when all over Greece it is traditional to serve a whole, spit-roasted lamb. As it cooks, the lamb is basted using rosemary branches dipped in olive oil. Not that Easter is lamb's fifteen minutes of fame. The meat is everywhere—in tavernas it shows up as souvlaki, chunks of leg of lamb skewered and grilled until they're black and crusty on the outside and juicy within; or baked with preserved lemons in clay; in spicy stews with mint, rice, raisins, and walnuts; and in casseroles with honey (the thyme-scented honey of Crete is renowned), raisins, cinnamon, vinegar, and capers. But above all, there is moussaka, ground lamb layered with eggplant, tomatoes, cinnamon, and feta, topped with béchamel sauce, and baked in clay pots.

Finally there are sweets. Greeks may be able to give up meat for long periods of time, but when it comes to sweets, forget it. The Greek passion for sweet things could give you a toothache just thinking about it. When guests arrive unexpectedly, they are often served syrupy preserves meant to be eaten with a spoon and made from quince, walnuts, pistachios, bergamot (the citrus that flavors Earl Grey tea), figs, or oranges. There are all manner of ultra-sweet phyllo-based pastries soaked with honey—baklava, for example—plus *thiples*, fried pieces of dough dipped in honey and nuts, which are supposed to appease any malicious spirits lingering around the household. Lest anyone feel unsatisfied, most Greek homes also have an ample supply of cookies, tarts, and biscuits, often made with sesame seeds, almonds, or walnuts and—what else?—honey.

juice, and broth. When the broth is chicken, the sauce can become the basis for *kotosoupa avgolemono*—chicken soup.

As for salads, the custom of ending a meal with a refreshing green salad probably originated in ancient Greece (sorry, France), but today, salads are more commonly served first. None is better known than the classic Greek salad, a dish that ranges from awesome to appalling. Done right, it has juicy, vine-ripened tomatoes, cucumber that is almost crunchy it's so crisp, tangy fresh feta cheese, rich briny kalamata olives, good anchovies, snappy green peppers, pungent oregano, and a dressing of piquant, green-gold extra virgin olive oil, with a splash of spunky red wine vinegar. Lettuce is optional.

Greece's thousands of miles of coastline and numerous islands make it a logical haven for seafood. Sitting in a no-frills harborfront taverna, you can grow faint smelling all the immaculately fresh, delicious whole grilled fish being whisked out of the kitchen. Greece has dozens upon dozens of different fish, and besides being grilled, they are baked in salt,

The Greek Wines to Know

SPARKLING

KARANIKA

BRUT | CUVÉE SPÉCIALE | AMYNDEON, MACEDONIA

100% xinomavro

Karanika, made by the husband-and-wife team of Laurens Hartman and Annette van Kampen, is not only the best sparkling wine in Greece, but a stunning example of an artisanal sparkling wine made anywhere in the world from grapes other than chardonnay and pinot noir. And while the red grape xinomavro may seem a very surprising choice (it's boldly tannic and acidic), the grape's naturally high acidity is pitch perfect for a good sparkler. The wine—made according to the traditional (Champagne) method— is distinctive and fresh, with a frothy, creamy mousse that's delicious. Amyndeon (named after the grandfather of Alexander the Great) is an area in the far northwest of Greece, toward the border with Albania. Far inland and blocked off from the Aegean Sea by mountains, it has the coolest climate in Greece.

WHITES

TSELEPOS

MOSCHOFILERO | MANTINIA, PELOPONNESE

100% moschofilero

Tselepos's moschofilero has a bright, aromatic richness that seems evocative of the Peloponnese landscape itself. With its wonderful, super-fruity lemon character and hints of spicy pepperiness, it's a tight, refreshing wine ready to spring open at the merest suggestion of an interesting food companion. (Grilled octopus salad? Pot stickers?) Giannis Tselepos studied wine at the University of Dijon, in Burgundy, and worked for several Burgundian domaines before starting his own winery in southern Greece with his wife, Amalia, in 1989.

DOMAINE GEROVASSILIOU

MALAGOUSIA | MACEDONIA

100% malagousia

The best Greek whites carry you away with them to a sunny, wild-herb-scattered, windswept ancient landscape, and no wine does that better than Gerovassiliou's Malagousia, based on the ancient native grape malagousia, which was saved from extinction in the 1980s, in part due to the efforts of Vangelis Gerovassiliou. The wine opens with a rush of exotic lemon, bergamot, pear, and mango aromas and flavors, and then takes on a delicious, resiny herb quality. Tight, pristine, and focused, it's mouthfilling and rich. Domaine Gerovassiliou, about 15 miles (24 kilometers) southeast of the ancient city of Thessaloniki, in Macedonia, makes wines that span a huge creative range—from malagousia to viognier and from syrah to limnio.

GENTILINI

ASPRO | CEPHALONIA, IONIAN ISLANDS

40% tsaoussi, 30% sauvignon blanc, 30% muscat

Aspro (the name means "white" in Greek) tastes like an island wine—it's one big burst of freshness, as if the blue ocean and fresh fruit were somehow melded together. With its beautiful notes of green fig (that's the sauvignon blanc talking) and the touches of exotic fruitiness (muscat), Aspro is the kind of wine you'd find in a seaside taverna in Greece. As for tsaoussi, this Greek variety, with its light melon and peach flavors, is thought to have originated on Cephalonia (*Kefaloniá* in Greek), the largest of the Ionian Islands. (Cephalonia was the island in the bestselling novel *Captain Corelli's Mandolin*, by the English author Louis de Bernières.)

KTIMA BIBLIA CHORA

OVILOS | PANGEON, MACEDONIA

50% assyrtiko, 50% sémillon

Located on the slopes of Mount Pangeon, in Macedonia, the Ktima (which means "estate") Biblia Chora was founded by two famous Greek enologists, Claus Tsaktsarlis and Vangelis Gerovassiliou. Their top wines are stunningly creative. Ovilos, for example, combines the freshness of assyrtiko with the broad, honied character of sémillon (who knew there was a single sémillon vine in Greece?), and the result is a sensational wine that seems like the lost cousin of white Bordeaux. With its beautiful sweeping flavors of dried wild herbs, chamomile, roasted nuts, sea salt, cardamom, and the classic candle wax character of sémillon, Ovilos is both rich and sophisticated. The name Ovilos is a reference to the ancient people of the region and their refusal to pay a tax, or *obulus* (ancient silver coin), in order to plant vineyards on the land. Over centuries, this refusal of an *obulus* came to be known as *ovilos*.

HIGH PEAKS

DRY MUSCAT OF SAMOS | SAMOS, AEGEAN ISLANDS

100% muscat blanc à petits grains

For several centuries, the mountainous island of Samos, just a little over a mile (1.6 kilometers) off the coast of Turkey, has been one of the most famous islands in the Aegean. The word *samos* is thought to come from the Phoenician word for heights. Here, muscat grapes, planted in rocky, terraced vineyards rising to 2,500 feet (760 meters) in altitude, make wines that are stunningly aromatic and redolent of flowers and fruits. While some muscat of Samos wines are sweet and fortified, High Peaks (*Psilés Korfés* in Greek) is a fascinating dry wine with edgy marmalade-like bitterness plus exotic notes of lychee, ginger, and kumquat, as well as the dry, resiny shrub character that adds a special "Mediterranean island" aroma and flavor. High Peaks is one of the top wines of the Union of Viticultural Cooperatives of Samos.

ROSÉ

KIR-YIANNI

AKAKIES | DRY ROSÉ | AMYNDEON, MACEDONIA

100% xinomavro

The bright red/blue color of a cherry Popsicle, Kir-Yianni's dry rosé is ravishingly fresh, with a sophisticated, slight edge of bitterness. Think juicy strawberries splashed with Campari. You can immediately imagine yourself on some sun-drenched Greek island overlooking the cobalt blue Mediterranean and drinking this ice-cold. While Greece has a way to go to challenge southern France as the European capital of dry rosé, this wine is poised for the mission, and indeed, Amyndeon is the only Greek appellation approved for rosé wines. Akakies is made in part by skin contact, and in part by the *saignée* or "bleeding" method, giving it a deep concentration. The name *Akakies* means "acacia trees" in Greek and refers to the acacia trees with their bright pink flowers that line the road from the town of Amyndeon to the small village of Agios Panteleimon, where the vineyards and the winery are located.

*D*ry red wine
Protected Geographical Indication *"Letrini"*

2009

Domaine
Mercouri

Produced & bottled at the estate
MERCOURI ESTATE S.A.
Korakochori Ilias, Greece

contents 750 ml   L.E.   09   Alc. 13.5% by vol
Wine of Greece

RAMNISTA

DRY RED WINE/PROTECTED DESIGNATION OF ORIGIN NAOUSSA
XINOMAVRO

2010

KIR·YIANNI

NET. CONT. 750 ML   ALC. 13.5% BY VOL
PRODUCED AND BOTTLED AT KIR-YIANNI ESTATE NAOUSSA,GR · PRODUCT OF GREECE

REDS

DOMAINE MERCOURI

LENTRINI, PELOPONNESE

85% refosco, 15% mavrodaphne

Domaine Mercouri's simple but delicious red has a cocoa-y, dusty character that's just right for a country wine. Although refosco is rare in Greece, family-owned Domaine Mercouri is well known for pioneering the variety. Indeed, after the estate was founded in 1864, Theodoros Mercouri brought back refosco cuttings from northern Italy, where he had business dealings. Like refosco from the Friuli-Venezia Giulia region of Italy, this has a sleek body and an attractive salty/spicy character. Here, it's blended with mavrodaphne, which adds a bitter cherry lift.

KIR-YIANNI

RAMNISTA | NAOUSSA, MACEDONIA

100% xinomavro

Xinomavro is in full form in Ramnista, the Naoussa wine from Kir-Yianni. (In local dialect, *ramnista* means "down there." It's also the name of the area within Naoussa where the grapes for this wine were grown.) For starters, there's an onslaught of tannin and acid that lash around on the palate like leather straps. But with some air (actually, a lot of air), Ramnista's firmness begins to yield, and the wine reveals a sexy, earthy aroma and powerful flavors of bitter cherries, dark chocolate, and espresso. Never for the faint of heart, xinomavro benefits from decanting to open it up, and from roast lamb to mollify its impact. Yiannis Boutari, of the large Boutari wine company, founded Kir-Yianni in 1997 as a small estate devoted to super-premium wines.

DRIOPI ESTATE

RESERVE | NEMEA, PELOPONNESE

100% agiorgitiko

If you have ever walked into an old men's club, you know this smell: a comingling of old leather, old books, old cigars, old coffee, even old men. It's a very attractive aroma, and Domaine Driopi's Nemea exudes it. But then come the juicy, fruity, and bitter flavors—something like raspberries soaked in Campari—that give this wine its delicious "center." Together, the two ideas combine to create a sophisticated red wine. Driopi is the brainchild of Giannis Tselepos, founder of Tselopos Estate in Peloponnese. The winery was opened in 2004 and focuses solely on agiorgitiko.

GAIA ESTATE

NEMEA, PELOPONNESE

100% agiorgitiko

GAIA Wines was founded in 1994 by Yiannis Paraskevopoulos, an agriculturalist and PhD in enology from the University of Bordeaux, and Leon Karatsalos, also an agriculturalist. The two decided to work with indigenous Greek varieties and establish two wineries, one to makes wines from Santorini, and the other to make Nemea wines from agiorgitiko, in the Peloponnese. GAIA's agiorgitiko is more complex than most—a sleek, firm wine with slightly spicy, wild chaparral aromas and then flavors of raspberries, violets, minerals, and sea salt that come crashing onto the palate in a wonderful combination of severity and sensuality.

BOUTARI

GRANDE RESERVE NAOUSSA | NAOUSSA, MACEDONIA

100% xinomavro

As I've noted in this chapter, it isn't easy to fall in love with xinomavro, but certain wines—such as Boutari's Grande Reserve Naoussa—are captivating for their sheer force and impact. (Wine drinkers who eschew the use of the word *masculine* to describe wine should try this.) And there's more than just power here. I love the wine's cherry/anise/salty character and the way it exudes numerous types of bitterness—from strong espresso to wild herbs to something like the medicinal-tasting bitterness of Fernet Branca. At the table, carnivores will be happy.

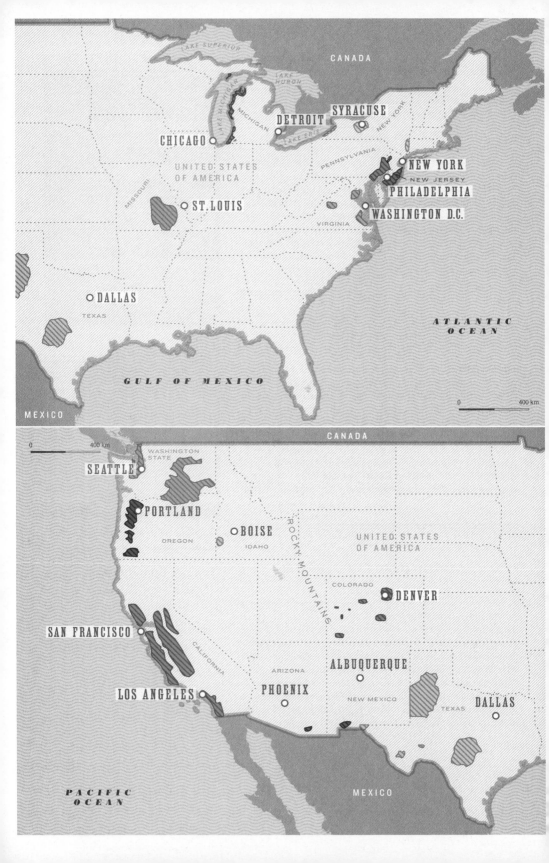

THE UNITED STATES

CALIFORNIA | WASHINGTON STATE | OREGON | NEW YORK STATE | TEXAS | VIRGINIA

ARIZONA | MISSOURI | NEW MEXICO | PENNSYLVANIA | IDAHO | MICHIGAN | COLORADO | NEW JERSEY

THE UNITED STATES RANKS FOURTH AMONG WINE-PRODUCING COUNTRIES WORLDWIDE. AMERICANS DRINK AN AVERAGE OF 3 GALLONS (12 LITERS) OF WINE PER PERSON PER YEAR.

It's often said that the United States possesses a pioneering spirit, a vestige of its beginnings. Nowhere is that pioneering spirit more alive than in the world of wine. The United States now ranks fourth worldwide in wine production; wine is made in every U.S. state; and year after year, the number of new producers continues to climb—as of a recent survey, there were nearly 8,400 wineries in the country.

Amazingly, the United States is now the world's largest wine-consuming market,

having taken the title from France in 2010. More than 780 million gallons (29.5 million hectoliters) of wine is drunk in the U.S. each year, but this impressive amount is, in fact, the result of the country's large population. By per capita consumption, the U.S. ranks not first, but fifty-seventh. Indeed, more than 40 percent of all American adults don't drink alcohol in any form, principally for religious reasons. (Such abstinence has few parallels in the western world. Germany, for example, has a 5 percent abstinence rate, France, a little more than 6 percent, and the U.K., 12 percent.) Wine, alas, remains the passion of only a small percentage of Americans. As of 2012, just 25 percent of adult Americans consumed 93 percent of the wine sold in the United States.

But changes have begun to take place. Since the mid-1990s, shifting lifestyles and mounting evidence of wine's health benefits caused

EXPLOSIVE GROWTH

The number of wineries in the United States has increased dramatically. This is very clear when, for the leading wine-producing states, the number of wineries in 1960 is compared to that in 2012.

STATE	1960	2012
California	256	3,406
Washington State	15	786
Oregon	0	441
New York State	15	366
Texas	1	283
Virginia	0	250

Gainey Vineyards' "Evan's Ranch" is nestled in the cool western appellation known as the Sta. Rita Hills—a two-hour drive along the Pacific Coast north of Los Angeles, and perfect for pinot noir and chardonnay.

wine consumption to rise. The most significant evidence of that shift: By 2011, for the first time in U.S. history, among people who drank alcohol, wine slightly edged out beer as the preferred alcoholic beverage.

Finally, for most wine drinkers, California is the driving force behind wine in the United States (and indeed, more than 90 percent of all American wine is produced there). But Oregon and Washington State now make wines of national renown, and New York State and Virginia are producing some of the best wines they ever have in their long histories. Plus, some surprisingly good wines come from places as far-flung as Texas. We'll take a good look at all of these and glance at several even more unexpected locations. For an explanation of the United States' wine laws, see the Appendix on Wine Laws, pages 927–928.

THE UNITED STATES: AN OVERVIEW

The United States is a vast country—the fourth largest in the world, spread over more than 3.5 million square miles (9 million square kilometers). Given the country's size, it comes as little surprise that the history of viticulture in the United States is really two separate histories, each independent of the other and centered on a separate coast.

On the East Coast, the first attempts at producing wine from European grapes occurred in the early decades of the seventeenth century. Most ended in failure, including the multiple efforts of third president Thomas Jefferson, who was convinced that Virginia possessed the perfect environment for making fine wine. For Jefferson and others it was especially frustrating to note that wild American vines grew in hearty profusion all around the colonies. Unfortunately, the wine made from these native vines tasted pretty odd (at least to

AMERICA THINKS BIG

The largest winery in the United States, Gallo, is also the largest winery in the world. According to winemaker Gina Gallo, the family-owned company produces 75 million cases a year—for comparison's sake, this is somewhat more wine than the entire country of Portugal produces.

The Gallo company beginnings, however, could not have been more humble. In 1933, in the aftermath of the Depression and Prohibition, Ernest and Julio Gallo, aged twenty-four and twenty-three, respectively, decided to start a winery in the then dusty farm town of Modesto, in California's Central Valley. There were, they realized, a few problems with their plan. The brothers had no experience with winemaking, no equipment, no vineyards, no winemaker, and no money.

But by reading pamphlets on winemaking in the Modesto public library, by borrowing equipment, and by taking out loans to buy grapes, Ernest and Julio managed to make their first batch of wine. Today, at any given moment, more people in the United States are drinking a Gallo wine or one of its sixty sister brands, than any other brand. And while most of those wines will be among Gallo's numerous inexpensive wines, the company also makes many fine wines, most of which come from grapes grown in Sonoma County.

"Wine is one of the most civilized things in the world and one of the natural things of the world that has been brought to the greatest perfection, and it offers a greater range for enjoyment and appreciation than, possibly, any other purely sensory thing."

— ERNEST HEMINGWAY,
Death in the Afternoon

those who had developed a European palate). And so wave after wave of immigrants persisted in bringing European vines with them to the East Coast. And those European vines, for their part, continued to die of various diseases and pests, including the most virulent pest of all, and one the immigrants could not have known about—phylloxera (see page 30).

Undeterred by such setbacks, settlers in New York and Virginia soon began to reexamine native grapes, hoping to come up with ways

VIRGINIA DARE

Thought to be the oldest branded wine in the United States (dating from circa 1835), *Virginia Dare was named after the first child born of English parents in America. The white Virginia Dare was originally called Minnehaha; the red, Pocahontas. The wine was made from scuppernong, a variety of native grapes that were found growing off the coast of Virginia and North Carolina. (The grapes are named after the Scuppernong River). During Prohibition, the company that made Virginia Dare stopped making wine and instead manufactured flavorings (which depend on alcohol during extraction). Today, Virginia Dare is a Brooklyn, New York–based flavor and extract company.*

AMERICA'S WINE CULTURE–PROHIBITED

More than any other political event in the history of the United States, the nearly fourteen-year period called Prohibition shaped America's current drinking patterns. Prohibition quashed the budding wine culture, and the U.S. became, almost overnight, a society that found pleasure and solace in hard liquor. The Eighteenth Amendment's constitutional ban on the manufacture, sale, and transport of all beverages containing alcohol officially took effect January 16, 1920 (although various Prohibition laws were on the books of individual states earlier), and ended December 5, 1933. It was enforced by a set of rules known as the Volstead Act, which was named after its sponsoring Minnesota congressman, Andrew J. Volstead.

At the time the law was enacted, California had roughly the same number of wineries it would have some seventy years later—slightly more than seven hundred. By the end of Prohibition, only 140 wineries remained. Most were destitute, having barely survived by making sacramental and kosher wine for priests, ministers, and rabbis (a rash of new religious groups had also formed) as well as making nonprescription medicinal wine "tonics" (blends of wine, salt, and beef broth) for the infirm and convalescent (whose numbers had greatly increased).

The decades before Prohibition had been a golden age for wine in the United States. Founded by ambitious German, Swiss, and Italian immigrants, the wine industry had grown rapidly, unfettered by European laws and land rights. American wine had won awards in dozens of international competitions, including the prestigious Paris Exhibition of 1900. A vibrant culture of wine with food—not unlike Europe's—was just beginning to take hold. But the Prohibitionists had been gaining power for a decade, led, in many cases, by women empowered by their newfound right to vote. In the face of growing antagonism, vintners remained surprisingly optimistic. Surely wine, the beverage of the Bible and Thomas Jefferson, would be exempt, they rationalized. After all, weren't immoral saloons and public drunkenness—and not the moderate consumption of wine with meals—the Prohibitionists' real targets? In what can only be described as naïveté or denial, even after Prohibition was signed into law, many

of making the wine from them taste better. By crossing certain native grapes with others, they succeeded. Later these crosses were joined by French-American hybrid grapes, created mostly by French scientists and quickly adopted in the United States. By the time of the Civil War, the East Coast had a well-established, if small, wine industry based primarily on native grape varieties, crosses, and hybrids.

Meanwhile, out west, another wine-making culture was emerging. In 1629, two Spanish clergymen—a Capuchin monk named Fray Antonio de Arteaga and a Franciscan priest named Fray Garcia de San Francisco y Zúñiga—founded missions near present-day

Busted, circa 1930. A policeman uncovers a stash of liquor and wine in a New York hotel.

winemakers believed it would be suspended so that the 1920 crop could be harvested. To the architects of Prohibition, of course, alcohol was alcohol.

Ironically, during this time grape production and home winemaking increased. A veiled provision in the Volstead Act allowed citizens to make up to 200 gallons annually of nonintoxicating cider and fruit juices. Nonintoxicating, however, was never actually defined. Brokers and wineries immediately began shipping crates of grapes, grape concentrates (the most famous one, called Vine-Glo, came in eight varieties), and even compressed grape "bricks" to home winemakers around the country. Along with the bricks came the convenient admonition: "Warning. Do not place this brick in a one gallon crock, add sugar and water, cover, and let stand for seven days or else an illegal alcoholic beverage will result."

Meanwhile, the bootlegging of powerful high-proof spirits became a thriving industry, and the local drinking establishment formed a new order for what and how people drank. *Speakeasy* was the name given to the raucous illegal saloons that sprung up during Prohibition. The word derived from the English underworld term "speak softly shop"—a smuggler's house where one could buy cheap liquor. By the end of Prohibition,

it was clear that the social experiment in forced abstinence had failed. New York at the time had more than 32 thousand speakeasies—twice the number of saloons that had closed.

The hard drinking and notorious behavior inside speakeasies set a new tone for alcohol consumption in the United States. A glass of cabernet with roast chicken it was not. At the same time, home winemaking, however clandestine and resourceful, would ultimately prove detrimental to whatever crippled wine industry was left. By the end of Prohibition, the best California vineyards had been torn out and replanted mostly with inferior, tough-skinned varieties that would not rot in the boxcar during the long haul back east. Over time, an affinity for fine wine was lost, supplanted by a taste for sweet, cheap, fortified wine. Even after repeal, the desire for sweet, cheap, and strong remained. It was not until 1967 that fine table wine, rather than inexpensive sweet wine, once again led production in California.

By this time, most of the winemakers in America had no historical knowledge and no traditions to rely on. Even Robert Mondavi and Ernest and Julio Gallo—three of the most successful vintners of the second half of the twentieth century—had to teach themselves to make wine by reading books.

San Antonio, Texas, and Albuquerque, New Mexico, and, in order to have wine to celebrate the Eucharist, planted the grape listán prieto, which had been grown for a century in Mexico as misión. Farther west, Franciscan fathers and Spanish soldiers, moving north from the peninsula of Baja ("Lower") California, Mexico, into Alta ("Upper") California in the mid-1700s, established a string of missions, each a day's horseback ride from the next. Each mission had its own vineyard, again based on the Spanish grape listán prieto, rechristened as mission. These first California vines were the descendants of vines brought to Mexico two centuries before by explorers including Hernan Cortés. As the eighteenth century drew to a

close, the Alta California missions and their tiny vineyards stretched beyond San Francisco as far north as Sonoma. They were all property of the Spanish crown (as was Alta California itself) until 1821, when Mexico won its independence from Spain, and Alta California became part of Mexico. It wasn't until 1846 that Alta California—henceforth known simply as California—was ceded to the United States, ultimately becoming a state in 1850.

The next big push came with the discovery of gold, in 1849, in the Sierra Foothills. The Gold Rush brought risk-taking, hard-working, poor, young European adventurers to California. But when the mines dried up, thousands of European immigrants who

WHERE THE VINEYARDS ARE

There are 1 million acres (404,700 hectares) of vineyards planted in the U.S.

State	Approximate Acres (Hectares)
California	543,000 (219,744)
Washington State	43,800 (17,725)
New York State	37,000* (14,973*)
Oregon	20,400 (8,256)
Texas	3,500 (1,416)
Virginia	2,600 (1,052)

*20,000 of these 37,000 acres (8,100 of 15,000 hectares) are planted with Concord grapes, most of which are destined to become grape juice or jelly, not wine.

after founding a prosperous fur trading company, went on, in 1879, to build one of Napa Valley's most impressive château-style wineries—Inglenook (today owned by film director Francis Ford Coppola).

As a result of the efforts of such men as these, viticulture in northern California experienced its first boom. By the 1880s, the West Coast had a thriving wine industry, and the United States as a whole seemed poised to become a wine-drinking nation, much like the countries of Europe. But it was not to be. Over the next half century, the United States wine industry on both coasts crumbled under the cumulative devastation of phylloxera, followed by Prohibition, followed by World War I, the Great Depression, and World War II. Although a few wineries managed to hang on and a few others began operating, the spirit of wine in America was substantially subdued. Wine production was modest at best. Fairly large wineries controlled most of that production, and most of what they made—huge blends of cheap, generic, sweet wines—tasted just about the same no matter whose wine it was or what you bought.

But a new era was about to dawn, and it would begin in California. In the 1960s and early 1970s, a wave of wealthy, well-educated, independent-minded men and women came to northern California with the idealistic notion of starting wineries. In a number of cases, these individuals—who typically knew little about grape growing—had other lucrative careers in publishing, medicine, education, technology, banking, or law. Many wanted a simpler life. Few knew just what kind of life they were in for.

As the newcomers—the Cakebreads, Shafers, Jordans, and Davieses (of Schramsberg)—joined by the then established vintners, such as the Martinis, de Latours (of Beaulieu), Mondavis, and Gallos, the California wine industry boomed for the second time. Meanwhile, thanks to the financial support provided by an exciting newfound industry, the enology and viticulture school of the University of California became one of the leading institutions of its kind anywhere. The quality of California wine soared.

did not strike it rich turned to the occupations they knew: viticulture and agriculture. California at the time was already home to a number of rugged individualists from all over the world, who had come to America's western frontier to seek their fortunes. Two of the most successful were the Hungarian aristocrat Agoston Haraszthy and the Finnish sea captain Gustave Niebaum. The dashing Haraszthy not only founded Sonoma's Buena Vista winery in 1857 (making it the oldest continually operating winery in the United States), but also promoted winegrowing with such fervor that for years he was called the Father of California Wine. In his first year at Buena Vista, Haraszthy is said to have imported 165 different varieties of grapes. And Niebaum,

Older vintages of Simi are often still in exquisite condition. The winery was founded in 1876 in the town of Healdsburg in Sonoma.

Then, in 1976, in Paris, an event occurred that would forever change the California (and American) wine industry. In a blind tasting, renowned French judges were asked to rank a group of the greatest Bordeaux and Burgundies, along with several unknown California cabernet sauvignons and chardonnays. When the scores were tallied, the top-ranked red and white were both California wines. The judges were stunned (and appalled). The news spread around the world. The Judgment of Paris Tasting of 1976, as it became known, proved to be a turning point for the culture of wine in the United States. By 1980, most wine professionals around the world agreed that California wines should be considered in the same company as the finest wines of Europe.

LABELS AND POLITICS

In 1989, the U.S. Bureau of Alcohol, Tobacco, and Firearms (BATF) issued a controversial regulation requiring wine bottles to carry the warning: "(1) According to the Surgeon General, women should not drink alcoholic beverages during pregnancy because of the risk of birth defects. (2) Consumption of alcoholic beverages impairs your ability to drive a car or operate machinery and may cause health problems." No other country except Mexico has ever mandated a warning label on wine, and the Mexican label stipulates that abuse (as opposed to use) is not good for health.

Soon after the rule was enacted, a well-known California-based wine importer named Kermit Lynch proposed balancing the warning with a statement about wine's benefits. He suggested Louis Pasteur's declaration that wine was the most hygienic beverage known to man. The bureau ruled that the quote was unacceptable. Lynch tried again, suggesting a biblical quote about wine's healing properties. Again, the bureau rejected the text.

Finally, Lynch proposed two quotes from Thomas Jefferson. The first was turned down because, according to the BATF, Jefferson had implied that wine was healthy. The second read, "Good wine is a necessity of life for me." That quote was considered acceptable long enough for Lynch to print 50,000 labels. Upon reconsideration, however, the bureau rescinded its decision, and Lynch was out the printing costs.

When Bill Clinton was elected president in 1992, Lynch decided to try one last time. He wrote to the BATF arguing that the phrase "necessity of life" did not imply that wine was healthful, merely that it was pleasurable. He also questioned whether it was the role of a governmental agency to censor Thomas Jefferson. Lynch's persistence paid off. Later that year the BATF finally approved Lynch's request. All bottles of wine imported by Kermit Lynch now carry Jefferson's statement affirming that wine was, for him, a "necessity of life."

AMERICAN VITICULTURAL AREAS

In the United States, the process of defining wine regions was begun in 1978, when the then Bureau of Alcohol, Tobacco, and Firearms (today, the Tax and Trade Bureau) began to draw up requirements for establishing the first American Viticultural Areas or AVAs. An AVA is defined as "a delimited grape growing region, distinguished by geographical features, the boundaries of which have been recognized and defined." On United States wine labels, such place-names as Napa Valley, Finger Lakes, Willamette Valley, and Columbia Valley are all AVAs. The first American Viticultural Area was, curiously enough, Augusta, Missouri, approved in June 1980. The smallest AVA is Cole Ranch, in Mendocino, California, which comprises just a quarter square mile. The largest AVA is the Upper Mississippi River Valley. At 29,914 square miles (77,477 square kilometers; an area larger than Vermont), it is located in parts of four states—Minnesota, Wisconsin, Illinois, and Iowa. In total, there are now just over two hundred AVAs in the United States.

At first, it might seem as though American Viticultural Areas and European appellation systems are similar constructs. In fact, they are immensely different in critical ways. The appellation rules in European countries do not simply define the boundaries of a region. They also legally mandate a sweeping array of details, including which grape varieties can be used in the wine and in what percentages; vineyard and farming practices; how long and in what type of vessel the wine must be aged; the minimum and maximum alcohol of the final wine; and so on. By comparison, winemakers in the United States are free to plant whatever they want and to make wine in almost any way they want.

Such freedom has one drawback. The premise behind an AVA or an appellation is that the wines of a given area will share certain characteristics of flavor. However, this has been difficult to demonstrate in the U.S., where winemakers often treat wines in vastly different ways. So in the U.S., it can be very hard to determine exactly what is contributing to any given flavor: some characteristic of the place—or something the winemaker did.

Many of the wine regions in the United States are beautifully rural places, where old farming families work the land using traditional methods.

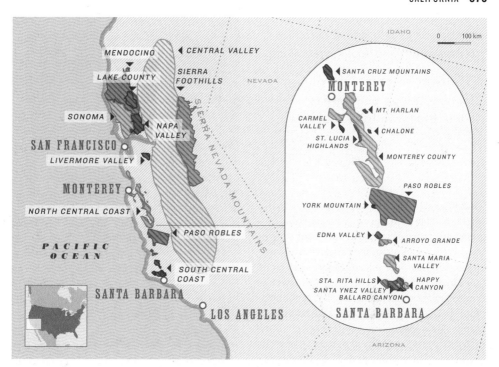

CALIFORNIA

NAPA VALLEY | SONOMA | MENDOCINO | SIERRA FOOTHILLS | NORTH CENTRAL COAST | LIVERMORE VALLEY | PASO ROBLES AND YORK MOUNTAIN | SOUTH CENTRAL COAST

California is wine's Camelot—a place of awesome beauty and high ideals; a wine region where the realm of possibility knows no bounds. The third largest state in the United States and not quite three-fourths the size of France, California produces more than 90 percent of all wine made in the country. The state's wine history goes back more than two centuries to the Spanish explorers and Franciscan fathers who moved north from Mexico and painstakingly built rustic missions, surrounding them with small vineyards. From those tentative beginnings, the industry progressed, becoming one of the most successful in the world.

Today, the conviction that anything is achievable is as irrepressible as ever in the Golden State. Fine wines are being made from a steadily expanding range of grapes. At the same time, better and better classics are being made, including—to name two strong suits— sumptuous, elegant pinot noirs and gorgeously rich and powerful cabernet sauvignons.

California's nearly 3,500 wine producers range from extremely large (the family-owned

Partimque figuras rettulit antiquas,
partim nova monstra creavit.

(Partly we recovered the old,
familiar things, partly we created
something wondrous and new.)

— OVID,
Metamorphoses 436–7

THE QUICK SIP ON CALIFORNIA

MORE THAN 90 PERCENT of the wine made in the United States is made in California.

THE STATE'S INCREDIBLY DIVERSE yet largely beneficent climate and geography allow California wines to be made in a profusion of styles from dozens of different grape varieties.

WHILE WINEMAKING in the state has spanned four centuries, California is one of the most modern, technologically oriented wine regions in the world.

winery Gallo is the largest wine producer in the world) to tiny commercial wineries that buy grapes and make a handful of barrels of wine in the garage. About 120 grape varieties are grown in the state, but just 8 lead the production of fine wines. In order, they are: chardonnay, cabernet sauvignon, zinfandel, merlot, pinot noir, pinot gris/pinot grigio, syrah, and sauvignon blanc. The state's wine regions cover more than 540,000 acres (218,500 hectares), stretching more than 700 miles (1,100 kilometers) from the redwood forests of Mendocino in the north to the sun-drenched hills of Temecula, south of Los Angeles. The climate, soil, and geology over so vast a territory are markedly different. Still, overall California is considered to be the New World's Mediterranean, for the state's vineyards are blessed by such generous, bright sunlight that winemakers almost never worry about whether grapes will ripen. Sunlight and ripeness mean that California wines are all about cream, not about skim milk. The wines have a natural richness and core of delicious fruit. They are, in the words of one vintner, "Here-I-am wines."

BEGINNING AND BEGINNING AGAIN

The California wine industry would seem to owe its beginnings to divine providence. As noted previously, the Spanish explorers and missionaries who moved north from Mexico in the mid-1700s secured their new territory—known as Alta (Upper) California—with a string of missions, each a day's journey from the next. Wine was needed for the Catholic mass, not to mention for the friars and explorers themselves, who depended on it both for nourishment (wine was an important source of calories) and as solace amid the harshness of daily life. According to the historian Thomas Pinney, the Spanish clerical authorities initially decided that the California missions would be perfectly well off with Mexican wine, which could be shipped north. But accidents and difficulties along the supply route ultimately led California's Franciscan fathers to plant vineyards of their own.

The cuttings they brought from Mexico were of the Spanish grape listán prieto, and were descended from those brought to Mexico some two centuries earlier by explorers such as Hernán Cortés. In Mexico, listán prieto had become known simply as misión, and later, in California, was spelled "mission," after the missions where it was planted.

As the nineteenth century dawned, California settlers began planting small vineyards of their own, all initially based on the mission grape alone. By the 1830s, commercial

Expansive, 100-year-old oak trees and rolling dry hills frame many vineyards in California. Here, the syrah and viognier vineyards of Fess Parker in the Santa Ynez Valley.

wineries had begun in Los Angeles, and a decade later, in Sonoma and Napa counties.

From the 1850s onward, California's future looked bright. The Gold Rush of 1849 pumped up the local population (in the two years from 1848 to 1850, San Francisco alone went from 800 inhabitants to 25,000) and created both a new demand for wine and a pool of potential

CHINESE CONTRIBUTIONS

With the Gold Rush of 1849, Chinese immigrants began to come to California in large numbers. Many were poor laborers and farmers who, after working on the transcontinental railroad, immediately went to work for the wealthy new winery owners in Sonoma and Napa. From the 1860s to the 1880s, Chinese vineyard workers cleared fields, planted vineyards, built wineries, harvested grapes, and dug by hand many of northern California's most impressive underground cellars. What is now the golf course of Napa Valley's prestigious Meadowood resort was once a Chinese camp where several hundred Chinese vineyard workers lived in barracks. A few miles away, at the grand old winery Inglenook, handwritten payroll ledgers from the 1870s show Chinese winery workers were paid an hourly wage that was a fraction of what their fellow Caucasian workers were paid. According to the historian Jack Chen, an economic crisis in the late 1870s resulted in agitation against Chinese labor, and ultimately in the Chinese Exclusion Act, passed by Congress in 1882. By 1890, hoping for better, safer conditions, most of the Chinese in wine country had fled.

CALIFORNIA'S BIGGEST WINE-PRODUCING REGION

*T*he Central Valley, a vast, hot, fertile, 300-mile (480-kilometer)-long expanse extending from the Sacramento Valley in the north to the San Joaquin Valley in the south, produces a full 60 percent of all the agricultural products in California and crushes 75 percent of all the wine grapes. There are numerous large growers here, wineries are huge; and the wines themselves are mostly super-inexpensive generic blends. Such well-established firms as Gallo dominate the region.

vintners. Better-tasting zinfandel began to supplant mission as the variety of choice, and the wine industry shifted north, first to Sonoma and then to Napa, both valleys being better suited to viticulture than Los Angeles.

Some of the great wineries were founded just after the Gold Rush, including Buena Vista (1857), Charles Krug (1861), Schramsberg (1862), and Inglenook (1879). As if this boom was not enough, California's future soon took on international possibilities, for the mildew odium and the root-eating insect phylloxera had already begun to destroy the vineyards of Europe.

Excitement over burgeoning markets notwithstanding, winemaking at the time was tough business. The early California vintners had no schools, no technical help, little or no knowledge of exactly what grape varieties they were planting (the identification of imported grapevines was hit or miss), very little equipment (even bottles were scarce until a bottle-making factory was founded in 1862), and few traditions on which to rely. Ever willful, Californians forged full speed ahead until the mid-1880s, when phylloxera finally made its way to California. By 1890, the insect had wrought havoc throughout the state, for California's vineyards were, at that time, planted with *Vitis vinifera* varieties grown on their own roots.

But by the turn of the century, the solution—planting *Vitis vinifera* varieties on tolerant American rootstock—was well known.

PHYLLOXERA—
THE DEVASTATION RETURNS

*T*he most painful and shocking event in the modern history of California winemaking happened in Napa Valley in the mid-1980s. Phylloxera returned. This time around, the insect had mutated into so-called Biotype B, and it destroyed grapevines planted on AxR1 rootstock at an astonishing clip. Vintners were stunned and despondent. Over the next decade, every vineyard planted on AxR1 (the rootstock had been especially prevalent in Napa Valley) had to be replanted

from scratch, at a cost estimated, in the 1990s, to be $3 billion. However agonizing this was, there was a silver lining. With decades' worth of experience and scientific data behind them, California's vintners changed the grape varieties they planted (and the clones of those varieties) to be better suited to their vineyard sites. Napa Valley, in particular, went from a region known for a score of white and red varieties to a place highly specialized in (and internationally regarded for) superb cabernet sauvignon.

The name California was used officially in Spanish documents as early as 1542. It is believed to come from the description of a fabled island called California in the sixteenth-century Spanish novel *The Exploits of Esplandián.*

The California industry rebuilt itself quickly. Soon, some three hundred named grape varieties were being grown in California, and there were nearly eight hundred wineries.

To the vintners at that time, the idea that such hard-won success could vanish overnight must have seemed unreal. But on the sixteenth day of January, in 1920, when the Volstead Act took effect, Prohibition became the law. Almost fourteen years later, when Prohibition finally ended, in December of 1933, only 140 wineries remained. Ironically, many had managed to hang on by making what the very first California winemakers had—sacramental wines.

California vintners were down but not out. It would take until the late 1960s and early 1970s for winemaking to build momentum again, but once it did, it soared ahead with startling speed. Within a decade, California became one of the most advanced and accomplished wine regions in the world. The enormity of the transformation is captured by the juxtaposition of two facts. In 1966, the best-selling California wines were cheap, sweet "Ports," often made primarily from carignane or Thompson seedless, both of which were

THE MOST IMPORTANT CALIFORNIA WINES

LEADING WINES	WINES OF NOTE
CABERNET FRANC red	ALBARIÑO white
CABERNET SAUVIGNON AND BORDEAUX-STYLE BLENDS red	BARBERA red
CHARDONNAY white	GRENACHE red
MERLOT red	MUSCAT/MOSCATO white (dry and sweet)
PINOT GRIS white	PETITE SIRAH red
PINOT NOIR red	PETIT VERDOT red
RHÔNE BLENDS red and white	PORT-STYLE WINES red (fortified; sweet)
SAUVIGNON BLANC white	RIESLING white (dry and sweet)
SPARKLING WINES white and rosé	VIOGNIER white
SYRAH red	
ZINFANDEL red	

THE WHITE GRAPES OF CALIFORNIA

ALBARIÑO: Plantings are small but growing. The grape makes fresh, lively whites evocative of the famous albariños of northwest Spain.

CHARDONNAY: The most widely planted white grape; it is the source of wines that range from bland to extraordinary. Most of the best come from cool areas and are made by winemakers who prize balance over oak.

CHENIN BLANC: Historically used for jug wines; it is capable of making very tasty wines, although plantings have been in decline for some time.

FRENCH COLOMBARD: Widely planted in less-than-ideal locations; it is grown at very high yields for jug wines.

GEWÜRZTRAMINER: A very minor grape in terms of production, but some surprisingly delicious wines come from it, causing fans to wonder why more isn't planted.

MARSANNE: A minor grape in terms of production but it makes good, simple wines on its own and is a leading component, with roussanne, in white Rhône-style blends.

MUSCAT CANELLI, BLACK MUSCAT, AND ORANGE MUSCAT: These are three different varieties, all of which share the word *muscat* in their names, thanks to their pronounced aromas. All are used primarily to make delightful semisweet and sweet wines. What is called muscat Canelli in California, the same as muscat blanc à petits grains, is the most frequently used of the three and is made into dry wines as well as sweet.

PINOT GRIS: A major grape, also known in California by its Italian name, pinot grigio. It is turned into light quaffing wines, as well as more serious wines of substance.

RIESLING: California's dry rieslings pale by comparison to those made in the Old World or even in New World places like Australia and Washington State. But, more successfully, the grape is turned into a small number of late-harvest dessert wines, some of which are very good.

ROUSSANNE: A minor grape in terms of production, but prized for its elegance and aroma; it is sometimes blended with marsanne in white Rhône-style blends.

SAUVIGNON BLANC: A major grape; it makes simple dry wines that are snappy and citrusy, as well as more complex wines modeled on dry white Bordeaux. It is also used to make botrytized dessert wines. Sometimes blended with sémillon.

SÉMILLON: A very minor grape in terms of production, despite its high quality; it is used primarily for blending with sauvignon blanc for white, Bordeaux-style dry wines and botrytized dessert wines.

VIOGNIER: The leading white Rhône variety, it makes opulent, rich, full-bodied whites, evocative of honeysuckle and melons. Since the mid-1990s, plantings have increased.

widely grown grapes at the time. Just ten years later, the state's fine wines were so good that French judges were left reeling when, in the now legendary Judgment of Paris Tasting of 1976, two wines—Stag's Leap Wine Cellars' cabernet sauvignon and Chateau

Montelena's chardonnay—took the first places for red and white wine, respectively, beating out such exalted wines as Château Mouton-Rothschild, Château Haut-Brion, and Domaine Roulot Meursault-Charmes. (Chateau Montelena, like a number of wineries in the United States, spells *château* "New World" style—without the circumflex on the *a*.) In the end, the French judges explained away California's victory, saying that, for wines so young, of course the California wines—so showy and full of fruit—would indeed be expected to outshine their more restrained French counterparts; but the ultimate superiority of the French wines would be clear, the judges argued—just give the French wines time to age.

The organizer of the original Paris tasting, British wine expert Steven Spurrier, did just that. In 2006, thirty years after the Paris tasting, he held a reenactment of the tasting with all the same wines, but that time, each wine was at least thirty years older. Two panels of British, French, and American judges tasted the aged wines. This time, all of the top five places were awarded to California wines. The 1971 Ridge Monte Bello Vineyard Cabernet Sauvignon came in first, followed by (in second to fifth places, respectively) Stag's Leap Wine Cellars Cabernet Sauvignon 1973, Heitz Martha's Vineyard Cabernet Sauvignon 1970, Mayacamas Cabernet Sauvignon 1971 (a tie for third), and Clos du Val Cabernet Sauvignon 1972.

> "Age gives a wine a sense of beauty and satisfaction that it could never have had before when it was young. In our minds, we intuit that beauty and satisfaction as a feeling of completeness. Because so much of life is incomplete, an old wine is remarkable and moving."
>
> — **WARREN WINIARSKI**, founder of Stag's Leap Wine Cellars

Mariah Vineyards' zinfandel grapes, surrounded by giant redwoods, grow in Mendocino.

THE LAND, THE GRAPES, AND THE VINEYARDS

Millions of years ago, as large tectonic plates under the Pacific Ocean repeatedly grated against and smashed into the continent of North America, California was formed. It became a place of amazing geologic and climatic diversity. Almost every kind of climate, land formation, vegetation, and animal life that can be found anywhere else in the United States can be found in California. Much of the state, however, is either too bone-chillingly cold or too torridly hot to be ideal for wine grapes. Close to the 840-mile-long (1,350-kilometer) Pacific coastline, people often wear goose-down jackets in the summer. Eighty miles (130 kilometers) inland, the immense, oval cradle of the Central Valley can be as blistering as an oven. Most of the top wine regions are poised between these two extremes—close enough to the ocean to benefit from its cooling effects, yet inland enough to benefit from the warmth needed for ripening. Thus, the major wine regions are stacked, one

THE RED GRAPES OF CALIFORNIA

BARBERA: Fairly widely planted for use primarily in jug wines; harvested at lower yields, it can make a fine wine with appealing red cherry and red raspberry flavors.

CABERNET FRANC: Generally blended in small amounts with cabernet sauvignon or merlot in California's Bordeaux-style blends, although cabernet franc is sometimes found as a stellar wine on its own.

CABERNET SAUVIGNON: The most important of all red grape varieties and the most widely planted, it is capable of making powerful and complex wines that are also ageworthy. Wines made from cabernet sauvignon were the first to put California on the international wine map.

CARIGNANE: The California spelling of the French grape carignan, it was historically used in jug wines but is increasingly grown at lower yields to make wines that can contribute solidly to fine-wine blends. Often blended with syrah, mourvèdre, and grenache to make Rhône-style blends.

GRENACHE: Historically planted for use primarily in jug wines, but increasingly, better clones have been planted and grown at lower yields to make high-quality, spicy, juicy wines that are often blended with syrah, mourvèdre, and carignane to make Rhône-style blends. Also the source of numerous delicious rosés.

MALBEC: A minor grape currently, but it shows considerable promise and plantings are on the rise. It is often blended with cabernet sauvignon, cabernet franc, and merlot to make Bordeaux-style blends.

MERLOT: A major grape; many solidly good red wines and occasionally some very expensive sensational wines are made from merlot. It is used alone and blended with cabernet sauvignon.

on top of the other, up and down the length of the state, from Santa Barbara County in the south to Mendocino in the north.

But there's more to the story. California's fine wine regions exist only because of a unique climatic phenomenon, itself the result of the state's distinct topography. As the days warm up and the heat in the interior intensifies and rises, cool winds and fog are sucked in from the Pacific, either directly into wine valleys (as is the case in the Santa Maria and Santa Ynez Valleys) or through gaps in the low coastal mountain ranges. The big, yawning mouth of San Francisco Bay, for instance, acts like a funnel for cool winds that are drawn in off the ocean and then pulled into Carneros and from there up into Napa and Sonoma Valleys. All along the coast, a similar cycle of warming and cooling is at work. Admittedly, this wondrous climatic yin-yang is more dramatic in some wine regions than in others. Still, it is an essential and crucial aspect of California's overall viticulture, for without it the state would be full of areas too hot to produce fine wine.

Unlike most European winemakers, California winemakers have always been free to plant whatever grape varieties they want. Accordingly, everything from albariño and Friulano to petit verdot and carmenere is planted in California. But the top eight varieties—in order of tons crushed: chardonnay, cabernet sauvignon, zinfandel, merlot, pinot noir, pinot gris/pinot grigio, syrah, and sauvignon blanc—are still, by a wide margin, the dominant grapes in the state. You'll find brief portraits of them (whites first, followed by reds,

MISSION: California's historic grape and the one that dominated all plantings until the Gold Rush. It was brought to California in the eighteenth century by Spanish explorers and friars via Mexico (where it was called misión). According to DNA typing, it is the same as the Spanish grape listán prieto.

MOURVÈDRE: A minor grape in terms of production but an essential part of the blend in many top Rhône-style wines.

PETITE SIRAH: Makes delicious, robust, highly tannic wines. DNA testing in the late 1990s confirmed that what grape growers and wineries have traditionally called petite sirah could be one of (or even a blend of) several different grapes, the most likely singular of which is Durif, a cross of the Rhône variety peloursin and true syrah. Also spelled petite syrah.

PETIT VERDOT: A minor but increasingly important grape for its vivid "black/blue" flavor and impressive structure. Like malbec, tiny amounts of petit verdot are often blended with cabernet sauvignon, cabernet franc, and merlot to make Bordeaux-style blends.

PINOT NOIR: A major grape; it is capable of making complex, earthy, supple wines, especially when grown in cool areas. Also used in sparkling wines.

SANGIOVESE: One of the leading Italian varieties in California, but making great wine from it remains a challenge.

SYRAH: The most prestigious and most successful of the red Rhône varieties; it makes concentrated, deeply colored, earthy wines that can be rich and complex. It is often blended with mourvèdre, grenache, and carignane to make Rhône-style blends.

ZINFANDEL: The second most widely planted red grape variety, it is an enormously versatile grape, used for everything from the sweetish pink wine known as white zinfandel to rich, jammy, robust wines that are almost purple in color. DNA testing reveals it is Croatian in origin and the same as the grape tribidrag, also known as crljenak kaštelanski.

Pride Winery at the top of Spring Mountain. The billowing fog in the distance sits like a blanket on the Napa Valley 2,000 feet (609 meters) below.

in alphabetical order) and my recommendations for some of their best producers starting on page 683.

CHARDONNAY

With nearly 95,000 planted acres (38,400 hectares) as of 2013, chardonnay is the leading variety in California. More than 758,000 tons (687,600 metric tons) are now harvested every year (more than any other variety), and chardonnay alone accounts for over 16 percent of all the wine made in the state.

By all rights, chardonnay should be one of the state's most exciting wines. Sadly, it often isn't. Many examples are simply clumsy wines that taste overwrought, overoaked, and overdone. What about elegance?

HOW TO MARRY RICH

From Thanksgiving well into the winter, when much of America is dining on the sort of hearty roasts and hot stews that could easily figure into a Dickens novel, Californians are feasting on a wholly West Coast indulgence: huge Dungeness crabs. Accompanied by crusty loaves of sourdough bread and washed down with glasses of cold chardonnay, Dungeness crab may well be the best use California chardonnay is ever put to. Although there are more than four thousand species of crabs in the world (and more of these live off the coasts of North America than anyplace else), there are only a few that serious eaters need to know about, and the most delicious among these is arguably the Dungeness, 38 million pounds (17 million kilograms) of which are landed, on average, every year. More than 20 percent meat by weight and weighing about four pounds each, Dungeness crabs are prized for their pure, succulent, sweet flavor. As a result, they're often served cold, with nothing more than warm melted butter as a dipping sauce plus fresh lemons. Which is where chardonnay comes in. Rich, sweet on its own, and even sometimes a touch minerally, chardonnay's flavors mirror a lump of butter-drenched crabmeat like no other wine can.

Chateau Montelena, built in 1882, made one of the first California chardonnays to receive international acclaim.

In fairness, great chardonnay is not easy to make, and the sites where the grapes are grown are critical. Generally, the best-balanced chardonnays in California come from cool regions (the Santa Maria and Santa Ynez Valleys of the South Central Coast, for example) or at least cool pockets within a given viticultural area, such as the coolest sites within the Russian River Valley and the Sonoma Coast.

Style, of course, is exceedingly important with chardonnay, and California makes a variety of styles—from full-bodied, ripe, low-acid, ultra-creamy styles evocative of crème brûlée, to extremely buttery/toasty styles, to lean, racy, crisp styles that are made without the influence of new oak or malolactic fermentation. The latter, now on the rise, are commonly known as "unoaked" chardonnays, and there are stunning examples, such as Williams Selyem's unoaked chardonnay—a wine with flavors as pristine as a mountain stream. The predecessor of these was Napa Valley's iconic and highly sought after Stony Hill, an almost Chablis-like chardonnay, sold by a private mailing list. When the first vintage of Stony Hill chardonnay—vintage 1952—was released (at the then steep price of $1.95), there were fewer

In the morning, looking down at the Napa Valley from Cakebread Cellars' vineyards on Howell Mountain is like looking down on the foam atop a cappuccino.

than 200 acres (80 hectares) of chardonnay planted in the entire state.

In terms of plant material, most of the chardonnay in California is known as clone 4, derived from one of the original Wente selections that were brought to California from France's University of Montpellier by the Wente winemaking family in the early twentieth century (see page 731). In addition, there are numerous chardonnay field selections (groups of clones that are replicated when a new vineyard is established). Among the most famous are the Hyde, Hudson, Robert Young, See, Rued, Mount Eden, and Spring Mountain field selections. And finally, many new clones of chardonnay from Burgundy (the so-called Dijon clones 76, 95, 96, and 548) have been planted in the past decade but have met with mixed results in California, since such clones ripen early and lose acidity (which is beneficial in a cool climate such as Burgundy's, but not in warmer ones).

SOME OF THE BEST PRODUCERS OF CHARDONNAY

Au Bon Climat • Brewer-Clifton • Cakebread • Clendenen Family • Diatom • DuMOL • Edna Valley • Fantesca • Far Niente • Franciscan • Hanzell • Heitz • J. Rochioli • Kistler • Kongsgaard • Liparita • Littorai • Mayacamas • Melville • Mount Eden • Navarro • Newton • Paul Lato • Peay • Peter Michael • Ridge • Scribe • Shafer • Stony Hill • Williams Selyem

PINOT GRIS

In California, the names pinot gris and pinot grigio are used interchangeably for easy-drinking, dry white wines that fall into two camps. First are no-fuss, basic wines that are fairly neutral in character, in the manner of most versions of Italian pinot grigio. (This is not necessarily a bad thing; who doesn't need

Sunset over the Pacific Ocean casts a feathery light over the coastal vineyards of Seaview Ranch in Sonoma County.

the wine equivalent of a basic white T-shirt, especially if it's inexpensive?) And second are more flavorful versions that involve better grapes from better sites and more-involved winemaking. So far, no one region in California has emerged as the key location for pinot gris, and while the top examples are tasty, the California wines made from pinot gris are rarely complex.

SOME OF THE BEST PRODUCERS OF PINOT GRIS/ PINOT GRIGIO

Arbe Garbe • Chalk Hill • Etude • FEL • Gargiulo • Hahn • J Vineyards • Navarro • Palmina • Pavi • Robert Sinskey • Swanson • Wind Gap

SAUVIGNON BLANC

Despite huge leaps in quality over the past decade, California sauvignon blancs are still remarkably underappreciated. In the past few years, the very finest ones (Araujo, Rudd Estate, Arietta, Illumination, Vineyard 29, and Merry Edwards, for example) have broached the top whites of Bordeaux in sophistication and aging potential. As for the good, well-priced, every-night sauvignon blancs, they're racy, keen-edged, refreshing, and arguably the best California whites for serving with food, thanks to their acidity and clean, fresh flavors.

Why the recent quality shift in California sauvignon blanc? The answer lies in the vineyards—and in economics. Historically, it is much more expensive to farm great sauvignon blanc than chardonnay. Sauvignon blanc, a vigorous variety that has the potential to grow out of control, must be carefully and continually trained, hedged, leafed, and so on, requiring crews of workers to be sent into the vineyard scores of times to keep the vines' growth in balance. In the past, many growers simply weren't willing to spend the money it took to grow great sauvignon blanc, and as a result, many sauvignons tasted weedy and cabbage-like. Today, that view has changed radically. All of the good and top growers now commit far more financial resources to sauvignon blanc than at any other time in California history. They do so because wineries will pay more for sauvignon blanc grapes than they have in the past. And wineries are paying more because wine drinkers have shown a new willingness to spend more on sauvignon blanc—if it's good.

Most every-night sauvignon blancs in California are simply made in stainless-steel tanks which, because they protect against oxygen exposure, help the sauvignon blanc retain its beautiful, fresh green aromas. More complex, expensive sauvignon blancs are often made by blending small lots of wine that have been made in a variety of containers (new oak barrels, used oak barrels, concrete eggs, and stainless-steel drums, for example), giving the final wine greater depth and character on the palate.

As for plant material, almost all of the sauvignon blanc grown in California is a single clone (now named clone 1), thought to have been brought to California from Bordeaux. Many of California's top sauvignon blanc producers also grow a more aromatic clone of sauvignon blanc called sauvignon musqué, as well as a tangy-tasting clone from the Loire Valley called clone 530.

Finally, sauvignon blanc in California is sometimes called fumé blanc (a term coined in the 1960s by Dry Creek Vineyard, in Sonoma's Dry Creek Valley, and later adopted and popularized by Robert Mondavi). As a group, California sauvignon blancs are not stylistically different from wines labeled fumé blanc. Vintners simply use the name they think you'll like best and want to buy.

SOME OF THE BEST PRODUCERS OF SAUVIGNON BLANC AND WHITE BORDEAUX-STYLE BLENDS

Araujo • Arietta • Cakebread • Crocker & Starr • Flora Springs • Frog's Leap • Grassini • Groth • Illumination • Kamen • Lail • Lambert Bridge • Margerum • Merry Edwards • Peter Michael • Robert Mondavi • Rochioli • Rudd Estate • Spottswoode • Vineyard 29

CABERNET SAUVIGNON

The grape that put California on the international map as one of the world's top wine regions, cabernet sauvignon is arguably the state's single most compelling variety, capable of producing wines of enormous power and grace, as well as structure and concentration. Since the late 1980s, the best California cabernets have gotten lusher, richer, and more complex by the year as winemakers and viticulturists have continued to refine their methods for growing the grape and making the wine. One of the key elements has been a new understanding of ripeness and the necessity of letting grapes high in tannin, such as cabernet sauvignon, hang on the vine long enough—not just for the sugar to mature, but also for the tannin to mature. Tannin that is ripe feels softer on the palate. Thus, an ideal California cabernet sauvignon has a significant amount of tannin so that the wine has a majestic structure and longevity, but at the same time, the character of the tannin is ripe, so that the wine avoids having a ragged, sandpaper-like texture, and an exceedingly drying mouthfeel.

In California, cabernet sauvignon is often the leading component in Bordeaux-style blends, joining merlot, cabernet franc, malbec, and/or petit verdot.

THE ORIGIN OF CALIFORNIA'S TOP CABERNETS

For more than a century, some of the most riveting and powerful cabernets throughout California have all traced their parentage back to three clones (genetic subtypes), simply known as 07, 08, and 11. The three were imported from Bordeaux (allegedly from Château Margaux) by Irish immigrant James Concannon, who had founded Concannon Vineyard in the Livermore Valley, east of San Francisco, in 1883 (he was the first Irishman to own a California winery). Concannon's agent in Bordeaux was the legendary San Francisco lawyer-turned-grapevine-dealer Charles Wetmore, who himself had founded a winery he called Cresta Blanca. While many grape clones died out during Prohibition, the "Bordeaux/Concannon clones" survived the thirteen-year ban on wine thanks to Concannon's reinvention of itself as a supplier of altar wine to the Archbishop of San Francisco. In the 1960s, cuttings from the three clones were brought from Concannon to the Foundation Plant Services department at the University of California, Davis, where they were replicated as virus-free plants. A decade later, 07, 08, and 11 vines were planted by now-famous wineries throughout the state, and subsequently became legendary wines.

ADAMVS • Araujo • Arkenstone • Baldacci BOND • Brand • Cardinale • Caymus • Chappellet • Chateau St. Jean • Colgin • Continuum • Corison • Corra • Dalla Valle • Dana • Dancing Hares • Diamond Creek • Dominus Estate • Dunn • Far Niente • Gandona • Gargiulo • Grace Family • Groth • Harlan • Heitz • Jordan • Joseph Phelps • Kapcsandy • Kelly Fleming • La Jota • Lail • Laurel Glen • Lokoya • Long Meadow Ranch • Louis Martini • Mayacamas • Melka • Mount Veeder Winery • Opus One • O'Shaughnessy • Outpost • Ovid • Paradigm • Paul Hobbs • Peter Michael • PlumpJack • Quintessa • Reverie • Ridge • Robert Mondavi • Rudd • Scarecrow • Schrader • Screaming Eagle • Shafer • Silverado • Silver Oak • Sloan • Spottswoode • Spring Mountain Winery • Staglin Family • Stag's Leap Wine Cellars • Turnbull • Venge • Vérité • Vineyard 29

In the Red Hills of Lake County, Beckstoffer Vineyards' high-elevation cabernet sauvignon vines have a view of Snow Mountain.

> "When it's good, pinot noir doesn't knock your socks off. It slips them off—slowly."
> —ROBERT MONDAVI,
> founder of Robert Mondavi Winery

MERLOT

California merlot's reputation has been on a seesaw for more than a decade. On the one hand, there are serious, top-notch producers (Duckhorn, Chappellet, Shafer, and Gargiulo, for example) who make intensely flavored, big-structured complex wines. On the other side are oceans of innocuous, unstructured merlot that is little more than inexpensive red wine marketed as "soft." These fairly bland merlots bear almost no resemblance to the top versions.

Interestingly, in California the top merlots are almost never soft per se, many of them having been produced from grapes grown in the mountains or on volcanic soils. These top merlots can be, and often are, as magnificently structured and captivating as top cabernet sauvignons.

Beringer • Chappellet • Crocker & Starr • Duckhorn • Gargiulo • Happy Canyon • Lewis • Liparita • Markham • Newton • Nickel & Nickel • Pahlmeyer • Paloma • Paradigm • Pride Mountain • Robert Foley • Robert Sinskey • Shafer • Stags' Leap Winery • Switchback Ridge • Twomey • Whitehall Lane

PINOT NOIR

Pinot noir gets my vote for the California wine that has experienced the most immense and remarkable increase in quality over the past decade. The sheer number of lusciously textured pinots that are complex and deeply

Old gnarly zinfandel vines—a precious part of California's viticultural heritage—appear especially poignant in spring when all around them in the Napa Valley, the delicate yellow mustard flowers bloom.

to Oregon by Oregon State University in 1987 and 1988, and planted there before being taken south to California.

SOME OF THE BEST
PRODUCERS OF PINOT NOIR

Alma Rosa • Ancien • Aubert • Au Bon Climat • Belle Glos • Bien Nacido • Bonaccorsi • Brewer-Clifton • Calera • Cambria • Capiaux • Ceja • Chamisal • Chanin • Davis Bynum • Dierberg • Domaine Carneros • Dragonette • DuMOL • Etude • Failla • Fess Parker • Fiddlehead Cellars • Flowers • Foursight • Foxen • Gainey • Hanzell • Hartley Ostini • Hirsch • Joseph Swan • J. Rochioli • Laetitia • Lafond • Kosta Browne • Littorai • Marcassin • McIntyre • Melville • Patz & Hall • Paul Hobbs • Paul Lato • Peay • Pisoni • Presqu'ile • Radio-Coteau • Rhys • ROAR • Saintsbury • Samsara • Sandhi • Sanford • Saxon Brown • Sea Smoke • Scribe • Siduri • Talisman • Talley • Truchard • Williams Selyem • Wrath

---

flavored but also refined and elegant is frankly astounding, for the grape is notoriously difficult to grow and make into fine wine. Best of all, the very top California pinot noirs possess a sense of beauty and precision—their flavors are not muddled or diffuse, but rather, what I like to call the flavor equivalent of the sound of a church bell in the mountains.

Amazingly, pinot noir is grown over a 500-mile (800-kilometer) coastal span in California, from the Anderson Valley in Mendocino County, in the far north of the state, to the Santa Ynez Valley, relatively near Los Angeles, in the south. In between are stunning appellations for the grape—all of which are highly influenced by cold Pacific breezes and fog. These include Sonoma Coast, Russian River Valley, Carneros, Santa Lucia Highlands, Arroyo Grande Valley, Sta. Rita Hills, Santa Ynez Valley, and Santa Maria Valley.

With pinot noir, clones (different genetic variations) can have a huge impact on the flavor of the wine, and within California's top pinot noir growing areas, a vast array of clonal material is now planted. This includes historic clones such as Pommard (sometimes called UC Davis 4) and Wadenswil (which came to California and Oregon from Burgundy, via Switzerland) plus an assortment of the so-called Dijon clones of pinot noir (113, 114, 115, 667, 777, and others), which were first brought

SYRAH

The best French syrahs (from appellations like Côte-Rôtie and Hermitage) are distinctive wines (gamy, minerally, white peppery, sometimes sweaty and bloody). Similarly, the best Australian shirazes (from appellations like Barossa Valley and McLaren Vale) are quite unique (peppery, eucalyptus-y, spicy, licoricey, with a rich core of fleshy fruit). But the syrahs of California are not as easy to categorize. They can lean in either a French or an Australian direction (and sometimes—intriguingly—in both at the same time).

Syrah is, for the most part, not a beginner's wine. The wine is never shy or tame; it howls out of the glass. The bloody-sweaty-gamy flavors can be something of an acquired taste (but like all acquired tastes, once you've got it, you're mad for it). And at least some of the time, syrah shows a propensity to be what is called "reduced," that is, it initially smells a little funky until you swirl the glass vigorously and work oxygen into the wine, whereupon the wine emerges smelling just fine. Syrah lovers are used to this and it presents no problem, but a novice can easily be caught off guard.

Syrah is often a component in California's Rhône-style wines, where it is joined by grenache, mourvèdre, carignane, and sometimes cinsault. Such wines are increasingly popular in the state. Indeed, from next to nothing in the 1980s, the acreage of Rhône varieties has grown to more than 30,000 acres (12,141 hectares) currently; and nearly two hundred California producers belong to an organization called the Rhone Rangers.

SOME OF THE BEST
PRODUCERS OF SYRAH
AND RHÔNE-STYLE BLENDS

Alban • Alta Colina • Andrew Murray • Araujo • Arnot-Roberts • Bonny Doon • Calera • Colgin • Copain • Edmunds St. John • Failla • Fess Parker • Jonata • Joseph Phelps • Kongsgaard • Landmark • Margerum • Ojai • Paul Lato • Peay • Piedrasassi • Qupé • Radio-Coteau • Samsara • Sanguis • Sans Liege • Saxum • Sean Thackrey • Shafer • Sine Qua Non • Stolpman • Tensley • Zaca Mesa

---

ZINFANDEL

Until cabernet sauvignon superseded it in 1998, zinfandel was the most widely planted red grape in California. Although a large percentage of these grapes are turned into slightly sweet, mild tasting, inexpensive white zinfandels, the very best grapes are made into the real stuff: jammy, briary, mouthwatering, big-fruited, dry red zinfandels that can be as lovable and irresistible as puppies.

Some of the most prized vineyards in California are those planted with old zinfandel vines. These gnarled, twisted vines have low productivity, but the grapes often make for wines of richness and depth. Although the term *old vines* has no legal definition, if you see

The famous Bien Nacido Vineyards of Santa Maria Valley coated in morning fog.

it on a label, it generally signifies that the wine came from vineyards in continual production for at least forty years, and occasionally more than a hundred.

While zinfandel still grows throughout the state (and is California's third leading variety, after chardonnay and cabernet sauvignon), the wine regions where it excels are usually warm (notably the Dry Creek area of Sonoma County; the Gold Rush counties of Amador and El Dorado; and the inland AVAs within Mendocino County).

Zinfandel is both loved (by some) and criticized (by others) for its high alcohol content. In fact, it's hard to make zinfandel that doesn't have a lot of alcohol. The variety is notorious for uneven ripening on the same cluster. Thus, come late summer, while some grapes on the cluster will be perfect, others could be raisins and still others could be hard and unripe. If you press a cluster like this, you end up with something that tastes more like sweet-and-sour sauce than wine. As a result, most winemakers are forced to wait for the unripe grapes

SYRAH IN CALIFORNIA: MYSTERIOUS BEGINNINGS

Though story of how syrah came to grow in California illustrates just how labyrinthine and complex grape introductions can be. Often records are lost (if they were kept in the first place), and memories fade. So the history of syrah in California is spotty, but here's what is known.

Syrah (the progeny of two fairly obscure French grapes—dureza and mondeuse blanche) emerged on the California viticultural scene at least four main times. The first was in 1936, when University of California at Davis professor Dr. Harold Olmo brought in cuttings from the University of Montpellier, in southern France (there's no record of the source of the Montpellier cuttings). This "Montpellier" syrah remained at UC Davis until 1959, when Dr. Olmo convinced the Christian Brothers winery to plant some in their vineyards in Napa Valley. Along with the syrah, Christian Brothers reportedly planted other varieties in the same vineyard, including (probably) petite sirah and carignan. Although that vineyard has long since been pulled out, Joseph Phelps Vineyards purchased some of the syrah grapes in 1974 (along with syrah cuttings). Since field blends were very common back then, it's possible that what Phelps purchased was not syrah alone, but a blend of several varieties. Nonetheless, Phelps subsequently came out with the first varietally labeled syrah, vintage 1974, and using the cuttings, planted 20 acres (8 hectares) of syrah in their vineyards.

Meanwhile, in 1970, cuttings of shiraz were brought to California from the Victoria Plant Research Institute, in Victoria, Australia. This shiraz was what winemaker/nurseryman Doug Meador planted in his Meador Estate within Ventana Vineyards, in Monterey County, in 1978. Some wineries subsequently got their syrah (shiraz) cuttings from Meador. In 1973, three years after shiraz arrived from Australia, more syrah was brought in from France, from the French national plant materials laboratory, *L'Etablissement National Technique pour l'Amélioration de la Viticulture,* commonly known as ENTAV, situated at Domaine de l'Espiguette. Thus, the "Espiguette clone" was added to the syrahs available in the state. But a fourth clone was also available, thanks to Dr. Harold Olmo and Gary Eberle, who was then a doctoral student at UC Davis. Olmo gave Eberle eighteen cuttings from vines growing at UC Davis, vines Olmo had received years earlier from Max Chapoutier, part of the family that owned the famous Chapoutier vineyards in Hermitage and Côte-Rôtie, in the northern Rhône. After enlisting Meador's help to propagate the cuttings, Eberle planted the "Chapoutier clone" at Estrella Vineyards (where he was the winemaker), in Monterey. In subsequent years, Chapoutier cuttings were given to winemakers all over the state. Finally, as you might imagine, with winemakers driven to establish the best syrah possible in California, there have also been many reports (always unconfirmed) that some of the state's best syrah can be traced back to—*shhhhh*—"Samsonite clones" (something recently and illegally carried back in a suitcase).

to ripen, by which time many of the ripe grapes have begun to raisin. With a high percentage of sugar in the bunches, the inevitable result is a wine of high alcohol.

Curiously, zinfandel is rarely blended, although starting in 1966, Ridge began making some fantastic zinfandels that were blends of zinfandel, petite sirah, and carignane. Today,

NAME A GROWER

Most avid wine drinkers could name a famous California winery—maybe even a famous California winemaker. But a grower? The men and women who grow grapes in most U.S. states are virtually anonymous, even though their talents are the fulcrum on which great wine hinges. Then there's Andy Beckstoffer, without a doubt the best-known grape grower in northern California, and a man whose farming company now owns over 5,000 acres (2,000 hectares) of prime vineyard land, from Mendocino County to Napa Valley. Dozens of leading wineries, including Stag's Leap Wine Cellars, Cain, Schrader, and Paul Hobbs, use Beckstoffer grapes for their luxury wines. In 2010, to secure a vineyard he considered exemplary, Beckstoffer paid one of the then-highest prices ever for a vineyard in the United States—$300,000 per acre ($750,000 per hectare). By comparison, the highest price then paid for a vineyard in Monterey County, just 150 miles (240 kilometers) south of Napa Valley, was about a tenth of the price.

the most monolithic and massively concentrated example of a zinfandel blend is The Prisoner, in which zinfandel is blended with cabernet sauvignon, syrah, petite sirah, charbono, grenache, and others. Not for the faint of heart, The Prisoner has a cult following.

Although few people actually cellar them, the top zinfandels can age beautifully. I was stunned by the almost Burgundy-like refinement of a 1988 Sutter Home zinfandel that I took from my cellar and drank twenty-five years later, in 2013. And a 1995 Kunde Century Vines zinfandel (made from vines planted in 1882!) taken from my cellar later that same week was, at seventeen years old, achingly good.

Finally, while zinfandel is often called America's grape (no place in Europe produces a wine by that name), it is of European (*Vitis vinifera*) descent. In the late 1990s, DNA typing revealed that zinfandel is the Croatian grape historically called tribidrag and now called crljenak kaštelanski in Croatia. In Italy, it's also known as primitivo, and is traditionally grown in Apulia, the "heel" of the Italian boot. The grape found its way to the United States in the mid-nineteenth century, when Croatia was part of the Austro-Hungarian Empire. For reasons no one has discovered, it became known by variations of the name zinfandel.

SOME OF THE BEST PRODUCERS OF ZINFANDEL

Alex Sotelo • A. Rafanelli • Bedrock • Brown • Carlisle • Dashe • Eberle • Green & Red • Joseph Swan • Kunde • Martinelli • Miner Family • Outpost • Paraduxx • Ravenswood • Ridge • Rosenblum • Runquist • Seghesio • Steele • St. Francis • Storybook Mountain • Sutter Home • Ted Bucklin • The Terraces • Turley • Vineyard 29

SPARKLING WINES

In the 1970s and 1980s, a knowledgeable drinker easily could have distinguished California sparkling wine from Champagne. Today, doing so would be a lot harder, for the top California sparklers have complexity, richness, and length.

The wines, of course, do not taste like Champagne. For one thing, the soils in California are rarely based on limestone, as are the soils in Champagne. But what the best California sparkling wines do possess is what I call the contrapuntal tension of great sparkling wine and Champagne—the fascinating sensory

CALIFORNIA SPARKLERS AND FRENCH CHAMPAGNE: COMPARISONS

The temptation to compare California sparkling wines and French Champagnes is inevitable. Here is a look at the two types of wine, the styles in which they are produced, the aging on the yeasts each undergoes, and a host of other factors that influence how each tastes. This chart considers only California's traditional (Champagne) method producers, not wines made by the Charmat (bulk) process.

LOCATION	California	France
WINEMAKING TECHNIQUE	Champagne method	Méthode champenoise
GRAPES	Chardonnay, pinot noir, and occasionally but rarely pinot meunier	Chardonnay, pinot noir, and pinot meunier
TYPES OF SPARKLING WINE	Nonvintage, vintage, and sometimes prestige cuvée	Virtually all firms make nonvintage and, in exceptional years, vintage and prestige cuvée wines
STYLES OF WINE	Golden, *blanc de blancs,* rosé, and *blanc de noirs*	Golden, *blanc de blancs,* and rosé
DEGREES OF SWEETNESS	Levels not regulated by law but most top producers follow the European standards.	Extra brut: 0–6% sugar Brut: less than 1.2% sugar Extra-dry: 1.2–1.7% sugar Sec: 1.7–3.2% sugar Demi-sec: 3.2–5% sugar
NUMBER OF WINES IN A NONVINTAGE BLEND	As many as 50 and as few as 2 base wines	Dozens—possibly hundreds—of base wines
NUMBER OF DIFFERENT YEARS IN A NONVINTAGE BLEND	Usually 1 to 4 years	Usually 3 to 6 years
LENGTH OF AGING ON YEASTS BEFORE RELEASE	18 months to 3 years for most nonvintage bruts; up to 10 years for prestige cuvées	15 months minimum for nonvintage; 3 years minimum for vintage; prestige cuvées are aged for up to 10 years
YEARLY PRODUCTION	Approximately 29 million bottles	Approximately 324 million bottles
SOURCE OF GRAPES	Most firms grow a substantial amount of their grapes	Most firms buy the majority of their grapes from the region's 15,000 growers
VINEYARD CLIMATE	Generally cool	Extremely cool
SOILS	Varies considerably, depending on the vineyard	Mainly chalky limestone and marl

The late Jack Davies, who, with his wife Jamie, began Schramsberg Vineyards in Napa Valley in 1965. In the process, the Davieses ushered in a new era of fine sparkling wines in the U.S.

yin/yang between creaminess and acidity that erupt on the palate simultaneously.

I'm talking here of California sparkling wines made by the traditional (Champagne) method, in which the fermentation that causes the bubbles takes place inside each individual bottle. (California does make oceans of cheap fizzies, such as André, Tott's, and Cook's, which are made in large tanks by faster, cheaper methods such as the Charmat process. These are definitely not in the same class.)

For the best California sparklers, the path to excellence was neither simple nor straightforward. The story begins in Sonoma in the mid-1890s, when three brothers, Czechoslovakian immigrants named Korbel, made California's first sparkling wines. Old ledgers indicate that the Korbels used several grapes, including chasselas, riesling, traminer, and muscatel, and that they made their sparkling wine by the traditional (Champagne) method.

Despite this promising beginning, the period from Prohibition to the 1960s was a kind of Dark Ages for California sparkling wine. Most of the sparklers produced were cheap, frothy, Charmat-method wines. Only Korbel and the Napa Valley winery Hanns Kornell continued to make traditional-method sparklers. But with the founding of the then tiny Schramsberg winery, in the mid-1960s, a new age for California sparkling wine dawned. The first Schramsberg wines were made with chardonnay—a grape that was scarce in the 1960s.

Quickly outclassing every other California sparkling wine being made, Schramsberg's sparklers, and the emerging fine wines of California in general, did not go unnoticed by the Champenois themselves. Not only were certain parts of California well suited to growing chardonnay and pinot noir, but land in California—unlike land in Champagne—was both available and, at that time, affordable. (Champagne is a delimited area. Virtually all of the best land has already been planted.) In 1973, the famous Champagne house Moët & Chandon purchased 200 acres (80 hectares) in Napa Valley and, with an initial $2.5-million investment, established Domaine Chandon. Over the next fifteen years, some half dozen of the top Champagne firms, plus the Spanish sparkling wine giants Freixenet and Codorníu, would set up joint ventures or subsidiaries in California. Today, most of the wineries in California that make traditional method sparkling wine also specialize in still (non-bubbly) pinot noir and/or chardonnay.

Finally, a few other facts. California's largely benevolent climate allows vintage sparkling wines to be made every year (unlike in Champagne, where vintage wines are made only three or four times per decade). However, as is true in Champagne, sparkling wine producers in California make several styles of bubbly, including *blanc de blancs* made entirely from chardonnay grapes, and/ or *blanc de noirs* made entirely from the red grape pinot noir. (Interestingly *blanc de noirs* are rarely, if ever, made in France, where, if you want a wine with a fuller-bodied character, you drink rosé Champagne.) And lastly, most California sparkling wine firms also make a top-of-the-line sparkling wine that would be equivalent to a prestige cuvée in Champagne. These may be aged for up to ten years on the yeast lees before being disgorged. Among the best are Roederer Estate's L'Ermitage, Schramsberg's J. Schram, and Domaine Carneros's Le Rêve.

SOME OF THE BEST CALIFORNIA SPARKLING WINE HOUSES

Domaine Carneros • Domaine Chandon • Gloria Ferrer • Iron Horse • J Vineyards • Mumm Napa Valley • Roederer Estate • Schramsberg

---

DESSERT AND PORT-STYLE WINES

California's dessert wines and Port-style wines are like gems kept hidden in the jewelry box. Quietly, over the past few decades, while seemingly few people were taking notice, some have become simply extraordinary.

Dessert wines in California generally fall into one of three broad groups:

BOTRYTIZED WINES made from sauvignon blanc and sémillon, and modeled on Sauternes

---

LATE-HARVEST WINES, usually made from riesling

WINES FROM THE MUSCAT FAMILY of grapes, modeled on southern French and Italian dessert wines

---

Sauternes-style wines are rare and very difficult to make in California, since the state tends to be either too dry and hot or too cool for the perfect formation of noble rot, *Botrytis cinerea*. However, in 1957, Beringer's famous winemaker Myron Nightingale made California's first botrytis-induced sweet wine by inoculating already harvested grapes with botrytis spores in a laboratory. Because Beringer Vineyards' "Nightingale" is still handcrafted in much the way Nightingale himself made the first such wine, only sixty to three hundred cases of half-bottles are made each year. Even so, that's more than many other botrytized dessert wines in California.

Then there's Dolce, considered by many to be California's most hedonistic wine, made from sémillon and sauvignon blanc grapes botrytized as they grow in the vineyard (this was once considered impossible in California— or at least not reliably possible). First made in 1985 by the same owners as Far Niente, Dolce comes from a low-lying, sheltered vineyard in Coombsville, in the southeastern corner of Napa Valley, where fog and humidity collect each morning. The grapes are harvested some two months after most Napa Valley grapes have been made into wine, and they are harvested painstakingly over six weeks by specifically trained workers who go into the vineyard over and over again. Using special shears, all berries that are not botrytized are cut away. Sometimes a cluster will have just one single berry deemed worth keeping. Needless to say, the wine deserves to be rather expensive—in 2013, the half-bottle cost $85.

As for riesling, California's late-harvest versions are generally made by letting the grapes hang for an extended period of time on the vine and then stopping the wine's fermentation early, thereby leaving some natural sweetness in the wine. Great late-harvest rieslings are, like botrytized wines, rare in California and exceptionally hard to make (many turn out to be dull, sweetish wines without verve, grip, lushness, or complexity). One of the best has been a knockout for two decades—Chateau St. Jean's Special Select Late Harvest Riesling, from the renowned Belle Terre Vineyard, in Alexander Valley.

Sweet wines from southern France and Italy are the inspiration for many easy-to-love, dazzlingly aromatic California dessert wines made from muscat grapes. A large, ancient group of grape varieties (only some of which are genetically related), wines with the word *muscat* in their names were spread throughout the Mediterranean by the Phoenicians (the present-day Lebanese) and Greeks. In California, the leading muscat varieties are muscat of Alexandria, muscat blanc à petits grains (also known as muscat blanc and muscat Canelli), orange muscat (muscat fleur d'oranger), and black muscat (muscat of Hamburg). Muscat wines are usually not as syrupy or voluptuous as other dessert wines, but instead are riotously fresh and full of racy mandarin orange, melon, and apricot flavors. They are some of the most charming (if underappreciated) sweet wines from the state. The leading California wineries for world-class sweet muscats are Navarro (in Anderson Valley), whose Cluster Select Late Harvest Muscat Blanc is sensational and refined; and Quady (in the Central Valley), which specializes only in dessert wines. In 1980, Quady produced a sweet orange muscat called Essensia, and then, in 1983, a black muscat called Elysium. Each is an epiphany of pleasure.

California Port-style wines are a mixed bag. In the past, many were simply inexpensive syrupy-sweet wines made from rather poor-quality, overripe grapes. While such "Ports" still exist, the best California Port-style wines are made by a handful of wineries that generally use traditional Portuguese grape varieties, such as touriga nacional, tinta cão, and tinta roriz. There are also, however, some excellent examples made from zinfandel and petite sirah. Again, Quady is a leader, with a magnificently rich, citrusy, mocha-y Port-style wine called—playfully—Starboard. (In 2006, out of respect for European place names, the U.S. signed an agreement with the European Community on the use of semi-generic foreign geographic names on alcoholic beverages. The result is that any U.S. wine created since 2006 cannot legally use the word *Port* on its label. However, U.S. wines that were called Port before 2006 can still use the term, provided

> "The simple physical act of opening a bottle of wine has brought more happiness to the human race than all the collective governments in the history of the earth. Even organized religions are mere spiritual mousetraps compared to the 'pop' of a cork, the delicious squeak when you loosen it from the firm grip of the corkscrew. And then the grandeur of the burble as we fill the glass, the very same sound we hear at the source, the wombs of all the rivers on earth."
>
> — JIM HARRISON,
> American poet and writer,
> from the essay "Wine"

that their brand name has not changed and the proprietary name of the wine has not changed. Thus, Prager Royal Escort Port is legally compliant, since this wine predates 2006.)

THE VINEYARDS AND MAJOR WINE REGIONS

From a scientific standpoint, California's vineyards are immensely varied, from computer-enhanced vineyards that incorporate NASA technology to scraggly vineyards dotted with hundred-year-old, untrellised zinfandel vines standing like solitary Rumpelstiltskins, their thick trunks bent and long tresses of leaves sprouting from their heads.

What follows is a look at the major wine regions of California. (As of 2013, California had 120 American Viticultural Areas, ranging from tiny to large.) First we'll explore the familiar

WHEN YOU VISIT . . . NAPA VALLEY

NAPA VALLEY WINERIES love visitors, the tasting room staffs are well trained, and it's easy to get around, since there are just two main roads— Highway 29 and the Silverado Trail. Make reservations well ahead.

CULTURAL EVENTS abound here; many tastings involve food pairings; and the usually well-earned "detoxifying" massages at the many fantastic spas are obligatory.

RESTAURANTS ARE NUMEROUS and excellent, including the restaurant many consider the single best in the United States: The French Laundry, in the little hamlet of Yountville.

SUMMERTIME IN GENERAL, as well as harvest time in September and October, mean traffic lines on these small roads. On the other hand, the valley is beautiful and a joy to visit in the winter and spring, when the number of visitors is far smaller.

regions of Napa Valley, Sonoma County, and Carneros, the region that straddles them. Then we'll travel more or less north to south, beginning with Mendocino and Lake counties; followed by the Sierra Foothills; followed by the North Central Coast (composed of the Santa Cruz Mountains, Monterey, Chalone, Mt. Harlan, Carmel Valley, and the Santa Lucia Highlands). Then it's on to Livermore Valley, Paso Robles, and York Mountain, as well as Edna Valley and Arroyo Grande. And, finally, there's the magnificent South Central Coast wine regions of Santa Barbara County, Santa Ynez Valley, Santa Maria Valley, Sta. Rita Hills, Ballard Canyon, and the fittingly named Happy Canyon.

NAPA VALLEY

 bout 48 miles (77 kilometers) north of San Francisco, Napa Valley is California's best-known and most renowned wine region, even though it is responsible for an astoundingly small amount of all the wine produced in the state— just 4 percent. Its fame (and infamy) is derived from an eventful commingling of history and humanity. For almost a century and a half, the valley has attracted a majority of the most ambitious, talented, driven, and outspoken vintners in the United States.

Where else but in the Napa Valley would a palatial wine estate (Inglenook) be built by an adventurous Finnish sea captain and fur trader named Gustave Niebaum, then sold, more than a hundred years later, to a superstar film director named Francis Ford Coppola? Where else but in the Napa Valley would an Olympian monolith called Opus One be built by two of history's most iconic vintners, Robert Mondavi and Baron Philippe de Rothschild? Where else but in the Napa Valley would the first California wine to cost $100 a bottle be made (in 1989), not to mention the first to cost $200 (in 1994), not to mention the first wine that cost more than $300 (in 2006)? The first two wines were Diamond Creek Cabernet Sauvignon Lake Vineyard 1987 and 1992, respectively; the third wine, the 2004 Harlan Estate.

Critics say Napa Valley has an ego. But what it really has is a gargantuan appetite for life and success. You can taste it in the wines. While Napa Valley is not the only California region to make great wine, it consistently makes a good share of the most polished, classy, and complex wines in the state—especially the cabernet sauvignons.

Named as California's first AVA in 1981, the valley proper is small and neatly framed. Stretching in a banana shape from northwest to southeast, it is 30 miles (48 kilometers) long (similar to the length of Burgundy's Côte d'Or) and ranges between just 1 and 5 miles (1.6 and 8 kilometers) wide. It begins at a bay (San Pablo) and ends at an extinct volcano (Mount

Four thousand years ago, Napa Valley was home to many thousands of Wappo Indians, although there is almost no trace of a Native American population in the valley today. The word *napa* comes from the Wappo dialect and means "plenty."

St. Helena). On each side, the valley is flanked by mountain ranges—the Vaca Mountains on the eastern side; the Mayacamas Mountains on the western side. The general climate is quite Mediterranean, with dry, warm summers and wet, cool winters.

Although, to the untrained eye, the valley looks geographically uniform, nothing could be further from the truth. The volcanic eruptions that occurred here millions of years ago—which caused the valley floor to rise and then collapse; plus the quashing together of the North American and Pacific plates; plus the sedimentary soils that have been deposited here, conveyer belt fashion, from what was once the Pacific Ocean floor; plus the cyclical flooding and receding of the Napa River—have, taken together, left the valley with a huge diversity of soils. Soil scientists categorize all of the world's soils into twelve orders, for example, and Napa Valley has six of them—an astounding array for such a small place. Within those orders are almost three dozen different soil series and over a hundred soil variations. The topography itself is also irregular, with numerous benches, canyons, and what geologists call "toes" that have formed as a result of landslides off the mountains, plus vast alluvial fans of soils conveyed by water flowing down from the tops of mountains to the valley below. This geologic potpourri, coupled with highly independent winemaking styles (there are more than four hundred wineries in Napa Valley, and most are small and family owned), means that wine estates next door to one another often make wines that taste totally different.

The valley's geologic diversity is underscored by its variable climate. In summer, a person standing at the cool southern end, which is open to San Pablo Bay, might be pulling on a sweater at the very same minute someone in the north, near Calistoga, might be stripping down to a bathing suit. In the early morning, the vineyards at 2,600 feet (800 meters), in the mountains, may be swathed in warm sunshine, while vineyards at 200 feet (60 meters), near the valley floor, are sitting under a cold, gray layer of fog. In addition, vineyards on the eastern hills, along the Vaca mountain range, receive copious amounts of late afternoon heat and light, as the sun sets beyond the Pacific. Thus, grapes on this side of the valley (especially in Howell Mountain, the Stags Leap District, and the eastern sides of Oakville and Rutherford) can get very ripe, and the wines can be very full-bodied. By contrast, wineries on the western side of the valley, along the Mayacamas Mountains (Mt. Veeder, Spring Mountain, St. Helena, and the western sides of Oakville and Rutherford), get the cooler morning sun and generally make balanced wines that aren't as mammoth. North/south, east/west, high altitude/low altitude, the factors that effect a given vineyard's mesoclimate are almost holographic.

What virtually all of the valley shares (thanks to the nearby Pacific Ocean) is a huge diurnal temperature fluctuation. Nighttime temperatures can be 30° or even 40°F (17° to 22°C) lower than daytime temperatures. This allows the vines to grow according to a nearly ideal rhythm of nighttime rest and daytime photosynthesis. In the best vintages, the result are grapes that are ripe, but contain the acidity needed for pure flavors and a sense of elegance.

Napa Valley vineyard land is thought to be the most expensive agricultural land in the United States. As of 2013, a planted vineyard in a prime location would cost in the neighborhood of $350,000 or more per acre ($875,000 per hectare), making the valley the most expensive agricultural land of any type in the United States. Vineyards cover just over 43,500 acres (17,600 hectares) of the 485,000 acres (196,300 hectares) that constitute the valley.

THE LEGENDARY ROBERT MONDAVI

Napa Valley's reputation as the premier wine region in the United States is due not only to the quality of its wines, but also to the relentless will of its vintners, including the late Robert Mondavi. Born in Virginia, Minnesota, in 1913, Mondavi grew up with hardworking Italian immigrant parents and got into Stanford University during the Great Depression. From owning a fruit packing business during Prohibition, the family eventually went on to become winery owners by purchasing Napa Valley's Charles Krug winery in 1943. Robert was in charge of the business and marketing; his older brother, Peter, was in charge of winemaking. But after his brother fired him during a severe quarrel in 1965, Robert Mondavi moved six miles south to the hamlet of Oakville and, at the age of fifty-three, started his own winery, naming the venture after himself. Despite years of subsequent lawsuits with his brother, and what appeared to be endless family infighting, Mondavi succeeded in making the Robert Mondavi Winery an international emblem of a top California estate. Throughout, Mondavi was a tireless crusader for California's place in the wine empyrean. His credo—that California wines belonged in the company of the greatest wines of the world—became a refrain he repeated endlessly to anyone who would listen. Countless did, and Mondavi rose to international fame, eventually forming some of the wine world's first global joint ventures. (Mondavi reportedly struck the deal with Baron Philippe de Rothschild, of Château Mouton-Rothschild, in the baron's bedroom, with the baron still in his pajamas.) In his later years, Mondavi, with his wife, Margrit, brought wine together with art, music, and cuisine as an exploration of culture and living well. In 2004, amidst fractious disagreements among Mondavi's children and among the winery's investors, Constellation Brands was able to launch a takeover, and eventually acquired the Robert Mondavi Winery for $1.36 billion in cash, and assumed the winery's debt.

Although Napa Valley is planted with numerous varieties, no grape captures the success of the valley better than cabernet sauvignon. Chardonnay, sauvignon blanc, merlot, and zinfandel can all become very good, and occasionally brilliant, wines in Napa Valley, but the top cabernets are phenomenal. No other wine region in the country makes as many stunningly rich and complex cabernets year after year.

Some of these top-notch cabernet sauvignons are made from 100 percent cabernet. But others have small amounts of merlot, cabernet franc, petit verdot, and/or malbec— the so-called Bordeaux varieties—blended in. Some of these wines are given a proprietary name if the percentage of cabernet is less than 75 percent. (In 1974, Joseph Phelps was the first to release a proprietarily named "Bordeaux blend"—Insignia.) Today, even more commonly, top estates in Napa Valley simply refer to the wine by the estate name. So, for example, Harlan Estate's cabernet sauvignon-based wine is labeled simply Harlan Estate; Dalle Valle is just Dalla Valle, and so on. This, of course, truly mirrors Bordeaux, where the top wine of Château Margaux is labeled simply Château Margaux.

NAPA VALLEY AVAS

In addition to the American Viticultural Area Napa Valley, there are sixteen smaller AVAs within the valley. Some of these AVAs are in

AFTER THE SIXTIES:
NOTHING WAS EVER THE SAME

1966. The Beatles had just released *Yellow Submarine*. The first episode of *Star Trek* aired. *Doctor Zhivago* played in movie theaters. The most sought-after Napa Valley wine was Inglenook Cask Cabernet Sauvignon; at $5 a bottle, it was the most expensive wine in the state. There were one or two women winemakers in Napa Valley, but they were self-taught; no viticultural school in the U.S. had yet enrolled women. And it was the first year the Napa County Agricultural Commission reported the exact acreage of grapes grown in the valley. Astoundingly, and even though Napa Valley had only about a third as much vineyard acreage as it has today, eighty different varieties of grapes were grown (forty-two reds and thirty-eight whites).

In 1966, the valley's most planted reds (in order of prominence) were petite sirah, zinfandel, gamay, carignane, and cabernet sauvignon. The most planted whites: French colombard, sauvignon vert, sauvignon blanc, golden chasselas, and the unfortunately named white grape burger. But as popular a crop as grapes were, the leading agricultural industry in Napa Valley in 1966 was livestock (especially cattle), and not far behind were prunes (public schools started late so that Napa Valley children like Michael Mondavi could help pick prunes) and dairy (more than 4.5 million dozen Napa Valley eggs were sold that year). It would be six more years before Napa Valley's main town, St. Helena, got its first stoplight.

the mountains, others, on the valley floor and lower hillsides. (A word about the so-called "valley floor." The term is useful because it distinguishes these vineyards from mountain vineyards. Yet Napa's "valley floor" isn't really the floor of the valley, but rather undulating benches of land that, in a series of steps, are a few hundred feet higher than the small Napa River that flows essentially north/south through the valley.)

In terms of the prestige of their wines, the most important of the mountain AVAs are: Howell Mountain, Diamond Mountain District, Spring Mountain District, and Mount Veeder. The most important valley floor/lower hillside AVAs are Stags Leap District, Oakville, Rutherford, and St. Helena. The AVA Carneros, at the southern tip of the valley, straddles both Napa and Sonoma counties, and is covered on page 705.

Napa's mountain AVAs, and the

vineyards that comprise them, are highly prized, for the wines from them can be superbly concentrated and structured, yet elegant at the same time. At up to 2,400 feet (730 meters) in elevation, the mountains provide an environment where grapes ripen slowly, yet because these vineyards are above the fog line, the grapes are also drenched in luminosity for long hours each day. Additionally, mountain soils are nearly always shallow and infertile, leading to smaller vines that produce tiny grapes. If the grapes are red, their small size means there's a larger skin-to-juice ratio, leading to mountain wines with impressive tannic structures.

Examples of high-quality Napa mountain wines are numerous, and some wineries make several different wines from the grapes of different mountains. Among those not to be missed:

FROM HOWELL MOUNTAIN: the merlots from Beringer and the cabernet sauvignons from Dunn, O'Shaughnessy, and Ladera, and Adam's

FROM MOUNT VEEDER: the cabernets from Mayacamas, O'Shaughnessy, and Mount Veeder Winery; the syrahs from Lagier Meredith; the sauvignon blanc from Rudd

FROM DIAMOND MOUNTAIN DISTRICT: the cabernets from Diamond Creek

FROM SPRING MOUNTAIN DISTRICT: the zinfandels from Ridge's York Creek; the cabernets from Cain, Pride, Newton, Lokoya, and Spring Mountain Vineyard; and one of the most legendary of all California chardonnays, Stony Hill's

Napa's valley floor and lower hillside AVAs are some of the oldest AVAs in the valley. Perhaps the two best known are Oakville and Rutherford, which, geologically speaking, are either primarily large alluvial fans (on the west side) or volcanic landslide slippages (on the east side). The areas sit side by side and spread out north and south from the towns of Rutherford and Oakville, smack in the heart of the valley. Some of the most famous and historic of all Napa wineries are found here, including, in Oakville: Far Niente, Harlan, Screaming Eagle, Rudd, Gargiulo, Groth, Dalle Valle, Opus One, Ovid, Silver Oak, and Robert Mondavi Winery. And in Rutherford: Caymus, Dana Estate, Quintessa, Staglin, Grgich Hills, Scarecrow, Cakebread Cellars, and the two old grande dames: Beaulieu Vineyard (BV) and Inglenook.

Stags Leap District, a small pocket of land on the lower hillsides in the southeast corner of the valley, is about the same size as New York City's Central Park. The district is named for what looms above it—majestic, sun-dappled outcroppings of tortured rock, over which, as fable has it, stags have leapt to escape hunters. The vineyards have a more auspicious existence, sprawled as they are on the rocky foothills below.

The district is known mainly for cabernet sauvignons from such leading wineries as Shafer, Stag's Leap Wine Cellars, Stags' Leap Winery, Silverado Vineyards, Chimney Rock, and Clos du Val.

Finally, among the valley floor/lower hillside appellations is St. Helena, ringing the small town of St. Helena, the heartbeat of the valley proper. St. Helena is where the valley constricts, like the center of an hourglass. Indeed, at the tightest spot, it's no more than a mile (1.6 kilometers) from the west side to the east side. The constriction traps warmth, ensuring even and full ripeness. Most St. Helena vineyards hug the western foothills and many are sited on alluvial fans. Again, cabernet sauvignon reigns here, especially from top wineries such as Corison, Spotteswoode, Crocker & Starr, Newton, and Vineyard 29.

THE TOP NAPA VALLEY CABERNET SAUVIGNONS

The quality of Napa Valley cabernet sauvignon is very high across the board, but following are the estates that I would put in the highest ranks.

Araujo · BOND* · Colgin · Corison · Dalla Valle · Diamond Creek · Gargiulo · Grace Family · Groth · Harlan Estate · Heitz · O'Shaughnessy · Ovid · Quintessa · Rudd Estate · Scarecrow · Screaming Eagle · Shafer

---

*BOND is made up of five separate estates: St. Eden, Melbury, Quella, Vecina, and Pluribus

---

The Napa Valley Wines to Know

SPARKLING WINE

SCHRAMSBERG VINEYARDS

J. SCHRAM | PRESTIGE CUVÉE, VINTAGE BRUT | NORTH COAST

Approximately 80% chardonnay, 20% pinot noir

J. Schram is the prestige cuvée (top of the line) of Napa's historic Schramsberg winery, credited with initiating, in the mid-1960s, California's modern era of sophisticated sparkling wines made by the traditional (Champagne) method. While just under half of the grapes for this wine are sourced in Napa Valley, I've included Schramsberg here because this is where the estate is, and because the wine is not to be missed. This is California's answer to Krug Champagne—a sparkler that is caramelly-rich, toasty, creamy, and nothing short of voluptuous on the palate. The wine is named for Jacob Schram who, in 1862, established Schramsberg, then the first winery on the hillsides of the Napa Valley.

WHITES

STONY HILL

CHARDONNAY | NAPA VALLEY

100% chardonnay

From Stony Hill's volcanic hillside vineyards comes Napa Valley's most historic chardonnay. When it was first made, by novice wine-makers Fred and Eleanor McCrea in the mid-1940s, there were fewer than 200 acres (80 hectares) of chardonnay planted in the entire state. (The first vintage of Stony Hill chardonnay—the 1952—was released at the then significant price of $1.95.) Their wine's reputation rests on its absolutely amazing ability to age. Stories abound of twenty-five- and thirty-year-old Stony Hill chardonnays that still tasted gorgeously bright thanks to the wine's exquisite acidity. Oblivious to fashion, Stony Hill continues to make its chardonnay not in an oaky, buttery style, but rather in a leaner, purer one.

ROBERT MONDAVI

FUMÉ BLANC | RESERVE | TO KALON VINEYARD | NAPA VALLEY

100% sauvignon blanc

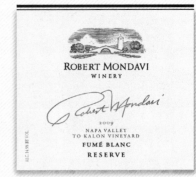

The To Kalon (the name means "the highest beauty" in Greek) vineyard sits right behind the Robert Mondavi Winery, up on a bench of land at the foothills of the Mayacamas Mountains. Within the vineyard is one of the oldest plots of sauvignon blanc in Napa Valley, the source of this unusually distinctive, exotic, exquisite wine. Unlike most sauvignon blancs, it doesn't taste vividly "green." Instead, it's fresh and stony—like the air in a dry creek bed after it rains. The late Robert Mondavi was one of the first vintners to use the name fumé blanc (now a synonym for sauvignon blanc), which he felt sounded more sophisticated than sauvignon blanc and was reminiscent of the Loire Valley village Pouilly-Fumé, where sauvignon blanc is the leading grape.

VINEYARD 29

SAUVIGNON BLANC | NAPA VALLEY

100% sauvignon blanc

Just a tiny amount of Vineyard 29's sauvignon blanc is made, but it's hugely significant, for it reveals a whole new side of what is possible in the Napa Valley—namely, to make a complex, luxurious, age-worthy Napa white on par with the great, famous white Bordeaux. The wine is a showstopper, with the faintest hints of meadows and hedgerows, and a distinct earthiness and minerality. But more than anything, it's the texture that gets you—a yin-yang between creaminess and spikiness . . . as if you were getting a Swedish and a shiatsu massage at the same time. In California, fascinating sauvignon blancs like this don't usually happen by themselves, and indeed, the winery uses innovative, painstaking techniques like chilling the harvested whole clusters of grapes to just above freezing for several days to soften the skins, and then fermenting the wine in three vessels—concrete eggs, stainless-steel drums, and new French oak barrels that have been bent into shape by immersion in hot water rather than by toasting, since toasting would leave too much of a toasty impact on the wine. As with Château Haut-Brion Blanc, I could drink this wine all day (if only such were possible).

REDS

KONGSGAARD

SYRAH | HUDSON VINEYARD | NAPA VALLEY

100% syrah

John Kongsgaard is a legendary winemaker in Napa Valley—known for making incredibly distinctive wines packed with personality (and for blasting classical music so loud that neighbors miles away can hear what he's listening to). Kongsgaard (formerly the wine-maker for Newton Vineyards) started his own winery in 1996, and among all of his immaculate wines, I may love this one the best. For starters, it's like smelling Christmas—pine boughs, mulling spices, cranberries, a wood fire. But then come the flavors—layers and lay-ers of fruit, black pepper, black olives, and violet-like flowers, and a salty minerality that makes syrah so compelling. Needless to say perhaps, but roast lamb is in order.

SHAFER

HILLSIDE SELECT | STAGS LEAP DISTRICT

100% cabernet sauvignon

Made from blueberry-sized grapes grown on hillside outcroppings of scrappy rock in the tiny Stags Leap District, Shafer's Hillside is one of the most powerful, lush cabernets in California. For all its gravitas and massiveness, the wine is impeccably balanced and so sensual it's impossible to resist. The texture is like cashmere; the flavors and aromas a complex interplay of cassis, dark chocolate, worn leather, sweet tobacco, bitter espresso, and black licorice. I have tasted every vintage of Hillside back to the first one, made in 1983, and remain thoroughly impressed year by year.

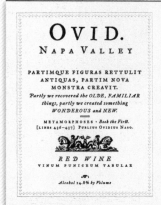

OVID

NAPA VALLEY

Approximately 60% cabernet sauvignon, 25% cabernet franc, plus merlot and petit verdot

Ovid (the name of both the winery and the wine) takes its name from the Roman poet Ovid (43 B.C. to c. A.D. 18), who wrote about the enigma of metamorphosis (everything changes, yet everything stays the same . . . an apt way of thinking about a vineyard). These vineyards sit high on a red volcanic rock promontory, a few hun-dred feet above Oakville, on the warm, luminous eastern side of the valley. You can taste the hardness of the rock and the energy of the sun in the wine. Scrumptious and rich, this is a cabernet blend with vivid, rapier-like intensity, its concentrated cranberry/chocolate/spice fruitiness pierced by a sense of minerals and licorice. Drinking this wine always reminds me of hand developing a photograph in the old days, and watching with wonder as the picture radiates into focus.

O'SHAUGHNESSY

CABERNET SAUVIGNON | HOWELL MOUNTAIN

Approximately 85% cabernet sauvignon, 5% merlot, 5% St. Macaire, 3% malbec, and 2% petit verdot

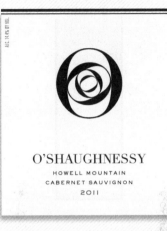

O'Shaughnessy is a great example of dozens of tiny production cabernets made by family-owned wineries often located high up in the mountains, a 30-minute drive, but a world away, from the valley's main road—Highway 29. (In the case of O'Shaughnessy, even a GPS won't help you find it.) This is black bear, mountain lion, rattlesnake, and hawk territory, and the wines often smell and taste of the rugged wild landscape that surrounds the small vineyards. O'Shaughnessy makes two mountain cabernet sauvignons—one from Mount Veeder and one from Howell Mountain, the latter on a site appropriately called El Rancho del Oso ("Ranch of the Bear"). And while I have been astounded by the deliciousness of both, the Howell Mountain, with its deep exotic spiciness, almost furry texture, and vivid black fig and cassis flavor, is the more hedonistic of the two. O'Shaughnessy may be the only winery in the United States to have plantings of the rare ancient Bordeaux grape St. Macaire.

SCARECROW

RUTHERFORD

100% cabernet sauvignon

Named after the scarecrow in *The Wizard of Oz*, Scarecrow comes from the historic J. J. Cohn estate, next door to Inglenook, tucked up against the hills of the Mayacamas Mountains in Rutherford. The land was bought out of bankruptcy in the 1930s by Joe Cohn, an immigrant Russian Orthodox Jew who made his way from Harlem, New York, to Hollywood, eventually becoming the first head of MGM (the studio that produced the movie *The Wizard of Oz*). The vines—planted in 1945—produced grapes that went into many of Napa Valley's most prestigious wines until 2003, when Cohn's grandson, Bret Lopez, began making the first Scarecrow wines with the help of consulting winemaker Celia Welch. From the first vintage, the wines have taken on near legendary status for their beauty (a rare term in the world of powerful cabernet), immaculate purity, textural tenderness, and savory quality, not unlike the wines of First Growth Château Haut-Brion.

HARLAN ESTATE

OAKVILLE

Cabernet sauvignon with small amounts of merlot, cabernet franc, and petit verdot sometimes added

Founded by Bill Harlan in 1984, Harlan Estate lies over the soft crests and slopes of a set of small hills edged up against the Mayacamas Mountains, in the western part of Oakville. The hills form a silent promontory (with 360 degrees of exposition) poised above Napa Valley, 225 to 1,225 feet (69 to 373 meters) below. Standing in these vineyards, you're overtaken by the feeling that you have found yourself in an enchanting and spiritual place. The wine is justifiably considered one of the greatest—if not the greatest—in the United States. Since it was first made, it has garnered numerous 100-point scores by critics. It's a subtle, immaculate wine of astounding beauty—a wine that seems to insinuate itself into your senses so completely that you are left without words, but craving more. Wines like this do not seem to be made as such, but rather, like Michelangelo's *Pietà,* to emerge into the physical world as everything nonessential is sculpted away.

SWEET WINE

DOLCE

NAPA VALLEY

80% sémillon, 20% sauvignon blanc

When it was created in 1985, by the late Gil Nickel and his partners (Nickel also founded Far Niente), Dolce became a Napa Valley sensation—first, because the wine was so mind-bendingly decadent, and second, because creating a late-harvest, botrytized wine in the manner of a great Sauternes was considered virtually impossible in the dry climate of California. Nickel was not only undeterred, he was galvanized by the challenge. Today, Dolce is the only winery in Napa Valley devoted exclusively to a single dessert wine. Great sweet wines are defined not by their sweetness (a given) but by their balance and acidity. Dolce's impeccable balance means the wine rolls over your palate in waves of lusciousness. The wine is exceedingly difficult to make. It starts with a vineyard tucked into a sheltered corner, so that fog settles and huddles there for hours each day (moisture is necessary for botrytis to form). At harvest, vineyard workers using special shears cut out all berries that are not infected with botrytis mold (sometimes a cluster provides a mere single usable berry). Because of the high sugar content of the juice, fermentation takes half a year. But Dolce, with its grand Art Nouveau–inspired label and 22-karat gold lettering, is a wine worthy of the complexity required to usher it into existence.

CARNEROS

About 40 miles (64 kilometers) north of San Francisco, the AVA Carneros (also known as Los Carneros) spans the southern ends of Napa and Sonoma counties, and includes just over thirty wineries and some 8,000 acres (3,200 hectares) of vineyards. It is a serene place. No towns, just softly loping, windswept hills that, now vine-covered, were once the exclusive domain of sheep. (The word *carneros* is Spanish for "rams.")

What makes Carneros special is its proximity to San Pablo Bay, which is the most northern part of San Francisco Bay. It acts as a giant funnel for the cool ocean air and fog that surge through Carneros as they are pulled up into the warmer Napa and Sonoma Valleys. The effect on the region's vineyards is profound. The grapes, while getting plenty of sun, rarely get too much warmth. Because of the constant caress of cool air, the risk of flavors being baked out of the grapes is virtually nonexistent. As a result, the wines—especially pinot noirs and chardonnays—often have gorgeous balance. While rich, the wines are rarely fat, flaccid, or overwrought. One sip of Shafer's Red Shoulder Ranch Chardonnay (from their vineyard in Carneros) shows just how complex and lusciously refined the wines can be.

The greatest number of the grapes grown in Carneros are either chardonnay or pinot noir, although merlot, syrah, and several other grapes also grow here in warmer pockets. There are also two very famous large vineyards here—the Hyde Vineyard (owned by Larry Hyde and Aubert de Villaine, of Burgundy's famous Domaine de la Romanée Conti) and Hudson Vineyards (owned by Lee Hudson). Among the top-rated California wineries that buy grapes from one of these two prestigious vineyards are: Marcassin, Kistler, Aubert, Paul Hobbs, Ramey, DuMOL, and HdV (the Hyde/deVillaine partnership.

Not surprisingly for a cool region that specializes in chardonnay and pinot noir, some fantastic sparkling wines are also made here, including several of the best in California. Among the sparkling wine firms that are either located in or buy grapes from Carneros are Domaine Carneros, Mumm Napa Valley, Gloria Ferrer, Domaine Chandon, and Schramsberg.

The top two Carneros sparklers I find most impressive are both the California equivalents of prestige cuvées and have spent six or more years aging on their yeast lees. They are: Domaine Carneros Le Rêve, (*le rêve* is French for "the dream"—an apt name for this pristine and elegant bubbly) and the rich, full-bodied Schramsberg J. Schram Reserve.

Finally, historically, the wineries and grape growers of Carneros have undertaken an ambitious amount of research, including research on dozens of different clones of pinot noir. In fact, as early as 1986, an investigation into Carneros pinot noirs revealed that they shared specific flavor characteristics, namely those of cherries, berry jam, cherry cola, and spice.

My favorites among the top wineries in Carneros include: Acacia, Ancien, Ceja, Cuvaison Carneros Estate, Domaine Carneros, Etude, Gloria Ferrer, HdV, Hudson Vineyards, Saintsbury, Schug, and Truchard.

SONOMA COUNTY

Directly north of San Francisco and bordering the Pacific Ocean, Sonoma County has 1 million acres (404,700 hectares) of land, making it more than two times bigger than its next-door neighbor, Napa Valley. Sonoma's size means, among other things, that the county is a geographical patchwork quilt of valleys, mountains, riverbeds, plains, and slight uplifts in the terrain, known as benchlands. Within this shifting landscape are sixteen viticultural areas that can be quite different in their nuances of climate and soil.

From a historical, psychosocial, and cultural standpoint, Sonoma County is rather different from Napa. Vineyards were planted here as the nineteenth century dawned, well before they were planted in Napa, and many vintners and winemakers are members of old, established farming families. A kicked-back country style pervades much of the region. People drive around in dusty pickups, no one puts on the ritz very much, and when Sonomans do get together, the talk is as likely to be about tractors as about wine sales in Tokyo. But be assured, among the top producers there's as much cutting-edge wine stuff happening in Sonoma as anywhere in California.

The county itself is beautifully pastoral, and is often called California's Provence. Vineyards alternate with apple orchards, vegetable farms, redwood forests, dairies (cheese is a local specialty), sheep ranches, nurseries (including dozens of Christmas tree farms), and even aquaculture fisheries along the rugged coast. Sonoma boasts one of the best bakeries west of the Mississippi (the Downtown Bakery, in Healdsburg), the first commercial shiitake mushroom farm in the United States, plus the Dry Creek General Store, a funky, old-fashioned general store, but on Saturday night, if you're single and in the wine industry, count on it being the place to hang out (everyone sits on the front porch and drinks beer).

Perhaps the nearest I come to gluttony is with wine. As often as possible, when a really beautiful bottle is before me, I drink all of it I can, even when I know that I have had more than I want physically. That is gluttonous.

But I think to myself, when again will I have this taste upon my tongue? Where else in the world is there just such a wine as this, with just this bouquet, at just this heat, in just this crystal cup? And when again will I be alive to it as I am this very minute, sitting here on the green hillside above the sea, or here in this dim, murmuring, richly odorous restaurant, or here in this fisherman's café on the wharf? More, more I think— all of it to the last exquisite drop, for there is no satiety for me, nor ever has been in such drinking.

—M.F.K. FISHER,
An Alphabet for Gourmets, 1949.
Fisher lived in the Sonoma Valley
for much of her life.

A morning in Sonoma reveals why the region is special climatically. Soft white fog rises in massive banks off the coast and drifts inland, wrapping itself around mountains, filling the valleys and riverbeds with pillows of cool vapor. Sonoma is well known for the daily ebb and flow—almost a yin and yang—of fog and sunshine. Of course, areas closer to the coast (especially the AVAs Sonoma Coast and parts of the Russian River Valley) tend to be somewhat cooler, while areas farther

Northwestern face of Camp Meeting Ridge—a chardonnay vineyard at 1,200 feet (400 meters) in the appellation known as the Sonoma Coast. The vineyard belongs to Flowers Vineyard and Winery, one of the early pioneers of the appellation which, as the name implies, is strung out along Sonoma's Pacific coast.

THE NAME SONOMA

There are many legends concerning the origin of the name Sonoma. According to Arthur Dawson, in *The Stories Behind Sonoma Valley Place Names,* the most frequent of these is that the word *sonoma* means "valley of the moon." This was the translation given by General Mariano Vallejo, the Mexican commander of the northern territories in the 1840s, when what is now California was taken over by the United States. Vallejo reportedly said that *sono* meant "moon" in Suisan, the language of a Native American tribe that lived not in Sonoma but in Napa Valley. It appears that Vallejo may have simply liked the idea of this meaning, since the general wrote admiringly of how full moons seemed to rise and set several times over Sonoma's eastern hills. Then there's the Pinocchio version: *Sono* supposedly also means "nose." As this legend goes, a Native American servant in the Vallejo household told of a time long before the arrival of Spaniards and Mexicans in California, when a baby with an especially large nose was born. The baby grew up to be chief of the tribe, and thus *sonoma* came to mean "the land of Chief Big Nose." The most likely interpretation, according to Dawson, is based on the work of early twentieth-century anthropologists, who noted that *sonoma* is a common Wappo suffix appearing at the end of village names. The Wappo tribe is thought to have occupied Sonoma before being pushed out by other tribes and relocating in what became known as Napa Valley. According to Laura Somersal, the last fluent speaker of Wappo, who died in 1990, *sonoma* meant "abandoned camping place."

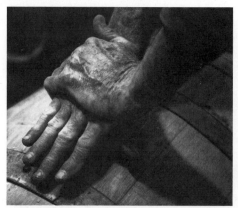

A winemaker's hands tell the story of painstaking work. Here, Don Van Staaveren, who helped his wife, the winemaker Margo Van Staaveren, create the famous Chateau St. Jean cabernet blend called Cinq Cépages.

inland are warmer. But overall, what makes Sonoma Sonoma is its pendulum-like climate of warm days and cool nights, the classic scenario for grapes with the potential to mature evenly and fully.

Sonoma County is not known for one or two grape varieties in the way Napa is renowned for cabernet sauvignon, or Amador County is noted for zinfandel. Instead, Sonoma's size and generally propitious climate, coupled with its highly variable topography and changes in altitude, mean that many different varieties do well here—in fact, fifty different grapes are grown in the region. Which place they are grown in, of course, is the key. Over the past two decades, Sonoma's viticultural areas—like viticultural areas throughout much of California—have become increasingly specialized as vintners understand the fine points of matching grape variety to site. Today, Alexander Valley, a warm interior valley, is prized for its soft cabernet sauvignons; and the county's cooler coastal areas, such as Russian River Valley and Sonoma Coast, are known for what, in great years, can be elegantly complex pinot noirs, as well as chardonnays; and no one would dispute that Dry Creek Valley is one of California's centers for zinfandel.

According to some historians, Sonoma's first vineyards were not planted by Spaniards but by Russian fishermen who, around the beginning of the nineteenth century, hunted otters and seals and established a community on the coast near Fort Ross (said to be derived from their name for their homeland—Rossiya).

By 1820, the Spanish were in on the act. Franciscan fathers planted vineyards surrounding their northernmost mission, the Mission San Francisco Solano, which today still stands in the town of Sonoma. The missions were eventually appropriated by the Mexican government (Mexico won its independence and laid claim to California in the Mexican War of Independence in 1821), but in just over two decades, in 1846, the whole of California was annexed by the United States and made a state in 1850. During this time of political instability, cuttings from Sonoma's vines were planted throughout northern California.

But Sonoma's role as the cradle of northern viticulture was to be even more solidly established once Agoston Haraszthy (HARASS-thee), the "Father of the California Wine Industry," arrived on the scene. Haraszthy—a cross between Indiana Jones, James Bond, and Thomas Jefferson—was a Hungarian wheeler-dealer who made and lost his fortune multiple times. Haraszthy thought big, and in 1857 he established Buena Vista, which, with 300 acres (120 hectares) of vineyards, was the largest winery in the state at the time. One of Haraszthy's other coups was to convince the nascent California legislature to send him to Europe, where he studied viticulture, ultimately returning to Sonoma in 1861 with 100,000 French, German, Spanish, and Italian vine cuttings. Haraszthy considered Sonoma a viticultural paradise, and his promotion of it was so effective that within a few years, land prices jumped from $6 to $150 an acre as waves of French, German, and Italian winemakers moved into the region.

Among the Italians who ultimately moved into Sonoma were a couple of brothers who, after reading a book on winemaking borrowed from the public library, went on to build America's best-known and largest wine brand—E. & J. Gallo. As poor, hardworking young men coming of age at the end of Prohibition,

THE KNIGHT OF KNIGHTS VALLEY

Next door to Sonoma's Alexander Valley is Knights Valley, which has its own knight, Sir Peter Michael. One of England's early tech entrepreneurs, Michael founded Micro Consultants Group and UEI Plc, as well as Cosworth Engineering. In 1972, he opened shop in California's Silicon Valley, founding Quantel, a digital special effects company, whose product Paintbox revolutionized television and film graphics. While in Silicon Valley, Michael fell in love with California, ultimately buying 600 acres of land in Knights Valley in 1982 and establishing his namesake winery. In 1989, Michael was knighted by Queen Elizabeth II, joining the ranks of former president George Bush, Hollywood director Steven Spielberg, and software tycoon Bill Gates. The winery, tucked up into the steep, twisting, volcanic canyons on the western face of Mount St. Helena, has developed a cult following for its six expensive but immaculately precise and complex vineyard-designated chardonnays, all of which are considered among the most extraordinary in California, and all of which have French names—Belle Côte ("Beautiful Slope"), Mon Plaisir ("My Pleasure"), La Carrière ("The Quarry"), Ma Belle-Fille ("My Daughter-in-Law"), Cuvée Indigène ("Indigenous Blend"), and Point Rouge ("Red Dot"). The winery's main Bordeaux-style red blend, Les Pavots ("The Poppies"), is often mistaken for a Napa Valley cabernet because of its depth, complexity, and structure.

Ernest and Julio Gallo began their winery in the farm town of Modesto, in California's hot Central Valley. Early on, however, the brothers became convinced that Sonoma was where the state's best wines would eventually be made. Year by year, they bought increasing amounts of Sonoma grapes to use as top-flight blending material in their regular wines. By the time the Gallos launched their expensive, ultrapremium, small-production wines in 1993 (a $60 cabernet and a $30 chardonnay; extraordinary prices at the time), they owned 4,000 acres (1,600 hectares) in Sonoma.

Sonoma County's long history lives on today in the old vineyards to be found there. Sonoma, along with the Sierra Foothills, is home to more old vineyards than any other wine region in California. Such vineyards are extremely special and historically important, for they were planted with clones of grapes—especially clones of zinfandel—that have, as a result of more than a century of natural adaptation, developed their own personalities and unique flavors.

SONOMA COUNTY AVAS

Of the sixteen AVAs within Sonoma, the most important are Alexander Valley; Russian River Valley (within which are the AVAs Green Valley and Chalk Hill); Dry Creek Valley; Sonoma Coast (inside of which is the AVA Fort Ross-Seaview); and Sonoma Valley (with its smaller AVA Sonoma Mountain). Carneros (which straddles Sonoma and Napa counties) is addressed on page 705.

Alexander Valley, at the northern end of Sonoma County, is a long, warm, inland corridor of vines. If you arrived there for the first time around 3:00 p.m. on a summer afternoon, you'd swear the valley was one of the hotter places in northern California. But you'd be right only until twilight. As night approaches, the valley cools down considerably, thanks to the Russian River (which runs through the valley) and the fog that snakes its way up and down the river's basin. Generally, the fog wallows along the river until it is burned off by the strong morning sun. This is cabernet sauvignon territory, although some powerful,

WHEN YOU VISIT . . . SONOMA

BEFITTING ITS NICKNAME as California's "Provence," Sonoma County is full of small towns that sell local cheeses, olive oils, honey, fruits, and vegetables. In particular, don't miss both Healdsburg and Sonoma, wonderful historic towns built around charming squares filled with boutiques and great small restaurants like The Girl & the Fig, a Sonoma must.

THE WINERIES OF SONOMA are not neatly lined up along a single main road, but instead are spread all over the county, so count on following lots of twisting country roads. Reservations at wineries are suggested.

TO GET A GREAT understanding of the impact of viticulture on wine flavor, visit the Benziger Family Winery, which has what is possibly the state's best tour geared specifically to biodynamic viticulture.

speaking, these regions are quite cool (parts of both are less than 10 miles/16 kilometers from the Pacific Ocean), and as a result, pinot noir and chardonnay are the prominent grape varieties.

Pinot noir, of course, is difficult, moody, delicious. But despite the grape's irascible nature, the pinots from this part of Sonoma can have extraordinary balance and complexity, as one sip of Williams Selyem, Kosta Browne, DuMol, or Rochioli—all Russian River pinots to die for—will attest. As for chardonnay, very good versions abound here, and those from Williams Selyem and Lewis can be spellbinding. Finally, while the Russian River Valley isn't famous for sauvignon blanc, two of the best sauvignon blancs in the state come from here: Merry Edwards and Rochioli.

Pinot noir and chardonnay are king and queen in Russian River Valley, together making up a whopping 70 percent of all plantings. The cool climate and coastal fog that travel from the Pacific directly through the Petaluma wind gap provide an ideal climate for making distinct, expressive wines. Indeed, once the evening fog rolls in, the air temperature in Russian River Valley can drop 35° to 40°F (20° to 22°C). This natural air conditioning slows ripening and lengthens the growing season by as much as 20 percent compared to neighboring areas. The soils in Russian River Valley are varied, but the most prized is Goldridge—a fine, sandy loam with excellent drainage and low soil fertility. The central part of the region contains clay, and the river benchlands are alluvial soil.

full-bodied chardonnays are also made here, including Stonestreet and Chateau St. Jean's Belle Terre Vineyard chardonnay. Among the wineries that make top cabernet sauvignons from Alexander Valley are Silver Oak (which also makes cabernet sauvignon in Napa Valley), Lancaster Estate, Jordan, and for good value, Geyser Peak.

After flowing down through Alexander Valley, the Russian River makes a few hairpin turns and then starts flowing westward through the valley that takes its name. Most of Russian River Valley and the smaller viticultural area inside it, Green Valley, is the opposite of Alexander Valley. Generally

Given so much high-quality pinot noir and chardonnay, plus the region's cool temperature, it comes as no surprise that some of Sonoma County's finest sparkling wines, including the two best, those from J Vineyards and Winery and Iron Horse, are also made from Russian River or Green Valley grapes.

Among the top wineries making wines from the Russian River Valley and Green Valley are Davis Bynum, Joseph Swan, Merry Edwards, Iron Horse, Lewis, Paul Hobbs, Rochioli, Kistler, Kosta Browne, Marimar Estate, DeLoach, DuMOL, and Williams Selyem.

Perhaps the most charming viticultural area of all in Sonoma County is Dry Creek Valley. Time seems to have stood still here. The gently rolling, blond hills are dotted with old, gnarled vines (there are many old vineyards) that lift their twisted black arms skyward as though they were imploring heaven. Due west of Alexander Valley, Dry Creek Valley is a zinfandel paradise. Other wines are made here—including some good cabernets and Rhône blends—but zinfandel is the variety through which the earth speaks most compellingly. Some Dry Creek zinfandels are big and meaty, others, soft and graceful. What the best of them share is a sensual richness of flavor that can be irresistible. Among the Dry Creek producers to look for: A. Rafanelli, Seghesio, Mauritson, and Ridge.

Sonoma's largest appellation (750 square miles/1,940 square kilometers), but the one least planted with vineyards, is Sonoma Coast, which stretches south from Mendocino all the way to just north of San Francisco, and from the Pacific coastline inland for 40 miles (64 kilometers) at its widest point. Importantly, several prominent, small vintners opposed the boundaries of this AVA, saying that it was too large to be meaningful. They then formed an association called West Sonoma Coast Vintners, made up of wineries within what they call the "true" Sonoma Coast, an area west of local Highway 16, from the town of Petaluma north to Annapolis. Here, on the edge of the Pacific Ocean, some of the coolest (and best) vineyards

have an ocean view, although many sit on rocky hillsides above the fog line—a critical fact, for this close to the ocean, it's important to catch every possible ray of sun if grapes are to ripen. Even so, Sonoma Coast viticulture is risky. As a result of the ocean's proximity, there's twice as much rainfall here as in other parts of Sonoma.

Once grazing land buffeted by high winds, the western part of Sonoma Coast was historically thought to be too cold for grapes. But in the 1990s and 2000s, several pioneers in the region—Mike Bohan (Bohan Ranch), David Hirsch (Hirsch Vineyards), Ted Lemon (Littorai), Burt Williams (Williams Selyem), Steve Kistler (Kistler Vineyards), Greg La Follette (then at Flowers), Ehren Jordan (Failla), and Andy Peay (Peay Vineyards), among others, began planting pinot noir and chardonnay, with beautiful results. Today, syrah is also planted here, and those wines can be stunning and packed with spice.

Within Sonoma Coast is the especially prestigious, small AVA of Fort Ross-Seaview, a high-altitude coastal area that's home to some of Sonoma's best wineries, including Peay, Hirsch, and Flowers. In addition, the top wineries Failla, Marcassin, Peter Michael, and Martinelli all have vineyards here.

Finally, the AVA Sonoma Valley and its smaller AVA Sonoma Mountain are in the southern part of Sonoma County, edged up against the Mayacamas Mountains. This is where viticulture in northern California began. Sonoma Valley is anything but your conventional valley. The topography, much of it spread over the foothills of the Mayacamas Mountains, rises and dips over knolls and glens with such fanciful names as Valley of the Moon and Glen Ellen. Sonoma Valley is a wonderful mishmash, both geographically and climatically. Given the total variability of the region, many different varieties of grapes are grown here and made into a scrumptious grab bag of wines. Among the best things to taste are the structured, complex cabernets from Laurel Glen, the zinfandels from Ridge, the pinot noirs from Hanzell, and the chardonnays from Kistler.

The Sonoma Wines to Know

WHITES

SCRIBE

RIESLING | SONOMA

100% riesling

The number of great rieslings in California could charitably be counted on two hands, leading many wine professionals to conclude that the Golden State just isn't very golden when it comes to riesling. That certainly was my opinion, too. Until I tasted Scribe. Here is a bone-dry riesling of restraint, elegance, and purity, recalling the dry rieslings of Australia. How the three young men who started Scribe packed this Sonoma wine with such Audrey Hepburn–like grace is a mystery, but they did. (Don't miss their elegant pinot noir, either.)

HANZELL

CHARDONNAY | SONOMA VALLEY

100% chardonnay

Founded in 1953 by Ambassador James Zellerbach (who helped craft the Marshall Plan for Europe after World War II), Hanzell has been a Sonoma blue-chip estate for decades. The chardonnays have special renown—and deservedly so. They are not modern in style—no obvious oak, heavy butter, or discernible sweetness. Instead, the wine is one beautiful sweep of cream and minerals, seamlessly stitched together. The wine's enticing choreography starts quietly, then builds with luscious intensity. I can't resist thinking of this as Sonoma's version of a Puligny-Montrachet.

PETER MICHAEL WINERY

CHARDONNAY | MON PLAISIR | KNIGHTS VALLEY

100% chardonnay

Peter Michael has a stellar reputation for its six separate chardonnays, each from a different vineyard, the most lovely of which is often the Mon Plaisir (French for "my pleasure"). Although, I would never pass up a glass of La Carrière or Belle Côte, its sisters. In top years Mon Plaisir is hauntingly elegant and seamless, with rich, high-definition fruit. A chardonnay of exquisite style.

REDS

FAILLA

PINOT NOIR | HIRSCH VINEYARDS | SONOMA COAST

100% pinot noir

Business partners Ehren Jordan and Anne-Marie Failla (FAY-la), owners of Failla winery, make a handful of exquisite pinot noirs from high-elevation, ocean-air-cooled vineyards along the "true" Sonoma Coast. These are wines of purity and pinpoint elegance, with mouthwatering juiciness. (This graceful pinot noir from the Hirsch Vineyards is a knockout, and a favorite.) Neither Jordan, whose degrees are in art history and classical architecture, nor Failla, whose background is in banking, have formal credentials in winemaking. But they appear to have something even better—a genius for their craft.

WILLIAMS SELYEM

PINOT NOIR | EASTSIDE ROAD NEIGHBORS | RUSSIAN RIVER VALLEY

100% pinot noir

I've followed Williams Selyem from its early days, when Burt Williams and Ed Selyem—down-home, seemingly run-of-the-mill guys—were making a few hundred cases of decidedly not run-of-the-mill pinot noir (and astounding the pinot noir universe in the process), to the winery's purchase by John and Kathe Dyson in 1998. For a while then, Williams Selyem lost its way. But for the past half decade the winery (now making fourteen pinot noirs) is back in top form. Evidence: this Eastside Road Neighbors pinot, a long, structured, sensual, nicely sweaty red, laced with spicy notes. When you drink this pinot, its flavors just keep coming at you like waves on the beach. ("Eastside Road Neighbors" refers to the four vineyards along Eastside Road in the Russian River Valley, from which the grapes are sourced.) The winery also makes a delicious chardonnay—the unoaked one—that's as fresh as a cold-moving mountain stream.

ROCHIOLI

PINOT NOIR | RESERVE | RUSSIAN RIVER VALLEY

100% pinot noir

Generally one of the most massive, saturated, and intense pinot noirs in Sonoma, Rochioli's reserve, with its opulent, dark, almost brooding berry flavors and utterly supple texture, can be a mind-blower. The Rochioli family has been growing grapes in Sonoma since the 1930s, but it wasn't until the 1980s that they began making their own wines. The grapes for this wine come from the family's West Block vineyard—about 500 yards (460 meters) from the Russian River—as well as from their Sweetwater Vineyard, named for the many natural springs in the area.

RADIO-COTEAU

SYRAH | LAS COLINAS | SONOMA COAST

100% syrah

Every time I drink Radio-Coteau, I picture—what else?—an old-style radio, and indeed, with Las Colinas ("the hill"), the volume dial is turned on very high. There's a gorgeousness to this syrah, and its vivid, spiced and peppery raspberry character is intense. Of course, the wine has richness and superb density, but it's the way the flavor appears to float, without weight, that's magical. This is always one of the best syrahs in California. The name Radio-Coteau, by the way, is an expression from the northern Rhône region of France that literally means "broadcasting from the hillside," and when used colloquially, means "word of mouth."

A. RAFANELLI

ZINFANDEL | DRY CREEK VALLEY

Mostly zinfandel with a touch of petite sirah

The Rafanelli family's zinfandels have a way, over time, of making you crave them. The best are deep, generous, totally alive with flavor, and have a sensual softness that you could lose yourself in. Yet despite their obvious textural appeal, these are zinfandels of structure and ageworthiness. The Rafanellis own zinfandel vineyards that have been in existence for close to a century.

RIDGE

ZINFANDEL | PONZO | RUSSIAN RIVER VALLEY

Approximately 95% zinfandel, 5% petite sirah

Zinfandel is compelling for many reasons—but one of them is not elegance, not usually. But with Ponzo, Ridge (a winery that makes twelve separate zinfandels) has achieved the nearly impossible—a wine of exquisite beauty, dimension, and structure. This is a zinfandel that soars with vivid strawberry, cranberry, and spice flavors, a zinfandel that has complex herb and savory notes. It's a bit like drinking Thanksgiving. Ponzo is a reference to Bob Ponzo, the owner of Ponzo Vineyard, who has proven that a so-called warm-climate grape like zinfandel can be magically refined when grown in a slightly cooler place, like the Russian River Valley.

RIDGE 2011
PONZO
ZINFANDEL

97% ZINFANDEL, 3% PETITE SIRAH   SONOMA COUNTY
RUSSIAN RIVER VALLEY   14.1% ALCOHOL BY VOLUME
PRODUCED AND BOTTLED BY RIDGE VINEYARDS   BW 4798
650 LYTTON SPRINGS RD, HEALDSBURG, CALIFORNIA 95448

SILVER OAK

CABERNET SAUVIGNON | ALEXANDER VALLEY

100% cabernet sauvignon

Although the winery itself is located in Napa Valley, Silver Oak makes two different, famous cabernet sauvignons, one from Napa Valley (the more structured) and the other from its vineyards in Sonoma's Alexander Valley (possibly a shade more plump and hedonistic). Immensely popular and stamped with lots of vanilla (thanks to its aging in American oak), the Alexander Valley cabernet is captivating, full of energy, and easy to love. Year in and year out, the texture of this cabernet is as irresistible as homemade jam that's just been taken off the stove.

SILVER OAK
2009
Alexander Valley Cabernet Sauvignon

CHATEAU ST. JEAN

CINQ CÉPAGES | SONOMA COUNTY

Differing percentages each year of cabernet sauvignon, merlot, cabernet franc, petit verdot, and malbec

Cinq Cépages (French for "five grape varieties") is so big that I'm often tempted to dismiss it as too much. But then, like some huge, adorable sheepdog that keeps putting its nose in your hand, it just won't go away. For all of its ripeness and power, the wine fills the palate and moves with great waves of fruit, spice, and briaryness. It is a slam-dunk kind of cabernet and one that would meet filet mignon head on. Chateau St. Jean, founded in 1973 near the tiny town of Kenwood, is one of the most impressive estates in Sonoma. The 1920s-era château on the property (once a private family home) is on the National Trust for Historic Preservation. Cinq Cépages, and all of Chateau St. Jean's distinctive wines, have been made for the past thirty-three-plus years by Margo Van Staaveren.

CINQ
CÉPAGES

CLASSICALLY CRAFTED TO
HONOR FIVE TRADITIONAL
GRAPE VARIETALS, THIS
BORDEAUX-STYLE WINE BLENDS
RICH TEXTURE WITH THE
ELEGANCE OF SONOMA

CHATEAU ST JEAN.
SONOMA COUNTY

The old village of Mendocino in Mendocino County was once a small whaling port. Today it is a very low-key artists' hamlet.

MENDOCINO

California's two most northern wine regions, Mendocino and Lake County, are just north of Sonoma and Napa counties, but they are light-years away in temperament and style. The vast, ravishing wilderness here, and tranquil, almost reckless beauty is the California of a century ago. Rolling mountains covered in golden grasses and wild oats alternate with immense stands of giant redwoods. In Mendocino, more than a million acres (more than 400,000 hectares) of forest stand majestically amid the vine-covered, sun-dappled hills. Orchards and ranches are sprinkled over the landscape. On the coast, the windswept town of Mendocino is an artists' hamlet. Mendocino has the largest percentage of organic vineyards of any county in California—nearly 30 percent are certified by the California Certified Organic

The word *mendocino* is a diminutive of de Mendoza, the name of one of the earliest Spanish explorers to come ashore in Mendocino, in the late sixteenth century.

AMERICA'S FINEST BRANDY

In 1982, American Ansley Coale and Frenchman Hubert Germain-Robin founded the artisanal distillery Germain-Robin near the town of Ukiah, in Mendocino. Today, Germain-Robin's brandies are considered the best brandies made in the United States and have, in multiple blind tastings, repeatedly bested a host of Cognacs.

To make these brandies, Hubert Germain-Robin, a master Cognac distiller whose family has produced Cognac since 1782, uses an antique alembic still. Each year, he hand-distills eighty barrels of brandy from such premium grapes as pinot noir and sauvignon blanc (in Cognac and elsewhere in Europe, brandies are usually distilled from lesser grape varieties). Of the five brandies Germain-Robin makes, the most stunning is the XO Reserve, a brandy so smooth, elegant, and lush it can leave you speechless.

LAKE COUNTY

Taking its name from Clear Lake (the largest natural lake in California), Lake County is smaller, drier, and less diverse than Mendocino. There are 8,400 acres (3,400 hectares) of vineyard in Lake County, but just over thirty wineries, most of which focus on relatively inexpensive cabernet sauvignons and sauvignon blancs that are often just simple and serviceable. On the other hand, this is where stunning bargains can be found—like Six Sigma's Cuvée Diamond Mine, a delicious blend of cabernet sauvignon and tempranillo that tastes like it ought to cost a whole lot more than it does. Other wineries have paid close attention to the deals that can be made here. Indeed, Lake County is primarily a provider of grapes to a number of huge wineries, including Beringer, Sutter Home, and Kendall-Jackson (which began here).

Lake County's first important vineyards were cultivated by the enterprising English actress Lillie Langtry, who planted the hillsides of her remote estate in the 1880s, intending to make what she hoped would become "the greatest claret in California." The vineyards ultimately became a part of the winery called Guenoc, now known as Langtry Estate & Vineyard. The other notable Lake County winery, Steele Wines, is owned by Jed Steele, a well-known and highly respected winemaker who, as the winemaker at Kendall-Jackson in the 1980s and early 1990s, established the Kendall-Jackson style of soft, round, easy-drinking chardonnay. Under four different labels, including Steele and Shooting Star, Steele makes some fifty different wines from varieties as diverse as aligoté and counoise, as well as exciting, well-priced old-vine zinfandels.

Farmers—and countless others are organic but not certified.

Mendocino's jagged, almost menacing coastline has been carved out over eons by icy, dark-blue waters. Farther inland, in the middle of Lake County, the grand body of water known as Clear Lake is the largest natural lake in California. On any given day in these two regions you're more likely to see a whale, mountain lion, or rattlesnake than someone in a business suit. Indeed, when the sixties ended in San Francisco, some "flower children" simply dropped out of city life and moved north to the backwoods of Mendocino (today, besides grapes, marijuana is a popular crop). In this section, I'll focus on Mendocino, the more significant of the two wine regions. Lake County is addressed in the box above.

The first small wineries in Mendocino were established in the 1850s by failed prospectors turned farmers, in the wake of the

Mendocino's simple beauty remains unspoiled. A large percentage of vineyards here are farmed organically.

California's giant redwoods—a state treasure. Many of Mendocino's best vineyard areas are surrounded by these majestic trees, which can reach 367 feet (112 meters) in height and have a width of 22 feet (7 meters) at the base.

WHEN YOU VISIT . . . MENDOCINO

BESIDES BEING HOME to a slew of laid-back wineries, Mendocino in particular is full of zany things to do. You may want to crack, slurp, and sip your way through the Mendocino Crab and Wine Days festival (in January), check out the whale festival (usually in March, when the whales are running off the coast), taste through the self-proclaimed world's largest salmon barbecue (in July), take in the Paul Bunyan parade (on Labor Day), or go for a vegetarian lunch at the City of Ten Thousand Buddhas, the largest Buddhist monastery in California. For a full calendar of events, contact the Fort Bragg Mendocino Coast Chamber of Commerce.

Gold Rush. But by the end of Prohibition, virtually every winery had disappeared, and pear orchards or nut trees stood where vineyards had once flourished. The two counties, so rugged and remote, were not quick to be reborn as wine regions. As of 1967, there was only one winery in Mendocino (Parducci), even though the wine business was beginning to take off in both Napa and Sonoma. The next year, however, proved to be a turning point. In 1968, Mendocino's Fetzer Vineyards was founded by lumber executive Barney Fetzer. Fetzer's growth was meteoric. During the decade of the 1980s, ten of Barney Fetzer's eleven children built the family winery into one of the largest in California. Although Fetzer Vineyards is now owned by Chile's huge wine firm Concha y Toro, the Fetzer family continues to hold prime vineyard land in Mendocino.

Thus, Mendocino became home to one of California's most technologically sophisticated large wineries. Surrounding it are some ninety smaller wineries, plus about 345 grape growers who range from modern, large-scale operators to tiny, one-man operations where the last technological innovation might well have been replacing the horse with a tractor. Today there are just over 17,000 acres (6,880 hectares) of vineyards in Mendocino, and the leading grape varieties are chardonnay and cabernet sauvignon. That said, some terrific pinot noir is beginning to be made here, too (especially in Mendocino's Anderson Valley). Mendocino is also where you'll find one of the producers of California's most stunning, complex sparkling wines—Roederer Estate—plus Germain-Robin brandy, considered the finest brandy made in the United States.

Mendocino stretches from the cool Pacific coast inland to several warmer wine valleys tucked between the coastal mountain range and the Mayacamas. The headwaters of the powerful Russian River are located here and flow down through Mendocino and much of Sonoma County before curving abruptly and spilling into the Pacific Ocean. Within Mendocino are several smaller AVAs, the most important of which is Anderson Valley.

Winter blankets Mariah Vineyards' high-elevation zinfandel vines.

ANDERSON VALLEY

Slicing like a fjord inland from the cold sea, Anderson Valley, especially its northwestern end, is one of the chilliest grape-growing areas in California. Chardonnay and pinot noir are the leading grapes, with, in particular, wineries such as Goldeneye, Baxter, Williams Selyem, Littorai, and Husch making fantastic pinots from Anderson Valley grapes. Not surprisingly, pinot and chardonnay are blended by Roederer Estate (owned by the Champagne house Louis Roederer) to make some of the raciest sparkling wines in California.

Before it bought land in Anderson Valley in 1981, the house of Louis Roederer searched for several years for the perfect sparkling wine site in California. Roederer was so convinced

that Anderson Valley was that place that it waited seven years—until its own vineyards matured—before making its first sparkler, instead of buying grapes from someplace else.

Anderson Valley's dramatic coolness means the region is also ideal for two grapes that other parts of California have largely given up on, gewürztraminer and riesling. The most hedonistic and exciting gewürztraminers and rieslings in California are made here by Navarro Vineyards.

Like Sonoma's Russian River Valley, Mendocino's cool Anderson Valley has some warm spots. High above the chilly and often foggy valley are mountain ridges directly exposed to the warm sun. The grapes for some of Mendocino's top berry-and-spice zinfandels come from vineyards here, especially Mendocino Ridge, composed of disparate mountain areas, and the first noncontiguous AVA in California.

The Mendocino and Lake County Wines to Know

SPARKLING WINE

ROEDERER ESTATE

BRUT | ANDERSON VALLEY, MENDOCINO

Approximately 60% chardonnay, 40% pinot noir

I drink this wine about once a week, and would happily drink it every day if there weren't so many other wines in the world to taste. The wine's wonderful play of creamy yet spiky textures, the apple Danish, limey flavors, and the overall impeccable focus and clarity of the wine all add up to a completely satisfying experience and one of the best ways possible to greet six o'clock after a long workday.

WHITES

LA FOLLETTE

CHARDONNAY | MANCHESTER RIDGE | MENDOCINO COUNTY

100% chardonnay

From a coastal plateau 2,000 feet (610 meters) above the adjacent Mendocino shoreline comes this beautifully elegant chardonnay with its lovely custard and crème brûlée notes, and merest hint of enticing spice. I especially love the wine's vividness—the result of a fresh, tactile backdrop of acidity. And that, in turn, probably comes from the cold Pacific breezes that cool this vineyard every day.

NAVARRO VINEYARDS

GEWÜRZTRAMINER | ANDERSON VALLEY, MENDOCINO

100% gewürztraminer

Navarro makes the most sophisticated, complex, and delicious dry gewürztraminers in California. Vintage after vintage, they are wines of remarkable clarity, precision, and pizzazz. Pears, tangerines, stones, minerals, and lychees come at you in what can only be described as a driving rainstorm of flavor. Navarro first planted gewürztraminer grapes in 1974, and has since developed a cult following for the wine it produces.

REDS

PHILLIPS HILL

PINOT NOIR | OPPENLANDER VINEYARD | MENDOCINO COUNTY

100% pinot noir

Here's a beautiful pinot noir for people who like pinot noir the old-fashioned way—earthy and graceful. And in the case of this wine, with a subtle exotic character, not unlike Darjeeling tea. Phillips Hill is owned by Toby Hill, a formally trained artist whose study of composition in the abstract eventually found its physical grounding when Hill decided to reinvent himself by making wine. The Oppenlander Vineyard is just 10 miles (16 kilometers) from the ocean.

GOLDENEYE

PINOT NOIR | ANDERSON VALLEY, MENDOCINO

100% pinot noir

Goldeneye, owned by the same partners that own Napa Valley's Duckhorn Vineyards, began making pinot noir in Anderson Valley in 1997, and they quickly set about making a style that's different from that of most of their neighbors. This is not delicate, ethereally light pinot noir, but rather, dense, saturated pinot with a texture that's thick and velvety, with spicy, wood-smoke aromas and flavors. To me, this is pinot noir for the wintertime, when there's a fire in the fireplace and a roast in the oven.

LANGTRY

PETITE SIRAH | SERPENTINE MEADOW | GUENOC VALLEY, LAKE COUNTY

100% petite sirah

Langtry's petite sirah smells like chocolate truffles dusted in dirt—it's a great smell! Black in color, dense in flavor, packed with fruit, gripped by tannin and bold in intent, this wine is classic petite sirah. Serpentine Meadow—a vineyard at 1,000 feet (305 meters) in elevation—is just a tiny part of the 21,000-acre (8,500-hectare) Langtry Estate.

STEELE

PERSONA NON GRATA | LAKE COUNTY

50% syrah, about 20% each of zinfandel and petite sirah,
plus barbera and petit verdot

As one might imagine, Persona Non Grata has something to say—
even something to prove. This wine soars all over the palate. It's
bold and rugged and the flavors come fast and dense, with no elegance whatsoever—just a dagger of intense fruit. When I first
tasted this wine I thought of the miners during the Gold Rush,
and thought that this was the kind of wine they might have drunk.
But on reflection, I think the miners would have felt they'd died
and gone to heaven if they had something this good lying around
ready to gulp down. The back label of this wine acknowledges that,
despite the quality of the grapes grown in Lake County, the region
remains unknown. Steele writes, "In drinking and enjoying this
wine, you will be helping us to shed the chains that have for so
long bound us in the role of 'Persona Non Grata.'"

SWEET WINE

NAVARRO VINEYARDS

MUSCAT BLANC | CLUSTER SELECT LATE HARVEST | ANDERSON VALLEY, MENDOCINO

100% muscat blanc à petits grains

This may well be the most lovely dessert wine made in the United
States. It's not super syrupy, not opulent, not oozing with honey.
It's more like the Audrey Hepburn of dessert wines, the liquid version of pure, pristine, sweet fresh fruit. I love the sense of minerals
in this wine and the way it lifts off the palate with zesty tangerine
and lime flavors. A sensational bottle to have at the end of a meal
with nothing more than some soft cheese.

THE SIERRA FOOTHILLS

Until the mid-nineteenth century, California's wine industry was centered around Los Angeles. But in 1849, with the discovery of gold near the town of Coloma, in the Sierra Nevada foothills, the wine industry took off in a new direction. Mining camps sprang up everywhere, and in their wake, so did vineyards and small wineries begun mostly by immigrants seeking their fortunes. By the 1860s, there were nearly 200,000 vines growing in the "gold counties" of northern California, and wineries there outnumbered those in other parts of the north. These were the first wineries in the state to forgo the common mission grape in favor of better varieties, such as zinfandel.

In time, the gold supply diminished and eventually dried up. The population shrank. Winemaking and grape growing slowed considerably and then, following the double blows of phylloxera and Prohibition, virtually disappeared in some areas. By the end of World War II, the Sierra Foothills were home mostly to ghost wineries and abandoned vineyards. Only one winery managed to remain continuously in operation, the D'Agostini Winery, now the Sobon Estate, in Amador County.

A renaissance began in the 1970s, and today there are some one hundred wineries in the Sierra Foothills and more than 6,400 acres (2,600 hectares) planted with vines.

The region known as the Sierra Foothills is a strip of eight remote counties roughly stacked one on top of the next, from north to south. California's capital, Sacramento, is to the west, the Nevada border to the east. Of the eight counties, the two most important are El Dorado and Amador, ruggedly beautiful regions where the spirit of the Old West and a strong sense of individualism live on.

El Dorado, a mountainous region with mostly volcanic and granitic soils, has some of the highest-elevation vineyards in California, including what is thought to be the highest of all, Madroña Vineyards, at an elevation of

> El Dorado County took its name from a mythical being— El Dorado, the golden one. According to legend, Spanish conquistadores searched for El Dorado believing he would lead them to a place of gold and riches.

3,000 feet (900 meters). Thanks to the breezes that sweep down off the 10,000-foot (3,000-meter) peaks of the Sierra Nevada, nights here are very cool. Amador County, warmer than El Dorado, is spread over lower foothills composed of granite with some sandy loam. Amador first came onto the modern scene in the 1970s with gutsy, teeth-staining, King Kong–size zinfandels that lots of red wine drinkers immediately fell in love with. The intensely flavored grapes came from very old (often pre-Prohibition) vineyards that had been kept in production as a source of fruit for home winemakers. One of the first wineries to realize the value of these old Amador vineyards was Sutter Home, in Napa Valley. In 1971, the winery released its first Amador County zinfandel, a stunning wine made from grapes from the now highly regarded Deaver Ranch, in the Shenandoah Valley.

Most wineries of the Sierra Foothills are not yet well known, and many deserve to be, given the quality and distinct personality of the best wines. This is changing quickly, however. Domaine de la Terre Rouge, Montevina, Skinner, and Boeger, for example, have already developed followings nationally, and there are a half dozen more wineries poised to join them.

A remarkable number of grape varieties (more than thirty) are planted in the Sierra Foothills, but the best wines are almost invariably from red Mediterranean varieties. In particular, the zinfandels, barberas, syrahs, mourvèdres, and Rhône blends have a robust boldness that can be irresistible.

THE NORTH CENTRAL COAST:
SANTA CRUZ MOUNTAINS, MONTEREY, CHALONE, MOUNT HARLAN, CARMEL VALLEY, & SANTA LUCIA HIGHLANDS

Monterey County and those American Viticultural Areas north of it, up to San Francisco Bay, are often collectively referred to as the North Central Coast. The area includes the important wine regions of Santa Cruz Mountains, Chalone, Mount Harlan, Carmel Valley, Santa Lucia Highlands, and, of course, Monterey. These AVAs range in size from quite large (Monterey has about 40,000 acres/16,187 hectares of grapevines) to diminutive (Chalone has 300 acres/120 hectares of grapevines), and each has a distinct personality.

For more than forty-five years, winemaker Paul Draper has made one of California's most prestigious and age-worthy cabernet sauvignon–based wines—Ridge Monte Bello—from the Santa Cruz Mountains.

SANTA CRUZ MOUNTAINS

South of San Francisco, about an hour and a half's drive along California's iconic Highway 101, is the funky university town of Santa Cruz, a coastal haven for aging hippies and ardent surfers. Although it's right next door to Silicon Valley, Santa Cruz is, experientially speaking, about as far away as you can get. Here, the mountain air has a thrillingly sharp, close-to-the-ocean freshness to it. Ancient redwood forests soar up into a cerulean sky. The mountains themselves have been torn and thrust into beautifully rugged formations by the perilous San Andreas Fault, which lies below them.

Thanks to the tangle of mountain crevices, canyons, hilltops, craggy slopes, knolls, and valleys, plus varying altitudes and orientations to the sun, the vineyards of the Santa Cruz Mountains can have widely different mesoclimates. In general, the higher vineyards (some are more than 2,000 feet/600 meters in elevation) and those facing the Pacific Ocean are considerably cooler than lower vineyards and those facing east, toward the warmer interior valleys.

The individuality of the vineyards explains why the region is known, seeming paradoxically, not only for cool-climate varieties like pinot noir and chardonnay but also for those that like more warmth, including zinfandel and cabernet sauvignon. What all vines here do share is the beneficial struggle of growing in the region's thin, stony mountain soil.

Because vineyards here are neither easy to farm nor high-yielding, most of the district's seventy wineries are small-production companies making personality-driven wines. Heading the list are three wineries with stellar reputations—Ridge Vineyards, Mount Eden Vineyards, and David Bruce Winery.

Indeed, Ridge would be on most wine collectors' A-lists—especially after the winery came in first in the thirty-year retrospective of the famous Judgment of Paris Tasting of 1976 (see page 671). Year in and year out, Ridge's wines are exemplary, and their cabernet sauvignons are nothing short of majestic. They possess the utterly fascinating ability to be refined yet powerful in the same split second. No wine illustrates the idea better than the hauntingly rich, explosive Ridge cabernet sauvignon from

BORN TO RHÔNE

I first met Bonny Doon's owner, Randall Grahm, a ponytailed, MIT-educated intellectual, in the mid-eighties, a couple of years after he founded his vinous "dooniverse" in Santa Cruz. Even in the early days, Bonny Doon was full of idiosyncratic wines and zany ways of showcasing them. What other winery has owned two large spaceships? (Bonny Doon's current flying machine is suspended from the ceiling of the tasting room.)

Grahm's love of wine took hold in Los Angeles in the 1970s, while he worked as a wine shop sales clerk (mostly sweeping floors). With financial backing from his family, he eventually created Bonny Doon, initially conceived as a winery devoted to pinot noir. But within a decade, Grahm had come under the spell of Rhône varieties such as syrah, grenache, marsanne, and roussanne. Among his first wines was the inaugural vintage (1984) of Le Cigare Volant, a sexy, syrah-based red that catapulted Grahm to fame in California winemaking circles. It was an enological foot in the door, and Grahm (thereafter dubbed the "Rhone Ranger") went on to make dozens of successful wines from dozens of varieties that had theretofore been largely overlooked by other California winemakers.

the Monte Bello vineyard, first planted in the Santa Cruz Mountains in 1855 and purchased by Ridge in 1959.

David Bruce Winery has a cult following for its pinot noirs, which are pinots to the core—unpredictable (sometimes great, sometimes not so), but always full of character. And the estate chardonnays from Mount Eden Vineyards have almost mythic stature. The vineyards, on the crest of a mountain, were planted with chardonnay in 1948.

The super-creative winery known as Bonny Doon Vineyard is also located here, in a hamlet named Bonny Doon. In the 1980s and 1990s, the erudite (if madcap) owner/winemaker Randall Grahm was the first winemaker to produce a string of successful fine wines from obscure or never-before-tried-in-California grape varieties, and his impact on the California wine industry was profound.

MONTEREY COUNTY

Descending southeast from the vast arc of Monterey Bay lies Monterey County, the largest appellation within the northern part of the Central Coast. There are about 40,000 acres (16,200 hectares) of vines here, plus thousands upon thousands of acres of vegetables in the fertile garden known as the Salinas Valley. (Indeed, the Salinas Valley, nicknamed the "lettuce capital of the world," is also where more than 50 percent of all the United States' broccoli, strawberries, mushrooms, spinach, artichokes, and chile peppers are grown.)

Although there were Franciscan missions in Monterey in the eighteenth century, the area did not really emerge as a wine region until the 1960s and 1970s, when extensive urban development in Livermore and Santa Clara, plus rising land prices in Sonoma and Napa, caused many wineries to look elsewhere for suitable vineyard land. Monterey, an easily accessible, agricultural coastal region, was just waiting to be tapped.

The southern part of Monterey can be extremely hot, but the northern part of the county is a chilly tunnel for cold winds that whip in off the whitecapped waters of Monterey Bay (home to otters, seals, and migrating whales). The severity of the winds can be seen in the permanently bowed trees, many of which are stripped of growth on their ocean-facing side. While a little bit of wind is

The irrepressible Gary Pisoni, owner of Pisoni Vineyards in the Santa Lucia Highlands. Pisoni expanded the idea of just how luscious and rich California pinot noir could be.

generally good for vines (it cools them and helps guard against mildew and rot), extreme wind can cause the cells responsible for photosynthesis to shut down, inhibiting the ripening of the grapes. In a region that's already cool, anything that further constrains ripening is no blessing. Thus, the top vintners have had to be extremely careful in selecting protected vineyard sites. Even then, Monterey's cabernet sauvignons often have a green tobacco note to them, the result of borderline ripeness.

There are just under forty wineries in Monterey, and a considerable number of wineries located elsewhere buy Monterey grapes. Chardonnay and pinot noir are the dominant grapes in the county, especially in the cooler northern part, where wines of real character can be made. Caymus and Morgan are just two of the best producers making lively Monterey wines.

SANTA LUCIA HIGHLANDS, CHALONE, MOUNT HARLAN, AND CARMEL VALLEY

Within Monterey County and its neighbor, San Benito County, are several small AVAs,

the most significant of which are Santa Lucia Highlands, Chalone, Mount Harlan, and Carmel Valley.

In the past decade, Santa Lucia Highlands has come on as a stellar place for pinot noir—and not just any pinot noir, but rich, bold, flashy, scrumptious pinot. (Some Burgundy-loving arch-traditionalists say Santa Lucia Highlands' pinot noirs are, in fact, too rich and dense.) The nearly 6,000 acres (2,400 hectares) of vineyards here undulate along a single impressive southeastern-facing bank of the Santa Lucia mountain range. As you drive south through the Salinas Valley, the vineyards are easy to see, folded up into crevices 1,000 to 2,000 feet (300 to 600 meters) above the valley below, and gently exposed to cold fog that sweeps down from Monterey Bay morning and night. For all of its proximity to the sea, this is a very dry place (often no more than 15 inches/38 centimeters of rainfall a year) and the well-drained, sandy loam and decomposed granite soils have been carried down canyons in the hillsides on alluvial fans for centuries.

The name to know here is Gary—there are two of them, local childhood friends who reportedly shared tractors as toddlers. Gary Pisoni is the owner of Pisoni Vineyards and in many ways the ambassador of the Highlands. (In a family debate, to convince his farmer father to expand beyond growing vegetables and plant a vineyard, Pisoni challenged, "Have you ever been to a $250 lettuce tasting?" His father relented.) Pisoni's original 5 acres (2 hectares) of pinot noir vines, planted in 1982, are rumored to be "Samsonite cuttings" (that is, brought to the U.S. surreptiously in a suitcase) from a "famous domaine in Vosne-Romanée, Burgundy." Gary Franscioni (the other Gary) owns vineyards with Pisoni (Rosella's Vineyard, and one called simply Gary's), as well as a winery known as ROAR, which makes phenomenally complex, riveting pinot noirs that sell out instantaneously. Besides Pisoni Vineyards and ROAR, there are dozens of small producers making fantastic pinot noirs here, as well as wineries located elsewhere that make pinot noir from Santa Lucia Highlands grapes.

WHEN YOU VISIT . . . THE NORTH CENTRAL COAST

THE WINERIES of the North Central Coast are spread out over a large and diverse area. Several of the most beautiful are tucked into remote enclaves in the coastal mountains. They are not on a tourist route, so calling ahead for an appointment is a must.

IF MONEY IS NO OBJECT, don't miss an overnight stay, or at least dinner, at either the Highlands Inn, on Highland Drive in Carmel, or the Ventana Inn, on Highway 1 in Big Sur. Two of the most spectacular, secluded hotels on California's coast, each has stunning views of the Pacific Ocean.

In addition to pinot noir, Santa Lucia Highlands is known for chardonnay as well as impressive syrah. Many top wineries in other parts of California buy grapes from Santa Lucia Highlands, including Kosta Browne, Siduri, Peter Michael, Belle Glos, Capiaux, Copain, and others.

Chalone and Mount Harlan are two very tiny AVAs; indeed, Mount Harlan has but one winery: Calera. The Chalone appellation (the name comes from the Native Americans who lived there) is home to Chalone Vineyard. Both Chalone Vineyard and the Calera Wine Company were founded by individuals maniacally possessed by the conviction that chalky limestone (a major component in the best soils of Burgundy) was essential for world-class pinot noir and chardonnay.

In the case of Chalone Vineyard, that individual was Curtis Tamm, a Burgundian who, in 1919, found limestone in the Gavilan mountain range and planted a vineyard. This first Chalone Vineyard is the oldest still producing in Monterey County. Chalone today is owned by the drinks giant Diageo.

In the late 1960s and early 1970s, Yale- and Oxford-educated Josh Jensen also went looking for limestone in California. He, too, found it in the Gavilan mountain range where, on Mount Harlan, he established the Calera Wine Company in 1975. Calera's six pinot noirs, named after people who have been important to Jensen—Jensen (his father), Mills, Reed, Selleck, Ryan, and deVilliers—are handcrafted from single vineyards and made in what can only be described as a purist's manner. Like most of the best pinots, they are variable and capricious: Sometimes they're stunning, sometimes not quite so.

Carmel Valley is named for the postcard-quaint tourist town of Carmel nearby, and the Carmel River watershed. There are only a handful of wineries spread over this mountainous area, including, notably, Bernardus and Heller Estate. Most of the better vineyards sit on warm, east-facing benches and ridges. Unlike the rest of Monterey, which is known for white wine, this is prime cabernet sauvignon and merlot territory.

WHITES

CALERA

VIOGNIER | MT. HARLAN

100% viognier

Viognier is a tough-go in California. Too often the wine tastes like spongy orange Halloween candy. But since 1975, Calera has made one of the few excellent viogniers in the state. Long, distinctive, and elegant, its beautiful aromas are pure and floral—not cosmetic-y. There's also a lovely sense of tangerine juice and pith. But what's especially distinctive are the edgy, tactile hints of white pepper and minerality that give the wine dynamism. Calera, one of the blue chips of the North Central Coast, also has an illustrious track record with pinot noir.

DAVID BRUCE

CHARDONNAY | SANTA CRUZ MOUNTAINS

100% chardonnay

High in the Santa Cruz Mountains, David Bruce makes Meursault-like chardonnays. With their deep golden, nutty, luscious flavors, they are reminiscent of those Turkish pastries where layers of phyllo are drizzled with honey and walnuts. And as with good white Burgundy, the opulence and creaminess is beautifully balanced—in this case by a fresh line of crisp, appley flavor and little sparks of spice. David Bruce winery was founded in the early 1960s by David Bruce, a young doctor who had just completed his residency. Bruce purchased 40 acres (16 hectares) of remote land in the Santa Cruz Mountains and cleared it, by hand, himself. Bruce's chardonnay was one of the original eleven California wines to be included in the famous Judgment of Paris Tasting of 1976 (see page 671). The winery is also known for its stellar pinot noirs.

REDS

ROAR

PINOT NOIR | SANTA LUCIA HIGHLANDS

100% pinot noir

Saying ROAR to a pinot noir lover is a little like saying "Ferrari" to a person who loves cars. Some of the most luscious, complex, and rich pinots in the state are made by this small producer. Besides the regular (delicious) Santa Lucia bottling, there are two other, especially highly sought-after ROARs—Gary's Vineyard and, a fraction more expensive, Pisoni Vineyard. Both are phenomenal wines. Gary's Vineyard lifts off the palate like a rocket launcher and is infused with attractive peat and cranberry flavors (a great pinot for Scotch lovers). The Pisoni Vineyard pinot noir is dense, long, and almost muscular for pinot noir. But its tiny explosions of spice keep it fascinating and alive on the palate. ROAR gets its name from the sound of the Monterey Bay winds roaring through the winery's vineyards.

CALERA

PINOT NOIR | MILLS | MT. HARLAN

100% pinot noir

Calera makes six single-vineyard pinot noirs from vineyards on limestone soil in the heart of the Gavilan Mountains. Each year they are some of the most ethereal, delicate, refined pinots in California. Picking a favorite is next to impossible, for what they all possess is the seamless beauty of elegant fruit that drives pinot noir lovers mad. Calera's pinots are not superfruity, and they don't jump out of the glass with richness. Indeed, in a blind tasting, most professionals confuse them with subtle Burgundies for their contemplative character.

BONNY DOON VINEYARD

LE CIGARE VOLANT | RESERVE | CENTRAL COAST

Approximately 30% syrah, 30% grenache, 20% mourvèdre, 20% cinsaut

Randall Grahm's first (1984) and leading Rhône wine, Le Cigare Volant, is modeled after the wines of Châteauneuf-du-Pape and takes its name from a real law on that city's books prohibiting flying saucers—or "flying cigars," as they're called in France—from landing in the region's vineyards. Dark and savory, Le Cigare Volant is not a massive wine nor even a wine that's "Californian" in style. Rather, it's an homage to the delicious Rhône gestalt of flavors—wild herbs, roasted game, leather, salt, white pepper, and a wonderful gush of cherry preserves smack in the center. There is a "regular" Le Cigare Volant, but the Reserve—aged in large glass jars known as carboys in English and called, more beautifully, *bonbonnes* in French—is more compelling, more vivid, and the wine you want.

RIDGE 2011
MONTE BELLO®

MONTE BELLO VINEYARD 88% CABERNET SAUVIGNON, 8% MERLOT, 4% CABERNET FRANC
SANTA CRUZ MOUNTAINS   12.8% ALCOHOL BY VOLUME
GROWN, PRODUCED & BOTTLED BY RIDGE VINEYARDS
18100 MONTE BELLO ROAD, P. O. BOX 1810, CUPERTINO, CA 95015

RIDGE

MONTE BELLO | SANTA CRUZ MOUNTAINS

Approximately 70% cabernet sauvignon, with the remainder merlot and petit verdot

As structured, powerful, and impeccably balanced as a First Growth Bordeaux, the Ridge Monte Bello cabernet sauvignons are majestic wines. Opening one from a great vintage when it's young is almost criminal, for while the inky, dense, young version will knock you out with its flavor impact, older ones are mesmerizing. With a decade or more of age, Monte Bello unfurls into a hauntingly complex wine that is quite simply one of the greatest cabernets in the United States. For anyone who has tasted an older Monte Bello, it will come as no surprise that this was the wine that placed first in the thirty-year reenactment of the Judgment of Paris Tasting. Ridge was founded in 1959 by four Stanford Research Institute engineers, who still own it; the winery's famous winemaker, Paul Draper, is still at the helm after forty years.

LIVERMORE VALLEY

East and slightly south of San Francisco is one of California's most historically influential wine regions, the small, 15-mile-long-(24-kilometer) Livermore Valley. Some of the state's most important wineries were begun here over a century ago, including Wente, Concannon, and Cresta Blanca (now gone). Atypically for valleys in California, the Livermore Valley runs east-west. Although it can be brightly sunny and as hot as blazes during the day, the valley becomes an enormous wind tunnel by late afternoon. Temperatures can drop by a full 50°F (28°C) at night. The combination of bright light, heat, and strong winds, followed by nighttime cooling, plus the valley's shallow soil, is reminiscent of parts of southern France.

The current generations of Wentes: Phillip, Carolyn, Karl, Christine, and Eric. The Wente family brought some of the first chardonnay to California from France in 1912.

Among the top wineries here, Wente, in particular, has made remarkable contributions not solely to Livermore Valley but to the California wine industry as a whole—especially concerning chardonnay. Most of the chardonnay grapes grown in the state today, for example, are Wente clones or derived from Wente clones, including California's most planted chardonnay clone, known as clone 4 (technically, Foundation Plant Sciences Clone 04). The Wente clones, as well as other clones derived from these, were the result of painstaking genetic research that Ernest Wente conducted over his lifetime. Son of the winery's founder, Carl H. Wente, Ernest began experimenting with chardonnay in 1912, when the grape was all but unheard of in California and only a minuscule amount was planted, most of it in Livermore. Ernest imported his chardonnay from the nursery at the University of

> **Most of the sauvignon blanc in California came from cuttings brought initially to Livermore Valley from Bordeaux's famous Château d'Yquem.**

Montepellier, France, still considered one of the leading viticultural schools in France. Today Wente continues to make wonderful chardonnays in a variety of styles, from full and buttery to a fresh, unoaked style.

Livermore's other leading historic winery is Concannon, built in 1883 (the same year as Wente) by Irish immigrant and devout Catholic James Concannon. During his lifetime, Joseph, James Concannon's son, sent a barrel of the Concannon muscat de Frontignan to the pope every five years. Joseph's brother Jim was the first to introduce a varietal petite sirah in California, in 1961. Concannon is now owned by The Wine Group, the third largest wine company in the U.S. and makers of Franzia wine-in-a-box.

The Wentes and Concannons were helped significantly by the ambitions of another prominent Livermore figure, newspaper journalist turned winemaker Charles Wetmore. Just before founding Cresta Blanca in 1882, Wetmore persuaded the California legislature to establish the state viticultural commission. As the commission's first president and CEO, Wetmore headed straight for Europe, where he obtained cuttings from prestigious sources, including cuttings of sauvignon blanc and sémillon from no less than Bordeaux's Château d'Yquem. Those cuttings became the plant material for vineyards in Livermore, which, in turn, provided it to other vineyards all over the state. Thus, the leading clone of sauvignon blanc now grown in California (called clone 1) is Wetmore's acquisition from Château d'Yquem.

Early on, Livermore Valley thrived not only because of the dynamism of its first vintners and its suitability for viticulture, but also because of its close proximity to San Francisco. Sadly, the latter would also prove—almost—to be the valley's undoing. Housing divisions, industrial parks, and an endless stream of urban development throughout the 1960s, 1970s, and 1980s gobbled up Livermore's vineyards with frightening finality. By the late 1980s, thousands of acres of grapes had simply disappeared. The valley has initiated an innovative land-use comeback, and there are now some fifty wineries in the region.

Among the top Livermore wineries are Wente and Concannon, along with Steven Kent, McGrail, Kalin, Fenestra, Page Mill, and Darcie Kent.

PASO ROBLES AND YORK MOUNTAIN

About halfway between San Francisco and Los Angeles (but light-years away from the cosmopolitan way of life) is Paso Robles, with its rustic, country western feel. (If you've never seen a horse drinking beer in a bar—surely a seminal experience for anyone who appreciates beverages—you'll want to mark your calendar for the annual Pioneer Day celebration at the Pine Street Saloon in October.) Here, along California's quiet mid-Central Coast, are 26,000 acres (10,500 hectares) of Paso Robles vineyards and more than 230 wineries.

The AVA is the most dramatic exception to the generally cool climates of the middle and southern Central Coast. A generally very warm expanse of sun-baked, oak-studded hills (the original name, *El Paso de Robles,* means "the pass of oaks" in Spanish), Paso Robles is shielded from the cool, maritime influence of the Pacific Ocean by the almost solid curtain of the Santa Lucia Range on the AVA's western side. That said, producers here are quick to point out whether their vineyards are on the slightly cooler and hillier western side of Paso Robles, closest to the ocean (the "west side"—considered the better part of the region), or the flatter, hotter eastern part.

TABLAS CREEK

Tablas Creek Vineyard was established in 1989, when the Perrin family of Château de Beaucastel, in Châteauneuf-du-Pape, France, and Robert Hass, famed U.S. importer and founder of Vineyard Brands, purchased 120 acres (50 hectares) in Paso Robles after a four-year search throughout California for the optimal site to grow Rhône varieties. In 1990, the partners began the lengthy process of importing vines from the Château de Beaucastel estate, including several clones of mourvèdre, grenache noir, syrah, counoise, roussanne, viognier, marsanne, grenache blanc, and picpoul blanc. After a three-year, USDA-mandated indexing process to ensure the vines were virus-free, the vines were ready to be multiplied (eventually reaching some 200,000 annually) and planted at Tablas Creek, both for the winery's own use and to be sold to others. California producers who have planted Tablas Creek clonal material include Ridge, Bonny Doon, Qupé, Zaca Mesa, and Stolpman, among many others.

EDNA VALLEY AND ARROYO GRANDE

At 35 square miles and 67 square miles (91 square kilometers and 174 square kilometers), respectively, Edna Valley and Arroyo Grande may be small viticultural areas, but they are pinot noir and chardonnay edens. Located about 40 miles (64 kilometers) south of Paso Robles, both areas are close to the sea and profoundly influenced by its cool, damp breezes. These coastal effects temper Edna Valley's climate enough to create one of the longest growing seasons of any wine region in California. Arroyo Grande is even cooler, being blanketed in fog for most of the day (which begins to explain why pinot noir thrives here).

Edna Valley was one of the first areas where Spanish missionaries planted the mission grape, but the region lay neglected for centuries until the Goss family planted vineyards in 1973, and started Chamisal Vineyards. Arroyo Grande was similarly brought out of obscurity in the second half of the twentieth century, thanks to Maison Deutz, the California subsidiary of the Champagne house Deutz, which purchased land in Arroyo Grande in 1982, but sadly no longer makes wine there.

Today, the most well-known pinot noirs (and they are sensational) are from Chamisal and Laetitia, and the best chardonnays are made by Edna Valley Vineyards and Talley Vineyards. In addition, using grapes from Edna Valley, tiny Alban Vineyards makes one of the most sensual viogniers in California.

The significant variation between hot daytime and nighttime temperatures, often as great as 50°F (28°C), saves the best wines from being simply overripe and overwrought. In addition, many of the top wines are the result of vines planted in calcareous clays (limestones), which, in particular, can be found on the west side of Paso Robles, closer toward the ocean.

For years, the top wineries of Paso Robles felt that the region needed to be divided into smaller AVAs that would reflect the overall region's diversity. In 2014, that's exactly what happened. The Bureau of Tax and Trade approved the largest appellation proposal in U.S. history and established eleven new appellations within Paso Robles: Adelaida District, Creston District, El Pomar District, Paso Robles Estrella District, Paso Robles Geneseo District, Paso Robles Highlands District, Paso Robles Willow Creek District, San Juan Creek, San Miguel District, Santa Margarita Ranch, and the Templeton Gap District. It will undoubtedly be many years before the distinctive characteristics of the wines from these AVAs are known.

The rocky, limestone-laced vineyards of Tablas Creek in Paso Robles.

A winter sunset in the dry-farmed, wide-spaced, head-pruned zinfandel vineyards of Dusi Vineyard. The Dusi family has been farming zinfandel grapes in Paso Robles since 1924.

As for grapes, the most widely planted varieties in Paso Robles are cabernet sauvignon, merlot, syrah, zinfandel, and chardonnay (in that order). Indeed, some of the syrah planted in California is thought to be descended from syrah vines planted by Paso Robles's Eberle Winery in 1975. Later, in the late 1990s, the nursery at Tablas Creek was the source of 200,000 cuttings a year of Rhône varieties, much of which was syrah.

Although the Central Coast has a reputation for expansive vineyards yielding high volumes of grapes, nearly two-thirds of wineries in Paso Robles produce fewer than five thousand cases annually. Additionally, 95 percent of wineries are family owned and operated.

Among the top wineries of Paso Robles are Saxum, Turley, L'Aventure, and Daou Vineyards. Additionally, Ridge Vineyards (located in the Santa Cruz Mountains) makes one of its twelve exquisite zinfandels from Paso Robles grapes; and Andrew Murray Vineyards (located in the Santa Ynez Valley) makes devastatingly good grenache from Paso.

Just west of Paso Robles, on the eastern side of the Santa Lucia Range, the York Mountain AVA—the smallest in the mid-Central Coast—sits more than 1,500 feet (460 meters) high in the mountains, near a deep gash in the range known as the Templeton Gap. This cool-climate viticultural area is only 7 miles (11 kilometers) from the Pacific Ocean. Although today there are only 50 acres (20 hectares) of vineyards, the first winery on the Central Coast was established here. Originally known as Ascension Winery and later as York Mountain Winery, it was built by trailblazer Andrew Jackson York in the late nineteenth century using bricks that were hand-formed and fired onsite. Alas, the building was devastated by the 2003 Paso Robles earthquake, but it is being rebuilt by its new owner, Epoch Winery.

BIEN NACIDO

In the early 1980s, when I went to Santa Barbara wine country for the first time (amazingly enough, on assignment for *Playboy* magazine), Bien Nacido was already famous. At the time, it was highly unusual for an American vineyard to be well known, especially one in the Santa Maria Valley of Santa Barbara County (itself not well known then). But the name Bien Nacido, which means "well born," said it all. Indeed, it seemed like a majority of the greatest wines coming out of Santa Barbara County all had the words *Bien Nacido Vineyards* on their labels. The sloped vineyard, with panoramic views facing southwest, had been planted in 1973 by a multigenerational farming family named Miller. It was a huge vineyard—600 acres (240 hectares) of mostly chardonnay, pinot noir, and syrah—divided into small blocks that were named alphabetically. Winemakers, then and now, contracted for the fruit by specific *rows* of grapes. In 2007, after nearly thirty-five years of custom farming, the family decided to make their own wines as well. Bien Nacido pinot noir from Bien Nacido Vineyards (eight rows from Q block) is classically *bien nacido*: elegant and sumptuous.

THE SOUTH CENTRAL COAST:

SANTA BARBARA COUNTY, SANTA MARIA VALLEY, SANTA YNEZ VALLEY, STA. RITA HILLS, BALLARD CANYON, AND HAPPY CANYON

About an hour and a half's drive north of Los Angeles, the American Viticultural Area Santa Barbara County contains two large AVAs within it: Santa Maria Valley and Santa Ynez Valley. Telescoping down further within the Santa Ynez Valley, there are three smaller AVAs: Sta. Rita Hills, Ballard Canyon, and Happy Canyon. Collectively, these are called the South Central Coast, and they are among the most dynamic wine regions in the state. The sheer concentration of supertalented, independently minded winemakers here is astounding, from the wise old guard (men like Richard Sanford, Jim Clendenen, and Bob Lindquist) to younger winemakers crafting some of the most delicious, enticing wines in the state (Greg Brewer, Jenne Lee Bonaccorsi, Paul Lato, Steve Clifton, Gavin Chanin, Matt Murphy, Adam Lee, Sashi Moorman, and dozens of others).

Unlike the North Central Coast, where the viticultural areas are distinctly different, the South Central Coast's AVAs share an overriding style and character. As a result, I'll talk about them jointly, while noting some climatic differences.

In a state that is never at a loss for beauty, the Santa Ynez and Santa Maria valleys may be the most alluring wine regions. In the spring and fall, the sunlight has an unreal clarity to it, as if the light itself were looking at you. The hills are curved in feminine roundness. Immense mesas spread out magnificently, then stop and fall into the scarred arroyos that split them. Ancient oaks, with their tangled arms, seem twisted in their own embrace. Everywhere, cattle and horses graze. Fields of strawberries go on forever. Within an hour, you're so mellow that drinking really good pinot noir strikes you as a constitutional right, not to mention a necessary part of your life's work.

Paradoxically, the South Central Coast is one of the oldest wine regions in California—and, at the same time, among the hippest and newest. Spanish missions and vineyards were strung like beads on a necklace here in

THE WINE GHETTO

In distance, Santa Barbara County may be the closest wine region to Hollywood. But in style, you couldn't get farther away than the decidedly reverse-chic "wine ghetto." Located in the town of Lompoc, in the Sobhani Industrial Park, the ghetto is a confab of small, hip tasting rooms and wine production facilities. The first winemaker to set up shop here was Rick Longoria, who did so in 1998. Longoria didn't have the money to build an impressive winery (or any winery at all, for that matter), and he figured the industrial park's proximity to his vineyards would be advantageous. Today, the blue and white industrial buildings house more than twenty brands, including Evening Land, Samsara, Fiddlehead, Stolpman, and, of course, Longoria. The laid-back atmosphere, exuberant camaraderie, world-class wines, and ethno food trucks all add up to what has become, against the odds, a not-to-be-missed wine destination.

Jim Clendenen, one of the pioneers and most influential winemakers of the South Central Coast.

the eighteenth century. As of the early 1980s, the South Central Coast had become a haven for tiny, imaginative wine companies on shoestring budgets, headed by maverick winemakers who intuitively understood the region's potential (wineries like Sanford, Au Bon Climat, Qupé, Foxen, and Zaca Mesa, for example). By the late 1980s, however, so many delicious wines were coming out of the region that big companies like Robert Mondavi, Beringer, and Kendall-Jackson moved in and snapped up huge tracts of vineyard land at comparatively rock-bottom prices. It seemed like the indie character of the South Central Coast would be lost in a sea of corporate winemaking.

But that has not happened. If anything, these valleys continue to be a hotbed of young energy, originality, and a fervor to make great wine. Indeed, and not so surprisingly, some of the newest, tiny wine companies have been started not by trained winemakers but by sommeliers who taught themselves winemaking and for whom the South Central Coast is the place to be.

Despite a southerly latitude, parts of the South Central Coast are by far among the coolest wine areas in the state. The reason: the direction in which the main valleys lie. During California's tumultuous geologic past, most of the state's mountain ranges were formed in a north/south direction, tearing open valleys that also ran essentially north to south (think of Napa and Sonoma as well as the huge Central Valley, for example). Unusually for California, however, the wine areas of Santa Ynez and Santa Maria were formed so that the valleys run basically east to west, enabling them to become direct conduits for fog and cold offshore winds that barrel inland from the Pacific Ocean, making summertime temperatures hover around the low 70s (around 21°C). The soils here have also been influenced by the Pacific Ocean. Most are sedimentary soils left from ancient seabeds, now often covered by many feet of wind-blown sand. Indeed, in the far western parts of the valleys—in an area such as Sta. Rita Hills, for example—the soils are often fossilized, diatom-rich sand dunes that have been weathered by centuries of age.

Within an hour of being in the South Central Coast, you're so mellow that drinking really good pinot noir strikes you as a constitutional right, not to mention a necessary part of your life's work.

Of the two main regions, Santa Maria is the most northern and Santa Ynez is just southeast of Santa Maria. Within Santa Ynez, from west (coldest climate) to east (warmest climate) are: Sta. Rita Hills, Ballard Canyon, and Happy Canyon.

Sitting at the far western end, the small cluster of hills known as the Sta. Rita Hills was considered far too cold for grape growing until 1970, when maverick vintners Richard Sanford and his partner Michael Benedict decided to take the risk and plant pinot noir there. The vineyard they established—known as Sanford & Benedict—went on to become one of the most legendary vineyards in California, and proof that the Sta. Rita Hills, one of the coldest parts of the South Central Coast, was capable of producing pinot noirs with an elegance that rivaled Burgundy. Today, some fifty wineries are located in Sta. Rita Hills or make wine (primarily pinot noir and chardonnay) from vineyards here.

As you travel east, inland and farther from the ocean, you come to Ballard Canyon and eventually Happy Canyon. Both are known for some devastatingly good syrahs, more on which in a moment. Plus, in Happy Canyon, good cabernet sauvignons are now being made, along with wonderful sauvignon blancs (try the delicious sauvignons from Grassini Vineyards and from Margerum, especially the one called Sibarite). Finally, a piece of history that cannot go unmentioned: The evocatively titled Happy Canyon got its name because it was once a moonshine-making site for local dude ranches. It's also where Hollywood directors filmed feel-good westerns like *The Lone Ranger*. (And yes, the stallion Silver—as in "hi-ho Silver!"—lived here.)

WHEN YOU VISIT . . . THE SOUTH CENTRAL COAST

SANTAS YNEZ, MARIA, AND RITA are among the most charming, laid-back-but-sophisticated wine regions in the state, and hospitality here runs deep. Since the countryside itself is drop-dead beautiful, wandering around the countryside among wineries is a simply fantastic experience. Or, wander around in town. Santa Barbara County has a number of small towns virtually devoted to tasting. In Los Olivos, for example, the thirty plus tasting rooms can keep you busy for hours.

THE RESTAURANT not to be missed in this part of wine country is The Hitching Post II in Buellton, a no-frills local hangout (made famous in the movie *Sideways* and usually full of winemakers) where the specialty is grilled red meats.

As for grapes and the wines made from them, chardonnay makes up about 40 percent of the grapes grown in the Santa Maria Valley and Santa Ynez Valley. To me, the wines made from them are some of the most distinct, precise, and complex chardonnays in the state. Chardonnays like those from Diatom, Lafond, Sandhi, Au Bon Climat and its sister winery, Clendenen Family Vineyards, Melville Estate, and Paul Lato, for example, have pristine flavors thanks to their through-line of vibrating acidity. Yet, they are lushly textured at the same time. In this regard, they are like Burgundian Premier Crus. There's also a fantastic sense of exotic fruit about them (quince, bergamot, kaffir lime) plus a very apparent minerality or salinity—what longtime winemaker Rick Longoria calls a "chalky, rocky,

Many of California's top wine regions surround Catholic missions founded in the 1700s. From San Diego and Santa Barbara in the south to Sonoma in the north, the missions were strung out like pearls on a necklace, each a one-day horseback ride from the next.

salty" character, perhaps from the region's sandy seabed soils replete with marine fossils.

As for pinot noir, the South Central Coast makes, as I've said, some of the most elegant pinots in the state. They are absolutely driven by vividly bright fruit and spice flavors—a pinot lover looking just for earthiness won't find much in these wines. (I think of them as tasting like tiny wild woodland strawberries in the forest, not the forest itself.) And although they do not taste tart, South Central Coast pinot noirs have a structure that comes from cool fruit with lots of acid. As a result, the wines have a precise, silky, tight-knit character, almost as if the fruit is spring-loaded. Then, once you sip, all that fruit explodes into aromas and flavors. Many of these pinots benefit from very early budbreak, then a very long, gentle growing season (considered one of the core requirements for complexity in wine). Moreover, the absence

of heat spikes means the grapes retain their lovely aromatics and crisp acidity, giving them bright flavors. Says winemaker Greg Brewer, "Ripening in California is like a big and rapid heartbeat; except down here. Here, the heartbeat is slow and long."

Finally, a word about syrah. The South Central Coast may well be syrah's ultimate California home—that singular place where it consistently makes uncommonly good wine. For now, and for sure, this is true: Syrah here is huge, meaty, thick, and wild. The vivid, almost blueberry syrup-like character is slashed with spiciness and something like wild lavender. They are syrahs evocative of blood and strength. Indeed, one of the top syrah producers here is Sanguis—the Latin word for "blood" or "strength." Also fantastic and worth seeking out: Jonata, Refugio Ranch, The Ojai Vineyard, Stolpman, Margerum, Andrew Murray, Qupé, Sans Liege, and Zotovich.

WHITES

DIATOM

CHARDONNAY | MIYA | STA. RITA HILLS

100% chardonnay

After I tasted this wine for the first time (in 2012; it was the 2010 vintage), my view of California chardonnay changed forever. Frankly, I didn't think California's chardonnays would ever broach this level of exquisiteness. But Diatom's Miya (the name means "Beautiful Night") is as pristine and exact and pent up as a wave about to break in the early morning sea. Avant-garde winemaker Greg Brewer says he is motivated by "a Japanese aesthetic," "negative space," "the movement of the restricted voice," and a "dread for the explicit." This is not conventional winespeak, to be sure. But few words are needed anyway. The wine, in this case, actually does say it all.

MELVILLE

CHARDONNAY | INOX | STA. RITA HILLS

100% chardonnay

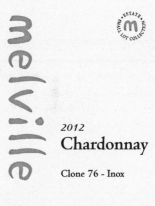

Over the past decade, Melville has quietly become one of the most exciting wineries on the South Central Coast. Indeed, the winery makes such soulful, sensual pinot noirs, it's almost a crime to write about anything else. But Melville's Inox (the name means "stainless-steel" in French) is an amazingly lush chardonnay—every molecule of which is based simply on the purity of the fruit (the wine is not exposed to oak barrels). Of course, dozens of chardonnays in California are now made in the "unoaked" style—but none of them comes close to the complexity and excellence of this one.

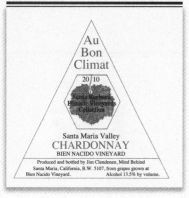

AU BON CLIMAT

CHARDONNAY | BIEN NACIDO VINEYARD | SANTA MARIA VALLEY

100% chardonnay

When he began his winery in 1982, Jim Clendenen, the owner and winemaker of Au Bon Climat, was an irreverent, irascible nonconformist with fierce opinions and colossal talent. Now, all these years later, he's exactly the same, with one added trait—he's inspired and mentored more young winemakers than perhaps any other winemaker in southern California. As such, his artistic impact on the region and its wines has been profound. As a young man, Clendenen immersed himself in the artisanal winemaking of Burgundy. Today, his wines still evoke that early love affair with Burgundian chardonnay and pinot noir. This chardonnay from the famed Bien Nacido Vineyard, for example, is as voluptuous, creamy, nutty, lees-y, and earthy as can be, and yet it's vibrant, precise, complex, and imbued with a pulsing force of acidity (hello, Bâtard-Montrachet). And for bigger-is-always-better drinkers, this wine's sister, Au Bon Climat's Nuits-Blanches au Bouge, steps it up just a notch. I asked Jim what Nuits-Blanches au Bouge meant, and here was his answer: "A *nuits-blanches* (white night) is a night without sleeping in French slang. A *bouge*, in the French dictionary, is a pig warren or den, or in slang, a brothel. So a Nuits-Blanches au Bouge is a sleepless passage in a decadent environment. Oenologically speaking, it is a multiple-*entendres* of nuanced but daunting complexity."

REDS

BREWER-CLIFTON

PINOT NOIR | MOUNT CARMEL | STA. RITA HILLS

100% pinot noir

Greg Brewer and Steve Clifton are, like many business partners, very different men. But when it comes to winemaking, both are poets, able to find the deep and the meaningful. Somehow, they always coax out an extra sense of purity, richness, and rhythm that then defines their wines. This Mount Carmel pinot noir, for example, is a bottomless pond of kirschlike fruit, framed by echoes of spice, violets, and sea salt, plus a wonderful umami character reminiscent of the savoriness of beef juices. All these hedonic flavors are carried on slow waves of sensation, giving the wine an unreal sense of length. The small Mount Carmel vineyard, right in the heart of Sta. Rita Hills, was first planted in 1992.

SIDURI

PINOT NOIR | CLOS PEPE VINEYARD | STA. RITA HILLS

100% pinot noir

Siduri is a tiny enterprise, which, in certain years and despite its size, makes an astounding twenty-five different pinot noirs. I love this one in particular, from the Clos Pepe Vineyard, named for the first vineyard Stephen and Catherine Pepe ever planted, which was in their backyard. Full of personality and refinement, it is a study in contrasts. In the same sip, it is silky yet charged with firecrackers of spice. Long swaths of earthiness are interspersed with flecks of espresso-like bitterness. There's a coolness here (like menthol) at the same time that the wine is infused with warm tones (like sun-baked raspberries).

SANFORD

PINOT NOIR | SANFORD & BENEDICT | STA. RITA HILLS

100% pinot noir

Year after year, the freshness, purity, beauty, lift, and sheer exquisiteness of this wine continue to amaze wine professionals and pinot noir lovers alike, for in many ways, this was the pinot noir that first inspired a whole generation of southern California winemakers. Established in 1971 by maverick vintners Richard Sanford and Michael Benedict, the Sanford & Benedict vineyard was the first vineyard in what today is the Sta. Rita Hills AVA. Countless advice at the time warned the two men that they were out of their minds, for the region was considered too close to the Pacific Ocean and therefore too cold to grow grapes. A few years later, Richard Sanford established his eponymous winery and began making pinot noir with the Sanford & Benedict grapes. Today, Sanford Winery is owned by the Terlato Wine Company, which continues to carefully make this crown jewel of the South Central Coast.

JONATA

SYRAH | LA SANGRE DE JONATA | SANTA YNEZ VALLEY

97% syrah, 3% viognier

Jonata is a great example of the bold, distinctive, artisanal syrahs coming out of Santa Ynez. With its flavors reminiscent of meat juices, charcuterie, and exotic spices, this wine clearly pays homage to Côte-Rôtie. Yet, with all of the beautiful blueberry and blackberry fruit, it is also definitively Californian. The complexity here is almost a kind of moodiness, as the wine explores the edges of bitterness, chalk, lavender, and violets. Jonata (pronounced ho-NA-ta; it's the Chumash Indian word for "live oak") comes from grapes grown on a small part of a 600-acre (240-hectare) ranch in Ballard Canyon. Winemaker Matt Dees has a degree in soil science, but is self-taught as a winemaker. The owner of Jonata, billionaire sports-team and real estate tycoon Stan Kroenke, also owns Napa Valley's Screaming Eagle winery, the NFL's St. Louis Rams, the NBA's Denver Nuggets, and the English soccer club Arsenal.

THE OJAI VINEYARD

SYRAH | SOLOMON HILLS VINEYARD | SANTA MARIA VALLEY

100% syrah

Syrah—unhinged. (I'm not sure how a wine can take on the character of a psychological thriller, but this one has.) The wild—almost savage—energy of flavors in this wine is mesmerizing: cedar, incense, sage, spice, and a deep, rich, red meatiness, like an oxtail stew that has simmered for hours. But as primordial as the aromas and flavors are, it's the choreography—the way this wine detonates on the palate—that leaves you most impressed. Among wine industry insiders, Adam Tolmach, the owner/winemaker of the tiny Ojai Vineyard, is considered one of the best winemakers in California.

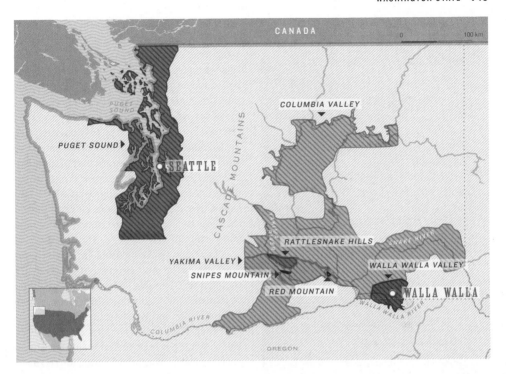

WASHINGTON STATE

ost of the world's classic grapes can grow in lots of places, but each has a kind of spiritual home—a place (or sometimes places) where that grape can ascend beyond what is merely good and be transformed into stunning wine. In the 1990s, Washington State, much to most wine drinkers' surprise, emerged as one of the great spiritual homes of cabernet sauvignon and merlot. The phenomenon was startling, for only a dozen or so years earlier most winemakers' hopes were pinned on gewürztraminer, chardonnay, and other white grapes that filled the vineyards. As it turns out, these grapes (which are still widely grown in Washington) make good wine there. But nothing like the top tier of cabernets and merlots.

By the late 1990s, with cabernet and merlot well established, two more grapes captured the imaginations of Washington wine-growers: riesling and syrah. By the late 2000s, Washington State made the best riesling in the country, and the state had become known as a hotbed of fantastic, rich, complex syrahs that were the equal of (and some would argue better than) syrah grown anywhere else in the United States.

What you notice immediately about the greatest Washington State cabernet sauvignons and merlots (or blends of the two) is the

THE QUICK SIP ON WASHINGTON STATE

WASHINGTON STATE is the second-largest wine-producing state in the United States (after California), and is known for highly structured, deeply flavored cabernet sauvignon, merlot, and syrah, as well as inspired rieslings.

WASHINGTON STATE is one of the few places in the U.S. (and indeed, in the world) where many vines grow on their own roots (not on phylloxera-tolerant rootstocks).

VIRTUALLY ALL of Washington's vineyards are in the dry, warm, eastern part of the state, separated from the rainy western part by the Cascade Range.

To the uninitiated, the idea that Washington can produce great wine seems, at first, nonsensical. After all, the state is best known for its rain—a factor that led to the rise of its famous coffeehouses (what else to do when it's pouring?), including Starbucks, which began here. However, virtually all of the state's grapes (there are more than thirty varieties) are grown not in the west, near Seattle, but in the arid, almost desertlike eastern part of the state. The massive Cascade mountain range, which divides the two areas, is so effective as a rain shield that eastern and western Washington are about as similar in appearance as Montana and Vermont.

There are thirteen AVAs in Washington State, the three most prominent of which are the gigantic Columbia Valley, and within it, the two smaller but highly thought of appellations Yakima Valley and Walla Walla Valley. Most of the other AVAs are also within the Columbia Valley AVA. They include Red Mountain, Horse Heaven Hills, Wahluke Slope, Rattlesnake Hills, Snipes Mountain, Lake Chelan, Naches Heights, and Ancient Lakes of Columbia Valley. Indeed there are only two appellations that fall outside of the Columbia Valley: Columbia Gorge, on the Oregon-Washington border (in 1805, the gorge was the route used by the Lewis and Clark Expedition to reach the Pacific), and the smallest appellation in the state and the only one on the western side of the Cascades—Puget Sound.

Although the first wine grapes were planted in Washington State by Italian and German emigrants in the 1860s and 1870s, the modern wine industry was born a hundred years later. Over the past few decades, the number of wineries in the state has increased rapidly. In 1960, Washington State had fifteen wineries; in 1995, it had eighty-eight. By 2012, there were just over 740.

The forerunners of Washington's powerful merlots and cabernets were three wines, pinot noir, grenache, and gewürztraminer, made in 1951 by a psychology professor in his basement. Humble as those wines must have been, they held a promise. Indeed, a little more than a decade later, the modern Washington wine industry began to take form. The professor,

concentration of the wines. It almost seems as though, by some magical osmosis, they've been infused with the primal, lush berryness of wild Northwest blackberries, boysenberries, raspberries, and cherries.

The high-elevation Cascade Mountains form a rain shield, insuring that the wine regions in eastern Washington State don't have Seattle's weather.

THE MOST IMPORTANT WASHINGTON STATE WINES

LEADING WINES	WINES OF NOTE
CABERNET FRANC red	FRUIT WINES MADE FROM RASPBERRIES, PEARS, AND OTHER FRUIT
CABERNET SAUVIGNON red	GEWÜRZTRAMINER white
CHARDONNAY white	LEMBERGER red
MERLOT red	MALBEC red
PINOT GRIS/PINOT GRIGIO white	SÉMILLON white
RIESLING white (dry and sweet)	SPARKLING WINES white
SAUVIGNON BLANC white	VIOGNIER white
SYRAH red	

DON'T CRY FOR ME WALLA WALLA

Wine and roses? That's already had its day(s). Wine and cheese? Been there, done that. Wine and onions? Okay, you're listening. Walla Walla Valley—the tiny wine region in southeastern Washington—is perhaps the only wine region in the world that is famous for both its delicious red wines and its delicious, jumbo-size sweet onions—24 million pounds (11 million kilograms) of which are harvested each year. Like the Vidalia from Georgia and the Maui from Hawaii, Walla Walla onions are low in sulfur (the compound that makes you cry) and so sweet they can be eaten out of hand, as you would an apple.

Dr. Lloyd Woodburne, was a home winemaker who was soon joined in his hobby by several of his university colleagues. They named themselves Associated Vintners and began making wine together. As their skills and production increased, the hobby turned serious. A commercial winery was built, and in 1967 the first wines—cabernet sauvignon, gewürztraminer, pinot noir, and riesling (then known as Johannisberg riesling)—were produced. In 1984, Associated Vintners became Columbia Winery, one of the first Washington State wineries devoted to premium wines.

Meanwhile, other wines were being produced in Washington, just as they had been for decades. Mostly they were cheap, sweet, and fortified. After Prohibition, for example, the companies Pommerelle and National Wine Company (NAWICO) made millions of gallons of such stuff from Concord and other native varieties. Pommerelle and NAWICO are now unknown names, but the company that they eventually became, after they merged, is the most well-known and largest winery in Washington State: Chateau Ste. Michelle, founded in 1965 under the name Ste. Michelle

CHATEAU STE. MICHELLE

The seventh-largest winery in the United States is also the godmother of the Washington State wine industry: Chateau Ste. Michelle. During the 1980s and 1990s, Chateau Ste. Michelle—with its considerable financial, enological, and viticultural resources—helped push Washington State into the limelight, and in the process created a market for the wines of countless top-notch small wineries like Leonetti Cellar, Cayuse, and Betz Family. Ste. Michelle, owned by the tobacco company Altria (the parent company of Philip Morris), farms more than 3,500 acres (1,400 hectares) of vineyards in the state and contracts with growers for another 17,000 acres (6,900 hectares); indeed, some 60 percent of all vineyard acreage in Washington State is devoted to grapes grown for Ste. Michelle. The winery, which produces 2 million cases a year of good to very good wine, also owns several other brands, including Columbia Crest (one of the best brands in the U.S. for inexpensive, easy-drinking, every-night wines), Northstar, Spring Valley, Col Solare (a joint venture with Italy's Piero Antinori), and Eroica (a joint venture with Germany's Dr. Loosen), plus two wineries in California's Napa Valley: Conn Creek and (famously) Stag's Leap Wine Cellars.

Vintners. Chateau Ste. Michelle immediately hired the most famous United States wine consultant of the postwar era, André Tchelistcheff. Cabernet sauvignon, pinot noir, sémillon, and grenache were the first varieties the winery produced.

For the next twenty years, the Washington State wine industry moved steadily along the quality track. Every winery, from Chateau Ste. Michelle to the smallest family-run operation, was on a steep learning curve, for Washington had almost nothing in common—climatically or geographically—with its neighbors to the south, Oregon and California. What it did share with the wine industries of these states was the discovery that the best teacher was trial and error.

THE LAND, THE GRAPES, AND THE VINEYARDS

Were it not for several cold mountain rivers—the Columbia, the Yakima, the Snake, and the Walla Walla—eastern Washington would be a desert. Rainfall here is no more than 8 inches (20 centimeters) per year on average (compared to western Washington's 48 inches/122 centimeters). But the river valleys and the irrigation they make possible have transformed the vast expanse into hauntingly beautiful rangeland, wheat fields, and orchards. Plus prime vineyards.

The dryness of the climate is only one of the factors that give Washington its distinct viticultural personality. Because of its northern latitude, the vineyards here get an average of two more hours of sun per day than vineyards in California's Sonoma County or Napa Valley. Temperatures are very warm but, again because of the latitude, not excessively hot. The extended hours of light and warmth (but not severe heat) help ripening progress evenly.

The day-to-night temperature contrast in eastern Washington can be remarkable—a difference of 50°F (28°C) or more in a single day is not uncommon. This diurnal temperature fluctuation is categorically good, for cool nights mean that grapevines can temporarily shut down and rest, thereby preserving acidity in the grapes.

Long Shadows Winery's vineyard, known as The Benches, is poised 1,400 feet (427 meters) above the grand Columbia River. The vineyard includes twenty-seven geologically created "benches" formed 20,000 years ago.

Sometimes, however, temperature drops can be lethal to vines. Brutal winters with fast-moving, subzero arctic winds are one of the most severe threats in eastern Washington. Temperatures may go from 40°F (about 4°C) to well below zero (–18°C) in a matter of a few hours. In situations such as this, water in the plants' system freezes so quickly, the vines can literally explode.

Soils in Washington are a mix of sand, silt, gravel, and volcanic ash—the result of two cataclysmic events. First, some 140 million years ago, the crashing together of the tectonic plate beneath the Pacific Ocean and the North American Plate resulted in an uplifted chain of highly pressurized volcanoes (consider Mount St. Helens) parallel to the coast. These systematically and repeatedly erupted all along the northern part of the western United States. Then, about 15 million years ago (during the last Ice Age), the repeated freezing and melting of a colossal ice dam resulted in massive floods—known as the Missoula Floods—covering the entire Columbia Basin of Washington, along with much of Oregon, Idaho, and Montana, in fast-moving water and depositing nutrient-poor sand, silt, and gravel as the water traveled toward the Pacific Ocean.

Indeed, perhaps because of the state's sandy soils and very cold winter climate, phylloxera—the deadly insect that, in the late nineteenth century, damaged most of the vineyards in the world, including those in California and Oregon—has never destroyed vineyards in Washington State (the pest has occasionally shown up for a few days at a time, probably brought in on farm equipment). As a result, 99 percent of the vineyards here are planted on their own roots, not on phylloxera-tolerant rootstock. Does that make a difference in flavor? Some winemakers believe it does, arguing that slight differences in *any* aspect of a wine's terroir affect flavor. Other winemakers disagree, saying that, in a blind tasting, no one has ever been able to differentiate wines grown on their own roots from wines grown on rootstock.

THE GRAPES OF WASHINGTON STATE

WHITES

CHARDONNAY: A major grape; a source of wines that are dependably good but rarely extraordinary.

CHENIN BLANC: A minor grape that can become a delicious or merely decent wine.

MADELEINE ANGEVINE: A very minor variety but appealing for its pleasing, offbeat floral character. Most of what is grown in the world is found in England.

MUSCAT CANELLI: A minor variety, the same as muscat blanc à petits grains. It can turn into simple but delightful sweet wines.

RIESLING: A very important grape; the top wines made from it are extraordinary, and even more modest versions can be very attractive, snappy, peachy, and minerally. It is made into dry, off-dry, and sweet wines.

SAUVIGNON BLANC: A minor grape; the top wines are appealingly fresh, clean, and herbal-tasting.

SIEGERREBE: A very minor grape, but a curiosity, grown in the Puget Sound region. It is thought to be a cross of Madeleine Angevine and gewürztraminer, bred in Germany in 1929.

REDS

CABERNET FRANC: A minor grape, but it shows potential, especially in blends with merlot and/or cabernet sauvignon.

CABERNET SAUVIGNON: A major grape capable of making powerful, rich, balanced wines with structure and depth. It is used alone and blended with merlot.

LEMBERGER: A very minor but interesting grape, traditionally grown in Germany and Austria (where it's known as blaufränkisch). Washington State has the only significant plantings in the United States.

MERLOT: A major grape and the source of many of the state's most lush, concentrated, beautifully balanced wines. It is used alone and blended with cabernet sauvignon.

SYRAH: A major grape that has achieved impressive success over the past ten years, making Washington State one of the best places in the U.S. for this variety.

As for grapes, while cabernet sauvignon, merlot, chardonnay, riesling, and syrah (in that order) clearly lead production, with cabernet franc, malbec, pinot gris, and sauvignon blanc following, winemakers here also grow tiny amounts of grapes that almost no one has ever heard of, such as Madeleine Angevine (grown mostly in England), siegerrebe (a German cross), and Lemberger (grown mostly in Germany and Austria as blaufränkisch). Despite having a name that makes marketing executives wince, Lemberger can make rich, dark, spicy reds; Madeleine Angevine makes easy-to-like, very floral white wines; and siegerrebe grows in the Puget Sound wine region, where rainfall can broach 48 inches (122 centimeters) a year.

With 43,800 acres (17,700 hectares) of grapevines, Washington State is a far smaller wine producer than California, where there are 543,000 acres (219,700 hectares) of vines. Of Washington's thirteen appellations, Columbia Valley, as we noted, is the largest. It extends over one third of the state's entire landmass—some

WHEN YOU VISIT . . . WASHINGTON STATE

A MAJORITY of Washington State's wineries are in rural eastern Washington. The Yakima Valley, for example, is about a two-and-a-half-hour drive from Seattle; Walla Walla, five hours. That said, the drive over the Cascade Mountains can in itself be an exhilarating part of the journey.

DESPITE THE FACT ABOVE, several small top wineries have tasting rooms in Woodinville, less than an hour from Seattle, and Chateau Ste. Michelle, Washington's largest winery (very much worth visiting), is also here.

FINALLY, a food lover alert: The icy bays and estuaries around Puget Sound are home to a wide variety of Pacific Northwest oysters, from the thumbnail-size Olympias to those named after the bays from which they come, such as Penn Cove, Westcott Bay, and Shoalwater Bay. Pacific Northwest oysters, generally more briny and minerally than East Coast or Southern varieties, are a perfect match for Washington State's crisp, minerally dry rieslings.

Washington wine country. Here, some of the state's most established wineries, including Hogue, are clustered fairly close together, and many other wineries buy Yakima grapes. Within Yakima Valley are three smaller AVAs: Rattlesnake Hills, Snipes Mountain, and Red Mountain.

Despite its small size, Walla Walla Valley, within Columbia Valley, boasts some of Washington's best wineries, including historic ones such as Leonetti Cellar, Woodward Canyon, and L'Ecole No 41, all of which helped put Washington State and Walla Walla on the map—as well as newer, top-notch wineries like Cayuse, Gramercy Cellars, K Vintners/Charles Smith Wines, and Long Shadows.

Finally, a word on Puget Sound, which could seem more of a curiosity than a wine region. The area, close to Seattle, spreads over islands in the Pacific Ocean and over Washington State lands that adjoin the sound itself. The climate in this western part of the state is very wet, and thus the forty-five wineries that are located here generally buy their grapes from the eastern (dry) side of the Cascades. That said, some wineries maintain a buy-local focus, growing Madeleine Angevine, siegerrebe, and pinot noir.

SOME OF THE BEST PRODUCERS OF WASHINGTON'S BIG REDS: CABERNET SAUVIGNON, MERLOT, AND SYRAH

Andrew Will Winery • Betz Family • Boudreaux Cellars • Cadence • Cayuse • Chateau Ste. Michelle • Col Solare • DeLille Cellars • Den Hoed • Doubleback • Fidelitas • Force Majeure • Gorman • Hestia • Januik • L'Ecole N° 41 • Leonetti Cellar • Long Shadows (Pirouette, Sequel) • Mark Ryan • Matthews Cellars • Owen Roe • Pepper Bridge Winery • Quilceda Creek Vintners • Rasa Vineyards • Reynvaan • Sheridan • Sleight of Hand • Sparkman • Woodward Canyon • Zero One

---

11 million acres (4.5 million hectares). The appellation is bordered on the north by the Okanagan wilderness, near Canada, on the south by Oregon (the appellation is actually shared by the two states), and on the east by the Snake River and Idaho. Almost 99 percent of the state's total production comes from this single appellation. Like large appellations in premium winegrowing areas everywhere, Columbia Valley contains smaller appellations, including Yakima Valley, Horse Heaven Hills, Walla Walla Valley, and many others.

The Yakima Valley, within Columbia Valley, is generally considered the heart of

RIESLING

POET'S LEAP

RIESLING
COLUMBIA VALLEY

WHITES

CHATEAU STE. MICHELLE AND DR. LOOSEN

RIESLING | EROICA | COLUMBIA VALLEY

100% riesling

Eroica (the name means "heroic" in Italian) is a joint venture between Washington State's Chateau Ste. Michelle and Germany's Weingut Dr. Loosen. While commonplace today, joint ventures were relatively new in 1999, when the Eroica project began, and time has proved the collaboration a huge success. Stunning nectarine and peach aromas lure you in to a flavor that's minerally and beautifully refined. Although the grapes were grown in Washington State's Columbia Valley, Eroica has the Mosel's penchant for clarity, lightness, and freshness. *Eroica* was the name Beethoven gave to his passionate Third Symphony, a musical metaphor for this wine.

POET'S LEAP

RIESLING | COLUMBIA VALLEY

100% riesling

This is wine masquerading as a butterfly. Ethereally light and lacy, it dances (hovers) on the palate with great delicacy. The aromas and flavors of pear, green apple, and orange citrus are as sheer as possible. Exquisite lightness like this is, in a sense, the spiritual side of wine, and is hard to achieve in fine wine. Poet's Leap is part of the Long Shadows portfolio (all of which are joint ventures between visionary businessman and former CEO of Chateau Ste. Michelle Allen Shoup, and notable winemakers from around the world). Poet's Leap was made by the German winemaker Armin Diel.

WOODWARD CANYON

CHARDONNAY | WASHINGTON STATE

100% chardonnay

Founded in Walla Walla in 1981 by Rick and Darcey Fugman-Small, Woodward Canyon has always been known for its well-structured reds—especially its cabernet sauvignons. But the beauty of their chardonnays is indisputable. And while many wineries make very good cabernets in Washington State, it's a rare artistic achievement to make very good chardonnay. The wine moves from stone fruit to star fruit, from the familiar to the exotic. It's lovely, balanced, and long—so long you feel like someone has thrown a stone in a pond, and you're watching the endless circles of ripples that flow from the center.

REDS

SPARKMAN

DARKNESS | SYRAH | YAKIMA VALLEY

100% syrah

The name of this wine, Darkness, says it all. Drinking it was like being in some dark, shadowy coffeehouse drinking espresso. The gaminess, the spices, the coffee and cocoa, the sense of black licorice and black pepper—it's all dark. Wines like Darkness are tailor-made for dark winter nights. Sparkman, a relative newcomer on the Washington scene, makes wines from a number of varieties, red and white. But by far its best wines are syrahs.

K VINTNERS

PHEASANT VINEYARD | WAHLUKE SLOPE

100% syrah

As animal as it gets. Every carnivorous thing you can think of seems woven together here—the fatty, cured smells of salami . . . the tantalizing, umami-rich flavors of meat juices . . . the gamy, savory, sexy flavor of roast lamb. And woven through all that are whiplashes of minerals and stones. Outrageous, almost foreboding syrah like this is more often the product of the Rhône Valley of France than it is of the New World, but K Vintners has captured it. The winery, begun in 2001 by self-taught winemaker Charles Smith (a former rock band manager), initially focused on syrah, hence the "K" in its name (*que sera, sera;* get it?). But the way I see it, K could also stand for "killer" syrah.

PRODUCED AND BOTTLED BY DeLILLE CELLARS
WOODINVILLE, WASHINGTON
750ml, RED MOUNTAIN RED WINE, Alc. 14.0% by vol.

DELILLE CELLARS

CHALEUR ESTATE | RED MOUNTAIN

Approximately 65% cabernet sauvignon, 25% merlot,
and tiny amounts of cabernet franc and petit verdot

For more than a decade, DeLille's Chaleur Estate has been one of the top Bordeaux-style blends in Washington State. The wine's refinement and structure look toward Bordeaux, but the intense cassis fruit and the creamy echo of melted chocolate speak to Washington. Best of all, and for all of its richness, the wine has lift and grace on the palate. Chaleur Estate's baby brother—known as D2—is packed with juicy, spicy black cherry flavors threaded with notes of stones, savory herbs, and sea salt.

LEONETTI CELLAR

RESERVE | WALLA WALLA

Approximately 50% cabernet sauvignon, 30% merlot,
plus cabernet franc and malbec

Founded by Gary and Nancy Figgins in 1977, on their family's farm begun in 1906, Leonetti Cellar was the first commercial winery in the then unknown appellation of Walla Walla. The quality of its initial wines was shockingly good. Now, more than three decades later, the winery continues its reputation as one of the greatest wine estates not only in Washington State but on the entire West Coast. Indeed, it was hard to choose which Leonetti wine to write about, for they are all magnificent. In the end, the Reserve won out for the sheer number of exclamation marks in the margins next to my original notes. Leonetti's Reserve is both elegant and mighty at the same time, rather like a Gothic arch that can both be exquisitely graceful and hold up the cathedral.

LONG SHADOWS

PIROUETTE | COLUMBIA VALLEY

Approximately 55% cabernet sauvignon, 25% merlot,
plus cabernet franc and malbec

This is quite simply an extraordinary wine made by some of the best wine pros in the United States. Refined, yet full of pent-up raw power, it's cabernet sauvignon at its exquisite best. The wine comes onto the palate with classic First Growth Bordeaux-like cassis flavors, then slowly unleashes itself in a torrent of savory deliciousness. The minds behind this remarkable wine are the joint-venture team of Allen Shoup (founder of Long Shadows), Agustin Huneeus Sr. (founder of Quintessa), and the remarkable Napa Valley-based winemaker Philippe Melka.

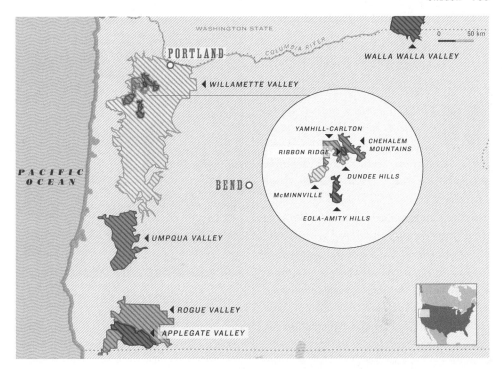

OREGON

I f Oregon had been established as a wine region during the Middle Ages, it would undoubtedly have been the work of monks, for only those with an ascetic temperament (and considerable faith) could find joy in the nail-biting, nerve-racking reality of Oregon viticulture. Growing grapes here is fraught with challenges. Sunlight and heat can be in short supply; ripening, as a result, is never a given. Rain (about 40 inches/102 centimeters a year in the Willamette Valley) and frost can be threats during spring and fall—the two times when grapes are most vulnerable. Weather patterns can be erratic (you need sunglasses one minute, an umbrella the next)— a stressful scenario for vines, which, like all plants, love constancy and stability.

And yet it's precisely the marginality of Oregon's climate, along with the state's unique geologic past, that forms the cradle of

its success as a wine region. Grapes here cannot burst into ripeness, but instead must make their way slowly and methodically toward maturity and complexity. Each year is a gamble, but when the forces of nature align with skilled winemaking, Oregon wines of utter beauty, focus, and finesse emerge.

When I wrote about Oregon in the first edition of *The Wine Bible*, the wine industry there was tiny, and the wines were sometimes surprisingly wonderful, sometimes sadly wanting. Then, in the first decade of the twenty-first century, Oregon turned the big corner. It had long since given up California as a viticultural and winemaking role model. Next, France, too, was abandoned. As Oregon winemakers set out on their own vinous course, they began to forge a new way of working with the unique demands of their land. The result has been a mega-leap in quality—especially for the state's signature

THE NINETY PERCENT LAW

While Oregon, of course, abides by U.S. wine laws, the state has opted to make some wine regulations stricter. For example, according to state regulations the leading Oregon wine types—pinot noir, chardonnay, and pinot gris—must contain at least 90 percent of whatever grape variety is named on the label (as opposed to the U.S. law, which mandates a minimum of 75 percent). Several grapes, however, are excepted from the Oregon 90 percent rule: Cabernet sauvignon, cabernet franc, merlot, syrah, sauvignon blanc, and several others that are thought to benefit from greater blending need only be 75 percent of the grape named.

The late David Lett (left) with son Jason. David Lett is considered the father of Oregon pinot noir.

THE QUICK SIP ON OREGON

OREGON'S SPECIALTY is pinot noir, a delicate and temperamental grape considered by many to make the most sensual red wines in the world.

OREGON'S RELATIVELY COOL, marginal climate is a major factor in the elegance that characterizes its top wines.

MOST OF THE STATE'S best wines come from a group of small appellations that make up the Willamette Valley, in the northwest corner of the state.

pinot noirs. If wines can be graceful *and* luscious, if they can have richness without heaviness, then Oregon is the place to find them.

Although a number of small wineries struggled along prior to Prohibition, the modern Oregon wine industry takes 1961 as the date of its birth. In that year, Richard Sommer, a graduate in agronomy from the University of California at Davis, planted riesling and other grapes at Hillcrest Vineyard in the Umpqua Valley. Four years later, David Lett, another UC Davis graduate, planted the state's first pinot noir at Eyrie Vineyards, in the long valley south of Portland known as the Willamette (rhymes with *dammit*, as locals are fond of saying). Both men were warned by university professors that *vinifera*-species grapes would not fare well in Oregon. And with that piece of advice unheeded, the Oregon wine industry was born.

Today there are more than 20,000 acres (8,100 hectares) of grapes and more than three hundred wineries in the state. Most of them grow pinot noir, the great (if fragile) red grape of Burgundy, France. Indeed, Oregon is one of only a few regions in the New World to be manically focused on a single grape variety.

While the story of Oregon is definitively the story of pinot noir, other grape varieties are also grown, albeit in far smaller amounts. Most are white. Among these whites, chardonnay is thought to have the most potential. Pinot gris is appreciated as a no-fuss local favorite that, as one winemaker puts it, "you drink while you're deciding which pinot noir to have." And finally, there's riesling. A dry riesling renaissance has swept Oregon, with several dozen winemakers now making small-production lots of this cool-climate grape.

Oregon wine country comprises four major regions, but the Willamette Valley is certainly the most important. Tucked into the northwest corner of the state, just south of Portland, and running north-south for 100 miles (160 kilometers), this corridor of soft, green hills could be visually described as the Vermont of the West. Here, more than two-thirds of the state's wines, including most of the best, are made. This one place—Willamette Valley— has put Oregon on the international wine map and indeed, has become virtually synonymous with "Oregon wine." So while some good wines are indeed made in the Umpqua, Rogue, and Applegate valleys, as well as in eastern Oregon in the Walla Walla region (which Oregon shares with Washington State), this chapter will focus on the Willamette Valley. Lastly, Oregon winemakers are a story in themselves. Independently minded farmers at heart, a surprising number of them are dropouts or exes. Dropouts from big-city life. Ex-high-tech execs. Dropouts from college. Ex-professors. Dropouts from the counterculture. Ex-theologians. A growing number are even ex-California winemakers.

Of course, many Oregon winemakers have enology degrees, but it doesn't always matter, for in Oregon, the greatest (most demanding) teacher remains Nature herself.

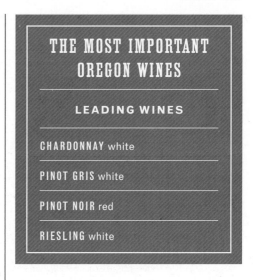

THE MOST IMPORTANT OREGON WINES

LEADING WINES

CHARDONNAY white

PINOT GRIS white

PINOT NOIR red

RIESLING white

THE (INCONCEIVABLE) LAND

Like California's, Oregon's geologic history is fascinating and violent. Here's a quick window into that past.

In a brutal collision some 140 million years ago, the tectonic plate beneath the Pacific Ocean crashed against the North American Plate and began to subduct, or plunge, underneath it. The massive crunch thrust up the sea bottom, creating the mountainous western coast of the United States, including much of Oregon. The mountainous landmass of uplifted seabed lay relatively still for millennia. Then, some fifteen million years ago, the volcanoes that formed Idaho's Blue Range Mountains erupted in a fury of wicked and immense activity. Hot lava spewed from the epicenter, covering the seabed with molten rock 1,000 feet (300 meters) deep. Such was the force behind the lava that it quickly oozed across the entire state of Oregon a potent flood of fiery volcanic sludge. Once cooled, the lava became a type of rock called basalt.

It was just the beginning. Some 15,000 years ago, during one of the earth's coldest periods, at the end of the last Ice Age (15,000 to 25,000 years ago), massive ice dams in Montana were breached, sending walls of water rushing toward the Pacific Ocean at a speed of 60 miles (97 kilometers) per hour. The entire Columbia River basin flooded. Over two thousand years, the Missoula Floods, as they became known, occurred again and again, each time creating a huge glacial lake where the Willamette Valley is today. The floods broke down the basalt in places and, in the process, deposited hundreds of feet of rich sediment on the floor of the valley.

OREGON, WOMEN, AND PINOT NOIR

Oregon has more women winemakers than California does, despite having one-twenty-seventh the grape acreage. Indeed, in the one U.S. state devoted to pinot noir, women account for 10 percent of all winemakers. The question seems obvious: Do women choose pinot noir? Or does *it* choose them?

I asked Lynn Penner-Ash, who in 1988 became the first female winemaker in Oregon, her view. Recounting the early days, she says, "Oregon was made up of small family-owned wineries and was just starting to understand the business of making and selling wine. Winemakers were eager to learn and eager to help establish Oregon as a place for world-class pinot noir. Female or male, if you were willing to work hard at making pinot, you were welcome." But Penner-Ash says there are also more subtle powers at work. "Pinot noir is a reflective grape. We strive to be guardians of it, but not dominators, which some might say reflects a more feminine sensibility."

Fast-forward to our time. All of the top vineyards of Willamette Valley exist above that fertile valley floor. The vineyards exist on "islands" of basalt (cooled lava), or ancient, uplifted marine seabed (sandy sediment), or windblown sand and silt (loess). Or sometimes a little of all three. From any one of the hilltops of the Willamette, this part of the distant past can be sensed immediately. The rich valley floor, barren of grapes, is lush with (and perfect for) grass. The vineyards—impeccably manicured—all begin rolling at about 200 feet (60 meters) up the slopes of numerous hills.

I will never forget the stark yet somehow gentle beauty of these vineyards. To reach them, you often wind along roads that are still dirt. Rare breeds of sheep graze. Swollen, slate-colored clouds drifting in off the Pacific Ocean sometimes hang in ponderous skepticism above the grapes.

As in Tuscany, there are no straight lines in the Willamette Valley. To drive is to meander up and down and around not just vineyards, but endless hazelnut orchards (more than 95 percent of the hazelnuts in the U.S. are grown here); forests of fir, oak, and maple; plus fields and fields of Christmas trees—an employment boon if you're an agricultural worker with little vineyard work in winter. (In the 1970s, land here cost $1,000 an acre; approximately $2,500 a hectare. Today prices broach $30,000 an acre; $74,000 per hectare).

Befitting this pastoral landscape, the wineries themselves are modest and farmlike. No châteaus, not even ranchettes. The state's progressive land-use laws stipulate that wineries must be true working wineries—each winery must earn a minimum of 75 percent of its revenue from the sale of wine (not baseball caps, jams, aprons, etc.). Plus there's a legal ratio of

Stoller Vineyards, in the Willamette Valley's Dundee Hills.

WHEN YOU VISIT . . . OREGON

THE MAJORITY OF OREGON'S wineries are in the verdant Willamette Valley, an easy drive from Portland. Most of these wineries are as welcoming and down-to-earth as they come. Often the owner is also the winemaker, tour guide, and tractor operator. It's best to call ahead for an appointment.

OVER THE MEMORIAL DAY and Thanksgiving weekends, Oregon wineries host massive open houses. Virtually every winery, no matter how tiny, is open for tastings and tours, and there are usually heaps of food and music, to boot.

WHENEVER YOU VISIT, don't miss a dinner at the Joel Palmer House, in Dayton, in the Willamette Valley. Owned by Jack and Heidi Czarnecki, two of the leading wild-mushroom experts in the United States and authors of several mushroom cookbooks, the Joel Palmer House specializes in (what else?) mushroom dishes paired with Oregon pinot noirs.

AS FOR PLACES TO STAY, my favorite B and B is the charming Black Walnut Inn in Dundee, and the best hotel by far is the Allison, a sophisticated luxury property with great food, a phenomenal spa, and a fantastically long list of exciting Oregon pinot noirs.

land to gallons produced. For example, anyone producing 50,000 to 150,000 gallons (1,900 to 5,700 hectoliters) of wine must have a corresponding parcel of 40 acres (16 hectares) of land. Mansions with "lifestyle vineyards" don't fit the bill.

THE CLIMATE

The vineyards of Willamette Valley are, for the most part, protected from the wet, cold onslaughts of the Pacific Ocean by a small chain of mountains known as the Coast Range. Winemakers here call it the first line of defense. The only gap in the range—the Van Duzer Corridor—is the one Achilles' heel. Still, while rain on the coast is often in excess of 80 inches (200 centimeters) a year, it's less than half that in Willamette Valley. Nonetheless, the region is generally cooler and wetter than its wine-producing neighbors, California and Washington State.

Importantly, however, most of the rain falls in winter—when the vines are dormant. And thus, the best growing seasons in Oregon are sunny—light at this northern latitude lasts until 10:00 p.m. in summer—but still relatively cool. (Locals report that, more than once, they've worn a down jacket to Fourth of July fireworks celebrations.) A cool growing season allows grapes to ripen slowly. And slow ripening, in turn, is the critical criterion for making Oregon's elegant style of top-notch pinot noirs. These pinots have a hum of acidity—a brightness and delicacy that defines them. They are just-ripe fruity, but not hot-sun jammy.

As for chardonnay, pinot gris, and riesling, the same cool climate that lends itself to well-balanced, earthy pinot noirs gives these white grapes a natural restraint. Of course, any winemaker with money to spare could override this inherent "quietness" with rap-music-like winemaking (lots of extraction) and a million dollars' worth of new oak barrels. Whether for philosophic or economic reasons (or both), this usually doesn't happen in Oregon. But there are some exceptions.

THE APPELLATIONS WITHIN WILLAMETTE VALLEY

I n the early 2000s, the winemakers of Willamette Valley came together and collectively mapped out six small areas within the valley that were ultimately given their own status as AVAs (American Viticultural Areas) in 2004, 2005, and 2006.

Each of these appellations begins about 200 feet (60 meters) above the valley floor and rises to about 1,000 feet (300 meters; above that, the climate here is too cool for grapes). Here is a short sketch on each, with a quick—but in no way complete—list of producers to seek out. Keep in mind that many top producers—Ken Wright and Bergström,

for example—make excellent wines from virtually every AVA, and thus aren't listed below.

CHEHALEM MOUNTAINS

This is a single, 20-mile-long (32-kilometer) landmass made up of several hilltops and ridges lifted up from the Willamette Valley floor. Parts of these hills (the south and southeast slopes) are mostly basalt and marine sediment; the more northern-facing slopes tend to be covered in loess. At more than 68,000 acres (27,500 hectares), this is the largest AVA within the Willamette. My top picks among the best producers include Adelsheim, Chehalem, and Ponzi.

DUNDEE HILLS

A small group of hills, Dundee is where the Willamette Valley's first pinot noir was planted, in 1965, by David Lett of Eyrie Vineyards. The area has unique red soils formed from ancient volcanic basalt. My top picks among the best producers include De Ponte, Domaine Drouhin, Stoller, and Domaine Serene.

EOLA-AMITY HILLS

This AVA is due west of the Van Duzer Corridor, a gap in the Coast Range, and thus is cool, thanks to exposure to air flowing in from the Pacific Ocean. Soils are a combination of volcanic basalt and marine sediment. My top

THE DIJON CLONES

O ne of the key drivers behind the vast improvement in Oregon wine in the 2000s was the widespread implementation of so-called Dijon clones. The University of Oregon was the first entity in the United States to bring in these clones of pinot noir and chardonnay (clones are genetic subtypes of a variety; for more information, see page 30). Named after Dijon, the city in Burgundy where France's ONIVINS plant materials laboratory is located, the numerous Dijon clones (with exciting names like 115, 667, and 777) are heralded for their complex flavors and ability to ripen fully in cool climates. In addition to Dijon clones, Willamette Valley pinot noirs are also often made from the Pommard clone, another well-suited clone from Burgundy.

Evesham Wood Winery, in the Willamette Valley's Eola-Amity Hills.

THE GRAPES OF OREGON

WHITES

CHARDONNAY: Considered the leading white grape in terms of potential; wines made from it range in quality from good to very good.

PINOT GRIS: The leading white grape in terms of production. A white variant of pinot noir, in Oregon it's usually made into popular, easy-to-like crisp whites.

RIESLING: An up-and-coming white, mostly made into light, fresh, dry wines, although there are some stunning examples of sweet dessert rieslings.

REDS

CABERNET SAUVIGNON, SYRAH, AND MERLOT: Minor grapes in Oregon, these are grown in the southern and eastern parts of the state. Their success is highly dependent on mesoclimates and producers.

PINOT NOIR: Oregon's most prestigious grape—virtually every winery in Willamette Valley grows it. It makes aromatic, elegant, earthy wines with supple textures.

---

picks among the best producers include Bethel Heights and Cristom.

MCMINNVILLE

Just west of the famous wine town of McMinnville, the AVA sits in a rain shadow of the Coast Range and is thus relatively warm and dry. It has shallow, uplifted marine sedimentary soils. My top picks among the best producers include Brittan and Yamhill Valley.

RIBBON RIDGE

The smallest of the AVAs, Ribbon Ridge is contained within the Chehalem Mountains AVA. It is an "island" of old silty/clay sedimentary soils, well protected by geographical features on all sides and thus a relatively moderate climate. My top picks among the best producers include Beaux Frères and Brick House.

YAMHILL-CARLTON

The AVA surrounds the hamlets of Yamhill and Carlton on coarse-grained, ancient marine

sedimentary soils. Top producers include Shea, Soter, Penner-Ash, and Elk Cove. In addition, the highly important Burgundy firm Louis Jadot, which bought vineyard land here in 2013, will be a producer to watch.

PINOT NOIR

Because Oregon, and the Willamette Valley in particular, is so strongly associated with pinot noir, a few words on the character of these wines is in order.

The best Oregon pinots possess what might be called a complex and quiet compellingness. They are rarely (if ever) dense, alcoholic blockbusters. Instead, the best of them offer a unique richness of supple fruit, without weight—the kind of pinot noir that would make a Burgundian monk genuflect. In fact, the kind of pinot noir that follows more in the tradition of Vosne Romanée than Santa Lucia Highlands.

PAPA PINOT

A photo in the February 16, 1967, *Newberg Graphic Farm News* shows a smiling young couple in heavy jackets and work boots, standing behind a wheelbarrow heaped with roots. The caption reads, "David and Diana Lett, who recently purchased the John Marner place in Dundee, pause with their European wine grape rootings. The Letts plan to remove prunes from the 20-acre farm and put in quality wine grapes."

The town's farmers thought David Lett was crazy, of course. And, in a way, he was possessed—by an idea. Namely, that finesse and complexity in wine were related to the marginality of the climate where the grapes were grown. In other words, grapes that had it easy, that ripened effortlessly thanks to unmitigating sun, would never make elegant wine. On the other hand, grapes that lived on the edge, that received barely enough sun to help them cross the finish line of ripeness, had at least a chance of making graceful wine.

Lett had earned a degree in viticulture at the University of California at Davis, but his thinking had been shaped even more pivotally by wandering around French vineyards for a year. The lesson out there, among the vines, seemed to be that grapes were sort of like life: No pain, no gain.

Lett had his mind set on pinot noir, and he planted it, along with pinot gris, riesling, and several other grapes that do well in cool, marginal climates. Eventually, other pioneer winemakers joined him. In the process, Oregon established itself as a wine region built not on trends, not on marketing strategies, not on the personal wine preferences of the vintner, but on the simple reality of its own terroir. David Lett, whose nickname was Papa Pinot, is today considered the father of Oregon pinot noir. Lett passed away in 2008.

The flavors of these pinots often seem to mirror the land itself, with their forest floor, wild mushroom, and brambly characteristics, circling a core of sweet, ripe berries. These aromas and flavors often get more vivid with time. Indeed, some of the most spellbinding Oregon pinot noirs I've tasted have been fifteen to thirty years old (this sort of ageworthiness is especially remarkable given that the entire Oregon wine industry is still quite young).

Then there's the issue of what I call "cool-climate lag time." Which is to say that almost no really good Oregon pinot noir tastes full-on the minute it's poured. In my experience, the best of these wines hit their stride and open up to a plethora of flavors twenty or more minutes after that. I wonder how many people have missed the beauty of a given Oregon pinot simply because they took one quick sip, then moved on.

But above all, the story of Oregon pinot is the story of texture. The best wines have a gentle feel of succulence—a sweet, palate-clinging character that is sometimes described as "sappy."

> "[Great Oregon pinot noir] . . . is about the complete power of gracefulness. When I'm drinking a pinot noir, I want it to taste like Grace Kelly just walked into the room."
>
> —ROLLIN SOLES,
> winemaker, Argyle Winery

A PARTNER FOR PINOT

In the United States, the sumptuous combination of grilled salmon and Oregon pinot noir was the first well-known food and wine marriage to forsake the old chestnut: white wine with fish; red wine with meat. And that it did brilliantly, for as anyone who has tasted grilled salmon and Oregon pinot noir together knows, the two are a consummate match. The rich fattiness and light char of the grilled salmon could have no better partner than an earthy Oregon pinot noir, with its relatively high (for red wine) acidity. Also critical to the partnership is the fact that pinot noir is very low in tannin, and thus doesn't interfere with the beautiful flavors of the fish. (By contrast, wines that are high in tannin, such as cabernet sauvignon, often make fish taste dry or metallic.) The biggest testament to the success of Oregon pinot noir and salmon happens each year on the final night of the wild and fantastic International Pinot Noir Celebration, when 600 pounds (272 kilograms) of chinook salmon are consumed with no one knows how many bottles of pinot noir.

SOME OF THE BEST PRODUCERS OF WILLAMETTE VALLEY PINOT NOIR

Adelsheim • Amity • Anam Cara • Argyle • Beaux Frères • Belle Pente • Bergström • Bethel Heights • Brick House • Brittan • Broadley • Carter • Chehalem • Cristom • De Ponte • Domaine Drouhin • Domaine Serene • Elk Cove • Erath • Et Fille • Evening Land • Evesham Wood • Ken Wright • Panther Creek • Penner-Ash • Ponzi • Raptor Ridge • REX HILL • Shea • Soter • St. Innocent • Stoller • The Eyrie Vineyards • Yamhill Valley

road to success has been rocky, and the state is just beginning to produce the kind of stop-you-in-your-tracks chardonnays that will command top dollar. I have to admit that, as of this writing, I'm only cautiously optimistic.

For the few really fabulous chardonnays, the quality surge has been largely the result of new Dijon clones brought to Oregon from Burgundy and now widely planted. (Originally, most Oregon chardonnay was made from a

The Willamette (rhymes with dammit) Valley is lush and serene.

CHARDONNAY

In Oregon—as in Burgundy and Champagne—chardonnay is considered pinot noir's cool-climate sister. When asked which white grape has the most potential for excellence here, most Oregon winemakers name it. But Oregon chardonnay's

PEAR EXCELLENCE

Although traditional in Europe for centuries, the making of handcrafted eaux-de-vie and fruit brandies is rare in the United States. Only a handful of tiny American distillers now practice the craft; among these is Clear Creek Distillery in Portland, Oregon. Clear Creek makes a pear brandy and an *eau-de-vie de poire* Williams that are two of the most extraordinary eaux-de-vie in America—indeed, in the world. To make them, perfectly ripe Williams pears (as the French call them; they're Bartletts in the United States) from orchards in Parkdale, Oregon, are fermented and then distilled in German-made pot stills. Although the process sounds straightforward, enormous skill is required to achieve an *eau-de-vie* with intense fruit concentration that is smooth and elegant at the same time. Clear Creek's *eau-de-vie de poire* Williams is especially renowned (and difficult to make) because it has an actual pear inside each bottle. To achieve this, empty bottles are carefully attached to tree limbs just after flowering. The pears actually grow inside the glass. After being rinsed with a special citric solution to sterilize the pears, the bottles are then filled with 80-proof pear *eau-de-vie*.

In Oregon, the moody vineyards of Maresh Red Hills in winter have a special charm.

warm-climate California clone that didn't ripen well in Oregon's cool climate, and thus produced thin, lean, bland wines.) Over the coming decade, Dijon clones are expected to be the chardonnay equivalent of a rising tide that lifts all boats.

There are already a few stunning examples—chardonnays that are elegant yet thoroughly rich, with waves of citrus, quince, and nut and mineral flavors. In style, they are closer to Burgundy than to California or Australia, and are rarely dominated by planky, sweet oak flavors.

Domaine Drouhin's Edition Limitée, Bergström's Sigrid, and Adelsheim's Stoller are already three of the best chardonnays in the United States.

The Oregon Wines to Know

WHITES

PENNER-ASH

RIESLING | WILLAMETTE VALLEY

100% riesling

Lynn Penner-Ash makes such beautiful pinot noirs that it might seem unusual to write about her riesling. But this delicious wine attests to just how good Oregon rieslings can be. Minerally and snappy, it's got a thrilling purity of pear and star fruit flavors. Refreshing? Kind of like a cold slap on a hot day.

CHEHALEM

SEXT | RIBBON RIDGE

100% riesling

In 1990, Harry Peterson-Nedry, one of the early winemakers in Willamette Valley, founded Chehalem (a Native American word meaning "valley of the flowers"). The winery makes beautiful pinot noirs and racy dry rieslings, but you should also know about Sext, Chehalem's fantastic, semi-sparkling dry riesling. It's a hailstorm in your mouth. Fresh, light flavors bolt around like electrons circling a core of apricots and other stone fruits. Liveliness is the wine's middle name.

BERGSTRÖM

CHARDONNAY | SIGRID | WILLAMETTE VALLEY

100% chardonnay

Josh Bergström, winemaker and co-owner, with his father and mother, John and Karen, named this extraordinary wine after Josh's Swedish grandmother. In luscious waves of golden richness, the flavors evoke images of quince, buttery pie crust, baking spices, and roasted nuts. The texture—utterly creamy yet framed by precise acidity—is reminiscent of great white Burgundy.

PONZI

PINOT GRIS | WILLAMETTE VALLEY

100% pinot gris

Drinking this wine, it seemed as though perfectly ripe pears and juicy tangerines were being transmogrified right then and there in the glass. Many wines, of course, are *like* fruit, but this wine seemed to *be* fruit. I like the wine not only for its exquisite fruitfulness but also because of its distinctiveness. It is far, far away from whispy pinot grigio, and neither does it manifest an Alsace pinot gris' gravitas. Instead, this good and beautiful wine has captured a split second of pure flavor that is Oregon.

REDS

BEAUX FRÈRES

PINOT NOIR | THE BEAUX FRÈRES VINEYARD | RIBBON RIDGE

100% pinot noir

Michael Etzel, winemaker and co-owner (with his brother-in-law, the wine critic Robert M. Parker Jr.) of Beaux Frères, makes gorgeous pinot noirs. Sweetly ripe and lushly textured, they are at the same time majestically refined and complex. To taste a great Beaux Frères pinot is to ride on wave after wave of sophisticated, sexy flavor. Impossible to resist such hedonism.

ADELSHEIM

PINOT NOIR | CALKINS LANE VINEYARD | CHEHALEM MOUNTAINS

100% pinot noir

David Adelsheim was among the pioneers of pinot noir in Willamette Valley and was instrumental in bringing new clones to the state. His wines continue to stand out for their beauty, balance, and integration. Suppleness and earthiness are their signatures. And yet, waves of delicate cherry fruit are woven, like ribbons, through the wines. Adelsheim makes many different pinots, but this one from Calkins Lane is a favorite.

DOMAINE DROUHIN

PINOT NOIR | LOUISE CUVÉE | DUNDEE HILLS

100% pinot noir

Famous Burgundy vintner Robert Drouhin planted vineyards in Willamette Valley in 1988 and put his winemaker daughter, Veronique, in charge. Louise Cuvée is named for Véronique's daughter. Not surprisingly, this wine possesses the finely tuned sensibilities of great Burgundy. It sways with the deep, primordial aromas of damp earth, wild herbs, warm rocks, fall leaves, and the most "earthy" aroma of all—the sweet, sweaty smell of men (not a pejorative by any means). The silky, supple texture here is enticing, and a marker for the top Oregon pinot noirs.

KEN WRIGHT

PINOT NOIR | SAVOYA | WILLAMETTE VALLEY

100% pinot noir

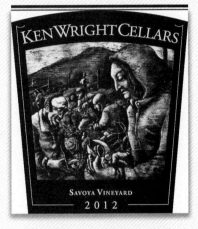

I have always thought that a prerequisite for great pinot noir is precision—a sense that the wine's flavors are crystal clear . . . like the sound of a church bell in the mountains. Ken Wright makes mind-blowing pinots like that. Savoya (a phonetic reference to the wild onions the Spanish-speaking workers found in the vineyard) crests along a perfect wave of suppleness, with sonorous flavors that are deeply earthy, berried, and spicy.

SOTER

PINOT NOIR | MINERAL SPRINGS | WILLAMETTE VALLEY

100% pinot noir

Winemaker Tony Soter began California's Etude Winery, and made more than a decade's worth of luscious Carneros pinot noir before selling Etude and moving to Willamette Valley. The man knows how to coax gorgeous fruit and spice from the earth. Soter's pinots have an extra dimension and depth of flavor—like the puddle of berry filling that oozed out of the pie while it baked, then fell onto the baking sheet, getting more and more concentrated until you swiped it up with your finger and ate it.

STOLLER

PINOT NOIR | SV ESTATE | DUNDEE HILLS

100% pinot noir

Stoller's exquisite pinot noirs are a testimonial to texture. Sappy, supple, silky, sensual, succulent (have I missed any other *s* words?). It was a Stoller pinot noir that first drove home for me the idea that pinot noir could have richness without ponderous weight. The exotic aromas and flavors are reminiscent of things like anise and sarsaparilla, with a smoky, peat bog kind of earthiness. Stoller is one of the biggest vineyards in the state, and many top producers (besides the Stollers themselves) make wine from this vineyard.

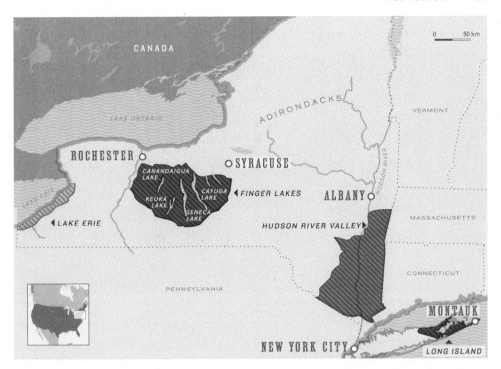

NEW YORK STATE

T he words *New York* generally evoke glamorous images of one of the world's most high-powered cities. But there is another New York as well, the New York of cornfields and potato barns, of rolling farmland and flowing rivers, of sapphire-colored lakes and graceful mountains. Much of New York State is, in fact, utterly and magnificently rural.

What would become New York State was formed during the Ice Age, as receding glaciers gouged out the Adirondack and Catskill mountains and carved deep passageways that would become the Hudson and Mohawk river valleys. As the glaciers retreated north, more than eight thousand lakes and ponds were created in the state. Eventually, these same glaciers would hollow out the five massive Great Lakes, including Lake Erie and Lake Ontario, which form parts of the northern and western borders of the state. In their wake, the glaciers not only left behind bodies of water but also deep, well-drained soil. By the time the colonists arrived, the area, already full of wild, indigenous vines, seemed naturally poised to become an important place for grapes. And so it would become; by the latter part of the twentieth century, New York State would have three major wine regions: the Hudson River Valley, the Finger Lakes, and Long Island. These remain the three important New York wine districts today.

In the Finger Lakes region, the grapes themselves have the best views of the deep lakes created by receding glaciers. Native Americans believed the stunning lakes—shaped like fingers—to be the hand of the Great Spirit.

THE QUICK SIP ON NEW YORK STATE

NEW YORK STATE'S modern wine industry, like all of the other major state wine industries, is based on fine wines made from *vinifera* species grape varieties. But up until two generations ago, the state was also known for a fascinating array of native American grapes and hybrids.

NEW YORK'S COOL northern climate makes it well suited to producing not only dry, still table wines, but also lively sparkling wines, plus some excellent late-harvest and icewines.

OF NEW YORK'S three major wine regions, the Finger Lakes is the fastest growing and accounts for almost half of the total wineries in the state.

Although Dutch colonists attempted to grow grapes on Manhattan Island as early as 1647, viticulture and winemaking did not take serious hold until the nineteenth century, when French, Dutch, and English immigrants began planting vineyards on the rolling hills of the Hudson River Valley. From there, the immigrants pushed westward into the state's stunning, remote, lake-clad interior. In particular, the Finger Lakes benefited from waves of German, French, and Swiss immigrants who were experienced at both grape growing and winemaking, and by the 1870s the Finger Lakes had become the heart of the New York wine industry. Steamboats laden with grapes and wine cruised back and forth doing a brisk business among the wineries that ringed the lakes. With the founding of the Geneva Experiment Station in the early 1880s, significant advances in grape breeding and viticulture led to leaps in quality among Finger Lakes wines.

The southern shores of Lake Erie, now one of the largest grape belts in the United States, were also planted with grapes around this time. The region, however, soon became a political stronghold for America's nascent temperance movement. All too soon, growers who might have planted wine grapes were focusing on table grapes instead. Indeed, because grapes

POLITICAL BEGINNINGS

*T*wo of the most culturally sig-nificant political movements in the history of the United States began in the wine regions of New York State: the temperance movement and the women's rights movement. The temper-ance movement began in Saratoga Springs and quickly spread to the Lake Erie region as early as 1808, eventually culminat-ing in national Prohibition in 1920. The women's rights movement began in Seneca Falls, in the Finger Lakes, with the first Women's Rights Convention in 1848.

grown in the Lake Erie region today are mainly destined for jelly and juice (not wine), I've left the region out of this chapter.

From the end of Prohibition until the mid-1970s, the New York wine industry was con-trolled by a few powerful companies. As of 1976, there were only nineteen wineries in the state, most of them specializing in native American grapes, crosses, and hybrids. Small growers, their hands tied by exorbitant New York State licensing fees and bureaucratic red tape, grew grapes for a handful of big wineries rather than creating fine-wine brands of their own. By the middle of the 1970s, New York's reputation as a producer of high-quality wines seemed to be sliding downhill fast.

In 1976, the critical turnaround came with the passage of the Farm Winery Act, which made operating a small winery economically feasible by permitting direct sales to restau-rants, wine stores, and consumers. Within seven years, nearly fifty small farm winer-ies had opened for business. Today, with the exception of the state's sole very large win-ery, Canandaigua Wine Company (itself part of Constellation Wines), the majority of New York's 283 wineries are small to medium in size.

THE MOST IMPORTANT NEW YORK STATE WINES

LEADING WINES

CABERNET FRANC red

CABERNET SAUVIGNON red

CHARDONNAY white

MERLOT red

RIESLING white (dry and sweet)

SPARKLING WINES white

WINES OF NOTE

BACO NOIR red

CATAWBA red and rosé

CAYUGA white

GEWÜRZTRAMINER white

NIAGARA white

RKATSITELI white

SEYVAL BLANC white

VIDAL white (dry and sweet)

VIGNOLES white (dry and sweet)

THE GRAPES AND THE WINES

s noted, New York's modern wine industry is based on familiar European (*Vitis vinifera*) grapes—especially riesling, chardonnay, merlot, and

THE GRAPES OF NEW YORK STATE

Crosses and hybrids have been included in this list for reference purposes, although today they constitute a small part of the modern industry.

WHITES

CAYUGA: A French-American hybrid, Cayuga is often used in off-dry blends and for dessert wines.

CHARDONNAY: A major grape; the good to very good wines it becomes are leaner in style than California chardonnays.

GEWÜRZTRAMINER: One of New York's best-kept secrets, it can be turned into delicious wines reminiscent of the gewürztraminers of Alsace.

NIAGARA: Foxy-tasting American cross that is often made into off-dry and dessert wines. It was first bred in the 1860s by growers in Niagara County, New York.

RIESLING: A major grape that makes many dynamic, vibrant dry wines, as well as delicious off-dry and dessert wines. Most of the best examples of riesling come from the Finger Lakes.

SEYVAL BLANC: A major French-American hybrid that is used on its own and in blends. Can make good-tasting, dry wines.

VIDAL: A French-American hybrid; a source of dry wines and some exceptional icewines.

VIGNOLES: A somewhat rare French-American hybrid also known as Ravat 51; used for dry wines and some tasty icewines.

REDS

BACO NOIR: A French-American hybrid that makes simple, fruity red wines that aren't particularly foxy.

CABERNET FRANC: A major grape that is often blended with merlot and cabernet sauvignon for Bordeaux-style reds.

CABERNET SAUVIGNON: Often blended with merlot to create Bordeaux-style reds. Only a modest number of producers, notably on Long Island, use it as a single varietal.

CATAWBA: A cross or hybrid (the genetic history is unclear) that was very popular in the American Northeast in the nineteenth century (back then, sparkling catawba was a specialty of the Finger Lakes). It makes spicy, grapey, high-acid, light red and rosé wines.

CONCORD: A native grape belonging to the *labrusca* species, it was first grown from seed in Massachusetts along the Concord River. It is the most widely planted grape in New York State, although most of the production is used for grape juice and jelly, not wine. The remainder is used to make sweet kosher wines and fortified wines.

MERLOT: A major grape, merlot can become sleek, berried wines that range from good to delicious, especially those produced on Long Island.

PINOT NOIR: Generally used for New York's numerous sparkling wines.

HYBRIDS AND CROSSES IN AMERICA

From the mid-1800s to the mid-1900s, French scientists and horticulturists attempted to develop grape varieties that would taste similar to *vinifera* varieties, yet be more hardy and disease-resistant, like native American varieties. To come up with these new "super" grape varieties, hundreds, if not thousands, of hybrids of *vinifera* and native American varieties were bred. (Reminder: A hybrid is not the same as a cross. A hybrid is a grape variety created by breeding two grapes of *different* species—for example, by breeding a *vinifera*-species grape with a grape that belongs to an American species. A cross is a grape created by breeding two varieties from *within* the same species.)

Many of the hybrids created by the French scientists (such as seyval blanc, vignoles, Vidal, and Baco noir) turned out to be fairly successful. They were indeed hardy in the vineyard, and their flavors, while not absolutely *vinifera*-like, also usually did not have the pungent grapey/animal fur character referred to as "foxy." Some of these French-American hybrids were initially widely planted in France, although all hybrids were ultimately outlawed in that country. Such hybrids are, however, still grown today in New York State (and other northeastern U.S. states, as well as Canada).

The history behind New York's French-American hybrids revolves around an assumption that later proved to be false. For centuries, European grapes were wrongly presumed too fragile to withstand New York's cold winters—especially in the Finger Lakes. But as the 1970s and 1980s progressed, more and more vintners took the risk of planting *vinifera* varieties, and consumers grew far more comfortable with New York wines based on them. The *vinifera* revolution was imminent.

---

cabernet franc (in that order). But as a historical aside, it's worth noting that New York's vinous genetic scope was once quite broad. Two generations ago, the state was also known for grapes that belonged to native American species (Concord is an example; today these go into jelly and jam); dozens of crosses of grapes within various American species (the grape catawba may be an example); and numerous hybrids, such as seyval blanc, Vidal, vignoles, and Cayuga (grapes created by breeding two different varieties that belong to different species). It made for a fascinating world of flavor.

As of the early 2010s, about 60 percent of all the wine produced in New York State was white, but red wines continue to show leaps in quality and sophistication. In particular, the Bordeaux varieties cabernet franc and merlot are the hot varieties to watch—especially on Long Island, which has the longest growing season in the state and a climate warm and sunny enough to bring these red varieties to ripeness. Sleek and medium-bodied, these reds are far more like Bordeaux wines than they are like California wines.

With all due respect to the state's increasingly solid reputation for fine red wines, New York's rieslings are among the most evanescent rieslings made in the United States (only a few rieslings of the Pacific Northwest can compare). Utterly light in body but concentrated in flavor, they have what the Germans—riesling specialists, after all—would approvingly call precision and transparency (meaning they reflect the character of their site). New York's rieslings come in all styles: dry, off-dry, slightly sweet, late-harvest, and icewines. The dry versions are wonderfully crisp, even austere; the off-dry rieslings, harmonious and mellow; the sweet rieslings, luscious yet exquisitely balanced.

CABERNET FRANC AND THE ISSUE OF COOL

Some 500 years ago, cabernet franc and sauvignon blanc had a nice moment in nature and cabernet sauvignon was born. Like cabernet sauvignon, parent cabernet franc has always been associated with relatively cool or maritime climates—the Loire Valley and Bordeaux, in France, for example, and New York State, in the United States. The reason is completely practical.

Cabernet franc vines bud late in the season (decreasing the chances that a catastrophic spring frost will kill the tender green growth and thus destroy the crop), and at the same time, cabernet franc grapes ripen early (avoiding potential fall rains and freezes that could decimate the harvest). Growers of cool-climate cabernet franc also argue that cool temperatures are what give the grape its distinct, sleek purity and nuanced flavors (including, often, violets, lavender, and a pleasing, resiny, green chaparral quality). But in a fascinating shift in the 2000s, cabernet franc plantings began increasing in numerous warm areas, such as California's Napa and Sonoma valleys. Winemakers in these warmer areas say there's a different side to the grape—a rich side that's evocative of dark chocolate, blueberry, and black olive. So, while warm-climate cabernet franc is now cool, don't forget, if you're in France or New York, that cool-climate cabernet franc is still hot.

There are numerous New York rieslings that shouldn't be missed, including those from Dr. Konstantin Frank, Hermann J. Wiemer, and Sheldrake Point, to name three producers.

Speaking of sweet wines, New York makes some of the best in the country—and not only from riesling but also from French-American hybrids, such as Vidal and vignoles. Sweet wines in the state come in two styles: late-harvest wines made with the help of *Botrytis cinerea,* the noble rot that gives French Sauternes its character, and icewines. Like the magnificent *eisweins* of Germany, Austria, and Canada, New York's icewines are made naturally from frozen grapes that have been left on the vines until well into winter.

VINIFERA VARIETIES SWEEP INTO THE STATE

Two prescient European immigrants are credited with ushering in a modern era for New York State wines. Charles Fournier, a former Champagne master at the house of Veuve Clicquot and later the head of New York's Gold Seal Wine Company, and Dr. Konstantin Frank, a Ukrainian-born professor with a PhD in viticulture and plant sciences, ultimately changed the course of New York's viticultural history by initiating, in the 1950s, what would become a *vinifera* revolution. Frank, who spoke nine languages but no English, came to New York City as an immigrant in 1951, at the age of fifty-four, and took the only job he could find—washing dishes. Later, Charles Fournier hired him at Golden Seal and allowed him to plant whatever European varieties he wished. Frank knew that *vinifera* grew in Ukraine, where winter temperatures were well below those in the Finger Lakes. By employing some careful and, at the time, sophisticated viticultural techniques, Frank was successful at growing the species, and Fournier at making it into good wine. By the early 1960s, Frank had established his own winery and was growing chardonnay, riesling, rkatsiteli

Dr. Konstantin Frank, a Ukrainian-born professor of viticulture and plant sciences, changed the course of winemaking in New York State by successfully growing Vitis vinifera *varieties in the 1950s.*

(are-cat-si-TELL-ee; a leading grape still grown in Georgia, Ukraine, and the Republic of Moldova), and some sixty other European grapes theretofore considered impossible to cultivate in New York State.

This triumph inspired other leading-edge winemakers. By 1996, there were 4,000 acres (1,600 hectares) of *vinifera* grapes in New York State, a 1,200 percent rise over the acreage of 1980, and such wines as riesling, chardonnay, and merlot were breathing new life into New York's wine industry.

THE LAND

I f you subtract the grapes grown for juice and jelly, New York has approximately 17,000 acres (6,890 hectares) of wine grapes, a small amount compared to California's 543,000 acres (219,700 hectares).

New York is, perhaps needless to say, very cool. Winter comes soon after Thanksgiving and can last until April, well after vines in California are already budding. Long hours and months of continuous sunshine are definitely not the norm, and achieving total ripeness can be an iffy proposition. Of course, there is

L'CHAIM

W*ine is central to the religious rites of Jews, and especially to such profoundly important Jewish holidays as Passover. Historically, in the United States, most of the wine used in Jewish ceremonies was made in New York State, relatively near large urban centers of Jewish populations, including New York City. While today dry kosher wines are made all over the world (and many are very sophisticated), sweet kosher wine remains a New York tradition and is made from native American varieties, particularly Concord grapes. Today, the leading brands of sweet kosher wine are Manischewitz, Kedem, and Mogen David.*

WHEN YOU VISIT . . . NEW YORK STATE

THE WINERIES of New York are set into some of the most charming, "small-town-America" landscapes in the United States. Many are housed in converted barns or colonial farmhouses, and the wine districts are full of old-fashioned inns, bed-and-breakfasts, and country restaurants. Because of their proximity to waterways, many wineries have panoramic views of stunning lakes or bays.

IF YOUR VISIT INCLUDES the Finger Lakes, be sure to experience the New York Wine and Culinary Center in the town of Canandaigua, on Lake Canandaigua—an educational tasting room, restaurant, and bar devoted to exploring the state's many wines and artisanal beers. And a word of travel advice: No bridges exist on the lakes, so plan on long, scenic, rural drives around them to get from place to place.

The English naval explorer Henry Hudson (1565 to 1611), after whom the Hudson Valley is named.

a blessing buried within this imperfect situation. New York State, like other areas with cool climates, has the potential to make some lovely, elegant wines.

The state's three major wine regions are fairly distant from one another, but share an important common denominator. All are adjacent to large bodies of water, which help moderate extremes of temperature, protecting the vines from severe cold snaps in spring and fall and fanning them with refreshing breezes during hot summers.

During the Ice Age, the glaciers that created New York's myriad lakes also left behind an amalgam of well-drained soils, from shale, schist, and limestone in the Finger Lakes to silt and loam on Long Island. Taken together, the combination of a cool but water-moderated climate, the variety of soil types, and individual sites that, geographically, can deviate considerably, means that New York State wines are highly influenced by the specific place where the grapes are grown.

Below are short profiles of the three major wine-producing regions.

THE HUDSON RIVER VALLEY

The Hudson River, the first great passageway into the New World, was explored in 1609 by the Englishman Henry Hudson who, on behalf of the Dutch East India Company, searched for a water route across North America to the Pacific. The deep, navigable river quickly became so important to trade that the harbor at its mouth is credited with helping New York City become one of the world's most prominent cities.

The vineyards of the Hudson River Valley, first planted in 1677 by French Huguenots, are the oldest in New York State. They begin just 40 miles (64 kilometers) north of Manhattan. Of the region's thirty-nine wineries, most are small or medium size, and production focuses on *vinifera* and some hybrid varieties. Perhaps the most forward-thinking winery in the region is Millbrook, owned by John Dyson, the former

Wish you were here! A postcard circa 1950 from the Finger Lakes, then (as now) a great rural vacation destination, especially for East Coast city dwellers.

state commissioner of agriculture and markets and also the owner of the prominent Sonoma pinot noir-oriented winery Williams-Selyem.

THE FINGER LAKES

U pstate New York's Finger Lakes region has been the center of the New York wine industry since the Civil War. Today, 118 wineries call this area home. The region fans out from eleven finger-shaped lakes, the four major ones called Seneca, Cayuga, Canandaigua, and Keuka, all Native American names. These narrow, deep lakes (some deeper than the sea floor) were considered by the Iroquois to be formed by the hand of the Great Spirit. Many wineries are within sight of the lakes, which are considered some of the most beautiful in New York State.

Originally planted with *labrusca* varieties and American crosses to make sweet wines, the vineyards of the Finger Lakes were where the state's French-American hybrids and *vinifera* varieties got their start. Today, the region

THE GRAPES OF (WELCH'S) WRATH

N ew York produces more grape juice than any other state. That rich, purply, aromatic juice includes the famous brand Welch's Concord grape juice, invented by Dr. Thomas Welch in 1869. Like most other grape juices, Welch's is made from native Concord grapes grown along the banks of Lake Erie, a huge viticultural region spanning not only New York but also parts of Ohio and Pennsylvania. Were it not for Dr. Welch, an ardent Prohibitionist, the Lake Erie region might have developed as an important producer of wine grapes rather than juice grapes.

is abuzz with familiar activity. All types of modern varieties are made here, from tasty chardonnays to sheer rieslings to lightly spicy gewürztraminers. Not to be missed are the region's excellent late-harvest and icewines, some based on hybrids.

Among the Finger Lakes' most famous historic wineries are Dr. Konstantin Frank Vinifera Wine Cellars, Hermann J. Wiemer, Wagner Vineyards, and the off-the-wall, highly idiosyncratic Bully Hill Vineyards. The Finger Lakes region is also home to a number of newer, exciting wineries, including Standing Stone Vineyards, Ravines, Knapp Winery, Fox Run, and Sheldrake Point.

LONG ISLAND

About 95 miles (150 kilometers) from New York City, the eastern end of Long Island is New York State's youngest wine region. The wine boom began here in earnest in the late 1970s and early 1980s, after John Wickham, a farmer in the small hamlet of Cutchogue, successfully grew *vinifera* grapes in the mid-1960s. Although Wickham never made a commercial wine, it was only a matter of a decade before someone did.

In 1973, Louisa and Alex Hargrave founded Hargrave Vineyard in a former Cutchogue potato field. Several years later, the Hargraves' cabernets were generating waves of surprise and excitement throughout the state. Other would-be Long Island vintners soon followed. By the late 1990s, Long Island had twenty-four wineries, and today it boasts sixty-three.

Shaped like a lobster claw, Long Island begins close to the mainland of New York State and then thrusts out into the sea on a northeast angle, roughly parallel to the Connecticut coast. The end of the island splits into two slivers of land, called the North Fork and the South Fork. The North Fork was historically known for its orchards, potato fields, and small farms; the South Fork for its white-duned beaches and whaling ports. Today, the South Fork is probably best known for the Hamptons, a string of chic, small villages where well-to-do Manhattanites spend summer weekends.

Although there are a sprinkling of wineries in the Hamptons, most of Long Island's vineyards are on the more protected and less populated North Fork. While it is surrounded by water (Long Island Sound to the north, Peconic Bay to the south, and the Atlantic Ocean to the east), the North Fork is not exposed broadside to the ocean, as is the South Fork. Thus, the North Fork benefits from the moderating influences of the waters around it, yet at the same time remains fairly well sheltered from severe saltwater storms and the area's not-infrequent hurricanes. As an additional boon, the North Fork of Long Island is the sunniest part of New York State, an obvious advantage for ripening grapes.

A viticultural threat both forks share, however, is birds. Long Island is on the Atlantic flyway, a migratory route for numerous species of birds who can decimate a vineyard within days. Many Long Island vineyards must be netted, at considerable expense to vintners.

Long Island's Atlantic maritime climate led early vintners to look at another Atlantic maritime climate for inspiration and guidance: Bordeaux. As a result, Long Island is now commonly planted with the Bordeaux red varieties merlot and cabernet franc.

Many Long Island wineries are among the most expensively and technically well equipped in the state. The island's proximity to Manhattan also means that vineyard land here is the most expensive in New York—far more expensive than that in the Finger Lakes, for example. Top Long Island wineries include Channing Daughters, Shinn, and Paumanok.

WHITES

CHANNING DAUGHTERS WINERY

MEDITAZIONE | SOUTH FORK OF LONG ISLAND

38% muscat ottonel, 27% sauvignon blanc,
26% pinot blanc, 6% chardonnay, 2% pinot grigio,
1% malvasia bianca

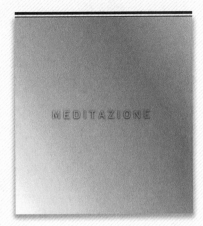

Among the wines that Channing Daughters makes are two extraordinary and unusual wines—called Meditazione and Envelope—both of which are reminiscent of the so-called "orange wines" made in Georgia, Slovenia, and the Friuli-Venezia Giulia region of northern Italy. The Meditazione (of which just four barrels are made) is a beautifully lush wine, exuberant with apricot and peach marmalade flavors and laced with notes of bitter orange zest. The grapes for the wine were grown in Bridgehampton, on the South Fork, where the winery is located, as well as on the North Fork, and the wine takes its vivid amber-orange color from eighteen months' aging in Slavonian hogsheads (a barrel slightly larger than a standard barrel). One of Long Island's most avant-garde wineries, Channing Daughters bases many of its wines on northern Italian grape varieties, many of which are fairly rare. Cofounder Walter Channing named the estate for his four daughters.

DR. KONSTANTIN FRANK

DRY RIESLING | FINGER LAKES

100% riesling

The late Dr. Konstantin Frank—a Ukrainian viticulturist who came to the U.S. in 1951 and specialized in cold-climate varieties—was one of the pioneers of viticulture in New York's Finger Lakes region. Today, the winery's experience shows, especially with temperamental varieties like riesling. The Konstantin Frank rieslings have a tactile sense of aliveness—a kind of kinetic edginess that makes them super refreshing. They are also delicate, and laced with spiciness. But more than any other quality, they demonstrate fruity concentration without weightiness.

Hermann J. Wiemer

Est. 1979

Riesling
Dry
2011

Estate Bottled and Grown

FINGER LAKES   ALC. 11.5% BY VOL.

HERMANN J. WIEMER

DRY RIESLING | FINGER LAKES

100% riesling

Of all Finger Lakes rieslings, the one from Wiemer is perhaps most like the vibrant, dry rieslings from Germany. Maybe this is no surprise, since the late Wiemer emigrated to New York from the Mosel village of Bernkastel and planted his vineyards in 1976. There's an exquisite sense of peach and tangerine fruit at the core of the wine, framed by delicate floral notes and a slight, zesty lime bitterness. I can't help imaging the clear, glacial waters of the lakes themselves when drinking this.

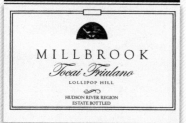

FOX RUN

V I N E Y A R D S™

Riesling 12
*Hanging Delta
Vineyard*

FINGER LAKES

FOX RUN

RIESLING 12 | HANGING DELTA VINEYARD | FINGER LAKES

100% riesling

From sites all along Seneca Lake, Fox Run makes a score of rieslings from dry to sweet and every permutation in between. Riesling 12 is the winery's name for their light-bodied off-dry riesling with a touch of gentle sweetness. Hanging Delta Vineyard is a reference to the ancient glacial deltas (now planted with vines) that formed thousands of years ago when a far larger lake drained to become Seneca Lake. This is an utterly delicate wine, and one that captures riesling's evanescent sense of beauty. As noted, it's also a bit sweet, but not in an ultrarich, viscous, or candied way. Rather, you have the sense that you've drunk the lightest essence of apricots, peaches, and strawberries—and that you could drink it all day long.

MILLBROOK
Tocai Friulano
LOLLIPOP HILL

HUDSON RIVER REGION
ESTATE BOTTLED

MILLBROOK

TOCAI FRIULANO | LOLLIPOP HILL | HUDSON RIVER VALLEY

100% Friulano

Millbrook's Friulano (at the time of this writing, the winery still used the old name for the grape, tocai Friulano) totally captures the essence of the delicious Friulanos from the northern Italian province Friuli-Venezia Giulia. It's light, zesty, and spicy, and has just the merest spin of something green, like dried sage or the way hedges smell in spring. Yet, like all good Friulanos, it also has a beautiful, creamy middle that makes the wine irresistible. Millbrook is owned by David Bova and his brother-in-law, John Dyson, a former agricultural commissioner of New York.

REDS

PAUMANOK

CABERNET FRANC | GRAND VINTAGE | NORTH FORK OF LONG ISLAND

100% cabernet franc

Paumanok makes some of the top reds on Long Island. The wines are beautiful expressions of their grape varieties, and are always juicy and dead-on delicious. My favorite is the winery's cabernet franc—a woodsy, violety, wild-berried wine that exudes a lip-smacking "red" quality—almost like grenadine. The wine couldn't be easier to drink. Imagine a farmers' market stand of Long Island berries. Yet there's structure and firmness here, too. A serious, sophisticated Hampton party red.

SHINN ESTATE

NINE BARRELS | MERLOT | RESERVE | NORTH FORK OF LONG ISLAND

96% merlot, with small amounts of malbec and petite verdot

From the husband-and-wife team of David Page and Barbara Shinn (former New York City restaurateurs) comes Nine Barrels—a merlot that's neither heavy nor lean, but beautifully mid-prance between the two (not unlike a Cru Bourgeois Bordeaux). The fascinating combination of raspberry, pomegranate, and rhubarb pie aromas and flavors has a cool purity that's true to Long Island's relatively cool climate. The savory whoosh of spice, black tea, and mineral flavors at the end is unusual for merlot, and deliciously distinctive. Needless to say, just nine barrels of this wine (about 225 cases) are made each year.

SWEET WINES

SHELDRAKE POINT

ICEWINE | FINGER LAKES

100% riesling

Upstate New York is famous for its icewines, dessert wines made by allowing the grapes to remain on the vine well into the winter. When the frozen grapes are finally picked, the juice that slowly oozes from them is completely luscious. Sheldrake Point's stunning icewine engulfs your senses with slow-motion tidal waves of dense apricot flavor. Although massively concentrated and quite sweet (28.3 percent residual sugar—or 283 grams of sugar per liter), the wine soars on the palate with a Zen-like lightness of being. A totally sensual experience.

STANDING STONE

RIESLING ICE | FINGER LAKES

100% riesling

Sweet wines can be bold and intense or ethereally exquisite and delicate. Standing Stone's the latter. With its beautifully pensive flavors (apricots, peaches, lemon curd), this is the "quiet music" of sweet wine. Even the sweetness itself seems to come at you in whispers. And the achingly long finish is just the way a great dinner should end. Technically speaking, Riesling Ice is not a traditional icewine, since the grapes were not fully frozen on the vine (the grapes were picked after they began to freeze, but were then placed in very cold storage until they were frozen solid). The grapes come from the remarkable, old Gold Seal Vineyard, planted with riesling in 1974.

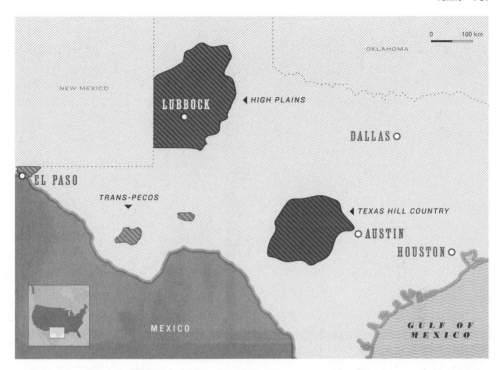

TEXAS

Some wine drinkers may find it surprising that good wine—or any wine at all, for that matter—can be eked out of dusty lands that even the cowboys found trying. Perhaps more surprising is the idea that Texas may have been one of the earliest places in the United States to produce wine. Historians theorize that Franciscan priests planted vineyards possibly as early as 1660, at missions in what is now far west Texas. Today, winemaking continues in the Lone Star State, and it's definitely not cowboy juice.

Texas is the largest of the forty-eight contiguous states. In landmass, it is bigger than France, although all of the vineyard acreage in the state, some 3,500 acres (1,400 hectares), could easily fit into the confines of the small French appellation of Sancerre. There are three broad grape-growing areas—the Texas Hill Country, the High Plains, and the vast Trans-Pecos region (more on all to follow). Within each region, wineries are not grouped closely together but scattered across hundreds of miles/kilometers of differing mesoclimates and terrains. Neighboring wineries are often more than an hour's drive apart.

As was true in California, the first grapes planted in Texas were mission grapes, a Spanish variety (known in Spain as listán prieto) that was the same as Chile's país grape, and that was one of the parents of Argentina's criolla grape. However serviceable mission wine might have been, it was only that—serviceable. By the nineteenth century, as new immigrants from Germany, Italy, and France came to Texas, they brought more European grape varieties. Generally, the vines succumbed to the severities of the climate and disease. Texas's immigrant winemakers were undeterred. When their new European vines

Fall Creek Vineyards in the Texas Hill Country near Austin. In the mid 1970s, owners Ed and Susan Auler were among the first in Texas to take a serious approach to grape growing and winemaking.

failed, they made wine from native Texas grapes, including one called, appropriately enough, mustang.

While there were at least sixteen commercial wineries operating in Texas prior to Prohibition, after it, only Val Verde Winery, near the border city of Del Rio, on the Rio Grande, remained. Almost four decades passed. Then, in the 1970s, the modern wine boom boomed—and it did so in a peculiarly Texan way.

In 1973, Ed Auler, a Texas cattle rancher and lawyer, went to France with his wife, Susan, to further his knowledge of cattle breeds. A few days of looking at cattle metamorphosed into several weeks of looking at vineyards and tasting wine. When the Aulers stood outside Clos de Vougeot, one of Burgundy's most famous vineyards, they noticed how much the topography and the limestone soil reminded them of their ranch in the Texas Hill Country. The Aulers thought the Texas thought: *We can do that.* Fall Creek Vineyards was born ten years later.

Meanwhile, out on the High Plains, in Lubbock, other vineyards were being planted.

In 1974, after noticing how exuberantly the grape trellis over his patio was growing, Texas Tech professor Bob Reed teamed up with another professor, Clinton McPherson, and

THE QUICK SIP ON TEXAS

TEXAS IS ONE OF THE OLDEST wine regions in the United States.

ALTHOUGH CABERNET SAUVIGNON and chardonnay are the most widely planted grapes in the state, dozens of varieties—from tempranillo and syrah to viognier and roussanne—are now grown, as Texans continue their search to determine which grapes will excel.

TEXAS'S NEARLY 250 WINERIES are scattered across thousands of miles, with differing mesoclimates.

A TEXAS HERO

Texas horticulturist T. V. Munson (1843–1913) played a central role in saving the vineyards of Europe from phylloxera devastation in the nineteenth century. In 1876, Munson began studying grapes, traveling from his home north of Dallas, in Denison, some 75,000 miles (120,700 kilometers) throughout the United States and Mexico (often on horseback), collecting native American grape varieties as he went. Using these as parents, Munson developed more than three hundred disease-resistant varieties of grapes. Based on his research, he wrote the classic text *Foundation of American Grape Culture* in 1909.

When phylloxera struck the vineyards of Europe, Munson was among those who shipped supplies of native rootstocks to European vintners. By grafting their vines onto the Texas-grown rootstocks, Europeans were ultimately able to salvage what remained of their vineyards. For his work, Munson was awarded the French Legion of Honor Cross of Mérite Agricole in 1888.

the two scientists planted one hundred varieties intended merely as a fun science project for their students. Within a few years, the project had become the highly successful Llano Estacado Winery, currently the largest winery in the state.

Segue to 1976. The University of Texas began to ponder the future of its 2.1 million acres (849,800 hectares) of land scattered across nineteen counties in the West Texas desert. Early in 1921, the Santa Rita oil well struck lucky, helping the university to become one of the richest in the world. But oil was a limited resource. The university's manager of lands and property, Billy Carr, proposed a mind-blowing idea: plant vineyards. In 1981, the first vines belonging to what would later become Ste. Genevieve Winery (named after a fifth-century nun who is the patron saint of Paris) were planted beside a giant mesa in the middle of the West Texas desert. By 1992, the winery was producing more than 100,000 cases of wine each year. And so the stories went. Texans thinking about cattle, about land, about oil, about agricultural innovation found their way to wine grapes. The movement had begun.

SPAIN'S GIFT

No alcoholic beverage made from grapes appears to have been produced in the Americas before the arrival of the Spanish conquistadores in the sixteenth century, according to Tim Unwin in Wine and the Vine: An Historical Geography of Viticulture and the Wine Trade. *Instead, the indigenous peoples of Mesoamerica made such alcoholic drinks as* pulque, *the forerunner of mescal, from the maguey or agave plant;* tesgüino, *from the sprouted kernels of maize; and* balche, *from mead, flavored with the leaves of the* Lonchocarpus, *a tropical tree or climbing shrub with colorful flowers. What makes this all the more fascinating is that numerous native species of the grape genus* Vitis *were to be found in the Americas, including in the Rio Grande Valley of Texas.*

THE GRAPES OF TEXAS

WHITES

BLANC DU BOIS: A hybrid developed at the University of Florida in 1968 and now grown in Florida, Texas, and the Gulf States because of its tolerance of humidity and resistance to Pierce's disease. It makes fresh, clean, fruity wines.

CHARDONNAY: A major white grape; the styles and quality of the wines made from it are variable and in flux.

CHENIN BLANC: A minor grape that is often made into good off-dry wines as a counterpoint to the region's chile-rich cuisine.

MUSCAT CANELLI: A minor grape, the same as muscat blanc à petits grains. It is made into very good off-dry wines.

SAUVIGNON BLANC: A major grape that can be the source of good, tasty, often peachy-herbal-flavored wines.

VIOGNIER: Plantings are small but growing. Many viticulturists believe Texas's future lies in Rhône varieties.

REDS

CABERNET FRANC: A modest amount is grown, often used for blending, but it is sometimes made into very good wine on its own.

CABERNET SAUVIGNON: A leading red grape; makes good wines.

LENOIR: An American-species grape, also known as "black Spanish" because of its incredibly dark color. Native to Texas, it is appreciated for its resistance to Pierce's disease and is usually used in blends.

MALBEC: A minor grape currently, but plantings are increasing significantly and the wines show promise.

MERLOT: A significant amount is grown, but it's mostly blended into cabernet sauvignon-based wines.

SANGIOVESE: A minor grape, but plantings are increasing a bit as vintners experiment with Italian varieties.

SYRAH: An important grape; increasingly planted, with growing success.

TEMPRANILLO: Plantings are small but growing. Expectations are high for the eventual success of this variety in Texas.

THE LAND AND THE GRAPES

There may be a Texas spirit, a Texas accent, a Texas cuisine, a Texas way of considering things, maybe even a Texas ego—but there is not a Texas land.

Texas covers more than 267,000 square miles (691,500 square kilometers). Geologically and climatically, the state is enormously varied.

The three broad grape-growing regions—Texas Hill Country, in the center of the state; High Plains, on the Texas Panhandle; and Trans-Pecos, a large winegrowing area in the southwest bordering Mexico—all encompass

A country highway leads through a field of Texas bluebonnets in the Texas Hill Country. The dazzling wildflowers of central Texas were seeded several decades ago as a gift from Lady Bird Johnson, wife of 36th U.S. president Lyndon Johnson.

numerous smaller AVAs. Texas Hill Country is a concatenation of rolling hills and color. The white limestone and pink granite soil stares out from the rough rock faces it clings to. In the spring, these hills are covered with scratchy olive-green mesquite and awash in bluebonnets and wagon-red wildflowers called Indian paintbrushes. By comparison, the High Plains are precisely that: majestic, flat plains some 3,600 feet (1,100 meters) above sea level, carpeted with wild grasses as far as the eye can see. The Trans-Pecos, in the West Texas desert, is yet again different, full of awe-inspiring, isolated mountainscapes; vast, barren red mesas; canyons; and, occasionally, fertile river valleys. Within the Trans-Pecos region, the Escondido Valley viticultural area is made up of limestone-laced hills and mountains full of marine sedimentary rock.

What is viticulturally critical in each of these regions are the well-drained soils, the high altitude of the best vineyards, and the fact that hot days usually don't end in equally hot nights. Without some temperature drop at night, Texas would not be able to produce good wine. Still, Texas is a comparatively warm place for grape-growing. The vines often wake up from their winter dormancy early in the year, and are sometimes ready to be harvested by the end of July—a full two to three months before

THE MOST IMPORTANT TEXAS WINES

LEADING WINES

CABERNET SAUVIGNON red

CHARDONNAY white

SAUVIGNON BLANC white

WINES OF NOTE

BLANC DU BOIS white

CHENIN BLANC white

MUSCAT white

SYRAH red

TEMPRANILLO red

VIOGNIER white

WHEN YOU VISIT . . .
TEXAS

THERE'S SOMETHING indescribably charming about watching winemakers wearing cowboy boots as they explain the intricacies of their "whyyyyyne..." (a multisyllabic word in the Lone Star State). Many Texas wineries welcome visitors, although it's a good idea to look up specific directions, since most wineries are deep in the countryside. It's often the owners themselves who will take you around.

so many Texas wines are simple and good— but not complex. (A long hang time and a progressive but slow pace en route to ripeness are thought to be some of the factors behind complexity in wine.)

THE FOODS OF TEXAS

For most of its history, Texas was better known for its cowboy boots than for its culinary bounty. That changed radically in the 1980s when, just as the modern wine industry was forming, a handful of dynamic young chefs began to piece together a maverick new style of cooking deemed Southwestern cuisine. Although it had no tidy parameters, Southwestern cuisine did have deep historical roots. They begin with the native Hopi and Pueblo Indians, who roasted corn to bring out its sweetness, used chiles to heighten flavor, grilled fish over hot-burning Texas woods, and smoked game.

the harvest in California and most European wine regions. As a result of this shortish, immediately warm growing season, grapes in Texas sometimes lack sufficient hang time at cooler temperatures. This, in turn, may be why

Aging wine at Caprock Winery, on the High Plains of the Texas Panhandle near the town of Lubbock. Vineyards here are planted on a vast plateau 3,600 feet (1,000 meters) above sea level.

Cowboys, too, left their culinary mark. With only a sack of pinto beans, a bucket of lard, a dozen eggs, chiles, garlic, a sack of masa harina (ground corn), a sack of flour, and coffee as provisions, cowboys set off to uninhabited ranch lands for weeks at a time. They hunted and grilled wild turkey, quail, and venison and made rough homemade biscuits or camp bread cooked over coals in black cast-iron pots. Biscuits, in fact, were a cowboy's silverware.

Although both are Texas specialties, grilling is not the same as barbecuing. Grilled food is cooked quickly over an open flame. The American word *barbecue* comes from *barbacoa*, the word Spanish explorers used to describe meats cooked extremely slowly in a pit, so that the meat was cooked by smoke as much as by flame, if not more so. In the end, the meat would be so tender and succulent it would fall off the bone. Pit barbecue restaurants are still found all over the state.

Texas shares 1,240 miles (2,000 kilometers) of border with Mexico. From the Mexicans, Texans learned how to cook with avocados, tomatoes, vanilla, and chocolate. Texas salsas (rough, uncooked sauces made from diced tomatoes, other vegetables, tropical fruits, and spices) are Mexican-inspired, as are flan desserts. Mexican home cooks taught Texans how to make food refreshing by using lime juice in marinades and as a seasoning. (Today, many Texans still drink beer as Mexicans do, with fresh lime squeezed in.) Mexican tortillas—thin, unleavened corn or flour disks—are the unofficial Texas bread.

The greatest commingling of Mexican and Texan cooking has been the development of Tex-Mex cuisine. Gutsy, homey, and inexpensive, Tex-Mex was created by Mexican Americans living in Texas and working with limited ingredients and a limited budget. The most famous Tex-Mex dishes (tacos, burritos, chiles rellenos, fajitas) are all based on tortillas, usually wrapped around some combination of beans, melted cheese, and ground

Chicken-fried steak with cream gravy. Not chicken; not steak exactly, and no cream. But a Texas specialty nonetheless and great with a Texas sauvignon blanc.

or sliced beef or pork, all spiked up with a fiery-hot dipping sauce. Texans say that if your forehead does not break out in beads of sweat, you are in the wrong Tex-Mex restaurant.

Texas, however, is as much the South as it is the West. Chicken-fried steak with cream gravy—a Southern dish—could almost be called the official Texas state dish. The name makes little sense, for the dish has nothing to do with chicken, and there is no cream in the gravy. To make it, an inexpensive cut of beef is seasoned with black pepper, flattened into a thin patty, coated in a flour, milk, and egg batter, and then deep-fried until it is crunchy. Over it, Texans pour the cream gravy, a dense, gray-brown sauce made by mixing flour with nutmeg, black pepper, and a little milk and then cooking the mixture until it is thick and lumpy. If anything begs for a glass of Texas cabernet, it's chicken-fried steak.

The Texas Wines to Know

WHITES

PEDERNALES

VIOGNIER | RESERVE | TEXAS

100% viognier

Viognier, the great aromatic white grape of France's minuscule Condrieu region, in the northern Rhône Valley, would seem one of the least likely candidates for vinous residency in Texas. But viognier made in the Lone Star State can be surprisingly good, and Pedernales is one of my favorites. With its deep floral/honeysuckle aromas and fresh apricot and vanilla flavors, this viognier is spot-on in terms of personality, but a steal in terms of price. Pedernales was founded in 2008 by the fifth, sixth, and seventh Texas generations of the Kuhlken family (just about everybody in the family works at the winery).

HAAK VINEYARDS & WINERY

BLANC DU BOIS | TEXAS

100% blanc du bois

No doubt about it—a winery located on the way to Galveston from Houston deserves to show up as the subject of a country western song. Especially Haak Vineyards—whose owner made the first blanc du bois in Texas back in the early 1980s. This wine is fruity and fresh—the kind of tasty, crisp white you might imagine would be perfect on a hot southern Texas night. Indeed, Texas vintners are pretty keen on this little grape—a complex hybrid developed in 1968 at the University of Florida. Blanc du bois is now grown all over the Gulf States, thanks to its amazing ability to tolerate humidity, pests, and fatal vine diseases like Pierce's disease.

LLANO ESTACADO

VIVIANA | TEXAS

An ever-changing blend of gewürztraminer, muscat canelli, viognier, riesling, and chardonnay

The winery's name, Llano Estacado, means "staked plains," which is what the area was called by Francisco Coronado, the early explorer who marked his way across the High Plains searching for the legendary cities of gold. Startling as the thought of northern European aromatic varieties planted in Texas may be, Llano Estacado's Viviana is a lively, fresh, thirst-slaking quaff that's beautifully aromatic and fruity. It's got some great crispness (perhaps from the riesling) and a wonderful, marmalade-like hint of bitterness (that's gewürztraminer talking).

2 0 0 8

SUPERIORE CUVÉE

TEXAS

REDS

RED CABOOSE

CABERNET FRANC-TEMPRANILLO | TEXAS HIGH PLAINS

70% cabernet franc, 30% tempranillo

Texans boast that they can cook a mean steak, and this cabernet franc-tempranillo blend would be just the right partner. With the very first sip, you know you're in for something dramatic and flavorful. Slightly rugged in an attractive way, this blend has terrific structure and appealing aromas and flavors reminiscent of woodsmoke, graphite, tobacco, and roasted coffee beans. Indeed, this wine recently won "Class Champion" at the Houston Livestock Show and Rodeo (eat your heart out, Château Margaux). Founded in 2003, Red Caboose is the effort of father-son team Gary and Evan McKibben. Gary, an architect, specializes in sustainable structures, and thus Red Caboose uses geothermal power for heating, cooling, refrigeration, and all other electricity, and the winery is built to harvest rainwater (1 inch of rainfall = 16,000 gallons; 2.54 centimeters = 606 hectoliters), which is used to irrigate the vineyards. The winery also makes a fun syrah/tempranillo/cabernet sauvignon blend called Range Rider.

R CW

Cabernet Franc 30%
Tempranillo 70%

Texas

RED CABOOSE
Winery & Vineyards

Alc.14.8% by Vol.   750 ml

FALL CREEK

SALT LICK VINEYARD | TEMPRANILLO | TEXAS

100% tempranillo

Fall Creek, one of the early pioneers of the modern Texas wine industry, made this rugged tempranillo from the vineyards at The Salt Lick—a famous down-home barbecue joint in Driftwood, Texas (don't plan on leavin' after the pork ribs without takin' a whole homemade pecan pie home, y'all). Back to the wine, this is tempranillo reminiscent of the center of Spain—juicy yet edgy, with a good grip of bitterness that makes you want meat charred on the grill.

SWEET WINE

CAP ROCK

ORANGE MUSCAT | TEXAS HIGH PLAINS

100% orange muscat

Muscat may well be the most beloved variety of grape. Indeed, the intense fruitiness of muscat wine is like the liquid version of a tropical fruit salad. And this one, from Cap Rock, is true to the *orange* in its name, for the wine also bursts with tangerine, kumquat, and mandarin flavors. This is a wine to be iced down cold and served all by itself on a hot weekend afternoon. (Orange muscat is a cross of muscat blanc à petits grains and chasselas.)

VIRGINIA

Among the first wines produced in America were those made around 1607 by Jamestown colonists, from wild, musky-tasting scuppernong grapes. The wines were so poor—even by colonial standards—that in 1619 the Virginia Company sent French vine cuttings and eight French winemakers to Jamestown to help establish proper vineyards and make decent wine. That same year, by legislative act, each colonist was required to plant at least ten grapevines. French help proved futile. The maiden vineyards soon died from fungal diseases and pests.

▲ *Barboursville Vineyards, a plantation, vineyard, and mansion founded in 1821 by James Barbour, former governor of Virginia and secretary of war (1825–1828) under President John Quincy Adams. The estate was purchased and restored in 1976 by the Italian winemaking family Zonin.*

THE QUICK SIP ON VIRGINIA

ATTEMPTS TO MAKE WINE in Virginia began in 1607—the earliest record of wine production in the United States.

DISEASES, PESTS, and difficult weather destroyed most of the early vineyards, including those planted by third U.S. president, Thomas Jefferson.

THE MODERN ERA of Virginia winemaking started in the late 1970s with the planting of chardonnay, cabernet sauvignon, and other grapes.

The old barn at Early Mountain Vineyards, along the Monticello Wine Trail in the pastoral Blue Ridge Mountains of Virginia. The mostly small family wineries here continue to be inspired by Thomas Jefferson's vision of an American wine culture.

WHEN YOU VISIT . . . VIRGINIA

JUST OVER 60 PERCENT of Virginia wine is sold in-state, and much of that is sold directly from the wineries themselves. As a result, even the tiniest of Virginia wineries welcomes (with considerable Southern hospitality) visitors and conducts tours and tastings.

VIRGINIA WINE COUNTRY is among the most beautiful in the United States, and many wineries have pick-your-own apple orchards, picnic areas, wine festivals, and even, should you be spontaneously swept away, wedding facilities.

Remarkably, the early Virginians were undeterred. For almost two centuries they continued to plant vines, and the vines, for their part, continued to perish. By President Thomas Jefferson's time, the prospects for a Virginia wine industry appeared nonexistent. Not that this stopped Jefferson (see box, page 793); he planted his Monticello vineyard in 1807. Alas, the vines eventually died because of diseases and pests.

Then, in the late nineteenth and early twentieth centuries, the picture changed radically. The devastation wrought by severely cold winters, plus vine diseases and phylloxera, caused plant breeders to develop (and import) a number of new crosses and hybrid grapes (for information about crosses and hybrids, see page 771). These crosses and hybrids became quite successful, even though, compared to European wines, some were still an acquired taste because of their grapey/animal fur character, known as "foxy." As time went on, however, several hybrids—including

AMERICA'S FIRST WINE EXPERT

Thomas Jefferson, third president of the United States and author of the Declaration of Independence, was an accomplished architect, scientist, musician, philosopher, scholar, and farmer in addition to being a politician. He was also America's first wine expert.

Born in Albemarle County, Virginia, on April 13, 1743, Jefferson was appointed ambassador to France at the age of forty-one, and moved to Paris. There he became deeply impressed by the French—especially their love of food and wine. Subsequently, he arranged for his slave James Hemings to take lessons from a French chef, promising Hemings his freedom if he would teach French cooking to the other slaves at Monticello.

During his time in Europe, Jefferson became profoundly curious about viticulture. In 1787 and 1788, he toured the wine regions of France, Germany, and northern Italy, visiting the top producers and taking detailed notes in hopes of growing European (vinifera) grapes and making wine at Monticello. When he returned in 1789, wines from the most prestigious vineyards of Europe were included in his eighty-six packing cases. He also came back zealously enthusiastic, convinced that, in moderation, wine was an integral part of healthful living. Alas, Jefferson's own attempts at establishing a vineyard in Virginia and making wine repeatedly failed.

Consuming great wine was, luckily, easier than producing it. Not surprisingly, the White House cellar was amply stocked—especially with French wines—during the Jefferson presidency. Indeed, Jefferson personally spent many thousands of dollars on wine—a feat in and of itself, given what wine cost in 1800. But Jefferson had an impact on the White House cellar well before and long after his terms. From Washington's presidency through Monroe's, Jefferson positioned himself as the unofficial presidential wine adviser, always ready with recommendations, even when none were requested.

No president since Jefferson has ever taken such a profound interest in wine and wine's beneficial role in society. The White House cellar remains, however, well stocked—today, mostly with American wines.

Vidal, Maréchal Foch, and chambourcin—were singled out as higher in quality, thanks to their relative lack of foxiness. Each is still grown (in small quantities) in Virginia today.

But the real birth of the state's modern wine industry came in the 1980s, with the widespread planting of *vinifera* grapes such as chardonnay and cabernet franc. A new period of optimism ensued. In 1979, there had been just 286 acres (116 hectares) of vineyards and six wineries in Virginia. By 2011, there were 2,600 acres (1,052 hectares) and 250 wineries. And, helpfully, some of the modern families who now own those wineries have a lot of experience with new ventures. Real estate magnate Donald Trump and AOL founder Steve Case, for example, both own wineries in Virginia.

THE LAND, THE GRAPES, AND THE VINEYARDS

The state's wineries are scattered over seven appellations, from Shenandoah Valley, in the northwest, between the Allegheny and Blue Ridge Mountains; to Monticello (named after the nearby home of Thomas Jefferson); to Northern Neck (George Washington's

VIRGINIA COUNTRY HAM

Arguably the quintessential Southern food, country ham has been produced in Virginia and its neighboring states from the earliest Colonial times. As the number of artisanal producers has declined, however, production of true country ham has diminished sharply.

Unlike the baked ham often eaten at Easter, Virginia country ham has a very dramatic, sweet, meaty flavor and can be quite salty. Like Italian prosciutto, it's meant to be sliced paper thin.

The best country hams—such as those produced near the town of Smithfield—come from peanut-fed hogs. The hams are dry-cured with sugar and seasonings, then smoked over hickory wood and aged from three months to up to one year. The longer the aging, the saltier the meat.

Salty foods often work best with either high-acid wines or sweet wines. Or, if you're up for an adventure, try a juicy, fruity red that's uniquely Virginian: Norton.

Here are three top Virginia ham producers: Smithfield Packing Co., Gwaltney of Smithfield, and S. Wallace Edwards & Sons.

---

birthplace); North Fork of Roanoke; Rocky Knob; and the Eastern Shore.

Eastern Virginia's vineyards tend to be planted mostly in clay and loam soils, while soils in the western part of the state are more granite based. Despite these soil differences, and although the vineyards are scattered across the entire state, all of them share a dramatic continental climate. Winters can be so bitingly cold that the trunks of the vines can freeze and split open. Springtime frosts can kill new buds. In summer, excessive heat can make the grapes ripen too quickly, which detracts from the elegance of the final wine. Humidity during the growing season can lead to rot, mildew, and disease. And as if all of this wasn't enough, hurricane season overlaps with the harvest, posing a threat of torrential rains. In Virginia, winemakers and viticulturists need to be extremely well skilled, and it's critical to plant vineyards only in sites where threats and problems are minimized.

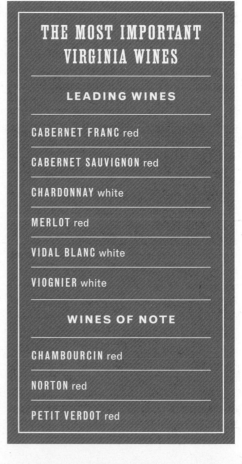

THE MOST IMPORTANT VIRGINIA WINES

LEADING WINES

CABERNET FRANC red

CABERNET SAUVIGNON red

CHARDONNAY white

MERLOT red

VIDAL BLANC white

VIOGNIER white

WINES OF NOTE

CHAMBOURCIN red

NORTON red

PETIT VERDOT red

Monticello, the Virginia estate of Thomas Jefferson, third President of the United States. Had Jefferson's hopes come true, the United States would have had a thriving wine industry by the turn of the 19th century, for Jefferson considered wine the most healthful and civilized of beverages.

THE GRAPES OF VIRGINIA

WHITES

CHARDONNAY: A widely planted grape; virtually every winery makes a chardonnay.

VIDAL BLANC: An important French-American hybrid that can make very good wines.

VIOGNIER: The second-leading white grape in the state; its quality can be very good.

REDS

CABERNET FRANC: An important grape that shows promise. It makes lean reds that are smoky and slightly spicy.

CABERNET SAUVIGNON: Generally less successful than cabernet franc; the wines from cabernet sauvignon vary in quality.

CHAMBOURCIN: An important hybrid with very good success in Virginia. It makes lean reds.

MERLOT: An important grape; most examples are fairly light and lean.

NORTON: A hybrid that makes simple, fruity wines with a lot of berry flavors. Although only a small amount is planted, the quality can be high.

PETIT VERDOT: An up-and-coming grape that makes lean, slightly spicy reds, sometimes with a lot of tannin.

The Virginia Wines to Know

WHITES

CHATEAU MORRISETTE

VIOGNIER | MONTICELLO

100% viognier

Chateau Morrisette, founded in the Blue Ridge Mountains in 1978, is owned by the Morrisette family, who are clearly dog lovers (the corks are branded "woof woof," the wine's back label is in the shape of a dog bone; the website is thedogs.com; and many of their wines are named after dogs: Black Dog, Frosty Dog, and Our Dog Blue). But canines aside, viognier is one of the family's strong suits. It's full of floral aromas (though thankfully it's not excessively perfumey) and tastes of dried apricot, quince, and citrus. Viognier fans, this is for you.

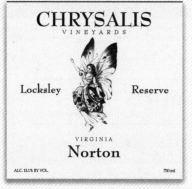

REDS

CHRYSALIS

NORTON | LOCKSLEY RESERVE | VIRGINIA

100% Norton

Made from the American hybrid called Norton, this juicy, light-bodied wine has a strawberry preserve quality, plus the hint of a good, bitter, Campari-like edge. Chill it just a bit (as if it were Beaujolais) and serve with some good Virginia country ham. Chrysalis has the largest plantings of Norton grapes in the world.

BARBOURSVILLE VINEYARDS

CABERNET FRANC | RESERVE

95% cabernet franc, 5% cabernet sauvignon

Barboursville, a historic Virginia landmark located between Monticello and Montpelier, boasts the ruins of the elegant 1814 brick house that Thomas Jefferson designed for his friend, the governor of Virginia and U.S. Senator James Barbour. The winery was founded in 1976 by Gianni Zonin, heir to one of the largest wine companies in Italy, and grows more than a dozen varieties of grapes. In particular, the winery's cabernet franc shows fine character and the potential for this variety in Virginia. With a distinct cedar/earth/cassis-like aroma and flavor, plus a significant structure, the wine is reminiscent of an easy-drinking but sophisticated Cru Bourgeois Bordeaux.

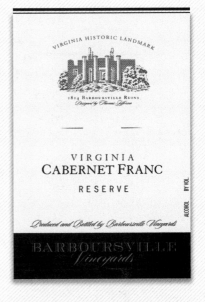

LINDEN

HARDSCRABBLE | VIRGINIA

Approximately 70% cabernet sauvignon, 15% cabernet franc, and small amounts of petit verdot and merlot

Linden, a small winery in the Blue Ridge Mountains, about an hour's drive west of Washington, D.C., has made cabernet-based wines since 1987, and their experience shows. Hardscrabble (named for a difficult plot of rocky, arid land) is the real deal—a Bordeaux-style wine with a solid core of licoricey/cocoa-y fruit, and a wonderful barklike character reminiscent of sophisticated bitters.

FLYING FOX

PETIT VERDOT | MONTICELLO

Approximately 80% petit verdot, with merlot

This inky wine is a surprise for Virginia, and perhaps an indication of good things to come from this variety. The wine is classic petit verdot—black in color, packed with rich red currant flavors, smoky, chocolaty, and very structured. Flying Fox, a small family winery, takes its name from the fox-topped weathervane on the property.

KING FAMILY

MERITAGE | MONTICELLO

Approximately 50% merlot, plus petit verdot, cabernet franc,
and malbec

The King family make very good Bordeaux-style wines from their
estate in Monticello (the term *meritage* refers to wines made from
a blend of varieties historically grown in Bordeaux). These are
medium-bodied, easy-drinking wines that have a nice sleekness to
them and terrific structure. Their sophisticated flavors and aromas
lean toward dark chocolate, licorice, and tar. Like many Virginia
wineries, this one is beautiful and has a deep sense of Southern
hospitality. Every Sunday in summer, polo matches are held at the
winery's polo field.

MICHAEL SHAPS

TANNAT | MONTICELLO

100% tannat

It's hard to know if tannat has a future in Virginia (or in the U.S.),
but this wine gives a hopeful glimpse of what might be possible.
Bold and packed with tar and dark chocolate flavors, it's a wine
that needs a shivery night and snow on the ground. Indeed, the
savory/salty/bitter flavors and sleek but mouthfilling texture are
just waiting for a roast leg of lamb to be taken from the oven.
Michael Shaps, a veteran of the Virginia wine scene, studied in
Burgundy before making wine for several Virginia wineries, including, as of 2007, his own.

OTHER IMPORTANT
WINE
REGIONS

ARIZONA | MISSOURI | NEW MEXICO | PENNSYLVANIA
IDAHO | MICHIGAN | COLORADO | NEW JERSEY

cabernet from New Jersey with dinner? It's no longer a completely far-fetched idea. As of the early twentieth century, most states in the U.S. had wine industries. But a combination of Prohibition, vine diseases for which there was then no remedy, and the Great Depression led farmers to pursue other crops in place of wine grapes. Today, the situation has completely turned around. All fifty states now have established wine industries. We've covered California, Washington State, Oregon,

---

▲ *Casa Rondena Winery in the Rio Grande Valley, Albuquerque, New Mexico.*

New York, Texas, and Virginia earlier in this chapter. Here are eight other states that make wines I think you'll want to taste and know about.

ARIZONA

Whatever the Apache warrior chief Cochise envisioned as the destiny of his homeland, it probably wasn't as wine country. But on the parched, blindingly bright high desert of southeast Arizona where Cochise once reigned, that's exactly what has happened. Just 20 miles (32 kilometers) from the Mexican border, the cactus-ringed villages of Sonoita, Sedona, and Wilcox (John Wayne westerns were filmed here) have sprouted the improbable: small green vines that clutch the earth with true grit.

Arizona's three major winegrowing areas are all on high deserts, and although a scorching desert climate would seem to preclude grape-growing, sixty-three wineries now exist, thanks to irrigation. All is not quite perfect, however. As it turns out, the state's coyotes and javelinas not only adore grapes but also possesses a special fondness for the flavor of

A horse-drawn wagon may still be the best way to experience the vineyards of Arizona. Here, Sonoita Vineyards.

irrigation hoses, without which no Arizonan winery could survive.

The first attempts to grow grapes in Arizona were made by Franciscan missionaries in the late seventeenth century, but the state's modern wine industry didn't emerge until the 1980s, when Dr. Gordon Dutt, who has a PhD in soil science from the University of Arizona, planted grapes near Sonoita. Today, the leading wineries include Callaghan Vineyards, Lawrence Dunham, Alcantara, Pillsbury, Javelina Leap, and Bitter Creek, several of which make good red wines based on Mediterranean and Spanish varieties such as tempranillo, mourvèdre, and grenache.

MISSOURI

With 119 wineries, Missouri is one of the most prominent up-and-coming wine regions in the United States. Until relatively recently, Missouri's was a riches-to-rags story. In 1866, George Husmann, a professor at the University of Missouri, prophesied that the United States would one day be the world's greatest wine-producing country. At the time, it seemed as if his home state might lead the way; it ranked second in the nation in grape-growing, and wines from Missouri quite frankly stunned critics in wine exhibitions in Paris, Vienna, and elsewhere in Europe. The grape variety Norton, a hybrid, was especially highly regarded—it was compared by one British wine expert to no less than French Burgundy "without the finesse." (As descriptions go, this was probably a bit fanciful; Norton's deep color, full body, and jammy fruit flavors are more reminiscent of zinfandel than pinot noir.) Ultimately and unfortunately, a combination of disease (especially mildew and rot), overproduction, and local Prohibition laws took their toll on Missouri's wine industry. By the 1880s, most vineyards were dying or abandoned. Those that survived national Prohibition did so by reinventing themselves as juice and jelly manufacturers.

Stone Hill Winery in Hermann, Missouri, on the banks of the Missouri River. Before Prohibition, Hermann was one of the flourishing centers of wine in the United States, and Stone Hill Winery was one of the five largest wineries in the world.

A rebirth came in the 1970s and 1980s, with new laws that helped jump-start a modern wine industry, and by 2010, Missouri was spawning nearly a dozen new wineries every year. The top three producing wineries in Missouri are St. James, Stone Hill, and Les Bourgeois.

NEW MEXICO

In the 1990s, a sparkling wine named Gruet developed a cult following in knowledgeable wine circles around the United States. On the face of it, there was nothing remarkable about this; there were, after all, many terrific California sparkling wines made according to the traditional (Champagne) method.

But Gruet wasn't from Napa or Sonoma, or for that matter from anyplace else in California. Gruet was from Truth or Consequences, a small town in New Mexico, and as surprising as *that* was, another surprise was in store when you called the winery looking for the owner. A Frenchwoman got on the line.

In 1983, Nathalie Gruet, her brother Laurent Gruet, and her husband, Farid Himeur, moved from France to Truth or Consequences, a stark plateau 150 miles (240 kilometers) south of Albuquerque, with the intention of making sparkling wine. As tourists years before, they'd fallen in love with the American Southwest and instinctively felt that it was wine country waiting to be discovered. Land prices were cheap. They figured that if the wine they made turned out bad, they wouldn't be out a lot of capital; if it turned out well, the notoriety would launch them. And that's exactly what happened. The first Gruet brut was released in 1989 to amazing press reviews. Crisp, frothy, and elegant, it's easily the equal of many California sparklers.

As in Arizona, New Mexico's first grapes were planted in the seventeenth century by Franciscan fathers who required wine for the Mass (this was earlier than in California by a few decades). But as in so many other states, disease, severe weather, and national Prohibition proved the New Mexican wine industry's undoing. At least until the 1980s. Today, New Mexico boasts fifty-two wineries, including two meaderies (wineries that make mead, or wine from honey), proving that truth, consequences, and wine can be a formidable combination.

PENNSYLVANIA

With hundreds of chardonnays made in California, you don't expect to find one of your favorites in Pennsylvania, but many wine lovers have. The state has more wineries than most of us would guess—123. Pennsylvania was the location of one of the first successful commercial winegrowing ventures in the United States: the Pennsylvania Wine Company, which began in 1793 but closed soon thereafter, its vineyards decimated by disease. Today, more advanced viticultural knowledge promises a brighter future for the state.

Pennsylvania has highly diversified climates, and thus a wide variety of wines are made. On the one hand, *vinifera* varieties such as chardonnay, pinot gris, and cabernet sauvignon are quite successful here, but so are hybrids such as catawba, Cayuga, chambourcin, seyval blanc, and Vidal blanc. In Pennsylvania's far north, near Lake Erie, icewines are made. As is true in New Jersey, Pennsylvania has a very active vintners' alliance dedicated to improving quality—the Pennsylvania Wine Quality Initiative—which is credited with raising wine quality dramatically in the past decade. Among Pennsylvania's top wineries: Chaddsford Winery, Windgate Vineyards, Mazza Vineyards, and Twin Brook Winery.

IDAHO

The first wineries in the Pacific Northwest were not in Oregon or Washington State but in Idaho, the oft-forgotten third member of the Pacific Northwest triad. German and French immigrants planted grapes here as early as 1864, but as with so many states, national Prohibition took a debilitating toll on the industry and brought production to an absolute halt.

Today, the Idaho wine industry is in the process of a whirlwind rebirth. Just ten years

Harvesting grapes in the Snake River Valley of southwestern Idaho.

ago the state had eleven wineries; today it has forty-nine.

That rebirth first began in the 1970s, when wine grapes were planted along the Snake River Valley, in the southern part of the state. Indeed, the Snake River Valley—an 8,000-square-mile (20,700-square-kilometer) expanse—was Idaho's first American Viticulture Area (AVA), having been approved in April 2007. The Snake River Valley is part of a larger southwestern Idaho area that today has the highest density of vineyards and wineries in the state.

From a geographical standpoint, southern Idaho has several viticultural assets. The area is at the same latitude as many European winegrowing regions, yet is sunnier and has far less rainfall. The characteristic cold winters, which might at first seem a disadvantage, are in fact quite conducive, allowing the vines to go completely dormant, thus conserving important carbohydrates for the coming season and at the same time ridding the vines of bugs and discouraging disease. In addition, the region's summer combination of cold nights and warm days helps create a good balance of sugars and acid, resulting in well-balanced wines.

Among the wineries to seek out: Cinder Winery, Coiled Winery, and Clearwater Canyon Cellars.

MICHIGAN

The first time I tasted a Michigan wine—it was a riesling from the small wine district Old Mission Peninsula—I was pretty astounded. But perhaps I shouldn't have been. Michigan has had a well-established wine industry for decades, and the state's climate is perfect for varieties such as riesling, pinot gris, and gewürztraminer, that thrive in cool temperatures.

The Michigan wine industry took its first formal step as far back as 1939, with the establishment of the Michigan Wine Institute, a trade association formed to benefit local grape growers. For many of these early decades, the industry revolved, as it did in nearby New York, around French-American hybrid grapes such as Vidal blanc. But in 1969, Carl Banholzer and Leonard Olson, owners of Tabor Hill Winery, in Buchanan, Michigan, took the next step and planted the state's first documented *vinifera* grape varieties—in this case, chardonnay and riesling.

There was no turning back. Lake Michigan's temperate shoreline and the bounty of cherry orchards and farmland enticed would-be winemakers By the late 1970s, many of Michigan's important wineries were founded, including Leelanau Cellars, Fenn Valley Vineyards, L. Mawby Vineyards, and Good Harbor Vineyards. Most importantly, large-scale plantings of *vinifera* varieties began, notably at Chateau Grand Traverse, one of the state's important wineries on Old Mission Peninsula.

That peninsula, by the way, is now one of Michigan's most important AVAs. Old Mission Peninsula extends north for 19 miles (31 kilometers) from Traverse City into the Grand Traverse Bay of Lake Michigan, ending at Old Mission Point. The climate on the peninsula is moderated by the surrounding waters, helping to prevent frost during the growing season. Today, there are ninety-three wineries in Michigan. Among the most influential: St. Julian Winery, Tabor Hill Winery, and Leelanau Cellars.

Punching down the "cap" of red grape skins at Chateau Grand Traverse on Old Mission Peninsula. One of Michigan's most important wineries, Chateau Grand Traverse introduced vinifera *varieties to Michigan in the 1970s.*

COLORADO

When you visit a hip city like Boulder, Colorado, it seems entirely logical that the state has an enthusiastic wine culture. That comes as no surprise. What is surprising, however, is viticulture in Colorado. The Rocky Mountain state's 105 wineries are mostly nestled in high-elevation river valleys and on mesas—many of which are at elevations of 4,000 to 7,000 feet (1,200 to 2,100 meters) above sea level, making Colorado's vineyards some of the highest in the world.

At such elevations, nights are cold, but during the ripening season in late summer, days are 30°F (17°C) warmer, dry, and sunny. Indeed, as in Argentina (where vineyards are often 4,000 to 5,000 feet/1,200 to 1,500 meters in elevation), the grapes experience an intense luminosity during ripening. In Colorado, that luminosity is coupled with long daylight hours. The combination of these factors bodes well for an industry that is just now beginning to get some traction. Among the most highly thought of wineries are Winery at Holy Cross Abbey, Two Rivers Winery, Bookcliff Vineyards, Creekside Cellars, and Garfield Estates Vineyard.

Striking palisades loom over the vineyards of Palisade, near Grand Junction, in northwest Colorado.

NEW JERSEY

The Garden State is often the butt of less-than-genteel jokes. But one thing that's no joke: New Jersey makes surprisingly good wines.

The first time I tasted a group of New Jersey wines, I figured it would take a few minutes and no more (very simple wines = fast tasting). But a half hour later, my tasting group and I were still discussing how much the reds (especially merlot, cabernet sauvignon, and cabernet franc) reminded us of Bordeaux.

And speaking of Bordeaux: In New Jersey, an audacious tasting occurred in 2012 that immediately put New Jersey wine on a whole new level. Called "The Judgment of Princeton," the tasting was modeled on the famous Judgment of Paris Tasting of 1976, which put California wine on the international map. The Princeton Tasting was led by none other than George Taber who, as a *TIME* magazine reporter in 1976, broke the Paris Tasting story. For the Judgment of Princeton, nine judges from France, Belgium, and the U.S. blind-tasted New Jersey wines against top Bordeaux—indeed, against the same top Bordeaux as were included in the 1976 tasting: Château Mouton-Rothschild, Château Haut-Brion, and others of high status. In the end, the highest-scoring white and red were both French wines (a Joseph Drouhin Beaune Clos des Mouches and Château Mouton-Rothschild, respectively). But—and here's the astounding part—three of the four top whites were from New Jersey, and the best New Jersey red ranked third.

You could be cynical. You could make a dozen arguments about the questionable validity of taste-offs. But, OMG. New Jersey rests her case.

Among my favorite New Jersey wineries: Hawk Haven, Unionville Vineyards, Ventimiglia Vineyard (which makes a stunning wine from the hybrid grape chambourcin), Heritage Estate, Working Dog Winery, and Bellview.

MEXICO

s an important wine region, Mexico may seem unlikely. Yet this is where the history of wine in the Americas began. Indeed, the first winery in the New World—Casa Madero—was established in 1597 in the Mexican town of Santa Maria de las Parras ("Holy Mary of the Grapevines"), and the winery continues to thrive today.

Like many wine drinkers, I once assumed that most Mexican wine would be cheap, rough-and-ready stuff sold in supermarkets. Admittedly, such wines do exist in Mexico (as they do nearly everywhere else). But beginning in the 1990s, and building on the success of already established wineries like Monte Xanic, Santo Tomás, and L.A. Cetto, a group of creative young winemakers quietly began making small lots of surprisingly delicious wines.

Today, Mexico's rapidly growing fine wine industry is bursting with energy, and the top wines are astonishing in quality.

Mexico has some 7,660 acres (3,100 hectares) of vineyards, and wine is produced in three principal areas—in the northwest, specifically in the Baja Peninsula, immediately south of California; in the north central states of Coahuila, Durango, and Chihuahua, all just south of Texas and New Mexico; and in the center of Mexico, in the states of Zacatecas, Aguascalientes, and Queretaro. Of these three regions, more than 90 percent of all fine wine is produced in Baja.

The 1,012-mile-long (1,629-kilometer) Baja Peninsula is divided lengthwise by the

▲ The shaded areas of this map indicate entire states where wine is made. The actual vineyard areas are smaller and scattered throughout the state.

The vineyards of Adobe Guadalupe in Mexico's Guadalupe Valley on the Baja Peninsula. Besides making excellent wine, the estate breeds prize-winning Azteca sport horses and has a stunning small hacienda-like inn.

> "Wine is our path of life. It is not what we do; it's our path to who we are."
>
> —JOSÉ LUIS DURAND,
> winemaker and owner,
> Durand Viticultura

mineral-rich Sierra de Baja California mountain range, which effectively divides the climate of the peninsula in half. All of the vineyards lie in arid valleys to the west of these mountains, where the climate is Mediterranean-like and cold air from the Pacific Ocean acts as a giant air conditioner, cooling the grapes. The main valleys extend, from the thriving port city of Ensenada on the Pacific Ocean. (A gastronomically oriented city, Ensenada is famous for its fish tacos, in which Pacific lobster or shark are deep-fried in lard, then wrapped in fluffy, homemade flour tortillas.)

The main valleys include Guadalupe, San Antonio, Ojos Negros, Santo Tomás, San Vicente, and Llano Colorado. But of these, Guadalupe Valley is, by far, Mexico's Napa Valley. Here, along the largely unpaved Ruta del Vino ("Wine Route") are some seventy wineries, several of which also boast stellar avant-garde restaurants (Laja has exquisite food), and small hacienda-like hotels (Adobe Guadalupe is a spiritual haven). The number of physical wineries, however, does not directly reflect the booming industry here, for many boutique wineries are brands that buy grapes and, lacking their own facilities, rent space in other wineries. Many of these boutique wineries began as a result of La Escuelita ("The Little School")—part trade school, part wine boot camp, where locals are trained to make artisanal wines by one of the most passionate Mexican enologists, Hugo d'Acosta, owner of Casa de Piedra winery. (D'Acosta's minerally, creamy chardonnay, called Piedra de Sol, is one of the best chardonnays in Latin and South America.)

At 231 square miles (598 square kilometers), Guadalupe Valley is almost as big as Chianti Classico. Thanks to irrigation, green vineyards dot a ranching landscape that otherwise is so dry that little besides chaparral and desert shrubs grow. The lack of water is a concern for every vintner here and the leading limitation to further growth of the valley's wine industry. The soils are divided into those that are extremely sandy and infertile, near the now-dry river and streams that once ran through the valley, and those that are made up of eroded, decomposed granite washed down millennia ago from nearby mountains. Salinity in these soils often adds an unusual, attractive "minerality" to the flavor of the wines. Interestingly, the Guadalupe Valley wines that come from grapes grown in the sandy soils often display the greatest elegance.

As for grapes, Guadalupe Valley is a seemingly incongruous whirlwind of diversity. The three main grapes used in top wines are tempranillo, nebbiolo, and cabernet sauvignon, but many other varieties appear to do well here, including syrah, merlot, cabernet franc, malbec, pinot noir, mourvèdre, grenache, and petite sirah among reds; and among whites, sauvignon blanc, chardonnay, viognier, and chenin blanc. Rarely are the grapes made into monovarietal wines. Instead, virtually all of the

In Mexico, as in California, the harvest is often done in the cool of night.

wines are blends—often blends that have no precedent anywhere in the world (imagine, if you can, the flavor of a wine based on a combination of nebbiolo, petite sirah, petit verdot, merlot, and cabernet sauvignon).

A word on Mexican nebbiolo. As delicious as wines made from it can be, the morphology of the leaves and clusters, as well as the character of the wine itself, indicate that it's not nebbiolo from Piedmont. (As of this writing, DNA analysis had not yet been performed to determine the grapes' genetic identity.) Indeed, leading enologists here believe that Mexican nebbiolo is probably not a single variety, but several varieties that were brought from Italy after World War II by the Italian winemaker Esteban Ferro, then at Santo Tomás winery. Ferro's cuttings were apparently stalled at the port of Veracruz for a long period of time, and the identification tags, wet and disintegrating, were eventually lost. But the cuttings were planted and collectively called nebbiolo.

Mexican wines run the gamut from ethereally elegant and refined to powerhouses of intensity. Like Mexican culture, the wines often seem to simultaneously possess fragility and resilience. Among the best wines are Adobe Guadalupe's Gabriel (a vividly alive and rich Bordeaux-like blend of cabernet sauvignon, merlot, and malbec); La Lomita's Singular (always a dramatic, spicy, and distinctive red, although the blend changes completely every year); and José Luis Durand's Ala Rota and Ícaro (the first, a mostly cabernet sauvignon and petite sirah blend that's mindblowingly elegant, minerally, and delicious; the second, an intense, vivid, almost gamy wine based on nebbiolo and Bordeaux varieties).

Finally, because Mexico has no system of denominations of origin, many Mexican wines are simply labeled "product of Mexico," although some indicate the valley in which most of the grapes grew. Additionally, no regulatory wine laws means that the varieties listed on a label may or may not be listed in the order in which they dominate in the blend. A wine labeled tempranillo, cabernet sauvignon, and syrah, could be mostly syrah.

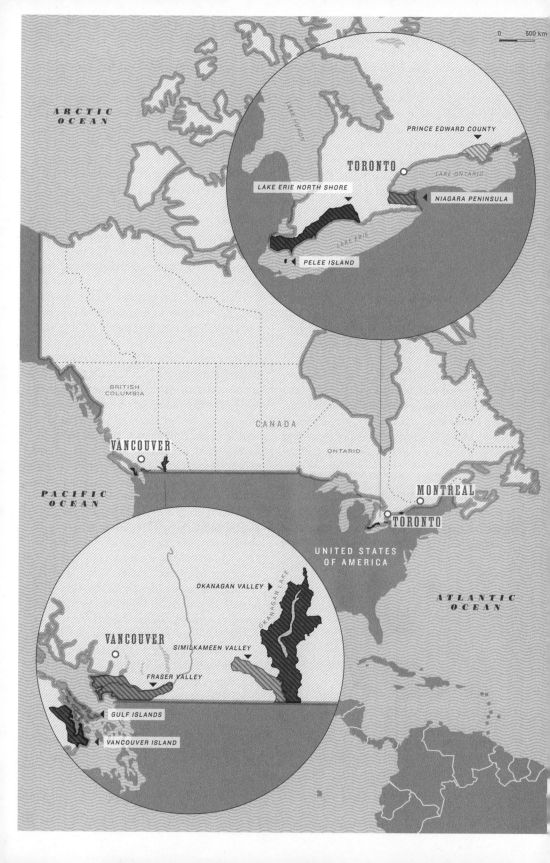

0   500 km

ARCTIC
OCEAN

PRINCE EDWARD COUNTY

TORONTO

LAKE HURON

LAKE ERIE NORTH SHORE

LAKE ONTARIO

NIAGARA PENINSULA

LAKE ERIE

PELEE ISLAND

BRITISH
COLUMBIA

CANADA

ONTARIO

VANCOUVER

PACIFIC
OCEAN

MONTRÉAL

TORONTO

UNITED STATES
OF AMERICA

ATLANTIC
OCEAN

VANCOUVER

OKANAGAN VALLEY

OKANAGAN LAKE

SIMILKAMEEN VALLEY

FRASER VALLEY

GULF ISLANDS

VANCOUVER ISLAND

CANADA

CANADA RANKS SIXTEENTH AMONG WINE-PRODUCING COUNTRIES WORLDWIDE. CANADIANS DRINK AN AVERAGE OF 4 GAL-LONS (15 LITERS) OF WINE PER PERSON PER YEAR.

anada is one of the newest wine regions in the New World. And like its southern neighbor, the United States, the country possesses a pioneering spirit thanks to its early days as a vast wilderness. Today, from seemingly out of nowhere, an exciting wine industry has sprung, and the top Canadian wines—dry and sweet—are now turning heads in competitions internationally. Though the industry is small, in the ten years between 2003 and 2013, the number of wineries here quadrupled. Today, there is no doubt that the wine industry in Canada is on a roll and that many distinctive, exciting dry wines are being made. As for Canada's renowned, sweet icewines—prepare to be devastated by their deliciousness.

Many Americans, and, indeed, many Canadians, may never have tasted a Canadian wine (the modern industry is still in its infancy), but grape-growing actually began here in the 1860s, when grapes intended for sacramental wine were planted near the Okanagan Mission in British Columbia, as well as on Lake Erie's Pelee Island, at a winery with what, at the time, was the evocative name Vin Villa. Yet for more than a century,

As the harvested grapes arrive, winemakers at Malivoire Winery in Ontario sort out any that aren't perfect.

Hillside vineyards in the sunny, dry Okanagan Valley of British Columbia. Millions of years ago, the hillsides were formed by receding glaciers.

the development of a prosperous wine industry was hampered by a complex series of political and economic barriers, including the creation of government monopolies that controlled the sale and distribution of alcoholic beverages. It was not until the late 1980s and early 1990s that a modern wine industry finally took hold.

It is still a very tiny industry by world standards. As of 2012, there were approximately 29,000 acres (11,700 hectares) of vineyards in Canada. That's less than the grape acreage in Switzerland, for example, and even the small Napa Valley in California has one and a half times as much vineyard acreage as Canada does.

For an explanation of Canadian wine law, see the Appendix on Wine Laws, page 928.

THE QUICK SIP
ON CANADA

CANADA'S TINY WINE industry is one of the newest and most exciting in the New World.

CANADA MAKES surprisingly excellent dry wines—especially rieslings and pinot noirs—as well as what has become one of the country's superstars—icewine, a rich, sweet nectar made from grapes frozen on the vines and harvested in the dead of winter.

CANADA'S TWO most important wine regions are on opposite sides of the country—in the west, British Columbia (principally the Okanagan Valley); in the east, Ontario (principally the Niagara Peninsula).

THE LAND, THE GRAPES,
AND THE VINEYARDS

I think of the wine regions of Canada as existing in a state of refrigerated sunlight. The country's cool, sunny, mostly dry climate and northern latitude come together to create an ideal environment for

THE GRAPES OF CANADA

WHITES

CHARDONNAY: A major grape, it can make very good wines ranging from lean, cool-climate styles to wines that are reminiscent of white Burgundies.

GEWÜRZTRAMINER: One of Canada's best-kept secrets. Can make beautifully aromatic, refreshing wines.

PINOT GRIS: A major grape; it makes crisp, distinctive, high-quality whites.

RIESLING: A major grape, made into sensational, concentrated, dry wines that are crisp and lively, as well as beautifully elegant icewines.

SAUVIGNON BLANC: An important grape; combined with sémillon, it makes good Bordeaux-style whites.

VIDAL BLANC: A major French-American hybrid created in the 1930s in France. It makes what many consider to be among Canada's best icewines, as well as good dry table wines.

VIOGNIER: A minor grape, but it can make amazingly beautiful, fresh wines in the Okanagan Valley in particular.

REDS

BACO NOIR: A French-American hybrid; it makes simple, fruity wines in Ontario, Quebec, and Nova Scotia.

CABERNET FRANC: A major grape; it is made into sleek, dry reds in the manner of Chinon, from France's Loire Valley, and also red icewines.

CABERNET SAUVIGNON: Often blended with merlot to make good, if usually lean, Bordeaux-style blends.

GAMAY: A minor grape, but it can make some amazingly fruity, fresh wines evocative of good Beaujolais.

MERLOT: Made as a single variety and combined with cabernet sauvignon and cabernet franc to make some good Bordeaux-style blends.

PINOT NOIR: Canada's star red grape, especially in the Okanagan Valley, where it makes elegant, silky pinot noirs reminiscent of those made in Burgundy and Oregon.

SYRAH: A minor grape in terms of production, but growing. Thus far, it is made into some exciting wines reminiscent of those of France's northern Rhône Valley. Shows promise.

making pristine wines with highly precise, pure flavors. Indeed, the first research center dedicated to cool-climate grape-growing and winemaking—the Cool Climate Oenology and Viticulture Institute—was established in Ontario in 1997.

In particular, white varieties seem to soar with elegance and freshness here. The best Canadian rieslings could fool you into thinking you're drinking something from the Mosel region of Germany; the best chardonnays have a sense of precision that white Burgundies possess; the pinot gris are terrific wines—reminiscent of Alsace pinot gris; and the aromatic varieties gewürztraminer and viognier may have their best New World homes in Canada.

The Niagara Peninsula (best known for the Falls of honeymoon fame) makes surprisingly good wines.

> "I liken making pinot noir to waking up a woman at three in the morning. You never quite know what you're going to get."
>
> —LUKE SMITH,
> owner and winemaker, Howling Bluff Winery, British Columbia

this writing, perhaps not as evolved, although cabernet franc shows promise.

Canada's vineyards and wineries are concentrated in just two provinces: Ontario and British Columbia, which, although on opposite sides of the country, more than 1,900 miles (3,100 kilometers) apart, together account for 98 percent of the volume of premium Canadian wine made. (Wine is also made in Quebec, and a tiny amount of sparkling wine is made in Nova Scotia, although neither region yet makes wine in commercially significant amounts.)

As for red wines, pinot noir is the absolute star, making wines of world-class stature. Red wines based on Bordeaux varieties are, as of

Of the two states, most of the wineries (299 as of 2014) are located in British Columbia and are small-production, family-run businesses.

COLD WINES AND HOT NIGHTS

If you're reading this book, you're probably the kind of person who'd want to go to Niagara to taste some of Ontario's top wines. But it's worth noting that you could honeymoon there, too. Each year, more than fifty thousand people do. The tradition of honeymooning at Niagara Falls began in 1801, with the then-famous couple of Joseph Alston and Theodosia Burr, the daughter of U.S. Vice President Aaron Burr. Three years later, Napoléon's younger brother, Jérôme Bonaparte, honeymooned there with his American bride, Elizabeth Patterson. The falls, which are composed of two major sections, the Horseshoe Falls on the Canadian side and the American Falls on the American side, were formed when glaciers receded at the end of the last Ice Age, and water from the newly formed Great Lakes carved a path through the Niagara Escarpment to the Atlantic Ocean. Today, more than 6 million cubic feet (169,900 cubic meters) of water falls over the crest line every minute in high flow. Interestingly, that water appears unusually green thanks to the 66 tons (60 metric tons) a minute of embedded dissolved salts and very finely ground rock generated by the erosive force of the Niagara River itself. Indeed, currently, the falls erode at a rate of about 1 foot (30 centimeters) a year. Scientists believe that, fifty thousand years from now, the remaining 20 miles (32 kilometers) to Lake Erie will have been undermined, and the falls will cease to exist. Presumably honeymoons will continue to endure.

THE VQA SEAL
OF APPROVAL

*M*ost top Canadian wines carry a government seal with the letters VQA, which stand for *Vintners Quality Alliance. Used on wines from Ontario and British Columbia (the tiny vineyards of Quebec and Nova Scotia are not yet included in the program), the VQA seal ensures that the wine has been professionally tasted and adheres to standards set forth by a board of Canadian vintners and growers. The VQA also stipulates how and when appellation names such as Okanagan Valley or Niagara Peninsula can be used, plus the percentages of grape varieties required in making the wine.*

Despite their size, many wineries make six to twelve different wines. It's quite common for the lion's share of these wines to be sold from the wineries' own tasting rooms.

Of the two regions, Ontario, despite having fewer wineries, is the larger producer, accounting for more than 50 percent of all the wine made in the country. Ontario's four wine districts—Niagara Peninsula (the largest, with 14,000 acres/5,700 hectares of grapes), Lake Erie North Shore, Prince Edward County, and Pelee Island—all lie along the shores (or just offshore) of two of the Great Lakes, Lake Ontario and Lake Erie. Within the Niagara Peninsula are fifteen smaller sub-appellations, many of which, like Beamsville Bench and the Niagara Escarpment, have gained quite a bit of prestige for their wines.

Ontario's wine districts are Canada's most southerly, but the icy arctic winds that sweep across the region would render viticulture nearly impossible were it not for the warming and moderating effect of the lakes. Like the

THE MOST IMPORTANT
CANADIAN WINES

LEADING WINES

CABERNET FRANC red

CHARDONNAY white

GEWÜRZTRAMINER white

ICEWINE white and red (sweet)

PINOT GRIS white

PINOT NOIR red

RIESLING white

SAUVIGNON BLANC and white
BORDEAUX-STYLE BLENDS

SYRAH red

VIDAL BLANC white

WINES OF NOTE

BORDEAUX-STYLE BLENDS
(merlot and cabernet sauvignon) red

GAMAY red

SPARKLING WINE white

VIOGNIER white

lakes themselves, the wine districts of Ontario were carved out by retreating ancient glaciers that left behind a variety of deep, well-drained soils.

British Columbia, at the 50th parallel in latitude, is Canada's most westerly viticultural area, and one of the newest top wine regions of the New World. It's also one of the most

On the Niagara Peninsula, the gentle sloping vineyards of the Beamsville Bench district sit on an elevated escarpment. Though it may not look like it, the region benefits from warming breezes during winter (and cooling breezes in summer).

northern. Close your eyes when you taste, and you could be in the Mosel (if the wine is riesling) or in Burgundy (if it's pinot noir). British Columbia is made up of five wine districts— the Okanagan Valley, Similkameen Valley, Fraser Valley, Gulf Islands, and Vancouver Island. Of these, the 150-mile-long (240-kilometer) Okanagan Valley (known as the "fruit bowl" of Canada) is where most of British Columbia's wineries are located and where any wine lover will be most impressed (and impressed you will be).

Although British Columbia is considerably farther north than Ontario, the temperatures in the region are often warmer thanks to its climate and geography. This is especially true of the sunny Okanagan Valley, which, while quite close to the Pacific Ocean as the crow flies, is sheltered behind the curtain of the Coastal Mountain range. Rainfall here is scant, and the southern end of the valley is in fact the northern tip of the Sonoran Desert. Days are consistently bright with sunlight; nights are very cool—a viticulturist's dream scenario.

The name *Okanagan* has two possible origins: Historians tell us it means "rendezvous" and refers to the meeting place on Lake Osoyoos where the Native Americans of Washington and British Columbia gathered annually to stock up on supplies, while a local legend has it that the name means "big head" and refers to an ancient native people of exceptional bravery.

In the center of the Okanagan Valley is the long, narrow, pristine Okanagan Lake, carved out by receding glaciers and so deep that the distance from the bottom of the lake to the top of the surrounding mountains exceeds the depth of the Grand Canyon. All around the lake, orchards and vineyards flourish, many

WHEN YOU VISIT . . . CANADA

GETTING MARRIED at Niagara Falls aside, one of the best ways to experience Canada is to visit its small wineries. Many offer not only tastings and tours but also breathtakingly beautiful scenery, and some have terrific cafés or restaurants. In addition, numerous festivals and concerts are held throughout the year.

of them located on lateral outcroppings or "benches" created when the sides of the lake were scoured by giant blocks of ice that repeatedly froze and melted. In the winter, this is ski country, but the very warm, dry summers are perfect for growing all manner of fruit, including of course, grapes. As such, the Okanagan is not exactly a "cool climate" in the traditional viticultural sense, but, more accurately, a northern latitude with a short, warm growing season. As a result, the wines, while displaying ripe, bright flavors, never have a flaccid, overripe character. This fact is, of course, crucial for making British Columbia's elegant pinot noirs and rieslings.

ONE OF CANADA'S BEST (FROZEN) ASSETS—ICEWINE

Thanks to Canada's reliably bone-chillingly cold winters, icewines are produced here every year, and the wines are so ethereal, they have near mythic status and an international following. Indeed, Canada is now the leading producer of icewine in the world.

As is true in Austria and Germany, in Canada, icewine (or *eiswein,* as it is written in Europe) is made only in the traditional, centuries-old manner, by allowing the grapes—usually riesling or Vidal—to freeze naturally on the vine (as opposed to a shortcut sometimes used elsewhere: freezing grapes in huge industrial freezers). When the outside ambient temperature is no higher than 17.6°F (-8°C; a Canadian legal requirement), the grapes are picked by hand, one frozen grape at a time. As the frozen grapes are pressed (the yield of juice for icewine is a mere 15 percent of the yield of juice for regular table wine), the sweet, high-acid, concentrated juice is separated from the ice. The ice is thrown away and the resulting wine is made solely from the hyperconcentrated juice. (Usually, no botrytis is involved.) By law, Canadian icewine must be 12.5 percent residual sugar (125 grams per liter), but there is no maximum, and indeed many are 20 percent or more. The painstaking process is, needless to say, fraught with numerous difficulties, from the exigencies of harvesting in subzero-degree weather to the challenge of dealing with hungry bears, coyotes, deer, and birds, who can quickly strip the vines of every last sweet, frozen grape.

Virtually every top producer in Canada tries to make icewine at some point or another, and many producers are renowned for them, including Cave Spring, Inniskillin, and Mission Hill.

In Ontario, frozen grapes, soon to be made into icewine, are netted to protect them from being eaten by wildlife.

CANADA'S OTHER GREAT ICE CAPADE

The lusciousness of Canadian icewine has inspired another cool, delicious phenomenon in Canada—ice cider. Made principally in the province of Quebec, ice ciders can be produced in two ways: The apples (many different varieties) can be left on the tree to freeze and are then pressed, or the apples can be picked at the height of ripeness, pressed, and the juice set outside over the winter to freeze. In both cases, the concentrated juice is fermented for six months into a cider containing 7 to 13 percent alcohol. The purity and freshness of a sip is like biting into a hundred fresh apples at once. Some of the best producers include Neige, Domaine Pinnacle, and Clos St.-Denis.

Snow-capped heirloom apples. Once frozen, they are destined to become ice cider.

As you can imagine, the greatest Canadian icewines possess an almost otherworldly contrapuntal tension between acidity and sweetness, making drinking them an ethereal sensation. That's saying it in an intellectual way. But here's the kid-in-you version: You'll want to lick the bowl.

They forgot to write "Please Don't Touch!" on the sign.

SOME OF THE BEST PRODUCERS IN CANADA

BRITISH COLUMBIA

Blue Mountain • Burrowing Owl • Church and State • Culmina • Gray Monk • Hawthorne Mountain • Hester Creek • Howling Bluff • Konzelmann • Lake Breeze • Liquidity • Meyer Family • Mission Hill • Nk'Mip • Orofino • Osoyoos Larose • Painted Rock • Quail's Gate • Red Rooster • Road 13 Vineyards • Sandhill • Sumac Ridge Estate • Summerhill • Tantalus • Tinhorn Creek Vineyards • Wild Goose

ONTARIO

13th Street • Cave Spring Cellars • Château des Charmes • Colaneri • Fielding Estate • Flat Rock • Henry of Pelham Estate • Inniskillin • Jackson Triggs • Le Clos Jordanne • Malivoire • Pillitteri Estates • Ravine Vineyard • Stratus • Tawse • Thirty Bench • Trius at Hillebrand • Vineland Estates

The Canadian Wines to Know

Canadian wine is, of course, not a single thing; the wines of British Columbia and Ontario are distinctly different from one another, thanks to the great distances that separate the two regions. What unifies the wines, however, is their amazing progress. Barely thought about in the twentieth century, the wines of Canada are now deliciously established "players" in the New World.

WHITES

COLANERI

ALLEGRIA | NIAGARA-ON-THE-LAKE, ONTARIO

52% gewürztraminer, 36% sauvignon blanc,
7% chenin blanc, 5% riesling

This fascinating and delicious wine was made *appassimento* style, an Italian term that means the grapes were partially dried in order to concentrate their juices before they were pressed and fermented. The result is Allegria, a wildly aromatic wine that is off-dry and beautifully fruity, with notes of white peaches, exotic oranges, and dried apricots. In 1967, the Colaneri family came to Canada from Italy, and today, three generations are involved in working on the vineyard.

CAVE SPRING

RIESLING |
BEAMSVILLE BENCH, NIAGARA PENINSULA, ONTARIO

100% riesling

Whenever I taste this wine, I can't help but think the word *spring* in the name is apt, for this riesling is as spring-loaded as wine gets. The beautiful tangerine, peach, and star fruit flavors rush at you with such energy, it's almost as though the wine can't talk fast enough. Founded by the Italian Pennachetti family in 1978, the winery is named for the limestone caves and mineral springs discovered on the property by European settlers in the eighteenth century.

CAVE SPRING

RIESLING
Estate Bottled
VQA BEAMSVILLE BENCH VQA

CAVE SPRING VINEYARD

OLD VINES RIESLING

BC VQA OKANAGAN VALLEY

TANTALUS

RIESLING | OLD VINE | OKANAGAN VALLEY, BRITISH COLUMBIA

100% riesling

The first buzz in the wine world that phenomenal wines were being made in Canada occurred in the 1990s, and Tantalus' dry riesling was invariably named as evidence. Made from vines planted in the 1970s, the wine has a pure, crystalline focus and effusive exotic citrus flavors—like icicles of limeade. Darting around inside the main flavor are shooting-star-like notes of apricot, peach, spices, and star fruit. This is a riesling lover's riesling, and a wine that's both elegant and formidable.

MISSION HILL FAMILY ESTATE

RIESLING | MARTIN'S LANE |
OKANAGAN VALLEY, BRITISH COLUMBIA

100% riesling

Mind-blowing in its sorbetlike intensity, Martin's Lane dry riesling from Mission Hill ranks with the top rieslings of the New World. Pure and vivid in flavor, it has an enticing, languorously silky texture. In great vintages, the fruit is so dense it seems combustible. The wine is named after proprietor Anthony von Mandl's father, Martin, and the grapes are grown on the steepest slope on the estate.

MARTIN'S LANE RIESLING
OKANAGAN VALLEY 2012

PERPETUA

CHARDONNAY | OSOYOOS VINEYARD |
OKANAGAN VALLEY, BRITISH COLUMBIA

100% chardonnay

Perpetua, a brand owned by Mission Hill, makes fantastic cool-climate chardonnays that have a precision and distinctiveness not often found in New World chardonnay. This wine begins with high soprano notes of tangerine and citrus, then descends in long sweeps to deep bass notes of earth and tarte Tatin. The Osooyos Vineyard, named for nearby Odoyood Lake, is located in Canada's only desert.

MEYER FAMILY

CHARDONNAY | OLD MAIN ROAD | OKANAGAN VALLEY, BRITISH COLUMBIA

100% chardonnay

Meyer Family Vineyards

Tribute Series - Pat Quinn
Chardonnay
Okanagan Valley   2013
Old Main Road Vineyard

The Meyer Family chardonnays have beautiful richness wrapped around a core of freshness. The grapes for this wine are often picked late into the fall, contributing perhaps to the wine's "warm baked pears and cool whipped cream" character. There's also a deep earthiness to this and all of the four other Meyer Family chardonnays—a nod to Burgundy, where the winemaker worked for a time.

LIQUIDITY

VIOGNIER | OKANAGAN VALLEY, BRITISH COLUMBIA

100% viognier

Viognier is not easy to make. The wine often gets bogged down in its own full body and heavy perfume. But Liquidity manages to make one of the best in the New World. Fresh, humming with lovely acidity, and nearly kinetic with light wisps of energy, the wine's floral and peach flavors are like tiny lights twinkling on and off. Liquidity, perched on an outcropping over Okanagan Valley, also makes very good pinot noir and has a fantastic restaurant.

WILD GOOSE

GEWÜRZTRAMINER | OKANAGAN VALLEY, BRITISH COLUMBIA

100% gewürztraminer

It wasn't easy deciding which Wild Goose to write about—the pinot gris, the pinot blanc, or this gewürztraminer, for these three Wild Goose whites are all exciting, deeply flavorful, elegant wines (the pinot blanc may be the single best New World pinot blanc I've ever tasted). But I chose the gewürztraminer for its sheer beauty and utter deliciousness. Wild Goose channeled Alsace on this one. The wine seems to lift out of the glass on aromatic waves of rose petals, peaches, and spice. The flavors are finely etched and pure—peaches again, plus star fruit and minerals. But best of all, the wine shows pedigree of place—gewürztraminer this refined can come only from a cool climate and high latitude. Canada appears to be tailor-made.

Malivoire
COURTNEY GAMAY
VQA Beamsville Bench VQA

REDS

MALIVOIRE

GAMAY | COURTNEY | NIAGARA ESCARPMENT,
NIAGARA PENINSULA, ONTARIO

100% gamay

Until I tasted this wine, I felt there was no delicious gamay in the Americas. But here it is: a magenta-colored gamay with all the cool, vibrant freshness of a great Beaujolais. The wine's exuberant fruitiness is laced with hints of spice. Malivoire is owned by Martin Malivoire, a director of special effects for several Hollywood movies.

HOWLING BLUFF

SUMMA QUIES | PINOT NOIR |
OKANAGAN VALLEY, BRITISH COLUMBIA

100% pinot noir

If I were tasting this wine blind and you told me it was Chambolle-Musigny, Burgundy, I'd believe it. Former investment banker Luke Smith left his day job to build his modest winery by hand and plant every grapevine himself. This wine—a testament to how good pinot noir in the Okanagan can be—has a sumptuous red fruitiness and freshness, a sexy saddle-leather character, and an evocative earthy quality—like the smell of warm rocks after a rainstorm.

STRATUS

CABERNET FRANC | NIAGARA-ON-THE-LAKE, ONTARIO

100% cabernet franc

If cabernet sauvignon is about power, cabernet franc is about mystery. It doesn't rush out of the glass and overwhelm you with flavor. It waits, and draws you in. At least that is what the excellent Stratus cabernet franc seems to do. As you might expect from a cool-climate cabernet franc, the wine is sleek and pretty, with notes of tar, minerals, and grenadine. I am not surprised that winemaker Jean-Laurent Groux is a native of the Loire Valley, France, where cabernet franc excels.

HOWLING BLUFF

2013 PINOT NOIR
BC VQA OKANAGAN VALLEY
Summa Quies
13.9% alc./vol.   750ml
RED WINE / VIN ROUGE PRODUCT OF CANADA / PRODUIT DU CANADA

stratus

CABERNET FRANC

BURROWING OWL

ATHENE | OKANAGAN VALLEY, BRITISH COLUMBIA

50% cabernet sauvignon, 50% syrah

Big red grapes like cabernet sauvignon and syrah generally don't do well in cool climates like much of Canada's. But in the warmer pockets of the dry, sunny Okanagan Valley, it's a different story. The rich aroma of this wine is completely evocative of both varieties—a mélange of tobacco and cassis, plus spiced plums, menthol, and a tiny nuance of gaminess. And the powerful structure gives the wine good grip on the palate. It's definitely worthy of slow-roasted game on a cold Canadian winter night.

SWEET WINES

CAVE SPRING

RIESLING ICEWINE | NIAGARA PENINSULA, ONTARIO

100% riesling

Mindlessly good. Cave Spring's Riesling Icewine, at 22 percent residual sugar, starts with exquisite, sweet fruit that seems charged by minerals. As in all great dessert wines, savoriness and acidity lurk just below the surface and counterbalance the sweetness, giving the wine its complexity and mental intrigue. The grapes were allowed to raisin on the vine, then were frozen solid by the cold winds of Lake Ontario, then hand-picked and pressed at temperatures below 14°F (–10°C); a phenomenal achievement.

INNISKILLIN

CABERNET FRANC ICEWINE | NIAGARA PENNINSULA, ONTARIO

100% cabernet franc

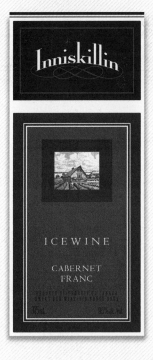

This is a hard wine to make. . . . Cabernet franc (like all of the red Bordeaux varieties) has tannin, after all, and tannin can taste drying and bitter (in the manner of espresso). So, can one make a luscious, sweet icewine from cabernet franc? Inniskillin does. The wine, distinctive and unusual, is sweet, but then bitterness and acidity kick in, giving it fantastic play between components. As for the fruits, one might imagine one is in the Canadian forest, where tiny berries—black, red, and blue—thrive naturally. Inniskillin also makes a riesling icewine, of course, and it's drop-dead gorgeous.

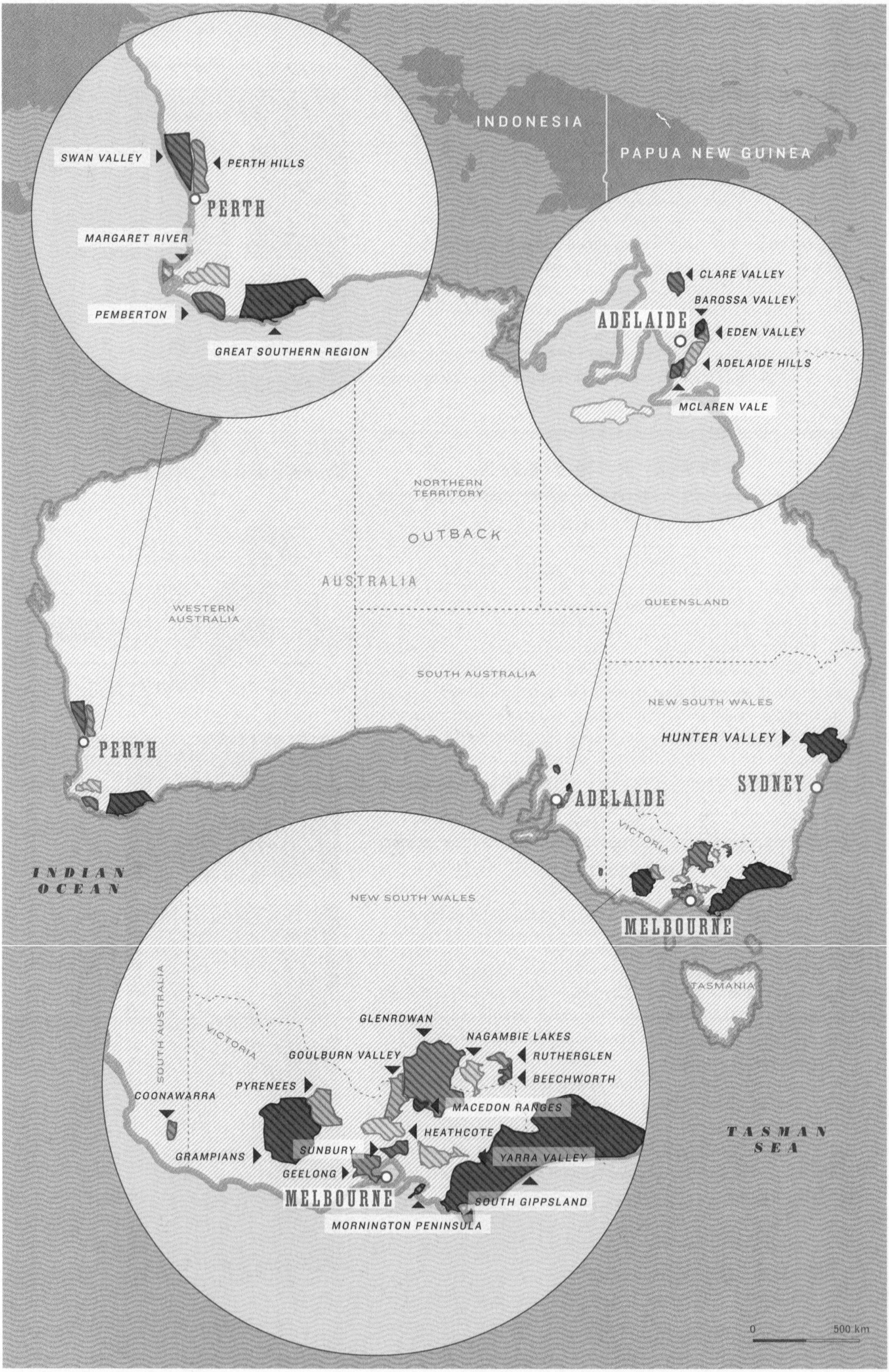

INDONESIA

PAPUA NEW GUINEA

SWAN VALLEY
◄ **PERTH HILLS**

PERTH

MARGARET RIVER

PEMBERTON

GREAT SOUTHERN REGION ▲

CLARE VALLEY ►

BAROSSA VALLEY

ADELAIDE
◄ **EDEN VALLEY**

◄ **ADELAIDE HILLS**

McLAREN VALE

NORTHERN
TERRITORY

OUTBACK

AUSTRALIA

WESTERN
AUSTRALIA

QUEENSLAND

SOUTH AUSTRALIA

NEW SOUTH WALES

HUNTER VALLEY ►

PERTH

ADELAIDE

SYDNEY

VICTORIA

INDIAN
OCEAN

MELBOURNE

NEW SOUTH WALES

TASMANIA

SOUTH AUSTRALIA

VICTORIA

GLENROWAN

NAGAMBIE LAKES

GOULBURN VALLEY
RUTHERGLEN

PYRENEES
BEECHWORTH

COONAWARRA
MACEDON RANGES

HEATHCOTE

GRAMPIANS
SUNBURY
YARRA VALLEY

GEELONG
MELBOURNE
SOUTH GIPPSLAND

MORNINGTON PENINSULA

TASMAN
SEA

0   500 km

AUSTRALIA

SOUTH AUSTRALIA | NEW SOUTH WALES | VICTORIA | WESTERN AUSTRALIA

AUSTRALIA RANKS SEVENTH AMONG WINE-PRODUCING COUNTRIES WORLDWIDE. AUSTRALIANS DRINK AN AVERAGE OF 8 GALLONS (30 LITERS) OF WINE PER PERSON PER YEAR.

I f it were superimposed over Europe, Australia—a huge landmass of 3 million square miles (7.8 million square kilometers)—would stretch from London to the Black Sea. The wine industry within this large country is one of the most dynamic and cutting-edge in the world.

The past few decades have been a period of phenomenal growth for Australian wine. According to Wine Australia (formerly known as the Australian Wine and Brandy Corporation), during the ten years from 1995 to 2005 alone, the number of wine companies more than doubled (to more than two thousand); the grape crush more than doubled to 2 million tons (1.8 million metric tons); and vineyard plantings tripled to 390,000 acres (157,800 hectares). Exports during this period quadrupled in value, and for two countries—the United Kingdom and the United States—Australian wine, especially good-value Australian wine, became a comfortable mainstay on the wine scene.

High-tech could be the Australian wine industry's middle name. Most wineries use state-of-the-art equipment and employ winemakers trained in the most advanced techniques. Virtually every vineyard task, from pruning to harvesting, is automated. Yet, for all this industrial sophistication, most Australian wines are rather like the Australians themselves: charismatic and outgoing. This is certainly true of the country's simple, inexpensive wines. But even Australia's most prestigious and complex wines, like Penfolds Grange and Henschke's Hill of Grace, have a hedonistic charm that makes them disarmingly approachable.

For a large part of the twentieth century, the majority of the wine made in Australia was either cheap and sweet or had a substantial level of alcohol. But, as was true in the

THE QUICK SIP ON AUSTRALIA

AUSTRALIA BOASTS hundreds of small, top-notch producers of complex, age-worthy wines. But it's also known for simple, good-value white and red wines that are mouthfilling and easy to drink.

THE MOST RENOWNED, best-loved, and most widely grown grape is shiraz (the same as the French grape syrah), which is turned into irresistible red wines with deep berry flavors laced with spice.

THE MAJORITY of Australia's vineyards are clustered in the southeastern part of the continent, relatively near the major cities of Sydney, Melbourne, and Adelaide. However, one of the newest fine wine regions in the world, Margaret River, is on Australia's west coast.

More than forty varieties of grapes are grown, but the five most important (by tonnage harvested) are shiraz (it alone accounts for 30 percent of the total wine grape acreage), chardonnay, cabernet sauvignon, merlot, and sémillon. To that list, I'll add grenache and riesling, which, while produced in smaller amounts, are nonetheless important by virtue of their quality and distinctiveness.

The first Australian vineyards were planted in New South Wales at the end of the eighteenth century, more than one hundred years after the first vineyards were planted in other parts of the New World, including Colonial Virginia, in the United States, and Cape Town, in South Africa. The men who planted them were Australia's first European settlers, mainly Englishmen who knew a lot about drinking wine but little about growing grapes. The vines they planted were cuttings of European (*vinifera*) varieties, generally brought from the South African Cape of Good Hope, where ships stopped for provisions en route to Australia.

Unfortunately, the area where the first tiny vineyards were planted—part of a penal colony—was so hot and humid that the grapes rotted and the vines died. Today, ironically, Sydney's botanical gardens are just across the road from that same spot. The Australian settlers were undeterred. They moved slightly inland, to what is now the Hunter Valley, and with practice, grew more adept at grape-growing. Between the 1850s and 1870s, as new, more viticulturally savvy immigrants arrived, vineyards began to thrive.

In 1877, phylloxera was discovered in Australia, specifically in the state of Victoria. Although the pest did not spread to every other wine region, it effectively crippled some important vineyards (especially in Victoria) before the vines could be replanted on tolerant American rootstocks. Replanting resulted in the production of fine wines by some producers, but others rebounded by doing the opposite—making cheap, sweet fortified wines of passable quality, often from large tracts of hot, fertile, irrigated valley land.

With the 1960s and 1970s, a new era dawned. Changing tastes, changing economic forces, and the development of new wine

United States, the industry here changed radically in the 1970s, as high-quality dry wines became the focus. By the mid-1980s, Australia had a well-developed modern industry made up of small, top-notch producers, as well as big brands focused on creamy chardonnays and soft shirazes.

Hollywood's portrayal of Australia as an untamed outback populated mainly by sheep, crocodiles, and kangaroos doesn't quite square with most people's idea of a top-class wine region. Of course, vineyards are not planted in the desertlike center of the country, nor in the steamy, tropically hot north. The greatest number are located in the cooler, southern part of the continent, within a few hours' drive of the coast.

Today, there are just under 2,500 wineries in Australia, and they make every style of wine: dry, sweet, still, sparkling, and fortified.

THE MOST IMPORTANT AUSTRALIAN WINES

LEADING WINES

APERA white (fortified, Sherry-style wine; dry and sweet)

CABERNET SAUVIGNON red

CABERNET-SHIRAZ BLENDS red

CHARDONNAY white

FORTIFIED TAWNY red (fortified, Port-style wine; sweet)

GRENACHE-SHIRAZ-MOURVÈDRE BLENDS red

MUSCAT white (fortified; sweet)

PINOT NOIR red

RIESLING white (dry)

SÉMILLON white (dry and sweet)

SHIRAZ red

SHIRAZ-CABERNET BLENDS red

TOPAQUE white (fortified; sweet)

WINES OF NOTE

CHARDONNAY-SÉMILLON BLENDS white

SPARKLING white and red

VERDELHO white

VIOGNIER white

---

technologies all propelled Australia toward the modern wine industry that exists there today. Production statistics tell the story in a snapshot. In 1960, only 1 million cases of dry table wine were produced. By 2010, the amount had shot up to 134 million cases. (Alas, stupendous growth can have a downside. Australia now produces so much wine that the Australians themselves only consume about 40 percent of what is made each year. Even the country's well-established export markets, such as Great Britain and the United States, cannot absorb it all. In 2010, Australia's wine industry leaders, including the Winemakers' Federation of Australia, concluded that in 2009 the country produced 20 million to 40 million more cases of wine than it sold. Part of the solution has been to voluntarily reduce vineyard acreage. In 2010, for example, nearly 20,000 acres/8,100 hectares of vineyards were pulled out.)

In 1970, every single winery in Australia was family-owned, and today, scores of

> "Great wine is born not in the vineyard, but in the brain."
> — **BRIAN WALSH,**
> director of winemaking, Yalumba

small, high-end wineries—Clarendon Hills, Henschke, Grosset, Torbreck, Jim Barry, Jasper Hill, and many others—still are. That said, the industry is now dominated by a handful of very large, influential companies that together are responsible for the lion's share of all Australian wine. Two notable ones are Pernod Ricard, owner of the brands Jacob's Creek and Wyndham, and Treasury Wine Estates, which owns Penfolds, Lindemans, Rosemount, Wynns, Mildara, and Wolf Blass (as an aside, they also own the prominent California wineries Beringer, Stags' Leap Winery, Etude, and Chateau St. Jean).

For an explanation of Australian wine law, see the Appendix on Wine Laws, page 928.

[YELLOW TAIL]: THE CRITTER THAT STARTED A CRAZE

In 2001, a little Australian brand named [yellow tail]—the company stylizes [yellow tail] with brackets and lowercase letters—entered the U.S. market with the goal of selling 25,000 cases. By the end of that first year, the wine with the yellow kangaroo on the label had sold eight times that amount. It was only the beginning. [yellow tail] sold two million cases in the U.S. in its second year and an incredible eight million cases by its fifth year. By 2012, it was the single largest-selling imported wine in the U.S. and the fastest-growing brand in the history of the U.S. wine industry.

Why did a simple wine—so undistinguished in terms of quality—achieve such success? The critter was, of course, cute. But [yellow tail] somehow captured a craving for the uncomplicated. It was easy to understand and easy on the wallet, and it ushered in a whole new wave of wine consumers. Wine's "critter era" had begun. Today, labels around the world sport not only kangaroos but also scores of other animals, including elephants, frogs, wild boars, bobcats, chickens, alligators, buzzards, butterflies, beavers, bees, aardvarks, and eagles (screaming, of course).

TWO PHILOSOPHIES OF WINEMAKING

Conventional European wisdom holds that good wine comes from specific sites that have distinctive terroirs. Accordingly, some of Australia's very best wines come from single vineyards in top regions such as Coonawarra, Barossa Valley, Margaret River, and others.

However, many Australian winemakers believe that good wine needn't derive from a single terroir, or even from a small number of them. Instead, these Australian winemakers arrive at a good wine through an extensive process of selection and blending.

For example, the grapes for many Australian wines are grown over vast stretches of territory. Wines labeled South Eastern Australia, for instance, may be made with grapes grown anywhere within the southeastern part of the entire continent. (This philosophy is not at work quite as much in the United States, where it would be unusual to blend, say, a batch of chardonnay from southern California with a batch from Washington State and then label it Western U.S.A. Chardonnay.)

The process of selecting and blending is practiced mostly for the production of lower- and moderately priced wines. The goal here is to make brands of wine that have fairly consistent flavors year after year, in the manner of beer. Simple, inexpensive wines like Jacob's Creek and Yalumba's "Y" Series, for example, are dependably tasty no matter the vintage.

What's surprising (at least to a traditionalist) is that, in addition to low-priced, everyday wines, some of the most prestigious wines in Australia are also made by the process of selecting and blending. Australian winemakers know they may lose a bit of the sense of place when they blend wines from different sites, but they are hoping to achieve more complexity. As an Australian winemaker once said to me, "How interesting would a perfume be if it was just one aroma?"

One of the best examples of the selecting and blending philosophy is Australia's most legendary and expensive wine, Penfolds Grange—a blend of shiraz grapes (sometimes with small amounts of cabernet sauvignon) grown in various vineyards as many as

600 miles (970 kilometers) apart. To make Grange, winemakers at Penfolds start out with tanks and barrels holding the equivalent of 40,000 cases of wine. After selecting the very best lots and blending them together, fewer than 7,000 cases of Grange are made. The remaining lots go down the ladder to make progressively more humble-quality and less expensive Penfolds wines.

THE LAND, THE GRAPES, AND THE VINEYARDS

Australia, along with India and Africa, is one of the oldest landmasses. The ancient, weathered soil here is impoverished and, in many places, highly eroded. In the center of the continent is the vast, flat, arid area known as the Outback, where it often fails to rain for

Kangaroo Island scallops—a sure sign you're in Oz. Especially good with a glass of brisk, cold sémillon.

BINS AND SHOWS

Australian wines are labeled varietally, making label reading easy enough. But there are two idiosyncracies that will be helpful for a wine drinker to know about: bin numbers and designations such as Show Reserve.

Bin numbers are used by many Australian wine companies as the names of various wines. Penfolds, for example, makes three cabernet sauvignons—Bin 407, Bin 707, and Bin 389—each of which is a different blend and is priced differently. Probably the most recognized bin number is Lindemans Bin 65 chardonnay, one of the biggest-selling brands of chardonnay in the world. Bin numbers were put on Australian wine labels as early as the 1930s, although it's not clear exactly when the practice began. Originally the numbers were probably a winemaker's way of tracking the wines through blending and aging, and signified the underground cellar bin or place in the winery where a given wine was typically stored year after year. The shorthand stuck, and now countless Australian wines are known by their bin numbers.

Special designations, such as Show Reserve, frequently appear on wine labels, but such terms have no legal definition. Rather, they refer to the fact that the wine has won an award in one of Australia's many wine shows or competitions. More than wine drinkers elsewhere in the world, Australians take wine competitions seriously and have a good deal of faith in their results.

THE GRAPES OF AUSTRALIA

WHITES

CHARDONNAY: The leading white grape, made into wines that span all levels of quality, from simple, fruity quaffers to lush, complex, elegant wines.

MUSCADELLE: Renowned in the Victoria wine district of Rutherglen, where it makes the rare but renowned sweet, fortified wine known as topaque, once called Australian tokay.

MUSCAT BLANC Á PETITS GRAINS: Considered the best of the different varieties with the word *muscat* in their names. It makes the rare but extraordinarily sweet, fortified muscat wines of Rutherglen in Victoria.

RIESLING: A major grape with a long history in Australia, it makes dry, racy wines evocative of exotic citrus. It also ages beautifully into wines with creaminess and almost Danish pastry–like characters.

SAUVIGNON BLANC: A minor grape, but some excellent examples exist. It is often blended with sémillon in the manner of white Bordeaux.

SÉMILLON: A major grape and a signature of Australia, especially in the Hunter Valley, of New South Wales and in the Margaret River area of Western Australia. It makes snappy, tightly wound wines when young. With age, the wines undergo a magical transformation, becoming honeyed, with rich lanolin textures.

VERDELHO: A minor grape, but fascinating, since it was brought to Australia directly from the Portuguese island of Madeira in the 1820s. Grown mostly in Western Australia, it makes good, tasty wines with soft, fruity flavors.

VIOGNIER: A minor grape, but surprisingly excellent examples exist—especially in the Barossa Valley.

years. Yet water surrounds the continent on all sides—the Timor and Arafura Seas and the Gulf of Carpentaria to the north, the Coral Sea and the Tasman Sea to the east, and the Indian Ocean and Southern Ocean to the west and south, respectively. Antarctica is about 2,380 miles (3,830 kilometers) away.

Virtually all of the vineyard land—some 417,000 acres (168,800 hectares) as of 2012—(not to mention most of the population) is clustered in the southeastern or southwestern corners of the continent. In the southeast, wine is made in three important states: South Australia (nearly half of all the vineyards in the country are planted in this one state), New South Wales, and Victoria. In the southwest is the lone wine state of Western Australia.

Whether they are in the southeast or southwest, most of these regions share a sunny,

A cherished old vine in what is probably the oldest cabernet sauvignon vineyard in the world—Penfolds's legendary Block 42 in the Barossa Valley.

REDS

CABERNET SAUVIGNON: A major grape that can make delicious, powerfully structured wines with notes of green tobacco, especially in Coonawarra and Margaret River. It is considered by some Australian vintners to be more sophisticated than shiraz, with which it is sometimes blended.

GRENACHE: An important, distinctive grape that makes rich, concentrated red wines with a core of cherry jam character, especially when made from grapes grown in older vineyards. It is also commonly blended with shiraz and mourvèdre to make Rhône-style blends and is used as a main part of the blend in many of the country's sensational Australian fortified tawnies.

MERLOT: Significant in terms of production, but largely undistinguished in quality. It is grown mostly for use in cabernet sauvignon-merlot blends.

MOURVÈDRE: An important grape, especially for Rhône-style blends, in which it's combined with shiraz and grenache. Also used along with grenache as part of the blend in Australia's fortified tawnies. Also referred to as mataro.

PINOT NOIR: On the rise in production, although the jury is out on eventual success. It is grown especially in the cool areas of Victoria and makes good and occasionally great still pinot noir, and is used as well for sparkling wines.

SHIRAZ: The leading red grape, the same as the French grape syrah. At its best, it makes seductive, lusciously textured, complex wines. It is sometimes blended with cabernet sauvignon, or with grenache and mourvèdre in Rhône-style blends, and is also used in Australia's top fortified tawnies.

---

fairly stable, Mediterranean-like climate. In some parts, however, despite warm days, nighttime temperatures can be quite cold. Which is how Australia can, paradoxically, be known for great dry riesling (a cool-climate grape) at the same time as it is known for great cabernet sauvignon (a warmer-climate grape). The harvest takes place during the southern hemisphere's summer, February through May.

Naturally, there are challenges. Rot, frost, drought, and strong, salt-laden winds all take their toll in various districts. Not to mention kangaroos, which jump (literally, of course) at the chance to feed on the soft leaves and buds of young vines. High fences topped with barbed wire surround some vineyards to keep the herbivorous marsupials out.

Given its fairly limited population, Australia lacks a ready supply of harvest workers. As a result, viticulture here is the most mechanized in the world. While some small, prestigious vineyards are cared for by hand, often by Southeast Asian field workers, in most Australian vineyards, machines perform almost every critical task, including picking the grapes, pruning the vines, spraying for disease, trimming leaves during the growing season, and so on.

Here is a quick look at some of Australia's signature grapes and the wines made from them, starting with white grapes, then progressing to red.

RIESLING

In Australia, riesling goes back to the 1840s, predating chardonnay by more than a century. Today, most Australian wine experts

Chardonnay grows on gentle slopes in the Adelaide Hills. With its creamy, mouthfilling character, Australian chardonnay first took the world by storm in the 1980s.

consider riesling and sémillon to be the two great Australian whites. Most of the country's top rieslings come from either Eden Valley or Clare Valley (named after County Clare in Ireland), both of which are north of the city of Adelaide, in the state of South Australia. That said, some terrific rieslings are also to be had from Victoria, Western Australia, and even the large island of Tasmania.

The first time I tasted a group of top Australian rieslings, I was struck by two things. First, they didn't taste anything like the rieslings of Germany, Austria, or Alsace. Second, they didn't taste conventionally Australian, by which I mean they weren't big, soft, dense, or any of the other descriptors that have come to be widely associated with Australian wine.

Indeed, Australian rieslings are as unique as they are counterintuitive. These are snappy, frisky rieslings with an electrical current of acidity. Bracing and bone dry, they are usually light to medium in body and very elegant. Most are aromatic, minerally, and especially evocative of citrus zest and citrus marmalade. Because they are so pure, fresh, crisp, dry, citrusy, and light, they are enchanting with seafood, and are terrific with dishes that incorporate aromatic Asian ingredients like Kaffir lime, lemongrass, and

ginger. Lastly, like riesling from all great areas, Australian riesling ages beautifully and gracefully. I love the rieslings from Pewsey Vale (especially The Contours), Petaluma (especially Hanlin Hill), Grosset (especially Polish Hill), Kilikanoon (especially Mort's Reserve), Henschke (especially Julius), Leo Buring, Craigow, and De Bortoli.

CHARDONNAY

Chardonnay is so popular in Australia (a 500 percent increase in production occurred between 1986 and 1996 alone), you'd think the Aussies invented it. Virtually every firm now makes the wine, yet as late as 1967 there was only a minuscule number of chardonnay vines in the entire country. (Tyrrell's, in the Hunter Valley of New South Wales, made the first chardonnay in 1971, calling it Vat 47 Pinot Chardonnay.)

When Australian chardonnays first burst onto the international scene in the early 1980s, there were few white wines like them anywhere. They were so creamy, it seemed as if a spoon would stand up in them. Chardonnay lovers went mad. Today, Australia's greatest chardonnays take a more elegant approach. Although the wines are

OLD, OLDER, OLDEST

Amazingly, many of the oldest cabernet, syrah, and grenache vines in the world are in Australia. It's no surprise, then, that the words *old vines* often show up on wine labels. Yet, as is true in other countries, the term is not legally defined in Australia. In the beginning of the 2000s, the family winery Yalumba sought to clarify the issue by creating an Old Vine Charter that defines just how old an old vine is. In 2009, this was adopted and expanded by other Barossa winegrowers to create the Barossa Old Vine Charter. It designates the following age classifications:

OLD VINE

A vine at least thirty-five years of age. Vines of this age are beyond adolescence and have a fully mature trunk and root system.

SURVIVOR VINE

An antique vine, defined as a vine of at least seventy years of age. Such vines have weathered significant fluctuations in climate, as well as social and political changes that have influenced Australia's wine industry.

CENTENARIAN VINE

An exceptionally old vine of at least one hundred years of age. These vines have thick, gnarly trunks and were planted at a time before irrigation or trellising were possible.

ANCESTOR VINE

A vine at least 125 years old. These vines are considered living tributes to Australia's European settlers.

---

certainly rich, they are refined as well. Among the very best of these are Leeuwin Estate's Art Series, Penfolds Yattarna, Vasse Felix, Giaconda Estate, Domaine Epis, Mount Mary, and Rosemount Estate's Roxburgh, all phenomenal wines suffused with flavor.

SÉMILLON

The most novel white grape in Australia, however, is sémillon, which the Australians pronounce SEM-eh-lawn and spell *semillon*—without the accent used in France; for consistency's sake, I've kept the accent here. Australia is sémillon's second-most-famous home, after Bordeaux (the dry whites of Bordeaux, as well as sweet Sauternes and Barsac, are traditionally made by blending sémillon with sauvignon blanc).

When young and when grown in top vineyard sites, Australian sémillon is as tight, tart, and edgy as white wine gets. It's a wine for acid freaks (the nickname for wine drinkers—and I'm one—who love acidity). This young, dagger-sharp style evolved in Australia's Hunter Valley, in the state of New South Wales. There, the unusually cloudy, rainy climate compelled winemakers to pick sémillon early (when it was barely ripe), before the onset of autumn rains. With time, these young sémillons became famous for their dramatic, kinetic snap.

Today, though, delicious young sémillon is also grown in the Adelaide Hills of South Australia and in the Margaret River region of Western Australia, where it is blended with sauvignon blanc to make sophisticated white blends not unlike a good Pessac-Léognan, from the Graves region of Bordeaux (try Cape Mentelle's version).

BUBBLES AND THE BARBIE

About 10 percent of Australian wine production are sparkling wines. These are made by the traditional (Champagne) method, from pinot noir and chardonnay, and are brut (dry) in style. In character, most are fresh, lively, and unfussy, lacking the complexity of Champagne. It's easy to imagine oceans of such bubbly being downed while yabbies (freshwater Australian crawfish) are searing on the barbie (barbecue). Among the best Australian producers is the French Champagne house of Moët & Chandon, whose subsidiary, Domaine Chandon Australia, makes a whole range of sparklers, from *blanc de blancs* to rosés.

And finally, although it's not particularly sophisticated, sparkling shiraz must be mentioned. Spunky, fruity, and vividly red, sparkling shiraz is an Aussie signature. The wines are intense with raspberry, strawberry, blackberry, and spice notes. Generally, the *dosage* (approximately 3.5 percent, or 35 grams of sugar per liter) is twice that of standard brut sparkling wine in order to balance the tannin in a bubbly made with red grape skins. The first red sparklers in Australia were made in the 1840s and called sparkling Burgundies. Seppelt, still a leading producer, has made red sparklers on a continual basis since the 1890s.

Interestingly, with aging time in the bottle, Australian sémillon displays radically different characteristics than young sémillon. After five years or more, the best wines take on honey, brioche, and roasted cashew flavors, plus a wonderful, lanolin-like texture. No one who loves Australian wines should miss the magnificent sémillons of Tyrrell's (Tyrrell's Vat 1 is possibly the most awarded Australian wine ever made), Hart & Hunter, Vasse Felix, Rothbury Estate, Thomas Wines, and Tim Adams.

CABERNET SAUVIGNON

Many winemakers consider cabernet sauvignon the elite red grape of Australia, although shiraz may be closer to many Australians' hearts. Cabernet is not new to Australia. Indeed, the grape was planted here in the mid-nineteenth century. In fact, the cabernet vines planted in 1888 in Penfolds's famous 10-acre (4-hectare) Block 42 parcel within the Kalimna Vineyard, in the Barossa Valley, are thought to be the oldest cabernet sauvignon vines in the world. The vines are on their own roots,

not grafted on rootstock. (With the 2004 vintage, Penfolds held back a tiny portion of the wine from the Block 42 vineyard and kept it separate from their main blends. After aging it for several years, the company released just twelve bottles of the wine in 2012. Each bottle of Block 42 was packaged in a handblown glass sculpture and sold for about $168,000.)

The simplest cabernets are blackberry flavor-packed bargains. But at the very top, Australian cabernets are refined and complex. Cabernets such as Henschke's Cyril Henschke, Wendouree, and Penfolds Bin 707 bring together the gripping structure of a good Bordeaux with pure, concentrated black currant flavors, graced by notes of green tobacco and a green chaparral character. Many of these top cabernets come from either Coonawarra, a small region in South Australia known for its red, clay-over-limestone soils, or the Margaret River region, of Western Australia.

Not surprisingly, cabernet is also often blended with shiraz—an inspired idea, especially when the blend captures cabernet's prodigious structure and at the same time has shiraz's succulent core of fruit. Yalumba's Signature Cabernet Sauvignon/Shiraz, from the Barossa Valley, and Penfolds Bin 389 Cabernet Sauvignon/Shiraz, from South Australia, are both fantastic examples.

SOME OF THE BEST PRODUCERS OF AUSTRALIAN CABERNET SAUVIGNONS

Several of the following producers are large and make wines at many price levels. Their top cabernets are generally their most expensive wines.

Cape Mentelle • Cullen • Greenock Creek • Hardys • Henschke • Leeuwin Estate • Moss Wood • Noon • Penfolds • Vasse Felix • Wendouree • Yarra Yering

---

Kangaroos in the vineyards of South Australia.

GRENACHE

Grenache was probably brought to Australia in the late 1820s and 1830s by James Busby, known as the father of Australian and New Zealand viticulture. (Having studied viticulture and winemaking in France and Spain, Busby arrived in Australia in 1824 and helped establish the Hunter Valley as one of the country's premier wine regions.) It's thought that Busby brought the grenache directly from Spain, the variety's ancestral home. Yet, despite the direct link, Australians call the grape by its French name, grenache, rather than its original Spanish name, garnacha. Today, one-hundred-year-old grenache vineyards still exist in Australia, and the grapes are used to make sensational table wines. Interestingly, much of this now treasured grenache would have been pulled out in the early and mid-twentieth century, except for the fact that grenache was (and still is) the "secret sauce" that made many of Australia's fortified wines taste so good.

Much of the great grenache in Australia is grown in the state of South Australia, in particular in McLaren Vale and the Barossa Valley. The grapes are sometimes made into single-varietal wines, and sometimes into blends of grenache with syrah, or with syrah and mourvèdre (the so-called "GSM" wines).

A top Australian grenache is a vibrant, spicy, kirschlike wine with a rich core of boysenberry and cherry confiture flavor. While not as massive as shiraz or cabernet, it is nonetheless more full-bodied than pinot noir, making it, for many Australians, the perfect red wine.

Grenaches like d'Arenberg's The Beautiful View, or Kilikanoon's The Duke, or Yalumba's Bush Vine are not to be missed.

SHIRAZ

And finally, there's shiraz, which is to Australia what cabernet sauvignon is to Bordeaux—the signature. Australians are chauvinistically crazy about it, and not surprisingly it's the leading variety in terms of production. The sheer number of spellbinding small-production shirazes in Australia is dizzying.

Shiraz is another name for the grape syrah. Interestingly, until the 1980s, Australians called syrah "hermitage" and occasionally "shiraz." But because Hermitage is an official, protected appellation in the northern Rhône Valley of France, use of that term was ultimately deemed unfair to French vintners. Thus, for the past two decades in Australia, syrah has been known almost exclusively as shiraz, although the derivation of the name remains something of a mystery. One myth—that the grape originated in the Persian city

EUCALYPTUS ELUCIDATED

O*ne of the signature aromas and flavors of many Australian wines (especially shiraz and cabernet sauvignon) is eucalyptus— a fresh, cool, minty, and even medicinal character. How is this possible? The presence of eucalyptus-like aromas and flavors is directly related to a vineyard's proximity to eucalyptus trees (which are native to Australia). The closer the trees to the vineyard, the stronger the character in the wine. It is believed that the compound responsible for this distinct character (1,8-cineole, commonly referred to as eucalyptol) accumulates on the skins of the grapes and from there, combines with the juice during maceration. This may explain why white wines (which are quickly pressed and separated from their skins) generally have little eucalyptus character, but red wines (which are often macerated with their skins) can have moderate to even high levels.*

of Shiraz—has been shown by DNA typing to be exactly that: a myth. (Syrah/shiraz is indigenous to east-central France.) But myths aside, what is known is that syrah has several closely related names in France. There, it's been known as schiras, sirac, syra, syrac, serine, and sereine. Indeed, prior to the mid-nineteenth century, Australians sometimes called the grape scyras. In the end, the term *shiraz* is probably yet another linguistic variation on the name of a grape with a long line of similar-sounding names.

There is no doubt that shiraz helped establish Australia as one of the world's top wine-producing countries. The

wine's seductive aromas, up-front, unctuously soft texture, and saturated berry flavors are impossible to ignore. The best of these wines are a hedonistic puddle of flavor—dark plum, boysenberry, blueberry, and mocha, with hints of spice, violet, and black pepper, plus an echo of gaminess and often an iron (ferrous) quality. By comparison, they are much more saturated with fruit than the syrahs of the Rhône. Which is not to say they are all the same. Australian shirazes can differ considerably depending on the region(s) where the grapes were grown. In general, cooler-climate Australian shirazes are more spicy and savory than their warmer-climate cousins. And shiraz is often blended with grenache to make sensational, complex wines (labeled shiraz/grenache) with dark, sappy, rich cherry confiture and chocolate flavors, often overlaid by a sense of minerals and tar. S.C. Pannell Shiraz/Grenache, from McLaren Vale, and Charles Melton Nine Popes Shiraz/Grenache, from the Barossa Valley, are impressive, delicious examples.

The most iconic—and expensive— Australian shiraz is Grange (once called Grange Hermitage), made by the powerful wine firm Penfolds. Dr. Christopher Rawson Penfold, an Englishman, emigrated to South Australia and, in 1844, established Penfolds to make Port-style wines for his anemic patients. Grange was first made in 1951 by Penfolds's then winemaker Max Schubert, who, after a trip to Bordeaux during which he tasted the wines of several great châteaux, wanted to make a wine of similar intensity, structure, depth, and ageability—but using shiraz grapes.

With the 1953 vintage, the wine was released to the market. Alas, critics were not kind. One belittled it as "a concoction of wild fruits and sundry berries with crushed ants predominating." Today, Grange is widely praised for its power, concentration, elegance, and beautiful flavors and aromas of leather and tobacco mingled with boysenberries and mint. To make Grange, Penfolds winemakers blind-taste hundreds of different shirazes from vineyards they own or have contracts with all over Australia. In the end, fewer than seven thousand cases of Grange

The wrinkled, purple skins of shiraz grapes left behind after wine is made at Jim Barry winery, one of the top family estates in the Barossa Valley of South Australia.

are made each year. And while the wine may be 100 percent shiraz in some years, it isn't always so. Depending on the character of the shirazes in any given year, small amounts of cabernet sauvignon may be added to the final blend. The wine is always aged in brand-new American oak.

STICKIES

Australia makes some of the world's most wickedly exquisite fortified sweet wines. To me, they are nothing short of ravishing. Just the thought of drinking one gives me a rush. And while Australia has made them for centuries, they remain largely unknown (a crime to be sure).

Australians call them stickies—a catchall term for both sweet fortified wines and their sweet, but not fortified, cousins. There are several types. The most sensational and rare of the stickies are Australia's sweet fortified muscats and topaques, made in Rutherglen, in the northeast corner of Victoria. (Topaques were formerly known as tokays, but the name was changed in 2010 as a result of an agreement between Australia and the European Union, in which Australia agreed to recognize Tokay—or

Tokaji, as it is written in Hungarian—as the name reserved exclusively for a historic appellation in Hungary.) Muscats and topaques have an almost primordial character. Nearly black in color, with slashing glints of orange and green, they ooze around the sides of a wineglass, taking their time. Drinking them is a mind-blowing experience; indeed, it seems to take forever for the languorous sensation of flavor to end.

The muscats are made from a brownish-tinged version of the white grape muscat blanc à petits grains; the topaques, from the white muscadelle grape (the latter is sometimes listed on wine labels as topaque muscadelle). The best are usually made in tiny quantities and are rarely exported. To make the wines, the grapes are left on the vine long after the normal harvest, until they begin to shrivel and their sugar intensifies. During fermentation, the soupy mass of crushed grapes is fortified with neutral grape spirits, which stops the fermentation, leaving a wine with natural residual sugar. The wine is then aged for ten to twenty years or more in small, used oak barrels (not brand-new) set up like a Sherry solera (see page 458), until the wine takes on unreal, hard-to-describe flavors reminiscent of toffee, brown sugar, vanilla, chocolate, fig syrup, miso, molasses, and honey. Among the best sweet, fortified muscats and topaques are those

The second vintage (1952) of Penfolds Grange—its label still mostly intact—being poured for a guest.

produced by Chambers Rosewood Vineyards, Campbells Wines, and Morris.

Next are Australian Port-style wines, now called Australian fortified tawnies. Australian fortified tawnies, most of which are made in South Australia, are made in a way roughly approximate to that used for Portuguese tawny Ports, although the Australian versions are sometimes vintaged wines, and shiraz, grenache, and mourvèdre (which fortified wine producers often call "mataro") are used instead of native Portuguese grapes. The finest Australian fortified tawnies are as complex (if not more) as Portuguese tawny Ports and are surging with dramatic, rich, nutty, caramelly, espresso, citrus, and spice flavors, and unreal colors that often seem flecked with neon orange. The two blockbusters of the genre are Seppeltsfield DP 90 and Seppeltsfield Para—with luscious fortified tawnies also made by Penfolds, Yalumba, Reynella, and Stanton & Killeen.

As for Australian Sherry-style wines (now called "apera"), they are made using two Spanish grapes, palomino and Pedro Ximénez, sometimes with muscat gordo blanco blended in. Made in minute quantities, the best come pretty close to having the finesse, complexity, and flavor of true Spanish Sherry. Again, Seppeltsfield makes a very fine one.

In addition to topaques, muscats, fortified tawnies, and aperas, Australia also boasts numerous nonfortified sweet wines made from late-harvested grapes, usually riesling or sémillon, that have been affected by *Botrytis cinerea* (just the way Sauternes is).

THE WINE REGIONS

Here are thumbnail sketches of Australia's major wine states and some of the best-known wine regions within them. Remember that for multiregional blends labeled South Eastern Australia, the grapes will probably have come from disparate regions, possibly quite far apart. For such wines, the most important guide to quality is the producer's name.

SOUTH AUSTRALIA

ADELAIDE HILLS | BAROSSA VALLEY | EDEN VALLEY | CLARE VALLEY | MCLAREN VALE | COONAWARRA

South Australia is the driest state in Australia (which is the driest continent). More than half of all Australian wine is produced in this state, including many of the country's best cabernet sauvignons, shirazes, chardonnays, rieslings, and sémillons.

The wine regions of South Australia span out from the city of Adelaide. Among the top regions are Adelaide Hills, Barossa Valley, Eden Valley, Clare Valley, McLaren Vale, and Coonawarra. These districts were founded by men whose names have become synonymous with Australian wine: Hamilton, Seppelt, Penfold, and so on. And today, a Who's Who of large Australian wine companies is located here, including Hardys, Penfolds, Peter Lehmann, Seppeltsfield, Wolf Blass, Wynns, and Yalumba. But the region is also a hotbed of small and medium-size avant-garde producers such as Henschke, Jim Barry, Grosset, Torbreck, Shaw & Smith, and Tim Adams.

A cool-climate region just east of the city of Adelaide, the Adelaide Hills is one of

SOUTHERN COMFORT—SORT OF, MATE

Many Australian wines are labeled South Australia or South Eastern Australia. Are these designations essentially the same? The answer is no. In fact, they could not be more different. South Australia is one of the five Australian states. (These are comparable to states in the United States, although Australian states are much larger.) Within the state of South Australia are some of the country's most famous wine regions, including the Barossa Valley (renowned for shiraz), the Clare Valley (remarkable for dry riesling), and Coonawarra (known for cabernet sauvignon). By contrast, South Eastern Australia is not a state, and in a sense, not a place. It's a legal designation that means the wine in the bottle is a blend of wines made from grapes grown thousands of miles apart, often in three different states—New South Wales, Victoria, and South Australia. To give a New World analogy, a wine labeled South Eastern Australia is the rough equivalent of a wine hypothetically made from a blend of grapes grown in California, Oregon, Washington State, and Texas and then called "Western United States." Not surprisingly, South Eastern Australia wines are often inexpensive wines meant for everyday drinking, while wines from South Australia are among the most expensive in the country.

the largest geographical regions in Australia, and one of the most diverse. A wide range of grape varieties—everything from riesling, sauvignon blanc, and chardonnay to shiraz and cabernet sauvignon—grows here. Viticulture in the Adelaide Hills began in the 1840s, but a modern industry took hold only after the 1970s.

Eden Valley and Clare Valley are both known for exquisite rieslings, although both also make very precise shirazes. Eden Valley (actually a plateau above the Barossa Valley) is known for more floral, exotic, medium-bodied rieslings, while those of Clare Valley (again, not a true valley, but an elevated plateau) are more citrusy, with driving acidity. It is commonly assumed that the rieslings from these two areas are picked early to achieve their dizzying crispness, but they are not. Rather, the regions' extremely cold nights and water-holding, limestone-laced soils are credited with preserving riesling's backbone of inherent acidity.

In a blind tasting, the shirazes from McLaren Vale always seem relatively easy to pick out, first for their powerful and ripe character but sleek structure, and second for their dramatic lift of spiciness, black olive, menthol, and dark chocolate. Both Clarendon Hills' Astralis Shiraz and d'Arenberg's The Dead Arm Shiraz are perfect examples. The small region, a mix of hills and valleys with ironstone and loamy clay soils, is just 22 miles (35 kilometers) south of Adelaide, on the Fleurieu Peninsula. It is bounded on the northwest by the Onkaparinga River, and on the west by Gulf St. Vincent, giving at least some of the vines a bit of cooling maritime influence, which may help account for the wine's structure and elegance. Grapes were first planted here in 1838, by John Reynell and Thomas Hardy, who started Seaview and Hardy Wine Company, respectively. Shiraz accounts for more than 50 percent of the wine made in McLaren Vale.

Coonawarra (the name is Aboriginal for "honeysuckle") is considered (along with Western Australia's Margaret River) one of the best places in the country for structured cabernet sauvignons. The region, about 230 miles (370 kilometers) south of Adelaide, is a cigar-shaped strip

THE ABORIGINES

Many of Australia's wine districts have Aboriginal names, such as Coonawarra ("honeysuckle"), Mudgee ("nest in the hills"), and Padthaway ("good water"). The Aborigines, Australia's native inhabitants, are a distinct race that has no close affinity with any other people. They have lived in Australia for more than thirty thousand years and are the oldest race on earth today.

just 7.5 miles (12 kilometers) long and 1.2 miles (1.9 kilometers) wide of terra rossa soil, porous reddish clay soil overlaying limestone. The climate, not surprisingly, is maritime, like that of Bordeaux.

I find these cabernets evocative of black currants, with a discernible note of something green—not unripe green bell pepper, but rather a more sophisticated suggestion of chaparral.

But for all of the deserved excitement of the regions above, the best-known wine region in the state of South Australia—indeed, perhaps the best-known wine region in all of Australia—is the Barossa Valley. The wide, fertile valley is made up of biscuit-colored rolling hills, with vineyards planted in the best sites, where the soils are laced with ironstone, red clay, quartz, and limestone, and everywhere else, fields of corn, wheat, barley, legumes, and orchards as far as the eye can see. Sheep meander in paddocks, and the small hamlets are full of old stone cottages. The Barossa (as it is simply known) was settled in the early 1800s by a handful of Englishmen, as well as a large Lutheran Silesian community (Silesia, today part of Poland, was then part of Germany, and German is still regularly spoken in the Barossa). The Silesians were an insular community of hardworking, frugal farmers with a

strong food culture. Baked, pickled, preserved, and smoked foods were—and still are—local specialties, as evidenced by the hugely popular Barossa Farmer's Market and the annual dill gherkin and pickled onion championships.

Great cabernet is made in the Barossa, and I've loved many grenaches and grenache blends from here, as well as the superb Australian fortified tawnies made in the region. But above all, the Barossa is known for shiraz—rich, sappy shiraz with a concentrated core of vivid "berriness" overlaid by wild lavender, spice, brambly, and licorice notes. Yet, for all their dramatic richness and bigness, the best Barossa shirazes also have a superb structure, balance, and sense of precision.

NEW SOUTH WALES

HUNTER VALLEY

New South Wales is Australia's second-leading state in wine production, after South Australia. (A lot of this is very inexpensive wine.)

The most famous wine district in the state is the relatively small Hunter Valley, 75 miles (120 kilometers) north of Australia's oldest and largest city, Sydney. The Hunter Valley was the first wine area in Australia, vineyards having been planted here at the beginning of the nineteenth century by the country's earliest European settlers. Around 1960, Penfolds moved to an area slightly north of the original vineyards, initiating the distinction between what is now known as the Upper Hunter and the Lower Hunter.

The whole Hunter Valley region is something of an anomaly. Being one of the most northerly of Australia's wine districts, it is closer to the equator and its weather patterns are influenced by warm ocean currents coming from the tropics. As a result, it is very warm and almost too humid for grapes. Nonetheless, and almost against all odds, several top chardonnays and shirazes come from here.

But if the Hunter Valley has an ace in the hole, it's sémillon, a wine that starts out as bracing, limey, white peppery, and as high in acid as wine gets. Drinking it is like being slapped. But with age—five to ten years or more—something startling happens: The wine turns into a honey pot of rich, nutty, buttery fruit. Great examples are found from Tyrrell's, McWilliam's, Mount Pleasant, Hart & Hunter, Thomas Wines, and Brokenwood.

VICTORIA

BEECHWORTH | GEELONG | GLENROWAN | GOULBURN VALLEY | GRAMPIANS | HEATHCOTE | MACEDON RANGES | MORNINGTON PENINSULA | NAGAMBIE LAKES | PYRENEES | RUTHERGLEN | SOUTH GIPPSLAND | SUNBURY | YARRA VALLEY

Just as northern California's wine industry was jump-started by the gold rush of 1849, the discovery of gold in Victoria, in 1851, paved the way for a fledgling wine industry in the state. As Victoria's economy and population boomed, the ambitions of vintners soared every bit as high as those of the gold diggers. Eventually, as the supply of gold dwindled, vintners were known to hire out-of-work miners to dig underground wine cellars.

But when the gold ran out completely, Victoria's fortunes began to spiral downward. The picture grew especially gloomy for wineries as phylloxera, economic decline, competitive wines from South Australia, and changing land use all took a toll. (As an aside, while phylloxera did affect a small number of vineyards in Victoria, the country as a whole has largely escaped the pest, and most vineyards are on their own roots rather than grafted onto tolerant rootstock.) By the 1960s, Victoria's

Fermentation—a family affair at Torbreck.

TASMANIA

Tasmania, the smallest state of the Commonwealth of Australia, is a triangular, mountainous island in the Southern Ocean, about 150 miles (240 kilometers) south of Victoria. With its mild, sunny, cool, maritime climate, the island is an up-and-coming wine region, known especially for its pinot noir, as well as chardonnay, sauvignon blanc, riesling, and sparkling wines. While most of its 160 wine producers are small, winemaking here has exploded, especially in the past decade. From a mere 100 acres (40 hectares) of vines in the 1950s, Tasmania now has some 3,700 acres (1,500 hectares) of vineyards.

Tasmania (or "Tazzy," as it is often called locally) is named for the Dutch explorer Abel Tasman, who discovered it in 1642. The island's vast array of plant and animal life includes the Tasmanian devil, a not very devilish, doglike creature, which, like the kangaroo, is a marsupial.

wine industry was a shadow of its former self. When the Australian wine industry as a whole began to take off in the 1970s and 1980s, however, a new period of growth ensued for the state.

Of all of mainland Australia's wine regions, Victoria is the smallest and most southern (only the island of Tasmania, off the Victorian coast, is smaller and farther south). The region includes more than 820 producers, spread over more than a dozen small wine districts that fan out directly from the city of Melbourne.

Victoria's wine districts vary considerably in climate, terrain, and soil, thanks in part to the Great Dividing Range, which cuts through Victoria, creating mountainous and hilly terrain over more than a third of the state. Several of the most renowned wine districts—the

WHEN YOU VISIT . . . AUSTRALIA

AUSTRALIA'S WINERIES are generally well set up for visitors, and the larger wineries often have multiple facilities and attractions, including restaurants, galleries, concerts, and so forth. The small wineries are far more humble, but chances are you'll have the opportunity to taste with the owners themselves.

MANY WINERIES are within easy driving distance of Australia's major cities: Sydney, Melbourne, Adelaide, and Perth. In each of these cities, there are a number of wine bars worth visiting to get you started on the right foot.

WHEN YOU VISIT THE STATE of South Australia, don't miss the extraordinary Seppeltsfield where, for a small fee, you can taste the wine of your birth year, going back to the early 1950s.

Yarra Valley, Geelong, and Mornington Peninsula, for example—are very close to the sea and benefit from cool breezes that sweep in off the Great Southern Ocean. In these cool areas, chardonnay and pinot noir grapes thrive. Farther inland, in slightly warmer pockets like Beechworth, the chardonnays that are made can again be stellar, if richer (Giaconda Estate's fantastic chardonnay comes from here). Victoria is also known for cabernet sauvignon and shiraz, with some producers—such as Yarra Yering and Mount Mary—making delicious red blends.

One of Victoria's specialties is the captivating, sweet muscats and topaques made in northeastern Victoria, in the district of Rutherglen, by producers such as Chambers Rosewood Vineyards and Campbells Wines. Spellbinding and unctuous, these wines are deliciously unique (see Stickies, page 835).

Finally, Victoria has always been associated with sparkling wine because Seppelt, one of Australia's oldest and most important sparkling producers, is located in the district of Grampians. And in 1986, the French house Moët & Chandon founded Chandon Australia here in the Yarra Valley.

WESTERN AUSTRALIA

MARGARET RIVER | GREAT SOUTHERN REGION | PEMBERTON | PERTH HILLS | SWAN VALLEY

Far on the other side of the Australian continent, 3,000 miles (4,800 kilometers) away from the power centers of winemaking in the southeast, is the remote state of Western Australia. The first known sighting of the western coastline was in 1622, by the Dutch vessel *Leeuwin,* meaning "lioness." The name would later be adopted by one of the state's most prominent wineries.

Western Australia's several wine districts, which include Margaret River, Great Southern Region, Pemberton, Perth Hills, and Swan Valley, stretch out from the coastal city of Perth. Vines were planted in this area in 1829, some years before the first plantings in either South Australia or Victoria. But the state's isolation and limited population hampered the industry's growth and scope until the 1980s.

The Swan Valley, north of Perth, was Western Australia's first wine district. It became known for table grapes as well as wine grapes, and the leading wines were mostly sweet and/or fortified, and were sold in bulk. It was here that Houghton White Burgundy, once Australia's most recognized white wine, was born in the years just before World War II. Although it is slightly more polished now (and renamed Houghton White Classic), it was originally a rustic, powerfully alcoholic wine made from chenin blanc, muscadelle, and chardonnay. Amazingly, the Swan Valley is also where the Portuguese grape verdelho was planted—almost two centuries ago, in 1829. It was brought by one of Western Australia's first colonists, a botanist named Thomas Waters, who took cuttings from the island of Madeira, off the African coast (a stopping point to pick

The Margaret River wine region, where the cold Southern Ocean and the warm Indian Ocean splash together.

up provisions on the long voyage out). Among the best verdelhos to try are Ashbrook Estate, Chestnut Grove, and Capel Vale.

Take a three-hour bus ride south from Perth, and you'll come to the corner where the great, warm Indian Ocean and the cold Southern Ocean collide. This is where you'll find the most renowned and ambitious of all the Western Australian districts: Margaret River. Originally known for its timber, Margaret River is one of the world's newer fine wine regions. Vines weren't planted here until the late 1960s, more than a century after grapes were planted in the Napa Valley, for example. The region is still extremely remote and is best known for its hypnotic giant waves. (Many of the local winery staff surf daily before work.)

One of the key pioneers of the Margaret River region was David Hohnen, a modest but smart farmer who moved to California briefly to learn winemaking, then cobbled together bank loans to found Cape Mentelle winery in 1970. (The prescient Hohnen is also credited with being one of the first to recognize the potential of Marlborough, in New Zealand; he founded Cloudy Bay there in 1983.)

Given Margaret River's maritime location and gravelly soils, Hohnen and several other pioneers focused not on shiraz, but on Bordeaux varieties. Today, the region is considered something of a "little Bordeaux" for the loveliness of its sémillon/sauvignon blanc

blends and the structure and elegance of the cabernet sauvignons—especially those from the leading wineries, among them the afore-mentioned Cape Mentelle, plus Leeuwin Estate and Vasse Felix.

All of this said, chardonnay, too, has an almost magical affinity for the region. Leeuwin Estate, in particular, makes its Art Series Chardonnays—wines of depth that with several years' aging grow even richer and more expansive. They are among the best produced in all of Australia.

Despite a nearly ideal sunny/ocean-cooled climate in Margaret River, there is one huge problem: birds. As harvest approaches and the grapes begin their final push toward ripeness, each row of vines must be netted. Before net-ting was used, three crops out of five would be lost because the grapes would be eaten by the omnivorous birds called silvereyes. Finally, in addition to Margaret River, the cool subdis-tricts within the Great Southern Region are generating excitement. Wineries to watch here include Howard Park, Houghton, and Plantagenet.

SOME OF THE BEST PRODUCERS OF AUSTRALIAN SHIRAZ AND SHIRAZ BLENDS

Several of the following producers make wines at many price levels. Their top shiraz or shiraz blends are their most expensive wines.

Charles Melton • Clarendon Hills • Clonakilla • Craiglee • d'Arenberg • Giaconda • Grant Burge • Hardys • Henschke • Jasper Hill • Jim Barry • Kilikanoon • Leasingham • Mitchelton • Mount Langi Ghiran • Ngeringa • Noon • Penfolds • Peter Lehmann • S.C. Pannell • Shaw & Smith • St. Hallett • Torbreck • Tyrrell's • Vasse Felix • Wendouree • Wynns • Yabby Lake • Yalumba

WHITES

TYRRELL'S

SÉMILLON | VAT 1 | HUNTER VALLEY, NEW SOUTH WALES

100% sémillon

Dry sémillon (or as the Australians write it, *semillon*) is one of Australia's great treasures, and no winery is more lauded for it than Tyrrell's, which has made sémillons back to 1963 from a site memorably called Short Flat Vineyard. When young, Tyrrell's Vat 1 is like a flash of moonlight . . . a hauntingly stark, bright wine that's racy, limey, and needle-sharp on the palate. With time, however, the wine undergoes a magical transformation for which it is famous. The edginess melts away to reveal a great white wine of beauty and strength—a wine evocative of brioche, whipped butter, and cashews. In these older Tyrrell's Vat 1 sémillons, the butteriness and vibrancy are like oppositely charged molecules in total attraction.

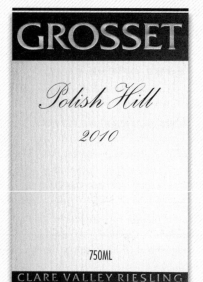

GROSSET

RIESLING | POLISH HILL | CLARE VALLEY, SOUTH AUSTRALIA

100% riesling

Jeffrey Grosset is the patriarch of riesling in Australia . . . a man who has helped put Australian riesling on the international map; a man who has spent his life exploring finesse in a wine country often better known for power. The Grosset rieslings are spot-on for Clare Valley—sharp and vivid, with intense, citrusy notes, but a lightness of being that defines them. With age, the wines take on richness, creaminess, plus brioche notes, and a weathered rock character, but their vivacity and focus never leave.

PEWSEY VALE

RIESLING | THE CONTOURS | EDEN VALLEY, SOUTH AUSTRALIA

100% riesling

The Contours is perhaps Australian riesling's most sacred site. Planted in 1961, high up on the limestone-laced Eden Valley plateau above the Barossa Valley, the undulating vineyard is planted on terraces contoured to the sway of the hills, an early method of catching precious rainfall. Unlike most dry rieslings worldwide, The Contours is released only after five-and-a-half years of aging, when it has taken on a lanolin-like texture, as well as the mesmerizing and unusual aromas and flavors of marzipan, pistachio, Kaffir lime, and Danish pastry. This is one of Australia's most sophisticated whites and a must for riesling lovers.

LEEUWIN ESTATE

CHARDONNAY | ART SERIES | MARGARET RIVER, WESTERN AUSTRALIA

100% chardonnay

Seemingly at the end of the world in far Western Australia, 3 miles from the Indian Ocean, Leeuwin Estate makes extraordinary, age-worthy, rich chardonnays that, in top vintages, are suffused with complex and mysterious nuances. Never heavy or ponderous, despite their intensity and concentration, these are chardonnays that, sip after sip, draw you into them, revealing something new each time. Leeuwin's Art Series wines (so called to distinguish them from the regular Leeuwin wines) are blends of the top lots. Each year, labels for the Art Series are commissioned from leading Australian artists.

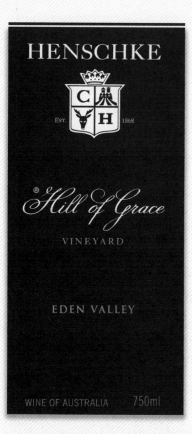

REDS

HENSCHKE

SHIRAZ | HILL OF GRACE | EDEN VALLEY, SOUTH AUSTRALIA

100% shiraz

Year in and year out, Hill of Grace, as it is known, is one of Australia's most voluptuous and impressive shirazes. Named after a local church and made from vines that, amazingly, are over 130 years old, it is a rich, aromatic, impossibly sensual wine suggestive of black raspberry, bitter chocolate, boysenberries, cedar, leather, and cigar boxes. The density and power behind the wine is indelible. Vintages many decades old take on complex camphor and cedar chest aromas, with deeply satisfying, savory umami flavors. Hill of Grace's sister shiraz, Mount Edelstone (these vines were planted in 1912), is equally captivating, with waves of exotic spices and plush fruit and a long, peppery tail of a finish.

JIM BARRY

SHIRAZ | THE ARMAGH | CLARE VALLEY, SOUTH AUSTRALIA

100% shiraz

Pure hedonism in a bottle, The Armagh (named after a county in Northern Ireland) is a majestic and distinctive wine—one that shocks you with its masculine force of dark rock, iron, and mineral flavors, then, the next minute, spreads over the palate like velvet jam. In the middle is the kind of "corruption" only syrah is capable of: flavors that swirl around the ideas of blood, hung game, cigars, and sweat. Jim Barry began his career in 1959, a contemporary of Max Schubert at Penfolds. Today, the vineyards are cared for by Jim's son, the feisty, irrepressible Peter Barry, who has been known to tell if shiraz is ripe by sticking his balding pate between the vines and seeing how quickly his head feels warm.

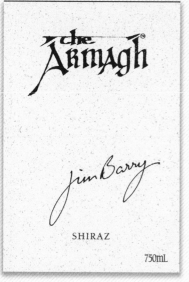

TORBRECK

SHIRAZ | THE LAIRD | BAROSSA VALLEY, SOUTH AUSTRALIA

100% shiraz

The world has many excellent fruity wines with notes of spice and minerals—but not many spicy/minerally wines with notes of fruit. This is the latter—a masculine wine of incredible rockiness, angularity, firmness, and precision. It's the iron fist, with only the merest velvet glove. Torbreck (named after a forest in Scotland) was founded by the indomitable, insatiable David Powell, a man who seems like he could stare down the end of a gun barrel . . . and chuckle. The wine is aged in wood for three years, in special barrels made of staves 1.8 inches (45 millimeters) thick (an average stave is only about half as thick— .87 to 1.1 inches (22 to 27 millimeters) and then never topped up, since the thicker staves serve to inhibit evaporation. Unusual winemaking, but the proof is in the pudding.

CHARLES MELTON

SHIRAZ GRENACHE | NINE POPES | BAROSSA VALLEY, SOUTH AUSTRALIA

Approximately equal parts shiraz and grenache, with 5% mourvèdre

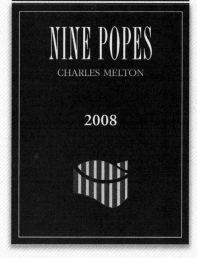

Nine Popes is an homage to Châteauneuf-du-Pape. The famous appellation in the Rhône Valley of France translates as "new castle of the pope," a reference to the time in the thirteenth century when the papacy was located here. However, Charlie Melton's French skills being modest, he thought the name meant "home of nine popes," and named his wine accordingly. The wine, intense and complex, proves just how riveting Rhône-style blends can be in Australia. Lashings of leather, tar, and espresso-like bitterness hit the palate in between herb-scented notes of wild lavender and thyme, salty notes of minerals, and fruit flavors that are more blue (blueberry) than red (cherry). Today, Charlie Melton is considered one of the protectors of old-vine Rhône varieties in the Barossa.

KILIKANOON

SHIRAZ | ATTUNGA 1865 | CLARE VALLEY, SOUTH AUSTRALIA

100% shiraz

It's hard to choose a Kilikanoon wine to write about, as the winery makes killer riesling and grenache in addition to several extraordinary shirazes. Attunga shiraz (the word means "high place" in the Aboriginal language) won out for its sublimeness. Made only in extraordinary years, the wine comes from a low-yielding, old vineyard just 2.5 acres (1 hectare) in size. Lushly textured but not immediately effusive, Attunga is a shiraz that reveals its menthol character slowly on the palate. And that choreography sneaks up on you as it can only in great wines.

PENFOLDS

GRANGE | SOUTH AUSTRALIA

Mostly shiraz, occasionally with a tiny bit of cabernet sauvignon

Grange is widely considered to be Australia's most famous shiraz and the country's most famous wine, comparable in status to a First Growth Bordeaux. A wine of exquisite balance, it embodies power and elegance simultaneously. When the wine is young, the texture is velvet-on-velvet, and the lush berry flavors are infused with vanilla (thanks to long aging in American oak). With time, Grange becomes deliriously supple, with aromas and flavors suggestive of violets, black figs, cedar, and spices. Grange has one of the longest track records when it comes to long aging. Wines from the 1950s, made by the master winemaker Max Schubert, are still in amazing condition.

FORTIFIED SWEET WINES

CHAMBERS ROSEWOOD

TOPAQUE MUSCADELLE | CLASSIC | RUTHERGLEN, VICTORIA

100% muscadelle

In a tasting of Rutherglen topaques not long ago, I was tempted—maybe compelled—to score the wines. They were *so* good, so distinctive, so unique, so emotion-inducing. I wrote 100 repeatedly. Chambers (as it's usually simply known) was one of those 100-point wines—a wine that has a plumb line deep into figs, chocolate, and molasses. The texture was unreal . . . like some ethereal combination of honey and melted chocolate. Most remarkable of all, despite its luxuriousness, the wine was alive with energy, and very vivid on the palate.

SEPPELTSFIELD

PARA | AUSTRALIAN FORTIFIED TAWNY | BAROSSA VALLEY, SOUTH AUSTRALIA

Matro (mourvèdre), shiraz, grenache, in varying combinations each year

Each year, tiny amounts of this mind-blowing wine are released when the wine is a century old (in 2010, the 1910 was released; in 2012, the 1912 was released, and so on). And the wine is a steal (in 2012, the small, 3- to 4-ounce/100-milliliter bottle of the 1912 Para cost $300—a bargain given its age). The complexity of Para is astounding. The wine's flavors seem to spread through your body like a hypnotic drug. And what flavors! Surges of sweet licorice, molten chocolate cake, dried fruit soaked in liqueur, molasses, citrus peel, anise, toffee, bark, and peat. Wines like this have no reference point. They are simply plunges into a netherworld of sensory pleasure. Seppeltsfield has made Para since 1878. The name Para refers to a small river in the Barossa Valley.

CHAMBERS
Rosewood Vineyards
RUTHERGLEN

Established
1858

Muscadelle

PRODUCED AND BOTTLED BY
CHAMBERS ROSEWOOD VINEYARDS
BARKLY STREET RUTHERGLEN
VICTORIA 3685 AUSTRALIA

Alc. 18.5% by vol. WINE PRODUCT OF AUSTRALIA 375mL

SEPPELTSFIELD
- EST 1851 -
PARA
PRODUCT OF AUSTRALIA
750mL

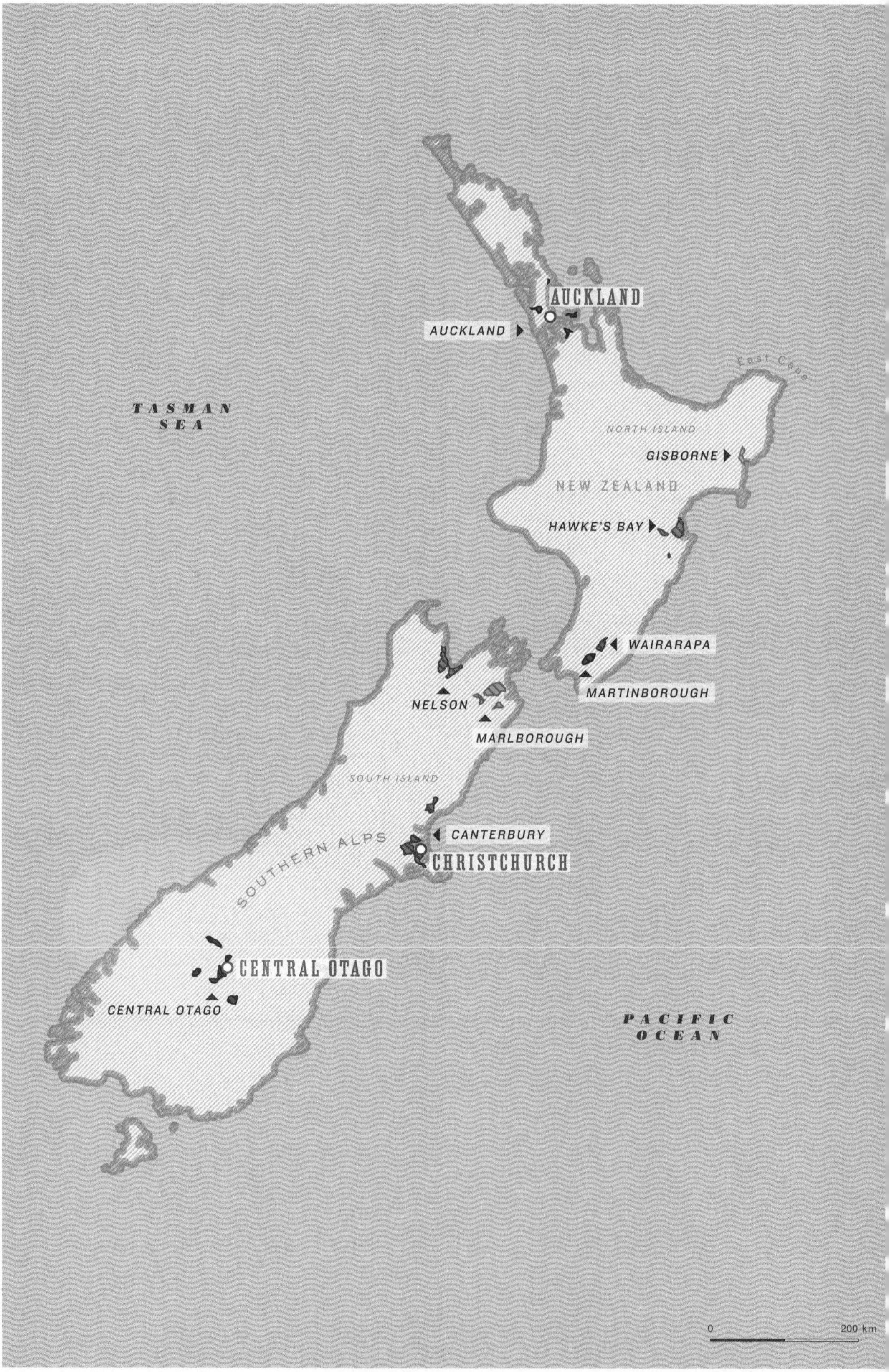

TASMAN
SEA

AUCKLAND

AUCKLAND ▶

East Cape

NORTH ISLAND

GISBORNE ▶

NEW ZEALAND

HAWKE'S BAY ▶

WAIRARAPA ◀

MARTINBOROUGH

NELSON ▲

MARLBOROUGH

SOUTH ISLAND

CANTERBURY ◀

SOUTHERN ALPS

CHRISTCHURCH

CENTRAL OTAGO

CENTRAL OTAGO

PACIFIC
OCEAN

0   200 km

NEW ZEALAND

NEW ZEALAND RANKS FOURTEENTH AMONG WINE-PRODUCING COUNTRIES WORLDWIDE. NEW ZEALANDERS DRINK AN AVERAGE OF 4 GALLONS (14 LITERS) OF WINE PER PERSON PER YEAR.

ocated roughly midway between the equator and the South Pole, New Zealand lies isolated in the middle of the South Pacific Ocean. The nearest landmass, Australia, is 1,000 miles (1,600 kilometers) to the northwest. The country is composed of two long main islands, called simply the North Island and the South Island, plus numerous small off-shore islands. New Zealand's vineyards are the southernmost in the world. They are also the first vineyards on earth to see the sun each day, thanks to New Zealand's location close to the International Date Line.

In the 1970s, when so many wine-producing countries were moving toward modern wine industries, New Zealand was still far better known for lamb than wine (indeed, the country had more sheep than people at the time). Then, in the mid-1980s, and almost against all odds, one wine rose to extraordinary fame—Cloudy Bay Sauvignon Blanc. The first few vintages put the whole of New Zealand on the international wine map. It was the first time a single wine had ever had such impact—a feat made even more surprising by the fact that sauvignon blanc was, at the time, considered something of a second-string variety. But Cloudy Bay's sauvignon blanc was startlingly different. It rocked the wine world by opening the door to a whole new galaxy of flavor. Every adventurous wine drinker in the world had to taste it because it expanded the known realm of what wine *could* taste like. Since that time, countless

> "New Zealand is the youngest nation in the world, both geologically and in terms of human settlement. It's four million people, still wandering around in dazed wonder at its beauty, still trying to figure out what they want to do with it all."
>
> —NIGEL GREENING, proprietor of Felton Road

THE QUICK SIP ON NEW ZEALAND

NEW ZEALAND is best known for its racy, vibrant sauvignon blancs and earthy, elegant pinot noirs.

NEW ZEALAND'S wine industry, while growing and infused with excitement, remains tiny by global standards. Wine production here accounts for less than 1 percent of the world's total.

ONE OF THE COOLEST maritime wine regions in the New World, New Zealand boasts vineyards that are the most southerly on the globe.

wine drinkers have had the same oh-my-god experience with other New Zealand sauvignon blancs. The wines are, quite simply, outrageousness in a bottle. And they've flung the door wide open to other exciting New Zealand varietals—especially pinot noir.

The remote islands of New Zealand were unknown to the western world until Abel Tasman, the Dutch sea captain after whom Tasmania was named, landed on the northern tip of the South Island in 1642. There, Tasman encountered a violent group of native peoples—the Maori—and promptly left. More than a century would pass before the next westerner ventured onto New Zealand's shores. In 1769, the English explorer Captain James Cook circumnavigated the islands. His explorations resulted in the British colonization of New Zealand, and in the bond between the two countries that still exists today. Almost fifty years later, in 1819, the first New Zealand vines were planted by an Anglican missionary named Samuel Marsden, although there is no record of wine being produced from the grapes. Then, in 1839, Scotsman James Busby successfully made the country's first wines. Both Marsden and Busby had written of New Zealand's promise as a wine producer, for the climate and terrain appeared exceptionally well suited to grapevines.

Despite this auspicious beginning, it would be a century and a half before a solid wine industry would take hold. From the 1840s to the 1980s, the obstacles to success were pervasive. To begin with, many of the pioneering New Zealand winemakers were English immigrants who had no history or experience with grape-growing. To make matters worse, for decades before and after the turn of the twentieth century, New Zealand came under the influence of a relentless temperance movement, which severely handicapped the establishment of any sort of wine culture. For most of the 1800s, wineries could not sell wine to consumers; they could only sell to hotels for banquets, and then only if certain conditions were met. It wasn't until after World War II that wine was permitted to be sold by the bottle from wine shops, and selling wine in restaurants became legal only in the 1960s. Even then, there was a 10:00 p.m. cutoff after which no wine or alcohol could be sold.

None of this fully deterred the young country's would-be winemakers. In the late 1800s, immigrants from the Dalmatian coast, now in Croatia, intending to make their fortunes in New Zealand's gum fields, eventually turned to

The snowcapped Kaikoura Ranges are a stunning backdrop for vineyards in Marlborough.

farming and grape growing instead. Although many of these immigrants were experienced winemakers, they were powerless against oidium (powdery mildew) and phylloxera, which soon decimated their young vineyards. In the wake of these diseases and the economic downturn that followed, the industry turned for a time to hardy hybrid grapes and the production of poor-quality, sugary, fortified concoctions roughly modeled on inferior brandy and ersatz Sherry.

Today, New Zealand is a vastly different place. The fine wine industry that began to take hold in the mid-1980s has boomed. Between 1994 and 2013, for example, the number of wineries skyrocketed from just thirty to over seven hundred. More recently, between 2003 and 2013, vineyard acreage doubled, and now stands at 88,300 acres (35,700 hectares). And despite a global financial crisis in the late 2000s, New Zealand's wine production grew by more than 50 percent in the four years between 2007 and 2011.

New Zealand's seven hundred wine producers range from tiny family operations to large, global companies (Pernod Ricard, for example, owns several New Zealand brands, including Brancott Estate and Church Road). While some producers do grow all their own grapes, the majority of New Zealand wineries buy grapes from the country's 833 independent grape growers. Increasingly, of course, these grape growers are making wine and coming out with their own small brands.

Of the twenty-five or so grape varieties grown in New Zealand today, sauvignon blanc and pinot noir are the most renowned and, respectively, the most widely planted. While it's true that 78 percent of the vineyards are planted with white grape varieties (primarily sauvignon blanc), pinot noir has had a stellar rise to fame in this country. In addition, pinot gris and riesling (the latter, both as a dry wine and as a late-harvest dessert wine) are creating a great deal of excitement, especially on the South Island, in Marlborough and Canterbury/ Waipara Valley.

For an explanation of New Zealand's wine laws, see the Appendix on Wine Laws, page 928.

THE MOST IMPORTANT NEW ZEALAND WINES

LEADING WINES

CHARDONNAY white

PINOT GRIS white

PINOT NOIR red

RIESLING white (dry and sweet)

SAUVIGNON BLANC white

SPARKLING WINES white and rosé

WINES OF NOTE

CABERNET SAUVIGNON and **BORDEAUX-STYLE BLENDS** red

GEWÜRZTRAMINER white

SYRAH red

THE LAND, THE GRAPES, AND THE VINEYARDS

The factor that most influences New Zealand's grapes, and hence its wines, is the coolness of the climate. New Zealand has some of the coolest maritime wine regions in the New World. Because of the long, narrow shape of the two main islands, no vineyard is more than 80 miles (130 kilometers) from the sea. This cool, steady climate allows the grapes to ripen evenly and gently over the course of a long growing season, culminating in a harvest that can take place anytime from March to May (this is, after all, the Southern Hemisphere). In the

THE GRAPES OF NEW ZEALAND

WHITES

CHARDONNAY: The third-most widely planted grape in New Zealand, chardonnay is a source of wines of character. The wines can be found in a variety of styles, from lush to lean and Chablis-like. Also used for sparkling wine.

GEWÜRZTRAMINER: While acreage is still small, gewürztraminer shows considerable promise here.

PINOT GRIS: An important variety creating lots of excitement. Plantings have multiplied more than sixfold in the past decade.

RIESLING: An up-and-coming variety with lots of promise. It can make delicious dry wines and sensational botrytized dessert wines.

SAUVIGNON BLANC: The grape that focused world attention on New Zealand wines, sauvignon blanc makes outrageously good wines with full-throttle green and lightly tropical fruit flavors.

REDS

CABERNET SAUVIGNON: Planted in the warmest pockets around the country and often blended with merlot and other varieties to make Bordeaux-style blends. Plantings are in decline as cool-climate varieties like pinot noir move ahead.

MERLOT: Almost always blended with cabernet sauvignon.

PINOT NOIR: The most widely planted red grape in New Zealand, and the country's red specialty. Pinot noir can make delicious, earthy, still wines; it is also used for sparkling wines.

SYRAH: A minor but potentially important grape, viewed as having significant potential.

---

best of circumstances, the length of the growing season can lead to elegant wines with wonderfully pure flavors. It's often said that New Zealand vegetables and fruits, including grapes, have an intensity of flavor rarely found in produce grown elsewhere. Of course, a cool climate also means that, generally speaking, the grapes boast a good amount of natural acidity. For the best New Zealand whites, this can translate into a dazzling sense of crispness.

All of this said, New Zealand is not without viticultural hurdles. Principal among these is rain. In the past, rainy weather often led to moldy grape bunches, dense vine canopies, and wines that tasted like stewed green vegetables. In the 1980s, however, top viticulturists—including the internationally famous Australian Dr. Richard Smart—developed trellising systems and viticultural techniques that help promote ripeness and maturity. In New Zealand, such techniques led to a whole different sort of green character—a ripe, complex, fresh green flavor rather than a vegetative one. Needless to say, many of these techniques have been copied around the world and are used to grow numerous different grape varieties.

New Zealand's two main islands stretch more than 900 miles (1,400 kilometers) in length. Both islands boast extensive and beautiful mountain ranges (the glacier-laced Southern Alps, with twenty-three peaks that are more than 10,000 feet/3,000 meters in height, are located here). But the mountain slopes are so steep and erosion is such a problem that the country's vineyards are mostly planted on flat plains or gently rolling hills. Soil varies considerably, from clays interspersed with particles of volcanic rock to fertile river-basin types. Such diversity is the result of New Zealand's tumultuous geologic past. The country lies at the active juncture of two of the world's great tectonic plates, the Indo-Australian Plate and the Pacific Plate.

On New Zealand's North Island, two of the largest and most important wine districts are Gisborne and Hawke's Bay. Gisborne, near the International Date Line and the small, easternmost landmass in the country (an area known as the East Cape), is the site of the world's easternmost grapes and is known for numerous tasty chardonnays, often with light honey and tropical fruit flavors. Hawke's Bay is the second largest wine region in the country and is considered one of the best. Its complex and varied soil patterns allow for many types of vines to thrive here. Gimblett Gravels, an area within Hawke's Bay, is particularly known for producing high-quality merlot, syrah, cabernet franc, and cabernet sauvignon. (The wine known as Dada 2, which is made from these varieties, is stunning.) Gimblett Gravels soil,

called Omahu soil, was deposited in the area by the Ngaruroro River, and its layers of sand and stony gravel drain water well, creating ideal growing conditions for these red varieties. Additionally, merlot, syrah, and cabernet sauvignon thrive in warm summer weather, and by virtue of its long hours of sunshine, Hawke's Bay is one of the warmer regions in New Zealand. I'm sure that if I was poured blind the sleek Mission Estate Reserve Cabernet Sauvignon, with its fine cassis and tobacco aromas and flavors, I'd think I was drinking good Bordeaux.

The third major wine district on the North Island is often simply called Auckland, although what is really meant is the territory around Auckland, New Zealand's largest city. Far smaller than Gisborne or Hawke's Bay in terms of wine production and vineyard acreage, Auckland nonetheless boasts the greatest number of wineries. Many of New Zealand's top wine companies are headquartered here,

Cloudy Bay, one of the wineries that put New Zealand on the international map, is known for sauvignon blanc and pinot noir.

THE MAORI

New Zealand was originally inhabited by the Maori, a Polynesian people who, over centuries, migrated from subtropical Pacific islands. The Maori developed a concept called *kaitiakitanga,* which means "guardianship." When westerners arrived in large numbers at the end of the eighteenth century, they quickly adopted the Maori way of thinking. Today, one-third of the island nation's land is owned by the government and protected against development.

Although the Maori had no written language, Christian missionaries in the nineteenth century recorded the words the Maori spoke. Today, many towns, wineries, and even vineyards have Maori names. The Maori name for New Zealand, *Aotearoa,* means "land of the long white cloud."

In Central Otago, pinot noir vines are covered in nets to prevent birds from eating the grapes.

even though their vineyards are located elsewhere in the country. And there are several first-rate small family producers, such as Kumeu River. Auckland encompasses a handful of smaller, well-known wine districts, including Kumeu/Huapai, Henderson, and Waiheke Island. Because the Auckland area is somewhat warmer than other districts, the focus here is chardonnay and Bordeaux blends.

Finally, in the southeast corner of the North Island, relatively near New Zealand's capital, Wellington, is the small wine region Wairarapa/Martinborough. The two dozen or so high-quality producers here make a variety of good wines. However, their most noteworthy—and hard-won—successes have been with pinot noir. In just a few short years, Ata Rangi, Martinborough Vineyard, Dry River, Schubert Wines, Craggy Range, and others have produced remarkable pinot noirs with international reputations.

Compared to the North Island, the South Island is even cooler and was

very rural until relatively recently. There were no commercial vineyards on the South Island until 1973. In that year, the company known as Montana Wines planted vines in Marlborough, on the northeastern tip of the South Island, and pioneered what was to become the most prestigious wine district in the country (in 2005, Montana Wines was absorbed into the large French conglomerate Pernod Ricard and renamed Brancott Estate). Today, more than 60 percent of all New Zealand vineyards are in Marlborough alone, and the region produces 70 percent of all New Zealand wine and 80 percent of all New Zealand sauvignon blanc. Indeed, Marlborough is quintessential sauvignon blanc territory, as wines from wineries like Cloudy Bay, Greywacke, Wairau River, and Villa Maria demonstrate. Yet, fantastic pinot gris and riesling are also on the rise here (Forrest's botrytized riesling is a beautiful wine), and Marlborough is also one of the country's main regions for top pinot noir (more on this in a moment).

Other wine districts on the South Island include Nelson, a small but beautiful wine region about 40 miles (64 kilometers) west of Marlborough, and Canterbury, a cool region midway down the length of the island. But the most southerly and important of all is Central Otago, a small region within Otago that, in Maori, means "place of red earth," referring to the region's ocher-colored soils. It was here that New Zealand's Gold Rush occurred in the 1850s, but today Central Otago is best known as one of the hubs of great pinot noir in New Zealand, and is home to such wineries as Felton Road, Burn Cottage, and Amisfield.

SAUVIGNON BLANC

If any grape is central to New Zealand's wine identity, it's sauvignon blanc, now the leading variety in the country and the wine that dominates exports. New Zealand sauvignon blancs have no parallel anywhere in the world. Explosive yet taut, they evoke a spectrum of fresh greens: limes, wild herbs, watercress, gooseberries, green olives, green figs, green tea, green melons, plus a host of green vegetables

THE OTHER KIWI

Because of New Zealand's prolonged isolation, which lasted until the eighteenth century, it has both unusual vegetation and a high proportion of species found nowhere else. The only native mammals, for example, are two species of bats. In the absence of predatory mammals, New Zealand became home to several rare species of flightless birds. One of these, the kiwi (about the size of a large hen), is also the nickname for a New Zealander.

---

from snow peas to green beans. (So ubiquitous are these flavors that one might well wonder if some Narnia-like green netherworld exists under New Zealand.)

But, of course, greenness is a double-edged sword. Green can also be gawky, acrid, and vegetal, and come at you like an assault rifle firing asparagus. For the top estates, the key has been to harness sauvignon's freshness and zing but leave out any strident, raw, unripe flavors. And greenness isn't the whole story. New Zealand sauvignons also have an exotic tropical backdrop. They often hint at mango, papaya, or passion fruit. The combination can be dynamite, making for untamed, unleashed wines that are true to their name—sauvignon, from the French *sauvage*, means "wild."

Finally, two notes on how New Zealand sauvignon blancs are made. First, most are fermented in stainless steel so that their green/tropical flavors don't get bogged down by oak. That said, some estates now ferment a tiny portion of the wine in older oak barrels and blend that portion back in, to give the wine a subtle sense of roundness. And second, the top New Zealand sauvignon blancs are dry. It's something of a desperate move (and a cheap trick) to try to mask unripe, vegetal wine by leaving residual sugar in it.

THE GUMBOOT CLONE

The Gumboot Clone (*gumboot* is the New Zealand term for a rain boot), also known as the Abel Clone, is the Kiwis' secret weapon for rich, balanced pinot noir, but it is also a story of intrigue. As it goes, in the 1970s a New Zealand rugby player returning from France tried to sneak pinot noir cuttings into the country in his rain boot (in which case he must have had huge feet). The rumor is that they were cuttings from the Domaine de la Romanée-Conti, in Burgundy. The plants were found by a fastidious customs agent named Malcolm Abel, who also just happened to be a grape grower in Auckland. Abel suspected he might have something of real value, and after passing them through customs and quarantine, he planted the cuttings in his vineyards (we can't vouch for the legality of all this), and shared them with his friend Clive Paton, of Ata Rangi. Abel passed away shortly afterward, but Paton continued to grow the Abel Clone and began turning out stunning pinot noirs. The clone eventually spread across the country, and now accounts for some of the best pinot noirs in New Zealand.

PINOT NOIR

As mentioned, pinot noir has proven hugely successful in New Zealand, and in a very short period of time. (Plantings of pinot doubled in the decade between 2003 and 2013.) Indeed, winemakers at top estates like Cloudy Bay, Ata Rangi, and Dry River began experimenting with pinot noir clones only as of the late 1980s, and pinot noir represents such a new phenomenon

WHEN YOU VISIT . . . NEW ZEALAND

NEW ZEALAND'S WINERIES and vineyards are often surrounded by beautifully pastoral rolling hills, majestic mountains, and unspoiled coastlines. Don't miss one of the country's most breathtaking features, the Southern Alps on the South Island, with twenty-three peaks that are more than 10,000 feet (3,000 meters) in height, including Mount Cook.

MOST NEW ZEALAND WINERIES— small and large—are well set up for tours and tastings, and a number of wineries have restaurants and picnic facilities.

MUTTON NO MORE

Once known culinarily as the land of lamb and little else, New Zealand now boasts some of the most exciting food in the Pacific. Auckland alone has dozens of wildly creative restaurants where the dramatic, boldly seasoned dishes are a spin on European ideas infused with the complex flavors of Southeast Asia, Polynesia, and the South Pacific islands. And on every restaurant table, it seems, is a bottle of New Zealand wine. But then, not just any wine will work when it comes to dishes uninhibitedly laced with chiles, lime, and tropical fruits. What do work are New Zealand's burstingly fresh pinot gris and rieslings, and the country's racy, herbal, tropical sauvignon blancs.

in New Zealand that growers and winemakers are still discovering the best sites to plant vineyards and the best methods for winemaking.

New Zealand pinot noir is planted throughout the entire country, but the lion's share is grown on the South Island. Almost half of this is grown in Marlborough alone, and a significant amount of the rest comes from Central Otago, in the far southern part of the South Island. In general, Marlborough pinot noirs appear to be the fruitier of the two, with nuanced red fruit flavors. They are often used to make sparkling wines, which are very popular in New Zealand, although not often exported. Central Otago pinot noirs, on the other hand, often display an earthiness and wild herb character, which places them stylistically between Old World and New World pinot noirs.

On the North Island (at the southern tip), the small region of Martinborough also produces stellar pinot noirs whose concentration and depth can be spellbinding. After a 1978 New Zealand government report found the soils of Martinborough to be very similar to the soils of Burgundy, a rush to plant pinot noir vines swept the region, and it now produces some of the best pinot noirs in New Zealand.

SOME OF THE BEST PRODUCERS OF NEW ZEALAND SAUVIGNON BLANC

Astrolabe • Ata Rangi • Auntsfield • Brancott • Clos Henri • Cloudy Bay • Craggy Range • Dada • Dog Point • Giesen • Greywacke • Mahi • Man O' War • Martinborough Vineyard • Misha's Vineyard • Mud House Wines • Neudorf • Palliser Estate • Pegasus Bay • Saint Clair • Seresin Marama • Spy Valley • Te Mata • Villa Maria • Wairau River • Wither Hills

The New Zealand Wines to Know

WHITES

GREYWACKE

SAUVIGNON BLANC | MARLBOROUGH

100% sauvignon blanc

New Zealand sauvignon blanc is never about delayed gratification. It generally comes hurtling at you, arms wide open. But Kevin Judd's Greywacke sauvignon blanc is, like his pinot noir, a very sophisticated wine. It starts out with intriguing, spicy green notes reminiscent of baby arugula, then moves to mango, then to something deep and foresty. The texture, meanwhile, is alive, bouncy and brisk, and the finish lingers for a long while (a rarity with sauvignon blanc). In summer especially, I could drink this all day long.

CLOUDY BAY

SAUVIGNON BLANC | MARLBOROUGH

100% sauvignon blanc

When Cloudy Bay Sauvignon Blanc was first released in 1985, it became an overnight sensation and, for the first time, focused world attention on the wines of New Zealand. The wine is a torpedo of intensity. Lime zest, newly mown grass, green tea, grapefruit, mint, wheatgrass, seawater, green peppercorns, caraway, and a flurry of exotic green flavors go off like grenades in your mouth. But it is not the green explosion that makes Cloudy Bay so compelling. It's the way all of these flavors are intricately woven together to create a complex, round, mouthfilling wine with a sophisticated, long finish. Cloudy Bay was founded in 1985 by David Hohnen (who, earlier, had founded Western Australia's Cape Mentelle winery), and today it is owned by Moët Hennessy-Louis Vuitton.

WAIRAU RIVER

SAUVIGNON BLANC | MARLBOROUGH

100% sauvignon blanc

The Wairau River sauvignons are often seized tight when you first open them, but then their spring-loaded acidity and wild flavors burst on the scene and everything gets fascinating. I love this wine's ocean-fresh saline/briny aromas, and the pithy, spicy "bite" of peppery greens like arugula, dandelion leaf, and tomato leaf. Lest the sophisticated, salty/bitter flavors get too much, there's also a beautiful richness here, as if someone drizzled lemon crème anglaise over everything. Wairau River was founded in 1978 by Phil and Chris Rose, who run the estate with their children today.

MUD HOUSE

SAUVIGNON BLANC | THE WOOLSHED VINEYARD | MARLBOROUGH

100% sauvignon blanc

Named after the shed where wool was stored on the sheep farm that occupied the land before Mud House purchased it in 2002, the Woolshed Vineyard sauvignon blanc is saturated with tropical fruit flavors—pear, passion fruit, melon, and lime—and a luscious texture. A clean, linear thread of acidity keeps the wine fresh and lively, and a hint of herbaceousness arrives at the last minute, delivering that classic Marlborough greenness in the form of thyme and green tea. Founded in 1996, Mud House is owned by the Australian-based wine group Accolade.

VILLA MARIA

DRY RIESLING | ESTATE CELLAR SELECT | MARLBOROUGH

100% riesling

Villa Maria, founded in 1961 by Sir George Fistonich, was one of the early, pioneering wineries in New Zealand and, for many wine drinkers, their well-known and widely praised sauvignon blanc has been an initiation into "New Zealand flavor." But I have decided to write about their cutting-edge dry riesling, for it demonstrates the beauty this variety can achieve in New Zealand. Flashy and vibrant, the wine has lovely notes of apricots, peaches, yellow fruits, and citrus. It's cleansing and brisk, with a cool mineral finish that makes it a perfect counterpoint to many foods, but bold-flavored dishes like spicy Southeast Asian crab or pad thai with lots of mint are especially terrific matches.

KUMEU RIVER

CHARDONNAY | KUMEU

100% chardonnay

Year in and year out, Kumeu River makes two of the most impressive chardonnays in New Zealand—the "regular" Kumeu River and the vineyard-designated Maté's Vineyard. Both are fascinatingly distinctive and artisanal, and seem to have more in common with white Burgundies than with other New World chardonnays. The regular Kumeu is rich, leesy, and nutty, and has an earthy/salty character. A vibrant line of acidity holds it all together so that the wine tastes both rich and elegant. The Maté's Vineyard is the more powerful and the more expensive. Kumeu River is owned by the Brajkovich family, who came to New Zealand from Croatia in 1937. Winemaker Michael Brajkovich was also New Zealand's first Master of Wine.

REDS

ATA RANGI

PINOT NOIR | MARTINBOROUGH

100% pinot noir

My tasting notes on Ata Rangi's pinot noirs always include the word *beautiful*. "Beautiful harmony." "Beautiful spiced tea flavors." "Beautiful silky texture." Beauty is indeed a concept that reverberates through these lovely pinots, which draw you in with their pure cranberry/raspberry flavors and the soft echo of something earthy. Ata Rangi (the name in the Maori language means "dawn sky" or "new beginning") was founded in 1980 by Clive Paton, a former cattle farmer. To make ends meet when the vines were young (and not yet producing grapes), Paton sold pumpkins and garlic, which he grew between the rows until the new vines began producing the quality fruit that has made Ata Rangi one of the best pinot producers in New Zealand.

GREYWACKE

PINOT NOIR | MARLBOROUGH

100% pinot noir

In 2009, Kevin Judd, the super-talented original winemaker for Cloudy Bay, started his own brand, Greywacke (named for the round greywacke river stones found in the soil). The man has a golden touch. It takes years of experience to get pinot noir right, but Judd's Greywacke is dead-on—a complex, spicy, earthy, cranberry-scented pinot noir with an underlying quiet freshness that pinot noir holds onto in cool climates. The wine's delicacy and arc of flavor are simply beautiful.

CRAGGY RANGE

PINOT NOIR | TE MUNA ROAD VINEYARD | MARTINBOROUGH

100% pinot noir

Ripe cherry and spiced cranberry aromas pull you in, but it's the delicious wave of black cherry, raspberry, bitter earth, and white pepper flavors in Craggy Range's Te Muna pinot noir that take over your senses (*te muna*, in Maori, means "the secret"). The wine's telltale earthiness and enticing spiciness are hallmarks of Martinborough, but the richness of this wine is probably the result of the elevated terraces in the vineyard, which cause the vines to struggle. Craggy Range was founded in 1997 by Terry Peabody, an American businessman, and Steve Smith, a leading viticulturalist in New Zealand. In 1999, when the pair planted a vineyard off Te Muna Road, a local Aboriginal woman named Aunt Sally buried a piece of the Peabody family's silver in the vineyard as a good luck omen. Nice move, Aunt Sally. Craggy Range also makes a stellar syrah called Le Sol from Gimblett Gravels, in Hawke's Bay.

DRY RIVER

PINOT NOIR | MARTINBOROUGH

100% pinot noir

Quiet beauty can be *very* delicious. In top vintages, Dry River's pinot noir opens with a gentle spicy aroma and a fine spicy "frame" within which all sorts of delicious fruit flavors congregate—pomegranate, cranberry, vanilla. These are the elegant clouds of flavor that form the core of Dry River's exquisite, distinct pinot noir. Then there's that silken softness—a texture that pinot noir lovers around the world crave. Neil and Dawn McCallum planted their first vineyard in 1979, and Dry Creek became one of the first wineries in Martinborough. It was also one of the five pioneering wineries that defined and created the Martinborough Terrace appellation, based on the area's low rainfall and free-draining soils. This wine's oxymoronic name comes from one of the first sheep stations in the area, which was called Dry River and was later renamed Dyerville.

WILD EARTH

PINOT NOIR | CENTRAL OTAGO

100% pinot noir

This is certainly a well-named wine, for Wild Earth's pinot is full of delicious, wild, earthy aromas and flavors—peat, bark, damp earth, and wild herbs. But against that background come other flavors . . . currants, cranberries, raspberries, and spices (like an exotic Christmas cranberry sauce). And then, something leathery or gamy, almost Rhône-like. When pinot noir takes you on a journey through different worlds of flavor, you know you are in the midst of something complex, artisanal, and very captivating.

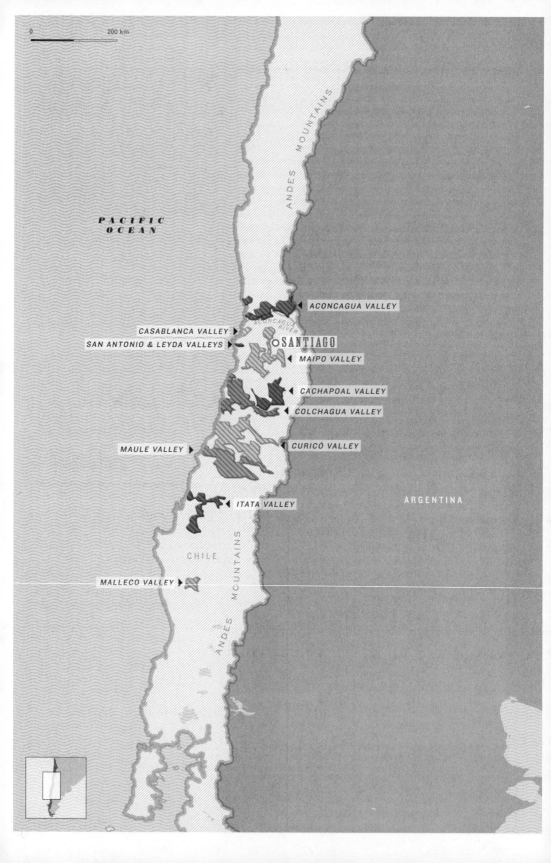

CHILE

hile exists in near perfect seclusion. On the west is the Pacific Ocean; on the east, the massive Andes Mountains; to the north, the Atacama Desert; and to the south, about 400 miles (640 kilometers) across the water, frozen masses of Antarctic ice. The country, squeezed in between these barriers, is roughly 2,700 miles (4,300 kilometers) long, but at its narrowest point, only 96 miles (155 kilometers) wide. Within these formidable natural boundaries exists an almost Eden-like environment for grapes and other crops. The warm, dry, brightly sunny days recall the Mediterranean. Irrigation is easy thanks to snow melting on the Andes, which feeds roaring rivers, themselves the products of melting ancient glaciers. And thanks to the country's physical isolation, there are very few vine diseases and pests, obviating the need for almost all sprays and chemical treatments. In short, grape-growing conditions are so ideal, the cost of vineyard land and labor is so reasonable, and serviceable wines are so easy to make that Chile has become one of the world's leading producers of value wines.

Those bargains have built an enviable export empire. From a negligible monetary value in 1980 (when less than 2 percent of Chile's wine production was exported), the value of Chilean wine exports rose to $50 million in 1990, then a staggering $1.5 billion in 2010. Indeed, today, 70 percent of Chilean wine is exported. But there's a dark side, too. Chile's early reputation for the $6.99 steal has inhibited the development of a vibrant upscale wine industry founded on more complex, higher-quality wines. Even now, few wine lovers with $50 to spend on a bottle of wine head straight for the Chile aisle in the wine shop. Or at least, until recently they

> "The beauty of great wine is revealed not by adding adornment, but by removing it."
> —ALEXANDRA MARNIER LAPOSTOLLE,
> Lapostolle

In winter, Chile's vineyards look stark and somber against the backdrop of the magnificent Andes Mountains.

THE QUICK SIP ON CHILE

CHILE'S MODERN WINE industry achieved international recognition in the early 1980s for bargain-priced wines (especially chardonnay and cabernet sauvignon) intended for export. Today, many top Chilean winemakers are focused on producing higher-quality, more expensive wines while continuing to maintain a reputation for value quaffs.

WHILE THERE IS VASTLY more cabernet sauvignon planted in Chile than any other grape variety, the country's signature grape is carmenère, a red grape variety indigenous to Bordeaux but now virtually extinct there.

CHILE'S MOST NOTABLE wine area is the vast Valle Central ("Central Valley"), where a majority of the most important appellations are to be found, including the two most renowned: Maipo Valley and Colchagua Valley.

haven't. But Chile is changing, and fine wine is becoming a part of its future.

The first European vines (*Vitis vinifera*) in Chile were Spanish varieties planted in the mid-sixteenth century by Spanish missionaries and conquistadores, who carried them directly to Chile (and later, overland to Chile from Peru and Mexico). The important first of these varieties was listán prieto, which went on to form the foundation for the entire wine industry in the Americas. Listán prieto was originally known in Chile as criolla chica ("creole girl"), but by the nineteenth century, the variety was so common it was rechristened simply as país ("country"). It was the same variety as the grape known as misión in Mexico, and eventually, as it was brought north, known as mission in California, New Mexico, and Texas.

Despite Spain's historic and political hegemony in Chile, France, not Spain, has had the greatest influence on the country's wines. In the mid-nineteenth century, rich Chilean landowners and mining barons showcased their wealth by building wine estates modeled after Bordeaux châteaux. Bordeaux, after all, was the wine superpower of the era, and after the 1855 Classification, grapes from Bordeaux's top communes were held in almost religious esteem. The Chileans planted vineyards with

THE CURIOUS ABSENCE OF PHYLLOXERA

As of this book's writing, Chilean vineyards have never been victims of the lethal insect phylloxera, which devastated most of the world's vineyards in the mid- and late-nineteenth century. Chile, in fact, is the only major wine country in the world where no phylloxera exists. Although Chile's physical isolation, dry soil, and use of flood irrigation may all have helped to protect the country, phylloxera's absence is not fully understood—especially given the fact that phylloxera is present right next door, in Argentina. Some scientists speculate that it's only a matter of time before the pest finds a route in, despite the Chilean government's strict quarantine requirements for plant materials. As a result of that fear, some of Chile's modern vineyards are based on vines grafted onto phylloxera-resistant rootstock—but not all of them. Chauvinistic Chileans argue that the flavor of wine from vines planted on the vine's own (*vinifera*) roots is better, somehow more authentic. This has never been demonstrated, nor have blind tastings revealed ungrafted vines to produce superior wine. What is known comes down to cold hard cash. Between the cost of the rootstock itself and the labor cost of grafting, a vineyard on rootstock costs four times more to plant than a vineyard where the vine is planted with its own roots.

imported French grapes, most notably cabernet sauvignon, merlot, and (although they probably didn't know it at the time) carmenère. And whenever possible, they hired French winemakers, who, by the latter part of the century, were easy to lure from their homeland thanks to a twist of fate. The deadly insect phylloxera had just begun its sweep through France. As vineyard after vineyard was destroyed, unemployed winemakers looked to other wine regions, including the wine frontiers of the New World. (Although phylloxera ultimately ravaged vineyards in virtually every wine-producing country, Chile has never been affected.)

For much of the twentieth century, Chilean wine was unexceptional and serviceable, rarely more. The combined impact of political instability, bureaucratic red tape, high taxes, low wages, and a local market that seemed perfectly satisfied with (if not thankful for) inexpensive quaffing wine effectively handcuffed Chilean winemakers and limited the scope of their ambitions.

Alexandra Marnier Lapostolle, owner of Lapostolle, and the woman who, more than any other, ushered into Chile a fine-wine revolution.

Then, in the late 1980s, vast changes in the country's political, economic, and social climate led to considerable domestic and foreign investment in the wine industry. In less than two decades, Chile went from being a Third World wine producer to being dubbed the

THE GRAPES OF CHILE

WHITES

CHARDONNAY: Along with sauvignon blanc, chardonnay is one of the two most important white grapes. It makes good, drinkable wines that rarely achieve complexity or sophistication.

SAUVIGNON BLANC: Many Chilean winemakers consider this grape better suited to Chile than chardonnay. It makes sassy, fresh wines with an unmistakable bolt of greenness.

SAUVIGNON GRIS: A gray-colored mutation of sauvignon blanc that tastes less herbal. Small amounts are grown in Chile.

SAUVIGNON VERT: Not related to sauvignon blanc, despite its name; rather, the grape is the same as sauvignonasse and northern Italy's friulano. In Chile, it makes a wine with light herbal and almond flavors.

REDS

CABERNET SAUVIGNON: Chile's major grape; it makes a full range of styles, from quaffing wines to quite extraordinary wines. It is often blended with carmenère and merlot to make Chile's greatest wines.

CARMENÈRE: A variety brought to Chile in the late-nineteenth century from Bordeaux, where, for all practical purposes, it no longer exists. Originally misidentified as merlot, it is today considered Chile's signature grape, and plantings are on a dramatic rise. The highest-quality examples are fascinating, soft, plush wines redolent of green tobacco, coffee, and leather.

MERLOT: Chile's second-most-planted fine-wine grape after cabernet sauvignon, merlot makes good to very good wines.

PAÍS: A major grape, país is Chile's historic mass-production grape, brought in the sixteenth century from Spain, where it is known as listán prieto. It is still widely planted for use in jug wines.

PINOT NOIR: A minor grape, but plantings are on the rise thanks to export demand for inexpensive pinot noir. So far, it makes mostly undistinguished wine, except in the hands of a very few producers.

SYRAH: An up-and-coming Chilean grape, syrah makes surprisingly good wines, with classic gamy/spicy aromas and flavors. It is sometimes blended with carmenère to very good result.

Bordeaux of South America. Among the first leading European wine families to invest were the Torres family from Spain and the Rothschilds from Château Lafite-Rothschild, in Bordeaux, who bought land in Curicó and Colchagua (Kohl-CHA-gwa), respectively. Within a few years, Paul Pontallier, director of Bordeaux's Château Margaux, and Bruno Prats, the former owner of Château Cos d'Estournel, founded a Chilean winery called Domaine Paul Bruno (and later renamed Viña Aquitania). From the United States, Chilean-born vintner Agustin Huneeus, owner of the prestigious Napa Valley winery Quintessa, jumped into the game, buying land in the cool, coastal valley of Casablanca and founding Veramonte winery in 1990. But perhaps no outsider has accelerated the reputation of Chilean wine more than

The largest winery in South America and one of the Chilean "old guard," Concha y Toro was founded in 1883 by Don Melchor de Santiago Concha y Toro, who brought vines to Santiago from Bordeaux.

THE ANDES

Rising up behind many of Chile's vineyards are the majestic Andes, the longest mountain chain in the world. The Andean peaks reach 22,000 feet (6,700 meters) and are exceeded in elevation only by the Himalayas. When the mountain chain was formed, sedimentary rocks were folded and bent into ridges, creating many of the sheltered valleys in which Chile's vineyards lie. Today, no visitor to Chile's wine country (or to the wine country of Argentina, just on the other side of the Andes) can help but be awed by the sheer beauty of vineyards framed by these magnificent, snow-laden peaks.

Frenchwoman Alexandra Marnier Lapostolle (owner, with her family, of the famous French liqueur firm Grand Marnier). In 1994, Marnier Lapostolle bought property in the Colchagua Valley and immediately hired French enologist Michel Rolland (the world's most famous consulting winemaker) to help make world-class wine at the Lapostolle winery.

Simultaneously, Chile's historic, grand wine firms, such as Cousiño-Macul, Concha y Toro, Canepa, Errázuriz, Santa Rita, Undurraga, and Santa Carolina, spent millions modernizing their wineries and buying both new equipment and new French and American oak barrels. Moreover, for many of these firms, a whole new avenue of business sprang to life: the international joint venture.

In the early 1990s, Errázuriz partnered with California's Robert Mondavi Winery to create Seña, a Bordeaux blend that cost a startlingly high $55 in 1998, when it was first released. A year later, the joint-venture team of Château Mouton-Rothschild and Concha y Toro debuted their Bordeaux-style blend, Almaviva, at $70 a bottle.

THE SPIRIT OF THE DESERT

On several trips to Chile, I've felt it culturally imperative to start the evening with a pisco sour (strictly for research purposes, of course). Chile's famous and traditional distilled spirit, pisco, was first developed in Peru by Spanish settlers in the sixteenth century. By the mid-eighteenth century, however, northern Chile had become an important center of pisco production, and today, Chile ranks as the leading producer of the yellowish-colored brandy. Chilean pisco is made from grapes that, by law, can be grown only in the desertlike, high-altitude regions of Atacama and Coquimbo, in the northern part of the country. (In some parts of the Atacama Desert, no measurable rainfall has ever been recorded.)

Pisco can be made from any one or a combination of muscat of Alexandria, torontel, and Pedro Ximénez grapes, which can grow only because snowmelt from the Andes creates small rivers that can be tapped for irrigation. The wine is aged for a few months in oak barrels and then distilled with mountain water.

Momentum had begun to build. And at the same time, as all of the above was happening, a new type of winery was also quietly emerging in Chile—the small wine estate owned by a grower who, instead of selling his grapes, decided to market his own brand.

Remarkably, the success of Chile's wine revolution hinged on a bet that the United States and Great Britain would become the major markets for all of these new wines—from the better-quality bargain wines to the new class of what the Chileans call "icon" wines. To help ensure this would be the case, Chilean producers initially focused their exports on wines that were already extremely popular, especially chardonnay, sauvignon blanc, merlot, and cabernet sauvignon. By the early 2000s, the red Bordeaux variety carmenère was also part of that list.

As it turned out, the United States and Great Britain have not only become the leading export markets for Chilean wine, but many of the more expensive wines are sold almost exclusively in the two markets. During the fiscal year 2010 to 2011, for example, more than eight million cases of Chilean wine were exported to the U.S., and more than ten million to Great Britain.

For an explanation of Chilean wine laws, see the Appendix on Wine Laws, page 929.

HUMPHREY BOGART DID NOT SLEEP HERE

Casablanca . . . ah, yes. Humphrey Bogart steamily kissing Ingrid Bergman. Morocco in the 1940s. WAIT—wrong Casablanca. The pastoral, vineyard-filled valley of Casablanca in Chile is not related to the iconic World War II movie of the same name. Chile's Casablanca Valley is named after the Chilean town of Casablanca (the word means "white house"), founded in 1753 under the original name Santa Barbara Queen of Casablanca (that's the English version) in honor of Doña Barbara de Braganza, wife of Fernando VI, King of Spain. Understandably, with the passage of time, the town's name was shortened simply to Casablanca.

Some Chilean vineyards are harvested by machine, but the top grapes are still picked by hand.

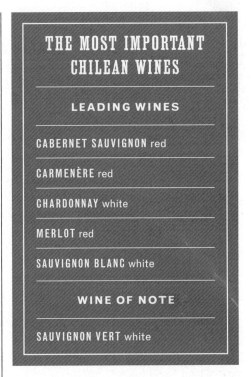

THE MOST IMPORTANT CHILEAN WINES

LEADING WINES

CABERNET SAUVIGNON red

CARMENÈRE red

CHARDONNAY white

MERLOT red

SAUVIGNON BLANC white

WINE OF NOTE

SAUVIGNON VERT white

THE LAND, THE GRAPES, AND THE VINEYARDS

Unlike the arid, extremely high-altitude vineyards in Argentina, on the other side of the Andes, Chile's main wine regions are low in altitude and relatively close to the sea. But while they are cooled by the Pacific, Chilean vineyards are largely protected from extreme maritime weather by a low-lying range of mountains, called the Coastal Range, just inland from the coast.

If you flipped Chile over into the northern hemisphere, the best vineyards would fall roughly at the latitude of North Africa or southern Spain. But this image skews the reality of Chilean climate and viticulture. Thanks to the Pacific Ocean's Humboldt Current, which brings ice-cold water and air up the coast from Antarctic waters, temperatures in Chile's wine country rarely rise above 90°F (32°C) and summertime nights are cool. Indeed, in very cool regions like Casablanca Valley, harvest (theoretically the warmest time of the year) can be so nippy that everyone is wearing fleece vests.

Chile's 506,000 acres (204,800 hectares) of vineyards and two hundred plus wineries are located in five major *Denominacions de Origen* (DOs). From north to south, they are: Atacama, Coquimbo, Aconcagua, the Valle Central, and the Southern Regions. The northernmost DOs of Atacama and Coquimbo are desert-like; the DO Southern Regions is the coldest. But the DOs to know are the ones in the middle—Aconcagua (ah-kon-KAH-gwa) and the Valle Central ("Central Valley"). These make up Chile's historic wine center, and they are still today the areas where most of Chile's best wine districts are to be found. Indeed, a lion's share of all of the wine exported from Chile comes from these two areas.

Aconcagua, which takes its name from the nearby Aconcagua River, includes the warm-ish Aconcagua Valley (home to Errázuriz, one of Chile's prominent wine producers) and the more coastal, cool, avant-garde districts

BRAZIL AND PERU

If you've been sidetracked by caipirinhas and pisco sours over the last few years, you're forgiven. But while you were "spiritually" preoccupied, the wine industries of both Brazil and Peru have been working hard to become players on the South American wine scene.

Brazil now boasts 213,000 acres (86,200 hectares) of vines, and Peru has 43,000 acres (17,400 hectares), although in both countries, per capita wine consumption is low and a modern wine-drinking culture is in its infancy. Indeed, for both Brazil and Peru, a good share of their future success may hinge on their ability to develop international export markets for their wines.

The largest country in South America, Brazil has a long, though difficult, history of grape growing. The first vines were brought here in 1532 by the Portuguese explorer Martim Afonso de Souza, who planted them in the southeastern state of São Paulo. But even far away from the tropical jungles of the north, the vines perished from disease in the hot, humid climate. Over the next century, many more attempts at grape growing were made, with patchy success, by Jesuit priests hoping to make wine for Mass. A solid wine industry finally took form in the late-nineteenth century, when Italian immigrants began planting American hybrid grapes such as Isabella, as well as Italian *Vitis vinifera* varieties and tannat in the drier mountainous region of the Serra Gaúcha near the border with Uruguay and Argentina, still the key region for fine wines.

Brazil's most important wines include the reds syrah, tannat, malbec, cabernet sauvignon, and tempranillo, but the category that's been hot for decades is sparkling wine. Every type of sparkler is made in Brazil—from traditional-method (Champagne) sparkling wines based on chardonnay and pinot noir to Brazil's version of simple prosecco to tank-fermented fizzy moscato.

Thanks to its high altitude and dry, desertlike climate, Peru has many of the viticultural assets of Argentina and northern Chile. Indeed, this may be the most exciting undiscovered wine country in South America, not to mention the most dynamic culinarily.

In 1528, the Spanish explorer Francisco Pizarro and his troops arrived at the northern border of the vast Inca empire, which then included not only Peru but parts of Equador, Chile, and the Amazon basin. By 1572, the henceforth named Viceroyalty of Peru belonged to the Spanish crown, and in the years in between, grapevines were introduced both by explorers and priests. Over the next century, as the city of Lima grew and as a mining industry took hold, the production of Peruvian wine increased substantially.

But an enormous earthquake in the late 1600s, religious suppression in the mid-1700s, the rise in popularity of the spirit pisco, and the demand for cotton, all contributed to the ripping out of vineyards and wine's general decline.

In the 2000s, the Peruvian wine industry initiated a comeback. The industry is centered around the towns of Pisco and Ica on the Central Coast. Numerous types of red and white wine are made primarily from cabernet sauvignon, malbec, grenache, and barbera, as well as sauvignon blanc and torontel, which, like Argentine torrontés, is a cross of mission and muscat of Alexandria.

Chile's dry climate and geographic isolation have meant that many wineries farm organically using an integrated, sustainable approach. Here, friends of Cono Sur winery check out the vines.

of Casablanca Valley and San Antonio Valley (and within San Antonio Valley, the very upcoming zone of Leyda Valley). In the 1990s, these regions experienced the wine equivalent of a mini gold rush, as investors swooped in, bought land, and began planting sauvignon blanc and chardonnay.

Southwest of Chile's capital, Santiago, lies the large Valle Central, an expanse of fertile and fairly flat land lying between the Andes and the Coastal Range, low-lying mountains just inland from the Pacific. The most fertile part of the Valle Central (the center of the valley, where the soils are deepest) is indeed fertile. There, an abundance of crops, from wheat, corn, and beans to nuts, fruits, and sugar beets, are grown. By contrast, it's in the less fertile, granitic soils that wine grapes are grown. These soils often hug the hillsides, and span five distinct sub-valleys

within the Valle Central: Maipo, Cachapoal, Colchagua, Curicó, and Maule. (Wine label readers note: Sometimes the Cachapoal and Colchagua valleys are referred to together as the Rapel Valley.) Many of these sub-valleys are separated by rivers that begin high in the Andes and flow to the Pacific Ocean.

Of all of the important central valleys, perhaps the two most renowned are Maipo Valley and Colchagua Valley. It's from these two

Dancing the cueca, *a family of traditional dances from Chile, Argentina, and Bolivia.*

WHEN YOU VISIT . . . CHILE

A NUMBER OF CHILE'S top wineries are in the Maipo Valley, just minutes from the capital, Santiago, or a few hours' drive south in the Colchagua and Cachapoal regions, or north of the city, in Casablanca. Do not miss, for example, Lapostolle's stunning estate in the Colchagua Valley or the palatial Cousiño-Macul just minutes from the heart of Santiago. For all wineries, it is best to make an appointment in advance.

districts that most of Chile's so-called icon wines are sourced.

Edged up against the city limits of Santiago, the Maipo Valley is one of Chile's oldest wine regions and, because of its proximity to the capital, many wineries are headquartered there. This is where the huge wineries Concha y Toro and Cousiño-Macul are located, the latter with its massive, cavernous cellars and stately 125-acre (50-hectare) park, a dreamlike expanse of private gardens tended by fifteen full-time gardeners.

Colchagua is fast becoming the Napa of Chile, especially the tiny district of Apalta, a small, moon-shaped internal valley hard up against the Coastal Range. This is where Neyen, Viña Montes's Alpha M, and Lapostolle's Clos Apalta wines are sourced, and all three are among the most iconic of the icon wines of Chile, each with dozens of international awards and high scores from critics.

Soils in Chile's top vineyards within the major valleys are often a type of well-drained, friable granite. As one moves closer to the deepest center parts of the valleys, the soils get more fertile and granitic stone is interspersed with loam, sand, and clay. In addition, on the eastern side of these valleys, below the Andes, many vineyards have alluvial fans, essentially rocky streams that have washed down mountainsides through the force of water.

Speaking of which, the easy availability of water is one of Chile's leading viticultural assets. But it can also be a downfall as far as the quality of the wine is concerned. Snow melting on the Andes provides a steady supply of water that is channeled to the vineyards through a system of dikes and canals. Growers who want huge crops to make bland wine that can be sold for peanuts have no problem achieving such wines by literally flooding the vineyards. The top wine producers eschew such practice, using controlled drip irrigation—or even watering by hand—instead.

Approximately fifteen varieties of wine grapes are grown in Chile—everything from riesling and sémillon to pinot noir and malbec. But most wines are based on just five major grapes: cabernet sauvignon, chardonnay, merlot, sauvignon blanc, and carmenère.

Of all the grapes grown in Chile, cabernet sauvignon is by every account the star. Moderately priced Chilean cabernets are usually very easy to drink,

Chilean empanadas are a traditional dish. Usually made from chopped beef or pork plus black olives, hard-cooked eggs, and raisins, they are especially delicious hot, when right out of a brick oven.

with soft, minty, black currant, and olive flavors. The newer, high-priced icon cabernets and cabernet blends are polished wines, with much more concentrated and complex flavors and firmer structure.

In the 1990s, chardonnay was extensively planted in response to the seemingly bottomless demand for inexpensive chardonnay in the United States and Great Britain. Today, most Chilean chardonnay is exactly that—bargain-priced, uncomplicated, and with a few exceptions (such as Lapostolle and Montes), unremarkable. Chilean sauvignon blanc is definitely the more exciting white grape. Zesty and bold, the best Chilean sauvignons have surprisingly vivid flavors. Chile is also known for the milder-tasting sauvignon vert, which is not related to sauvignon blanc at all, but rather is a grape called sauvignonasse (or, in Italy, friulano).

But by all accounts the grape to watch is carmenère, which holds a signature position in Chile, similar to that of malbec in Argentina. Carmenère (which the Chileans pronounce car-men-AIR) has a fascinating story.

The grape is indigenous to the Bordeaux area of France, but it ripens so late in the year that, in Bordeaux, it barely ever achieved ripeness, producing wines that tasted more like rhubarb juice than a *grand vin*. After the nineteenth-century phylloxera epidemic in France, it was almost never replanted.

In Chile, however, carmenère found a hospitable home. Chile's warm, long growing season was perfect for the grape, and thus, after being brought to Chile, probably in the 1850s with the great influx of "noble" grapes from Bordeaux, carmenère thrived. Not that anyone

Chilean huasos ("cowboys") are skilled horsemen. Here, they rope a bull during a rodeo competition. Rodeo was declared Chile's national sport in 1962.

knew it was carmenère, exactly. Grapevine importation was at an all-time high—and at a time before any reliable method of grapevine identification existed in Chile. Over the next 145 years, carmenère was generally misidentified as a late-ripening type of merlot. Indeed, it wasn't until the mid-1990s that many producers discovered that the "merlots" they were exporting were, in fact, something else.

The word *carmenère* comes from the Latin *carmin* ("crimson") and is a reference to the bright reddish color of the variety's leaves come harvest time. In a stroke of perfect coincidence, carmenère was "rediscovered" at Viña Carmen, a winery in the Maipo Valley in the mid-1990s. Álvaro Espinoza, Viña Carmen's winemaker at the time, had brought in Jean-Michel Boursiquot, a famous French ampelographer (grapevine identification specialist) to determine why some merlots ripened so much later and tasted so different from others. Boursiquot hypothesized that what Chile had in at least some of its "merlots" was an entirely different grape called carmenère. DNA typing later confirmed that Boursiquot was right.

Subsequently (and sadly), some producers tore out their old carmenère vineyards and replanted with true merlot. Others saw an opportunity—a chance to carve out a unique position for Chile in the world of wine.

Very low in acid, and lower in tannin than cabernet sauvignon, carmenère grapes—when grown in great sites at low yields—make wines with a naturally plush texture (in this they are like the top malbecs) that boast a mocha, coffee, green tobacco, and spice character. But quality is the key. For as fascinating as top Chilean carmenères are, the basic ones are definitely a yawn.

Similarly, with top wines, when carmenère is blended with cabernet, it provides a nice "fatness" to the final wine. Carmenère/cabernet blends like Neyen's Espiritu de Apalta can be stupendous wines—fleshy and spicy thanks to the carmenère, structured and majestic thanks to the cabernet.

Genetically, carmenère is a natural cross of cabernet franc and gros cabernet—the latter an old Bordeaux variety, not the same as cabernet sauvignon, that is no longer cultivated.

The Chilean Wines to Know

WHITES

LAPOSTOLLE

CHARDONNAY | CUVÉE ALEXANDRE | CASABLANCA VALLEY

100% chardonnay

Lapostolle makes one of the great chardonnays of the New World. The wine is extraordinarily fresh and lively as well as rich and opulent—loaded, in fact, with beautifully precise tropical fruit flavors. Unlike virtually all New World wineries making chardonnay, Lapostolle goes through the vineyards multiple times at harvest. The early pickings give bright, snappy fruit flavors, and the later pickings give deeper, more opulent, riper fruit flavors. The process is expensive, to be sure, but the effort shows in the beauty and complexity of this wine.

COUSIÑO-MACUL

SAUVIGNON GRIS | MAIPO VALLEY

100% sauvignon gris

This is a simple white, but it's so delicious I wanted you to know about it. The historic, family-owned producer Cousiño-Macul (founded in 1856) is one of the few producers in the world to make a 100 percent sauvignon gris (an entirely different variety from sauvignon blanc). With its gorgeous tangerine aromas and lovely, minerally, spicy flavors, this is the kind of fresh, pure wine you just can't stop drinking on a summer night. Sauvignon gris is more mouthfilling and fruity than sauvignon blanc, and has less of sauvignon blanc's "greenness."

REDS

NEYEN

ESPIRITU DE APALTA | COLCHAGUA VALLEY

Approximately 80% carmenère, 20% cabernet sauvignon

In the indigenous language of central Chile, *neyen* (which, curiously, can be read forward or backward) means "spirit." And the wine is certainly soulful. Dense and concentrated on the palate, Neyen has a texture that's almost furry. In great years, it has majestic power and a thundering, immediate impact of flavor. Spicy and minerally, it's evocative of espresso and bitter chocolate, with notes of violets and kirsch. The hand-watered Neyen vineyard (which includes 120-year-old cabernet vines) is tucked into a serene cul-de-sac in Apalta—a tiny, prestigious area within the very important region of Colchagua.

LAPOSTOLLE

CLOS APALTA | COLCHAGUA VALLEY

Percentages vary, but typically 40% to 80% merlot, with carmenère, cabernet sauvignon, and petit verdot

Lapostolle's greatest wine is one of the icon wines of Chile, and it is stunning. Owner Alexandra Marnier Lapostolle (of the Grand Marnier family) likes elegance in wine; her consultant, the famous French enologist Michel Rolland, likes power. Together they've created a wine that bridges both worlds. No expense is spared in making the wine: Among other nuances, the grapes are even de-stemmed by hand, by women. Clos Apalta's flavors are unique—a fascinating swirl of cocoa beans, vanilla, woodsmoke, and chaparral, along with something almost piquant, like cayenne pepper. The texture is soft, almost syrupy. But what really gets to you is the finish . . . the long, slow waves that don't stop.

TERRANOBLE

CARMENÈRE | COSTA | CA2 | COLCHAGUA VALLEY

100% carmenère

From vineyards near the Coastal Range comes this fantastic carmenère that won't require anyone to hock the family jewels. Highly structured and sleek, in great vintages it's got amazingly vivid violet and white pepper flavors offset by whooshes of mocha and minerality. Terranoble winery, which specializes in carmenère, believes that two different expressions of the grape exist in Colchagua. Their wine designated CA1 is from carmenère vineyards on the eastern side of the valley, near the Andes. CA2 is the name of their wine from carmenère vineyards on the western side of the valley, near the Coastal Range.

VERTICE

APALTA VINEYARD | COLCHAGUA VALLEY

Approximately 51% carmenère, 49% syrah

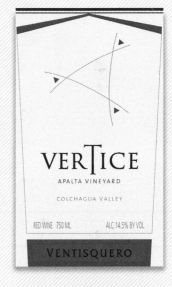

The Vertice (VER-tea-say) wines are a partnership between the large Chilean wine company Viña Ventisquero and renowned Australian winemaker John Duval (formerly the winemaker of Penfolds Grange). And what a win-win. Ventisquero's quartz-, granite-, and iron-rich vineyards and Duval's sheer talent come together in a dramatic, sumptuous, dark cocoa-y/spicy/earthy wine with a texture like a velvet pillow. But in top years, there's also breathtaking complexity and length here, making Vertice (the word *vértice* means "apex") a showstopper.

MONTES

ALPHA M | COLCHAGUA VALLEY

80% cabernet sauvignon, 10% cabernet franc, 5% merlot, 5% petit verdot

From the steep hillsides of their Finca de Apalta vineyard comes Montes's Alpha M, a Bordeaux blend that, when it was first made in the mid-1990s, ambitiously sought to be Chile's equivalent of a First Growth. The wine is massively intense and often closed when it is released. But a few years later (or after an hour or two in a decanter), the wine unfurls into an amazing, richly structured beauty packed with cassis, woodsmoke, and graphite flavors. The small, half-moon-shaped Apalta region—the best area in Chile for ageworthy reds—has long, warm days, but it lies just 18 miles (29 kilometers) from the sea and thus benefits from cool ocean breezes.

PACIFIC
OCEAN

CHILE

PARAGUAY

BRAZIL

URUGUAY

◄ SALTA

◄ CATAMARCA

◄ LA RIOJA

ANDES MOUNTAINS

◄ MENDOZA

◄ SAN JUAN

MENDOZA ○

◄ LUJAN DE CUYO

◄ UCO VALLEY

BUENOS AIRES ○

ARGENTINA

NEUQUÉN

RIO NEGRO

◄ PATAGONIA

ANDES MOUNTAINS

ATLANTIC
OCEAN

0   200 km

ARGENTINA

ARGENTINA RANKS FIFTH AMONG WINE-PRODUCING COUNTRIES WORLDWIDE. ARGENTINIANS DRINK AN AVERAGE OF 10 GALLONS (36 LITERS) OF WINE PER PERSON PER YEAR.

Of all the wine-producing countries that have come of age in the past twenty years, none has come quite so far so fast as Argentina.

As of the late 1980s, much of the wine Argentina produced was, as it had been for centuries, dirt cheap and dead ordinary. Sometimes oxidized and occasionally microbial, it was funky but serviceable. The Argentines had grown used to it. And, with a big national population and no major export markets, they drank virtually all of it themselves.

Which, as it turns out, was a lot of wine. Until the late 1990s, Argentine per capita consumption had hovered for decades at around 26 gallons (98 liters) a year. It's now about 9.5 gallons (36 liters) per year. (In the U.S., the figure is about 2.4 gallons/9.1 liters per year.) Argentina not only drank a lot of wine, it also produced a lot. Indeed, since the mid-1960s, in wine production volume, Argentina has ranked between fourth and sixth place in the world; fifth is where it currently sits.

Today, Argentina is a wine country transformed. The best wines (mostly malbecs) are distinct in character and spellbinding in flavor. Even the simple wines have a delicious charm. In less than a generation, Argentine wine has gone from run-of-the-mill to remarkable.

What prompted this profound shift in quality? A single answer is hard to come by. But vintners point out that by 2000, Argentina had come to the end of nearly a century's worth of political instability and economic depression, during which time inflation often soared over 1,000 percent and the country wobbled under dictators and a series of power-hungry military governments. With the new economic, political, and social climate of the twenty-first century came vast new business opportunities. A stellar wine industry was one.

Then, within the new business-friendly climate, two other influences emerged as added incentives.

First was what might be called the "Chile factor." Throughout the 1990s, Argentina had watched as its neighbor Chile virtually reinvented its wine industry by improving

The stunning, 22,800-foot-high (6,960-meter) Andes Mountains—snow-covered year-round—frame the vineyards of Mendoza. Here, the vineyards of Catena Zapata, a winery at the forefront of the new era for top-class wine in Argentina.

the quality of its basic wines, pricing those wines higher, and then exporting them at a good profit, especially to the United States and Great Britain. Many of Argentina's most forward-thinking wineries figured (correctly): *If Chile can do it, why can't we?*

Second was the astounding success of one man—Nicolás Catena. Catena grew up in an Argentine winemaking family but graduated with a PhD in international economics from Columbia University in New York, and had been a visiting professor at the University of California at Berkeley. During his time in northern California, Catena developed a strong friendship with Robert Mondavi, ultimately, he says, preferring Mondavi's wines over those of his own family. When it came time for Nicolas to take over the reins of the family business, he did so with a resolute determination to make the sort of wines he had experienced in Napa and Sonoma. During the 1980s and 1990s, Nicolas turned the family wine business inside out—in the process, creating the winery he called Catena Zapata

(the sum of his parents' surnames). By the late 1990s, it was the most innovative and successful winery in the country. Nicolas Catena's huge success in export markets like the United States inspired other Argentine vintners, who hoped they could get a piece of the pie.

Fairly quickly, a new Argentine wine industry bloomed. Sometimes with the help of foreign investment or via joint ventures, Argentine wineries hired French, Italian, and American consultants (notably Michel Rolland, Alberto Antonini, and Paul Hobbs, respectively) to help them modernize. New French oak barrels and temperature-controlled stainless-steel tanks (the indispensable tools of modern winemaking) were purchased. Most significantly, vineyards were often completely overhauled, with the old *parral* system of overhead canopies replaced by modern trellising and modern farming techniques that minimized yields and maximized quality.

Importantly, Argentina quickly aimed higher than Chile, and sought to compete in world markets not only with modestly

THE QUICK SIP ON ARGENTINA

THE MODERN ARGENTINE wine industry came of age at the turn of the twenty-first century. After centuries of producing copious amounts of cheap quaffing wine, Argentine winemakers are increasingly focused on producing world-class wine.

MALBEC IS ARGENTINA'S signature grape. Nowhere else in the world does malbec rise to such heights of quality and richness as it does in Argentina.

ARGENTINA'S MOST NOTABLE wine region is Mendoza, made up of vast, very high-altitude, steplike plains below the peaks of the Andes.

priced, every-night wines, but also with fine, ageworthy wines that could command $50 or more a bottle. Export figures told the story best. In 1994, Argentina exported 389,000 gallons (14,700 hectoliters) of wine to one of its lead customers, the United States. Four years later that figure was 3.3 million gallons (124,900 hectoliters). And by 2010, Argentina way outpaced even Chile, with a record export to the U.S. of nearly 40 million gallons worth just shy of $230 million.

At more than 1 million square miles (2.6 million square kilometers), Argentina is the second-largest country in South America, after Brazil. From the hot jungles of the Tropic of Capricorn in the north, the country extends southward to the icy habitat of penguins at the tip of the continent, just a few hundred miles from Antarctica. Argentina's western border with Chile lies along the crest of the Andes. From these majestic peaks, the highest in the Americas, the country slopes downward until it meets the Atlantic Ocean in the east.

Winemaking began here, as it did in Chile, in the latter part of the sixteenth century,

with Spanish missionaries and conquistadores who brought grape seeds and cuttings with them from Spain. Some vines landed in Chile or Peru first and were later brought overland to Argentina. And some vine varieties may have been born spontaneously—the result of natural crossings of European varieties that occurred in Argentina itself. Initially, the most significant of these grapes was criolla grande ("big Creole"), an Argentine-born, pink-skinned member of the group of vines with criolla in the name, but a grape whose parents are not known. It made (and makes) the most bland of bland rosé and white red wines.

But there was also another criolla—the so-called criolla chica ("Creole girl")—which came to Argentina directly from Spain. From DNA typing, we know that this was the Spanish grape listán prieto—the same grape as Chile's país and California's mission. (For the full story of the intersection between these grapes, see the criolla and listán prieto entries in Getting to Know the Grapes, pages 81 and 86, respectively). In time, in Argentina, listán prieto crossed naturally with muscat of Alexandria (which had also been brought from Spain). One result was a pink-skinned grape called cereza (cherry), still Argentina's most widely planted grape but used only for the most basic supermarket rosés and whites. Another spontaneous cross of these two parents resulted, however, in something quite amazing: the white grapes torrontés Riojano and torrontés Sanjuanino. (More on this in a moment.)

Although the early Spanish settlers planted vines on the Argentine coast as well as inland, it soon became apparent that the high-altitude, sunny, bone-dry plains below the Andean peaks were an ideal location. Employing a system of dams and canals begun hundreds of years before by the Incas and local Huarpe Indians, the early missionaries learned to use snowmelt from the mountains to irrigate what otherwise would have been a virtual desert. With a constant supply of water, vineyards flourished.

In the 1820s, with the end of Spanish colonial rule, waves of European immigrants—mostly from Italy, France, and Spain—came to Argentina, bringing vines with them. (The first malbec in Argentina dates from this time.) They were followed in the 1890s by a second wave of Italians, French, and Spaniards, many of whom were from wine-producing regions and were escaping the phylloxera epidemic, which had ravaged the vineyards of the Old World. (Today, Argentine winemakers often joke that roughly half of them are Italian by descent, half are Spanish, but the wines they produce virtually all come from—*oh, no!*—French varieties.) For all of these immigrants, wine was an integral part of daily life. In Argentina, they found a place where wine could play a similar role.

One of the most important early events in the formation of the Argentine wine industry happened in 1853, with the founding of the Quinta Nacional, the national vine nursery. Its creator, the Frenchman Michel Aimé Pouget, established the nursery by bringing numerous vine cuttings from France, including the reds malbec, cabernet sauvignon, pinot noir, gamay, grenache, and petit verdot, as well as the whites sémillon, malvasia, and muscat. Criolla grande and cereza now had serious competition.

Then, in 1885, the first railway linking Argentina's premier wine region, Mendoza, with its capital city, Buenos Aires, was finished, opening access to a huge new market of wine drinkers. By 1900, Argentina had the beginnings of a massive wine industry.

There are now some 1,400 wineries in Argentina, according to the Instituto Nacional de Vitivinicultura, including a few very large players who make wine (often sold not in bottles, but in cartons like milk) primarily, if not exclusively, for the domestic market. But the wineries we are most concerned with here are Argentina's fine wine producers—a growing number of well-capitalized, often family-owned or joint-venture companies making some of the most spellbinding wines in South America. Among them: Alta Vista, Achaval Ferrer, Bodega Noemia, Catena Zapata, Cheval des Andes (a joint venture between Bordeaux's famous Château Cheval Blanc and Terrazas de los Andes, a winery owned primarily by Moët & Chandon),

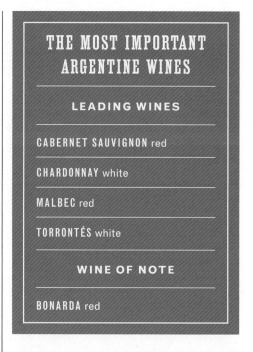

THE MOST IMPORTANT ARGENTINE WINES

LEADING WINES

CABERNET SAUVIGNON red

CHARDONNAY white

MALBEC red

TORRONTÉS white

WINE OF NOTE

BONARDA red

Clos de los Siete (a partnership that includes the world's most famous wine consultant, Michel Rolland), Viña Cobos (begun by famous U.S. winemaker Paul Hobbs and partners), Dominio del Plata, Fabre Montmayou, Bodega Piedra Negra, Nieto Senetiner, O. Fournier, Renacer, Salentein, Terrazas de los Andes, Tritono, Trivento, and Vistalba, among others.

Almost unilaterally, their star grape is malbec, a variety that, in Bordeaux (where it is also grown), ranks well below cabernet sauvignon and merlot in quality. In Argentina, however, malbec can broach magic.

For an explanation of Argentine wine laws, see the Appendix on Wine Laws, page 929.

THE LAND, THE GRAPES, AND THE VINEYARDS

A rgentina's 545,000-plus acres (220,600 hectares) of vineyards are found in seven important wine provinces in the west central part of the country, scattered

TANGO LESSONS

"If music be the food of love, play on," says Duke Orsino in Shakespeare's *Twelfth Night.* If the music had been tango and the duke had been drinking malbec, well, the romance part would have fallen quickly (and deeply) in place.

Indeed, while wine tasting seems romantic the world over, it's only in Argentina that you could find yourself at a winery at midnight, sipping a soft, saturated red wine while watching a man and a woman, entwined in each other, move, in raw desire, across a sweeping marble floor. (If nothing else, the provocativeness of wine takes on a whole new meaning here.)

The national dance of Argentina, the tango, is thought to have originated in working-class slums in Buenos Aires, as well as in Montevideo, Uruguay, in the late 1800s. While many styles of tango now exist, the dance is characterized by a palpable sexiness and the close embrace of the partners, who often seem joined at the hip, thighs, and chest. According to Ernesto Catena, one of the country's leading vintners, the tango is all about "desireability"—not unlike Argentine wines themselves. Maybe more winemakers around the world need tango lessons.

---

across the foothills of the Andes at elevations ranging up to 5,000 feet (1,500 meters) above sea level, making these some of the highest-altitude wine areas in the world. (Chile's major wine regions are directly across the Andes; close to the Pacific coast, they are therefore considerably lower in elevation.)

The provinces are often grouped, north to south, into three main areas:

THE NORTHWEST, generally the warmest region; includes the provinces Salta, Catamarca, and La Rioja

---

CUYO, the largest region, in the middle; includes Mendoza and San Juan

---

PATAGONIA, the farthest south, coolest, and smallest region; includes Neuquén and Río Negro

---

Of these, Mendoza, in the Cuyo region, is by far the largest and most important province. We will examine it in more detail later in this section.

With the exception of Patagonia, Argentina's wine regions all have a dry,

Yes, there was a llama in this vineyard—a whole goofy flock of them, in fact. Llamas migrated to South America from the plains of North America some three million years ago.

desertlike climate, with copious amounts of intense sunlight—some 320 days per year on average—and rainfall that rarely exceeds 8

THE GRAPES OF ARGENTINA

WHITES

CHARDONNAY: A major grape, especially for exported wines. Wine styles range from simple to toasty and oaky, in the manner of many California chardonnays.

TORRONTÉS: An Argentine specialty, although there are three distinct varieties with torrontés as part of their names. The most famous and widespread is torrontés Riojana, which makes delightful, dry, spicy, aromatic wines with a lightly unctuous texture. It is a centuries-old natural crossing of muscat of Alexandria with the red grape listán prieto. More rare is torrontés Sanjuanino, also a natural cross of muscat of Alexandria and listán prieto. And the final variety, torrontés Mendocino, is generally not as aromatic or high in quality; only one of its parents (muscat of Alexandria) is known.

REDS

BARBERA, SANGIOVESE, AND TEMPRANILLO: Planted by early Italian and Spanish immigrants, these varieties are used mainly in inexpensive blends that are sold in jugs and cartons, although sometimes they are made into varietal wines.

BONARDA: Once Argentina's main red grape, bonarda is now second to malbec. It makes tasty, bold wines that can have some complexity with age. Despite its name, it is not related to the Italian bonarda Piemontese. DNA analysis reveals that Argentine bonarda is the French grape douce noir, which originated in the Savoie region of France. In California, douce noir (bonarda) is called charbono.

CABERNET SAUVIGNON: An important red mainly intended for the export market. Its wines can range from simple to powerful and sleek.

CEREZA: The most widely planted variety, it is used for inexpensive wines sold in cartons on the domestic market. Like two of the torrontés varieties, it is a cross of listán prieto and muscat of Alexandria, but is not as successful. The word means "cherry" in Spanish.

CRIOLLA CHICA: The same grape as listán prieto, the original grape variety brought to Argentina from Spain.

CRIOLLA GRANDE: A widely planted if undistinguished pinkish-skinned grape related to other criollas, but its parents are not known. It is used to make coarse, bland white and rosé wines sold on the Argentine domestic market in jugs or cardboard cartons, or in bulk.

MALBEC: Argentina's most important and impressive red. The grape originated in southwestern France, near the region of Cahors, where it is known by its proper name, côt. The first malbec vines were brought to Argentina in the 1830s, and better selections arrived in the 1890s. In the top sites and in the hands of the best winemakers, the grape makes wines of surprising grip, depth, concentration, and velvety texture.

MERLOT: While less prestigious and less successful than cabernet sauvignon, merlot is still a source of good-value wines mainly for the export market.

The Argentine asado *is a barbecue built for carnivores. Every cut of beef imaginable is thrown on the grill along with sausages, ribs,* chivito *(baby goat), and a few, ahem, surprises. This is malbec territory, big time.*

to 10 inches (20 to 25 centimeters) per year. Amazingly, despite the strong sunlight, temperatures are generally mild thanks to the high elevation of the vineyards. Indeed, during the long grape-growing cycle, vineyard temperatures are surprisingly just 60°F to 75°F (16°C to 24°C).

Immense luminosity—but without immense heat—creates a unique environment for photosynthesis and ripening. The top Argentine malbecs, for example, are often lush and rich in flavor, yet never ponderous, fat, and alcoholic in the way wines from very warm regions can be. As an aside, the bone-dry air means that Argentine vineyards are mostly free of diseases, virtually eliminating the need to spray preventive chemicals.

Of course, the lack of rain means irrigation is essential. For new vineyards, that means drip irrigation, which uses water sparingly. But some older vineyards are still irrigated by the historic old canal system. Interestingly, vineyard properties do not automatically come with water rights; even water from the narrow canals must be licensed and paid for by the vintner.

SPEAKING OF *MALBEC* . . .

*A*lthough it is now famous in Argentina, malbec's ancestral home is Cahors, a tiny, ancient wine region in southwest France. Here, the wine is known as le vin noir, "the black wine," not only because of its dark color, but also because of its severe, tannic, "dark" flavors. The word malbec is actually a nickname for the grape's true ampelographic name: côt. In the nineteenth century, malbec was a slang term for someone who spoke badly of others (from the French mal, or "bad," and bec, or "mouth"). There must have been a lot of malbecs in Cahors, for the word became a common surname—and an affectionate term for the local grapes.

While no winemaker here worries about rain, there is one type of moisture that can be frightening and ruinous: hail. The legendary hailstorms that can build off the Andes in March and April (right during harvest) have, all too many times, wiped out entire vineyards. (Local wisdom says there's a one in ten chance every year of complete devastation.) Just a few decades ago, Argentine vintners hired "witch doctors" to cast spells to protect against the ice balls. Today, many vineyards are protected with expensive hail netting. The netting (which does reduce the direct light of the sun on the grapes) must be replaced every five or so years—a cost that most other vineyard owners around the world don't have to worry about.

A word about soils. While Argentina is a huge country, the wine districts are all in well-drained areas of very low soil fertility—a good thing for grapevines, as lack of water and low fertility lead to small yields. Many vineyards are visibly gravelly and rocky, thanks to deposits from glaciers and rivers millennia ago.

Many also contain significant amounts of sand, clay, and limestone.

Like Chile, Argentina has never been the victim of phylloxera, the insect that decimated many of the world's vineyards in the mid- and late-nineteenth century and showed up again in the 1980s and 1990s, destroying many vineyards in the western United States. As a result, many Argentine wines are made from vines that still grow on their own roots (not on pest-tolerant rootstocks, as has been typical throughout the world for a century). It's not that phylloxera doesn't exist here—it does, in spots. But for reasons no one seems to fully understand, the insects here do not have a fully functioning "fly cycle" (phylloxera are airborne during part of their lives), causing difficulty in reproduction. In addition, phylloxera have a hard time thriving in sandy, dry soils and in soils that can be flooded via irrigation if need be. Still, most modern Argentine winemakers say they don't plan to press their entomological luck, and thus, new vineyards are almost always planted on rootstock.

PERFECTING THE RED-WINE-WITH-MEAT RULE

In no other country in the world is beef as celebrated, or as much a part of daily life, as it is in Argentina. Argentines eat beef in every form— breaded, fried, rolled, stuffed, chopped, and combined with raisins, olives, and eggs in empanadas. But perhaps most irresistible of all is beef right off the *parilla,* or grill, as part of the Argentine *asado,* a no-holds-barred barbecue for which ribs, *chorizo* (sausage), *chivito* (baby goat), and *vizchaca* (why didn't someone tell me this was chinchilla before I ate it?) are also obligatory. But it's the beef, above all, that counts. Beef is so much a part of Argentine cuisine that Argentines eat more of it than almost any other people in the world. In 2010, consumption was an enthusiastic 124 pounds (56 kilograms) per person per year. (In the United States, itself no slouch in the beef department, per capita consumption was approximately 60 pounds/27 kilograms in 2010.) Argentine beef is relatively lean, with a pronounced flavor that Argentines say is the true beef flavor, attributable to the fact that the cattle feed on grasses as they roam over enormous expanses of land, rather than being fattened in feed lots and fed growth hormones. And what do the Argentines drink with their national culinary treasure? Their national vinous treasure: malbec. (Wine, incidentally, was actually signed into law as Argentina's national beverage by President Cristina Fernández de Kirchner in 2010.)

The most famous grape in Argentina—and specifically in Mendoza—is malbec. While widely associated with Bordeaux (it's one of the permitted red varieties there), malbec is native to the area around Cahors, slightly south of Bordeaux, in southwest France.

In Cahors, malbec is known by its original name, côt. But while the grape may be the same, the wine has hugely different characteristics depending on where the grapes are grown. Cahors' côt, for example, is extremely hard, sleek, and tannic. Argentine malbec, on the other hand, is usually remarkably soft, rich, and palate-coating. And in Bordeaux, the grape makes a wine somewhere in the middle of those flavor bookends.

Not that there's much malbec left in Bordeaux. The variety is prone to certain fungal diseases, and thus, after the phylloxera epidemic of the late 1800s, very little was replanted in Bordeaux, a wet climate at risk for fungal problems. Today, a typical Bordeaux wine has less than 10 percent malbec, if it has any at all.

In arid Argentina, however, the grape variety thrived and continues to do so. Indeed, Argentina may now have the deepest DNA pool of malbec and malbec clones in the world.

Malbec also does very well in California, where it is increasingly planted and used to add richness and dark, cocoalike flavors to many top-notch California cabernet blends.

MENDOZA

Mendoza is the name of Argentina's leading wine province, and the name of the province's capital city, founded in 1561. The province and city were named for Don García Hurtado de Mendoza, a sixteenth-century Chilean governor (Mendoza was once a Chilean colony and belonged to what was called the Captaincy of Chile).

Huddled in the high desert foothills of the Andes, the province covers more than 36 million acres (14.6 million hectares)—yes, *million*. Indeed, at more than 57,000 square miles (147,600 square kilometers), Mendoza is about the size of New York State. Not all of this huge area is covered by vineyards, however.

WHEN YOU VISIT . . . ARGENTINA

ASIDE FROM BEING the best-known wine region in Argentina, Mendoza is also the most accessible and rewarding for wine-tasting experiences. You'll need a car to travel between destinations, but with so many new wineries and boutique hotels, you won't have to drive far. Many of the wineries, like Familia Zuccardi, have fantastic restaurants that specialize in Argentine cuisine.

Given the prominence of wines from Mendoza, it's interesting to know that less than 5 percent of the surface area of the province is planted with grapevines.

Nonetheless, Mendoza is more than just the leading wine region—it is the heartbeat of the Argentine wine industry. Virtually all of the wineries of any importance are to be found here, and a map of the province reads like a Who's Who of wineries. Indeed, of the approximately 1,400 wineries in Argentina, nearly 1,000 are in this one province, and a majority of all Argentine wine, including the vast majority of all malbec, is grown here.

The region lies directly west of Buenos Aires, roughly 1,000 miles (1,600 kilometers) inland from the Atlantic Ocean. The vineyards, at 4,000 feet (1,200 meters) and more above sea level, are framed by the snowcapped Andes, and are the highest in the country. The climate is, as I've noted, extremely dry. But it's the light one never forgets. What the Mendozans call "sunlight density" is nothing short of riveting.

Within Mendoza province, the most important subregions fall south of Mendoza city along the Ruta 40 (Highway 40) corridor. These include the two well-known subregions Luján de Cuyo and the Uco Valley, the latter made up of the three well-known wine districts Tupungato, Tunuyán, and San Carlos.

URUGUAY

In the language of the indigenous people, the Guaraní, *Uruguay* means "river of birds" thanks to their more than 450 species of birds. There are far fewer species of grapes, of course, but Uruguay is nonetheless one of the most exciting emerging wine regions in the Americas. Grapevines were first brought there in the 1870s by Basque immigrants, but a serious wine industry began only as of the 1980s and 1990s. Today, the country has 22,000 acres (8,900 hectares) of vineyards and 270 wineries, most of which are small and family-run and sometimes helped by one of several famous international wine consultants, among them the American Paul Hobbs, the Italian Alberto Antonini, and the Frenchman Michel Rolland.

Uruguay (which lies at the same latitude range as Argentina, South Africa, and Australia) has a gentle maritime climate due to its location on the edge of the Atlantic Ocean. The country also boasts the purest vineyard environment in the world, according to the Environmental Sustainability Index published by Yale and Columbia Universities in the United States (Finland and Norway rank higher for total environmental purity, but good luck trying to grow grapes in either country).

The signature grape of Uruguay is tannat, a tannic grape that originated in southwest France, although today more tannat is grown in Uruguay than in the entire rest of the world. Aged in oak to soften it, tannat (whose name refers to the dark color of the grapes) can be rich and mouthfilling, with black cherry, chocolate, and espresso flavors. In Uruguay, it is considered the perfect accompaniment to the popular local *asados,* wood-fired barbecues devoted to Uruguay's high-quality beef. Other promising grape varieties include merlot, cabernet sauvignon, chardonnay, sauvignon blanc, and the unusual French white variety petit manseng, which was brought to Uruguay at the same time as tannat, and makes dry, floral wines. Some of the best producers of Uruguayan wine include Stagnari, Bouza, Pizzorno, Pisano, and Juanicó.

SALTA

While nowhere close to Mendoza in terms of the volume of wine produced, the province of Salta, in northernmost Argentina (a two-day drive north of Mendoza), is a place any wine lover should know. The region itself was founded in the fifteenth century by Incas moving out of Peru. It is warm and more moist this far north, with cold nights thanks to altitudes of 5,600 feet (1,700 meters) and higher. And it is here that Argentina's best torrontés (specifically, the variety known as torrontés Riojana) is grown.

Torrontés Riojana is, of course, Argentina's top white wine—a wine of dazzling aromatics with a dry, snappy flavor, and a curious, unctuous feel. The top torrontés wines tend to come from Salta's wine capital, the town of Cafayate. Most of the torrontés here is grown using the *parral* system of pergolas that lift the vines high overhead, keeping the clusters cool, free of sunburn, and dry of evaporating dew.

Among my favorite torrontés wines are those made by Alta Vista, Terrazas de los Andes, and Tomero.

The Argentine Wines to Know

WHITES

TERRAZAS DE LOS ANDES

TORRONTÉS | SALTA

100% torrontés Riojana

Terrazas de los Andes is making some of Argentina's most intriguing and complex wines, including this beautifully vivid, fresh torrontés, with its cooling aromas and flavors of lime blossom, lychee, and tangerine. But what really escalates the deliciousness here is an intriguing touch of citrusy bitterness (like grapefruit pith), which gives the wine its exotic distinctiveness.

REDS

RENACER

MALBEC | GRAN RESERVA | MENDOZA

100% malbec

One look at the electric purple color of this wine and you can't help thinking you're in for something good. In point of fact, you're in for something *great*. Waves of exotic aromas and flavors—black figs, spices, minerals, cocoa—fill your senses. At the same time, the texture of the wine knocks you out with its yin-yang of rockiness and lushness. But the aspect I love most about Renacer's Gran Reserva is its vividness and precision. It's as if every molecule of flavor is pulsing with intensity. Renacer makes Gran Reserva only in exceptional years, and the wine tastes like it.

CATENA ZAPATA

MALBEC | NICASIA | MENDOZA

100% malbec

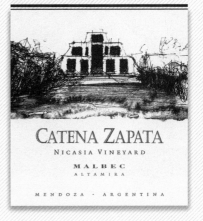

I love many of the Catena Zapata wines, but Nicasia, named for the small area where the vineyard is located, is a favorite. From a vineyard that gives less than 1 ton per acre, it's a massively structured malbec, with its sappy texture and explosive flavor. Yet for all of the wine's ripe fruit and black licorice flavors, there's also a beautiful hum of acidity here. Indeed, it's the wine's impeccable balance between ripe fruit and acidity that gives always-powerful Nicasia a sense of gracefulness.

TERRAZAS DE LOS ANDES

MALBEC | LAS COMPUERTAS | MENDOZA

100% malbec

Spellbinding precision and structure. That's what Terrazas de los Andes's top wine from the single vineyard Las Compuertas possesses in great years. Indeed, this wine comes from vines that are more than eighty years old, and it soars with a sense of majesty. The flavors are all about dark fruits, black licorice, charred meat, and spice, all overlaid by a sprinkling of something deliciously dusty, like cocoa. The vineyard Las Compuertas ("the floodgates") is considered one of the top vineyards in Mendoza, and it's the vineyard that inspired famous winemaker Pierre Lurton, from Bordeaux's Château Cheval Blanc, to begin making wine in Argentina.

CHEVAL DES ANDES

MENDOZA

Approximately 50% malbec, 45% cabernet sauvignon, 5% petit verdot

Cheval des Andes makes only one wine—an expensive wine, intended to be among the very greatest wines of the world. And like great Bordeaux, the wine is named simply by its estate; no designation of grape variety is given on the label. The wine is a blend that includes fruit from malbec vines planted on their own roots in 1929. Like Château Cheval Blanc (the wine to which it is an homage), Cheval des Andes defines the intersection of grace and power. Complex and sumptuous, it's got the full complement of Mendozan malbec aromas and flavors: spices, grilled meat, licorice, espresso, dark fruits, dried herbs . . . and a texture like ribbons of black velvet. But at the same time, there's a sustained minerally, rocky character here that's mesmerizing.

NIETO SENETINER

MALBEC | CADUS | MENDOZA

100% malbec

With its fine precison and concentration, Cadus (the word means "amphora") from Nieto Senetiner is a beauty. Sleek and less syrupy than many top malbecs, it is a structured wine, with wonderful violet aromas and flavors evocative of spices, cassis, cocoa, and blackberries. And its finish lingers and lingers. Nieto Senetiner is one of the larger wineries in Argentina, and it makes an inexpensive, simple malbec that's fine for quaffing. But Cadus is their top of the line, and it's the one you want.

TOMERO

MALBEC | GRAN RESERVA | MENDOZA

100% malbec

This small-production malbec is as dark and saturated as they come. With aromas and flavors evocative of Christmas pudding or Fig Newtons, Tomero has an impression of sweetness thanks to the rich ripeness of the grapes. Wonderful spice notes and a distinct minerality give the wine complexity. Tomero is owned by Carlos Pulenta, one of the key figures in the Argentine industry and the scion of the family that built Argentina's first massive-production wine company—Peñaflor.

ACHAVAL FERRER

MALBEC | FINCA BELLA VISTA | MENDOZA

100% malbec

The soaring, savory aromas of this wine can cause you to imagine that you're standing on the high Andean plain, surrounded by chaparral. With intense and complex flavors of black figs, black licorice, peat moss, grilled meats, minerals, and spices, Achaval Ferrer's malbec is dramatic and lively. Less soft than many other malbecs, it is monolithic in structure and intensity and delicious to drink with a thick grilled steak that's crusty black on the outside and pinkish red on the inside.

ALMA NEGRA

MISTERIO | MENDOZA

Grape varieties never revealed

Alma Negra is owned by Ernesto Catena, son of Nicolas Catena, the father of the modern Argentine wine industry. Rather iconoclastic and highly spiritual, Ernesto Catena never reveals the grapes in the logically named Misterio (mystery). No matter, the wine is sensational. Incredibly spicy with loads of black licorice and blackberry flavors, it's also minerally, indeed almost salty, on the palate. The commanding structure is impeccable, and the texture, grippy and almost furry, is fascinating. All in all, this is a sensational wine. (After much journalistic pressing, Mr. Catena hinted that the mystery in question might involve cabernet franc, cabernet sauvignon, malbec, bonarda, and syrah.)

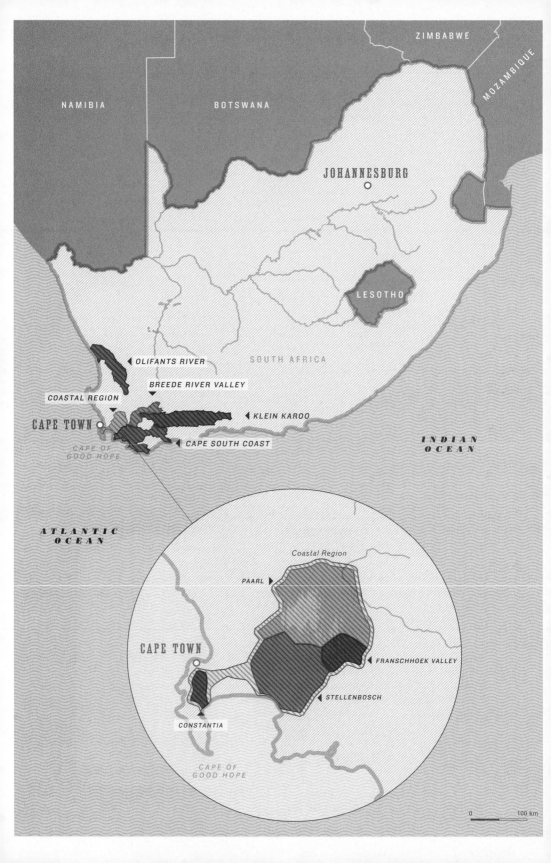

SOUTH AFRICA

SOUTH AFRICA RANKS EIGHTH AMONG WINE-PRODUCING COUNTRIES WORLDWIDE. SOUTH AFRICANS DRINK AN AVERAGE OF 2 GALLONS (7.5 LITERS) OF WINE PER PERSON PER YEAR.

 f the more than fifty countries on the African continent, only eight are wine producers: South Africa, Morocco, Algeria, Tunisia, Egypt, Libya, Zimbabwe, and Kenya. Most make only minuscule amounts of bland wine. South Africa, by comparison, is both a leading wine producer (eighth in the world by volume) and the source of the continent's finest wines.

Not quite twice as large as Texas, South Africa is bordered on the north by Namibia, Botswana, and Zimbabwe, and on the east by Mozambique and Swaziland. The country has about 323,000 acres (130,700 hectares) of planted vines, cared for by just over 3,500 grape growers who supply nearly six hundred wineries (known in South Africa as "wine farms"). With about 1,800 miles (2,897 kilometers) of coastline, South Africa is one of the only wine regions in the world sandwiched between two oceans—in South Africa's case, the Atlantic and the Indian.

The first South African wines were made more than three centuries ago by Dutch colonists who vinified the wild grapes they found growing on the southwestern tip (known as the Western Cape) of the African continent. The colonists, employees of the Dutch East India Company, planned to establish the Western Cape as a restocking station for food and provisions for ships, halfway between Europe and the spice-rich East Indies.

Although the presence of native grapes was encouraging to the colonists, the wine made from them was not. The commander of the small settlement, Jan van Riebeeck, immediately sent word back to Holland, imploring his employers to send European vine cuttings on the next ship out. Within a decade, French vine cuttings—most probably chenin blanc and muscat of Alexandria—were thriving in Western Cape soil.

The closely spaced vineyards were too narrow to be worked by animal-drawn plows and too extensive to be worked by the colonists alone. The colony relied, regrettably, on slaves—at first Malay, and then, in 1658,

A baobab tree in the middle of the renowned vineyards of Groot Constantia, where the extraordinary dessert wine Vin de Constance is made. Native to Africa and Madagascar, baobab trees are oddly shaped and long-lived (up to 2,000 years).

THE QUICK SIP ON SOUTH AFRICA

SOUTH AFRICA has a more than three-hundred-year-old history of grape growing.

THE BEST SOUTH AFRICAN wines come from an emerging group of small private estates devoted to making artisanal, high-quality wine. That said, a large percentage of South African wine is still utterly simple stuff made by large cooperatives.

MOST DRY WINES are based on five well-known grapes: sauvignon blanc, chardonnay, cabernet sauvignon, merlot, and syrah. Along with these, the country is known for an unusual red wine specialty: pinotage. Some stunning (and famous) sweet wines are also made—often from muscat blanc à petits grains.

Dutch ships brought two hundred slaves from Madagascar and Mozambique to the settlement. The very next year, on the first day of the harvest, February 2, 1659, van Riebeeck recorded in his journal: "Today, God be praised, wine was pressed for the first time from Cape grapes."

Despite the long history of Western Cape winemaking, South African wines were virtually unknown in the United States and in many European countries before the 1990s, as a result of trade sanctions imposed in response to the South African policy of racial apartheid. When apartheid ended and the bans on South African goods were lifted (mostly in 1991), the doors of commerce swung open. By mid-decade, Western Cape wines had begun to turn up in wine shops in Europe, as well as in the United States.

South Africa has five major wine zones—referred to as geographical units. Of these, only one is important for fine wine: the Western Cape, located in the most southwesterly part of the country. Telescoping down further, within the Western Cape, one region is more important than all others: the Coastal Region. All of South Africa's top wine districts are here. One of the smallest of these districts,

THE DESSERT WINE OF KINGS, POETS, AND PARTYGOERS

During the nineteenth century, Constantia winery, nestled in a serene valley south of Cape Town, South Africa, was known for its sweet wine; during the twentieth century, it was known for throwing one hell of a party.

Founded in 1685 by then governor of the Cape Simon van der Stel, Constantia was one of South Africa's first "wine farms" (the local term for winery). Constantia produced Vin de Constance, a luscious dessert wine made from muscat blanc à petits grains grapes. The wine rose to become one of the most sought-after dessert wines in all of Europe, ordered by the case by Napoléon Bonaparte and never absent from the table of King Frederick the Great of Germany.

In addition to being a royal preference, Vin de Constance was immortalized by some of the most well-respected authors and poets of their day. Jane Austen reflects on the wine's "healing powers on a disappointed heart" in *Sense and Sensibility,* while Charles Dickens enshrines it as the cure-all in *The Mystery of Edwin Drood.* The wine even made its way into Baudelaire's poetry: "Even more than Constantia, than opium, than Nuits, I prefer the elixir of your mouth, where love performs its slow dance." Now, who could argue with that?

With the death of van der Stel in 1712, Constantia was broken up into three entities—two wineries: Groot Constantia (Big Constantia) and Klein Constantia (Little Constantia); and a farm called Bergvliet (Mountain Stream).

During the Roaring Twenties, Klein Constantia hosted the most extravagant parties on the African continent. After American heiress Clara Hussey de Villiers purchased and restored the Klein Constantia manor house in 1913, guests strolled the lawns alongside peacocks, while enjoying live orchestras and feasting on oysters and Russian caviar laid on barrels of ice arranged around the gardens. Jay Gatsby would have been proud.

Today, both Groot Constantia and Klein Constantia continue to operate, and each continues to produce the fabled Vin de Constance. And while the courtly glamour of Constantia's past may have waned slightly, the wine remains extraordinary. Klein Constantia, in particular, makes a Vin de Constance that is one of the greatest and most spiritual wine experiences to be had.

Constantia, was already so well established by the mid-1700s that a sweet, muscat-based wine named simply Constantia was renowned throughout Europe and was reportedly a favorite of Napoléon.

If there is one factor that, more than any other, shaped the current state of South African wine, it was the establishment of extremely powerful cooperatives at the turn of the twentieth century. The cooperative movement began after the combined devastation of the Anglo-Boer War and phylloxera, a root-killing insect (see page 30), left the country's vineyards in near ruins. In the aftermath of these destructive forces, South African vineyards were replanted with a vengeance. Overproduction ensued, and grape prices hit rock bottom. In 1905, the South African government appointed a commission to examine the widespread financial depression in the wine industry. The result was the formation of the first South African

IS THE TABLECLOTH ON?

outh Africa's Coastal Region includes one of the most impressive sights to be found in wine country anywhere—the 3,563-foot-high (1,086-meter), flat-topped, granite-based mountain known as Table Mountain. Singular and dramatic, with a plateau more than 2 miles (3.2 kilometers) long, Table Mountain forms an amphitheater around the charming, bustling seaside city of Cape Town. The mountain was formed approximately 250 million years ago as a result of massive geologic eruptions that resulted in plutons, domelike protrusions of hot lava that rose from deep within the earth to penetrate its crust. After cooling, the plutons of the Western Cape eroded into unusual, flat-topped mountains like Table Mountain. Fascinatingly, the top of Table Mountain is often covered by clouds, forming what the locals call the "tablecloth."

co-op, funded with huge government grants. The stage was set.

Almost a dozen co-ops sprung up over the next several years, but many of these were unsuccessful. Grape prices plummeted again after World War I. In desperation, 10 million vines were uprooted, and grape growers planted alfalfa fields to feed ostriches—ostrich feathers being highly fashionable in Europe during the (roaring) 1920s. But when the feather fad faded and growers went back to planting grapes, overproduction loomed yet again.

In 1918, one of the most massive, mighty cooperatives in the world was formed—the KWV, or *Koöperatieve Wijnbouwers Vereniging van Zuid Afrika* (the Cooperative Wine Growers' Association of South Africa). Over the next few decades the KWV became omnipotent. No wine could be made, sold, bought in South Africa, or exported from it, except through the KWV. After the end of apartheid in 1991, wine surpluses disappeared and wine sales and exports increased. The KWV was mostly dismantled, and today the much-reduced company is focused largely on producing inexpensive brandy. Most importantly, the grape growers and small wineries who had relied on the KWV to buy their excess grapes and distill them have now turned their focus toward lowering yields and making better, higher-quality wine instead.

With the end of the KWV era, South Africa began moving toward the production of quality wines. At first, the pace of change was modest. For example, even as late as 1990, 70 percent

THE MOST IMPORTANT SOUTH AFRICAN WINES

LEADING WINES

CABERNET SAUVIGNON red

CHARDONNAY white

CHENIN BLANC white (dry and sweet)

SAUVIGNON BLANC white

SYRAH/SHIRAZ red

WINES OF NOTE

PINOTAGE red

SPARKLING WINES white

A monkey sits contentedly among the vines.

THE CAPE OF GOOD HOPE

On a momentous day in 1488, the Portuguese navigator Bartolomeu Dias became the first European to sail through tempestuous seas past the rocky headland of the Cape Peninsula. He named the area Cabo Tormentoso, the Cape of Storms. Later, Portugal's king, fearing that mariners would refuse to sail around the Cape to the Far East to trade, renamed it Cabo de Boa Esperança, the Cape of Good Hope. Dias's achievement was stunning, for traveling south down the coastline of Africa, the Cape of Good Hope marked the point where a ship began to travel more eastward than southward, and thus on a direct course for Asia. Despite its importance, the Cape of Good Hope is not the southern tip of Africa. The southernmost point is Cape Agulhas, about 90 miles (145 kilometers) to the east-southeast.

of all South African grapes were still being distilled into cheap brandy, sold as table grapes, or even simply discarded. Only 30 percent were used to make wine intended for consumers. Today, that picture is entirely reversed, with nearly 80 percent of all grapes being made into wine.

Still, South Africa is a wine region caught in a protracted struggle to modernize. On the one hand, the country is blessed with an abundance of geological and climatic factors that bode well for fantastic wine. On the other, South Africa remains economically strained and technologically challenged. Too many wine companies, large and small, are still working with poor-quality, outdated equipment, and are short on modern wine-making expertise. Harvesting in South Africa is often inefficient, and the industry is fraught with labor problems as well as occasional labor abuses.

For example, South Africa still suffers from the vestiges of the so-called tot system, whereby workers were paid in distilled alcohol in lieu of wages. Although the system was officially declared illegal in 1962, the practice persisted for years, furthering the rampant alcoholism and misery that have existed for generations among the poorest laborers, virtually all of whom are black. In addition, in 2011, Human Rights Watch reported that some laborers in the Western Cape's wine and fruit industries were subject to appalling conditions. In response, the top wineries with ethical labor practices have formed an organization called the Wine and Agriculture Industry Ethical Trade Association (WIETA) and have created much-needed fair labor standards.

At this writing, South Africa still produces large quantities of undistinguished, cheap wine. Most wine is still made by co-ops. But there is also a growing cadre of ambitious small estates who are making remarkable

THE GRAPES OF SOUTH AFRICA

WHITES

CAPE RIESLING: A minor grape when it comes to the production of fine dry wines, but it can make some delicious, old-style sweet wines. It is not related to riesling, despite its name, but is the same as the French grape crouchen blanc.

CHARDONNAY: An important and very popular grape that is made into good everynight wines as well as stunningly complex, creamy wines.

CHENIN BLANC: A major grape, although production is in decline. Historically it was often called steen. Small producers working with old vineyards are making stellar dry and sweet wines, although a lot of very neutral-tasting chenin blanc is also made by co-ops.

MUSCAT OF ALEXANDRIA: One of the many grapes with the word *muscat* in the name, it is used, along with other muscat varieties, for sweet fortified wines, some of which can be very appealing.

MUSCAT DE FRONTIGNAN: The South African name for the grape muscat blanc à petits grains, the leading muscat variety. It is used in the extremely famous dessert wine Vin de Constance.

SAUVIGNON BLANC: A very important major grape used to make delicious, smoky, grassy, minerally, snappy dry wines with high acidity and lots of personality.

REDS

CABERNET FRANC: A minor blending grape, generally used with cabernet sauvignon.

CABERNET SAUVIGNON: A prestigious red grape planted in the best regions and often made into Bordeaux-style blends.

CINSAUT: A southern French variety; in South Africa it's often called hermitage. It is the source of light reds and is often used in blending.

MERLOT: Gaining in popularity, although it is not yet as successful as cabernet sauvignon. Merlot is made as a varietal wine and is used for blending.

PINOTAGE: A South African cross, in 1925, of cinsaut and pinot noir. It makes rustic reds that are rarely complex.

PINOT NOIR: A minor grape; historically not very successful in South Africa, but its quality is improving. It is used primarily for sparkling wines.

SYRAH/SHIRAZ: The grape goes by both names in South Africa, and shows considerable promise here. It is the source of popular, big-fruit wines with lots of smoky chocolate flavors. It is used for varietal wines as well as for blending.

wines, and in some cases pioneering entirely new, cool coastal areas. Increasingly, there's also much-needed foreign investment—not only of capital, but also of expertise. While we've perhaps had only a small "taste" of it so far, the South African wine revolution is clearly in full swing.

For an explanation of South African wine laws, see the Appendix on Wine Laws, page 929.

Men punch down the cap of grape skins by hand at Kanonkop winery in the Stellenbosch district of the Western Cape.

THE LAND, THE GRAPES, AND THE VINEYARDS

As noted earlier, grape growing and wine making in South Africa are spread out over five huge areas known as geographical units, but most of these areas have the barest minimum of a wine industry. For all practical purposes, the single area that matters most (and the one to know) is the Western Cape—an area concentrated in the southwestern part of the country, bordered on the west by the Atlantic Ocean and on the south by the Indian Ocean.

The geology of the Western Cape is ancient and remarkable. Massive geologic upheavals over millions of years resulted in majestic mountain ranges on the southern tip of the Cape. The enormous pressures exerted during these upheavals caused folding and uplifting, creating high peaks and deep valleys. On these slopes and in these valleys, South African viticulture takes place today. About 250 million years ago, an intensive period of folding and uplifting occurred, followed by massive erosion that "flat-topped" the mountains. The results were dramatic sandstone mountains like Table Mountain (3,563 feet/1,086 meters high) and Simonsberg (4,590 feet/1,399 meters high).

NELSON MANDELA

Elected in 1994, Nelson Rolihlahla Mandela was South Africa's first black president and the first to be elected with voter participation from all races. Mandela's release from Victor Verster Prison in Paarl in 1990, after more than twenty-seven years in confinement, signaled a new era in South African politics and paved the way for the lifting of trade sanctions and the importation of South African wine into the United States. Nelson Mandela's connection to wine grew even more substantial in 2010, when his daughter Makaziwe and granddaughter Tukwini launched the House of Mandela wine brand, which includes a chardonnay, cabernet sauvignon, shiraz, and a sparkling wine. For the Mandela family, who are part of the royal abaThembu lineage and the Madiba clan, honoring the ancient wisdom of one's ancestors and honoring the earth gives meaning and purpose to life. Upon the release of their wines, the family wrote, "We have chosen wine as a bridge into the future."

The Western Cape is divided into five areas: Breede River Valley, Klein Karoo, Coastal Region, Olifants River, and Cape South Coast. As mentioned earlier, the most established of these (and the area from which the best wines to date have come) is the Coastal Region. Spreading out like a fan from the charming city of Cape Town, the Coastal Region includes the fine wine districts of Constantia, Franschhoek Valley, Paarl, and Stellenbosch. Here the climate is largely Mediterranean, with a beautiful growing season free of frost and rain. What occasionally could be scorching heat is kept at bay by the comingling of cooling maritime

RICH BEYOND GRAPES

South Africa has the largest known reserves of gold in the world, and is the foremost supplier (accounting for about 35 percent of total world production). Johannesburg, in fact, began as a gold-mining camp in the 1800s. Indeed, in 1961, South Africa's modern currency was named the rand after a gold-mining region—Witwatersrand ("ridge of white waters" in Afrikaans). The ridge is a north-facing scarp 35 miles (56 kilometers) long, over 2 miles (3 kilometers) deep, and traversed by several north-flowing rivers that form impressive waterfalls. Forty percent of all the gold ever mined from the earth has been mined from this one place.

In 1867, the country's diamond industry began with a young boy who found a transparent "pebble" on his father's farm. The pebble turned out to be a 21-carat diamond, and so began South Africa's diamond rush. South Africa also has the largest known reserves of chromium, platinum, vanadium, manganese, andalusite, and fluorspar, as well as substantial deposits of many other minerals, such as coal, uranium, iron ore, antimony, asbestos, nickel, and phosphates.

---

breezes off the Atlantic and Indian Oceans. The best vineyard sites in these districts are often on slopes, sheltered from the late afternoon sun.

As seems logical, given so much geologic activity in this part of South Africa, soils vary considerably in the top wine districts. Some of the most prominent types include gravel, granite, clay, sand, schist, shale, and hutton, a deep, rich red soil also known as Cape sandstone.

KANONKOP
ESTATE WINE
Pinotage
2009
GROWN, PRODUCED & BOTTLED ON THE ESTATE
WINE OF ORIGIN SIMONSBERG STELLENBOSCH
PRODUCE OF SOUTH AFRICA

Historically, more white grapes than red were grown in South Africa—a reflection of the past importance of South African "sherry" and brandy. Indeed, brandy was so important in the past that even as of 1993, more than 80 percent of all grapes planted were white, and most of those were destined for distillation. By 2011, the percentage of white grapes was down to 55 percent. Chenin blanc (the leading grape that had been grown at high yields for brandy) accounted for much of what was lost.

Although official viticultural statistics track the acreage of more than ninety grape varieties in South Africa, the vast majority of the vineyards are planted with just seven varieties: chenin blanc, chardonnay, sauvignon blanc, cabernet sauvignon, merlot, shiraz, and pinotage. The most planted of these seven is still chenin blanc (although, as noted, its acreage is in decline). Lots of South African chenin blanc is pleasant and simple at best. But treasure troves of old chenin blanc vineyards can still be found, and the grapes from these vineyards are often turned into amazingly delicious wines—both dry and sweet.

Then there are sauvignon blanc and chardonnay, which are key grapes for top producers.

South African sauvignons are some of the most distinctive and bold in the world. Wildly tangy, citrusy, minerally, and smoky, they have a gunflint character that's extremely appealing, as the terrific sauvignon blancs from Neil Ellis, Fairview, Saxenburg, and others demonstrate. South African chardonnay, when at its best, is creamy, sophisticated, and rich, without the overwrought buttery or oaky flavors that can often mar New World chardonnays. Hamilton Russell is a perfect example.

The leading red grape is cabernet sauvignon, followed by syrah and merlot. At a basic level, South African cabernets, syrahs, and merlots are unfussy, straightforward wines, often with a smoky character balanced by cherry, plum, and coffee flavors. Higher-priced, higher-quality South African reds are a different story. Wines like Anwilka (a syrah-cabernet

---

WHEN YOU VISIT . . . SOUTH AFRICA

MOST OF THE TOP wine estates in South Africa are located in the Coastal Region, an easy drive from Cape Town. Many of them have beautifully restored buildings in the whitewashed Cape Dutch style, tasting rooms, and exciting restaurants. In fact, some of the best restaurants in the Coastal Region are part of wineries, and the Franschhoek Valley is often called the culinary capital of the Cape.

IF YOU HAVE TIME to visit just one winery, consider making it Groot Constantia. Groot (the word means large) Constantia, with its classic Cape Dutch architecture, embodies South Africa of the past, while its sister winery next door, Klein (which means little) Constantia is a good example of the modern wine-making now taking place in South Africa.

THE NEDERBURG AUCTION

Held each September in Paarl, the Nederburg Auction of rare Cape wines is one of the leading wine auctions in the world, along with Burgundy's Hospices de Beaune, Germany's Kloster Eberbach, and Napa Valley's Auction Napa Valley. The first Nederburg Auction, which was held in 1975, was intended both as a showcase for South African wine and as an incentive for vintners to produce higher-quality wine. Today, the Nederburg Auction is actually two separate auction events—one for the public, and the other a commercial auction, which can only be attended by wine producers. Three community-based charities are the beneficiaries.

---

blend), Saxenburg's Private Collection Shiraz, or Mullineux's Syrah are sophisticated, classy, and could easily be mistaken for high-quality French wines.

And then there's pinotage. Produced almost nowhere else in the world, pinotage was created in 1925 when Cape cinsaut was genetically crossed with pinot noir in a South African laboratory. The grape was first bottled by the Stellenbosch Farmers' Winery in 1959. Today, pinotage has a sort of second-class status in South Africa, and many examples, made without a lot of care or attention to cleanliness, taste lackluster at best (and are packed with brettanomyces—see page 112).

While it may seem surprising, South Africa produces a small quantity of tasty sparkling wines made by the traditional (Champagne) method. South Africa's official name for these traditional-method sparklers is Cap Classique. They are usually made from chardonnay, pinot noir, and pinot meunier, although sometimes from a blend that includes sauvignon blanc and chenin blanc.

THE FOODS OF SOUTH AFRICA

Once, as a young child, I saw a vivid photo in *National Geographic* of a South African ostrich egg. It was frighteningly large. Around it were even more frightening-looking tribesmen. On my first trip to South Africa's wine regions, I wondered if I'd be eating anything other than ostrich omelets. In fact, Cape cooking goes far beyond egg dishes. The culinary bold strokes are a curious blend of Dutch, English, and Malay cookery, Malays having been brought to the earliest Cape settlements as slaves.

Well-loved dishes include *bredie,* a humble Malay stew often made with lamb neck bones and *waterblommetjie,* water lilies. These are a popular South African vegetable and taste like a cross between artichokes and green beans. They grow wild on the surface of roadside ponds. Somewhat more exciting than *bredie* is *bobotie,* best described as Malay shepherd's pie. In the tastiest *boboties,* chopped meat is spiked with cinnamon, curry, and raisins, and it is frequently served with a chutney of dried peaches and apricots.

South Africa is, not surprisingly, a land of extraordinary game. All sorts of deer and antelope are roasted and made into pies. During the famous South African *braai* (rhymes with cry), a traditional, outdoor Sunday barbecue, an amazing number of meats are grilled—guinea fowl, several types of antelope and deer, plus pork, Karoo lamb, beef, and ostrich, which tastes remarkably like sirloin steak but is leaner and lower in fat than chicken. (The Cape alone has almost three hundred ostrich farms.) In the wine regions, the meats are grilled over a fire fueled with branches pruned from grapevines. A *braai* may also include *potjiekos* (pot food), layers of vegetables, onions, and beef, cooked all afternoon in a pot over the fire; and *potbrood,* bread baked in a cast-iron pot over the fire.

In restaurants, the bread that is virtually always served is a sprouted wheat bread that harkens back to the Cape's Dutch heritage. Any number of dishes will be accompanied by chips (potato chips) or slap chips (French fries).

Poised as it is between two oceans, South Africa is famed for its seafood, including what outsiders call South African lobster tails and the South Africans call crayfish. Both are incorrect. The creature in question is actually a type of spiny lobster with a wide tail but no claws. Then there are *perlemoen* (abalone), mussels, calamari, clams, oysters, and several kinds of deep-sea fish, such as *snoek* (pronounced snook), a large fish related to the barracuda family. Smoked *snoek* pâté shows up everywhere.

South African desserts are humble—even now in keeping with the customs of the earliest settlers, for whom things like cream, chocolate, and fresh fruit were rarities. The two homiest desserts are *koeksusters* (a dish that definitely requires careful pronunciation)—deep-fried dough, recooked in sugar syrup—and milk tarts, essentially rich pastry tarts filled with cinnamon-spiked milk custard.

On South Africa's beloved public holiday—National Braai Day (September 24)—just about every meat you can think of gets thrown on the grill.

The South African Wines to Know

WHITES

FAIRVIEW

SAUVIGNON BLANC | DARLING

100% sauvignon blanc

The vivid, briny, oceanic aroma of Fairview's remarkably inexpensive sauvignon blanc reminds me of cracking open a fresh, minerally oyster. But then waves of other cooling aromas and flavors follow—limes, snowpeas, grapefruits, guava, hedgerows, and that distinctive gunflint character that so many South African sauvignons possess. Fairview is owned by the Back family, originally immigrants from Lithuania who arrived in South Africa in 1902.

NEIL ELLIS

SAUVIGNON BLANC | GROENEKLOOF

100% sauvignon blanc

Decades ago, some of the original Neil Ellis sauvignon blancs were bullet trains of outrageous, smoky green flavors. But the winery has matured and its style has evolved. Now these sauvignons are among the most lovely and sophisticated in South Africa. They open with fresh mineral flavors and then take on a crisp, salty, tangy character (rather like good Sancerre), and finally finish with an ever-so-gentle creaminess. The vines that produce the grapes for this wine are planted in decomposed red granite as "bush vines" (without trellising).

HAMILTON RUSSELL VINEYARDS

CHARDONNAY | HEMEL-EN-AARDE VALLEY

100% chardonnay

A wonderful example of a full-bodied, New World–style chardonnay, with custard and crème brûlée-like flavors and a toasty, nutty edge. And while the wine is palate-coating and long, a background of crisp citrus and fresh pear notes keeps the creaminess in check. One of the most southerly wine estates in Africa, and one of the closest to the sea, Hamilton Russell is located in the cool, maritime Hemel-en-Aarde Valley, just behind the old fishing village of Hermanus, southeast of Cape Town.

DeMORGENZON

CHENIN BLANC | WESTERN CAPE

100% chenin blanc

In a sea of commercial chenin blancs, this one from DeMorgenzon is an artisanal beauty. The rich, caramel-apple flavors are laced with notes of whipped cream, roasted nuts, spices, and sea salt. A beautiful crispness underlies the wine, lifting it up and giving it incredible vibrancy. And don't miss the lush DeMorgenzon chardonnay, another of the winery's several exemplary wines. Owners Wendy and Hylton Appelbaum pipe Baroque music through their vineyards twenty-four hours a day, believing that the music exerts a powerful positive influence on the ripening process. The winery is named after DeMorgenzon, a small, high-altitude area (now the location of one of its vineyards) that is the first place within the Stellenbosch Valley to see the sun each day. DeMorgenzon means "the morning sun" in Afrikaans.

REDS

MULLINEUX

SYRAH | SWARTLAND

100% syrah

Mullineux's fantastic syrah could easily appear in a blind tasting of Rhône Valley syrahs and never be caught out. Wildly gamy, smoky, and peppery, it's packed with the vivid charcuterie flavors that many syrah lovers go mad for. But that's just for openers. Next, loads of briary chaparral flavors appear, plus notes of resiny sage, dried lavender, and black licorice. Yet for all this unleashed, untamed wildness, the wine also has a rich core of soft blackberry fruit. Like most great syrahs, this one loves to unwind in the presence of oxygen, so it will be even more charming if poured from a decanter. Husband and wife Chris and Andrea Mullineux (their surname is an adaptation of Moulineaux, French for "water mill") are both winemakers.

ANWILKA

STELLENBOSCH

48% shiraz, 42% cabernet sauvignon, 10% merlot

Quite possibly the single best red of South Africa, Anwilka has a majestic structure and is a distinctive synthesis of two great grapes (with a little merlot thrown in to knit the flavors together). From the cabernet, the wine gets its rich, red currant, green tobacco, and black plum aromas and flavors. From the syrah come sweet, meaty flavors, like skirt steak sitting in a pool of meat juices. Begun in the late 1990s, the winery had an impeccably talented team of owners: Lowell Jooste (the former co-owner of Klein Constantia), Hubert de Boüard (co-owner of Bordeaux's Château Angélus, in Saint-Emilion), and Bruno Prats (former owner of Bordeaux's Château Cos d'Estournel, in Saint-Estèphe). All three men remain involved with the project, although Anwilka has since merged with Klein Constantia and has new owners: Czech-born Zdeněk Bakala, a United States investment banker, and Charles Harman, a British investment banker.

SWEET WINES

MULLINEUX

STRAW WINE | SWARTLAND

100% chenin blanc

The chenin blanc grapes for this artisanal wine come from thirty-plus-year-old vines growing in stony schist and shale soils on Riebeek Kastel Mountain, and forty-plus-year-old vines growing in decomposed granite soils on Paardeberg Mountain. The young husband-and-wife winemaking team of Chris and Andrea Mullineux place the harvested grapes on racks outdoors and allow them to dry and partially shrivel in the South African sun for three weeks. The result is an exquisite straw wine that is a poem to apricots—not to mention to orange marmalade, quince, and papaya. The wine's dizzying vividness keeps it remarkably light and fresh on the palate, setting it apart from many sweet wines.

KLEIN CONSTANTIA

VIN DE CONSTANCE | CONSTANTIA

100% muscat de Frontignan

Klein Constantia (Little Constantia) is part of the famous Constantia wine estate founded in 1685. Constantia has historically been known for Vin de Constance, a luscious dessert wine made from muscat blanc à petits grains grapes (known as muscat de Frontignan in South Africa). The wine rose to become one of the most sought-after dessert wines in all of Europe, ordered by the case by Napoléon Bonaparte. And the wine remains extraordinary today. To begin, the color is unreal. Filaments of orange and amber light glint off the surface of the wine like tiny bolts of lightning. The ethereal apricot sweetness and citrus-skin bitterness detonate on the palate, then seem to float up in clouds of lingering richness. Yet for all its opulence, Klein Constantia is impossibly light and fresh. It is wine as a halo.

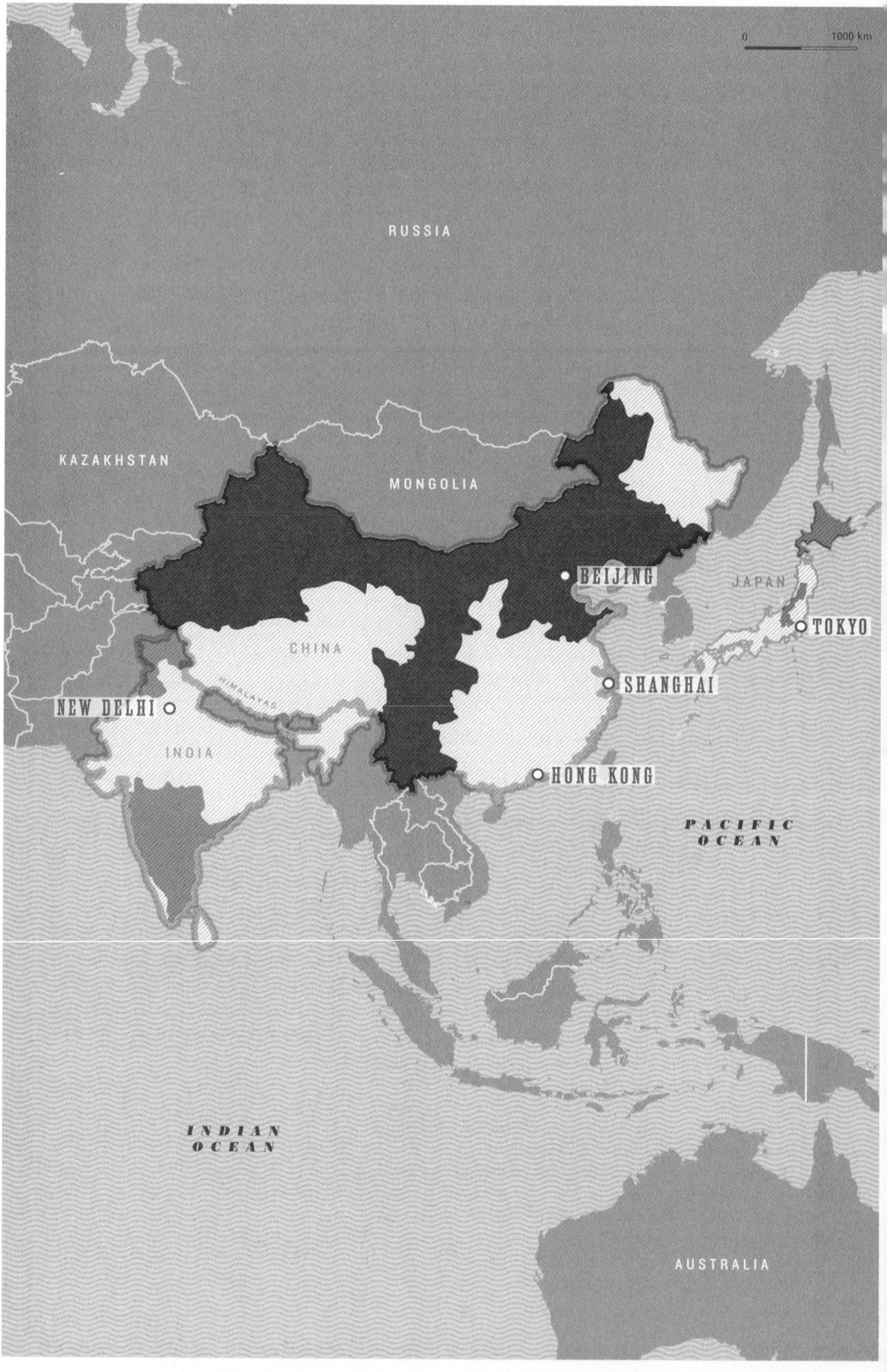
0
1000 km
RUSSIA
KAZAKHSTAN
MONGOLIA
BEIJING
JAPAN
TOKYO
CHINA
SHANGHAI
HIMALAYAS
NEW DELHI
INDIA
HONG KONG
PACIFIC OCEAN
INDIAN OCEAN
AUSTRALIA

ASIA

sia's modern wine industries have sprung on the scene so quickly and, in some cases, are evolving so fast that they almost defy a book author's ability to write about them. Yet wine is produced in China, Japan, and India, as well as in rather astonishing places such as Thailand, Vietnam, Iran, Taiwan, Myanmar, Cambodia, Korea, and even Kazakhstan, Kyrgyzstan, and several of the other "stans." In the pages that follow, I have done my best to explore Asia's three main wine-producing countries, for these are places—China especially—that knowledgeable wine drinkers will increasingly want to know about. No entity has stated the case more succinctly than the prestigious London-based wine firm Berry Brothers & Rudd, which predicts that within fifty years, the quality of Chinese wine will rival that of Bordeaux.

◄ The shaded areas of this map indicate entire areas where wine is made. The actual vineyard areas are smaller and scattered throughout them.

Female construction workers carry rocks on their backs in Yunnan Province, one of China's newer wine regions.

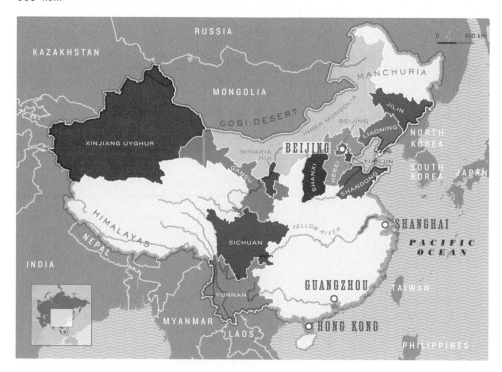

CHINA

A decade ago, most wine drinkers in the Western world rarely would have come across the words *China* and *wine* in the same sentence. Times have changed. As of 2012, China was already, in volume, the fifth leading wine-consuming nation, according to the OIV (*L'Organisation Internationale de la Vigne et du Vin*), the intergovernmental organization that tracks global wine statistics. That, perhaps, was not entirely surprising; China, with fully 19 percent of the world's population, is the most populous country on earth. But the fact that, by 2012, China was also fifth in world wine *production*—now, that was something almost no Westerner saw coming.

For all of its newness on the modern wine scene, China has had a long history of wine-making. Numerous archaeological findings have revealed evidence of an ancient wine culture here, and in the mid-1990s, a joint American-Chinese archaeological team uncovered yet more evidence—this time, dating wine production in Shandong Province back to 2500 B.C. At two sites near the city of Rizhao, more than two hundred clay vessels contained the residue of wines made from grapes, as well as from rice and from honey (mead).

But by the end of the Bronze Age in China (around 700 B.C.) grape-based wines (known as *pútáojiŭ*) had been almost completely overshadowed by a range of alcoholic beverages made from grains like millet and sorghum and from fruits like lychees and Asian plums, and these beverages remained cultural mainstays

▲ The shaded areas of this map indicate entire provinces where wine is made. The actual vineyard areas are smaller and scattered throughout the province.

until modern times. Even as of the 1970s, China was a devoted beer- and spirits-drinking society. The World Health Organization estimated that beer and spirits made up 99 percent of alcohol consumed in China in 1970. Today, along with beer, the two most popular alcoholic drinks are *baijiu* and *huangjiu*. The first, distilled principally from sorghum, is the world's most consumed spirit, and, at 40 to 60 percent alcohol by volume, packs a powerful punch. The second, popularly known as "yellow wine," is usually fermented from rice and millet.

How, then, to account for the current explosion of the modern Chinese grape-wine industry? Here is an extremely brief sketch of China's history, to put that wine revolution in context.

The Chinese Empire was established around 221 B.C., when the Qin Dynasty first conquered several states and peoples, uniting them into a single entity. Numerous dynasties followed, over the next two thousand plus years, until 1911, when the Republic of China overthrew the last dynasty, the Qing Dynasty (also known as the Manchu Dynasty), which had ruled since 1644. The Republic of China went on to govern the mainland until 1949. After the defeat of the Empire of Japan in World War II, the Republic of China devolved into fractious internal fighting between its two main parties—the Communist Party and the Kuomintang nationalist party. The Communist Party prevailed, forming the People's Republic of China (PRC) in Beijing on October 1, 1949 (the Kuomintang relocated the Republic of China government to Taiwan). In 1978, the PRC initiated a series of major economic reforms, as a result of which China has become one of the world's fastest-growing major economies.

In the 2000s, China's rapid modernization shifted into warp speed. Living standards among the country's 1.35 billion people soared, and the percentage of wealthy Chinese sky-rocketed. (Of the ten countries with the most millionaires, China is third—after the U.S. and Japan—and Taiwan ranks seventh; Hong Kong, tenth.) With their burgeoning wealth, Chinese consumers grew increasingly fascinated by Western culture, Western lifestyle,

THE NAME CHINA

*T*he word China *(中国)is derived from the Persian word Chin (چین), which is the Sanskrit word Cīna (चीन). It was first recorded in 1516, in the journal of the Portuguese explorer Duarte Barbosa, and later translated into English by Richard Eden, in 1555. It is commonly thought that the word is derived from the name of the Qin Dynasty, the first imperial dynasty of China, lasting from 221 to 206 B.C.*

and Western luxury goods. The stage was set for fine wine.

Since 2008, China's almost over-the-top passion for wine has been head-spinning.

WINE CONSUMPTION doubled in five years between 2008 and 2013.

IN 2011, A CHINESE BUYER paid a record $541,000 for twenty-five cases of Château Lafite Rothschild at a Christie's auction.

CHINA IS ON TARGET to be the world's largest consumer of wine by volume as of 2016.

ACKER MERRALL & CONDIT, the world's largest auction house for wine, set 483 new world records in Hong Kong for the prices paid for wines sold at auction in 2013. The majority of these new records were related to the sale of Burgundy wines, as Hong Kong has, since 2011, become the most important auction market worldwide for both Bordeaux and Burgundy.

As for its own domestic production, the statistics are equally stunning. From 2000 to 2012, wine production in China nearly doubled, to 393 million gallons (14.9 million hectoliters). That made China, as noted, fifth in the world in wine production. Importantly, these statistics come from the authoritative

LOST IN TRANSLATION—
THE CASSIS CONUNDRUM

In the late 1990s, my wine classes in California often included a handful of students from Asia. They were studious, attentive, and polite. But the teacher in me knew something wasn't clicking. Finally one young Chinese man confided he'd never tasted a raspberry or blackberry in his life, and by the way, what was cassis? For days, I'd been comparing the flavor of wines to fruits, flowers, and foods he'd never even heard of.

For wine professionals in the Asian headquarters of the big auction houses, such as Sotheby's and Christie's, the lack of a universal wine language is painfully apparent. Not only is it next to impossible to translate the names of European wineries into Chinese characters based on the Mandarin pronunciations of the syllables in the names, but tasting notes written by European wine experts often make no sense to Chinese buyers. Accordingly, some Chinese wine experts have now begun the daunting task of reinterpreting the descriptions of famous wines using locally understood flavors. So, a great Burgundy? Forget the cherries and earth. Think, a hint of *dang gui* (a traditional Chinese medicinal herb), a suggestion of fermented cabbage, and maybe some notes of Chiuchow stock (an aromatic, soy-based liquid for poaching meats).

OIV, which counts only *grape* wine production. (Independent Chinese statistics are next to impossible to come by, and those that are available don't appear to distinguish between wine made from grapes and wine made from rice or from other fruits like plums.) But even the OIV numbers must be taken with a grain of salt, for there's another problem, too—and it exists everywhere in Asia. The wine that producers bottle (and thus the wine that is counted as "production") doesn't come from Chinese grapes exclusively. China, like all Asian wine-producing countries, buys a considerable amount of bulk wine and grape concentrate from its Pacific Rim neighbors, Australia, South America, and North America, not to mention from parts of Europe as well. As a result, Chinese wine production—while certainly enormous—is not entirely related to Chinese-grown grapes.

The Chinese wine industry is currently made up of approximately seven hundred wineries that fall into two camps: extremely large producers of inexpensive, utterly basic wine (companies such as Dynasty, China Great Wall, and Changyu) and newer estates making expensive wines targeted at affluent Chinese consumers (in 2012, Chateau Hansen, based on the edge of the Gobi Desert, in Inner Mongolia, released the first vintage of its top cabernet sauvignon—called Red Camel—for just under $700 a bottle). As for quality, the cheap wines from the very large producers have mostly verged on dismal. Wines from the cutting-edge wineries are far better. Indeed, some of these wines are so good they could easily pass for a California or Bordeaux wine in a blind tasting.

China's love affair with fine wine began as, and remains, mostly a love affair with Bordeaux and Burgundy (the Chinese mania for Château Lafite-Rothschild has no equal, and the Domaine de la Romanée-Conti could easily sell its entire production here). Accordingly, many of the newer, high-end wineries are aesthetically influenced by France. Some, for example, are designed to look like Bordeaux châteaux and have the word *château* in their

All over China, impressive wineries (and the roads to them) are being built by tens of thousands of people working around the clock. Wine regions that would have taken centuries to develop in Europe have often sprung up within five years in China.

names; others are French-Chinese joint ventures. A prominent example is a partnership announced in 2009 between Château Lafite-Rothschild and Citic Group (China's largest state-owned investment company), to make wine in Shandong Province. Another is the joint venture between Champagne producer Moët Hennessy and SOE Nongken, which resulted in a $5.5 million sparkling wine facility (and impressive wine) in Ningxia in 2013.

THE LAND, THE GRAPES, AND THE VINEYARDS

At 3.7 million square miles (9.6 million square kilometers), China is the fourth largest country on Earth. Its borders stretch from its 9,000 miles (14,500 kilometers) of Pacific Ocean coastline in the east to the border with Kyrgyzstan, Tajikistan, and Pakistan, 3,100 miles (5,000 kilometers) away in the west. In the north, China touches Russia, Mongolia, and Kazakhstan, and in the south, the (contested) Chinese territory of Tibet lies along the border with India. Within this vast country are

some twenty-two provinces, five autonomous regions, and two self-governing special administrative regions (Hong Kong and Macau).

Collectively, these possess virtually every type of climate and geography—from subtropical forests to subarctic scrubland, and from flat deserts to some of the tallest mountains in the world (the Himalayas include ten of the tallest mountain peaks on earth). As you can imagine, much of the country is either too muggy and hot (monsoons are a problem) or too excruciatingly cold to sustain viticulture. Even in several existing wine regions, vines must be "weather-protected"—that is, banked up with soil in winter to prevent the roots and some of the trunk tissue from being fatally damaged by deep freezes. In parts of Inner Mongolia and Ningxia, where vines must often survive temperatures as low as −20°F (−29°C), a local viticultural technique goes a step further. Called deep-ditch cultivation, it starts with vines planted in trenches 3 to 5 feet (.9 to 1.5 meters) deep. Each year, soil is added to the trench in order to more deeply bury the newest roots, which are closest to the surface of the land. Meanwhile, the deepest, main roots are progressively buried deeper and deeper, allowing them to resist the damage caused by subzero soil temperatures.

Women tending the roses at Changyu Global Winery outside of Bejing. All over China's wine regions, women do a large share of the agricultural and landscaping work.

As of 2012, vineyards were spread over 1.41 million acres (570,600 hectares) in China (double the area in 2000). By comparison, Spain had 2.5 million acres (1 million hectares, the world's most); France, 1.97 million acres (797,200 hectares); while the U.S., with 1 million acres (404,700 hectares), had fewer than China. (But here's a critically important fact: The vineyard acreage for China includes table grapes—not just wine grapes.

China's vineyards are planted with only a small number of grape varieties that would be recognized in the West. New plantings are often of red grapes (a culturally preferred color), including cabernet sauvignon, merlot, cabernet franc, syrah, and what is called cabernet gernischt (DNA profiling reveals this to be identical to carmenère) for still wines and pinot noir for sparkling wines. Among whites, chardonnay (largely for sparkling wines) is planted along with a small amount of chenin blanc, sémillon, and a few other whites. Cold-climate varieties such as rkatsiteli and saperavi, both successful in Russia and the Republic of Georgia, are also planted. In addition to these classic wine grapes, a number of table grapes are planted and used for wine, including muscat Hamburg, niunai ("cow's nipples"), kyoho, Thompson seedless, and longyan ("dragon eyes"). And new hybrid grape varieties are being developed to withstand central and northern China's brutal winters.

As of this writing, China does not have a formal system of delineating appellations. (Because of that, most of the key wine regions are actually administrative provinces.) The top wine regions are clustered in five parts of the country:

THE NORTHEAST (including the wine regions Shandong, Hebei, Beijing, Tianjin, Liaoning, Jilin, and Shanxi)

EAST CENTRAL (Ningxia Hui and Gansu)

NORTH CENTRAL (Inner Mongolia)

FAR WEST (Xinjiang Uyghur)

FAR SOUTH (Yunnan and Sichuan)

Here are brief notes on each, as well as wineries located in each. (Note that many wineries have a presence in several regions.)

SHANDONG PROVINCE

Located on the Shandong Peninsula, on Bohai Bay in northeastern China, Shandong has a maritime climate and, despite summer storms, is fairly well suited to European *Vitis vinifera* grapes. This is China's main wine region by both volume and value of the wines produced, and it was the first well-established region in the modern Chinese wine era. Importantly, this is where Château Lafite Rothschild established its joint venture with the state-owned investment firm Citic Group, and there are a number of other cutting-edge wineries (Chateau Reifeng-Auzias and Qingdao Great River Hill Winery) as well as large players like Changyu Pioneer Wine Company and China's largest wine producer, the China Great Wall Wine Company.

HEBEI PROVINCE

Relatively near Shandong, and also benefiting from a maritime climate thanks to Bohai Bay, Hebei is China's second region in terms of sales. This is where some of the first dry whites and dry reds were made. Historically, off-dry reds made from longyan table grapes were also local specialties. Well-known wineries

The ornate gates outside the city of Yinchuan, the capital of Ningxia, which intends to be the "Napa Valley of China" by 2020.

here include China Great Wall Wine Company, Chateau SunGod, Chateau Red Leaf, and Sheng Tang Winery.

BEIJING

Beijing is geographically located within Hebei Province, but it is considered its own "direct controlled" municipality. Because of Beijing's prominence as the political and cultural capital of China, it has attracted small wineries with strong orientations to wine tourism. However, if land were not scarce, this could well be an important larger wine region, for the climate is fairly dry and sunny in summer. Wineries include Dragon Seal, Chateau Bolongbao, and Fengshou Wine Co.

TIANJIN

Located just south of Beijing, Tianjin is well known as the location of one of the first Chinese-French joint ventures—the Sino-French Joint-Venture Dynasty Winery Ltd. (Cognac producer Rémy Martin was the French partner). Opened in 1980, the company makes wines and brandies. The Dynasty wines, as they are simply known, have been served at countless Chinese state banquets.

LIAONING PROVINCE

North of Beijing, on the border with North Korea, Liaoning Province is known, amazingly enough, for icewines made from Vidal grapes in the Golden Ice Wine Valley, notably by the wine company Changyu. Otherwise, the province is one of China's most industrial, with heavy industries built on iron, steel, coal mining, petroleum, and natural gas.

JILIN PROVINCE

Jilin Province, located north of Liaoning, in what was once called Manchuria, is known for native grapes of the species *Vitis amurensis*. This species of grapes is amazingly cold-tolerant, and thus has been the source of plant-breeding material for Chinese scientists hoping to cross it with *Vitis vinifera* varieties.

Gansu Province, on the ancient "Silk Road" of central China, has a small number of wineries, though the rugged terrain and hot climate present challenges.

Wineries include Tonghua Grape Wine Co. and Changbaishan Wine Holding Co.

SHANXI PROVINCE

Vineyards here are concentrated in the Taiyuan Basin, and the wineries are small. But Shanxi rose to fame on the success of Grace Vineyard, perhaps China's first "cult winery." Founded in 1997 by industrialist C. K. Chan, Grace Vineyard was taken over by Chan's daughter, Judy Chan Leissner, when she was just twenty-four years old. Grace Vineyards makes more than a dozen wines, including cabernet sauvignon, cabernet franc, and merlot, the vines for which were brought in from a Bordeaux nursery. The top wine—called Chairman's Reserve—is a mainstay on expensive hotel and restaurant wine lists in China. In addition to Grace Vineyard, Shanxi is the location of another high-end winery—Chateau Rongzi. Founded in 2007, Rongzi achieved almost instant credibility by convincing Jean-Claude Berrouet (former winemaker of Bordeaux's ultrafamous Château Petrus) to be its wine consultant.

NINGXIA HUI AUTONOMOUS REGION

Sometimes referred to as the Napa of China, Ningxia (as it is simply known) has a semi-arid climate conducive to growing grapes, and water from the nearby Yellow River provides irrigation. Considerable investment in the region—both by wineries large and small and by the Chinese government in the form of infrastructure—have placed Ningxia (especially the region within it, known as Helan Mountain East Foothills) at the top of the hierarchy of China's most impressive wine regions. Wineries here include Moët Hennessy's Chandon China (the first Chinese sparkling wine house), Helan Qingxue, Zhi Hui Yuan Shi, Silver Heights, Lux Regis, Domaine de Arômes, Chateau Yunmo, Chateau Changyu Moser XV, Lanny Chateau, Domaine Helan Mountain, and many others.

GANSU PROVINCE

A fairly isolated, cool region, Gansu has several wineries, although the province is not thought to be among those with the most promising futures. Ripening can be a difficult process here. The main wineries include Mogao Winery, Qilian Wine Company, Zixuan Wine, and Grand Dragon.

THE DARK SIDE: COUNTERFEIT WINES

In the 2000s, the Chinese frenzy to buy ultra-expensive wines created another sort of frenzy—a whirlwind counterfeit industry, more extensive and skilled than anything that has ever before existed in the global wine industry. As of 2013, industry analysts estimated that as much as 50 percent of the foreign wine sold in China may have been fake. Certain individuals among a small army of Chinese bottle scavengers (aka "professional bottle recyclers") have been known to pay over $300 for a single empty bottle of Château Lafite-Rothschild or Château Pétrus. After their tasting events, auction houses in China now routinely smash empty bottles with a hammer, to prevent the bottles from ending up on the black market and being refilled with cheap wine or worse, a concoction of citric acid, flavoring essence, and food coloring. Of course, skillful counterfeiters have also taken another tack. Instead of using authentic bottles with real labels, many have simply bought facsimile bottles and then replicated the labels of great estates, dispersing the fakes among genuine bottles in wine shops all over Asia.

INNER MONGOLIA

Inner Mongolia has a long history of raisin production and winemaking, especially in the area near Wuhai. The days during the short growing season are hot; the nights, cold. Sunlight is intense and humidity is low. So far so good. But the extremely cold, snowless winter means that the ground freezes hard and deep. As a result, much of the leading research on winter-hardy grape varieties and cold-climate viticultural techniques like deep-ditch cultivation have happened here. As is easily imagined, researchers in Inner Mongolia are also at the forefront of developing new, extremely cold-tolerant hybrids, especially of grapes belonging to the species *Vitis vinifera* and *Vitis amurensis* (thus far, the resulting grape varieties have been given names like Red Wine Grape #1 and Inner Mongolia #1). There also exists here a fascinating *Vitis vinifera* variety called Tuo Xian, thought to be one of the most cold-tolerant *vinifera* varieties in existence. Its pink berries and huge, foot-long clusters are amazing, but the wine from these grapes is rather basic. Finally, Inner Mongolia is known for a special drink—Tuo Xian white wine infused with fresh flowers of the *Osmanthus fragrans* shrub. The drink, said to have a strong, floral cherry aroma, is usually sweet and is served

Wa Ta Si—*The Temple of the Five Pagodas in Inner Mongolia, where there is a long history of winemaking.*

Walking among the tall flowers in Yunnan Province. Some vineyards in the province are planted at an altitude of 10,000 feet (3,000 meters).

as a highly aromatic dessert wine. Among the top wineries here are Chateau Hansen, Viction Winery, and In the Clouds Winery.

XINJIANG UYGHUR AUTONOMOUS REGION

Originally famous for its raisins (frequently used culinarily by the largely Muslim population), Xinjiang (as it is simply known) now has the largest wine grape production in China. The region—in far western China—is extremely remote, and while vineyard acreage has grown quickly over the past several years, transporting products out of the region is difficult and expensive. Still, it was through Xinjiang—one of the ancient Silk Road transit points—that *Vitis vinifera* vines (and many foods) came into China from Europe. The region is also noteworthy for a special drink of the Uyghur people—*musailaisi* wine. Local *Vitis vinifera* table grapes (munage and

hashihaer) are cooked with roses, wild berries, saffron, and cloves, along with (sometimes) velvet antler, pigeon blood, and roasted lamb. After cooking, the mixture is strained, poured into jars, and allowed to ferment for about forty days. Brownish in color, and both sweet and bitter, *musailaisi* is considered to have very positive health benefits, and it certainly seems like an antidote to a cold night on the edge of Mongolia. But of course, it is also a treasured part of the local Uyghur heritage, and to accept some upon being offered a cup is to be a courteous (not to mention adventurous) guest.

Main wineries in Xinjiang include Citic Guoan Wine, Xinjiang Xiangdu Winery, Chateau Loulan, Niya, Skyline of Gobi, Château Zhongfei Winery, China Great Wall Wine Company, and others.

YUNNAN PROVINCE AND SICHUAN PROVINCE

The two wine provinces of Yunnan and Sichuan are often mentioned together because of their proximity along the border with Tibet. Despite their low latitude in southern China, both regions have altitude in their favor. Altitude with a capital A. Vineyards here on the 10,000-foot (3,000-meter) Diqing Plateau are more than twice as high as the highest vineyards in the foothills of the Andes in Argentina. Thus, the climate in these provinces tends to be cool. Also because of altitude, both areas benefit from intense luminosity, leading to efficient photosynthesis and ripe grapes. The hilly terrain is a challenge, however, so vineyards exist as small fields dotting the mountains, rather than large tracts of land. Yunnan and Sichuan are very new wine regions in China, but they have attracted a considerable amount of investment. Wineries include the Shangri-La Winery, the Spirit of Highland Winery, Kangding Hong Winery, Hongxing Leader Winery, and AoYun by Moët Hennessy.

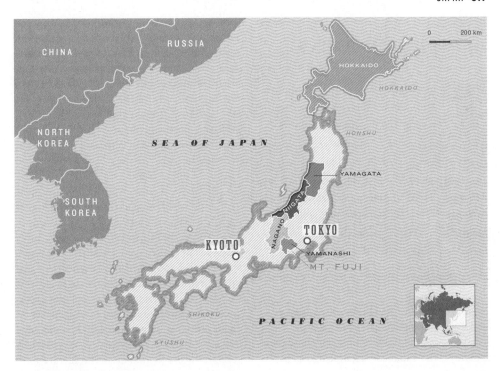

JAPAN

onsidered one of the most gastronomically sophisticated countries in the world, Japan was the first Asian country to fully embrace European wines and develop a strong connoisseurship of them. In contrast to China, where wine education is growing but still in its infancy, Japan boasts countless wine schools, numerous wine experts, a flourishing wine book industry, and a thriving sommelier association (ten thousand strong). Indeed, as far back as 1995, Japanese sommelier Shinya Tasaki was named the most knowledgeable and skillful sommelier in the world when he won the Sommelier World Championship.

Thanks to their strong affinity for Western luxury goods (including fine wine), Japan and China do share spiraling wine consumption. Between 2000 and 2013, Japan's total wine consumption increased 28 percent, according to the OIV, although, on a per-person, per-year basis, the amount remains relatively small. Yet Japanese consumption has historically been somewhat higher than Chinese consumption (.72 gallons/2.73 liters per capita in Japan versus .35 gallons/1.32 liters per capita in China).

In fact, for many urban Japanese, the culture of consuming wine is now fully integrated into modern living. Imported wines from across the world and of every level of quality are now widely available at diverse locations from high-end restaurants and standing wine bars to conveyor-belt sushi restaurants, convenience stores, and roadside vending machines.

But despite its early and avid adoption of imported wine, Japan has struggled to

▲ The shaded areas of this map indicate entire prefectures where wine is made. The actual vineyard areas are smaller and scattered throughout the prefecture.

THE NAME JAPAN

*T*he English word **Japan** *derives from the Chinese pronunciation of the Japanese name,* 日本, *which in Japanese is pronounced Nippon (formally) or Nihon (more casually). Japanese people refer to themselves as Nihonjin (*日本人*) and to their language as Nihongo (*日本語*). Both Nippon and Nihon mean "sun-origin," and are often translated as* **Land of the Rising Sun.**

establish its own domestic wine industry—and for good reason. At 145,925 square miles (377,900 square kilometers; about the size of Norway), the Japanese archipelago is made up of 6,852 islands that sit between a huge landmass (China) and a huge body of water (the Pacific Ocean). As a result, Japan is buffeted by erratic extremes of climate. When it isn't freezing cold, it's often humid or rainy. Indeed, Siberian winds and typhoons (along with occasional monsoons and hurricanes) all take their toll—often during the growing season or at harvest time. And then there's the topography itself. Japan, the product of volcanoes, is so steeply mountainous that little usable land is available. Take some of that for cities and towns to support the dense (126 million) population, and some of it for other types of agriculture (such as rice), and what's left for vineyards is tiny and massively expensive, if it's even suitable for viticulture. Yet, for all of this, Japan does have a domestic wine industry, and we will explore it in a moment.

It is commonly believed that the first wines were brought to Japan in the sixteenth century by Portuguese Jesuit missionaries, as gifts for the feudal lords of Kyushu. However, the modern wine industry takes its beginnings from the 1860s, during the so-called Meiji Restoration, when the state was centralized under one emperor, and Japan began to seek out Western ideas and emulate Western lifestyles. The consumption of alcohol evolved to become a more regular custom, even for those outside the leisure classes. Most importantly, the development of commercial agriculture other than rice (or mulberry for the declining silk industry) became a focus. Establishing fruit growing—and later winemaking—became a stated national priority. The Japanese government sent technicians to the United States and Europe to collect hundreds of grape varieties for trials and to study winemaking practices. The amount of land planted with table grapes rapidly expanded. In the Kofu Basin north of Mount Fuji in Yamanashi Prefecture, table grape farmers using earthenware containers and second-hand sake tanks began fermenting their harvested but unsold grapes to make wine for personal consumption. Many of these operations were later legitimized to collect tax revenues, and thus began a small Japanese wine industry. Mercian and Suntory—the two biggest producers in Yamanashi Prefecture (still one of the most important locations for vineyards)—began making wines in 1877 and 1909, respectively.

The grapes used during the late nineteenth century included koshu (more on this soon) and hardy varieties grown in cold, wet areas

The proud Mt. Fuji, which can be seen from the vineyards of Yamanashi Prefecture.

Nagano Prefecture, west of Tokyo, one of Japan's newer wine regions. Here, the prefecture's Matsumoto Castle, officially a "National Treasure of Japan."

on the East Coast of the United States, such as the French-American hybrid Delaware and the American cross Niagara. Later, grapes that could adapt to the Japanese climate were developed in Japan. The best known of these—muscat Bailey A—is a red table grape developed in 1927 by Zenbei Kawakami, at the Iwanohara Winery in Niigate Prefecture. A cross of Bailey and muscat Hamburg (both of which are crosses themselves), muscat Bailey A produces a sweet, candy-ish, grape-juicy red wine that is popular on the domestic market. Drier versions are often blended with imported bulk wine (such as cabernet sauvignon and merlot) to make simple red wines. (Like all Asian wine-producing countries, Japan imports a considerable amount of bulk wine and grape concentrate.)

By the 1970s and 1980s, however, Japan had at least some success in developing sophisticated viticultural techniques that allowed for the production of Japanese-grown merlot, chardonnay, and other popular *Vitis vinifera* varieties, even in humid conditions and in areas without significant periods of sun.

Among these techniques were planting vines like hedges on steep mountain terraces for maximum sun exposure and constructing high, elevated trellises or pergolas that kept the fruit as much as 10 feet (3 meters) off the ground for maximum air ventilation. Alas, for the most part, both techniques encouraged quantity over quality, and thus met with only partial success. As a result, in the last two decades, grape-growing for fine wine continues to shift beyond traditional areas and toward cool but sunnier and somewhat drier areas such as Nagano Prefecture and Yamagata Prefecture, as well as on the far northern island of Hokkaido.

One grape that has been quite successful in Yamanashi Prefecture, however, has been koshu, a *Vitis vinifera* pinkish-hued, humidity-tolerant white grape with a long, somewhat mysterious history in Japan. Before it was possible to identify grapes by DNA typing, legend had it that koshu was a cross of a native, wild Japanese grape with a *vinifera* variety brought from the Caucasus to China and then, approximately a thousand years ago, by Buddhist

Yamagata Prefecture is a wine region facing the Sea of Japan. Here, the prefecture's Yamadera Temple, reachable by a thousand-step climb, is where the famous haiku poet Matsuo Bashō wrote and worked.

monks, to Japan. But DNA typing has revealed no relationships with other known varieties, and thus koshu's origins remain unknown. Today, koshu is experiencing a newfound popularity as the hip wine of young professionals. Still versions are dry, delicate, and crisp (not unlike Muscadet), and there are sparkling versions as well, which I find even more attractive.

Ranking forty-seventh in the world in vineyard land, Japan has some 45,000 acres (18,200 hectares) of vines, most of which are planted on two islands—Honshu, the largest island, where Tokyo is located; and Hokkaido, the most northern island. The wine districts of Honshu include the prefectures of Yamanashi, Nagano, and Yamagata. As noted, in Yamanashi, southeast of Tokyo, most of the vineyards are planted in the Kofu Basin, with spectacular views of Mount Fuji towering above. The growing season here is one of the longest in Japan, and the relatively low level of rainfall is a huge asset (Mount Fuij provides the convenient rain shadow effect). Nagano, northwest of the capital, is located farther inland, on mountain foothills over 2,000 feet (600 meters) in altitude. Yamagata, in the far northern part of Honshu, is a mountainous region facing the Sea of Japan. Despite its humid summers, the

autumns are dry, and the region has begun to produce good-quality merlot and chardonnay. Then there's Hokkaido, Japan's northernmost and coldest island. Despite the cold, it is fairly well suited to viticulture, in part because the growing season is not dominated by bouts of rain. Interestingly, cool-climate grapes associated with northern Italy, Germany, and Austria have done well here, including Kerner, Müller-Thurgau, riesling, and Zweigelt.

Finally, a few words about the structure of the domestic wine industry. Japanese vineyards—especially in the traditional areas—are usually small and owned by independent growers, each of whom farms numerous noncontiguous, tiny plots of vines, along with other crops. These farmers typically concentrate on higher-valued table grapes, but also sell their wine grapes to large drinks companies which then ferment the grapes to make Japanese wines sourced from Japanese grapes (often koshu). Though a source of local pride, such wine is, however, only a small part of the total amount of wine produced in the country, for large drinks companies such as Suntory, Mercian, Sapporo, and Asahi also make wine from grape juice purchased on the international market.

INDIA

henever I imagine wine in India, I invariably picture British colonists during the Raj (the word means "reign" in Hindi, and denotes the period between 1858 and 1947) sitting under fans in the sweltering humidity, drinking Madeira and Port. But that image is only one part of the complex, on-again-off-again story of wine on the Indian subcontinent.

Viticulture in India has been estimated to date back as far as the fourth millennium B.C., when traders from Persia (modern-day Iran) are said to have introduced grapevines to the subcontinent. The date would mean that Indian viticulture (although not necessarily wine making) was established significantly earlier than viticulture in China, and the idea is indeed conceivable. Biomolecular archaeologist Patrick McGovern's considerable findings on wine in the ancient world include Neolithic jars containing winelike residues dating from 5400 to 5000 B.C. at the site of Hajji Firuz Tepe, in the Zagros Mountains of Iran. It is possible that from there, grapevines were brought to the Indus Valley civilization (an area that extends from what is today northeast Afghanistan to Pakistan and northwest India) between 3300 and 1300 B.C. The Indus Valley civilization is considered one of the three great early civilizations of the Old World, along with Ancient Eygpt and Mesopotamia.

Evidence specifically of winemaking comes much later in India, however. As of the fourth century B.C. (just two hundred years after wine began to be made in France), grape-based

▲ *When you need a bottle of wine, even the most humble shop will do.*

wines known as *madhu* were among the popular indulgences of the Emperor Chandragupta
Maurya, and were chronicled, along with the
emperor's revelries, by his chief minister,
Chanakya. Wine became, as it did in Europe,
the drink of the privileged and noble classes,
while the poor drank alcoholic beverages made
from millet, barley, and wheat.

But India soon entered one of its many anti-
alcohol eras. During the otherwise enlightened
and artistic era known as the Muslim Mughal
Empire (A.D. 1526 to approximately 1700), wine
was banned in accordance with Islamic teachings. It wasn't until the British Raj, during the
Victorian era, that views on alcohol made an
about-face. Vineyards were planted throughout the Baramati, Kashmir, and Surat regions
and winemaking was strongly encouraged,
largely so that British colonists would have a
domestic supply, lest the imported Madeira
run out.

But just as it was reaching some measure of
critical mass, at the end of the nineteenth century, the wine industry in India was devastated
by phylloxera. In the early part of the twentieth
century, the industry barely recovered, and it
didn't help that another growing temperance
movement in India resulted in several Indian
states banning all alcohol outright.

Still, by the 1970s, India, like many of its
Asian neighbors, had a growing middle class
for whom wine was a sign of Westernization
and sophistication. A new, modern wine era
began. In the mid-1980s, in the state of Goa,
for example, the Tonia Group (originally producers of fennys—high-alcohol spirits distilled from coconuts and cashews) imported
varieties like cabernet sauvignon, chardonnay, chenin blanc, and pinot noirs and began
making wine. About the same time, based
on research by Champagne Technologies
of France, Chateau Indage was founded in
Narayangaon, in Maharashtra state. Today,
the large winery makes high-end cabernet
sauvignon and chardonnay under the brand
Chantilli. There are numerous other small,

high-end Indian wineries, including Sula
Vineyards, begun by Rajeev Samant, a Mumbai-
born, Stanford University-educated former
executive with Oracle corporation (the winery is known for sauvignon blanc and chenin
blanc); as well as Chateau d'Ori (known for
its merlot) and Grover Vineyards (known for
its cabernet sauvignon-shiraz blend). All told,
in 2011, India had an estimated 10,000 acres
(4,000 hectares) of grapevines (about a quarter of the number of vineyard acres in the tiny
Napa Valley), according to the organization
Indianwine; the exact number of wineries is
not tracked and remains unknown.

Establishing a modern wine industry in
India has been fraught with challenges—the
first of which is climate. The southern half
of India lies squarely in the tropics, thus the
summer growing season is extremely hot,
humid, and prone to monsoons. As a result,
vineyards must be planted in cooler, higher-
altitude areas, or viticultural techniques to
mitigate the effects of heat and humidity have
to be employed. Among the coolest wine-
producing regions are the states of Kashmir
and Punjab, in the north, near the Himalayas.
But wine is also made in the southern states
of Maharashtra (the area around Nasik is
considered the heart of Indian wine country), Andhra Pradesh, Karnataka, Goa, and in
the farthest southern state of Tamil Nadu.
In these areas, vines are often trained on tall
pergolas, creating a large canopy to protect
the grapes from sunburn and simultaneously
lifting the vines up to provide maximum air
circulation.

Finally, grapes intended for wine represent
just a small fraction of all the grapes grown in
India, many of which, like anabeshahi, arkavati,
and arkashyam, are indigenous table grapes.
And although they can be used for wine, the
three most widely planted grapes of all—sul-
tana (known in California as Thompson seedless), Bangalore blue (the American hybrid
Isabella), and gulabi (black muscat)—are far
more often eaten out of hand.

WINE LAWS

M aybe you'd like to pour yourself a glass of wine and get comfortable before reading further. What follows are overviews of the (sometimes complex) wine laws of each wine-producing country included in this book. We'll start with France, and because it is often considered a model for the rest of the world, we'll go into it in some depth. In addition, be sure to see the box on European Union Wine Laws (page 142) for how EU law intersects with specific national regulations.

FRANCE

In 1935, the Institut National de l'Origine et de la Qualité (previously the Institut National des Appellations d'Origine—INAO) was created with the mission of setting up the French *Appellation d'Origine Contrôlée* (AOC) system. Today, the AOC is still administered and periodically revised by the INAO. The AOC is equivalent to the European Union designation PDO, Protected Designation of Origin.

The system sets standards for specific categories of wine as well as various foods, including Grenoble walnuts, Bresse chickens, Isigny butter, Puy lentils, Nyons olive oil, and Brie, Cantal, Roquefort, and Reblochon cheeses.

Under the AOC system, the two main categories of wine, in descending order of quality, are:

VINS D'APPELLATION D'ORIGINE CONTRÔLÉE

The category *Vins d'Appellation d'Origine Contrôlée*—AOC—includes the finest wines of France. Each wine must abide by a strict set of regulations. Among other issues, the regulations cover:

AREA OF PRODUCTION: Each area is precisely defined. Only wines made from vines growing within the borders of the appellation have the right to use that appellation.

VARIETY OF GRAPE: Each area has permissible grape varieties, which may be used only in given proportions. If a producer makes wine from grapes other than those permitted, or uses a ratio of grapes that is not permitted, he or she must forfeit the appellation.

YIELD PER HECTARE: The basic yield allowed is set, although in some years it may be increased. In Bordeaux, for example, the yield permitted for red wine is 55 hectoliters per hectare, or 1,452 gallons of wine for every 2.47 acres. The legal yield for white wine is slightly higher.

VINEYARD PRACTICES: How and when the vines can be pruned, the type of trellising system, and whether the use of irrigation is permitted are regulated. For some AOCs, even the start date of the harvest is specified.

DEGREE OF ALCOHOL: All AOC wines have a required minimum level of alcohol content, and some have a maximum level.

WINEMAKING PRACTICES: Winemaking practices, such as chaptalization and acidification, are regulated, as are, in some cases, aging requirements.

TASTING AND ANALYSIS: All AOC wines must go through a chemical analysis and pass a taste test for typicity—that is, they must taste true to their kind. Those wines that fail must be declassified.

VARIETAL LABELING: All French wines may now put the grape variety on the label, but only if 85 percent of the wine constitutes the variety mentioned. Some AOCs are even more strict, specifying that a grape variety can be listed only if the wine is 100 percent of that variety.

While it may seem that such detailed rules are unfairly strict (especially compared to the New World, where winemakers have vastly more creative rein), a majority of French wine producers support such regulations (as do their counterparts in other European countries). Why?

The answer can be summarized this way. By holding all variables constant, French and other European producers are able to determine which vineyard plots consistently produce the greatest wines. In other words, since all producers make essentially the same kind of wine in essentially the same way from the same grapes grown in essentially the same manner, the only thing left that might account for quality differences is the exact plot of land where the grapes were grown. The French/European approach highlights the terroir of the place where the grapes were grown.

VINS DE PAYS

France's so-called country wines—*vins de pays*—are defined by region. Like AOC wines, they must meet certain rules, although these rules are usually far less strict than for AOC wines. Permissible yields are higher, and the rules concerning grape varieties are more flexible. Vins de Pays must carry the logo/stamp for the European Union designation PGI—Protected Geographical Indication or, in French, Indication Géographique Protégée (IGP). They may choose to be known by the EU designation rather than the French Vin de Pays.

ITALY

Italian wine regulations are roughly similar to the French *Appellation d'Origine Contrôlée* laws. The Italian Ministry of Agriculture and Forestry oversees the regulations. There are four categories. In ascending order they are: VDT, IGT, DOC, and DOCG. You'll find an overview of these laws below. However, as Italy is a member of the European Community (EU), some Italian wineries use EU wine designations as well as (or in place of) Italy's national wine laws. To understand how EU regulations intersect with Italian and other national regulations, see PDO, PGI—The European Union Wine Laws on page 142 in the French chapter.

VDT (*Vino da Tavola*): These are simple, generic table wines that may list only the type of wine inside—red, white, or rosé. Sometimes, a varietal name is also listed, for example, Merlot, Italy.

IGT (*Indicazione Geografica Tipica*): Roughly equal to the French designation Vin de Pays, IGT wines are "country wines" that must meet certain rules regarding the area of production, the permissible grape varieties, the maximum yield of grapes per hectare, and so forth, but these rules are generally much less stringent than for DOC or DOCG wines. There were 118 IGTs as of 2013.

DOC and DOCG (*Denominazione di Origine Controllata and Denominazione di Origine Controllata e Garantita*): There are more than 330 areas where wine is produced that have been given DOC status, and 73 have DOCG status. In these regions, the DOC and DOCG laws govern the area of production, the permissible grape varieties, the maximum yield of grapes per hectare, the minimum degree of alcohol the wines must possess, such vineyard practices as pruning and trellising systems, winemaking practices, and the requirements for aging. In addition, all wines must pass chemical analysis and taste tests for typicity. The rules for DOCG wines are somewhat stricter than those for DOC wines. And, interestingly, most DOCGs are found in the northern part of the country, with Tuscany, Piedmont, and the Veneto accounting for the lion's share of them. A full list of Italy's DOCGs can be found on page 967.

SPAIN

The Spanish *Denominación de Origen* (DO) laws, first enacted in 1932 and revised since, are similar to France's *Appellation d'Origine Contrôlée* laws, which define and protect wines from specific geographic areas. You'll find an overview of these laws below. However, as Spain is a member of the European Union (EU), some Spanish wineries use EU wine designations as well as (or in place of) Spain's national wine laws. To understand how EU regulations intersect with Spanish and other national regulations, see PDO, PGI—The European Union Wine Laws, on page 142 in the chapter on France.

Spanish regulations currently cover sixty-nine DOs, or officially recognized and geographically defined wine regions. An even higher designation—the *Denominación de Origen Calificada* (DOCa, or Qualified Denomination of Origin)—was created in 1991. To qualify for DOCa status, a region's wines must have demonstrated exceptional quality over a long period of time, and the region must have had DO status for at least ten years. Currently, only two regions in Spain have DOCa status: Rioja and Priorat.

Each DO and DOCa has its own *Consejo Regulador,* a governing control board that enforces specific viticultural and winemaking standards and regulates the total acreage that may be planted, the types of grapes planted, the maximum yield, the minimum length of time wines must be aged, plus the information that may be given on the label. In addition, each *Consejo Regulador* maintains a laboratory and tasting panel. Every wine awarded DO or DOCa status must be tasted, evaluated, and found to be true to type.

Since 2003, Spanish law also allows for a status that many consider higher than DOCa—Pago. The word *pago* means "single estate." Thus, estates of exceptional merit (the Spanish equivalents of *grand crus*) may each have their own Pago DO if they meet certain guidelines. The bodega must make wines only from grapes grown on the estate, and the wine must be made and bottled on the estate. Interestingly, to be awarded Pago status, the estate must also have an international reputation for quality, as measured by receiving high scores from the world's top wine critics and placements on the wine lists of the world's most famous restaurants. The first estate in Spain to receive its own Pago DO was the Dominio de Valdepusa estate, in Castilla-La Mancha. The estate, owned by well-known Spanish vintner Carlos Falcó, makes wines under the name Marqués de Griñón (Falcó's title). Today, some ten estates have Pago DO status, most of them in the regions of Castilla-La Mancha and Navarra.

If a grape variety is listed on a Spanish label, the wine must be composed of at least 85 percent of the variety named.

The term *Vino de Pago* may be used for an estate wine of recognized prestige that comes from a certain place or site within a recognized DO. Such wine must be made and bottled at the winery of the specific vineyard named.

As for aging, the terms below, when used, carry the following national requirements. A DO or DOCa region—Ribera del Duero or Rioja, for example—may choose to make their local requirements more strict than what follows, but not more lenient.

Vino de Crianza: May be used for red wines aged a minimum of twenty-four months, six of which must be in oak containers of a maximum capacity of 330 liters. White and rosé wines must be aged at least eighteen months.

Reserva: May be used for red wines aged a minimum of thirty-six months, twelve of which must be in oak and twenty-four of which must be in bottle. White and rosé wines must be aged eighteen months, six of which must be in oak.

Gran Reserva: May be used for red wines aged a minimum of sixty months, eighteen of which must be in oak. White and rosé wines must be aged forty-eight months, six of which must be in oak.

PORTUGAL

Portugal was one of the first European countries to have wine laws. As early as 1756, Portugal's then prime minister, the Marquis da Pombal, established the legal boundaries of the Douro River Valley to protect the authenticity of Port wine. Portugal's wine industry was dramatically modernized after the country joined the European Economic Community (later renamed the European Union) in 1986. Below, you'll find an overview of Portuguese wine law.

As Portugal is a member of the European Union (EU), some Portuguese wineries use EU wine designations as well as (or in place of) Portugal's national wine laws. To understand how EU regulations intersect with Portuguese and other national regulations, see PDO, PGI—The European Union Wine Laws on page 142.

Today, the country has more than fifty DOPs (*Denominação de Origem Protegida,* or Designations of Protected Origin) within its eleven major wine regions. These designations, similar to France's AOC (*Appellation d'Origine Contrôlée,* or Appellations of Controlled Origin) are set forth by Portugal's Instituto da Vinha e do Vinho (Institute of Vines and Wines), as well as by numerous local commissions. The regulations not only determine the physical boundaries of a wine district, but also set forth strict requirements for the wines made there, including the total acreage that may be planted, the types of grapes and their maximum yield, the methods of vinification, the minimum length of time wines must be aged, and the information given on the label. As for labeling, most Portuguese table wines are named according to the geographic area from which they come: Douro, Dão, Alentejo, and so forth. However, some wines are also labeled according to grape variety. If the grape variety is given, at least 85 percent of the grapes for that wine must be of that variety.

GERMANY

The vineyards and wines of Germany are governed by a monumental set of laws that took effect in 1971 and were aimed at simplifying German wine. The 1971 law established the eleven original German *anbaugebiete* or wine regions (which, in 1989, with the reunification of Germany, became thirteen) and their subdivisions—the thirty-nine districts known as *bereiche* and 167 collections of vineyards known as *grosslagen.* The 1971 law also effectively collapsed the then-existing 30,000 individual named vineyard sites down to some 2,600 individual vineyard sites, or *einzellagen.*

The most basic category of German wine is called, by law, *Deutscher wein* (formerly this was called *tafelwein*). *Deutscher wein* must be made from German grapes in Germany.

For *Deutscher wein* as well as the higher quality category, *Qualitätswein bestimmter Anbaugebiete* (QbA) and higher still, *Prädikatswein,* Germany's detailed wine laws regulate where the grapes can

be grown, the maximum yield of wine per hectare, the minimum alcohol level the wine must attain, whether chaptalization is permissable, what methods of fermentation may be used, and what information must appear on the label. The laws also specify how ripe the grapes must be (measured in Oechsle) in order to be considered a QbA, or a *Prädikatswein* and its subdivisions of *kabinett, spätlese, auslese,* and other even greater ripeness levels. Finally, the law requires that each wine be examined, tasted, and found to be true to type. For more comments on the requirements for QbA and Prädikat wines, see the German and Austrian glossary, page 963.

AUSTRIA

Austria's wine laws are among the strictest in Europe. They stipulate precise requirements for every wine, including the minimum sugar content of the grapes at harvest and the maximum alcohol level.

Basic, neutral wine, referred to as *Landwein,* is not ripe. One step up, so-called quality wine (*Qualitätswein*) is a bit riper. But fine wine falls into a higher category still, called *Prädikatswein.* These are high-quality wines that must achieve higher levels of ripeness and may not be chaptalized or sweetened after fermentation. Thus, in a dry table wine, any tiny amount of residual sugar in the wine may only result naturally (that is, the fermentation stopped on its own before every trace of residual sugar was gone). For sweet wines, fermentation can be stopped, leaving natural residual sugar in the wine, but again, the sweetness cannot be added after the fact (i.e., after fermentation). For *Prädikatswein,* there are also detailed laws regulating where the grapes can be grown, the maximum yield of wine per hectare, what methods of fermentation may be used, and what information must appear on the label. If a wine lists a specific grape, for example, it must contain at least 85 percent of that grape. If a wine has a vintage on the label, it must contain a minimum of 85 percent of that vintage. If a wine region is listed, all of the wine (100 percent) must come from that region.

The laws also require that each wine be examined, tasted, and found true to type. Finally, each wine must be scientifically tested and given an official test number. Indeed, all Austrian wines have a red-and-white striped "banderole" around the neck or on top of the cork or screwcap, which must be purchased by the producer to ensure that official regulations are not breached.

HUNGARY

Hungarian wines are governed by a set of national laws last revised in 1997. Roughly similar to the *Appellation d'Origine Contrôlée* (AOC) laws of France, Hungary's regulations define the boundries of wine regions, stipulate the grape varieties that can be planted, designate allowable winemaking and viticultural processes, and govern how wines are labeled.

GREECE

When Greece joined the European Union in the 1980s, it revised its regulations along the lines of the *Appellation d'Origine Contrôlée* (AOC) laws of France. The laws defined the boundaries of wine regions, stipulated which grape varieties could be planted, designated allowable winemaking and viticultural processes, specified aging regimes, and governed how wines were labeled. However, after the European Union established its own set of wine laws in 2009, Greece adopted these in place of its national laws. (All twenty-seven EU member countries are free to do this, or any member country may institute a hybrid system that recognizes both EU wine law and the country's own national laws.) Following are the designations you will find on Greek wines:

PROTECTED DESIGNATION OF ORIGIN (PDO) WINES

The European Union designation PDO is the highest designation and is equivalent to what, in France, would be a wine designated as AOC, or *Appellation d'Origine Contrôlée*. In essence, a PDO indicates a historic top wine-producing area. In Greece, twenty-nine wines carry PDO status. They fall into two categories:

- AOQS (Designation of Origin of Superior Quality) for dry wines. These must carry a red band on the neck of the bottle.

- AOC (Controlled Appellation of Origin) for sweet wines. These carry a blue band on the neck of the bottle.

PROTECTED GEOGRAPHICAL INDICATION (PGI) WINES:

The European Union designation PGI falls below PDO. Historically, these were the table wines of a country. (In France, for example, PGI is equivalent to Vin de Pays.) In Greece, the PGI designation covers all local wines (before the EU law was adopted, these were called *topikos oenos*) and traditional wines such as retsina.

UNITED STATES

Although winemakers in the United States have considerable creative freedom to make whatever sort of wine they want, there are several important federal rules and regulations wine producers must abide by. These are administered by the TTB (Alcohol and Tobacco Tax and Trade Bureau), under whose jurisdiction wine falls. Here is a quick summary of the most important laws.

- When a wine is labeled with an American Viticultural Area (AVA), at least 85 percent of the grapes that make up the wine must come from that AVA.

- In place of an AVA, a wine can be labeled by county—Sonoma County, Mendocino County, and so on. When a wine is labeled by county, at least 75 percent of the grapes must come from that county.

- In place of an AVA, a wine may be labeled by state. Wines labeled by state must contain at least 75 percent wine from that state. Some states, however, require higher percentages. In California, 100 percent of the wine must be from California. In Washington State, 95 percent of the wine must be from Washington State.

- When a grape variety is named on the label, the wine must be composed of at least 75 percent of that variety. Again, some states have stricter rules. In Oregon, this percentage has been raised to 90 percent for the most-planted grapes, such as pinot noir and chardonnay. (But for wines made from many varieties grown in small amounts in Oregon—cabernet sauvignon, cabernet franc, merlot, malbec, sauvignon blanc, and others—the percentage remains at 75 percent.)

- When a vintage is declared on the label, 95 percent of the wine must be from that vintage.

- All bottles of wine made in the United States are required to carry a warning about the dangers of alcohol and to indicate that the wine contains sulfites (see page 41).

CANADA

The Vintners Quality Alliance (VQA) is the agency responsible for the creation and administration of the rules and regulations that govern quality wine in Canada's two main wine regions, British Columbia and Ontario. There are slight variations to the rules between the two regions, but the major points are the same. Like the regulations set forth in most of the New World, the VQA laws are far less stringent than the laws governing most European regions. Some of the most important regulations in Canada are as follows:

- If a grape variety is named on the label, at least 85 percent of the wine must be composed of the grape named.

- If two varietals are listed, they must comprise at least 90 percent of the blend.

- If a vintage is indicated on the label, 85 percent of the wine must be composed of grapes from that vintage.

- If a vineyard is named on the label, 100 percent of the grapes must be from that vineyard.

- In order for a wine to be labeled 'British Columbia' or 'Ontario' 100 percent of the grapes must be from the corresponding region.

- The regulations for icewine are Canada's strictest. Among them: only certain grape varieties are allowed, the grapes must be naturally frozen on the vine, and the external temperature must reach -8°C (17.6°F) before the grapes can be picked.

AUSTRALIA

Australia, like the United States, does not have a strict system of laws regulating grape growing and winemaking. There are no rules similar to the French *Appellation d'Origine Contrôlée* laws, which govern the varieties of grapes that can be planted in specific areas, the yield produced from those grapes, how the grapes are vinified, how long the wines are aged, and so on.

However, there are regulations that govern labeling and define viticultural areas. These areas, known as Geographic Indications (GIs), are similar to American Viticultural Areas (AVAs) in the United States. All of Australia's wine regulations are set forth by the governmental agency Wine Australia, and notably stipulate the following:

- If a grape variety is named on the label, 85 percent of the wine must be composed of the grape named.

- If two or more varieties are listed, they together must comprise at least 85 percent of wine, must be the major contributing varieties of the blend (each must contribute at least 5 percent of the blend), and must be listed on the label in order of percentage. Thus, a wine labeled Cabernet-Shiraz has more cabernet than shiraz; a wine labeled Shiraz-Cabernet has just the opposite.

- If a vintage is indicated on the label, 85 percent of the wine must be composed of grapes from the vintage indicated.

- If a Geographical Indication (GI), state, zone, region, subregion, or vineyard is named on the label, 85 percent of the wine must come from that place.

NEW ZEALAND

There is no strict system of laws regulating grape-growing and winemaking for New Zealand—nothing comparable to the French *Appellation d'Origine Contrôlée* laws, governing such matters as the varieties of grapes that can be planted in specific areas, the yield produced from those vines, how the grapes are vinified, or how long the wines are aged. New Zealand does have regulations that govern labeling and certain aspects of wine production. These rules are part of the country's official Food Act and Food Regulations, and they mandate that:

• If a grape variety or varieties are named on a label, 85 percent of the wine must be composed of the variety or varieties named. In practice, many New Zealand wines are 100 percent the variety or varieties named.

• If two grapes are named on the label, they must be listed in order of percentage. When you see a wine labeled Cabernet-Merlot, it contains more cabernet than merlot; a wine labeled Merlot-Cabernet has just the opposite.

• When an area, district, or region appears on a label, 85 percent of the wine must come from that place.

CHILE

Like most New World countries, Chile does not have a strict system of laws that regulate grape-growing and winemaking—nothing comparable to the French *Appellation d'Origine Contrôlée* laws, which govern which grape varieties can be planted in which areas, as well as myriad other details concerning how the vines are grown and how the wine is made and aged. In 1994 and 1995, for the first time, however, new laws went into effect establishing each key viticultural region as a *Denominacion de Origen* (DO). These were established jointly by the Servicio Agricola Ganadero, the Ministerio de Agricultura, and the wineries themselves. The laws define not only the key appellations but also the subregions and zones within those regions.

The 1995 laws also mandated that:
• If a wine is labeled with a viticultural region, at least 75 percent of the wine must come from that region.

• If a grape variety is named on the label, the wine must be composed of at least 75 percent of the grape named.

• In wines with labels specifying a vintage, at least 75 percent of the wine must come from that vintage.

In practice, most Chilean wineries observe an 85 percent minimum for all three categories

above, to comply with European Union standards for export.

Finally, while there are no legal aging requirements for terms like *Reserva Especial* and *Gran Reserva,* Chilean law does mandate that wines that use these designations must spend at least some time in oak. That said, labeling a $14 wine as a *Gran Reserva* (as is often done in Chile) seems, if nothing else, a little misdirected.

ARGENTINA

Although wine exports are monitored by its Instituto Nacional de Vitivinicultura, Argentina does not have a well-defined system of appellations, and thus, where wine regions begin and end is more a matter of common opinion than law. Nor are there laws regulating grape growing and wine-making. There are, for example, no rules similar to the French *Appellation d'Origine Contrôlée* laws, governing what grapes may be planted in which regions, with details for their cultivation and how wine should be made from them.

All of this said, Argentina's rapid evolution has meant that the wine industry itself has begun to attempt to define specific viticultural regions, especially within the main large wine-producing region, Mendoza.

As for labeling regulations, if a grape variety is named on the label, 85 percent of the wine must consist of that grape. You will also find label terms such as *reserva* and *gran reserva* on Argentine wine labels, but neither of these terms is defined by law. Either term can be used by a winery to mean whatever the winery intends.

SOUTH AFRICA

In 1973, South Africa's Wine of Origin (WO) legislation was enacted, defining the geographical boundaries of wine regions and regulating labeling. The system, which is administered by the Wine and Spirit Board (WSB), does not impose strict grape-growing and winemaking regulations in the manner of, say, France's *Appellation d'Origine Contrôlée* system. But it is more strict than most New World systems and requires, for example, that all wines be analytically tested, as well as tasted by a professional panel, before the wine can be certified to be sold. Once certified, the wine receives the official seal of the WSB (locally known as a "bus ticket"), which is affixed to the neck of the bottle.

The WO system establishes four nested categories of appellations. The largest category is a geographical unit. There are five of these, the most important of which is the Western Cape. Within each geographical unit is a region, followed by a district, followed by the smallest geographical entity, a ward. So, for example, within the Western Cape is the Coastal region and within that, the district Stellenbosch and within that, the ward of Papegaaiberg.

Most wines in South Africa are labeled by grape type. A wine labeled with a variety must be composed of at least 85 percent of that variety. And if a single area is named as the appellation, then 100 percent of the grapes must come from that area. If the grapes come from multiple areas, that, too, must be indicated on the label.

GLOSSARIES

I 've provided here a main glossary with a comprehensive set of definitions for common English wine words and extensive glossaries for French, Italian, Spanish, and German and Austrian wine terms. You'll also find glossaries for the most important Portuguese, Hungarian, and Greek terms. Words appearing in all capital letters are cross-referenced within the main glossary or the glossaries for individual countries. The French glossary begins on page 950, the Italian on page 954, the Spanish on page 957, the Portuguese on page 959, the German and Austrian on page 960, the Hungarian on page 964, and the Greek on page 965.

MAIN GLOSSARY

A

ACETALDEHYDE: Produced naturally during FERMENTATION, acetaldehyde is a colorless volatile component with a pungent ODOR. It is an asset in flor-based (see FLOR, Spanish Glossary) wines, such as Sherry, but a detectable amount in table wine is considered a flaw. Also occurs in coffee and ripe fruit.

ACETIC: A negative description for a wine with an unpleasant, sharp, vinegarlike smell and taste. A wine becomes acetic as a result of the presence of acetobacter, a bacteria that causes the natural conversion of wine to vinegar by producing acetic acid in the presence of air. See VOLATILE ACIDITY.

ACID: A natural component of wine; responsible for the zesty, refreshing qualities of some, acidity also helps wine to age. Wines with the proper amount of acid relative to their ALCOHOL content are vibrant and lively to drink. Wines with little acid relative to the alcohol are the opposite: FLAT and blowsy. Wines with excess acid taste sharp and biting. There are multiple acids in wine, the three most important of which—tartaric, malic, and citric—all come from the grapes. Other acids may be produced during FERMENTATION.

ACIDIFICATION: A process practiced in warm wine regions whereby a winemaker adds ACID to grape MUST before or during FERMENTATION in order to boost its naturally low level of acidity, in hopes of creating a more balanced wine. Acidification is legal and widely practiced in many parts of the world, including California. Also called *acidulation*.

ACIDITY: See ACID.

AERATION: The process of intentionally exposing wine to oxygen to "open up" and soften it. Aeration occurs during the winemaking process, as when wine is poured or racked (see RACKING) from barrel to barrel, but it may also take place at serving time, such as when a young wine is poured into a carafe or a decanter or even just swirled in the glass.

AFTERTASTE: See FINISH.

AGING: The process of intentionally holding a wine for a period of time so that the components in it can integrate and the wine can grow softer and possibly more COMPLEX. Wines are generally aged first in a barrel and later in bottles, since wines evolve differently in each vessel. The length of time any wine is aged is initially up to the producer, though many of the top European wines by law must be aged a certain minimum number of months or years. Most wines worldwide are aged only briefly before release.

AH-SO: A wine opener often used by sommeliers to remove corks that have begun to crumble, as with very old wines. The device does not penetrate the cork, but instead two flat metal blades are inserted down the sides of the cork and then the device is gently twisted while pulling upward, to remove the cork. It was originally named the Magic Cork Extractor and patented in 1879, but it has been called the Ah-So since the 1960s.

ALCOHOL: During FERMENTATION, yeasts convert the natural sugar in grapes to alcohol (also known as ETHANOL or ETHYL ALCOHOL) and CARBON DIOXIDE. The riper the grapes, the more sugar they contain and the higher the potential alcohol content of the wine will be (see How Wine Is Made, page 37). Wines with low alcohol (German rieslings, for example) are LIGHT-BODIED wines. With high alcohol (many California chardonnays) are FULL-BODIED and almost CHEWY. When a high alcohol wine has too little FRUIT and a low ACID content, it tastes out of BALANCE and gives off a HOT or slightly burning sensation in your mouth.

ALCOHOL BY VOLUME: The percentage of the ALCOHOL content by volume in a wine must, by United States law, appear on every wine label. However, because alcohol can be difficult to measure precisely and because wineries often need to print their labels before they know the exact alcohol content, the percentage stated on the label need only be accurate within 1.5 percent as long as the total amount is not more than 14 percent. If greater than 14 percent, it must be accurate to within 1 percent. For example, a wine labeled 12 percent alcohol by volume may contain anywhere from 10.5 to 13.5 percent alcohol.

ALDEHYDES: Produced as FERMENTATION converts sugar to ALCOHOL, aldehydes have pungent odors that contribute to the flavor and quality of wine but in excess are undesirable.

AMPELOGRAPHY: The science of the identification and classification of grapevines according to their physical properties, such as the size and shape of their leaves and grape clusters. Increasingly, grapevines are also being identified by DNA typing.

AMPHORAE: Earthenware vessels, ranging in size from that of a milk can to a refrigerator, used by the ancient Greeks and Romans to store and ship wine. An amphora was oval in shape, with two large handles at the top for carrying and a pointed bottom so that the vessel could be pushed into the soft earth, where it would remain upright.

ANTHOCYANINS: The red pigments in grape skins and wine.

APPEARANCE: One of the categories by which a wine can be judged by sensory evaluation, generally including an assessment of clarity and COLOR.

APPELLATION: In general conversation the word *appellation* is often used simply to indicate the place where the grapes for a given wine were grown and subsequently made into wine. Technically, however, the word has much broader significance and importance. For this we must turn to the French for whom the full term is *Appellation d'Origine Contrôlée,* often abbreviated as AOC (see page 137). France's AOC regulations have become the world's model for laws that define and protect geographically named wines, spirits, and even certain foods. For any given wine the AOC laws stipulate, among other things, the precise area where the grapes that make the wine can be grown, the grape varieties that the wine can be made from, the permissible YIELD, aspects of VITICULTURE, such as PRUNING and irrigation, the minimum alcoholic strength of the wine, plus various details of how the wine can be made. For a given French wine to carry an appellation, it must meet all of the criteria set down in the AOC laws. Multiple appellations can exist within a larger appellation. For example, Margaux is an AOC within the AOC Haut-Médoc, which itself is an AOC within the larger AOC Bordeaux. The AOC laws evolved progressively, beginning in the 1930s. Today, most European wine-producing countries have similar, fairly stringent systems that define and govern the wines produced. In the NEW WORLD, including the United States, regulations defining the geographic boundaries of wine-producing areas are more recent. While New World regulations may specify the boundaries of a given place such as the Napa Valley, they rarely specify or regulate details, such as grape varieties, permissible yields, or how the wine can be made. See also AVA.

AROMA: A term broadly used to describe a wine's smell. Technically, however, the smell of any wine is divided into the aroma, the smell that derives from the grapes, and the BOUQUET, a more complex smell that a wine acquires after AGING.

AROMATIC: A positive description, indicating that a wine has a pronounced AROMA. Some VARIETAL wines, such as muscat and gewürztraminer, are well known for being especially aromatic, often having SPICY and/or floral (see FLOWERY) scents.

ASTRINGENT: A term describing the drying MOUTHFEEL of a wine with a considerable amount of TANNIN: a dry sensation provoked by some wines and certain foods, such as walnuts. Often used negatively to describe red wines with a lot of green or unripe tannin. Excess astringency is unpleasant and causes the mouth to pucker.

AUTOLYSIS: The decomposition of spent yeast cells by enzymes they contain. When a wine is SUR LIE, or on the LEES, it is left in contact with the spent yeasts that performed the FERMENTATION. As the yeast cells break down, they impart, for reasons not fully understood, an extra dimension of flavor, texture, VISCOSITY, and complexity to the wine.

AVA: The acronym for American Viticultural Area. An AVA is defined as "a delimited grape growing region, distinguished by geographical features, the boundaries of which have been recognized and defined." On United States wine labels, such place names as Napa Valley, Sonoma Valley, Columbia Valley, and so on, are all AVAs. There are now more than 203 AVAs in the United States.

B

BAKED: Negative term used when a table wine's AROMA and/or flavor seems overripe, caramel-like, or even burnt. Poorly made table wines allowed to get too warm or to become oxidized often taste baked (see OXIDATION). For certain wines, such as Sherry and Madeira, however, some "bakedness" is considered appropriate and positive, especially when combined with the wines' tangy nuttiness.

BALANCE: A harmonic equilibrium among the components of a wine (ACID, ALCOHOL, FRUIT, TANNIN, and so on) such that no one characteristic stands out like a sore thumb. Great wines have balance.

BARREL-FERMENTED: Used to describe a wine—usually a white—that has undergone FERMENTATION in small oak barrels as opposed to in more neutral large casks, cement vats, or stainless-steel tanks. Fermentation in a small barrel can impart a richer flavor and creamier texture to some wines, though these characteristics may be acquired at the expense of the wines' FRUIT. To mitigate against too intense a barrel-fermented character, winemakers can use older barrels, and/or ferment only a portion of the wine in barrels and then BLEND this portion with wine that has not been barrel-fermented.

BENTONITE: A type of light clay, usually from the United States or Africa, mixed into wine to clarify it by removing tiny suspended protein molecules that can cause a hazy appearance (see FINING). As the bentonite settles, it absorbs and carries the particles suspended in the wine along with it to the bottom of the vessel. The clear wine is then racked off the settled material.

BIG: A descriptive term used for FULL-BODIED, robust wines that are usually high in ALCOHOL.

BIODYNAMIC VITICULTURE: See box, page 34 in the chapter Where It All Begins.

BITTER: A harsh flavor in wine, often derived from stems and seeds that have been carelessly or inadvertently crushed along with the grapes. Bitterness can also be caused by unripe grapes or unripe TANNIN. In certain big red wines, a slight bitterness is considered a positive nuance, just as it would be in a good espresso.

BLEND: To combine two or more lots of wine in hopes of enhancing flavor, BALANCE, and/or complexity. Often these are wines from different grape varieties (cabernet sauvignon and merlot, for example). However, blends may also be made up of wines that come from grapes grown in different soil or microclimates, wines that come from vines of different ages, wines from different CLONES, or wines made by different winemaking methods (some aged in one kind of oak, some in another, for instance). Virtually all Bordeaux wines and Champagnes are blends, as are wines from France's southern Rhône Valley and numerous other wines from elsewhere around the world.

BODY: The perceived weight of a wine in your mouth. The perception is dependent on ALCOHOL—the higher the alcohol content, the more FULL-BODIED the wine. As a point of reference, consider the relative weights of skim milk, whole milk, and half-and-half. Light-bodied wines feel like skim milk, medium-bodied ones like whole milk, and full-bodied ones like half-and-half.

BOOZE: Once spelled "bouse," the term comes from a medieval Dutch word, *büsen,* meaning "to drink to excess."

BOTRYTIS CINEREA: A beneficial fungus, also known as noble rot, which is necessary to produce many of the world's great sweet wines, including Sauternes. In certain years, when the degree of humidity is just right, *Botrytis cinerea* will attack grapes, covering them with a gray mold. The mold lives by penetrating the grapes' skins and using up the available water in the juice. This concentrates the sugar, flavor, and ACID so that a COMPLEX wine of exceptional sweetness can be made. Botrytis is unique in that, unlike other molds, it produces flavors that harmonize with the flavors of particular grapes.

BOTRYTIZED: Affected by BOTRYTIS CINEREA.

BOTTLE: Initially, the amount glass bottles held was not consistent. From the fifteenth to the seventeenth century, bottles held anywhere from 16 to 52 ounces. Today a standard wine bottle holds 25.36 ounces (750 milliliters). Restaurants generally pour five to six glasses of wine from a single bottle.

BOTTLE AGING: The process of allowing a wine to rest for a considerable period of time (usually years) in a bottle. Wines that have been bottle aged taste more mature, and their flavors can become so integrated that it's no longer easy to identify such specific fruit flavors as lemon, raspberry, or cherry. Bottle aging adds to the complexity of a wine (see AGING).

BOTTLE SICKNESS: A temporary condition that occurs following the bottling process, during which wine is exposed to large amounts of oxygen as it is transferred from barrels or tanks to bottles. A wine with bottle sickness, sometimes called bottle shock, can temporarily taste FLAT, dull, or out of BALANCE. The condition usually goes away in a few weeks, occasionally after months.

BOUQUET: Technically, bouquet refers specifically to the aspects of a wine's scent derived from BOTTLE AGING (see AROMA).

BRIARY: A term used to describe a briar patch or barklike taste in a wine. Often briary wines have a slightly scratchy texture, rather than being soft and round.

BRILLIANT: When applied to a wine's color, it means the wine is absolutely clear.

BRIX: A measure of the sugar content of grapes before they are harvested. Used to estimate the ALCOHOL content of the resulting wine.

BRUT: French term indicating a Champagne or sparkling wine that is dry to very dry, with less than 1.5 percent residual sugar.

BUD: The small node on a grapevine shoot that carries within it the grape clusters for the year to come. In the early spring, these buds open, allowing the frail green SHOOTS and tiny clusters to emerge.

BUDDING: The act of grafting buds of one vine onto an existing planted vine. When buds from the scion variety are grafted onto the rootstock, the process is known as "field budding."

BULK PROCESS: An inexpensive and quick way of making SPARKLING WINE. The bulk process, also called the Charmat method, involves placing wine in large, pressurized tanks for its SECONDARY FERMENTATION. In an alternative and far more expensive method, known as the MÉTHODE CHAMPENOISE (see French glossary), the secondary fermentation takes place inside individual bottles.

BULK WINE: Literally, wine not in a bottle. Wineries of all types, sizes, and levels of quality buy and sell wines in bulk. Some sell all of their production that way. Most large producers buy significant amounts of bulk wines from other wineries and then BLEND, bottle, and distribute those wines under their own labels. Small prestigious wineries, however, may also sell small amounts of high-quality wine in bulk to producers who will use it to enhance their own wines. In harvest years when the size of the crop is small, the prices for bulk wine go up.

BUNG: A plug for stoppering a wine barrel.

BUSHVINE: A vine that is free-standing with no trellis system that looks like a bush. It is also known as a goblet-trained vine, and many of the world's oldest vines are trained in this manner.

BUTTERY: Used to describe a wine that has an AROMA and flavor reminiscent of butter. Buttery aromas and flavors in wine are the result of DIACETYL, which is a by-product of MALOLACTIC FERMENTATION.

C

CANE: A SHOOT (stem) that has turned from green to tannish brown and has become hard and fibrous. Shoots turn to canes in the fall in order to withstand the oncoming winter. The canes will ultimately be pruned back, usually in the late winter. See PRUNING.

CANE TRAINING: The process of training a vine along a structure such as a trellis.

CANOPY: The "umbrella" formed by the leaves and SHOOTS of the grapevine.

CAP: The crusty layer—up to two feet or more deep, of grape skins, pulp, stems, and seeds—that rises and floats on top of the juice during a red wine's FERMENTATION. The cap must be kept in contact with the juice by one of several methods. It may be frequently PUNCHED DOWN into the juice, or the juice can be PUMPED OVER—that is, drawn up from the bottom of the tank and then showered over the cap. As a result of being punched down or pumped over, the ALCOHOL in the fermenting juice can extract COLOR, AROMA, flavor, and TANNIN from the cap. In addition, if the cap is not broken up and kept wet with the juice, it dries out and becomes a haven for bacteria that will ultimately mar the wine.

CAPSULE: The molded plastic, bimetal, or aluminum sheath that fits over the cork and top part of the neck of a wine bottle. Historically, capsules were made of lead to keep animals and bugs away from the cork. Today lead is banned because of potential health risks.

CARBON DIOXIDE: Along with ALCOHOL, the gas carbon dioxide (CO_2) is a by-product of FERMENTATION. Sometimes the small amounts of CO_2 remaining in a wine make it slightly SPRITZY. If fermentation occurs in a closed vessel, such as a bottle, the CO_2 becomes trapped in the wine and will ultimately form bubbles.

CARBONIC MACERATION: More accurately called semicarbonic maceration, carbonic maceration is a type of FERMENTATION in which bunches of uncrushed grapes are placed whole inside a closed tank. The weight of the bunches on top crushes those on the bottom, releasing juice that ferments in the standard manner. For the intact bunches on top, however, fermentation takes place inside each grape, leading to an extremely juicy style of wine. Carbonic maceration is used extensively in Beaujolais, where it heightens the wine's already grapy flavor.

CARTOUCHE: The raised glass logo or emblem embossed on a bottle of wine, most often found on the wines from the region of Châteauneuf-du-Pape. A cartouche is added to a wine bottle by pressing a mold filled with molten glass to the already-finished bottle. The word *cartouche* comes from the oval symbol used in ancient Egyptian hieroglyphics to indicate that the name written within the oval was a royal name.

CHAPTALIZATION: The addition of cane or beet sugar to wine MUST before or during FERMENTATION in order to increase the total amount of sugar and hence raise the potential ALCOHOL content (see page 932). Chaptalization is legal and widely practiced in many cooler northern European wine regions, where cool vintage years can lead to grapes that aren't fully ripe and, in turn, to wines that are thin and lacking in BODY. By increasing the alcohol content of such wines, the winemaker can make them fuller bodied and therefore make them seem more substantial. Chaptalization is not permitted in many warm wine regions, including California, where it is not needed but could be used to produce cheap wines high in alcohol but with virtually no flavor.

CHARMAT METHOD: See BULK PROCESS.

CHEWY: A term for mouthfilling, FULL-BODIED wines, chunky and viscous enough to seem almost chewable. Certain grape varieties, such as zinfandel, produced in very warm areas like Amador County, California, often take on a chewy character.

CLONE: The verb *to clone* means to propagate a group of vines from a "mother" vine that has desirable characteristics. The noun *clone* refers to plants of the same species that have identical physical characteristics and hence probably can be traced to a common "mother" plant. Clones are the result of natural genetic mutations, with each mutation then being replicated via cuttings. For example, pinot noir, a variety of grape, has many clones thanks to natural genetic mutations that have occurred over hundreds, possibly thousands, of years. Clones are critical in VITICULTURE because two clones of the same grape variety can taste remarkably different. Because clones occur spontaneously in nature, there is no way of knowing how many clones of a given variety exist at any one time.

CLOSED IN: Refers to a wine that seems to have considerable potential, yet its AROMAS and flavors are temporarily muted. A wine can be closed in for a variety of reasons. Two common ones: It's young or it's densely concentrated and needs time and/or oxygen to open up. In the first instance, the closed in wine may need additional BOTTLE AGING before it opens up; in the second case, pouring the wine into a carafe or decanter and giving it an hour or so to breathe will help.

CLOUDY: Descriptive term, not necessarily negative, for a wine that looks hazy rather than brilliantly clear. A wine can be slightly cloudy because it has not undergone FINING or filtration (see FILTER). Some wines, however, are cloudy as the result of faulty winemaking.

CLOYING: Describes a wine with unbearable, candy-like sweetness. Dessert wines should not be cloying.

CLUSTER: An entire bunch of grape berries.

CLUSTER THINNING: During the vine's growth cycle, the act of removing the fruit to enhance the quality of the fruit left on the vine.

COARSE: Descriptive term for a harsh, unsophisticated wine, lacking in FINESSE.

COLD FERMENTATION: A type of FERMENTATION that takes place in a vessel that can be cooled, usually a stainless-steel tank. Because cool fermentations are slower and more gentle than those that occur at warm temperatures, they help preserve the wine's fresh FRUIT AROMAS and flavors. Many light- and medium-bodied white wines are cold-fermented.

COLD STABILIZATION: A common winemaking technique whereby harmless TARTRATE crystals and small protein molecules are intentionally precipitated out of the wine. This is done by quickly chilling it. Unstabilized wines sometimes become hazy or form snowflake-like crystals, which are odorless and tasteless but look a bit unnerving.

COLOR: One of the distinguishing characteristics of wine, color is derived primarily from grape skins. White wines vary from pale straw to greenish yellow to yellow-gold amber; reds from garnet to crimson to brick red to lipstick red to purple. While the color of a wine is a tip-off to its variety (zinfandel is usually purplish in color, for example) and an indication of its age (white wines get darker as they get older; red wines get lighter), color is not a predictor of a wine's flavor or quality.

COMPLEX: Describes a multifaceted wine with compelling nuances and character. Importantly, in a complex wine, the multiple AROMAS and flavors reveal themselves subsequently over time. Thus, a complex wine is unknowable in one sip. All great wines are complex.

CONCRETE EGGS: Large egg-shaped concrete vessels (usually 5 to 6 feet tall) used to ferment white wine. Fermenting in concrete eggs has been practiced in France for decades, and the technique is now also used in the New World. There are distinct advantages to fermenting wine in concrete eggs instead of oak barrels or stainless-steel tanks. As fermentation gets underway, the oval shape of the egg helps create a vortex, causing the wine to roll in circular arcs, assuring a thorough, active fermentation. The concrete itself holds heat well, so the warmth created by fermentation is not quickly dissipated, and the wine doesn't experience wide temperature swings. Lastly, concrete is porous like wood, which allows for the gentle introduction of air, which softens the wine.

COOPERAGE: Containers a winery uses for storing wine, usually barrels or wood casks, though the term cooperage can also apply to concrete or stainless-steel vessels.

CORDON: A permanent woody arm that is trained horizontally from the trunk of the vine. The cordon will support the SHOOTS and grape clusters.

CORKED: A term used to describe a wine that smells like a wet dog in a basement or, sometimes, like wet cardboard. Wines become corked when certain bacteria in the cork cells interact with minute amounts of chemical residues that may remain in corks or wine bottles after they are cleaned. A corked wine has a defective AROMA and flavor, although it will not harm the drinker. Corked wine cannot be predicted. Any wine, regardless of its quality or price, can be corked.

CROSS: A grape created by fertilizing one genetic variety of grape with another genetic variety that belongs to the same species. While a cross may be the result of breeding, most crosses occur spontaneously in nature. Within the European species VITIS VINIFERA two highly regarded man-made crosses are scheurebe (riesling × silvaner) and pinotage (pinot noir × cinsaut). A cross is different than a HYBRID.

CRUSH: Used as a verb, *to crush* means to break the grape skins so that the pulp oozes out and FERMENTATION can more easily begin. As a noun, *crush* is the general term used for all of the steps (e.g., harvesting) that take place just prior to fermentation.

CUTTING: A segment of a dormant CANE 14 to 18 inches long that is cut off a growing vine and used to propagate a new plant through GRAFTING or direct planting.

D

DECANT: The act of pouring a wine (generally an older wine) off any SEDIMENT or deposits that may have precipitated out and settled in the bottle. Sometimes the term is used to describe the action of pouring a young wine into a decanter or carafe to

mix it with oxygen and open it up, but this is more correctly called AERATION.

DECLASSIFY: With European wines, the decision to place a wine in a category that is lower in status than seems appropriate given the quality of the wine. European wines may be declassified for a variety of reasons. In France, for example, wines that do not meet the strict requirements of AOC laws are declassified, usually to TABLE WINE.

DEMI-SEC: Literally, half-dry in French. Term used for a SPARKLING WINE or Champagne that is moderately sweet.

DEPTH: Intensity and concentration. An especially intense and concentrated cabernet sauvignon, for example, might be described as having depth.

DESSERT WINE: General term for a wine that is sweet and, as such, could accompany, or be, dessert. In the United States, such wines often fall into the category of LATE HARVEST. There are many ways of making dessert wines (see page 693). Two of the world's most famous dessert wines, French Sauternes and German trockenbeerenauslesen, are the result of grapes that are infected with the noble rot BOTRYTIS CINEREA.

DESTEMMER: A machine that separates the stems from the grapes. When combined with a crusher, it is called a crusher-destemmer.

DIACETYL: Buttery-tasting compound created as a by-product of MALOLACTIC FERMENTATION. Chardonnays that have gone through malolactic fermentation often have noticeable diacetyl.

DIRTY: A negative description of wines with off flavors and odors resulting from faulty winemaking. The implication is that something is present in the wine that shouldn't be.

DISGORGING: Referred to in French as DÉGORGEMENT (see French glossary), this is the process used in the making of Champagne or SPARKLING WINE by which yeasty sediment is removed from the bottle after the second bubble-forming FERMENTATION.

DIURNAL TEMPERATURE FLUCTUATION: The difference in temperature from the coolest point in the morning to the warmest point in the afternoon. A large difference between these two temperatures is ideal for wine-growing regions, as it allows the sugars to ripen during the heat of the day while the natural acids are preserved thanks to the coolness of the night. In regions such as central Spain and Mendoza, Argentina, the diurnal temperature fluctuation can be as much as 30°F to 40°F (-1°C to 4°C).

DNA PROFILING: The practice of using DNA markers to identify the parentage of a vine. Also called DNA typing or fingerprinting.

DRY: Commonly used to describe any wine that doesn't contain significant grape sugar. Technically, a dry wine is one fermented until less than 0.2 percent of natural (RESIDUAL SUGAR) remains. A wine can be dry and taste FRUITY at the same time.

DUMB: Describes a wine that temporarily has little taste. This can be a wine, usually white, that is served so cold that it tastes as though it's not altogether there. Or it can be a wine, usually red, in an awkward stage of its development when it tastes neither full of FRUIT and young, nor mature. In this strange state, sometimes called adolescence, the wine seems dull, ungenerous, almost mute. Why some wines go through dumb phases is not fully understood.

E

EARTHY: Used to describe a wine the AROMA or flavor of which is reminiscent of the earth. It usually refers to flavors that evoke soil or the forest—moss, dried leaves, bark, mushrooms, and the like. The term is sometimes extrapolated to include the pleasant, sensual aromas of the human body.

ELEGANT: A descriptive term for a wine with such FINESSE and BALANCE that it tastes refined rather than rustic.

ENOLOGY: The science and study of winemaking, differentiated from VITICULTURE, the study of grape growing. Also spelled oenology.

ESTATE BOTTLED: Exact definitions of estate bottled differ depending on the country from which the wine comes. In the United States, the term may be used by a winery only if 100 percent of the wine came from grapes grown on land owned or controlled by the winery, and both the land and winery must be in an authorized viticultural area. The winery must produce 100 percent of the wine, age it, and bottle it at the winery. While the winery and vineyard must be within the same viticultural area, the parcels do not need to be contiguous.

ESTERS: Aromatic compounds produced by yeasts and bacteria primarily during FERMENTATION. Esters may be complementary or deleterious to the wine.

ETHANOL OR ETHYL ALCOHOL: Commonly referred to simply as alcohol. ALCOHOL results when yeasts convert the natural sugar in ripe grapes during FERMENTATION.

EXTRACT: The soluble particles in wine that would remain if all the liquid was drawn off.

EXTRA DRY: A confusing designation, extra dry actually refers to Champagne or SPARKLING WINE that is slightly sweet, containing 1.2 to 2.0 percent residual sugar.

F

FAT: A descriptive term for the texture of a FULL-BODIED wine with saturated fruit. Although being fat is generally considered a positive wine trait, being flabby is not. A flabby wine is a fat wine that lacks acidity so that it seems gross and unfocused.

FERMENTATION: Also known as primary fermentation, the process whereby yeasts convert the natural sugar in the grapes into ALCOHOL and CARBON DIOXIDE. The alcohol will remain a constituent of the wine that results, but in most cases, the carbon dioxide will be allowed to escape as a by-product.

FIELD BLEND: An old method of VITICULTURE whereby different grape varieties are planted within a single vineyard. The grower then harvests all of the grapes at the same time and ferments them together. Thus, the final blend of the wine is based on the percentages of the varieties in the vineyard. If about 20 percent of the vineyard was planted with syrah, then the final wine will be composed of about 20 percent syrah. Before the twentieth century, most blended wines were based on field blends. Today, vineyards (or at least blocks within a vineyard) tend to be planted with a single variety. The grower can then harvest that variety when it is optimally ripe and ferment it separately in order to evaluate it before using it in the final blend.

FIELD SELECTION: Known in French as *selection massale,* a field selection is made up of a group of clones within a given vineyard. When a grower wants to create a new vineyard using field selection, he takes cuttings not from one mother vine (which would be a single clone) but rather from a series of different "mothers" in the vineyard, hoping to replicate the clonal diversity with that site.

FILTER: A filter is a porous membrane or other device used to remove selected particles from a liquid. In winemaking, a filter can be used to remove yeast cells and bacteria from the wine. Winemakers may filter a wine extensively, not at all, or to any degree in between. Some critics contend that some wines are filtered excessively, thereby stripping them of positive flavors and textures.

FINESSE: Used to describe a wine with elegance and BALANCE. The term implies that the wine is polished and sophisticated. Hearty, rustic country wines would not be described as having finesse, while a well-made Champagne or top white Burgundy might be.

FINING: A process of softening the texture of a wine by adding one or more protein coagulants, such as gelatin, egg whites, or ISINGLASS, to the wine. The coagulant attaches itself to TANNIN molecules, then settles to the bottom of the container, carrying tannin along with it. Fining can also be done to clarify the color of a wine, as when BENTONITE, a clay, is used to remove unwanted particles suspended in the wine that are making the wine appear hazy.

FINISH: The impression that a wine leaves in your mouth even after you have swallowed it. A finish may be almost nonexistent, fairly short, or extremely long. It may be smooth and lingering or rough and choppy. A finish may also be dominated by one component in the wine, such as ALCOHOL (a HOT finish), ACID (a tart finish), or TANNIN (an ASTRINGENT finish). A great wine, as opposed to a good wine, always has a pronounced, very long, lingering, well-balanced finish. In some judgings, officials actually measure the length of time that the wine can still be tasted after it has been swallowed.

FLAT: Refers to wines that taste dull and uninteresting. Often this is because the wine lacks ACIDITY.

FLOWERY: Used to describe AROMAS and flavors, usually present in white wines, that are reminiscent of flowers.

FORTIFIED: A wine, such as Sherry or Port, that has had its ALCOHOL content increased by the addition of distilled grape spirits (clear brandy). Most fortified wines contain 16 to 20 percent ALCOHOL BY VOLUME.

FOXY: An odd descriptive term (having nothing to do with foxes, or sex appeal, for that matter) for the wild, candylike aroma and flavor associated with wines that come from native American grapes of the VITIS labrusca species, such as Concord. The flavor is derived from an ESTER, methyl anthranilate.

FREE RUN: The juice that runs—freely—simply as the result of the weight of the grapes, before any mechanical pressure is applied in a PRESS.

FRUIT: The part of a wine's AROMA and flavor that comes from grapes. The fruit in a wine is distinguished from the wine's ALCOHOL or ACID.

FRUITY: A catchall term for the pronounced flavor or AROMA that comes from the wine grapes themselves. Wines are generally most fruity when they are young. In addition, certain VARIETAL wines (gewürztraminer, gamay, zinfandel) seem more fruity than others.

FULL-BODIED: Having pronounced weight on the palate. Full-bodied wines are to LIGHT-BODIED wines as half-and-half is to skim milk. All other things being equal, the higher a wine's ALCOHOL content, the more full-bodied it will seem.

FUTURES: See EN PRIMEUR in the French glossary.

G

GENERIC: A category of inexpensive wine that has been given a general generic name that is not controlled by law. In the United States, terms such as "chablis," "rhine," "sherry," and "burgundy" are all considered generic terms because they are not controlled by United States law. Note that in Europe these are stringently defined terms. Thus, any inexpensive blended wine in the United States may be called "chablis" even though the wine itself will bear no resemblance to its namesake.

GLYCERINE: Also called glycerol, glycerine is a colorless, odorless, slightly sweet, oily substance that is a minor by-product of FERMENTATION. Though often commented upon by tasters, glycerine probably makes no more than a negligible contribution to a dry wine's viscosity and it is not responsible for a wine's so-called "legs" or "tears." The wines with the highest glycerine levels are sweet botrytized wines. In these wines, glycerine may contribute slightly to the wine's sweetness and unctuous feel.

GRAFT: To splice one grape species (say, *vinifera*) onto another species (say, *rupestris*). Grafting makes it possible to grow, say, chardonnay, (which belongs to the species *vinifera*), onto a native American species ROOTSTOCK. Without the ability to graft, many of the great vineyards of the world would have long ago succumbed to the insect PHYLLOXERA.

GRASSY: A descriptive term for the green flavors and AROMAS reminiscent of just-cut grass, meadows, fields of hay, and the like. The VARIETAL most often described as grassy is sauvignon blanc.

GREEN: A flavor in wine generally associated with those of grass, moss, or vegetables. Also a flavor found in wines made from underripe grapes. A certain amount of greenness can be characteristic of, and therefore positive in, some varietals like sauvignon blanc. With most red VARIETALS, however, obvious greenness is considered a fault.

GUNFLINT: The taste or smell suggested by wet metal. Often used to describe sauvignon blancs, particularly OLD WORLD ones.

H

HERBAL: When used to describe a wine with flavors or AROMAS slightly reminiscent of herbs, herbal is positive. Good sauvignon blanc, for example, is considered slightly herbal. When herbal flavors become extreme, they are often described as herbaceous, a quality some wine drinkers like and others don't. Herbal is different than VEGETAL, a term used negatively to describe a wine with a dank green OFF ODOR.

HOGSHEAD: A modern hogshead, quite a bit larger than a small barrel, holds 79.25 gallons (300 liters). Winemakers use hogsheads when they want the wine to be less stamped by oak, as may be the case with such delicate varieties as sangiovese and pinot noir.

HOT: Refers to a wine with a level of ALCOHOL that is out of BALANCE with its ACID and FRUIT. The impression of excessive alcohol produces a slight burning "hit" at the top of the nasal passages and on the palate.

HYBRID: A new grape variety developed by breeding two or more genetically distinct varieties from different species. When the hybrid is a cross of a European species (VITIS VINIFERA) grape and a grape from any one of several American species, it is referred to as a French-American hybrid. These hybrids were developed by French plant breeders after the massive PHYLLOXERA infestation in the late nineteenth century, but are now banned in most French appellations. Well-known hybrids include baco noir, villard blanc, and seyval blanc, all of which are grown in the eastern United States.

I

IRF SCALE: A scale created to indicate how dry or sweet a riesling tastes. Created by the International Riesling Foundation (IRF) in 2007, the chart (which appears on the back label of many riesling wines globally) shows a spectrum from dry to medium dry to medium sweet to fully sweet. It then pinpoints where that wine falls. The IRF scale is based on sophisticated technical guidelines, including the ratio of sugar to acid in the wine. Wines with very high acid, for example, may still taste dry even though they have some amount of residual sugar.

ISINGLASS: A gelatinous material, obtained from the air bladders of sturgeons and other fish, that is used in FINING to clarify and/or soften the texture of wine; happily enough, it is removed before bottling.

J

JAMMY: Having the thick, concentrated berry AROMA or flavor of jam. Also, the thick, rich, mouthfilling texture of jam. Full-bodied, ripe red zinfandel is often described as jammy.

JUG WINES: Inexpensive wines sold in large bottles. Jug wines can be GENERIC blends or made from one variety of grape.

L

LABRUSCA: See VITIS LABRUSCA.

LATE HARVEST: As the term suggests, a wine that comes from grapes picked after the normal harvest and therefore contains a greater percentage of sugar. Late-harvest wines may also be infected with the noble rot, BOTRYTIS CINEREA. DESSERT WINES are usually late harvested.

LEES: The remnants of yeast cells and bits of grape skin that settle to the bottom of the container after FERMENTATION is complete. Leaving the fermented wine in contact with its lees (SUR LIE), rather than removing the lees right away, often adds complexity and nuance. See AUTOLYSIS.

LEGS: Also known as tears in Spain and cathedral windows in Germany, legs are the rivulets of wine that have inched up the inside surface of the glass above the wine, then run slowly back down. Myth has it that the fatter the legs, the better the wine. This is not true. The width of legs is determined by the interrelationship of a number of complex factors, including the amount of ALCOHOL, the amount of glycerol (see GLYCERINE), and the rate of evaporation of the alcohol and the surface tension between solids and liquids. But the most important point is this: Legs have nothing to do with quality. It is irresistible to point out that wines—like women—should not be judged by their legs.

LIGHT-BODIED: The term that describes a wine that has very little weight on the palate. A light-bodied wine literally feels light in your mouth, while a FULL-BODIED wine feels just the opposite. Light-bodied wines are low in ALCOHOL.

LUXURY WINE: The top category within the widely accepted hierarchy of wine prices established by Gomberg, Fredrickson & Associates. Luxury Wine is defined as wine that costs more than $25 per bottle.

M

MADERIZED: A term for a wine that has been subject to a long period of OXIDATION and heat. The best-known example is Madeira, from which the term maderized comes. TABLE WINES should not be maderized. See OXIDATION.

MAGNUM: A 1.5-liter bottle, which contains the equivalent of two normal (750 milliliter) bottles. *Magnum* means "large" in Latin.

MALOLACTIC FERMENTATION: This process has nothing to do with primary FERMENTATION, since it does not involve yeasts or the production of ALCOHOL. Rather, malolactic fermentation is a chemical conversion of ACID instigated by beneficial bacteria. During the process, the sharp malic acid in grapes is converted to softer lactic acid. As a result, the wine tastes less crisp and more creamy. During malolactic fermentation, the by-product DIACETYL is created, giving the wine a buttery character. Malolactic fermentation can either occur naturally or be prompted by the winemaker. All red wines go through malolactic fermentation, rendering them more microbially stable. White wines may or may not. If the winemaker wants to achieve a soft MOUTHFEEL in the white wine, then malolactic fermentation is induced. If he or she prefers to retain dramatic, snappy acidity, then malolactic fermentation is prevented, usually by the use of SULFUR.

MASSALE SELECTION: An ancient method (literally "mass selection") of establishing a new vineyard or replanting an old one by selecting numerous older vines throughout an existing vineyard, propagating and planting them. Mass selection can help to maintain the consistency of style of the wine from a particular vineyard. The opposite of massale selection would be to replant a vineyard using specific clonal material from a nursery.

MERCAPTANS: Offensive-smelling compounds that result from poor winemaking when hydrogen sulfide combines with components of the wine. The AROMAS can include putrid food, skunk, and burnt rubber.

MERITAGE: A United States trademarked designation, adopted in 1988 by the Meritage Association, for California wines that are a blend of the varieties of grapes used in Bordeaux. A red Meritage might be made up of cabernet sauvignon, merlot, and cabernet franc. A white Meritage would be a blend of sauvignon blanc and sémillon. Meritage wines are usually moderately expensive and are often given fanciful proprietary names. Such wines as Opus One, Insignia, Cain Five, and Magnificat would all qualify as Meritage if their producers chose to have them so designated. Producers may choose not to use the term Meritage even if their wine meets the qualifications.

MICROOXYGENATION: A process winemakers use to add oxygen to wine in a controlled fashion. Adding oxygen changes the chemistry of the wine and, depending on the timing of the introduction, can have several different effects. Microoxygenation is most commonly used to assist fermentation, and/or accelerate maturation.

MOUTHFEEL: The tactile impression of a wine in your mouth. Like clothing, wine can feel soft, rough, velvety, and so on.

MUST: The juice and liquidy pulp produced by crushing or pressing grapes before FERMENTATION.

MUSTY: A dank, old-attic smell in a wine, attributed to unclean storage containers and sometimes to grapes processed when moldy.

N

NÉGOCIANT: See the French glossary.

NEW WORLD: A descriptive term encompassing all of those wine-producing countries that do not belong to the OLD WORLD. The most important New World wine producers are the United States, Australia, New Zealand, South Africa, Argentina, and Chile. By extension, New World techniques generally refer to modern viticultural and winemaking methods that rely heavily on science. Avantgarde Old World wine producers are often said to use New World techniques.

NOBLE ROT: See BOTRYTIS CINEREA.

NONVINTAGE: When applied to Champagne, a blend of wines from different vintage years. (A more correct term would be *multivintage*.) The majority of Champagnes are nonvintage. Sherry, Port, and Madeira are also usually nonvintage.

NOSE: The smell of a wine, including both the AROMA from the grape and the BOUQUET from AGING.

O

OAKY: A descriptive term for the toasty, woody, and vanilla smells and flavors contributed to wine during its FERMENTATION and/or AGING in oak barrels. The newer the oak barrel, the greater the potential for the wine to have a pronounced oaky character. Often (but not always) the longer the wine is left in oak, the greater the oaky influence. A wine that has an oak flavor that dominates all natural fruit flavors is considered over-oaked.

ODORS: The panoply of smells that may emanate from a wine. These include a whole range of fruits and berries (apple, lemon, peach, apricot, cherry, raspberry, cranberry, plum, and so on); plus flowers (honeysuckle, rose, violet, geranium, and so forth); plus assorted other smells reminiscent of the earth, yeast, beer, leaves, herbs, vegetables, mushrooms, truffles, straw, wet wool, caramel, pepper, spices, nuts, oak, wood, meat, game, mold, cigar boxes, dust, mint, pine, eucalyptus, olives, fuel oil, and rubber boots.

OENOLOGY: See ENOLOGY.

OFF-DRY: Ever so slightly sweet. In the U.S., there is however, no legally defined amount of sugar a wine must have to be considered off-dry.

OFF ODORS: Unpleasant smells (chemicals, dankness, moldiness, rotten eggs, burnt rubber, sauerkraut, and so on) that suggest that the wine was stored in unclean containers or poorly made.

OIDIUM: A vine disease also known as powdery mildew.

OLD WORLD: As applied to wine, Old World refers to those countries where wine first flourished, namely Western or Central European countries and others ringing the Mediterranean basin and in the Near East. Old World techniques, by extension, refer to ways of growing grapes and making wines that rely more on tradition and less on science. The Old World is usually talked about in contrast to the NEW WORLD. Wine producers in the New World, however, are often fond of saying that they employ Old World techniques as a way of establishing that their wines are made at least in part by traditional methods.

OLFACTION: The process of perceiving smells. In order to smell things—that is, in order for olfaction to occur—humans use two separate sensory areas. The first is the nasal cavity. AROMAS smelled via the nose are said to occur by orthonasal olfaction. The other area is at the cavity at the back of the palate. Aromas perceived this way—retronasally—happen as a result of wine first being warmed in the mouth and mixed with saliva.

ORGANIC VITICULTURE: See box, page 35, in the chapter "Where It All Begins."

OXIDATION: The process of exposing wine to air, which changes it. A little oxidation can be positive; it can help to soften and open up a wine, for example. Too much exposure to air, however, is deleterious. It can make a wine turn brown and take on a tired flavor. When too much exposure to air occurs, the wine is described as oxidized.

P

PH: A measure of the strength of the relative acidity versus the relative alkalinity of wine (or any liquid) on a logarithmic scale of 0 to 14. The lower the number is below 7 (the neutral pH of water), the greater the relative acidity. Winemakers consider the pH of a wine in relationship to other factors (ALCOHOL, TANNIN, EXTRACT, and the like) to determine if the wine is in BALANCE. As grapes mature, plotting the change in the pH of their pulp is a way of determining ripeness.

PHENOLS: A group of chemical compounds occurring naturally in all plants. In wine, phenols are derived from grape skins, stems, and seeds, as well as from oak barrels. Among the most important phenols are TANNIN, COLOR pigments, and some flavor compounds, such as VANILLIN. Depending on their chemical structure, some phenols are known as polyphenols.

PHYLLOXERA: A small, aphid-like insect that attacks the roots of vines belonging to the species VITIS VINIFERA. Phylloxera slowly destroys the vine by preventing the roots from absorbing nutrients and water. Native American vines, such as those belonging to the species VITIS LABRUSCA or Vitis riparia, tolerate the insect without adverse consequences. In the latter part of the nineteenth century, a phylloxera epidemic swept through Europe and eventually around the world. By the time a remedy was discovered, millions of acres of vines had been destroyed. The remedy, still the only known solution, was to replant each vineyard, vine by vine, with native American ROOTSTOCKS, then graft VITIS VINIFERA vines on top.

PIPE: In Victorian England, where a pipe of Port was commonly given to a newborn child as a gift, a pipe held 141.13 gallons (534.24 liters). Today, a pipe holds a volume ranging from 145.29 gallons (550 liters) to 166.42 gallons (630 liters), depending on the country they come from and whether they are used for maturing or shipping a wine. Pipes commonly contain Port, Sherry, Madeira, Marsala, or Cognac.

POMACE: The mashed-up solid residue (skins, stems, seeds, pulp) that is left after grapes are pressed. When pomace is distilled, it can be made into GRAPPA (Italy), MARC (France), or EAU-DE-VIE (France and the United States).

PREMIUM WINES: In the 1980s, the California-based wine consulting and management company of Gomberg, Fredrickson & Associates established a hierarchy of wines according to price. The hierarchy includes four levels of premium wine—Popular Premium ($3–$7), Mid Premium ($7–$10), Super Premium ($10–$14), and Ultra Premium ($14–$25).

PRESS: To press means to exert pressure on grapes to extract their juices. A press is a device used to do that. There are many kinds; one of the simplest and oldest is the hand-operated wooden basket press. A more modern press—the bladder press—is essentially a horizontal tank with an inflatable membrane running through its middle. As the membrane swells, it gently squeezes the grapes against the side of the revolving tank. Grape bunches can be put whole into a press, but more often they are crushed and the stems are removed first.

PRIVATE RESERVE: A term found on some NEW WORLD wine labels for which there is no legal definition. Sometimes a wine labeled Private Reserve is truly special and of high quality (such as Beaulieu Vineyards' Georges de Latour Private Reserve). Other times, however, the phrase is simply a hackneyed way of marketing an ordinary wine. Similar terms include Proprietor's Reserve and Grand Reserve.

PRODUCED AND BOTTLED BY: A term found on U.S. wine labels indicating that not less than 75 percent of the wine was fermented at the address on the label and that the wine was bottled at that address. See VINTED AND BOTTLED BY.

PRUNING: The removal of living canes, shoots, leaves, and other vegetative growth. Vines are usually pruned in winter when the plant is dormant (and thus less susceptible to diseases that could infiltrate the vine via the pruning wounds). Pruning is generally severe. About 90 percent of the previous season's growth is removed each year. Pruning keeps vines manageable and affects how the vine will grow in the following year. Thus, pruning can be used to regulate the size and quality of the next year's crop. Pruning is usually done by hand with shears, but mechanical pruners do exist to speed up pruning in large vineyards, especially in countries like Australia, where agricultural workers are in short supply.

PUCKERY: Used to describe a wine that is so high in TANNIN that it causes your mouth to pucker with dryness. Most often the wine will have been made from insufficiently ripe grapes.

PULP: The soft, fleshy part of the grape, which is infused with juice.

PUMPING OVER: A process during the FERMENTATION of red wine in which the juice is pumped from the bottom of the container to the top and then sprayed over the CAP of skins to break it up and keep it wet. By trickling through this mass of skins, the juice picks up even more COLOR, flavor, and TANNIN. Pumping over also helps prevent the growth of undesirable bacteria that might spoil the wine or create off flavors.

PUNCHEON: Modern puncheons, commonly used for wines like sangiovese that don't benefit from a lot of wood contact, come in two sizes: 79.25 gallons and 132.08 gallons (200 and 500 liters, respectively).

PUNCHING DOWN: The opposite of PUMPING OVER, this process accomplishes the same goals. During punching down, the CAP is pushed down with a paddle into the fermenting grape juice. Punching down, despite its name, is a gentle process.

PUNT: The indentation found in the bottom of most wine bottles. The punt may be shallow or, as in the case of Champagne bottles, quite pronounced. The punt adds stability by weighting the bottom of the bottle and strengthens the glass at its weakest point.

PYRAZINES: Molecular compounds in certain wines that give them a distinct green bell pepper flavor. Pyrazines are found in high concentrations in the skins of cabernet sauvignon, sauvignon blanc, merlot, and cabernet franc in particular. When these grapes do not get fully ripe, the pyrazine flavor is highly apparent.

Q

QVEVRI: A large earthenware vessel originating in Georgia around 6000 B.C. Lined with beeswax and sunk into the ground to control temperature, it was traditionally used to ferment and store wine.

R

RACKING: A method of clarifying a wine that has SETTLED by siphoning or pumping off solids and particulate matter, such as yeast cells and bits of grape skins, and pouring it into a different clean barrel. Racking also AERATES a wine.

RAISINY: A descriptive term for a wine (generally a red) that tastes slightly like raisins because the grapes were overripe when picked. A small bit of this quality can add an interesting nuance to the wine, but too much is a flaw.

RESERVE: Many producers the world over make a reserve wine in addition to their regular offering, the reserve being of higher quality (theoretically) and higher price (dependably). In the United States, a reserve wine may be a selection of the best lots of wine from grapes grown in the best vineyards, and/ or it may be a wine that has been allowed to age longer before release. But since the term *reserve* is not actually defined by United States law, an embarrassing number of producers use it purely as a marketing ploy to get you to buy wine that is, in fact, of cheap quality and rather pedestrian. The one exception to this is Washington State, where in 1999, an industry group, the Washington Wine Quality Alliance, set forth its own stipulations regarding the term *reserve*. Members of the alliance—virtually all of the top wine producers in the state—agreed to use the term *reserve* only for 10 percent of a winery's production or 3,000 cases, whichever is greater. Additionally, a wine labeled reserve must be among the higher-priced wines the winery produces, and all of the grapes for the wine must be grown in Washington State. In contrast to the United States, most European countries strictly define the terms reserve, RISERVA (Italy), RESERVA (Spain), and the like.

RESIDUAL SUGAR: Natural grape sugar that remains in wine because it has not been converted into ALCOHOL during FERMENTATION. Wines that taste dry can nonetheless have a tiny amount of residual sugar in them. Winemakers often leave small amounts of sugar in wine to make it seem rounder and more appealing (sweetness has a slight fat feeling to it). Wine producers are not required to list residual sugar content on labels.

RIDDLING: Called RÉMUAGE in French, riddling is the process during the making of Champagne or SPARKLING WINE whereby the bottles are individually rotated and tilted a small bit day after day in order to concentrate the yeast sediment in the necks prior to DISGORGING. In the past, bottles held in A-shape frames called pupitres were riddled by hand. Today, it may also be done by a computerized machine called a gyropalette.

ROOTSTOCK: The part of the grapevine that is planted directly in the soil. Rootstocks from different varieties have different tolerances to disease and climatic stress and will be more or less suitable to a given type of soil. The variety of rootstock also affects how slowly or quickly the vine itself will grow. A vine need not grow from its own roots. In fact, most vines are not grown from their own roots but instead are grafted onto select rootstocks that have been bred for their disease-resistant properties (see PHYLLOXERA and VITIS).

ROTTEN EGG: The term most often used to describe a wine that exhibits the fault of having excessive hydrogen sulfide.

ROUGH: Used to describe the coarse texture of a (usually young) tannic red wine before it has begun to round out. AGING can sometimes soften a rough wine.

S

SCION: The portion of the vine that is grafted onto the rootstock and determines the type of fruit grown by the plant.

SEC: French for DRY. In wine, however, the opposite is usually true. Champagne that is labeled sec, for example, is medium sweet to sweet.

SECONDARY FERMENTATION: A FERMENTATION that takes place after the first fermentation, either spontaneously or by intention. In the making of top Champagnes and SPARKLING WINES, the secondary fermentation takes place inside the bottle and produces the gas that eventually becomes the wines' bubbles (see CARBON DIOXIDE). In table wine, a secondary fermentation is undesirable.

SECOND CROP: Fruit that matures after the first crop has been picked. This is usually not picked because the quantity is too small to be economically viable and the grapes may not be sufficiently ripe.

SECOND WINE: The term for a secondary and usually less expensive wine made by a winery. In Bordeaux, for example, Château Latour's second label is Les Forts de Latour. Most wineries that make a second label are highly respected for their primary label and may not want to actively market (or be known for) their second label. The wine that is sold under the second label is never as high in quality as wine of the primary label. The grapes may come from younger vines and/or lesser vineyards.

SEDIMENT: The particulate matter (usually harmless) and color pigments that may precipitate out of a wine as it ages. The presence of sediment is not negative; many of the best wines in the world throw off sediment as they age.

SETTLING: The precipitation (settling out) of solid matter in wine. SEDIMENT, for example, settles out of a mature wine.

SHATTER: A phenomenon that can occur in the spring whereby individual grape berries become separated from the stem and fall to the ground. May be caused by cool, wet weather during early grape development, which tends to prevent the tiny cap on each fertilized berry from falling off. Then as the berries start to grow, they push against the cap and shatter, significantly reducing yields.

SHOOT: A new green stem that springs from the CORDON of the vine as it begins to grow in the spring. The shoots will ultimately sprout leaves and clusters of grapes.

SHOOT THINNING: The act of removing some shoots in order to improve the quality of the fruit, as well as to reduce vine stress. By thinning the shoots, the winegrower attempts to get the vine to put its energy into ripening its clusters rather than growing green vegetative parts.

SKIN CONTACT: In a sense, all red wines experience skin contact since in red wine FERMENTATION the juice and skins of the grapes are in contact. But in contemporary winemaking, the term skin contact generally refers to the process of letting crushed white grapes sit with the skins and the juice together, rather than immediately separating them. This process helps add flavor and AROMA to the final wine. A white wine may be given anywhere from a few hours to a couple of days of skin-contact time.

SMALL BARREL: Although first used as a general term to describe any wooden container, barrels are now used as specific measures. Three types of small barrels are standard around the world. French oak Bordeaux barrels, known as *barriques*, are used for many types of wine, including cabernet sauvignon, merlot, and Bordeaux. They hold 59.43 gallons (225 liters). French oak Burgundy barrels, known as pieces, are generally used for pinot noirs worldwide, including Burgundies. They hold 60.2 gallons (228 liters). And American oak barrels, used for all types of wine, are made in both sizes.

SMOKY: A smoky smell and taste found in both white and red wines. Though wines can take on smoky characters from the barrels in which they are aged, certain wines just have a naturally smoky character as a result of their TERROIR (see the French glossary). Many Pouilly-Fumés and Sancerres from France's Loire Valley are smoky, for example.

SOMMELIER: The French term for a wine steward, which has also been appropriated by the English language. In American slang, the word *sommelier* is sometimes contracted to *somm*.

SOUR: A descriptive term, generally used negatively, for a wine with a flavor that, as far as the taster is concerned, is too sharp and acidic.

SPARKLING WINE: A wine with bubbles. The most famous sparkling wine is Champagne, made in the region of the same name in France. Other types of sparkling wine include CAVA (from Spain), SEKT (from Germany), and PROSECCO (from Italy).

SPICY: A descriptive term for a wine with an AROMA or flavor suggestive of aromatic spices. Spicy wines are also often peppery and can have a slight, pleasantly scratchy texture.

SPLIT: A small wine bottle containing 6.4 ounces (187.5 milliliters), one fourth of a standard 750 milliliter bottle.

SPRITZY: Wines with a small amount of sparkle from carbonation left or trapped in the wine. In a still wine, this is usually undesirable.

STARTER: Commercial YEASTS used to initiate and ensure fermentation.

STEMMY: A descriptive term for a wine with the green odor or flavor of stems or, sometimes, wet grain.

STILL WINES: All wines that are not SPARKLING WINES.

SULFUR: A natural chemical compound that has been used as a wine preservative since antiquity. The most common form of sulfur used in wine making is sulfur dioxide (SO_2), which is formed when elemental sulfur is burned in air. Added to wine (usually as a gas), sulfur dioxide prevents OXIDATION as well as bacterial spoilage, and it inhibits the growth of YEASTS. As a result of this, sulfur dioxide can be used to stop FERMENTATION in order to produce a sweet wine, and it can be used to prevent MALOLACTIC FERMENTATION. A form of sulfur dioxide known as metabisulfite is often added to freshly picked grapes (and fruit juices in general) as a preservative. Sulfur dioxide's disadvantage is that it has an unpleasant, burnt-match odor, which can be smelled at low concentrations, although people vary widely in the thresholds at which they can detect it. The ability to detect sulfur dioxide also varies based on the type of wine, since in some wines the compound reacts to or combines with other compounds, rendering it more difficult to perceive. In any case, during the last few decades, winemakers the world over have sought to minimize the amount of sulfur dioxide they use in winemaking, mostly in response to health concerns voiced by wine drinkers. Nonetheless, it's virtually impossible to produce a wine that is entirely sulfur-free, because a small amount of sulfur dioxide is a byproduct of the metabolic action of yeasts during fermentation (this is why bread, too, contains sulfur dioxide). As a result, United States law mandates that the term "contains sulfites" appear on all wine labels that contain more than 10 parts per million of sulphur dioxide (and most do), even when the wine has been produced without the addition of any sulfur dioxide. The word *sulfites* in the warning is a catchall term for sulfur in all its various forms, including sulfur dioxide, sulfurous acid, bisulfite ion, and sulfite ion, as well as other complex forms. Sulfur in all its forms is harmless to people except for the tiny number of individuals who are severely allergic to it.

SUR LIE: Literally, "on the lees." Some white wines, notably white Burgundies, are, for a period of time, left in contact with the lees (spent YEAST) after FERMENTATION is complete. Wines that have been left take on a creamy, rounder MOUTHFEEL and generally display more complex flavors.

SUSTAINABLE VITICULTURE: See box, page 35 in the chapter "Where It All Begins."

T

TABLE WINE: The term used around the world to describe wines of moderate alcoholic strength (usually 9 to 15 percent ALCOHOL BY VOLUME) as opposed to FORTIFIED wines, which have grape spirits added to them and thus are stronger in alcoholic strength (usually between 16 and 20 percent alcohol by volume). In common speech, however, the term table wine is often used to indicate dry, STILL WINES served to accompany dinner, rather than sweet wines intended for dessert or SPARKLING WINES.

TANNIN: A PHENOL (a kind of compound) derived from the skins, seeds, and stems of grapes and from barrels. The presence of tannin is beneficial, for it gives red wines a firm structure as well as the potential for aging. Tannin is both tasted and felt. When young, highly tannic wines have a slight bitterness (like espresso or chocolate) and a drying, astringent feel. If the wine has been made from mature grapes with ripe tannin, the bitter, dry quality will be ameliorated. Excessively dry, harsh, scratchy tannin is a negative and may never ameliorate. Harsh tannin, often called green or unripe tannin, most often results when grapes have been picked before they are completely physiologically mature. Most white wines have only tiny amounts of tannin because they are not fermented on their skins.

TARTRATES: Tasteless, odorless, harmless bits of tartaric ACID that can precipitate out of a wine that has not been COLD STABILIZED. Tartrates look like small white snowflakes.

TASTEVIN: See the French glossary.

TERPENE: An organic compound that is produced by a variety of plants, including grapevines, which can produce a strong aroma. It is found in higher concentrations mostly in gewürztraminer, muscat, riesling, and other German crosses. Muscat has one of the highest concentrations of terpenes, and, therefore, its characteristic aroma can often be said to smell of "terpene."

TERROIR: See the French glossary.

THIN: Used to describe a wine lacking body, because it is low in ALCOHOL, as well as lacking fruit flavors, possibly because it was made from grapes produced at a very high YIELD. An extremely thin wine tastes watery.

TOASTING: Charring the inside of new barrels over an open flame. Charring caramelizes the staves of the wood. Wine stored in barrels treated this way will pick up a VANILLIN, toasty character.

TOPPING UP: To add more wine to a barrel or container to replace any wine lost through evaporation, and thereby prevent the wine from experiencing OXIDATION. The term is also used in more general circumstances to mean adding wine to a glass in which there's only a sip or two left.

TRANSFER PROCESS: A less expensive way of making SPARKLING WINE than the traditional MÉTHODE CHAMPENOISE (see the French Glossary). In the transfer process, the SECONDARY FERMENTATION takes place in the individual bottles (as it does in Champagne), but then instead of RIDDLING and DISGORGING each bottle, the wine is emptied into large tanks where these two processes take place under pressure. Finally, the wine is filtered, a DOSAGE (see the French glossary) is added, and the wine is rebottled.

TRUNK: The vine's permanent vertical stem, which grows out of the ground.

TYPICITY: A quality that a wine possesses if it is typical of its region and reflects the characteristics of the grape variety from which it came. Whether or not a wine demonstrates typicity is pretty subjective. It also has nothing to do with how good the wine tastes. A wine can be quite delicious and nonetheless show no typicity. A rich, full-bodied, buttery, oaky Sancerre, for example, would not have typicity, since Sancerres are typically lean, minerally, and zesty, and have tangy flavors. In certain OLD WORLD countries, an evaluation of typicity, even though it's subjective, is required by law in order for a wine to obtain APPELLATION status.

U

ULLAGE: The space that develops near the neck and shoulder inside a wine bottle or container because wine has been lost through leakage or evaporation. In a bottle with significant ullage, the wine will often be OXIDIZED and spoiled. In a wine auction, a wine with ullage will not command top dollar.

UNFILTERED: Used to describe a wine that has not been FILTERED to clarify it and remove any unwanted YEASTS or bacteria. Winemakers who believe that filtering strips wine of some flavors and texture may leave their wines unfiltered and may even label them as such. An unfiltered wine will often undergo FINING to remove large particles in suspension as well as coarse TANNIN. Unfiltered wines are sometimes less than brilliantly clear.

UNFINED: A wine that has not gone through FINING to remove large particulate matter and some tannins.

As with FILTERING, many winemakers believe fining can harm the flavor and texture of the wine. An unfined wine may still be filtered.

UNOAKED: A wine that has been fermented and aged in stainless-steel or concrete vessels, instead of oak. This style gives the wine more clarity and purity of fruit.

V

VANILLIN: A compound in oak barrels that is ultimately imparted to wine as a flavor and smell reminiscent of vanilla. New barrels have more vanillin than older barrels, and hence wine stored in new barrels has a more pronounced vanilla character.

VARIETAL: Wine made from a particular variety of grape. Chardonnay, riesling, pinot noir, cabernet sauvignon, and so on are all varietal wines. In general, each varietal has a unique flavor, distinct from other varietals. When a wine has a pronounced varietal flavor, it is said to have varietal character. On January 1, 1983, United States law established that a wine named after a grape—a varietal—must contain 75 percent or more of that grape variety and must have been grown in the appellation of origin appearing on the label. Prior to that date, a varietally labeled wine had to contain 51 percent or more of the named grape.

VEGETAL: Used to describe a wine with off-putting AROMAS and flavors reminiscent of stewed or canned green beans, asparagus, artichokes, and the like.

VERAISON: The change of color of the grape berries, signaling the onset of ripening. White grapes go from green to yellow, and red grapes go from green to red.

VINEGARY: Describes a wine with the harsh aroma of vinegar, usually produced by ACETIC acid. Considered a major fault in a wine.

VINICULTURE: The science of winemaking. The term is used much less frequently than ENOLOGY.

VINIFERA: See VITIS.

VINOUS: Winelike. Europeans sometimes criticize California wines as being too fruity and so not vinous enough.

VINTAGE: The year the grapes were grown and harvested. A vintage year appears on the labels of most wines, though some famous wines—nonvintage Champagne, Sherry, and many styles of Port, for example—never carry a vintage date because they are blends of wines from several different years. In the United States, most wines bottled with a vintage date are made up entirely of grapes from that year. Technically, however, United States law requires only that 95 percent of the wine comes from grapes harvested in the year appearing on the label.

VINTAGE CHAMPAGNE: Champagne made from a single year's harvest. Aged a minimum of three years and often four or five. Called MILLÉSIME in French.

VINTED AND BOTTLED BY: A term found on United States wine labels, indicating that the wine was bottled at the address on the label and that some cellar treatment (such as aging) was performed at the address on the label. However, vinted and bottled by does not mean that the wine was necessarily fermented at the address on the label. See PRODUCED AND BOTTLED BY.

VINTNER: A person who makes or sells wine. Often used to describe the owner of a winery who may also employ a winemaker.

VISCOSITY: The character some wines possess of being somewhat syrupy and slow to move around in the mouth. A spoonful of honey, for example, is more viscous than a spoonful of water, and ALCOHOL, by its nature, is viscous. Thus both sweet wines and wines with high alcohol are more viscous than dry wines and wines low in alcohol.

VITICULTURE: The science of growing grapes.

VITIS: The genus of the plant kingdom to which grapevines belong. Within the genus *Vitis* there are some sixty separate species. The most famous species—and the only one to have originated in Europe—is VITIS VINIFERA, which includes all of the well-known wine grapes: chardonnay, pinot noir, cabernet sauvignon, and so on (and accounts for virtually all of the wines made today). Most species of vines, however, originated in North America. These include VITIS LABRUSCA, *Vitis riparia*, *Vitis rupestris*, *Vitis rotundifolia*, and *Vitis berlandieri*, among others.

VITIS LABRUSCA: American vine species that generally produces wines that are far less sophisticated and complex than *vinifera* varieties. In particular, labrusca grapes are easily recognizable by their pungent, candylike aroma and flavor, usually described as FOXY. Concord, for example, is a grape variety that belongs to the species *Vitis labrusca*. Over centuries, many American species have hybridized by chance. In addition, from 1880 to 1950, plant scientists in both France and the United States intentionally created HYBRIDS by crossing *vinifera* varieties with hardier, more disease- and pest-resistant American varieties. While their use for wine is declining, hybrids remain critically important as ROOTSTOCKS. Two other North American vine species are *Vitis riparia* and *Vitis rotundifolia*. Although no well-known wines are made from these species, they are very resistant to PHYLLOXERA and so are frequently used for rootstocks. French/American hybrids such as *baco noir* are also made with these species.

VITIS VINIFERA: A vine species accounting for most of the wines made in the world today. Such grapes as chardonnay, cabernet sauvignon, pinot noir, syrah, and riesling are all *Vitis vinifera* varieties. *Vitis vinifera* originated in Europe and the Middle East.

VOLATILE ACIDITY: All wines have a tiny amount of volatile acidity, usually, with any luck, imperceptible. In excess, V.A., as it is known, causes a wine to have an unpleasantly sharp, vinegary aroma. Volatile acidity occurs because unwanted bacteria have produced ACETIC acid, the result of poor winemaking.

Y

YEASTS: Single-celled microorganisms used to convert sugar to alcohol and carbon dioxide during fermentation.

YEASTY: In STILL WINES, yeasty describes an AROMA suggestive of the yeasts used in FERMENTATION. The quality should not be pronounced. In Champagne and SPARKLING WINES, it refers to the aroma of bread dough, considered positive and often the result of long aging on the LEES.

YIELD: The measure of how much a vineyard produces. In general, very high yields are associated with low-quality wine, and low yields are associated with high-quality wine. However, the relationship of yield of grapes to wine quality is extremely complex and not linear. Thus, a yield of 2 tons per acre does not necessarily produce better wine than a yield of 3 tons per acre, which doesn't necessarily portend better wine than if the yield were 4 tons per acre. Every vineyard is different, and yield must always be considered in light of multiple other factors, including the variety of grape, the type of CLONE, the age of the vine, the particular ROOTSTOCK, and the TERROIR. In Europe, yield is measured in hectoliters per hectare (one hectoliter equals 26.4 gallons; one hectare equals 2.47 acres). The unofficial French dictum is that great red wine cannot be made from yields of more than 50 hectoliters per hectare. In the United States, yield is generally measured in tons of grapes per acre. Roughly speaking, 1 ton per acre equals 15 hectoliters per hectare. Yields in the United States can range from less than 1 ton per acre to 10 or more. This said, the way yield is thought about in the United States is changing as a result of new vineyards, many of which are now planted so that the vines are much more closely spaced than they were in the past. With such vineyards, viticulturists talk of pounds of grapes per vine, rather than tons per acre.

FRENCH WINE TERMS

A

APPELLATION D'ORIGINE CONTRÔLÉE (AOC): See page 137.

ASSEMBLAGE: A Champagne or SPARKLING WINE term that refers to the blending, or assembling, of still wines before the SECONDARY FERMENTATION, which creates the bubbles.

B

BAUMÉ: The scale used in France and much of the rest of Europe for measuring sugar in grapes and, hence, their ripeness. Other scales for measuring sugar include BRIX (used in the United States) and OECHSLE (used in Germany).

BAN DES VENDANGES: Literally, "opening of the harvest"—the official date when harvest can begin. Growers can choose to begin harvest anytime after the *ban des vendanges* but not before it. A *ban des vendanges* is mandatory in some (but not all) AOCs, including Champagne and Burgundy. Within a given area, the ban des vendanges differs depending on the grape variety and location of the vineyard.

BLANC DE BLANCS: Literally, "white from whites." A golden Champagne or SPARKLING WINE made entirely from white grapes, usually chardonnay grapes.

BLANC DE NOIRS: Literally, "white from blacks." A golden Champagne or SPARKLING WINE made from black (*noir*) grapes. (The French refer to red grapes as black.) It is possible to make a white wine from red grapes because the juice and PULP of red-skinned grapes is white. *Blanc de noirs* are usually made from pinot noir, but pinot meunier may be used in some cases. Very few Champagne houses produce blanc de noirs Champagnes. The practice is more common among makers of Californian sparkling wines.

BOUCHON: A type of restaurant in Lyon, France, known for serving traditional Lyonnaise dishes, which are heavy on meat and fat. The goal of a *bouchon* is not haute cuisine but a friendly and personal atmosphere. There are about 20 certified bouchons in Lyon, although many more proclaim themselves to be. Bouchon also refers to a stopper for the mouth of a wine bottle, most often a sparkling wine, as it prevents the bubbles from escaping.

BOTRYTIS CINEREA: See Main Glossary.

BRUT: A DRY to very dry Champagne or SPARKLING WINE containing less than 15 grams of sugar per liter (equal to 1.5 percent residual sugar). EXTRA BRUT is slightly drier than brut.

C

CÉPAGE NOBLE: *Cépage* means "grape variety." The so-called noble grape varieties—*cépages nobles*—are those that consistently make fine wine, such as cabernet sauvignon, pinot noir, or chardonnay.

CHAI: Above-ground facility used to store wine.

CHAPTALIZATION: See Main Glossary.

CHÂTEAU: A building where wine is made and around which vines grow. Despite the images most of us have of palatial estates, such as Bordeaux's regal Château Margaux, a château can be as humble as a garage. The names of most Bordeaux estates are preceded by the word *château*, though the word is used infrequently elsewhere in France and never in Burgundy, where the roughly equivalent term would be DOMAINE.

CLIMAT: The term used especially in Burgundy to mean a specific field or plot. Each *climat* is distinguished by its own soil, climate, orientation to the sun, slope, drainage capacity, and so on.

CLOS: A term used especially in Burgundy to indicate a vineyard enclosed by a wall. One of Burgundy's largest and most famous walled vineyards is Clos Vougeot.

COMMUNE: A small village that is often an APPELLATION. In Bordeaux, the communes of Margaux, Pauillac, St.-Julien, and St.-Estèphe are famous appellations. Communes are also the lowest level of administrative division in France, and as such, are the equivalent of incorporated cities in the United States.

COULURE: The failure of grapes to develop after flowering occurs. Weather conditions during the spring, such as clouds and cold temperatures, wind, rain, and high temperatures, can cause the flowers to stay closed or drop off the vine, and therefore not become fertilized. Each flower represents a potential grape, and vines that experience *coulure,* sometimes called SHATTER in English, often have irregular bunches that are missing grapes.

CRAYÈRES: Deep chalk pits used by Champagne houses to age Champagne. Originally dug by the Romans in A.D. 300 to source stones for building the city of Reims, these cold, dark, humid chambers are as deep as 60 feet underground and are shaped like a pyramid, with the bottom of the pit being the widest.

CRÉMANT: Today the word *crémant* is reserved for French SPARKLING WINES made outside the Champagne region using the MÉTHODE CHAMPENOISE. Important examples include Crémant d'Alsace,

Crémant de Bourgogne, and Crémant de Loire. Since 1994, the term has not been permitted to be used in Champagne. It was once used to describe a Champagne with about half the usual effervescence, often called a creaming wine. These half-sparkling Champagnes are still made, but today they are given proprietary names.

CRU: Translated in English as "growth," the word *cru* can mean a vineyard or an estate, usually a superior one, that has been classified geographically or by reputation. A classified *cru* is known as a *cru classé*. Within any given classification (such as those in Bordeaux and Burgundy), there are *Premiers Crus* (first growths), *Grands Crus* (great growths), and so on. The word is the past participle of the French verb *croître,* meaning "to grow."

CUVÉE: The wine from a selected barrel or vat (the term is derived from the French *cuve*, meaning "vat"). In Champagne, however, the word *cuvée* is used to describe a blend of wines. A Champagne cuvée is often made up of different varieties of grapes, or grapes from different vineyard plots, or both. The term prestige cuvée is used in Champagne to refer to a house's most expensive and prestigious wine. Dom Pérignon, for example, is the prestige cuvée of Moët & Chandon.

CUVERIE: The building that houses FERMENTATION tanks or vats. The place where the wine ferments.

D

DÉGORGEMENT: Disgorgement (see DISGORGING in Main Glossary)—the process of removing the yeasty sediments from a Champagne bottle after the second, bubble-forming FERMENTATION.

DEMI-SEC: A sweet Champagne or SPARKLING WINE containing 33 to 50 grams of sugar per liter (equal to 3.3 to 5 percent residual sugar). Demi-sec is sweeter than EXTRA DRY, which is sweeter than BRUT.

DE PRIMEUR: Wines that are sold and drunk very young. The most famous of these is Beaujolais Nouveau, although dozens of French wines are allowed by law to be sold the year the grapes were harvested. Not to be confused with EN PRIMEUR.

DOMAINE: A wine-producing estate. Many wineries throughout France incorporate the word in their names, especially Burgundian estates, the most famous of which is the Domaine de la Romanée-Conti.

DOSAGE: The degree of sweetness of the LIQUEUR D'EXPÉDITION, which is used to top up Champagne before its final corking. The *dosage* is what determines whether a Champagne will be BRUT, EXTRA DRY, DEMI-SEC, and so on.

E

EAU-DE-VIE: Literally, water of life. Eaux-de-vie (the plural) are grape spirits, or clear brandies, that have been made by distilling wine or POMACE.

ENCÉPAGEMENT: The various grape varieties used in any given wine.

EN COTEAUX: Vines planted on slopes, usually making superior wine.

EN PRIMEUR: A method of buying wherein the wine is bought before it is released. Also known as buying futures. Buying wine *en primeur* allows collectors to be more certain of securing given wines. The wines most likely to be sold *en primeur* are Bordeaux wines from top châteaux.

EXTRA BRUT: A very DRY Champagne or SPARKLING WINE, with minimal (less than 0.6 percent) added sweetness. Drier than BRUT.

EXTRA DRY: Slightly sweeter than BRUT, contains extra dry Champagne or SPARKLING WINE. Do not confuse extra dry with EXTRA BRUT, which is the driest dosage level.

F

FOUDRE: Large wooden vat used to age wines.

G

GARIGUE: A word used to describe the arid landscape of Provence and the southern Rhône, which is covered with dry scrub and tough, resiny wild herbs, such as rosemary, thyme, and lavender. The wines of Provence and the southern Rhône are said to smell and taste of garigue (*garrigue* in French).

GOÛT DE TERROIR: The distinctive taste of a given grape variety grown in a specific TERROIR.

GRANDE MARQUE: A member of a particular association of about thirty of the longest-established Champagne HOUSES. The Syndicat de Grandes Marques is devoted to upholding a written charter of high standards in the production of Champagne.

H

HOUSE: As used in the Champagne region, house refers to a producer who sells Champagne under its own brand name. The grapes may come from its own vineyards, from independent growers, or most often from a combination of the two. Such firms as Veuve Clicquot, Moët & Chandon, and Taittinger are all referred to as houses.

L

LEFT BANK: The term refers to all of the appellations of Bordeaux that are on the left side of the Gironde River as it flows out to the Atlantic Ocean. The main grape variety used for Left Bank wines is cabernet sauvignon. Many famous communes are on the Left Bank, such as Margaux, St.-Julien, Pauillac, St.-Estéphe, Graves, and Sauternes.

LIQUEUR D'EXPÉDITION: The wine added to the Champagne bottle after DISGORGING to top it up. The *liqueur d'expédition* is often made up of wines reserved from previous years and it contains some sweetness (known as the DOSAGE).

LIQUEUR DE TIRAGE: The mixture of wine and sugar added along with YEASTS to the blend of still wines in a Champagne bottle in order to induce the second, bubble-forming fermentation.

M

MACÉRATION CARBONIQUE: CARBONIC MACERATION, as it is referred to in English, is a type of FERMENTATION in which uncrushed grapes are placed whole into vats that are then closed. As the weight of the grapes on top crushes grapes on the bottom, juice is released and fermentation begins. This in turn releases the gas CARBON DIOXIDE (CO_2), which causes other grapes to ferment, in effect, within their skins. Carbonic maceration is commonly used to ferment fruity red wines for early drinking, typically in Beaujolais and sometimes in the Loire.

MARC: The French term for an EAU-DE-VIE made specifically by distilling the POMACE (grape skins, stems, and seeds) left over after pressing, not by distilling wine. *Marc* is generally a slightly more powerfully flavored spirit than eau-de-vie.

MAS: The southern French term for a DOMAINE, sometimes translated as "farm."

MÉTHODE CHAMPENOISE: The labor-intensive method used to make Champagne and other fine SPARKLING WINES. In this method, the wine undergoes a SECONDARY FERMENTATION, which creates the bubbles, in its individual bottle rather than in one large cask or vat.

MILLERANDAGE: A viticultural problem caused by abnormal pollination and fruit set. It results in differently sized berries with different numbers of seeds within one bunch. The yield of the crop is reduced, although some winemakers believe the smaller berries can increase the quality of the wine.

MILLÉSIME: A vintage Champagne.

MOELLEUX: A term commonly used in the Loire for very sweet, luscious white wines that can be almost syrupy.

MONOPOLE: Used most frequently in Burgundy and to a lesser extent in Champagne, a *monopole* is a vineyard owned entirely by one estate.

MOUSSE: The French term for the snowy layer of bubbles that form on the top of a poured glass of Champagne or SPARKLING WINE.

MOUSSEUX: French for "sparkling." Some VIN MOUSSEUX are made by the MÉTHODE CHAMPENOISE (with SECONDARY FERMENTATION taking place in the bottle); other less expensive *mousseux* are made in large tanks.

MUSELET: Meaning "muzzle" in English, a muselet is the wire cage that holds a Champagne or SPARKLING WINE cork in place. It is important when opening a bottle of bubbly safely. The *muselet* should not be removed before the cork is eased out. Rather, it should be loosened and then removed with the cork at the same time.

N

NÉGOCIANT: An individual or firm that buys grapes and/or ready-made wine from growers and/or cooperatives. The *négociant* then blends, bottles, labels, and sells the wine under its own brand or name. The first *négociant* houses were established in France around the time of the French Revolution. The sudden profusion of peasant growers who were inexperienced in sales created the need for firms that could bottle and sell the production from many small properties.

NOUVEAU: A young wine meant for immediate drinking, usually seven to ten weeks after being made. The most famous wine made in a nouveau style is Beaujolais Nouveau.

O

OEIL DE PERDRIX: Literally, "partridge eye," *oeil de perdrix* is the term used to describe the color of a pale rosé.

P

PRISE DE MOUSSE: Literally, "capturing the sparkle," a term for the SECONDARY FERMENTATION in Champagne. The secondary fermentation takes place inside each individual bottle. It is this secondary fermentation that creates Champagne's bubbles.

R

RÉMUAGE: The RIDDLING (rotating and tilting) of Champagne bottles to concentrate yeast sediments in their necks. Riddling is done by hand in A-shape frames called *pupitres* or by a computerized machine called a gyropalette.

RIGHT BANK: The term refers to all of the appellations of Bordeaux that are on the right side of the Gironde River as it flows out to the Atlantic Ocean. The main grape varieties used for Right Bank wines are merlot and cabernet franc. The well-known communes of Pomerol and St.-Emilion reside on the Right Bank.

ROSÉ CHAMPAGNE: A pink Champagne. The rosé color, which actually ranges from translucent pink to coppery salmon, is obtained either by blending a bit of still red wine into the Champagne blend before the SECONDARY FERMENTATION or by leaving the base wines in contact with the grape skins for a brief period of time to absorb color. Because rosé Champagnes are difficult and risky to make, production is limited and the wines are generally more expensive than golden Champagnes.

S

SAIGNÉE: A process used to make rosé by drawing pink-colored juice off fermenting red grapes. This process also results in concentrating the remaining red wine, since the ratio of skins to juice in the tank is increased when some juice is drawn off.

SEC: DRY. However, when sec appears on a Champagne or SPARKLING WINE label, the wine inside will be medium sweet to sweet.

SÉLECTION DE GRAINS NOBLES: In Alsace, the term for wines made from very-late-picked berries that have been affected by BOTRYTIS CINEREA.

SUR LIE: Literally, "on the LEES." For a period of time after fermentation is complete, some white wines, notably white Burgundies, are left in contact with the lees (spent YEASTS). Wines that have been left *sur lie* take on a creamy, rounder MOUTHFEEL and generally display more COMPLEX flavors.

T

TASTEVIN: A shallow, silver tasting cup used by a SOMMELIER. The cup was designed with dimpled sides that would reflect candlelight in dark cellars and thereby allow the sommelier to see the color of the wine.

TERROIR: French term for the sum entity and effect (no single word exists in English) of every environmental factor on a given piece of ground. Included within *terroir,* for example, are a vineyard's soil, slope, orientation to the sun, and elevation, plus every nuance of climate: rainfall, wind velocity, frequency of fog, cumulative hours of sunshine, average high temperatures, average low temperatures, and so on. Each vineyard is said to have its own terroir.

V

VENDANGE TARDIVE: In Alsace, the term for wines made from late-picked, very ripe grapes. VT wines, as they are called, are not as sweet as SELECTION DE GRAINS NOBLES nor are they botrytized.

VIGNERON: Literally, "vine grower." Many French winemakers refer to themselves as *vignerons*.

VIN DE GARDE: A wine to save—in other words, a wine that can and should receive AGING.

VIN DE PAYS: Country wine—an everyday wine from a specific region, but less rigorously controlled than a wine with an APPELLATION D'ORIGINE CONTRÔLÉE.

VIN DE TABLE: Table wine. Generally used to indicate a simple wine without APPELLATION D'ORIGINE CONTRÔLÉE status.

VIN GRIS: A very pale rosé wine, sometimes light gray in color.

VIN LIQUOREUX: A very sweet, syrupy white wine, generally made from grapes affected by BOTRYTIS CINEREA.

VIN MOUSSEUX: SPARKLING WINE, made either by SECONDARY FERMENTATION in bottle or in tank, or by the addition of carbon dioxide for inexpensive wines.

VIN ORDINAIRE: Literally, "ordinary wine"—a plain wine with no regional or VARIETAL characteristics. An everyday drinking wine, *vin ordinaire* is the opposite of VIN DE GARDE, a wine to save; that is, a wine with aging potential.

ITALIAN WINE TERMS

A

ABBADIA: The term for "abbey," sometimes shortened to just *badia*. Buildings that were once abbeys have often been converted into renowned Italian wine estates, such as Tuscany's Badia a Coltibuono.

ABBOCCATO: Slightly sweet.

AMABILE: A little sweeter than **ABBOCCATO**.

AMARO: Bitter. Many Italian wines, both white and red, have a slight *amaro* character, which is considered a positive attribute by Italians.

ANNATA: The year of the vintage.

APPASIMENTO: The process of drying grapes on mats or shelving (or hanging them in the air) in protected cool, dry lofts. There, the grapes shrivel and raisinate, concentrating their sugars.

ASCIUTTO: Totally **DRY**.

AZIENDA AGRICOLA: Wine estate—this term, sometimes abbreviated Az. Ag., often appears on wine labels, along with the actual name of the wine estate, when the grapes were grown on that estate, and the wine that was produced there as well.

AZIENDA VINICOLA: The term for a winery. It often appears on wine labels.

AZIENDA VITIVINICOLA: Grape-growing and wine-making company. Like **AZIENDA AGRICOLA** and **AZIENDA VINICOLA**, the term often appears on wine labels.

B

BIANCO: White, as in *vino bianco*: white wine.

BOTTE: Cask or barrel.

BOTTIGLIA: Bottle.

BRICCO: The sunny slope of a hill.

C

CANTINA: Wine cellar, or yet another term for a winery.

CANTINA SOCIALE OR COOPERATIVA: A growers' cooperative cellar. Italy, like France and Spain, has hundreds of wine co-ops, some of which make good but rarely great wine.

CASA VINICOLA: A wine firm, usually making wine from wine or grapes it has purchased (as opposed to grapes grown on its own estate). The word *casa* means "house."

CASCINA: Northern Italian term for a farmhouse or estate.

CASTELLO: The word for "castle." Several famous Italian wine estates are housed in what were once castles—Castello dei Rampolla in Tuscany, for example.

CHIARETTO: A very light red or even a rosé wine.

CLASSICO: An official designation, referring to the heart of a DOC zone—by implication the classic or best part. In Chianti, the *classico* zone is so highly regarded that it has a DOC of its own—Chianti Classico.

CONSORZIO: A consortium of producers of a certain wine, who join forces to control and promote it.

COOPERATIVA: See **CANTINA SOCIALE**.

D

DENOMINAZIONE DI ORIGINE CONTROLLATA (DOC): See page 328.

DENOMINAZIONE DI ORIGINE CONTROLLATA E GARANTITA (DOCG): See page 328.

DOLCE: Fully sweet. Italy produces countless sweet wines from many different grape varieties.

E

ENOTECA: Wine library; a place where bottles of wine from different regions are displayed. Often these wines are also available for tasting. The most famous enoteca in Italy is in Siena. Today, enoteca is also used to indicate a wine bar.

ETICHETTA: Label.

F

FATTORIA: Tuscan term for a farm or wine estate. Many top Chianti producers use this term as part of their names—Fattoria di Felsina, for example.

FIASCO: Literally, "a flask"; more often used for the straw-encased Chianti bottle that was a fixture of the bohemian lifestyle in the 1960s in the United States. Chiantis sold in *fiaschi* (the plural) were usually pretty thin and quite cheap. Today, very few Chiantis are sold in straw-covered bottles.

FRIZZANTE: Slightly fizzy, but less so than SPARKLING WINE.

G

GRADAZIONE ALCOOLICA: Percentage of ALCOHOL BY VOLUME.

GRAN SELEZIONE: Highest-quality category in Chianti Classico. Wine must be made from estate-grown grapes and aged at least 30 months before it is sold.

GRAPPA: A clear brandy (EAU-DE-VIE in French) made by distilling the POMACE left over after MUST or wine is pressed. *Grappa di monovitigno* is a grappa from a single grape variety, such as moscato or picolit. Because grappas made this way have a subtle suggestion of the AROMA and flavor of the original grapes, they are considered superior.

I

IMBOTTIGLIATO ALL'ORIGINE: Bottled at the source; the term may be used only by estates that produce and bottle the wine on the property where the grapes were grown.

IMBOTTIGLIATO DA: Bottled by, which will be followed by the producer's name; does not denote an ESTATE BOTTLED wine.

IMBOTTIGLIATO DAL VITICOLTORE: Bottled by the grower; may be used only by growers bottling their own wines.

INDICAZIONE GEOGRAFICA TIPICA (IGT): See page 328.

L

LIQUOROSO: Strong wine, often but not necessarily FORTIFIED, which can be sweet or not.

M

METODO TRADIZIONALE: The Champagne method (MÉTHODE CHAMPENOISE) for making SPARKLING WINE; also referred to as *metodo classico*. Most top Italian sparkling wines are made this way.

N

NERO: Black or very dark red; said of both grapes and wines.

P

PASSITO: The general term for wines made from intentionally raisinated grapes.

PASTOSO: Medium (not very) dry.

PODERE: A small farm, often turned into a wine estate. These often use the word *podere* in their names, as in the Tuscan Podere Il Palazzino.

PRODUTTORE: Producer.

R

RECIOTO: A word indicating the wine is sweet (as in recioto di Soave and recioto di Valpolicella). To make a recioto wine, the grapes are left for months to dry and raisinate, usually on mats or shelving in cool, dry lofts (a process called APPASSIMENTO). In Italy, the general term for wines made from intentionally raisinated grapes is *passito*. The word *recioto* comes from *recie* in the Venetian dialect, meaning "ears"—a reference to the little lobes or ears on a grape cluster that usually get very ripe because they are the most exposed to the sun.

RISERVA: A wine that has been matured for a specific number of years, according to DENOMINAZIONE DI ORIGINE CONTROLLATA regulations.

ROSATO: Rosé.

ROSSO: Red. Vino rosso is distinguished from vino bianco (white wine) and vino rosato (rosé wine).

S

SECCO: DRY.

SEMISECCO: Semidry; in reality, medium sweet.

SORI: The sunny top of a hill where the snow melts first.

SPUMANTE: Sparkling; literally, "foaming."

STRAVECCHIO: Very old; a term more frequently applied to spirits than wine.

SUPERIORE: Generally indicates a wine of higher quality, often because it has more alcohol than the minimum required and/or it has been aged longer than regulations stipulate. Valpolicella Superiore, for example, is a Valpolicella with at least one year of aging, in contrast to basic Valpolicella, which has no minimum.

T

TENUTA: Holding or estate. Wine estates often incorporate the word *tenuta* into their names, as in the Tuscan estate Tenuta San Guido.

U

UE: A softer, lighter type of GRAPPA achieved by distilling actual grapes rather than POMACE.

UVA: Grape.

V

VECCHIO: Old; said of mature wines.

VENDEMMIA: The vintage; can be used in place of ANNATA on labels.

VIGNA: Vineyard, also referred to as a *vigneto*.

VIGNAIOLO: Grape-grower, also called a *viticoltore*.

VILLA: Country manor; often one where wine is produced.

VINO DA ARROSTO: Wine for a roast, implying a red that is FULL-BODIED and has a deep COLOR.

VINO DA PASTO: Everyday wine.

VINO DA TAVOLA: Table wine—the regulation term for non-DOC wines.

VINO NOVELLO: The wine of the current year, now used in the same sense as Beaujolais Nouveau, though Italy's *vino novellos* are not as highly promoted as France's Beaujolais Nouveau.

VITE: Vine.

VITICOLTORE: Grape grower.

VITIGNO: Grape variety.

SPANISH WINE TERMS

A

AÑADA: See VENDIMIA.

AÑO: Year.

B

BODEGA: Wine cellar or wine-producing company. Curiously, a single wine company may nonetheless use the plural form *bodegas* in its name, as in Bodegas Ismael Arroyo.

C

CAVA: The name for Spanish SPARKLING WINE made by the Champagne method (MÉTHODE CHAMPENOISE). Cava is a specialty of the Penedès region of north-central Spain near Barcelona. The two largest cava producers, Freixenet and Codorníu, each produce far more sparkling wine by the Champagne method than any Champagne house makes.

CONSEJO REGULADOR: Local governing body that enforces wine policy for a given area, including the boundaries of the area, the grape varieties permitted, maximum YIELD, and so forth. Every Spanish wine region with a DENOMINACIÓN DE ORIGEN has a *Consejo Regulador*.

COSECHA: Year of harvest, or vintage.

CRIADERA: Literally, "nursery." *Criadera* refers to a layer of Sherry casks, all of which contain wine of approximately the same age and blend. Multiple criaderas, sometimes more than a dozen, make up a SOLERA.

CRIANZA: The basic-quality wine produced by each BODEGA. *Crianzas* are considered every-night drinking wines. They are less prestigious, less costly, and aged for shorter periods than RESERVAS or GRAN RESERVAS. While national law stipulates that crianzas must be aged for a minimum of six months in oak barrels, each DENOMINACIÓN DE ORIGEN or DENOMINACIÓN DE ORIGEN CALIFICADA can set higher standards. In Rioja, for example, a crianza must be aged for at least two years, one of which must be in oak barrels.

D

DENOMINACIÓN DE ORIGEN (DO): See page 925.

DENOMINACIÓN DE ORIGEN CALIFICADA (DOCA): See page 925.

DULCE: Sweet. Spain has less of a reputation for making top-quality sweet wines than France, Italy, or Germany, although several styles of Sherry, Spain's extraordinary FORTIFIED wine, can be sweet.

E

ELABORADO POR: Produced by.

EMBOTELLADO POR: Bottled by.

EN RAMA: Literally, "in an unrefined state." The name of fino or manzanilla Sherries drawn from barrels in the spring when the *flor* is thickest, then immediately bottled—usually unfined and without stabilization. *En rama* Sherries are extremely fresh and vivid and last mere months because they are so fragile. The equivalent of drinking Sherry directly from the cask, *en rama* Sherries are extremely rare on the commercial market.

EXTRA SECO: SPARKLING WINE that is not quite as dry as BRUT (SECO).

F

FLOR: Literally, "flower." A layer of YEAST cells that forms naturally on top of manzanilla and fino Sherries as they age in the cask. Flor acts to prevent OXIDATION and also contributes a unique flavor to the wine.

G

GRAN RESERVA: A BODEGA'S top wine, produced only in excellent years and then subject to lengthy AGING. Though national law stipulates that red *gran reservas* must be aged two years in oak barrels, each DENOMINACIÓN DE ORIGEN or DENOMINACIÓN DE ORIGEN CALIFICADA can set higher standards. In Rioja, for example, red gran reservas must be aged for two years in barrel followed by three years in bottle, and in practice, many Rioja producers exceed that.

L

LÁGRIMA: Literally, "tears." *Lágrima* also refers to a wine made from free-run juice without any mechanical pressing.

M

MÉTODO TRADICIONAL: Spanish term denoting SPARKLING WINE made by the Champagne method (MÉTHODE CHAMPENOISE). CAVA, by law, must be made this way.

P

PAGO: Term commonly used for a single estate. In 2003, the government of Spain also gave the term a legal definition and status, incorporating it into the official denominación system. Thus, in addition to Spain's DOs, (DENOMINACIÓN DE ORIGEN) and DOCAs (DENOMINACIÓN DE ORIGEN CALIFICADA) there exists the status DO *Pago*. These are denominations of origin awarded to just a single estate considered exemplary. So, for example, the estate Dominio de Valdepusa has its own DO Pago called Dominio de Valdepusa. Many Spanish equate a DO Pago with a French Grand Cru. As of 2012, there were about ten DO Pago estates in Spain.

PASADA: Term used to describe a well-aged Sherry.

R

RESERVA: A wine produced only in excellent years. Though national law stipulates that red *reservas* must be aged for one year in oak barrels, each **DENOMINACIÓN DE ORIGEN** or **DENOMINACIÓN DE ORIGEN CALIFICADA** can set higher standards. Red reservas from Rioja, for example, must be aged for a minimum of three years, one of which must be in barrel. Many Rioja producers nonetheless exceed these requirements.

ROBLE: Oak. Despite Spain's proximity to France, many Spanish producers age their wines in American oak.

ROCIOS: Literally, "morning dew." The name of the process of transferring Sherry between the **CRIADERAS**. The name is a reflection of the gentleness with which the process is done.

ROSADO: Rosé. It's still a well-kept secret that Spain makes some of the best rosés in Europe. The rosés from Navarra are especially well regarded.

S

SECO: Dry.

SEMISECO: Medium dry.

SOBRETABLE: In Sherry production, the term for the period of time a new wine spends before it goes into the **SOLERA**. The sobretable is usually six to eight months, but occassionally up to a year.

SOLERA: Complex network of barrels used for aging Sherry by progressively blending younger wines into older wines. Since the barrels are not completely filled, the wine is allowed to be gently subjected to **OXIDIZATION** during the process. Wine held in a solera is said to undergo the solera process.

V

VENDIMIA: Vintage.

VIEJO: Old.

VIÑA: Literally, "vineyard," but the word *viña* is often used as part of a brand name as, for example, in Viña Arana.

VINO DE MESA: Table wine.

VINO ESPUMOSO: General term for **SPARKLING WINE**.

VINO GENEROSO: **FORTIFIED** wine developed under **FLOR**.

PORTUGUESE WINE TERMS

B

BRANCO: Denotes a white wine.

C

COLHEITA: Literally, "harvest." However, *colheita* is also the name for an aged tawny Port from a single harvest. Colheita Ports are rare.

CUBA DE CALOR: A method of making fortified base wine for inexpensive Madeiras that involves heating the base wine in large vats fitted with serpentine-shaped, stainless-steel heating coils very slowly over a period of three to six months.

D

DENOMINAÇÃO DE ORIGEM CONTROLADA (DOC): See page 926.

E

ESCOLHA: Translated as "choice," *escolha* is used on labels to denote special selection wines in Portugal.

ESTUFAGEM: The step in the process of making Madeira that involves heating the wine. Depending on the quality of the Madeira being produced, there are several *estufagem* methods. The most basic involves placing the **FORTIFIED** base wines in containers that are then heated to an average temperature of 113°F/45°C (with a maximum temperature of 131°F/55°C allowed) for three to six months. To make the very finest Madeiras, however, the containers may be placed in a warehouse attic, which builds up tremendous heat thanks to the intense

Madeiran sun. There, the Madeira-to-be may be left for twenty years or more.

G

GARRAFEIRA: Used in reference to Portuguese still wines, the word *garrafeira* indicates a wine of especially high quality. But the word also means "wine cellar" or "bottle cellar" (from the Portuguese *garrafa*—"bottle"). In addition, garrafeira is a style of Port, albeit a rare one. Rich and supple, garrafeira Ports are usually from a single outstanding year and are aged briefly in wood and then for as many as twenty to forty years in large glass bottles. After aging, the garrafeira is decanted and transferred into standard 25-ounce (750-milliliter) bottles and sold.

L

LAGAR: A shallow stone or cement trough in which grapes are trodden by foot (usually for several hours) in order to crush them and mix the skins with the juice. Treading grapes by foot, an ancient practice, is still widely practiced in Portugal, and thus many wineries have *lagares*.

P

PIPE: A traditional Port barrel holding the equivalent of sixty cases of wine. Historically, Port was shipped by the PIPE to importers who would then bottle it for sale to consumers.

Q

QUINTA: Literally, "farm." In Portugal, the word *quinta* is used to refer both to a specific vineyard and to a wine estate. Quinta do Noval, for example, is the name of a highly regarded wine estate in the Douro region. Ports known as single-vintage *quinta* Ports come from grapes grown on a single estate in a single year.

T

TINTO: Denotes a red wine.

GERMAN AND AUSTRIAN WINE TERMS

A

ALTE REBEN: The term used in Germany and Austria for old vines.

AMTLICHE PRÜFUNGSNUMMER: A quality-control test number (the AP number) signifying that a wine has passed official analytical and taste tests. It appears on every bottle of quality German wine in the category of QUALITÄTSWEIN BESTIMMTER ANBAUGEBIETE (QBA) or QUALITÄTSWEIN MIT PRÄDIKAT (QMP).

ANBAUGEBIET: One of thirteen specified winegrowing regions in Germany. Plural: *anbaugebiete*.

AUSBRUCH: A category of wine made in Austria, in Burgenland. *Ausbruche* (the plural) are slightly more opulent than BEERENAUSLESEN, and must be made from overripe, BOTRYTIZED and/or naturally shriveled grapes.

AUSLESE: Plural: *auslesen*. Literally, "select harvest." A level of full ripeness according to the traditional German system. In the modern VDP system in Germany, denotes a wine with significant sweetness.

B

BEERENAUSLESE (BA): Plural: *beerenauslesen*. Literally, "berry select harvest." A level of considerable ripeness and sweetness in both the traditional and modern German systems. Beerenauslesen have often been the product of at least some BOTRYTIZED grapes.

BEREICH: One of thirty-nine official districts. Germany's thirteen wine regions (ANBAUGEBIETE) are officially broken down into thirty-nine *bereiche* (the plural of *bereich*), which in turn are broken down into 167 GROSSLAGEN, which are broken down into approximately 2,658 EINZELLAGEN.

BERG: Hill or mountain.

BLAU: Blue; when used to describe grapes, it means red.

BOCKSBEUTEL: Flagon-shaped bottle used for the wines of Germany's Franken region.

BURG: Fortress.

BUSCHENSCHENK: In the southern Austrian countryside, this is the name for a rustic restaurant that elsewhere is called a HEURIGE. A *buschenschenk* is easily identified by the *buschenschenk* (also the name for a swag of fir branches) tied to its doors.

D

DAC: *Districtus Austriae Controllatus,* or protected Austrian declaration of origin. Instituted in 2001, this system organizes Austrian wine into regions with specific laws on which grapes are allowed to be grown and other viticultural and winemaking regulations. It was modeled after France's AOC system in an effort to increase quality and put the focus on TERROIR.

DEUTSCHER WEIN: German table wine, the humblest category of wine. Although the ALCOHOL content, acidity level, and origin of grapes are all controlled by law, *Deutscher wein* is usually so light, it's often just a step above water. The term *Deutscher* means "of Germany." Absent that designation, the wine may be a "Euroblend" based on grapes that may come from one of several other European Union countries.

E

EDELFÄULE: BOTRYTIS CINEREA; Germany's and Austria's luscious DESSERT WINES—BEERENAUSLESEN and TROCKENBEERENAUSLESEN—are made with the help of *edelfäule.*

EINZELLAGE: The official name for an individual vineyard site. There are approximately 2,658 of them in Germany. Germany's thirteen wine regions are officially broken down into thirty-nine BEREICHE, which in turn are broken down into 167 GROSSLAGEN, which are broken down into *einzellagen,* the plural of *einzellage.*

EISWEIN: A rare and especially intense DESSERT WINE made by pressing frozen grapes that have been left hanging on the vine into midwinter, sometimes February. (*Eiswein* carries the vintage date of the main harvest year, so even if, for example, *eiswein* grapes were harvested in January 2015, the bottle would carry the vintage date 2014.) When *eiswein* grapes are harvested in late winter, they are gently pressed while still frozen so that the ice is separated from the remaining concentrated, very sweet, high-acid juice. Because of their ACIDITY, *eiswein* are usually less unctuous but more vibrant than BEERENAUSLESEN or TROCKENBEERENAUSLESEN. *Eisweins* age for decades and are extremely expensive.

ERSTE LAGE: Designation that indicates a first-class vineyard, similar to the designation *Premier Cru* in Burgundy. The designation used by the 200 plus members of the VDP. The term *Erste Lage* generally appears on the neck label. See description of the VDP system on page 553.

ERSTES GEWÄCHS: An old term meaning first growth. Used before 2006 in the Rheingau for high-quality dry wines made from riesling and pinot noir. Today, used less frequently as producers adopt VDP terms instead.

ERZEUGERABFÜLLUNG: Wines produced and bottled by a grower or a cooperative. You won't see *erzeugerabfüllung* on the labels of well-known estates.

F

FEDERSPIEL: A term used in the Wachau region of Lower Austria to indicate natural unchaptalized wines with at least 11.5 but no more than 12.5 percent ALCOHOL.

FEINHERB: An unofficial term used in Germany as a synonym for *halbtrocken* or half-dry wines—defined as less than 1.8 percent residual sugar. Wines called *feinherb* usually still taste extremely DRY because of the high corresponding ACIDITY in German wines.

FLASCHE: Bottle—the English word *flask* is derived from *flasche.*

G

GROSSLAGE: One of approximately 167 collections of vineyards. Germany's thirteen wine regions are officially broken down into thirty-nine BEREICHE, which in turn are broken down into 167 *grosslagen* (the plural of *grosslage*), which are broken down into approximately 2,658 EINZELLAGEN.

GROSSE LAGE: A term used by members of the VDP in Germany to indicate a vineyard that is of the highest quality. The term roughly corresponds to the Burgundian term *Grand Cru*. The term *Grosse Lage* will appear on the neck label. See description of the VDP system page 553.

GROSSES GEWÄCHS: The VDP term for a dry wine from a vineyard designated GROSSE LAGE, or of the highest quality.

GUTSABFÜLLUNG: Estate bottled.

GUTSWEIN: A term used by members of the VDP to indicate the wine comes from a good- but not great-quality vineyard owned by the winery. See description of the VDP system, page 553.

H

HALBTROCKEN: Literally, "half-dry"—defined as less than 1.8 percent residual sugar. The term is used in Germany, but rarely in Austria. Wines labeled *halbtrocken* usually still taste extremely DRY because of the high corresponding ACIDITY in German wines. The term FEINHERB is often used as a synonym.

HEURIGE: In Austria, a rustic type of restaurant often attached to a winemaker's home. Traditionally, all of the food at a *heurige* is made from scratch by the winemaker and his family. Similarly, the wine offered (which is also referred to as *heurige*) is the winemaker's.

K

KABINETT: A level of ripeness indicating that the wine was not completely ripe according to the traditional German system. *Kabinett* wines are drunk by Germans as every-night wines and their dependable presence in the family's kitchen or living room cabinet gave them their name. In the modern German system adopted by members of the VDP, *kabinett* is a level of minor sweetness. The term was also once used in Austria to indicate a table wine of modest ripeness, but ripeness designations now rarely appear on Austrian wines unless the wines are sweet (i.e. AUSBRUCH, BEERENAUSLESEN, etc.).

KELLER: Cellar.

KMW: Acronym for Klosterneuburger Mostwage. In Austria, the KMW scale is used to measure sugar in grapes and hence their ripeness. In Germany, sugar is measured in OECHSLE; in France, in BAUMÉ; and in the United States, in BRIX.

L

LESE: Harvest. Harvest dates generally range from September to December, according to the variety of grape, weather conditions, and the kind of wine being produced. One exception is EISWEIN, which can be harvested in January of the year following the main harvest.

LIEBLICH: Semisweet. The term used to describe German wines with discernible sweetness. *Lieblich* wines, therefore, are those that taste sweeter than HALBTROCKEN (half-dry). They can have up to 4.5 percent residual sugar (45 grams per liter).

O

OECHSLE: Scale used in Germany to indicate the ripeness of grapes. Developed in the nineteenth century by the physicist Ferdinand Oechsle, Oechsle measures the weight of the grape juice or MUST. Since the contents of the must are primarily sugar and ACIDS, the must weight is an indication of ripeness. According to traditional German law, ripeness categories are based on Oechsle levels that are specified for each grape variety and wine region (meaning they can change region to region). For example, for a riesling wine in the Mosel to be considered a SPÄTLESE, it must have 76 degrees Oechsle; in the Rheingau, a riesling must have 85 degrees Oechsle to be a spätlese. These adjustable levels reflect the fact that in some very cold regions like the Mosel, ripeness is harder to achieve.

ORTSWEIN: Designation that indicates the wine comes from a good but not great vineyard—roughly the equivalent of a Burgundian village wine. The designation used by the 200-plus members of the VDP. See description of the VDP system page 553.

P

PRÄDIKAT: The word roughly translates as "superior quality" or "possessing special attributes." *Prädikatswein* therefore is the general term for high-quality wine.

Q

QUALITÄTSWEIN BESTIMMTER ANBAUGEBIETE (QBA): A broad category of basic everyday wine under German law. QbA wines must come from one of the official thirteen winegrowing regions (Anbaugebiete), and the region must be shown on the label. QbA wines are made from grapes that have attained only a low level of ripeness, though there must be at least enough sugar in the grapes to produce a wine with 7 percent ALCOHOL BY VOLUME. CHAPTALIZATION (adding sugar to the unfermented grape juice to boost the body and final alcohol level) is permitted and often used. QbA wines range from dry to semisweet.

QUALITÄTSWEIN MIT PRÄDIKAT (QMP): Translated as "quality wine with specific attributes," this is the top level of German wines. In the traditional German system, QmP wines prominently display a ripeness level on the wine label (from KABINETT up to TROCKENBEERENAUSLESE) and a sweetness level, from dry (TROCKEN) to extremely sweet. Unlike QbA wines, QmP wines may not be CHAPTALIZED. QmP wines must be produced from allowed grape varieties in one of the 39 subregions (BEREICH) of one of the 13 wine-rowing regions, although it is the region rather than the subregion that is mandatory information on the label.

R

ROTWEIN: Red wine; Germany and Austria are famous for their whites, but a good deal of red wine is made in each and consumed locally.

S

SCHILCHER: Austrian name for a high-acid rosé made from the blauer wildbacher grape, which grows almost exclusively in west Styria.

SCHLOSS: Castle—many German wine estates are housed in what were once medieval castles.

SEKT: SPARKLING WINE.

SMARAGD: Austrian term used in the Wachau region of Lower Austria for the ripest grapes and hence are the fullest-bodied wines. *Smaragd* wines must have a minimum of 12.5 percent alcohol, but most have considerably more. The word *smaragd* is also the name of a bright green lizard that suns itself in the Wachau vineyards.

SPÄTLESE: Plural: *spätlesen*. Literally, "late harvest." A level of ripeness indicating that the wine was just ripe according to the traditional German system. According to this traditional system, a spatlese could be dry, half-dry, or semisweet. In the distinctly different modern German system adopted by members of the VDP, spätlese is a level of sweetness above KABINETT.

STEINFEDER: In the Wachau region of Lower Austria, natural unchaptalized wines with no more than 11.5 percent alcohol are referred to as *steinfeders*. These come from the least ripe grapes and hence are the lightest bodied of Wachau wines.

STRAUSSWIRTSCHAFT: German wine pubs, often attached to growers' homes, where they can sell their own wines and light foods for a total of only four months of the year, so as not to take business away from full-fledged restaurants open twelve months a year. A *strauss*—"wreath"—is usually hung over the door.

SÜSSRESERVE: Grape juice that has been held back from the harvest and unfermented so that it has all of its natural sweetness. In Germany, small amounts of *süssreserve* may be added to some high-ACID wines in order to BALANCE them.

T

TROCKEN: Dry. Wines labeled trocken from both Germany and Austria must have less than 0.9 percent RESIDUAL SUGAR.

TROCKENBEERENAUSLESE: Plural: *trockenbeeren-sauslesen*, but usually referred to as TBA. Literally, "dry berry select harvest"—an indication that the grapes had hung so long on the vine that they had shriveled almost to raisins before being picked. TBA is the ripest and sweetest level of both German and Austrian wine. The grapes for the wine are often BOTRYTIZED.

V

VDP: *Verband Deutscher Prädikatsweingüter,* or Association of German Prädikat Wine Estates. An organization of some 200 prestigious estates throughout Germany that are revising the traditional concepts of ripeness and sweetness in the country. The VDP has also instituted a Burgundian-like ranking system for vineyards, from GROSSES LAGE (Grand Cru) down to GUTSWEIN (village wine).

W

WEINGUT: Wine estate.

WEINKELLEREI: Winery that buys grape MUST or wine from a grower, then bottles and markets the wine.

WEINSTUBE: German for "wine tavern;" a comfortable, casual restaurant where Germans go for simple food and a bottle of wine.

WEISSHERBST: In Germany, a rosé wine of at least QUALITÄTSWEIN BESTIMMTER ANBAUGEBIETE (QBA) status made from red grapes of a single variety. A specialty of Baden.

WINZER: Grape farmer.

HUNGARIAN WINE TERMS

A

ASZÚ: The term for shriveled grapes that have been attacked by the beneficial mold BOTRYTIS CINEREA. More commonly, however, you'll encounter *aszú* as part of the name of Hungary's most famous wine: Tokaji Aszú. Luscious and honeyed, Tokaji Aszú is to Hungary what Sauternes is to France—a renowned sweet wine that is both difficult and expensive to make.

E

EDES: Slightly sweet, a term usually applied to Szamorodni, the type of wine made in Tokaj from vineyards where the grapes have not been sufficiently affected by BOTRYTIS CINEREA to make Tokaji Aszú. Szamorodni may be slightly sweet or dry (SZÁRAZ).

G

GÖNCI: The traditional barrels (named after the village of Gönc, known for its barrel makers) used in making Tokaji Aszú. *Gönci* hold about 37 gallons (140 liters) of wine.

P

PRIMAE CLASSIS: Literally, "first class." A Latin designation used by the Hungarians since around 1700 to indicate a Tokaj vineyard of first-class stature. The Tokaji Aszú wines produced from grapes grown in such a vineyard would by extension be considered top flight.

PRO MENSA CAESARIS PRIMUS: Around A.D. 1700, two Tokaj vineyards were given this designation, which means chosen for the royal table. These vineyards, Csarfas and Mézes Mály, ranked above those designated PRIMAE CLASSIS.

PUTTONY: The traditional basket in which ASZÚ grapes were gathered. The word *puttony* has given rise to puttonyos, the manner by which the sweetness of Tokaji Aszú is measured. Tokaji Aszú wines are labeled from two to six puttonyos; the more puttonyos, the sweeter the wine.

S

SECUNDO CLASSIS: "Second class" in Latin, first used in Hungary around 1700 to indicate a Tokaj vineyard considered second-best. Hence, a Tokaji Aszú wine that is second in quality compared to wines made from grapes grown in PRIMAE CLASSIS vineyards, but still well above most other vineyards.

SZÁRAZ: Dry. The term is usually applied to Szamorodni, the type of wine made in the Tokaj region from vineyards where the grapes are not sufficiently affected by BOTRYTIS CINEREA to make Tokaji Aszú.

GREEK WINE TERMS

A

AMPHORA: An earthenware vessel used by the ancient Greeks and Romans to store and ship wine. An amphora was oval in shape, with two large handles at the top for carrying, and a pointed bottom so that the vessel could be pushed into the soft earth, where it would remain upright. Amphorae range in size from that of a milk can to a refrigerator.

ARCHONDIKO: A word appearing on the labels of TOPIKOS OENOS, or PGI, wines. *Archondiko* roughly translates as CHÂTEAU.

E

EPITRAPEZIOS OENOS (E.O.): The simplest category of Greek wine, equivalent to VIN DE TABLE, or TABLE WINE, in France.

K

KRATER: A shallow bronze or pottery bowl used in antiquity to hold wine; wine would be poured from an AMPHORA into a krater for serving.

KTIMA: Estate; can appear on the labels of TOPIKOS OENOS wines.

KYLIX: A shallow, two-handled, often beautifully decorated cup from which wine was drunk in antiquity.

KYTHOS: In antiquity, a ladle used to scoop wine from the KRATER and transfer it into a KYLIX.

M

MONASTIRI: Monastery; several Greek wine estates are located in former monasteries, and several Greek monasteries still produce wine. The word *monastiri* sometimes appears on the labels of TOPIKOS OENOS wines.

S

STEFÁNI: A way of training grapevines that is especially common on windswept Greek islands. The vines are trained in a circle low to the ground (*stefáni* means "crown"), so that the grapes grow in the center, protected from the wind.

T

TOPIKOS OENOS (T.O.): One of the simpler categories of Greek wine, equivalent to PGI in European Union wine laws, or VIN DE PAYS, France's country wine.

THE CHÂTEAUX RANKED IN THE 1855 CLASSIFICATION OF BORDEAUX

THE MÉDOC

In the Médoc, the 1855 classification was based on the reputation of the châteaux (not on the ground where the vines grew) and did not take into account whether the châteaux produced red or white wines. In point of fact, virtually all of the Médoc châteaux listed below make red wines exclusively.

FIRST GROWTHS
(Premiers Crus)

CHÂTEAU HAUT-BRION (Pessac-Léognan, in Graves, not the Médoc)

CHÂTEAU LAFITE-ROTHSCHILD (Pauillac)

CHÂTEAU LATOUR (Pauillac)

CHÂTEAU MARGAUX (Margaux)

CHÂTEAU MOUTON-ROTHSCHILD (Pauillac)

SECOND GROWTHS
(Deuxièmes Crus)

CHÂTEAU BRANE-CANTENAC
(Margaux)

CHÂTEAU COS D'ESTOURNEL
(St.-Estèphe)

CHÂTEAU DUCRU-BEAUCAILLOU
(St.-Julien)

CHÂTEAU DURFORT-VIVENS
(Margaux)

CHÂTEAU GRUAUD-LAROSE
(St.-Julien)

CHÂTEAU LASCOMBES (Margaux)

CHÂTEAU LÉOVILLE-BARTON
(St.-Julien)

CHÂTEAU LÉOVILLE-LAS CASES
(St.-Julien)

CHÂTEAU LÉOVILLE-POYFERRÉ
(St.-Julien)

CHÂTEAU MONTROSE (St.-Estèphe)

CHÂTEAU PICHON-LONGUEVILLE
(Pauillac)

CHÂTEAU PICHON-LONGUEVILLE,
COMTESSE DE LALANDE (Pauillac)

CHÂTEAU RAUZAN-GASSIES
(Margaux)

CHÂTEAU RAUZAN-SÉGLA
(Margaux)

THIRD GROWTHS
(Troisièmes Crus)

CHÂTEAU BOYD-CANTENAC
(Margaux)

CHÂTEAU CALON-SÉGUR
(St.-Estèphe)

CHÂTEAU CANTENAC-BROWN
(Margaux)

CHÂTEAU DESMIRAIL (Margaux)

CHÂTEAU D'ISSAN (Margaux)

CHÂTEAU FERRIÈRE (Margaux)

CHÂTEAU GISCOURS (Margaux)

CHÂTEAU KIRWAN (Margaux)

CHÂTEAU LAGRANGE (St.-Julien)

CHÂTEAU LA LAGUNE
(Haut-Médoc)

CHÂTEAU LANGOA-BARTON
(St.-Julien)

CHÂTEAU MALESCOT ST.-EXUPÉRY
(Margaux)

CHÂTEAU MARQUIS D'ALESME
(Margaux)

CHÂTEAU PALMER (Margaux)

FOURTH GROWTHS
(Quatrièmes Crus)

CHÂTEAU BEYCHEVELLE
(St.-Julien)

CHÂTEAU BRANAIRE-DUCRU
(St.-Julien)

CHÂTEAU DUHART-MILON (Pauillac)

CHÂTEAU LAFON-ROCHET
(St.-Estèphe)

CHÂTEAU LA TOUR-CARNET
(Haut-Médoc)

CHÂTEAU MARQUIS-DE-TERME
(Margaux)

CHÂTEAU POUGET (Margaux)

CHÂTEAU PRIEURÉ-LICHINE
(Margaux)

CHÂTEAU ST.-PIERRE (St.-Julien)

CHÂTEAU TALBOT (St.-Julien)

FIFTH GROWTHS
(Cinquièmes Crus)

CHÂTEAU BATAILLEY (Pauillac)

CHÂTEAU BELGRAVE
(Haut-Médoc)

CHÂTEAU CANTEMERLE
(Haut-Médoc)

CHÂTEAU CLERC-MILON (Pauillac)

CHÂTEAU COS LABORY
(St.-Estèphe)

CHÂTEAU CROIZET-BAGES
(Pauillac)

CHÂTEAU D'ARMAILHAC (Pauillac)

CHÂTEAU DAUZAC (Margaux)

CHÂTEAU DE CAMENSAC
(Haut-Médoc)

CHÂTEAU DU TERTRE (Margaux)

CHÂTEAU GRAND-PUY-DUCASSE
(Pauillac)

CHÂTEAU GRAND-PUY-LACOSTE
(Pauillac)

CHÂTEAU HAUT-BAGES-LIBÉRAL
(Pauillac)

CHÂTEAU HAUT-BATAILLEY
(Pauillac)

CHÂTEAU LYNCH-BAGES (Pauillac)

CHÂTEAU LYNCH-MOUSSAS
(Pauillac)

CHÂTEAU PÉDESCLAUX (Pauillac)

CHÂTEAU PONTET-CANET (Pauillac)

SAUTERNES AND BARSAC
(Also part of the 1855 Classification)

These châteaux in Sauternes and Barsac make mainly sweet white wines.

FIRST GREAT GROWTH
(Premier Cru Supérieur)

CHÂTEAU D'YQUEM (Sauternes)

FIRST GROWTHS
(Premiers Crus)

CHÂTEAU CLIMENS (Barsac)

CHÂTEAU COUTET (Barsac)

CHÂTEAU DE RAYNE-VIGNEAU
(Sauternes)

CHÂTEAU GUIRAUD (Sauternes)

CHÂTEAU LAFAURIE-PEYRAGUEY
(Sauternes)

CHÂTEAU LA TOUR BLANCHE
(Sauternes)

CHÂTEAU RABAUD-PROMIS
(Sauternes)

CHÂTEAU RIEUSSEC (Sauternes)

CHÂTEAU SIGALAS-RABAUD
(Sauternes)

CHÂTEAU SUDUIRAUT (Sauternes)

CLOS HAUT-PEYRAGUEY
(Sauternes)

SECOND GROWTHS
(Deuxièmes Crus)**

CHÂTEAU BROUSTET (Barsac)

CHÂTEAU CAILLOU (Barsac)

CHÂTEAU D'ARCHE (Sauternes)

CHÂTEAU DE MALLE (Sauternes)

CHÂTEAU DE MYRAT (Barsac)

CHÂTEAU DOISY-DAËNE (Barsac)

CHÂTEAU DOISY-DUBROCA (Barsac)

CHÂTEAU DOISY-VÉDRINES
(Barsac)

CHÂTEAU FILHOT (Sauternes)

CHÂTEAU LAMOTHE (Sauternes)

CHÂTEAU LAMOTHE-GUIGNARD
(Sauternes)

CHÂTEAU NAIRAC (Barsac)

CHÂTEAU ROMER (Sauternes)

CHÂTEAU ROMER-DU-HAYOT
(Sauternes)

CHÂTEAU SUAU (Barsac)

**When Sauternes and Barsac were classified in 1855, twelve *Deuxièmes Crus Classés* were designated. Since then, some of these have split into more than one château. The *Deuxièmes Crus Classés* now number fifteen.

THE DOCGS OF ITALY

ABRUZZI

MONTEPULCIANO D'ABRUZZO

APULIA

CASTEL DEL MONTE BOMBINO NERO

CASTEL DEL MONTE NERO DI TROIA RISERVA

CASTEL DEL MONTE ROSSO RISERVA

PRIMITIVO DI MANDURIA DOLCE NATURALE

BASILICATA

AGLIANICO DEL VULTURE SUPERIORE

CAMPANIA

AGLIANICO DEL TABURNO

FIANO DI AVELLINO

GRECO DI TUFO

TAURASI

EMILIA-ROMAGNA

ALBANA DI ROMAGNA

COLLI BOLOGNESI CLASSICO PIGNOLETTO

FRIULI-VENEZIA GIULIA

COLLI ORIENTALI DEL FRIULI PICOLIT

RAMANDOLO

ROSAZZO

LAZIO

CANNELLINO DI FRASCATI

CESANESE DEL PIGLIO

FRASCATI SUPERIORE

LOMBARDY

FRANCIACORTA

OLTREPÓ PAVESE METODO CLASSICO

SCANZO

SFORZATO DI VALTELLINA

VALTELLINA SUPERIORE

MARCHE

CASTELLI DI JESI VERDICCHIO RISERVA

CONERO

OFFIDA

VERDICCHIO DI MATELICA RISERVA

VERNACCIA DI SERRAPETRONA

PIEDMONT

ALTA LANGA

ASTI

BARBARESCO

BARBERA D'ASTI

BARBERA DEL MONFERRATO SUPERIORE

BAROLO

BRACHETTO D'ACQUI

DOLCETTO DI DIANO D'ALBA

DOLCETTO DI DOGLIANI

DOLCETTO DI OVADA SUPERIORE

ERBALUCE DI CALUSO

GATTINARA

GAVI

GHEMME

NIZZA

ROERO

RUCHÉ DI CASTAGNOLE MONFERRATO

SARDINIA

VERMENTINO DI GALLURA

SICILY

CERASUOLO DI VITTORIA

TUSCANY

BRUNELLO DI MONTALCINO

CARMIGNANO

CHIANTI

CHIANTI CLASSICO

ELBA ALEATICO PASSITO

MONTECUCCO SANGIOVESE

MORELLINO DI SCANSANO

SUVERETO

VAL DI CORNIA ROSSO

VERNACCIA DI SAN GIMIGNANO

VINO NOBILE DI MONTEPULCIANO

VENETO

AMARONE DELLA VALPOLICELLA

ASOLO PROSECCO

BAGNOLI FRIULARO

BARDOLINO SUPERIORE

COLLI DI CONEGLIANO

COLLI EUGANEI FIOR D'ARANCIO

CONEGLIANO VALDOBBIADENE-PROSECCO

LISON

MONTELLO

PIAVE MALANOTTE

RECIOTO DELLA VALPOLICELLA

RECIOTO DI GAMBELLARA

RECIOTO DI SOAVE

SOAVE SUPERIORE

UMBRIA

SAGRANTINO DI MONTEFALCO

TORGIANO ROSSO RISERVA

INDEXES

GENERAL INDEX

Page numbers in **bold** refer to grape profiles and descriptions.

PHOTO CREDITS

STOCK PHOTOGRAPHY: **AGE FOTOSTOCK**—César Lucas Abreu: p. 224; Jerûnimo Alba: p. 316; Galyna Andrushko: p. 718; Arco/J. Kruse: p. 355; Eric Baccega: p. 173; Rua Castilho: p. 483; Angelo Cavalli: pp. 656, 812; CCOphotostock_KMN: p. 744; Jean-Marc Charles: p. 370; Gianalberto Cigolini: p. 363; Classic Vision: p. 774; CSP_Nneirda: p. 37; J. D. Dallet: pp. 159, 167, 314; Danilo Donadoni: p. 342; Danny Lerner Studio, Ltd.: p. 168; Steve Dunwell: p. 380; Food Image Source: p. 118; Patrick Forget: p. 293; Robert Francis: p. 841; Owen Franken/ CORBIS: p. 220; Funkystock: p. 620; Giovanni Gagliardi: p. 382; André Gonçalves: p. 406; Christian Goupi: p. 215; Henning Hattendorf/imageBROKER: p. 575; Hoffmann Photography: p. 559; Hendrik Holler: pp. 552, 621; Herve Hughes: p. 232; Danuta Hyniewska: p. 619; Keller & Keller Photo: p. 787 (top); Christian Kober: p. 916; Javier Larrea: p. 490; Herbert Lehmann: p. 340; Nicolas Leser: p. 289; Horst Lieber: p. 377; Sabine Lubenow: p. 353; Melba: p. 440; Andrew Michael: p. 357 (bottom); Philippe Michel: p. 416; Paolo Gallo Modena: p. 332; Martin Moxter/ imageBROKER: p. 551; Domingo Leiva Nicolas: p. 505; George Ostertag: p. 761; Lynne Otter: p. 358; Aldo Pavan: p. 915; Carlos S. Pereyra: pp. 9, 473; Jordi Puig: p. 495; Jose Fuste Raga: pp. 388, 564, 914; Mike Randolph: p. 445; Rivière: p. 120; Norbert Scanella: p. 305; James Schwabel: p. 768; Shaffer Smith Photography: p. 40; Hans-Peter Siffert: p. 357; Andreas Strauss: p. 620; SuperStock: p. 786; K. Thomas: p. 618; Lucas Vallecillos: p. 617; White Star/Monica Gumm/imageBROKER: p. 540; Peter Widmann: p. 615; Jochem Wijnands: p. 469; Wilmar: p. 74; Hans Zaglitsch: p. 921; Zoonar/Rostislav Gli: p. 336. **ALAMY**—AA World Travel Library: p. 479; Aflo Co. Ltd.: pp. 918, 919; Rossella Apostoli: p. 391; Aurora Photos: p. 79; Paul Bernhardt: p. 537; Cephas Picture Library: pp. 237 (bottom), 272, 368, 387 506, 726, 816 (bottom); Maria Galan Clik: p. 452; Cosmo Condina North America: p. 814; Richard Cummins: p. 75; Luis Dafos: p. 642 (top); Fine Wine Stock: p. 736; Rob Greebon: p. 785; Arina Habich: p. 804; Hackenberg-Photo-Cologne: p. 131; Peter Horree: p. 396; Isifa Image Service s.r.o.: p. 477; Niels van Kampenhaut: p. 255; Per Karlsson/Robert Landau: p. 717; LOOK Die Bildagentur der Fotografen GmbH: p. 474; LS Black and White Collection:

p. 284; Malcolm Park Wine and Vineyards: p. 250; Werner Otto: p. 562; Magdalena Paluchowska: p. 643; Nicolas Paquet: p. 816 (top); Sean Pavone: pp. 512, 920; Really Easy Star/Tullio Valente: p. 367; REDA &CO srl: p. 328; Edwin Remsberg: p. 795; Robert Harding Picture Library Ltd.: p. 523 (top); RosaIreneBetancourt 6: p. 803; Ian Shaw: p. 150; Universal Images Group (Lake County Discovery Museum): p. 775; Michael Ventura: p. 799. **FOTOLIA**— alexpoison: p. 279; ChantalS: p. 301; Martin Ferrier: p. 154; Sergii Figurnyi: p. 324; ImageArt: p. 294; julia252: p. 308; Kondor83: p. 403; PHB.cz: p. 280; samott: p. 392; Pavlo Vakhrushev: p. 349. **GETTY IMAGES**—Peter Adams/Photolibrary RM: p. 401; Jean-Marc Barrere/hemis.fr: p. 320; Bosca78/ E+: p. 369 (top); Fabrice Dimier/Bloomberg: p. 318; Hill Street Studios/Blend Images: p. 802; Paul S. Howell: p. 782; Francesco Iacobelli/AWL Images RM: p. 414; Owen Lexington: p. 833; Lonely Planet Images: p. 364; Michael Melford/National Geographic Creative: p. 524; New York Daily News Archive: p. 668; Chris Parker/Design Pics: p. 795; Peopleimages: p. 115; Photononstop RM: p. 315; Alex Robinson/AWL Images RM: p. 485; John Storey/The LIFE Images Collection: p. 692; Vetta: p. 313.

COURTESY PHOTOGRAPHY VIA KAREN MACNEIL: Alana-Tokaj: p. 626. Bob Adler: p. 913. Kurt Ammann, Star Lane Vineyard: p. 688. Antinori family: p. 329. Archive CRDOQ Priorat: p. 497. Christian Arial: pp. 248, 256. Jim Auchew: pp. 378, 384. Ballochdale Estate Ltd: p. 850. Susana Bates for Drew Altizer: p. 671. Miha Batič: p. 4. Batič Vineyards-Slovenia: pp. 54, 61. Bertani Winery, courtesy of Palm Bay International: p. 350. Bodega Alta Vista: p. 16; Bodega Catena Zapata, Courtesy of Winebow: p. 880 (top). Don Brice: p. 835. Brittany Ferries: p. 297. Kimberly Burfiend: pp. 907, 913. Elizabeth Caravati: pp. 18, 502, 625, 738. Stacey Carlo: pp. 327, 393, 411, 418, 419, 420. Ana Paula Carvalho: p. 539. Casa Madero: p. 807. Beth Cash: pp. 180, 271. Castello di Bossi, Courtesy of Winebow: p. 395. Castello di Fonterutoli, courtesy of Palm Bay International: p. 379, 385. Ceretto, Courtesy of Winebow: p. 337 (top). chrisshanahan.com: p. 834. Cloudy Bay Vineyards: pp. 72, 853, 856. Cono Sur: pp. 864, 871 (top). Consejo Regulador de las Denominaciones de Origen Jerez-Xerez-Sherry: pp. 46 (left), 431, 456, 461. Consejo Regulador Rias Baixas: p. 486. Conti Costanti: p. 390. Creation Wines: p. 128. Mark Davidson: p. 830 (top). Gilles

Deschamps: pp. 298, 300. Diageo Chateau & Estate Wines: p. 214. Domaine Clarence Dillon: pp. 149, 156. Domaine de L'Arlot (AXA Millesimes Gestion): pp. 206, 211. Domaine Select Wine Estates: p. 325. Domaine Trevallon: p. 308. Domane Wachau: pp. 122, 604, 605. Dan and Vicki Dooling: pp. 679, 719. Joanne Dow: pp. 488, 657, 658. Dr. Konstantin Frank Wine Cellars: p. 773. Ernesto Catena Vineyards: p. 883. F. X. Pichler, courtesy of Palm Bay International: p. 593. Faber & Partner: pp. 59, 63, 71. Faber & Partner Duesseldorf: pp. 68, 599, 595, 611. Farnese Group: p. 60. Farnese Vini SrL: p. 413. Fernando Fernandez: pp. 429, 448, 449, 450. Ferrari Winery, courtesy of Palm Bay International: pp. 326, 404. Rebecca Fletcher: pp. 11, 15, 19, 104, 113, 126, 130. Owen Franken: pp. 164, 191, 228, 410. Georgian Wine Association: p. 641. German Wine Institute, www.germanwines.de: pp. 553, 557, 560, 563, 585. Greek Wine Bureau: pp. 646, 647, 650, 655. Simi Grewal: p. 287. Groot Constantia: pp. 894, 897. Jason Haas, Tablas Creek Vineyard: p. 733. Steve Haider: p. 610. Timothy Hartley, British Chancellor of the Jurade: p. 162. Hotel Marques de Riscal, a Luxury Collection Hotel, Elciego: p. 435. Richard Humphrys: pp. 828, 836. Hype House: p. 672. Gene Iverster/Studios on Main: pp. 2, 101, 111. J. Boutari & Son Wineries: pp. 648, 652. Robert Janover: pp. 684, 707. Kanonkop Wine Estate: p. 899. Andy Katz: pp. 666, 686. Katie Keeley: pp. 489, 503, 504. Eric Kelley, for Early Mountain Vineyards: p. 792. Kermit Lynch Wine Merchant: p. 230. Amanda Klein, Hearts and Horseshoes: p. 734. Kobrand Wine & Spirits: pp. 178, 283, 422, 510, 511, 515, 516, 517, 683. Valerie Lailheuge: p. 157. Domaine Laroche: p. 216. Jai Yin Liu, Chateau Palmer: p. 148. Valenti Llagostera: p. 23. Long Shadows Vintners: p. 474. Cecile Loqmane: p. 153. Patria E. Lopez Lozano:

p. 806. Steve Lumpkin, "Under Prairie Skies": p. 53. MAAL: p. 20. Karen MacNeil: pp. 32, 38, 124, 139, 140, 183, 185, 186, 188, 218, 219, 221, 262, 265, 266, 267, 269, 270, 273, 274, 464, 501, 509, 518, 827, 885. Madeira Wine Company: p. 531. Maisons Marques & Domaines: pp. 191, 281. Marchesi de' Frescobaldi: pp. 330, 394. Marques de Caceres Winery: p. 438. Curtis John Marsh: pp. 157, 242, 576. Mas Doix: p. 496. Janis Miglavs www.jmiglavs.com: pp. 911, 912. Moët & Chandon: p. 177. Jean-Marie Muron: p. 208. National Braai Day: p. 902. Michael Newsom, courtesy of Blue Danube Wine Co: p. 425. Northwest Wines Ltd: pp. 589, 756, 758, 762, 574, 586. Numanthia: pp. 430, 432, 507. Kathy A. O'Neal: p. 73, 681. RGA: p. 116. Riedel Crystal: pp. 45, 121. Rob Brown Photography, Fess Parker Winery: p. 675. Romantischer Rhein Tourismus GmbH: p. 581. Royal Tokaji: pp. 630, 633, 634, 636. Rudi Wiest Selections: pp. 566, 567, 580 (top), 587. Scala Dei Winery: pp. 56, 106, 495. Meredith Schlacter: pp. 867, 872 (top). Schweiger Vineyards: p. 29. Seguin Moreau: pp. 46, 47. Sogrape Vinhos S.A.: pp. 525, 526. Taylor Fladgate & Yeatman: p. 519. The Eyrie Vineyards: p. 754. The Symington Family Estate: p. 520 (bottom). Ahin Thomas, Vintners' Alliance: p. 70. Jamey Thomas: p. 724 (top). Zabrine Tipton: pp. 27, 708 (top). Torbreck: p. 839. Vietti Winery: p. 339. Roberto Voerzio, Courtesy of Winebow: p. 335. David Waitz: p. 436. Lauren Watters: pp. 28, 199, 203, 237, 252, 345. Weingut Loimer: p. 598. Weingut Sattlerhof: p. 616. Weingut Selbach-Oster: p. 568 (bottom). Williams Selyem Winery: p. 43. Matt Wilson: p. 865. winebc.com: p. 810. Wines of Chile: pp. 869, 873 (top), 874. winesofontario.org: pp. 809, 815. Wooing Tree Vineyard: p. 854 (top). www.kvevri .org: p. 642 (bottom). www.vienna-unwrapped.com: p. 602. Joco Žnidaršič: pp. 424 (top), 426, 427.